NORTH DAKOTA
STATE UNIVERSITY

JUL 0 7 1997

SERIALS DEPT.
LIBRARY

WITHDRAWN

THE BOWKER ANNUAL

42nd Edition • 1997

THE BOWKER ANNUAL

Library and Book Trade Almanac™

Editor • Dave Bogart
Consultant • Jane Williams

R.R. Bowker®
New Providence, New Jersey

Published by R. R. Bowker,
a division of Reed Elsevier Inc.
Copyright © 1997 by Reed Elsevier Inc.
All rights reserved
Printed and bound in the United States of America
Bowker® is a registered trademark of Reed Elsevier Inc.
The Bowker Annual Library and Book Trade Almanac™ is a trademark of Reed Elsevier Properties Inc., used under license.

International Standard Book Number 0-8352-3906-3
International Standard Serial Number 0068-0540
Library of Congress Catalog Card Number 55-12434

No part of this publication may be reproduced or transmitted in any form or by any means, or stored in any information storage and retrieval system, without prior written permission of R. R. Bowker, 121 Chanlon Road, New Providence, NJ 07974.

No copyright is claimed for articles in this volume prepared by U.S. government employees as part of their official duties. Such articles are in the public domain and can be reproduced at will.

ISBN 0-8352-3906-3

Contents

Preface ix

Part 1
Reports from the Field

News of the Year
LJ News Report: Public Library Budgets Brace for Internet Costs *Evan St. Lifer* 3
SLJ News Report: 'Are We *There* Yet?' An Impatient Librarian Recaps 1996
Renée Olson 9
PW News Report: The Year of Living Dangerously
John F. Baker, John Mutter, Jim Milliot, and *Daisy Maryles* 15

Federal Agency and Federal Library Reports
National Commission on Libraries and Information Science *Jane Williams* 37
National Technical Information Service *Janet E. Wooding* 43
National Archives and Records Administration *Lori A. Lisowski* 52
United States Information Agency *Cynthia Borys* 57
National Center for Education Statistics Library Statistics Cooperative Program
Adrienne Chute 60
Library of Congress *Audrey Fischer* 74
Center for the Book *John Y. Cole* 84
Federal Library and Information Center Committee *Susan M. Tarr* 88
National Agricultural Library *Brian Norris* 102
National Library of Medicine *Robert Mehnert* 110
Educational Resources Information Center *Ted Brandhorst* 116
United States Government Printing Office *Francis W. Biden* 125
National Library of Education 133

National Association and Organization Reports
American Library Association *Mary R. Somerville* 141
Association of American Publishers *Judith Platt* 149
American Booksellers Association *Carol Miles* 163
Association of Research Libraries *Julia C. Blixrud* 173
Commission on Preservation and Access, Council on Library Resources
Maxine K. Sitts 185

v

International Reports

International Federation of Library Associations and Institutions
Edward J. Valauskas 197
Special Libraries Association   *Jennifer L. Stowe* 205
World Trade and World Fairs, 1996: King Frankfurt and His Minions
Herbert R. Lottmann 216
Trends and Issues in Library and Information Services in Canada, 1996
Ken Haycock and *David Chow* 220

Special Reports

Copyright 1996: Fleshing Out the Issues   *Robert L. Oakley* 229
Library Networking and Cooperation in 1996
David H. Brunell 239
Evolution of School Library Media Programs in the 1990s
Paula Kay Montgomery 248
Recent Changes for Three Federal Library and Information Agencies:
Lessons to the Field, from the Field, or Neither?   *Jane Williams* 258

Part 2
Legislation, Funding, and Grants

Legislation

Legislation and Regulations Affecting Libraries in 1996
Carol C. Henderson and *Anne A. Heanue* 273
Legislation and Regulations Affecting Publishing in 1996   *Judith Platt* 284

Funding Programs and Grant-Making Agencies

National Endowment for the Humanities   *Thomas C. Phelps* 293
U.S. Department of Education Library Programs, 1996   *Robert Klassen* 302

Part 3
Library/Information Science
Education, Placement, and Salaries

Guide to Employment Sources in the Library and Information Professions
Maxine Moore 337
Placements and Salaries, 1995: Beginner's Luck—A Growing Job Market
C. Herbert Carson 360
Accredited Master's Programs in Library and Information Studies 372
Library Scholarship Sources 375
Library Scholarship and Award Recipients, 1996 379

Part 4
Research and Statistics

Library Research and Statistics
Research on Libraries and Librarianship in 1996 *Mary Jo Lynch* 405
State Library Agencies: What Do the Numbers Tell Us?
Mary Jo Lynch and *Keith Curry Lance* 420
Number of Libraries in the United States, Canada, and Mexico 426
Highlights of NCES Surveys 430
Library Acquisition Expenditures, 1995–1996: U.S. Public,
Academic, Special, and Government Libraries 435
Price Indexes for Public and Academic Libraries
Kent Halstead 444
State Rankings of Selected Public Library Data, 1995 460
Library Buildings, 1996: Beating the High Cost of Libraries
Bette-Lee Fox and *Erin Cassin* 461

Book Trade Research and Statistics
Prices of U.S. and Foreign Published Materials *Gay N. Dannelly* 479
Book Title Output and Average Prices: 1995 Final and 1996
Preliminary Figures *Gary Ink* 505
Book Sales Statistics, 1996: AAP Preliminary Estimates 512
United States Trade in Books: 1996 *William S. Lofquist* 514
International Book Title Output: 1990–1994 *William S. Lofquist* 520
Number of Book Outlets in the United States and Canada 522
Book Review Media Statistics 523

Part 5
Reference Information

Bibliographies
The Librarian's Bookshelf *Sandy Whiteley* 527

Ready Reference
Publishers' Toll-Free Telephone Numbers 539
How to Obtain an ISBN *Emery Koltay* 573
How to Obtain an ISSN 577
How to Obtain an SAN 579

Distinguished Books
Best Books of 1996 583
Best Young Adult Books of 1996 584
Best Children's Books of 1996 586
Notable Recordings for Children 587
Notable Children's Films and Videos 588
Notable Children's Software 588
Quick Picks for Reluctant Young Readers 589
Bestsellers of 1996 *Daisy Maryles* and *Judy Quinn* 591
Literary Prizes, 1996 *Gary Ink* 629

Part 6
Directory of Organizations

Directory of Library and Related Organizations
Networks, Consortia, and Other Cooperative Library Organizations 639
National Library and Information-Industry Associations,
United States and Canada 669
State, Provincial, and Regional Library Associations 734
State and Provincial Library Agencies 746
State School Library Media Associations 751
International Library Associations 759
Foreign Library Associations 767

Directory of Book Trade and Related Organizations
Book Trade Associations, United States and Canada 779
International and Foreign Book Trade Associations 783
NISO Standards 791
Calendar 795
Acronyms 801
Index of Organizations 805
Subject Index 817

Preface

Welcome to the 42nd edition of *The Bowker Annual*, a compilation of thoughtful analysis and practical information on the rapidly evolving library and book trade industries.

This edition chronicles a year during which the ever-expanding "Information Superhighway" continued to grow in influence in virtually every aspect of librarianship and publishing, presenting new challenges and offering new opportunities.

The pace of change accelerated during 1996. As our report from the Washington, D.C., office of the American Library Association notes, "Significant legislative and regulatory issues on the public agenda made 1996 one of the busiest and most important years for libraries in recent history."

Our Special Reports in this edition look closely at developments in four spheres:

- Robert L. Oakley, Director of the Law Library and Professor of Law at Georgetown University Law Center, examines the evolution of copyright during 1996, particularly in regard to information created, published, or used in the electronic environment.
- Jane Williams of the National Commission on Libraries and Information Science looks into the numerous challenges confronting three federal library and information agencies, the Government Printing Office, the Library of Congress, and the National Archives and Records Administration—noting that the problems they face are the same in nature as those faced by libraries at all other levels.
- David H. Brunell, Executive Director of the Bibliographical Center for Research, assays the year's developments in library networking and cooperation, noting a greatly heightened emphasis on implementation of Internet-based services.
- Paula Kay Montgomery, publisher of *School Library Media Activities Monthly*, weighs the revolutionary changes school library media programs are facing in the 1990s.

Our reports from federal agencies and libraries describe a year of continuing efforts to prepare for the information demands of the new millennium while, in many cases, coping with shrinking resources.

Also in Part 1 are reports from national and international information agencies and examinations of the year's developments from *Library Journal*, *Publishers Weekly*, and *School Library Journal*.

Part 2 features analyses of legislation affecting libraries and publishing as well as reports from grant-making and funding agencies.

Professional information for librarians is found in Part 3, including our annual look at placements and salaries, a listing of scholarship and award winners, and guides to employment and scholarship sources.

Part 4 is dedicated to research and statistics on libraries and publishing, from detailed materials price indexes to surveys of library construction and book title output and sales.

Reference information makes up Part 5: expanded listings of the year's best books and bestsellers, literary prize winners, updated reports on how to obtain an ISBN, ISSN, or SAN, and much more. Among new features here is "The Librarian's Bookshelf," a bibliography of professional reading that reflects the radical changes the profession has undergone in recent years.

Part 6 is our Directory of Library and Related Organizations at state, regional, national, and international levels, plus a calendar of events and indexes of organizations and subjects covered.

As always, *The Bowker Annual* is the work of many. We are thankful to all those who contributed articles and reports and helped us to update and expand our directories. Special thanks are due Consulting Editor Jane Williams and editor/consultants Catherine Barr and Linda Durfee.

We are confident that this edition of *The Bowker Annual*, like its predecessors, will prove to be a valuable resource. We welcome your comments and suggestions.

Dave Bogart
Editor

Part 1
Reports from the Field

News of the Year

LJ News Report:
Public Library Budgets Brace for Internet Costs

Evan St. Lifer
Senior Editor, News, Library Journal

Public libraries have had to negotiate a budgetary obstacle course in the 1990s. First they had to endure an economic downturn at the beginning of the decade, before surviving a nationwide tax revolt in the 1994 elections that froze local property taxes in many venues across the nation. Now comes their latest hurdle: how to handle the cost of becoming their communities' access point to the Internet.

Not only are libraries having to contend with the surging cost of installing and maintaining net technology; they also are having to employ financial legerdemain to figure out how they can squeeze the additional funds from their already stretched-to-the-limit budgets. According to *Library Journal*'s 1997 Public Library Budget Report, based on a comprehensive survey answered by 352 public libraries nationwide, public libraries (PLs) have seen their technology-related costs skyrocket by almost 85 percent in the last two years. Put in perspective, libraries starting from scratch just two or three years ago account for the high percentage jump in technology spending.

Three Reasons to Smile

Still, librarians' angst over dealing with runaway Internet costs should be mitigated by three pieces of encouraging news:

- First, data from *LJ*'s report indicate that public library budgets remained relatively healthy across the board. Total budgets rose by 6.4 percent, up from a 6 percent increase last year; materials budgets saw a 7.1 percent jump, matching last year's increase, and salary/personnel budgets are up 6.3 percent, an improvement over last year's 5.6 percent growth.
- Second, telecommunications rates could be discounted substantially for PLs by the end of this year if the Federal Communications Commission (FCC) heeds recommendations by its Federal-State Joint Board. The

Note: Adapted from *Library Journal*, January 1997

board, appointed to advise FCC on how best to implement telecommunications discounts to the nation's libraries and schools and to what degree, has recommended deep discounts ranging from 20 to 90 percent that would save libraries an estimated $2.25 billion.
- Third, the recent reauthorization of federal funding for libraries under the Library Services and Technology Act (LSTA) provides it with a much brighter future in its new home under the Institute of Museum and Library Services, a relatively safe haven, according to Washington insiders. Library funding was less secure in its former incarnation as the Library Services and Construction Act (LSCA) under the Department of Education, an area of government that many Republicans in Congress continue to target for drastic cuts.

The Local Story

Despite the promising national news, libraries still receive the bulk of their funding from local sources. Thus they remain beholden to their local tax base, economy, and politicians to support their endeavors. Said a staffer at a Connecticut public library serving 16,000, "We are limping along the 'highway' like a medieval pilgrim on crutches." While that library is going to request "town funds" in its fiscal year (FY) 1997–1998 budget for technology-related equipment, the staffer characterized her town as "very wealthy but very conservative." A librarian at a county library in South Dakota has seen her technology costs jump by 100 percent in the last year. However, she is having difficulty getting the extra funding she needs from the county commissioners, who are responsible for appropriating 100 percent of the library's funding. "The public uses [the library], but [the county commissioners] don't see the need," she said. "They think you should pay for your information."

Contrast those fiscally beleaguered libraries with one where residents combine with local and state officials to support the library, and the outlook is drastically different: "The financial outlook is excellent," said Stephen Wood, director of the Cleveland Heights–University Heights PL. "We get good financial support from the state, and the Ohio PL information network (OPLIN) is providing commercial databases and T1-line connectivity to all 250 library systems in Ohio. That makes a difference!"

Still, even on a local level, the *LJ* Budget Report found that PLs are holding their own, particularly in the area of library referenda. Voters supported bond issues nearly 80 percent of the time, according to *LJ* survey respondents, an improvement even on last year's lofty success rate of 72 percent. The good news at the polls comes on the heels of a slew of Election Day victories last November. Financially strapped California libraries made the biggest splash, winning seven of 11 contests.

Perhaps the most direct evidence of public library service continuing to garner enthusiastic support from local residents and officials comes in the form of another increase in per capita funding. Public libraries projected an average of $23.41 for FY 1997 vs. their reported FY 1996 per capita funding average of $22.23, a 5.3 percent jump.

Offering a glimpse of the way a public library's funding base is broken down, the *LJ* survey found that municipal funding accounted for 45.25 percent, followed by county (32.06 percent) and state (15.35 percent), with fee-based services contributing 3.08 percent, fund-raising 1.81 percent, grants 1.77 percent, and federal funding trailing with a .68 percent contribution.

Emerging Net Costs

Two telling statistics illustrate how quickly Internet-related costs are emerging as an essential line item, vying with other basic PL services for an increasingly larger piece of the budgetary pie. Public libraries reported spending an average of $100,213 to provide some form of Internet access to patrons and staff (for average Internet expenditures by library size, see Table 1). Meanwhile, technology expenditures as a proportion of total budgets have edged up, from 5.7 percent in FY 1995 to 6.8 percent in FY 1996.

Public libraries' added emphasis on providing net access and publishing community information on the Web has forced library staffs to reevaluate their fiscal priorities as well as their role in the community. Almost four out of ten respondents said they would have to cut back spending in other areas to fund Internet-related initiatives. Of those having to cut back, nine out of ten public libraries are taking funds from their materials budgets. In fact, every librarian from a library with a population served of under 50,000 who responded to the *LJ* survey said they had to cut from their materials budgets to fund some type of net-based service.

Table 1 / The Cost of Plugging In
How much PLs have spent to integrate the Internet

Size (Patrons served)	Average Expenditure
Fewer than 10,000	$3,480
10,000–24,999	6,405
25,000–49,999	11,073
50,000–99,999	58,334
100,000–999,999	151,150
More than 1 million	375,000

Source: *Library Journal* Budget Report 1997

In Search of ... Additional Funds

While 40 percent of PLs have forged ahead by using funds extracted from their existing budgets, 60 percent are aggressively pursuing funding from outside sources to foot their technology bills. Determined not to cut from traditional services and resources, PLs reported having sought out additional funding via state (57 percent) or federal government (43 percent), corporate or private philan-

Table 2 / Public Library Snapshots
Changes in Budgets from FY 1996 to FY 1997 *(cont.)*

Library	Pop. Served	Total Budget FY 1997	Materials	Salaries	Total Budget
Serving 100,000–999,999					
Muskegon County Library, MI	112,974	$1,237,345	+9.4%	+1.3%	+7.2%
Schaumburg Twp. District Library, IL	124,500	8,276,500	+6.4%	+3.1%	+2.4%
Pueblo Library District, CO	127,353	4,437,351	+18.3	+9.7%	+10.2%
First Regional Library, Hernando, MS	180,306	1,924,676	+5.6%	+8.5%	+7%
Wheeler Basin Reg. Lib., Decatur, AL	196,716	1,270,428	+4%	+9.8%	+5.7%
Lake County PL, Merrillville, IN	199,453	7,180,992	+5.1%	+4.5%	+5.4%
Finger Lakes Lib. System, Ithaca, NY	311,393	1,397,598	-16.4%	+2.2%	-5.2%
Mesa PL, AZ	338,117	8,635,177	+11.8%	+11.2%	+8.8%
Ocean County Library, Toms River, NJ	406,759	15,720,500	+9.3%	+4.1%	+5.1%
Long Beach PL, CA	436,800	11,071,845	+31.3%	+8.9%	+.07%
Mid Continent PL, Independence, MO	582,063	20,250,000	+5.2%	+6%	+3.5%
Kern County Library, Bakersfield, CA	624,000	10,500,000	NC	+10.7%	+19.1%
Baltimore County PL, Towson, MD	713,949	23,850,000	+10.6%	NC	+9.1%
Las Vegas-Clark Cty. Lib., NV	820,000	24,000,000	-10%	+16.7%	+16.7%
Serving More Than 1 Million					
Detroit PL	1,027,000	$26,515,430	NC	+2.1%	+2.7%
Harris County PL, Houston	1,047,000	10,300,000	+6.3%	+6.7%	+3.9%
King County Lib. System, Seattle	1,100,000	44,619,000	-5.1%	+6.7%	+5%
Hawaii State Lib. System, Honolulu	1,178,600	19,906,624	+19.1%	+.04%	-4.5%
San Antonio PL	1,200,000	32,000,000	+11.2%	+2.5%	+6.3%
Broward Cty. Lib., Fort Lauderdale, FL	1,364,168	32,143,820	NC	-.03%	+2.4%
Phoenix PL	1,200,000	19,425,000	+5.5%	+5%	+5%
Sacramento PL, CA	1,200,000	17,500,000	+6.8	+14.5%	+2.9%
Orange County PL, Santa Ana, CA	1,250,000	19,100,000	+20%	-10%	-6.9%
Miami-Dade PL Sys., FL	1,663,113	34,733,000	-3.3%	+4.8%	+4.8%
Queens Borough PL, Jamaica, NY	2,000,000	59,000,000	NC	NC	NC
Brooklyn PL	2,300,000	5,900,000	+7.2%	+2.9%	NC
Los Angeles PL	3,607,700	44,000,000	-2.9%	+1.1%	+4.1%
New York PL	12,000,000	200,000,000	+5.9%	+3.3%	NC

NC—No Change   NA—Not Available
Source: *Library Journal* Budget Report 1997

SLJ News Report: 'Are We *There* Yet?' An Impatient Librarian Recaps 1996

Renée Olson
News and Features Editor, *School Library Journal*

"Are we *there* yet?" You're usually in a car when you hear that question, and it's normally uttered with a whine by someone not yet in possession of a driver's license.

But not this time. Instead, it's me, a stubborn librarian tapping her foot, waiting for faxes and e-mail announcing more library funding, more library hours, and let's face it, more libraries. After all, this is the year that "Kids Can't Wait," compliments of American Library Association (ALA) President Mary Somerville.

But somehow, the enthusiasm that librarians effortlessly muster for kids doesn't always reach the people who manipulate purse strings and policies: the mayors, the school administrators, the library directors, the legislators on Capitol Hill.

I'll restrain myself from burdening you with a long laundry list, but I'll indulge myself with a few 1996 crimes against librarians and their customers.

Exhibit One: The recently deceased piece of legislation that earmarked federal funds for media center materials, otherwise known as the Elementary and Secondary Education Act III–Part F. This fall it was excised, slashed, sliced from the books. Why? It had never been funded. ALA and librarians worked hard to get the legislative language in place, but all for naught. That means we'll continue to hear about school libraries that have books predating the voyage to the moon.

Exhibit Two: In January we ran a news story about a Missouri survey that asked principals to prioritize the responsibilities of media specialists. The principals gave high ratings to materials selection and reference help, but curriculum planning struck them as only of average importance. Too bad Missouri kids have principals of only average intelligence.

Exhibit Three: In November Margie Klinck Thomas wrote an opinion piece for us that put a 1996 study by the National Association of Secondary School Principals under a magnifying glass. She searched in vain among more than 80 recommendations to reinvent high schools for a single mention of the media center. Someone needs to stick Keith Lance's Colorado study under the principals' noses.

Enough griping. There are good stories to tell as well. High-profile initiatives, such as the American Association of School Librarians' Library Power program and ICONnect/KidsConnect, are excellent ways to change people's perceptions of school libraries. And angels in Philadelphia are definitely paying attention to the "Kids Can't Wait" message. In late October the Philadelphia Free Library announced that the William Penn Foundation had donated $18 million

Adapted from *School Library Journal*, December 1996

for youth services. News like that is enough to make even an impatient librarian pause for a smile.

Somerville Backs Clinton's Reading Challenge

On his way to the 1996 Democratic Convention, Bill Clinton announced "America Reads." The five-year, $2.75–billion plan is designed to boost fourth graders' reading scores. According to a recent national reading assessment, 40 percent are not cutting the mustard.

Note to Clinton: For best results, deposit the money directly into library and media center bank accounts.

Tragically, that's not the plan. Nevertheless, ALA President Somerville took the high road and called for the profession to make libraries the heart of tutoring initiatives in each community.

"America Reads," Somerville wrote in an open letter, "represents a tremendous opportunity to demonstrate how our nation's libraries and librarians make a difference. I urge all of you to join me in taking up this challenge."

If approved by Congress, "America Reads" would

- Create America's Reading Corps, a group of one million volunteers trained to tutor K–3 students at a cost of $2.4 billion. A reading specialist and supervising tutors would assist volunteers in each community.
- Distribute $300 million through "Parents as First Teachers." That's a challenge grant fund for states, local governments, organizations such as the Urban League, and community or nonprofit groups that run programs stressing parental involvement in teaching kids to read. ALA is watching the fund's development to make sure libraries will be eligible.
- Expand Head Start to reach more eligible three- and four-year-olds

According to an *Education Week* article, some educators wonder whether "the money might be better spent on professional development for early elementary teachers, the hiring of reading specialists, and the implementation of programs with successful track records."

Still, well-placed attention is a start. The Department of Education's Web site tells us that "a focus on reading can pay off. Our nation's 15-year emphasis on students taking higher-level math and science courses is paying off in ongoing improvements in math scores. More attention to reading can stimulate similar reading gains."

In a prompt letter to Clinton, Somerville urged him to make libraries eligible for program funds. She also lobbied the polished public speaker "to take every opportunity to remind parents and caregivers that our nation's libraries are a source of empowerment for all children and their families."

What Ever Happened to ...

School Librarians in Kansas? Despite a blizzard of angry letters from Kansas media specialists, the state board of education still plans to drop teacher certification for media specialists, according to Joanne Proctor, president of the Kansas Association of School Librarians. The change, part of a plan to update education standards, would allow new librarians to work without a teaching degree, but still require outcomes that depend on that degree (*SLJ*, May 1995, p. 14). The next step is a series of hearings and then a vote by June 1997.

Family-Friendly Libraries? Karen Jo Gounaud, founder of the Virginia-based group that emerged last year, has spent her time ricocheting from one speaking engagement to another. Her most recent appearances were at library conferences in Virginia, New York, and New England. Gounaud told me that she has used these occasions to practice honing the group's message, which, she said, is a call for "age-appropriate" policies for library materials. She believes that library collections should carry titles such as the picture book *Daddy's Roommate* (Alyson, 1990), but that these should be interfiled with adult books, not in children's collections.

Librarians already overwhelmed by shrinking materials budgets, using the Web to find just one lone authoritative reference source, and staring at outdated six-month-old computer equipment may not take kindly to Gounaud's belief that there are not enough materials challenges. To her, the ratio of complaints to the number of schools and libraries nationwide is low. She'd like to see more parents start a dialogue with librarians: "I think there's not enough use of the First Amendment."

The Library in the Supermarket? Last spring the Adams Memorial Library in Latrobe, Pennsylvania, signed a three-year lease and opened a 6,000-foot branch in a busy supermarket (*SLJ*, September 1996, p. 110). But by August the owner had put the store up for sale, leaving the library unsure as to whether it had a future among the cold cuts and cream cheese. The latest news is good. The new owner, according to Assistant Director Nancy Okonak, is happy to honor the original lease.

Communications Decency Act

While the Telecommunications Act of 1996 gives libraries a shot at discounted rates, it also brought with it the Communications Decency Act (CDA). In June a panel of federal judges ruled it unconstitutional; the case has been appealed to the U.S. Supreme Court.

The CDA would have made it a felony to display or transmit to minors material that is "patently offensive by contemporary community standards." The vagueness of the word "offensive" alarmed librarians, many of whom feared that they could be held responsible if, for instance, a minor found four-letter words while searching a catalog via the Web.

"We are ecstatic. The decision was everything we could have wished," said Judith Krug, Director of ALA's Office for Intellectual Freedom, of the June decision.

The fervor with which ALA chased a legal remedy to the CDA this year was impressive, as was the speed with which the association took a leadership role. ALA filed suit in March against the CDA as lead plaintiff in a coalition of 36 groups, including America Online, Families Against Internet Censorship, the

American Booksellers Association, the Association of American Publishers, and Microsoft.

But the initial victory came at a price. Attorney fees for the case, apparently the association's most expensive legal action in history, total $400,000 to date: ALA's piece of the pie comes to $250,000, while the Freedom to Read Foundation has contributed $100,000, and the Public Library Association $50,000. In September the Connecticut Library Association donated $500 and challenged each state association to pledge the same or better.

Krug told me she feels that both the lower court's decision and the increased stature the suit has given ALA were worth the expense. "When legal issues are at stake, you want your concerns accommodated," she explained. "We opened our mouths. We put our money where our mouths were. We went [to court] as equals." ("I was not a poor cousin," she added, referring to clout often handed to corporate interests.)

When the case is closed, Krug estimates that ALA, the online community, and the remaining coalition members will have split the cost approximately in thirds. ALA's attorney has capped fees at $1.1 million; anything beyond that will be pro bono.

One of the coalition's legal arguments was that the CDA violates the free-speech rights of adults without protecting children from explicit materials. To achieve the latter, some librarians have installed software that blocks access to certain sites. ALA's Office for Intellectual Freedom does not see that as a solution. "Blocking software is appropriate for the home," said Krug. "This is not appropriate technology for libraries because it blocks everyone's access."

The U.S. Department of Justice appealed the lower court decision and the Supreme Court will have to make a ruling by the end of session in June 1997. ALA believes that the high court will rule the CDA unconstitutional.

The City of Hills

Running a library in San Francisco sure has its share of ups and downs. In April actor Robin Williams read to kids at the opening of the new San Francisco Public Library. At the same time, Library Director Ken Dowlin took flack for what some librarians and customers called snuggling up to benefactors, including opening the "Chevron Teen Center." The shift to the new building also prompted *New Yorker* writer Nicholson Baker to accuse San Francisco Public Library of pell-mell weeding.

Slightly Fattened Federal Education Purse

The 1996 presidential campaign brought a dollop of increased federal funding for schools and media centers. Both Democrats and Republicans doled out goodies in the hope of keeping the electorate happy.

With the federal fiscal year (FY) 1997 budget in place, Mary Costabile, Assistant Director of ALA's Washington Office, said that school librarians should grab Elementary and Secondary Education Act funds while they're around, especially those for technology and instructional and library materials (see *SLJ*, November 1996, p. 14). "It's coming," she said of the current funding, "and [media specialists] have to figure out how to get it."

And be quick about it, she adds. Like most people who overindulge at the holiday table, Congress may have to pay later for its largesse. "They're probably going to have to cut back next year," Costabile said. "It's a good thing that money for [the Library Technology and Services Act or LSTA] gets sent out right away."

Congress's determination to pass a budget also meant that the aforementioned LSTA (formerly the Library Services and Construction Act) was reauthorized for six years, a move for which ALA had lobbied hard.

Senior Year Blues

While President Clinton makes noise about the inadequate reading skills of K–3 students, he should also get worked up about the scores of high school seniors. The National Assessment of Education Progress, the country's report card on schools, announced this year that its "most striking finding" is that the average reading proficiency of 12th-grade students declined significantly from 1992 to 1994. Only 36 percent of 12th-grade students reached the "proficient" reading level and only 3 to 7 percent reached the "advanced" level. The study showed that the decline in reading proficiency "was evident at all levels of parental education."

The Unwired Masses

Those still waiting to be wired to the Internet might actually be blessed. The Federal Communications Commission (FCC) may pave the way for new wireless communication equipment (called NII/SUPERNet devices). According to the FCC, these devices could support new wireless local area networks, as well as provide access to the Internet without the expense of wiring. The commission sees them as a solution for schools and libraries lacking the funds to wire buildings, especially those loaded with asbestos.

Headaches in Hawaii

The next time you meet a Hawaiian public librarian, say thanks. Thank him or her for playing guinea pig for the rest of the country's libraries by living day to day with a $11.2 million outsourcing contract with wholesaler Baker & Taylor.

Hawaii State Librarian Bart Kane handed over selection, acquisitions, cataloging, and processing for all public libraries to B&T (see *SLJ*, June 1996, p. 10, and November, p. 10). At the Hawaii Library Association's October conference, Kane explained that his decision to shift selection to a vendor was necessary to comply with the governor's request for deep budget cuts. Kane responded by moving most behind-the-scenes staffers to public-service positions, and having B&T take on their duties.

While the man has his supporters, namely those who appreciate extra time for customer service and believe that his plan streamlines selection, his detractors (many of whom serve young people) are vocal in and outside Hawaii. Criticism of the plan landed as far afield as *Newsweek*'s October 28 issue, making it the first time I can remember reading, albeit very briefly, about an internal library concern in a national newsweekly.

The complaints? Too many to list, but here are a few: call numbers that don't jibe with what the library uses, dissatisfaction with new titles (one Hawaiian librarian called them "shelf sitters"), and charges of a lack of communication between library administrators and staff.

While Hawaii's librarians are understandably less than overjoyed at the prospect of testing Kane's reengineering plan—especially when faced with complaining customers—they're performing a valuable service for the profession. If Kane and B&T fail, it'll sound a death knell for outsourcing on this scale and librarians will decide whether the practice, like the school privatization wave of a few years ago, needs to expire. If, however, some new way to handle selection emerges from the experiment, then the profession benefits.

While thanking a Hawaiian librarian, consider giving him or her a large bottle of pain relievers; B&T's contract has another five years before it runs out.

Ahhh, the Future

Once the dust settles on President Clinton's preelection welfare reform bill, we'll want to monitor how it affects children from low-income homes over the next few years. Hunger has a way of putting a damper on the desire to learn.

We'll also have front seats to watch Microsoft continue to cultivate a cozy relationship with librarians in the interest of marketing its products. I'm concerned that the decision made this summer by the executive board of the American Association of School Librarians to team up with Microsoft's Family Technology Nights puts librarians at risk of being associated with what some call merely infomercials for Microsoft.

If the Internet doesn't crash from heavy traffic jams, we'll start to see multimedia electronic publications that arrive via e-mail (meaning you're relieved of the burden of remembering to go to a Web site), searchable rating labels on Web sites that may alleviate parental concern about content, fewer CD-ROM titles and more original content on the Web, and . . . in May, a final FCC decision on what constitutes "affordable" telecommunications rates for school and libraries.

Perhaps my impatience to see more progress in library services for kids is due to the pressure that the impending end of a millennium brings, the intensification of the need to get everything done by the year 2000. (After all, none of us has gone through this before.) But if I can glue myself in my chair long enough for reflection, I'd venture to say that my anxiety comes from the simple belief that great libraries are a timeless gift society owes its kids.

PW News Report:
The Year of Living Dangerously

John F. Baker
Editorial Director, *Publishers Weekly*

Last year at this time we observed that 1996 was likely to be a year of considerable uncertainty. That turned out, in hindsight, to be an understatement of some magnitude: 1996, in fact, turned out to be a kind of watershed year for the book business, in which a number of issues that had long been simmering came to a rather painful head.

For a start, it was for many a decidedly rugged year economically, with much higher-than-usual returns, flat or declining sales in most categories, and a pervasive sense of uncertainty about the direction the marketplace was heading. An increasingly volatile readership made some surprising bestseller choices, stampeded madly off after Oprah's book club anointments, new and old, and sat on their wallets for all too many big-budget items. Publishers still trying to come to terms with the seat-of-the-pants approach of just-in-time delivery found they were also hamstrung by never quite knowing where their sales efforts were and were not working, often until it was too late.

The suits that the American Booksellers Association (ABA) had brought against publishers over the years—as well as the long-running Federal Trade Commision (FTC) investigation—were all wrapped up, in the booksellers' favor, and a more level playing field was certainly achieved; but meanwhile many sturdy independents had gone under, and the industry's great annual get-together, the newly christened BookExpo America, seemed to be falling apart—or at very least seeking a new role—as more and more big publishers abandoned it. The retail marketplace was falling increasingly under the sway of the big chain superstores and non-book outlets, with the jury still out as to how effective these were likely to be over the long haul in genuinely extending the market for books—or even selling them. And what of the bestsellers? What worked and what didn't during the year, who moved up or down in the bestseller ratings, and what do these changes portend for 1997?

These and other outstanding issues are all explored exhaustively in the pages that follow, with leading publisher and bookseller voices expressing their hopes, fears—and sometimes mutual suspicions—to *Publishers Weekly (PW)* reporters and writers. It may not always be comfortable reading, but as we all head into what will certainly be a highly challenging year it should be at least salutary and, we hope, instructive.

Adapted from *Publishers Weekly* January 6, 1997

what was surely an understatement. He described a "rather mediocre" manuscript on a rock celebrity of a previous generation (who shall be nameless) that one of his publishers had costed out and was prepared to offer $100,000 for, only to see a big national house pre-empt for a million. "I don't see how any math could justify that," he commented. Arlene Friedman acknowledged that she had overpaid on occasion, "but not overprinted," and that in any case, with BDD's insistence on foreign rights wherever possible, foreign sales had earned out many advances before the books were even published. Bob Miller finds overpayment "a story that repeats itself each year with more intensity," and though Hyperion enters many auctions, "we don't always feel the need to win." "We all have to decide what to go to the mat for," said Carolyn Reidy at S&S. According to Egen, "It's hard sometimes not to overpay. You don't want to lose authors you care about, and it's harder to refuse authors who have been successful. It's troublesome."

The Question of Readership

Concerns were expressed frequently about the size, and dedication, of the readership for books. Arlene Friedman and Carolyn Reidy had somewhat similar takes on where readers' heads were in 1996. Reidy: "I think readership is contracting a little. The conventional wisdom is that everyone is distracted by the Net, but last year had a lot of other distractions: the election, the Olympics." "Yeah, they were distracted—by the conventions, the Olympics," said Friedman, "but then along came the 'Oprah' factor, and a book you've virtually forgotten about [in her case, Jane Hamilton's *The Book of Ruth*, a choice for Winfrey's "book club"] goes through the roof."

Romanos at S&S was concerned about the "confused" marketplace, with the growth of superstores, the decline of independents "and the almost overnight collapse" of the ID market. "The marketplace we planned to publish into in 1996 does not exist," he declared. He is convinced that in future it will be harder for "small" books to be discovered, and "the inability of such books to justify meaningful print runs will call into question whether some books should be printed at all." For Jonathan Galassi at FSG the question was rather one of connecting with the right readers, the ones he is convinced are still out there. "One of the obstacles to reaching those readers is that there are fewer bookstores that really know what they've got on the floor . . . It's not a problem with the numbers of books in the stores, it's a question of how the reader connects with what's in the store."

Winton voiced concern about a distribution question. "Are we 'just-in-time'-ing ourselves to death?" he asked, referring to the system of frequent reprints designed to match up more closely with the rate of orders. "How much do you lose in the ability to merchandise properly by always being right on the edge? I don't think this approach is quite as responsive as we would like it to be." He is expecting 1997 to be a year of "medicine-taking, more conservative buying, higher returns again," and as a result is planning, "for things still being mediocre; there's not much optimism in there." Despite all the added square footage in the new superstores, Winton feels the book market "seems to have arrived at some sort of plateau. from which it may be difficult to advance."

Random House CEO Alberto Vitale outlined Random's approach to 1997: "We have basically cut our trade list about 10 percent to 15 percent for next year. And that is in addition to the cuts we've made over the last few years." As for the issue of just-in-time, he said, "Hopefully just-in-time inventory will work, but it's a total system. If we reserve inventory at the warehouse but the bookstores or chains forget to reorder, then it doesn't work."

Bob Miller's worry was that of a largely frontlist publisher depending on big hits. Big-budget nonfiction titles, especially those linked to celebrities, have an ever-shrinking window of opportunity to make their mark, he observed. "Timing is crucial, orchestrating the laydown carefully with advertising and publicity, and it's all-consuming: all your eggs are in one basket for a few days." He agonizes about books that need to establish themselves very strongly, very quickly, but often need more time than is readily available to accomplish this.

The Impact of Superstores

Concerns about the retailing scene were common, and there was a confused mingling of appreciation and anxiety about the impact on the scene of the ever-growing number of superstores. Carolyn Reidy feels that in many cases they have created a stronger market, but "it is a regional story, not a national one, it's happening on a region-by-region basis," and she wants to work with the chains on a regional basis to merchandise her books more effectively. Elaine Koster worries about the financial health of the chains: "I see that each quarter they're still losing money, and though it's less than it was, I'd really like to see them in profit, because the whole business depends so much on their health." The consolidation of mass market distribution too, has been "a real concern."

Bill Shinker summed up a general feeling succinctly: "I am simultaneously exhilarated and anxious about the continued rapid expansion of superstores," he declared. "Their growth has been very positive for readers, authors, and publishers, and I am sure there are still parts of the country that do not have enough bookstores to meet demand, but I am concerned that superstore growth has been overheated." Vitale said that he's "very concerned" about the independents. "The ABA should use all their money to teach them how to be better and not to compete with chains. They need to establish themselves as an entity that caters to a specific group." Anthea Disney is unsure: "There are certainly persuasive statistics that the superstores have expanded the market. However, we are all seeing store closings, and we know we are facing a very competitive environment with regard to title selection. Certainly the '96 returns rate and the decrease in releases suggest the reading public is changing its patterns."

But just how? Publishers asked to analyze the nation's current reading habits often confessed themselves bewildered by seemingly paradoxical responses to their offerings. Lou Aronica wanted to spend "more time out in the marketplace seeing what customers are buying," and to re-examine his packaging and marketing techniques. He adds: "I don't think the readership is contracting. I just think people aren't buying books right now." Egen, ever optimistic, has a sense that "people may be rediscovering books; they're trying to find quality downtime, and reading is a good way to achieve this. I think the growing market for better books is a way for people to reward themselves." "The audience is giving us a thousand messages," said Paul Fedorko, Morrow's new publisher. "We can listen to all of them, then decide which ones we can answer." Arlene Friedman thinks there really is a new audience for books: "They're the ones who used to meet in bars, and now they're in Barnes & Noble coffee shops." Bob Miller, too, sees expansion in readership. "Even beyond the big splashy titles, our sales are now over a wider range, and that's a healthy trend." "There's every indication," said Irwyn Applebaum, "that the hunger of readers is just as broad as the number of topics out there. There's been an explosive growth of sales in hardcover, and there are probably more hardcovers being sold in every town in this country than ever before. And the buyers are probably more various than they used to be. If you go into superstores, you'll see they're quite democratic places."

"People's lifestyles are different these days, and we need to attract their attention in different ways, to experiment with different kinds of marketing, from guerrilla niche marketing to big, splashy consumer marketing," is Anthea Disney's view. "We need to pay more attention to shifting public tastes."

Tracking Book Sales

In past such surveys, the book distribution system, and its many inefficiencies, was often a prime source of publisher discontent. Not so this time, for, though prompted, hardly anyone thought this worthy of attention. What is of far greater concern is the accurate tracking of sales out of the stores, to the point where printings and shippings can be sensibly adjusted. "Regrettably, the flow and the sources of sales information are so many and so fragmentary that we are still struggling with a way to efficiently consolidate and model sales data," said Shinker. "We get better at this, but we are still a long way from having sales tracking that would give us a complete and real-time model of what is happening with our titles in the marketplace." Disney concurred: "Our systems are doing a good job of tracking our shipments out the door, but we need to track point-of-sale data to get true sales figures." Applebaum: "Our systems have gotten better and better at tracking sales, but just because we get more and better reports, it's hard to make relevant sense out of them. What does a regional spurt of sales really mean, for instance?"

"Hollywood has the best system: literally overnights," said Fedorko. "But what we currently have is just what people have on hand in what outlets. It's a little colonial. Also, the gathering of information from so many outlets, with their different reporting structures, is complex. We could use a clearinghouse to report all sales figures to one source." Bob Miller could use more analyses of trends; for Chip Gibson, "our actual title/region/store-specific/point-of-sale knowledge is woefully lacking. It is a huge objective in the coming year to improve our management of inventory."

"Tracking sales remains our biggest problem; we still can't get proper figures out of our second-biggest customer," laments Winton.

Two houses are actually doing something about the question, rather than just worrying about it. Elaine Koster said Penguin is changing systems in the new year, to "something that will address our present shortcomings," mostly involving sales through independents. "We get good information from the major chains." And Doubleday's Friedman said the company is going into a "totally new sales tracking system, called S.A.P, and I believe we're the first American company to have it, though it's been extremely successful in Europe."

The year 1996 did feature one radically new form of distribution, noted by Vitale: the Internet. "Amazon has proved they can successfully reach people with book information. Does everyone need a book instantly? Or can you wait a week or so for it?" Vitale cited a Knopf title that sold 76 copies by featuring it on their Web site, while during the same period, Borders sold only 10 more copies nationwide. Vitale went on to point out that "Amazon did no business a year and half ago and had barely begun selling in April. Now it looks like they will be finishing the year off with about $15–$17 million dollars in book sales."

And what would a New Year's report be without resolutions? At *PW*'s prompting, our chosen publishers were asked to share them. There were plenty of variations on the theme of "Buy (or publish) only books that sell" and "Publish only great books, and sell them well." A few were more idiosyncratic—and perhaps more realistic. Samples:

- "To believe in the positives of the business—though it does get harder and harder when there are people losing faith, getting laid off."—Irwyn Applebaum.
- "To be careful of the big titles and pay more attention to the ones that have regional and niche opportunities."—Bob Miller.
- "Not to get disheartened in the face of tough conditions in the marketplace, and not to lose our enthusiasm for books and our courage to publish them well."—Bill Shinker
- "Try and have fun."—Charlie Winton.

And finally, one that acknowledges the current perils while retaining the sometimes irrational optimism that characterizes publishing at its best (and has a nice literary turn to it too):

- "1997 is not going to be a year for the faint-hearted. Perhaps silence, exile, and cunning is the answer, but I prefer to just keep believing."—Jonathan Galassi.

One Size Doesn't Fit All

John Mutter
Executive Editor, Bookselling, *Publishers Weekly*

In 1996 even the most fervent supporters of superstores began to wonder if the book retailing market might be reaching saturation.

Certainly the numbers looked ominous. During a year of high returns, retail space devoted to books once again increased much faster than book sales. The top four chains expanded the space in their stores devoted to books by an estimated 3.35 million square feet, or 20 percent, and increased sales by 19 percent; meanwhile total retail book sales rose about 3 percent over 1995.

This year the chains will continue to open superstores at a torrid pace, adding about as much space for books as they did last year; on the other hand, no one is predicting that book sales growth will jump appreciably.

The ramifications of the continued growth of book retail space out of proportion to sales growth are wide-reaching. The effects are already apparent:

- Many more books sit on bookstore shelves unsold and are returned as they "age," a factor in this year's heavy returns.
- The emphasis on cramming as many titles as possible into superstores and competitive independents means that most books are shelved spine-out and are stocked only in ones and twos, making publishers and distributors despair that their titles can be marketed and merchandised properly.
- With chains' sales growth paralleling their expansion of square footage devoted to books—and that expansion continuing—independents should continue to lose market share.
- As independents lose ground and nontraditional book retailing outlets account for more than half of the market, many publishers and distributors are shifting focus to reach nontraditional markets.

Superstore Growth Spurt

Altogether, the top four bookstore chains opened some 190 superstores during the year; they now operate more than 800 superstores, all but a handful of which were opened since 1990. Many industry observers, including some chain executives, predict that the current expansion frenzy won't end until there are about 1,500 superstores, a little less than double the number that exist today. (If that target is reached and superstores' configurations don't change drastically, the extra 700 stores would increase the amount of retail square footage devoted to books by about 14 million, almost doubling the amount of space provided in the chains for books.)

The largest chain, Barnes & Noble, has almost 440 superstores, 91 of which opened during 1996.

Owner of the best-stocked and merchandised stores, Borders Books & Music, operates nearly 160 superstores, 41 of which opened during the year.

Crown Books, which rebounded somewhat in 1996, has 110 superstores after adding about 30 during the year.

Troubled Books-A-Million opened some 25 superstores in 1996, giving it a total of 90.

While many industry members have focused simply on the vast superstore numbers in and of themselves, another aspect of superstore growth vividly points out the dramatic changes taking place as a result of the chains' expansion.

Assuming conservatively that each superstore devotes an average of 20,000 square feet to books, the gross gain in book retail space nationwide last year was about 3.8 million square feet.

However, while the chains have been adding superstores at a rapid rate, they have also been closing mall stores. During 1996 they closed an estimated 180 mall stores, roughly equal to the number of superstores opened. Some of the closed mall stores were victims of cannibalization, losing business to new, nearby superstores owned by the same company. Others were closed because of stagnant mall business.

Mall stores are much smaller than superstores, giving only about 2,500 square feet of space to books. Thus the closed stores represented 450,000 square feet of book retail space. The net gain is 3.35 million square feet devoted to books in the chains. This net gain amounted to an increase of 20 percent.

In dollars, sales for the top four bookstore chains grew during the year in roughly the same proportion as the growth in book retail space: from February through October 1996, the first three quarters of the chains' fiscal year, sales for the top four chains grew 19 percent to $3.2 billion from $2.7 billion.

Estimates of trade book sales growth during the first half of the year amounted to 2.5 percent. If chain sales were rising at a 19 percent pace, then independents' sales had to be down by as much as 8 percent.

During 1995, the most recent year for which complete figures are available, the unit sales of adult books through independent bookstores fell to 19.5 percent from 21.4 percent in 1994, according to the *1995 Consumer Research Study on Book Purchasing*. At the same time, the chains' share jumped to 26.2 percent from 24.2 percent. Nontraditional outlets garnered 54.3 percent of the market, up from 54 percent.

Is Too Much Not Enough?

While independents, of course, have suffered most because of the clash of the chains, the chains are mainly fighting each other. That is why, in area after area around the country, new superstores continued to open down the block—even across the street—from each other.

As a result, over the past five years, chain superstores have doubled and tripled the amount of retail space devoted to books in the major and secondary markets. In Chicago, for example, Barnes & Noble, Borders, and Crown compete in both the city and suburbs. In some areas, like Diversey Parkway in Chicago's Lakeview district, the three chains have major stores within a five-minute walk of each other.

In New York City, hometown chain Barnes & Noble has expanded preemptively, opening stores very close to one another. For example, in 10 minutes one could walk the distance between the flagship store on lower Fifth Avenue and a newer store on Union Square and on Avenue of the Americas in Chelsea. Borders was finally able to obtain a lease in Manhattan, opening its first Big Apple store this year in the World Trade Center.

During 1996 the battle became so fierce that chains began expanding into tertiary markets, which many had thought were immune from the superstore onslaught because of their smaller size.

In an oft-quoted case of chains going overboard in a seemingly limited location, both Borders and Barnes & Noble opened superstores in 1995 in Omaha, Nebraska, which has a metropolitan area of 350,000 people. (The stores helped shut down independent Combs & Combs, once hailed as the only literary bookstore in the state of Nebraska.)

But there were many other examples of superstore arrivals that made the Omaha situation pale in comparison. In Fargo, North Dakota, Boise, Idaho, Greenville, South Carolina, and Santa Rosa, California, all areas with fewer than 150,000 people, at least two chain superstores have opened. In High Point, North Carolina, where the surrounding county has all of 71,500 inhabitants, five superstores have arrived. Columbia, South Carolina, and Gainesville, Florida, each have three superstores.

In Columbia, South Carolina, the state capital and home of the University of South Carolina, bookstore square footage tripled, to 120,000 from 42,000, in the space of two years, as Books-A-Million opened two stores and Barnes & Noble opened one. The area has a population of 98,000.

In Gainesville, home of the University of Florida, bookstore space doubled to 84,000 square feet in three years at the same time that average sales in the county grew 7 percent. Gainesville has a population of 94,000.

Again and again, local independents note that book customers may be drawn to the large stores out of curiosity, but they probably will not continue to buy books at the rate necessary to make one superstore, let alone several, profitable.

Merchandising Mess

Of course, 1996 was the year when many publishers and distributors reported a huge increase in returns, on average about double the usual rate, largely because of higher returns from chain stores. Literary presses suffered the most; publishers of reference and information books did relatively well.

Gone are the days when university and poetry presses rejoiced when they received large orders from chains wanting to fill the vast shelves of their superstores. Those same chains this year sent many presses their largest returns shipments ever.

Publishers and distributors see several reasons to be concerned about chain superstores. Among them: buyers, publishers complain, tend to use computers to weed out slow-selling titles no matter what their long-term potential. Chains, all of which are publicly owned now, fiddle with inventory levels to make their balance sheets look better. But perhaps most crucially, publishers and distributors say that chains have lost the fine art of in-store merchandising.

Face-out display is probably the most effective passive in-store bookselling method. But in today's crammed stores, this technique, still used with great success in nontraditional stores, has become rare indeed. Many fear that the only way they can get face-out display and other in-store attention is by paying for it. In fact, some of the chains have become as mercenary about product promotion as grocery stores. Consider some of Books-A-Million's in-store programs, whose terms contradict any sense of traditional bookselling.

Monthly endcap positions cost publishers $1,500 in Books-A-Million stores, $850 in BAM's smaller Bookland stores and $2,300 chainwide. To be featured in the new and notable books sections, publishers must pay $750 for trade titles and $500 for mass market books. Children's publishers who want to have a book selected for BAM's children's storyteller hours must pay $450 per book.

Further, BAM "breakout books"—books that the stores' employees must read and that are promoted in a variety of ways in-store—cost $7,500. The supreme category of "handselling" at BAM is Clyde's Picks, on which Clyde Anderson, president of BAM, "puts his stamp of approval," according to explanatory literature. Among the bonuses of Clyde's Picks: galleys of the favored books are given to all store managers; the titles are featured in BAM's edition of *BookPage;* the authors do signings; the titles appear in BAM's print advertising. The cost to be "picked" by Clyde: $12,000.

When's the Shakeout?

Media Play and On Cue, the all-media retail divisions of Musicland, may well be the first casualties of expansion arithmetic that doesn't add up. Already last December, Media Play announced that it was abandoning some key markets and closing a total of 29 Media Play stores, leaving it with 69. As recently as 1995, Musicland opened 43 Media Plays, each of which stock 75,000 book titles; it had planned to open 30 last year. Together with On Cue, which are smaller stores geared to smaller markets, the two divisions sold enough books to make Musicland the fifth-largest bookseller in the country.

Of all the major chains selling books, Musicland was most hurt by the relatively poor Christmas in 1995 and heavy discounting early in 1996. It never seemed to recover, with comparable sales at Media Play and On Cue stores open at least a year down during the first six months of the year. (Musicland was not helped by the fact that its music retail divisions, Musicland and Sam Goody, suffered from the music business's worst season in many years. The poor sales elsewhere in the company did not give Media Play and On Cue any breathing space.)

Among the top four bookstore chains, Books-A-Million is considered the most likely candidate for closing, merger or severe cutbacks, à la Media Play and On Cue.

In a key sign of poor prospects, BAM's comparable store sales dropped 1.4 percent at its superstores and 2.3 percent overall during BAM's most recent quarter, ended November 2, 1996. The company appears to be emphasizing bargain books at its superstores, a move that gives publishers little solace.

Moreover, publishers and distributors who sell to Books-A-Million continue to report several disturbing trends at the company. For one, BAM's buyers and others who work with publishers and distributors have become extremely adversarial; some go so far as to call them downright hostile. The company continues to return books at a significant level, and payments are few and far between, often delayed even beyond what's customary for traditionally late booksellers.

In another sign of financial difficulties at Books-A-Million, the company appears to be trying to draw as much profit as possible from publishers in new and roundabout ways. Several publishers have said BAM is "very aggressive" about demanding marketing and promotional allowances and payments for other services that go far beyond those of Barnes & Noble, some of which were cited in the American Booksellers Association's lawsuit against six publishers.

Several publishers have complained that they are afraid not to participate in BAM's "management seminars," at which BAM employees gather at headquarters in Birmingham, Alabama, for a book exposition funded by the publishers. Non-appearances, publishers worry, could mean even less exposure and promotion at BAM stores.

Typical "meal sponsorships" offered to publishers for the October 13–17, 1996, seminar ranged from $1,000 for a morning break to $6,000 for either lunch or a cocktail reception to $8,000 for dinner. Each "section" or table at the vendor booth per day cost $1,000, or $2,550 for three.

For inclusion on Books-A-Million's "product knowledge videos"—videotapes that are produced by BAM and shown to its booksellers ("required viewing")—publishers can obtain a 60-second spot for $600 or a 90-second spot for $900. In addition, publishers can buy a five-minute spot on a "training video" about selling new and backlist titles, for $2,500. In material about the two video offers, BAM states clearly that "funds for this program should not be considered as part of regular co-op dollars." Placement in the BAM Christmas catalog costs $3,000.

In fact, it seems just about everything is up for sale at BAM. Advertisements on the sides of BAM trucks cost $1,500 for one truck, $3,500 for four and $6,200 for eight. Books promoted on "marquee posters" at the exits of all stores cost $3,500 per month. For 100,000 BAM bags printed with a publisher's logo or title, the cost is $3,500. Book or publisher images on the side of 100,000 coffee cups in BAM cafes cost $3,000; the same images on "table talkers" cost $2,000. In a category that makes some publishers feel especially stepped upon, welcome mats with company information at entrances to BAM stores cost $150 per store for three months.

Clouded Crystal Ball

For better or for worse, the new fact of publishing life is that because of difficulties in marketing effectively through chains and because of independents' declining market share, publishers are focusing increasingly on nontraditional markets. These outlets range from warehouse clubs to Internet sites, from gardening and home-supply stores to all-media stores. While these venues offer plenty of opportunities to reach people who might never be made aware of books via traditional bookselling avenues, this is a diffuse, decentralized kind of business, where a few titles can sell a handsome number of copies but where a publisher's full list can rarely be sold in one outlet.

Some fear that in this new book world, the good old corner bookstore, whether chain or independent, will be overlooked. Independents, who have proved especially effective at doing what is after all the core of the business—selling books, particularly non-bestsellers—could wind up victims of the current oversaturation. Stretched thin already and without the financial resources of the chains, they may not be able be survive as the corporate titans battle fiercely with one another.

Looking for the Peace Dividend

Jim Milliot
Editor, Business and Finance, *Publishers Weekly*

The November settlement between the American Booksellers Association and Random House in the ABA's antitrust lawsuit filed against the largest trade house almost exactly one year ago means that for the first time in some 20 years the book publishing community is beginning a new year with no publishers involved in litigation with the American Booksellers Association or having the specter of a Federal Trade Commission (FTC) investigation hang over the industry. The FTC dismissed its 17-year investigation against six publishers in September without ruling on whether the publishers had violated the Robinson-Patman Act, leaving it to the ABA to "level the playing field."

From the ABA's point of view, the lawsuits and settlements reached in late 1995 and early 1996 achieved the goal of publishers adopting flatter discount schedules that put independent booksellers in a better competitive position not only with chain bookstores, but with other retailers that sell books. In addition, publishers involved in the lawsuits agreed to make any promotional allowances proportionally available to all competing customers eligible for such allowances. In agreeing to the settlements, which all feature a 10-year consent decree, publishers admitted to no wrongdoing.

A major difference between the agreements reached with the five publishers involved in the original ABA suit—Hugh Lauter Levin, Houghton Mifflin, Penguin USA, Rutledge Hill, and St. Martin's—and the Random House agreement is that the five publishers involved in the lawsuit had the terms of their discount policies spelled out in their respective consent decrees. Under its agreement, Random House will adhere to its already existing terms. But an important point gained in all settlements is that publishers' retail schedules treat bookstores, both independents and chains, in the same fashion that they treat nonbookstore retailers.

ABA executive director Bernie Rath estimated that with Putnam now falling under the consent decree with its acquisition by Penguin (which closed late in December), publishers that represent close to 40 percent of trade book sales will be covered by consent orders. "We may not be able to save all independents, but we've given them more revenue and a better chance to survive," Rath said. He noted that even publishers that are not subject to consent decrees have moved to flatter discount schedules, and that most publishers have a better understanding of the issues of discount schedules and promotional allowances.

Publishers are happy to have the litigation behind them and generally feel that their relationship with booksellers is good. John Sargent, president of St. Martin's Press, told *PW* that there "certainly is no ill will on our part. We are delighted to move forward in partnership." He noted that the settlements have created a more "structured" environment in which to work, but said he has no problems with the new terms. Jack Romanos, president of the Simon & Schuster consumer group, said the lawsuits and FTC investigation "never interfered with the company's day-to-day business." He described S&S's relationship with booksellers as "fine." Romanos acknowledged that while there continues to be "a tug between chains and independents, publishers need both to be successful."

Bantam Doubleday Dell spokesperson Stuart Applebaum called BDD's relationship with booksellers "reasonably positive and purposeful." He noted that even when BDD had disagreements with its customers, it was always able to discuss business. "Everyone realizes warfare is not going to do anyone any good," Applebaum said. Brenda Marsh, president of general book sales for Harper-Collins, said bookseller-publisher relations are better than a year ago. "Everyone is concentrating on their business realities, and publishers and retailers seem to have a healthier respect for each other's businesses," Marsh said.

Booksellers were of a slightly more mixed mind. Barbara Bonds Thomas, owner of Toad Hall Inc. in Texas and president of ABA, believes bookseller relationships with publishers have improved. She said that the publishers ABA has settled with are in constant communication with the association. And even more importantly, Thomas observed, "we all have the goal of selling as many books as possible." Bill Petrocelli, co-owner of Book Passage, said he was "guardedly optimistic" that independent booksellers' relationships with publishers will improve in 1997. Petrocelli noted that in theory the various settlements should improve the independents' chances for competing against the chains, but he added that the independent sector still appears to be losing market share. His strongest hope for improved relations with publishers is that he thinks some publishers "are finally showing some concern about the power of the chains, and are not thrilled with their growing domination. Some publishers are coming to the conclusion that they need the independents to give some balance."

ABA's Rath thinks the bookseller-publisher relationship is poor, although he does not feel the strain is due to the lawsuits. Rather, Rath believes the flashpoint has been the high rate of returns this year, with everybody looking for a scapegoat as to the cause. While some publishers blame bookstores, Rath feels the high rate of returns has been caused by a breakdown in the publishing economic model. According to Rath, more people are involved with the publishing process, each demanding a bigger piece of the pie. The problem is that publishers are finding themselves squeezed between demands from ownership for higher profit margins and higher advances for authors and larger commissions for agents. This situation forces publishers in turn to wring as much advantage as they can from booksellers. Rath feels the answer to the problem is a move to net pricing, which would permit publishers to set a price that would give them a profit, and give booksellers the opportunity to set prices based on market demand.

The breakdown in the economic model is seen by some as one reason why a growing number of publishers are pulling out of the BookExpo America (BEA, formerly ABA) convention. While some publishers (notably Penguin and Random House) withdrew from the convention in past years as a protest against the lawsuits, others have pulled out of the 1997 show for economic reasons. The list of those not attending BEA in 1997 includes a wide range of publishers: Random House, Bantam Doubleday Dell, Simon & Schuster, William Morrow, HarperCollins, Penguin USA, Houghton Mifflin, Farrar, Straus & Giroux, Kensington Publishing, Harvard University Press, and Oxford University Press. In pulling out of the show, many of the larger publishers said they felt the show was not cost effective, and that they would instead devote more resources to attending regional shows in the fall. Other publishers, however, made no assertion that they would give greater attention to the regionals, but found attending the BEA to simply be too expensive.

Many publishers who will not be attending BEA in 1997 said they would reevaluate attending in 1998. Some industry members feel that a number of publishers who have pulled out of the show have done so because they see it has an easy way to save some money in what has been a difficult year. Attending BEA can easily cost the larger publishers between $200,000 and $600,000. Many feel they can reach their customers without attending the show, and with independent booksellers becoming less important to publishers, the incentive to attend BEA is missing. For smaller and medium-sized publishers, however, attending BEA still provides the best opportunity to meet customers and even write some orders. But without the large publishers in attendance (and therefore few major authors, and probably fewer overseas visitors), the 1997 show will likely be quieter than in past years.

The directors of several regional bookselling associations are skeptical about seeing a large increase in publisher attendance at their 1997 shows. "There have been a number of publishers who haven't attended the national show in the past and they have never attended our show in greater numbers," Thom Chambliss, executive director of Pacific Northwest Booksellers Association, noted. If publishers are going to get more involved with the regionals, "it's not demonstrable yet," New England Booksellers Association executive director Rusty Drugan noted. Ginnie Thorpe, executive director of Norther California Independent Booksellers Association, told *PW* that it's "too early to tell" what the changes for the regional and national shows will be. "I don't think whatever is going to happen is going to all happen in 1997. This is an evolving process, and it could take several years for BookExpo to become what it will become."

The executive directors agreed that the regional shows and the national convention were never in competition with each other, but are designed to be complementary. "Regionals are not alternatives to the national show," Chambliss said. "Publishers do a good job promoting their titles locally at our show, but it is not a national networking opportunity." "You need both the regionals and the national convention," Thorpe agreed. Chambliss noted that he attends BookExpo America to look for speakers and authors for his two regional events and generally finds one-quarter to one-third of his speakers at BEA. If the major publishers aren't there with their authors, Chambliss expects he'll end up with authors from smaller houses, noting, "there is nothing wrong with that."

Chambliss maintained that the national show has never really been a place where orders were written. According to Chambliss, the major publishers usually sent few sales reps, instead sending public relations and rights people. Chambliss said he thinks the major publishers won't send sales reps to the national show because independents represent such a small percentage of their business. Drugan took a similar approach when talking about the future of the regionals. "The question that needs to be answered is how important do publishers think the bookstore market is, and how important is it for them to listen to their customers?"

What does this all mean for the future of BEA? Few publishers say they want to see the national show end, but agree that the show needs to be "reinvented." One publisher noted that "publishers became their own worst enemies in driving up the cost of attendance" by taking huge booths, engaging in expensive giveaways and throwing elaborate parties. With the costs increasing and fewer booksellers in attendance, "the lines crossed somewhere where going to BEA didn't make sense," this publisher said.

There was a consensus among other publishers contacted by *PW* that the most important thing the show organizers can do to lure companies back is to focus the convention more on business. "The days of going to BEA just because it's good public relations for the industry—and it *is* good PR for the industry—are gone," S&S's Romanos said. "You can't keep going back to the same well if it is not working." In addition to attracting more booksellers, Romanos thinks bringing in more aspects of the industry might make a workable fair.

St. Martin's John Sargent said he would be interested in returning to BEA "if there was less hoopla and more opportunities to do business." BDD's Applebaum told *PW* that BEA "wouldn't have to work very hard to interest us in thinking about returning," adding that BDD still is willing to support "an industry conclave."

For its part, ABA is still very much behind the convention, although Barbara Bonds Thomas acknowledged that things appear unsettled for the 1997 show. Nevertheless, Thomas said, "booksellers are always interested to see what's new." Attending the show also gives one a chance to "come up with new things serendipitously."

Settlement Terms with ABA

These are the terms of the November settlement of ABA's antitrust suit:

- Hugh Lauter Levin Associates—Sells all titles to independent bookstores on same terms as to other buyers. Settlement was early in litigation; no payment toward ABA's legal fees.
- Houghton Mifflin—Flat 47 percent discount on orders of 15 assorted copies. Removed distinction between trade and non-trade customers. Nonreturnable option available. Warehouse discount of an additional 2 percent for carton quantities shipped to a single location. Paid $275,000 toward ABA's legal fees.

- Penguin—Flat discount of 46 percent on minimum order of 10 assorted copies. Free freight continues. Nonreturnable discount available. 48 percent retail distribution center discount. Paid $450,000 toward ABA's legal fees.
- Rutledge Hill—47 percent discount on orders of 1–499; 48 percent discount on orders of 500 or more; 49 percent distribution center discount. Broadened definition of "retailer." Paid $60,000 toward ABA's legal fees.
- St. Martin's Press—46 percent discount on orders of 10 or more frontlist titles; 47 percent discount on backlist; distribution center discount of 48 percent for orders of 100–499, and 49 percent discount on orders of 500 or more frontlist titles; 49 percent discount on orders of 100–499, and a 50 percent discount on orders of 500 or more on backlist titles. Made nonreturnable option available. Paid $1.2 million toward ABA's legal fees.
- Random House—47 percent discount on orders of 25 assorted books to Selective Distribution customers; 45 percent discount for non-Selective Distribution customers; 50 percent nonreturnable option; 49 percent discount on qualifying Retail Distribution Center orders. All stores classified as "retailers." Settlement was early in second-phase litigation; no payment toward ABA's legal fees.

How the Winners Made It To the Top

Daisy Maryles
Executive Editor, *Publishers Weekly*

On the bestseller front, competition was even keener than in past years, especially for those publishers who depend on big books for their coffers and their stature. In a year in which returns kept rising for frontlist books (and even backlist returns intensified), publishers looked for some big windfalls to compensate for the shortfalls.

In hardcover fiction, veteran bestselling authors dominated; approximately 90 percent of the top fiction titles were by writers who have enjoyed bestsellerdom in previous years. Considering the ever-higher contracts that these authors command, this is a good thing. Still, many found themselves in the limelight for shorter periods of time than in previous years, and with even briefer stays at the top of the charts.

The nine books by writers with no time spent on the charts prior to 1996 included eight first novels, clearly indicating that it's often easier to get sales attention for a debut than for a second or third novel by a midlist author. The media certainly helped Anonymous's *Primary Colors* in its run: the considerable hoopla about which political insider wrote the seemingly authentic novel kept print and broadcast media buzzing for months in early 1996. For first-timers like Jacquelyn Mitchard and Jane Mendelsohn, it was Oprah and Don Imus who got them big attention for *The Deep End of the Ocean* and *I Was Amelia Earhart*, respectively. For Warner's two big buys—$2 million for David Baldacci's *Absolute Power* and $1 million for Nicholas Sparks's *The Notebook*—lots of media attention and well-executed pre- and post-publication marketing helped the books' landings and long runs. And at a time when shorter novels seem to have the sales edge, the 1,079-page, forbiddingly dense experimental novel *Infinite Jest* by David Foster Wallace was enough of an oddity to create a sales buzz.

Continuing a long-standing trend in bestselling nonfiction, the 1996 winners included books by and about people in the news, plus the ever-popular how-to category. But a disturbing reality, noted by publishing pundits, occurred frequently this past year: there is a shrinking window of opportunity for big nonfiction titles, especially those by and about celebrities. And, not surprisingly, these are the very titles for which publishers usually pay the big bucks. Autobiographies by Montel Williams and Brett Butler earned their publishers, Warner and Hyperion, respectively, only a one-week bestseller run each.

The O. J. Simpson trial inspired a large number of bestsellers and, perhaps, some of the year's bigger disasters. Christopher Darden's *In Contempt* clearly won the bestseller verdict with 20 weeks on the lists, six of them in first place. Robert Shapiro's five-week run for *In Search of Justice* may have been a bit too short to earn back its seven-figure advance. But Johnnie Cochran's *Journey to Justice* never even got a chance to travel on the national bestseller charts to help sell its 500,000-copy first printing.

Oprah's Magic Touch

Each year, we note the importance of the media, especially broadcast, in making a bestseller. One of the most influential members of the media has been Oprah Winfrey. But in 1996 her influence became the headline story. A look at the charts for just one week indicates her colossal impact on a book's ascendence: back on November 11, all of the number-one titles on *PW*'s four lists were there because of Oprah. In fiction, *The Deep End of the Ocean* knocked Stephen King off the charts after Oprah chose it as the first selection for her on-air reading club—total in print quickly climbed from 100,000 copies to 640,000. In nonfiction, *The Soul's Code* by James Hillman even knocked Oprah's own *Make the Connection* off the number-one spot; the book went from 45,000 copies to almost 200,000 in a few weeks. Toni Morrison's *Song of Solmon* jumped onto the trade paper list when it was announced as the second book for Oprah's reading program. Plume rushed an additional 540,000 copies to the stores. And *The Rules* led the mass market list; an Oprah appearance deserves the lion's share of credit for its run at the top of the charts during the very busy final two months of the year.

Comparing the Numbers

In 1996, 308 titles hit the bestseller charts for the first time. This was a bit less than in 1995 and 1994, when the final tally was 317 and 310, respectively. The only list that gained new members was mass market, where 113 books landed, a bit better than the 109 in 1995. In fiction, there were 85 novels debuting on the charts, three less than in 1995 but five more than in 1994. In nonfiction, there were 63 new players, compared to 68 in 1995 and 60 in 1994.

Since 1993 the number of trade paperbacks that get on *PW*'s weekly lists has been in a downward spiral. The numbers have gone from 60 in 1993 to 55 in 1994 and 52 in 1995. This past year, that trend continues, with only 47 books making a first appearance on the charts. Much of this downward slope can be ascribed to the longevity that certain books enjoy on this list; last year there were nine books that had runs of more than six months, and four of them were fixtures on the trade list.

There is both good news and bad news in the analysis of how many books landed the top slot on the charts during 1996. The good news is that 51 books, a new record, had a shot at the number-one position in the course of the year. In hardcover, 14 fiction titles and 14 nonfiction books—again, the highest figures ever—made it to number one.

The bad news? It was also the first time that not one of these titles enjoyed a double-digit run. The best was nine weeks at the top for any hardcover and only two books reached that number—*Primary Colors* by Anonymous (aka Joe Klein) and *Make the Connection* by Bob Greene and Oprah Winfrey. Contrast that with how well Oprah's personal chef, Rosie Daley, did back in 1994 when *In the Kitchen with Rosie* had a 20-week run in the number-one position. John Grisham's *The Runaway Jury* had a seven-week run in the number-one slot. The only other hardcover bestseller that performed better was Dennis Rodman, whose *Bad as I Wanna Be* had an eight-week run in the number-one spot.

In mass market there were also 14 books that made it to the top (the same number as in the previous two years), but six of those were the installments for Stephen King's serial novel *The Green Mile*. The only book that had a double-digit run was John Grisham's *The Runaway Jury,* with 12 weeks. While the author also enjoyed one more week in the lead with the movie tie-in edition of *A Time to Kill*, Grisham was not the author who dominated the number-one slot. That feat was left to King as *Green Mile*'s six titles enjoyed the number-one position for 22 weeks. The only other mass title to get the lead slot for more than a month in the course of 1996 was *The Rules* by Ellen Fein and Sherrie Schneider.

In trade there were nine books that enjoyed a run in the number-one spot, most for only one or two weeks. That was because the dominant player was the acclaimed literary novel *Snow Falling on Cedars* by David Guterson. One of three trade paperbacks to achieve a spot on the list every week throughout the course of last year, it hogged the number-one position for a whopping 35 weeks. The next best performer was Toni Morrison's *Song of Solomon,* in the lead for five weeks.

The Big Seven

For the last four years we have been tracking how much bestseller clout is wielded by the seven publishing conglomerates. In analyzing the 1996 number, the answer would be a lot. In hardcover, the mighty seven held 87.9 percent of all available spots on the hardcover weekly charts, a record number, overtaking the 1993 record of 85.8 percent.

For paperbacks, the same group of publishers had 80 percent of the available slots, a number that is lower than in the three years prior to 1996. But on the trade list there are two niche players—Health Communications and Andrews & McMeel—that once again had a stellar year; their combined tally added up to 11 percent (so that means there were eight corporations taking 91 percent of all trade paper spots). Health's four Chicken Soup titles took up 12.4 percent of all available slots on the trade list. Andrews & McMeel owned the humor category in trade paper; in the last 12 months eight such titles made it onto the weekly charts for a total of 75 weeks, accounting for 9.6 percent of trade paper slots.

In assessing which publishing empires are garnering the largest percentage of bestseller chart territory, the leader continues to be Random House Inc. In the last four years, it has had the highest share of hardcover bestseller slots, and, except for 1995 when it was bested by Bantam Doubleday Dell, the Random House paperback imprints also led on that side of the ledger sheet. Random House improved its paperback share this past year by almost eight percentage points. Much of that gain can be credited to the stellar performance of Vintage; its nine titles on the trade paperback list had a combined run of 125 weeks, enough to grab a 16.2 percent share of available spots in trade paper. Random didn't fare as well in the hardcover sweepstakes, where it lost almost 9 percent of its share of the weekly slots and had its worst performance since we began these calculations in 1993. Perhaps some of this loss was due to a slower year for Knopf in 1996; its tally for 1996 was 16 books with a total of 105 weeks on *PW*'s weekly charts, down quite a bit from 1995, when it had 23 books on the weekly bestseller charts for a total of 204 weeks.

The other publishing conglomerate to lose some percentage points this past year was Simon & Schuster. Its 11.3 percent of hardcover bestseller slots and 11.8 percent of paperback slots were the publisher's lowest in the last four years. The drop was more significant in softcover; S&S had fewer trade paperbacks with long tenures on the charts. In 1996 the perennial bestselling 7 *Habits of Highly Effective People* was the only S&S bestseller to enjoy a run of more than 15 weeks on the 1996 charts; in 1995, the firm's trade paper imprints Fireside and Touchstone had three on the "Longest-Running" charts (7 *Habits*, plus *The Shipping News* and *Driven to Distraction*).

The other five publishers that dominated the bestseller charts all had gains in their share of paper or hardcover spots and two—Penguin USA and Time Warner—gained in bestseller share for both paper and hardcover. Warner certainly increased the number of bestsellers on the charts in 1996, going from a cloth/paper total of 16 in 1995 to 23 books last year. And 1996 marked the house's first long-tenured nonfiction bestseller since 1986; that year it was Harvey and Marilyn Diamond's *Fit for Life*; this time it was Sarah Ban Breathnach's *Simple Abundance*.

The publisher with the largest increase in market share for both paper and hard was Penguin USA. The publisher can credit just about its entire 6.3 percent gain in paper to King's *The Green Mile*. Signet's masterful distribution and marketing of its signature author amounted to a total run of 89 weeks for the books, with all but the sixth title enjoying double-digit tenures on the weekly charts. If you factor in the eight weeks King's *Rose Madder* spent on the weekly charts, the author's books had a total of 97 weeks on the mass market charts, amounting to a 12.4 percent share. That's a higher percentage than any mass paperback imprint garnered for all of its authors combined.

Next year, the big players decrease with the merger of Penguin/Putnam. A strong year for the new corporation could easily put it in the number-two position for paperback share of market and perhaps number-two, more likely number-three, for hardcover. But anything goes in this high-stakes deep-pocket game. And there is always the Oprah factor, which can turn the tide for any given book in just one hour of airtime. Other developments, as yet unknown, can also have a significant impact at the cash registers. Call this *The X-Files* meets The $ Files.

Federal Agency and Federal Library Reports

National Commission on Libraries and Information Science

1110 Vermont Ave. N.W., Suite 820, Washington, DC 20005-3522
202-606-9200; fax 202-606-9203
World Wide Web: http://www.nclis.gov

Jane Williams
Research Associate

Highlights of the Year

Jeanne Hurley Simon continued as chairperson of the National Commission on Libraries and Information Science (NCLIS) and Peter R. Young continued as executive director. Nominated in late 1995 by President Clinton, Abe Abramson of Montana and LeVar Burton of California were confirmed as commissioners by the Senate in 1996. They replaced Barbara J. H. Taylor and Kay Riddle, respectively.

Diane Frankel, director of the new Institute of Museum and Library Services, became the 16th commissioner with September 30 legislation (P.L. 104-208). Her position is as an ex officio, nonvoting commissioner.

In December President Clinton announced his intent to nominate Jose-Marie Griffiths to the commission. A well-known and respected information scientist, Dr. Griffiths is the University of Michigan's Chief Information Officer. Previous positions include director of the School of Information Sciences, University of Tennessee–Knoxville, and vice president of King Research, Inc.

Continuing commissioners are NCLIS Vice Chair Martha Gould, Joan Challinor, Mary Furlong, Frank Lucchino, Bobby Roberts, Gary Sudduth, Joel Valdez, and Robert Willard. Winston Tabb represents James H. Billington, the Librarian of Congress, a permanent NCLIS member. The terms of Shirley Adamovich and Carol DiPrete expired in July, but they continue to serve until successors are confirmed, or until July 1997.

In some respects 1996 was an active and event-filled year. First, NCLIS celebrated its 25th anniversary. Second, the commission was fully involved in three major program areas: libraries and the Internet/National Information Infrastructure, policy for disseminating federal information, and the proposed Library

Services and Technology Act (LSTA). NCLIS also established a Web site to disseminate information—including the contents of its reports—electronically.

In other respects fiscal year (FY) 1996 was difficult and uncertain, with over half the year under continuing resolutions and an 8 percent budget reduction. The commission met only twice and other activity and initiatives were restricted as well.

FY 1996 ended on an upbeat note, however. September 30 brought a budget of $897,000 for FY 1997 (the same as for FY 1995). Also, the new Museum and Library Services Act was in the omnibus spending bill, making important changes in federal programs for libraries and making NCLIS responsible for advising on the programs. NCLIS commissioners and staff advised on the transition and planned for longer-range work with the director of the Institute of Museum and Library Services (IMLS). The commission's responsibility for general policy advice on LSTA was a major topic at its December 1996 meeting.

Support for Executive and Legislative Branches

In 1996 NCLIS advised on major issues of federal policy concerning libraries and information services: federal support for libraries as proposed in LSTA and IMLS copyright/intellectual property access to government information.

NCLIS had frequent contact in 1996 with the Senate Labor Committee and the House Economic and Educational Opportunities Committee on bills incorporating LSTA and IMLS. NCLIS's consultation on the Workforce Development Act (S. 682) and the CAREERS Act (H.R. 1617) was the most extensive of any with Congress in recent years.

There was much activity late in the legislative session to see if the library portions of the bills could be introduced and passed separately. The library sections were incorporated in the omnibus spending bill for FY 1997 (H.R. 3610), passed September 30, 1996, and signed by the president that same day (P.L. 104-208).

LSTA consolidates library funds for technology and services, retains state-based programs for most of the funds, and removes federal targeting of funds for public libraries. The law itself states no priorities among the purposes it serves. The law moves administration of LSTA programs and money from the Department of Education to the new IMLS, to which NCLIS is to provide general policy advice.

In other legislative matters, Chairperson Simon testified before the House Judiciary Committee's Courts and Intellectual Property Subcommittee on copyright as provided for in H.R. 2441, the National Information Infrastructure (NII) Copyright Protection Act of 1996. In June she testified before the Senate Rules and Administration Committee on access to government information in the 21st century. Plans proceeded for NCLIS-led and joint initiatives on public access to government information. One such initiative is with the Government Printing Office, for an NCLIS-directed study regarding standards for government information in electronic formats.

The commission also commented to the House Commerce Committee on the Communications Decency Act provisions of the Telecommunications Act of

1966 and endorsed the recommendation of the NII Advisory Council regarding free speech in a digital environment. NCLIS objected to S. 1961's provision to move the Copyright Office from the Library of Congress to a U.S. Intellectual Property Organization.

NCLIS commented on the Telecommunications Act, the CAREERS Act, and the National Technical Information Service to the Legislative Reference Division in the Office of Management and Budget. Commissioners and staff met, consulted, and cooperated with officials in such other departments and agencies as the Department of Commerce and the National Archives and Records Administration.

As usual, NCLIS related to various offices and functions in the Department of Education. The commission commented on the Office of Educational Research and Improvement's draft of research priorities plan, the National Library of Education's roles and responsibilities, and the proposed replacements for the Library Services and Construction Act (LSCA). The commission and the National Center for Education Statistics cooperatively operated the Library Statistics Program. NCLIS also kept in contact with the National Institute for Postsecondary Education, Libraries, and Lifelong Learning.

Library and Information Services in a Networked Environment

In August 1996 the commission published a new research report, *The 1996 National Survey of Public Libraries and the Internet: Progress and Issues*. This survey was the third NCLIS-sponsored study of public libraries and the Internet. The 1996 edition was done in part to gain longitudinal data on public libraries' Internet connectivity. Findings are summarized as follows:

- Overall increase of 113 percent (from 20.9 percent to 44.6 percent) in public library Internet connectivity since 1994
- Differences in connectivity with respect to size of population served
- Significant regional differences
- No plans to connect to the Internet in the next 12 months for 39.6 percent of the 55.4 percent of public libraries without Internet connections, with those serving smaller populations less likely to be planning connections in the next year
- The chance that public library Internet connectivity could exceed 60 percent by 1997
- Differences related to the extent, type, and costs of connectivity and to the provision of public access to the Internet
- The possibility that public libraries serving 25,000 or fewer are the only public Internet access available to a community

In a "Progress and Issues" section, the authors identified issues for further discussion, including the remaining disparities, connectivity versus services, the goal of universal service, quality of network services, life cycle of public library Internet development, and preparing for the next survey. NCLIS will cooperate with the American Library Association and others to sponsor a 1997 study of public libraries' Internet connections and services.

NCLIS used the results of its 1994 and 1996 public library/Internet studies to advise the Federal Communications Commission on universal service provisions for libraries. NCLIS filed three sets of comments, on May 7, August 2, and December 19. With the American Library Association, NCLIS planned and carried out a forum on affordable telecommunications rates for libraries; the forum was held in New York City on July 8.

The commission conducted a hearing, "Libraries, Interactive Services, and the Information Superhighway," July 22, 1996, in San Diego, where it met in conjunction with the conference of the Interactive Services Association. Witnesses included corporate representatives and library supporters, directors, and librarians, along with local officials. Many testified to libraries' important role as information equalizers for access to interactive services.

NCLIS spent much time in 1996 preparing to lead a study for the Government Printing Office (GPO) on standards for creating and disseminating government information in electronic formats. In a June 1996 report, GPO noted that a successful transition to a more electronic Federal Depository Library Program depends in part on more information about agencies' publishing plans, the cost-effectiveness of various formats, and the standards used in and out of the federal government. Through an interagency agreement with GPO and using its contracting authority, NCLIS will be responsible for assessing standards to facilitate improved public access to government information. It is expected the agreement will be signed and work begun early in 1997.

Commissioners discussed with legislative and executive officials the need for a broader policy study of federal government printing and publishing—in other words, the federal government's information policy regarding its own information.

Library Statistics

For the ninth consecutive year NCLIS and the National Center for Education Statistics (NCES) operated the Library Statistics Program through a memorandum of understanding. A small task force of experts was established and met in the fall of 1996 to advise on output measures for electronic library services.

Data for FY 1994, from the first national statistical survey of state library agencies, were published in FY 1996, and FY 1995 data were collected. A steering committee recommended revisions and improvements for these annual data collections.

A national survey of library cooperatives was prepared. Cooperatives include library networks, systems, and consortia with formal arrangements to support library and information services for the mutual benefit of participating libraries. A universe file of library cooperatives was compiled and a survey instrument drafted.

For the seventh consecutive year, data on public libraries were collected, reviewed, and distributed. The 1994 data were collected in the summer of 1995 and distributed in paper and electronic forms in late 1996. The annual workshop for state data coordinators for public library data was held in March 1996.

Academic library data are collected biennially as part of the Integrated Postsecondary Data System. The American Library Association's Office for Research and Statistics and a committee of academic library specialists advises NCLIS and NCES on improving the biennial survey. A training workshop on academic library statistics for state library representatives and institution coordinators was held in September.

On May 20 and 21, 1996, NCLIS and NCES cosponsored the fourth annual Forum on Library and Information Services Policy, "The Impact of Information Technology and Special Programming on Library Services to Special Populations." Highlights are on NCLIS's Web site. The forums' objectives are to ensure that statistics about libraries and information services meet the needs of policymakers and to help guide development of public policy on libraries and information services.

International Activities

The commission completed its 11th year of cooperation with the Department of State to coordinate and monitor proposals for International Contributions for Scientific, Educational, and Cultural Activities (ICSECA) funds and to disburse the funds. The allocation for ICSECA, included in the State Department's International Organizations and Programs account, was formerly under International Conventions and Scientific Organizations Contributions (ICSOC). The amount decreased from $175,000 in FY 1995 to $35,000 for FY 1996.

NCLIS was not represented at the summer 1996 meeting of the International Federation of Library Associations (IFLA) in Beijing. The commission did, however, continue to host sessions to orient and share information with librarians and other officials visiting the United States, usually under the auspices of the U.S. Information Agency or Meridian House International. In 1996 visitors were from Australia, China, France, Germany, Nigeria, Romania, Singapore, South Africa, Turkey, and Venezuela.

25th Anniversary

The official anniversary was from July 20, 1995, the anniversary of enactment of NCLIS's enabling legislation (P.L. 91-345), to September 21, 1996, the anniversary of the first meeting of the commission.

In April 1996 the commission announced the winners of 25 Silver Awards, given to celebrate NCLIS's 25th anniversary and to honor representatives of all the people who have made noteworthy and sustained contributions to the strength of libraries and information services in the past 25 years at the national, state, or local levels.

The awards were presented, to the extent possible, at events of the award winners' choosing. Eleven were presented at the July 1996 American Library Association conference in New York City; others were awarded at state or local events.

To close the anniversary celebration, in September NCLIS announced a second set of Silver Awards to former NCLIS commissioners and staff and to one U.S. Senator, Mark Hatfield of Oregon.

Publications

Annual Report 1994-1995.

Bertot, John Carlo, Charles R. McClure, and Douglas L. Zweizig. *The 1996 National Survey of Public Libraries and the Internet: Progress and Issues.*

Paper copies of the above are available free of charge from the NCLIS office. These and other reports are also available on the commission's Web site at http://www.nclis.gov. The following are available only on the Web site:

Hearing on Libraries and Interactive Services on the Information Superhighway July 22, 1996, San Diego, CA

Proceedings of the Library and Information Services Policy Forum (May 19–20, 1996)

Young, Peter R. "Librarianship: A Changing Profession." *Daedalus* (Fall 1996), 103–125.

National Technical Information Service

Technology Administration
U.S. Department of Commerce, Springfield, VA 22161
703-487-4650
World Wide Web: http://www.NTIS.gov

Janet E. Wooding
Writer/Editor
Marketing Communications

The National Technical Information Service (NTIS), a relatively small government organization, located on the outskirts of Washington, D.C., proudly serves as the nation's largest central resource and primary disseminator of information produced by the U.S. government and by worldwide, primarily governmental, sources. NTIS collects scientific, technical, engineering, and business-related information, then organizes, maintains, and disseminates that information in a variety of formats. NTIS is a key participant in the world of information exchange and is the United States' partner for prosperity.

The mission of NTIS is to improve the efficiency and effectiveness of the U.S. research and development enterprise; increase productivity and innovation in the United States; and increase U.S. competitiveness in the global economy. The public can be assured of the availability of the most current information on numerous subjects.

Although categorized as a government agency by its mere creation and the terms of its mission, NTIS operates very much like a private business and is somewhat unusual in that it pays its own way. NTIS is a self-supporting federal agency within the Technology Administration of the Department of Commerce. All costs associated with operating NTIS are paid for by revenue generated from the sale of the products and services it offers. Therefore, costs and the continuing operation of NTIS are considered when setting prices. NTIS's goal is to set the most reasonable prices possible for its products and services.

The vast NTIS collection of nearly three million titles contains products available in various formats. The information in its collection includes reports describing research conducted or sponsored by federal agencies and their contractors; statistical and business information; U.S. military publications; audiovisual products; computer software and electronic databases developed by federal agencies; and technical reports prepared by research organizations worldwide. Approximately 100,000 new titles are added and indexed into the NTIS collection annually. A permanent repository is maintained of all material available for sale to its customers.

NTIS recognizes the evolution taking place in the "electronic world" and the needs of the people who reside in it. Today's rapid advances in technology allow more information to be processed at a much greater speed than previously. Users of this information may want or need to locate, access, and receive it in a much different way than tradition dictates. To accommodate the requirements of all of its customers, NTIS continues as a key participant in the electronic arena.

U.S. Government Contributors

More than 200 U.S. government agencies contribute to the NTIS collection, including the National Aeronautics and Space Administration, the Environmental Protection Agency, the National Institute of Standards and Technology, the National Institutes of Health, and the Departments of Agriculture, Commerce, Defense, Energy, Health and Human Services, Interior, Labor, Treasury, Veterans Affairs, Housing and Urban Development, Education, and Transportation. Numerous independent agencies also contribute.

The American Technology Preeminence Act (ATPA) of 1991 (P.L. 102-245) requires all federal agencies to submit their federally funded unclassified scientific, technical, and engineering information products to NTIS within 15 days of the date the product is made publicly available. With the passage of this act, NTIS's wealth of information increased dramatically. NTIS is now able to provide its customers with timely access to a more diverse and practical range of information.

The primary purposes of ATPA are to help U.S. industries accelerate the development of new processes and products and to help the United States maintain a leading economically competitive position worldwide. Under ATPA, information products include technical reports, articles, papers, and books; regulations, standards, and specifications; charts, maps, and graphs; software, data collection, datafiles, and data compilations software; audio and video products; technology application assessments; training packages; and other federally owned or originated technologies.

Worldwide Source Contributors

NTIS is a leading U.S. government agency in international technical and business information exchange. It actively acquires and distributes valuable information produced by a large number of international government departments and other organizations. In 1996 approximately one-fourth of NTIS's total product offerings came from worldwide sources.

NTIS continues to negotiate agreements to improve the coverage of reports from major industrialized countries, as well as from newly industrialized countries producing advanced technologies. NTIS focuses its acquisition efforts on topics of major interest to NTIS customers.

NTIS National Audiovisual Center

In late 1994 the National Audiovisual Center (NAC) joined NTIS to consolidate most of the U.S. government's activities in the duplication of audio, visual, and multimedia products. This merger provides the opportunity to make federally produced media products available to a wider audience.

NAC's collection includes approximately 9,000 active titles covering 600 subject areas from more than 200 federal agencies. Included in the collection are language training materials, occupational safety and health training materials, fire service training materials, drug education programs for schools and industry, travelogues, fine-arts programs, and documentaries chronicling American history.

Award-winning World War II films from many of Hollywood's most celebrated directors are included in the NAC collection. *December 7th—Long Version* is the full-length version of John Ford's *December 7th*. This film, made in collaboration with famed cinematographer Gregg Toland, explores the history and re-creates the events of the attack on Pearl Harbor in 1941. A shorter version was made and won an Academy Award for Best Short Documentary. Another important film in NTIS's NAC collection is one entitled *The Negro Soldier*, directed by Frank Capra and Stuart Heisler, which shows the enormous contributions and sacrifices made by African Americans in all of our nation's armed conflicts from 1776 to 1944.

Videos on current concerns cover such topics as AIDS. For example, *Nobody's Immune* is a color video by the Walter Reed Institute of Research, Department of the Army, that discusses how AIDS can be contracted and the impact it has on the lives of the patient and the patient's family. *Olga's Story* is about one woman's personal experience with AIDS, how she contracted it, and how it is affecting her life and her family's. The video is also available in Spanish. *At Home with AIDS* was produced by a VA Medical Center and provides help to caregivers of HIV-positive patients.

FedWorld, the NTIS Online Information Network

In 1992 NTIS began experimenting with online information dissemination and created FedWorld to test customer reaction to this type of service. As a result of overwhelming demand, FedWorld—which provides a user-friendly, central electronic resource for government information—has become a central and growing component of the suite of information dissemination services NTIS offers to the public. FedWorld recognizes the fact that there still are many people without sophisticated technology and the luxury of being able to access the Internet. Currently serving more than 25,000 customers daily, FedWorld offers a choice of user platforms: dial-up, file transfer protocol, and the World Wide Web. Anyone with a computer and a modem can access valuable government information.

As demand for government information increases, so too does the need for government entities to make their information readily available. FedWorld offers solutions for those agencies that do not have the know-how or that have limited funding to disseminate information electronically to the American public.

The NTIS Online Information Network provides a free, seamless channel of access to several hundred U.S. government computer systems.

To connect to FedWorld by modem: Set modem parity to none, data bits to 8, and stop bit to 1. Set terminal emulation to ANSI. Set duplex to full. Then set communication software to dial FedWorld at 703-321-3339.

To connect to FedWorld via the Internet: Telnet to fedworld.gov. For Internet file transfer protocol services, connect to ftp.fedworld.gov. For World Wide Web services, point the Web browser to http://www.fedworld.gov.

FedWorld access is free. For more information on FedWorld, call 703-487-4223.

NTIS on the World Wide Web

The World Wide Web serves as an ideal armchair access point for customers to easily and quickly identify and order information available from NTIS. Because the NTIS collection is large and varied (nearly three million titles), NTIS created a product-oriented site for specific needs. Users can easily browse for government-produced information—from U.S. and worldwide sources—on such high-interest subjects such as business, environment, health and safety, and more. Or if interests are broader, simply click on links to other pages on the NTIS Web site. Currently, the NTIS Web site is organized into 11 core areas: Products, Information Tools, News, Search, Our Organization, Services for Federal Agencies, FedWorld, Ordering, Catalogs, Comments, and About This Site.

Information on the NTIS Web site (http://www.NITIS.gov) is accessible from multiple points. New-product information, for example, is available directly from the Product Announcements section under News and through the Business, Environment, and Health and Safety pages via our Products section. Users can also browse Special-Interest Collections and Featured Products and access catalogs from the Business, Environment, and Health and Safety pages. NTIS's most requested catalogs can be viewed online or downloaded by way of the core Catalogs link. A list of key telephone numbers and corporate information can be reached through both the Our Organization and the Comments sections. The Services for Federal Agencies link points federal agencies to a multitude of support services offered by NTIS. The FedWorld link is a central electronic resource for locating and acquiring government information. About This Site provides a site map for easy navigation.

NTIS Order Now Catalog on CD-ROM

As publishing environments change, so too must NTIS. Over the past several years, production, printing, and postage costs for the popular *Government Reports Announcements and Index* have skyrocketed. To keep this product accessible to its customers, NTIS needed to find an affordable solution to the high cost of print dissemination. As a result, NTIS developed the *NTIS Order Now Catalog on CD-ROM* as an alternative to the printed *Index*.

The NTIS Order Now CD-ROM offers quick and easy searching for novice, intermediate, and expert users. With the NTIS Order Now CD-ROM, customers can quickly identify and purchase valuable government research findings added to the NTIS collection within the previous two years. The CD-ROM gives descriptions of more than 100,000 quality products and provides a built-in ordering module. Each user can electronically fill in an order form and fax or e-mail it to NTIS.

Developed in cooperation with the National Information Services Corporation (NISC), the user-friendly NTIS Order Now CD-ROM includes NISC's powerful ROMWright software, supporting novice, intermediate, and expert searchers. NTIS Order Now CD-ROM requires a 386 (or higher) IBM-compatible computer.

NTIS Order Now CD-ROM is affordably priced: single issue, order number SUB-5398LOS, $39 plus handling; $78 plus handling outside the United States, Canada, and Mexico; one-year subscription with quarterly updates for customers in the United States, Canada, and Mexico, order number SUB-5398LOS, $124; $248 for all other subscribers (prices are subject to change). To subscribe, call the NTIS Subscriptions Department at 703-487-4630.

NTIS Order Now Online

It's easy to find out what has been recently added to the NTIS collection. NTIS offers a free, convenient online service called NTIS Order Now Online. Via the World Wide Web, this service allows users to quickly locate and purchase the most recent products added to the NTIS collection. One can access NTIS Order Now Online at http://www.ntis.gov/order now.

Secure Online Ordering Via the Internet

NTIS understands the concerns a customer may have about security when placing an order on the Internet and encourages customers to register their credit card at NTIS, thus avoiding the need to send an account number with each order. To register, customers should call 703-487-4682 and leave their card number and expiration date, and we will automatically charge their card when their e-mail order is processed. Orders may be placed through the Internet 24 hours a day.

The NTIS Database

The NTIS Database (listings of information products acquired by NTIS since 1964) offers unparalleled bibliographic coverage of U.S. government and worldwide government-sponsored research. Its contents represent hundreds of billions of research dollars and covers a range of important topics, including agriculture, biotechnology, business, communication, energy, engineering, the environment, health and safety, medicine, research and development, science, space, technology, transportation, and much more.

Each year, NTIS adds approximately 100,000 new entries (most including abstracts) to the NTIS Database. Database summaries describe technical reports, datafiles, audiovisuals, and software. These titles are often unique to NTIS and generally are not available from any other source. Whether you are looking for information about state-of-the-art technology or practical applied research or you want to learn about available government-sponsored software, the NTIS Database is your answer. It provides instant access to approximately 1.8 million records.

The NTIS Database is available through several commercial services or can be leased directly from NTIS. The commercial vendors are

DATA-STAR	800-221-7754
DIALOG	800-334-2564
European Space Agency	39-6-9418-0777

Ovid Technologies, Inc. 800-950-2035
Questel-Orbit, Inc. 800-456-7248
SilverPlatter Information, Inc. 800-343-0064
STN International/CAS 800-848-6533

To lease the NTIS Database directly from NTIS, contact the Office of Product Management at 703-487-4929.

Federal Research in Progress Database

As the U.S. government's central technical and scientific information service, NTIS is responsible for providing access to summaries of current and ongoing projects via the Federal Research in Progress (FEDRIP) database. FEDRIP provides advance information about the more than 150,000 research projects currently under way. The U.S. government funds billions of dollars for R&D and engineering programs annually. The ongoing research announced in FEDRIP is an important component of the technology transfer process in the United States.

The FEDRIP database focuses on health, physical sciences, agriculture, engineering, and life sciences. There are many reasons to search FEDRIP: to avoid research duplication, locate sources of support, identify leads in the literature, stimulate ideas for planning, identify gaps in areas of investigation, and locate individuals with expertise.

For more information, contact the NTIS Office of Product Management at 703-487-4929.

World News Connection

The World News Connection (WNC) is an NTIS online news service accessible via the World Wide Web. WNC was developed as a companion news source to help individuals obtain information they could not find elsewhere, particularly in English. WNC provides English-language translations of time-sensitive news and information from thousands of non-U.S. media sources.

Particularly effective in its coverage of local media sources, WNC enables users to identify what is really happening in a specific country or region. Compiled from such non-U.S. media sources as speeches, television and radio broadcasts, newspaper articles, periodicals, and books, the information covers significant socioeconomic, political, scientific, technical, and environmental issues and events.

The information in WNC is provided to NTIS by the Foreign Broadcast Information Service (FBIS), a U.S. government agency. For more than 50 years, analysts from FBIS's domestic and overseas bureaus have monitored timely and pertinent open-source material, including "gray literature." Uniquely, WNC allows subscribers to take advantage of the intelligence-gathering experience of FBIS.

The information in WNC is obtained from full texts and summaries of newspaper articles, conference proceedings, television and radio broadcasts, periodicals, and nonclassified technical reports. New information is entered into WNC every government-business day. Generally, new information is available within 48 to 72 hours from the time of original publication or broadcast.

WNC incorporates a powerful search engine designed to make it easy for subscribers to get to the information they want regardless of their online search skills. Subscribers can conduct unlimited interactive searches and can set up automated searches known as profiles. When a profile is created, a search is run against WNC's latest news feed to identify articles relevant to a subscriber's topic of interest. Once the search is completed, the results are automatically sent to the subscriber's Internet e-mail address. Additionally, anyone who receives profile results does not even have to log into WNC to view the articles. Profiles can help reduce the amount of time spent on research activities and are useful for tracking the latest international news and information. Users also can change their profiles at any time.

WNC is a valuable research tool for anyone who needs to monitor non-U.S. media sources. For additional information on WNC's individual pricing and subscription plans, connect to the WNC Web site at http://wnc.fedworld.gov or call NTIS Fax Direct at 703-487-4140 and enter product code 8645.

NTIS Alerts

More than 1,600 new titles are added to the NTIS collection every week. *NTIS Alerts* were developed in response to requests from customers to search this new source of information. NTIS prepares a list of search criteria that is run against all new studies and R&D reports in 16 subject areas. An *NTIS Alert* provides a twice-monthly information briefing service covering a wide range of technology topics. It is an efficient, economical, and timely way to stay in touch with the latest information in your field of interest. A subscription to the *NTIS Alert* provides numerous benefits:

- Access to the latest U.S. government technical studies
- Concise, easy-to-read summaries
- Information not readily available from any other source
- Contributions from more than 100 countries
- Subheadings within each copy designed to identify essential information quickly

Published Searches

Published Searches are bibliographies that provide the most current research data available from both the U.S. government and worldwide sources. Each Published Search contains the 50 to 250 most recent abstracts of reports and studies on a given topic. An emphasis is placed on (but not limited to) scientific, technical, and engineering information. Materials dealing with business, law, security issues, manufacturing, mathematical sciences, and much more are also available.

Published Searches are jointly produced through an agreement between NTIS and NERAC, Inc. With this agreement, NTIS and NERAC can provide abstracts of completed research literature derived from one of approximately 40 specialty databases. With each Published Search order, a new database search is run and an updated bibliography is produced.

Published Searches are available in paper copy or microfiche. For a listing of over 2,000 Published Search titles, view or download a copy of the *Published Search Master Catalog* (PR-186) from the Web address http://www.ntis.gov/pubscrch.htm or by calling the NTIS sales desk at 703-487-4650.

Continuous Acquisition and Life-Cycle Support Information Center

The NTIS Continuous Acquisition and Life-Cycle Support (CALS) Information Center is the largest single resource for current and historic hard-copy and electronic CALS and related-topic reports from international government and industry sources.

CALS was originally conceived by the U.S. Department of Defense and private industry as a strategy to streamline acquisition of weapons systems. It has since become a major government and industry initiative to speed the transition from a paper-intensive environment to a highly automated and integrated operation.

The CALS Information Center was formed at NTIS in 1991 to provide a public resource of CALS and CALS-related information. The center hosts a large inventory of CALS information products, including standards and specifications, technical reports, and training materials, in both hard copy and electronic formats. From the early days of the CALS initiative to today's most recent test reports and standards, the CALS Information Center represents a publicly available repository of CALS and related reports from domestic and international government and industry sources.

The CALS Information Center home page on the World Wide Web is accessible at http://www.fedworld.gov/edicals/calsinfo.html. From here, users can learn more about the center, access the electronic library via Telnet to FedWorld or file transfer protocol (ftp) to the CALS or the CALS-STD Libraries, or send e-mail directly to the manager of the CALS Information Center.

The electronic collection is available on the CALS electronic bulletin board (BBS) on FedWorld. To access the CALS BBS and online collection via dial-up or Telnet, users must first connect from the FedWorld main menu and type "/go cals" at the prompt.

The EC/EDI and CALS Resource Locator Web Page is intended to help users identify, locate, and link to Internet World Wide Web, ftp, gopher, Telnet, and mailing lists relating to Electronic Commerce, Electronic Data Interchange and CALS information sites. The Web address is http://www.fedworld.gov/edicals/locator.html.

NTIS Fax Direct

Information on NTIS products or services is also available by fax through NTIS Fax Direct, a free information service that distributes directly to the user's fax machine subject-specific listings of NTIS's most frequently requested titles, detailed product descriptions for those products, and general information on NTIS services and events. Call NTIS Fax Direct at 703-487-4300 and follow the voice prompts to receive requested information within minutes.

Premier Customer Service

Newly installed automated systems at NTIS have achieved dramatic improvements in the service provided to customers. Electronic document storage is now fully integrated with NTIS's order-taking process, which allows NTIS to provide same-day reproduction for the most recent additions to the NTIS document collection. For materials NTIS has in electronic storage or that are available from shelf stock, orders are usually shipped within 24 hours.

As of January 1997 NTIS automatically ships all larger domestic-order packages by express carrier with two-day delivery. Later in 1997 NTIS expects to ship all orders by a fully traceable carrier so that undelivered orders can be immediately located.

To provide easier order placement, NTIS also has introduced a simplified flat-rate document-handling fee that will reduce costs for many of its customers. The new fee will replace the multiple-rate shipping and handling fee with a flat-rate fee of $4 per order for delivery to any location in the United States, Canada, or Mexico. Orders outside North America will carry a flat-rate handling fee of $8 per order.

Key NTIS Contact Numbers

Order by phone
8:30 A.M.–5:00 P.M., Eastern time, Monday–Friday
Sales desk: 703-487-4650
TDD: 703-487-4639

Order by fax
24 hours a day, seven days a week 703-321-8547
To verify receipt of fax, call 703-487-4679
7:00 A.M.–5:00 P.M., Eastern time, Monday–Friday.

Order by mail
National Technical Information Service
5285 Port Royal Road
Springfield, VA 22161
RUSH Service (available for an additional fee) 800-553-NTIS (6847)

NTIS Order Now Online
Order the most recent additions to the NTIS collection at the NTIS Web site http://www.ntis.gov/order now

Order by e-mail
24 hours a day at orders@ntis.fedworld.gov
If concerned about Internet security, users can register their credit card at NTIS by calling 703-487-4682

National Archives and Records Administration

Seventh and Pennsylvania Ave., N.W., Washington, DC 20408
202-501-5400
World Wide Web: http://www.NARA.gov

Lori A. Lisowski
Office of Human Resources and Information Services

The National Archives and Records Administration (NARA), an independent federal agency, ensures for the citizen, the public servant, the president, the Congress, and the courts ready access to essential evidence that documents the rights of American citizens, the actions of federal officials, and the national experience.

NARA is singular among the world's archives as a unified federal institution that accessions and preserves materials from all three branches of government. NARA assists federal agencies in documenting their activities, administering records management programs, scheduling records, and retiring noncurrent records to Federal Records Centers. The agency also manages the Presidential Libraries system; assists the National Historical Publications and Records Commission in its grant program for state and local records and edited publications of the papers of prominent Americans; publishes the laws, regulations, presidential documents, and other official notices of the federal government, and oversees classification and declassification policy in the federal government through the Information Security Oversight Office. NARA constituents include the federal government, a history-minded public, the media, the archival community, and a broad spectrum of professional associations and researchers in such fields as history, political science, law, library and information services, and genealogy.

The size and breadth of NARA's holdings are staggering. Together, NARA's 33 facilities hold approximately 21.5 million cubic feet of original textual material documenting the activities of the federal government. In addition, NARA has extensive multimedia collections, including 9.2 million aerial photographs; 13.8 million still pictures; 5.2 million maps, charts, and architectural and engineering plans; almost 340,000 motion picture, sound, and video recordings; more than 400,000 microforms; and more than 23,000 computer files.

Strategic Directions

John W. Carlin became the eighth Archivist of the United States in June 1995. Carlin launched a campaign to reshape NARA that includes sharpening NARA's mission and developing and implementing a new strategic plan. The plan, *Ready Access to Essential Evidence: The Strategic Plan of the National Archives and Records Administration, 1997–2007* (August 1996) lists several action items the agency will pursue to reach its broad long-range goals:

- To determine what evidence is essential for documenting the rights of citizens, the actions of federal officials, and the national experience

- To ensure that government creates such evidence
- To make it easy for users to access that evidence regardless of where it is or where they are for as long as needed

A copy of the plan is available on the NARA web site at http://www.nara.gov/nara/vision/naraplan.html or by calling the Policy and Communications staff at 301-713-7360.

Records and Access

Archives II

NARA's state-of-the-art archival facility, located on 33 acres in College Park, Maryland, houses a research complex, 21 stack areas with a total capacity of two million square feet, preservation and conservation laboratories, administrative offices, and conference facilities. Records began moving from the National Archives Building in downtown Washington, D.C., and the Washington National Records Center in Suitland, Maryland, in November 1993, and the move was completed in November 1996. All nontextual records and several clusters of textual records have been moved to Archives II. Although much of the archives' holdings will be consolidated at College Park, the following clusters of records will be stored in the National Archives Building: genealogy, American Indian, District of Columbia, New Deal/Great Depression, World War I agencies, maritime, old Army, old Navy, judicial, and general records of the U.S. government.

CLIO

CLIO is the NARA information server available via the Internet. Construction of CLIO began in May 1994, and it is now accessed an average of 1,900 times an hour. CLIO—accessible by gopher clients at gopher.nara.gov and by World Wide Web browsers at www.nara.gov—offers immediate access to more than 10,000 files, including the NARA Archival Information Locator, the John F. Kennedy Assassination Records Collection Reference System, publications, on-line exhibits, teaching packets, digital documents, links to Internet information servers maintained by the Presidential Libraries, and pointers to related Internet resources.

Fax-on-Demand

This is an interactive fax retrieval system in which a single digital copy of a document is stored on the hard drive of a computer, where it can be selected and retrieved by any customer with access to a fax machine. The system receives about 2,000 calls and sends more than 5,000 documents each month. There is no charge for the service except for any long-distance telephone charges the user may incur. Documents are updated or added regularly and include General Information Leaflets, press releases, training bulletins, records finding aids, regional archives and presidential library fact sheets, NARA library news, preservation reports, and *Federal Register* notices. The system can be reached at 301-713-6905.

Presidential Libraries

The Presidential Libraries have made finding aids and other historical materials—such as the Ford Museum's "A Day in the Life of a President" and the Roosevelt Library's "New Deal Network"—available on the Internet. Colleges and universities near the libraries have assisted in many of these automation initiatives. This information is accessible through the NARA Internet server, CLIO.

As part of the effort to fulfill the requirements of Executive Order 12958, NARA and the interagency External Referral Working Group implemented the Remote Archives Capture Project. The project was created to optically scan the estimated seven million pages of classified materials more than 25 years old held by the Presidential Libraries and to make digital copies available to all of the classifying agencies for declassification review. Pilot projects were conducted at the Johnson and Kennedy libraries, where more than 200,000 pages were scanned. At the Johnson Library, more than 6,000 items already have been declassified.

On April 12, 1996, NARA reached an agreement with three other parties to lift obstacles to the release of White House audiotapes from the Richard M. Nixon administration. Consequently, 201 hours of conversations were opened on November 17, 1996. Additionally, the parties instituted a formula that would result in the acceleration of the processing and public opening of 3,700 hours of taped conversations over a four-year period and resolved the issue of transcription and public availability of the tapes.

The Reagan Library opened its remodeled Presidential Gallery permanent exhibit in February 1996. The new gallery features hands-on interactive exhibits and a sample of Reagan humor on a bank of computer kiosks. The Truman Library completed the first phase of a major multiyear renovation of its museum with the opening in December 1995 of its new White House Gallery and its greatly enhanced Oval Office replica.

The George Bush Presidential Library and Museum in College Station, Texas, which is being constructed with private funds, will reside on 90 acres of land on the campus of Texas A&M University. Until the facility opens in November 1997, NARA will continue to oversee the storage and preservation of the records of the Bush presidency and associated personal papers in the Bush Presidential Materials Project. NARA personnel are providing staff access to the digitized images of approximately two million pages of President Bush's correspondence in a document tracking system to facilitate quick reference and retrieval.

Online Federal Register

The *Federal Register*, the daily newspaper of the federal government, includes notices of meetings, regulations, reorganizations, and other governmental activities of wide interest to the public. Publication and distribution of the *Federal Register* is the responsibility of the Government Printing Office (GPO), which has made electronic access to the *Federal Register* one of the keystones of its own electronic delivery system, GPO ACCESS. Free access to the full text of the electronic version of the *Federal Register* is available through federal depository libraries or via the Internet. The full text of the *United States Government*

Manual, another publication of the Office of the Federal Register, is also available through GPO ACCESS and through CLIO. In addition to these publications, NARA publishes the *Weekly Compilation of Presidential Documents* and the *Public Papers of the President.*

Electronic Access Project

In 1994 NARA teamed with the National Institute of Standards and Technology (NIST) to explore systematically the information needs of citizens in locations remote from a NARA facility. In March 1995 the NIST team produced the blueprint for the design of electronic-access systems to meet the needs of NARA customers. The blueprint described access points and information retrieval techniques, formats for the dissemination of information, and the extent to which the digitization of documents would meet the public's needs. The blueprint provided a draft strategic road map for the future development of the agency's information systems.

NARA received funding for two follow-on projects that became available to the public via the Internet in 1996. The first, the Gallery of the Open Frontier, is a digital-image library of still pictures and supporting documentary materials that pertain to the history of the American West. The gallery was created in partnership with the University of Nebraska Press. The second project, the NARA Archival Information Locator (NAIL), is a prototype for an on-line catalog of archival holdings linked to selected digital images. The prototype contains many post-Civil War records relating to the settlement of the West.

In 1997 NARA will be expanding this prototype in preparation for the full-scale development of a comprehensive on-line catalog that will provide improved access to NARA holdings nationwide. During the next two years, NARA will digitize 200,000 images with links to catalog descriptions to illustrate the breadth and value of NARA's holdings and bring them directly to classrooms, public libraries, and the homes of the American people. This expansion of NARA's public-access capability will play a key role in achieving NARA's mission of ready access to essential information.

Customer Service

Customers

Few archives serve as many customers as NARA. In fiscal year (FY) 1996 there were 286,000 research visits made to NARA facilities nationwide, including Presidential Libraries. At the same time, customers made 819,000 requests by mail and by phone. The National Personnel Records Center in St. Louis, Missouri, received two million requests for information from military and civilian government service records. In addition to providing research and reference services, NARA provides informative exhibits for almost one million people each year in the National Archives Rotunda in Washington, D.C., and 1.2 million more visit the Presidential Library museums. NARA also serves the executive agencies of the federal government, the courts, and Congress by providing records storage, reference service, training, advice, and guidance on many issues relating to records management. The agency's current *Customer Service Plan* and first *Customer Service Performance Report*, both available free in the research rooms nationwide, list the many types of customers NARA serves and describe the agency's goals for customer service standards. These publications, available on the Internet, may also be ordered from the National Archives and Records Administration, Product Sales Section, Room G9, Seventh and Pennsylvania Ave. N.W., Washington, DC 20408; toll-free at 800-234-8861; or by fax at 202-501-7170.

Customer Opinion

NARA cares about what its customers think of its services. Major surveys of National Personnel Records Center researchers, the Office of the Federal Register customers, at several Presidential Library museums, and among other groups of frequent customers have been conducted in the past year. Results are published in the *Customer Service Performance Report*. NARA continues to survey, hold focus groups, and meet with customers in order to evaluate and constantly improve services.

Centers Information Processing System

The Centers Information Processing System (CIPS) allows federal agencies to make electronic reference requests for records stored at a Federal Records Center. CIPS improves customer service by reducing reference preparation time and cost, delivery delays, and turnaround times. Begun as a pilot project in October 1993, CIPS processed more than 875,000 electronic requests in FY 1996, and turnaround times have been reduced from 10–12 days to 2–3 days. NARA's service improvement allows other federal agencies to provide faster service to their public customers as well.

Administration

NARA employs approximately 3,000 people, of whom about 2,000 are full-time permanent staff members. For FY 1996, NARA's budget was $195 million, with $5 million to support the National Historic Publications and Records Commission (NHPRC). An annual description of the activities and finances of NARA can be found in the *Annual Report of the National Archives and Records Administration*. For a copy of the report or for further information about NARA, call the Policy and Communications staff at 301-713-7360.

United States Information Agency

Bureau of Information
Room 130, 301 Fourth St. S.W., Washington, DC 20547
202-619-4225

Cynthia Borys
Information Resource Center

The United States Information Agency (USIA), an independent organization within the executive branch, is responsible for the U.S. government's overseas information, educational exchange, and cultural programs. The work of the agency is carried out by a staff of foreign service officers assigned to U.S. missions abroad and by a professional staff of career civil servants in Washington, D.C. Known abroad as the United States Information Service (USIS), the agency has more than 200 posts in 146 countries that are grouped in six geographic areas: Africa; Western Europe; Eastern Europe and the Newly Independent States; East Asia and the Pacific; the American Republics; and North Africa, the Near East, and South Asia. Posts in these areas report to area offices in Washington, D.C.

History of USIS Library Programs

Today's worldwide system of USIS libraries evolved from a matrix of programs. First, in Latin America, came libraries associated with President Franklin Roosevelt's "Good Neighbor" program. In 1941 the coordinator of inter-American affairs, Nelson Rockefeller, contracted with the American Library Association (ALA) to establish and operate a library in Mexico City, the now-famous Biblioteca Benjamin Franklin. Under similar contracts, ALA opened and operated on behalf of the U.S. government two other libraries in Latin America: in Managua, Nicaragua (1942), and Montevideo, Uruguay (1943).

Beginning in 1942 the Office of War Information (OWI) began to establish reference libraries as part of its overseas information program. These were separate and distinct from U.S. Embassy reference libraries at the outset. Later, parts of many embassy collections were turned over to USIS libraries. The American Library in London started operations in December 1942 and officially opened in April 1943. The London library was the first overseas library directly under U.S. government control. Between 1942 and 1945 OWI established libraries in 40 more locations throughout the world. In 1945 the Department of State assumed responsibility for overseas libraries.

Shortly after World War II the U.S. Military Government began opening Information Center (Amerika Häuser) libraries and reading rooms in Germany, throughout the American Zone and in the major cities of the British and French zones. At the same time Information Center libraries were started under the auspices of the United States Forces in Austria, Japan, and Korea. The State Department assumed responsibility for these centers when civilian control was restored in each country. Nine centers came under the department's auspices in

January 1949, and ten centers in Austria were added in 1950. These centers were initially transferred to the State Department and finally, on August 1, 1953, to the newly created United States Information Agency. Since that time USIS libraries and information resource centers have been opened in virtually every country with which the United States maintains diplomatic relations.

Current Programs

Although USIS library and information centers vary significantly from country to country, all advance two mutually supportive functions:

- To provide the most current and authoritative information about official U.S. government policies
- To serve as a primary source of informed commentary on the origin, growth, and development of American social, political, economic, and cultural values and institutions

Activities of USIS libraries and information resource centers are carried out by host country staff. They provide a vital communication link between USIS posts and local audiences. A corps of 20 American information specialists periodically travels to overseas posts to provide professional guidance and to define the roles of libraries and information centers in relation to American foreign policy objectives. As greater emphasis is placed on current awareness and outreach services to foreign opinion leaders, USIS staff rely on direct, electronic access to the wealth of information sources in the United States. In places where information about the United States is extremely limited or virtually nonexistent, USIS libraries provide a balanced cross section of outstanding American contributions in the social sciences and humanities, which promote appreciation and understanding of American intellectual and cultural history, American economic and social institutions, and American political traditions. Book collections at these places usually range from 3,000 to 10,000 volumes.

USIA Washington continues to operate one of the federal government's most dynamic special libraries. Annually, the Information Resource Center (IRC) fields over 18,000 research and reference requests from USIA Washington staff and overseas posts. The IRC maintains a collection of 50,000 monographs, 800 journals, and access to 1,000 online and CD-ROM sources. USIA headquarters is also responsible for the professional development of field librarians.

Public Diplomacy Query Database

USIA also produces and maintains a family of databases called Public Diplomacy Query (PDQ), to index, store, and make available to USIS libraries most program and foreign policy materials acquired and produced by USIA. PDQ is available online and via CD-ROM.

Book Programs

USIA also supports the publication of American books abroad, both in English and in translation. The agency, through its field posts abroad, works with publishers to produce a variety of translated books in the humanities and social sciences that reflect a broad range of American thought and serve to explain American life and institutions.

Through programs of book translation and through a variety of seminars, conferences, and short-term professional publishing workshops, USIA seeks to encourage respect for and adherence to international standards of intellectual property rights protection. The agency works closely on this issue both with foreign governments and with domestic and foreign nongovernment organizations.

American publishers seeking additional information about the agency's book program should direct their inquiries to Print Publications (I/TPP), Bureau of Information, USIA, 301 Fourth St. S.W., Washington, DC 20547. Foreign publishers should turn for assistance to the Public Affairs Office of the U.S. Embassy in their country.

National Center for Education Statistics
Library Statistics Cooperative Program

U.S. Department of Education, Office of Educational Research and Improvement
555 New Jersey Ave. N.W., Washington, DC 20208-5652

Adrienne Chute
Surveys and Cooperative Systems Group

The mandate of the National Center for Education Statistics (NCES) to collect library statistics is included in the Improving America's Schools Act of 1994 (P.L. 103-382) under Title IV, the National Education Statistics Act of 1994. The Library Statistics Cooperative Program is administered and funded by NCES, which regularly collects and disseminates statistical information on libraries under six surveys. These surveys include the Public Libraries Survey, the Academic Libraries Survey, the School Library Media Center Survey, the State Library Agency Survey, the Federal Libraries Survey and the Library Cooperatives Survey. The U.S. National Commission on Libraries and Information Science (NCLIS) and the U.S. Bureau of the Census work cooperatively with NCES in implementing the Library Statistics Cooperative Program.

The six library surveys provide the only current, comprehensive, national data on the status of libraries. They are used by federal, state, and local officials, professional associations, and local practitioners for planning, evaluation, and making policy, and drawing samples for special surveys. These data are also available to researchers and educators to analyze the state of the art of librarianship and to improve its practice.

Public Libraries

Descriptive statistics for nearly 9,000 public libraries are collected and disseminated annually through a voluntary census, the Public Libraries Survey. The survey is conducted by the National Center for Education Statistics (NCES) through the Federal-State Cooperative System (FSCS) for public library data. In 1996 FSCS completed its eighth data collection.

Data files on diskette that contain 1993 data on about 9,000 responding libraries and identifying information about their outlets were made available in 1995. The 1993 data were also aggregated to state and national levels in an E.D. Tabs, an NCES publication designed to present major findings with minimal statistical analyses. The 1994 FSCS data were collected in August 1995, with release scheduled for winter 1997. The 1995 data were collected in July 1996, with release scheduled for summer 1997. The 1996 data will be collected in July 1997, with release scheduled for summer 1998.

Note: Carrol Kindel, Jeffrey Williams, Elaine Kroe, Rosa Fernandez, and Martha Hollins of NCES and Chris Dunn of Library Programs contributed to this article.

The 50 states and the District of Columbia participate in data collection. Beginning in 1993 the following outlying areas joined the FSCS: Guam, Northern Marianas, Palau, Puerto Rico, and the Virgin Islands. However, for the 1994 data collection, the respondents again were the nearly 9,000 public libraries, identified by state library agencies in the 50 states and the District of Columbia.

The Public Libraries Survey collects data on staffing; type of governance; type of administrative structure; service outlets; operating income and expenditures; size of collection; service measures such as reference transactions, interlibrary loans, circulation, public service hours, library visits, circulation of children's materials, children's program attendance, and interlibrary relationship; and other data items. Beginning with 1996 for the collection of 1995 data, six technology-oriented data items were added to the Public Libraries Survey. These are:

- Does the public library have access to the Internet?
- Is the Internet used by library staff only, patrons through a staff intermediary, or patrons either directly or through a staff intermediary?
- Does the library provide access to electronic services?
- The number of library materials in electronic format
- Operating expenditures for library materials in electronic format
- Operating expenditures for electronic access

In general, both unit response and response to specific items are very high. Efforts to improve FSCS data quality are ongoing. For example, NCES has sponsored a series of studies on coverage, definitions, finance data, and staffing data These studies were conducted by the Governments Division, Bureau of the Census. Over the past several years the clarity of FSCS definitions, software, and tables has been significantly improved.

At the state level and in the outlying areas, FSCS is administered by data coordinators, appointed by each state or outlying area's chief officer of the state library agency. FSCS is a working network. An annual training conference is provided for the state data coordinators and a steering committee that represents them is active in the development of the Public Libraries Survey and its data-entry software. Technical assistance to states is provided by phone and in person by state data coordinators, by NCES staff, by the Bureau of the Census, and by NCLIS. NCES also works cooperatively with NCLIS, the U.S. Department of Commerce's Bureau of the Census, the Institute of Museum and Library Services' Office of Library Programs, the Chief Officers of State Library Agencies (COSLA), the American Library Association (ALA), and the U.S. Department of Education's National Institute on Postsecondary Education, Libraries, and Lifelong Learning.

FSCS is an example of the synergy that can result from combining federal/state cooperation with state-of-the-art technology. FSCS is the first national NCES data collection in which the respondents supply the data electronically. The data can also be edited and tabulated electronically at the state and national levels through NCES-developed software. All eight FSCS data collections have been collected electronically.

To enhance the Public Libraries Survey, NCES developed the first comprehensive public library universe file (PLUS) and merged it with existing software into a revised software package called DECPLUS. DECPLUS has been used to collect data since 1992. DECPLUS collects identifying information on all known public libraries and their service outlets, all state library agencies, and some library systems, federations, and cooperative services. This resource is now available for use in drawing samples for special surveys on such topics as literacy, access for the disabled, library construction, and the like. A historical change-tracking mechanism has also been established beginning with DECPLUS. Closings, additions, and mergers of public libraries and public library service outlets, for example, are tracked in a historical file. DECPLUS software is cost-effective and has improved data quality.

The following are highlights from *E.D. TABS Public Libraries in the United States: 1993* released in June 1995.

Number of Public Libraries and Their Service Outlets and Governance

- 8,929 public libraries (administrative entities) were reported in the 50 states and the District of Columbia in 1993 (Table 1).
- Fewer than 11 percent of the public libraries serve over 71 percent of the population of legally served areas in the United States (derived from Tables 1A and 1B).[1] Each of these public libraries has a legal service area population of 50,000 or more (Table 1B).
- 1,454 public libraries (over 16 percent) reported one or more branch library outlets, with a total of 7,017. The total number of central library outlets reported was 8,887. The total number of stationary outlets reported (central library outlets and branch library outlets) was 15,904. Nearly 10 percent of reporting public libraries had one or more bookmobile outlets, with a total of 1,035 (Table 2).
- Nearly 56 percent of public libraries were part of a municipal government; 12 percent were part of a county/parish; nearly 7 percent had multijurisdictional governance under an intergovernmental agreement; nearly 10 percent were non-profit association or agency libraries in a given state; nearly 4 percent were part of a school district; and nearly 6 percent were separate government units known as library districts. Less than 1 percent were combinations of academic/public libraries or school/public libraries. Over 5 percent did not report or reported a form of governance not mentioned here (Table 17).
- Over 80 percent of public libraries had only one direct service outlet (Table 18).

---

[1] The percent distribution was derived from Tables 1A and 1B of *E.D. TABS Public Libraries in the United States: 1993*. The sum of the five columns on table 1A where the population of the legal service area is greater than 49,999 is 10.9 percent. The sum of the five columns on table 1B where the population of the legal service area is greater than 49,999 is over 71 percent.

Income, Expenditures, and Staffing
- Public libraries reported that 78 percent of total operating income of over $5.0 billion came from local sources, nearly 13 percent from the state, about 1 percent from federal sources, and over 8 percent from other sources, such as gifts and donations, service fees and fines (Table 10).
- Per capita operating income from local sources was under $3 for nearly 14 percent of public libraries, $3 to $14.99 for over 52 percent, and $15 or more for 34 percent of public libraries. Per capita income from local sources varies considerably, with a percentage distribution of about 10 percent in each of 10 categories reported (Table 11).
- Total operating expenditures for public libraries were over $4.7 billion in 1993. Of this, over 65 percent was for paid FTE staff and 15 percent for the library collection (Table 12). The average U.S. per capita operating expenditure was $19.16. The highest average per capita operating expenditure in the 50 states was $31.66 and the lowest was $7.85 (Table 13).
- Nearly 41 percent of public libraries reported operating expenditures of less than $50,000 in 1993. Just over 38 percent expended between $50,000 and $399,999, and just over 21 percent exceeded $400,000 (Table 14).

Staffing and Collections
- Public libraries reported a total of nearly 111,945 paid full-time equivalent (FTE) staff (Table 8).
- Nationwide, public libraries reported over 656 million books and serial volumes in their collections or 2.7 volumes per capita. By state, the number of volumes per capita ranged from 1.6 To 4.9 (Table 6).
- Nationwide, public libraries reported collections of over 22 million audio materials, 535,000 films, and nearly 7.9 million video materials (Table 6).

Circulation and Interlibrary Loans
- Total nationwide circulation of library materials was nearly 1.6 billion or 6.5 per capita. Highest statewide circulation per capita was 11.9 and lowest was 3.2 (Table 4).
- Nationwide, nearly 7.6 million library materials were loaned by public libraries to other libraries (Table 4).

Children's Services
- Nationwide circulation of children's materials was nearly 462.9 million or over 29 percent of total circulation. Attendance at children's programs was nearly 35.6 million (Table 5). Information on public library service to children is included in the E.D. TABS for the first time.

Per capita figures in these highlights are based on the total unduplicated population of legal service areas in the states, not on the total population of the states. Population of legal service area means the population of those areas in the state or nation where public library service is available. It does not include the population of unserved areas.

Additional information on FSCS may be obtained from Adrienne Chute (202-219-1772), Surveys and Cooperatives Systems Group, National Center for Education Statistics, Room 311A, 555 New Jersey Ave. N.W., Washington, DC 20208-5652.

Academic libraries

NCES surveyed academic libraries on a three-year cycle between 1966 and 1988. Since 1988, the Academic Libraries Survey (ALS) has been a component of the Integrated Postsecondary Education Data System (IPEDS) and is on a two-year cycle. ALS provides data on about 3,500 academic libraries. In aggregate, these data provide an overview of the status of academic libraries nationally and statewide.

The survey collects data on the libraries in the entire universe of accredited higher education institutions and on the libraries in nonaccredited institutions with a program of four years or more. ALS produces descriptive statistics on academic libraries in postsecondary institutions in the 50 states, the District of Columbia, and the outlying areas.

The first release of ALS 1994 data was in spring 1996 over the Internet. Several data products will follow—an ED Tabs and a diskette of the data.

NCES has developed IDEALS, a software package for states to use in submitting ALS data to NCES. Its model was DECTOP, the predecessor of DEC-PLUS, the software developed for the collection of public library data in the FSCS program. IDEALS was used by 46 states in the collection of 1994 data.

ALS, using FSCS as a model, has established a working group comprised of representatives of the academic library community. Its mission is to improve data quality and the timeliness of data collection, processing, and release. This network of academic library professionals works closely with state IPEDS coordinators (representatives from each state who work with NCES to coordinate the collection of IPEDS data from postsecondary institutions in each of their states). NCES also works cooperatively with ALA, NCLIS, the Association of Research Libraries, the Association of College and Research Libraries, and numerous academic libraries in the collection of ALS. ALS collects data on total operating expenditures, full-time-equivalent library staff, service outlets, total volumes held at the end of the fiscal year, circulation, interlibrary loans, public service hours, gate count, reference transactions per typical week, and online services.

The following are highlights from *E.D. TABS Academic Libraries: 1992*, released in November 1994.

- In 1992, total operating expenditures for libraries at the 3,274 institutions of higher education totaled $3.6 billion (Table 1A).
- The three largest individual expenditure items for all academic libraries were salaries and wages, $1.9 billion (51.8 percent); current serial sub-

scription expenditures, $639 million (17.5 percent); and print material expenditures, $421 million (11.5 percent) (Tables 2A and 3A).
- The libraries of the 500 doctoral-granting institutions (15.3 percent of the total institutions) accounted for $2.3 billion, or 62 percent of the total operating expenditure dollars at all college and university libraries. This included $1.1 billion for salaries and wages, $467 million current serial subscription expenditures, and $253 million print material expenditures (Tables 2B and 3B).
- The number of volumes held at all academic libraries at the end of FY 1992 totaled about 749 million (Table 5A).
- Libraries at institutions granting doctoral degrees held about 471 million volumes, or 63 percent of the total volumes held (Table 5B).
- The total number of full-time-equivalent (FTE) staff members in college and university libraries equaled 96,000, including about 26,000 librarians and other professional staff, 40,000 other paid staff, 29,000 student assistants, and 404 staff who contributed their services (Table 4A).
- Libraries at institutions granting doctoral degrees accounted for 52,000, or half of all, FTE staff at all academic libraries. This included about 14,000 librarians and other professional staff, 24,000 other paid staff, 14,000 student assistants, and 128 staff who contributed their services (Table 4B).
- Academic libraries had 229 million circulation transactions; 78.8 percent from general collections, and 21.2 percent from reserve collections (Table 9A).
- Libraries at institutions granting doctoral degrees accounted for more than half of this total circulation with 129 million circulation transactions (Table 9B).

Additional information on academic library statistics may be obtained from Jeffrey Williams, Surveys and Cooperative Systems Group, National Center for Education Statistics, 320A, 555 New Jersey Ave. N.W., Washington, DC 20208-5652 (202-219-1362).

School Library Media Centers

In 1991 a small amount of data on school libraries was collected as embedded items from a sample of public and private elementary and secondary schools as part of the NCES 1990–1991 Schools and Staffing Survey (SASS). Data collected included number of students served, number of professional staff and aides, number of full-time equivalent librarians/media specialists, number of vacant positions, number of positions abolished, number of approved positions, and amount of librarian input in establishing curriculum. NCES released a short report on these data in November 1994.

The following are highlights from this report, titled *Survey Report School Library Media Centers in the United States 1990–91.*

Historical Overview

- In 1958 only 50 percent of public elementary and secondary schools in the United States had a library or library media center. As of 1990–1991, 96 percent of public and 87 percent of private elementary and secondary schools in the United States had a library or library media center (Table 3).
- From 1960 to 1980 the number of public school librarians/media specialists in the United States nearly tripled, from 17,363 to 48,018, outstripping increases in student enrollments. Since 1980, expansion in the number of public school librarians/media specialists substantially slowed, and in the early 1990s school library media center staffing levels did not keep pace with increases in student enrollments (Table 4).

The Availability of School Library Media Centers

- In the public sector, small schools (those with fewer than 300 students) and combined schools (those jointly offering both elementary and secondary levels) were the least likely to be equipped with library media centers in 1990–1991. Ten percent of small public schools and 15 percent of combined public schools did not have library media centers (Table 6).
- In the private sector, small schools, elementary schools, combined schools, and non-Catholic private schools, both religious and nonsectarian, were the least likely to be equipped with library media centers in 1990–1991. The percentages of schools in these groups without library media centers ranged from 14 to 23 percent (Table 6).

Staffing Levels of School Library Media Centers

- In the public sector, 8 percent of schools with library media centers did not employ some kind of library media center staff, neither a professional librarian/media specialist nor a library aide, in 1990–1991. Four percent of public school students attended such schools. Elementary schools, combined schools, and small public schools were the most likely to have employed no library staff. One third of small public schools had no librarian/media specialist, and one-fifth of those same schools had neither a librarian/media specialist nor an aide (Table 9).
- The proportion of private schools with unstaffed library media centers was far greater than for public schools in 1990–1991. Over half of smaller, elementary, and non-Catholic religious private schools employed neither a librarian/media specialist nor a library aide. Overall, a quarter of all private school students were enrolled in schools with no employed library media center staff (Table 9).

The Role of School Library Media Specialists

- Teachers in public schools were slightly more likely than teachers in private schools to strongly agree that the materials in their school library media centers were supportive of their instructional objectives (Table 15).

- Few school principals (16 percent) reported that school librarians/media specialists had a great deal of influence over decisions concerned with establishing the curriculum in their schools. Librarians/media specialists in private schools were more frequently reported to have a great deal of influence over curricular decisions than in public schools (Table 17).

A national survey on school library media centers was conducted in school year 1993–1994, the first since school year 1985–1986. NCES, with the assistance of the U.S. Bureau of the Census, conducted this survey as part of the 1994 Schools and Staffing Survey (SASS). The survey consisted of two questionnaires. The school library media specialist questionnaire data will provide a nationwide profile of the school library media specialist workforce. The school library media center questionnaire data will provide a national picture of school library collections, expenditures, technology, and services. This effort will be used to assess the status of school library media centers nationwide and to assess the federal role in their support. Two publications are planned using data from the 1993–1994 survey. The first will be released in early 1997.

Additional information on school library media center statistics may be obtained from Jeffrey Williams, Surveys and Cooperative Systems Group, National Center for Education Statistics, 320A, 555 New Jersey Ave. N.W., Washington, DC 20208-5652 (202-219-1362).

Surveys on Children, Young Adults

In spring 1994, under the sponsorship of the U.S. Department of Education's Library Programs Office, NCES conducted two fast response surveys—one on public library services and resources for children and another on public library services and resources for young adults. These surveys updated similar surveys from 1989 and 1988, respectively. The two surveys collected data directly from two different representative samples of public libraries.

The Survey on Library Services and Resources for Children in Public Libraries included questions regarding the availability of specialized staff and resources for children and the adults who live and work with them, use of available services, prevalence of cooperative activities between public libraries and other organizations serving children, and barriers to providing increased library services for children.

The Survey on Library Services and Resources for Young Adults in Public Libraries obtained information on services for young adults, use of available services, cooperation between libraries and other organizations, ways in which libraries interact with schools, and factors perceived as barriers to increasing young adult services and their use. The data from the two surveys were consolidated into one report.

The following are highlights from the report *Services and Resources for Children and Young Adults in Public Libraries* (1995).

- Sixty percent of the 18 million people entering public libraries during a typical week in fall 1993 were youth—children and young adults.

- The percentage of libraries with children's and young adult librarians has not changed since the late 1980s. Thirty-nine percent of libraries employ a children's librarian, 11 percent have a young adult librarian, and 24 percent have a youth services specialist on staff.
- Librarians report that ethnic diversity of children and young adult patrons has increased in over 40 percent of U.S. public libraries over the last five years. Seventy-six percent of public libraries currently have children's materials and 64 percent have young adult materials in languages other than English.
- Although computer technologies are among the most heavily used children's and young adult resources in public libraries, they are also among the most scarce. Only 30 percent of public libraries reported the availability of personal computers for use by children and young adults. However, 75 percent of libraries having this resource report moderate to heavy use by children, and 71 percent report moderate to heavy use by young adults.
- Less than half of all public libraries (40 percent) offer group programs for infants and toddlers. These programs are more prevalent now than in 1988, when only 29 percent of libraries offered group programs for infants to two-year-olds. Eighty-six percent of libraries offer group programs, such as story times, booktalks, puppetry, and crafts, for preschool and kindergarten age children; 79 percent of libraries offer group programs for school-age children.
- Seventy-six percent of public libraries report working with schools; 66 percent work with preschools and 56 percent with day care centers.
- While almost all libraries provide reference assistance, only about 1 in 7 libraries offer homework assistance programs for children or young adults. However, fairly large percentages of libraries with homework assistance programs report moderate to heavy use by children and young adults. Sixty-four percent report moderate to heavy use by children and 58 percent report moderate to heavy use by young adults.
- Librarians report that insufficient library staff is a leading barrier to increasing services and resources for both children and young adults. Sixty-five percent of librarians consider this a moderate or major barrier to increasing services for children, and 58 percent consider lack of staff a barrier to increasing services for young adults.

Additional information on these surveys may be obtained from Edith McArthur, National Center for Education Statistics, 402K, 555 New Jersey Ave. N.W., Washington, DC 20208-5652 (202-219-1442).

Federal Libraries and Information Centers Survey

The Federal Library Survey is designed to obtain data on the mission and function, administrative and managerial components (e.g., staff size and expenditures), information resources (e.g., collection size), and services of federal libraries and information centers. The Federal Library Survey is a cooperative effort between NCES and the staff of the Federal Library and Information Center Committee (FLICC) of the Library of Congress. The survey has established a nationwide profile of federal libraries and information centers. This survey has made available the first national data on federal libraries since 1978. NCES plans to conduct the survey every five years.

The survey was pretested in 1993 and 1994 and the full-scale survey conducted in 1995. Four data products are planned from this survey: an E.D TABS with the 1994 data (released July 1996), an analytical report on the health of federal libraries (planned for 1997), the survey data base (released 1996), and a directory of federal libraries (planned for 1997).

Additional information on the Federal Libraries and Information Centers Survey may be obtained from Martha Hollins, Surveys and Cooperative Systems Group, National Center for Education Statistics, 315B, 555 New Jersey Ave. N.W., Washington, DC 20208-5652 (202-219-1462).

State Library Agency Survey

NCES conducted a new survey on state library agencies in 1994–1995. Two data products were released on the Internet through the NCES Website: an E.D. TABS, with 28 tables for the 50 states and the District of Columbia (also available in print), and the survey data base (also available on diskette). The state library agency survey is a cooperative effort between NCES, COSLA, and NCLIS and is planned to be conducted annually. A study evaluating the new state library survey including the comparison of these data with other sources is planned for 1997.

Additional information on the state library agency survey may be obtained from Elaine Kroe, Surveys and Cooperative Systems Group, National Center for Education Statistics, 315A, 555 New Jersey Ave. N.W., Washington, DC 20208-5652 (202-219-1361).

Survey of Library Cooperatives

A new Survey of Library Cooperatives moved forward in fiscal year (FY) 1996 with completion targeted for FY 1997. It is expected to be conducted every five years. A working group was organized and met in December 1995. Topics discussed by this committee included definitions, developing a universe file and survey design. The Steering Committee also reviewed a preliminary list of existing library cooperatives, which was compiled by the Bureau of the Census from several sources.

Additional information on the Interlibrary Cooperation Survey may be obtained from Rosa Fernandez, Surveys and Cooperative Systems Group, National Center for Education Statistics, 317, 555 New Jersey Ave. N.W., Washington, DC 20208-5652 (202-219-1358).

Library Statistics Surveys—Plans

NCES plans to continue the Public Libraries Survey. NCES provides technical assistance and training to states and outlying areas for public library data collection. In 1996 this program was expanded to include academic libraries as well.

Opportunities for expanded electronic data collection from states are now being offered in the Public Libraries Survey. For example, some data collection is being done via the Internet. NCES has also implemented an early release policy for these data. Data provided by states are released over the Internet when received by NCES. These are preliminary data and subject to revision until replaced by a final fully edited data file.

NCES is continuing to sponsor its series of studies on data quality. In 1997 the Governments Division of the Bureau of the Census will complete a report on data collection processes and technology, the sixth in the series for public libraries. Data quality reports will also be completed for the School Library Media Centers, State Library Agencies, and Federal Libraries and Information Centers surveys.

For the first time, the Public Libraries Survey is imputing data for nonresponse beginning with FY 1995 data. NCES also plans to impute three to four years of earlier Public Libraries Survey data and release it on a CD-ROM in 1998. The CD-ROM will also include trend analysis on key variables and software for making tabulations and peer comparisons.

NCES has also fostered the use and analysis of FSCS data. A Data Use Subcommittee of the FSCS Steering Committee has been addressing the dissemination, use, and analysis of FSCS data.

Several analytical projects are currently under way. NCES has sponsored a project through the American Institutes for Research that has developed indices of inflation for public libraries, a cost index, and a price index. A report of the project will be available in 1997. NCES has been exploring the potential of geographic mapping for public libraries. In September 1996 NCES sponsored a two-year project through Westat, Inc. to develop the capability to link census demographic data with Public Libraries Survey data through geographic mapping software.

Work is under way to geocode public library service outlets nationwide and map and digitize the boundaries of the almost 9,000 public library legal service area jurisdictions, so that they can be matched to Census Tiger files and to Public Libraries Survey data files. The project will also produce a public use data file linking Public Libraries Survey data, with key census demographic variables and a user's guide. A technical report will describe the methods of geocoding and public library mapping.

Public library questions are also being included as parts of other NCES surveys. For example, in 1996 questions about frequency of use and the purposes for which households use public libraries were included on an expanded household screener for the NCES National Household Education Survey. Over 55,000 households nationwide were surveyed in such a way as to provide state- and national-level estimates on library items. A Statistics in Brief reporting the survey results will be published in 1997. A CD-ROM and user's manual will also be made available in 1997. NCES also plans to include some library-oriented questions on their new Early Childhood Longitudinal Study. Questions are being field tested in 1997. Data collection is scheduled for 1998 and 1999, with data release scheduled for 2000.

Data dissemination for the library surveys has also been broadened with electronic release of both current and back years data and E.D. TABS on the Internet. In addition an information service called the National Education Data Resource Center (NEDRC) has been set up. The NEDRC helps customers obtain reports and data files and also responds to requests for tabulations on library and other NCES studies and surveys. (See below for ways to contact the NEDRC.)

The collection of academic library data through IPEDS will also be continued. NCES plans to improve the quality of the data by promoting the use of IDEALS software for data collection. New data elements focusing on electronic access and other new technologies may be added to the survey. A descriptive report of changes in academic libraries between 1990 and 1992 is in process and will be released in 1997.

Several questions about the role of academic libraries in distance education were included as part of another survey sponsored by the National Institute on Postsecondary Education, Libraries, and Lifelong Learning. The Survey on Distance Education Courses Offered by Higher Education Institutions was conducted in fall 1995 under NCES's Postsecondary Education Quick Information System (PEQIS). A report of this survey is in process and will be released in 1997.

NCES will continue school library data collection. Surveys are planned for once every five years.

The Library Statistics Program also sponsors activities that cut across all types of libraries. For example, in 1993 NCES sponsored an invitational forum on policy analysis using library data from all types of libraries. The 1994 forum focused on electronic technology. The 1995 forum topic was "Changes in Library and Information Services in the Next Five Years." The fourth forum topic was "Impact of Information Technology and Special Programming on Library Services to Special Populations." A fifth forum is planned for fall 1997. Beginning in 1993 and 1994 NCES has also sponsored the attendance of librarians from all sectors at NCES training opportunities, including the semiannual Cooperative System Fellows Program. In fall 1995 the scope and title of the former *FSCS Memo* was broadened to cover statistical news of all library sectors—public, state, academic, school, and special. Its title has been changed to *Library Statistics Program Memo*.

Publications

Public Libraries in Forty-Four States and the District of Columbia: 1988; An NCES Working Paper (November 1989). o.p.

E.D. TABS: Academic Libraries: 1988 (September 1990). o.p.

E.D. TABS: Public Libraries in Fifty States and the District of Columbia: 1989 (April 1991). o.p.

E.D. TABS: Public Libraries in the U.S.: 1990 (June 1992). o.p.

E.D. TABS: Academic Libraries: 1990 (December 1992). Government Printing Office No., 065-000-00549-2. o.p.

Survey Report: School Library Media Centers in the United States: 1990–91 (November 1994). For sale through the Government Printing Office, No. 065-000-00715-1. $4.25.

E.D. TABS: Public Libraries in the United States: 1991 (April 1993). Government Printing Office, No. 065-000-00561-1. o.p.

E.D. TABS: Public Libraries in the United States: 1992 (August 1994). Government Printing Office, No. 065-000-00670-7. o.p.

E.D. TABS: Academic Libraries: 1992 (November 1994). Government Printing Office, No. 065-000-00717-7. $3.75

Data Comparability and Public Policy: New Interest in Public Library Data; papers presented at Meetings of the American Statistical Association. Working Paper No. 94-07. National Center for Education Statistics, November 1994.

Report on Coverage Evaluation of the Public Library Statistics Program (June 1994). Prepared for the National Center for Education Statistics by the Governments Division, Bureau of the Census. Government Printing Office, No. 065-00-00662-6. $11.

Finance Data in the Public Library Statistics Program: Definitions, Internal Consistency, and Comparisons to Secondary Sources (1995). Prepared for NCES by the Governments Division, Bureau of the Census. Government Printing Office, No 065-000-00794-9. $5.50

Report on Evaluation of Definitions Used in the Public Library Statistics Program (1995). Prepared for the National Center for Education Statistics by the Governments Division, Bureau of the Census. Government Printing Office, No. 065-000-00736-3. $6.

Staffing Data in the Public Library Statistics program: Definitions, Internal Consistency, and Comparisons to Secondary Sources (1995). Prepared for NCES by the Governments Division, Bureau of the Census. Government Printing Office, No. 065-000-00795-9. $5.

Statistical Analysis Report: Services and Resources for Children and Young Adults in Public Libraries (August 1995). Prepared for NCES by Westat, Inc. Government Printing Office, No. 065-000-00797-5. $9.

E.D. TABS: Public Libraries in the United States: 1993 (September 1995). Government Printing Office, No. 065-000-00800-9. $8.

Public Library Structure and Organization in the United States. NCES No. 96-229 (March 1996).

E.D. TABS: State Library Agencies, Fiscal Year 1994 (June 1996). Government Printing Office No. 065-000-00878-5. $12.

E.D. TABS: Federal Libraries and Information Centers in the United States: 1994 (July 1996).

More recent publications may be available through the Superintendent of Documents (GPO). Write to: New Orders, P.O. Box 371954, Pittsburgh, PA

15250-7954. Credit card orders may be placed by fax at 202-512-2250. Call the GPO Order Desk at 202-512-1800 for additional ordering information or to place an order by telephone.

Data Files Released on Computer Diskette

Public Libraries in Forty-Four States and the District of Columbia: 1988 (March 1990).
Public Libraries in Fifty States and the District of Columbia: 1989 (May 1990).
Academic Libraries: 1988 (October 1990).
Public Libraries Data, 1990 (July 1992).
Academic Libraries: 1990 (February 1993).

The NCES data files above are generally available on computer diskette through the U.S. Department of Education, Office of Educational Research and Improvement, National Library of Education, 555 New Jersey Ave. N.W., Washington, DC 20208-5725.

Public Library Data 1992 (September 1994). Government Printing Office, No. 065-000-00675-8.
Academic Libraries: 1992 (November 1994). Available through the NEDRC.
Public Library Data FY 1993 on Disk (July 1995). Government Printing Office, No. 065-000-00790-8. $17.
State Library Agencies Data, FY 1994 on Disk (May 1996).

The NCES data files above are generally available through the Government Printing Office. Attn: Electronic Products, P.O. Box 37082, Washington, D.C. 20013-7082. Telephone: 202-512-1530. Fax: 202-512-1262. Upon request, the National Education Data Resource Center (NEDRC) will provide the data files and some publications free of charge. The NEDRC also responds to requests for tabulations on NCES studies and surveys. (See below for ways to contact the NEDRC.)

Electronic Releases of Publications and Data Files

Many NCES products are also available on the Internet.
To reach NCES library products on the Department of Education NCES World Wide Web site, type the URL address http://www.ed.gov/NCES, then select "Data and Surveys," then "Libraries," then choose from a list of options.
To reach NCES products on the Department of Education OERI Gopher Server, point to *gopher.ed.gov: 10,000* and choose from a list of options.
For more information about obtaining NCES reports and data files through the Internet, GPO, or NEDRC, contact NEDRC. Send your request by Internet to: nedrc@inet.ed.gov, or send a fax to 703-820-7465, or write to NEDRC at 1900 N. Beauregard Street, Suite 200, Alexandria, VA 22311-1722, or call 703-845-3151.

Library of Congress

Washington, D.C. 20540
202-707-5000, World Wide Web http://www.loc.gov

Audrey Fischer
Writer-Editor, Library of Congress

The Library of Congress was established in 1800 to serve the research needs of the U.S. Congress. For nearly two centuries the library has grown both in the size of its collections and in its mission. The largest library in the world, with collections totaling more than 111 million items, it serves not only Congress but also government agencies, libraries around the world, and scholars and other citizens in the United States and abroad. At the forefront of technology, the library now serves patrons on-site in its 22 reading rooms and at remote locations through its highly acclaimed World Wide Web site on the Internet. Throughout 1996 an average of more than 20 million transactions were recorded monthly on all of the library's public electronic systems. Given the library's stature as a major information provider, it was appropriate that the Telecommunications Act of 1996, aimed at strengthening the nation's "Information Superhighway," was signed by President Clinton in the library's Main Reading Room on February 8, 1996.

In fiscal year (FY) 1996 (October 1, 1995–September 30, 1996) the library operated with a budget of $352,399,000, an increase of $3,929,000, or 1.1 percent, over FY 1995, including authority to spend $27,699,000 in copyright receipts and cataloging-data sales.

Donald L. Scott, retired Army brigadier general and former vice-president and national director of the AmeriCorps National Civilian Community Corps, was appointed Deputy Librarian of Congress on September 30, 1996. He supervises day-to-day internal operations; the library's service unit heads report to him.

A newly developed Management Improvement Plan (MIP) was put in place to track progress in implementing institutional priorities. The MIP incorporates many of the recommendations contained in two reports commissioned by the General Accounting Office for Congress—a management review conducted by Booz-Allen & Hamilton and a financial audit conducted by Price Waterhouse LLP—which were completed in April 1996.

Service to Congress

The Congressional Research Service (CRS) delivered nearly 500,000 research responses to members and committees of Congress in 1996. An upgraded Inquiry Status and Information System (ISIS 96) was implemented on November 13, 1996, to track these requests. CRS staff supplied timely, objective analysis across a wide spectrum, including welfare reform, changes in immigration law, and revision of the 1934 Communications Act. Some 690,000 copies of CRS reports and related products were delivered to Congress. Of this number, approximately 30,000 products were distributed electronically through a fax-on-demand system (an online system that provides access to the full texts of CRS products) or via the CRS home page on the World Wide Web, which provides CRS Issue Briefs online to congressional offices.

Other direct assistance to Congress was provided by the Law Library, which answered nearly 5,100 reference requests from congressional users. Many of these queries were answered via the Law Library's "congressional hotline" telephone that operates when either chamber is in session. Law Library research staff produced 931 written reports for Congress, including comprehensive multinational studies on such issues as abortion, victims' rights, computer security, and intellectual property.

Working with the Committee on House Oversight, the Senate Committee on Rules and Administration, in consultation with the House and Senate subcommittees on legislative-branch appropriations, the Library of Congress developed a plan for a single integrated legislative information retrieval system to serve Congress. The proposed system, called the Legislative Information System (LIS), would reduce duplication of efforts within the legislative branch and improve the quality and timeliness of information to Congress. By the end of FY 1996 development was under way, with a first release of the system planned for the start of the 105th Congress.

Service to the Nation

The library continued to reduce its arrearage of unprocessed materials, as demonstrated by another cut of 1.5 million items during FY 1996—a cumulative 47.2 percent decrease since the initial arrearage census in September 1989. Arrearage reduction efforts have most recently made available to researchers the Altshuler Jazz Collection of 264,327 78-rpm sound records, a pamphlet collection of Americana consisting of 10,630 titles, and a Finnish collection of 1,000 titles.

Major progress was achieved in processing print materials, including cataloging a record 289,509 volumes. Building on the momentum generated in FY 1995 through the Program for Cooperative Cataloging, member libraries reached a high of 213 participants and contributed record-breaking totals in FY 1996: 14,173 bibliographic records, 97,964 name authorities, 8,074 series authorities, 2,026 subject authorities, and 780 classification numbers.

Linked to the library's arrearage reduction project is the development of a secondary storage site to house processed materials and to provide growth of the collection during the first part of the 21st century. During 1996 the Architect of the Capitol (AOC) contracted with an architectural firm to plan for the development of the Fort Meade, Maryland, campus and to design the initial collection storage module for the library. Plans call for the initial module for paper-based collections, primarily books, to be ready for occupancy in 1999.

The National Library Service for the Blind and Physically Handicapped (NLS/BPH) distributed more than 23 million items to some 777,000 readers in 1996. When President Clinton signed Public Law 104-197 on September 16, 1996, NLS/BPH received its most significant improvement in the national reading program since passage of the Pratt-Smoot Act more than 60 years earlier. Sponsored by Sen. John Chafee (R-R.I.), this amendment to Title 17 of the U.S.

Code grants nonprofit agencies automatic permission to reproduce nondramatic literary works in special formats. Books can now be converted into braille and audio formats as soon as they appear in print, without securing permission from the copyright holder.

On September 18, 1996, the American Folklife Center (AFC) celebrated its 20th anniversary. In 1996 AFC received a two-year congressional reauthorization, as well as private funding for the second year of the Montana Heritage Project and for the continuation of the Appalachian Forest Project.

Copyright

The Copyright Office received more than 620,000 claims and made some 550,000 registrations in 1996. Through its Web site, the Copyright Office disseminated public information and provided electronic access to its registration and recordation databases.

Effective January 1, 1996, the Copyright Restoration Provision of the GATT Uruguay Round Agreements Act restored the copyrights of a vast number of foreign works that were previously in the public domain in the United States. Through October 1996 the Copyright Office processed a total of 2,162 documents containing 7,632 restored titles.

Following the 125th anniversary of the Copyright Office's placement in the Library of Congress in 1995, legislation was introduced to join the Copyright Office with the Patent and Trademark Office in a new intellectual property organization within the Department of Commerce. The Librarian of Congress voiced his opposition to this measure in a written statement to the Senate Committee on the Judiciary: "The strength of the Library of Congress and its ability to serve the Congress and the nation depend on the presence of the Copyright Office in this institution. The effective administration and protection of our copyright laws depend on the retention of both copyright practices and policy within the Copyright Office, within the Library of Congress, and within the Legislative Branch." Ultimately, the copyright provisions were removed from the bill, which died in the 104th Congress.

Electronic Access

Usage of the library's electronic resources grew exponentially during 1996. In April the library recorded more than 24 million monthly transactions on all of its computer systems—triple the number recorded in April 1992. The library's Internet home page was redesigned in June 1996 to facilitate public searching. The hours of online availability of the Library of Congress Information System (LOCIS) were extended to 24 hours per day to accommodate users in all time zones. In December the library enabled public access to Internet on ten workstations located in the Computer Catalog Center and five reading rooms (Prints and Photographs in the Madison Building; Hispanic, Local History and Genealogy, and the Main Reading Room in the Jefferson Building; and the Science Reading Room in the Adams Building).

The library's Internet-based systems were continually cited for excellence in 1996: (1) Point Communications, an Internet rating service, placed the library's Web site among the "Top 5% of All Web Sites"; (2) The *Atlantic Monthly* cited the library's exhibitions as "the most compelling area"; (3) *Time* magazine cited the library's American Memory historical collections among "the best Web sites of 1996"; (4) the National Information Infrastructure (NII) Awards Program chose the library as one of the six finalists in the education category; and (5) *PC Magazine* rated the library's Web site among the top 100 best sites.

Advancements made in 1996 to increase electronic access to the library's resources include the National Digital Library Program, THOMAS, the Global Legal Information Network, the Geographic Information System, and Technology Projects in Test Status.

National Digital Library Program

During 1996 the library gained momentum toward its ambitious goal of digitizing millions of items by the year 2000, the library's 200th anniversary. To date, more than 350,000 digital files are available online or in digital archives. In addition, more than 1.7 million digital files are in production or under contract for digitization. To support the effort, fund-raising for the National Digital Library program reached $22.2 million in cash and pledges from the private sector and $7 million toward the $15 million in public funds pledged by Congress.

The number of online multimedia American history collections more than doubled to 17 during the year. The two most recent additions were made available in October: *American Variety Stage: Vaudeville and Popular Entertainment, 1870–1920* contains the heavily referenced Houdini collection, and *Inside an American Factory: The Westinghouse Works* provides a glimpse of turn-of-the-century industrial life, including early motion picture footage of period machinery. The library also increased the number of online exhibitions to 12 with the addition of *Dresden: Treasures of the Saxon State Library*.

The National Digital Library effort continued to reach out to the education community with the March 6, 1996, launch of the Learning Page, a World Wide Web service designed for teachers and students. In September, a "Back to School Special" on the Learning Page added teacher-generated suggestions from the Center for Children and Technology on how to use the library's primary source materials in the classroom.

THOMAS

Named in honor of Thomas Jefferson, THOMAS is a database designed to make legislative information more accessible to the public. Inaugurated January 5, 1995, THOMAS is available 24 hours per day, free to Internet users. During 1996 THOMAS was expanded to include bill summary and status information, Major Legislation, House and Senate committee reports, Featured Items (from House committees), Congress This Week (floor actions), and the *Congressional Record Index* for the 103rd Congress and both sessions of the 104th Congress. In June 1996 the THOMAS home page was redesigned to facilitate system usage and to improve links to other Internet resources, such as House and Senate home pages and to the text of such historical documents as the Declaration of

Independence and the Constitution. As of September 30, 1996, more than 30 million transactions had been processed by the THOMAS system since its inception.

Global Legal Information Network (GLIN)

GLIN is a cooperative international network in which member nations contribute the full texts of statutes and regulations to a database hosted by the Law Library of Congress. GLIN made its debut on the library's home page in July 1996. Although only member countries can retrieve images of legal documents, nonmembers are able to search the database and retrieve citations. To date, 11 member nations are contributing abstracts and full texts at the rate of 15 entries per day.

Geographic Information System

The Geography and Map Division (G&M) established itself as a leader in the cartographic and geographic communities through its work in geographic information systems. Working closely with private-sector partners, G&M is developing the capability to create large-format digital images and transmit and display these images through the Internet. Donated computer hardware and software, valued in excess of $700,000, was installed and put into operation during 1996. More than 700 rare American maps have been scanned, and G&M successfully completed testing of a new file compression technology that will allow the library to transmit these images worldwide.

Technology Projects in Test Status

The Copyright Office Electronic Registration, Recordation and Deposit System (CORDS), a major new system for digital registration and deposit of copyrighted works over the Internet, is being developed by the Copyright Office in collaboration with the Advanced Research Projects Agency and the Corporation for National Research Initiatives. The Library of Congress successfully tested the registration and deposit components of the prototype system with Carnegie Mellon University in February 1996. Four applications and accompanying copyright works (unpublished computer science technical reports) were successfully transmitted over the Internet and processed by the Copyright Office.

The Electronic Cataloging in Publication (ECIP) project is testing the feasibility of electronically transmitting manuscripts for cataloging via the Internet to reduce the number of keystrokes needed to create a record, eliminate mail time and postage costs, and enhance the quality of cataloging. Using this system, completed catalog records can be transmitted via e-mail to the publisher for inclusion on the copyright page of the printed book. Fifty-three publishers are now participating in this project. Staff have cataloged 707 titles, bringing the cumulative total since the experiment's inception to 1,082.

Collections

The Library of Congress is using the results of the GAO management review, financial audit, and comprehensive survey of collections security by the

Computer Sciences Corporation to develop a centralized security program. Major security accomplishments during 1996 include (1) an automated reader registration system to identify readers using the Thomas Jefferson Building Reading Rooms; (2) an antitheft gate to prevent unauthorized removal of library materials from the Newspaper and Current Periodicals Reading Room; (3) restriction of personal belongings in reading rooms upon the installation of cloakrooms; (4) antitheft targets placed in an additional one million books, bringing the total to four million targeted volumes; (5) activation of the electronic system controlling stack access in the Adams Building; (6) assignment of a full-time, on-site security officer and implementation of a new electronic access system at the Landover Annex; and (7) implementation of an item-level inspection program before and after public use for material designated "vulnerable."

The library receives millions of pieces each year, from copyright deposits, federal agencies, and purchases, exchanges, and gifts. Notable acquisitions during FY 1996 include the personal library of writer and educator Ralph Ellison, author of *Invisible Man*; large additions to the National Association for the Advancement of Colored People Collection, 1919–1996; the personal papers and several hundred original drawings of cartoonist, playwright, and screenwriter Jules Feiffer; the first installment of the papers of Robert McNamara, former Secretary of Defense under Presidents John F. Kennedy and Lyndon B. Johnson; the papers of modern architect I. M. Pei; and *Ars Moriendi*, a 15th-century incunabulum.

The library's growing collection of music by jazz masters was enriched by a deposit of 10,000 music scores from the late jazz singer Ella Fitzgerald, including arrangements by Nelson Riddle and Billy May; 1,300 original compositions and arrangements and 6,000 printed scores from Louis Bellson; and an additional 6,000 scores from Bellson's wife, singer Pearl Bailey.

The Marian S. Carson Collection—believed to be the most extensive private collection of Americana and totaling about 10,000 manuscripts, broadsides, pamphlets, photographs, prints, and drawings dating from before the American Revolution to the late 19th century—was acquired by the library through a gift from Mrs. Carson, appropriated funds, and contributions from the James Madison Council.

The Samuel Breeze Collection of 110 manuscript maps, original printing plates, proof pulls, and business records documenting the development of the cerographic (wax-engraving) process for map printing developed in the United States in the 1830s was also acquired.

Publications

The Publishing Office produced more than 40 books, calendars, and other products describing the library's collections—many of them through cooperative agreements. Five new copublishing agreements were signed with major trade publishers; and by the end of 1996, 19 cooperative agreements were in effect with such publishers such as Crown, Harry N. Abrams, Viking/Penguin, Pomegranate Artbooks, Scott Foresman/Addison Wesley, and Fulcrum Publishing. Highlights of these copublishing agreements were the release of *The*

Millennium Book of Days, published by Crown Publishers; *Witnessing America: The Library of Congress Book of Firsthand Accounts of Life in America, 1600–1900*, published by Penguin Reference; and two in a series of seven multimedia CD-ROMs called *AuthorWorks*. The series, aimed at grades 6–12, was produced in conjunction with the Scott Foresman/Addison Wesley Literature and Integrated Studies textbook series.

The Publishing Office won two awards for overall design excellence. The award winners, from Washington Book Publishers, were *Dresden: Treasures from the Saxon State Library*, companion catalog to the exhibition, and *Library of Congress Geography and Maps: An Illustrated Guide*. This guide, along with others in the series—such as *Library of Congress Hispanic and Portuguese Collections: An Illustrated Guide*—were funded in part by the Madison Council, the library's private-sector advisory body.

At year's end the latest in a series of subject area resource guides was released: *Many Nations: A Library of Congress Resource Guide for the Study of Indian and Alaska Native Peoples in the United States* was the result of a six-year effort by a team of library staff members.

Exhibitions and Literary Events

The library's collections were shared with tens of thousands of Americans through exhibitions, special events, symposia, and traveling exhibitions. The major exhibition of the year was *Dresden: Treasures from the Saxon State Library* (April 11–July 13, 1996), which drew 70,000 visitors. Celebrating the 440th anniversary of the illustrious Sachsische Landesbibliothek (Saxon State Library), the exhibition includes priceless manuscripts of classical literature by Horace and Ovid; original musical scores by J. S. Bach, Vivaldi, Wagner, von Weber, and Schumann; illuminated and religious works; a sketchbook of Albrecht Durer; and images from life in Dresden.

Other exhibits included *Space and Place: Mapmaking East and West, 400 Years of Western and Chinese Cartography* (July 11–October 11); *Drawing the Iron Curtain: Cold War Cartoons, 1946–1960* (May 23–August 21); *Pablo Neruda: Absence and Presence* (September 4–October 18); *Jules Feiffer: Cartoons and Manuscripts* (October 18, 1996–January 31, 1997); and *Frank Lloyd Wright: Designs for an American Landscape, 1922–1932* (November 14, 1996–February 15, 1997).

The Gutenberg Bible and the Giant Bible of Mainz (both prepared in Mainz, Germany, in the 1450s) were returned to permanent display in the Great Hall of the Jefferson Building in November. They had been on display in the Madison Building during the renovation of the Jefferson Building.

Six traveling exhibits—on subjects as diverse as the history of the spiritual and cultural creativity of the Jewish people and literary maps of American states—extended the riches of the library's collections to 21 venues in 17 states.

Robert Hass, the library's eighth poet laureate consultant, served for the 1995–1996 season, and was reappointed for 1996–1997. He received national attention, appearing regularly on the "NewsHour with Jim Lehrer," with a weekly column in the *Washington Post*'s "Book World" section, and featured in articles about his own work and that of other poets in major media outlets. In cooperation with *Orion* magazine, Mr. Hass organized a week-long exploration of nature writing that brought together 31 poets, essayists, novelists, science writers, and ecologists under the theme "Watershed: Writers, Nature, and Community."

Historian Martin E. Marty of the University of Chicago delivered the fourth annual Joanna Jackson Goldman Memorial Lecture on April 13. The title of his lecture was "America After Its Trauma: Tribalism, Totalism, and the Common Good."

Under the terms of the National Film Preservation Act, each year the Librarian of Congress names 25 "culturally, historically or aesthetically" significant motion pictures to the National Film Registry. Each list serves to increase public awareness of the richness of American cinema and the need for its preservation. The films selected for the registry in 1995 toured in eight cities.

The following 25 films were named to the National Film Registry in 1996, bringing the total to 200:

The Awful Truth (1937)
Broken Blossoms (1919)
The Deer Hunter (1978)
Destry Rides Again (1939)
Flash Gordon serial (1936)
The Forgotten Frontier (1931)
Frank Film (1973)
The Graduate (1967)
The Heiress (1949)
The Jazz Singer (1927)
The Life and Times of Rosie the Riveter (1980)
*M*A*S*H* (1970)
Mildred Pierce (1945)
The Outlaw Josie Wales (1976)
The Producers (1968)
Pull My Daisy (1959)
Road to Morocco (1942)
She Done Him Wrong (1933)
Shock Corridor (1963)
Show Boat (1936)
The Thief of Baghdad (1924)
To Be or Not to Be (1942)
Topaz (1943–45)
Verbena Tragica (1939)
Woodstock (1970)

Preservation

The library took action during 1996 to improve the preservation of its vast and diverse collections by (1) completing the installation of a state-of-the-art audio system to preserve and restore at least 80 percent of the library's audio collections, including audio cylinders; (2) developing a design for protective casing to house the library's "Top Treasures"; (3) implementing the emergency response plan; (4) completing the mass deacidification treatment of the first 25,000 books from the general collections using the Bookkeeper limited-production contract; (5) training staff to use the computer-driven, automated box-making machine; (6) refining procedures for the preparation, treatment, and scanning of collection material as part of the National Digital Library effort; (7) developing environmental specifications for the secondary storage facility at Fort Meade; and (8) refurbishing the display cases for the Gutenberg Bible and the Giant Bible of Mainz.

Restoration and Renovation

The Architect of the Capitol completed interior renovation and restoration of the Thomas Jefferson and Adams buildings (except for the Coolidge Auditorium and Whittall Pavilion, to be completed in October 1997) and reopened the west front entrance of the Jefferson Building on January 2, 1996. A Visitors' Center is under construction, to be completed for the May 1, 1997, reopening of the whole building, which coincides with the 100th birthday of the Thomas Jefferson Building.

Human Resources

The trend toward a downsized staff continued with 4,114 permanent library employees on board during 1996, a 10 percent reduction over the past two years. A library-wide reorganization in November 1996 involved the merger of three service units (Collections Services, Constituent Services, and most of Cultural Affairs) into one unit (Library Services), which assumed the functions of acquisitions, cataloging, public service, and preservation. A National Services unit within Library Services assumed responsibility for areas of library outreach, such as the Federal Library and Information Center Committee and the National Library Service for the Blind and Physically Handicapped.

On November 14, 1996, the U.S. Court of Appeals for the District of Columbia Circuit authorized the library to begin implementing the $8.5 million settlement in the *Cook* class action suit, which began as an Equal Employment Opportunity complaint in 1975.

In October 1996, 29 affirmative-action interns completed the 1994–1996 program and were placed in GS-7 or GS-9 positions with promotion plans to the GS-11 or GS-12 level.

In March 1996 the first ten participants graduated from the new Leadership Development Program after a 15-month training program. All filled Library of Congress positions. Forty staffers received the Affirmative Action Tuition

Support Award. The award carries a stipend of up to $1,200 for education in eight job series: social science analyst, economist, foreign affairs analyst, computer science specialist, administrative officer, copyright examiner, librarian, and technical information specialist.

In August 1996 the first ten participants completed the Hispanic intern program. The library also welcomed its first class of ten interns from the Hispanic Association of Colleges and Universities National Internship Program, a nonprofit national education association representing 127 Hispanic-serving institutions of higher education. Interns received ten-week work assignments in various library offices.

Award-Winning Magazine

During its second year of publication, *Civilization: The Magazine of the Library of Congress* won the 1996 National Magazine Award for general excellence in its circulation class. On January 15, 1997, Capital Publishing (a subsidiary of Boston-based Fidelity Investments) signed a formal purchase agreement to buy the award-winning publication and pledged a major investment to boost circulation, which numbered some 218,000 paid subscribers at year's end.

Additional Sources of Information

Library of Congress telephone numbers for public information:

Main switchboard (with menu)	202-707-5000
Reading room hours and locations	202-707-6400
General reference	202-707-5522
	202-707-4210 TTY
Exhibition hours/visitor information	202-707-8000
	202-707-6200 TTY
Research advice	202-707-6500
Sales shop	202-707-0204
Copyright information	202-707-3000
Copyright hotline (to order forms)	202-707-9100

Center for the Book

John Y. Cole
Director, The Center for the Book
Library of Congress

With its network of 32 affiliated state centers and more than 80 national and civic organizations serving as reading-promotion partners, the Center for the Book is one of the Library of Congress's most dynamic and visible educational outreach programs. Since 1977, when it was established by Librarian of Congress Daniel J. Boorstin, the center has used the prestige and resources of the Library of Congress to stimulate public interest in books, reading, libraries, and literacy and to encourage the study of books and the printed word.

The center is a successful public-private partnership; the Library of Congress supports its four full-time positions, but its projects, events, and publications are funded primarily through contributions from individuals, corporations, foundations, and government organizations.

1996 Highlights

- The addition of three states—New Mexico, South Carolina, and Tennessee—to the center's national network of affiliated state centers for the book
- "Library-Head Start-Museum Partnership" workshops in Austin, Phoenix, and Denver that brought together more than 250 Head Start teachers and administrators, librarians, and museum specialists to develop cooperative, community-level projects to promote reading and family literacy
- The launching of "Books and Beyond," a continuing series of talks at the Library of Congress by authors of recently published books
- The inaugural presentation of "Read More About It" lists of suggested readings on the National Digital Library's Learning Page on the World Wide Web
- The creation of a Center for the Book home page on the Library of Congress's World Wide Web site, with links to state center affiliates and other resources
- Cosponsorship, at the Library of Congress, of the Bradley Lecture series about "books that mattered to Western citizenship, statecraft, and public policy"
- Publication of *Books Change Lives*, a report on the center's 1993–1994 national reading promotion campaign; *Libraries: The Drama Within*, a volume of photographs of readers in libraries published in association with the University of New Mexico; and *Even Anchors Need Lifelines: Public Libraries in Adult Literacy*, by Gail Spangenberg, a study sponsored by the Center for the Book in cooperation with the National Center for Literacy and the American Library Association

Themes

The Center for the Book establishes national reading-promotion themes to stimulate interest and support for reading and literacy projects that benefit all age groups. Used by state centers, national organizational partners, and hundreds of U.S. schools and libraries, each theme reminds Americans of the importance of books, reading, and libraries in today's world. "Shape Your Future—READ!" continued as the theme for 1996 and served as the focal point for the center's reading-promotion activities. "Building a Nation of Readers" was announced as the center's national reading promotion theme from 1997 through 2000.

Reading Promotion Partners

The center's partnership program expanded the range of its projects in 1996. The importance of letters, language, and design in promoting reading and literacy is the emphasis of "The Alphabet Project," a cooperative effort with the American Institute of Graphic Arts (AIGA). A primary focus is on nurturing joint projects among the 32 state center affiliates and the 37 AIGA chapters of graphic designers across the country. The partnership with "Everybody Wins," which emphasizes adults reading with young children on a weekly basis, involves three state centers in pilot projects. The national "Letters About Literature" essay contest for young people organized by Weekly Reader Corporation's *Read* magazine, received more than 14,000 entries in 1996, with 19 state centers participating in the selection of state winners.

State Centers

When James H. Billington became Librarian of Congress in 1987, the Center for the Book had ten affiliated state centers; at the end of fiscal year (FY) 1996 there were 32. The newest state centers are in New Mexico, located at the New Mexico State Library; South Carolina, based at the South Carolina State Library; and Tennessee, located with the Tennessee Humanities Council.

Each state center works with the Library of Congress to promote books, reading, and libraries as well as the state's own literary and intellectual heritage. Each center also develops and funds its own operations and projects, using Library of Congress promotion themes when appropriate and occasionally hosting Library of Congress-sponsored events and traveling exhibits. When its application is approved, a state center is granted affiliate status for three years. Renewals are for three-year periods.

On May 6, 1996, representatives from 28 state centers participated in an idea-sharing session at the Library of Congress. State center representatives discussed such topics as developing partnerships and coalitions, strengthening new state centers, fund-raising, and making effective use of reading-promotion themes. Growing interest in electronic communications and in books and their relationship to new technologies was apparent. State literary heritage projects also remain popular. Other state center projects discussed included Arizona's promotion of reading clubs and a monthly literary luncheon; Colorado's successful Rocky Mountain Book Festival; Vermont's "Mother Goose Asks Why?" science reading project; Virginia's use of teleconferencing; and Wisconsin's author database on CD-ROM. In FY 1996 the traveling exhibit "Bonfire of Liberties: Censorship of the Humanities" was seen in Arizona, California, and Oregon.

Projects

The Library-Head Start-Museum partnership project continued into FY 1996 with three state workshops. Funded with a transfer of funds from the U.S. Department of Health and Human Services to the Center for the Book and carried out in collaboration with the Association for Library Service to Children (ALSC), a division of the American Library Association, and the Association of Youth Museums, the Library-Head Start-Museum partnership demonstrates in American communities how libraries, museums, and Head Start programs can work together to promote reading and family literacy. State workshops were hosted by the Texas Center for the Book in Austin December 7–8, 1995, by the Arizona Center for the Book in Phoenix February 29–March 1, 1996, and by the Colorado Center for the Book in Denver September 5–6, 1996.

In January 1996 the Center for the Book became the on-the-air producer of "The Sound of Writing," a National Public Radio (NPR) program of short-story readings that is broadcast on more than 100 NPR affiliates. In September 1996 director John Y. Cole began a series of guest appearances on "The Book Guys," an NPR program about the world of books and book collecting that is broadcast by 20 NPR affiliates.

In cooperation with the American Folklife Center, the center continued to represent the Library of Congress in the "Montana Heritage Project," a community-based project for Montana high school students.

As part of its mission of stimulating public interest in books and reading, the center began cooperating closely with Discovery Communication's The Learning Channel in the production of its "Great Books" series of one-hour specials about classics of world literature. The center formed an advisory panel to help select books to be included in the series and continues to offer advice and other kinds of help. Each "Great Books" program carries the acknowledgment "Produced in Cooperation with the Center for the Book in the Library of Congress."

Outreach

In 1996 the center created a home page on the Library of Congress's World Wide Web site. The Web pages, established and maintained by Maurvene D. Williams, include an overview of the center's purpose; information about projects and other activities; a calendar of selected forthcoming events; recent press releases; news from the center provided through a link to the library's *Information Bulletin*; a list of state centers with contact information, including links to Web sites; a bibliography of Center for the Book publications; the full text from the current reading-promotion theme brochure; the history of the community of the book prior to the founding of the center; a list of community of the book organizations, with links where available; and a list of book fairs and literary festivals. The Center for the Book's home page address is http://lcweb.loc.gov/loc/cfbook.

In 1996 the Center for the Book prepared six new reading lists for the Library of Congress/CBS Television "Read More About It" project. The 30-second messages appeared during several major prime-time telecasts, including the U.S. Open tennis championship and the special "Aladdin on Ice," which was seen by five million viewers. The "Read More About It" project is now in its 17th season. Since 1979 these reading messages from the Library of Congress, which direct viewers to their local libraries and bookstores, have been telecast on more than 400 CBS Television programs.

Five issues of the newsletter *Center for the Book News* and one issue of the briefer *Center for the Book Quick Takes* were produced in 1996. A new edition of the state center handbook was produced in May 1996. The Library of Congress issued 24 press releases about Center for the Book activities, and a two-page "News from the Center for the Book" feature appeared in each issue of the Library of Congress's *Information Bulletin*.

Events

Sponsorship of events, symposia, and lectures—at the Library of Congress and elsewhere—is an important Center for the Book activity. Through such special events, the center brings diverse audiences together on behalf of books and reading and publicizes its activities nationally and locally. Examples of events at the Library of Congress in 1996 include 12 talks by authors; a reception and program marking the 20th anniversary of the National Commission on Libraries and Information Science; two programs cosponsored with the library's Preservation Directorate: Preservation Awareness Day on April 30 and the symposium "Preservation Selection for 19th Century Books," held on September 30; and a program and reception in the library's Great Hall to promote the "Great Books" television series, cosponsored with The Learning Channel.

Federal Library and Information Center Committee

Library of Congress, Washington, DC 20540
202-707-4800
World Wide Web: http://lcweb.loc.gov/flicc

Susan M. Tarr
Executive Director

Highlights of the Year

During fiscal year (FY) 1996 the Federal Library and Information Center Committee (FLICC) worked to meet the changing professional and service needs of the federal library and information center community. FLICC's annual information policy forum featured expert panelists exploring the balance between open access to and protection of government information. FLICC also reinstituted its annual symposium on the information professional, focusing on the importance of forming liaisons with computer professionals.

FLICC working groups finished reviewing the results of the FY 1994 nationwide survey of federal libraries and information centers and worked with the National Center for Education Statistics to publish the tabulations; developed new educational initiatives for advocacy, library technicians, and distance learning; updated the five-year-old FLICC bylaws; initiated an information technology listserv; and published a background paper on qualifications requirements for federal librarian positions. FLICC sponsored 26 seminars and workshops for 1,282 participants. Staff also conducted 108 Online Computer Library Center (OCLC) and Internet training classes for 1,122 students.

FLICC's cooperative network, FEDLINK, continued to enhance its fiscal operations, successfully passing a General Accounting Office (GAO) audit and completing a productive systems compliance review by an outside contractor. FEDLINK Network Operations (FNO), with advice from the FLICC Information Technology Working Group, implemented the FLICC/FEDLINK Web site (http://lcweb.loc.gov/flicc), with links to FEDLINK vendor home pages. FEDLINK completed the year with 101 vendors, including two new service areas—technical processing services and copyright clearance. In addition, FEDLINK initiated subscription options with many of its online database vendors.

Quarterly Membership Meetings

At the year's first FLICC quarterly membership meeting, FLICC Executive Board members led small group brainstorming sessions to reconsider FLICC's Vision 2000 statement, and to identify crucial issues for FLICC members and specific actions for FLICC and FEDLINK for the next five years. Crucial issues fell into four general categories: technology, personnel/staffing, funding/service, and shifting organizations.

The second quarterly membership meeting featured FLICC member Phyllis Christenson, director of the Information Services Center, GAO, who initiated

FLICC's year-long focus on library advocacy by reporting on her recent experience in defending the Information Services Center in GAO downsizing actions. Small group discussions highlighted strategies (such as home pages, focus groups, user-group presentations, initiatives to agency management, and library committees) for promoting federal libraries and information centers.

The third FLICC quarterly membership meeting continued the advocacy focus with a panel on both internal and external library committees. Laurie Stackpole, chief librarian, the Ruth H. Hooker Research Library and Technical Information Center, Naval Research Laboratory (NRL), described NRL's reconstituted, proactive library committee. Comprised of research division heads, this committee has raised the NRL library's visibility and status. Nancy Cavanaugh, acting director, Collection Development and Technical Services Division, National Library of Education (NLE), discussed the formation and accomplishments of the NLE Task Force, an external committee mandated in the law that established the NLE. Finally, Carol Watts, director, National Oceanographic and Atmospheric Administration (NOAA) Library, traced the development of NOAA's Library Advisory Council, which includes library champions from line, staff, and program offices who are appointed for two-year terms. In addition, each of NOAA's 30 libraries in the field has its own advocacy group. Other FLICC members also shared their experiences with "user" committees.

The fourth membership meeting featured a guest lecture on "Making the Case for Library Support" by Betty Turock, professor, School of Communication, Information and Library Studies, Rutgers University, and immediate past president of the American Library Association (ALA). Turock presented several methods for evaluating a library's success and stressed the importance of constructing a mission statement to use as a planning and measuring device.

Working Groups

Education Working Group

In addition to program-planning activities, the FLICC Education Working Group concentrated developmental efforts in three areas: advocacy, library technician training, and distance learning. The results of these efforts will be evident in FY 1997 programs.

In FY 1996 the Education Working Group directly sponsored the 1996 FLICC Forum on Federal Information Policies, "The Public's Information: Striking a Balance Between Access and Control" on March 19; a CD-ROM Instruction discussion on February 12; "Just in Time: Making Real Choices—Interlibrary Loan vs. Document Delivery" on July 22; "Clause and Effect: Negotiating License Agreements for Digital Publications" on August 1; the 1996 FLICC Symposium on the Information Professional, "Dangerous Liaisons? Partnering with Computer Professionals to Create Digital Information Services" on September 24; and a series of three "brown-bag discussions" on copyright issues, culminating in an all-day symposium, "Copyright in the Digital Age: Issues and Applications for Federal Libraries" on May 21. Once again, the Education Working Group sponsored a downlink site for a second series of "Soaring to Excellence" programs for library technicians. In addition, the working group cosponsored five programs: "This Library Is Closed..." on November 13 (with the District of Columbia Library Association); the Joint Spring Workshop on April 26; "Technical Services Workstations: The State of the Art in Cataloging" on April 29 (with the Association for Library Collections and Technical Services and the CAPCON Network); the Federal Law Librarians' "Agency Day" on June 17 (with the Law Librarians Society of Washington, D.C.); and "Electronic Journals Today" on September 10 (with the CAPCON Network).

Budget and Finance Working Group

The FLICC Budget and Finance Working Group began meeting in February to develop the FY 1997 FEDLINK budget. This budget ultimately held FEDLINK service fees to FY 1996 levels and reduced FEDLINK program costs by 2 percent relative to the FY 1996 budget. The FLICC and FEDLINK voting members unanimously supported the FY 1997 budget proposal.

Information Technology Working Group

In FY 1996 the recently established Information Technology Working Group focused on the three areas identified by FEDLINK members as of greatest concern to the federal library community: information sharing, the Internet, and licensing/acquisitions agreements. To increase information sharing, the group worked toward the development of a database identifying the automated systems used by federal libraries and information centers. With the help of an Army librarian on detail, FLICC staff created a questionnaire to collect this information; following review by the Survey Working Group, the questionnaire will be distributed and the database created in FY 1997. To better use Internet resources, the group initiated its own information technology listserv, FEDLIBIT, moderated by a working group member. The working group has also assumed responsibility for planning FLICC's annual *Information Technology Update*, which in 1997 will highlight intranet issues. To explore licensing issues, a subgroup held several meetings; they outlined problems and opportunities and then presented a half-day symposium, "Clause and Effect," on August 1, in cooperation with the Education Working Group.

Membership and Governance Working Group

Beginning in FY 1994 the FLICC Membership and Governance Working Group has been reexamining the FLICC bylaws, in effect since 1991. During FY 1996 the group completed its review of the bylaws and presented its proposed revisions to the FEDLINK Advisory Council and the FLICC Executive Board (FEB). The proposed revisions include substantial language clarification, updates, and changes to the election process. After reconsidering its proposal to accommodate FEB comments, the working group will submit a modified package for approval by the FLICC membership and the Librarian of Congress in 1997.

Nominating Working Group

In FY 1996 the Nominating Working Group oversaw the 1996 election of the following three FLICC rotating members who will serve a three-year term

(1997-1999): Ann Parham (National Defense University), Jewel Player (Army Materiel Command), and Mary Augusta Thomas (Smithsonian Institution). The group also managed the election of the following five FEDLINK members to FLICC for the 1997-1999 term: Nancy Cavanaugh (National Library of Education), Barbara Huckins (Veterans Administration), Bonnie Klein (Defense Technical Information Center), Denise Lomax (Federal Bureau of Prisons), and Janet Wright (National Agricultural Library). The three achieving the highest number of votes (Klein, Lomax, and Wright) will also serve for three years on the FEDLINK Advisory Council.

Personnel Working Group

The Personnel Working Group edited its 1993 background paper to support the master's degree qualifications requirement for federal librarian positions. At the end of FY 1996 FLICC published the document, titled "Qualification Needs for Federal Librarians: A Position Paper Prepared for the Office of Personnel Management," and made it available to federal libraries and information centers.

Preservation and Binding Working Group

The FLICC Preservation and Binding Working Group hosted a downlink site at the Library of Congress (LC) for the two-hour teleconference "Mass Deacidification for Paper-Based Collections" in October 1995. In April the group sponsored a symposium on "Preserving Federal Depository Library Materials for Today's User and Users in the 21st Century," to coincide with the spring meeting of the Government Printing Office Depository Library Council as it considered the congressional initiative to convert to electronic distribution and archiving. For the June issue of *FEDLINK Technical Notes*, working group member Karma Beal wrote an assessment of "Preservation on the Worldwide Web." At year's end the working group was updating preservation reference and resource listings to provide complementary information on FLICC's own Web site.

Policy Working Group

In FY 1996 FLICC reconstituted its Policy Working Group to include seven federal information policy experts and leaders in addition to the members of the FLICC Executive Board. The group agreed to abandon on-site meetings and develop communications via a closed listserv maintained by FLICC staff to share information on such topics as GILS (Government Information Locator System), the electronic Federal Depository Libraries proposal, appropriations status, documents exchange and surplus policies, and the role of chief information officers vis-a-vis federal libraries and information centers.

Reference/Public Services Working Group

The FLICC Reference/Public Services Working Group continued communications over FEDREF-L, FLICC's open listserv for reference librarians. The group also supported four brown-bag lunch discussions about reference issues relating to the Internet and another lunchtime discussion of CD-ROM user training.

Survey Working Group

Organized in FY 1991 to update the 1978 federal library statistics, the FLICC Survey Working Group (formerly the FLICC Statistics Working Group) continued working with the National Center for Education Statistics (NCES) and the Bureau of the Census to review results from the FY 1994 census of federal libraries and information centers. Chaired by Elizabeth Yeates (Nuclear Regulatory Commission), the FLICC Survey Working Group assisted the Census Bureau and NCES in interpreting responses and determining how to display tabulations for publication. Yeates and FLICC Executive Director Susan Tarr participated on the NCES publications review board. The survey tabulations, available from NCES in print and via their Web site (http://www.ed.gov/NCES), comprise 34 tables covering 18 distinct topics; 16 of the topic areas are analyzed both by government organizational unit and by library type. The working group is also working with NCES to review a consultant's extended analysis of the survey results, to be available in 1997.

Publications and Education Office

Publications

In FY 1996, despite the resignation of editor-in-chief Darlene Dolan in March, the FLICC Publications and Education Office (FPE) supported an ambitious publications schedule with the help of a temporary writer-editor and the addition of a permanent editorial assistant in June. During FY 1996 FPE produced ten issues of *FEDLINK Technical Notes* and five eight-page issues of the *FLICC Quarterly Newsletter*. FPE also published a 20-page summary of the 1995 FLICC Forum, "The Cycle of Government Information: Challenges of Electronic Innovation," and (in conjunction with FEDLINK staff) a fourth edition of the *Checklist of Microcomputer-Based Library Systems* and the first edition of the *FLICC/ FEDLINK Education Catalog*, to be updated quarterly. FPE published expanded and enhanced materials to support the FEDLINK program, including the FY 1997 *FEDLINK Registration Booklet*, the looseleaf FY 1997 *FEDLINK Member Handbook*, and the FY 1996 FEDLINK Books Package, as well as 11 *FEDLINK Information Alerts* and a comprehensive FLICC/FEDLINK information packet. FPE also produced the FY 1995 *FLICC Annual Report*, minutes of the FY 1996 FLICC quarterly meetings and bimonthly FEB meetings, and all FLICC Education Program promotional and support materials including the four-color FLICC forum announcement, forum attendee and speaker badges, press advisories, speeches and speaker remarks, and forum collateral materials. In addition the office produced 29 FLICC meeting announcements to promote FLICC education programs, FEDLINK membership, vendor, and OCLC user meetings.

Education

In conjunction with the FLICC Education Working Group, FLICC offered a total of 26 seminars, workshops, and lunchtime discussions to more than 1,280 members of the federal library and information center community. The FY 1996 FLICC education schedule underscored cooperative relationships as FLICC sponsored programs with other organizations in the library, education, and association community, including the CAPCON Library Network; the National

Institute for Library Personnel; the Learning Resources Center and Library Technical Assistant Program at the College of DuPage; the Federal Librarians Special Interest Section of the Law Librarians Society of Washington, D.C.; the Potomac Valley Chapter of the American Society for Information Science; the District of Columbia Library Association; the D.C. Online Users Group; the Special Libraries Association, D.C. Chapter; and ALA's Association for Library Collections and Technical Services (ALCTS).

FLICC also provided organizational, promotional, and logistical support to FEDLINK meetings and events, including the FEDLINK fall and spring membership meetings, two FEDLINK OCLC Users Group meetings, the FEDLINK FY 1996 vendor briefing, and a program on how to use FEDLINK in FY 1997. The latter program was repeated in Denver for 35 FEDLINK users in that region. FLICC continued and expanded its videotaping of FLICC programs and developed an arrangement with the National Library of Education to make FLICC videotapes more readily available to federal libraries through interlibrary loan.

FEDLINK (Federal Library and Information Network)

In FY 1996 FEDLINK provided federal agencies with cost-effective access to an array of automated information retrieval services for online research, cataloging, and interlibrary loan. FEDLINK member agencies also procured such publications as serials, electronic journals, CD-ROMs, and books via LC/FEDLINK contracts with major vendors.

The FEDLINK Advisory Council (FAC) met monthly (excluding November and August) during FY 1996. During the year, FAC approved the FY 1997 FEDLINK budget, assisted in the spring and fall FEDLINK membership meetings, and reported on its 1995 member survey. Survey respondents were particularly interested in having FEDLINK offer the following services: more training in information technology, assistance in handling staff shortages, consultation services to support decision making, and help in communicating the value of library services to agency officials.

The fall FEDLINK membership meeting was held on November 8, 1995. The principal speaker was Lisa Weber of the Policy and Information Resources Management Services, National Archives and Records Administration, who addressed "Talking about GILS from a Library/Archives Point of View." The spring membership meeting was held on May 1, 1996. Barbara Polansky of the American Chemical Society addressed "Copyright Issues and Concerns in Electronic Publishing: A Scholarly Publisher's Perspective."

FEDLINK Network Operations: OCLC Network Activity

During the first quarter of the fiscal year 60 FEDLINK OCLC users attended the 1995 fall FEDLINK OCLC Users Group meeting at which the OCLC team outlined new and upcoming products and services. FLICC Executive Director Tarr hosted Susan Olson of OCLC and three other OCLC staff on October 26 for the annual review of FEDLINK as a regional OCLC network. OCLC deemed FEDLINK's performance and dedication of resources satisfactory. On December 4 a luncheon program on interlibrary loan and document delivery provided members with the opportunity to discuss the many options offered by OCLC and other providers.

During the second quarter Fedlink Network Operations (FNO) staff helped OCLC make a telecommunications shift of dial-access libraries from the OCLC Sprint hubs to CompuServe to take advantage of lines that will allow access to OCLC at up to 28.8 bps. Staff introduced the new OCLC telecommunications software, Passport for Windows, by conducting eight classes in the spring and a special "Passport for Windows for Catalogers" session at the Smithsonian libraries in July. The focus of the training shifted from installation and configuration to how to better use the software to assist the library in serving its mission.

In the third quarter FEDLINK held the spring OCLC users meeting. On May 1, 1996, Anita Reeb, OCLC account manager for FEDLINK members, provided an overview of the SiteSearch software and WebZ. On May 10 Patti Fields delivered a one-hour overview on Format Integration Phase 2 changes at the Army Library Institute in Carlisle, Pennsylvania, as part of her afternoon program, "OCLC Cataloging Update."

In the fourth quarter FEDLINK staff worked with the Library of Congress Technical Processing and Automation Instruction Office to present the first FLICC/FEDLINK Cataloging Institute, July 29–August 2. Attended by 60 students, the event provided 30 contact hours of training in cataloging concepts relevant to the participants' workplaces; it provided a structured grounding in the most basic concepts of description and access in the Anglo-American Cataloguing Rules, using CDS's publication *Cataloging Concepts: Descriptive Cataloging*. Afternoon sessions furnished instruction in OCLC MARC applications. In August and September FNO staff conducted significant regional OCLC training in the field, traveling to the following Air Force base (AFB) libraries: Fairchild AFB, Washington; Vance AFB, Oklahoma; Goodfellow AFB, Texas; Randolph AFB, Texas; Laughlin AFB, Texas; Scott AFB, Illinois; Columbus AFB, Mississippi; and Maxwell AFB, Alabama.

Executive Director Tarr continued to attend the quarterly meetings of the Regional OCLC Network Directors Advisory Council (RONDAC). At the spring meeting, Tarr was elected vice-chair/chair elect of RONDAC; her term as chair will begin in May 1997.

FEDLINK Internet/Technology Program

The FLICC/FEDLINK Web site was inaugurated in June 1996. The site provides access to FLICC/FEDLINK publications, information about FEDLINK services (including training and education, events, OCLC support, and contracting), and the FY 1996 FEDLINK Services Directory. During the year, new listservs were created for the FLICC Information Technology Working Group and the Policy Working Group, and a listserv was "loaned" to the National Biological Survey to assist with the integration of that service into the Geological Survey. Also, at the request of the FEDLINK Advisory Council (FAC), FEDLIB was converted to an interactive listserv to enable FAC to increase its contact with FEDLINK members. Members of FAC will moderate the listserv on a rotating basis. FEDLINK Network Operations staff continue to maintain three subject-oriented listservs: FEDCAT-L, FEDREF-L, and FEDACQ-L. At the beginning of FY 1996 staff converted the basic Internet class from a two-day course to multiple one-day specialized courses. In early 1996 Fedlink Network Operations (FNO) further redesigned the intermediate and advanced World Wide Web courses. FNO staff conducted six free Internet brown-bag discussion sessions during 1996: "Providing Reference Service by E-mail," "Tools for Searching the Internet," "Technical Services on the Internet," "Reference Service by E-mail: Part II," "GPO Pathway Service," and "Evaluating Internet Reference Resources." On April 29, 104 librarians attended the ALA/ALCTS Institute on Technical Services Workstations, a technology that brings the tools of cataloging together on a single computer. FEDLINK initiated this program for the D.C. area and cosponsored it with the CAPCON Network.

Exhibits Program

For the first time in its history, FLICC/FEDLINK created an exhibit booth and unveiled it at the Special Libraries Association conference in Boston in early June. FLICC/FEDLINK exhibited via the LC booth at the ALA Annual Conference in New York in July.

FEDLINK Training Classes in FY 1996

One hundred and eight OCLC and Internet classes were conducted, with 1,122 students. Staff introduced the new OCLC telecommunications software, Passport for Windows, and held a special training session at the Smithsonian libraries.

Procurement Services

Database Retrieval Services: In June FEDLINK announced the availability of subscription pricing for online and CD-ROM database services. Members were able for the first time to subscribe to an online system for a fixed period of time—a finite amount of service at a fixed price. Also, FEDLINK kept its database solicitation open during most of the year, resulting in the addition of four new vendors.

Publications Acquisitions: In May FEDLINK created and distributed to members a 60-page package containing a full-scale comparison of the services and costs for FY 1996 FEDLINK books jobbers/publishers. To acquaint members with the expanding world of electronic journals, staff held meetings with Academic Press to explore its pilot project, IDEAL, and invited the Johns Hopkins University Press to demonstrate and discuss its Project MUSE electronic journals system at a program on April 23. On September 10, FLICC and CAPCON cooperated to produce a full-day program on electronic journals. Publishers, librarians, and intermediaries explained how they are meeting the challenges posed by moving from print to electronic media.

Library Support Services: In August five contractors signed agreements to conduct technical processing services through the FEDLINK program. These services include original cataloging, copy cataloging, retrospective conversion, and physical processing. During the summer FEDLINK concluded negotiations on a sole-source agreement with the Copyright Clearance Center, an organization that can provide an agency with an annual license to photocopy from the works of more than 9,000 publishers.

FEDLINK Fiscal Operations

FEDLINK enjoyed another successful year of operating performance. During FY 1996 FEDLINK Fiscal Operations (FFO) processed 12,005 member service transaction requests for current and prior years, representing $53.3 million for transfer-pay and $66.2 million for direct-pay FY 1996 service dollars; expanded vendor services for FY 1997 to include five new technical processing vendors, four new electronic information retrieval vendors, and the Copyright Clearance Center; vouchered 67,583 invoices for current year and prior year orders; incurred virtually zero net interest expense for late payment of FEDLINK vendor invoices; completed FY 1991 member service dollar refunds to close out obligations for expired appropriations; successfully passed the GAO audit of FY 1995 transactions performed by Price Waterhouse; successfully completed work associated with the FY 1995 Price Waterhouse task order to conduct a compliance review of FEDLINK's financial system and identify opportunities for electronic commerce; ensured that administrative expenditures and obligations did not exceed program fee projections; and implemented plans to have Abacus Technology Corporation perform strategic reviews of the FEDLINK program to enhance customer service, program planning, and execution. During FY 1996 FEDLINK saved its member agencies an estimated $10.3 million in discounts and contracting cost avoidance.

FEDLINK Vendor Services

Total FEDLINK vendor service dollars for FY 1996 represent $53.3 million for transfer-pay customers and $66.2 million for direct-pay customers. Database retrieval services represent $15.3 million and $49.2 million, respectively, for these customers. Within this service category, online services comprise the largest procurement for transfer-pay and direct-pay customers, representing $14.0 million and $48.1 million, respectively. Publications acquisition services represent $31.9 million and $16.9 million, respectively. Within this service category, serials subscription services comprise the largest procurement for transfer-pay and direct-pay customers, representing $25.4 million and $16.0 million, respectively. Library support services represent $6.1 million and $0.1 million, respectively, for transfer-pay and direct-pay customers. Within this service category, bibliographic utilities are the largest procurement representing $5.1 million and $0.1 million, respectively.

Value of the FEDLINK Procurement Program

Based on FFO analysis of discounts offered through LC/FEDLINK basic ordering agreements (BOAs), FEDLINK discounts saved members at least $2.2 million in gross service dollars in FY 1996. Analysis of comparable contracting costs for establishing 101 BOAs and providing competition for 333 individual serials orders over $50,000 suggests that FEDLINK's centralized contracting activity saved the government approximately $8.1 million in cost avoidance (estimating $20,000 per contracting action). Thus, through discounts and contracting cost avoidance alone (and not considering FEDLINK's invoice processing, education, and other services), the FEDLINK program saved agencies an estimated $10.3 million, more than twice the FEDLINK annual operating budget.

Accounts Receivable and Member Services

FFO accounts receivable processed FY 1996 registrations from federal libraries, information centers, and other federal offices, which resulted in 775 signed FY 1996 interagency agreements (IAGs). In addition, FFO processed 3,641 IAG amendments (1,353 FY 1996 and 2,288 prior year adjustments) for agencies that added, adjusted, or terminated service funding. These IAGs and IAG amendments represented 12,005 individual service requests to begin, move, convert, or cancel service from 101 FY 1996 FEDLINK vendors. FFO executed service requests by generating delivery orders that were issued to vendors by LC/Contracts and Logistics. For FY 1996 alone, FEDLINK processed approximately $53.3 million in service dollars for 2,824 transfer-pay accounts and approximately $66.2 million in service dollars for 245 direct-pay accounts. Included in the above member service transactions are 694 member requests to move prior-year (no-year and multi-year) funds across fiscal year boundaries. These service request transactions represented a contracting volume of $3.0 million comprised of 1,161 delivery orders.

The FEDLINK Fiscal Hotline responded to a wide variety of member questions, ranging from routine queries about IAGs, delivery orders, and account balances to complicated questions regarding FEDLINK policies and operating procedures. In addition, Internet e-mail addresses were established for FFO, to give FEDLINK members and vendors 24-hour access to fiscal operations. FFO continued the practice of scheduling appointments with FEDLINK member agencies and FEDLINK vendors to discuss complicated account problems, and assigned senior staff to concentrate on resolving complex current year and prior year situations. FEDLINK ALIX-FS maintained 2,824 accounts in FY 1996 and continued to provide members early access to their monthly balance information throughout the fiscal year. FFO prepared monthly mailings that alerted individual members to unsigned IAG amendments, deficit accounts, rejected invoices, and delinquent accounts.

Transfer-Pay Accounts Payable Services

On behalf of transfer-pay users, FFO vouchered 67,583 invoices for payment during FY 1996 for both current year and prior year orders. FFO accounts payable efficiently processed vendor invoices and earned $100 in discounts in excess of interest payment penalties levied for the late payment of invoices to FEDLINK vendors. FFO continued to maintain open accounts for three prior years to pay publications service invoices ("bill laters" and "back orders") for members using books and serials services. FFO reviewed 68,302 invoices for current and prior fiscal years and rejected the following: 2,402 invoices for having no delivery orders; 885 invoices due to duplicate vendor submissions; 1,304 invoices for having no signed IAG; 1,905 invoices for overdraft/insufficient funds; and 2,412 invoices for inadequate vendor information.

FFO issued 87,878 statements to members (24,439 current year and 63,439 prior year). FFO continued to generate current fiscal year statements for database retrieval service accounts on the 30th or the last working day of each month, and publications and acquisitions account statements on the 15th of each month. FFO issued final FY 1991 statements in support of closing obligations for expired FY 1991 appropriations. FFO issued quarterly statements for prior fiscal years, including FY 1992, and supported reconciliation of FY 1992 FEDLINK vendor services accounts.

Financial Management

Retirement of Prior Year Service Obligations: FFO completed all unfinished work associated with reconciling FY 1991 vendor obligations and payments and collaborated with LC/Financial Services to refund member remaining account balances. This facilitated member agency compliance with statutory requirements for retiring obligations associated with FY 1991 expired appropriations.

GAO FY 1995 Library Audit: During FY 1996 FEDLINK successfully passed the GAO audit of FY 1995 transactions conducted by Price Waterhouse. During the May 7 congressional hearing of the Joint Committee on the Library, GAO Director of Corporate Audits and Standards Robert W. Gramling reported that LC had done a good job of cleaning up problems identified in the 1991 audit with regard to FEDLINK accounts. FEDLINK's success with the GAO is attributed to staff efforts to revise program finance and procurement policies and procedures in response to the previous audit findings.

Price Waterhouse Compliance Review: FFO completed the task order with Price Waterhouse to perform a compliance review of FEDLINK's automated system, SYMIN. The system test and compliance focused on the SYMIN automated system, its inputs and outputs, its data, and its procedures. Price Waterhouse acknowledged the many enhancements and modifications made to SYMIN to improve its functionality and performance since the 1992 compliance review. Both the system test and the compliance review revealed areas for improvement or further evaluation. These findings confirmed management's assessment to evolve SYMIN from a DOS-based to a Windows-based operating system. Price Waterhouse also provided guidance on issues that should be considered when designing the next version of SYMIN. All major recommendations are being incorporated into the SYMIN system plans to develop the successor financial system.

Budget and Revenue

During FY 1996 FEDLINK ensured that administrative expenditures/obligations did not exceed the program fee projections. By year's end FEDLINK realized a $380,000 surplus, due to fee revenue exceeding budgeted volume and to unanticipated personnel cost savings. Because the surplus was not realized until the last month of FY 1996, FLICC management did not have sufficient time to rebate members prior to the end of the year. The fee surplus will be distributed to FEDLINK members' accounts and refunded upon reconciliation of their FY 1996 account activity.

Systems Planning

In FY 1996 FLICC management and systems staff used a formal process to review all outstanding task requests, and group and categorize them by priority; they set directions for automation in FLICC/FEDLINK for the next five years. Much of the focus was on the next generation of the SYMIN financial management system; the plan deferred as many tasks as possible to that resystemization. Included in the preparations for the next five years was the decision to migrate to 32-bit Windows-based software from the current 16-bit DOS systems. Technology acquisitions during the year began establishing the infrastructure for the new system with Windows 95, Borland Delphi systems, Oracle database management, and Windows NT file servers to host the Oracle system. An additional programmer was added to help develop the new software. Windows 95 was implemented on selected desktops to evaluate the impact and identify problems in migration; the last obstacle to Windows 95 implementation was resolved by year's end.

One high priority enhancement to SYMIN could not wait for the next generation system—delivery order check-in at LC/Contracts and Logistics. This enhancement was accomplished by upgrading the communications line between the FLICC offices and LC and by developing software to enable FEDLINK contracting officers in Landover, Maryland, to check delivery orders directly into the SYMIN system at FLICC. This enhancement eliminates the three- to five-day lag that existed when the paper delivery orders were transported from Landover to the FLICC office before check-in.

Strategic Reviews

During FY 1996 FEDLINK implemented plans to have Abacus Technology Corporation perform strategic reviews of the program in the following areas: program cost/benefit analysis; program cost allocation/accounting for transfer-pay and direct-pay activity; and development of a formal five-year business plan. These studies will be finalized in FY 1997.

Executive Summary

During fiscal year (FY) 1996 the Federal Library and Information Center Committee provided a variety of innovative educational and networking opportunities to the federal library community. FLICC's annual Forum on Federal Information Policy featured expert panelists exploring the balance between open access to and protection of government information. FLICC also reinstituted its annual symposium on the information professional, focusing on the importance of forming liaisons with computer professionals. In all, FLICC sponsored 26 educational events—on such topics as interlibrary loan vs. document delivery, database licensing, CD-ROM instruction, preservation of electronic federal depository library documents, and copyright in the digital age—for 1,282 members of the federal library and information center community.

The FY 1996 FLICC education schedule underscored cooperative relationships as FLICC sponsored programs with other organizations in the library, education, and association community, including the CAPCON Library Network; the National Institute for Library Personnel; the College of DuPage; the Law Librarians Society of Washington, D.C.; the Potomac Valley Chapter of the American Society for Information Science; the District of Columbia Library Association; the D.C. Online Users Group; the Special Libraries Association, D.C. Chapter; and the ALA Association for Library Collections and Technical

Services (ALCTS). FLICC continued and expanded its videotaping of FLICC programs and developed an arrangement with the National Library of Education to make FLICC videotapes more readily available to federal libraries through interlibrary loan.

At the first FLICC quarterly membership meeting, FLICC Executive Board members led small group brainstorming sessions to reconsider FLICC's Vision 2000 statement and to identify crucial issues for FLICC members and specific actions for FLICC and FEDLINK for the next five years. In calendar 1996 the FLICC membership meetings focused on federal library advocacy. At the February meeting FLICC member Phyllis Christenson (Director of the Information Services Center, General Accounting Office), described her initiatives to convey the importance of the Information Services Center during GAO downsizing actions. In May a panel on library committees—at the Naval Research Laboratory, the National Library of Education and the National Oceanographic and Atmospheric Administration—discussed the benefits of such user advocate groups. In September Betty Turock (professor, School of Communication, Information and Library Studies, Rutgers University, and immediate past president of the American Library Association) presented several methods for demonstrating a library's success; her lecture was titled "Making the Case for Library Support."

FLICC working groups had many accomplishments. They finished reviewing the results of the FY 1994 nationwide survey of federal libraries and information centers and worked with the National Center for Education Statistics to publish the tabulations; developed new educational initiatives for advocacy, library technicians, and distance learning; updated the five-year-old FLICC bylaws; initiated an information technology listserv; established a closed listserv to consider federal policies related to information service; and published a background paper on qualifications requirements for federal librarian positions.

FLICC supported an ambitious publications schedule, producing ten issues of *FEDLINK Technical Notes*, five eight-page issues of the *FLICC Quarterly Newsletter*, a 20-page summary of the 1995 FLICC Forum, a fourth edition of the *Checklist of Microcomputer-Based Library Systems*, and the first edition of the *FLICC/FEDLINK Education Catalog*. FLICC also published expanded and enhanced materials to support its cooperative network, FEDLINK; these materials include the FY 1997 *FEDLINK Registration Booklet*, the looseleaf FY 1997 *FEDLINK Member Handbook*, the FY 1996 *FEDLINK Books Package*, 11 *FEDLINK Information Alerts*, and a comprehensive FLICC/FEDLINK information packet.

FLICC/FEDLINK inaugurated its own Web site in June 1996. The site provides access to FLICC/FEDLINK publications, information about FEDLINK services (including training and education, events, OCLC support, and contracting), and the FY 1996 Services Directory, with hot links to FEDLINK vendors. During the year new listservs were created for the FLICC Information Technology Working Group and the Policy Working Group and a listserv was "loaned" to the National Biological Survey to assist with the integration of that service into the Geological Survey. Also, at the request of the FEDLINK Advisory Council (FAC), FEDLIB was converted to an interactive listserv to enable FAC to increase its contact with FEDLINK members.

FAC met ten times during FY 1996 to plan the spring and fall FEDLINK membership meetings and to follow up on member needs identified in the 1995 FEDLINK member survey: more training in information technology, assistance in handling staff shortages, consultation services to support decision making, and help in communicating the value of library services to agency officials.

In FY 1996 FEDLINK staff conducted 108 OCLC and Internet classes, attracting 1,122 students. Staff introduced the new OCLC telecommunications software, Passport for Windows, by conducting eight classes, as well as a special training session at the Smithsonian libraries. In April 104 librarians attended the ALA/ALCTS Institute on Technical Services Workstations, to confer about a technology that brings the tools of cataloging together on a single computer; FEDLINK initiated this program for the D.C. area and cosponsored it with the CAPCON Network.

FEDLINK staff also worked with the Library of Congress Technical Processing and Automation Instruction Office to present the first FLICC/FEDLINK Cataloging Institute. Attended by 60 students, the event provided 30 contact hours of training in basic concepts of description and access based on Anglo-American Cataloguing Rules; afternoon sessions furnished instruction in OCLC MARC applications. In August and September FEDLINK staff conducted significant regional OCLC training in the field, traveling to eight Air Force libraries.

For the first time in its history, FLICC/FEDLINK created an exhibit booth and unveiled it at the Special Libraries Association meeting in Boston in early June. FLICC/FEDLINK also exhibited via the LC booth at the American Library Association Annual Conference in New York in July. In June FEDLINK announced the availability of subscription pricing for online and CD-ROM database services. Members were able for the first time to subscribe to an online system for a fixed period of time—or a finite amount of service—at a fixed price. FEDLINK completed the year with 101 vendors, including two new service areas: technical processing services and copyright clearance.

FEDLINK Fiscal Operations enjoyed another successful year of operating performance. During FY 1996 fiscal staff processed 12,005 member service transaction requests for current and prior years, representing $53.3 million for transfer-pay and $66.2 million for direct-pay FY 1996 service dollars; vouchered 67,583 invoices for current year and prior year orders; incurred virtually zero net interest expense for late payment of FEDLINK vendor invoices; completed FY 1991 member service dollar refunds to close out obligations for expired appropriations; successfully passed the General Accounting Office audit of FY 1995 transactions performed by Price Waterhouse; successfully completed work associated with the FY 1995 Price Waterhouse task order to conduct a compliance review of FEDLINK's financial system and identify opportunities for electronic commerce; ensured that administrative expenditures/obligations did not exceed program fee projections; and implemented plans to have Abacus Technology Corporation perform strategic reviews of the FEDLINK program to enhance customer service, program planning, and execution. During FY 1996 FEDLINK saved its member agencies an estimated $10.3 million in discounts and contracting cost avoidance.

National Agricultural Library

U.S.Department of Agriculture, NAL Bldg., 10301 Baltimore Ave.,
Beltsville, MD 20705-2351
E-mail: agref@nal.usda.gov
World Wide Web: http://www.nal.usda.gov

Brian Norris
Public Affairs Officer

The National Agricultural Library (NAL) is the primary agricultural information resource for the nation and is the largest agricultural library in the world with a collection of over 2.2 million volumes. Established in 1862 under legislation signed by Abraham Lincoln, NAL is part of the Agricultural Research Service (ARS) of the U.S. Department of Agriculture (USDA). The NAL collection includes books and journals, audiovisuals, reports, theses, software, laser discs and artifacts. The library receives over 25,000 serial titles annually.

In addition to being a national library, NAL is the departmental library for USDA, serving thousands of USDA employees around the world. NAL is a keystone of USDA's scientific and research activities.

As the nation's chief resource and service for agricultural information, NAL has a mission to increase the availability and use of current and accurate agricultural information for researchers, educators, policy makers, farmers, consumers, and the public at large. NAL also serves a growing international clientele.

The NAL staff numbers about 200 and includes librarians, computer specialists, administrators, information specialists, and clerical personnel. A number of volunteers, ranging from college students to retired persons, work on various programs at the library. NAL also has an active visiting scholar program that allows scientists, researchers, professors, and students from universities worldwide to work on projects of mutual interest.

NAL works closely with land-grant university libraries on programs to improve access to and maintenance of the nation's agricultural knowledge.

AGRICOLA (AGRIcultural OnLine Access) is NAL's bibliographic database, providing quick access to the NAL collection. AGRICOLA contains more than three million citations of agricultural literature and is available online and on CD-ROM. NAL's online catalog is available over the Internet.

The library maintains specialized information centers in areas of particular interest to the agricultural community. These centers provide a wide range of customized services ranging from responding to reference requests and developing reference publications to coordinating outreach activities and setting up dissemination networks. Subjects covered by the information centers are agricultural trade and marketing, alternative farming systems, animal welfare, food and nutrition, plant genome, rural information (including rural health), technology transfer, and water quality.

The NAL homepage on the World Wide Web is accessible at http://www.nal.usda.gov.

Some of the major NAL activities that occurred in 1996 follow.

Network Engineering Continues

NAL continues to expand its networking capabilities. The library has completed the backbone and desktop cabling of its system and will upgrade the backbone networking equipment to enable users to access network resources more quickly. A new set of high-speed modems was purchased that will allow employees to connect more quickly to resources on NAL's local area network. The library also completed the first step in connecting to the Wide Area Network of its parent agency, the Agricultural Research Service.

NAL installed a new solution for backup of network servers consisting of a network-accessible tape drive and a tape library with network backup software. It is used to provide backups of all of NAL's multi-user, mission-critical, and server-based resources. NAL set up a prototype server to provide network access to several databases. A production server was purchased to provide network and World Wide Web access to additional databases. The NAL Web server underwent a hardware upgrade and storage expansion in 1996.

AgNIC Goes on the Web

NAL established a World Wide Web site for the library's Agricultural Network Information Center (AgNIC) pilot project in 1996. AgNIC provides a focal point for Internet access to agriculture-related information, subject area experts, and other resources. To achieve its goal of facilitating access to these resources, AgNIC provides value-added services. First, the library developed a prototype database, called AgDB, of more than 500 descriptions of agriculture-related resource databases, datasets, and information systems that can be viewed alphabetically or searched by keyword. Next, NAL set up a directory of experts in agriculture-related subjects. Third, an Agricultural Conferences, Meetings, and Seminars Calendar was set up, providing information on agricultural conferences. Finally, NAL established five "centers of excellence" that provide on-line reference assistance for specific areas of agriculture. Participating are Cornell University (providing reference assistance in the area of USDA economic statistics), Iowa State University (animal science), Nebraska State University (plant sciences), University of Arizona (rangeland management), and NAL (food and nutrition, and rural information).

ISIS Improved

Access to NAL's ISIS (Integrated System for Information Services) became available worldwide in 1996 via a telnet connection. In addition, NAL expanded the hours of operation for the ISIS OnLine Public Access Catalog (OPAC) to Monday through Saturday from 6:00 A.M. to 9:00 P.M., Eastern Time. The OPAC telnet address is opac.nal.usda.gov. The ISIS homepage on the World Wide Web was established at http://www.nal.usda.gov/isis, and provides a description of ISIS, links to ISIS search commands, and a link for telnet sessions. NAL will make complete Web access to ISIS available in 1997.

CALS Goes Electronic

The Current Awareness Literature Service (CALS), which provides ongoing literature searches to USDA researchers, made its products available electronically in 1996. Of the 12 databases offered by CALS, all but NAL's AGRICOLA were outsourced to DIALOG (Knight-Ridder Information). This allowed for electronic delivery of search results as well as enhancements to search strategy development. The new AGRICOLA system is also available electronically and features searching enhancements. Almost a third of the nearly 1,000 USDA researchers who have CALS profiles receive their literature searches electronically.

NATDP Rolls On

NAL's National Agricultural Text Digitizing Program produced several new CD-ROMs. The *Nicoll's Birds of Egypt CD-ROM*, produced through a cooperative training program with the Egyptian National Agricultural Library (ENAL), was sent to the land-grant university libraries and ENAL late in 1995. NAL also released its *Food Irradiation 2* disc early in 1996. With funds from the American Society of Agronomy, NAL produced the third *Agronomy Journal (Volumes 23–28) CD-ROM*. NAL completed scanning and review of the database for the first *American Journal of Agricultural Economics CD-ROM*. Plans for 1997 include continuing the *Agronomy Journal* and the *American Journal of Agricultural Economics CD-ROM* series, scanning a collection of U.S. Forest Service photographs for the World Wide Web, and publishing a collection of botanical and plant pest prints on CD-ROM.

NAL Joins Latin American Project

NAL joined with more than 30 other research libraries in the United States and Canada in a project to make scholarly resources from Latin American countries more accessible worldwide. In agreeing to participate in the "Latin Americanist Research Resources Pilot Project" of the Association of Research Libraries and the Association of American Universities, NAL will provide access to selected Latin American serials on agriculture and related subjects. This will be done by acquiring and cataloging the serials into the NAL collection, and making materials from the serials available through NAL's document delivery service. The project gives participating libraries the responsibility for acquiring, cataloging, and making accessible specific scientific literature from Latin America. The libraries share information on the literature through an electronic database.

Bulletin Board System Ended

Effective September 30, 1996, NAL discontinued its ALF (Agricultural Library Forum) Bulletin Board System. The Internet and the World Wide Web are now the primary vehicles for access to NAL's computer-based collection and delivery of NAL materials to customers. Although ALF provided excellent service from its beginning in 1987, most data services offered by ALF became available on NAL's Internet-accessible information servers.

Public Exhibits Highlight Special Collections

NAL's Special Collection Section prepared exhibits highlighting a variety of agricultural topics. One exhibit focused on the work of Beverly T. Galloway and the development of the Bureau of Plant Industry. The basis of the exhibit was an album of photographs donated to NAL by Dr. Galloway's grandson. Special Collections also prepared displays and exhibits highlighting the William Prestele horticultural watercolors, the USDA Pomology Watercolor Collection and the Smokey Bear Collection. Special Collections lent material to the Maryland Historical Society for an exhibit, "Where the Wild Things Are: The Nature of Maryland," and to the U.S. Forest Service for a year-long exhibit at the Historical Museum at Fort Missoula, Montana. Two exhibits focused on the contributions of immigrant communities to U.S. agriculture. These were "Contribution of German Immigrants to American Agriculture," displayed at the German Embassy, and "Belgian Emigration to the United States," displayed at the Belgian Embassy.

Collection Management Section Established

The year saw NAL's Document Delivery Services Branch establish a separate Collection Management Section and appoint a collection management librarian. NAL houses over 2.2 million volumes of vital importance to the agricultural community and this section is responsible for organizing, maintaining, and storing this vast collection of books, journals, audiovisuals, photographs, software, microforms, historical documents, manuscripts, and rare materials. The section head will work with NAL's preservation officer and the head of NAL's Special Collections Section to ensure that NAL's collections are housed properly and that policies are established to ensure the availability and usability of the collection now and for the future.

Funding Allows Start of Preservation Program

NAL received congressional appropriations to create a Preservation Office and initiate an NAL Preservation Program. This will insure preservation of resources, many of which are held only at NAL, and provide for long-term and wider access to these materials. NAL detailed a librarian to coordinate program development and to perform an analysis of preservation plans and organizations in other national and federal libraries. Following this analysis, NAL began recruiting nationally for an NAL Preservation Officer, who is expected to be on staff early in 1997. NAL has already initiated a number of important preservation projects and activities to preserve and conserve the collection. These include a detailed analysis of the results of prior cooperative archival microfilming, NAL's first venture into archiving the collection digitally, and a three-year cooperative agreement with Cornell University to begin implementing an Agricultural Information Digital Archive.

AWIC Celebrates Anniversary

On September 12, 1996, NAL's Animal Welfare Information Center (AWIC) and the Animal Care Unit of USDA's Animal and Plant Health Inspection Service sponsored a symposium to celebrate the 30th anniversary of the Animal Welfare Act and the 10th anniversary of AWIC. The symposium provided a retrospective look at the development and impact of animal welfare regulations in the United States since the passage of the Laboratory Animal Welfare Act in 1966. Leaders from government, industry, and animal protection groups offered unique viewpoints on the impact of the regulations and insights on the future of animal welfare for animals used in research, testing, education, and in exhibits. Approximately 200 people attended.

Customer Service Continues to Improve

NAL made significant changes and additions to its collection of CD-ROM database titles available for public access in 1996. CD-ROM titles now include over 30 resources. Additional end-user workstations were installed, with multi-disk CD-ROM towers. Also, networked access for use of NAL's bibliographic database AGRICOLA by WinSPIRS (a Windows-based search software used for accessing certain databases) was provided for all end-user workstations in the library's Main Reading Room. NAL also implemented Windows access to databases, allowing faster searching for NAL users. At the NAL branch at USDA headquarters in Washington, D.C., a new public computer workstation with Internet connectivity was added and another workstation was upgraded to provide customers with the ability to search CD-ROMs faster.

Document Delivery 2000 Takes Shape

NAL's Document Delivery Services Branch began providing document delivery service directly to USDA employees at all USDA field locations in the United States and Puerto Rico. The new procedure enhances an earlier program that provided photocopies of articles and loan of materials through arrangements with 38 land-grant university libraries in 34 states and Puerto Rico. USDA employees now can send requests to NAL via fax or electronic mail and receive materials by fax or over the Internet via Ariel. These methods are efficient, more cost-effective for the library and fast—85 percent of requests filled are delivered within two working days.

NAL's commitment to electronic document delivery has resulted in significant increases over the past year, both in terms of the number of requests received and materials delivered. During 1996, 24 percent of all document delivery requests were received electronically and 16 percent of all document delivery requests filled by NAL were delivered electronically. The number of requests received electronically (via fax, e-mail and Ariel) grew 46 percent while the number of documents delivered electronically (via fax and Ariel) rose 40 percent.

Risk Assessment Notebook Completed

At the request of USDA's Office of Risk Assessment and Cost-Benefit Analysis, NAL assembled a five-volume compilation of information related to *Risk Assessment in Agriculture*. Subtitles include (1) methodologies, organizations, communication, and education; (2) food safety and health assessment; (3) environment and rural issues; (4) organisms, plants, and germplasm importation and movement; and (5) trade/import and export issues. Each volume contains articles, reports, bibliographies, lists of electronic information sites and organizations, and current USDA research programs and research results on risk assessment. The volumes are a "work in progress" and will be updated as needed.

Electronic Media Center Established

NAL developed plans to established an Electronic Media Center. Equipment for the center, including network servers, was purchased, and a center coordinator was recruited. With a view to improving service to both internal and external customers, NAL purchased OCLC's SiteSearch software, a client server technology, to provide seamless access to NAL information products, databases, and full text resources. This package will help the library analyze who uses the NAL resources and what resources are the most valuable.

NAL Works with NIH on Nutrition

The National Institutes of Health and NAL's Food and Nutrition Information Center have agreed to work together to develop a searchable bibliographic database of international scientific literature on the World Wide Web that will provide the nutrition community with improved access to the scientific research on dietary supplements. NAL will employ its expertise in the use of new information management technology to make the International Bibliographic Information on Dietary Supplements database an important resource for the scientific and education community.

Laboratory Animals Publication Completed

Through a cooperative agreement with the United Kingdom's Universities Federation for Animal Welfare, NAL's Animal Welfare Information Center produced the publication *Environmental Enrichment Information Resources for Laboratory Animals—1965–1995: Birds, Cats Dogs, Farm Animals, Ferrets, Rabbits, and Rodents*. The 289-page document contains summaries of current practices related to laboratory animal use, extensive bibliographic listings, listings of relevant journals, organizations, enrichment devices and suppliers. The document will eventually be available on the Web.

TEKTRAN Database Now on the Internet

NAL worked with the Agricultural Research Service Technology Transfer Office to put the ARS TEKTRAN database on the Internet. TEKTRAN contains interpretive summaries of articles recently submitted for publication and should be an asset to librarians, researchers, and companies trying to find recent, unpublished agricultural research results. A task force of ARS and NAL staff was established to work of the project. By early 1996 a prototype database was on the Internet and searchable using WAIS and Glimpse software. NAL staff demonstrated 'TEKTRAN LIVE' on the Internet on April 25 at an NAL's Technology Demonstration Day on Capitol Hill.

Soros Fellow Completes Internship at NAL

In 1996 an official from the Central Food Library in Prague, Czech Republic, completed an eight-week internship at NAL as part of the Soros Foundation–Library of Congress Librarian Intern Program. The program supports democratic change and development in Central and Eastern Europe by promoting the concept of free-flowing information and accessible library services. The program gives participants the opportunity to see and experience librarians working in technologically advanced environments, to develop professional contacts and establish relationships that can be useful in their work. The NAL intern furthered her experiences in acquisitions including international exchange of publications and cataloging. She also assisted the NAL cataloging branch in preparing and inputting cataloging records of Czech monographs. Additional experiences included learning about MARC format, searching OCLC for cataloging purposes and assigning LC Subject Headings and call numbers.

Need for Terrestrial Database Investigated

NAL received a grant from the National Aeronautics and Space Administration to investigate the feasibility of USDA taking the lead in establishing a World Data Center for Terrestrial Ecosystems. Interest is high in this project, particularly from the National Academy of Sciences and the International Council of Scientific Unions. Currently, there is no centralized data center to coordinate the inventory, quality control analysis, documentation, long-term archival storage, or clearinghouse functions for datasets and information on terrestrial ecosystems. NAL conducted a survey over the Internet requesting that interested people indicate their interest in and need for data on the subject. A planning meeting was held with participants from the public and private sector. Those attending the meeting recommended that USDA develop a strategic plan to implement a USDA National Center for Terrestrial Ecosystems and assist in developing a World Data Center for Terrestrial Ecosystems. It was proposed that the center be a "virtual library" with Internet access to the data and information, as well as providing traditional services for low-end technology users.

Computer Training Program Completes Fifth Year

The NAL computer training program completed its fifth year with an on-site computer instructor. The program provides NAL staff with hands-on instruction for microcomputers and the Internet. Training classes are scheduled regularly and range from short 90-minute sessions to all-day workshops. The training room contains ten student workstations and an instructor's workstation, which are networked. In addition to training NAL staff, sessions have been held for various USDA staffs and international visitors to NAL.

National Library of Medicine

8600 Rockville Pike, Bethesda, MD 20894
301-496-6308, fax 301-496-4450
E-mail: publicinfo@nlm.nih.gov
World Wide Web: http://www.nlm.nih.gov

Robert Mehnert
Public Information Officer

The National Library of Medicine (NLM), a part of the Department of Health and Human Services' National Institutes of Health in Bethesda, Maryland, is the world's largest library of the health sciences. The director, Donald A. B. Lindberg, is a physician with wide experience in developing systems that use computer and communications technology to improve health science research, education, and health care delivery.

NLM has two buildings containing more than 420,000 square feet. The older building (1962) contains the collection, public reading rooms, catalog area, and library staff and administrative offices. The ten-story Lister Hill Center Building (1981) contains the main computer room, auditorium, audiovisual facility, offices, and research/demonstration laboratories.

The library received an unusual amount of attention in the public press in 1996. Newspapers, magazines, and television stations around the country carried items related to the Internet Grateful Med, the Visible Human Project, 19 awards for telemedicine projects, and the Human Gene Map.

Internet Grateful Med

On April 16, 1996, NLM announced the Internet Grateful Med, a program for searching MEDLINE via the World Wide Web. (The URL for Internet Grateful Med is http://igm.nlm.nih.gov.) The introduction was made at a press conference presided over by Michael E. DeBakey, M.D., of Baylor University (a member of the library's Board of Regents), and U.S. Senator Bill Frist (R-Tenn.), also a surgeon and a long-time user of Grateful Med and MEDLINE. Senator Frist showed how the Internet Grateful Med presents to searchers an interface that lets them employ such useful limiters as language, age group, and year of publication and, even more remarkable, lets them take full advantage of the more than 500,000 terms in the Unified Medical Language System in formulating searches for MEDLINE.

Soon after the Internet Grateful Med was introduced in April, the library announced several added features. In June the ability to register online was instituted, in effect allowing anyone around the world with access to the World Wide Web to join the NLM network of MEDLINE users. In August the library added three databases to Internet Grateful Med's search capability: AIDSLINE, HealthSTAR, and PreMEDLINE (a new working file that contains a daily update of citations and abstracts *before* they are indexed and added to MEDLINE). Other databases, including the suite of NLM files on toxicology and environmental health, will be added in the future.

Publicity about the Internet Grateful Med got a great boost in July when Ann Landers's syndicated newspaper column included a laudatory letter from Dr. DeBakey. Many new users were enrolled into the system as a result of this publicity: By the end of the year, there were more than 150,000 user codes in effect.

Online Network

The 150,000 users of NLM's online network conducted 7.4 million searches in fiscal year (FY) 1996. Many more health professionals, students, educators, and, increasingly, members of the public also made use of NLM's databases through commercially available CD-ROM products and online vendors.

NLM's largest and most widely consulted database, MEDLINE, continued to grow, with 336,000 references added in the fiscal year ending September 30, 1996. Because of the federal furlough, snow shutdowns, and a problem with contract indexers, this figure is about 14 percent lower than the previous year's. About three-quarters of the references currently being added include an English-language abstract. The database is updated weekly; in most cases, references are added within 30 days of a journal issue arriving at the library. It is estimated that altogether NLM's 50 databases contain more than 20 million records, including not only the latest in published medical findings but historical materials dating back to the 11th century. As the result of a special project, late in 1996 the library expanded MEDLINE's coverage with the addition of 307,000 references from the period 1964–1965.

Internet- and World Wide Web-Based Programs

The Internet and the World Wide Web figure prominently in many NLM programs. The library recently completed a survey of its online database users and discovered that 75 percent have access to the Internet and that of the remaining 25 percent, more than half plan to upgrade to the Internet within 12 months. Eighty-five percent of users have computer platforms that can support Internet applications.

The library's Internet Connections Program provides small amounts of money to help medical organizations connect to the Internet. The awards are $30,000 for single institutions and $50,000 if the institution reaches out to other organizations. A wide variety of organizations have been funded over the last several years, including small hospitals, free-standing clinics, and large medical centers. These grants are administered by NLM's Extramural Programs, which also is responsible for awarding a variety of research, resource, training, and publication grants under the Medical Library Assistance Act and the Public Health Service Act.

The library's World Wide Web site (http://www.nlm.nih.gov) is home to much health-related information and it continues to be a popular destination for those using the Internet. Daily, some 40,000 users gain access to NLM databases, download the texts of such publications as NLM newsletters and fact sheets, and view a variety of visual materials.

Some of the most interesting Web-accessible visual materials are in NLM's high-profile imaging activity known as the Visible Human Project. This program has resulted in two computer-generated cadavers, one male (15 gigabytes in size) and one female (40 gigabytes). The male was a 39-year-old convicted murderer, executed in Texas by lethal injection. The female, from Maryland, was 59 years old when she died of a heart attack. The two were selected by researchers at the University of Colorado, under contract to NLM. The Colorado scientists then carried out the photographic and electronic imaging that resulted in the large files of images. These data can be converted into full-color, three-dimensional images that can be manipulated and viewed in an infinite variety of ways.

Over the last several years, NLM has signed agreements with 600 researchers in 25 countries (the datasets are made available without charge). In October 1996 the library hosted a two-day conference to look at how some of these medical researchers are making use of the datasets. Most of the applications discussed at the meeting involve using computers to reconstruct the images into tissues, organs, and other body systems that can be rotated, dissected, and reassembled on the computer screen.

Another area with Internet implications is telemedicine. In October NLM announced the funding of 19 telemedicine-related projects. In making the announcement, Health and Human Services Secretary Donna Shalala said that "telemedicine offers us some of our best and most cost-effective opportunities for improving quality and access to health care." The projects should serve as models for evaluating the impact of telemedicine, for example, on cost, quality, and access to health care. We hope also to learn about various approaches to ensuring the confidentiality of health data transmitted via electronic networks. The 19 multiyear projects, located in 13 states and the District of Columbia, total some $42 million.

These projects are tied closely to the recommendations from two National Academy of Sciences (NAS) reports. The first, released by NAS in October, is a guide to assessing telecommunications in health care. The second, which was scheduled for release early in 1997, is a study on preserving confidentiality and security of electronic health data. NLM contributed to the funding of both.

The Gene Map

The National Center for Biotechnology Information, a research component of NLM and an important component of the national Human Genome Program, creates and maintains systems for storing, analyzing, and retrieving information on molecular biology, biochemistry, and genetics. The GenBank database is doubling every year both in size (it now contains 620,000 sequences) and in use. There are now more than 30,000 GenBank queries every day from scientists around the world.

On October 24 the library held a press conference to announce a publicly accessible "Human Gene Map." The map represents the most extensive effort so far to locate and identify the 80,000 genes in the human genome. More than 16,000 are included in the map, giving scientists about a 1 in 5 chance that a gene they are looking for is on the map.

The map is notable both for the science it represents and for the clever application of technology that makes the knowledge visually accessible in all its detail on the World Wide Web. Now this information—in pictures, text, and graphics—can be examined by anyone with access to the Internet: the high school biology student, the general public, and the scientist. The creation of the gene map resulted from a remarkable voluntary, collaborative effort by 18 leading research institutions around the world. Coordination was provided by NLM's National Center for Biotechnology Information. The URL for the Human Gene Map is http://www.ncbi.nlm.nih.gov/science96.

The center has also taken the lead in creating a new experimental system that will enable users to search the biomedical literature through MEDLINE and link from MEDLINE records to the corresponding full-text Internet version of recent articles as provided directly by publishers over the World Wide Web. Because of its role as a public biomedical information provider, NLM is uniquely positioned to create linkages from the publishers' articles, not only to MEDLINE abstracts, but also to gene sequences, protein structures, disease descriptions, and clinical-practice guidelines. The center has demonstrated the feasibility of this concept by linking a subset of MEDLINE in the area of molecular biology to several online journals.

The Collection

In FY 1996 NLM received and processed 175,000 modern books, serial issues, audiovisuals, and computer-based materials. Preservation microfilming was completed for 2,400 volumes (1.2 million pages). A net total of 83 journals were added to those indexed for MEDLINE (the number indexed is now 3,868).

Table 1 / Selected NLM Statistics*

Library Operation	Volume
Collection (book and nonbook)	5,186,000
Items cataloged	20,400
Serial titles received	22,600
Articles indexed for MEDLINE	336,000
Circulation requests filled	585,000
For interlibrary loan	348,000
For on-site users	237,000
Computerized searches (all databases)	7,397,000
Budget authority	$149,846,000
Full-time staff	575

*For the year ending September 30, 1996

Outreach

Recognizing that more health professionals should be using the library's computer-based information services, Congress has directed that NLM undertake an outreach program to scientists, health care providers, and students. The goal of this outreach activity is to let American health professionals know that modern computer-based information services can be of inestimable help in their work and that no matter where they live or practice they have convenient and inexpensive (sometimes free) access to NLM's immense data resources. Outreach has been a high priority of NLM's Board of Regents since 1989, when a special planning panel under the leadership of Dr. DeBakey published *Improving Health Professionals' Access to Information*. This report has served the library as a blueprint for outreach ever since.

A key role in providing information services to health professionals is played by the 4,500 member institutions in the National Network of Libraries of Medicine. The network, coordinated by NLM, consists of basic health science libraries (mostly at hospitals), resource libraries (medical schools and major health institutions), eight Regional Medical Libraries, and, as backup for the entire network, NLM itself. The mission of the 30-year-old network is to make biomedical information readily accessible to U.S. health professionals irrespective of their location. The largest network activity—providing books, audiovisual productions, and copies of journal articles on interlibrary loan—is also heavily dependent on electronic transmission of requests to and from network libraries. Some three million such lending transactions are recorded annually in the United States.

The activities of the Regional Medical Libraries are supported, in part, by contracts from NLM. In 1996 the library awarded new contracts totaling nearly $34 million over a five-year period. One emphasis in the new contracts is to make greater use of the National Information Infrastructure in providing information services to health professionals. Because this will involve access to the Internet by both member network libraries and health professionals, the Regional Medical Libraries will increase the substantial efforts they are already making to facilitate connectivity for institutions and health professionals alike. Special efforts will be made under the new contracts to reach underserved groups of health professionals in both rural and inner-city areas. There will be increased emphasis on demonstrations, training, and exhibits at professional meetings.

Another area of outreach emphasis is to increase the usage of NLM's three HIV/AIDS online databases: AIDSLINE, AIDSDRUGS, and AIDSTRIALS. These files are made available to all users without charge, and NLM, with the help of the Regional Medical Libraries, has helped community organizations around the country to hook up electronically to the information.

The eight Regional Medical Libraries and the regions they serve are:

- New York Academy of Medicine (Delaware, New Jersey, New York, Pennsylvania)
- University of Maryland at Baltimore, Health Sciences Library (Alabama, Florida, Georgia, Maryland, Mississippi, North Carolina, South Carolina, Tennessee, Virginia, West Virginia, District of Columbia, Puerto Rico, U.S. Virgin Islands)
- University of Illinois at Chicago Library of the Health Sciences (Iowa, Illinois, Indiana, Kentucky, Michigan, Minnesota, North Dakota, Ohio, South Dakota, Wisconsin)

- University of Nebraska Medical Center, Leon S. McGoogan Library of Medicine (Colorado, Kansas, Missouri, Nebraska, Utah, Wyoming)
- Houston Academy of Medicine, Texas Medical Center Library (Arkansas, Louisiana, New Mexico, Oklahoma, Texas)
- University of Washington Health Sciences Center Library (Alaska, Idaho, Montana, Oregon, Washington)
- University of California, Los Angeles, Louise Darling Biomedical Library (Arizona, California, Hawaii, Nevada, U.S. Territories in the Pacific)
- University of Connecticut Health Center, Lyman Maynard Stowe Library (Connecticut, Massachusetts, Maine, New Hampshire, Rhode Island, Vermont)

Several long-term outreach projects, reported previously, are continuing. These include the joint program with the Montgomery County (Maryland) public library system to provide the public with free access to NLM's AIDS and environmental-health databases. Another project is with the Historically Black Colleges and Universities (HBCUs) to provide training to health professionals affiliated with the HBCUs in the use of NLM's databases as well as other electronic resources. A five-year summary of outreach efforts was published in 1996 and is available from the library's Public Information Office.

In 1996 NLM convened the first of three meetings of a long-range planning panel to review the library's international programs. The 24-member panel will prepare a report to the Board of Regents advising the library on the relative priority of its various international activities and to develop strategies for meeting its responsibilities. It will complete its work in 1997. At present, NLM has formal arrangements with 20 governmental institutions in other countries to provide access to MEDLINE and the other NLM databases. The Chinese University of Hong Kong became NLM's most recent international partner in 1996.

Educational Resources Information Center

ERIC Processing and Reference Facility
1100 West Street, Laurel, MD 20707-3598
301-497-4080, 800-799-3742, fax 301-953-0263
E-mail: ericfac@inet.ed.gov
World Wide Web: http://ericfac.piccard.csc.com

Ted Brandhorst
Director

ERIC Budget (FY 1997)

The fiscal year (FY) 1997 appropriation for the Educational Resources Information Center (ERIC) was $9 million, the same amount that was ultimately appropriated in FY 1996 after considerable delay. This amount represents an increase of $1 million over the annual funding level of $8 million in the immediately preceding fiscal years.

The increase is widely regarded as a vote of confidence for ERIC's programs to make use of the Internet and the World Wide Web to disseminate information and for ERIC's programs to prepare and disseminate large numbers of ERIC Digests, brief two-page syntheses on education-related topics of high current interest.

ERIC's budgetary challenges in the year ahead will likely be threefold: (1) keeping up with the phenomenal growth of the Internet/World Wide Web and coping with the resultant high volume of electronic user contacts; (2) putting into electronic page image form the full text of the thousands of documents entering the ERIC bibliographic database and the development of products to enable public access to this full text; (3) developing techniques to achieve bibliographic control for reference purposes over the many new electronic/non-print forms in which education-related information now comes.

ERIC Annual Report, 1996

For the last several years ERIC has produced an annual report "summarizing the recent accomplishments of the Educational Resources Information Center." These reports are available free of charge from ACCESS ERIC (800-538-3742) and are regularly entered into the ERIC database.

Because 1996 was ERIC's 30th anniversary year, the annual report for 1996 was prepared as an attractive multi-color brochure containing a wide variety of useful reference information, including all ERIC-sponsored listservs and ERIC-sponsored World Wide Web sites.

The current report, covering 1995–1996, includes the following highlights:

- The ERIC database now contains nearly 900,000 records of education-related documents and journal articles, including abstracts of 6,000 published books [920,172 records through 1996, to be precise].

- More than 900 journals are indexed in the ERIC database, some cover-to-cover and others on a more selective basis [990 journals, as of the end of 1996].
- ERIC ensures the timely addition of high-quality education-related materials through standing acquisition arrangements with some 1,900 universities, research centers, professional organizations, and federal and state agencies [2,106 organizations, as of the end of 1996].
- Four private online database vendors and six CD-ROM vendors offer the ERIC database. The ERIC database is also accessible in whole or in part via the Internet at several library online public access catalogs and at the AskERIC World Wide Web site, http://ericir.syr.edu.
- More than 1,000 institutions in 27 countries provide access to the ERIC database, ERIC documents on microfiche, and other ERIC resources.
- Four hundred ERIC Partner organizations promote ERIC, disseminate ERIC information through their newsletters and journal articles, help build the database, and undertake joint projects. (In return, Partners receive VIP handling of information requests, advance notification and discounts on publications, and technical assistance and support.)
- ERIC looks to the private sector to provide access to the database, documents and article delivery, and publishing services. Companies such as DynCorp I&ET, Apple Computer, Sun Microsystems, and Personal Librarian have provided generous contributions to support technological advances. Such relationships enable ERIC to provide enhanced products and services at no additional cost to the government or to taxpayers.
- ERIC staff answer more than 50,000 toll-free calls, 80,000 letters, and 500,000 e-mail questions per year.
- The ERIC system maintains a network of award-winning Internet sites, including AskERIC, an electronic question-answering service and "Virtual Library" begun in 1992, all linked through one systemwide site, http://www.aspensys.com/eric
- More than 300,000 individuals use ERIC's continually updated Internet sites each week.
- ERIC fosters communication on such topics as parenting, early childhood education, independent schools, and school library and media services through 27 listservs hosted by seven ERIC Clearinghouses, with a total subscriber base of 16,414.
- Each year, ERIC Clearinghouses produce more than 250 original, high-quality publications on such important topics as assessment, reading instruction, and education technology.
- ERIC Clearinghouses distributed more than 1.5 million copies of their publications in 1995, many of them at no cost.
- More than 625,000 copies of ERIC-produced publications were distributed by various non-ERIC organizations in 1995.

ERIC Database Size and Growth

The ERIC database consists of two files, one corresponding to the monthly abstract journal *Resources in Education* (*RIE*) and one corresponding to the monthly *Current Index to Journals in Education* (*CIJE*). *RIE* announces education-related documents and books, each with an accession number beginning "ED" (for "educational document"). *CIJE* announces education-related journal articles, each with an accession number beginning "EJ" (for "educational journal").

Document records include a full abstract and are approximately 1,800 characters long on average. Journal article records include a brief annotation and are approximately 650 characters long on average.

Through 1996 the ERIC database includes 391,305 records for documents and 528,867 records for journal articles, for a grand total of 920,172 bibliographic records. Approximately 13,000 document records and 20,000 article records are added annually, for a total of 33,000 records per year. Overall, the ERIC database through 1996 is approximately 1,050 million bytes (1.050 gigabytes) in size and is growing at a rate of around 35 million bytes per year.

File	1966–1995	1996	Total
Resources in Education (*RIE*)—ED Records	378,625	12,680	391,305
Current Index to Journals in Education (*CIJE*)—EJ Records	509,434	19,433	528,867
Totals	888,059	32,113	920,172

Number of Records

ERIC Document Reproduction Service (EDRS)

The ERIC Document Reproduction Service (EDRS) is the document delivery arm of ERIC, handling all subscriptions for ERIC microfiche and on-demand requests for reproduced paper copy or microfiche. During 1996 the number of Standing Order Customers (SOCs) subscribing to the total ERIC microfiche collection (about 12,000 titles on 16,000 fiche cards, priced at approximately $2,500 annually) rose to 980. SOCs include over 100 overseas addresses.

EDRS prices usually increase about 3 percent annually, due to increases in the cost of basic materials and labor. The following table presents prices in effect for the period January 1–December 31, 1997.

Product	1997 Prices
Microfiche	
Annual subscription (approximate)	$ 2,500.00
Monthly subscription (price/fiche)	$ 0.2822 (silver)
	$ 0.1379 (diazo)
Back collections (1966–previous month) (price/fiche)	$ 0.1623
Clearinghouse collections (price/fiche)	$ 0.2971
On-demand Documents, per title	
Microfiche (MF) Up to 5 fiche (5 fiche = 480 pages)	$ 1.38
Each additional fiche (up to 96 pages)	$ 0.25
Reproduced Paper Copies (PRC) First 1-25 pages	$ 4.08
Each additional 25-page increment (or part thereof)	$ 4.08
1996 Cumulative Indexes (on Microfiche)	
Subject, Author, Title, Institution, Descriptor, and Identifier Indexes	$ 75.00

The EDRS five-year contract, awarded in December 1995 to DynCorp Information & Engineering Technology, contained a requirement to scan, capture, store, and disseminate electronic page images of documents added to the ERIC bibliographic database. This activity began with the documents announced in the January 1996 issue of *Resources in Education* (*RIE*). It is the first step in eventually shifting the archival storage of ERIC documents from microfiche to high technology electronic media, though traditional products such as ERIC microfiche collections and on-demand microfiche and paper copy blowbacks will continue to be provided for some time to come.

EDRS's plan is to create a World Wide Web site at which users will be able to search the ERIC database and then, in the same session, place orders for the items they wish to obtain. Full text documents will be received back either by downloading an online file or by a fax-back service. A prototype of the planned online access system is currently available for user exploration and testing. (Contact EDRS customer service at 800-443-3742).

ACCESS ERIC

ACCESS ERIC is responsible for system-wide outreach, marketing, publicity, and promotion for the ERIC system. One major outreach activity is staffing exhibits and giving presentations on ERIC at education and library conferences. In 1996 these included the meetings of the American Library Association (ALA), Association for Supervision and Curriculum Development (ASCD), National School Boards Association (NSBA), and Special Libraries Association (SLA).

ACCESS ERIC works closely with the ERIC Clearinghouses to produce *The ERIC Review*, a free journal on current education issues. Recent issues focused on the themes of "School-to-Work-Transition," "Inclusion," and "Information Dissemination." The Clearinghouses also provide material for a series of Parent Brochures, which included the following titles in 1996: *How Can We Provide Safe Playgrounds? How Can We Help Make Schools Safer for Students? How Can I Receive Financial Aid for College? How Can I Help My Gifted Child Plan for College?* and *Homeschooling Resources for Parents and Students*. Several of these titles were also available in Spanish.

Many ACCESS ERIC activities in 1996 focused on the celebration of ERIC's 30th anniversary. Free posters and bookmarks were produced and distributed. With support from the EDRS contractor, DynCorp Information & Engineering Technology, ACCESS ERIC assisted the ERIC Program Office with the production of a special *ERIC Annual Report, 1996*, available free from ACCESS ERIC by calling 800-LET-ERIC. The ERIC systemwide Web site (http://www.aspensys.com/eric) was completely redesigned to reflect the anniversary motif, including a special "treasure hunt" featuring some of the best material on the various ERIC Web sites.

ACCESS ERIC continues to produce a number of information and referral databases and publications, including 1996 editions of the *Catalog of ERIC Clearinghouse Publications*, the *ERIC Directory of Education-Related Information Centers*, the *Directory of ERIC Resource Collections*, and the *Calendar of Education-Related Conferences*.

Plans for 1997 include introduction of an Online ERIC Publications Catalog on the systemwide Web site that will enable users to browse, search, and place online orders for print copies of ERIC Clearinghouse publications (or to download information for traditional ordering). Publications activities will include *Striving for Excellence (Volume 3)*, a compilation of more than 60 ERIC Digests related directly to the National Education Goals. ACCESS ERIC is also assisting the Department of Education with development of the Education Resources Organizations Directory, available on the department's Web site: http://www.ed.gov

AskERIC

AskERIC, a project of the ERIC Clearinghouse on Information & Technology (IR), is an e-mail-based reference and referral system providing question answering, help, and referral to K–12 educators through the Internet. Some 31,430 educators, students, parents, and other individuals received personalized responses to questions via AskERIC's Question Answering Service in 1996, an average of about 600 per week, reaching 900 per week during peak periods of the school year. AskERIC, which celebrated its fourth anniversary in November 1996, is currently receiving an average of 700 electronic mail inquiries weekly. AskERIC draws on the total resources of the ERIC system to generate and send Internet responses to all inquiries within 48 hours.

In addition, AskERIC has established a growing file of full-text resources on its gopher/ftp site (ericir.syr.edu) and its World Wide Web site (http://ericir.syr.edu). This full-text data bank, referred to as the AskERIC Virtual Library, includes hundreds of lesson plans, news and information about ERIC and AskERIC, ERIC Digests in full text, completed searches on current topics, resource guides, popular questions and answers, and the archives of some education-related listservs. This resource currently is accessed by the public at the phenomenal rate of 122,893 electronic "visits" per week.

The AskERIC Virtual Library continues to grow and evolve. In April 1996 AskERIC introduced newly designed look for its Web site, including the addition of the following resources: (1) Crossroads: K–16 American History Curriculum Unit, (2) 86 new lesson plans; (3) *Newton's Apple*: Seasons 10, 12, 13, and 14; (4) 11 new AskERIC InfoGuides, and (5) the ERIC bibliographic database (latest six years), with easy-to-use search interface using PLWEB retrieval software.

National Parent Information Network (NPIN)

The ERIC Clearinghouse on Elementary and Early Childhood Education and the ERIC Clearinghouse on Urban Education continue to jointly operate the National Parent Information Network (NPIN). This award-winning Internet-based project includes an expanding World Wide Web site (http://ericps.ed.uiuc.edu/npin/npin-home.html); a question-answering service for parents (as part of the AskERIC program, parenting questions are sent to askeric@ericir.syr.edu and responded to by a parent educator); a discussion group on parenting; and presentations and workshops on use of the Internet to support parenting. NPIN is specifically devoted to providing high quality, noncommercial information on child development, care, and education, and the parenting of children from birth through adolescence, to parents and those who work with parents.

During 1996 the National Parent Information Network Web site nearly doubled in size. The site is updated bi-monthly and provides links to many other Internet sites on parenting and related issues. "Parent News," a monthly electronic newspaper that includes summaries of research and resources on parenting and education written specifically for parents, has become a major feature of the site.

NPIN was awarded four Internet awards during 1996.

ERIC on NISC DISC CD-ROM

Beginning in April 1995 the ERIC Facility offered a robust CD-ROM product providing access to the entire ERIC database, including the full text of around 1,500 ERIC Digests. This product is prepared by the National Information Services Corporation (NISC) and is sold exclusively to ERIC for re-sale to users at an economical price aimed at bringing the product within the financial reach of all parts of the educational community ($100 per year for four quarterly updated discs).

During its first year of operation this project sold discs to some 400 different customers and acquired approximately 300 subscribers (20 percent of which were individuals). Because the project was planned on a break-even basis, marketing efforts consist of using targeted mailing lists and whatever publicity ERIC newsletters, journal columns, and Web sites can generate.

Beginning with the first discs sent out in 1997, the ERIC database will be reallocated across the two discs, in order to provide for future expansion on the "Current" disc: the "Archival" disc will contain the 1966–1984 data; the "Current" disc will contain data from 1985 to the present, i.e., initially, the last 12 years.

Also beginning with 1997, the ERIC on NISC DISC project assumed fulfillment responsibility for the former subscribers to the Oryx Press CD-ROM product (now discontinued) that contained only the journal article half of the ERIC database.

ERIC Database Changes

In 1997 the ERIC Facility will convert its database-building operations from a 30-year-old mainframe "legacy" system to an internal database management system called STAR, operating on a Sun Sparcstation.

This changeover will involve many operational changes for the ERIC Facility, but will be largely transparent to the ERIC Clearinghouses that feed bibliographic data to the Facility and to the many users of the ERIC database who receive monthly or quarterly updates via tapes or ftp (file transfer protocol) download process.

The major database changes will be new separate fields for International Standard Book Number (ISBN) and for International Standard Serial Number (ISSN) and an expansion of the Personal Author field to accept as many authors as may be cited on a document or article. In addition, certain redundancies that now exist (e.g., pagination data in two locations) will be eliminated and codes and their textual translations will be associated explicitly rather than, as formerly, by relative position. Obsolete data fields will be deleted. All calendar-year data in the Publication Date field will be converted from two to four characters to eliminate the "year 2000" problem.

Distribution of ERIC bibliographic data to subscribers will gradually evolve from the distribution of physical tapes to an ftp downloading process for all subscribers that can accept data in this way.

OERI National R&D Center Documents

Since the early 1970s the National R&D Centers have been one of the foremost initiatives of the research arm of the U.S. Department of Education (and its predecessors). Across the years approximately 70 organizations have held the prestigious, competed contracts to operate these centers. The ERIC database contains records for over 8,000 documents prepared by these centers from their beginnings through 1996.

A "Digitization Project" was launched in late 1996 to prepare a CD-ROM product that will contain searchable bibliographic records for all R&D Center documents (1966–1996) and the full text of R&D Center documents entered into the database from 1980 through 1996. This multi-disc product will be prepared by the ERIC Document Reproduction Service (EDRS), with scanning of the document full text being based on the microfilm masters held by EDRS. The retrieval engine has yet to be selected. When available, this product will be publicly announced.

The Most Popular (Top 25) ERIC Documents Ordered From EDRS in 1996 (Paper Copies)

Title	ED Number	Clearinghouse
1 Teaching Mathematics with Understanding to Limited English Proficient Students	ED 322 284	Urban Education
2 Storyboarding: A Brief Description of the Process	ED 384 171	Disabilities and Gifted Education
3 A Social Foundations Approach to Educational Policy Analysis	ED 383 052	Educational Management
4 Serving More Than Students:A Critical Need for College Student Personnel Services	ED 267 678	Higher Education
5 Guidelines and Recommended Practices for the Individualized Family Service Plan	ED 336 907	Disabilities and Gifted Education
6 Synthesis of Existing Knowledge and Practice in the Field of Educational Partnerships	ED 362 991	Educational Management
7 More than the Sum of the Parts: Using Small Group Learning in Adult Basic and Literacy Education	ED 368 905	Adult, Career, and Vocational Education
8 Violence Prevention for Young Adolescents: The State of the Art of Program Evaluation	ED 356 441	Counseling and Student Services
9 Training in the Use of the Internet	ED 378 953	Information & Technology
10 Methodologies of Reading and Writing in Kindergarten	ED 302 834	Reading, English, and Communication
11 Violence Prevention for Young Adolescents: A Survey of the State of the Art	ED 356 442	Counseling and Student Services
12 The Community College of the Future	ED 381 191	Community College
13 Encouraging Your Junior High School Student To Read	ED 333 362	Reading, English, and Communication
14 Applications in Educational Assessment: Future Technologies	ED 340 773	Assessment and Evaluation
15 Evaluation of a High School Block Schedule Restructuring Program	ED 384 652	Assessment and Evaluation
16 What Twenty Years of Educational Studies Reveal about Year-Round Education	ED 373 413	Educational Management
17 Ethical Use of Information Technologies in Education	ED 348 989	Information & Technology
18 America Goes Back to School: A Place for Families and the Community	ED 383 483	Elementary and Early Childhood Education
19 What Young Adolescents Want and Need from Out-of-School Programs	ED 358 180	Urban Education
20 Teaching Technical Writing in the Secondary School	ED 243 111	Reading, English, and Communication
21 Perceived Effects of Block Scheduling on the Teaching of English	ED 382 950	Reading, English, and Communication
22 Redesigning High School Schedules. A Report of the Task Force on Block Scheduling	ED 391 391	Languages and Linguistics

The Most Popular (Top 25) ERIC Documents Ordered From EDRS in 1996 (Paper Copies) (cont.)

Title	ED Number	Clearinghouse
23 Full-Day Kindergarten: A Summary of the Research	ED 345 868	Elementary and Early Childhood Education
24 Creating Inclusive Adult Learning Environments: Insights from Multicultural Education and Feminist Pedagogy	ED 384 827	Adult, Career, and Vocational Education
25 Policy Considerations in Conversion to Year-Round Schools	ED 357 476	Educational Management

ERIC on the World Wide Web

All ERIC components now have Web sites, some of them prize-winners. In order to coordinate ERIC Web sites, Access ERIC has been mandated to maintain a system-wide Web site with hyperlinks to all the other ERIC system sites. This central site is the best place to begin any exploration of ERIC's resources on the Web: http://www.aspensys.com/eric

United States Government Printing Office

North Capitol and H Streets N.W., Washington, DC 20401
202-512-1991
E-mail: fbiden@gpo.gov
World Wide Web: http://www.access.gpo.gov

Francis W. Biden
Director, Office of Congressional, Legislative and Public Affairs

The United States Government Printing Office (GPO) produces or procures printed and electronic products for Congress and the agencies of the federal government. GPO also disseminates printed and electronic government information to the public through the Superintendent of Documents' sales and depository library programs. It hosts a major government World Wide Web home page, featuring the award-winning GPO Access service, which provides free public access to major government information databases.

GPO's primary facility is in Washington, D.C. Across the country, 14 regional printing procurement offices, six satellite procurement facilities, one field printing office, a major distribution facility, a retail sales branch, and 24 bookstores complete the GPO printing and sales structure.

This report focuses on GPO's expanding role as the producer, disseminator, and coordinator of U.S. government information in electronic formats. Previous reports have detailed GPO's printing services to the federal government.

Superintendent of Documents

GPO's original job when it opened in 1860 was to handle printing. Responsibility for the sale and distribution of government documents was added in 1895. Today, through its documents program, overseen by the Superintendent of Documents, GPO disseminates one of the world's largest volumes of informational literature, distributing more than 100 million government publications every year in print and electronic formats.

Library Programs

Most products produced by or through GPO are available to the public for reference through nearly 1,375 depository libraries located in the United States and its possessions. Depository libraries are public, academic, or other types of libraries designated by members of Congress or by law as official depositories. The Federal Depository Library Program (FDLP) is administered by the Library Programs Service (LPS), under the Superintendent of Documents. The mission of FDLP is to provide equitable, efficient, timely, and dependable no-fee public access to government information within the scope of the program.

Transition to Electronic Offerings

In August 1995 GPO, at the direction of Congress, initiated the "Cooperative Study to Identify Measures Necessary for a Successful Transition to a More Electronic Federal Depository Library Program." The study was concluded in March 1996, and a draft study report was released for public comment. The final study report was issued in June 1996.

The key findings of the study report addressed the following issues:

- Scope of the Federal Depository Library Program
- Notification and compliance
- Permanent access to authentic information
- Locator services
- Timetable for implementation
- Assessment of standards for creation and dissemination of electronic government information products
- Cost of electronic information dissemination
- Legislative changes

Conclusions drawn in the study report reflect the views and advice of the library community, federal publishing agencies, and users of government information. Strong support emerged in the working-group discussions about two major issues concerning the Federal Depository Library Program as a whole. The first issue concerned the value of having the authority for a broad-based public information program rest in the legislative branch. Nearly all of the participants felt that this model has served the public well. High value was placed on the presence of the FDLP in nearly every congressional district, to directly serve the public in local library settings.

There was also strong support for the value and utility to the library community of having a single entity in the Superintendent of Documents to coordinate library-related information dissemination activities. The depository library community has consistently affirmed the utility and cost-effectiveness of a "one-stop shopping" approach to acquiring government information.

Permanent access to government information is a critical issue in the electronic environment. GPO will ensure, through the mechanism of FDLP, that electronic government information products are maintained for permanent public access, in the same spirit in which regional depositories provide permanent access to print products. This requires the development of a distributed system that includes all of the institutional program stakeholders: information-producing agencies, GPO, depository libraries, and the National Archives and Records Administration (NARA).

Usage of the Federal Depository Library Program and GPO Access

The Federal Depository Library Program continues to be a principal mechanism to meet the government information needs of the American public. Responses from the *1995 Biennial Survey of Depository Libraries* yielded an estimate that 189,000 to 237,000 persons used FDLP information each week. The transactions included both on-site usage in libraries and remote electronic usage, such as reference service via e-mail.

In addition, users are also electronically accessing free government information available from the GPO Access service at a rapidly growing rate. Users are downloading nearly three million documents per month from more than 70 databases. System usage has expanded significantly since the user fee requirement for GPO Access was eliminated in December 1995.

Federal Depository Library Program

Depository libraries receive government information products at no cost in return for providing free public access to the information. The information products are sent in a variety of formats, including paper, microfiche, and CD-ROM. An increasing number are available as online files. While the federal publishing environment is in a period of transition to decentralized printing and online dissemination, LPS is working to ensure that federal information content, regardless of format, is available to the public through the Federal Depository Library Program.

In fiscal year (FY) 1996, 15.5 million copies of 55,100 titles in all formats were distributed to depository libraries under authority of the Superintendent of Documents. A total of 1.8 million of these copies were distributed in microfiche by the Department of Energy. U.S. Geological Survey and Defense Mapping Agency maps are distributed by those agencies under agreements negotiated with LPS.

LPS acquires government documents, determines the format of publications distributed to depository libraries (paper, microfiche, or electronic), and assigns Superintendent of Documents (SuDocs) classification numbers. LPS also acts as the documents distribution agent to foreign libraries in the International Exchange Service Program, on behalf of the Library of Congress.

LPS administers the designation and termination of depository libraries and monitors the condition of depository libraries through periodic inspection visits and a biennial survey. LPS also organizes continuing education efforts for documents librarians. In 1997 the annual Federal Depository Conference (scheduled for April 14–17), which attracts a large audience of information professionals, was to present new federal electronic information products. The annual Interagency Depository Seminar (scheduled for May 28–June 4), familiarizes new depository library staff with major federal information products and services.

LPS identifies, assesses, and implements information technology solutions as the FDLP moves toward a more electronic future. LPS coordinates the LPS World Wide Web applications, including the suite of Pathway Services, which facilitate access to federal information on the Web. It also coordinates efforts to establish partnerships with federal agencies, depository libraries, and the National Archives and Records Administration.

Sales

The sales program currently offers approximately 10,000 federal information products on a wide array of subjects. These are sold principally by mail order and through U.S. government bookstores across the country. The program operates on a cost recovery basis, without the use of tax dollars.

Publications for sale include books, forms, posters, pamphlets, and maps. Subscription services for both dated periodicals and basic-and-supplement services (comprising an initial volume and supplemental issues) are also offered. A growing selection of electronic information products, including CD-ROMs, computer disks, and magnetic tapes are now available in the sales program.

U.S. Fax Watch offers customers in the United States and Canada free access to information on a variety of sales products, electronic products and services, and depository library locations. To use the service, customers call in from a Touch-Tone telephone or the handset of their fax machine, follow voice prompts to select the document they want, and then have the requested information faxed back to them in minutes. U.S. Fax Watch is available 24 hours a day, seven days a week, at 202-512-1716.

Express service, which includes priority handling and Federal Express delivery, is available for orders placed by telephone for domestic delivery. For only $8.50, orders placed before noon Eastern Time for in-stock publications and single-copy subscriptions will be delivered within two working days. Some quantity restrictions apply. Call the telephone order desk at 202-512-1800 for more information.

Certain consumer-oriented publications are also sold through the Consumer Information Center, which GPO operates on behalf of the General Services Administration.

U.S. Government Bookstores

Publications of particular public interest are made available in government bookstores. In addition, to meet the information needs of all customers, a bookstore can order any government information product currently offered for sale and have it sent directly to the customer. Customers can order by phone, mail, or fax from any government bookstore.

Government bookstores are located in major cities throughout the United States. Their addresses, hours, and a map are available on the GPO Web site.

Catalogs

GPO publishes a variety of free catalogs that cover hundreds of information products on a vast array of subjects. The free catalogs include:

- *U.S. Government Information*: new and popular information products of interest to the general public
- *New Information*: bimonthly listing of new titles, distributed to librarians and other information professionals

- *U.S. Government Subscriptions*: periodicals and other subscription services
- *Subject Bibliographies* (*SBs*): nearly 200 listings, each containing titles relating to a single subject or field of interest
- *Subject Bibliography Index*: lists all *SB* subject areas
- *Catalog of Information Products for Business*: GPO's largest catalog for business audiences

(*U.S. Government Subscriptions* and *Subject Bibliographies* are also available from U.S. Fax Watch at 202-512-1716 and via World Wide Web at http://www.access.gpo.gov/su_docs.)

Publications Reference File

The Superintendent of Documents issues the GPO *Sales Publications Reference File* (*PRF*), a guide to current U.S. government information products offered for sale through the Superintendent of Documents. The fully searchable *PRF* database, which is updated every working day, is available online via GPO's Web site.

The *PRF* is also available online through DIALOG (File Code 166). DIALOG service offers online ordering, retrieval, and research capabilities.

PRF is available on subscription on 48X microfiche format or on machine-readable magnetic tape. The microfiche service consists of bimonthly mailings of the complete master file and monthly mailings of a single fiche containing new information products. The magnetic tape service provides biweekly mailings of the complete file.

Monthly Catalog of United States Government Publications

More than two million bibliographic records for government information products have been published in the *Monthly Catalog of United States Government Publications*. This catalog is the most comprehensive listing of government publications issued by more than 250 federal departments and agencies within the legislative, judicial, and executive branches.

The full cataloging records are available online through the Online Computer Library Center (OCLC) at approximately 17,000 libraries worldwide. Additional dissemination occurs through commercial vendors and via online catalogs of many public and university libraries.

Monthly Catalog records are also published on the GPO Web site, as soon as three days after original production. A locator application links *Monthly Catalog* records with the names and locations of depositories that selected each title. Records for online titles contain links to the actual electronic texts.

In 1996 GPO introduced a CD-ROM edition of the Monthly Catalog. This version, which replaces the microfiche edition, features both DOS and Windows user interfaces. The CD-ROM edition cumulates complete records on a monthly basis and includes multiple years on a single disc. The CD-ROM edition is available for $245 per year (12 discs).

An abridged paper edition of the *Monthly Catalog*, including abbreviated records and a single key word title index, also is available. Each monthly issue consists of discrete monthly data sets and is intended as a ready-reference paper adjunct to the complete *Monthly Catalog* edition on CD-ROM. This edition is available for sale as a subscription service for $65 per year.

GPO Access

GPO provides free public access to important government information over a unique online information delivery system called GPO Access.

GPO Access is a free service through which users can

- Access and obtain copies of official government documents such as the *Federal Register, Congressional Record*, and congressional bills, on the day of publication, exactly as they appear in print
- Locate and research other government information products
- Locate government publications in a federal depository library
- Place an electronic order to purchase a paper copy

Recognizing the various needs and technological capabilities of the public, GPO Access supports a wide range of dissemination technologies, from the latest client-server applications through the Internet to dial-up modem access, including methods compatible with assistive technologies. Gateway libraries provide convenient off-site access to users from their homes or offices. Even those without computers can use GPO Access through public access terminals located in federal depository libraries throughout the country.

The GPO Access service currently provides access to 72 databases through a Wide Area Information Server (WAIS). Several databases were added late in 1996, including a number of Code of Federal Regulations (CFR) titles. Additional titles will be added incrementally until a complete set is available.

Searchability

The Library Programs Service (LPS) at GPO provides a number of Pathway Services on the Internet via the GPO Access World Wide Web site at http://www.access.gpo.gov/su_docs/aces/aces760.html. Pathway Services are designed to provide a variety of useful pathways to anyone who uses government information. A short description of each Pathway service's focus and intended audience follows.

Browse Topics classifies government and military Internet sites under approximately 170 subjects, based on the subject terms used in GPO's *Subject Bibliographies*. A brief annotation describes the general contents of each site. Browse Topics is useful for anyone who wants an overall knowledge of what is available on the Internet from the federal government on one topic, or who simply wants guidance in identifying possible topics and sites for more in-depth research.

Browse Pathway GILS provides a directory of Government Information Locator Service (GILS) records prepared by LPS that describe the information policies and provisions of cabinet-level and other major federal agencies. The services include interactive links to agency home pages and agency-specific information locators. Browse Pathway GILS is useful for locating agency-specific information sources or contacting an agency's information specialists.

Browse Titles lists electronic government information products available on federal government servers, arranged alphabetically by agency. Listed are products that have previously been in the FDLP or new titles that are available only on the Internet.

Search the Web contains a simple search form that enables users to query a database of information collected on a regular basis from official government sites. Be it .gov, .mil, or even part of a cooperative agreement between the government and an outside partner, the Pathway Indexer will have already searched and indexed the information. The user types in search terms and receives a list of results ranked by relevance, complete with a list of lines containing the search term(s) and a link to the exact page needed.

Search MoCat links directly to the online *Monthly Catalog* search page. The online version of the *Monthly Catalog* offers full-text and fielded searches of GPO cataloging records from 1994 onward; it provides fielded displays of MARC cataloging, identifies any depository libraries that can provide access to the product, and it links the user to electronic versions, if available. Search MoCat is useful for locating government information products regardless of format.

Commerce Business Daily

GPO recently entered into an alliance with the U.S. Department of Commerce to handle all facets of the day-to-day operation of the *Commerce Business Daily* (*CBD*). The new electronic portion of the *CBD* project, named CBDNet, appears on GPO Access and the Internet. While CBDNet utilizes new and exciting electronic means to improve the CBD process, GPO has also provided for the continued use of *CBD* by those not yet equipped to participate electronically. Agencies still are able to submit notices in manuscript form, if necessary, and the public can still purchase printed copies of *CBD* or use a copy without charge in participating federal depository libraries.

Federal Bulletin Board

GPO Access also includes the Federal Bulletin Board (FBB), maintained by GPO. The FBB provides immediate self-service access to more than 7,000 files from more than 25 agencies and organizations in all three branches of the federal government.

The Storage Facility component of GPO Access permits GPO to retain electronic files for extended periods of time after their short-term use for production of print products or active electronic dissemination is completed. In addition to its permanent-access function, in the future the Storage Facility will be used as the original point for storing and providing on-demand access to data files that are anticipated to have limited usage and/or are not appropriate for dissemination through the online services.

FDLP Administration World Wide Web Page

News, information, and communication for and about the Federal Depository Library Program are provided on the FDLP Administration Web page on GPO Access. Users can link to online electronic versions of *Administrative Notes*, *Administrative Notes Technical Supplement*, *LPS Contacts*, and various FDLP instructions, manuals, and guides. New material is continually added as this page develops.

Improved Search and Retrieval

In 1997 Phase II of GPO Access online search and retrieval capabilities will be implemented. Phase II uses open-text build/search/retrieval software to support online and CD-ROM distribution of data. It also includes many types of applications built upon the comprehensive adoption of Standard Generalized Markup Language (SGML) as a data standard.

Accolades

In 1996 GPO Access was named Best Government Site by *legal.online*, a monthly newsletter for legal professionals using the Internet. Additionally, The WebCrawler Select Editorial Team chose the Code of Federal Regulations available through GPO Access as an Outstanding Web Site. Also in 1996, Harcourt Brace Professional Publishing selected the GPO Access GILS site as one of its Top Five Web Sites for the week of October 28–November 3.

User Support

Questions or comments regarding the GPO Access service can be directed to the GPO Access User Support Team by Internet e-mail at gpoaccess@gpo.gov, toll-free via telephone at 888-293-6498, by phone locally at 202-512-1530, or via fax at 202-512-1262.

National Library of Education

555 New Jersey Ave. N.W., Washington, DC 20208-5721
202-219-1692, Internet: library@inet.ed.gov, World Wide Web: http://www.ed.gov

The National Library of Education (NLE) is the largest federally funded library in the world devoted solely to education. An expansion of the former U.S. Department of Education Research Library, NLE houses on-site more than 200,000 books and about 750 periodical subscriptions in addition to studies, reports, Educational Resources Information Center (ERIC) microfiche, and CD-ROM databases. NLE's holdings include books on education, management, public policy, and related social sciences; dictionaries, encyclopedias, handbooks, directories, abstracts, indexes, and legal and other research sources in print and CD-ROM; current and historical journals and newsletters; and more than 450,000 microforms.

Special collections include rare books published before 1800, mostly in education; historical books, 1800–1964; early American textbooks, 1775–1900; modern American textbooks, 1900–1959; U.S. Department of Education reports, bibliographies, and studies; archived speeches, policy papers, and reports; and children's classics.

Mission

The mission of the National Library of Education is to ensure the improvement of educational achievement at all levels by becoming a principal center for the collection, preservation, and effective use of research and other information related to education. NLE will promote widespread access to its materials, expand coverage of all education issues and subjects, and maintain quality control. NLE will also participate with other major libraries, schools, and educational centers across the United States in providing a network of national education resources.

Organizational Structure

NLE reports to the Office of the Assistant Secretary for the Office of Educational Research and Improvement (OERI) and is organized into three divisions: Reference and Information Services, Collection and Technical Services, and Resource Sharing and Cooperation.

History

The U.S. Department of Education was established by an act of Congress in 1867 for the purpose of

> collecting such statistics and facts as shall show the condition and progress of education in the several states and territories, and of diffusing information as shall aid in the establishment and maintenance of efficient school systems and otherwise promote the cause of education throughout the country. (Statutes at Large 14 [1867]: 434)

The prominent educator Henry Barnard was named commissioner of education. After one year of independent operation, however, the Department of Education was transferred to the Department of the Interior, where it was known as the Bureau of Education. When Barnard, who was interested in establishing an education library, resigned as commissioner in 1870, he left his own extensive private collection of books on education with the bureau. During the 70 years of its operation in the Department of the Interior, the Bureau of Education administered an independent library serving the specialized needs of its employees.

In 1939 the Bureau of Education became one of the five constituent agencies of the new Federal Security Agency, forerunner of the Department of Health, Education, and Welfare (HEW). The Bureau of Education library then became part of the Federal Security Agency library, which eventually became the HEW library.

As a result of a 1973 management study of the HEW library, which recommended decentralization of the library, the education collection was transferred to the newly established (1972) National Institute of Education (NIE). NIE agreed to maintain an educational research library in an effort to fulfill its mandate to "provide leadership in the conduct and support of scientific inquiry in the education process." (Education Amendments of 1972, U.S. Code, vol. 20, sec. 1221 a [1972])

From 1973 to 1985 the NIE Educational Research Library was the recipient of several fine education collections, including the education and library and information science collections of the HEW library, the library of the Center for Urban Education (formerly in New York City), the National Education Association library, the Community Services Administration library, and the former Central Midwest Regional Education Laboratory (CEMREL) library.

A major reorganization of OERI, which had included NIE as a component, occurred in October 1985. The name of the library was changed to U.S. Department of Education Research Library and it operated as part of Information Services, one of the five units of OERI. More recently, it operated under OERI's Library Programs.

In March 1994 Congress authorized the establishment of the National Library of Education, with specific charges. By law, two other units in OERI—the former Education Information Branch and the former Education Information Resources Division—have joined forces with the library staff to form NLE, boosting services to department employees and other clients. The Educational Resources Information Center (ERIC) is a major U.S. Department of Education program that serves the community, the government, and the general public with ready access to education information nationwide (See the article titled "Educational Resources Information Center—*Ed.*).

This new designation as National Library and the expansion of functions meant a broader range of services and a larger staff. NLE now has approximately 50 staff members compared to the former Education Research Library's staff of seven.

Functions

NLE provides a central location within the federal government for information about education; provides comprehensive reference services on education to employees of the U.S. Department of Education and its contractors and grantees, other federal employees, and members of the public; and promotes cooperation and resource sharing among providers and repositories of education information in the United States.

Major Themes and Goals

Among the major themes and goals of NLE are to establish and maintain a one-stop, central information and referral service to respond to telephone, mail, electronic, and other inquiries from the public on:

- Programs and activities of the U.S. Department of Education
- ERIC resources and services of the 16 clearinghouses and ERIC Support Components, including the ERIC database of more than 850,000 records of journal articles, research reports, curriculum and teaching guides, conference papers, and books
- U.S. Department of Education publications
- Research and referral services available to the public, including ERIC, the OERI Institutes, and the national education dissemination system
- Statistics from the National Center for Education Statistics
- Referrals to additional sources of information and expertise about educational issues available through educational associations and foundations, the private sector, colleges and universities, libraries, and bibliographic databases

In addition, NLE aims to:

- Provide for the delivery of a full range of reference services (including specialized subject searches; search and retrieval of electronic databases; document delivery by mail and fax; research counseling, bibliographic instruction, and other training; interlibrary loan services; and selective information dissemination) on subjects related to education
- Promote greater cooperation and resource sharing among libraries and archives with significant collections in education by establishing networks; developing a national union list of education journals held by education libraries throughout the United States; developing directories and indexes to textbook and other specialized collections held by education libraries; and cooperating to preserve, maintain, and promote access to educational items of special historical value or interest

Current Activities

During its first year, the library focused on selecting the National Library of Education Task Force and planning for its 1996 meetings, creating a budget, establishing collection assessment and collection development policies, producing a commemorative poster, designing outreach and promotion programs, setting up and monitoring a toll-free customer-service line, creating a World Wide Web home page and site, organizing a quarterly lecture series, creating and carrying out a customer service survey, and establishing near- and long-term goals and objectives.

The library also continues to provide legislative reference services through a branch library in the department's headquarters building. Further, NLE is establishing liaisons with the OERI Institutes and other offices within OERI, participating in the orientation of new department employees, and undergoing an internal management review and evaluation.

Future Plans

NLE's future plans include:

- Establishing a networking/resource-sharing program
- Developing a three-year plan to eliminate the arrearage of uncataloged books and other materials in the library's collection and to preserve and maintain their usability
- Expanding NLE's presence on the Internet through INet (the U.S. Department of Education's Internet) and ERIC
- Initiating a digitization program
- Carrying out a functional analysis of the library

Publications

NLE's primary publication is *The Open Window*, a quarterly newsletter of the library. Flyers and other informational material are available on request.

Primary Collections

NLE's primary collections include its circulating, reference, serials, and microform collections. The circulating collection largely includes books in the field of education published since 1965. The broad coverage of the collection includes not only education but such related areas as law, public policy, economics, urban affairs, sociology, history, philosophy, and library and information science. The reference collection includes current dictionaries, general and specialized encyclopedias, handbooks, directories, major abstracting services, newspapers and journals related to education and the social sciences, and indexes.

Current periodical holdings number more than 750 English-language journals and newsletters. The collection includes nearly all of the primary journals indexed by *Current Index to Journals in Education* (*CIJE*) and *Education Index*. The library subscribes to eight major national newspapers and maintains back issues in microform of four national newspapers.

The microform collection consists of more than 450,000 items, including newspapers, the *Federal Register*, the *Congressional Record*, *Newsbank*, college catalogs, the William S. Gray Collection on Reading, the Kraus Curriculum Collection, and various education and related journals. It also includes the complete microfiche collection of ERIC documents, a program funded by the U.S. Department of Education. NLE's ERIC collection contains complete sets of the ERIC indexes and recent ERIC clearinghouse publications and products. ERIC research publications are in varied formats—bibliographies, state-of-the-art papers, reviews, and information analyses in the 16 areas of education presently covered by the ERIC system.

Special Collections

The earliest volumes of NLE's special collections date to the 15th century and include early American textbooks, children's books, and books about education. Some restoration has taken place; items are housed in controlled space, and a catalog—*Early American Textbooks, 1775–1900*—has been issued. This collection began with Henry Barnard's private collection of American schoolbooks, was nurtured by Commissioner John Eaton during his tenure (1870–1886), and was further enriched by several private donors. Other special collections maintained by the library are (1) material from the former National Institute of Education, the former U.S. Office of Education, and the U.S. Department of Education, including reports, studies, manuals, and other documents; (2) archives of the former U.S. Office of Education and the former National Institute of Education, including speeches, policy papers, and other documents.

Interlibrary Loan

NLE offers an active interlibrary loan service and is a member of the Online Computer Library Center (OCLC). Through the OCLC database, library staff can tap the resources of a large number of research library collections throughout the United States and draw on their holdings, as well as offer interlibrary loan service to other libraries.

Technology Resources

NLE's Technology Resources Center offers users an opportunity to explore what is available in technology, use the equipment, and look at hundreds of programs designed for use in classrooms. The center has computer programs, CD-ROM, videotapes, and videodiscs. It offers a range of hardware and software for all levels of education and training.

The center is open to visits from all educators, researchers, administrators, curriculum specialists, teachers, librarians, and anyone else interested in the effective use of technology in education and training. Publishers of computer materials have provided over 400 programs from preschool to postgraduate levels. The collection of computer programs is strong in science, reading, mathematics, and word processing. Programs on art, music, science, biology, history, mathematics, chemistry, and employment skills are included. Many of the titles are chosen from programs listed in the Association for Supervision and Development's "Only the Best."

Equipment represents state-of-the-art computer technology available for use in schools. Included are Apple, IBM, and Compaq systems, as well as Kodak Photo CD and Philips Full-Motion CDi systems. Several models of CD-ROM units are demonstrated for both MS-DOS and Macintosh. Interactive videodiscs using computers and barcode readers are also shown; and videotape, electronic mail, online data services (including the Internet), and closed-captioned decoders are all on display.

The Technology Resources Center regularly provides programs on the use of technology in education. Special presentations and demonstrations are arranged on request. Tours of the facilities and demonstrations of materials are given for visiting educators and the public. Center staff work with school systems, software publishers, and vendors to arrange special demonstrations related to individual school system needs.

Copies of commercially published software evaluations and an index of software programs are available for use in the center. Software lists from state and local education agencies are welcomed. The center does not evaluate, recommend, or endorse hardware or software, nor does it lend software or equipment. Equipment is used solely for demonstration.

OERI Online Access

NLE maintains an electronic repository of education information and provides public access through two electronic networks:

- INet. An Internet-based service, INet makes information available through World Wide Web, gopher, and ftp servers.
- OERI Toll-Free Bulletin Board System. For educators who do not yet have access to the Internet, the bulletin board provides access to most of the same information as INet.

How to Access the U.S. Department of Education via Internet

The U.S. Department of Education maintains several types of Internet servers and tries to make all its holdings accessible to the public through channels commonly used by educators.

- *World Wide Web*. NLE's World Wide Web server can be accessed at http://www.ed.gov/.
- *Gopher*. The gopher server's address is gopher.ed.gov; or select North America—>USA—>General—>U.S. Department of Education from the All/Other Gophers menu on your system.
- *Ftp*. Ftp users can access the information by ftping to ftp.ed.gov (log on anonymous).

- *E-mail.* E-mail users can get a catalog and instructions for using the NLE mail server by sending e-mail to almanac@inet.ed.gov. In the body of the message, type: send catalog<M>. Avoid the use of signature blocks.
- *Telnet.* No public telnet access is available. Users must either have an appropriate WWW, gopher, or ftp client at their site or be able to telnet to a public access client elsewhere.

Questions and Comments

Suggestions or questions about the contents of the WWW, gopher, ftp, and mail servers should be directed to one of the following:

E-mail	webmaster@inet.ed.gov
	gopheradm@inet.ed.gov
	wwwadmin@inet.ed.gov
Telephone	202-219-2266
Fax	202-219-1817
Mail	INet Project Manager
	U.S. Department of Education
	Office of Educational Research and Improvement
	National Library of Education/RSCD
	555 New Jersey Ave, N.W., Rm. 214
	Washington, DC 20208-5725

How to Access the OERI Toll-Free Bulletin Board System

Virtually any computer with telecommunications software can be used to access the OERI Toll-Free Bulletin Board System.

For any computer, set the following parameters in the communications software before dialing the bulletin board:

- speed up to 14,400 baud
- 8 data bits
- 1 stop bit
- no parity
- full duplex

The BBS toll-free number is 800-222-4922 (within Washington, DC, area, 202-219-1511). Call 202-219-1526 with any system access problems.

How to Find Out What's New Online

The INet World Wide Web, gopher, ftp, and e-mail servers are continuously updated with new press releases, grant announcements, publication summaries, full-text documents, and statistical data sets. New material on major U.S. Department of Education initiatives such as Goal 2000, School-to-Work,

Technology, and Elementary and Secondary Education Act (ESEA) Schoolwides is added frequently.

To find new items on the INet World Wide Web Server, select News near the top of the home page to display a list of recent additions.

To find new items on the gopher server, follow the path:

What's New in This Gopher/
What's New (Format: nn=#days back or mm/dd/yy=since date)<?>

and enter a search string in one of the formats indicated (e.g., "7 days" or "12/31/94"). The gopher will quickly build and present a menu of items added or changed during that time.

To find new items on the OERI Toll-Free Bulletin Board System, type G to select [G]opher from the main menu. Then follow the instructions for gopher above.

NLE Telephones

Library Administration	202-219-1884
Reference/Research/Statistics	202-219-1692
Outside Washington, DC, area	800-424-1616
Fax	202-219-1696
Circulation/Interlibrary loan	202-219-2238
Collection Development/Technical Services	202-219-1883
Legislative Reference Service	202-401-1045
Fax	202-401-9023
Technology Resources Center	202-219-1699
ACCESS ERIC	800-LET-ERIC

National Association and Organization Reports

American Library Association

50 E. Huron St., Chicago, IL 60611
312-944-6780, 800-545-2433
World Wide Web: http://www.ala.org

Mary R. Somerville
President

In the second year of ALA Goal 2000, a five-year initiative to position the association for the 21st century, the American Library Association (ALA) claimed a number of major victories: among them, a favorable ruling in its legal challenge to the Communications Decency Act, passage by Congress of the Library Services and Technology Act (LSTA), and the historic designation of libraries as universal service providers under the new Telecommunications Act.

Founded in 1876, ALA is the voice of U.S. libraries and the millions of people who depend on them. The oldest and largest library association in the world, ALA has 56,703 members: librarians, trustees, publishers, and other supporters.

ALA's mission is to promote the highest-quality library and information services and to protect public access to information. Activities are focused in four areas: advocating the public's right to a free and open information society; developing innovative programs to help libraries acquire new information technology and train the public in its use; supporting libraries as centers for culture, literacy, and lifelong learning; and promoting excellence in libraries and librarianship.

The association encompasses 11 membership divisions focused on areas of special interest. They are the American Association of School Librarians, the American Library Trustee Association, the Association for Library Collections and Technical Services, the Association for Library Service to Children, the Association of College and Research Libraries, the Association of Specialized and Cooperative Library Agencies, the Library Administration and Management Association, the Library and Information Technology Association, the Public Library Association, the Reference and User Services Association, and the Young Adult Library Services Association.

In addition to its headquarters in Chicago, the association maintains a legislative office and the Office for Information Technology Policy in Washington, D.C., and an editorial office in Middletown, Connecticut, for *Choice*, a review journal for academic libraries.

Washington Report

Led by its expanded Washington Office and new Office for Information Technology Policy, ALA focused its legislative efforts on issues that will shape public access to information in the 21st century.

Major successes included designation of libraries for the first time as universal service providers in the Telecommunications Act of 1996 and a preliminary recommendation by the FCC Federal-State Joint Board that libraries receive discounts from 20 to 90 percent on a full range of telecommunications services. Libraries in high-cost and low-income communities would receive deeper discounts. The FCC is scheduled to act on the recommendation in May 1997.

The Library Services and Technology Act (LSTA), developed by ALA and other library groups to replace the expiring Library Services and Construction Act (LSCA), was passed by Congress and signed into law by President Clinton on September 30, 1996. The act focuses on technology innovation and outreach services, with some funding for training and research in library science, preservation and digitization, and model library and museum projects. The act also provides that library programs formerly administered by the Department of Education will be transferred to a new Institute of Museum and Library Services (formerly the Institute of Museum Services). Federal library programs were funded at $136.4 million, an increase of $4 million, including the highest ever for LSCA. [For further information on LSTA and other legislative matters, see the article "Legislation and Regulations Affecting Libraries" in Part 2—*Ed.*]

ALA was among the most vocal of groups urging substantial revision of international copyright proposals that would have severely limited fair use of copyrighted materials on the Internet by students, researchers, small businesses, and other members of the public.

At copyright treaty negotiations at the World Intellectual Property Organization (WIPO) held in December 1996 in Geneva, Switzerland, ALA Executive Board member James Neal served as a technical advisor to the U.S. delegation. Adam Eisgrau, legislative counsel for the ALA Washington Office, served as one of three representatives for the International Federation of Library Associations and Institutions (IFLA). Some 125 governments participated. The final treaties reflect significant progress over earlier proposals in balancing the rights of copyright proprietors with the interests of users. ALA will continue to work toward copyright legislation that protects public access to information as well as the rights of copyright holders.

The ALA Washington Office celebrated its 50th anniversary on May 6, 1996, with a gala dinner as part of National Library Legislative Day activities. Guests of honor receiving honorary ALA membership included U.S. Senators Mark Hatfield, Nancy Kassebaum, Paul Simon, and Claiborne Pell; Representative Pat Williams; and former ALA Washington Office Director Eileen Cooke. Some 500 library advocates from across the country met with legislators on Capitol Hill to urge support for key issues.

The ALA-led Coalition on Government Information presented its 1996 James Madison Award to the National Information Infrastructure Advisory Council for its efforts to promote broad and equitable public access to the emerging "Information Superhighway." The coalition, founded by ALA in 1986, presents the annual award in connection with Freedom of Information Day (March 16) to recognize outstanding efforts to protect and promote public access to information.

The Washington Office and Office for Information Technology Policy added a toll-free telephone number for calls from outside the Washington, D.C., metropolitan area: 800-941-8478.

Intellectual Freedom

The successful legal challenge to the Communications Decency Act, led by ALA, was before the U.S. Supreme Court at year's end. The historic case is the first to consider how freedom-of-speech rights guaranteed by the First Amendment will apply to cyberspace.

The act was struck down as unconstitutional by a special three-judge federal court panel on June 12. ALA is the lead plaintiff in a suit filed by the Citizens Internet Empowerment Coalition, which includes the Freedom to Read Foundation, online providers, publishers, parents, and other groups.

The suit challenged the act on the grounds that it violated the constitutionally protected right of free speech for adults without effectively protecting children from inappropriate content on the Internet.

The coalition's challenge was consolidated with a separate lawsuit brought by the American Civil Liberties Union (ACLU) and 20 other plaintiffs. The cases were argued together before the federal panel in Philadelphia, and the ACLU and coalition legal teams continued to work together as coplaintiffs in the Supreme Court phase.

The association's Office for Intellectual Freedom again recorded hundreds of challenges to library materials during 1996. In addition to providing counsel to individual librarians and others working to protect the freedom to read, the office sponsored a series of regional Leadership Development Institutes to educate librarians about intellectual-freedom principles and how to deal with challenges.

"Banned Books Week: Celebrating the Freedom to Read" in September again focused attention on the dangers of censorship with displays of challenged books in libraries and bookstores and news reports in the media. The observance drew opposition from some conservative groups that maintain that preventing children from exposure to materials they deem harmful is protection, not censorship. The annual event is sponsored by ALA, the American Booksellers Association, the American Booksellers Foundation for Free Expression, the Association of American Publishers, the American Society of Journalists and Authors, and the National Association of College Stores. The 1997 observance is set for September 20–27.

Children's Book and Media Awards

Karen Cushman, author of *The Midwife's Apprentice*, won the 1996 Newbery Medal for the most distinguished contribution to American literature for children. The Caldecott Medal for the most distinguished American picture book went to Peggy Rathman, illustrator of *Officer Buckle and Gloria*. The awards are presented annually by the Association for Library Service to Children, a division of ALA.

The 1996 Coretta Scott King Awards for outstanding children's books by African American authors and illustrators went to author Virginia Hamilton for *Her Stories* and to Tom Feelings for his illustrations for *The Middle Passage: White Ships Black Cargo*.

A new award honoring Latino writers and illustrators of children's books was presented for the first time in 1996 to Judith Oritz Coffer, author of *An Island Like You: Stories of the Barrio*, and Susan Guevara, illustrator for *Chato's Kitchen*. The award bears the name of Pura Belpre, a children's librarian at the New York Public Library known for her pioneer work in preserving and disseminating Puerto Rican folklore.

The Andrew Carnegie Medal for Excellence in Children's Video went to Paul R. Gagne for *Owen*.

Houghton Mifflin Company, publisher of *The Lady with the Hat* by Uri Orlev, received the 1996 Mildred L. Batchelder Award for the most outstanding children's book published first in another language and then in English in the United States.

Judy Blume, author of *Forever*, received the Margaret A. Edwards Award for her lifetime contribution to literature for young adults. The award is sponsored by *School Library Journal* and administered by the Young Adult Library Services Association, an ALA division.

Technology Initiatives

Ensuring that all people have access to the "Information Superhighway" via public and school libraries is a key component of ALA Goal 2000.

In February 1996 ALA hosted a six-hour summit meeting aimed at placing libraries in the forefront of the national debate over information technology policy. Titled "A Nation Connected: Defining the Public Interest in the Information Superhighway," the summit was held February 20 at the Annenberg Center in Rancho Mirage, California. The forum brought together 18 experts from a variety of fields, including legal scholar Charles Ogletree, Nobel Prize winner Arno Penzias of AT&T Labs, *HotWired* founding Executive Editor Howard Rheingold, EDventure Holdings President Esther Dyson, U.S. Rep. Major Owens, and Pulitzer Prize winning essayist Richard Rodriguez.

The summit was sponsored with support from the Annenberg Center for Health Sciences, the John D. and Catherine T. MacArthur Foundation, the W. K. Kellogg Foundation, and the H. W. Wilson Foundation. A videotape of highlights and *A Nation Connected*, white papers by library leaders who attended the summit, are available.

In partnership with the Microsoft Corporation, the association launched Libraries Online!, a one-year, $3 million pilot program to research and develop innovative approaches to extending information technologies to underserved populations through libraries. Nine libraries received cash grants, computer hardware, software, and technical support. Libraries participating were the Seattle Public Library, Pend Oreille County (Washington) Library, Charlotte-

Mecklenberg County (North Carolina) Public Library, Brooklyn Public Library, Tucson-Pima Public Library, Mississippi Library Commission, South Dakota State Library, Baltimore County Public Library, and Los Angeles Public Library. Following the success of the pilot project, Microsoft founder and CEO Bill Gates announced plans to give an additional $10.5 million to expand Libraries Online! to a total of 41 library systems in the United States and Canada.

KidsConnect, an online service to help children learn how to use the Internet, made its debut in 1996. Underwritten by Microsoft, the project is administered by the American Association of School Librarians, a division of ALA. Answers to e-mail questions are provided by a national network of volunteer school library media specialists. KidsConnect is part of ICONnect, a three-year technology initiative to develop the online skills of school library media specialists, teachers, and students through online Internet training, a minigrant program, and curriculum connections on the Internet.

Nine libraries were selected to participate in the second year of the LibraryLINK program administered by ALA in partnership with MCI Telecommunications Corporation. These included libraries in Austin, Texas; Baltimore, Maryland; Cedar Falls, Iowa; Dallas, Texas; Portland, Oregon; Richmond, Virginia; Springfield, Missouri; and Tampa, Florida. Each received a cash grant of up to $30,000 to implement a technology-based project to enhance reference and information services.

A half-century after adoption of the first Library Bill of Rights, ALA Council adopted "Access to Electronic Information, Services and Networks: An Interpretation of the Library Bill of Rights," aimed at protecting the rights of library users in cyberspace. The association also called on Congress to protect public access to government information in print formats during the shift to electronic publishing.

LISAN, the Libraries on the Information Superhighway Network, was established by ALA's Library and Information Technology Association and Office for Information Technology Policy, with collaboration from several library associations. The national network includes about 100 specially trained librarians who are available to address issues related to development of the National Information Infrastructure.

The American Library Association's Web site (http://www.ala.org) provides a comprehensive, up-to-the-minute look at association activities, including the latest news and information on legislative issues, technology initiatives, conferences and events, awards, and products. The site earned a "Top 5 percent" ranking from the editors of *Point*, a respected rating and review service.

Public Awareness

Spearheaded by 1995–1996 ALA President Betty J. Turock, ALA focused its public-awareness efforts on alerting the public to the promise and pitfalls of new information technology and promoting libraries as "on-ramps" to the "Information Superhighway."

As ALA president, Turock conducted a ten-city media tour in connection with her theme "Equity on the Information Superhighway." In more than 150 newspaper, radio, and TV interviews—including "ABC Evening News," The *New York Times*, and *U.S.A. Today*—Turock urged support for libraries as information centers where all people, not just those who can afford computers, can obtain online information.

An op-ed article by Turock explaining the association's opposition to the Communications Decency Act appeared in the *Chicago Tribune* under the title "The Big Chill on the Internet."

National Library Week—April 14–20, 1996—continued the popular theme "Libraries Change Lives" with the addition of the tagline "Call. Visit. Log-on" to focus attention on the new role of libraries in delivering electronic information. On April 16 the association sponsored "Log-on @ the Library Day" with libraries across the country conducting "tours" of the "Information Superhighway." A special interactive Web site, designed by Adam Curry's new media company *On Ramp*, demonstrated the wide range of information available online and let the public register its support for libraries on an Equity Petition that was delivered to the members of the Federal Communications Commission (FCC).

National Library Week 1997 (April 13–19) will focus on library services to youth with the theme "Kids Connect @ the Library."

ALA's acclaimed celebrity READ poster series, now in its 12th year, featured actors Tim Allen, Antonio Banderas, Danny Glover, Michelle Pfeiffer, and the Lawrence Brothers—Joey, Andrew, and Matthew—reading from their favorite books.

Award-winning country singer and literacy advocate Faith Hill urged adults to get help learning to read in television public service announcements produced for ALA.

A new ALA Library Advocacy Now! listserv was launched to provide library supporters with updates and action alerts on key legislative issues.

Special Projects

The association and its divisions continue to develop a wide array of programs, exhibits, and activities to support libraries as centers for culture, literacy, and learning, often with the help of major foundations and corporations.

The Fund for America's Libraries, a new foundation established to support the work of the association, received $8.4 million in grants and contributions, far surpassing its first-year goal of $4 million. Charter board members are former U.S. Senator Paul Simon (chair), director/choreographer Debbie Allen, former First Lady Barbara Bush, Nashua President and CEO Gerald Garbacz, Americans for Indian Opportunity Executive Director LaDonna Harris, former FCC Chair Newton Minow, former NTC Publishing Group CEO William Pattis, Ominigraphics Inc. Publisher Fred Ruffner, Viburnum Foundation executive director Molly Lazear Turner, and author and historian David McCullough.

Lucille Clifton, Reginald Gibbons, and Luis J. Rodriguez were among the noted authors who conducted readings and workshops during the second year of "Writers Live at the Library," sponsored with $415,000 from the Lila Wallace-Reader's Digest Fund. Libraries in ten Midwestern cities with populations under 150,000 hosted programs.

"It's US: A Celebration of Who We Are in America Today," a framed collection of 48 photographs representing the nation's cultural diversity, traveled to 74 public libraries across the country, with funding from Time Warner Inc.

A traveling exhibit titled "The Frontier in American Culture" began a 45-library tour in September 1996 in connection with the PBS broadcast of the new Ken Burns documentary "The West." Sponsored in cooperation with Chicago's Newberry Library and funded by the National Endowment for the Humanities (NEH), the exhibit uses photographs, maps, cartoons, and other materials to explore how stories and images of the Old West have shaped American identity and values.

Twenty libraries were selected to host a series of discussions about the workplace as part of a "national conversation" titled "The Nation That Works: Conversations on American Pluralism and Identity," funded by a $373,000 NEH grant. The association also received a $390,000 grant from NEH for a series of library-sponsored radio programs titled "Following the Back Road Home: Looking for American Identity through Regional Writing." The programs, to be broadcast in the Southwest and Northwest, will feature scholar-led discussions of regional literature.

The Lila Wallace-Reader's Digest Fund gave $1.3 million to expand and improve literacy instruction available to adults in public libraries. The grant was part of a package of grants totaling more than $6 million awarded to 13 public libraries in five states. The ALA Office for Literacy and Outreach Services will provide training and technical support.

Other grants include $250,000 from the Emily Hall Tremaine Foundation for "Roads to Learning," a project to raise awareness among librarians and the public about learning disabilities, administered by the Association of Specialized and Cooperative Library Agencies.

The Sutter County Library in Yuba City, California, and the Memphis/Shelby County (Tennessee) Public Library and Information Center each received $30,000 grants, for a total of five libraries selected as national "Born to Read" demonstration sites. Funded by the Prudential Foundation and administered by the Association for Library Service to Children, the project creates model partnerships between libraries and health care providers to help "at-risk" parents raise children who are healthy and ready to learn.

In its ninth year, the Library Fellows program, supported by the United States Information Agency, placed ten U.S. library professionals in assignments in Brazil, the Czech Republic, Egypt, Ethiopia, Ghana, Israel, Jordan, Kazakhstan, and Ukraine. The program also welcomed five International Library Fellows who came to the United States for three to ten months to work in American libraries.

Publishing Highlights

ALA Editions enjoyed a record-breaking year in revenues and profit, boosted by the bestselling *Guide to Reference Books*, 11th Edition. Other new titles included *Building the Service-Based Library Web Site, Black Heritage Sites: An African-*

American Odyssey and Finder's Guide, and *Library Fundraising: Models for Success.*

Irrepressible Reformer, Wayne Wiegand's long-awaited biography of Melvil Dewey, won critical raves and the coveted "Nota Bene" of the week in the *Chronicle of Higher Education.*

A stand-alone electronic publication, *The Searchable Internet,* offered a "Quick-Bib" on disk. The ALA Editions Web Site was established at http://www.ala.org/ala.editions.html.

Under new editor Leonard Kniffel and associate publisher Stuart Whitwell, *American Libraries* acquired an attractive new design and editorial direction focused on the association's role as the center of the profession's interests and concerns.

In addition to reviewing more than 8,000 books, CD-ROMs, software programs, and videos, *Booklist,* the ALA review magazine for public and school libraries, created a Web site at http://www.ala.org/booklist.html.

Officers and Staff

Mary R. Somerville, director of the Miami-Dade Public Library System in Florida, assumed the 1996–1997 presidency of ALA at the end of the 1996 Annual Conference in New York. Barbara Ford, executive director of library services at Virginia Commonwealth University in Richmond, is vice-president/president-elect. Bruce Daniels, director of the Onondaga County Public Library in Syracuse, New York, was elected treasurer.

Elizabeth Martinez announced her resignation as ALA Executive Director in July. She will serve the remainder of her contract, through August 15, 1997.

New staff appointments in 1996 included Carol A. Erickson, director of the International Relations Office; Jacqueline Mundell, executive director of the Library Information and Technology Association; Greta Southard, executive director of the Public Library Association; Judith O'Malley, editor of *Book Links*; and Coleen J. Sullivan, director, Office for Library Personnel Resources.

Association of American Publishers

71 Fifth Ave., New York, NY 10003-3004
212-255-0200
1718 Connecticut Ave. N.W., Washington, DC 20009
202-232-3335

Judith Platt
Director of Communications and Public Affairs

The Association of American Publishers (AAP) is the book publishing industry's national trade association, with approximately 200 corporate members, including university presses and other nonprofit publishers. AAP members publish hardcover and paperback books in every field, including journals; instructional materials for the elementary, secondary, postsecondary, and professional markets; computer software, and electronic products and services, such as online databases and CD-ROMs. Many of these products are sold in the global as well as the domestic market. AAP also represents about 500 smaller regional publishers through formal affiliations with the Rocky Mountain Book Publishers Association, the Publishers Association of the South, and the Florida Publishers Association. AAP maintains two offices, in New York and in Washington, D.C.

AAP was created in 1970 through the merger of the American Book Publishers Council, a trade publishing group, and the American Educational Publishers Institute, a group of educational textbook publishers. The association was established under a system of confederation, with divisions created to deal with issues in specific markets and industrywide "core" committees assigned the task of dealing with larger issues that affect all publishers across market boundaries. In the years since its founding, AAP's divisional structure has been refined, as the interests of various market segments have shifted and converged.

The restructuring process accelerated over the past 18 months as the AAP leadership conducted a strategic review to pinpoint issues of overriding concern to the AAP membership and to channel fiscal and human resources accordingly. The strategic review highlighted several areas of primary importance:

- The protection of intellectual property rights at home and abroad for content published in any format, with special attention to the emerging information technologies
- Support and protection of freedom of expression
- Promotion of funding for instructional materials as an important component of educational reform
- Development and expansion of global markets for AAP members' products in all formats

As a result of the strategic review, at its September 1996 meeting AAP's board of directors approved several organizational changes designed to strengthen AAP's work in priority areas. The divisional structure was largely discontinued, with only the School Division and the Professional and Scholarly Publishing

Division retaining fiscal responsibility for budgets and programs. The Trade, International, and Higher Education divisions became industrywide committees, with project funding coming directly from the board.

Highlights of 1996

- Richard Robinson, CEO of Scholastic, Inc., was elected to a two-year term as AAP chairman.
- AAP continued to take the lead in the search for electronic commerce solutions for the publishing industry.
- Ruling in the Michigan Document Services case, the full 6th Circuit Court of Appeals reaffirmed the need to obtain permission to use copyrighted materials in college course packs.
- A School Division survey that revealed nationwide shortages of textbooks helped increase funding for instructional materials in several states.
- AAP and its coplaintiffs won a significant victory in the first round of a legal fight over the Communications Decency Act when a federal court struck down the act as unconstitutional.
- Allan R. Adler joined the AAP staff as Vice President for Legal and Governmental Affairs.
- AAP joined with three partners to create a new Pubnet joint venture.
- AAP was a major participant in the Conference on Fair Use (CONFU), which is seeking consensus on fair-use guidelines for use of copyrighted materials in the digital environment.
- With support from AAP, the "Reach Out and Read" literacy program is being introduced in pediatrics clinics all over the country.
- AAP went onto the World Wide Web with its own home page.
- The Florida Publishers Association became the third regional publishing group to establish formal ties with AAP.
- Two former AAP chairmen were singled out for honors in 1996: publisher and human rights activist Robert Bernstein, the recipient of the Curtis Benjamin Award for Creative Publishing, and Richard Morgan, recipient of the Mary McNulty Award for distinguished contributions to educational publishing.

Government Affairs

AAP's Washington office is the industry's front line on matters of federal legislation and government policy. The Washington office keeps AAP members informed about developments on Capitol Hill and in the executive branch to enable the membership to develop consensus positions on national policy issues. AAP serves as the industry's voice, communicating these positions to Congress, government officials, and the media.

A number of AAP houses maintain a corporate presence in Washington, either through their own Washington office or through representation by legal counsel. These comprise the "Washington Representatives" group, which meets periodically to share information and coordinate legislative strategy.

On April 1, 1996, attorney Allan R. Adler, who had worked closely with AAP as outside Washington counsel, joined the AAP staff as Vice President for Legal and Governmental Affairs.

Communications and Public Affairs

The Communications and Public Affairs Program is AAP's voice. It tells the trade press and other media, the AAP membership, and the general public how AAP works to advance and protect the interests of American publishers. Through the program's regular publications, press releases and advisories, op-ed pieces, and other means, AAP expresses the views of the industry it represents, and provides up-to-the-minute information on subjects of concern to its members. Senior AAP staff address many interested audiences throughout the United States and abroad to ensure that the AAP message is heard and understood.

AAP's public affairs activities include outreach and cooperative programs with such organizations as the Center for the Book in the Library of Congress; the Commission on Preservation and Access (with ties to the National Endowment for the Humanities); the Arts Advocacy Alliance (supporting the National Endowment for the Arts and other federal arts programs); PEN American Center and its International Freedom to Write Program (AAP was a founding member of the U.S. Rushdie Defense Committee); a host of literacy and reading promotion efforts, including a highly praised pediatric literacy initiative, "Reach Out and Read"; and liaison with affiliated regional publishing organizations (the Publishers Association of the South, the Rocky Mountain Book Publishers Association, and the Florida Publishers Association).

The AAP Communications and Public Affairs Program is responsible for a number of publications. The *AAP Monthly Report*, the primary means of communication, went online this year, substantially increasing its readership; *An Introduction to AAP*, a general brochure, describes the structure and function of the association; the *AAP Annual Report* provides a yearly detailed report on AAP's activities.

Copyright Committee

The Copyright Committee coordinates AAP efforts to protect and strengthen intellectual property rights and to enhance public awareness of the importance of copyright as an incentive to creativity. Peter Jovanovich (McGraw-Hill) is chair of the committee.

A major concern of the Copyright Committee in 1996 was the ongoing dialogue among various groups representing educators, libraries, and copyright owners to establish guidelines for a variety of new digital uses of copyrighted materials in schools, colleges, and libraries. AAP played a prominent role, presenting the views of the U.S. publishing industry at the Clinton administration-sponsored Conference on Fair Use (CONFU) and in negotiations sponsored by the Consortium of College and University Media Centers. At year's end, a degree of consensus had been reached on proposed guidelines for multimedia, image archiving, and distance learning.

The committee also coordinated AAP's support for the publisher plaintiffs in their copyright infringement suit against Michigan Document Services (MDS). Although the year started with a disappointing ruling in the 6th Circuit (in which two members of a three-judge panel found MDS's unauthorized use of copyrighted works in college course packs to be fair use), the court granted the plaintiffs' petition for a rehearing by the full court, and on November 8, by an 8–5 vote, the 6th Circuit ruled that MDS's activities are *not* fair use and reaffirmed the need for copy shops creating college course packs to obtain permission to use copyrighted materials.

AAP joined the Information Industry Association and the American Medical Association in an *amicus* brief in the *Pro CD* case, asking the 7th Circuit Court of Appeals to reverse a lower court finding that copyright law preempts private contracts, in particular contracts restricting the redistribution of uncopyrightable material. The appellate court reversed the lower court ruling in June.

AAP continued to play a leading role in the international copyright arena in 1996. At the 25th Congress of the International Publishers Association (IPA) in Barcelona in April, AAP's Vice President for Copyright and New Technology presented a position paper on "Libraries, Copyright and the Electronic Environment," urging publishers and libraries to recognize the profound differences between the digital and print environments and to commit themselves to cooperative efforts that will allow them to function effectively while safeguarding copyright. The paper was formally adopted by the IPA International Committee and forwarded as an IPA document to the International Federation of Library Associations for its consideration and response.

Digital Committee

Originally set up as a special subcommittee of the Copyright Committee, the Digital Committee, chaired by Richard Rudick (John Wiley & Sons), worked on copyright issues in the context of the digital environment, with special emphasis on the National and Global Information Infrastructures. The group spent considerable time coordinating AAP's response to legislation introduced to implement the administration's White Paper recommendations and to crafting congressional testimony presented by AAP Vice Chairman Richard Robinson in February 1996.

One of AAP's major objectives was to secure enactment of National Information Infrastructure (NII) copyright legislation that would effect minimum changes in the copyright law while at the same time clarifying its application in cyberspace. Efforts to pass such legislation were thwarted by various groups, including the Digital Future Coalition, which saw the legislation as somehow threatening the free flow of information in cyberspace. Working independently and through the Creative Incentive Coalition, a group dedicated to protecting intellectual property in cyberspace, AAP tried to convey the message to Congress and the public that cyberspace can accommodate free speech, free information, and commercial endeavors; that all three components are crucial to the NII's success, and that the commercial component must be safeguarded by effective intellectual property (IP) protection. [For a full report on legislative and regulatory issues, see the article "Legislation and Regulations Affecting Publishing" in Part 2.—*Ed.*]

Education Program

In late 1995 AAP inaugurated a program to provide educational opportunities for publishing industry personnel. The first course was an intensive "Introduction to Publishing," designed to give entry-level employees an overview of the industry and a better understanding of the publishing process. Highly successful, "Introduction to Publishing" was offered a second time in March 1996.

In fall 1996 the Education Program sponsored a seminar on the human resources and legal issues related to work-for-hire, contracted services, and freelance work. In November AAP sponsored a two-day tax seminar in Washington, D.C., covering recent state, local, and federal developments affecting the publishing industry and on tax issues relating to the Internet and new media.

Enabling Technologies Committee

The Enabling Technologies Committee focuses on publishing in the electronic networked environment and serves as a steering committee, directing AAP's efforts to promote the development of workable systems for managing copyright in the digital environment. Tim King (John Wiley & Sons) was chairman of the committee from its inception until August 1996, when Craig Van Dyck (Springer-Verlag) assumed the chairmanship.

During the second phase of the Enabling Technologies project, four roundtables were convened to facilitate discussions between developers of various copyright management systems technologies (including CD-ROM, Internet browsers, metering systems, infringement prevention and deterrence systems, and encryption technology) and publishers representing the major market segments of the AAP membership. A report on the roundtables, *Publishers and Technology: Face to Face*, describing the various technologies and their applicability to copyright protection for different types of content, was published in spring 1996.

During its early work in 1995 the committee recognized a fundamental need for a unique, unambiguous way to identify digital materials—a type of "electronic license plate" for a "digital vehicle" traveling the "Information Superhighway." AAP issued a Request for Proposal to develop a "digital object identifier" (DOI) system for the publishing industry. On September 9 AAP announced selection of the team that will carry the work forward: R. R. Bowker and the Corporation for National Research Initiatives. The team will focus on developing a system for publishers to use in identifying digital objects, and developing a network-based directory to link DOIs to the publisher. Since the DOI system uses open standards, publishers and other companies can build their own products and services based around DOIs.

AAP's groundbreaking work on the DOI system is getting a good deal of attention, recognition, and support in the international community. The DOI project was featured prominently at a meeting in November as part of the European

Union's effort to facilitate standards of interoperability on the Global Information Infrastructure. AAP's proposed DOI was officially recognized at that meeting as a model for an industry-developed project that will work as an open international standard. In addition, a special committee of the American National Standards Institute is working on development of the DOI to ensure its adoption as an American and then an international standard.

Freedom to Read Committee

The Freedom to Read Committee coordinates AAP's efforts to promote and protect First Amendment rights and intellectual freedom. In fulfilling its mandate, the committee provides guidance on possible AAP intervention in First Amendment court cases, lobbies on free-expression issues at the national and state level, and conducts educational programs. The Freedom to Read Committee works closely with allied organizations—especially the American Library Association's Office for Intellectual Freedom and the American Booksellers Foundation for Free Expression—and coordinates AAP participation as a member of the Media Coalition, a group of trade associations formed to fight censorship. Lisa Drew (Lisa Drew Books/Scribner) is committee chair.

In February 1996 AAP joined the American Library Association (ALA), the American Booksellers Association (ABA), and a broad range of groups representing Internet users, content providers, and access providers, in a lawsuit charging that the Communications Decency Act (CDA), which bans "indecent" speech on the Internet, violates the First Amendment. Filed in federal court in Philadelphia, the suit was heard by a special three-judge panel which ruled unanimously on June 12 that the CDA violates constitutional free-speech guarantees. The court issued a preliminary injunction barring the government from enforcing the act. As expected, the Justice Department appealed to the U.S. Supreme Court, and on December 6 the Supreme Court accepted the case for review.

Working closely with AAP's government affairs program, the Freedom to Read Committee examines First Amendment legislation and recommends AAP action at the state and national level. Through the Media Coalition, AAP joined in an unsuccessful effort to secure a gubernatorial veto of the "little CDA" passed by the New York State legislature, which bans dissemination of "indecent" speech that may be "harmful to minors" on the Internet. AAP plans to join in a legal challenge to the New York statute. Together with interested authors' representatives, AAP spearheaded legislative efforts in Albany to broaden New York's "press shield" law to encompass the activities of book publishers and their authors. In the area of federal legislation, AAP was concerned about the Child Pornography Prevention Act of 1996, which raises serious constitutional questions. In the course of the legislative process, Media Coalition testimony and joint lobbying efforts succeeded in convincing Senate sponsors to remove what were seen as the most blatantly unconstitutional provisions from the bill prior to its passage.

With ALA, ABA, and others, AAP cosponsors Banned Books Week, an annual celebration of the freedom to read. Held each year in early fall, the observance calls attention to books that have been banned or challenged and turns the spotlight on special interest groups that try to impose their views and ideological agendas on public schools and libraries. In addition to the CDA challenge, the Freedom to Read Committee was involved in a number of court cases in 1996:

- The committee submitted letter briefs in two separate cases in California, pitting privacy guarantees in the state constitution against First Amendment free-press guarantees, arguing that state guarantees of privacy cannot trump the First Amendment.
- AAP was one of the friends-of-the-court that protested a restraining order issued by a Cincinnati judge against *Business Week*. The order was resoundingly struck down by the 6th Circuit Court of Appeals.
- AAP joined in asking the U.S. Court of Appeals for the District of Columbia to refuse to enforce the libel judgment of a British court in the United States.
- The Freedom to Read Committee joined with other First Amendment and media organizations in an *amicus* brief asking for dismissal of a civil suit brought by the families of three murder victims against the publisher of the book *Hit Man*. The suit accused the publisher of being an accessory to the crimes because the confessed killer allegedly used information found in the book. The case was dismissed August 30 on the finding of a federal judge that the material in the book was protected by the First Amendment. The case is now on appeal.
- On May 2 a federal judge in Cincinnati ruled that the Hamilton County (Ohio) prosecutor violated the First Amendment when he sent Barnes & Noble a letter warning that a display containing *Playboy* and five other magazines violated Ohio's "harmful to juveniles" display law. The prosecutor had been sued by AAP and other Media Coalition members, who charged him with prior restraint of First Amendment-protected materials. On December 23, 1996, the judge refused a request to rehear the case. Late in 1995 AAP filed an *amicus* brief in the Supreme Court in the *Alliance for Community Media* case, arguing against the inherent vagueness of an "indecency" standard in regulating cable programming. Making only passing reference to AAP's legal analysis, the Supreme Court decision issued June 28 failed to resolve definitively the important First Amendment questions raised by the case.
- In November AAP signed an *amicus* brief in *Khawar* v. *Globe International*, a California defamation suit. The brief asks the California Supreme Court to overturn a defamation judgment that holds that a "re-publisher" of previously published information is obligated to take further steps to ascertain the truth in the face of "extravagantly improbable" allegations.

Higher Education Division

AAP's Higher Education Division, which was restructured into an industrywide committee by the board, continues to serve the needs and interests of AAP members who publish for the postsecondary educational market. The new Higher Education Committee is chaired by June Smith (Houghton Mifflin).

The Higher Education group again coordinated AAP's participation at the National Association of College Stores Annual Meeting and Campus Exposition in San Diego in April. AAP's higher education publishers gathered in Chicago in May for a two-day annual meeting to discuss corporate innovation with the leaders of other copyright industries (including motion pictures, sound recordings, and computers). At the Chicago meeting, the James Leisy Higher Education Achievement Award was presented to Worth Publishers founder Robert Worth.

Campus Copyright Education Program

AAP's Campus Copyright Education Committee works to encourage and improve copyright law compliance in the higher education community by offering copyright education, assisting members of the academic community in achieving compliance, and working for continued improvement in various systems that facilitate compliance. The program inaugurated a series of luncheon seminars in 1996. AAP and the Software Publishers Association (SPA) developed a new video aimed at increasing copyright awareness and respect for intellectual property rights in the higher education community. Titled *A Shared Set of Values: Copyright and Intellectual Property in the Academic Community*, the video will support the efforts of AAP, SPA, and allied groups to promote respect for copyright law and the ethical use of intellectual property in the academic community.

International Division

The International Division was restructured by the board into an industrywide committee serving the breadth of the AAP membership. Deborah Wiley (John Wiley & Sons) chairs the International Committee.

AAP's international activities in 1996 included a major presence at the 16th Paris Book Fair in March. The Salon du Livre featured an impressive American collective exhibit and numerous panel discussions involving U.S. industry leaders. AAP President Nicholas Veliotes and AAP Heads of House Charles Ellis (John Wiley), Peter Mayer (Penguin), Paul Gottlieb (Abrams), Bruno Quinson (Holt), and Alberto Vitale (Random House) were awarded medals by the French government.

AAP's popular international seminar at the American Booksellers Association (ABA) Conference in Chicago in June focused on the Italian market in 1996, with the director of the Bologna Children's Book Fair and a number of noted Italian publishers as featured speakers. The AAP International Rights and Sales Center was a popular meeting place at ABA for publishers and their international customers. Among the educational programs in 1996 was a seminar on the impact of immigration and the "official English" movement on publishing.

AAP again cosponsored the International Rights Directors meeting at the Frankfurt Book Fair, this year focusing on the growing importance of the book-to-film rights process. Also at Frankfurt, for the fourth year, AAP member publishers cosponsored an internship program that brought publishers from central and eastern Europe to the fair and gave them an opportunity to work at U.S. booths.

In July AAP hosted a luncheon and organized three on-site visits to AAP member houses for a delegation of senior officials from the People's Republic of China who were in the United States to discuss ongoing intellectual property problems.

Antipiracy Program

AAP continued its vigorous efforts to combat international copyright piracy. Working with other U.S. copyright industries in the International Intellectual Property Alliance, AAP continued to press the U.S. government to protect American copyrights overseas and encourage the elimination of market access barriers for U.S.-copyrighted works. AAP participated in the alliance's annual filing to the U.S. Trade Representative (USTR) targeting countries whose failure to protect American copyrights warrants attention under the "Special 301" provisions of the Trade Act. China's failure to live up to its obligations under the 1995 U.S.-China Agreement on Enforcement of Intellectual Property Rights prompted the United States to move toward imposing massive trade sanctions in spring 1996. At USTR public hearings on June 7 AAP President Nicholas Veliotes reported that AAP members were increasingly discovering some of their most valuable works in Hong Kong and elsewhere on illegal, Chinese-made CD-ROMs. Veliotes applauded the U.S. government's tough stance on Chinese piracy. Trade sanctions were averted by a last-minute agreement reached June 17 in Beijing under which the two governments laid out a new plan to enforce the 1995 accord.

At the Frankfurt Book Fair, AAP coordinated a meeting for international sales representatives from both AAP and the British Publishers Association member houses to discuss joint antipiracy activities in various markets. At the meeting, AAP distributed its latest *Status Report on Copyright Reform and Publishing Antipiracy Activities in 70 Countries*. The report is available from the AAP Washington office.

AAP continued its overseas enforcement campaign. Efforts in 1996 centered on Argentina, Bolivia, Korea, Malaysia, Puerto Rico, Singapore, and Taiwan.

International Freedom to Publish Committee

AAP's International Freedom to Publish (IFTP) Committee defends and promotes worldwide freedom of written communication. The committee monitors human rights issues and provides moral support and practical assistance to publishers and authors outside the United States who are denied basic freedoms. The committee carries on its work in close cooperation with other human rights groups, including Human Rights Watch and PEN International. Wendy Wolf (Penguin USA) is committee chair.

A delegation of publishers, writers, academics, and human rights activists, under the sponsorship of the IFTP Committee, visited Indonesia in September to discuss restrictions on freedom of expression. During their week-long visit, the delegation sponsored a two-day conference with writers, publishers, academics, and other intellectuals. Scores of individuals and organizations met to discuss censorship, focusing on four themes: politics, religion, sexuality, and academic freedom. Ending the visit at a press conference in Jakarta, IFTP chair Wolf said the group was "both encouraged and troubled" by its meetings—encouraged by the willingness of many individuals to discuss openly the restrictions on free expression, but discouraged that more than 2,000 books are banned from circulation, that three journalists are currently imprisoned for reporting the news, and that writers such as Prameodya Ananta Toer are not allowed to travel or publish. One of the mission's primary objectives was to establish alliances with Indonesian colleagues and to foster continued direct exchanges between Indonesian and U.S. publishers, writers, and scholars. Through a series of meetings with U.S. and foreign government officials and with U.S. businesses with interests in Indonesia, and also through published reports, the committee hopes to bring free expression issues in Indonesia to public attention.

Publisher and human rights activist Robert Bernstein, who was instrumental in creating the IFTP Committee and served as its first chair, received the 1996 Curtis Benjamin Award for Creative Publishing. In a moving acceptance speech at the AAP Annual Meeting in Palm Beach, Bernstein discussed the continuing struggle for human rights and free expression in China, and reminded his audience of the special responsibility of writers and publishers in exposing human rights abuses wherever they occur.

Among the ways in which the committee aids foreign writers and publishers is by issuing invitations to visit the United States. In 1996 the committee sent a second letter of invitation to Vietnamese novelist Duong Thu Huong, who has been subjected to harassment by the government of Vietnam. It was hoped that she could visit the United States in the fall of 1996, but as of January she had not received permission to travel abroad. The IFTP Committee continued to voice protests on behalf of writers, journalists, and publishers who are denied basic rights of free expression. In 1996 letters were sent to Fidel Castro, regarding the forced exile of Cuban journalist Rafael Solano; to the prime minister of Turkey, protesting the conviction and sentencing of writer/journalist Yasar Kemal; to Turkish and U.S. government officials, regarding charges against Turkish publisher Aysenur Zarakolu; to the first prime minister of Cambodia, regarding the killing of opposition journalist Thun Bun Ly; to the president of Peru, regarding the detention of broadcaster Jesus Alfonso Castiglione Mendoza; to Boris Yeltsin, protesting the killings of correspondents in Chechnya and Siberia; to the prime minister of India, regarding the abduction and murder of Kashmiri newspaper editor Ghulam Rasool Sheikh; and to top government officials of the People's Republic of China, protesting the sentencing of Wang Dan.

The committee occasionally provides modest financial support to assist publishers and writers overseas. In 1996 a small grant was made to the New York-based Committee to Protect Journalists for the purchase of Spanish-language books needed by the newly formed Cuban Press Club, an organization of independent news agencies. The books will be sent to Cuba for use by journalism students. Among the guest speakers who addressed IFTP meetings in 1996 were Xiao Qiang, Executive Director of Human Rights in China, who spoke about dissidents and political prisoners, especially Wang Dan; Tom Gjelten, National Public Radio foreign correspondent, who provided an update on Bosnia since the peace accords; and a delegation from the Vietnamese Writers Association, a quasi-governmental group that visited the United States in the fall of 1996.

New Media Committee

AAP's New Media Committee was established in 1994 to provide publisher support in the CD-ROM marketplace and to assist booksellers entering this new market. From its inception, the committee was chaired by Randi Benton (Random House).

In 1996 the committee cosponsored (with *Publishers Weekly* and Association Exposition Services) a second study of new media market trends among independent bookseller members of ABA. The survey, which found a market penetration virtually unchanged from 1995, highlighted a number of interesting trends among independent booksellers, including heightened interest in the Internet as a business tool.

The New Media Committee hosted a presentation on books in cyberspace featuring representatives of Amazon.com and Book Stacks Unlimited.

In fall 1996, having accomplished what it set out to do and in light of dramatic changes in the marketplace, the New Media Committee was disbanded.

Postal Committee

The Postal Committee coordinates AAP activity in the area of postal rates and regulations, monitors developments at the U.S. Postal Service (USPS) and the independent Postal Rate Commission, and intervenes on the industry's behalf in formal proceedings before the commission. The committee also directs AAP lobbying activities on postal issues. Stephen Bair (Time-Life Books) continued to serve as chair in 1996.

In spring 1996 AAP wrote to the Postmaster General urging USPS to pursue a reclassification initiative, eliminating the current 10-pound weight limitation and implementing other changes that will assist publishers in using the "Bound Printed Matter" class of parcel service.

Much of the committee's energy was devoted to developing AAP's testimony on the Postal Reform Act of 1966 presented to the House Postal Service Subcommittee. Efforts to ensure that the Postal Reform Act reflects the concerns of AAP's members will continue in the 105th Congress.

Professional and Scholarly Publishing Division

The Professional and Scholarly Publishing (PSP) Division is concerned with the publication of technical, scientific, medical, and scholarly materials. Division members produce books, journals, computer software, databases, and CD-ROM products. Professional societies and university presses play an important role. Eric Swanson (John Wiley & Sons) is division chair.

PSP's 1996 annual meeting was held in Washington in March. Outstanding achievements in professional and scholarly publishing were honored in the annual PSP awards program; Charles Scribner's Sons Reference Books, publisher of *Civilizations of the Ancient Near East*, edited by Jack M. Sasson, received the R. R. Hawkins Award. In addition, book awards were presented in 28 subject categories, in design and production, and in journal and electronic publishing.

With funding and support from PSP, the AAP home page was inaugurated on the World Wide Web in early 1996. The PSP Electronic Information Committee will publish its second Internet White Paper early in 1997. Covering the traditional and changing role of the publisher, trends and tools in Internet publishing, and key issues such as archiving and copyright, White Paper II was written and edited entirely online on a secure Web site.

In August PSP and ABA released the results of a new joint study examining the market for professional and scholarly books sold through traditional bookstores.

Among PSP's educational programs in 1996 were a Journals Committee seminar highlighting Internet publishing case studies, a program on the changing role of subscription agents, and an Electronic Information Committee "satellite" seminar that preceded the PSP Annual Meeting.

Pubnet

Pubnet, AAP's electronic data interchange service for book ordering, continued to grow in 1996. More than 3,700 bookstores, library jobbers, wholesalers, schools, and exporters and some 90 companies (representing more than 500 publishers) are now on the system. Originally established to serve the college publishing community, Pubnet has successfully expanded in recent years to trade, mass market, and academic publishing, and has enlarged its membership to include other book suppliers, with several wholesalers and small-press distributors now processing orders.

On June 15, 1996, AAP, R. R. Bowker, the National Association of College Stores, and ABA announced their intention to form a joint venture to direct Pubnet's future operations. The aim of the new joint venture, which is to be officially established in 1997, is to "reinvent" Pubnet, providing lower-cost fulfillment solutions and increased ordering capabilities for publishers, as well as enhanced information and communications capabilities for booksellers. The joint venture plans to introduce major new systems changes in 1997.

School Division

The School Division is concerned with publishing for the elementary and secondary school (K–12) market. The division works to enhance the role of instructional materials in the education process, to maintain categorical funding for instructional materials and increase the funds available for the purchase of these materials, and to simplify and rationalize the process of state adoptions for instructional materials. The division serves as a bridge between the publishing industry and the educational community, promoting the cause of education at the national and state level, and it works closely with the AAP Washington office and an effective lobbying network in key adoption states. William Wisneski (Houghton Mifflin) chairs the division.

The School Division, with help from the National Education Association, surveyed teachers across the country on the availability of up-to-date instructional materials in their classrooms. The results of the survey, released in February 1996 at a press conference with Florida Governor Lawton Chiles and given extensive nationwide media coverage, showed that school children are being hampered by severe shortages of textbooks and the use of outdated teaching materials in all parts of the country. The division produced a video, *Crisis in the Classroom*, highlighting the survey's results, and made it available to school boards, education officials, lawmakers, and parent-teacher organizations across the country. The AAP survey was cited in budget debates in a number of state legislatures; it has been credited with playing an important role in the 46 percent increase in instructional materials funding approved by the Florida state legislature, and in record appropriations of $298 million for instructional materials purchases in California. The survey was also cited in a CNN report on the textbook crisis in New York City schools, raising public awareness of the situation and leading to the November announcement by New York's mayor that an additional $70 million would be allocated to buy books for the city's schools.

AAP school publishers are serving on a new task force convened by the Florida education commissioner to study the instructional materials funding process and the issue of categorical funding. At the school division 1996 meeting in Washington, D.C., Richard T. Morgan, former CEO of Harcourt Brace and a former chairman of AAP and the School Division, received the division's highest honor, the Mary McNulty Award.

In June the School Division and the Library of Congress cosponsored a symposium on public/private partnerships and the National Digital Library, exploring opportunities for educational publishers to tap into the library's new digitized Americana collections.

Trade Publishing

Restructured by the board into an industrywide committee, AAP's Trade Publishers Committee met for the first time in November to discuss its role in the new AAP organizational scheme. At that meeting it was decided that the Libraries Committee will continue its liaison work with ALA through a joint committee with ALA's Association for Library Collections and Technological Services (ALCTS). At the ALA Annual Conference in New York in July, the ALCTS/AAP committee sponsored a program designed to familiarize publishers and librarians with Standard Generalized Markup Language (SGML), an encoding system used for publishing. The Libraries Committee is moving forward with plans to conduct a new library marketing and acquisitions survey (earlier surveys were done in the mid-1970s and mid-1980s). The Trade Publishers Committee also plans to continue the AAP Book Preview video presentation at the National Association of College Stores.

Three years ago, AAP's trade publishers voted to allocate funds to support a new, innovative early childhood literacy program, "Reach Out and Read." Developed and pioneered at Boston City Hospital, the program utilizes pediatrics clinics and personnel to integrate reading promotion into a "well baby" program in inner city and rural clinics serving economically deprived populations. Over the past year, with AAP's help and with special support from several AAP regular and affiliate members, the "Reach Out and Read" training manual, informational brochures, and ancillary materials were printed and distributed to pediatrics facilities all over the country. The program was given a national send-off in Washington on May 8 at a major international gathering of pediatricians, and a special interest group meeting on pediatric literacy was held to introduce pediatricians to the program and to encourage them to initiate programs of their own. At its November meeting, the Trade Publishers Committee voted to continue its involvement in "Reach Out and Read," in line with AAP's commitment to improving educational opportunities for America's children.

Administrative Committees

Lawyers Committee

The Lawyers Committee is composed of both in-house and outside counsel of AAP member companies. It meets periodically to discuss legal issues under review by AAP's committees and divisions. Ellis Levine (Random House) is committee chair.

Compensation Survey Committee

The Compensation Survey Committee, chaired by Christine Names (Random House), functions in alternate years. It coordinates and supervises preparation of the *AAP Survey of Compensation and Personnel Practices in the Publishing Industry*. Prepared and published every two years, the report is designed to provide current, accurate information on prevailing compensation levels for representative management and professional positions in the industry. The 1997 survey is being prepared by Buck Consultants, a compensation firm with extensive experience.

American Booksellers Association

828 S. Broadway, Tarrytown, NY 10591
914-591-2665
World Wide Web: http://www.bookweb.org

Carol Miles
Director of Research

In late 1996 the concluding chapter was written in the American Booksellers Association's ongoing litigation against six publishers who were charged with price discrimination, promotional allowance discrimination, and illegally favoring certain kinds of retail booksellers. Of the five defendants in the original antitrust lawsuit, brought by ABA and six bookseller coplaintiffs in mid-1994, three (Hugh Lauter Levin Associates, Houghton Mifflin, and Penguin USA) had settled by the end of 1995. The remaining two defendants (Rutledge Hill Press and St. Martin's Press) settled in late July and early August of 1996, respectively.

Meanwhile, ABA and five bookseller coplaintiffs began the year by filing a similar antitrust discrimination lawsuit against Random House Inc., the largest trade book publisher in the United States, on January 3. That suit, which also alleged violations of the Robinson-Patman Act, was, in turn, settled in late November. In each case, while admitting no wrongdoing, the publishers agreed in consent orders to comply with a set of rules assuring nondiscrimination in pricing and co-op policies when selling to competing book retailers.

Despite the successful resolution of the litigation and concomitant evidence that other publishers were also beginning to adopt terms of sale equitable to bookstores and other retailers, indicators tracked by ABA and released during 1996 continued to suggest that the industry is facing a multitude of challenges. Notably, the 1995 Consumer Research Study on Book Purchasing—jointly sponsored by ABA, the Association of American Publishers (AAP), and the Book Industry Study Group (BISG) and published by BISG—revealed a virtually flat market for adult books. The unit growth rate slowed to just 1 percent between 1994 and 1995 from a much healthier 16 percent between 1991 and 1992.

Unpublished data collected for the study and analyzed by the ABA research department showed that bookstores in general and independents in particular have continued to decline in importance as distribution channels for books. Specifically, the total 1995 bookstore share of the market for adult books dropped to just below 50 percent (49.7 percent of units for independents, chains, and used-book bookstores combined), compared to 57.3 percent in 1991. Looking only at bookstores selling predominantly new books, the situation is even bleaker: independents and chains combined accounted for well under half (45.7 percent) of the unit purchases of adult books in 1995, down from 54.6 percent in 1991. As all bookstores lost share to all other types of adult book retailers, so did independents continue to lose market position to chains in 1995. By the end of the year, chains held 26.2 percent of the adult book market, while independents accounted for only 19.5 percent.

Consistent findings based on dollar sales of bookstores selling predominantly new books and periodicals emerged from an analysis of data from the *Current*

Retail Census and financial reports of the four largest bookstore chains (Barnes & Noble, the Borders Group, Crown Books, and Books-A-Million) and were published in *Bookselling This Week* in 1996. These data showed that calendar year bookstore sales increased 3 percent between 1994 and 1995 (compared to a 4.9 percent increase for the entire retail sector), reaching an estimated total of $10.3 billion in 1995. It is noteworthy, however, that when inflation is taken into account, year-to-year bookstore sales were essentially flat.

In order to assess relative dollar market share of the four largest chains and all other new-book bookstores, total bookstore sales figures were compiled for the period corresponding to the fiscal years of the four leading chains (approximately February 1 through January 31). The results showed that total dollar bookstore sales for the 12 months ending January 31, 1996, had increased just 0.6 percent; however, sales of the four largest chains grew 17.4 percent, while sales for all other bookstores declined 8.6 percent during that fiscal period. Similarly, estimated dollar market share of the four largest bookstore chains rose in 1995. During their 1994 fiscal year, market share of the top chains amounted to 35.6 percent, but by the end of the 1995 fiscal year the comparable figure was 41.5 percent.

In addition to bringing the antitrust lawsuits to a successful conclusion, other major actions taken by the association in 1996 to address the competitive challenges being faced by booksellers included entering into a partnership with AAP, R. R. Bowker, and the National Association of College Stores (NACS) to revise and relaunch Pubnet. The new Pubnet will feature an online version of Bowker's *Books In Print* (*BIP*) database and improved front-end internet access, among other capabilities designed to benefit trade booksellers. Finally, as the year drew to a close, Executive Director Bernie Rath and President Barbara Bonds Thomas announced that ABA would enter into a strategic planning process designed to lead the association into the 21st century and beyond.

Membership

Membership in the association at the end of 1996 declined slightly to just over 7,000, consistent with the trends reported above resulting in continuing independent bookstore closings and exacerbated somewhat by the dues increase approved by the membership in 1995 and implemented during 1996.

All five of ABA's specialty membership segments (Scientific/Technical/Professional, Science Fiction, Travel, African American, and Gay/Lesbian) held roundtable discussion sessions at the 1996 ABA Convention, and members of each segment also continued to receive a tabloid-sized specialty newsletter published quarterly by ABA's periodicals publishing division. In addition, the African American booksellers segment and the Scientific Technical/Professional group each held a full-day conference. As part of the latter event, results of the ABA-PSP Professional and Scholarly Book-Buying Study, sponsored jointly by ABA and AAP's Professional and Scholarly Publishing Division (PSP), were presented.

Capitalizing on the enthusiastic response of members to the BookWeb, ABA's site on the World Wide Web inaugurated in 1995, the association moved to encourage expanded member presence on the Internet. In return for updating their membership information, members were offered a free business description appended to their listing on ABA's Web site. In addition to a fully searchable database of ABA-member bookstores, the site—designed to promote member booksellers to consumers—also includes articles from *Bookselling This Week* (*BTW*) and *American Bookseller* magazine, a monthly contest through which consumers can win a gift certificate to the member bookstore of their choice, and other ABA news and information of interest to consumers. Since its inception, the BookWeb has received more than one million visits, and as of December 1996 it was averaging in excess of 500,000 "hits" per month. The address is http://www.bookweb.org.

In addition, ABA is currently leasing space on the BookWeb to any ABA-member bookseller wishing to have a home page, and is building hyperlinks to any member home pages that are already in existence. By the end of 1996 approximately 350 booksellers had availed themselves of this opportunity and the number was growing daily. Many had the opportunity to see the BookWeb demonstrated at ABA's booth at the 1996 ABA Convention and Trade Exhibit in Chicago, where ABA also held many live online author chats. Featured guest "speakers" were Louise Erdrich, Senator Jim Wright, Tanya Melich, Raymond Feist, Martin Keating, H. Ross Perot, Senator Paul Simon, Burt Ward, and Ray Bradbury.

The free Fax-on-Demand service was also expanded in 1996 to include more business-related information about an array of ABA services. The association is now utilizing e-mail, as well as fax, for instantaneous communication with members.

Responding to requests from the membership, ABA established a health insurance program and a low-cost, small-package shipping program, as well as putting in place a new bank-card processing provider. These services are available to the associate category of members and to main store (bookstore) members. (Associate members are publishers, wholesalers, distributors, and all who provide goods or services that might be of interest to booksellers.)

1996 Convention and Trade Exhibit

The 1996 ABA Convention and Trade Exhibit was held at Chicago's McCormick Place from June 15 to 17. ABA's second convention in its new Chicago home attracted some 38,000 attendees. Of these, 10,205 were book buyers (up from 9,548 in 1995, a 7 percent increase), including booksellers, wholesalers/distributors, libraries, and schools. There were more than 2,500 exhibiting companies and 16 special exhibit sections on the trade floor, including children's, new media, remainders, small press, gay/lesbian/feminist, scientific/technical/professional, and sidelines.

The trade show was once again managed by ABA's joint venture partner, Reed Exhibition Companies' Association Expositions and Services. As it turned out, this was the last "ABA Trade Exhibit," as ABA sold its remaining 51 percent interest in the trade show to Reed in the latter half of 1996. (Starting in 1997 it will be rechristened "BookExpo," with ABA participating as a sponsor.) At the

1996 show, the convention portion was once again managed by ABA, as it will continue to be in the future. The exceptionally popular convention educational program was once again designed and managed by ABA's department of education and professional development. Some 70 seminars, workshops, and roundtable discussions were conducted. Those events with particularly high attendance and enthusiastic response were indicative of the areas of most concern to booksellers. They included a full-day paid session on "The Bookstore of the 21st Century," which demonstrated much of the new technology now available and actually in use in several bookstores, and a seminar titled "Value Migration," which focused on the need for strategic planning. Also highly rated were three very practical sessions in the area of financial management, one of which was titled "Analyzing and Controlling Your Store's Cash Flow." Another was called "Using and Understanding Financial Documents to Make Management Decisions," and the third was termed "Determining the Proper Level of Inventory and Using a System to Control the Dollar Volume of Purchases." Other highlights of the convention program included 12 roundtable discussions for bookstores of various types and sizes, a full-day session for children's booksellers on "Nurturing Your Inventory from a Financial Perspective," and a full-day conference for African American booksellers, half of which was devoted to a seminar on financial management.

As usual numerous authors were present at both book-signings and numerous events featuring authors-as-speakers, all of which were heavily attended. On Saturday morning a new and well-received auditorium-based "Wake Up" format was introduced. "Wake Up with Children's Writers" began with the presentation of the Children's American Booksellers Book of the Year (ABBY) award (for the book booksellers most enjoyed handselling during 1996) to Sam McBratney and Anita Jeram for *Guess How Much I Love You*, (Candlewick). Following that, the Lucile Micheels Pannell Award was presented to children's specialty bookseller Kay Remick of Edward T. Rabbit in Richmond, Virginia, and to general booksellers Julia Barron and Kathy Patrick of Barron's Books in Longview, Texas. Featured speakers were authors Eve Bunting, Floyd Cooper, and Brian Jacques.

Sunday's "Wake Up with Writers" event in the Arie Crown Theater showcased authors Eleanor Clift, John Grisham, Mia Farrow, and Art Buchwald. Also during the Sunday morning program an ABBY Award was presented to David Guterson for his *Snow Falling on Cedars* (Harcourt Brace/Vintage), and Virginia Hobson Hicks was honored as the winner the Charles S. Haslam Award for Excellence in Bookselling.

On Monday morning, featured speakers were Andrew Young, Neil Simon, Louise Erdrich, and David Mixner. In addition, two bookselling awards were presented. The 1996 Charley Haslam International Scholarship Award went to Kelly Grant of Pages for All Ages, and there were several 1996 Blackboard Awards honorees. The nonfiction award was won by Iyanla Vanzant's *Value in the Valley* (Simon & Schuster); the fiction award by E. Lynn Harris's *Just As I Am* (Doubleday); and the children's award by Virginia Hamilton's *HerStories* (Scholastic). Blanche Richardson accepted the Blackboard Bookseller of the Year award on behalf of her father, Julian Richardson, of Marcus Books.

Sunday's "Poetry and Literature in Everyday Life" luncheon was moderated by U.S. Poet Laureate Robert Haas. Speakers were Ivan Doig, Susan Power,

Donald Hall, and John Edgar Wideman. GiGi Bradford, literature director at the National Endowment for the Arts (NEA), also spoke briefly about NEA.

Finally, Saturday and Sunday evening Reading Rooms offered convention attendees the opportunity to listen to a number of authors reading excerpts from their own works. This year's featured readers were Robert Olen Butler, William Kotzwinkle, Jill McCorkle, Diane McKinney-Whetstone, Larry Brown, Mary Kay Zuravlef, and Christopher Leland.

American Booksellers Foundation for Free Expression

The American Booksellers Foundation for Free Expression (ABFFE) maintained its role as a leading defender of First Amendment and free expression rights for booksellers and others throughout 1996. When the much-heralded Telecommunications Act of 1996 was passed, ABFFE joined the coalition spearheaded by the American Library Association (ALA) in forming a new entity, the Citizens Internet Empowerment Coalition (CIEC), to challenge the so-called communications decency provisions of that legislation. The coalition won a unanimous victory before a special three-judge panel in June, and the Supreme Court is scheduled to hear CIEC's arguments in 1997.

ABFFE was a signatory and supporter of the successful "No on Censorship, No on 31" campaign committee in response to an Oregon referendum. The foundation was also a plaintiff in a successful effort in Cincinnati to uphold the rights of booksellers to display constitutionally protected materials, and it lent support against a constitutional amendment in Colorado dealing with parental rights. Furthermore, ABFFE joined as an amicus curiae on behalf of Paladin Press and its book *Hit Man*, supporting the principle that booksellers and publishers cannot be held responsible for criminal acts. It similarly supported the rights of booksellers to distribute a new edition of *The Turner Diaries*.

ABFFE once again sponsored special events at the ABA Convention and Trade Exhibit as a means of drawing attention to First Amendment concerns. A panel discussion titled "Campaign '96: The Candidates, the Conflicts and the Constitution" featured political experts Tom Brazaitis, David Brock, Stephen Carter, Eleanor Clift, Gary Hart, Tanya Melich, Richard Reeves, Ed Rollins, Theodore Sorenson, and Jim Wright. Chicago's well-known comedy troupe The Second City and special guests Roger Ebert and Michael Moore presented two performances of a new revue, "Debate '96."

Other ABFFE activities in 1996 included continued cosponsorship of Banned Books Week. To enhance its Banned Books Week activities, the foundation provided more than 1,000 booksellers and others with educational and promotional materials geared to this annual event.

Education and Professional Development

A high priority of the education department during 1996 was making professional education more accessible to booksellers. An intensified effort was placed on reducing the cost of schools and seminars for member booksellers. Although several four-day schools for prospective booksellers were held at venues around the country, professional-level schools for experienced booksellers have now been shortened by a day and are being held at less-expensive facilities than previously. These "Econ-o-Schools" were often held in tandem with regional trade shows, thereby helping to save participants several hundred dollars in travel and hotel expenses.

Response to another innovation, the adaptation to a night-school format of the professional bookselling curriculum, was very enthusiastic. On five consecutive Monday nights in the fall of 1996, classes were held at the G. Royce Smith Education Center on ABA's Tarrytown campus, and on five consecutive Monday, Tuesday, or Wednesday evenings in February and March, classes were held in Denver, Dallas, and Austin. It is anticipated that this night-school format will be continued in the spring of 1997 in Berkeley, Portland, and Seattle.

In other initiatives, many requests for information directed to the education department are now being received and answered through electronic mail, and the booksellers schools' curriculum outline posted on ABA's Web site is drawing numerous inquiries.

Rental of ABA's training videos continues to provide "in-house" educational opportunities for many member businesses. To further aid booksellers in providing lower-cost training for more of their staff, a series of self-paced, open-learning workbooks is being developed, incorporating the same subject matter covered in the professional-level booksellers schools. The first of these materials will be ready by the summer of 1997.

Publications

As in the past, the ABA publications department strove, through a wide variety of utilitarian books and periodicals, to keep booksellers current with respect to both information and business skills. A particularly notable achievement of 1996 was the publication of the all-new fifth edition of *Manual on Bookselling: Practical Advice for the Bookstore Professional*. The book, which received an overwhelmingly positive response, includes extensive discussion of the critical leadership skills so necessary in today's competitive environment, as well as a number of chapters (for example, "Building a Bookselling Future on the World Wide Web") to assist booksellers as they navigate the technologies that continue to change day-to-day bookstore life. This edition also offers detailed, realistic, and informative articles on bookstore finance, as well as a wealth of creative and practical ways to differentiate a bookstore from its competition.

Booksellers Publishing, Inc. (BPI), the book-publishing subsidiary of ABA, expanded its list of professional titles available for people in the book community. New additions to the list of BPI offerings in 1996 were *Display and Visual Merchandising*, a new retail action guide by renowned bookstore planners Ken White and Frank White. This volume is designed to help booksellers establish and implement successful in-store merchandising programs. BPI also published a new edition of *ABACUS Expanded*, which reports the operating results of ABA-member independent booksellers participating in an annual financial survey. The 1996 edition, once again compiled by the ABA research department, is based on 1994 operations of more than 200 bookstore businesses and offers a range of new income statement and balance sheet results. Additions and enhancements include comparative analysis of participants' results by inventory productivity groupings based on gross margin return on inventory (GMROI) and trended composite income statements and balance sheets for the past three years for the group of companies participating in each of the corresponding three surveys. Other additions include the quick ratio (a liquidity measure) and an average monthly inventory figure used to calculate inventory turnover and GMROI. Also among the 1996 innovations are a separate breakdown of the proportion of sales generated by combined audio and electronic books, and an index to assist readers in finding key topics and terms used throughout the book.

ABA's expanded news weekly *Bookselling This Week* (*BTW*) entered its third year of publication in April 1996. Catering to the needs of ABA-member booksellers and readers across the book industry, *BTW* delivers breaking news, interviews, features, and columns, as well as extensive coverage of books in the media, author tours, and timely announcements for booksellers. *Bookselling This Weekend*, an offshoot of *BTW* and the official publication of the 1996 ABA Convention and Trade Exhibit in Chicago, was published and distributed daily to attendees of that convention. ABA's publications department also continued to publish quarterly specialty newsletters in a tabloid format similar to that used by *BTW* for members of ABA's five specialty membership segments. In addition, *Free Expression*, ABFFE's four-page newsletter covering free speech and First Amendment issues, was inserted quarterly into *BTW* during 1996.

On the cusp of its 20th year, *American Bookseller* (*AB*) worked throughout 1996 to help booksellers and others in the industry cope with the increasing complexity of today's business landscape. Recognizing the key changes resulting from technological advances, *AB* introduced a new column, "Web World," a monthly update on bookstores that have successfully begun to negotiate the challenges of commerce in cyberspace. In addition, *AB* changed the name and the emphasis of the monthly technology column from "New Media Update" to "BiblioTech" to accommodate the changing environment in which booksellers find themselves. *AB* also improved electronic access to key magazine features available on ABA's Web site, thereby increasing the speed with which members can receive news.

Throughout the year, with such features as "Guerrilla Marketing On-Line," by noted business writer Jay Conrad Levinson, *AB* worked to expand coverage of new and timely ways for improving business operations. With an eye toward helping readers analyze key market forces and trends, the magazine published such pieces as ABA executive director Bernie Rath's examination of the changing nature of co-op, and *AB* editor Dan Cullen's 1996 keynote speech to the Australian Booksellers Association. To offer readers deeper coverage of titles and publishing category trends, *AB* expanded its "Bookstore Bestsellers" department, adding both profiles of bookstores and booksellers and a reproducible book-group discussion guide for stores to share with customers.

As it ended its second decade, the magazine carried on many of its well-known features, with an expanded children's "Pick of the Lists" (a selection by children's bookselling experts of the best titles of the selling season), more "Conversations" with industry leaders (this year including Broadway Books publisher Bill Shinker), and in-depth coverage of the 1996 ABA Convention and

Trade Exhibit. More and more publishers, especially small presses, are taking advantage of "Check It Out," a free service that lists complimentary promotional materials for booksellers to order directly from the publisher for use in their stores. Finally, the magazine once again published the *Bookstore Source Guide*, a directory to everything a bookstore needs except books; the *Bookstore Merchandising Calendar*; and a comprehensive excerpt from BPI's *ABACUS Expanded*.

Research

As in the past, during 1996 the ABA research department produced and disseminated a wide variety of both benchmark and trend data pertinent to bookselling. Among the findings published were those from the *1995 Consumer Research Study on Book Publishing* and the *Current Retail Census*; some of these data have been reported above. In addition, the research department compiled and made available such detailed information as retail outlet market share and book subject category share, as requested by regional booksellers associations, individual booksellers, other members of the industry, and the media. The department routinely prepared material for *Bookselling This Week*'s regular bookstore sales, personal consumption expenditures (PCEs) on books and maps, and "In Fact . . ." features, and also analyzed results of various ABA studies for press releases and articles.

The 1996 *ABACUS Expanded*, reporting the results of ABA's annual financial survey of member independent bookstores (based on 1994 operations), confirmed the difficulties of independents as discussed above. Average net income before taxes for the 201 participating businesses amounted to just 0.6 percent of sales. Among the 88 businesses participating for three consecutive fiscal years (1992, 1993, and 1994), however, the results were somewhat more encouraging, with average results for those years coming in at 2.7 percent, 2.75 percent, and 2.46 percent, respectively. Other results showed that the high profitability group of booksellers (the top 25 percent of businesses based on total return on assets) enjoyed a relatively higher average net income of 8.71 percent of sales. This group shared four traits: lower operating expenses; higher inventory productivity (including higher gross margin, higher inventory turnover, higher GMROI, and a lower rate of returned products to vendors); higher employee productivity; and more favorable balance sheets. Independent booksellers participating in the survey experienced a modest average book returns rate to vendors of 10.3 percent of purchases.

The results of the 1995 ABA Book Buying Study, an annual tracking study conducted by the Gallup Organization for the association, were released during 1996. Among other findings, on the combined basis of four quarterly telephone surveys, nearly two out of every three adults (63 percent) had purchased one or more books during the previous three months, with 18 percent being characterized as "light buyers" (1–3 books), another 18 percent as "moderate buyers" (4–6 books), and the remaining 27 percent as "heavy buyers" (7 or more books). The study, which also tracks audio and multimedia purchasing, showed that purchasing books in those formats was similar in 1994 and 1995. Asked specifically about such purchases in the previous three months, 8 percent of all adults claimed to have bought an audio book (compared to 9 percent in 1994), while 7 percent purchased a multimedia book (versus 6 percent in 1994).

Findings of the ABA-PSP Professional and Scholarly Book-Buying Study, conducted by Wirthlin Worldwide, were not only presented at the Scientific/Technical/Professional conference at the 1996 convention but were also reported in *Bookselling This Weekend* and later in the summer in more detail in *Bookselling This Week* and other industry publications. A major finding of the multiphased study is that booksellers want more accurate and timely information from publishers about new titles, covering, for example, their contents, intended market, and status. Likewise, publishers want more information from booksellers, such as feedback on which marketing tactics work best. The study also indicated that selection, accuracy of information, the ability to examine books, and convenience are the major factors determining where consumers purchase professional and scholarly books. Buyers of professional and scholarly books interviewed for the study spent an average of $750 on such books (compared to an estimated annual average of $263 for all books), while nearly one respondent in three spent more than $500 annually.

Key results of the 1995 ABA Member Survey were presented to the membership at the annual meeting held during the 1996 ABA Convention and Trade Exhibit. Among other things, the annual tracking study found that technology of various types is increasingly being used by members, suggesting that ABA's concerted efforts in this area are beginning to pay off. Specifically, fax machines were reportedly being used by 66 percent (up from 57 percent in 1994), while personal computers were being used for word processing, desktop publishing, and so on, by 75 percent (up from 69 percent the previous year). In addition, use of computerized accounting systems increased from 51 percent to 56 percent, and use of CD-ROM technology jumped from 35 percent to 48 percent. The proportion of members selling CD-ROMs also increased (to 23 percent from 14 percent), but there was no significant change in extent of use of computerized inventory control (60 percent), electronic ordering (44 percent), or online services (26 percent).

Bookstore Promotion

In light of the difficult competitive environment persisting throughout 1996, ABA stepped up its marketing assistance to member bookstores. One high-profile event was the third annual National Independent Bookstore Week (NIBW), observed during the week of July 20–27. As in 1995 ABA joined forces in this promotion with Habitat for Humanity, a nationally recognized community-based organization. The event's theme, "Building Community Foundations," once again underscored the objective of raising public awareness of the fact that independent bookstores are an integral part of every community. In pursuit of this goal, booksellers raised money, donated books to needy families, and helped support local Habitat chapters. ABA provided participating member stores with an information kit filled with promotional and marketing ideas, case studies, and other supporting materials. In addition, bookmarks, posters, and T-shirts were available for in-store promotions. The 1997 NIBW is scheduled for July 19–26.

In another initiative, on April 23, 1996, 100 ABA-member booksellers took part in World Book Day, sponsored by the Department of Culture in Barcelona, Spain. Working with the Department of Culture, ABA arranged for the delivery of fresh-cut roses, bookmarks, and posters to its participating members. World Book Day evolved from the celebration of St. George's Day in Barcelona—a day when booksellers traditionally present a rose to anyone who buys a book—and ABA participants enjoyed surprising and thanking their customers by doing likewise.

In an effort to provide booksellers with an innovative and inexpensive way to reach new customers, ABA produced a 27-second generic advertisement ready to be personalized and aired on local television stations, cable and otherwise. The advertisement promotes the idea that "books make the greatest gift," by comparing them in an entertaining way to such alternatives as flowers, jewelry, teddy bears, and ties. A successful prior initiative, the "Appealing Book Accents" program, which makes available to booksellers low-tack stickers and eye-catching "wobblers," continued to add new designs in 1996. Innovations included a "Used" sticker and a variety of square stickers for pricing. "Autographed Copy" and "Local Author" continue to be the best sellers.

Booksellers Order Service

Booksellers Order Service (BOS) a wholly owned subsidiary of ABA, continued to offer, through its group buying program, advantageously priced products (most shipped freight-free) that could be sold or used by booksellers in their day-to-day operations. Several new products were introduced during 1996, including "I feel the need to read" enamel pins, "Books—The Greatest Gift" wrapping paper, and four new types of gift certificate. Other new 1996 offerings were Norman Rockwell book-related ties, two new T-shirt lines ("Attitude" and "Norman Rockwell"), and a jute shopping bag. In addition, the quotable T-shirt line was completely redesigned with added graphics.

BOS continues to stock a range of other products, including an expanded line of 3M security strips, adult gift-wrapping paper with a book design, children's gift-wrapping paper by renowned children's illustrator Thacher Hurd, and plastic and paper bags in three sizes imprinted with BOS's definition of a book on one side and of a bookstore on the other. Also available on a continuing basis are book lights and hand-painted animal bookmarks. Additional products offered by BOS include reprint editions of fine art books, heavyweight canvas totebags (plain or imprinted with the store logo), and recycled-paper shopping bags. All BOS T-shirts can be imprinted with the bookstore's name and logo.

These items are but a few among many featured in the ABA *Quarterly Merchandising Catalog*. Introduced in 1996, the catalog provides booksellers with a continually updated list of products and an easier way to order from BOS, ABA, BPI, and ABFFE. This full-color catalog highlights new products, in addition to listing stock items, and contains an order form for the convenience of booksellers.

Association of Research Libraries

21 Dupont Circle N.W., Suite 800, Washington, DC 20036
202-296-2296, e-mail arlhq@cni.org
World Wide Web http://arl.cni.org

Julia C. Blixrud
Senior Program Officer

The Association of Research Libraries (ARL) represents the 120 principal research libraries that serve major research institutions in the United States and Canada. ARL's mission is to shape and influence forces affecting the future of research libraries in the process of scholarly communication. ARL programs and services promote equitable access to and effective use of recorded knowledge in support of teaching, research, scholarship, and community service. The association articulates the concerns of research libraries and their institutions, forges coalitions, influences information policy development, and supports innovation and improvement in research library operations.

ARL fulfills it mission and builds its programs through a set of strategic objectives:

1 *Scholarly Communication and Information Policies*: to understand, contribute to, and improve the system of scholarly communication and the information policies that affect the availability and usefulness of research resources

2 *Access to Research Resources*: to make access to research resources more efficient and effective

3 *Collection Development*: to support member libraries' efforts to develop and maintain research collections, both individually and in the aggregate

4 *Preservation*: to support member libraries' efforts to preserve research collections, both individually and in the aggregate

5 *Technology*: to assist member libraries to exploit technology in fulfillment of their mission and assess the impact of educational technologies on scholarly communication and on the role of research libraries

6 *Staffing*: to identify on an ongoing basis the capabilities and characteristics required for research library personnel to best serve their constituencies, and to assist member libraries and educational programs in the recruitment, development, and effective use of staff

7 *Management*: to assist member libraries in augmenting their management capabilities

8 *Performance Measures*: to describe and measure the performance of research libraries and their contributions to teaching, research, scholarship, and community service

To meet these objectives, ARL resources are organized into a framework of programs and capabilities. For 1996 ARL established three priority activities: (1)

raising library and scholarly community awareness to issues associated with copyright and intellectual property management; (2) influencing copyright legislation; and (3) developing a capacity for research libraries to sponsor and support electronic publishing.

Scholarly Communication

The Office of Scholarly Communication (OSC) undertakes activities to understand and influence the forces affecting the production, dissemination, and use of scholarly and scientific information. These activities include promoting innovative, creative, and alternative ways of sharing scholarly findings, particularly through championing evolving electronic techniques for recording and disseminating academic and research scholarship. OSC also collaborates with others in the scholarly community to build common understanding of the challenges presented by electronic scholarly communication and to generate options for concerted action. OSC was initially created as the Office of Scientific and Academic Publishing; it was renamed in spring 1996.

One of the major OSC projects has been to address elements of the shared agenda of the Association of American Universities (AAU) and ARL. The AAU/ARL Research Libraries Steering Committee has addressed the needs for collective action in the area of electronic publishing projects, and in 1996 the committee encouraged the examination of issues related to content and conduit in Internet 2. ARL membership supported continuation of ARL's efforts to monitor the progress of electronic scholarly publishing and to facilitate discussion of the future of scholarly communication with the educational community. A series of action steps have been identified that include development of common vision statements, collaboration with higher education and scholarly organizations, and developing programs and services to support member library staffs engaged in licensing electronic resources.

Licensing electronic information is fast becoming standard business practice for information providers. A December 1996 program, sponsored by the OSC in cooperation with the Coalition for Networked Information (CNI), presented an overview of the many issues involved in licensing electronic resources. These issues included copyright, contract law, the economics of electronic information, consortial purchasing, and rights management technologies. Almost 150 people attended, and proceedings will be published in 1997. A series of hands-on licensing workshops is also under development.

OSC, CNI, and the Chief Officers of State Library Agencies (COSLA) will cosponsor a Web site and program on networked information consortia. OSC is also working with the Association of American University Presses (AAUP) and American Council of Learned Societies (ACLS) to develop a symposium on the future of the scholarly monograph.

OSC published the sixth annual edition of the *Directory of Electronic Journals, Newsletters, and Academic Discussion Lists,* which documents the advances in electronic/Internet publishing and has become the standard reference book in its area. An abridged electronic version of the publication is mounted on the ARL Web site. Quick surveys on trends in serials and monograph purchasing also are conducted by OSC and results are made available on the ARL Web site.

Federal Relations and Information Policy

The Federal Relations and Information Policy Program monitors activities resulting from legislative, regulatory, or operating practices of international and domestic government agencies and other relevant bodies on matters of concern to research libraries; prepares analysis of and responses to federal information policies; influences federal action on issues related to research libraries; examines issues of importance to the development of research libraries; and develops ARL positions on issues that reflect the needs and interest of members.

Copyright and intellectual property issues were a major focus for this and other ARL programs in 1996. ARL actively participated in information policy debates by responding to and shaping national and international legislative initiatives that impact research libraries. The restructuring of the telecommunications infrastructure due to the passage of the Telecommunications Act of 1996 shifted some of ARL's attention to working with agencies to implement National Information Infrastructure (NII) programs and responding to NII proposals, and collaborating with others in the education, library, and public-interest communities to promote common positions.

ARL reviewed and endorsed ALA filings before the Federal Comunications Commission on discounted telecommunications rates for schools and libraries. ARL also participated in the challenge to provisions included in the Telecommunications Act of 1996 that dealt with restrictive access to selected information resources. The association actively opposed provisions included in Title V (the Communications Decency Act [CDA]) that sought to prohibit access to indecent or patently offensive materials via the Internet.

ARL staff worked with several government agencies in designing and proposing network applications programs, such as the NASA Information Infrastructure Technology and Applications Program (IITAP), the NSF/ARPA/NASA digital-library initiative (DLI), and the NTIA/TIIAP program. ARL staff also participated in follow-up discussions to the conference "Higher Education and the NII—from Vision to Reality." This 1995 conference explored the steps required over the next few years to turn the potential of the advanced information infrastructure into reality for higher education. ARL also submitted or contributed to statements, provided testimony, and worked in support of budget requests for federal or congressional agencies to provide either funds or programs of interest to the research library community.

The Federal Relations Program provided regular updates on selected national and international legislative activities via regular monthly federal-relations electronic news reports to members.

The ARL GIS Literacy Project continues to expand and evolve. The Project, managed by the Federal Relations Program, seeks to educate librarians and users about Geographical Information Systems (GIS) and to develop GIS capabilities in research libraries. Background materials related to this project are available on the ARL server.

Intellectual Property and Copyright Issues

The ARL board of directors identified intellectual property and copyright as a defining set of issues for the future of scholarly communications. As part of the association's interest in raising library and scholarly community awareness of issues associated with copyright and intellectual property management, several activities were undertaken to advance the ARL agenda in these critical areas.

ARL is collaborating very closely with four other library associations on copyright and NII issues through the formation of the Shared Legal Capability (SLC). During 1996 SLC met with members of the U.S. administration and congressional staff to discuss many proposed changes to the Copyright Act; participated in negotiations with other interested stakeholders on copyright term extension legislation; submitted statements to the House and Senate regarding the NII Copyright Protection Act of 1995; with other groups drafted six alternative legislative proposals to the act; participated in congressional negotiations with online service providers and content owners on online-service liability issues; sent a joint letter with the Association of American Publishers and the National Humanities Alliance to the chair of the Senate Judiciary Committee expressing serious reservations with the PTO reform legislation; and agreed to explore the development of "best practices" issue briefs, in lieu of "fair-use guidelines," in selected areas.

With others in the public and private sectors, ARL formed the Digital Future Coalition (DFC), comprised of a diverse constituency of library, education, legal, scholarly, consumer, and public-interest associations; hardware and software manufacturers: and telecommunications providers that share concerns about pending legislation and the administration's "white paper," the Final Report from the Working Group on Intellectual Property and the National Information Infrastructure. The DFC submitted testimony; met with members of Congress, their staff, and the administration; sponsored a technology briefing for Senate staff; developed alternative proposals to those included in the legislation and submitted them to the World Intellectual Property Organization (WIPO); launched a campaign focused on the international dimensions of the NII bills; began a public-awareness campaign regarding the critical importance of this legislation; worked to change and/or delete a provision of the Copyright Clarifications Act of 1996 that would make ephemeral copies legal "copies," thus changing current law and presenting serious liability issues for all network service providers; and successfully influenced the U.S. administration's position submitted to WIPO.

ARL staff also participated in another copyright-related collaboration, the Ad Hoc Copyright Coalition, comprised of private-sector online service providers. This coalition, which shares many of the same concerns as the SLC and the DFC, is primarily focused on network liability issues and the expansion of the selected copyright owners' rights.

Discussions on defining fair use in the NII were conducted under the auspices of CONFU (Conference on Fair Use), and ARL staff participated in these discussions. After review and discussion of proposals put forward for educational fair use for distance education, digital images, and multimedia, ARL decided not to endorse any proposals for guidelines that do not fully protect the fair-use rights of the scholarly and education communities.

In July 1996 the ARL board of directors hosted a discussion of current issues in copyright and intellectual property as they relate to scholarly communication. Representatives of most sectors of the scholarly community participated, and the results indicated that the meetings were beneficial to develop understanding and exchange perspectives among the several constituencies. Follow-up meetings were hosted by the National Humanities Alliance.

ARL produced a number of copyright and intellectual property publications in 1996. The second NII copyright briefing packet, "Copyright and the NII: Resources for the Library and Education Community," was distributed in May. It is designed to help libraries and educators understand current copyright legislative reform and to encourage involvement in the debate. Segments of the publication are also available on the ARL server. Other publications include workshop materials, booklets, and flyers. Copyright materials are regularly added to the ARL Web site, with links to other relevant copyright and intellectual property sites.

Access and Technology

A centerpiece of the ARL access capability is the North American Interlibrary Loan and Document Delivery (NAILDD) Project. Established in 1993, the NAILDD Project promotes developments to maximize access to research resources while minimizing costs. The operating philosophy is to seek practical technical developments that enable libraries to redesign their interlibrary loan/document delivery (ILL/DD) services for a networked environment. The strategy is to seek actions on the part of private-sector developers that will respond to the priority needs of the library community.

The NAILDD Developers/Implementors Group (DIG), which met twice in 1996, seeks to accelerate collaboration between libraries and a broad constituency of private-sector players to advance the NAILDD Project's priority technical goals. Now representing 50 organizations, DIG is a source of information and a forum for major organizations that provide ILL/DD services. The ILL Protocol Implementors Group (IPIG) was established in 1995 to expedite implementation standards for ILL communication and in mid-1996 was broadened to welcome organizations and projects from outside North America that are also implementing the protocol. To facilitate the incorporation of new technical developments, the NAILDD Project pursues two kinds of training institutes to assist libraries in reconceptualizing their ILL/DD operations: a "redesigning" institute for library teams and a "rethinking" institute for individual librarians.

Funded by the Andrew W. Mellon Foundation, the two-year ILL/DD Performance Measures Study is collecting data on ILL/DD performance of research and academic libraries. One of the study goals is to identify and highlight best practices and effective ILL operations to encourage other institutions to improve their procedures. Data collection on turnaround time, fill rate, user satisfaction, and costs is under way. Results of the study will be published in 1997.

Collections and Preservation

Early in 1996 a four-year project on the state of foreign acquisitions in research libraries concluded with the publication of *Scholarship, Research Libraries and Global Publishing*. This project was funded by the Mellon Foundation, and more than 50 librarians from around the country were involved in various stages of the project. ARL's Research Collections Committee provided oversight for ARL/AAU demonstration projects on Germany, Japan, and Latin America, and, using the recommendations from the foreign-acquisitions study, developed a tactical plan for scaling up from the pilot project to a Global Resources Program. In December 1996 Mellon awarded funding to ARL to work in cooperation with the AAU to establish such a program.

The Global Resources Program will build on existing structures and initiatives, including North American consortia and institutions overseas. Two additional pilot projects (on Africa and Southeast Asia) will be established. Lead institutions will be identified to coordinate acquisitions from particular regions and electronic distribution of publications from each region. A Web-based clearinghouse to disseminate information on the different projects will be established. Symposia for faculty, both on campus and at meetings of learned societies, are also planned.

The demonstration projects that lead to the establishment of the Global Resources Program continued to evolve. The German Demonstration Project has 22 participating libraries. The Library of Congress (LC) made special arrangements so that libraries in the project have access to the cataloging records prepared by the Deutsche Bibliothek through the files mounted at the library. Access to the records is available to participants on a subscription basis via Z39.50. The Universitätsbibliothek in Göttingen has mounted an Internet-accessible test file of regional government documents. The project's top priority is to obtain funding to enable the participants to undertake cooperative activities, such as developing a common serials list, analyzing methods for increasing North American coverage of German monographs in political science and history, and stimulating the development of digital documents by German agencies and making them easily available.

The Japan Journal Access Project, which originally began as the Japanese Scientific and Technical Information Project, seeks to improve access to Japanese journal literature across all disciplines. Broadening the scope of the project was facilitated by the interest and support of the National Coordinating Committee on Japanese Library Resources. The project has thus far focused primarily on gaining access to Japanese journals available from Japan. This focus will continue, but the project is being expanded to also include improving access to Japanese-language journals available from U.S. sources.

The Mellon Foundation provided two grants to expand the range of materials available to Latin Americanist students and scholars. The original Latin American Demonstration Project focused on three categories of Argentine and Mexican resources: serials, government documents, and the publications of nongovernmental organizations (NGOs). Thirty-five ARL libraries participated in a variety of project activities in 1996: presidential messages from Argentina and Mexico were digitized; participants assumed collecting responsibilities for

Argentine and Mexican publications from NGOs, research institutions, and other noncommercial producers of research reports and discussion papers; participants tested and refined a process for managing the development of a table of contents (TOC) database of 300 journal titles; and a pilot interlibrary loan service was made operational to streamline the process of obtaining articles included in the TOC database. To determine the cost-effectiveness of cooperation, the University of Florida was funded to conduct an analysis.

The Preservation of Research Library Materials Committee encourages and strengthens broad-based participation in national preservation efforts in the United States and Canada, support for development of preservation programs within member libraries, advocacy for strengthening copyright legislation to support preservation activities in the electronic environment, support for effective bibliographic control of reservation-related processes, encouragement for developing preservation information resources, and monitoring technological developments that may have an impact on preservation goals.

The second edition of *Preservation Microfilming: A Guide for Librarians and Archivists* was published. This guide is considered one of the basic texts for preservation microfilming.

ARL member leaders and staff contributed to a series of meetings with representatives of the Modern Language Association, American Historical Association, Society of American Archivists, Commission on Preservation and Access/Council on Library Resources, and others to consider issues involved in the preservation of the artifact/primary resources. A joint working group was formed, with the first tasks including preparation of background documents on progress made in preservation and on identification of the intellectual issues that still face the scholarly community in preservation.

Diversity

ARL's Diversity Program has a two-fold charge: define and address diversity issues in ARL libraries and support activities that encourage broad participation in the field. This program seeks to encourage exploration of the rich gifts and talents diverse individuals bring to the library. Program staff work closely with a broad range of libraries, graduate library education programs, and other library associations to promote awareness of career opportunities in research libraries and support the academic success of students from groups currently underrepresented in the profession.

The program offers staff development seminars, presentations, and on-site, e-mail, and telephone consultations. During 1996 dozens of site visits were conducted across the United States and Canada. A special effort to identify diversity initiatives in Canada was conducted by Toni Olshen, York University Library, serving as a Visiting Program Officer with the Diversity Program. The findings were disseminated in several ways: a resource notebook, bibliographies available through the ARL Web site, presentations at meetings, and a newsletter article.

Information on successful diversity strategies from libraries participating in a Partnership Program was gathered in 1996 and will be published by ARL's Diversity Program in the coming year.

Office of Management Services

The Office of Management Services (OMS) supports large academic and research libraries in their efforts to employ the most effective leadership and management practices currently available. The office was established in 1970 to help large libraries develop better ways of managing their human and material resources and to work with librarians to determine the best way to meet the needs of their users. To achieve those ends, OMS staff stay abreast of current organizational and management theory and practice, seeking concepts and techniques that are applicable to, and have the potential for contributing to, the improved effectiveness of academic and research libraries. Three programs make up OMS: the Organizational Development and Consulting Program, the Training and Leadership Development Program, and the Information Services Program.

The OMS Organizational Development and Consulting Program includes activities related to the conduct of consultations and institutional studies. To assist libraries in their efforts to make the transition from an archival entity to an information gateway during these times of limited resources, this program provides a wide range of services, incorporating new research on service delivery, work design, promotion of services, and organizational effectiveness. There were three primary areas of activity: updating strategic planning processes, optimizing design, and supporting team planning and development. There continues to be interest in examining the provision of public services as libraries struggle with the need to provide quality services in an environment of shrinking resources.

OMS staff conducted projects in organizational design, leadership development, strategic planning and planning retreats, collection management, technical-services process improvement, facilitation, resource sharing, and assisted self-studies.

In 1996 approximately 800 library staff participated in OMS Training and Leadership Development Program events. Increases in this program continue to be in the areas of sponsored Training Institutes and Learning-on-Site Workshops. With reduced funding, libraries are seeking more cost-effective approaches to training and staff development; bringing OMS to their sites meets this need. Training Skills for the Implementation of an Integrated Library System (originally developed in 1995 for the University of Chicago) is also a program that is meeting the needs of those institutions migrating to new, more-advanced library systems. OMS staff facilitated discussions and training programs for teams, helped assess customer service levels, created a curriculum to assist in raising those levels, and led custom-designed workshops on communication and working together.

The OMS Information Services Program maintains an active publications program whose principal components are the Systems and Procedures Exchange Center (SPEC) and the OMS Occasional Paper Series. Through the OMS Collaborative Research Writing Program, librarians work with OMS staff in joint research and writing projects that are published by OMS. Participants and staff work together in all aspects of the publication process, from survey design, writing, and editing to seeking management perspectives on current academic concerns.

SPEC Kits organize and collect selected library documents concerning a specific area of library management. Kits are designed to illustrate alternatives and innovations used in dealing with particular issues. Documents describing both the administrative and operational aspects of the topic are included. SPEC Kits produced in 1996 covered the topics of technical services workstations, digitizing technologies for preservation, library reorganization and restructuring, the role of libraries in distance learning, and information technology policies.

Transforming Libraries, a new subseries of the SPEC program, debuted in October with the first issue focusing on electronic reserves. This series will address how institutions and individuals are pioneering or transforming themselves in a particular area. The publication takes a reportorial approach to its topics, seeking libraries that are trying new applications of technology and highlighting their experiences while they are still innovative. SPEC is also developing a Web-based resource center to accompany each issue of *Transforming Libraries*. This important feature allows continued learning on each topic. Future issues include overviews of geographic information systems, electronic scholarly publishing, and distance education.

Statistics and Measurement

The ARL Statistics and Measurement Program collects, analyzes, and publishes quantifiable information about library collections, personnel, and expenditures, as well as expenditures and indicators of the nature of research institutions. The program and its oversight committee are also developing new ways to describe and measure traditional and networked information resources and services. The program sponsors workshops to give library staff and others opportunities to develop skills for developing survey instruments and for handling and managing statistical data. Customized, confidential analyses can be provided from the program's data.

Five statistical compilations were produced during 1996: *ARL Statistics 1994–95*, *ARL Academic Law and Medical Libraries Statistics 1992–93 to 1994–95*, *Developing Indicators for Academic Library Performance: Ratios . . . 1993–94 vs. 1994–95*, *ARL Annual Salary Survey 1995–96*, and *ARL Preservation Statistics 1993–94*.

A new survey was conducted to gather information about new services available at research libraries, such as patron-initiated circulation, e-mail reference, and digital imaging. Results of the survey will be published in 1997. The Council on Library Resources awarded a grant of $11,800 to ARL to study "The Character and Nature of Research Library Investment in Electronic Resources." The project goal is to develop new definitions that support collection of information about the transformation of research library collections. Timothy Jewell, head of the Electronic Information Program at the University of Washington Libraries, was appointed Visiting Program Officer (VPO) from September 1996 to July 1997 to work on this project.

Office of Research and Development

The ARL Visiting Program Officer is managed by the ARL Office of Research and Development. This program provides an opportunity for a staff member from a member library to assume responsibility for carrying out part or all of a project for ARL. It provides a visible staff development opportunity for an outstanding staff member and serves the membership as a whole by extending the capacity of ARL to undertake additional activities. Since the program's beginning, 21 member libraries have sponsored a VPO. In 1996 they included: Mark Grover, Brigham Young University, who served as project coordinator for the ARL/AAU Latin American Demonstration Project; Deborah Jakubs, Duke University, who is developing the AAU/ARL Global Resources Program; Kendon Stubbs, University of Virginia, who developed a manual and designed a workshop for libraries to measure user satisfaction; Tim Jewell, University of Washington, who is investigating library investments in electronic resources; and Toni Olshen, York University, who addressed diversity issues in Canadian libraries.

The ARL Office of Research and Development consolidates the administration of grants and grant-support projects administered by ARL. The office identifies and matches ARL projects that support the research library community's mission with sources of external funding. Among the projects not previously mentioned in this report and under way in 1996 are:

Copyright Education Initiative

The H. W. Wilson Foundation awarded ARL funding to develop an educational initiative on copyright compliance. The initiative includes development of training resources to assist library managers and support for the design of workshops for librarians who have a training or spokesperson role in copyright compliance. Four workshops have been held in the United States and Canada. A notebook used in the workshops and a *Copyright Resource Handbook* also were published.

National Register of Microform Masters (NRMM) RECON Project: Non-Roman Reports and Musical Scores

In May 1996 the National Endowment for the Humanities awarded ARL a grant of $114,000 in support of the final phase of the NRMM RECON Project. In cooperation with the Library of Congress and the New York Public Library, ARL is managing a cooperative project for creating more than 13,800 online records for non-Roman reports and for other remaining NRMM reports. Records are produced by OCLC's conversion services. The project, scheduled to end in September 1997, will result in the completion of a complex multiyear effort to provide online access to more than 500,000 bibliographic records for preservation microform masters.

Communications and External Relations

The ARL Communications Program is designed to acquaint ARL members with important current developments of interest to research libraries, inform the library profession of ARL's position on these issues, influence policy and decision makers within higher education and other areas related to research and scholarship, and educate academic communities about issues related to research libraries. The program uses print and electronic publications and direct outreach to inform members and others about ARL positions on issues that affect the research library community.

Even as ARL promotes electronic publishing within the scholarly community, it is learning how to perform those processes. Many of its statements and publications are available on the ARL server, and the ARL-Announce service provides timely information about ARL and news items about ARL member library activities.

The ARL Web site grew substantially in 1996, with contributions from all program areas. Popular additions include the Career Resource Center and a Web version of the *Directory of Electronic Journals, Newsletters and Academic Discussion Lists.*

ARL sponsors more than 50 electronic discussion groups, including both private lists, such as the ARL-Directors and ARL Committee lists, and public lists, such as ARL-ERESERVES and ARL-EJOURNAL. Archives for the lists are updated monthly and made available on the ARL server.

Six issues of ARL's newsletter were published in 1996. Topics covered in those issues included copyright, fair use, and intellectual property rights; global resources; age demographics of academic libraries; diversity; statistics on library expenditures; keynote addresses from university leaders; and updates on the progress of ARL.

A special supplement, "Fair Use in Digital Environments: The Work of the Conference on Fair Use (CONFU)," written by Douglas Bennett, vice-president, American Council of Learned Societies, was included with the June issue.

The May 1994 meeting proceedings, *The Research Library the Day after Tomorrow,* were issued in print and electronic form in January 1996. The October 1994 meeting proceedings, *Renewing the ARL Agenda,* were issued in December.

Association Governance and Membership Activities

The spring meeting of the association was held May 15–17, 1996, in Vancouver, British Columbia. The theme, "Leading the Agile Organization," focused attention on the experiences of leading enterprises through the ongoing challenges of the 21st century. The fall ARL Membership Meeting was held October 16–18, 1996, in Washington, D.C. "Redefining Higher Education" was the theme of that meeting, and sessions addressed how research libraries will contribute to the emerging agendas for change in higher education.

At the conclusion of the ARL Business Meeting in October, ARL President Nancy Cline (Harvard College Library) handed the gavel over to President-Elect Gloria Werner (UCLA). During the business meeting, James G. Neal (Sheridan Director, Milton S. Eisenhower Library, Johns Hopkins University), was elected Vice-President/President-Elect. Shirley Baker (Washington University), Kenneth Frazier (University of Wisconsin–Madison), and William Gray Potter (University of Georgia) were elected to three-year terms on the ARL board of directors.

The ARL program plan for 1997, reviewed and approved by the ARL board at its February 1997 meeting, identified the following priority activities for the association for 1997:

- Accelerate and broaden copyright advocacy and education within the research and educational communities and to the general public
- Build partnerships to explore and promote cost-effective strategies and models for managing global scholarly communication
- Develop programs and products to help research libraries move into a transformed environment
- Influence the development of advanced networking applications and Internet 2

ARL program staff and the association's standing committees will address these priorities in the coming year.

Commission on Preservation and Access
Council on Library Resources

1400 16th Street N.W., Suite 715, Washington, DC 20036-2217
202-939-3400, 202-939-3370; fax 202-939-3407, 202-939-3499
World Wide Web: http://www-clr.stanford.edu/clr.html and
http://www-cpa.stanford.edu/cpa.html

Maxine K. Sitts

Program Officer

The Commission on Preservation and Access was established in 1986 to foster and support collaboration among libraries and allied organizations, to ensure the preservation of the published and documentary record in all formats and to provide enhanced access to scholarly information.

The Council on Library Resources is a private operating foundation established in 1956 to look toward the future on behalf of libraries, to address problems experienced by libraries in the aggregate, and to identify innovative solutions. It promotes research, organizes conferences, issues publications, and manages collaborative projects to bring about significant changes in its areas of interest.

Overview

Following a year of informal affiliation, the boards of the commission and council confirmed plans for an administrative merger and held their first conjoint meeting in October 1996. Consequently, this report combines the program activities of the two organizations into one narrative. The formal merger will be accomplished by July 1, 1997.

During this transition, the commission and council developed a set of programs that address the most pressing needs of libraries and other information organizations as they approach the next millennium. Building on their strengths, the commission and council sought to encourage new alliances and partnerships, form new types of working groups to study problems and recommend alternatives for the future, and develop models for institutional change.

This is a time to think about the information management structures that will be required for the 21st century.

- What must be in place to assure enduring and equitable access for scholars and researchers so that all that has been learned and thought and recorded becomes raw material for new knowledge in subsequent generations?
- What are libraries' and archives' obligations to society? Can we continue to think of the public library as the ubiquitous information resource for anyone with a question?

Note: Adapted from the Council on Library Resources, Commission on Preservation and Access *Annual Report 1995–1996*,[1] and Commission on Preservation and Access Newsletters nos. 85–94.[2]

- Can the investment in research libraries and archives be translated into access to resources for the general public at a reasonable cost?

To address these and other questions, the merged organization operated the following programs: Digital Libraries, Economics of Information, Leadership, Preservation and Access, Scholarly Involvement, and the International Program.

Digital Libraries

National Digital Library Federation

The National Digital Library Federation (NDLF), organized in May 1995, became a charter organization. Its membership includes 15 research institutions (including the Library of Congress and the National Archives) and the commission. The goal of NDLF is to advance coherent and enduring access to physically distributed sources of digital information supporting teaching, learning, and research.

The first planning phase ended June 1, 1996, with a final report from NDLF's Planning Task Force (http:/lcweb.loc.gov/loc/ndlf). Task force members concluded that a national digital library will be feasible only if it is founded on the principles of federation to ensure that the digital technologies employed are affordable and appropriate to the needs of the higher education community. The report identifies three areas in which NDLF could play a unique and important role in building a digital library infrastructure: discovery and retrieval, rights and economic models, and archiving.

The task force also concluded that much of the technology that would facilitate a federated approach to a national digital library is either already available or well advanced in development. If the individual work is to contribute to a greater whole, however—the construction of a national digital library—it will need to be based on a set of common structures and protocols.

Task Force on Archiving of Digital Information

The Task Force on Archiving of Digital Information completed its final report, *Preserving Digital Information*[3], on June 1, 1996 (http://www.rlg.org/ArchTF/). The 21-member task force (composed of librarians, archivists, information technologists, and government agency and publishing firm representatives) concluded that the preservation of digital information is not simply a matter of "refreshing" data or copying it to new media or formats; it entails a nexus of migration issues that must be addressed if the information is to remain useful.

The report's greatest contribution may be its analysis of what is involved if an organization or individual aims to provide indefinite access to records stored in digital electronic form. The report concludes with nine recommendations aimed at the library, archival, and higher education communities, generally. The recommendations are based on the premise that there should be a system to certify archives. These certified digital archives would have the legal right to take the necessary steps to save culturally significant digital information that is at risk of being inadvertently lost or intentionally destroyed.

Pilot Inventory of Scanning Projects

The council and commission jointly sponsored a "snapshot in time" inventory of projects employing digital scanning—or other electronic conversion methods—to make the content of library collections available in digital form[4]. The inventory was intended to be the first step toward comprehending the growing variety of conversion and dissemination projects planned or under way.

Vision 2010

Vision 2010, a two-year project funded by the Carnegie Corporation to study the implications of digital technology for higher education, concluded in May 1996. The School of Information and Library Studies, University of Michigan, was the project partner. Discussions with academic leaders revealed widespread concern about changes in higher education. All participants acknowledged that the academy no longer has the luxury of conducting its business as usual. The commission and council will address leadership development for the future as one of their primary program goals for the next few years. Vision 2010 proved instrumental in establishing many of the themes to be incorporated into the next stage of this program.

Digital Library Projects

The council and commission funded the following projects:

- In cooperation with Online Computer Library Center (OCLC), the council initiated a project to manage and coordinate the development of a Civil War Virtual Library as a pilot project in digital archiving. Working with Knox College and the Museum of the Confederacy, the council and OCLC assembled a selection of Civil War regimental histories and veteran memoirs to be made available online to segmented audiences, to study and measure user response and needs.
- The commission funded a pilot project on the preservation of digital information in the Yale Social Science Data Archive, one of the oldest university library collections of numeric information in digital form. The project will contribute to the development of best practices in areas of concern identified by the Task Force on Archiving of Digital Information. The project seeks to identify the best means of migrating data from a significant collection of public opinion polls. In addition, the codebooks, which are in paper form and are rapidly deteriorating, will be converted to digital form to enable continued discovery, retrieval, and use of the numeric data files.
- The commission and the council supported a proposal from Yale University to create an online tool that will assist academic research libraries in negotiating electronic licensing agreements. The tool will be created for use on the World Wide Web and will be widely accessible to any organization through a standard browser.

Economics of Information

As libraries move into the new age of electronic communication, data on the costs of both old and new systems of information management and delivery are necessary for planning and budgeting. The council's Economics of Information program completed several projects and began a two-year effort, funded by the Andrew W. Mellon Foundation, to provide small grants for projects to provide information on the costs of traditional and electronic library services.

Mellon Small Grant Program in the Economics of Information

The council's Small Grant Program in the Economics of Information, launched in January 1996, stimulates research, encourages the collection of needed data, and promotes economic analysis of library operations and services. Guided by the Economics of Information Advisory Committee, the council hopes to encourage research in several areas, including studies of cost and pricing issues related to the transmission of digital information, cost-benefit analysis of commercial documentary delivery services, life-cycle costing models for print and electronic media, and analysis of the scholarly information market. The Economics Advisory Committee awarded grants to the following projects:

- University of California at Berkeley Library, for a planning project to study "Performance Measures for Research Library Collection and Information Services"
- Association of Research Libraries, Washington, D.C., for a project to study "The Character and Nature of Research Library Investment in Electronic Resources"
- Johns Hopkins University, Milton S. Eisenhower Library, for a project to provide "Comprehensive Access to Print Materials" and investigate the costs of these various retrieval systems.

HighWire Press User Survey

To learn more about user reactions to electronic scientific journals, the council joined forces with HighWire Press of the Stanford University Libraries and commissioned the first phase of a project that will create an in-depth profile of users and their attitudes. Ultimately the study will provide the means for comparing user responses to free online information and fee-for-service information. Its Web address is http://highwire.stanford.edu.

Cost Centers and Measures in the Networked Information Value-Chain

The life cycle of scholarly and scientific communication is the subject of a policy paper commissioned by the council and being prepared by the Coalition for Networked Information. The project seeks to identify those activities, functions, and departments that will be most affected by the increasing use of networks and networked information.

Challenging Marketplace Solutions to Problems in the Economics of Information

On September 18 and 19 the council cosponsored a major conference on this theme. The proceedings are published in *The Economics of Information in the Networked Environment*, edited by Meredith A. Butler and Bruce R. Kingma (Washington, D.C.: Association of Research Libraries, 1996).

Leadership

As noted above, the development of leaders for the future has become a focus of the council's efforts. In its second year the leadership program has broadly addressed leadership in the profession, for today and for tomorrow.

The Kellogg Program

The council has created a framework and assessment tool to help the W. K. Kellogg Foundation evaluate the projects and organizations it has supported in its Human Resources for Information Systems Management program. The council also established a major project to analyze the ways in which public libraries are using technology in their communities. Leadership issues include:

- How public libraries have become leaders in serving their communities by using new technology
- How public library leaders have recast the function and purpose of their institutions in their communities
- How, in an era of accelerating technical change, leaders of public libraries can be cultivated and trained for the challenges that all libraries will face in the 21st century

The council has defined leadership as something that can be an individual characteristic and an institutional quality. Library directors can be leaders in their libraries, but libraries can also be leaders in their communities. Several projects and activities have grown out of the council's Kellogg initiative.

Public Libraries and Innovative Technology

The council prepared case studies of public libraries and their use of technology, as well as an analysis of the major issues that surfaced from its research. Teams visited 12 sites selected from more than 200 possibilities in 46 states, interviewing library directors, staff, and users (http://www.si.umich.edu/CLR/). The resulting case studies[5] describe how these libraries are working in and with their communities in the new era of electronic information.

Public Library Leaders Summit Meeting

With Kellogg funds, the council helped establish an agenda to address developing public library leadership for the future. The council contracted with the University of California, Los Angeles, School of Library and Information Science to hold a summit meeting of public library directors in August 1996 to frame a preliminary curriculum for training public library directors and information managers.

Libraries and Community Information Networks

Using information gathered during the above-described site visits, the council contracted with Northern Lights, Inc., to develop a framework for understanding the capabilities of systems that bring information, people, and technologies together to support community needs. The framework will be adapted and used as a tool for educating information leaders about how community information networks can enhance the democratic decision making process by facilitating access to information.

Distance Education in Library and Information Science

In October the council convened a meeting of deans from several schools of library and information science to discuss distance education philosophies, the educational options that distance learning affords the profession, and specific training needs to prepare librarians and library leaders for the future.

Transformation of the Public Library

With the John F. Kennedy School of Government at Harvard University and five other organizations, the council sponsored a public policy symposium titled "The Transformation of the Public Library: Access to Digital Information in a Networked World." The conference emphasized the challenges and opportunities that public libraries face in the information revolution, and the need for striking new partnerships and for building alliances.

Preservation

Academic and commercial sectors have focused on providing faster access to information in multiple formats to more people. During such times, continued emphasis on collaborative preservation strategies becomes even more essential for the survival of irreplaceable historical resources.

Advocacy for the Brittle Books Program and Permanent Paper

As has been the custom since 1988, the commission collaborated with the National Humanities Alliance and the Association of Research Libraries to provide written testimony in support of annual appropriations for the National Endowment for the Humanities.

Preservation Science Research Initiative

The Preservation Science Council (PSC) is a group of preservation administrators and scientists from 20 university libraries, archives, and laboratories. Convened in 1992, PSC emphasizes the needs of large collections of libraries and archives, and argues for research that leads to useful tools for strategic decision making and cost-effective management. Funding from the William and Flora

Hewlett Foundation enabled PSC to build a second research agenda in 1996. Each project was chosen for its ability to help preservation administrators serve as managers of information resources. The new projects address:

- The methods for providing an optimum storage environment at the lowest possible cost, using existing heating and air-conditioning equipment
- The longevity of adhesives now used or under development in library binding
- The creation of a management tool to allow preservation managers to predict how rapidly or slowly books, tapes, and films equilibrate to changes in temperature and relative humidity and to estimate how common enclosures (book stacks, encapsulations, boxes, and compact shelving systems) slow down the rate of equilibration
- The applicability of a life-cycle cost analysis tool for managing the longevity of existing collections of paper, film, and magnetic media
- The magnitude of the effects of repeated paper recycling on the strength and color of papers that will find their way into collections in the future
- The creation of software for an Environmental Management Information System—a low-cost, comprehensive system for delivering environmental data and assessments to preservation managers

Preservation Management and Technology

As digital technologies provide new ways to reformat and gain access to the collections of libraries and archives, it is important to establish an intellectual rationale for the centrality of preservation concepts and ethics. A thoughtful 1996 report, *Preservation in the Digital World*[6], suggests that many of the basic tenets of preservation management can be applied in a highly technological environment, but that some long-held principles may no longer apply. The publication urges that preservation planning, management, and action be carried out at the highest level, since information in digital form is far more fragile than the clay and papyrus that have survived through centuries.

For several years, the commission has investigated the preservation and access implications of scanning text and microfilm. To respond to new interest in the digitization of visual collections, the organization commissioned and published *Digital Image Collections: Issues and Practice*[7]. This report focuses on what sets the digitization of visual collections apart from other scanning projects. It provides basic suggestions about planning digitization projects, practical guidelines for working with images, and some final thoughts about the future systems and infrastructure needed to provide collections of images over the long term. One of the most telling conclusions is that it is difficult to accomplish a large-scale digitization project with the same level of speed, quality, and enthusiasm as for initial tests. If we are to use digitization as a tool to provide worthwhile, enduring access to cultural and historical resources, then we must take time at the outset to become informed, to establish guidelines, and to proceed in rational, measured steps to ensure that reformatting of visual matter is accomplished well and cost-effectively.

College Libraries Committee

The commission established the College Libraries Committee in February 1989 to consider the role of college libraries in the national preservation agenda. The committee sponsors a library journal column about preservation, and has developed a preservation management training seminar offered at various locations over the years. In July the seminar was held in Santa Fe, New Mexico, cosponsored by AMIGOS Bibliographic Council. The program covered digitization systems for preservation and access, along with administrative concerns of program management, selection, and environmental control.

To determine the current state of preservation activities in college libraries, the committee surveyed 200 colleges about preservation priorities, funding, staffing, collection assessment, environmental conditions, and institutional preservation needs and concerns. Over half of the surveyed institutions responded; results were made available on the commission's Web site and a 1997 article was planned.

The committee sponsored a workshop titled "Digitizing Texts and Images: A Workshop for College Library Directors" in Charleston, South Carolina, in April. The program, attended by nearly 100 individuals, included presentations on digital image quality during conversion projects; preservation in a digital world; lessons learned from digitizing one million pages; and the standards, training, costs, and uses of electronic texts and images on the Internet. Abstracts of the talks were made available on the commission's Web site.

Scholarly Involvement

The first group to be formed following the recommendations of the 1995 commission report (*Difficult Choices: How Can Scholars Help Save Endangered Research Resources?*[8]) was the Scholarly Task Force on Hispanic Literary Heritage, charged with articulating a strategy for identifying and preserving Hispanic materials in the United States. The task force includes a number of individuals from the Recovering the U.S. Hispanic Literary Heritage Project at the University of Houston.

To provide additional scholars' perspectives on digitizing visual collections, the commission published an abbreviated version of an article by a professor of art history[9]. The article makes a strong case for the involvement of scholars in influencing the directions of digital imaging projects.

The International Program

The International Program promotes preservation awareness abroad and establishes collaborative projects to improve the accessibility of research materials to scholars everywhere.

Shared Bibliographic Records of Preserved Materials

Since 1990 the International Program has collaborated, first with the Commission of the European Union and then directly with the institutions involved, to create the European Register of Microform Masters (EROMM). EROMM has become a model of multinational cooperation among libraries and archives. In addition to the four original partners (national libraries of France, Portugal, England, and the Staats- und Universitätsbibliothek Göttingen), the following have joined EROMM: the national libraries of Denmark, The Netherlands, and Belgium; the ETH Library, Zurich; and Deutsches Bibliotheksinstitut, Berlin. The national libraries of Poland, Hungary, Austria, and Sweden also expect to join this effort. Some 34 institutions in seven countries have contributed to the database of more than 325,000 items.

The International Program supported the development of a Latin American Register of Microform Masters with a project titled "Infrastructure for Automated Processing of Microform Holdings in Latin America and the Caribbean." In this collaborative effort, the National Library of Venezuela has assembled more than 15,000 bibliographic descriptions of microform holdings in 11 Venezuelan institutions.

Another project is converting bibliographic records of microform masters held by libraries and archives in Poland to machine-readable, U.S.-compatible format. This commission-supported effort will enable Poland to join EROMM and offer assistance to similar projects in other countries of Central and Eastern Europe.

Collaboration and Advocacy

In its investigations of preservation and access developments, the International Program often collaborates with other organizations and programs. A number of mass deacidification projects prompted the joint development, with the Preservation Science Council and the European Commission on Preservation and Access, of a scientific report reviewing techniques for mass deacidification. The report, written by Henk Porck of the Department of Library Research, Koninklijke Bibliotheek, The Hague[10], describes large-scale (rather than mass) technologies, which combine deacidification with paper strengthening (Bückeburg process, graft-copolymerization, paper splitting, and the Vienna process). The author does not present recommendations in favor of one or another technique, but in a final section discusses the main issues in a critical evaluation of the possibilities of mass deacidification in general.

The International Program continued its involvement with UNESCO's Memory of the World initiative to save our common cultural heritage, and worked with UNESCO to plan a new edition of its "General Guidelines to Safeguard Documentary Heritage."

Late in 1996 the commission assumed responsibility for an ongoing microfilming project at Fudan University in Shanghai. The project will microfilm and make available in the United States more than 4,000 titles of Chinese-language monographs published during Japan's occupation of China and the Sino-Japanese War (1932–1945). The project was initiated by the Committee on Scholarly Communication with China, which closed its office in June.

Publications

A continuing series of International Program publications acquaints readers with preservation and access activities around the world at a time when preservation activities are as varied as the countries in which they operate. The series began in

January 1995 with an overview and reports from Bulgaria, Europe, and Latin America.

The situations in Canada and Russia were explored in 1996 reports. Canada is a country of far-flung provinces and two official languages, yet its cultural heritage ties a vast land together. Similarly, preservation of its printed heritage provides a unifying theme for Canada's libraries, archives, and collections. *Preservation Activities in Canada: A Unifying Theme in a Decentralised Country*[11], describes Canada's preservation efforts within the context of this common purpose. The second 1996 report was written by the Deputy Director General of the Library for Foreign Literature in Moscow. *Preservation Challenges in a Changing Political Climate*[12] presents a distinctly Russian perspective on the ways in which libraries and archives are attempting to adapt to widespread changes while seeking to maintain their services and introduce new technologies, all with decreasing financial resources. The report illuminates how the substantial political, economic, and social changes in Russia today directly affect the preservation efforts of libraries and archives.

Education and Training

The Andrew W. Mellon Foundation funded a project, "Publication and Dissemination of Preservation Knowledge in Brazil," with the commission acting as U.S. coordinator. Phase I involved the selection and translation into Portuguese of more than 1,000 pages of current literature on preservation and conservation. In Phase II, this literature will be distributed to almost 1,500 libraries and archives in Brazil. The literature will support week-long workshops in five regions, where 70 participants will be trained in preservation and conservation concepts.

Conclusion

The commission and council are supported by private foundations, corporations, institutions, and individuals. The boards believe that an independent organization not confined by the needs of its members can be useful during this time of transition for libraries, archives, and academic institutions. Such an organization can bring thoughtful and creative individuals together to discuss information policies and their implications. It can also serve as an ever-present voice for the cause of preservation. In its communications efforts, the merged council and commission can identify the best individuals to produce reports on issues of substance, and can promote discussion of these issues by disseminating reports and results of studies to those in positions of influence and decision making. Although the small staff of the council and commission is not equipped to accomplish all the needed work, it is nonetheless is committed to facilitating cooperation among talented people to shape and transform the information agencies that serve the needs of scholarship and society.

Notes

1. Commission on Preservation and Access and Council on Library Resources. *Annual Report, 1995–1996*
2. Commission on Preservation and Access. *Newsletter* nos. 85–94 (January 1996–November/December 1996)
3. Waters, Donald, and John Garrett. *Preserving Digital Information: Report of the Task Force on Archiving of Digital Information.* May 1996.
4. McClung, Patricia A. *Digital Collections Inventory Report.* February 1996.
5. Council on Library Resources. *Public Libraries, Communities, and Technology, Twelve Case Studies.* November 1996.
6. Conway, Paul. *Preservation in the Digital World.* March 1996
7. Ester, Michael. *Digital Image Collections: Issues and Practice.* December 1996.
8. George, Gerald. *Difficult Choices: How Can Scholars Help Save Endangered Research Resources?* August 1995.
9. Rhyne, Charles S. *Computer Images for Research, Teaching, and Publication in Art History and Related Disciplines.* January 1996. A shortened version of an article in *Visual Resources: An International Journal of Documentation*, ed. Helene E. Roberts, vol. XI, no. 3 (1995). January 1996.
10. Porck, Henk. *Mass Deacidification: An Update on Possibilities and Limitations.* October 1996
11. Turko, Karen. *Preservation Activities in Canada: A Unifying Theme in a Decentralised Country.* February 1996.
12. Kislovskaya, Galina, *Preservation Challenges in a Changing Political Climate: A Report from Russia.* September 1996.

International Reports

International Federation of Library Associations and Institutions

Edward J. Valauskas

Nearly seven decades old in 1996, the International Federation of Library Associations and Institutions (IFLA) demonstrated its vitality last year with a wide variety of conferences, workshops, programs, publications, and digital documents, strengthening its leadership as an association for all librarians in the world. In its long and rich history, IFLA has never had a more popular or successful annual event as the 62nd Annual Conference in Beijing. But the conference was just one of many IFLA-sponsored events that demonstrated the association's commitment to serve the global library community in person, in print, and increasingly on the Internet.

Beijing Conference

With 2,384 delegates and 284 exhibitors from 91 countries, the 62nd IFLA conference (August 25–31, 1996) ranked as one of the largest events in IFLA's history. Given the well-documented interest of the host country in books, reading, and libraries (China was one of the founding members of IFLA in 1927), it was not surprising that the conference and its participants were the focus of much media attention in Beijing and China. The conference itself was professionally extended by several significant preconference programs that examined copyright and technology; issues that were often to be raised again during formal sessions sponsored by IFLA's sections, divisions, and roundtables.

Forty sections and roundtables sponsored programs during the course of the conference, where nearly 150 papers were presented on a wide range of topics. The variety of problems and issues addressed in these papers was broad; technology, copyright, preservation, and access were common themes. In addition, 14 posters, provided by 17 speakers, were presented along with nine contributed papers in invitational open sessions, and more than 20 workshops.

For many participants, the opening session remarks of Premier Li Peng of the State Council were memorable in his emphasis on libraries in China. For oth-

---

Note: Edward J. Valauskas, an IFLA member, is Principal, Internet Mechanics, Chicago, and Chief and Managing Editor, *First Monday*, a peer-reviewed journal on the Internet about the Internet (http://www.firstmonday.dk).

ers, a gala performance of dance and music, organized by the Ministry of Culture, was a major highlight of the conference. For many others, the distribution on CD-ROM of the contents of IFLA's Web site at the National Library of Canada was a momentous occasion. The conjunction of both the IFLA conference and the subsequent meeting of the International Council of Archives (ICA) provided an opportunity to meet with colleagues involved in preservation and conservation. Overall, the conference proved IFLA's continued commitment to encourage the professional development of libraries and to bring together librarians to address common problems by developing appropriate solutions.

Other Activities

CAIFE

IFLA's ad hoc Committee on Access to Information and Freedom of Expression (CAIFE) was established in 1995 to examine the association's own interests in promoting the free flow of information and in protecting freedom of expression. In her guest lecture at IFLA's 61st Council and General Conference in Istanbul, Frances D'Souza, Executive Director of Article 19, strongly suggested a more active role for associations like IFLA. This theme was again addressed in Beijing in a lecture by Marianna Tax Choldin of the University of Illinois, followed by an open forum for further discussion of IFLA's evolving policy. CAIFE, under the direction of Chair Tony Evans, has been developing, over the course of the past year, a draft IFLA policy statement. This document will outline IFLA's interests in these issues, provide examples of incidents from around the world, and propose activities, relative to information access and freedom of expression, that IFLA will follow in the near future. CAIFE will provide the IFLA membership with an opportunity to discuss and analyze this policy statement at the 63rd IFLA Council and General Conference in Copenhagen in 1997.

COPEARMS

In conjunction with the European Commission, IFLA's Core Program on the Universal Availability of Publications (UAP) began to work with organizations in Belgium, France, and Great Britain on the Coordinating Project for an Electronic Authors' Right Management System (COPEARMS). This project attempts to bring together different systems for monitoring the uses of copyrighted materials, allowing copyright owners to communicate with all parties on licensing uses of protected materials. UAP's role is to protect the interests of libraries, ensuring broader access to materials, and to promote the use of standards. This project is scheduled to last three years.[1]

Joint Committee on Preservation in Africa

Established at a meeting in February 1996 in Dakar, Senegal, the Joint Committee on Preservation in Africa (JICPA) attempts to educate librarians and government officials on the importance of preservation, encouraging training and research through cooperation with IFLA's Section on Conservation and ICA's Committee on Preservation of Archival Materials. JICPA will work in Africa to develop national commissions to increase awareness of preservation issues and develop training plans. The committee will be supported by IFLA and ICA, with additional assistance from IFLA's Regional Office for Africa in Dakar.[2]

Vologda Conference on Libraries and Reading

Organized by IFLA's Section on reading and Round Table on Library History, the "Libraries and Reading in Times of Cultural Change" conference was held June 18–22, 1996, in Vologda, Russia, some 350 miles north of the Russian capital.[3] An enthusiastic Russian and American audience attended the conference, at which there was a lively discussion on the "vulgarization" of literature with the growth of democracy and the removal of state controls on printing and literature; the increasing availability of religious materials in Russia; and censorship in obvious and less apparent ways. James Billington, Librarian of Congress, and others explained difficulties in the West during times of war and political unrest. Two translators were kept busy in the course of these dialogues, which featured in the audience the Russian Vice-Minister of Culture, Iuril Volegov; IFLA Second Vice-President Ekaterina Genieva; Director of the Library of Congress's Center for the Book, John Cole; American Library Association (ALA) President Betty Turock; editor of the *Cambridge History of the Book in Great Britain*, Ian Willison; and editor of the *Bulletin des Bibliothèques de France*, Martine Poulain. The conference showed the high level of interest in the ways publishers, readers, and their governments respond to change, and the manners in which libraries reflect these responses.

WIPO Conference

Stimulated by several well-attended workshops and seminars on copyright in Beijing, and the formal adoption of a copyright policy relative to digital information, IFLA was strongly represented at the World Intellectual Property Organization (WIPO) Diplomatic Conference in December 1996. This conference would have significantly altered copyright law to reflect the electronic distribution of information in networks and on digital media. IFLA, as an Non-Governmental Organization (NGO), enjoys observer status with WIPO, and used its position to organize a team to defend libraries, librarians, and readers in debate on access to information in electronic and networked forms. The team consisted of Sandy Norman, IFLA's copyright advisor; Adam Eisgrau of ALA's Washington, D.C., Office; and Jamie Wodetzki, formerly of the Australian Council of Libraries and Information Services (ACLIS).

IFLA, like many of the participants in the WIPO conference, has actively followed the debate surrounding modifications of copyright and intellectual property law relative to electronic information. IFLA's Copyright Committee initially stimulated much formal discussion of these issues within the IFLA community. These discussions led IFLA's executive and professional boards to adopt in Beijing the "IFLA Position Paper on Copyright in the Electronic Environment[4]," which encourages the use of electronic information in libraries and calls for no legal restrictions on the use of digital data. IFLA's team in Geneva at the WIPO conference made this position paper and responses to the WIPO draft proposals widely available.

The WIPO Committee of Experts created a number of draft proposals for consideration at the conference, of which several were critical to libraries and other parties. The draft version of Article 7 would have severely limited the use of temporary or transient copies of information, without the permission of the owners of the works. IFLA, online service providers, telephone companies, and other routine users of networked resources to transmit information were strongly opposed to a more constricted interpretation. This article was not included in the final treaty, thanks in part to IFLA's concern over the implications of granting more control to copyright owners.

Article 12 was designed to eliminate some of the exceptions or limitations (such as fair use in accessing and using information) granted by various states. Many were concerned that fair use as it is known in the United States would be subject to challenges as a trade issue, if Article 12, in its draft form, were adopted[5]. IFLA's criticism of Article 12 was supported in whole or in part at the WIPO conference by representatives from Denmark, India, Singapore, Korea, and by others, leading to a revised and less harsh version of Article 12 to be approved.

IFLA's work at the WIPO Diplomatic Conference, in conjunction with representatives from other countries and with other observers, proved to be effective in turning the final adopted treaty (which can be found at http://www.wipo.int/eng/diplconf/distrib/94dc.htm) into a fairer document for libraries and their users. The skill of IFLA's representatives in lobbying for changes in draft materials was noted by many representatives to the conference, including publishers. In addition, IFLA recognized the importance of making alliances with representatives from certain geographic areas, such as Asia and Scandinavia. Given that these issues will repeatedly emerge both on international and national agendas, IFLA's experience at the WIPO conference will be tested in different venues.

IFLANET

IFLA's presence on the Internet, maintained by the IFLA International Office for Universal Dataflow and Telecommunications (UDT) at the National Library of Canada, grew considerably in 1996. IFLA maintains three popular listservs and a highly used Web site (http://www.nlc-bnc.ca/ifla/), all of which provide a means for documents to be transmitted globally and for librarians and others to communicate efficiently and effectively.

In 1996 IFLA's Web server handled nearly 700,000 requests, or nearly 2,000 requests per day. Over 140,000 distinct hosts were served, with over 13,000 megabytes of data transmitted. On average, more than 37,000 kilobytes of information were transmitted each day (see Table 1). If we assume that a printed page of a document uses two kilobytes, then some 18,500 equivalent pages of IFLA documents are circulated around the world every day, or some 6.5 million pages a year.

Table 1 / Use of IFLA Web server (http://www.nlc-bnc.ca/ifla/) in 1996

Total data sent:13,366 MB	
Data sent, average/day:	37,397 KB
Total requests:	691,408
Requests, average/day:	1,889
Total distinct hosts:	140,389

Training information and documents related to copyright were highly popular. Documents concerning the Beijing and Istanbul conferences were in high demand, along with information from IFLA's Section on Information Technology and archives for IFLA's listservs (especially LIBJOBS). IFLA members and others from more than 106 countries accessed information from the IFLA site. Overall growth in use of the Web server in the course of one year indicates an increasing desire for information in this medium (see Table 2).

Table 2 / Growth in the use of the IFLA Web server, 1995–1996

	July 1995	July 1996	percent increase
Hosts served	5,318	12,637	138
Files transferred	19,926	51,845	160

IFLA's mailing lists processed some five million messages in 1996, read by 6,000 subscribers in some 60 countries (see Table 3). IFLA-L, the most basic IFLA listserv (with more than 800 subscribers in 60 countries), provides a means for librarians and others interested in IFLA to communicate and exchange information in issues related to international librarianship (see Table 3). LIBJOBS, dedicated to posting jobs around the world for librarians, is the most heavily viewed listserv, with over 3,500 subscribers in more than 50 countries. DIGLIB, dealing with the invention and development of digital libraries, includes over 1,700 subscribers in 53 countries. Other listservs restrict their circulation to IFLA officers and board members.

Table 3 / Usage of IFLA Listservs (as of January 1997)

	Total subscribers	No. of countries
IFLA-L	835	60
DIGLIB	1,761	53
LIBJOBS	3,598	52

IFLA's continued expansion of its Web site (with 14,778 distinct files and over 8,000 links to other sites and servers) will provide opportunities for IFLA's members and others to learn more about the association and its activities. In addition, the Web site will continue to act as an effective public relations tool in promoting the association digitally, proving to the global Internet community the digital savvy of librarians.

Some 2,000 Internet sites and servers are linked to IFLA's site, according to Digital Equipment Corporation's search tool, Alta Vista (http://www.altavista.digital.com/). IFLA's server and listservs additionally make it possible for the membership, officers, and staff to respond more quickly to critical issues needing member input and to develop policies and other positions quickly by consensus. Continued expansion of the server is expected in 1997, with documents for the Copenhagen conference already available. Traffic demands have led to the construction of a mirror of the server in France (http://ifla.inist.fr/) at the Institut de l'Information Scientifique et Technique (INIST) in Vandoeuvre-lès-Nancy. The number of documents available on the server in languages other than English will also increase over the course of 1997.

Awards and Grants

IFLA awarded several prizes and grants in the course of 1996. Keijing Liu of the Department of Information Management at the Central China Normal University in Wuhan won the Gustav Hofmann Grant for 1996. She will examine the impact of new technologies on freedom of expression.

In recognition of their contributions to IFLA, Thomas Tottie, University Librarian at Uppsala University in Sweden; Marianne Scott, National Librarian of Canada; and Ben G. Goedegebuure, formerly Executive Director of the International Federation of Documentation and Information, were presented with scrolls at the Beijing conference.

Marieke van Buytene, a recent graduate of the Department of Information Services and Information Management at the Haagse Hogeschool, University of Professional Education in the Hague, is the first Paul Nauta Residential Fellow. She works in the IFLA headquarters in the Hague with Winston Roberts, coordinating professional activities of the association, as well as with Carol Henry and other IFLA staff on membership issues.

At the Beijing conference, Dong Ming of the Sanwieshuwu Book Shop in Shenyang was recognized for his effort to attend the conference. Ming spent eight days riding his bicycle to the conference, promoting the event along the way with a banner signed en route by librarians.

Publications

With the growth of IFLA's presence on the Internet, it is not surprising that some of IFLA's traditional printed publications are appearing both in paper and digitally. *The International Directory of Art Libraries* first appeared on the Internet in November 1995 at http://aaln.org/ifla-idal and will appear in print this year. Text and html versions of the *IFLA Journal* appear on the IFLA server at http://www.

nlc-bnc.ca/ifla/V/iflaj/index.htm with back issues available to the beginning of 1993. Some sections and divisions of IFLA are making their newsletters available electronically; electronic versions of newsletters from several of the offices of the Core Programs are also available.

These experiences with electronic information will allow IFLA to update and supplement printed reports and documents. For example, the invaluable *National Libraries of the World: An Address List*, produced by the UAP Core Program, is available in an up-to-date digital form (last updated January 1997) on the IFLA server (http://www.nlc-bnc.ca/ifla/VI/2/p2/natlibs.htm).

IFLA released several significant reports and documents in 1996, published by K. G. Saur in Munich. The IFLA Section of Art Libraries released through Saur its second revised and enlarged edition of the *Multilingual Glossary for Art Librarians* (ISBN 3-598-21802-8). In English, with indices in Swedish, Spanish, Italian, German, French, and Dutch, this revision was a decade in the making; it includes references to new technologies and definitions of terms. The Section of University Libraries released its report on techniques for measuring the performance of academic libraries with its report *Measuring Quality* (ISBN 3-598-21800-1). The guidelines in the report apply to all kinds of academic libraries in measuring effectiveness, from the standpoint of users. Guidelines were also prepared for newspaper preservation microfilming (ISBN 9-070-91659-2), by the Section on Serial Publications and the Round Table on Newspapers. In addition, the sixth edition of the *World Directory of International Parliamentary Libraries* (ISBN 3-893-72014-6) appeared in 1996. In two volumes, the report provides information on 258 parliaments or chambers in 191 states; it is available from the Deutscher Bundestag in Bonn.

Future Prospects

IFLA's role in the professional development of libraries is especially important in this period of rapid technological change, with information resources increasingly becoming available in digital form. Some libraries, due to location, budgets, or bureaucracies, are finding themselves technologically isolated from new resources available only via the Internet.

Recognizing these rapidly evolving changes in the information landscape, IFLA's Medium Term Program, for the period 1998–2001, will concentrate on the digital environment "as it affects IFLA's objective to promote librarianship globally, particularly through . . . equal access to information, literacy programmes, and preservation of the world's documentary heritage[6]." In addition, IFLA plans to establish a technology assistance plan, to assist libraries with connectivity and training[7]. This program will benefit from IFLA's experiences with IFLANET, its technically sophisticated members in the Information Technology Section and other IFLA units, and the overall enthusiasm of IFLA as a whole. IFLA indeed seems to be growing in anticipation of developments in technology and in membership, while creating an overall strategic plan to address the needs of its members—from the most technologically sophisticated to the most technophobic. This plan should allow IFLA to continue well into the next century as the premier international library association.

Notes

1. "IFLA Programme for UAP to be Involved in COPEARMS Project," *IFLA Journal* 22, no. 1 (1996): 58.
2. "Joint Committee on Preservation in Africa Established in February 1996," *IFLA Journal* 22, no. 3 (1996): 258–259.
3. P. S. Richards and V. Stelmakh, "A View Toward Library Users," *IFLA Journal* 22, no. 4 (1996): 322–323.
4. "IFLA Position Paper on Copyright in the Electronic Environment," *IFLA Journal* 22, no. 4 (1996): 314–315. Also at http://www.nlc-bnc.ca/ifla/V/ebpb/copy.htm.
5. P. Samuelson, "Confab Clips Copyright Cartel: Big Media Beaten Back," *Wired* 5, no. 3 (1997): 180.
6. "IFLA Medium-Term Programme, 1998–2001," *IFLA Journal* 22, no. 3 (1996): 253.
7. Wedgeworth, R., "A View toward Library Users," *IFLA Journal* 22, no. 4 (1996): 279.

Special Libraries Association

1700 18th Street N.W., Washington, DC 20009-2514
202-234-4700, ext. 634; fax 202-265-9317, e-mail jenni-s@sla.org
World Wide Web http://www.sla.org

Jennifer L. Stowe
Director, Public Relations

Headquartered in Washington, D.C., the Special Libraries Association (SLA) is an international association representing the interests of more than 15,000 information professionals in 60 countries. Special librarians are information resource experts who collect, analyze, evaluate, package, and disseminate information to facilitate accurate decision making in corporate, academic, and government settings.

As of June 1996 the association had 56 regional chapters in the United States, Canada, Europe, and the Middle East; 25 divisions representing a variety of industries; and 12 special-interest caucuses.

The association offers myriad programs and services designed to help its members serve their customers more effectively and succeed in an increasingly challenging environment of information management and technology. Association activities are developed with specific direction toward achieving SLA's strategic goals: to advance the leadership role of its members in putting knowledge to work for the benefit of decision makers in their organization and the general public; and to shape the destiny of the information society.

The following are highlights of SLA's programs during 1995–1996.

Professional Development

The Professional Development Program serves the professional needs of SLA members through a variety of high-quality and cutting-edge educational training activities that meet member needs and respond to changes in information technology and corporate culture. During 1995–1996 more than 50 educational programs were offered.

In September 1995 SLA produced its first distance-learning program. Cosponsored by LEXIS-NEXIS, the program featured a panel discussion of copyright issues that was broadcast to seven sites throughout the United States and Canada. The program was so successful that a second program, on marketing, was produced in April 1996.

The 1996 Winter Education Conference, "Technology and Tools in the Information Age," offered ten workshops and courses dealing with various aspects of information technology. This year's conference also featured a presentation by Case Western Reserve University outlining its virtual-library project. In addition to the courses, 34 vendors participated in a technology fair that demonstrated the latest trends in information technology. The "Technology and Applications" unit of the Middle Management Institute (MMI) was also offered during the conference.

The SLA Annual Conference in Boston featured 35 continuing-education courses to more than 1,300 attendees. Of those courses, 12 were offered by divisions. Two MMI units, "Human Resources" and "Analytical Tools," were also offered, along with the "Principles of Accounting and Financial Management" segment of the Executive Management Course.

In addition to the courses, a career workshop on how to conduct job prospecting in the 1990s and beyond was held. Also available at the conference were the Employment Clearinghouse and the Career Advisory Service. More than 125 people registered with the clearinghouse to review 80 job postings. Fifty-two people received career counseling through the Career Advisory Service.

Some continuing-education courses were cosponsored by various SLA chapters and other organizations throughout the year. The Library of Congress cosponsored four SLA courses in conjunction with its Leadership Development Program. Cosponsored courses are arranged through headquarters and can be offered anywhere.

The self-study program currently has 13 titles from which SLA members can choose to learn in a self-paced environment. The latest workbook, "Control of Administrative and Financial Operations in Special Libraries," is the second book in a financial-management series.

The 1995 State-of-the-Art Institute, "Southeast Asia: The Information Age," attracted more than 40 people who learned about information marketing, information technology, and economic development in nine Southeast Asian countries.

Public Relations

The primary goal of the SLA Public Relations Program is to increase awareness and appreciation of the important role that special librarians play in their organizations and society.

To help accomplish this goal, SLA has hired Read-Poland Associates, a medium-sized but growing firm that is closely affiliated with Burson-Marsteller, one of the world's largest public relations and public affairs firms. Read-Poland has extensive experience representing diverse professions, from car dealers to plastic surgeons.

Read-Poland is focusing on getting coverage of special librarians in metropolitan newspapers and business publications. The target audience is organizational decision makers. As a result of the agency's initial efforts, articles featuring special librarians have been published in the *Chicago Tribune*, *Washington Post*, *Fort Worth Star-Telegram*, and *Denver Post*.

The "P.R. Update" column has been revised slightly to place more emphasis on positive articles about the profession. The column will be further revised and renamed for *Information Outlook*, which will become SLA's new monthly magazine in 1997.

Public relations materials were prepared for SLA's Web site. Because people unfamiliar with the profession will discover the site, a page was added on what a special librarian is, and it was linked to a page giving seven reasons to use a special library.

An annual public relations highlight is International Special Librarians Day, a time to gain recognition for the contributions of the profession in the global sharing of information. The 1996 theme was "Special Librarians: Partners in Global Information Management." To help members celebrate International Special Librarians Day, a free marketing kit containing camera-ready materials was prepared.

SLA mailed the marketing kit to all unit public relations chairs and offered the kit free to members. In addition, LEXIS-NEXIS helped sponsor the cost of producing the kit and sent it to many of its customers.

SLA awards and honors also are a part of the SLA Public Relations Program. To stimulate member interest, the awards program is getting increased publicity through coverage in information industry publications.

Research

The goals of SLA's Research Program are to provide methodologies, data, and analyses that address significant elements of the profession. SLA supports research through a variety of activities; for instance, it independently conducts research, works in collaboration with other organizations in conducting and sponsoring research, and funds research through the Steven I. Goldspiel Memorial Research Grant.

At the June 1996 meeting, the SLA Board of Directors approved the Research Committee's nomination of F. W. Lancaster and Linda C. Smith as recipients of the 1996 Steven I. Goldspiel Research Grant for their proposal "Potential Applications of Artificial Intelligence and Expert System Technologies in the Special Library of the Future." The primary objective of the project is to appraise the applicability of artificial intelligence/expert system (AI/ES) technologies to current and future special library operations.

Lancaster and Smith plan to comprehensively review the literature in all relevant disciplines, identify applications in both library and nonlibrary environments that are relevant to special library operations and services, determine the success or failure of relevant applications, and document the determinants of success or failure. Results will be presented at the 1997 SLA Annual Conference in Seattle. The findings will also be published by SLA in the fall of 1997, with highlights reported in *Information Outlook*.

SLA's third membership needs assessment survey, distributed to a random sample of 33 percent of SLA members, was conducted in March 1996. In conjunction with the "Super Survey," the first survey of nonmembers—defined for this survey as information professionals who had attended an SLA conference or continuing-education program but had not joined SLA—was conducted. Demographic highlights from the first two surveys were presented to SLA's board of directors in June 1996; the final report was presented during its October 1996 meeting. Highlights also were featured in *Information Outlook*. Data from both surveys will be used by all SLA program areas to refine existing programs and services and in the development of new programs and services.

Working in partnership with Association Research, Inc., SLA research staff revised, administered, and analyzed the *1996 Biennial Salary Survey*. The survey instrument was revised to capture additional relevant data and enable more-extensive analysis of the data. Results of the survey were published by SLA in October 1996.

SLA is sponsoring a new study on the value of information services in response to its identification at SLA's 1995 Research Forum as the number-one research priority. The objectives of the project are to identify and organize the dimensions of value of specific library services, to identify and test procedures for measuring the value of those services, and to develop a manual that demonstrates how to apply the research procedures at other organizations. The manual will contain samples of the research instruments used in the study and an explanation of how to modify the instruments for application in other libraries. The project director is Paul B. Kantor, director, Alexandria Project Laboratory, and professor, School of Communication, Information and Library Studies, Rutgers University. The coinvestigator is Tefko Saracevic, also a professor at the School of Communication, Information and Library Studies, Rutgers University. The project is expected to be completed by fall 1997.

Serial Publications

The Serial Publications Program is becoming increasingly member-driven as a renewed emphasis is placed on seeking member-written articles. News from chapter and division bulletins is also receiving more exposure as it finds its way into the pages of the monthly *SpeciaList* newsletter. Additionally, peer reviewers and book reviewers are crucial to the success of the quarterly *Special Libraries*. As a result of these member efforts, the publications are able to provide more timely information to the membership.

For example, *SpeciaList* has featured articles on such topics as the Texaco copyright case (*American Geophysical Union* v. *Texaco*), international librarianship, "knowledge mapping," Internet resources, information audits, global villages, the Telecommunications Act of 1996, marketing techniques, universal access to the National Information Infrastructure, and, of course, the Internet itself.

Articles in *Special Libraries* have focused on such topics as the research knowledge and activities of special librarians, indexing of editorial cartoons, information policy audits, strategic positioning/partnering, designing an Internet class, malpractice in the library setting, marketing library services, and building business cases. *Special Libraries* also served members by providing an update on the *1995 Salary Survey* and providing in-depth coverage of the 87th Annual Conference in Boston.

Building on the success of the two expanded issues of *SpeciaList* that SLA provided in 1995, six 20-page issues were published in 1996. The interest expressed by the membership in receiving more timely information management coverage, coupled with increased advertiser interest and a number of other researched factors, prompted the SLA board of directors to vote to discontinue the two existing serial publications, *SpeciaList* and *Special Libraries*, and create a new 48-page, four-color monthly magazine, *Information Outlook*. Although this monthly magazine was not to premiere until January 1997, work on this project began in October 1995. Content issues and design of the publication have been a strong focus of the Serial Publications Program in 1995–1996. With this exciting new endeavor, the Serials Program has an opportunity to provide members with even more timely and in-depth coverage of the news and events important to information professionals.

Who's Who in Special Libraries, the association's annual membership directory, now contains more than 420 pages and continues to expand as more features are added to make it an even better networking tool and information resource for the membership. For example, the 1995–1996 *Who's Who* contained SLA's first and quite successful "Buyer's Guide," containing information on providers of specific products and services. It now contains chapter and division officer and member information; member statistics; historical highlights; SLA's bylaws, strategic plan, and vision statement; awards and honors; and a schedule of future meetings and conferences.

Nonserial Publications

The philosophy of the Nonserial Publications Program (NSP) is to provide the information community, particularly SLA members, with competitive products that continue to meet their changing needs. In addition, the program endeavors to make a significant contribution to the literature of the information profession and to increase the influence of the professional and the field itself.

The program produces 10–15 publications each calendar year and remains committed to providing them at a savings to the membership. The member-pricing policy enables SLA members to purchase publications at a discount from the regular price, which is a significant benefit.

The NSP Program strives to anticipate member needs by keeping abreast of what's happening in the world of information and producing quality titles that meet those needs. SLA released ten titles in 1995, ranging from Internet resources to special librarianship as a career. Future acquisitions are focused on updating mainstay titles as well as new books on the "Information Superhighway" and advances in information technology.

Focused acquisition efforts combined with targeted marketing efforts produced NSP sales in excess of projections last year. This sales trend seems to be indicative of the continual need for publications that address the issues facing members and of SLA's commitment to provide members with timely, relevant, information-packed publications.

By publishing information kits, professional papers from the SLA Annual Conference, the proceedings from the State-of-the-Art Institute, special papers on timely topics, and books, the program ensures a balance of products available to meet the broad range of member needs.

Government Relations

SLA's Government Relations Program seeks to inform and educate government officials at all levels on issues that are pertinent to the special libraries community, while increasing member awareness of government relations activities that affect them as information professionals and citizens. SLA also solicits member involvement in monitoring and tracking governmental activities of interest to the library community and profession and assists in issue formulation.

In general, matters that are addressed by the Government Relations Program deal directly with information—how it is collected, maintained, and disseminated, as well as the rights of individuals, the end-users, to access information. The SLA Government Relations Committee annually formulates the association's Government Relations Platform for presentation to the SLA board of directors at its fall meeting.

Because SLA is opposed to censorship on the Internet, the association joined the Citizens Internet Empowerment Coalition, which filed a lawsuit challenging censorship provisions in the Communications Decency Act.

SLA joined with four other library associations in writing a letter to Carlos Moorhead (R-Calif.), chair of the House Subcommittee on Courts and Intellectual Property, commending him for calling interested parties together for negotiation and to recommend broadening these discussions to include all stakeholders.

Comments also were submitted on the Electronic Federal Depository Library Program (FDLP) Transition Plan, chiefly expressing a concern that the technology infrastructure necessary to support the nearly all-electronic FDLP described in the plan does not yet exist.

In examining the myriad issues that have been debated in the legislative, regulatory, and judicial arenas on the local, state, provincial, federal, and international levels, SLA determined, as the 1995–1996 association year came to a close, that it would modify the Government Relations Program somewhat. Although SLA will continue to focus on five core issues—copyright and intellectual property rights, telecommunications, global information infrastructure, access to information, and competitiveness—the program will address these issues more equally in the future. By increasing its efforts in areas getting less attention from other information groups, SLA will enhance its leadership role and visibility.

Membership Development

By working in partnership with all other program areas, the Membership Development Department continues to pursue member recruitment and retention as well as support the activities of chapters, divisions, caucuses, and student groups. In addition, the department maintains the membership database, including adding new and prospective members, processing renewals and address changes, and updating officer information. Further, the Membership Development Department promoted and administered the SLA scholarship program and student group activities.

Specific department projects included stepping up the invoicing process to balance any potential negative effects of the dues increase and increasing the overall accuracy and timeliness of the renewal notice mailings; sending membership information to prospects in a 24-hour turnaround time; disseminating an informative new member packet within one week of a member's join date;

adding a title space in the membership database to begin the collection of member titles; and providing assistance to association leaders through monthly mailings and leadership training sessions.

The Membership Development Department's retention efforts are supported at the grassroots level. The Membership Development Department provides membership chairs with monthly member notification reports, bimonthly new-member reports, and deactivated-member reports. Membership chairs also receive information in an electronic format. In addition, the membership chairs receive monthly mailings containing membership information and tips about recruitment and retention.

In an effort to attract students into the field of special librarianship, SLA offers a scholarship program and supports activities of student members. The Membership Development Department semiannually produces and mails *The Student Union*, the student group newsletter. The department works closely with the chair of the Student and Academic Relations Committee to build a partnership with the association leaders and the student members to increase retention. Activities of the SLA scholarship program included the disbursement of $24,000 in financial aid awarded to four students.

The Membership Development Department works together with all SLA staff to increase retention through quality services and increase recruitment through exceptional programs.

Conferences and Meetings

Membership commitment to careers and to the association was apparent when special librarians from the United States and around the world went to Boston to participate in SLA's 87th Annual Conference. Approximately 7,700 information professionals attended, making it the largest SLA conference ever.

Complementing this year's conference, which had the theme "Information Revolution: Pathway to the 21st Century," was an exhibit hall with more than 520 booths and tabletop displays from companies around the world. With a record number of vendors, the exhibit hall served as a one-stop marketplace for every product or service an information professional could need.

Under the guidance of Ellen Kuner, 1996 Conference Program Committee chair, SLA division program planners were responsible for implementing many of the program sessions. Conference attendees had the opportunity to choose from more than 500 programs, special events, continuing-education courses, meetings, and field trips to plan their personal conference itineraries.

As in past years, the most popular sessions at the conference dealt with the Internet and information technology. In addition, the Internet Room was again available for conference attendees to access their e-mail.

The general-session address was given by Allen Neuharth, founder of *USA Today* and current chair of the Freedom Forum. His presentation focused on the growing hunger for information and how information professionals can survive in this environment.

More than 1,300 information professionals took part in this year's pre- and postconference professional-development programs, which featured courses on topics ranging from strategic planning to the World Wide Web. The courses were geared toward professionals at all levels, from introductory to advanced.

Recognizing its civic responsibility, SLA worked with the Boston conference facilities to take maximum advantage of their recycling programs. In addition, excess banquet food was donated to local charities.

Information Resources Center

SLA's Information Resources Center (IRC) continues to respond to the large number of requests for information from members and nonmembers on a variety of aspects of special librarianship. There has been a significant increase in the number of requests made via the Internet; and with the introduction of the SLA home page, there should be an increase in the number of answers given directly from the Web site or via e-mail.

The majority of information requests are on library management, careers, and salaries. Other popular topics are library technology, setting up libraries or information centers, professional development, and marketing. The discussions on setting up special libraries often lead to referrals to the SLA Consultation Service or referrals from the CONSULT database.

Bibliographies have been updated on such topics as starting and managing a special library, library automation software, copyright, the value of the information center, contracting out and outsourcing library services, and space planning. These bibliograpies are now accessible to members and nonmembers from the SLA Internet home page.

The Management Document Collection (MDC) continues to be a popular resource for both members and nonmembers. Loans from the MDC of user surveys significantly outnumbered those of mission statements, collection development, library brochures, strategic plans, and fees for services. The IRC staff has sought to enhance the collection by soliciting additional model materials from members. A goal for the coming year is to develop and enhance services to members and staff by increased utilization of the Internet and other advances in library technology.

Fund Development

In the second year of its existence, SLA's Fund Development Program experienced continued success.

SLA's members were supportive of the Second Annual President's Reception, held in conjunction with the 1996 Annual Conference in Boston. Attended by more than 200 individuals, the event provided more than $10,000 to support SLA's public relations activities.

SLA's members were supportive of the association's established affinity programs, which provide members discounts on various products and services. The MBNA Visa program, the AT&T communication services program, and the Airborne Express overnight delivery program all grew substantially.

In addition, members encouraged and supported expansion of the list of available programs. As a result, SLA added four new affinity programs that provide discounts to members on products and services: the Hertz car rental program, the Mellon mortgage services program, the Enterprise Group investment services program, and the Information Today professional publications program.

Finally, SLA's members encouraged new programs in planned giving and annual giving, and the association obliged. The SLA Legacy Club was created in November 1995, in order to provide members with appropriate recognition for long-term giving through wills, insurance, property, stocks, bonds, and other instruments.

Also in November 1995, the SLA President's Appeal was introduced in order to provide members with a method for making a year-end gift to the association. More than 100 leaders and supporters participated in the program, which will be expanded in the future.

In addition, SLA's corporate supporters requested a method to support the association—both above the existing Patron level ($1,000) and below the existing Sponsor level ($500). In November 1995 SLA introduced its new investment categories: President's Circle ($10,000), Benefactor ($5,000), Contributor ($250), and Donor ($100). To date, there are already three charter members of the President's Circle, one charter member of the Benefactor giving category, and several new Contributors and Donors.

Corporate supporters also took advantage of the new, improved conference and meeting program. SLA's Technology Fair had a record 34 booths, and the Annual Conference exhibit hall produced an astounding 504 booths and 20 tabletop displays. For the first time ever, there were several sponsors of SLA's Winter Meeting and Winter Education Conference in Cleveland, raising more than $8,000 for SLA's leadership services and professional-development programs. Also this year, sponsorship levels tripled for SLA's Annual Conference, raising more than $82,000 in conference support.

Advertising sales were at or above projected levels in nearly all areas, including *SpeciaList*, *Who's Who in Special Libraries*, the *Buyer's Guide*, and the *Preliminary* and *Final Conference Programs*. Although advertising sales fell short of goal in *Special Libraries*, the introduction of *Information Outlook* in 1997 will provide a new and exciting medium.

Finally, corporate supporters expressed interest in partnerships. A number of customized programs were undertaken in this area, including Disclosure, Inc.'s sponsorship of SLA's home page and Knight-Ridder's and Teltech's sponsorship of the Executive Management Course. These partnerships have generated more than $125,000 in support in the first year alone.

Finance and Administration

The organizational structure and staff competencies continue to be a focus of the senior management and leadership in maintaining the direction set forth in the association's strategic plan and vision statement. Such focus has enabled the staff to develop and implement annual program philosophies and financial assumptions, the association program plan, and the association budget. In addition, the staff job descriptions and performance appraisal process have been reviewed and revised where necessary.

The staff development program was developed and organized by the Executive Office. The 1995 program incorporated various in-house training and professional sessions geared toward increasing staffing competencies and service to the membership. Topics include association leadership; managing time, stress, and priorities; financial forecasting; visioning; performance appraisals; the Internet; and marketing. The positive impact of this program is evidenced in the feedback received from staff and the requests for a similar program in 1996.

In addition, the Finance and Administration staff has implemented a customer service education series for the entire staff, with a focus on increasing operational efficiency and service to the membership. The Finance and Administration staff has also maintained its interdepartmental cross-training program to ensure maximum use of staffing resources.

Another means of maximizing resources is the implementation of a bank lockbox service for the collection of dues and registration fees. This service expedites the deposit of funds and the processing of member records.

A major focus in the Financial Services department has been the monitoring and implementation of various new laws and regulations affecting nonprofit organizations. The collection, recording, and dissemination of financial information has changed significantly in the past few years due to rulings issued by the Internal Revenue Service and the Financial Accounting Standards Board. In addition, the association has continued working with the Internal Revenue Service on its examination of the association's books and records. Staff is communicating the compliance issues of the Internal Revenue Code as it applies to tax-exempt organizations to the association's units.

The Administrative Services staff has also monitored the various laws and regulations affecting the general operations of SLA, including personnel management, salary administration, benefits compliance, and occupancy/building code compliance. Other administrative projects completed include the revision of the emergency procedures, an analysis of internal equipment needs, an update to the 15-year building plan and schedule of capital improvements, and a space requirements plan. As approved by the board of directors, the association completed the first major building renovation since 1985 in the fall of 1996.

Computer Services and Technology

The SLA Computer Services and Technology Program continues to focus on merging new and existing technologies to enhance the products and services provided by the association to address the growing needs of the membership.

The most significant event in 1996 was the expansion of the association's Internet access and services. This was accomplished by merging Internet server technology and services with the association's existing Internet access capabilities, by upgrading the telecommunications link to the Internet to T1 access, by providing full Internet access to staff from their workstations, and by hosting all of the association's Internet services, such as the Web site, gopher site, and listservs. Most important in this expansion, however, was the development of the association's new Web page, which is being sponsored by Disclosure, Inc., during the next four years. The address is http://www.sla.org.

In order to improve service to membership and customers, several modifications to the Association Management System (AMS) were implemented. AMS's record structure and operating system, which houses and manages the association's membership and financial records, was upgraded to increase system performance by 100 percent. This increase in performance significantly reduced processing time of all reports and processing tasks, improving the delivery time of products and services to membership and customers. In addition, the upgrade removed a memory limitation for the chapter and division notification report that allowed the report to be modified to incorporate business, home, and e-mail address changes.

An exhibitors module was added to AMS to support SLA's Advertising and Exhibits Section in managing exhibitor information for any association event. This new module was used to successfully manage exhibitor contracts, booth and tabletop sales, invoices, labels, and various other reports for the 87th SLA Annual Conference in Boston.

New services currently under development include implementation of batch server technology for AMS to provide efficient use of staff workstations and to improve office productivity by allowing staff to submit reports, processes, and label requests to the batch server for processing to free their workstations to perform other tasks; and the hosting of committee, chapter, division, section, and caucus listservs and Web pages at the association office to minimize the expense for the units to implement these services.

With the implementation of new services and technologies and the addition of a new Internet manager position, the association's Computer Services and Technologies Program will provide increased support to the growing business and information requirements of the association.

World Trade and World Fairs, 1996: King Frankfurt and His Minions

Herbert R. Lottman
International Correspondent, *Publishers Weekly*

Contrary to popular belief, there is no international book trade (or if there is, it's a negligible one), and this thanks to language barriers and local traditions. "Thank God for both!" a believer in native and national cultures must say. But finished books, especially in the major languages, can and often do move from country to country, and of course the licensing of translation rights has become big business. Much of the import-export and licensing takes place at book fairs, chiefly at *one* book fair held each autumn in Frankfurt (this year's dates are October 15–20).

Indeed, an argument could be made that there is room for only one international book and rights market, and Frankfurt has preempted the job just by being the first to offer its candidacy. It was launched in 1949 in a still-devastated postwar Germany—with a dismal cityscape and second-class comforts—by a publishing community eager to pick up the pieces. But Germany had a book fair tradition; foreign publishers and booksellers quickly saw the utility of planning coeditions at a given time and place each year, and the first "international" book fair was born.

For a long time after that Frankfurt had no rival; today it remains the single essential meeting place for publishers, distributors, and booksellers, a window open on the world for librarians. Last fall's 48th fair (October 2–7) drew 6,819 exhibitors from 110 nations, Germany alone accounting for 2,539. There were over 300,000 books on display, an estimated 75,000 of them new, on a total exhibition surface of 1.9 million square feet. Nearly 275,000 visitors were clocked (including some 50,000 professionals—among them publishers and agents, booksellers and librarians, authors invited by their local publishers, and of course the press).

Until the fair's expansion last year, Frankfurt management regularly turned away would-be exhibitors, just as the hotels in this year-round trade fair city have long proved inadequate to accommodate the tens of thousands of professional visitors who crowd in from all parts of the world. Among specialized shows only the Bologna Children's Book Fair (held this year in April) can claim similar universality. And note the peculiarity that neither Frankfurt nor Bologna advertises itself as an "international" book fair, while an increasing number of strictly domestic bookselling and promotional events make use of the I-word to increase public interest (even when they are international only because some of the books on display are imported).

Among the most important national book fairs—often called "salons"—are those in Paris, São Paulo, Turin, and Geneva, even Casablanca and Ramallah (where a first Palestine International Book Fair was held last November). Country-wide book weeks featuring indoor or outdoor street fairs take place in such widely separated areas as Spain, the Netherlands, and Israel. There may be urgent reasons for attending the Beijing International Book Fair (a sixth edition took place last summer), especially if one is selling finished books into China, or even the Moscow International Book Fair (for the same purpose). But East-West negotiations remain marginal in both places, and third-country trade (say negotiations in China between a Dutch and a French participant) most unlikely. Fairs in Spain, Britain, Japan, and major East European capitals are billed as international and some really are, but with few exceptions they could disappear from the calendar without undue pain. Hence Frankfurt. "Everybody goes there because... everybody goes there," is what they say; it's the best definition of a marketplace one can expect to hear.

The crowd at Frankfurt last fall was certainly encouraged by the health of the international book trade (which is not to say the health of each and every participating nation's trade). The host country could point to a stable business climate despite a slowing national economy: Germany's book market rose 2.7 percent in 1995, while overall retail business declined 1 percent. With a phenomenal 720,000 titles in print, German publishers were responsible for 74,000 new titles that year, and that despite serious reductions in library expenditures (down an estimated 7.5 percent in the former West Germany, 13 percent in the former East). Germans will tell you that their chief asset is a firm no-discount retail tradition, although the Germans also concede that the United States leads in market growth and the United States is considered by many European traders the worst example of price anarchy.

Seen from Frankfurt, the United Kingdom is the sick man of Europe. Germans sometimes attribute this to the collapse of Britain's publisher/bookseller fixed-price agreement, although in fact British publishing has been in recession for some time and abolishing a rigid price-fixing system was designed to help the trade out of its slump. Spain, Italy, and France are touch and go, Norway is bursting with oil money, and Finland is mired in what is now felt to be permanent depression because of the loss of traditional trading with its Russian neighbor.

Slumps Enliven Fair Business

But bad business at home never seems to trouble the trading at book fairs, certainly not at Frankfurt. On the contrary, the remedy for publishers in slow economies is to look even harder for best-selling fiction and non-fiction likely to help them out of the slump; invariably, the potential blockbusters come from Anglo-American authors (via their agents and publishers). In this way a slowdown in the book trade in a country or a region can lead to ever-higher bidding for the big Frankfurt books. The phenomenon has been observed in such countries as Argentina and Brazil at their worst moments, and in Sweden and elsewhere among Nordic states. At Frankfurt last autumn, prices obtained from countries with flat economies such as France were higher than ever, each bidder obviously hoping that the next commercial novel down the pike will make its fortune. Such thinking does keep Frankfurt lively, guarantees its survival, and probably dooms it to further growth.

In any case the biggest national contingent after Germany last year was (once again) Britain, sick man of Europe or not, with 871 imprints, up from 861 the previous year. The United States was runner-up with 819 companies—the largest American representation ever—calling for this comment by Frankfurt fair director Peter Weidhaas: "I am particularly pleased with the fact that U.S. participation has gone up consistently in the past five years."

Note that Japan, with a chronically ailing book trade, was present at the fair with 64 publishers representing all the trade leaders, and was paying higher advances for more rights from Western sources than ever before.

Many Fairs in One

Once again, Frankfurt turned out to be many fairs in one. If it is best known as a rights market—rallying-point for agents and publishers—and a book sales and promotion market for the German domestic trade, an export promotion market for countries like the United States, Britain, and Spain using world languages, it is also a remainder market and a showcase for printers and other book services.

This year two floors of one of the central pavilions were devoted to electronic media, and while exhibits there seemed oriented to the German retail trade and consumers, they did allow visitors both domestic and foreign an overview of the state of the art in which games—for once—played a secondary role. To the 488 exhibitors in the electronic publishing hall one could add over twice that many elsewhere at the fair, alongside or within the booths of traditional book houses, showing electronic projects or offering electronic rights. Thanks to these figures, Frankfurt's organizers were calling their event the world's number-one fair for electronic publishing. The unmentioned number-two fair was Milia, the annual winter new-media fair in Cannes, France; actually Milia remains the number-one fair for electronic rights. Frankfurt, of course, had its own Web site and distributed its catalog and "who's who" of the fair on a CD-ROM that also contained a "Rights-on-ROM" listing of titles available from 550 exhibitors.

Because major importing booksellers and librarians from every reading nation use the fair, the organizers sponsor an International Booksellers and Librarians Center, a welcome corner (actually not so small a corner) for visitors far from home without booths to call their own, featuring meeting rooms, chairs and tables, locker facilities, a snack bar, and advisory services. For the first time there was also a Library Forum, designed to allow German and foreign firms to show new products.

The fair has been particularly generous in its pro bono activities, offering stands and technical assistance to Third-World publishers back in the days when being to Frankfurt symbolized a step into the real world. Later it opened its doors—also with subsidized travel and booths—to the newly independent nations of the ex-Soviet bloc. The opening took the form of an East-West "meeting point," with panels and lectures designed both to familiarize East and Central European book traders with First-World publishing for profit and to provoke sympathy and support for the newcomers. Last fall the fair deemed the East Europeans ripe for going it alone, and indeed one found a critical mass of active traders present, including 56 exhibitors from Russia, 21 from Poland, 20 from Hungary, and 18 each from the Czech Republic and Romania. Among the most active participants—selling as well as buying rights and projects—was Andrzej

Chrzanowski, director of Poland's number-one book producer, educational publisher WSiP, who described the launching of a new data base and books in print developed by the Polish publishing community with the assistance of the Börsenverein (Germany's umbrella group for publishers, booksellers, and distributors).

In 1995 Frankfurt had hosted its first South-North Meeting Point, designed to repeat the experience of the East-West project; this time the meeting area was the centerpiece of a sector showing 183 exhibitors from Asia (not including Japan), 70 from Latin America, and 44 from Africa.

More Than Business

Alongside the main events at every Frankfurt Fair, one can count on finding conferences, seminars, round-table meetings, even general assemblies of major international groups concerned with the business of books (since one can be sure that their chief executives and key personnel are all in town). Each year, on the Tuesday afternoon immediately preceding the official opening, fair management—in collaboration with the Association of American Publishers—sponsors an international rights seminar. This time the subject was books-into-film, with contributions from both Hollywood agents and scouts and their European counterparts.

The International Publishers Association (IPA), whose membership consists of the national publishing associations of every significant book-producing nation, once again staged meetings of its executive bodies and panels (notably on electronic publishing, freedom to publish, and copyright). Two of the panels were open to the public, the IPA Copyright Forum (whose subject was "Netlaw: A Law for Cyberspace") and an Electronic Publishing Workshop focusing on marketing and distribution. Unlike IPA, the International Association of Scientific, Technical and Medical Publishers (STM) draws its membership directly from the principal companies in the field, and its annual meetings are attended by the owners and publishers of the world's leading academic, scientific, and professional groups. This year STM's retiring chairman, John F. Dill of Mosby, turned the floor over to incoming chairman Dietrich Gotze of Germany's scientific Springer-Verlag. Before leaving the rostrum Dill did a final good deed in giving STM's first annual Service Award to another retiree, Nicholas Veliotes, outgoing president of the Association of American Publishers.

Each year Frankfurt comes with a focal theme, designed to add meaning to the fair to the German public (admitted on weekends) and the non-professional press. This year the spotlight fell on "Ireland and its Diaspora," a theme designed to melt the hearts of even hardened professionals, with Ireland's president Mary Robinson walking about the fair, Irish Nobel poet Seamus Heaney reading and talking, the books of contemporary greats such as Yeats, Joyce, and Beckett on view, even Irish music floating through the halls and Guinness flowing in strategically located makeshift pubs. Twenty-six Irish publishers took stands.

Trends and Issues in Library and Information Services in Canada, 1996

Ken Haycock
David Chow
School of Library, Archival and Information Studies
The University of British Columbia
Vancouver, British Columbia

The key trends and issues affecting library and information services in Canada in 1996 remain the same as those mentioned in previous annual reports: challenges and opportunities presented by information technology; information access and rights; increased demands during periods of budget restraint; partnerships with other libraries, corporations and government; lobbying for tax and copyright exemptions for libraries; and the need for improved marketing and advocacy.

Information Technology

The National Library of Canada (NLC) continues to provide leadership in establishing standards. NLC held a number of sessions on Z39.50, the American standard for database searching and information retrieval. The sessions focused on multiple database searching across different networks using the search command interface of the client. The Future of Communication Formats conference held at NLC examined standards for data transfer and structuring to determine whether national standards need to be established. NLC also completed four digitization projects: the Index to Royal Commissions and special committee reports; the Canadian Music Periodical Index; The North: Landscape of the Imagination, which presents the works of artists and authors; and the Glenn Gould Website and Virtual Exhibition featuring the renowned pianist.

Technology continues to pose challenges as information becomes widespread and commercial. The Access '96: Innovative Technology in Libraries Conference was the fourth in a series held by Canadian academic libraries to address issues related to electronic publishing, the Web, and newer and emerging technologies. Specific topics included network access tools, digital document authentication and security, and electronic payment.

The Council of Prairie and Pacific University Libraries (COPPUL) offers the Current Contents service to its member libraries through the Internet, listing the tables of contents and bibliographic data of current issues of 7,000 scholarly periodicals and the names of member institutions that carry the journals. Requests can be made for interlibrary loan or document delivery. The next phase will see improved document delivery, joint acquisitions, full-text databases, and use of Z39.50 compliant software to link all member libraries.

Blackwell's launched a pilot project to test the feasibility of accessing electronic journals on the Web. Simon Fraser University and the University of Western Ontario are among 12 North American universities assisting in the design of the interface and determining access points.

The Canadian Association of Law Libraries/Association Canadienne des Bibliothèques de Droit has published a position paper outlining its concerns about publication of legal information in CD-ROM format, particularly pricing, production, and management issues.

Several administrative functions have been automated by various libraries this year: catalogs accessible through the Web; simple circulation tasks (renew, pay fines, place holds, check the status of a book, make changes to addresses and phone numbers); self-service check-out; automatic telephone systems that inform users that a book on hold is ready to be picked up. Other innovations include the University of British Columbia's Crane Resource Center making accessible recordings combining spoken text and audio recordings for blind students through computers using the DIGIDESIGN Session 8 System and the North York (Ontario) Public Library's Zoomtext Plus, software that enlarges text displayed on a computer screen (magnification of up to eight times is possible). The Nepean (Ontario) Public Library has NOLAView and NOLAVoice to help visually handicapped users and hard-of-hearing/deaf users: NOLAView can magnify print on a screen and change the background color of the screen, and offers three different screen views; NOLAVoice uses synthetic speech output of information displayed on the screen; by using keystrokes, users control the volume and speed of the reading voice, select either a male or female voice, and choose the type and amount of information.

Information Access and Rights

SchoolNet is a cooperative project of government, academia, and industry to link all private, public, and First Nations schools to the Internet. Stentor, the alliance of Canada's major telephone companies, intends to provide high-speed, affordable access during 1997 (if achieved, Canada will be the first country in the world to accomplish this). Stentor will also offer affordable rates to rural areas and financial assistance to libraries, museums, colleges, universities, and cultural institutions that wish to digitize their collections. LibraryNet was established to connect all public libraries to the Internet and provide an extended range of services by the year 2000. Developed as an offshoot of SchoolNet (whose name and focus was thought to limit library participation), LibraryNet's principal goal is to increase the skills of the general public in order to provide access to government services and information and to promote economic and community development.

Business is also becoming involved in helping libraries gain access to the Internet: Microsoft Canada launched its "Libraries On-line!" program to help establish computer centers in libraries by donating funds, software, and training in order to promote computer literacy for youth in particular. Total donations of $4.5 million have been given to libraries in Vancouver, Toronto, and Ottawa.

Industry Canada sponsored the Community Access Program, which provides matching funds of up to $30,000 to rural communities wishing to establish an Internet connection. The aim is to enable libraries to provide information to help create employment and promote economic development.

The Richmond (British Columbia) Public Library provides Internet access and free basic training on how to use it. In the future there will be fee-based services for users interested in learning about more sophisticated, narrow-focus searching. The Richmond librarians' expertise as information leaders brought recognition from their city council and chamber of commerce.

In spite of these successes, several issues remain. Access to government information is becoming more difficult as governments provide some information solely in electronic format, making it inaccessible to many. Government is increasingly requiring that information be provided only on full cost recovery for distribution and production. Further, the telecommunications companies whose telephone lines, ISDN cables, and satellites over which the information travels are applying for or have received permission to increase local telephone charges.

The federal government's Depository Services Program, a partnership between government and libraries to make government information available to the public, is looking at a new model that will change full depositories to resource centers, and the Canadian Library Association (CLA) has lobbied to ensure equitable access across the country, urban and rural, and to ensure that government departments and sources are accountable for distribution.

CLA has also been lobbying the Canadian Radio and Telecommunications Commission to reverse its decision to allow Stentor the right to increase local telephone rates without a corresponding decrease in monthly rates for long distance. CLA fears that those unable to afford these increases will be unable to access digital information sources over telephone lines. Furthermore, CLA opposes any attempt to charge telecommunications users by the minute, or by the byte as some commercial service providers propose. To ensure that communities in general have equitable access to information, CLA advocates that broadband, commercial-interest-free channels be established and administered by a not-for-profit community organization. There is also opposition to Industry Canada's plans to privatize CA*net, the Internet network of Canada, which is presently operated by a consortium of universities.

The Don't Tax Reading Coalition continues its fight to have books, magazines, and newspapers exempted from the Goods and Services Tax (GST). In Atlantic Canada, the provinces' agreement to harmonize their provincial taxes with the federal GST has meant that these materials would now be subject to a provincial tax as well, but there appears to be a good chance of reversing this in some provinces.

The British Columbia Supreme Court reached a decision in the court case initiated by Little Sister's, a bookstore that specializes in gay and lesbian materials, against Canada Customs. The court ruled that the way in which Canada Customs officials administer regulations covering obscene materials is in violation of the Charter of Rights and Freedom, but did not rule that the sections of the Customs Act are unconstitutional. The case is being appealed.

Library Advocacy Now! began to train librarians and trustees to be advocacy leaders who will, in turn, train others. The program concentrates on an understanding of the political environment in which libraries operate and effective strategies to promote and maintain support.

Intellectual Property

CLA and the Canadian Association of Research Libraries appeared at hearings to discuss the Act to Amend the Copyright Act, the proposed "phase two" amendments to deal with exemptions for educational, research, private study, teaching, and information dissemination purposes. Libraries support the sections of the bill that allow them to make single copies of works for collection management purposes and for interlibrary loan, and that grant them absolution of responsibility for customers' use of self-service photocopy machines. Public libraries are negotiating with CANCOPY, a national collective of copyright holders, to compensate creators for photocopying done outside the proposed amendments in Bill C-32.

The Internet continues to pose problems concerning protection of intellectual content for creators/producers who mount information on Websites: How can they be compensated when users download or e-mail documents to themselves? How do you compensate them directly if you do so? Will people have to subscribe to certain sites in order to view documents of interest to them?

Provincial Outlook

The federal government "off-loads" programs to the provinces without funding and the provinces, in turn, off-load programs to the municipalities, and libraries get caught in the financial squeeze.

Cuts in British Columbia will result in a decrease in funding for libraries, and thus reduced hours and services. The British Columbia Electronic Highway Accord calls for significant improvements to the telecommunications structure, an increase in rural Internet providers, and the establishment of a provincial learning network linking libraries, museums, universities, colleges, and schools, but an advisory council to receive the input of interested parties has yet to be established. The government will fund the development of the infrastructure, but institutions will have to fund their own connections to the network. Some small rural libraries were automated and $500,000 was set aside to train librarians in Internet access and provision, but the Vancouver FreeNet must become self-sustaining because the provincial government will not continue to finance it.

The Inuvik (Northwest Territories) Centennial Library opened with connections to the Internet, government library services, and Aurora College. The Yukon Libraries Cooperative Catalogue was inaugurated in CD-ROM format, enabling shared resources, improved interlibrary loan, and a coordinated acquisitions policy.

Alberta hopes to connect public libraries electronically over the next three years. Libraries ASAP (Alberta Strategic Alliance for Planning) received financial support, and a CD-ROM union catalog of regional libraries was released. The provincial government also announced that it will increase local authority for library boards and distribute funding through boards, except for Edmonton and Calgary; formulas for grants will be developed. The Calgary Public Library launched Business adVenture and fee-based services (faxing, information searching, document delivery, and online searching), and advertised and held seminars promoting these services.

In Saskatchewan, increasing numbers of libraries are joining the Saskatchewan Union Catalogue, which is accessible through the Web. However, rural libraries and small organizations are joining in smaller numbers, in part due to telephone rates and hardware, software, and staff requirements. SaskTel, in conjunction with Internet service provider Sympatico, has introduced a service that does not discriminate in pricing between urban and rural telephone rates. The province will undertake a review of regional libraries to determine what library services and needs will be in the future, and there is a new Saskatchewan Public Libraries Act. There have been a number of closures of special libraries.

Manitoba is continuing its program to automate the catalogs and circulation systems of rural public libraries. The Manitoba Public Libraries Information Network (MAPLIN) is a province-wide, integrated, automated library system. Its Manitoba Union Catalogue contains records from public libraries in rural and northern Manitoba, the Public Library Services central collection, and the Legislative Library. As more libraries automate they will be expected to join in order to gain the benefits of MAPLIN's databases and resources. Internet provision in rural public libraries is increasing, thanks in part to Industry Canada's funding of Blue Sky Community Networks, which provides access through freenets. Municipalities continue to establish libraries, either independently or as part of existing systems, increasing the number of library systems to 49, an increase of ten in four years.

Ontario is suffering devastating cutbacks in services; some libraries have even closed. The province is also considering making libraries entirely a municipal responsibility. The Ontario Library Trustees Association has launched an advocacy program to demonstrate that the government should not abdicate its leadership responsibilities. Northern Ontario, where libraries cover a wide geographic area, has been particularly hard hit. The Savings and Restructuring Act gives municipalities and local boards the right to impose fees or charges for non-core services, prompting a review of what is a core service and whether province-wide guidelines are possible.

A Nova Scotia study examined how the public could access the holdings of all libraries in the province and recommended use of the Z39.50 standard in conjunction with the Web. The EdNet Wide Area Network was launched, linking 135 schools, museums, and regional libraries; the network will be phased in over the next few years. School districts have amalgamated into fewer, larger ones resulting in teacher-librarians now serving several schools.

The New Brunswick Library Service (NBLS) is undergoing a provincial government review with respect to quality of service. The government also created a single New Brunswick Public Libraries Board to replace five regional boards. The new board includes representatives of public, university, and college libraries as well as provincial government. Despite the decrease in funding, library closures and increased rural taxation have been ruled out as options, but fees to rent recreational videos and CDs are being considered. Under a new revenue scheme donations from the public of up to $100,000 will be matched by the provincial government. The Canada-New Brunswick Infrastructure Program granted $1.3 million to connect all provincial libraries to the provincial catalog. NBLS monitors the Literacy Program for Kids in which university students are working one-on-one with children at 25 public libraries.

Prince Edward Island's access-to-information legislation failed second reading, leaving PEI the only province without such a bill. PEI also does not require that government documents be deposited in public libraries. There are no freenets in the province, but three library sites now have access to the Internet.

In Newfoundland, a project is under way to connect libraries to the Internet, and 19 have been connected so far. In St. John's and its environs, two libraries were closed due to a 17 percent decrease in the public library system's budget. Amalgamations and combining of services have occurred as well. Memorial University of Newfoundland has also had its budget reduced, by 7 percent, due to a decrease in the amount of money granted by the province.

Public, Academic, Special, and School Libraries

Public Libraries

There is universal recognition that the public library is a vital community resource and an integral element of the total education process, but this does not translate into dollars for service. Budget cutbacks continue to occur across the country: the Metro Toronto Reference Library, for example, laid off 17 librarians, reduced operating hours, and merged some divisions. A further erosion of almost $4 million is expected.

Continuing decreases in funding mean that new sources of revenue must be found. The Edmonton Public Library renamed its main branch after a donor, and like the Vancouver Public Library's acceptance of corporate donations for library-card advertising and the Toronto Public Library's acceptance of corporate funds for summer reading programs, the Edmonton action generated considerable controversy. CLA has now created a Task Force on Corporate Sponsorship of Libraries. Edmonton also hopes to raise the $4 million needed to open two new branch libraries. Further revenue-raising activities include levying a "registration" fee for new library cards and operating an on-site espresso bar.

The Richmond (British Columbia) Public Library benefited from donation of almost 6,000 Chinese-language books for its large Chinese Canadian population. Another Chinese Canadian donated $10,000 after reading about the book donations. The Regina Public Library inaugurated the Great Plains Freenet by providing specially designated terminals as a result of a federal-provincial infrastructure program. And the Canadian Association of Public Libraries persuaded Stentor to include public libraries in its definition of educational institutions; this allows public libraries to be charged a preferential rate for telecommunications services.

The role of the public library trustee is becoming more complex and demanding. More trustee organizations are providing professional development programs and resources to meet new challenges, and are struggling to ensure that government understands their unique role and importance to quality services.

Academic Libraries

As is the case for public libraries, there is less money overall for higher education (Canadian universities are public institutions with government restrictions on enrollment and tuition fees), and academic libraries are being hit particularly hard. Some institutions in Nova Scotia have been closed down entirely, some have merged, some have dropped programs or departments available elsewhere in the province. To help cope with all the changes, Halifax University Services Limited was formed by institutions in the Halifax area to reduce expenditures in a wide range of services, including library services. Community college libraries, particularly those with technical programs, may have received better funding because governments appear to believe that specific job-related skills are more useful than a liberal arts education.

The rush to acquire access to digital resources continues to generate controversy, particularly when funded from staff positions. With increased emphasis on electronic information retrieval, university librarians are offering more training sessions on how to conduct searches and use various kinds of electronic equipment. The British Columbia government gave the University of British Columbia a grant equivalent to half the sum needed to purchase 35 workstations for the new Walter C. Koerner Library's Teaching and Learning Center.

In British Columbia, the establishment of university colleges has meant that former college libraries have had to provide access to resources more appropriate for research. Improved resource sharing with the province's three universities has been achieved in part through the Electronic Library Network (ELN), which links all universities, university-colleges, and colleges in the province. ELN offers a shared serials database, media database, and union catalog of the holdings of colleges and public libraries. ELN's On-line Journal Access service combines database searching and document delivery.

The Tri-University Library Consortium (composed of the Universities of Guelph, Waterloo, and Wilfrid Laurier) has merged services and resources so that the three operate seamlessly as if one single large library. COPPUL extended reciprocal borrowing and interlibrary loan services to all faculty, staff, and students of member institutions in the west. The University of Ottawa and ISM Library Information Services have established a pilot project in which ISM will provide processed bibliographic records and resources to the university's libraries. The Faculty of Information Studies at the University of Toronto and ISM are jointly creating a shared cataloging database of Internet resources. The two will create and maintain MARC records of the Internet resources and investigate methods to maintain uniform resource locators (URLs).

The Royal Bank of Canada donated $250,000 to Dalhousie University Libraries to improve library services through technology. The money will be put toward the Dalhousie Desktop Library (DDELI) project, which mounts 500 journals online, accessible from every connected terminal in the library system. The project is to be complete by 2001.

Special Libraries and Information Centers

Restructuring and government downsizing continue to affect special librarians adversely. The Canadian Association of Special Libraries and Information Services annual conference highlighted current issues and concerns: advocacy, the value of corporate libraries, and entrepreneurship in order to promote the importance of special libraries in corporations and how they contribute to economic development and growth. As more public libraries add profit centers serving local business, tensions are expected to result between public librarians and information specialists in the corporate sector.

The National Research Council's Canada Institute for Scientific and Technical Information (CISTI) and the Canadian Agriculture Library have reached agreement to share technology, business services, and an integrated document delivery service and to allow each organization's users to access the other's resources. CISTI and the Conference des Recteurs et des Principaux des Universités du Québec have established a joint fee-based document delivery service.

School Library Resource Centers

As in 1995, nowhere is the "interface" of "Information Superhighway" hype and library services more evident than in schools. The result is an infusion of information technology, often divorced from the school's library resource center and teacher-librarian, and an increased lack of understanding of the role of the teacher-librarian on the part of educational decision-makers and school board members. Schools are now linking all classrooms to the school resource center in one large local area network (LAN) so that students can access information from servers and CD-ROM towers without leaving the classroom. Some schools are connected to wide area networks (WANs), which cover entire school districts.

Teacher-librarians, typically not protected by teacher union contracts, are being replaced by library technicians at both the school and district level; this represents a trend that should be closely monitored. In Ontario, the Ministry of Education released a report, "Information Literacy and Equitable Access: A Framework for Change," to outline changing roles and responsibilities of teacher-librarians and to encourage arrangements with public libraries, post-secondary institutions, and others to share resources.

The National Library of Canada conducted a survey of teacher-librarians, library technicians, and others and found that the most critical issues were budgets, staffing, and new technologies.

Education

Canadian schools of library and information studies continue to investigate distance education opportunities. Unlike their American counterparts, there is currently little incentive for them to attract students beyond the quotas set for them; nevertheless, it seems likely that the first graduate courses through distance education will be available in the new year. Most schools now have the infrastructure in place.

The University of Western Ontario Graduate School of Library and Information Science, Graduate School of Journalism, and parts of the Faculty of Part-time and Continuing Education will amalgamate to form the new Faculty of Communications and Open Learning. The new faculty emphasizes the relationship between information and technology. McGill University's Graduate School of Library and Information Studies joined the Faculty of Education, emphasizing the closer relationship among technology, learning, and information in both formal and informal education and social issues related to access.

Emerging Trends

Several trends seem evident and are certainly not unique to Canada. Previous reports noted partnerships with other institutions to share resources, partnerships with business and industry to support and exploit those resources, partnerships with government to make libraries the primary information access point for citizens, and partnerships with colleagues and citizens to advocate for libraries and librarians. There are again several examples of these. Newer challenges centered around electronic resources, funding for acquisition and access, adequate Canadian content, and equitable access, all in the context of decreasing government funding. There is increased evidence for each of these this year. Libraries are also becoming more like other businesses in the sense that they have to market and increasingly fund themselves.

Special Reports

Copyright 1996: Fleshing Out the Issues

Robert L. Oakley
Director, Law Library, and Professor of Law,
Georgetown University Law Center

Throughout 1996 there was a great deal of discussion—and remarkably little progress—on copyright issues, especially as they pertain to information created, published, or used in the electronic environment. The way in which these issues are resolved will have a direct effect on the ability of libraries and other educational institutions to fulfill their missions in the future. Indeed, the way in which these issues are resolved could, to some extent, determine whether libraries will even continue to exist in the future.

How will the libraries of the future obtain the information they need, for example, and what will they be able to do with it once they have access to it? Will libraries be able to lend an electronic copy of a work, as they would a print work today? Will they be able to make a copy of it for purposes of preservation? Or for a user? When? Under what constraints? Will they be able to make such a work available by means of an electronic network? To whom and where? Will they engage in interlibrary sharing of print works by electronic means, or of electronic works at all? Will they be able to preserve existing print works in digital form? What are the implications for libraries of information obtained through the World Wide Web? Do libraries commit an act of infringement merely by pointing to a site on the Web? Does the common practice of caching—storing the contents of a page in local memory—create any problems? Will libraries become obsolete—museums of an older print technology—while contemporary users get the latest information by going directly to electronic information providers for a fee? All these questions and more are part of the discussions now under way on copyright.

Despite the amount and intensity of the discussion, by the end of the year remarkably little consensus had been achieved. For all practical purposes, the discussions ended when Congress adjourned for the November elections. But in reality the discussion then just shifted from national level policy discussions in Washington, D.C., to international treaty discussions in Geneva, Switzerland, where the World Intellectual Property Organization (WIPO) was debating many of the same questions. Although many in the United States feared an end run at WIPO that would preclude a meaningful congressional debate on the issues, the WIPO delegates did leave room for member countries to create or maintain the kind of balance for libraries and information users that has long been an essential part of U.S. law. As a result, it is clear that virtually all of the same issues will be back in 1997 as part of the debates of the 105th Congress.

Most people do not expect a swift resolution to the issues. The debate so far has shown, if nothing else, the complexity of the problem. Moreover, most of the stakeholders are reluctant to make any concessions while the use of the network and other new technologies is still evolving. Publishers are anxious to protect any market, actual or potential, that might be available to them in the future. At the same time, libraries want to preserve their role as neutral information providers that level the playing field among users by avoiding fees for the use of information.

Term Extension

In 1995 a bill was introduced in Congress[1] to extend the term of copyright by 20 years.[2] For new works, such a change would result in a term of the life of the author plus 70 years. For many older works not yet in the public domain, the new maximum would be 95 years, and works published in the 1920s and 1930s would not come into the public domain for an additional 20 years. In effect, this proposal would create a 20-year moratorium on any new works entering the public domain.

The stated reason behind term extension was "international harmonization." A few European countries had begun to migrate to the longer term, and it was argued that without a similarly longer term in the United States, our authors would be disadvantaged in some overseas markets. Perhaps more important for U.S. political purposes was the fact that the film industry and the music industry are both strong supporters of the extension because without it some valuable properties from the 1920s will soon enter the public domain. With such powerful industries behind the proposal, it seemed clear at the outset that the bill would ultimately succeed.

From the library perspective, the longer term presents a number of problems. In general, the extension could interfere with a library's efforts to serve its clients, even when a work was old and out of print, and when the copying did not interfere with any identifiable market. Moreover, from the library perspective, the issue is closely linked to the preservation problem. Because of the uncertainties of copyright, many librarians working to preserve their collections choose to follow the secure path of preserving only those materials that are already in the public domain, i.e., published before 1922. A 20-year moratorium on new works entering the public domain would represent a 20-year setback to the library preservation effort.

With these issues in mind the library community sought an exemption from the extension "provided that such use is not undertaken for the purposes of direct or indirect commercial advantage to such library . . . and provided further that the copyright owner has not demonstrated that such use had had a material adverse effect upon the value of the copyrighted work."[3]

Extensive discussions were held throughout 1996 under the direction of the Copyright Office on term extension generally, and on the library proposal in particular. Copyright owners were concerned about the open-ended nature of the potential uses in the library proposal, and they also wanted stronger language to protect their markets. By the end of the Congress, compromise language was submitted by the Register of Copyrights to the Senate Committee on the Judiciary:

> For purposes of this section, during the last 20 years of any term of copyright of a published work, a library or archives may preserve, reproduce, distribute, display or perform in facsimile or digital form a copy or phono record of such work, or portions thereof, for purposes of scholarship or research if such library or archives has first determined on the basis of a reasonable investigation that the work: (1) is not subject to normal commercial exploitation, or (2) cannot be obtained at a reasonable price.

This language seemed to many to be a workable compromise. At the very end of the session, however, one of the owners' representatives stated that "normal commercial exploitation" would include works made available through a licensing program, whether or not the licensing agency actually had such works available. Such a provision seemed to the library community to make the whole proposal a nullity because anything could then be included on a list of works available by license and thereby negate the whole purpose of the proposal. The discussions foundered at the end on this issue. The 105th Congress is likely to pick up the proposal as it stands now and attempt to move it forward in 1997. The library community will almost certainly seek language to clarify the meaning of "normal commercial exploitation."

Copyright and the National Information Infrastructure

Following the release of the White Paper on Copyright and the National Information Infrastructure,[4] the National Information Infrastructure Copyright Protection Act[5] was introduced to implement the recommendations. The goals and basic substance of all of the proposed changes to the act were supported by the Register of Copyrights in a statement to the House Subcommittee on Courts and Intellectual Property on November 15, 1995.

The library community had some concerns with the proposal, however, and submitted a statement to the House Committee on February 8, 1996.[6] In that statement, the five major library associations argued that the bill would shift the historic balance in the copyright act to favor copyright owners' desires over the needs of consumers and users of information. If enacted, they said, the bill would have significant negative consequences for the future of education, research, and scholarship in the United States because it gave a high level of control over electronic information to copyright proprietors, without similarly protecting and advancing the needs of information users. The library groups cited a concern about the unintended consequences of the proposal on distance learning, on the ability of a purchaser (such as a library) to share an electronic work as they have always been able to share print works, and on privacy.

The library groups noted that the bill gave copyright owners what could be argued was an expansion of their rights through the addition of "transmission" to their enumerated rights. As a result of that change, the library groups proposed a parallel amendment to the fair use section to ensure that the goal of preserving and protecting fair use would carry forward into the electronic environment.[7]

The major library organizations were also charter members of the Digital Future Coalition (DFC), an activist organization of technology and telecommunications corporations, educators, school boards, libraries, and others that came together following the introduction of the NII bill to express their serious reservations about the proposals. Again stressing the importance of balance in the copyright law, the coalition testified before the Senate Committee on the Judiciary on May 7, 1996,[8] presenting a package of concerns and counterproposals to improve the bill overall, while recognizing the need for a "digital update" to the Copyright Act:

Browsing—DFC felt that the proposed legislation could have a serious negative impact on the ability of users to surf the Internet. In order to view such information, a temporary copy is made in the computer's Random Access Memory (RAM). If such temporary copies were considered to be "copies" for purposes of determining copyright infringement, DFC argued that the right and opportunity to browse information online would be seriously undermined or, at some point soon, precluded. The coalition suggested that the definition section of the act be amended to make clear that RAM and other ephemeral reproductions are not copies within the meaning of the statute.

Fair Use—The coalition endorsed the library community's proposal for an update to the fair use section of the act. It said that fair use provides the basis for many of the most important day-to-day activities in scholarship and education and that it is no less vital to American industries, which lead the world in technological innovation.

Preservation—DFC also endorsed a library proposal to strengthen the preservation sections of the act. The bill itself had made an effort on behalf of preservation but needed a few modifications to make it work the way libraries need. The proposals made by DFC would permit libraries to make three copies (instead of the one now permitted) for preservation, so long as no more than one of those copies could be used at the same time. They would also have made the preservation sections of the Copyright Act technology-neutral, thus permitting the use of digital technology, rather than limiting preservation to "facsimile form" as the act now provides.

"First Sale"—Under the current law, someone who has a lawful copy of a work may freely transfer possession or ownership of the work without risking liability for copyright infringement. This principle—known as the first sale doctrine—permits the existence of both public lending libraries and video rental stores. The White Paper argued that this doctrine applies only to the transfer of physical copies and does not apply in the electronic environment. DFC argued that someone who had a lawful version of a digital work should be permitted to pass that copy on to another, so long as no additional copies were made or retained in the process. It urged Congress to clarify the issue by making clear that the first sale doctrine applies to digital copies to the same extent—no more or no less—that it applies to physical analog copies.

Distance Education—The coalition pointed out to Congress that the proposed bill would have serious unanticipated negative consequences on the growing movement toward distance education in the United States. The current law accommodates distance education by permitting the performance or display of copyrighted works through a transmission to classroom-like settings. Inadvertently, through a technical drafting problem, the NII bill would have made such transmissions unlawful in the digital environment. DFC proposed a technical amendment to ensure that the proposed clarification of the proprietor's distribution right does not deprive students of the benefits made possible by new technologies. These concerns were well received on Capitol Hill because many states have developed strong distance-learning programs that are especially important to the poor and/or rural areas of their states.

Anti-circumvention—The proposed legislation would have outlawed "any device, product, or component, whose primary purpose or effect is to circumvent any technology used to protect a proprietor's rights." Such language is broad enough to outlaw other technologies that have now become common, including VCRs. It would, in effect, overrule the Supreme Court's holding in the Betamax case, which said that since the VCR was capable of "substantial non-infringing uses" the sale of such devices to the public did not make SONY contributorily liable. DFC did not support the use of black boxes whose sole purpose was to infringe copyright. But they also thought the legislation needed to be drafted far more narrowly in order not to defeat the development of new technologies whose purpose was to help consumers make lawful fair uses of copyrighted material.

Copyright Management Information—The NII bill would have prohibited the public distribution of a work containing false copyright management information. Such a proposal was intended to protect the rights of copyright owners and to ensure that they receive whatever royalty compensation is appropriate from subsequent distributions of their work. Unfortunately, the way the bill was written this provision could create serious problems for both librarians and secondhand booksellers who are both likely to be distributing older works whose copyright management information had changed, but where that fact was unknown. DFC proposed that the distribution of works with false copyright management information would only be actionable if it were done with the intent to infringe copyright.

Online Service Provider Liability—Finally, DFC supported a resolution to the problem of online service provider liability. Any digital update to the Copyright Act passed by Congress had to resolve that problem, it thought. Unfortunately, there was no such provision in this bill, although interested parties were carrying on discussions even as the bill was proceeding through Congress. DFC urged Congress not to deal with the issues piecemeal but rather to wait for a resolution to this issue so the whole package could be passed together.

Conference on Fair Use

The Conference on Fair Use (CONFU) was an outgrowth of the process that led to the White Paper[9] and the NII bill discussed above. In the preliminary hearings that led to the White Paper, the library community and other representatives of information users had stated that if there were to be any changes in the Copyright Act, it was important to maintain the existing balance between the rights of copyright owners and the needs of information users, especially as reflected in the

Fair Use doctrine.[10] The preliminary report of the working group, known as the Green Paper,[11] agreed that the principles of fair use should apply in the electronic environment, but declined to be more specific, preferring instead to convene a conference consisting of copyright owner interests and user interests to discuss fair use issues and, if appropriate and feasible, to develop guidelines on fair use in the digital environment for librarians and educators.

The initial meeting was held on September 21, 1994, and the group continued to meet approximately monthly throughout 1995 and 1996. The participants in these meetings were self-selecting, as the meetings were open to anyone who wanted to attend. The major library organizations were active participants throughout the process, as were the representatives of major copyright owner groups, including the Association of American Publishers, the Author's Guild, BMI, and so forth.

The earliest meetings were essentially brainstorming sessions at which a wide range of potential issues were discussed. From the various issues initially identified, several were selected for further discussion of specific scenarios that could provide examples of potential fair uses in the library and education context. These scenarios included distance learning, multimedia, electronic reserves, copying for the use of the visually impaired, preservation, visual-image archives, interlibrary loan/document delivery, downloading for personal use, and browsing.

Preservation copying was deemed to be important and legitimate, but the group could not agree that it was a fair use. Instead, a separate preservation proposal was drafted for an expansion of the preservation sections already in the act. That proposal was discussed at the CONFU meetings and eventually incorporated into the final White Paper and the NII bill. Similarly, separate legislation was introduced and passed to clarify the rights of the visually impaired.[12] Downloading for personal use was too contentious and was dropped from consideration at an early stage. Browsing was discussed at length, but the group found it difficult to define browsing in the Internet context with sufficient precision to arrive at any conclusions about what might or might not be "fair." It, too, was therefore dropped from further consideration.

Eventually, several working groups agreed to meet and try to negotiate fair use guidelines in some of the specific areas that were left. Under the strong leadership of one of the participants, an effort was made to develop compromise language on Electronic Reserves. Although the resultant proposed guidelines did win the support of at least two library associations and the American Association of University Presses, they did not win the support of enough of the participants to warrant inclusion in the Final Report of the Conference. Interlibrary lending and document delivery were also discussed at length. Eventually the working group agreed that it was premature to draft guidelines for the digital transmission of digital documents, and no conclusions were reached on the other dimensions of the issue.

By the end of 1996 three sets of proposed guidelines emerged from the process. They were each included with a common introduction and circulated for endorsement to members of the library and education community as part of the Interim Report of the Conference to the Commissioner of Patents and Trademarks. The final meeting of CONFU will be in May 1997, at which time it will be possible to tell which of the proposals have received sufficient endorsement to consider them workable. The guidelines circulating for endorsement as of this writing include:

Digital Images

Collections of digital images raise issues different from text collections, and one of the working groups agreed to draft guidelines in consultation with art librarians, photographers, and others concerned with the conversion of image collections to digital form. The draft provides guidance for the conversion of both newly acquired and existing analog collections, the creation of thumbnail images, and the display and distribution of such images on an institution's network. It also provides guidance on how long such images may be retained and when it is appropriate to seek permission from the copyright owner.

Distance Learning

The Copyright Act already supports distance learning using traditional technologies transmitting into a traditional classroom environment. The distance-learning guidelines extend the existing principles to the digital environment for live interactive classes and for instruction recorded for later transmission over a secure computer network. Under these guidelines, entire works may be transmitted for instructional use and subject to a number of restrictions, but they may not be retained for more than 15 days without the permission of the copyright owner.

Educational Multimedia

The proposed guidelines on educational multimedia were developed under the leadership of the Consortium of College and University Media Centers (CCUMC) outside the regular CONFU process, but were brought to CONFU for endorsement and support. These guidelines permit students to produce educational multimedia projects for a course and also permit educators to produce multimedia teaching tools for their own use. It also sets out time and portion limitations for such projects. Under the guidelines, for example, educators may retain a project for two years, after which they should get permission for further retention. They may also take up to 10 percent of many types of works, but in any event, no more than three minutes of a motion picture, 1,000 words of a text work, or 30 seconds of the music and lyrics of a musical work.

Databases

Late in the 104th Congress, a new bill for the separate protection of databases outside of copyright was introduced. Similar proposals had been under development in Europe for many years, and the European Union issued a directive on database protection[13] in March of 1996. Shortly thereafter, the same ideas were included in H.R. 3531, which was introduced by Rep. Carlos Moorhead (R-Calif.) in the House of Representatives.

Supported by the information industry, H.R. 3531 sought to legislatively overrule the Supreme Court Opinion in *Feist* v. *Rural Telephone Co.* (499 U.S.

340 [1991]). That opinion held that creativity was a bedrock requirement for copyright protection and that there was no such creative element in the white pages of the telephone directory. *Feist* itself had overruled the "sweat of the brow" rationale for copyright under which some courts had allowed protection based on the hard work or investment in compiling the information. Although the *Feist* decision dealt directly only with the white pages, it called into question the copyrightability of every other database, unless some level of creativity could be shown through the "selection, coordination, or arrangement of the information."

For its part, the industry believes that such legislation is critical to its survival. More and more the industry is investing in the compilation of large databases that could easily be pirated. If information industry companies are to make the necessary investments in such databases, they must have some assurance that their databases will not just be stolen by someone else.

Early reviews by the library community suggested a number of concerns. First, the definition of database in the bill is very broad. In fact, it is so broad that many fear the new form of protection would soon dominate, and copyright would soon be the exception rather than the rule. Second, in practical effect the bill would offer protection in perpetuity rather than for a limited term. The term specified in the bill is 25 years. But a new term begins anytime there is any change to the database. As a result, as long as the owner continues to maintain and update the database, protection is continuous, running until 25 years after the last update or change. Third, the bill does not contain a fair use provision or exemptions for libraries similar to the current provisions of the Copyright Act. Fourth, and finally, the library community was concerned that the bill would allow a proprietor to obtain public domain data (such as government information) at the source and eventually become a monopoly provider of material that should remain in the public domain.

The scientific community also had serious reservations about the bill. In a letter, the National Academy of Sciences and the National Academy of Engineering said, "We believe that these changes to the intellectual property law . . . would seriously undermine the ability of researchers and educators to access and use scientific data, and would have a deleterious long-term impact on our nation's research capabilities. Moreover, the proposed changes are broadly antithetical to the principle of full and open exchange of scientific data espoused by the U.S. government and academic science communities, and promoted internationally."

The database bill died at the end of the 104th Congress. However, the issue remains to be taken up again in 1997. After the close of the Congress, the issue was part of the discussions at a meeting of the World Intellectual Property Organization (WIPO). Although it was tabled there, it is scheduled for more international discussion in 1997, and new proposed legislation was also planned for early introduction in the 105th Congress.

WIPO Treaty Discussions

After Congress finished its business for 1996, the focus of attention on copyright issues shifted to Geneva, where a meeting of the World Intellectual Property

Organization was held in December. WIPO is the arm of the United Nations that administers the Berne Convention for the Protection of Literary and Artistic Works, the international treaty governing copyright issues. The purpose of the meeting in Geneva was to consider amending the Berne Convention by means of a new protocol that would then be sent back to the member states for ratification. The protocol proposed in Geneva would have had three parts, one on databases, one on NII, and one on sound recordings. The last of these did not attract much attention from the library community, but the other two did, since they were substantially the same as the proposals on databases and NII that had attracted so much attention in Congress.

Among the concerns of the library community as the conference began were:

- That the database proposal was over-broad and premature
- That the proposal would inhibit browsing on the World Wide Web by limiting RAM copying
- That the proposal would expand, not limit, the exposure of online service providers
- That many of the exceptions or limitations provided in the U.S. Copyright law to assure the rights of information users would be undermined
- That equipment manufacturers would be exposed to liability for the manufacture of devices that had substantial non-infringing uses

Because of these concerns, the library community and other members of the Digital Future Coalition worked hard before and during the Geneva meeting to make sure that the concerns raised during the domestic debate were not foreclosed as a result of an international treaty. By the end of the meeting, public interest groups felt that the results were substantially better than the proposals at the beginning of the meeting and that they did not foreclose any domestic debate.

First, there was so much opposition to the proposed treaty on databases that it was tabled until some time in 1997 when a working group could be convened to explore the issues more fully. Those meetings were subsequently scheduled for March and September 1997.

Second, the new proposed treaties and the record of the conference are the first international agreements that explicitly recognize and embody the fact that "balance" between the need of information proprietors for protection and the need of the public for access to information must be at the core of a successful legal regime for intellectual property. Specifically,

- The Preamble explicitly recognizes "the need to maintain a balance between the rights of authors, and the larger public interest, particularly education, research and access to information..."
- The proposal to treat temporary reproductions in RAM in the same manner as "hard copies" was deleted.
- The Conference Record contains an interpretive "agreed statement" that protects those who provide access to and facilitate use of the Internet from liability for copyright violations by their users.

- The Conference Record affirms that signatories are free to craft exceptions to rights granted to proprietors in the digital environment.
- The provision that would have outlawed VCRs and some other technologies was eliminated in favor of a more general provision to protect against the use of circumvention technologies for unlawful purposes.

These elements of the treaty ensure that the domestic debate will continue in 1997. The treaty will be submitted by the president for ratification early in the year, but it will require implementing legislation before it can be effective. Such legislation will set the stage for the copyright debates of 1997.

Notes

1. H.R. 989, 104th Congress.
2. The length of the period of protection is one of the most basic limits on the rights of creators. It started out as a 14-year renewable term, but over the years it has become longer and longer—first a 28-year renewable term, and then up to 75 years, total. The 75-year term still applies to most older works, but for new works the term is now still longer, at the life of the author plus 50 years.
3. Proposed "Library Exemption" to H.R. 989, September 19, 1995.
4. *Intellectual Property and the National Information Infrastructure, the Report of the Working Group on Intellectual Property Rights*, Washington, D.C., Information Infrastructure Task Force, September 1995. See preliminary analysis of the White Paper by James M. Sabina in the 1996 *Bowker Annual*, p. 248.
5. H.R. 2441 and S. 1284.
6. Statement on behalf of the American Association of Law Libraries, the American Library Association, the Association of Research Libraries, the Medical Library Association, and the Special Libraries Association on H.R. 2441, the NII Copyright Protection Act of 1995, before the Subcommittee on Courts and Intellectual Property of the House Committee on the Judiciary, 104th Congress, 2d Session, February 8, 1996.
7. Id. at 9.
8. Testimony of the Digital Future Coalition on the "NII Copyright Protection Act of 1995," United States Senate Committee on the Judiciary, Presented by Professor Robert L. Oakley, May 7, 1996.
9. See note 4, *supra*.
10. The Fair Use Doctrine is an equitable rule of reason that has been codified in Section 107 of the act. It contains a four-part test that allows users to make "fair use" of a work, so long as the interests of the copyright owner are not unduly affected. The four-part test includes (1) the purpose and character of the use, (2) the nature of the copyrighted work, (3) the amount and substantiality of the portion used in relation to the whole, and (4) the effect of the use on the market for the original work.
11. *Intellectual Property and the National Information Infrastructure, a Preliminary Draft of the Report of the Working Group on Intellectual Property Rights*, Washington, D.C., Information Infrastructure Task Force, July 1994.
12. P.L. 104-197
13. *1996 Official Journal* 77 (March 11, 1996)

Library Networking and Cooperation in 1996

David H. Brunell
Executive Director
Bibliographical Center for Research (BCR)

The dominant issues in U.S. library networking and cooperation in 1996 involved one aspect or another of the continuing move toward the delivery of library services over the Internet. Indeed, the trend toward planning and implementation of Internet-based library services that Nevins and Baughman noted in their 1995 survey of networking, and Segal identified in 1994, became a virtual stampede in 1996.[1] Three issues were of particular concern to networks in 1996:

- How can basic Internet connectivity for libraries be facilitated?
- What are the problems and implications of World Wide Web-based library services?
- How can the cost of delivering library services via the Internet be controlled?

This review will focus on how U.S. library networks are dealing with these key issues. Most of the examples come from the activities of the 16 large state and multistate networks represented in the Alliance of Library Service Networks. These networks and their URLs are listed in Fig. 1.

The alliance networks are only a small fraction of the total number of library consortia working with U.S. libraries. But their services are used by more than 7,000 libraries, and many of their interests can be seen as characteristic of the library networking community as a whole. These large regional networks negotiate group contracts with the major organizations that supply the most widely used library databases. They are best known for their work with OCLC's systems and services, but most of the networks also negotiate group contracts for access to a number of other major database providers such as SilverPlatter, Knight-Ridder, H. W. Wilson, OVID, and Gale. They commonly provide both technical support and training services for these systems as well. In addition, the regional networks are increasingly involved in providing services to and partnering with state library agencies, smaller consortia, library systems, and other ad hoc resource-sharing groups. Thus, the services and activities of the large regional library networks have a significant impact nationally both on the library community's use of database services and on the information industry's delivery of those services.

Libraries Rush to the Net

By the end of 1996 a very high percentage of the academic and public libraries in the United States had some sort of Internet connection. The *1996 National Survey of Public Libraries and the Internet* sponsored by the National Commission on Libraries and Information Sciences (NCLIS) indicated that the number of Internet connections in public libraries had grown more than 113 percent between mid-1994 and early 1996.[2] The study predicted that more than three quarters of public libraries would be connected by March 1997, and that 50 percent would be providing public access to the Internet. However, less than a quarter of the public libraries with Internet access provided Web-based services for patrons by February 1996.

It is interesting to note the results of a November 1996 Benton Foundation study comparing library leaders' vision of future libraries (with both extensive Internet-based digital resources and local print collections) with public opinion and support for this vision.[3] The Benton report concludes that "The public loves libraries but is unclear about whether it wants libraries to reside at the center of the evolving digital revolution—or at the margins."[4] Yet it is clear both from the comments of library directors in the Benton study and from the NCLIS survey that public libraries are moving rapidly ahead with the implementation of full Internet-based services in spite of any doubts that the public may have.

The American Library Association's involvement in converting LSCA (Library Services and Construction Act) legislation to LSTA (Library Services and Technology Act) with its focus on technological innovation, as well as the hard fight to include discounts for libraries in the Telecommunications Act of 1996, are clear indications that the creation of digital libraries and the associated costs are major concerns for the library community. And with good reason; the NCLIS survey documents significant expenses for even basic Internet connectivity. This finding is further verified by the *Library Journal* 1997 Public Library Budget Report showing that public library Internet expenses were averaging more than $100,000 a year.[5]

Regional Networks Offer Internet Connections

In 1996 the regional networks were involved in a number of significant efforts to help the library community with basic Internet connectivity. Several of the networks provided connectivity services of various sorts. SOLINET, for instance, offered such service through an agreement with SURAnet, one of the regional NSF (National Science Foundation) Internet providers.[6] OHIONET, CAPCON, and the Michigan Library Consortium (MLC) all offered full Internet service through their own servers, with more than 600 libraries getting access through these accounts.[7] PALINET provided discounted equipment and software contracts along with installation services for both local area networks and wide area networks.[8] The regional networks also provided a wide variety of basic-training classes, workshops, and seminars on how to use the Internet effectively in libraries, with a total of more than 250 such classes offered during the year.[9]

But establishing basic Internet connectivity is just the first faltering step toward the provision of high-quality Internet-based library services. In the 1996 NCLIS survey, Charles McClure describes a daunting developmental cycle for such services that begins with basic awareness of the Internet and connectivity for library staff and continues with the development of significant, customized information services accessible by remote patrons through the library Web site.[10] He goes on to point out that most public libraries have not gone much beyond making basic information resources available over the Internet, mainly moving patron access from print resources to electronic versions of the same indexes. It is clear, however, that the technological distance between that part of the library community that is beginning to offer Web-based services and the libraries that are just getting Internet connectivity has grown considerably in the last year.

Indeed, one of the key issues facing library networks as well as state library agencies in 1996 was how to support a library community that is becoming much more technologically diverse, with some well-funded institutions providing remote patron access services via elaborate Web sites while hundreds of other libraries have only the most basic dial-up capabilities. State library networking projects as diverse as ACLIN in Colorado, SILO in Iowa, SAILOR in Maryland, and the LOUIS/LLN projects in Louisiana all grappled with the problem of how to offer advanced Web-based services that are still accessible and usable by institutions with only dial-up Internet connectivity and low-end computers.[11] Regional networks faced similar problems and often used similar less-than-perfect solutions: the redundant maintenance of both Web and obsolete gopher-based information resources, and the use of Lynx textual browsing software with all its entertaining idiosyncrasies.

Upgrading Equipment

There was also a continuing effort to use grant funds to help libraries upgrade both equipment and connectivity band-width. For instance, 159 computers were awarded to institutions in Colorado through the ACLIN project, along with multiple awards for Z39.50 software and 56K Internet connectivity.[12] In Indiana, state technology funds were used to put 32 new computers and 11 new Internet connections into libraries, and LSCA funds were used to support the "Internetworked Librarianship" initiative. A cooperative effort between the INCOLSA network and the Indiana State Library, this initiative provided access to the Internet, space on an Internet server, software, and HTML and WWW management training for more than 175 libraries.[13] In Wyoming, 31 libraries received technology grants to upgrade computer equipment and/or telecommunications capacity.[14]

Some 381 public, school, academic, and special libraries in Illinois received grants totaling more than $700,000 for computer equipment for Internet use through the Illinois State Library.[15] And the Utah State Library received a networking grant as part of Microsoft Corporation's "Libraries Online" project, a major philanthropic effort to help 41 rural or disadvantaged library systems across the country. The Utah grant was typical of this project, providing cash, networking software, training, and technical support to connect three public library systems to the statewide Utah Library Network.[16]

Early in the year OCLC offered to replace the older computer workstations that are used in libraries to access OCLC services with more powerful machines at a relatively low cost, and more than 2,000 new computers were purchased and installed in libraries through this project.[17] The 16 regional networks that work with OCLC gave technical and administrative support for the project and offered software training for library staff to help ease the trauma of using WINDOWS operating system software for the first time. Several networks also offered alternative discount schemes for acquiring more powerful PCs for their member libraries that were not OCLC users.[18]

The World Wide Web: Geek Becomes Chic

The rapid development of World Wide Web sites by the library community, along with (finally) a number of useful information services that could be reliably accessed via the Web, meant that 1996 was a particularly chaotic period for library service networks in this country. We should note that this brisk implementation of WWW sites in libraries is being made in the absence of research that would convincingly demonstrate that Web-based resources are actually more effective than either local CD-ROM databases or more traditional online library services.

Indeed, if computer hardware is not upgraded, Web-based information systems will almost always have a slower response time and often have significantly less sophisticated search engines than older library information systems they replace.[19] In addition, the cute graphical interfaces and "hot links" that make Web sites so popular are relatively complex to set up and maintain, and are difficult for those with sight impairments to use.[20] A number of these issues are being investigated in a number of digital library testbed projects jointly funded by the National Science Foundation (NSF), the Defense Advanced Research Projects Agency (DARPA), and the National Aeronautics and Space Administration (NASA).[21]

Multimedia Web-based systems do overcome many of the platform and interoperability problems that have plagued the proprietary information systems long used by the library community. In doing so, they have facilitated the shared use of remote electronic information resources. And their colorful "way cool" interface features add a certain joie de vivre that was missing in traditional library systems. But the question of whether they add enough additional functionality to justify their substantial cost is still unanswered. This question may actually be irrelevant, since the overwhelming popularity of the WWW in the commercial sector makes it unlikely that the library community could locate the resources and support needed to develop an alternative technology. It is likely, however, that we will develop ways to meld the Web to the more sophisticated search engines and other tools that are already used effectively in libraries.

Indeed, as organizations such as OCLC, SilverPlatter, and OVID began to provide reliable WWW-based access to databases that have been widely used by the library community for some time, it could be argued that the Web has become a practical research tool. It is certainly easier for library administrators to justify the very significant costs of developing and maintaining library Web sites if they can show that both library staff and clientele are using the Web to access the same well-organized and indexed databases that the library has traditionally provided.

In this context, David Messerschmitt's discussion of "The Convergence of Telecommunications and Computing: What Are the Implications Today?" was one of the more significant articles of the year for library networkers.[22] His comments furnish a convincing rationale for Internet II funding and development, as well as a handy theoretical framework for the implementation of digital (i.e., Web-based) local library services. Crawford and Gorman's discussion of *Future Libraries: Dreams, Madness, and Reality* also offers a useful (and more balanced) perspective on some of the more significant electronic library issues.[23]

From a library perspective, providing reliable database services based on WWW software is still problematic for several reasons. Web servers are relatively expensive computers, and Web database services still require a significant amount of maintenance. Local libraries can avoid these two problems by having their Web site mounted on a remote server at a network, Internet provider, or state library. But even accessing the graphical Web interface with local computers requires either a full Internet connection or at least the use of either PPP or SLIP software on dial-up workstations. And both PPP and SLIP have interesting quirks that can make the installation process and ongoing maintenance less than a trivial task. In addition, without high-speed modems WWW comes to stand for "World Wide Wait." To make this adventure in technology even more interesting, the most common Web browsers are based on WINDOWS software, which is still not used in many smaller libraries because they do not have powerful enough PCs to work well in this environment (even in the older 3.1 version).

Technical and Support Training

All the regional library networks run relatively large-scale technical support operations, and these sorts of issues have led to a dramatic increase in both the workload and expense associated with these services. In 1996 library networks therefore significantly increased the number of workshops and courses designed to help the library community understand and cope with the issues related to WWW site design, implementation, and use. Web-related seminars became a staple for most network training programs, and a cursory look at training calendars for 1996 reveals that about 180 courses on Web-searching techniques, Web site design, HTML coding, and so forth were offered by the 16 regional networks.

Network Partnerships

Several networks were also engaged in major Web implementation projects. In addition to the INCOLSA "Internetworked Librarianship" program mentioned earlier, SOLINET continued work with the MONTICELLO project. MONTICELLO is an ongoing effort to promote regional access to electronic information, funded by major grants from the Telecommunications and Information Infrastructure Assistance Program (TIIAP) and the National Telecommunications and Information Administration (NTIA).[24] It is important to note that this project, like most other major network Web initiatives, is being undertaken in partnership with other major stakeholders in the information community. In the case of MONTICELLO, SOLINET is partnering with the Southeastern University Research Association (SURA), the Southern Growth Policies Board (SGPG), and OCLC. Similarly, the Bibliographical Center for Research (BCR) worked closely with the Colorado Library Resource Sharing and Information Access Board, the CARL Alliance, the Kansas State Library, and OCLC to provide OCLC's FirstSearch databases to hundreds of libraries in Colorado and Kansas via ACLIN and Kansas's Blue Skyways Web sites.[25]

The BCR multistate FirstSearch initiative is an example of a related trend toward large-scale consortia contracts for electronic information resources. As consortia and state libraries began looking for information resources to mount on

Figure 1: The Alliance of Library Service Networks and Their WWW Site Addresses

AMIGOS Bibliographic Council, Inc.	www.amigos.org/amigos
Bibliographical Center for Research (BCR)	www.bcr.org
CAPCON	www.capcon.net
FEDLINK	lcweb.loc.gov/flicc
ILLINET/OCLC Services	www.library.sos.state.il.us/isl/oclc/oclc.html
Indiana Cooperative Library Services Authority (INCOLSA)	www.palni.edu/incolsa
Michigan Library Consortium (MLC)	www.mlc.lib.mi.us
MINITEX Library Information Network	othello.lib.umn.edu
Missouri Library Network Corporation (MLNC)	www.mlnc.com
Nebraska Library Commission (NEBASE)	www.nlc.state.ne.us/netserv/nebase/nebserv.html
NELINET, Inc.	www.nelinet.net
OHIONET	ohionet.org
PALINET	www.palinet.org
Southeastern Library Network, Inc. (SOLINET)	www.solinet.net
SUNY/OCLC Network	sunyoclc.sysadm.suny.edu
Wisconsin Interlibrary Services (WILS)	milkyway.wils.wisc.edu

their Web sites, it became clear that joint negotiations with database vendors had the potential to significantly reduce the per-site costs. As a result, there has been a proliferation of statewide and multistate contracts for database use that provided access for thousands of smaller libraries for the first time. SOLINET's ongoing work on behalf of the GALILEO and VIVA projects, ILLINET's broad acquisition of reference databases for libraries across the state, and OhioLINK's ground-breaking group contract with Academic Press for access to full-text journals are all examples of the success of this sort of large-scale group negotiation in 1996.[26]

These large-scale group contracts have been so successful that smaller networks and consortia are commonly partnering with the larger networks to leverage both staff resources and buying power.[27] In effect, the use of large group contracts has substantially reduced the per-search price of using online databases for most libraries in the United States. At the same time, the move to Web-based systems that encourage patrons' direct use of databases (i.e., the trend toward "disintermediated" searching) has dramatically increased the overall use of such systems in most libraries.

The very scale of such group contracts substantially increases the complexity of the negotiations with database vendors. And the lack of a single, commonly acceptable model for pricing database services also adds to the difficulty of such agreements. Pricing schemes based on the number of potential users, or the number of users that can simultaneously access the data, or the number of total transactions, were all being used by various database vendors in 1996. These pricing methods are often modified further, depending on the number and type of libraries (e.g., academic, special) involved in a group, and by the type of database being used (e.g., index, full-text). Library demands for archiving prerogatives and interlibrary loan rights also impact the price that vendors now charge for database access.[28]

Conclusion

The regional library service networks have always played a significant role in negotiating group contracts for the database services used by the library community and in training librarians to use those services effectively. These activities continued in 1996, but the nearly universal availability of the Internet, along with the explosive growth of World Wide Web-based information systems, altered the scope and context of network operations significantly. The scale of negotiations for access to electronic information resources grew dramatically as consortia and state library agencies banded together in statewide and multistate partnerships. The content of almost every network workshop had to be altered to account for Internet and Web technology. The networks were involved in efforts to help upgrade Internet connectivity and computers in libraries throughout the country. And the basic terms of existing network agreements with database vendors were altered to fit a flood of new Web-based products and services designed for end-user access.

In 1996 the increasing importance of Web-based library services, along with the related trend toward using large group contracts for gaining access to online information resources, helped emphasize the significance of the role that regional networks play in the library community. The question of whether regional library networks can continue to play this role successfully in a rapidly changing new technological environment has yet to be answered.

Notes

1. Kate Nevins and Steven Baughman, "Library Networking and Cooperation in 1995," *The Bowker Annual Library and Book Trade Almanac*, 41st edition (New Providence, N.J.: R. R. Bowker, 1996) pp. 235–46. JoAn Segal's comments on the beginning of this trend are also interesting. See JoAn S. Segal, "Library Cooperation and Networking, 1994," *The Bowker Annual Library and Book Trade Almanac*, 40th edition (New Providence, N.J.: R. R. Bowker, 1995) pp. 46–65.
2. *1996 National Survey of Public Libraries and the Internet* (Washington, D.C.: National Commission on Libraries and Information Science, 1996). The full results are available on the NCLIS Web site (www.nclis.gov). For a clear, although slightly dated, summary of what university libraries are doing with Internet technology, see the text of Carol Tenopir's lecture on "Electronic Reference in Academic Libraries in the 1990s" in *The Annual Review of OCLC Research—1995* (Dublin, Ohio: Online Computer Library Center, Inc., 1996) pp. 66–68.
3. *Buildings, Books, and Bytes: Libraries and Communities in the Digital Age* (Washington, D.C.: The Benton Foundation, 1996). This is at www.benton.org/Library/Kellogg/buildings.html. See also the commentary on this report by Leigh S. Estabrook, "Polarized Perceptions," *Library Journal*, v.122, n.2 (Feb. 1, 1997) pp. 46–48.
4. *Ibid.* p. 4.
5. St. Lifer, Evan, "Public Library Budgets Brace for Internet Costs," *Library Journal*, v.122, n.1 (January 1997) p. 45.
6. See the SOLINET Web page (www.solinet.net/inetserv/iswhat.htm).
7. See information under "Internet Services" on the CAPCON Web site (www.capcon.net). Information on the MLC Internet services can be found both under the "Internet Services" section of its Web site, and in the *1995–1996 Annual Report*, also mounted on its site.

8. See the PALINET Web site (www.palinet.org) or Palinet News, no. 121 (April 1996) p. 6.
9. This conservative estimate is derived from information in the various network workshop calendars and Web sites. The actual number of classes is probably somewhat higher, since sessions are commonly added at the last minute on popular topics, and Internet training was clearly very popular. There were actually more network classes related to the use of the Internet and Web development than OCLC workshops. This is a dramatic change from three years ago. See David Brunell, "Training and Educational Programs Offered by the Regional Library Service Networks," in *Network Planning Paper 25: Education for Networking—Building New Partnerships* (Washington, D.C.: Library of Congress, 1994) pp. 93–98.
10. See the "Connectivity Versus Services" section of the 1996 *National Survey of Public Libraries and the Internet: Progress and Issues: Final Report.* The full text is available at www.nclis.gov.
11. See the Web sites of these projects; ACLIN (www.aclin.org), VIVA (www.viva.lib.va.us), GALILEO (www.peachnet.edu/galileo/status696.html), SAILOR (www.sailor.lib.md.us), and LOUIS/LLN (www.lsu.edu/ocs/louis).
12. See Web files entitled "About ACLIN" (www.aclin.org/about.html) and "ACLIN Expansion Grants" (www.aclin.org/grants.html).
13. *Library Networking Inside INDIANA*, v.2, n.3 (August/September 1996) pp. 4–5.
14. *The Outrider*, v.28, n.7–8 (July/August 1996) pp. 1–2.
15. See file entitled "Grants to Help Public and School Libraries Buy Computers," on the Illinet Web site (http://www.library.sos.state.il.us/news).
16. *Directions for Utah Libraries*, v.9, n.4 (November/December 1996) p. 2. This newsletter is available on the Utah State Library Web site (192.111.46.220/division/main-one.htm).
17. K. Wayne Smith, "The Growing Value of Your OCLC Membership," *OCLC Newsletter*, n.221 (May/June 1996) p. 3.
18. NEBASE, BCR, and PALINET are only three of the most obvious examples here. See *Ncubed*, v.2, n.2 (March/April 1996), pp. 10–12; *PALINET News*, n.124, July/August 1996, p.6, and BCR's newsletter, *Action for Libraries*, at the BCR Web site (www.bcr.org).
19. Tenopir, Carol. "Online Databases: Trends in End User Searching," *Library Journal*, v.121, n.20 (December 1996) pp. 35–36.
20. An interesting discussion of several of the more significant problems with Web-based search software can be found in two articles published in the electronic journal *D-Lib Magazine*. In the March 1997 issue (located at http://www.dlib.org/dlib/march97/03jones.html), Paul Jones argues in "Java and Libraries: Digital and Otherwise" that the use of Java programming language "applets" may help solve some of the more infuriating problems currently associated with the use of WWW sites in libraries. In "Z39.50 and the World Wide Web," Sebastian Hammer suggests that Z39.50 client/server software may be used to solve some of the problems inherent in WWW browsers. The Hammer article was published in the March 1996 issue of *D-Lib Magazine*, at http://www.dlib.org/dlib/march96/briefings/03indexdata.html.
21. Progress reports on several of these testbed projects can be found in the July/August *D-Lib Magazine*, at http://www.dlib.org/dlib/july96.
22. Messerschmitt, David G., "The Convergence of Telecommunications and Computing: What Are the Implications Today?" *Proceedings of the IEEE*, v.84, n.8 (August, 1996) pp. 1167–1186.
23. Crawford, Walt, and Michael Gorman, *Future Libraries: Dreams, Madness, and Reality* (Chicago: ALA, 1995).
24. See the background report as well as ongoing information on the MONTICELLO project on the SOLINET web site (www.solinet.net/monticello/monticello/backgrnd.htm).

25. See files on the BCR Web site (www.bcr.org) for information about the FirstSearch group contract for ACLIN, Blue Skyways, and SILO. The same site has May, June, and November back issues of *Action for Libraries* describing these projects.
26. See the BCR web site (www.bcr.org) for background on group purchases. The OhioLINK Web site (www.ohiolink.edu) includes a good briefing on OhioLINK programs, as well as back issues of the newsletter *OhioLINK Update*, the September 1996 issue of which is devoted to a description of the agreement with Academic Press. See also the latest status file on the Galileo (www.peachnet.edu/galileo/status696.html) and VIVA (www.viva.lib.va.us) Web sites.
27. See Brunell, David, "Cooperation Among Library Networks Benefits Both Libraries and Networks," *Action for Libraries*, v.22, n.2 (February 1996) pp. 1–2.
28. These issues were discussed at a meeting of the Library of Congress Network Advisory Committee (NAC), entitled "Electronic Publishing, November 17–19, 1996." The proceedings of this meeting are to be published electronically on the NAC Web site (www.loc.gov/nac).

Evolution of School Library Media Programs in the 1990s

Paula Kay Montgomery
Publisher, *School Library Media Activities Monthly*

When fifth-grade suburban Washington, D.C.-area students were asked during a February 1997 interview whether their school or public libraries had computers, they stared back in disbelief that such a question could be asked. None of the students had been in a public or school library media center without automated catalogs.

One young man stated his displeasure that one of the media centers had an "old" computer (nine years old); he said the computer was so slow that it was not even worth waiting for the information. His father helped him use the Internet, check the holdings of different libraries, and download encyclopedia articles. In that way, he said, he didn't waste time and he got what he needed for his reports.

The library media professional kept a straight face. Information access through computers in the late 1980s and early 1990s had been hard to implement in terms of initial funding, software acquisition, data entry of collection, and training and use of resources. The perceptions of the 52-year-old library media specialist about the value of the library media center resources did not match exactly those of the young recipients of those services.

What happened in so short a time and what continues to evolve? The job for which today's average-aged school library media specialist studied no longer exists, or will exist only in pockets of the country. Miller and Shontz reported that in 1993–1994 the mean years of experience of library media specialists in K–12 schools was 19 years with a median of 20 years (p. 476). Clearly, an experienced population is dealing with many new challenges. New standards, updated equipment, more resource format options that must be obtained under funding restraints, higher expectations from a diverse group of students and parents, and more levels of accountability are among the issues impacting the school library media center. In the midst of routine operation of library media programs, library media professionals find themselves either overwhelmed or exhilarated by visions of what appears to be ahead. What are the issues?

Societal Issues Impacting School Library Media Programs

The nonlinear qualities of life are becoming more acutely visible and acceptable. Society is both hierarchical and relational. People outline their ideas in organizational patterns that have been in use in industrial models for years. At the same time, the word "connectivity" takes a different meaning as people "network" rather than just communicate. There are electronic webs for information that allow connection because of a relationship seen between ideas, needs, or desires.

Note: Paula Kay Montgomery is the American Association of School Librarians' representative to the National Forum on Information Literacy, and former Chief, School Library Media Services, Maryland Department of Education.

Electronic search engines replace manual indexes. All this is made possible at a faster speed because of changes in technologies. Users of technologies are aware that differences exist in how people process or assimilate information and respond to the form in which information is presented. Understanding the common operators behind human thought is seen as pivotal to better use of technology and, in turn, to improvement of the human condition. All of this occurs within the context of the existing societal patterns. What are some of the major societal issues that are impacting school library media programs locally, regionally, and nationally?

Technology

Thirty years ago, sound filmstrips and films were lauded as examples of educational technology that would capture the interest of students. Videotapes followed with the promise of ease of use. The use of the electronic media to manage, manipulate, and transmit information has transcended the former views. New developments are announced almost daily. Technology itself seems to beget more innovations and more technology. It is not only individual technologies that support computers, fax machines, cellular telephones, and so forth, but the comingling of different technologies at faster and faster speeds that provides promise and dread. Technology from one field makes its way into use in other fields more quickly. Figures on the speed at which information doubles vary, but it is clear that these changes are pervasive and have affected every part of the school and workplace.

The appropriate use of each new technology is difficult to anticipate. Reading and transmitting text, sound, and visuals on computer screen seems to be more motivating than paper handout. On the other hand, banning "beepers" from schools because they might be used for illicit behavior affects those students whose parents want to have contact with their children for the sake of safety. With each innovation, new learning or training in procedures is required. Selecting the technologies or innovations that would provide the most benefit to learning requires greater expertise and access to technology in order to make wise and financially sound decisions.

Accountability

The public wants government to be accountable. Workplace expectations of what a literate adult worker might be in terms of competencies was reported by the U.S. Department of Education's Secretary's Commission on Achieving Necessary Skills (SCANS). Five workplace competencies that workers should possess included "Information—be able to acquire and evaluate data, organize and maintain files, interpret and communicate, and use computers to process information." Federal legislation related to welfare and library funding certainly provides some evidence of the perceptions of voters. The need to know where the population stands is reported routinely in newspapers in the form of charts and comparisons of school test scores.

Testing issues occupy national and state legislative agendas. In the midst of the politics, educators strive to find measures other than standardized tests that authentically assess achievement. Terms such as portfolio assessment, performance assessment, and direct assessment are cited as alternatives to measuring patterns of student achievement. Indicators for measuring success are rubrics.

The proliferation of national and state standards for what should be learned or achieved by students is apparent in most subject areas, including school library media. The American Association of School Librarians (AASL) developed a set of standards in 1996–1997 that will serve as the structures under which many school library media and information skills programs might function: Information Literacy (accesses, evaluates, and uses information); Independent Learning (pursues information, appreciates and enjoys literature, and strives for excellence in information seeking); and Social Responsibility (recognizes the importance of information, practices ethical behavior, and participates effectively in groups to pursue information). The movement for accountability in the field for students, library media specialists, and teachers is growing.

Equity of Resources

What happens when new schools are built to incorporate new technologies while aging buildings just down the road must continue to make do as they try to upgrade? In each state, schools are at the core of many political battles. Funding of schools is a major responsibility and problem of local and state government. Where should the money be spent, and for which technologies? In the 1990s, libraries are no longer sacrosanct. Changes in federal funding and the trend toward complete or partial school-based management have brought on a need for individuals to justify what is purchased. What is fair? Who makes the decisions and on what basis?

Diversity and Community Values

As communities have changed in racial, religious, and cultural mix, educators have worked to implement programs that deal with multicultural issues. Parent and community involvement has been sought, as has an emphasis on family values. This involvement brought with it the need for better understanding of the values of those varied populations. Decisions about local education issues are often decided by diverse populations that sometimes seem at odds. Diversity is also seen and discussed in terms of learning styles, ability levels, background knowledge, emotional intelligence, and so on. So much diversity can bring rancor as well as richness and creativity to the education system and, in turn, the school library media program. Skeele and Schall note that "a multicultural perspective must be an integral part of the total library media center mission. It is much too critical to relegate to the status of something extra—a few new books or an occasional ethnic celebration. School library media centers that foster climates of equality evolve from carefully examining and adapting collection development, user services, and the curriculum activities."

Learning Theory and Information Literacy

An interesting turn can be seen in fields of psychology, education, library and information science, and computer science (artificial intelligence) as the search continues for a better understanding of how the human brain works. The literature in each field emphasizes a different aspect. These emphases range from a desire to understand cognition, to the processes by which children develop and learn, to neurological pathways to how the computer can replicate thought. Abbott states, "The understanding of learning will become the key issue of our time. The creation of intellectual capital has been going on with every generation for millions of years, with perhaps one exception—and that is what has happened over the past five or six generations." Each field presents models or theories for learning, thinking, and information processing. Theories about what intelligence is (multiple intelligences, emotional intelligence, etc.) combine with the search for definitions of what literacy (information, visual, etc.) is.

Evolution of Traditional Functions of School Library Media Programs

These societal issues all impact the functions of the school library media center as it has been defined during the past 30 years. The issues combine to impact the library media center as it exists within the walls of local schools; in the context of acquisition and organization of materials to support instructional goals; in the perceptions of the community of students, teachers, administrators, parents, and library media specialists; in the development of competent teachers and staff; in the formation of information-literate children; and in the cooperative use of resources.

Collection

New options in technological delivery of information are changing the look of collections in schools. More formats, ranging from books to CD-ROMS to time on online services or the Internet, are available. The complication arises when the rising cost of materials meets shrinking financial resources. As of 1997, the average cost of a children's or young adult book was $15.65 as opposed to the 1996 price of $15.26. The concept of having "balanced collections" in which all subject matter is represented from multiple points of view can not be supported financially. Miller and Shontz reported a mean of $15,499 and median of $11,745 for expenditures of local, federal, and gift funds from a sample of 590 public and private schools in 1993–1994. These funds represent expenditures for books, periodicals, microforms, audiovisual materials, and computer software and equipment. Modest gains are shown, but differences between mean and median point to the gulf between schools with up-to-date technology and those with little. The authors reported that collections were becoming inadequate. Doll adds credence to this with data on the quality of collections: "Unfortunately there seems to be a pattern of neglect with regard to school library media collections."

Part of the neglect may be due to the multiple formats that must be purchased or added. The concept of what composes a school library media collection is changing. The mission statement that school library media collections exist to support the curriculum is being examined not only because the kinds of resources that will be needed to meet the diverse learning styles have expanded, but because the curriculum and objectives are changing. Selection is a more complex responsibility when communities are actively involved in school programs. The complexity requires added knowledge and sensitivity on the part of the library media specialist who cannot rely on a single judgment but must involve all staff members in a participatory model for collection development. Brennan noted the trend toward more collection management: "There is an increasing focus on collection management activities to enable libraries to better meet the general goals of institutions as well as specific needs of users." The library media specialist may find the need to embrace the concept that collection management is a more important job function.

The electronic environment is so new that teachers and library media personnel must cooperate to redefine or reaffirm the term "selection" as opposed to censorship. Evans notes that "The electronic environment creates several dichotomies . . . print versus electronic; ownership versus access; user versus institutional need; free versus fee; gatekeeper versus user selection. It is not a matter of either/or, rather it is a matter of determining the proper local mix" (p. 260). The school library media specialist will need to look for ways to re-examine selection criteria, acquire resources, justify spending, budget time and money, weed, and weigh the value of multiple formats. All this must be managed within the same time period.

Facility

Historically, the library has always been a place. Electronic access to information is changing that concept. If a student or teacher can locate and use information from home, "place" takes on a different meaning and the requirements change to meet the implications that distance and time formerly limited. If parents are more involved in the education of students, the spirit of community may be more apparent, and a library media center becomes more of a community in which communication takes different forms. If a major goal for the library media specialist is to facilitate learning through the use of information, then spaces must be arranged differently to accommodate different kinds of instruction. If it is accepted that learning is both an independent activity and a cooperative venture, spaces for accessing and using information require spaces for multiple multimedia interactions. That change can be seen when standards from the 1960s and 1970s that provided very specific square footage requirements for shelf space and functions are compared with new goal emphases.

Cochran and Gisolfi suggest renovation goals for the library media specialist and architect. The goals for the library media specialist are especially reflective of changes in understanding of place:

Renovation Goals
For the Media Specialist:

- A flexible facility that meets our current technology needs, and can grow and adapt to changes in educational technology
- An information center that enables the media specialists to teach
- A facility that allows access to tools necessary for a wide variety of presentation formats for student work
- A space that's warm and inviting for the entire school community

For the Architect:

- An inspirational space that captures the mood of learning, the sense of library
- A seamless integration of technology into the media center
- A clear, functional layout for a space that's logically organized and easy to supervise
- A design that ties the media center back to the rest of the school

These goals reflect the need to combine the spirit of what library has meant traditionally with a need for flexibility. Time on tasks, scheduling of type of student use, grouping of students for use, function of use, and learning modalities of students will become more apparent.

Services and Instruction

School library media specialists have always acknowledged and embraced the instructional or teaching role. It has been described in hundreds of documents as the role of facilitator, guide, support, team member. *Information Power: Guidelines for School Library Media Programs* (AASL/AECT) lists the activities in which the library media specialist engages when a teacher (p. 39). As a teacher, the library media specialist fulfills the following guidelines:

- The information curriculum is taught as an integral part of the content and objectives of the school's curriculum.
- The information curriculum includes instruction in accessing, evaluating, and communicating information and in the production of media.
- Library media specialists and teachers jointly plan, teach, and evaluate instruction in information access, use, and communication skills. Assistance is provided in the use of technology to access information outside the library media center.
- Teachers and other adults are offered learning opportunities related to new technologies, use and production of a variety of media, and laws and policies regarding information.
- Library media specialists use a variety of instructional methods with different user groups and demonstrate the effective use of newer media and technologies.

Implementation of these guidelines has gained ground as library media specialists work toward goals of planning for integration and flexible scheduling of instruction in the library media center. Van Deusen and Tallman noted that their study "supports the move away from fixed scheduling and underscores the value of collaborative climate in the school. These elements appear to facilitate implementation of the teaching and consultative roles described in *Information Power*." (p. 24) Library media specialists are making a shift to more instruction.

Technology properly applied and implemented offers the opportunity to spend more time on instruction. This instructional role may be seen as the library media specialist offers directed learning activities (teaches), serves as a member of a team that facilitates learning activities, or manages instruction by supporting other teachers with materials, ideas, time, or space for teaching.

The teaching role offers the most promise and shows the most impact of technology and learning theory. As models for learning have developed, so, too, have models for what used to be library and reference skills. Now one can see evidence of information-processing skills at local, state, and national levels. The

AASL Position Statement *Information Literacy: A Position Paper on Information Problem Solving* outlines problem-solving skills for information-literate individuals, and comments that "Information Literacy is the term being applied to the skills of information problem-solving." The *American Library Association Presidential Committee on Information Literacy Final Report* provides the following definition:

> Information literacy is defined as the ability to: know where there is a need for information, identify information needed to address a given problem or issue, find needed information, evaluate the information, organize the information, and use the information effectively to address the problem or issue at hand. (p. 1)
>
> Ultimately, information-literate people are those who have learned how to learn. They know how to learn because they know how knowledge is organized, how to find information, and how to use information in such a way that others can learn from them. They are people prepared for lifelong learning, because they can always find the information needed for any task or decision at hand. (p. 1)

A number of models are available to the practicing school library media specialist. The only formally researched model, by Kuhlthau, reflects the constructivists' concern for process and content. Other information skills models include Eisenberg's and Berkowitz's Big Six, Pappas's and Tepe's Pathway Model, Stripling's and Pitt's REACT Model, and the I-Search Method. All of the models look at the processes of pre-search, task identification, gathering of data, organization of information, and completion of product. These models are being used in library media centers and classrooms as both library media specialists and teachers attempt to help students think critically and successfully locate and use information. Evidence of the models appears in state and local library media curriculum documents. National and state association meetings include sessions in which library media specialists share their successes with the models.

The models are seen in terms of how instructional partnerships may be made. Planning with teachers is seen as a goal for which the library media specialist strives. Wolcott notes that "a successful instructional partnership hinges on the library media specialist's understanding of the planning process as teachers see and practice it. Collaborative planning is the library media specialist's survival skill—a skill that becomes even more important as the concept of information literacy, lifelong learning, and resource-based learning propel us into the third revolution."

Trends suggest that instruction and collaboration with teachers will continue to be a major force in the school library media profession.

Job Functions

When the AASL standards were published in 1988, three job functions were identified for the library media specialist: information specialist, teacher, and instructional consultant. The standards are being revised in 1996–1997 and implementation steps planned again. These three functions, when seen in terms of technology and new expectations, take on an urgency. The profession appears to be re-examining the way tasks have been performed. New requirements that put increased emphasis on running computer networks, working with parents, and collaborating with teachers shift the emphasis of skills. This also means that the job of library media specialist cannot be completed alone. The profession has tried to deal with the requirements of the job and the needs of other staff members in the years since 1988. Of note is the publication of AASL's *Competencies for Prospective Teachers and Administrators*. This brief publication recommended that:

- Teacher education programs require candidates to use available school library media centers, and a range of resources in developing curriculum units and lesson plans. Setting this expectation affords candidates opportunities to practice and develop many of the information literacy skills they will need to encourage their students.
- School districts expect beginning and experienced teachers to employ the instructional methods and the facilitator/coach roles that foster resource-based learning and the development of information literacy skills by students
- Pre-service and in-service teacher education programs be developed to assist prospective and practicing teachers to structure student tasks and assignments that go beyond information retrieval to the evaluation and application of information
- Pre-service and in-service teacher education programs be developed to assist prospective and practicing teachers to assess both process and product in evaluating student learning

AASL recognized the need for shared responsibility for teaching students effective information-processing skills. The curriculum in the "information" or "electronic" age cannot be supported by a sole library media specialist in a school; it is a joint venture.

Retooling the job requirements may be slower. Library media education institutions may not have responded to these changes as quickly as other sectors. Harada surveyed library schools to review a number of factors related to school library media programs. Required technology-related courses were seen in media or instructional technology. "Comparatively few courses were required in such areas as systems analysis, library automation, and information storage and retrieval." (pp. 217–218)

Anecdotal evidence on listservs such as LM_Net suggests that library media specialists are attending local or state staff-development workshops and courses to update their knowledge of searching and use of the Internet. It is also evident that there are frustrations at having to learn while on the job. In some cases, library media specialists are completing manuals while learning how to operate and manage computer "hubs" and still juggling "old" responsibilities.

Conclusion

In what direction do these trends carry us? The school library media profession is rebuilding the raft on which it sails while bobbing in the waves. The raft is being built from materials gathered as the winds continue to blow. Although skilled builders, library media specialists are studying the flotsam and jetsam in hope of sighting land.

In the articles and discussions published in professional journals in the last five years it is acknowledged that our information or knowledge base is expanding; however, there is little mention of the expansion of wisdom. The library media professionals on the raft express great hope and optimism for the future in letters to editors, e-mail messages, and especially on listservs. It is to be hoped that the combination of trends will invigorate the profession as authentic information needs of learners are served.

References

Abbott, John. "To Be Intelligent." *Educational Leadership* 54:6 (March 1997), pp. 6–10.

American Association of School Librarians. *Competencies for Prospective Teachers and Administrators.* Chicago: AASL, 1995.

American Association of School Librarians. *Information Literacy Standards for Student Learning. Draft 5.* http://www.ala.org/aasl/stndsdrft5.html.

American Association of School Librarians and Association for Educational Communications and Technology. *Information Power: Guidelines for School Library Media Programs.* Chicago/Washington, D.C.: ALA/AECT, 1988

American Library Association. American Association of School Librarians. Position Statement on *Information Literacy: A Position Paper on Information Problem Solving.* Chicago: American Library Association, 1993. http://www.ala.org/aasl/positions/PS_infolit.html.

American Library Association. *American Library Association Presidential Committee on Information Literacy: Final Report.* Chicago: American Library Association, 1989.

Brennan, Mary Alice. "Trends and Issues in Library and Information Science 1990." ERIC Digest. Syracuse, N.Y.: ERIC Clearinghouse on Information Resources, 1991. ED 340389.

Cochran, Sally, and Gisolfi, Peter. "Renovate It and They Will Come: Designing a Popular High School Library." *School Library Journal* 43:2 (February 1997), pp. 25–29.

Doll, Carol A. "Quality and Elementary School Library Media Collections." *School Library Media Quarterly* 25:2 (Winter 1997), pp. 95–101.

Eisenberg, Michael B., and Berkowitz, Robert E. *Information Problem-Solving: The Big Six Skills Approach to Library and Information Skills Instruction.* Norwood, N.J.: Ablex Publishing, 1990.

Evans, G. E. *Developing Library and Information Center Collections.* 3rd ed. Englewood, Colo.: Libraries Unlimited, 1995.

Harada, Violet. "School Library Media Preparation Programs in ALA-Accredited Schools." *Journal of Education for Library and Information Science* 37:3 (Summer 1996), pp. 210–228.

Joyce, Marilyn Z., and Tallman, Julie I. *Making the Writing and Research Connection with the I-Search Process.* New York: Neal-Schuman, 1997.

Kuhlthau, Carol C. *Seeking Meaning: A Process Approach to Library and Information Skills Instruction.* Norwood, N.J.: Ablex Publishing, 1993.

Miller, Marilyn L., and Shontz, Marilyn L. "Expenditures for Resources in School Library Media Centers, FY 1993-1994: The Race for the School Dollar." *The Bowker Annual Library and Book Trade Almanac.* New Providence, N.J.: R. R. Bowker, 1996, pp. 462-481.

Pappas, Marjorie L., and Tepe, Ann E. *Follett Information Skills Model Kit.* McHenry, Ill.: Follett Software Company, 1995.

Skeele, Rosemary W., and Schall, Patricia L. "Multicultural Education: An Action Plan for School Library Media Specialists." *School Library Media Quarterly* 22:2 (Winter 1994), pp. 83-86.

Stripling, Barbara K., and Pitts, Judy M. *Brainstorms and Blueprints: Teaching Library Research as a Thinking Process.* Englewood, Colo.: Libraries Unlimited, 1988.

Van Deusen, Jean Donham, and Tallman, Julie. "The Impact of Scheduling on Curriculum Consultation and Information Skills Instruction. Part One: The 1993-1994 AASL/Highsmith Research Award Study." *School Library Media Quarterly* 23:1 (Fall 1994), pp. 17-25.

Wolcott, Linda Lachance. "Understanding How Teachers Plan: Strategies for Successful Instructional Partnerships." *School Library Media Quarterly* 22:3 (Spring 1994), pp. 161-164.

Recent Changes for Three Federal Library and Information Agencies: Lessons to the Field, Lessons from the Field, or Neither?

Jane Williams
Research Associate, U.S. National Commission on Libraries and Information Science

Many excellent writings exist on actual or proposed changes surrounding the Government Printing Office (GPO), the Library of Congress (LC), and the National Archives and Records Administration (NARA), three of the largest and most complex federal library and information agencies. This report covers different ground, especially from reports on information policy per se, the subject of so much of the existing and excellent writing. This report summarizes recent, important events and trends, and poses possibilities for further consideration, in the following large areas:

- Mission-oriented and organizational challenges at the three agencies
- Source and nature of the scrutiny of each institution
- Possible future challenges to the historical missions of each institution
- Parallels with state and local library and information agencies

Backgrounds of the Agencies

The Library of Congress was established in 1800, GPO in 1860, and NARA in 1934. The Library of Congress has the biggest budget of the three; its fiscal year (FY) 1997 budget is $362 million, NARA's is $197 million, and GPO's is $111 million.

The Government Printing Office and the Library of Congress are in the legislative branch of the federal government. In 1985 the National Archives and Records Administration was separated from the General Services Administration and re-established as an independent agency (i.e., not one of the cabinet-level departments) in the executive branch.

Although two of the three agencies are in the legislative branch, all are headed by presidential appointees who are confirmed by the Senate. The current Librarian of Congress, appointed in 1987, has been in his job the longest. Next is the Public Printer (head of GPO), named in 1993. The newest is the Archivist of the United States (head of NARA), appointed in 1995. The Public Printer is the only appointee with a work history within his organization; the Librarian of Congress and the U.S. Archivist were appointed to their agencies' top posts and from positions in other fields.

Note: The author's views are not necessarily those of the National Commission on Libraries and Information Science or the U.S. government.

Missions

The missions of the three agencies are quoted from their public documents:

"...GPO's mission will be: To assist Congress and Federal agencies in the cost-effective creation and replication of information products and services, and to provide the public with the most efficient and effective means of acquiring Government information products and services."[1]

"The Library's mission is to make its resources available and useful to the Congress and the American people and to sustain and preserve a universal collection of knowledge and creativity for future generations."[2]

"NARA ensures, for the Citizen and the Public Servant, for the President and the Congress and the Courts, ready access to essential evidence."[3]

GPO's mission statement appeared in its 1991 strategic plan. The Library of Congress's statement is from 1996, NARA's from 1997. All three statements build on traditional missions of library and information organizations. The Government Printing Office's 1991 plan moved GPO from a printing shop to an information dissemination utility for the federal government and to the public. The National Archives and Records Administration also expands its traditional mission by using the term *essential evidence* "... to underscore the *particular* importance we attach to safeguarding *within* the body of federal and presidential record materials, among others, those materials that document the identities, rights, and entitlements of citizens; the actions for which federal officials are accountable; and the effects of those actions on the national experience."[4]

Common Challenges

There have been many fits and starts, as well as leaps ahead, in achieving these agencies' missions. All three have challenged themselves and been challenged by others on practically every front, including mission, management, economics, and technology. In short, like the rest of the federal government, they reflect major federal initiatives and trends in the 1990s:

- Examination/re-examination of the federal government's roles and functions
- Resulting streamlining and re-invention of how agencies meet their responsibilities and cutbacks in the role of the federal government
- Challenges from Congress, the White House, and other federal agencies to their missions
- Opportunity and threat posed by changing electronic information and communications technologies

Streamlining Government—the National Performance Review

President Clinton took office in 1993 vowing to make the government work better and cost less. The first report of the National Performance Review (NPR) came out in September 1993. It promised a five-year (1995–1999) savings of $108 billion and a reduction in the federal work force of 252,000 positions, to be achieved by improving management, streamlining control, transforming structures, budgeting for results, and improving customer services.[5]

Of the three agencies with which this report is concerned, only the Government Printing Office was directly addressed in the first NPR report, which included the recommendation to "Give the executive branch authority to make its own printing policy that will eliminate the mandatory printing source. Develop a new executive branch printing policy for the 21st century . . . Give the executive branch responsibility for distributing printed federal information to depository libraries. Require agencies to inventory the federal information they hold, and make it accessible to the public."[6]

On the other hand, all three agencies have been affected by the general push toward smaller, more accountable, customer-oriented government that does only what is necessary and proper for it to do. The effects of the movement to streamline are evident in the agencies' budgets and staff levels.

For example, at the House hearing on the FY 1998 budget, the Public Printer stated that GPO's workforce has been reduced 55 percent since the 1970s.[7] Obviously, that reduction has many causes, notably the decreased workload as agencies shift from printing to electronic publishing. The story for NARA is less dramatic. The agency went from an appropriation of $120 million for FY 1990 to $195 million in FY 1995 and from approximately 3,000 staff in 1990 to about 2,900 in 1995.

The situation for the Library of Congress is also less dramatic than that for GPO, although LC officials (like those at NARA) stress the need for more than minimal increases in appropriations so that the agencies can move ahead with new services while maintaining traditional ones. The Library of Congress's budget increased from approximately $322.2 million in FY 1992 to $362 million in FY 1997, but staff (full-time-equivalent positions) dropped by 10 percent (435 positions) from 1992 to 1997.

Government Performance and Results Act

While the administration was busy in 1993 beginning the National Performance Review, Congress passed the Government Performance and Results Act (GPRA),[8] requiring agencies in the executive branch to set strategic goals, measure performance against those goals, and report progress (or lack thereof). By September 30, 1997, agencies must submit five-year strategic plans. In 1999 annual performance plans are due that contain program performance goals, resource summaries, and explanations of methods used to verify and measure the values of program outcomes. By March 31, 2000, each agency must report on program performance the previous year, comparing actual program output and outcomes with the goals submitted for the previous year.

Implementation of the Government Performance and Results Act, like the National Performance Review, will have significant impact on all three agencies. As noted above, the legislative branch's Government Printing Office was most directly addressed in the initial recommendations of the executive branch's NPR.

However, NARA and LC are affected as well. Likewise, although the act applies only to executive branch agencies, the push to plan strategically and to measure outcomes is felt government-wide.

NARA, the executive agency of the trio, prepared a ten-year strategic plan, released in 1996, called *Ready Access to Essential Evidence*. The Archivist's preface says that the plan will be the basis from which NARA will develop performance measures in accordance with the Government Performance and Results Act.[9]

103rd and 104th Congresses

The 103rd Congress may not be remembered as vividly as the 104th, partly because it worked in the shadow of a new president and the majority was the same party as the new president. However, the 103rd presaged the 104th in many ways, only one of which was passage of the Government Performance and Results Act. Especially in 1994 the movement to streamline government gained followers and momentum with bills like H.R. 3400, the Government Reform and Savings Act of 1994.

Although H.R. 3400 had many iterations and was not enacted, it nevertheless both echoed and foreshadowed other recommendations. The House approved a version of H.R. 3400 that included executive agencies doing their own printing and moved the Superintendent of Documents from the Government Printing Office to the Library of Congress. The Senate had its own plans, such as those in S. 1824, the Legislative Reorganization Act of 1994, which would have required Congress periodically to reauthorize GPO and LC and to let executive agencies bypass GPO for printing orders of $1,500 or less.

The 104th Congress, 1995–1996, was a governmental body full of anti-government fervor. One saying in Washington, D.C., in 1995 was that "Congress shoots at anything that moves." The 104th Congress took aim at many targets, including the subjects of this report. In hindsight, however, the 104th did not enact many of the revolutionary changes it said it would, although it did slow the federal government down, and it did stop major parts of it temporarily (with shutdowns and furloughs in late 1995 and early 1996). The lasting legacy of the 104th may be the doubt it expressed about the nature, functions, and worth of services provided by the federal government.

Unique Challenges

To GPO from Office of Management and Budget

Through its Office of Information and Regulatory Affairs, the Office of Management and Budget (OMB) continues to entertain the question the administration first raised in its September 1993 report on the National Performance Review: that is, GPO's authority to procure printing for all agencies of the federal government. In April 1996 the president's chief of staff told executive agencies to continue using GPO for 12 months while OMB investigated matters. In May 1996 the Department of Justice issued an opinion that Congress's requirement that executive agencies use a legislative branch agency (GPO) violates the constitutional principle of separation of power.

In January 1997 OMB unveiled plans to survey printing needs of executive branch agencies by collecting baseline and trend data in order to develop business models for the future "which maximize the benefits of increased agency flexibility."[10] OMB has also said it is "committed to working with Congress to achieve a comprehensive reform of Title 44, consistent with Constitutional principles."[11] Title 44 of the U.S. Code governs printing for the federal government.

To GPO from National Technical Information Service

The National Technical Information Service (NTIS) is a self-supporting unit in the Technology Administration of the U.S. Department of Commerce. It is "the Nation's largest central clearinghouse and governmentwide resource for scientific, technical, engineering, and other business-related information."[12] NTIS has built services and products and the methods for delivering them, including FedWorld, an "electronic marketplace"[13] that provides public access to government documents, federal online systems, and electronic delivery of other selected products.

Meanwhile, the Government Printing Office Electronic Information Access Enhancement Act of 1993 was passed[14] June 8, 1993, and the title was soon informally shortened to "GPO Access." The law required GPO to provide the *Federal Register*, the *Congressional Record*, and other databases electronically, to operate the Government Information Locator System, to store electronic files, and to perform other related duties.

In addition to already-competing services with GPO, NTIS was advised in a 1996 consultant's study that its future growth would come from deals that NTIS could broker between agencies and the private sector to publish government information, since the Department of Commerce held that NTIS was not obligated to use GPO for printing services.[15] In January 1997 NTIS announced "NTIS Order Now—Your Government Research Companion," a free online service to identify and purchase government information products.

To LC from Government Accounting Office

In 1988 the new Librarian of Congress called for the first-ever audit of LC. An audit of fiscal year 1988 was done in 1991. Concerned about shortcomings, incomplete control and accounting systems, and other aspects of LC's operations, Congress called on the Government Accounting Office (GAO) again in 1995 to review LC's finances and management. The audit report on FY 1995 showed mixed results in LC's implementation of GAO's 1991 recommendations. Improvements were noted in the FEDLINK program and a new financial management system was in place. On the other hand, LC still did not have "processes necessary to generate complete, auditable financial statements."[16]

LC has requested funds for FY 1998 for an electronic integrated library system to provide inventory control and for additional security measures, both of which would respond to some of the 1995 audit report's concerns.

A management review of LC in 1996 got more attention and reaction than the financial audit, primarily because the reviewers challenged head-on the mission of the Library of Congress "to sustain and preserve a universal collection." The management review recommended that the Library of Congress consider alternative missions, including that of "collaborative information/knowledge broker," dispersing its collections and serving as a clearinghouse and referral agency.[17] At a hearing on May 7, 1996, the Joint Committee on the Library affirmed LC's historic mission.

Other events and new personnel were viewed as progress in LC's efforts to become more fiscally and managerially responsible. In 1996 the major class action racial discrimination case against LC was settled. The acting deputy librarian hired in 1995 and the deputy librarian brought on board in 1996 as LC's chief operating officer are retired Army generals. The acting and the current deputy gave and give the agency a sense of command, control, and direction.

To LC from Patent and Trademark Office

In 1995 and 1966 the administration and Congress backed several plans and bills to make the Patent and Trademark Office (PTO) a performance-based organization or a government corporation and/or to turn it into the United States Intellectual Property Organization, incorporating authority and responsibility for copyright, patents, and trademarks. No such bill or proposal was passed in the 104th Congress, but a bill (H.R. 400) to make the Patent and Trademark Office a government corporation was introduced in January 1997, very early in the 105th Congress. As of early March, no current bill called for relocating the Copyright Office.

The Library of Congress maintains that moving the Copyright Office elsewhere would seriously hamper LC's mission of maintaining a universal collection because the registration and deposit functions would move with the Copyright Office.

To NARA from GAO and Congress

In the late 1980s and early 1990s several sources severely and publicly criticized the National Archives and Records Administration for mismanagement, politicization, delayed deployment of information technology, and other shortcomings and misdeeds. For example, the archives was sued in March 1992 for delaying public access to tape recordings made by President Nixon. In November 1992 the Senate Committee on Governmental Affairs released a report prepared for it by the General Accounting Office. The report cited management problems, shortsighted actions, and questionable compliance with laws, regulations, and standards of conduct.

To NARA (and the White House) from U.S. District Court

The precipitating action was the January 1993 agreement by the then-Archivist giving the departing president exclusive legal control over the computerized records of his presidency. In May 1993 the court held the White House and the Acting Archivist in contempt for failing to protect and preserve computer records made in the Reagan and Bush administrations. The presiding judge said he would levy fines if the White House did not act immediately to preserve deteriorating tapes, repair damaged tapes, and issue new guidelines to protect them. (In February 1995 the presiding judge declared the 1993 agreement between the then-Archivist and the then-president null and void.)

To NARA from the White House

Also in May 1993 the President's Council on Integrity and Efficiency accused top NARA officials of mismanagement, suggested disciplinary actions, and told the Acting Archivist to take actions necessary to protect the integrity of the agency's programs and to prepare recommendations for the new Archivist to be appointed by the president. After May 1993 the press seemed to stop covering the charges from Congress, the administration, and the courts.

In December 1993 the Acting Archivist issued NARA's strategic plan covering 1994–2001,[18] a revision of the plan done in February 1993. Press reports in 1994 and 1995 note the new Archivist agreed on release of the Nixon tapes and also on new regulations for preserving electronic-mail records, so it appears that the earlier years' charges were satisfactorily addressed.

Other External Scrutiny or Oversight

Labor unions, employee unions, other trade groups, professional associations, watchdog organizations, press and freedom-of-information groups, and many others helped keep pressure on GPO, LC, and NARA to meet expectations, conform with laws and regulations and to demonstrate accountability and progress. The motives, dynamics, and events spawned by all those groups are important but are beyond the scope of this report, which deals mainly with internal federal challenges and pressures.

Major New Initiatives Exploiting Electronic Information Technology

While GPO, LC, and NARA dealt with the challenges outlined above, they also advanced new services and operations. However, it is difficult to say whether some of the new offerings were the initiative of the agency or resulted from the insistence of another body.

Government Printing Office

Some claim the Government Printing Office should have developed a clearinghouse for electronic federal information before Congress passed the 1993 law requiring GPO Access. In any case, GPO did indeed develop this service, pursuant to Public Law 103-40, the Government Printing Office Electronic Information Access Enhancement Act of 1993.

GPO Access provides free, online access to the full text of the *Congressional Record*, the *Federal Register*, congressional bills, reports of the General Accounting Office, public laws, the U.S. Code, the *Monthly Catalog of Government Publications*, and other databases. GPO Access handles the Government Information Locator System records, connecting to other federal agencies' information resources.

Some House members are promoting a "CyberCongress"[19] and early in the 105th Congress the Clerk of the House submitted a request for a new document management system. It is not clear how this new system might affect GPO Access or other components of the GPO, such as printing for Congress. It is also not clear how THOMAS, the legislative information system operated by the Library of Congress, might fit into a "CyberCongress." In the past two years LC has also worked on a single system of legislative information (see below), again with uncertain ramifications for GPO Access.

The 104th Congress called on GPO to study transition to an electronic Federal Depository Library Program (FDLP).[20] GPO produced a multi-year plan for the FDLP as well.[21] In August 1996 the Public Printer submitted to the Senate Committee on Rules and Administration suggested changes to the statutes governing the FDLP. A renamed and re-described Federal Information Dissemination and Access Program would "reflect the electronic information environment" and the key goal of timely, current public access and "permanent, future access to Federal government information at no cost."[22] While the 104th Congress enacted no changes to the Federal Depository Library Program, the 105th is expected to consider them.

Library of Congress

Late in 1994 new leaders for the 104th Congress called on LC to develop an online, Internet-based legislative information service for public access. THOMAS, named after Thomas Jefferson, resulted and was inaugurated January 5, 1995. THOMAS is a graphical World Wide Web site for bills and acts of Congress, summaries of bills and status of legislation, reports and schedules of House and Senate committees, floor actions, and indexes for the *Congressional Record*.There are links to other Internet services as well, such as the House and Senate Web home pages.

In 1995 and 1996 Congress asked LC to propose a single legislative or congressional information system, both to reduce duplication of effort in the legislative branch and to improve the quality and timeliness of information to Congress. LC developed the Legislative Information System (LIS). January 1997 saw the first release of the LIS retrieval component, which will be further developed in 1997 and 1998.[23] It is not clear how this system relates to THOMAS, or how it does or will affect GPO Access or vice versa.

The above electronic services reflect LC's first priority, supporting Congress. The second priority is preserving, securing, and sustaining a universal collection. The third is making LC's collections maximally accessible. The fourth is enhancing the educational value of the library's collections.[24] Serving the second, third, and fourth priorities are high-visibility electronic projects aimed to the general public.

First came the April 1993 worldwide availability of LC's bibliographic databases (35 files of 26 million records) via the Internet. In October 1993 LC's Marvel (Library of Congress Machine-Assisted Realization of the Virtual Electronic Library) system was unveiled, offering not only bibliographic information but also information about the LC services and facilities, the U.S. Congress, and so forth.

Next came the National Digital Library Program, started in 1994, funded mainly with private donations and aiming to digitize material from the library's special collections. It began with "American Memory," two dozen key American history collections in the public domain. In 1996 the National Digital Library Program also received private funds to award to local libraries and other organizations to digitize some of their important historical material, which LC would then post on its Web site.

Other electronic services at the Library of Congress include the Global Legal Information Network, the Geography and Map Division's work in geographic information systems, and the Copyright Office's new system for digital registration and deposit of copyrighted works over the Internet.

National Archives and Records Administration

The National Archives and Records Administration may have attempted the most challenging mix—all during the same years—of reacting to charges, changing top management, planning for new technology, overseeing construction of the largest archival facility in the world, and moving much of its operation from downtown Washington, D.C., to College Park, Maryland. The new building, dubbed Archives II, houses the Center for Electronic Records, on which may hinge NARA's future.

The Archivist stresses that NARA includes records administration as well as archives, although the agency has traditionally emphasized the latter.[25] According to the strategic plan for 1997–2007, "NARA must be involved in the management of records throughout their life cycle."[26] The agency would give more attention to the life cycle's front end, with design of record systems, creation of records and organization of filing systems, and one-time appraisal of records (at the front of the life cycle).[27]

The strategic plan also says that NARA will expand current efforts to build a nationwide, integrated online information delivery system.[28] Work on NARA's Internet information server began in 1994 and connects to files of publications, digital photographs, presidential libraries, and other related Internet resources.

Outlooks for the Agencies—into the Electronic Future

GPO's recent reports have centered on the Federal Depository Library Program. GPO has not published a strategic or long-range plan since 1991 nor an annual report since 1994. Of the three agencies reviewed by this report, GPO seems most at risk of losing major parts of its mission and operation—not necessarily through anything it has done or not done, but because the nature of printing and publishing have changed so dramatically and unalterably.

In the mid-1990s LC seems to be solving some major managerial and fiscal problems and to be assuming more visible leadership (and cooperative stances too) with online bibliographic and legislative information as well as with digitizing information. On the other hand, through the Copyright Office or other means, LC's continuing effort to build a universal collection will likely be challenged again, especially if discussions about more storage space for books heat up.

Nevertheless, despite the electronic emphases and despite the expense of housing so much material, it is clear for LC as well as NARA that physical presence remains important. The obvious example for LC is its recently renovated and restored 100-year-old Jefferson Building and the attention, awe, and use it attracts. The Library of Congress also seems well positioned to use its 200th anniversary in the year 2000 to maximum advantage for the library itself and for libraries nationwide.

Now that NARA has occupied Archives II, the success of its hopes, plans, and efforts may well hinge on how thoroughly it can carry out the vision and mission articulated in its new strategic plan. NARA has not caught up with agencies' production of electronic records, and still must tackle the start of the life cycle of agencies' electronic records. That challenge is complicated by the fact that even more because NARA is still receiving paper records that are 25-30 years old, so the explosion in electronic record-keeping will have even more impact in the future. NARA must not only catch up with agencies' current production of electronic records; it must prepare for an explosion in such records at the same time it continues to deal with huge amounts of paper records and to reduce the cost of its records centers so that storing paper doesn't indefinitely drain the agency's resources.

In short, GPO, LC, and NARA face continuous and evolutionary change. Whether they will face revolutionary, discontinuous change is another matter.

Lessons to or from the Field

The recent changes and challenges these huge federal agencies have faced may differ in size and scope from those they will face in the next few years. They may also differ in size and scope from those faced by library and information agencies at state and local levels, but they do not differ in nature. The changes and challenges also seem to have occurred at all levels at about the same time. In other words, it does not appear that the federal government's changes presaged state and local changes, or vice versa; or, if they did, that enough time intervened for one level of government to observe, take notes, and learn from the other. Most seem to be going through roughly the same transition at roughly the same time.

Furthermore, it does not appear that GPO, LC, and NARA are far enough into their re-inventions to provide any broad vision or detailed pattern of what library and information agencies need to do to address the challenges of the next century. Rather, examining their past and present actions produces the same list of organizational principles and values likely to produce success in the future as would be produced for a state or local institution with a similar mission. The list would include:

- Be clear about one's mission, goals, and objectives
- Streamline management
- Keep management and accounting systems in tip-top order
- Aggressively correct shortcomings or mistakes pointed out by oversight or governing bodies

- Innovate
- Take the initiative to partner with other governmental and non-governmental agencies
- Use technology innovatively, routinely, and widely
- Recruit, retain, support, and promote a diverse staff

Conclusion

This report has dealt with the traditional input measures of an agency's well-being: budget, staff, and the like. Major questions about an agency's customer base, customer service, quality of service, outputs and outcomes of the agency's programs, relationships with the private sector, intragovernmental competition, and so forth remain for other investigations and reports.

Another reporter might also explore whether the agencies will change their names. *Archives* and *library* and *printing* are, after all, very traditional terms.

Finally, this report does not look very far into the future. Perhaps others can report their visions for the Government Printing Office, the Library of Congress, and the National Archives and Records Administration—by whatever names they may be known—off into the next century.

Notes

1. U.S. Government Printing Office. *GPO/2001: Vision for a New Millennium.* Washington, D.C., U.S. Govt. Print. Off., 1991, p.1.
2. Statement of Dr. James H. Billington, the Librarian of Congress, before the Joint Committee on the Library of the U.S. Congress, May 7, 1996.
3. U.S. National Archives and Records Administration. *Ready Access to Essential Evidence: The Strategic Plan of the National Archives and Records Administration, 1997–2007.* Washington, D.C., U.S. Nat. Archives and Records Adm., 1996, p. 2.
4. *Ibid.*, p. 7.
5. Al Gore. *From Red Tape to Results: Creating Government that Works Better & Costs Less.* Washington, D.C., National Performance Review, 1993. pp. 160–161.
6. *Ibid.* p. 165.
7. Statement of Michael F. DiMario, the Public Printer, before the Legislative Branch Subcommittee of the House Appropriations Committee of the U.S. Congress, February 11, 1997.
8. Public Law 103–62
9. U.S. National Archives and Records Administration, *op. cit.*, p. 1.
10. Memorandum from Sally Katzen to Agency Chief Information Officers, "Reinventing Government Printing Management for the 21st Century," n.d.
11. Memorandum from Jacob J. Lew to heads of executive departments and establishments, "Procurement of Printing through the Government Printing Office," September 12, 1996.
12. U.S. National Archives and Records Administration. *The United States Government Manual, 1996/97.* Washington, D.C., U.S. Govt. Print. Off., 1996, p. 165.
13. *Ibid.*, p. 166.
14. Public Law 103–40

15. "Consultant Warns NTIS It Must Develop New Products," *Electronic Public Information Newsletter*, July 1966, p. 52.
16. Price Waterhouse, *Financial Statement Audit for the Library of Congress for Fiscal Year 1995*, GAO Contract No. 613003, Task Order 96-1, May 6, 1996, p. ii.
17. Booz Allen & Hamilton, *Management Review of the Library of Congress: Final Report*, prepared for the General Accounting Office, May 7, 1996, vol. 1.
18. U.S. National Archives and Records Administration. *The National Archives and Records Administration Strategic Plan for a Challenging Federal Environment, 1994–2001.* Washington, D.C., NARA, 1993.
19. "Rep. Vern Ehlers: The Future Role of the GPO Is Still be[sic] be Determined," *Electronic Public Information Newsletter*, 6:3, March 1996, p. 3.
20. U.S. Government Printing Office. *Report to the Congress: Study to Identify Measures Necessary for a Successful Transition to a More Electronic Federal Depository Library Program.* Washington, D.C., U.S. Govt. Print. Off., 1996.
21. U.S. Government Printing Office. *Federal Depository Library Program: Information Dissemination and Access Strategic Plan, FY 1996–FY 2001.* Washington, D.C., U.S. Govt. Print. Off., 1996.
22. "Changes to Chapters 17 and 19, Title 44," Attachment to letter of Michael F. DiMario, the Public Printer, to John Warner, Chairman, Committee on Rules and Administration, U.S. Senate, August 22, 1996.
23. Statement of Dr. James H. Billington, the Librarian of Congress, before the Subcommittee on Legislative Appropriations, Committee on Appropriations, U.S. House of Representatives, February 12, 1997.
24. *Ibid.*
25. "Archivist Carlin Sets New Course for NARA," *Government Imaging*, November/December 1995, p. 16.
26. U.S. National Archives and Records Administration, *op. cit.*, p. 7.
27. *Ibid.*, p. 8.
28. *Ibid.*, p. 12.

Part 2
Legislation, Funding, and Grants

Legislation

Legislation and Regulations Affecting Libraries in 1996

Carol C. Henderson
Executive Director, Washington Office, American Library Association

Anne A. Heanue
Associate Director, Washington Office, American Library Association

Significant legislative and regulatory issues on the public agenda made 1996 one of the busiest and most important years for libraries in recent history. Despite a challenging political environment, major legislative achievements for the library community were made during the final session of the 104th Congress. Congressional passage of the Library Services and Technology Act (LSTA), previously the Library Services and Construction Act (LSCA), was a critical success. The coordinated efforts of the American Library Association (ALA), the Chief Officers of State Library Agencies (COSLA), the Urban Libraries Council (ULC), and many other library organizations, furthered by strong and effective grassroots support, contributed to this success.

Congress's historic reform of the nation's Communications Act came to closure with the February passage of the Telecommunications Act of 1996. This was also historic for the library community. The new statute brought mixed news. For the first time, libraries were mandated to receive discounted telecommunications rates under universal service policies. At year's end the Federal Communications Commission (FCC) was considering favorable recommendations on how best to implement the discounted rates provision for libraries, K–12 schools, and rural health care providers. But the same law included the Communications Decency Act (CDA), which ultimately led ALA and others to pursue a major legal case to challenge the CDA's constitutionality.

The budget impasse between Congress and the president was finally resolved in March. As the November elections approached, Congress in the waning days of the session came to closure on the budget by funding education programs at or near the levels requested in President Clinton's fiscal year (FY) 1997 budget. As a result of hard work by library supporters, the highest ever amount for LSCA was appropriated for FY 1997: $128.9 million. Increases in elementary and secondary education programs provided many opportunities for school libraries to reap benefits, particularly from education technology programs.

On the intellectual property front, major threats to the delicate balance in American copyright law and the concept of fair use in a digital age were deferred when the 104th Congress adjourned without acting on several major bills. The library community was involved with the many national and international debates on intellectual property and copyright. Concerning government information, proposed legislative revisions of the Federal Depository Library Program were not enacted but likely preceded future debate on how access to government information will proceed in the digital age. There was also vigorous discussion about the transition to a more electronic depository library program with the release of a study by the Government Printing Office in June 1996.

By the end of 1996 the political climate was calmer than when the 104th Congress had been swept into office under the "Contract with America" and the major shift in power to a Republican-controlled Congress had taken place. The extremely important role of grassroots lobbying, a real strength within the library community, became even more clear as library supporters assessed the results of the 104th Congress and recognized the retirement of several longtime library champions from Congress.

Library Services and Technology Act

The landmark law LSTA ushered in a new phase in federal support of library services. Grassroots lobbying efforts and coalition support were critical to the success of this legislative effort. While local library advocates lobbied key congressional districts, the ALA Washington Office worked round the clock to ensure September passage of the LSTA conference agreement and final inclusion in the end-of-session omnibus measure. In the end, LSTA was the *only* education-related program up for reauthorization that was actually enacted in the 104th Congress.

LSTA replaced the former Library Services and Construction Act and some of the purposes of the former Higher Education Act Title II library programs. LSTA was designed to

- Consolidate federal library service programs
- Stimulate excellence and promote access to learning and information resources in all types of libraries for individuals of all ages
- Promote library services that provide all users access to information through state, regional, national, and international electronic networks
- Provide linkages among and between libraries
- Promote targeted library services to people of diverse geographic, cultural, and socioeconomic backgrounds; to individuals with disabilities; and to people with limited functional literacy or information skills

LSTA was authorized for six years at a total of $150 million (the ceiling for actual funding) for FY 1997 and "such sums" for each year through 2002. Most of the funds were allocated to state library agencies for statewide services or subgrants for technological innovation or electronic-linkage purposes and for outreach services. Any activity funded through the state-based program can involve public, school, academic, research, or, in some cases, special libraries. Up to 3 percent of appropriations may be used for federal administration, 1.5 percent for services to Indian tribes, and 4 percent for national leadership purposes, including education/training, research/demonstrations, preservation/digitization, and model joint museum/library projects.

A reauthorization and refocusing of the Library Services and Construction Act, the new LSTA brought to fruition a five-year effort by ALA, COSLA, and ULC, with participation by the U.S. National Commission on Libraries and Information Science (NCLIS) and observers from the Department of Education library programs represented on the interassociation "Task Force on LSCA Reauthorization." Unlike LSCA, which was administered by the Department of Education, LSTA will be administered by the independent Institute of Museum and Library Services (IMLS), along with existing museum grant programs. Following enactment, work by ALA, COSLA, and others began immediately to ensure an effective transition to the new LSTA and IMLS.

Appropriations

Fiscal Year 1996

The longest and most difficult budget impasse ever between Congress and the White House stalled final action on FY 1996 appropriations and caused two government shutdowns. Funding for FY 1996 was provided piecemeal through a series of short-term continuing resolutions. Although some funds were released to states for LSCA under each successive temporary measure, uncertainty over funding and inability to begin state library grant processes caused serious problems for state library agencies.

On April 25, seven months into FY 1996, H.R. 3019, an omnibus appropriations bill, passed and provided funding for the remainder of FY 1996 for several agencies for which regular appropriations bills had not been passed, including the Department of Education. Funds for LSCA and some Higher Education Act library programs were the same in both House and Senate versions of H.R. 3019 and much higher than earlier House-passed levels. For the NCLIS, H.R. 3019 provided $829,000, an 8 percent cut from the FY 1995 level, but more than the $450,000 passed earlier by the House.

Fiscal Year 1997

President Clinton submitted his FY 1997 budget request to Congress on March 19, about two months later than usual, due to the lack of final detail on FY 1996 funding. The administration requested $110 million "to support new library programs to be authorized under pending legislation." But by the time the appropriations process had been completed in late September, $128.5 million—the highest amount ever—had been appropriated for the LSCA and a total of $136.4 million for library programs. When education became an election issue in presidential and congressional campaigns, leaders in both parties were willing to increase funds for federal education and library programs.

Most proposed increases in funding were for large education programs such as Goal 2000, Title I, and Pell Grants. However, Title II Eisenhower Professional Development and Title VI (formerly Chapter 2), which some school districts use for school library resources, also received increases.

The Library of Congress received FY 1997 appropriations of $361.9 million, including the authority to spend receipts of $30.9 million. The bill reauthorized the American Folklife Center for two years and included current-level funding for the center, which had faced a possible 20 percent cut.

The Institute of Museum Services received an increase to $22 million, while the National Endowment for the Humanities received level funding of $110 million in FY 1997. Funding for the National Endowment for the Arts was set at $99.5 million, the same amount as in FY 1996.

The National Telecommunications and Information Administration's (NTIA) Telecommunications and Information Infrastructure Assistance Program (TIIAP) received $21.49 million in FY 1997. After Senator Robert Kerrey (D-Neb.) and 13 other senators sent a letter supporting TIIAP to Senate Majority Leader Trent Lott (R-Miss.), the Senate Appropriations Committee's slated $4 million funding was restored to $21.49 million in the omnibus appropriations package, P.L. 104-208.

The Denver Public Library ($524,492) and the New York Public Library ($500,000) were among the 67 grant recipients in 42 states and the District of Columbia selected in this year's TIIAP program. More than a dozen other libraries were also involved in partnerships with other organizations. The Department of Commerce's NTIA states that federal matching grants help bring the benefits of the information age to all Americans, particularly those living in rural and underserved inner-city areas.

Grant Opportunities Increased for School Libraries

The Improving America's Schools Act Title VI (program innovation, the former Chapter 2 block grant) received a $35 million increase to $310 million in FY 1997 appropriations. These funds were provided to school districts to carry out a broad range of educational-improvement activities. Purchase of school library materials is one of several allowed purposes of this block grant program. The U.S. Department of Education estimated that 40 percent of these funds are currently spent on school library resources. In part due to ALA efforts on the Improving America's Schools Act, the current School Technology Resources program specified providing training to school library media personnel and including them in the technology planning process.

English as the Official Language

The English Language Empowerment Act, H.R. 123, which ALA and others opposed, passed the House in August 1996. The bill would have made English the official language of the U.S. government and required that official government business be conducted in English. It would also have repealed a federal law requiring that states with large concentrations of non-English-speaking voters

Table 1 / Funding for Federal Library and Related Programs, FY 1996 and 1997
(figures in thousands)

	FY 1996 Appropriation	FY 1997 Appropriation
Library Programs		
GPO Superintendent of Documents	$ 30,307	$ 29,077
Higher Education Act	5,500	7,500
Title II-B: Library Education	2,500	2,500
Title II-B: Research and Demonstrations	3,000	5,000
Library of Congress	324,700[1]	361,896[2]
Library Services and Construction Act	127,005	128,869
Title I: Public Library Services	92,636	100,636
Title II: Public Library Construction	16,369	16,369
Title III: Interlibrary Cooperation	18,000	11,864
Title IV: Indian Library Services [3]	—	—
National Agricultural Library	19,000	19,000
National Commission on Libraries and Information Science	829	897
National Library of Medicine (and MLAA)	140,936	151,103
Library-Related Programs		
Adult Education and Literacy	259,583	354,562
ESEA Title I, Education for Disadvantaged	7,218,608	7,689,000
ESEA Title I-B, Even Start	101,997	101,997
ESEA Title II-A: Eisenhower Professional Development (Federal Activities)	17,984	13,342
ESEA Title II-B: Eisenhower Professional Development (State Grants)	275,000	310,000
ESEA Title III: Education Technology	78,475	305,000
Technology for Education	48,000	266,965
Star Schools, part B	23,000	30,000
ESEA Title VI: Innovative Education Program Strategies (State Grants; formerly Chapter 2: School Library Resources Eligible)	275,000	310,000
Education of Handicapped Children (State Grants)	3,000,000	3,783,685
Educational Research	56,021	72,785
Educational Statistics	46,227	50,000
Educational Assessment	32,623	32,623
Goal 2000	350,000	491,000
HEA Title III: Institutional Development	194,846	194,846
HEA Title IV-C: College Work-Study	616,508	830,000
HEA Title VI: International Education	56,151	59,751
Inexpensive Book Distribution (RIF)	10,300	10,265
Institute of Museum Services	21,000	22,000
NTIA Information Infrastructure Grants (TIIAP)	21,500	21,490
National Archives and Records Administration	199,633	196,963
National Endowment for the Arts	99,494	99,494
National Endowment for the Humanities	110,000	110,000
National Historical Publications and Records Commission	5,000	5,000
Postsecondary Education Improvement Fund	15,000	18,000

1 Includes authority to obligate $28.3 million in receipts.
2 Includes authority to obligate $30.138 million in receipts.
3 Funded at 2 percent of total for LSCA I, II, and III.
Source: American Library Association, Washington Office

provide bilingual ballots and voting information. The Senate adjourned without taking action on a similar bill, S. 352.

ALA was part of a coalition, under the auspices of the Leadership Conference on Civil Rights, that worked to defeat these bills. ALA President Betty Turock, during the first part of 1996, and ALA President Mary Somerville, in the second half, wrote letters to members of Congress urging them not to support any bill that would establish English as the official language of government. They said that ALA opposes all laws, legislation, and regulations relating to language that have the effect of restricting or abridging pluralism and diversity in library collections and services.

Fair Pay Act

ALA supported the Fair Pay Act, H.R. 1507, introduced in 1995 by Representative Eleanor Holmes Norton (D-D.C.), and a similar bill, S. 1650, introduced in 1996 by Senator Tom Harkin (D-Iowa). The bills—developed in cooperation with the National Committee on Pay Equity to which ALA belongs—were not passed.

Government Information Programs

Depository Library Program

In June 1996 the Government Printing Office (GPO) submitted to Congress a study titled *Study to Identify Measures Necessary for a Successful Transition to a More Electronic Depository Library Program*. Public Printer Michael DiMario initiated the study at congressional direction in 1995 to examine the functions and services of the Federal Depository Library Program in a shift to a more electronic program. GPO's first study on this transition, released in December 1995, projected a two-year transition to an almost entirely electronic depository library program.

GPO's second study in June responded to concerns that the first transition plan was based on an overly ambitious time frame. GPO recommended to Congress a five- to seven-year transition. Although long supportive of a more electronic depository library program, continuing concerns of librarians include

- Shifting costs from the government to libraries and the public
- Utilization of appropriate formats for government publications
- Long-term permanent access and preservation of electronic government files for continuing use

The Senate Rules and Administration Committee, chaired by Senator John Warner (R-Va.), conducted four hearings during the summer on "Public Access to Government Information in the 21st Century." ALA President Betty Turock testified on June 18 that the Federal Depository Library Program works extremely well and that Congress had already established the framework for providing public access to government information in the 21st century through this program. Turock warned of the need to know the costs and implications of changes before abandoning current systems and institutions.

Early in the 104th Congress, several bills were introduced to revise printing statutes of government publications but were not enacted. However, the most comprehensive revision of Title 44 *United States Code* was introduced as Congress adjourned by Representative Bill Thomas (R-Calif.). This bill, H.R. 4280, the Government Printing Reform Act of 1996, would have drastically changed the way government publications would be made available to the public by completely decentralizing printing and procurement in all three branches of government. The Government Printing Office had pointed out that if the bill became law as written, it might inadvertently give private vendors control over government information, and thus "the public could lose comprehensive and equitable access to it."

Electronic Records

On December 23, 1996, Public Citizen, joined by ALA and others, filed a complaint against John Carlin in his official capacity as Archivist of the United States in the United States District Court for the District of Columbia. The action challenges the archivist's promulgation of a "General Records Schedule" authorizing all federal agencies to destroy, at their discretion, the only electronic version of federal agency records stored on agency electronic mail and word-processing systems provided the agency has printed a hard copy of the electronic record on paper or microform. This lawsuit is a follow-up to *Armstrong* v. *Executive Office of the President* (Civil Action 89-142), in which ALA was a coplaintiff.

Freedom of Information Act

The Electronic Freedom of Information Act Amendments of 1996, H.R. 3802, were signed into law (P.L. 104-231) on October 2. This legislation clarified that federal government electronic records are subject to disclosure under the Freedom of Information Act (FOIA) and requires agencies to provide records in a requested format whenever possible. It encourages agencies to increase online access to government records. The law addresses the biggest complaint of FOIA requestors—delays in response—by doubling the previous ten-day agency response time. The legislation also requires better record management techniques, such as multitrack processing and expedited service, to those who demonstrate a compelling need for a speedy response.

Postal Service Kiosk Project

In June 1996 the U.S. Postal Service (USPS) began a pilot test in North Carolina of WINGS, the Web Interactive Network of Government Services. USPS plans to work with federal, state, and county government agencies to integrate government services around real-life events, enabling customers to complete government business online, either through the WINGS web site or from public-access kiosks in North Carolina. USPS indicated that lessons learned in the North Carolina pilot project would be used to expand the WINGS service into other locations across the nation.

Lobbying by Nonprofits

A provision in the FY 1997 Labor-HHS-Education Appropriations bill required organizations to disclose federal-funding dollar amounts and percentages on virtually all outgoing communications concerning programs funded through the bill, which was folded into the FY 1997 Omnibus Consolidated Appropriations Act (P.L. 104-208). Reportedly, the Departments of Education, Labor, and Health and Human Services are writing the provision into their grant requirements to give it teeth.

ALA worked with Let America Speak, a coalition of nonprofit organizations, to oppose various disclosure amendments. Leading organizations in the coalition include Independent Sector, a coalition to which ALA belongs.

Local Empowerment and Flexibility

The Local Empowerment and Flexibility Act (S. 88/H.R. 2166), was intended to improve the delivery of benefits and services under federal domestic-assistance programs at the state and local levels. However, nonprofit organizations had many concerns, among them that these bills would undermine the roles and responsibilities of authorizing and appropriations committees of Congress. State, local, or tribal governments, qualified nonprofit organizations, or a qualified consortium would have been able to use federal funds for programs and activities other than those for which those funds were distributed and without complying with certain federal requirements or mandates. In the end, Senator Mark Hatfield (R-Ore.) did not secure passage of S. 88.

Intellectual Property Issues

Fair Use Guidelines

In a time of rapid technological and policy evolution, the library community continued to emphasize that it is premature to formalize guidelines for the fair use of copyrighted materials in a digital-information environment. Fair use is an important element in maintaining the balance that the 1976 Copyright Act embodies and is the long-standing doctrine that allows the use of copyrighted materials without infringement under certain circumstances. ALA and others have always sought in copyright policy a balance between the legitimate needs of copyright proprietors and users of copyrighted materials in the interests of the development and spread of knowledge.

Representatives of library organizations participated in recent attempts to develop fair use guidelines in various areas through the Consortium of College and University Media Centers and the Conference on Fair Use. ALA and others stressed that for copyright policy to remain balanced, fair use must be fully protected and encouraged to evolve in the digital-information environment. To assist practitioners at this pivotal time, ALA, the American Association of Law Libraries (AALL), the Association of Research Libraries (ARL), the Medical Library Association (MLA), and the Special Libraries Association (SLA) committed to investigate the development of guiding principles and examples of current practices in the appropriate use of, and in licensing agreements for, digital-information resources. These organizations also committed to continue to promote respect for copyright law and the continued importance of fair use to the American public.

Intellectual Property Legislation

The ALA, AALL, ARL, MLA, and SLA, with substantial grassroots support, played an active role in attempting to shape major intellectual property legislation. All were involved with the creation of the Digital Future Coalition (DFC), a collaboration of private- and public-sector organizations dedicated to balanced intellectual property law and policies in both the domestic and international arenas.

ALA actively participated in the international treaty negotiation process and worked actively in concert with many other groups to help prevent the adoption of potentially disastrous new international law. Meeting in Geneva December 2–20, 1996, member nations of the World Intellectual Property Organization (WIPO) came together for the first time in 25 years to consider three international agreements to recalibrate copyright law for the digital age: (1) a treaty to update copyright law, especially with respect to works delivered in digital form; (2) a treaty to provide protections for performers in and producers of sound recordings; and (3) a treaty to broadly protect certain economically valuable databases. Delegates from more than 125 industrialized and developing countries attended, as did representatives from some 90 nongovernmental organizations.

The United States government advanced similar proposals for potential adoption by the member nations of WIPO at the Geneva conference. The proposed treaty on databases was not acted on, but the treaties pertaining to copyright broadly and to sound recordings were adopted at the diplomatic conference. The international debate over the new Copyright Treaty was preceded— and ultimately shaped—by intense domestic debate in the United States over the Clinton administration's "white paper" and associated National Information Infrastructure Copyright Protection Act (S. 1284/H.R. 2441), introduced to modernize copyright law to accommodate digital technology. That legislation ultimately was blocked from passage in the 104th Congress because of controversy that it engendered within both the public and private sectors. The treaties must now be ratified in the United States by a two-thirds vote in the Senate and are likely to require at least limited implementing legislation in both chambers of Congress.

The five library associations, acting with each other and through the Digital Future Coalition, also actively opposed the premature adoption of both H.R. 3531 regarding databases and the NII legislation as introduced. Similar efforts also were strenuously and successfully undertaken to prevent international adoption of the proposed Database Treaty and to substantially modify the proposed copyright and sound recordings treaties to facilitate the greatest possible public access to information through electronic networks.

The library community also was involved in debates on numerous other intellectual property issues. For example, ALA's other efforts in intellectual property concentrated on the Copyright Clarifications Act (H.R. 1861), the Copyright Term Extension Act (S. 483/H.R. 989), the Database Investment and

Intellectual Property Antipiracy Act (H.R. 3531), and the National Information Infrastructure Copyright Protection Act (S. 1284/H.R. 2441). Although none passed in the 104th Congress, the library community will monitor similar proposals expected in the 105th Congress and will continue to work with its library colleagues, proprietors' representatives, the Register of Copyrights, and key congressional staffs.

Telecommunications

Passage of Telecommunications Act of 1996

President Clinton signed the Telecommunications Act of 1996 (P.L. 104-104) on February 8 at the Library of Congress following passage by Congress at the end of January. Most people in the library community did not take a position on the bill as a whole, although library advocates actively worked to defeat the Communications Decency Act while supporting the discounted telecommunications provision sponsored by Senators Snowe, Rockefeller, Kerrey, and Exon. As with other issues, local library advocacy coordinated with lobbying at the federal level, was instrumental in the successes that were realized.

Lobbying on Telecommunications Issues

Lobbying efforts by all stakeholders in the telecommunications reform debate were extensive. In the first half of 1996 publicly available lobbying reports showed that local telephone companies spent $16 million and had 60 registered lobbyists to influence the outcome of telecommunications issues. For the same period, long-distance companies had 37 registered lobbyists and direct expenditures of $8 million for this purpose. In contrast, the National Education Association spent $470,000 and ALA spent $126,000; both organizations had two registered lobbyists.

Communications Decency Act

Unfortunately, the inclusion of the Communications Decency Act (CDA) in this historic telecommunications reform legislation prevailed in the final congressional vote. In advocating defeat of this provision, many librarians argued that the provision imposed criminal penalties for transmitting materials via the Internet that are perfectly legal on library and bookstore shelves. Others argued that the CDA would make criminals of adults sending e-mail messages to friends if they used a word that could be considered "indecent" or inappropriate for children. For example, libraries couldn't post their card catalogs for fear a book title might be found offensive. If implemented, this provision would have a tremendously chilling effect on libraries and on everyone who uses the Internet by restricting all communications to a level only appropriate for a child.

ALA and other library advocates, again with broad grassroots support from the library community and others, struggled to get the CDA provision removed or to remove or limit new criminal liability for libraries, educational institutions, and other providers in order to provide some protection for libraries and library workers. On February 26 ALA became the lead litigant, in conjunction with a broad coalition of service providers and others, in a lawsuit challenging the constitutionality of the CDA. *American Library Association* v. *Department of Justice* was consolidated with a separate lawsuit brought by the American Civil Liberties Union (ACLU) and 20 other plaintiffs, *ACLU* v. *Reno*. The cases were argued together in Philadelphia, where, on June 11, a special three-judge federal panel of the United States District Court for the Eastern District of Pennsylvania held that the CDA is unconstitutional. In December the United States Supreme Court agreed to hear the government's appeal of the legal challenge to the CDA. (For further information on the litigation, contact the ALA Office for Intellectual Freedom at 800-545-2433.)

Discounted Telecommunications Rates for Libraries

On the positive side, the provision mandating discounted telecommunications rates for libraries, K–12 schools, and rural health care providers was included in the Telecommunications Act of 1996. The Snowe-Rockefeller-Kerrey-Exon amendment recognized the critical role of libraries and schools as instruments of universal service by bringing advanced telecommunications and information services to their communities. By providing for discounted telecommunications rates, this amendment increased the opportunity for libraries, schools, and rural health care providers to provide these services to give all communities and learners access to the benefits of the "Information Superhighway."

Implementation of Discounted Telecommunications Rates and the Regulatory Proceedings

In March 1996 the FCC began its work on implementation of this part of the act by publishing a "Notice of Proposed Rulemaking" on universal service and having a Federal-State Joint Board on Universal Service hold proceedings to develop implementation recommendations. The joint board, comprised of state and federal regulators, was charged with making recommendations on universal service to the FCC, including recommendations on how state and federal policies could harmonize regulatory efforts. Many library groups participated in the various steps of the joint board and FCC regulatory proceedings. During one of the reply comment phases, libraries were the single largest group of stakeholders to submit formal comments in the proceedings. By the close of 1996 favorable recommendations were being considered by the FCC prior to their spring 1997 deadline for a final rule-making on universal service.

When the joint board issued its report on November 7, 1996, its recommendations included discounts worth up to $2.25 billion on a wide range of telecommunications services for libraries and schools. The participation of library associations, state library agencies, and other library supporters were a key contribution to the favorable recommendations submitted by the joint board to the FCC. These recommendations form the basis upon which the FCC must make its final rule-making, due before May 1997.

Legislation and Regulations Affecting Publishing in 1996

Judith Platt
Director of Communications and Public Affairs, Association of American Publishers

A number of bills affecting book publishing interests were the subject of legislative activity in the 104th Congress. The following is a brief summary of legislation of concern to publishers, and Association of American Publishers (AAP) activities related to these bills, along with a look at the prospects for reemergence of unenacted bills in the 105th Congress.

Intellectual Property

NII Copyright Protection Legislation

Proposed legislation to ensure protection of copyright in the digital environment was not enacted in 1996, but it is certain to be the subject of significant activity in the 105th Congress. Unable to resolve disputes over provisions in the National Information Infrastructure (NII) bill (H.R.2441/S.1284) to (1) limit copyright infringement liability for online service providers and Internet access providers, and (2) prohibit devices that circumvent copyright protection systems, the bill's sponsors could not advance the bill through committee. AAP testified on the legislation before the House Intellectual Property Subcommittee early in 1996, and AAP staff lobbied on Capitol Hill and met with White House, Copyright Office, and PTO personnel, individually and in coordination with representatives of other "copyright industries" as part of the Creative Incentive Coalition (CIC).

Copyright Exemption for the Blind

A provision originally included in the NII bill was ultimately enacted by Congress (P.L. 104-197) as an amendment to the Legislative Branch Appropriations Act. A compromise worked out through cooperation between AAP and representatives of the blind community, the measure adds a new exemption to the Copyright Act, allowing previously published nondramatic literary works to be reproduced and distributed in "specialized formats" (not including large print) exclusively for use by the blind, without the need to obtain permission from the copyright holder. AAP's contribution to the compromise was recognized on the floor of the Senate during consideration of the measure.

Copyright Term Extension

Legislation (S.483/H.R.989) to extend the basic terms of copyright protection by 20 years (to bring U.S. law into line with protection provided to member countries of the European Union) was reported out of the Senate Judiciary Committee but not enacted. The measure was held hostage to unsuccessful efforts by several House and Senate members to win statutory concessions on music licensing to benefit religious broadcasters and restaurant owners. AAP staff worked with

Congressional staff to ensure that provisions on "termination rights" were narrowly crafted. At the request of the bill's sponsors, they also worked with the Copyright Office and representatives of the library, educational, and archival communities in an unsuccessful effort to develop a limited exemption—to meet educational and archival needs—that would be acceptable to rights holders. At year's end it appeared this legislation undoubtedly would be reintroduced.

Copyright Clarifications Legislation

Although passed by the House in June as a non-controversial "technical corrections" bill, H.R. 1861 never moved in the Senate. The bill clarified current law with respect to restoration of copyright protection for certain foreign works (as required under GATT legislation) and broadened the authority of the Copyright Office to raise its fees. In addition, the bill would have reversed controversial court decisions holding, respectively, that automatically copying software into a computer's random access memory when the computer is activated constitutes infringing reproduction, and that the sale or distribution of recordings to the public prior to 1978 constituted publication of the underlying musical compositions. Last-minute disputes over the latter issues and efforts to transform the bill into a vehicle for enacting pieces of other stalled copyright measures blocked action on the bill in the Senate. Many of these legislative issues were considered likely to surface again.

Intellectual Property Organization Legislation

The legislative proposal (S. 1961) that would remove the Copyright Office from the Library of Congress and restructure it as a self-supporting component of a new U.S. Intellectual Property Organization drew such strong opposition that the bill's sponsor, Senate Judiciary Committee Chairman Orrin Hatch (R-Utah), conceded halfway through hearings September 18 that it was "probably not the time" to move the legislation forward. AAP and six organizations representing the library and scholarly communities voiced their alarm in a letter to Senator Hatch over reports that precipitous legislative action might sever the historic relationship between the Copyright Office and the Library of Congress and drastically recast the Copyright Office as a corporate administrative body with onerous obligations for cost recovery and revenue generation. Several of Senator Hatch's colleagues on the Commerce Committee voiced similar concerns. Among the potential negative consequences of such a move would be exorbitant increases in copyright registration and recordation fees and an inevitable reduction in the number of registrations and deposits, impeding the activities of the Copyright Office and damaging the Library of Congress's ability to maintain its collections. It was likely, however, that this proposal would resurface in the 105th Congress.

World Intellectual Property Organization (WIPO) Conference

With the International Intellectual Property Alliance and the Creative Incentive Coalition (CIC), AAP participated in discussions of the proposed "Digital Agenda" and other items that were to be considered in negotiations for a new Berne Convention Protocol and other agreements at the World Intellectual

Property Organization (WIPO) Diplomatic Conference in Geneva in December. Many of the same groups that have opposed the content industries' efforts to effect reasonable NII copyright protection legislation criticized U.S. participation in the WIPO conference, on the grounds that international agreements on the so-called "Digital Agenda" items, prior to resolution of the issues in the context of domestic legislation, would prejudice their interests in the latter process.

Conference on Fair Use

On November 25 the Conference on Fair Use (CONFU) met to work out certain details for concluding its proceedings. Participants agreed that an Interim Report—containing proposed guidelines for multimedia, distance learning, and image archives, as well as "scenarios" guidance on software use—would be issued and posted on the home page of the U.S. Patent and Trademark Office (http://www.uspto.gov). Guidelines (developed by a working group that initially undertook its task outside the CONFU process at the prompting of the Consortium of College and University Media Centers) for the creation of noncommercial educational multimedia projects were widely endorsed by CONFU participants and were lauded in a nonlegislative report drafted with AAP assistance and issued by the House Subcommittee on Intellectual Property. Although the interim report will describe the activities of CONFU working groups on "electronic reserves" and "interlibrary loan/document delivery," it will not contain any proposals for guidelines in these areas. CONFU participants will have until May 1998 to endorse or reject each of the proposed guidelines; at that time, a final CONFU meeting will be held to work out details for issuing a final report.

Freedom of Expression

Child Pornography Prevention Act of 1996

On September 30 the Child Pornography Prevention Act of 1996 was enacted as an amendment to the omnibus budget bill (Section 121 of P.L. 104-208). The new law prohibits visual depictions that "appear to be" of a minor engaging in sexually explicit conduct. The act reflects a radical departure from what the Supreme Court has seen as the key issue in denying First Amendment protection to sexually explicit materials involving children: the state's compelling interest in protecting real children from sexual exploitation. The law imposes massive penalties for giving the impression (through the use of computer simulation or adults posing as minors) that a child is involved. The act also creates an exception to laws restricting the search of newsrooms in cases involving child pornography. Although the final version has serious constitutional flaws, AAP staff along with the Media Coalition convinced Senator Hatch, the bill's chief sponsor, to narrow the bill before markup, eliminating some provisions of the original legislation that were of major concern.

Military Honor and Decency Act

Buried among provisions of the National Defense Authorization Act for fiscal year (FY) 1997, Congress enacted a new law (Section 343 of P.L. 104-201) requiring the Secretary of Defense to issue regulations prohibiting "the sale or rental of sexually explicit material on property under the jurisdiction of the Department of Defense." The new law also prohibits members of the armed forces, and civilian officers or employees of the Defense Department, acting in an official capacity, from providing for the sale, remuneration, or rental of such materials to another person. Although the definition of "sexually explicit material" does not appear to cover books, it clearly includes recordings, movies, and magazines "the dominant theme of which depicts or describes nudity, including sexual or excretory activities or organs, in a lascivious way." AAP, working through the Media Coalition, opposed the bill on First Amendment grounds.

Antiterrorism Act of 1996

Increasing concern about use of the Internet as an organizational tool by terrorist and militia groups initially led the Senate to adopt an amendment to its antiterrorism legislation to prohibit the distribution of information relating to explosive materials for a criminal purpose. The amendment, offered by Senator Dianne Feinstein (D-Calif.), would have made it a felony for any person to "teach or demonstrate the making of explosive materials, or to distribute by any means information pertaining to, in whole or in part, the manufacture of explosive materials" if the person "intends or knows" that the materials or information will be used to commit a federal crime. Although Feinstein's ostensible target was information disseminated on the Internet, the "by any means" language would have made the provision applicable to all distribution media, including books and other print materials. As a result of strong opposition by AAP and other groups on First Amendment grounds, Feinstein's amendment was replaced in the final legislation by a provision requiring the Attorney General to conduct a study to determine whether the establishment of such a criminal offense is necessary with respect to existing Federal law and permissible under the First Amendment (Section 804 of P.L. 104-132). The study, which was due six months after the legislation's April 24, 1996, date of enactment, also requires the Attorney General to develop an evidentiary record on the extent to which such instructive materials are available to the public "in any medium (including print, electronic, or film)," as well as the extent to which they have been or are likely to be used in terrorist incidents.

Electronic Freedom of Information Act Amendments

Congress approved amendments to the Freedom of Information Act to facilitate public access to federal agency records and information maintained in electronic formats (P.L. 104-231). The amendments (among other things) require agencies to make certain information available to the public by means of online access, CD-ROMs, and other electronic means, as well as in hard copy. Persons submitting requests for copies of agency records are now entitled to specify the form in which the materials will be provided, including electronic formats. In addition to addressing electronic record issues, the amendments should facilitate more timely responses to information requests by providing for multitrack processing of requests by agencies and expedited treatment of certain requests. AAP staff worked with newspaper groups and congressional sponsors in support of the legislation.

New Technologies

Encryption Legislation

Encryption—the use of complex numerical sequences to "scramble" electronic transmissions in order to preserve the confidentiality, integrity, or authenticity of communications—is generally viewed as a key tool for providing the privacy, security, and intellectual property protection necessary to achieve the promise of the Internet as a thriving medium for commerce, education, and entertainment. The government's fear that indecipherable encryption will be used to further terrorist or other criminal enterprises, however, has caused it to place export restrictions on the most advanced and secure forms of encryption, despite strenuous objections from American industry that such restrictions hamper their ability to compete in a global marketplace where strong encryption remains available to foreign competitors. U.S. software and hardware companies have been locked in a dispute with the Clinton administration over the latter's proposals to ease the export restrictions if makers (and, therefore, users) of encryption technology agree to a "key escrow" system, requiring them to give a government-approved agent the key to unscramble encrypted communications. U.S. industry opposes the plan as unworkable in the face of foreign availability of strong encryption and the risk of compromise and abuse of escrow authority. Hearings on the issue in the House and Senate produced several bills proposing to roll back export restrictions to the same level of encryption technology that is already generally available abroad and to limit the government's authority to impose key escrow requirements. Although no legislation was enacted before Congress adjourned, strong bipartisan support for House and Senate bills (S. 1726, S. 1587, and H.R. 3011)—and the link between strong encryption and the future of national and global information infrastructures—means that the issue will undoubtedly reappear in the 105th Congress.

Online Privacy Legislation

Apart from its implications for protecting proprietary digital communications, the issue of Internet privacy is a growing legislative concern with respect to the collection, dissemination, and use by commercial enterprises of personally identifiable information from and about Internet users. Online technology such as the so-called "cookies" associated with several popular browsing programs, facilitates tagging and tracking a user's activities in visiting different online sites, producing information that can be used for marketing purposes without the user's knowledge or consent. Prodded by alarming reports in the press and from various public interest groups, the Federal Trade Commission (FTC) and a number of individual legislators are looking critically at current online practices of many Internet entrepreneurs with a special focus on marketing efforts that target particular consumers, especially children.

Another sensitive area involves the proliferation of databases that compile extensive personal information about individuals, including Social Security numbers. Recent news stories regarding the Lexis-Nexis "P-Trak" database (which, until recently, included Standard Address Numbers or "SANs" among the personally identifiable data that could be accessed for a fee) have fueled concerns about the potential for abuse. A variety of businesses are scrambling to head off government regulation of these privacy issues by devising self-enforced industry guidelines and fair information practices. Several public interest groups are sponsoring certification and auditing programs that provide "seals of approval" to online merchants who meet optimal standards for privacy protection. But the FTC and Congress know a good consumer issue when they see it, and businesses are likely to face serious legislative and regulatory proposals in the 105th Congress. These issues are of concern to book publishers, since their ability to maintain copyright protection for their products may depend on technological measures and online practices that could raise additional privacy-related questions about the possible tracking and monitoring of their works and their customers. (Proposed legislation in 1996 included H.R. 3508/S. 1908, H.R. 3685, H.R. 4113, and H.R. 4299.)

FCC Rule-making Proceedings

AAP staff members continue to monitor a number of ongoing Federal Communications Commission (FCC) rule-making proceedings to implement certain provisions of the Telecommunications Reform Act of 1996 and provide for wireless access to the Internet. In brief summary, the proceedings and the related AAP interests are as follows:

- *Universal Service*—Originally designed to make "basic" telephone services available to all Americans at reasonable prices, the universal service system was revised by Congress to call for (among other things) the provision of "advanced telecommunications services" to elementary and secondary schools and libraries at "affordable" rates. The FCC proceeding will determine what services are to be delivered, who will deliver them, and how costs will be handled. Schools and libraries, with the backing of the White House, have used the proceeding to push for free access to the Internet. For AAP members, the issues addressed in this proceeding raise prospects for new marketing and distribution opportunities; they also raise the possibility of new costs, however, if the FCC determines that information service providers and other beneficiaries of broadband pipelines for schools and libraries should bear some of the costs of establishing the pipelines.
- *NII/SUPERNet Devices*—This proceeding anticipates wireless access to the Internet by responding to industry petitions to make spectrum available for use by new unlicensed equipment that will provide short-range, high-speed, wireless digital information transmission capabilities. Because aging school and library facilities in various degrees of obsolescence and disrepair constitute the most expensive obstacle to "wiring them up" to the Internet, the prospect of wireless access as an inexpensive networking alternative is extremely appealing and could speed up the process dramatically.
- *Electronic Publishing Competitive Safeguards*—The Regional Bell Operating Companies (RBOCs), once prohibited by the AT&T antitrust

consent decree from providing electronic publishing services, are now information service providers that may also create and control their own content products—provided they comply with certain competitive safeguards to ensure that they do not leverage their power as monopoly providers of local telephone exchange service to discriminate against competing electronic publishers who rely on local telephone services to deliver their products and services. The FCC proceeding will implement separate subsidiary requirements, as well as a variety of nonstructural safeguards, which are to remain in place for the next five years to prevent anticompetitive behavior by RBOCs in favor of their electronic publishing enterprises.

- *Customer Proprietary Network Information*—Referred to as CPNI, this is information about telephone customers' network services and their use of those services, collected by the telephone company in the course of providing the services. Because the information includes telephone numbers dialed by customers, exact times when customers made calls, and the length of such calls, CPNI provides a highly personalized account of the way customers use their telephones. Who has access to such information and for what purposes are key issues affecting two distinct interests: the privacy of telephone customers and competitive marketing by businesses in competition with the telephone companies. The FCC rule-making will implement congressional requirements to balance these considerations, while protecting both privacy and competitive interests.

Education Funding

Constant reorganization and renaming of programs, together with the "block grant" approach for increased state and local control over the spending of federal funds for education, have made it increasingly difficult to report accurately—let alone lobby—the extent to which federal funds for education are appropriated and authorized to support the purchase of books and other instructional materials.

A $3.5 billion (15 percent) increase in federal educational funding, provided in the Department of Education title of the omnibus appropriations measure for FY 1997 (Title I of P.L. 104-208) enacted shortly before adjournment, provided a surprising increase, however, in each of the major programs that are generally viewed as the main federal sources of funding for instructional materials.

Programs for Disadvantaged Students under Title I of the Elementary and Secondary Education Act (ESEA)—As the largest federal assistance program for poor school districts, Title I is still the largest source of federal funds used to acquire instructional materials. It received nearly $7.2 billion in basic and concentration grants to local educational agencies, an increase of some $464 million over the previous year's appropriations.

School Improvement Programs under Titles II and VI of the ESEA (formerly Chapter 2)—Another large source of federal funding for instructional materials, the consolidation of several funding programs to afford more discretion to state and local educational agencies was accompanied by an increase of more than $70 million over the previous year's appropriations of $550 million. In addition, a boost of over $150 million for the Safe and Drug-Free Schools and Communities programs under Title IV of ESEA may also benefit publishers, as it came with a $25 million increase for the state grant portion and a congressional admonition that "the best use of federal substance abuse prevention funds is in the classroom."

School Reform under the Goal 2000: Educate America Act—Although initially unfunded in the House version of the legislation, these programs, which provide funding that may be used for standardized tests, manuals, and curriculum guides, ended up with an additional $136 million over the previous year's $340 million in funding.

School Assistance in Federally Affected Areas under ESEA Title VIII's Impact Aid Program—This funding, providing compensation to school districts for revenues lost due to government property ownership and the absence of a tax base (such as schools on military bases and Indian reservations), is often the primary revenue source for school districts that use the money for textbooks and other basic necessities. Impact Aid grew by $37 million to some $730 million.

Education supporters were optimistic that, regardless of the outcome of the elections, they would not face a repeat in Congress of 1996's battle to cut back funding increases enacted during the previous year.

Postal Issues

Postal Reform Act of 1996

Less than a month before Congress adjourned, the House Postal Service Subcommittee held hearings on its chairman's postal reform bill (H.R. 3717). Testifying before the subcommittee, the chairman of AAP's Postal Committee called the bill "an important first step" in necessary reform efforts to improve the efficiency, competitiveness, and financial health of the U.S. Postal Service.

AAP's testimony focused on proposed changes to the rate-making process, praising those changes that would provide for negotiated rate agreements, market tests for experimental new products, the institution of price caps, and a five-year cycle for rate adjustments. The AAP witness expressed concerns, however, about proposals to downgrade the significance of "content" as a rate-making criterion, distinguish between competitive and noncompetitive product categories, and provide an "exigent circumstances" exception to the five-year rate-making cycle for noncompetitive products. Although the timing of the hearings made it clear that there would be no further action on the bill before adjournment, the process apparently signals an effort in the 105th Congress to consider changes in the legal framework for postal operations in the face of increasing challenges to the U.S. Postal Service from new technologies and private-sector competitors. Postal rates and reform remain important issues for many AAP members; notwithstanding the marketing potential of the Internet, it appears that distribution and delivery will, at least for the foreseeable future, remain an analog service.

Funding Programs and Grant-Making Agencies

National Endowment for the Humanities

1100 Pennsylvania Ave. N.W., Washington, DC 20506
202-606-8400, 800-634-1121
E-mail: info@neh.fed.us
World Wide Web: http://www.neh.fed.us

Thomas C. Phelps

> Democracy demands wisdom and vision in its citizens.
> —National Foundation on the Arts and Humanities Act of 1965

In order to "promote progress and scholarship in the humanities and the arts in the United States," Congress enacted the National Foundation on the Arts and the Humanities Act of 1965. This act established the National Endowment for the Humanities (NEH) as an independent grant-making agency of the federal government to support research, education, and public programs in the humanities. In the act, the term *humanities* includes, but is not limited to, the study of the following: language, both modern and classical; linguistics; literature; history; jurisprudence; philosophy; archaeology; comparative religion; ethics; the history, criticism, and theory of the arts; those aspects of the social sciences that have humanistic content and employ humanistic methods; and the study and application of the humanities to the human environment, with particular attention to reflecting our diverse heritage, traditions, and history and to the relevance of the humanities to the current conditions of national life.

The years 1995 and 1996 were years of change and challenge for the National Endowment for the Humanities. And 1997 will be little different. The NEH budget for fiscal year (FY) 1996 was drastically reduced by the U.S. Congress by more than one-third, and NEH faces the possibility of further reductions during the appropriations debates. NEH staff has been reduced accordingly, and, because of reduced appropriations, the agency has been reorganized. It is hoped, however, that it has been reorganized in such a way as to fulfill its mission and support its projects with even fewer resources, both human and financial. As the chairman of the endowment has written, "In spite of the reduced resources, the endowment is committed to continued support for projects that bring the humanities to the American people in the form of scholarly works, college and school teacher renewal opportunities, exhibitions in our cultural institutions, films, radio programs, library programs, newspaper and other material preservation, and other endeavors." For FY 1997, with an appropriation of $110 million (as opposed to approximately $172 million in FY 1996) NEH staff believe that, more than ever, the humanities have a crucial role to play in shaping America's future. At a time when sound bites take precedence over sound reasoning, it is urgent that the humanities lead the way to thoughtful discussion and careful listening.

To assist these endeavors and discussions, NEH, in its reorganized form, supports projects in three divisions: Preservation and Access, Public Programs, and Research and Education Programs. Through its Challenge Grant program, it supports institutions that in some way enhance the humanities in American life to raise needed resources. Through its Office of Enterprise, NEH works with other agencies, foundations, and corporations to bring a full compliment of programs to the American people in new and dynamic ways. And through its newly organized Office of Federal/State Partnerships, NEH fosters public understanding of the humanities throughout the nation, primarily through locally developed programs aimed at general audiences. To reach this goal, NEH provides support for state humanities councils in the 50 states, the District of Columbia, Puerto Rico, the U.S. Virgin Islands, the Northern Mariana Islands, America Samoa, and Guam. (See state council addresses and telephone numbers at the end of this article, or visit the NEH home page: http://www.neh.fed.us.)

What the Endowment Supports

NEH supports exemplary work to advance and disseminate knowledge in all the disciplines of the humanities. Endowment support is intended to assist cultural and educational institutions and complement private and local efforts. In the most general terms, NEH-supported projects aid scholarship and research in the humanities, help improve humanities education, and foster a greater curiosity about and understanding of the humanities.

Whom the Endowment Supports

NEH welcomes applications from nonprofit associations, institutions, and organizations. Applicants are encouraged to consult with NEH staff by phone or letter before submitting a formal proposal. Given enough lead time, staff will comment on draft proposals and assist applicants when appropriate.

How Applications Are Evaluated

Each application is assessed first by knowledgeable persons outside the agency who are asked for their judgments about the quality and significance of the proposed project. In FY 1995 about 1,200 scholars, professionals in the humanities, and other experts—such as librarians, curators, and filmmakers—served on approximately 225 panels. Panelists represent a diversity of disciplinary, institutional, regional, and cultural backgrounds. In some programs the judgment of panelists is supplemented by reviews from specialists who have extensive knowledge of the specific subject or technical aspects of the application.

The advice of evaluators is assembled by NEH staff, who comment on matters of fact or on significant issues that would otherwise be missing from the review. These materials are forwarded to the National Council on the Humanities, a board of 26 citizens nominated by the president of the United States and confirmed by the Senate. The council meets three times a year to advise the chairman of the endowment about matters of policy and about applications. The chairman, who is appointed for a four-year term by the president of the United States with consent of the Senate, takes into account the advice provided by panelists, reviewers, endowment staff, and members of the National Council on the Humanities, and, by law, makes the final decision about funding. A final decision can normally be expected about six months after the application deadline. Final decisions made by the chairman may not be appealed, but revised submissions are encouraged and accepted.

Grantmaking Programs

Public Programs

The division fosters public understanding and appreciation of the humanities by supporting projects that bring significant insights of the disciplines of the humanities to general audiences of all ages through interpretive exhibitions, radio and television programs, lectures, symposia, conferences, multimedia projects, printed materials, and reading and discussion groups.

Grants support projects that lead to the study of books, new technologies, and other resources found in collections housed in libraries and archives. Projects can be in many formats, including reading and discussion programs, lectures, symposia, and interpretive exhibitions of books, manuscripts, and other library resources. Useful supplementary materials—such as publications, media components, educational programming materials, and curricula guides—also receive support through grants from this division. The division also makes grants for the planning, scripting, and production of television and radio programs, as well as grants for exhibitions of cultural artifacts and other resources found in the collections of museums and historical sites.

Eligible applicants:	Nonprofit institutions and organizations including public television and radio stations and state humanities councils
Application deadline:	January 12, 1998
Information:	202-606-8267
	E-mail: publicpgms@neh.fed.us

Preservation and Access

In this division, grants are made for projects that will create, preserve, or increase the availability of resources important for research, education, and public programming in the humanities. Projects may encompass books, journals, newspapers, manuscript and archival materials, maps, still and moving images, sound recordings, and objects of material culture held by libraries, archives, museums, historical organizations, and other repositories.

Support may be sought to preserve the intellectual content and aid bibliographic control of collections; to compile bibliographies, descriptive catalogs, and guides to cultural holdings; to create dictionaries, encyclopedias, databases, and other types of research tools and reference works; and to stabilize material-culture collections through the appropriate housing and storing of objects, improved environmental control, and the installation of security, lighting, and fire prevention systems. Applications may also be submitted for national and regional education and training projects, regional preservation field service programs, and research and demonstration projects that are intended to enhance institutional practice and the use of technology for preservation and access. Proposals may combine preservation and access activities with a single project.

    Eligible applicants: Individuals, nonprofit institutions, and cultural organizations, associations, state agencies, and institutional consortia
    Application deadline: July 1
    Information: 202-606-8570
    E-mail: preservation@neh.fed.us

Research and Education

Through grants to educational institutions and fellowships to scholars and teachers and through the support of significant research, this division's programs are designed to strengthen sustained, thoughtful study of the humanities at all levels of education.

Education Development and Demonstration

Grants, including "next semester" Humanities Focus Grants, support curriculum and materials development efforts, faculty study programs within and among educational institutions, and conferences and networks of institutions. NEH is interested in projects that help teachers use new technologies to enhance students' understanding of the humanities.

    Eligible applicants: Public and private elementary and secondary schools, school systems, colleges and universities, nonprofit academic associations, and cultural institutions, such as libraries and museums
    Application deadlines: Education Development and Demonstration: October 1
    Humanities Focus Grants: September 15
    Information: 202-606-8380
    E-mail: research@neh.fed.us

Fellowships and Stipends

Grants provide support for scholars to undertake full-time independent research and writing in the humanities. Grants are available for a maximum of one year and a minimum of six weeks of summer study.

    Eligible applicants: Individuals
    Application deadlines: Fellowships: May 1
                                    Summer Stipends: October 1
    Information: 202-606-8467
                                    E-mail: research@neh.fed.us

Collaborative and Institution-Based Research

Grants provide up to three years of support for collaborative research in the preparation for publication of editions, translations, and other important works in the humanities and in the conduct of large or complex interpretive studies, including archaeology projects and the humanities studies of science and technology. Grants also support research opportunities offered through independent research centers and scholarly organizations and international research centers.

    Eligible applicants: Individuals, institutions of higher education, nonprofit professional associations, scholarly societies, and other nonprofit organizations
    Application deadlines: Collaborative Research: September 2
                                    Centers for Advanced Study and International Research: October 1
    Information: 202-606-8210
                                    E-mail: research@neh.fed.us

Seminars and Institutes

Grants support summer seminars and national institutes in the humanities for college and school teachers. These faculty development activities are conducted at colleges and universities across the country. Those wishing to participate in seminars submit their applications to the seminar director. Lists of pending seminars and institutes are available from the program.

    Eligible applicants: Individuals and institutions of higher learning
    Application deadlines: Seminar participants, 1997 seminars: March 1
                                    Seminar directors, 1998 seminars: March 1
                                    National institutes: March 1
    Information: 202-606-8463
                                    E-mail: research@neh.fed.us

Challenge Grants

Regular Challenge

Nonprofit institutions interested in developing new sources of long-term support for educational, scholarly, preservation activities and public programs in the humanities may be assisted in these efforts by an NEH Challenge Grant. Grantees are required to raise three or four dollars in new or increased donations for every federal dollar offered. Both federal and nonfederal funds may be used to establish or increase institutional endowments and thus guarantee long-term support for a variety of humanities needs. Funds may also be used for limited direct capital expenditures where such needs are compelling and clearly related to improvements in the humanities endeavors undertaken by the institution.

>   Eligible applicants: Nonprofit postsecondary, educational, research, or cultural institutions and organizations such as libraries working within the realm of the humanities

Special Initiative

A special initiative to assist public libraries in creating endowments to support humanities programming is available to libraries that have not previously held an NEH Challenge Grant. Awards made through this initiative have a maximum of $150,000 in federal dollars, and the recipient is required to raise two times the amount (rather than three) of federal funds offered. Applications will be accepted at the regular Challenge Grant deadline.

>   Application deadline: May 1
>   Information: 202-606-8309
>   E-mail: challenge@neh.fed.us

Enterprise

The Enterprise Office implements NEH special initiatives, creates partnerships with other federal agencies and private organizations, engages in raising funds for humanities activities, and explores other leadership opportunities for the agency.

Federal/State Partnerships

Each state council establishes its own grant guidelines and sets its own application deadlines. State humanities councils support a wide variety of projects in the humanities, including library reading programs, lectures, conferences, seminars and institutes for teachers and school administrators, media presentations, and museum and library traveling exhibitions. State councils on the humanities exist in every state, the District of Columbia, Puerto Rico, the U.S. Virgin Islands, the Northern Mariana Islands, American Samoa, and Guam.

Alabama Humanities Foundation
2217 Tenth Ct. S.
Birmingham, AL 35205
205-930-0540

Alaska Humanities Forum
421 W. First Ave., No. 210
Anchorage, AK 99501
907-272-5341

Arizona Humanities Council
The Ellis-Shackelford House
1242 N. Central Ave.
Phoenix, AZ 85004-1887
602-257-0335

Arkansas Humanities Council
10816 Executive Center Dr., No. 310
Little Rock, AR 72211-4383
501-221-0091

California Council for the Humanities
312 Sutter St., No. 601
San Francisco, CA 94108
415-391-1474

Colorado Endowment for the Humanities
1623 Blake St., No. 200
Denver, CO 80202
303-573-7733

Connecticut Humanities Council
955 S. Main St., Suite E
Middletown, CT 06547
860-685-2260

Delaware Humanities Forum
1812 Newport Gap Pike
Wilmington, DE 19808-6179
302-633-2400

D.C. Humanities Council
1331 H St. NW, No. 902
Washington, DC 20005
202-347-1732

Florida Humanities Council
1514 1/2 E. Eighth Ave.
Tampa, FL 33605-3708
813-272-3473

Georgia Humanities Council
50 Hurt Plaza S.E., No. 440
Atlanta, GA 30303-2915
404-523-6220

Hawaii Committee for the Humanities
First Hawaiian Bank Bldg.
3599 Wai'alae Ave., Rm. 23
Honolulu, HI 96816
808-732-5402

Idaho Humanities Council
217 W. State St.
Boise, ID 83702
208-345-5346

Illinois Humanities Council
203 Wabash Ave., No. 2020
Chicago, IL 60601-2417
312-422-5580

Indiana Humanities Council
1500 N. Delaware St.
Indianapolis, IN 46202
317-638-1500

Iowa Humanities Board
Oakdale Campus Northlawn
University of Iowa
Iowa City, IA 52242
319-335-4153

Kansas Humanities Council
112 S.W. Sixth Ave., No. 210
Topeka, KS 66603
913-357-0359

Kentucky Humanities Council
206 Maxwell St.
Lexington, KY 40508
606-257-5932

Louisiana Endowment for the Humanities
225 Baronne St., Suite 1414
New Orleans, LA 70112-1709
504-523-4352

Maine Humanities Council
371 Cumberland Ave.
Box 7202
Portland, ME 04112
207-773-5051

Maryland Humanities Council
601 N. Howard St.
Baltimore, MD 21201
410-625-4830

Massachusetts Foundation for the Humanities
One Woodbridge St.
South Hadley, MA 01075
413-536-1385

Michigan Humanities Council
119 Pere Marquette Dr., No. 3B
Lansing, MI 48912-1231
517-372-7770

Minnesota Humanities Commission
26 E. Ivy St.
Lower Level S.
St. Paul, MN 55106-2046
612-774-0105

Mississippi Humanities Council
3825 Ridgewood Rd., Rm. 311
Jackson, MS 39211
601-982-6752

Missouri Humanities Council
911 Washington Ave., No. 215
St. Louis, MO 63101-1208
314-621-7705

Montana Committee for the Humanities
Box 8036, Hellgate Station
Missoula, MT 59807
406-243-6022

Nebraska Humanities Council
Lincoln Center Bldg., No. 225
215 Centennial Mall S.
Lincoln, NE 68508
402-474-2131

Nevada Humanities Committee
1034 N. Sierra St.
Reno, NV 89507
702-784-6527

New Hampshire Humanities Council
19 Pillsbury St.
Box 2228
Concord, NH 03302-2228
603-224-4071

New Jersey Council for the Humanities
28 West State St., 6th flr.
Trenton, NJ 08608
609-695-4838

New Mexico Endowment for the Humanities
209 Onate Hall
University of New Mexico
Albuquerque, NM 87131
505-277-3705

New York Council for the Humanities
198 Broadway, 10th flr.
New York, NY 10038
212-233-1131

North Carolina Humanities Council
425 Spring Garden St.
Greensboro, NC 27401
919-334-5325

North Dakota Humanities Council
2900 Broadway E., No. 3
Box 2191
Bismarck, ND 58502
701-255-3360

Ohio Humanities Council
695 Bryden Rd.
Box 06354
Columbus, OH 43206-0354
614-461-7802

Oklahoma Foundation for the Humanities
Festival Plaza
428 W. California, No. 270
Oklahoma City, OK 73102
405-235-0280

Oregon Council for the Humanities
812 S.W. Washington St., No. 225
Portland, OR 97205
503-241-0543

Pennsylvania Humanities Council
320 Walnut St., No. 305
Philadelphia, PA 19106
215-925-1005

Rhode Island Committee for the Humanities
60 Ship St.
Providence, RI 02903
401-273-2250

South Carolina Humanities Council
1308 Columbia College Dr.
Box 5287
Columbia, SC 29250
803-691-4100

South Dakota Humanities Council
Box 7050, University Station
Brookings, SD 57007
605-688-6113

Tennessee Humanities Council
1003 18th Ave. S.
Nashville, TN 37212
615-320-7001

Texas Council for the Humanities
Banister Place A
3809 S. Second St.
Austin, TX 78704
512-440-1991

Utah Humanities Council
350 S. 400 E., No. 110
Salt Lake City, UT 84111
801-359-9670

Vermont Council on the Humanities
17 Park St., RR 1, Box 7285
Morrisville, VT 05561
802-888-3183

Virginia Foundation for the Humanities
145 Ednam Dr.
Charlottesville, VA 22903-4629
804-924-3296

Washington Commission for the Humanities
615 Second Ave., No. 300
Seattle, WA 98104
206-682-1770

West Virginia Humanities Council
723 Kanawha Blvd. E., No. 800
Charleston, WV 25301
304-346-8500

Wisconsin Humanities Council
802 Regent St.
Madison, WI 53715
608-262-0706

Wyoming Council for the Humanities
Box 3643, University Station
Laramie, WY 82071-3643
307-766-3142

American Samoa Humanities Council
Box 5800
Pago Pago, AS 96799
684-633-4870

Guam Humanities Council
272 W. Rte. 8, No. 2A
Barrigada, Guam 96913
671-734-1713

Commonwealth of the Northern Mariana Islands Council for the Humanities
AAA-3394, Box 10001
Saipan, MP 96950
670-235-4785

Fundación Puertorriqueña de las Humanidades
109 San Jose St., 3rd flr.
Box 9023920
Old San Juan, PR 00902-3920
809-721-2087

Virgin Islands Humanities Council
5-6 Kongens Gade, Corbiere Complex, Suite 200B
St. Thomas, VI 00802
809-776-4044

Applications

Guidelines and application forms are available from the program or from the Public Information Office, National Endowment for the Humanities, 1100 Pennsylvania Avenue N.W., Washington, DC 20506, telephone 202-606-8400 or 800-NEH-1121, e-mail info@neh.fed.us, or from the NEH home page at http:\\www.neh.fed.us. For the hearing impaired, the TDD is 202-606-8282. The Public Information Office does not maintain a general mailing list. Instead, NEH responds to specific requests for publications and guidelines.

Note: The applications deadlines listed in this article may change because of budget uncertainties. Until a full appropriations budget is adopted and enacted by the Congress and upheld without veto by the president, the endowment will operate on a continuing resolution at a reduction from the already reduced funding recommended by the Congress.

U.S. Department of Education Library Programs, 1996

555 New Jersey Avenue N.W., Washington, DC 20208-5571
202-219-2299, fax 202-219-1725

Robert Klassen
Director, Library Programs
Office of Educational Research and Improvement
U.S. Department of Education

Library Programs provides leadership to develop and improve the nation's libraries and library education by administering programs under the Library Services and Construction Act and the Higher Education Act, Title II. These programs support a wide range of projects in all types of libraries.

- Promoting access to local public library services for underserved and at-risk citizens
- Promoting access to the "Information Superhighway" for all citizens
- Constructing public library facilities
- Developing cooperation and resource-sharing opportunities
- Developing library services to Indian Tribes, Alaska Native Villages, and Hawaiian Natives
- Providing training and professional development
- Supporting public library-based literacy programs for adults

In addition, Library Programs serves the nation's libraries by

- Working with the states to plan and evaluate statewide library development
- Conducting research and demonstrations on current library issues
- Disseminating information about its programs and research

In fiscal year (FY) 1996 the Office of Library Programs continued an important special project, begun in FY 1994, to assess the role of school and public libraries in education reform. Westat, Inc., in cooperation with the American Library Association (ALA), is conducting the three-year, $1.3 million study funded under the Secretary's Fund for Innovation in Education.

Through national surveys and case studies of selected programs, this study is seeking to find out how school and public libraries are performing as education providers and how well they are responding to the country's urgent demands for

Note: The following Library Programs staff assisted in writing this article: Christina Dunn, Donald Fork, Jane Heiser, Evaline Neff, Kathy Price, Trish Skaptason, and Judy Stark.

school improvement. This combination of quantitative and qualitative data should provide a rich portrait of school and public libraries, offering current and reliable information to researchers, policymakers, and practitioners on six key issues:

- To what extent are school and public libraries contributing to education reform and to what extent can they contribute?
- What programs and services are school and public libraries providing to meet the needs of preschool and elementary and secondary (K–12) education providers?
- How well do these services and programs meet the needs of preschool and K–12 education providers?
- Do school and public libraries have the capacity—human and information resources, technology, and facilities—to adequately respond to identified needs and support systemic reform?
- What new technologies are promoting student opportunity to learn by improving services and resources in school and public libraries?
- What can we learn from successful school and public library programs and services designed to support preschool and K–12 education? Can these programs serve as models for the improvement of all school and public libraries? What are the barriers to effective services and programs?

In addition, the study will give special consideration to the issue of how school and public libraries can best serve the needs of disadvantaged students.

On September 30, 1996, the president approved legislation creating an Institute of Museum and Library Services, consolidating federal programs of support for libraries with programs of support for museums. This action renews and reorganizes the Library Services and Construction Act (LSCA) and Title II of the Higher Education Act (HEA II) into the Library Services and Technology Act (LSTA). LSCA and HEA II will operate in FY 1997; funding will become available under LSTA in FY 1998. LSTA, authorized for $150 million, streamlines federal library services programs to allow libraries to adapt new technologies to identify, preserve, and share library and information resources across institutional, local and state boundaries, and to extend outreach to those for whom library service requires extra effort or special materials. In addition, LSTA provides support for library services to Indian tribes, and for national leadership competitive grants and contracts for education and training, research and demonstration, preservation or digitization of library materials, and model cooperative programs between museums and libraries.

Higher Education Act (HEA, P.L. 99-498)

Title II of the Higher Education Act has been the backbone of federal financial assistance to colleges and universities for more than two decades. With the continuing expansion of information resources and the increasing demands on higher education libraries, Title II has been an important factor in helping these libraries to preserve, acquire, and share resources, and to use new technologies to improve services. In addition, it has assisted institutions of higher education in training and retraining personnel and conducting research and demonstrations in library and information science.

In FY 1996 only those programs under HEA II-B continued to be funded. They are Library Education and Training—Fellowships and Institutes, with an appropriation of $2,500,000, and Research and Demonstration, with an appropriation of $3,000,000.

Library Education and Human Resource Development Program (HEA II-B)

The Library Education and Human Resource Development Program (Title II-B of the Higher Education Act) authorizes a program of federal financial assistance to institutions of higher education and other library organizations and agencies to assist in training persons in library and information science and to establish, develop, and expand programs of library and information science. Grants are made for fellowships at the master's and doctoral levels, and for traineeships. Grants may also be used to assist in covering the costs of institutes, or courses, to upgrade the competencies of persons serving in all types of libraries, information centers, or instructional materials centers offering library and information services, and of those serving as educators.

Fellowships

In FY 1996 Congress appropriated $2,500,000 for the HEA II-B, Library Education and Human Resource Development Program. The U.S. Department of Education awarded $1,826,000 to 24 institutions of higher education to provide new and continuing fellowships in library and information science for academic year 1996–1997; a total of 37 grants were awarded to support 35 master's and 44 continuing doctoral fellowships. Between 1966 and 1996, institutions of higher education have received a total of $51,568,720 to support 1,503 doctoral, 282 post-master's, 3,365 master's, 16 bachelor's, and 53 associate's fellowships, and 77 traineeships.

Each grant provides funding to the school to cover the cost of training ($8,000 for master's-level and $10,000 for doctoral-level studies), allowing the school to waive all tuition fees. In addition, each grant provides fellowship recipients with a stipend of up to $14,000 a year, based on demonstrated need. The stipend amount is the same for master's and doctoral students. The institution receiving the grant has the sole responsibility for selecting fellowship recipients.

Areas of study reflect the Secretary of Education's priorities:

- To recruit, educate, train, retrain, and retain minorities in library and information science

- To educate, train, or retrain library personnel in areas of library specialization where there are currently shortages such as school media, children's services, young adult services, science reference, and cataloging
- To educate, train, or retrain library personnel in new techniques of information acquisition, transfer, and communication technology

In FY 1996 all fellowship awards focused on training library personnel in new techniques of information management. Of these awards, 11 supported recruiting and educating minorities in library and information science, while six supported educating personnel in areas of library specialization where there are currently shortages, primarily school and public librarians serving youth. Table 1 lists new and continuation grants, identifying the grantee institution, number of fellowships, level of study, and the purpose or area of study.

Institutes

In FY 1996 the U.S. Department of Education awarded $649,000 to support 10 institutes or training workshops primarily for school and public librarians. Nine institutions of higher education or library organizations received funding. Table 2 identifies these grantee institutions, describes the project, and gives the amount of each award. However, this amount does not necessarily reflect all of the resources devoted to an institute, as the grantee institution may provide additional support.

The institutes represent a variety of subject matter and approaches. However, all address at least one of the secretary's priorities:

- To recruit, educate, train, retrain, and retain minorities in library and information science
- To educate, train, or retrain library personnel in areas of library specialization where there are currently shortages such as school media, children's services, young adult services, science reference, and cataloging
- To educate, train, or retrain library personnel in new techniques of information acquisition, transfer, and communication technology
- To educate, train, or retrain library personnel to serve the information needs of the elderly, the illiterate, the disadvantaged, or residents of rural America, including Native Americans

Of the ten institutes funded in FY 1996, seven support training library personnel in information management; four, training in areas of library specialization where there are currently shortages; and two, training to serve the information needs of special populations. Most of the institutes focus on school and public librarians working with youth.

Table 1 / HEA Title II-B, Library Education and Human Resource Development Program, FY 1996 Awards

Grantee	Number and Level	Area of Study
University of Alabama	3 Doctoral	New techniques in information management; youth services; minorities
University of California, Los Angeles	2 Master's	New techniques in information management; youth services, cataloging, science reference; minorities
	3 Doctoral	Youth services—school and public libraries, science reference, cataloging; minorities
University of Central Arkansas	1 Master's	Youth services—school libraries; minorities
Florida State University	1 Doctoral	Youth services
Indiana University	2 Doctoral	New techniques in information management; youth services; handicapped services; adult services; literacy
University of Iowa	2 Master's	Youth services—school & public libraries
Kent State University	4 Master's	New techniques in information management; youth services—public libraries
Louisiana State University	3 Master's	Science reference; minorities
University of Maryland	5 Doctoral	New techniques in information management; youth services; information literacy
University of Michigan, Ann Arbor	3 Master's	New techniques in information management; youth services—school libraries, science reference; minorities
	6 Doctoral	New techniques in information management; minorities; library education and research
University of Missouri–Columbia	3 Master's	New techniques in information management; youth services—school libraries, science reference; minorities
University of North Texas	3 Doctoral	New techniques in information management; minorities
University of Oklahoma	4 Master's	Youth services—school libraries, cataloging; science reference; minorities
University of Pittsburgh	5 Doctoral	Cataloging; youth services; minorities; library education and research
Rutgers University	2 Doctoral	Library education, research, planning, and evaluation; minorities
University of South Florida	1 Master's	New techniques in information management; youth services, cataloging, science reference; minorities
Southern Connecticut State University	4 Master's	Youth services—public libraries; minorities
University of Southern Mississippi	2 Master's	New techniques in information management; youth services—school libraries, cataloging

Table 1 / HEA Title II-B, Library Education and Human Resource Development Program, FY 1996 Awards *(cont.)*

Grantee	Number and Level	Area of Study
State University of New York, Albany	2 Doctoral	New techniques in information management—research in the nature of information; library education and research
Syracuse University	5 Doctoral	New techniques in information management; library education and research
University of Texas at Austin	3 Doctoral	Cataloging in a computerized environment; readiness for school; health and engineering information; library education, planning, and research
Texas Woman's University	1 Master's	New techniques in information management; youth services—school and public libraries, cataloging; library education; minorities
	4 Doctoral	Youth services—school and public libraries; cataloging; minorities
Wayne State University	2 Master's	Youth services—school libraries, cataloging, science reference; minorities
University of Wisconsin–Milwaukee	3 Master's	Youth services—public libraries; minorities

Table 2 / HEA II-B, Library Education and Human Resource Development Program, FY 1996 Institute Awards

California

University of California
The Library
Berkeley, CA 94720-6000

$106,219
Janice H. Burrows
510-642-3778

This project represents Phase II of a partnership between the University of California, Berkeley (UCB) Library and the University of California Extension, with the participation of the UCB School of Information Management and Systems, to develop and test a replicable continuing education curriculum for librarians through a series of experimental institutes designed to significantly enhance the skills of currently practicing librarians. The project will result in the successful design of a model of professional education that will equip current information specialists to exercise leadership in meeting the information needs of 21st century society.

Florida

Pensacola Junior College
District Learning Resources
1000 College Blvd.
Pensacola, FL 32504

$55,620
Sandra Lockney-Davis
904-484-2010

The project will offer a series of five-day Institutes of instruction and hands-on training in new technology, specifically in searching and evaluating electronically-based information, to all levels of library personnel in academic, public, college, and school libraries in a tri-county area. Instruction will include teaching critical thinking skills and techniques for searching online or CD databases, evaluating retrieved information, and applying electronically-based information in library and classroom environments.

Table 2 / **HEA II-B, Library Education and Human Resource Development Program, FY 1996 Institute Awards** *(cont.)*

Georgia

Southeastern Library Network (SOLINET) $58,152
1438 West Peachtree St. N.W., Suite 200 Amy Bernath
Atlanta, GA 30309-2955 404-892-0943

The Southeastern Library Network (SOLINET) will design, implement, and evaluate a continuing education institute to develop rural public library leaders from 10 southeastern states in the management of new information technologies. The institute will give rural public librarians critical skills to enable them to effectively manage the use of information technology, foster development and support of community networks, and lead their libraries into the future. The institute will also serve as a model that can be easily replicated in individual states or in other regions.

Louisiana

Louisiana State University $51,630
School of Library and Information Science Beth H. Paskoff
267 Coates Hall 504-388-1480
Baton Rouge, LA 70803

This institute will train 70 librarians from all public libraries in Louisiana and the State Library of Louisiana to learn about appropriate science resources for adults, young adults, and children, and to acquire basic competencies in applying contemporary technologies to access this information. The institute will feature free and low-cost electronic resources available to all parish libraries through the Louisiana Library Network, as well as other electronic and print resources. Institute activities will include a combination of lecture, discussion, demonstration, and hands-on exercises, with opportunities for participants to prepare instructional modules for training other public library staff in electronic access to science information.

Louisiana State University $44,244
School of Library and Information Science Dana Watson
Baton Rouge, LA 70803 504-388-3158

School and public librarians in the southwest region will participate in a one-week intensive seminar on multicultural children's literature, its selection and evaluation within the collection management process, and related services. Participants will train/retrain in current theory and practice of collection management, including access to information using computer technology. Seminar activities will include a combination of lecture, discussion, field trips, role play, small group discussion, and hands-on experiences. Each participant will have the opportunity to complete a selected project.

New Jersey

Rutgers University $69,663
School of Communication, Information, Karen Novick
 and Library Studies, Professional Development Studies 908-932-7169
4 Huntington St.,
New Brunswick, NJ 08903

Because there are few formal educational programs for library paraprofessionals and few libraries provide broad-based training for their support staff, the Library Assistant Training Program is designed for paraprofessionals working in New Jersey libraries. The program consists of one module of required basic training and 12 other elective modules in areas including children's services, technology in libraries, technical services, reference services, and public services. The ultimate goal of the program is to provide library staff with the knowledge they need to deliver quality library services to the citizens of New Jersey.

New York

The New York Public Library $65,811
8 W. 40 St., 7th fl. Irene M. Percelli
New York, NY 10018 212-930-0639

Table 2 / HEA II-B, Library Education and Human Resource
Development Program, FY 1996 Institute Awards *(cont.)*

The collections of the New York Public Library's Research Libraries comprise over 39 million items; the library's collections of primary materials, such as manuscripts, archives, and ephemera, are as renowned as the size and scope of its holdings of secondary literature. Library staff must be prepared to meet the increasing and changing demands of users and embrace the technological capabilities to provide research library services in the 21st century. To prepare staff and management to provide library service with a strong service orientation and technology base, the library has embarked on a comprehensive staff development program. Staff in the Science, Industry and Business Library (SIBL) received training over a three-year period in technology competencies, service excellence, and professional development. The model of staff training developed at SIBL has provided the library with important prototypes for staff training and development throughout the organization. The proposed institute will play a critical role in the library's effort to provide staff the technological expertise necessary to teach a wide user base how to access information in digital formats and to create new electronic resources to make information more accessible to users, both on and off site.

Ohio

Kent State University $61,425
School of Library and Information Science Greg Byerly
Kent, OH 44242-0001 330-672-2782

This institute is designed to retrain and educate selected school library media specialists, public librarians, and academic librarians in the role that training must play in the effective use of information technology systems for young adults. The institute will provide an awareness and understanding of the need for effective training on new technologies; a structured opportunity for considering the local implications of a coordinated training program involving school media centers, public libraries, and academic libraries; an awareness and understanding of how training resources and facilities can be better utilized through cooperative efforts; and an understanding of how training on library, media, research, and information skills can be better utilized through cooperative efforts.

Oklahoma

Rose State College $79,098
6420 S.E. 19 St. Sharon Saulmon
Midwest City, OK 73110 405-736-0259

Rose State College proposes a two-week institute to train library staff, both professional and non-professional, in the use of new techniques of information acquisition, transfer, and communication technology on the Internet to better serve the information needs of their communities; and to train participants in how to teach their peers and library patrons in accessing the Internet. The participants will be selected from community libraries serving children, young adults, the illiterate, the elderly, and disadvantaged, rural, and minority populations.

Pennsylvania

University of Pittsburgh $57,138
School of Information Sciences Margaret Kimmel
Pittsburgh, PA 15260 412-624-9436

The institute will offer an innovative program designed to introduce new knowledge and skills or to upgrade existing knowledge and skills for librarians who serve the elderly or care givers for the elderly by providing a series of lectures designed to describe current research information seeking by seniors and their care givers. It will examine ongoing trends in service delivery that are targeted to the elderly and their care givers, and will highlight the roles that public and special libraries will play in this expanding area of service. Participants will learn about these current issues and strategies and resources, and the relevance of these topics to their work in specific types of libraries and social service agencies.

Library Research and Demonstration Program (HEA II-B)

The Library Research and Demonstration program (Title II-B of the Higher Education Act) authorizes grants and contracts for research and demonstration projects related to the improvement of libraries, training in librarianship, and the dissemination of information derived from these projects.

Title II, Part B, of the Higher Education Act was amended by the Higher Education Amendments of 1986. In 1987, by statutory mandate, "information technology" was deleted from the list of authorized research and demonstration purposes. This amendment precludes research on or about information technology but allows use of technology to accomplish the goals of a research or demonstration project.

In FY 1996 Congress appropriated $3 million for the HEA II-B Research and Demonstration Program. Funds supported three directed grants.

Survivors of the Shoah Visual History Foundation ($1,000,000). The foundation, created by Steven Spielberg to teach and promote racial, ethnic, and cultural tolerance, will videotape thousands of eyewitness accounts of the Holocaust and develop a comprehensive online multimedia archive of survivor testimonies. Each survivor interview will be approximately two hours, covering experiences before, during, and after World War II. The videotapes will be digitized, cataloged, and made available to educational institutions via state-of-the-art interactive network technology. The completed archive will show the richness of Jewish life in the early 20th century, the rise of Nazism, the horror of the Holocaust, the liberation of the concentration camps, and life for survivors today. By 1997 the online archive will be made available via computer network to five initial repositories—the Museum of Jewish Heritage in New York, the Simon Wiesenthal Center in Los Angeles, the U.S. Holocaust Memorial Museum in Washington, D.C., the Fortunoff Archive for Holocaust Testimonies at Yale University, and the Yad Vashem in Jerusalem—and ultimately to repositories throughout the world. The actual collection will be housed and maintained in Los Angeles.

The application of technology to the management of the massive amounts of digital material, combined with cross-reference cataloging methodology and online network technology make the archive immediately accessible and interactive. The technology being developed for this project can be applied to other historical events and subjects, combining videographic, photographic, and textual material into a multimedia format.

National Museum of Women in the Arts ($1,000,000). The National Museum of Women in the Arts offers the single most important collection of art by women. The core of the permanent collection is the donation of Wallace and Wilhelmina Holladay. In 1982, the Holladays donated their art and library to create a museum that brings recognition to women artists of all nationalities, working in all periods and artistic styles; it is the only institution in the world dedicated to this purpose. As such, it possesses unique and extensive resources that are of interest to scholars, other museums, and the general public.

To promote the study of women in the arts, the museum maintains a Library and Research Center (LRC) that supports activities directly associated with its mission of archiving works by women artists. Its collections include monographs, exhibition catalogs, periodicals, rare publications, artists' books, and special collections. In addition, the LRC maintains resource files on more than 10,000 artists from all periods and countries, including contemporary artists who have had at least one solo exhibition. The project, Archiving Works by Women Artists, will strengthen and improve the LRC, enhancing its services through effective and efficient uses of new technologies and promoting the widespread dissemination of unique archival materials on women artists. The project objectives include developing an integrated approach to collecting, archiving, and organizing information on women artists; applying new technologies to the broad dissemination of information on women artists; and testing the usefulness of the integrated archival system to scholars. The project's significance resides in the museum's ability to improve substantially its library and information services and to make widely available its unique visual, biographic, and bibliographic holdings on women artists.

The integrated approach to collection management and the technology being used for dissemination can be applied by other museums and libraries to other subjects. The project will be tested as a model for the integration of visual, biographic, bibliographic, and archival information.

Portland State University, PORTALS Project ($1,000,000). The PORTALS multistate consortium of public and private institutions provides information to the citizens of Oregon and Washington through a network of 14 major libraries. Through its gopher and World Wide Web structures, PORTALS organizes library catalogs, bibliographic databases, and other Internet-accessible resources. It has established a significant human/computing/ network infrastructure to support its information storage and dissemination mission. The PORTALS multistate consortium, Portland State University, Oregon State Library, Multnomah County Public Library, and Oregon Historical Society propose to build on the existing infrastructure and to extend the PORTALS mission to provide government and other information to the international networked community through the Internet.

The project will consolidate federal, state, and local agency, and state and local historical and archival information into a system that is oriented to the needs of users. Information resources will be assembled by agencies (Oregon State Library, Multnomah County Library, and Oregon Historical Society) whose primary and historical role has been to collect, organize, and present public and other information to users.

The system will be modular and feature non-proprietary software, vendor independent hardware and freely available documentation. All of the information encompassed by the system will be available over the Internet. Fourteen institutions will participate in a regional test and evaluation of multimedia information delivery to public graphic workstations over a wide-band network.

While the information collection will be valuable in itself, the greatest value of the project will be the construction and demonstration of a system architecture that can accommodate limitless yet coordinated and economical growth in the number and nature of new information modules. The fundamental objective of this project is to create an effective and efficient user-oriented system.

Library Services and Construction Act
Library Services for Indian Tribes and Hawaiian Natives Program (LSCA Title IV)

LSCA Title IV discretionary grants awarded in FY 1996 will improve public library services to 209 indian tribes and Alaska native villages and to approximately 170,000 Hawaiian natives. Funds, totaling $2,540,100, are being used in 31 states to support a variety of activities, including outreach programs to the community, salaries and training of library staff, purchase of library materials, and the renovation of library facilities.

Since FY 1985, 2 percent of the appropriations for LSCA Titles I, II, and III has been set aside as the available funding for LSCA Title IV (1.5 percent for indian tribes and 0.5 percent for Hawaiian natives). Only indian tribes and Alaska native villages that are federally recognized and organizations serving Hawaiian natives that are recognized by the governor of Hawaii are eligible to participate in the program. For the past 12 years, Alu Like, Inc. has been the only organization recognized to apply for the Hawaiian native set-aside.

Two types of awards are made: Basic Grants and Special Projects Grants. The Basic Grant is noncompetitive, and if an indian tribe or Alaska native village is eligible and pursues authorized activities, funding is guaranteed. In FY 1996 the established Basic Grant for indian tribes and Alaska native villages was $4,557, while Alu Like, Inc. received the entire Hawaiian native set-aside of $635,025. These funds continue to be used to support projects emphasizing outreach, collection development, and training of Hawaiian natives for librarianship.

Of the 547 indian tribes and Alaska native villages eligible to compete, 193 applied for and received Basic Grants. Of these, three were joint funding requests, involving 16 additional tribes. Approximately $952,537 was awarded under the Basic Grant Program (see Table 3 for Basic Grant Awards); the remaining $938,038 was used for Special Projects grants.

In FY 1996 the U.S. Department of Education supported 11 competitively awarded Special Projects grants to indian tribes for the improvement of public library services. Eleven tribes in seven states received grants ranging from $48,048 to $106,000.

All recipients are required to have a librarian, a three- to five-year long-range plan for public library development, and to contribute at least 20 percent of the total project costs. Grant funds are provided for assessment of community library needs, salaries and training of library staff, costs for transportation of community members without access to libraries, purchase of needed resource materials, and support of special programs offered to young and old. For example, projects will

- Implement technology-based initiatives that will lead to automation of library services, formation or expansion of regional networks, and improved learning opportunities for tribal members
- Train tribal members in library and information science
- Renovate deteriorating library facilities and improve accessibility for disabled patrons
- Expand services for both children and elders by initiating or expanding programs that address their particular needs

Table 4 provides a complete list of the Special Projects funded in FY 1996.

Table 3 / LSCA Title IV, Library Services for Indian Tribes and Hawaiian Natives Program, Basic Grants, FY 1996

State/Dollar Amount	Recipient	State/Dollar Amount	Recipient
Alabama		4,557	Haulapai Tribe
4,557	Poarch Band of Creek Indians	4,557	Kaibab Paiute Tribe
Alaska		4,557	San Jaun Souther Paiute Tribe
4,557	Akutan Traditional Council	4,557	The Hopi Tribe
4,557	Ambler Traditional Council	4,557	White Mountain Apache Tribe
31,899	Arctic Slope Regional Corporation	4,557	Yavapai-Apache Tribe
4,557	Buckland IRA Council	4,557	Yavapai-Prescot Indian Tribe
4,557	Cantwell Village Council	**California**	
4,557	Chugach Alaska Corporation	4,557	Barona Band of Mission Indians
4,557	Cook Inlet Tribal Council	4,557	Bear River Band of Rohnerville Rancheria
4,557	Copper River Native Association		
4,557	Deering Native village	4,557	Berry Creek Rancheria
4,557	Douglas Indian Council	4,557	Big Sandy Rancheria
4,557	Egegik Village Council	4,557	Blue Lake Rancheria
4,557	Elim Community Library	4,557	Bridgeport Paiute Indian Colony
4,557	False Pass Tribal Library	4,557	Campo Band of Mission Indians
4,557	Gulkana Village Council	4,557	Coyote Valley Tribal Council
4,557	Hoonah Indian Association	4,557	Cuyapaipe Reservation
13,671	IRA Council of Akiachak	4,557	Elk Valley Rancheria
4,557	Ivanof Bay Village Council	4,557	Fort Mojave Tribe
4,557	Kenaitze Indian Tribe IRA	4,557	Hoopa Valley Tribal Council
4,557	Lou Den Village Council	4,557	Karuk Tribe of California
4,557	McGrath Native Village Council	4,557	LaJolla Band of Luiseno Indians
4,557	Mentasta Traditional Council	4,557	La Posta Band of Mission Indians
4,557	Metlakatla Indian Community	4,557	Lytton Rancheria
4,557	Native Council of Kivalina	4,557	Mesa Grande Band of Mission Indians
4,557	Native Council of Port Heiden	4,557	Morongo Band of Mission Indians
4,557	Native Village of Atka	4,557	Morretown Rancheria
4,557	Native Village of Barrow	4,557	North Fork Rancheria
4,557	Native Village of Fort Yukon	4,557	Pala Band of Mission Indians
4,557	Native Village of Kotzebue	4,557	Pauma Band of Mission Indians
4,557	Native Village of Koyuk	4,557	Pinoleville Band of Pomo Indians
4,557	Ninilchik Traditional Council	4,557	Pueblo of Cochiti
4,557	Northway Village Council	4,557	Redding Rancheria Tribal Council
4,557	Ounalashka Corporation	4,557	Redwood Valley Little River Band
4,557	Ruby Native Council	4,557	Round Valley Indian Tribe
4,557	Selawik IRA Council	4,557	Sherwood Valley Rancheria
27,342	Shaktoolik IRA Council	4,557	Shingle Spring Ranchero
4,557	Village of Dot Lake	4,557	Sobaba Band of Mission Indians
4,557	Village of Perryville	4,557	Table Mountain Rancheria
4,557	Wrangle Cooperative Association, Inc.	4,557	Torress-Martinez Desert Cahuilla
		4,557	Tule River Tribal Council
Arizona		4,557	Tuolumne Band of Mewuk Indians
4,557	Colorado River Indian Tribes	4,557	Yurok Tribe

Table 3 / LSCA Title IV, Library Services for Indian Tribes and Hawaiian Natives Program, Basic Grants, FY 1996 (cont.)

State/Dollar Amount		Recipient	State/Dollar Amount		Recipient
Connecticut			4,557		Fort Peck Assiniboine and Sioux Tribes
4,557		Mashantucket Pequot Tribe	4,557		Northern Cheyenne
4,557		The Mohegan Tribe	**Nebraska**		
Florida			4,557		Winnebago Tribe of Nebraska
4,557		Seminole Tribe of Florida	4,557		Sautee Sioux Tribe of Nebraska
Hawaii			**Nevada**		
635,025		Alu Like, Inc.	4,557		Buckwater Shoshone Tribe
Idaho			4,557		Pyramid Lake Paiute Tribe
4,557		Shoshone-Bannock Tribes	4,557		Walker River Paiute Tribe
Kansas			4,557		Washoe Tribe of Nevada and California
4,557		Kickapoo Nation in Kansas	**New Mexico**		
Louisiana			4,557		Jicarilla Apache Tribe
4,557		Chitimacha Tribe of Louisiana	4,557		Picuris Pueblo
4,557		Tunica-Biloxi Indians of Louisiana	4,557		Pueblo of Acoma
Maine			4,557		Pueblo of Isleta
4,557		Aroostook Band of Micmacs	4,557		Pueblo of Jemez
4,557		Passamaquoddy Tribe	4,557		Pueblo of Laguna
4,557		Penobscot Nation	4,557		Pueblo of Sandia
Massachusetts			4,557		Pueblo of San Felipe
4,557		Wampanoag Tribe of Gay Head	4,557		Pueblo of Santa Clara
Michigan			4,557		Pueblo of Zia
4,557		Bays Mills Indian Community	4,557		Pueblo of Zuni
4,557		La Vieux Desert Band of Lake Superior Chippewa Indians	4,557		Santa Ana Pueblo
4,557		Little River Band of Ottawa Indians	**New York**		
4,557		Hannahville Indian Community	4,557		Oneida Indian Nation
4,557		Keweenaw Bay Indian Community	4,557		Seneca Nation of Indians
4,557		Nottawaseppi Huron Potawatomi	**North Carolina**		
4,557		Pokagon Band of Potawatomi	4,557		Eastern Band of Cherokee Indians
4,557		Saginaw Chippewa Indian Tribe of Michigan	**North Dakota**		
			4,557		Devils Lake Sioux Tribe
Minnesota			4,557		Standing Rock Sioux Tribe
4,557		Fond Du Lac Reservation	4,557		Three Affiliated Tribes
4,557		Red Lake Band of Chippewa Indians	4,557		Turtle Mountain Band of Chippewa Indians
Mississippi			**Oklahoma**		
4,557		Mississippi Band of Choctaw Indians	4,557		Caddo Tribe of Oklahoma
Missouri			4,557		Cherokee Nation
4,557		Eastern Shawnee Tribe of Oklahoma	4,557		Cheyenne Arapaho Tribe of Oklahoma
			4,557		Choctaw Nation of Oklahoma
Montana			4,557		Comanche Indian Tribe of Oklahoma
4,557		Blackfeet Tribe	4,557		Delaware Tribe of Western Oklahoma
4,557		Chippewa Cree Tribe	4,557		Fort Sill Apache Tribe of Oklahoma
4,557		Confederated Salish and Kootenai	4,557		Kaw Nation of Oklahoma
4,557		Crow Tribe	4,557		Kiowa Tribe of Oklahoma
			4,557		Lac du Flambeau

Table 3 / LSCA Title IV, Library Services for Indian Tribes and Hawaiian Natives Program, Basic Grants, FY 1996 (cont.)

State/Dollar Amount	Recipient	State/Dollar Amount	Recipient
4,557	Miami Tribe of Oklahoma	**Washington**	
4,557	Modoc Tribe of Oklahoma	4,557	Jamestown Skallam
4,557	Muscogee (Creek) Nation	4,557	Kalispel Tribe
4,557	Ooe Missouria Tribe	4,557	Lummi Indian Nation
4,557	Ottawa Tribe of Oklahoma	4,557	Muckleshoot Indian Tribe
4,557	Pawnee Tribe of Oklahoma	4,557	Nisqually Indian Tribe
4,557	Peoria Tribe of Oklahoma	4,557	Nooksack Indian Tribe
4,557	Sac and Fox Nation	4,557	Puyallup Tribe of Indians
4,557	Seneca Cayuga Tribe of Oklahoma	4,557	Port Gamble S'Klallam Tribe
4,557	Wyandotte Tribe of Oklahoma	4,557	Sauk Suiattle Indian Tribe
Oregon		4,557	Shoalwater Bay Indian Tribe
4,557	Burns Paiute Tribe	4,557	Skokomish Indian Tribe
4,557	Confederated Tribes of Coos	4,557	Spokane Tribe of Indians
4,557	Confederated Tribes of Grand Ronde	4,557	Squaxin Island Tribe
4,557	Confederated Tribes of Umatilla	4,557	Stillaguamish Tribe of Washington
4,557	Coquille Indian Tribe	4,557	Upper Skagit Indian Tribe
4,557	The Klamath Tribes	**Wisconsin**	
4,557	Warm Springs Confederated Tribes	4,557	Bad River Band of Chippewas
South Dakota		4,557	Forest County Pottawatom
4,557	Lower Brule Sioux Tribe	4,557	Lac Courte Oreilles Tribal Governing Board
4,557	Ogala Sioux Tribe		
4,557	Rosebud Sioux Tribe	4,557	Menominee Indian Tribe—Wisconsin
4,557	Sisseton Wahpeton Sioux Tribe	4,557	Oneida Tribe of Indians of Wisconsin
4,557	Yankton Sioux Tribe	**Wyoming**	
Texas		4,557	Arapahoe Business Council
4,557	Alabama Coushatta Tribe of Texas	4,557	Eastern Shoshone Tribe
4,557	Yselta Del Sur Pueblo		
Utah		Total	$1,587,438
4,557	Pauite Indian Tribe of Utah		

Table 4 / LSCA Title IV, Library Services for Indian Tribes and Hawaiian Natives Program, Special Projects Awards, FY 1996

Michigan
Saginaw Chippewa Indian Tribe of Michigan, Mt. Pleasant
Carla Sineway, Director, Tribal Education Department   Award Amount: $84,252
The tribe will use its first Special Projects grant to develop a reservation-based public library center to address tribal community needs. A librarian will be engaged and two tribal members will be enrolled in an accredited library science program. Funds will also be used to upgrade the library collection, to support special literacy programs, and to increase the community's awareness of the uses and benefits of library services as an integral part of daily tribal life.

Minnesota
Red Lake Band of Chippewa Indians, Red Lake
Kathryn J. Beaulieu, Director, Red Lake Tribal
Information Center Archives and Library   Award Amount: $48,048

Table 4 / LSCA Title IV, Library Services for Indian Tribes and Hawaiian Natives Program, Special Projects Awards, FY 1996 *(cont.)*

This grant will enable the tribe to continue its innovative contractual arrangement for the services of a professional librarian and to pursue additional training for its library technician. A second technician will also be hired and trained. In addition, existing programs aimed at children, young adults, and elders will be expanded, and new initiatives will be launched to improve the reading skills of younger children and to address issues confronting young adults. Funds will also be used to continue and expand links to statewide and regional library networks.

Nevada
Pyramid Lake Paiute Tribe, Nixon
Maxine Wyatt, Principal, Pyramid Lake High School					Award Amount: $98,062

With its first Special Projects grant, the tribe will implement a comprehensive plan to establish a community and high school library and educational facility for the isolated residents of the Pyramid Lake Paiute Reservation. Funds will be used to employ a full-time librarian and library assistant; to provide in-service training for the librarian, library assistant, student workers, and volunteers; and to purchase a wide variety of library materials. A monthly newsletter will inform tribal members about library activities, and transportation will be provided so that other reservation communities can use this library. A variety of special programs for tribal members of all ages will also be carried out.

New Mexico
Pueblo of Jemez
Judy Asbury, Librarian					Award Amount: $77,373

The primary focus of the Pueblo's first Special Projects grant is expansion and enhancement of popular technology-based programs. The Jemez Pueblo Community Library Special Technologies Project will continue and upgrade computer and library services that provide educational after-school programs for children and teenagers as well as computer classes for artists—including one on bookkeeping and tax records. In addition, the library will establish an Internet home page that will include a listing of Jemez Pueblo artists and craftspeople, and it is hoped that such programs will permit more businesses to operate from the village, thus discouraging movement away to the cities. The library will also be renovated internally and externally.

Santa Clara Indian Pueblo, Espanola
Teresa Naranjo, Librarian					Award Amount: $81,986

Designed to enhance the quality of library services and expand the technology resources available to Pueblo residents, this project will support the purchase of new equipment and materials and result in increased Internet services. Library staff will receive training in library technology, and a consultant will assist the pueblo in developing a long-range technology plan. In addition, a technology specialist will instruct fifth, sixth, and seventh graders in the use of laptop computers and will train key tribal personnel in information technologies. Monthly newsletters featuring information on library events will be disseminated, and special programs will be conducted for adults, seniors, and young adults.

Pueblo of Zuni, Zuni
Veronica Peynetsa, Librarian					Award Amount: $95,786

Greater accessibility for disabled patrons and safeguarding of the Zuni Public Library's valuable collection of books and rare archival material are among the projected outcomes of the pueblo's ambitious library renovation project. Funds will not only be used for structural restoration and repair of a facility deteriorating from cumulative weather damage, but will support employee training, hiring of two part-time staff members—including a bookmobile driver—and the purchase of computer equipment.

Table 4 / LSCA Title IV, Library Services for Indian Tribes
and Hawaiian Natives Program, Special Projects Awards, FY 1996 *(cont.)*

North Dakota
Turtle Mountain Band of Chippewa Indians, Belcourt
Margaret Kroll, Librarian   Award Amount: $106,000

As part of the tribe's long-range goals to expand its collection of culturally relevant resources that are responsive to the needs of the local population and to upgrade and expand youth library holdings, the Turtle Mountain Community College Public Library will launch the Children's Library Project. Grant funds will support the purchase of Native American materials and development of a young adult and children's library section. The project will also provide outreach services to the isolated, predominantly rural tribal population, by technologically networking all of the libraries on the Turtle Mountain Chippewa Reservation.

Oklahoma
Miami Tribe of Oklahoma, Miami
Karen Alexander, Librarian   Award Amount: $97,085

Building on the previously established CHARLIE (Connecting Help and Resources Linking Indians Effectively) network, the Miami Tribe of Oklahoma will continue enhancement of library services to tribal members and all other Native Americans residing in the Northeast Eight (NE-8) Oklahoma Tribes service areas. At present, this network unites the Miami with five of the NE-8, permitting them to share an online library catalog. The grant will permit an additional NE-8 tribe to join the network, and it will provide Internet access for all participating tribes and training in Internet use for tribal personnel and library patrons. Funds also will support an automated circulation system for more effective collection management.

Washington
Lummi Indian Nation, Bellingham
Nancy Carroll, Librarian   Award Amount: $83,873

With culturally relevant lifelong learning among their priorities, the Lummi are committed to developing library resources for their children who are often isolated and lack access to library services. Thus, the tribe will use this grant not only to continue employment of the children's librarian who will develop and implement programs at the library, but to add bookmobile services to take these programs to young people where they live. In addition, 700 new titles will be purchased for the children's collection, and the library will work to provide services to an additional 200 youngsters.

Nisqually Indian Tribe, Olympia
Maria Fletter, Education Director   Award Amount: $105,510

This grant will enable the tribe to build on the successes of earlier projects, while implementing a variety of new initiatives. For example, funds will support development of a correspondence course curriculum for the special field of Native American librarianship and will allow tribal members to receive formal training in librarianship through existing correspondence curricula. The Nisqually will also augment the community's access to networking technology and expand special programs and outreach efforts to nonusers by focusing programs and collection development on specific groups within the community.

Puyallup Tribe of Indians, Tacoma
Pauline Hanson and Ron Simchen   Award Amount: $62,585

With its first Special Projects grant, the Puyallup Tribal L.I.B.R.A.R.Y. Development Project will plan for tribal library needs, expand and update the Library's collections, and train tribal members as library personnel. In addition, funds will be used to develop efficient management and operations procedures and to introduce automation of library services. Young people and families will benefit from literacy tutoring and summer reading programs.

Library Literacy Program (LSCA Title VI)

This program was not funded in FY 1996.

LSCA State-Administered Programs

In FY 1996 nearly 94 percent of the Office of Library Programs's funding was allocated to the LSCA state-administered programs (Titles I, II, and III). An analysis of the annual state reports for FY 1995 indicates that the funds primarily were used for the following purposes under Titles I and III:

Public Library Services (LSCA, Title I)

- To upgrade local public library services
- To strengthen state library administrative agencies to improve statewide public library services
- To improve local library services to targeted populations
- To improve library services for targeted institutions

Interlibrary Corporation and Resource Sharing (LSCA, Title III)

- To operate library networks
- To increase the technological capacity of interlibrary cooperative efforts
- To support resource-sharing activities

To provide a more focused perspective for state-administered programs, the state administrative agency reports were reviewed primarily for FY 1995 to identify some of the innovative activities and trends in support of improved public library services for selected LSCA categories. Public Library Construction and Technology Enhancement (LSCA, Title II) is also reported.

In FY 1995, the year reported, the funds appropriated for these programs totaled $122,224,620. In FY 1996 the funds appropriated totaled $124,464,900. Table 5 gives a state-by-state breakdown for FY 1996 funding for LSCA Titles I, II, and III.

Table 5 / Funding for LSCA Titles I, II, and III, FY 1996
(Title I, Public Library Services)
(Title II, Public Library Construction and Technology Enhancement)
(Title III, Interlibrary Cooperation and Resource Sharing)

State	Title I	Title II	Title III
Alabama	$1,480,549	$271,603	$287,704
Alaska	384,026	124,661	75,597
Arizona	1,436,919	265,757	279,263
Arkansas	944,470	199,765	184,007
California	9,740,301	1,378,473	1,885,427
Colorado	1,309,615	248,697	254,638
Connecticut	1,194,152	233,224	232,304
Delaware	414,402	128,731	81,473
District of Columbia	373,068	123,192	73,477
Florida	4,435,130	667,540	859,222

Table 5 / Funding for LSCA Titles I, II, and III, FY 1996 *(cont.)*
(Title I, Public Library Services)
(Title II, Public Library Construction and Technology Enhancement)
(Title III, Interlibrary Cooperation and Resource Sharing)

State	Title I	Title II	Title III
Georgia	2,341,538	386,982	454,248
Hawaii	557,735	147,939	109,198
Idaho	543,915	146,087	106,525
Illinois	3,767,069	578,014	729,996
Indiana	1,945,953	333,971	377,728
Iowa	1,058,776	215,082	206,117
Kansas	975,241	203,888	189,959
Kentucky	1,361,564	255,658	264,687
Louisiana	1,509,777	275,520	293,357
Maine	576,446	150,447	112,818
Maryland	1,719,574	303,634	333,939
Massachusetts	2,033,689	345,728	394,700
Michigan	3,082,408	486,265	597,558
Minnesota	1,586,323	285,778	308,163
Mississippi	1,010,167	208,569	196,715
Missouri	1,801,946	314,673	349,872
Montana	459,840	134,821	90,262
Nebraska	692,593	166,011	135,285
Nevada	642,258	159,266	125,548
New Hampshire	545,064	146,241	106,747
New Jersey	2,599,114	421,499	504,072
New Mexico	701,901	167,258	137,085
New York	5,714,934	839,043	1,106,781
North Carolina	2,345,939	387,572	455,100
North Dakota	393,651	125,951	77,459
Ohio	3,569,900	551,592	691,856
Oklahoma	1,188,936	232,525	231,295
Oregon	1,136,765	225,534	221,203
Pennsylvania	3,858,309	590,241	747,645
Rhode Island	502,550	140,544	98,524
South Carolina	1,312,146	249,036	255,128
South Dakota	418,898	129,334	82,343
Tennessee	1,770,864	310,508	343,860
Texas	5,778,413	847,550	1,119,060
Utah	779,124	177,607	152,023
Vermont	376,113	123,601	74,066
Virginia	2,188,613	366,489	424,667
Washington	1,821,812	317,335	353,715
West Virginia	753,046	174,112	146,978
Wisconsin	1,742,459	306,701	338,365
Wyoming	344,477	119,361	67,947
American Samoa	54,197	21,903	12,746
Guam	80,416	25,416	17,818
Northern Marianas	53,157	21,763	12,545
Palau	33,075	15,525	8,414
Puerto Rico	1,269,060	243,262	246,793
Virgin Islands	70,903	24,141	15,978

Support for Library Services to Targeted Populations: Literacy and Limited-English-Speaking (LSCA Title I)

In FY 1995, a total of $7,581,701 was spent for literacy projects in public libraries. Of this amount, only $1,358,445 came from federal funds, representing a 34 percent decrease over the previous fiscal year and by far the greatest decrease in many years. The state and local share was $6,223,265, which represents a slight increase over the FY 1994 level.

Federal funding for Limited-English-Speaking activities totaled $944,307, a decrease of 25 percent from expenditures reported in FY 1994. State and local funding, totaling $176,622, increased by 109 percent over the previous fiscal year.

A review of the state annual project reports shows that while many individual libraries still focus on providing traditional Literacy and Limited-English-Speaking activities such as tutor training, one-to-one instruction, and provision of materials, there is a steady move away from library involvement in direct instruction and toward collaborative programs involving other community-based organizations. Collaborative activities allow participating organizations to share responsibilities while allowing each organization to make significant contributions by doing what it does best. In the case of the library, that includes coordinating programs, providing referral services, training tutors, and providing tutoring space and support materials.

Several trends, emerging over the last few years, are further evidenced by this year's reports:

- Cooperation between public libraries and community-based volunteer organizations such as Laubach Literacy International and Literacy Volunteers of America, continues to grow stronger.
- The role of state library agencies in statewide training and support activities, collaboration with other agencies, and participation in state literacy coalitions continues to increase.
- Literacy activities are more often integrated with services to targeted populations such as the elderly, incarcerated, job seekers, and youth at risk.
- Technology such as video and video captioning, computer-assisted instruction, and the Internet is more often used for independent and assisted instruction.

The following projects are examples of reported activities for FY 1995:

Oregon. The Independence Public Library in Polk County took a different approach to its Limited-English-Speakers effort this year when it developed the "Survival Spanish" program. With the Hispanic population in this rural community reaching nearly 20 percent, it became evident that English-speaking residents needed to learn at least a survival vocabulary in Spanish to communicate successfully at work and in the community.

Survival Spanish vocabularies developed by language consultants were designed for such target groups as teachers, law enforcement personnel, hospital workers, caregivers, store clerks, and librarians. Small classes were held for each group, with vocabulary lists audiotaped or put into Hypercard stacks for computer-assisted instruction. To disseminate the program, the audiotapes and Hypercard stacks were distributed to other libraries across the state.

Massachusetts. Two libraries in the state have been successful in reaching out to linguistic minorities by establishing coordinated programming for children and adults. The Sommerville Public Library conducted structured conversation groups for adults twice a week that ran concurrent with children's programming in order to encourage family attendance. Students from 14 countries as diverse as Sri Lanka, Egypt, and Bolivia spent close to five months with an English-as-a-second-language (ESL) teacher and members of the library staff. The 12 staff members involved in the project received training in conducting the classes, allowing content to be tailored to students' needs and interests. Many new materials were purchased to support the program; the most popular items were print materials accompanied by audiotapes, which allowed participants to improve their listening and comprehension skills between classes. At the end of the project, participants evaluated the program, requesting more classes and longer class times. As a result, the library has made a commitment to continue the ESL instructor.

The Lawrence Public Library implemented the "New Parents, New Horizons" project to strengthen the parenting skills of limited-English-speakers. Parents attended a series of "new parents" orientation programs at the library and brought their children to lap-sits and toddler story hour sessions. A parent information center called the Family Tree was established in the Children's Room, with more than 400 new books, periodicals, videotapes, and a collection of 30 take-home parenting kits. In addition, staff introduced parents to the use of the computer in 25 pre-school computer classes. The library exceeded its original target to serve 30 families; in the final quarter alone, it served 145 parents and children in the pre-school story hour and 153 in the infant/toddler story hours. Though intended as a one-year project, the success of this effort motivated the library to set aside 20 percent of its budget to continue the service. Additional support will come from contacts with community daycare providers, a local hospital and the Teen Parenting Program of the Greater Lawrence Community Action Council.

Indiana. The State Library of Indiana awarded nine mini-grants to public libraries for planning or implementing family and early-childhood literacy projects. As technology and computer literacy are important to today's literacy needs, priority was given to projects that incorporated use of technology. Items purchased by the participating libraries included "Kids Read," a read-to-me and read-along software program; several computer workstations; and a variety of multimedia software.

New York. The Buffalo & Erie County Public Library has been using the Internet since fall of 1994 to provide a means of sharing and communication, updating calendar information, and listing Internet resources for local literacy providers. This year the library focused on providing access to resources on the Buffalo Free-Net and training librarians and literacy tutors in the use of the Internet. Persons not having computers at home or work were encouraged to apply for Free-Net accounts in the Lifelong Learning Center at the library and to use the two computers dedicated to that purpose. During the project year more than 40 new accounts were initiated, terminals logged 813 users, and 93 individuals were trained in Internet use.

Support for Targeted Populations: The Handicapped (LSCA Title I)

Nearly all states and most outlying areas provide services on a statewide or territorial basis through a "regional" library for the blind and physically handicapped. Regional libraries function as service and distribution centers for audio-recorded materials and playback equipment available from the National Library Service (NLS) of the Library of Congress. In addition to services provided on a statewide basis, many states fund projects at the local level using LSCA funds to reach people whose disabilities prevent them from going to a library.

The types of services supported on a statewide basis include books and magazines recorded on disc, cassette, and magnetic tape, along with appropriate playback equipment, and materials in braille. Automation of collection inventories, patron records and loans is common practice.

Projects at the area and community levels focus on outreach activities, such as visits to shut-ins, programs for the deaf and hearing-impaired, summer reading programs for children, and radio reading services. In-house services include assistive devices for the visually and hearing impaired, and publications in formats other than in standard print.

The sum of federal, state, and local funds expended for services to the handicapped in FY 1995 was $33,481,302. Of this amount, $6,381,841 was federal funds, $25,029,382 was state funds, and $2,365,094 was from local sources for services to 763,389 persons with disabilities. Table 6 provides a state-by-state summary of expenditures.

Major trends continue to include:

- Automation of records concerning users, materials, equipment, and circulation, enabling libraries to serve increasing numbers of users with the same or fewer staff
- Greater use of assistive devices
- Projects whose specific purpose is to comply with the requirements of the ADA
- Disabilities awareness and sensitivity training for staff

Greater use of assistive devices has been by far the strongest trend since 1992 as libraries increased significantly their acquisition of devices such as reading machines (print-to-voice), print-to-braille, electronic magnifiers with up to 40X power, screen enlargers for computer monitors, closed-circuit television systems (CCTV), and text-on-computer-screen to large print, voice, or braille for the visually impaired; voice recognition and speech synthesizers for computers and radio reading programs for the blind; telecommunications devices for the deaf (TDDs); closed-captioned video and television programs for the hearing-impaired; and page-turners for the physically handicapped. This component of library services gained importance as a result of the enactment of the Americans with Disabilities Act (ADA) in 1990.

Table 6 / LSCA Title I Expenditures for the Blind and Physically Handicapped, FY 1995

	Federal	State	Local	Total	Population Served
Alabama	$17,298	$477,104	$0	$494,402	5,575
Alaska	0	84,567	0	84,567	833
Arizona	179,478	481,640	0	661,118	26,344
Arkansas	108,203	230,958	0	339,161	8,199
California	295,015	1,093,008	2,224,362	3,317,370	114,987
Colorado	130,812	262,293	0	393,105	12,063
Connecticut	318,873	176,830	0	495,703	9,000
Delaware	56,963	68,123	0	125,086	1,425
District of Columbia	41,562	116,877	0	158,439	9,840
Florida	209,511	580,321	59,591	849,423	72,570
Georgia	155,944	1,118,902	0	1,274,846	20,197
Hawaii	0	473,863	0	473,863	2,113
Idaho	0	250,000	0	250,000	3,600
Illinois	138,416	2,477,135	0	2,615,551	22,900
Indiana	344,498	229,455	0	573,953	21,009
Iowa	10,990	42,000	0	52,990	6,416
Kansas	122,500	320,000	0	442,500	14,703
Kentucky	88,000	200,000	0	288,000	5,521
Louisiana	172,331	220,845	0	393,176	5,279
Maine	153,943	118,387	0	272,330	3,502
Maryland	102,940	427,060	0	530,000	16,000
Massachusetts	33,743	1,100,251	0	1,133,994	19,250
Michigan	352,455	484,107	0	836,562	9,285
Minnesota	93,633	309,865	0	403,498	13,260
Mississippi	3,818	303,331	0	307,149	2,454
Missouri	94,034	424,402	0	518,436	14,200
Montana	146,237	1,797	0	148,034	2,600
Nebraska	118,890	369,120	0	488,010	5,808
Nevada	94,560	56,170	0	150,730	19,065
New Hampshire	60,286	133,729	0	194,015	3,160
New Jersey	687,372	353,696	0	1,041,068	13,000
New Mexico	0	151,250	0	151,250	4,343
New York	461,568	1,436,569	0	1,898,137	62,542
North Carolina	35,354	731,291	0	766,645	10,528
North Dakota	117,272	0	0	117,272	2,850
Ohio	298,810	1,700,230	81,141	2,080,181	26,295
Oklahoma	25,179	0	0	25,179	12,000
Oregon	0	242,299	0	242,299	7,025
Pennsylvania	48,800	2,202,000	0	2,250,800	22,888
Rhode Island	161,672	291,078	0	452,750	1,722
South Carolina	94,805	607,488	0	702,293	9,697
South Dakota	193,950	63,087	0	257,037	5,933
Tennessee	241,117	788,911	0	1,030,028	17,950
Texas	0	1,294,597	0	1,294,597	23,592
Utah	109,100	189,868	0	298,968	7,132
Vermont	43,957	3,054	0	47,011	1,843
Virginia	0	143,361	0	143,361	8,877
Washington	41,158	1,192,758	0	1,233,916	12,200
West Virginia	29,242	182,746	0	211,988	4,282
Wisconsin	93,429	597,420	0	690,849	30,045
Wyoming	0	55,383	0	55,383	1,000
Guam	3,000	34,525	0	37,525	16
Northern Marianas	615	250	0	865	50
Puerto Rico	36,048	85,829	0	121,877	1,421
Virgin Islands	14,460	49,552	0	64,012	5,000
Total	$6,381,841	$25,029,382	$2,365,094	$33,481,302	$763,3893

A change noted in work with the disabled is that hearing-impaired library users now tend to be older adults who have lost hearing later in life; thus, they tend to see their hearing loss as a disability, rather than as a culture.

A sampling of LSCA-funded projects for the handicapped illustrates some of the atypical services provided:

District of Columbia. The District of Columbia Public Library's Services to the Deaf Community offers sign language and deaf literacy programs to staff and residents of facilities for senior citizens and to the homebound. Major observations of the program indicate that senior citizens who have hearing disabilities are less likely to want to learn sign language because they have not accepted their hearing loss. Sign language programs in institutions succeed when seniors urge their neighbors to participate, when the programs are flexible, and when staff members participate as much as possible. Plans for the future include a computer with modem/TTY/fax capability and the installation of TTYs in pay phones in all of the library's branches.

California. San Francisco Public Library's Online Access in Braille supports workstations with scanning and voice output capabilities and a screen able to display enlarged fonts. The project added a paperless braille display that allows a braille reader to feel what is written on the computer screen (a method that is faster than voice output), and a braille embosser, used to produce text in braille from the computer. The project facilitates access to online databases by patrons who are blind or sight-impaired or who read only braille.

South Dakota. The state library's Services to the Physically Handicapped includes a diversity of programs. The Radio Talking Book, with volunteers reading local newspapers, is broadcast live one hour a day, Monday through Friday. A cooperative project with the South Dakota State Penitentiary has inmates assisting in the production of braille and large-print textbooks, while the Yankton (federal) Prison Camp records books and other materials, using prisoners trained as narrators. In addition, Yankton has six prisoners certified for the brailling unit who also repair braillers. The summer reading program for 137 blind or visually impaired children was co-sponsored by the Office of the Governor, among others. The top readers in the braille category and in the large print category received $50 savings bonds.

Support for Targeted Populations: The Elderly (LSCA Title I)

In 1971 Library Services to the Elderly became a priority under Title I of the Library Services and Construction Act (LSCA). Since then, states have annually funded this service using less than 2 percent of the total Title I allotment. Although Intergenerational Services was added as a priority under Title I in 1990, funding for both activities continues to remain a minor part of the program.

In the 1970s and early 1980s, LSCA funds were used primarily to support services to the homebound and institutionalized. While delivery projects have been common from the late 1980s to date, more emphasis is now being placed on development of special collections, especially large-print books. Acquisition of other special materials included talking books and videos as well as equipment for the visually impaired, such as magnifiers, special lamps, writing aids, and check-writing guides. Materials and equipment were delivered via bookmobiles, books-by-mail, and deposit collections in congregate sites.

Special programs, including multisensory programming and life-review kits, have become more popular over the years and represent the second most common type of activity. In addition to public libraries, programs were most often held at nursing homes and congregate sites.

While some intergenerational projects involve children visiting and reading to the elderly, most projects focus on the elderly aiding preschoolers and young school-aged children as they begin to learn to read or seek to improve reading skills. Seniors also have helped to run latchkey programs at libraries. These programs go beyond assistance with reading-skills improvement to encompass the social and emotional needs of the children as well as those of the elderly.

Statistics for projects completed in fiscal year 1995 (the latest year for which complete data is available) show that $850,281 in Title I funds was used for library projects designed to serve the elderly. This amount was matched by $203,524 in state funds and $378,119 in local funds for a total of $1,431,924 expended for projects serving the older reader. A breakdown of expenditures by state for FY 1995 are in Table 7. Following are examples of funded projects.

Development of Special Collections. Projects in Mississippi and Maine added to the large-print collections at the state library, which are often used to provide long-term or rotating collections in public libraries. Other large-print projects developed collections at the local level. The West Iron (Michigan) District Library added how-to books on hobbies and medical care. In addition to acquiring large-print books, the Payson (Arizona) Public Library added books-on-tape and TeleSensory computers with enlarging screen and voice capability. The Chester (South Carolina) County Library established a Senior Resource Center with special materials and equipment designed to meet the interests and needs of the elderly. For example, the library purchased a closed-circuit television that enlarges print up to 45 times and an Arkenstone "Open Book" that turns a personal computer into a reading machine and has a braille keypad to accommodate the severely vision impaired or blind.

Delivery of Materials and Services. Bookmobiles were used by the Nieves M. Flores Memorial Library (Guam) to deliver materials to the senior citizen housing community, and by the Martin Luther King Memorial Public Library in Washington, D.C., to visit the senior citizen centers. The Somerset County (Maryland) Public Library used the postal service to deliver materials to the elderly, while the Sun City (Arizona) Library used volunteers to deliver materials to the homebound and visit with them at the same time, and the Lee County (Florida) Library System included the caregivers of the homebound in their delivery program. The Santa Fe Springs (California) Library placed a deposit collection in a remodeled senior center, thus increasing the number of seniors with library cards at the center from 30 percent to 70 percent. A new trend in delivery of materials was typified by the Paducah (Kentucky) Public Library, which placed computers at local facilities for older adults, giving them access to the library's online catalog and making it possible for them to place holds on books that were then picked up and delivered by the staff of the host facility. Additional software was installed at these locations to allow for display of a family tree, interactive programs for use when grandchildren visit, and production of graphics.

Special Programming. Special programs aimed at audiences comprised of seniors are part of many projects for the elderly. The Argie Cooper (Shelbyville, Tennessee) Public Library established an audiovisual archive created from interviews with significant Shelby County residents who talked about their lives during the various eras of the 20th century. The "Especially for Seniors" program at the East Chicago (Indiana) Public Library focused on reminiscing, crafts, health, travel, read-aloud short stories, poetry, and songs, while a similar program at the Brillion (Wisconsin) Public Library purchased public performance videos of 30 minutes or less, a length found most suitable for the elderly in area senior housing units. The Miami-Dade (Florida) Public Library's "Programming Resources for the Elderly Project" (PREP) responded to the demand that cultural, recreational, and educational materials be developed for use with seniors and made available for loan to local agencies, organizations, and groups that serve older adults in a variety of settings.

Partnerships. Libraries undertaking projects aimed at the elderly frequently form partnerships with other organizations such as Meals on Wheels, Girl Scouts, and AARP, and with caregivers involved with this age group. For example, the Salt Lake (Utah) Public Library's partnership with Salt Lake County Aging Services to provide a lecture series entitled "Health and Aging—Not for Seniors Only" for both the elderly and their caregivers; the New Hampshire State Library worked with the New Hampshire Division of Elderly Affairs to determine the most appropriate services for the elderly populations; and the Beloit (Wisconsin) Public Library joined with the local school district so the library's adult and elderly volunteers could bring their outreach program to improve reading skills to the third graders of their district.

Intergenerational. The Davenport (Iowa) Public Library offered an intergenerational project with senior volunteers assisting in a program aimed at improving the reading skills of "at-risk" children in their community; "Reading in the Park," together with storytimes and workshop programs, reached 1,200 people of all ages. The Kirkwood (Missouri) Public Library established a storytelling collection and taught senior citizens and children the art of storytelling. Lastly, the Clinton-Essex-Franklin (New York) Library System joined with local scout leaders to promote a program of intergenerational reading between the elderly and young adults by matching reading pairs at five member libraries.

Support for Targeted Populations: The Institutionalized (LSCA Title I)

Library services to the institutionalized is one of the mandated priorities under LSCA. Added to the program in 1971, this priority supports improving public library services to populations that might not otherwise be receiving such services, specifically those unable to go to a local library because of their residence in a state-supported or locally-supported institution.

LSCA serves four main groups residing in institutions: prison inmates, the elderly, those in mental health/rehabilitation hospitals, and those in residential schools for the handicapped. While a small amount of the funds reported in FY 1995 went to serve those in local jails, the majority of the funding supported

Table 7 / LSCA Title I Expenditures for the Elderly, FY 1995

	Federal	State	Local	Total
Alabama	$3,000.00	$0	$0	$3,000
Alaska	0	0	0	0
Arizona	17,131	0	0	17,131
Arkansas	0	0	0	0
California	81,500	0	0	81,500
Colorado	0	0	0	0
Connecticut	0	0	0	0
Delaware	0	0	0	0
District of Columbia	600	70,271	0	70,871
Florida	70,699	0	0	70,699
Georgia	36,613	0	8,816	45,429
Hawaii	0	0	0	0
Idaho	2,606	0	0	2,606
Illinois	0	0	0	0
Indiana	12,908		0	12,908
Iowa	0	0	0	0
Kansas	0	0	0	0
Kentucky	63,942	0	0	63,942
Louisiana	12,356	8,057	0	20,413
Maine	344	43,431	0	43,775
Maryland	5,321	0	0	5,321
Massachusetts	0	0	0	0
Michigan	14,726	0	0	14,726
Minnesota	4,000	43,279	0	47,279
Mississippi	5,253	10,124	303,331	318,708
Missouri	31,044		0	31,044
Montana	0	0	0	0
Nebraska	0	0	0	0
Nevada	16,000	0	65,972	81,972
New Hampshire	5,792	0	0	5,792
New Jersey	0	0	0	0
New Mexico	0	0	0	0
New York	14,138	0	0	14,138
North Carolina	65,516	0	0	65,516
North Dakota	0	0	0	0
Ohio	1,704	676	0	2,380
Oklahoma	27,000	0	0	27,000
Oregon	0	0	0	0
Pennsylvania	8,049	0	0	8,049
Rhode Island	0	0	0	0
South Carolina	10,282	0	0	10,282
South Dakota	17,625	13,894	0	31,519
Tennessee	53,326	0	0	53,326
Texas	173,025	0	0	173,025
Utah	10,000	0	0	10,000
Vermont	0	0	0	0
Virginia	0	0	0	0
Washington	39,505	0	0	39,505
West Virginia	0	0	0	0
Wisconsin	44,276	0	0	44,276
Wyoming	0	0	0	0
Guam	2,000	2,000	0	4,000
Puerto Rico	0	11,792	0	11,792
Virgin Islands	0	0	0	0
Total	$850,281	$203,524	$378,119	$1,431,924

Table 8 / LSCA Title I Expenditures for the Institutionalized, FY 1995

	Federal	State	Local	Total
Alabama	$101,965	$305,429	$0	$407,394
Alaska	0	82,525	0	82,525
Arizona	6,312	226,865	0	233,177
Arkansas	82,525	9,809	0	92,334
California	0	4,089,381	0	4,089,381
Colorado	79,637	285,945	0	365,582
Connecticut	24,993	0	214,203	239,196
Delaware	0	19,291	0	19,291
District of Columbia	0	27,776	0	27,776
Florida	179,107	322,685	0	501,792
Georgia	68,625	9,498	8,816	86,939
Hawaii	0	275,000	0	275,000
Idaho	16,620	0	0	16,620
Illinois	12,716	3,262,111	0	3,274,827
Indiana	79,473	423,441	0	502,914
Iowa	48,901	419,008	0	467,909
Kansas	39,509	1,429	0	40,938
Kentucky	39,500	50,000	0	89,500
Louisiana	114,342	28,544	0	142,886
Maine	20,277	203,000	0	223,277
Maryland	100,750	239,431	0	340,181
Massachusetts	24,425	299,451	0	323,876
Michigan	95,166	0	0	95,166
Minnesota	43,279	985,449	0	1,028,728
Mississippi	1,663	2,155	303,331	307,149
Missouri	38,308	385,371	0	423,679
Montana	26,838	78,309	0	105,147
Nebraska	20,150	444,384	0	464,534
Nevada	18,500	17,000	65,972	101,472
New Hampshire	21,000	179,536	0	200,536
New Jersey	36,516	376,158	0	412,674
New Mexico	38,000	49,800	0	87,800
New York	90,346	2,267,844	0	2,358,190
North Carolina	46,000	210,103	0	256,103
North Dakota	36,620	78,649	0	115,269
Ohio	112,333	459,549	0	571,882
Oklahoma	119,645	230,068	0	349,713
Oregon	0	436,200	0	436,200
Pennsylvania	57,182	2,805,927	0	2,863,109
Rhode Island	3,694	229,500	0	233,194
South Carolina	31,817	568,183	0	600,000
South Dakota	55,106	202,585	0	257,691
Tennessee	50,000	25,000	0	75,000
Texas	59,460	0	365,912	425,372
Utah	30,000	87,930	0	117,930
Vermont	21,014	81,705	0	102,719
Virginia	0	260,000	0	260,000
Washington	52,662	1,557,292	0	1,609,954
West Virginia	40,012	158,441	0	198,453
Wisconsin	0	0	0	0
Wyoming	17,164	73,616	0	90,780
Guam	10,000	1	0	10,001
Puerto Rico	79,487	94,161	0	173,648
Virgin Islands	8,545	50,500	0	59,045
Total	$2,300,184	$22,976,035	$958,234	$26,234,453

grants to serve those residing in state-supported institutions (inmates, patients, or residents of penal institutions, reformatories, residential training schools, orphanages, or general or special institutions or hospitals operated or substantially supported by the state) or students (mentally retarded, hearing-impaired, speech-impaired, visually handicapped, seriously emotionally disturbed, orthopedically impaired, or other health-impaired persons who may require special education) in residential schools for the physically handicapped operated or substantially supported by the state.

An analysis of funding for projects completed in FY 1995 (the latest year with complete statistics), indicates that $2,300,184 in LSCA funds were expended. This amount was matched by $22,976,035 in state funds and $958,234 in local funds for a total of $26,234,453. For a state-by-state listing of expenditures, see Table 8.

For the most part, projects attempted to make the library service in an institution much like that in a local public library. Since reasons for institutionalization vary widely, each library focused on the special needs of its clientele through specially tailored programs and collection development. Penal institutions primarily used funds to develop better library collections. Hospitals and institutions for the mentally retarded purchased more self-help materials, including those aimed at teaching coping skills in preparation for life outside the institution. (Residential institutions for the deaf and for the blind continue to close as the number of residents continues to decline.)

Support for Public Library Construction and Technology Enhancement (LSCA Title II)

During FY 1994 the states obligated more than $20.6 million in LSCA funds for public library construction projects. Funding included more than $9.3 million from the total FY 1994 appropriation of $17.4 and $11.2 million carried over from previous year's allotments. This left $8 million from the FY 1994 allotment and over $3.5 million in carry-over funds available for approved projects in FY 1995.

During the same year, 26 states completed 112 public library construction or technology enhancement projects involving LSCA Title II funds. Table 9 lists the completed projects. There were 31 fewer completed projects than in FY 1993. The combined LSCA, state, and local funding for these projects totaled $80.4 million with about 10 percent of the funds coming from Title II.

The combined state and local matching funds totaled more than $72 million or 90 percent of the total costs for all completed public library construction projects in FY 1994. Of this amount, 88 percent came from local funds.

Text continues on page 333.

Table 9 / LSCA Title II Construction Projects Completed in FY 1994

Project	Federal	State	Local	Total
Alabama				
Troy Public Lib.	$75,000	$0	$90,436	$165,436
Alaska	0	0	0	0
Arizona	0	0	0	0
Arkansas	0	0	0	0
California				
Alpine County Lib.	3,200	0	3,721	6,921
Brawley Public Lib.	190,000	0	275,463	465,463
Newport Beach Central Lib.	727,387	0	7,782,190	8,509,577
San Marcos Branch	454,700	0	2,453,270	2,907,970
Colorado				
Center Public Lib.	7,264	0	7,561	14,825
Dolores Lib. District	7,333	0	9,282	16,615
Connecticut				
New Haven Free Public Lib.	100,000	350,000	16,972,768	17,422,768
Mystic & Noank Lib., Inc.	100,000	350,000	1,188,591	1,638,591
Wheeler School and Lib.	100,000	230,940	393,080	724,020
Delaware				
Division of Libraries	2,900	0	3,538	6,438
Millsboro Public Lib.	269	0	330	599
District of Columbia	0	0	0	0
Florida				
Clewison Public Lib.	400,000	0	478,795	878,795
Safety Harbor Public Lib.	400,000	0	748,995	1,148,995
Georgia	0	0	0	0
Hawaii	0	0	0	0
Idaho				
Buhl Public Lib.	68,373	0	148,700	217,073
Challis Public Lib.	20,000	0	62,000	82,000
Hailey Public Lib.	294,393	0	536,240	830,633
Mullan Public Lib.	75,000	292,235	186,500	553,735
Illinois				
Frankfort Public Lib. District	17,500	0	17,500	35,000
Galena Public Lib. District	75,000	0	190,733	265,733
Glenside Public Lib.	43,000	0	43,000	86,000
Lincoln Public Lib. District	60,000	0	60,000	120,000
Marrowbone Public Lib District	15,500	0	15,500	31,000
Indiana				
Grensburg Public Lib.	229,125	0	2,395,875	2,625,000
Iowa				
Dike Public Lib.	42,000	0	168,619	210,619
Jesup Public Lib.	171,889	0	193,837	365,726
Kansas	0	0	0	0
Kentucky	0	0	0	0
Louisiana				
Aududon Regional Lib.	3,760	0	3,892	7,652
East Carroll Parish Lib.	4,780	0	4,874	9,654
Franklin Parish Lib.	220,000	0	220,000	440,000
Jennings Canegie Public Lib.	2,500	0	2,545	5,045
Maine				
Cherryfield Public Lib.	2,000	0	2,391	4,391
East Blue Hill Lib.	500	0	500	1,000
Fort Fairfield Public Lib.	115,850	0	115,850	231,700
Hubbard Lib.	7,165	0	7,165	14,330
Hobbs Memorial Lib.	1,576	0	1,576	3,152
Salmon Falls Lib.	2,000	0	2,037	4,037

Table 9 / **LSCA Title II Construction Projects Completed in FY 1994** *(cont.)*

Project	Federal	State	Local	Total
Maryland				
Carroll County Pubic Lib.	29,000	0	43,500	72,500
Howard County Public Lib. (A)	20,584	0	30,166	50,750
Howard County Public Lib. (B)	6,804	0	10,206	17,010
Montgomery County Public Lib.	60,080	0	200,000	260,080
Wicomico Cnty Free Lib.	6,374	0	9,407	15,781
Massachusetts	0	0	0	0
Michigan				
Alpena County Lib.	26,055	0	36,711	62,766
Bad Axe Public Lib.	63,000	0	97,958	160,958
Cromaine Lib.	36,731	0	105,909	142,640
Elk Rapids District Lib.	33,637	0	62,995	96,632
Grand Rapids Public Lib. (A)	57,342	0	70,085	127,427
Grand Rapids Public Lib. (B)	15,400	0	18,823	34,223
Harrison Community Lib.	45,000	0	105,157	150,157
Hoyt Memorial Lib.	101,700	0	347,795	449,495
Muskegon County Lib.	120,000	0	487,863	607,863
Nottawa Township Lib.	39,150	0	50,657	89,807
Reed City Public Lib.	43,200	0	57,378	100,578
Rochester Hills Public Lib.	200,000	0	12,915,051	13,115,051
Willard Public Lib.	112,500	0	173,019	285,519
Minnesota	0	0	0	0
Mississippi	0	0	0	0
Missouri				
Kearney Branch Lib.	154,661	0	156,750	311,411
Salem Public Lib.	81,815	0	81,815	163,630
Montana	0	0	0	0
Nebraska	0	0	0	0
Nevada	0	0	0	0
New Hampshire				
NH State Lib. (Admin)	13,306	16,228	0	29,534
Amherst Town Lib.	7,140	0	7,140	14,280
Colebrook Public Lib.	8,784	0	12,000	20,784
Dudley-Tucker Lib.	22,612	0	246,000	268,612
Fuller Public Lib.	10,000	0	11,460	21,460
Hampstead Public Lib.	20,000	0	594,000	614,000
Keene Public Lib.	26,400	0	26,400	52,800
Laconia Public Lib.	15,000	0	15,000	30,000
Newmarket Public Lib.	30,000	0	3,339,400	3,369,400
NH State Lib. (Auto Info System)	8,500	0	12,447	20,947
Peterborough Town Lib.	3,198	0	3,211	6,409
Pillsbury Free Lib.	25,000	0	381,868	406,868
New Jersey	0	0	0	0
New Mexico	0	0	0	0
New York				
Canastota Public Lib.	43,750	0	81,250	125,000
Easton Lib. Association	36,750	0	68,250	105,000
The Field Lib.	2,975	0	5,525	8,500
Gates Public Lib. (A)	1,346	0	2,499	3,845
Gates Public Lib. (B)	14,920	9,045	17,980	41,945
Jefferson Public Lib.	6,860	0	103,340	110,200
Julia L. Bautterfield Memorial	14,000	0	26,000	40,000
Lyme Free Lib.	3,269	0	49,231	52,500
Marlboro Free Lib.	50,000	0	187,813	237,813
The Merrick Lib.	19,404	0	83,596	103,000

Table 9 / LSCA Title II Construction Projects Completed in FY 1994 *(cont.)*

Project	Federal	State	Local	Total
Montour Falls Memorial Lib	7,350	0	13,650	21,000
The Nyack Lib.	29,750	0	55,250	85,000
Olean Public Lib.	40,413	0	213,987	254,400
Olive Free Lib.	5,250	0	9,750	15,000
Ossing Public Lib.	1,953	0	3,627	5,580
Oswega City Lib.	7,680	0	15,853	23,533
Oyster Bay-E. Norwich Public Lib.	114,402	0	990,000	1,104,402
Patchogue-Medford Public Lib.	15,750	0	33,486	49,236
Rochester Public Lib.	190,587	0	1,394,159	1,584,746
Salamanca Public Lib.	700	0	1,300	2,000
Schenectady County Public Lib.	2,085	0	3,872	5,957
William K. Sanford Town Lib.	68,482	0	295,051	363,533
Youngstown Free Lib.	42,000	0	78,000	120,000
North Carolina				
Davie County Public Lib.	180,000	50,000	666,513	896,513
Henderson County Public Lib.	158,996	0	1,842,049	2,001,045
Hope Mills Branch Lib.	74,179	0	1,642,323	1,716,502
Rube McCary Memorial Lib.	100,375	0	188,258	288,633
North Dakota	0	0	0	0
Ohio	0	0	0	0
Oklahoma				
Atoka County Lib.	125,000	0	130,533	255,533
Oregon				
Driftwood Lib.	112,466	0	3,577,425	3,689,891
Pennsylvania	0	0	0	0
Rhode Island	0	0	0	0
South Carolina				
Pickens Branch	75,000	0	249,225	324,225
Tennessee				
Gray Branch Lib.	99,075	0	300,688	399,763
Macon County Public Lib.	69,353	60,784	52,583	182,720
Somerville-Fayette Cnty P. Lib.	99,075	35,784	179,058	313,917
Texas	0	0	0	0
Utah	0	0	0	0
Vermont				
Haston Lib.	45,600	0	53,750	99,350
Ruthland Free Lib.	57,641	0	59,822	117,463
Whiting Lib.	100,000	0	274,000	374,000
Virginia	0	0	0	0
Washington	0	0	0	0
West Virginia				
Administration	20,255	0	20,255	40,510
Pend Oreille Cnty Lib. Dist.	44,682	0	48,372	93,054
Wisconsin				
Clintonville Public Lib.	125,000	0	864,708	989,708
Deerfield Public Lib.	47,294	0	229,358	276,652
Kenosha Public Lib.	125,000	0	1,964,783	2,089,783
Mazimanie Public Lib.	48,600	0	404,017	452,617
Wyoming				
Platte County Lib.	3,876	0	5,813	9,689
Powell Branch Lib.	24,282	0	36,423	60,705
Guam	0	0	0	0
Puerto Rico	0	0	0	0
Virgin Islands	0	0	0	0
Total	$7,938,362	$1,395,016	$71,020,950	$80,354,328

Support for Technology and Networks (LSCA Title III)

The purpose of Title III is to assist states in planning and funding local, regional, and interstate cooperative networks involving public, academic, school, and special libraries for the general purposes of resource sharing. This includes assistance in developing the technological capacity of libraries for interlibrary cooperation and resource sharing. Title III also provides for statewide preservation programs for the systematic preservation of endangered library and information resources.

The 1995 appropriation for Title III was $23,226,000. Most of the $20,216,026 expended in FY 1995 (see Table 10) was for the establishment, expansion, and operation of cooperative library networks. Many of the projects took advantage of new technological advances in the fields of telecommunications and information retrieval. Other projects initiated Internet access or connections to other electronic resources. A few states funded projects for the preservation of significant historical documents.

A sampling of projects illustrates how Title III funds were used in beneficial ways:

Alaska. The Statewide Library Electronic Doorway (SLED) is a menu system that provides Alaskans access to library databases, state information resources, local community networks, and the Internet. It reaches more than 87 percent of the state's population via a local phone call in 40 communities and provides the only Internet access available to most communities. A cooperative effort of the Alaska State Library, the University of Alaska at Fairbanks, Rasmuson Library, and the University of Alaska Computer Network, SLED migrated from proprietary software to the World Wide Web mid-year and continues to add new connections.

Statistics show a 1,000 percent growth rate from 4,242 logins in May 1994 to 42,890 logins in March 1995, with Alaskans connecting most frequently to the World Wide Web, Weather Information, Economic Bulletin Board, Census Information, and library catalogs. For example, a practicing surgeon reports that he uses SLED at home in the evenings to look up medical information on Medline; an international business consultant says he uses SLED extensively to access the Economic Bulletin Board and other business-related databases (in fact, SLED played a primary role in the preparation of a recent Nigerian business-climate assessment completed for an Anchorage-based engineering firm).

Wisconsin. The 1995 catalog of the statewide database project known as WISCAT contains more than 4.95 million bibliographic records and more than 23 million holdings. A total of 1,084 libraries have holdings in the catalog, which now requires at least five CD-ROM drives to operate. Much consideration has been given to dealing with the size and continued growth of the catalog, resulting in a decision to split the database by continuing to separate out foreign-language and audiovisual titles onto supplement discs. Many libraries have commented on the usefulness of the supplement discs.

Many libraries continue to use WISCAT to extract USMARC records to support local automation projects. During 1994–1995, 50 libraries used the extraction services provided by the State Library. Several workshops were held on the topic, indicating that this type of training continues to be in demand as more and more libraries move toward automating their library operations.

More libraries are attempting to run WISCAT in a networked environment to reduce the cost of purchasing multiple workstations. Networking of a multi-disc package such as WISCAT can be very complex and often takes a great deal of expertise, patience, and time on the part of both the WISCAT staff and the local library staff. With the customization of the QuILL interlibrary loan software, staff also are being required to rethink how the interlibrary-loan process works. Specifications for software development and changes were created and new software was tested. The product is being installed in libraries and library systems, and is now operational in seven systems.

Table 10 / LSCA Title III Expenditures for Technology and Networks, FY 1995

State	Amount	State	Amount
Alabama	$355,623	New Hampshire	153,041
Alaska	114,578	New Jersey	543,730
Arizona	237,269	New Mexico	135,941
Arkansas	171,079	New York	1,278,531
California	2,075,714	North Carolina	455,153
Colorado	270,826	North Dakota	91,169
Connecticut	254,470	Ohio	532,392
Delaware	62,785	Oklahoma	273,511
District of Columbia	51,054	Oregon	211,039
Florida	937,092	Pennsylvania	1,081,367
Georgia	488,997	Rhode Island	120,599
Hawaii	107,758	South Carolina	286,514
Idaho	114,568	South Dakota	121,909
Illinois	716,218	Tennessee	374,178
Indiana	319,304	Texas	1,157,315
Iowa	239,141	Utah	121,609
Kansas	210,932	Vermont	68,258
Kentucky	322,570	Virginia	473,576
Louisiana	319,600	Washington	584,242
Maine	94,262	West Virginia	186,684
Maryland	366,492	Wisconsin	427,916
Massachusetts	508,627	Wyoming	66,943
Michigan	683,350	Guam	18,857
Minnesota	686,586	Northern Marianas	11,302
Mississippi	341,424	Puerto Rico	264,558
Missouri	535,384	Virgin Islands	18,205
Montana	233,761		
Nebraska	158,644	Total	$20,216,026
Nevada	179,379		

Part 3
Library/Information Science Education, Placement, and Salaries

Guide to Employment Sources in the Library and Information Professions

Maxine Moore
Office for Library Personnel Resources, American Library Association

This guide updates the listing in the 1996 *Bowker Annual* with information on new services and changes in contacts and groups listed previously. The sources listed primarily give assistance in obtaining professional positions, although a few indicate assistance with paraprofessionals. The latter, however, tend to be recruited through local sources.

General Sources of Library and Information Jobs

Library Literature

Classified ads of library vacancies and positions wanted are carried in many of the national, regional, and state library journals and newsletters. Members of associations can sometimes list "position wanted" ads free of charge in their membership publications. Listings of positions available are regularly found in *American Libraries, Chronicle of Higher Education, College & Research Libraries News, Library Journal,* and *Library Hotline*. State and regional library association newsletters, state library journals, foreign library periodicals, and other types of periodicals carrying such ads are listed in later sections.

Newspapers

The *New York Times* Sunday "Week in Review" section carries a special section of ads for librarian jobs in addition to the regular classifieds. Local newspapers, particularly the larger city Sunday editions, such as the *Washington Post, Los Angeles Times,* and *Chicago Tribune* often carry job vacancy listings in libraries, both professional and paraprofessional.

Internet

The many library-related electronic listservs on the Internet often post library job vacancies interspersed with other news and discussion items. A growing number of general online jobsearch bulletin boards exist; these may include information-related job notices along with other types of jobs. This guide includes information on electronic access where available through the individual organizations listed below. Two useful resources are: "Job Opportunities Glitter for Librarians Who Surf the Net" by A. Paula Azar, *American Libraries,* September 1996, and

Copyright © 1997 by the American Library Association. All rights reserved except those which may be granted by Sections 107 and 108 of the Copyright Revision Act of 1976.

"Library Jobs and Employment: A Guide to Internet Resources," compiled by Jeffery C. Lee, Texas Woman's University, and posted on the University of Michigan gopher (gopher.lib.umich.edu) under What's New & Featured Resources/Clearinghouse for Subject-oriented Internet Resource Guides (UM/All Guides/Library Employment; J. Lee; v.1.1; 1/29/95; URL: http://www.lib.umich.edu/chhome.html).

"Winning Résumé," by Scott Grusky in *Internet World*, February 1996, and "How to Find a Job Online" by Ann J. Van Camp (*Online* 12:26-34, July 1988) offer guidance on databases that might lead to library and information-related position listings.

A guide to other types of employment information on the Internet is available on the same gopher clearinghouse: "Job Searching & Employment; P. Ray, B. Taylor." Several articles in the Fall 1994 *Journal of Career Planning & Employment* discuss "Career Counseling in Cyberspace" and "The Job Search Goes Computer."

Library Joblines

Library joblines or job "hotlines" give recorded telephone messages of job openings in a specific geographical area. Most tapes are changed once a week, although individual listings may sometimes be carried for several weeks. Although the information is fairly brief and the cost of calling is borne by the individual job seeker, a jobline provides a quick and up-to-date listing of vacancies that is not usually possible with printed listings or journal ads.

Most joblines carry listings for their state or region only, although some will occasionally accept out-of-state positions if there is room on the tape. While a few will list technician and other paraprofessional positions, the majority are for professional jobs only. When calling the joblines, one might occasionally find a time when the telephone keeps ringing without any answer; this will usually mean that the tape is being changed or there are no new jobs for that period. The classified section of *American Libraries* carries jobline numbers periodically as space permits.

The following joblines are in operation:

Jobline Sponsor	Job Seekers (To Hear Job Listings)	Employers (To Place Job Listings)
American Association of Law Libraries	312-939-7577	53 W. Jackson Blvd., Suite 940, Chicago, IL 60604. 312-939-4764; fax 312-431-1097
Arizona Department of Library, Archives and Public Records (Arizona libraries only)	602-275-2325	Arizona State Braille & Talking Book Lib. Div., 1030 N. 32nd St., Phoenix, AZ 85008 fax 602-255-4312
British Columbia Library Association (B.C. listings only)	604-430-6411	Jobline, 110-6545 Bonsor Ave., Burnaby, BC V5H 1H3, Canada. 604-430-9633

Guide to Employment Sources in the Library and Information Professions / 339

Jobline Sponsor	Job Seekers (To Hear Job Listings)	Employers (To Place Job Listings)
California Library Association	916-443-1222 818-638-8057 (identical listings)	717 K St., Suite 300, Sacramento, CA 95814-3477. 916-447-8541
California Media and Library Educators Association	415-697-8832	1499 Old Bayshore Hwy., Suite 142, Burlingame, CA 94010. 415-692-2350
Cleveland (OH) Area Metropolitan Library System Job Listing Service	216-921-4702	CAMLS, 20600 Chagrin Blvd., Suite 500, Shaker Heights, OH 44122.
Colorado State Library[1] (includes paraprofessionals)	303-866-6741	Jobline, 201 E. Colfax, 3rd fl., Denver, CO 80203-1704. 303-866-6900; fax 303-866-6940; also via Libnet/listserv
Connecticut Library Association	860-889-1200	Box 1046, Norwich, CT 06360-1046
Delaware Division of Libraries (Del., N.J., and Pa. listings)	800-282-8696 (in-state) 302-739-4748 ext. 69 (out-of-state)	43 S. Dupont Hwy., Dover, DE 19901
Drexel University College of Information Sci. & Tech.	215-895-1672	College of Info. Sci. & Tech., Philadelphia, PA 19104. 215-895-2478
State Library of Florida	904-488-5232 (in state)	R. A. Gray Bldg., Tallahassee, FL 32399-0251. 904-487-2651
Library Jobline of Illinois[2]	312-828-0930 (professional) 312-828-9198 (support staff)	Illinois Library Assn., 33 W. Grand, Suite 301, Chicago, IL 60610. 800-665-5576; 312-644-1896; $40/2 weeks
State Library of Iowa (professional jobs in Iowa; only during regular business hours)	515-281-7574	East 12 & Grand, Des Moines, IA 50319. 515-281-7574
Kansas State Library Jobline (also includes paraprofessional and out-of-state)	913-296-3296	c/o Jana Ealy, 3rd fl., State Capitol, Topeka, KS 66612
Kentucky Job Hotline	502-564-3008 (24 hours)	Dept. for Libs. and Archives, Box 537, Frankfort, KY 40602. 502-564-8300
Long Island (NY) Library Resources Council Jobline	516-632-6658	516-632-6650; fax 516-632-6662
Maryland Library Association	410-685-5760	400 Cathedral St., 3rd flr., Baltimore, MD 21201. 410-727-7422 (Mon.–Fri., 9:00 A.M.–4:30 P.M.)

Jobline Sponsor	Job Seekers (To Hear Job Listings)	Employers (To Place Job Listings)
Medical Library Association Jobline	312-553-4636 (24 hours)	6 N. Michigan Ave., Suite 300, Chicago, IL 60602. 312-419-9094
Metropolitan Washington (D.C.) Council of Governments Library Council	202-962-3712	777 N. Capitol St. N.E., Suite 300, Washington, DC 20002. 202-962-3254
Michigan Library Association	517-694-7440	6810 S. Cedar, #6, Lansing, MI 48911. 517-694-6615 ($40/week)
Missouri Library Association Jobline	314-442-6590	1306 Business 63 S., Suite B, Columbia, MO 65201-8404. 314-449-4627
Mountain Plains Library Association[3]	605-677-5757	c/o I. D. Weeks Library, University of South Dakota, Vermillion, SD 57069. 605-677-6082, fax 605-677-5488
Nebraska Job Hotline (in-state and other openings during regular business hours)	402-471-2045 800-307-2665 (in-state)	Nebraska Library Commission, 1200 N St. 120, Lincoln, NE 68508-2023.
New England Library Jobline (New England jobs only)	617-521-2815	GSLIS, Simmons College, 300 The Fenway, Boston, MA 02115.
New Jersey Library Association	609-695-2121	Box 1534, Trenton, NJ 08607; 609-394-8032; nonmembers $25/4 weeks
New York Library Association	518-432-6952 800-232-6952 (in-state)	252 Hudson Ave., Albany, NY 12210-1802. 518-432-6952 (members $15/3 months, nonmembers $25/3 months)
North Carolina State Library (professional jobs in N.C. only)	919-733-6410	Division of State Library, 109 E. Jones St., Raleigh, NC 27601-2807. 919-733-2570
Ohio Library Council	614-225-6999	35 E. Gay St., Suite 305, Columbus, OH 43215. 614-221-9057; fax 614-221-6234
Oklahoma Department of Libraries Jobline (5:00 P.M.–8:00 A.M., Monday–Friday and all weekend)	405-521-4202	200 N.E. 18 St., Oklahoma City, OK 73105. 405-521-2502
Oregon Library Association (Northwest listings only)	503-585-2232	Oregon State Library, State Library Bldg., Salem, OR 97310. 503-378-4243 ext. 221
Pacific Northwest Library Association[4]	360-543-2890	c/o Graduate School of Library and Information Science, University of Washington, FM-30, Seattle, WA 98195. 360-543-1794

Guide to Employment Sources in the Library and Information Professions / 341

Jobline Sponsor	Job Seekers (To Hear Job Listings)	Employers (To Place Job Listings)
Pennsylvania Jobline[5]	717-234-4646	Pennsylvania Library Assn., 1919 N. Front St., Harrisburg, PA 17102. 717-233-3113 (weekly fee for nonmembers); fax 717-233-3121
Pratt Institute SILS Job Hotline	718-636-3742	SILS, Brooklyn, NY 11205. 718-636-3702
University of South Carolina College of Library and Information Science (no geographic restrictions)	803-777-8443	University of South Carolina, Columbia, SC 29208. 803-777-3887
Special Libraries Association	202-234-3632	1700 18th St. N.W., Washington, DC 20009. 202-234-4700
Special Libraries Association, New York Chapter	212-740-2007	David Jank, FIND/SVP, 625 Ave. of the Americas, New York, NY 10011. fax 212-645-7681
Special Libraries Association, San Andreas-San Francisco Bay Chapter	415-528-7766	415-974-3218; fax 415-974-3429
Special Libraries Association, Southern California Chapter	818-795-2145	818-302-8966; fax 818-302-8015
Texas Library Association Job Hotline (24 hours; Texas listings only)	512-328-0651	3355 Bee Cave Rd., Suite 401, Austin, TX 78746. 512-328-1518
Texas State Library Jobline (Texas listings only)	512-463-5470	Library Development, Box 12927, Austin, TX 78711. 512-463-5465; fax 512-463-8800
University of Toronto Faculty of Information Studies	416-978-7073	416-978-3035; fax 416-978-5762
University of Western Ontario Grad. School of Library and Information Science	519-661-3543	GSLIS, London, ON N6G 1H1, Canada. 519-661-2111 ext. 8494; fax 519-661-5506
Virginia Library Association Jobline (Virginia libraries only)	703-519-8027	669 S. Washington St., Alexandria, VA 22314

1. Weekly printed listing sent on receipt of stamps and mailing labels.
2. Cosponsored by the Special Libraries Association Illinois Chapter and the Illinois Library Association.
3. 800-356-7820 available from all MPLA states (includes listings for the states of Arizona, Colorado, Kansas, Montana, Nebraska, Nevada, North Dakota, Oklahoma, South Dakota, Utah, and Wyoming, and paid listings from out-of-region institutions—$10/week).
4. Alaska, Alberta, British Columbia, Idaho, Montana, Oregon, and Washington; includes both professional and paraprofessional jobs.
5. Sponsored by the Pennsylvania Library Association; also accepts paraprofessional out-of-state listings.

Specialized Library Associations and Groups

Advanced Information Management, 444 Castro St., Suite 320, Mountain View, CA 94041, 415-965-7799 (http://www.aimusa.com/aim@aimusa.com): Placement agency that specializes in library and information personnel. They offer work on a temporary, permanent, and contract basis for both professional librarians and paraprofessionals in the special, public, and academic library marketplace. They supply consultants who can work with special projects in libraries or manage library development projects. They maintain offices in Southern California (900 Wilshire Blvd, Suite 1424, Los Angeles, CA 90017, 213-243-9236) as well as in the San Francisco Bay Area. There is no fee to applicants.

American Association of Law Libraries Career Hotline, 53 W. Jackson Blvd., Suite 940, Chicago, IL 60604, 312-939-4764: The Hotline (312-939-7877) is a 24-hour-a-day recording, updated each Friday at noon. Any interested person may receive the complete Job Data Base free, by request. Ads may also be viewed on AALLNET, an Internet bulletin board (http://lawlib.wuacc.edu/aallnet/aallnet.html). To list a position contact AALL, Placement Assistant; fax 312-431-1097.

American Libraries, "Career LEADS," c/o *American Libraries*, 50 E. Huron St., Chicago, IL 60611: Classified job listings published in each monthly issue of *American Libraries* magazine, listing some 100 job openings grouped by type, plus "Late Job Notices" added near press time as space and time permits. Contains subsections: Positions Wanted, Librarians' Classified, joblines, and regional salary scales. Also contains ConsultantBase (see below) four times annually.

American Libraries, "Career LEADS EXPRESS," c/o Georgia Okotete, 50 E. Huron St., Chicago, IL 60611: Advance galleys (3-4 weeks) of classified job listings to be published in next issue of *American Libraries*. Early notice of approximately 100 "Positions Open" sent about the 17th of each month; does not include editorial corrections and late changes as they appear in the regular *AL* LEADS section, but does include some "Late Job Notices." For each month, send $1 check made out to AL EXPRESS, self-addressed, standard business-size envelope (4x9), with 55¢ postage on envelope.

American Libraries, ConsultantBase (CBase): An *AL* service that helps match professionals offering library/information expertise with institutions seeking it. Published quarterly, CBase appears in the Career LEADS section of the January, April, June, and October issues of *AL*. Rates: $5.50/line—classified; $55/inch—display. Inquiries should be made to Jon Kartman, LEADS Editor, *American Libraries*, 50 E. Huron St., Chicago, IL 60611, 312-280-4211.

American Library Association, ASCLA/SLAS State Library Consultants to Institutional Libraries Discussion Group, Institutional Library Mailed Jobline: Compilation of job openings in institutional libraries throughout the United States and territories. Send self-addressed, stamped envelope(s) to Institutional Library Jobline, c/o Gloria Spooner, State Library of Louisiana, Box 131, Baton Rouge, LA 70821-0131. Send job postings to same or call 504-342-4931; or fax 504-342-3547. Listings will appear for one month unless resubmitted.

American Library Association, Association of College and Research Libraries, 50 E. Huron St., Chicago, IL 60611-2795, 312-280-2513: Classified advertising appears each month in *College & Research Libraries News*. Ads appearing in the print *C&RL News* are also posted to *C&RL NewsNet*, an

abridged electronic edition of *C&RL News* that is accessible on the Web (http://www.ala.org/acrl/c&rlnew2.html).
American Library Association, Office for Library Personnel Resources, 50 E. Huron St., Chicago, IL 60611, 312-280-4281: A placement service is provided at each Annual Conference (June or July) and Midwinter Meeting (January or February). Request job seeker or employer registration forms prior to each conference. Persons not able to attend can register with the service and can also purchase job and job seeker listings sent directly from the conference site. Information included when requesting registration forms. Handouts on interviewing, preparing a resume, and other job search information are available from the ALA Office for Library Personnel Resources.

In addition to the ALA conference placement center, ALA division national conferences usually include a placement service. See *American Libraries* "Datebook" for dates of upcoming divisional conferences, since these are not held every year. ALA provides Web site job postings from *American Libraries*, *C&RL NewsNet*, and its conference placement services (http://www.ala.org) located in the library education and employment menu page.
American Society for Information Science, 8720 Georgia Ave., #501, Silver Spring, MD 20910-3602, 301-495-0900: There is an active placement service operated at ASIS Annual Meetings (usually October, locales change). All conference attendees (both ASIS members and non-members), as well as ASIS members who cannot attend the conference, are eligible to use the service to list or find jobs. Job listings are also accepted from employers who cannot attend the conference, interviews are arranged, and special seminars are given. Throughout the year, current job openings are listed in *ASIS JOBLINE*, a monthly publication sent to all members, and available to non-members on request. Please check ASIS for ad rates.
Art Libraries Society/North America (ARLIS/NA), c/o Executive Director, 4101 Lake Boone Trail, Suite 201, Raleigh, NC 27607, 919-787-5181; fax 919-787-4916 (74517.3400@compuserve.com): Art information and visual resources curator jobs are listed in the *ARLIS/NA UPDATE* (6 times a year) and a job registry is maintained at society headquarters. (Any employer may list a job with the registry but only members may request job information.) Listings also available on ARLIS-L listserv and Web site. Call headquarters for registration and/or published information.
Asian/Pacific American Libraries Newsletter, c/o Anna Wang, Ohio State University, 124 Main Library, 1858 Neil Ave. Mall, Columbus, OH 43210-1286, 614-292-6151: Quarterly. Includes some job ads. Free to members of Asian/Pacific American Librarians Association.
Association for Library and Information Science Education, c/o UM School of Information, 550 E. University Ave., Rm. 304, Ann Arbor, MI 48109-1092, 313-936-9812; fax 313-764-2475 (http://www.si.umich.edu/ALISE/ or e-mail: alise.si@umich.edu): Provides placement service at annual conference (January or February) for library and information studies faculty and administrative positions.
Association for Educational Communications and Technology, 1025 Vermont Ave. N.W., Suite 820, Washington, DC 20005, 202-347-7834; fax 202-347-7839; e-mail: aect@aect.org: AECT maintains a placement listing on the Internet

gopher (gopher_sunbird.usd.edu_72) and provides a placement service at the annual convention, free to all registrants.

Black Caucus Newsletter, c/o George C. Grant, Editor, Rollins College, 1000 Holt Ave. #2654, Winter Park, FL 32789, 407-646-2676; fax 407-646-1515; e-mail: bcnews@rollins.edu: Lists paid advertisements for vacancies. Free to members, $10/ year to others. Published bimonthly by Four-G Publishers, Inc. News accepted continuously. Biographies, essays, books, and reviews of interest to members are invited.

C. Berger And Company, 327 E. Gundersen Dr., Carol Stream, IL 60188, 708-653-1115; 800-382-4222; fax 630-653-1691; e-mail: c-berg@dupagels.lib.ilus. (www.cberger.com): CBC conducts nationwide executive searches to fill permanent positions in libraries, information centers, and related businesses at the management, supervisory, and director level. Professionals and clerks are also available from CBC as temporary workers or contract personnel for short- and long-term assignments in special, academic, and public libraries in Illinois, Indiana, Georgia, Pennsylvania, Texas, and Wisconsin. CBC also provides library and records management consulting services and direction and staff to manage projects for clients.

Canadian Association of Special Libraries and Information Services/Ottawa Chapter Job Bank, c/o CASLIS Job Bank Coordinator, 266 Sherwood Dr., Ottawa, Ontario, K1Y 3W4, Canada: Those looking for a job should send resume; employers with a job to list should call 613-728-9982.

Canadian Library Association, 200 Elgin St., Suite 602, Ottawa, Ontario, Canada K2P 1L5, 613-232-9625: Publishes career ads in *Feliciter* magazine. CASLIS division offers job bank service in several cities. Operates a "Jobmart" at the annual conference in June.

Catholic Library Association, 9009 Carter St., Allen Park, MI 48101: Personal and institutional members of CLA are given free space (35 words) to advertise for jobs or to list job openings in *Catholic Library World* (4/year). Others may advertise. Contact advertising coordinator for rates.

Chinese-American Librarians Association Newsletter, c/o Lan Yang, Sterling C. Evans Library, Texas A&M University, College Station, TX 77843-5000: Job listings in newsletter issued in February, June, October. Free to members.

Council on Library/Media Technicians, Inc., c/o Membership Chair, Julia Ree, PO Box 52057, Riverside, CA 92517-3057: *COLT Newsletter* appears bimonthly in *Library Mosaics*. Personal dues/U.S.: $35; Foreign, $60; Students: $30; Institutions/U.S.: $60; Foreign: $85.

Gossage Regan Associates, Inc., 25 W. 43rd St., New York, NY 10036, 212-869-3348; fax 212-997-1127: An executive search firm specializing in the recruitment of library directors and other library/information handling organization top management. About 50 nationwide searches have been conducted since 1983 for public, academic, and large specialized libraries in all regions of the U.S. Salary limitation: $60,000 up. Library Executive Recruiters: Wayne Gossage; Joan Neumann. And **Wontawk Gossage, Associates**, 25 W. 43rd St., New York, NY 10036, 212-869-3348; fax 212-997-1127; 304 Newbury St., No. 314, Boston, MA 02115, 617-867-9209; fax 617-437-9317: Temporary/long term/temporary to permanent assignments in the New York/NJ/CT and the Boston metropolitan areas in all types of libraries/information management, professional and support, all levels of responsibility, all skills. The original library temporaries firm, since 1980, as Gossage Regan. In charge: Nancy Melin Nelson, MLS; Gordon Gossage.

Labat-Anderson, Inc., 8000 Westpark Dr., No. 400, McLean, VA 22102, 703-506-9600; fax 703-506-4646: One of the largest providers of library and records management services to the federal government. Supports various federal agencies in 27 states, with many positions located in the Washington, D.C. area. Resumes and cover letters will gladly be accepted from librarians with an ALA-accredited MLS and records managers for part-time and regular full-time employment.

The Library Co-Op, Inc., 3840 Park Ave., Suite 107, Edison, NJ 08820, 908-906-1777 or 800-654-6275; fax 908-906-3562; e-mail: 71334-3036@compuserve.com: The company is licensed as both a temporary and permanent employment agency and supplies consultants to work in a wide variety of information settings and functions from library moving to database management, catalog maintenance, reference, retrospective conversion, and more. Recent developments include the forming of a new division, ABCD Filing Services, and the hiring of two specialists in space planning. Another new division, LAIRD Consulting, provides a full range of automation expertise for hardware, software, LANS, and WANS.

Library Management Systems, Corporate Pointe, Suite 755, Culver City, CA 90230, 310-216-6436; 800-567-4669; fax 310-649-6388; e-mail: lms@ix.netcom.com; and Three Bethesda Metro Center, Suite 700, Bethesda, MD 20814, 301-961-1984; fax 301-652-6240; e-mail: lmsdc@ix.netcom.com: LMS has been providing library staffing, recruitment, and consulting to public and special libraries and businesses since 1983. LMS organizes and manages special libraries; designs and implements major projects (including retrospective conversions, automation studies, and records management); performs high-quality cataloging outsourcing; and furnishes contract staffing to all categories of information centers. LMS has a large database of librarians and library assistants on call for long- and short-term projects and provides permanent placement at all levels.

Library Mosaics, Box 5171, Culver City, CA 90231, 310-410-1573: Magazine appears bimonthly and will accept listings for library/media support staff positions. However, correspondence relating to jobs cannot be handled.

Medical Library Association, 6 N. Michigan Ave., Suite 300, Chicago, IL 60602-4805, 312-419-9094: *MLA News* (10 issues a year, June/July and November/December combined issues) lists positions wanted and positions available in its "Employment Opportunities" column. The position available rate is $2.80 per word for non-members and for any advertisements received through an employment agency, advertising agency, or any other third party. Up to 50 free words for MLA members plus $2.45 per word over 50 words. Members and non-members may rerun ads once in the next consecutive issue for $25. All positions available advertisements must list a minimum salary; a salary range is preferred. Positions wanted rates $1.50 per word for non-members; $1.25 per word for members with 100 free words; $1.25 will be charged for each word exceeding 100. MLA also offers a placement service at annual conference each spring. Job advertisements received for *MLA News* publication are posted to the MLANET Jobline the week of receipt. The jobline can be accessed 9-5 (CST) by calling

312-419-9094 (ask for extension 343); 24-hour access is available by calling 312-553-4636. In the MLA jobline, positions are categorized by position type, salary range, and regional area.

Pro Libra Associates, Inc., 6 Inwood Pl., Maplewood, NJ 07040, 201-762-0070; 800-262-0070; e-mail: prolibra-2@mail.idt.net. A multi-service agency, Pro Libra specializes in consulting, personnel, and project support for libraries and information centers.

Music Library Association, c/o Elisabeth H. Rebman, MLA Placement Officer, Music Library, 240 Morrison Hall, University of California–Berkeley, Berkeley, CA 94720-6000, 510-643-5198; fax 510-642-8237 (http://www.music.indiana.edu/tech_s/mla/index.htm) or gopher: theme.music.indiana.edu: Monthly job list $15/year (individuals); $20 (organizations) to MLA Business Office, Box 487, Canton, MA 02021, 617-828-8450; fax 617-828-8915; e-mail: acadsvc@aol.com.

REFORMA, National Association to Promote Library Service to the Spanish-Speaking, Box 832, Anaheim, CA 92815-0832: Employers wishing to do direct mailings to the REFORMA membership (1,300+) may obtain mailing labels arranged by zip code for $100. Contact Al Milo, 714-738-6383. Job ads are also published quarterly in the REFORMA newsletter. For rate information contact Ed Erazo, 505-646-6930; fax 505-646-6940.

Society of American Archivists, 600 S. Federal, Suite 504, Chicago, IL 60605, 312-922-0140; fax 312-347-1452 (http://www.archivists.org or e-mail: info@archivists.org): The *Archival Outlook* is sent (to members only) six times annually and contains features about the archival profession and other timely pieces on courses in archival administration, meetings, and professional opportunities (job listings). The *SAA Employment Bulletin* is a bimonthly listing of job opportunities available to members by subscription for $24 a year, and to non-members for $10 per issue. Prepayment is required.

Special Libraries Association, 1700 18th St., N.W., Washington, DC 20009-2508, 202-234-4700 ext. 627; fax 202-265-9317 (http://www.sla.org or e-mail: sla@sla.org): SLA maintains a telephone jobline, SpeciaLine, which is in operation 24 hours a day, seven days a week, 202-234-4700 ext. 1. Most SLA chapters have employment chairpersons who act as referral persons for employers and job seekers. Several SLA chapters have joblines. The association's monthly magazine, *Information Outlook*, carries classified advertising. SLA offers an employment clearinghouse and career advisory service during the annual conference held in June. SLA also provides a discount to members using the resume evaluation service offered through Advanced Information Management. A "Guide to Career Opportunities" is a resource kit for $20 (SLA member, $15); "Getting a Job: Tips and Techniques" is free to unemployed SLA members. The SLA Job Bulletin Board, a computer listserv, is organized by Indiana University staff. Subscribe by sending message—subscribe SLAJOB first name, last name—to listserv@iubvm.ucs.indiana.edu.

TeleSec/Corestaff, 1160 Veirs Mill Rd., Suite 414, Wheaton, MD 20902, 301-949-4097, fax 301-949-7808; e-mail: telesec@clark.net: Offers many opportunities to get started in the metropolitan Washington, D.C., library market through short- and long-term assignments in federal agencies, law firms, corporations, associations, and academic institutions. Founded in 1948, TeleSec/Corestaff has

been performing library technical projects including cataloging, interlibrary loans, database design, and acquisitions since the late 1960s.
Tuft & Associates, Inc., 1209 Astor St., Chicago, IL 60610, 312-642-8889; fax 312-642-8883: Specialists in nationwide executive searches for administrative posts in libraries and information centers.

State Library Agencies

In addition to the joblines mentioned previously, some of the state library agencies issue lists of job openings within their areas. These include: Colorado (weekly, sent on receipt of stamps and mailing labels; also available via Libnet listserv); Colorado (via listserv and Access Colorado Library and Information Network—ACLIN; send SASE for access); Indiana (monthly on request) or access http://www.statelib.lib.in.us/do/posop16html; Iowa (*Joblist*, monthly on request); Massachusetts (http://www.mlin.lib.ma.us); Mississippi (*Library Job Opportunities*, monthly); and Ohio (*Library Opportunities in Ohio*, monthly, sent to accredited library education programs and interested individuals upon request).

The Colorado, Georgia, Nebraska, North Carolina, Oklahoma, Pennsylvania, South Carolina, and Texas state libraries have an electronic bulletin board service that lists job openings in the state. Colorado lists out-of-state jobs also (http://www.aclin.org) type JOBLINE as the code; for Georgia access (http://www.gpls.public.lib.ga.cis); Kentucky (http://www.kdla.state.ky.us/libserv/jobline.htm); Louisana access (http://smt.state.lib.la.us./statelib.htm); Nebraska can be accessed via Nebraska Online (402-471-4020; 800-307-2665 in Nebraska); North Carolina (http://hal.dcr.state.nc.us/jobs/jobs.htm) lists both professional and paraprofessional library positions; Texas (http://www.tsl.state.tx.us) can be accessed in-state and nationally by Internet; Oklahoma via computer and modem (405-524-4089); South Carolina via telnet (leo.scsl.state.sc.us, log in as "ebbs") or (http://www.state.sc.us/scs/lion.html); and in Pennsylvania listserv maintained by Commonwealth Libraries.

On occasion, the following state library newsletters or journals will list vacancy postings: Alabama (*Cottonboll*, quarterly); Alaska (*Newspoke*, bimonthly); Arizona (*Arizona Libraries NewsWeek*); Idaho (*State Library Newsletter*, monthly); Indiana (*Focus on Indiana Libraries*, 11 times/year, www.statelib.lib.in.us/ldo/posop16.html); Iowa (*Joblist*); Kansas (*Kansas Libraries*, monthly); Louisiana (*Library Communique*, monthly); Nebraska (*Overtones*, quarterly); New Hampshire (*Granite State Libraries*, bimonthly); New Mexico (*Hitchhiker*, weekly); Tennessee (*TLA Newsletter*, bimonthly); Utah (*Directions for Utah Libraries*, monthly); and Wyoming (*Outrider*, monthly).

Many state library agencies will refer applicants informally when vacancies are known to exist, but do not have formal placement services. The following states primarily make referrals to public libraries only: Alabama, Alaska, Arizona, Arkansas, California, Louisiana, Pennsylvania, South Carolina (institutional also), Tennessee, Utah, Vermont, and Virginia. Those who refer applicants to all types of libraries are: Alaska, Delaware, Florida, Idaho, Illinois, Kansas, Kentucky, Maine, Maryland, Mississippi, Montana, Nebraska, Nevada (largely public and academic), New Hampshire, New Mexico, North Carolina, North Dakota, Ohio, Pennsylvania, Rhode Island, South Dakota, West Virginia (on Pennsylvania Jobline, public, academic, special), and Wyoming.

The following state libraries post library vacancy notices for all types of libraries on a bulletin board: California, Connecticut, Florida, Georgia, Illinois, Indiana, Iowa, Kentucky, Michigan, Montana, Nevada, New Jersey, New York, North Carolina, Ohio, Oklahoma, Pennsylvania, South Carolina, South Dakota, Utah, and Washington. [Addresses of the state agencies are found in Part 6 of the *Bowker Annual* and in *American Library Directory—Ed.*]

State and Regional Library Associations

State and regional library associations will often make referrals, run ads in association newsletters, or operate a placement service at annual conferences, in addition to the joblines sponsored by some groups. Referral of applicants when jobs are known is done by the following associations: Arkansas, Delaware, Hawaii, Louisiana, Michigan, Minnesota, Nevada, Pennsylvania, South Dakota, Tennessee, and Wisconsin. Although listings are infrequent, job vacancies are placed in the following association newsletters or journals when available: Alabama (*Alabama Librarian*, 7 times/year); Alaska (*Newspoke*, bimonthly); Arizona (*Newsletter*, 10 times/year); Arkansas (*Arkansas Libraries*, 6 times/year); Connecticut (*Connecticut Libraries*, 11 times/year); Delaware (*Delaware Library Association Bulletin*, 3 times/year); District of Columbia (*Intercom*, 11 times/year); Florida (*Florida Libraries*, 6 times/year); Indiana (*Focus on Indiana Libraries*, 11 times/year); Iowa (*Catalyst*, 6 times/year); Kansas (*KLA Newsletter*, 6 issues/bimonthly); Minnesota (*MLA Newsletter*, 6 issues/bimonthly); Missouri (bimonthly); Mountain Plains (*MPLA Newsletter*, bimonthly, lists vacancies and position wanted ads for individual and institutions); Nebraska (*NLAQ*); Nevada (*Highroller*, 4 times/year); New Hampshire (*NHLA Newsletter*, 6 times/year); New Jersey (*NJLA Newsletter*, 10 times/year); New Mexico (shares notices via State Library's *Hitchhiker*, weekly); New York (*NYLA Bulletin*, 10 times/year; free for institutional members; $25/1 week, $40/2 weeks, others); Ohio (*ACCESS*, monthly); Oklahoma (*Oklahoma Librarian*, 6 issues/year); Rhode Island (*RILA Bulletin*, 6 times/year); South Carolina (*News and Views*); South Dakota (*Book Marks*, bimonthly); Tennessee (*TLA Newsletter*); Vermont (*VLA News*, Box 803, Burlington, VT 05402, 10 issues/year); Virginia (*Virginia Librarian*, quarterly); and West Virginia (*West Virginia Libraries*, 6 times/year).

At their annual conference the following associations have indicated some type of placement service although it may only consist of bulletin board postings: Alabama, California, Connecticut, Georgia, Idaho, Illinois, Indiana, Kansas, Louisiana, Maryland, Massachusetts, Mountain Plains, New England, New Jersey, New York, North Carolina (biennial), Oregon, Pacific Northwest, Pennsylvania, South Dakota, Southeastern, Tennessee, Texas, Vermont, and Wyoming.

The following associations have indicated they have no placement service at this time: Kentucky, Middle Atlantic Regional Library Federation, Midwest

Federation, Minnesota, Mississippi, Montana, Nebraska, Nevada, New Mexico, North Dakota, Ohio, Oklahoma, Utah, West Virginia, and Wisconsin. [State and regional association addresses are listed in Part 6 of the *Bowker Annual*.—*Ed.*]

The Pacific Northwest Library Association (PNLA) offers an electronic source for job postings in addition to its voice jobline. The listserv PNLA-L includes job postings in the PNLA region in addition to postings on other library issues. Send the following message: subscribe PNLA-L, your name to listserv@wln.com or listserv@idbsu.idbsu.edu. Questions may be addressed to listowner Bruce Ziegman at ziegman@fvrl.lib.wa.us or phone 360-699-8810.

Library and Information Studies Programs

Library and information studies programs offer some type of service for their current students as well as alumni. Most schools provide job-hunting and resume-writing seminars. Many have outside speakers representing different types of libraries or recent graduates relating career experiences. Faculty or a designated placement officer offer individual advising services or critiquing of resumes.

Of the ALA-accredited library and information studies programs, the following handle placement activities through the program: Alabama, Albany, Alberta, Buffalo (compiles annual graduate biographical listings), British Columbia, Dalhousie, Drexel, Hawaii, Illinois, Kent, Kentucky, Louisiana, McGill, Missouri (College of Education), Pittsburgh (Department of Library Science only), Pratt, Puerto Rico, Queens, Rhode Island, Rosary, Rutgers, Saint John's, South Carolina, Syracuse, Tennessee, Texas–Austin, Toronto, UCLA (compiles graduate profile booklets), Western Ontario, Wisconsin–Madison, and Wisconsin–Milwaukee.

The central university placement center handles activities for the following schools: California–Berkeley (alumni) and Emporia. However, in most cases, faculty in the library school will still do informal counseling regarding job seeking.

In some schools, the placement services are handled in a cooperative manner; in most cases the university placement center sends out credentials while the library school posts or compiles the job listings. Schools utilizing one or both sources include: Alabama, Albany, Arizona, Buffalo, Catholic, Clarion, Drexel, Florida State, Indiana, Iowa, Kent State, Long Island, Maryland, Michigan, Montreal, North Carolina–Chapel Hill, North Carolina–Greensboro, North Carolina Central, North Texas, Oklahoma, Pittsburgh, Queens, Rosary, Saint John's, San Jose, Simmons, South Florida, Southern Connecticut, Southern Mississippi, Syracuse, Tennessee, Texas Woman's, Washington, Wayne State, and Wisconsin–Milwaukee. In sending out placement credentials, schools vary as to whether they distribute these free, charge a general registration fee, or request a fee for each file or credentials sent out.

Those schools that have indicated they post job vacancy notices for review but do not issue printed lists are: Alabama, Alberta, Arizona, British Columbia, Buffalo, Catholic, Clark Atlanta, Dalhousie, Drexel, Florida State, Hawaii, Illinois, Kent State, Kentucky, Louisiana, Maryland, McGill, Montreal, North Carolina–Chapel Hill, North Carolina–Greensboro, North Carolina Central, Oklahoma, Puerto Rico, Queens, Rutgers, Saint John's, San Jose, Simmons,

South Carolina, Southern Mississippi, Syracuse (general postings), Tennessee, Texas Woman's, Toronto, UCLA, Washington, Wayne State, Western Ontario, and Wisconsin–Madison.

In addition to job vacancy postings, some schools issue printed listings, operate joblines, have electronic access, or provide database services:

- Albany (Job Placement Bulletin free to SISP students; $15/year fee for other subscribers)
- British Columbia (uses BCLA Jobline, 604-430-6411)
- Buffalo (listserv for entry-level N.Y. state positions; to subscribe, send message saying SUBSCRIBE LIBJOB-L first name last name to listserv.acsu.buffalo.edu)
- California–Berkeley (weekly out-of-state job list and jobline free to all students and graduates for six months after graduation; $55 annual fee for alumni of any University of California campus; call 510-642-3283)
- Clarion (free with SASE to alumni)
- Dalhousie (listserv for Atlantic Canada jobs, send message saying sub list-joblist to mailserv@ac.dal.ca)
- Drexel (job hotline listing local jobs only, 215-895-1672—changed each Monday) (http://www.cis.drexel.edu/placement/placement.html)
- Emporia (weekly bulletin for school, university, public jobs; separate bulletin for special; $42/6 months; Emporia graduates, $21/6 months)
- Florida State
- Hawaii
- Illinois (free online placement JOBSearch database available on campus and via access through telnet alexia.lis.uiuc.edu, login: jobs, password: Urbaign or http://carousel.lis.uiuc.edu/~jobs/)
- Indiana (free for one year after graduation; alumni and others may send self-addressed stamped envelopes or access http://www-slis.lib.indiana.edu/EDEN/JobPlacementBulletin/jobpage.htm)
- Iowa ($15/year for registered students and alumni)
- Michigan (free for one year following graduation, all other grads, $15/year for 24 issues; $20 to others)
- Missouri (http://tiger.coe.missouri.edu/placement.html; Library Vacancy Roster, mailed weekly, $15 per quarter)
- North Texas (free 24-hour job hotline listing for current students; $20 for former students)
- Oklahoma
- Pratt (free to students and alumni for full-time/part-time professional positions only)
- Rhode Island (monthly, $7.50/year)
- Rosary (*Placement News* every 2 weeks, free for 6 months following graduation, $15/year for students and alumni; $25 to others)

- Rutgers access http://www.scils.rutgers.edu or listserv@scils.rutgers.edu and subscribe
- Simmons (operates the New England Jobline, which announces professional vacancies in the region, call 617-521-2815)
- Southern Connecticut (printed listing twice a month, mailed to students/alumni free, also on gopher at scsu.ctstateu.edu)
- South Florida (in cooperation with ALIS; for $10/year to subscribers)
- Syracuse (lists selected jobs online through electronic mail to students)
- Texas–Austin (free to students and alumni for one year following graduation, *Weekly Placement Bulletin*, including *Classifacts*, $26/6 months or $48/year; *Texas Job Weekly*, $16/6 months or $28/year, some jobs available on new school-only listserv)
- Texas Woman's (electronic bulletin board for students)
- Toronto (jobline or access URL: http://www.fis.utoronto.ca)
- Washington (operates Pacific Northwest Library Association jobline, which announces professional vacancies, call 206-543-2890)
- Wisconsin–Madison (now sends listings from Wisconsin and Minnesota to Illinois for JOBSearch)
- Wisconsin–Milwaukee (sends selected jobs online through electronic mail to students)
- Western Ontario (http://www.uwo.ca/gslis/information) resources; to list positions call 519-661-2111 ext. 8495)

Employers will often list jobs with schools only in their particular geographical area; some library schools will give information to non-alumni regarding their specific locales, but are not staffed to handle mail requests and advice is usually given in person. Schools that have indicated they will allow librarians in their areas to view listings are: Alabama, Albany, Alberta, Arizona, British Columbia, Buffalo, California–Berkeley, Catholic, Clarion, Clark Atlanta, Dalhousie, Drexel, Emporia, Florida State, Hawaii, Illinois, Indiana, Iowa, Kent State, Kentucky, Louisiana, Maryland, McGill, Michigan, Missouri, Montreal, North Carolina–Chapel Hill, North Carolina Central, North Carolina–Greensboro, University of North Texas, Oklahoma, Pittsburgh, Pratt, Puerto Rico, Queens, Rhode Island, Rosary, Rutgers, Simmons, Saint John's, San Jose, South Carolina, South Florida, Southern Connecticut, Southern Mississippi, Syracuse, Tennessee, Texas–Austin, Texas Woman's, Toronto, UCLA, Washington, Wayne State, Western Ontario, Wisconsin–Madison, and Wisconsin–Milwaukee.

A list of accredited program addresses and phones can be requested from ALA or found in the *Bowker Annual*. Individuals interested in placement services of other library education programs should contact the schools directly.

Federal Employment Information Sources

Consideration for employment in many federal libraries requires establishing civil service eligibility. Although the actual job search is your responsibility, the

Office of Personnel Management (OPM) has developed the "Federal Employment Information Highway" to assist you along the way. The address for OPM's World Wide Web site is http://www.usajobs.opm.gov.

OPM's Career America Connection at 912-757-3000, TDD Service at 912-744-2299, is a telephone-based system that provides current worldwide federal job opportunities, salary and employee benefits information, special recruitment messages, and more. You can also record your request to have application packages, forms, and other employment-related literature mailed to you. This service is available 24 hours a day, 7 days a week. Request Federal Employment Information Line factsheet EI-42, "Federal Employment Information Sources," for a complete listing of local telephone numbers to this nationwide network.

OPM's Federal Job Opportunities "Bulletin" Board (FJOB) at 912-757-3100, is a computer-based bulletin board system that provides current worldwide federal job opportunities, salaries and pay rates, general and specific employment information, and more. You must have a personal computer with a modem to access this system. You may also contact OPM on the Internet via Telnet at FJOB.MAIL.OPM.GOV and file transfer protocol at FTP.FJOB.MAIL.OPM.GOV. Information about obtaining federal job announcement files via Internet mail should be directed to: INFO@FJOB.MAIL.OPM.GOV.

Federal Job Information "Touch Screen" Computer, is a computer-based system utilizing touch-screen technology. These kiosks, found throughout the nation in OPM offices, Federal Office Buildings, and other locations, allow you to access current worldwide federal job opportunities, online information, and more.

Once you have found an opportunity that interests you, you may obtain a copy of the vacancy announcement and a complete application package by leaving your name and address in one of the automated systems or, when available, by downloading the actual announcement and any supplementary materials from the FJOB. Although the federal government does not require a standard application form for most jobs, certain information is needed to evaluate your qualifications if you decide to submit any other format other than the OF-612 form.

Eligibility can be established in the Washington, D.C., metropolitan area by meeting specific education and/or experience requirements and submitting appropriate forms directly to federal agencies during designated "open" periods. Interested applicants should contact their local Federal Job Information/Testing Center (FJI/TC) periodically to find out what agencies are currently accepting applications. The FJI/TC will give contact numbers to request vacancy announcements and forms and to obtain the proper forms for filing. The FJI/TC is listed under "U.S. Government" in major metropolitan telephone directories. Current job openings in libraries in the Washington, D.C., area are on a recorded message with other federal jobs on 202-606-2700 (press 1, or 3). You may obtain information on jobs nationwide by visiting the Job Information Center in your area and by using the touch screen computers located in the FJI/TC.

The Federal Library and Information Center Committee operates a federal library electronic bulletin board listing professional and paraprofessional positions (telnet alix.loc.gov3000). Federal jobs are posted on the Dartmouth College FEDJOBSlist. Send a message to listserv@dartcms1 with command INDEX FEDJOBS; to get the librarian and government documents openings use command SEND LIBRARY TXT. *Washington Online: How to Access the Government's*

Electronic Bulletin Boards, by Bruce Maxwell (Washington, D.C., Congressional Quarterly, 1995), can lead to other services that may list library jobs among other government positions.

Applications are evaluated for the grade(s) for which applicants are qualified and will accept. Information on beginning salary levels can be obtained from the systems noted above. To qualify for librarian positions, applicants must possess: 1) a master's degree in library science; 2) a fifth-year bachelor's degree in library science; or 3) 30 semester hours of graduate study in library science. Note: If you have a combination of qualifying education and/or experience, you may qualify to take the written subject-matter test. This test is administered in the Washington, D.C., metropolitan area. To receive consideration for librarian positions and testing outside the D.C. metropolitan area, contact your local Federal Job Information/Testing Center.

Applicants should attempt to make personal contact directly with federal agencies in which they are interested. This is essential in the Washington, D.C., area where over half the vacancies occur. Most librarian positions are in three agencies—Army, Navy, and Veterans Administration.

There are some "excepted" agencies that are not required to hire through the usual OPM channels. While these agencies may require the standard forms, they maintain their own employee selection policies and procedures. Government establishments with positions outside the competitive civil service include: Board of Governors of the Federal Reserve System; Central Intelligence Agency; Defense Intelligence Agency; Department of Medicine and Surgery; Federal Bureau of Investigation; Foreign Service of the United States; General Accounting Office; Library of Congress; National Science Foundation; National Security Agency; Tennessee Valley Authority; U.S. Nuclear Regulatory Commission; U.S. Postal Service; Judicial Branch of the Government; Legislative Branch of the Government; U.S. Mission to the United Nations; World Bank and IFC; International Monetary Fund; Organization of American States; Pan American Health Organization; and United Nations Secretariat.

The Library of Congress, the world's largest and most comprehensive library, is an excepted service agency in the Legislative Branch and administers its own independent merit selection system. Job classifications, pay, and benefits are the same as in other federal agencies, and qualifications requirements generally correspond to those used by the U.S. Office of Personnel Management. The library does not use registers, but announces vacancies as they become available. A separate application must be submitted for each vacancy announcement. For most professional positions, announcements are widely distributed and open for a minimum period of 30 days. Qualifications requirements and ranking criteria are stated on the vacancy announcement. The Library of Congress Human Resources Operations Office is located in the James Madison Memorial Building, 101 Independence Avenue S.E., Washington, DC 20540, 202-707-5620.

Additional General and Specialized Job Sources

Affirmative Action Register, 8356 Olive Blvd., St. Louis, MO 63132: The goal is to "provide female, minority, handicapped and veteran candidates with an opportunity to learn of professional and managerial positions throughout the nation and to assist employers in implementing their Equal Opportunity Employment programs." Free distribution of a monthly bulletin is made to leading businesses, industrial and academic institutions, and over 4,000 agencies that recruit qualified minorities and women, as well as to all known female, minority, and handicapped professional organizations, placement offices, newspapers, magazines, rehabilitation facilities, and over 8,000 federal, state, and local governmental employment units with a total readership in excess of 3.5 million (audited). Individual mail subscriptions are available for $15 per year. Librarian listings are in most issues. Sent free to libraries on request.

The Chronicle of Higher Education (published weekly with breaks in August and December), 1255 23rd St. N.W., Suite 700, Washington, DC 20037, 202-466-1055; fax 202-296-2691: Publishes a variety of library positions each week, including administrative and faculty jobs. Job listings are searchable by specific categories, keywords, or geographic locations on the Internet (gopher at Chronicle.merit.edu or World Wide Web at http://chronicle.merit.edu).

Academic Resource Network On-Line Database (ARNOLD), 4656 W. Jefferson, Suite 140, Fort Wayne, IN 46804: This World Wide Web interactive database assists faculty, staff, and librarians to identify partners for exchange or collaborative research (http://www.arnold.snybuf.edu).

School Libraries: School librarians often find that the channels for locating positions in education are of more value than the usual library ones, e.g., contacting county or city school superintendent offices. Other sources include university placement offices that carry listings for a variety of school system jobs. A list of commercial teacher agencies may be obtained from the National Association of Teachers' Agencies, Dr. Eugene Alexander, CPC, CTC, Treas., c/o G. A. Agency, 524 South Ave., E., Cranford, NJ 07016-3209, 908-272-2080.

Overseas

Opportunities for employment in foreign countries are limited and immigration policies of individual countries should be investigated. Employment for Americans is virtually limited to U.S. government libraries, libraries of U.S. firms doing worldwide business, and American schools abroad. Library journals from other countries will sometimes list vacancy notices. Some persons have obtained jobs by contacting foreign publishers or vendors directly. Non-U.S. government jobs usually call for foreign language fluency. "Job-Hunting in the UK" by Diane Brooks, *Canadian Library Journal* 45:374-378 (December 1988), offers advice for those interested in the United Kingdom. *Career Opportunities for Bilinguals and Multilinguals: A Directory of Resources in Education, Employment and Business* by Vladimir F. Wertsman (Scarecrow Press, 1991, ISBN 0-8108-2439-6, $35), gives general contact names for foreign employment and business resources. "International Jobs" by Wertsman (*RQ*, Fall 1992, pp. 14–19) provides a listing of library resources for finding jobs abroad.

Council for International Exchange of Scholars (CIES), 3007 Tilden St. N.W., Suite 5M, Washington, DC 20008-3009, 202-686-7877; e-mail: cies1@ciesnet.cies.org org (http://www.cies.org/): Administers U.S. government Fulbright awards for university lecturing and advanced research abroad; usually

10–15 awards per year are made to U.S. citizens who are specialists in library or information sciences. In addition, many countries offer awards in any specialization of research or lecturing. Lecturing awards usually require university or college teaching experience. Several opportunities exist for professional librarians as well. Applications and information may be obtained, beginning in March each year, directly from CIES. Worldwide application deadline is August 1.
Department of Defense, Dependents Schools, 4040 N. Fairfax Dr., Arlington, VA 22203, 703-696-3033; fax 703-696-2697 (recruitment@odeddodea.edu): Overall management and operational responsibilities for the education of dependent children of active duty U.S. military personnel and DOD civilians who are stationed in foreign areas. Also responsible for teacher recruitment. For complete application brochure, write to above address. The latest copy of *Overseas Opportunities for Educators* is available and provides information on educator employment opportunities in over 191 schools worldwide. The schools are operated for the children of U.S. military and civilian personnel stationed overseas.
International Schools Services, Box 5910, Princeton, NJ 08543, 609-452-0990: Private, not-for-profit organization founded in 1955 to serve American schools overseas, other than Department of Defense schools. These are American, international elementary and secondary schools enrolling children of business and diplomatic families living abroad. ISS services to overseas schools include recruitment and recommendation of personnel, curricular and administrative guidance, purchasing, facility planning, and more. ISS also publishes a comprehensive directory of overseas schools and a bimonthly newsletter, *NewsLinks*, for those interested in the intercultural educational community. Information regarding these publications and other services may be obtained by writing to the above address.
Library Fellows Program, c/o American Library Association, 50 E. Huron St., Chicago, IL 60611, 312-280-3200: ALA administers a grant from the U.S. Information Agency for a program that places library professionals in institutions overseas for periods of 4–8 months. Assignments vary depending on projects requested by host countries. Persons with foreign language skills, technical expertise, and international interests or expertise are sought. Positions for the 1997/98 announced in March, interviews held in July and Fellows start assignments in September. 1997/98 project opportunities may be obtained from the ALA web (http://www.ala.org) or ALA's International Relations Office.
Peace Corps, 1990 K St. N.W., #9300., Washington, DC 20526: Volunteer opportunities exist for those holding MA/MS or BA/BS degrees in library science with one year of related work experience. Two-year tour of duty. U.S. citizens only. Living allowance, health care, transportation, and other benefits provided. Write for additional information and application or call 800-424-8580.
U.S. Information Agency (USIA), called the U.S. Information Service (USIS) overseas, seeks librarians with MLS and at least four years' experience for Regional Library Officer positions. Candidates must have a master's degree in librarianship from an ALA-accredited graduate program, proven administrative ability, and skills to coordinate the overseas USIS library program with other information functions of USIS in various cities worldwide. Some practical work experience in at least one of the major functional areas of adult library services is required. Additional relevant experience might include cooperative library program development, community outreach, public affairs, project management, personnel training. USIA maintains 160 libraries in 88 countries, 1 million

books, and 400 local library staff worldwide. Libraries provide reference service and publications about the United States for foreign audiences. U.S. citizenship is required. Benefits include overseas allowances and differentials where applicable, vacation leave, term life insurance, medical and retirement programs. Send standard U.S. Government application (SF-171), official transcripts, and 1,000-word autobiographical statement to USIA, Foreign Service Recruitment Officer, Office of Personnel, M/PDP Personnel Br., Rm. 518, 301 4th St. S.W., Washington, DC 20547.

Overseas Exchange Programs

International Exchanges, Most exchanges are handled by direct negotiation between interested parties. A few libraries have established exchange programs for their own staff. In order to facilitate exchange arrangements, the *IFLA Journal* (issued February, May, August, and November) lists persons wishing to exchange positions *outside* their own country. All listings must include the following information: full name, address, present position, qualifications (with year of obtaining), language, abilities, preferred country/city/library, and type of position. Send to International Federation of Library Associations and Institutions (IFLA) Secretariat, c/o Koninklijkebibliotheek, Box 95312, 2509 CH The Hague, Netherlands, fax 31-70-3834827 (ifla@nlc-bnc.ca) or (http://www.n.c-bnc.ca/ifla/).

ALA International Relations Committee/International Relations Round Table Joint Committee on International Exchanges, c/o Lucinda Covert-Vail, New York University Libraries, 70 Washington Square, S., New York, NY 10012: A database of U.S. and international libraries interested in international study visits or exchanges has been developed. The committee welcomes requests for information and inclusion in the database for and from all countries in the world.

LIBEX Bureau for International Staff Exchange, c/o A. J. Clark, Thomas Parry Library, University of Wales, Llanbadarn Fawr, Aberystwyth, Dyfed SY23 3AS, Wales, 011-44-1970-62247; fax 011-44-1970-622190; e-mail: parrylib@aber.ac.uk; URL http://www.aber.ac.uk/tplwww/parry.html. Assists in two-way exchanges for British librarians wishing to work abroad and for librarians from the United States, Canada, EC countries, and Commonwealth and other countries who wish to undertake exchanges.

Using Information Skills in Nonlibrary Settings

A great deal of interest has been shown in using information skills in a variety of ways in nonlibrary settings. These jobs are not usually found through the regular library placement sources, although many library and information studies programs are trying to generate such listings for their students and alumni. Job listings that do exist may not call specifically for "librarians" by that title so that ingenuity may be needed to search out jobs where information management skills are needed. Some librarians are working on a freelance basis, offering services to businesses, alternative schools, community agencies, legislators, etc.; these opportunities are usually not found in advertisements but created by developing contacts and publicity over a period of time. A number of information brokering businesses have developed from individual freelance experiences. Small companies or other organizations often need "one-time" service for organizing files or collections, bibliographic research for special projects, indexing or abstracting, compilation of directories, and consulting services. Bibliographic networks and online database companies are using librarians as information managers, trainers, researchers, systems and database analysts, online services managers, etc. Jobs in this area are sometimes found in library network newsletters or data processing journals. Librarians can also be found working in law firms as litigation case supervisors (organizing and analyzing records needed for specific legal cases); with publishers as sales representatives, marketing directors, editors, and computer services experts; with community agencies as adult education coordinators, volunteer administrators, grants writers, etc.

Classifieds in *Publishers Weekly* and *The National Business Employment Weekly* may lead to information-related positions. One might also consider reading the Sunday classified ad sections in metropolitan newspapers in their entirety to locate descriptions calling for information skills but under a variety of job titles.

The *Burwell World Directory of Information Brokers, 1995–96* ($99.50 + $5.50 s/h) is an annual publication that lists information brokers, freelance librarians, independent information specialists, and institutions that provide services for a fee. Individuals do not need to pay to be listed; the directory is available from Burwell Enterprises, 3724 FM 1960 West, Suite 214, Houston, TX 77068, 713-537-9051; fax 713-537-8332. Also published is a bimonthly newsletter, *Information Broker* ($40.00, foreign postage, $15.00), that includes articles by, for, and about individuals and companies in the fee-based information field, book reviews, a calendar of upcoming events, and issue-oriented articles. A bibliography and other publications on the field of information brokering are also available.

The Independent Librarians Exchange Round Table is a unit within the American Library Association that serves as a networking source for persons who own their own information businesses, are consultants, or work for companies providing support services to libraries or providing other information services outside traditional library settings. Dues are $8.00 in addition to ALA dues and include a newsletter, *ILERT Alert*. At the 1993 ALA Annual Conference, ILERT sponsored a program on "Jobs for Indexers," which is available on cassette #ALA332 for $24 from Teach'em Inc., 160 E. Illinois St., Chicago, IL 60611, 800-224-3775.

The Association of Independent Information Professionals was formed in 1987 for individuals who own and operate for-profit information companies. Contact AIIP Headquarters at 212-779-1855.

A growing number of publications are addressing opportunities for librarians in the broader information arena. "You Can Take Your MLS Out of the Library," by Wilda W. Williams (*Library Journal*, Nov. 1994, pp. 43–46); "Information Entrepreneurship: Sources for Reference Librarians," by Donna L. Gilton (*RQ*, Spring 1992, pp. 346–355; "Information Brokering: The State of Art" by Alice Sizer Warner, *Wilson Library Bulletin*, April 1989, pp. 55–57, and "The Information Broker: A Modern Profile" by Mick O'Leary, *Online*, November 1987, pp. 24–30, provide overviews on the practice of information brokerage. *The Information Broker's Handbook* by Sue Rugge and Alfred Glossbrenner (Blue Ridge Summit, Pa.: Windcrest/McGraw-Hill, 1992, 379p. ISBN 0-8306-

3798-2) covers the market for information, getting started, pricing and billing, and more. *Mind Your Own Business: A Guide for the Information Entrepreneur* by Alice Sizer Warner (New York: Neal-Schuman, 1987, 165 pp., ISBN 1-55570-014-4) describes planning for and managing an information business, including marketing, sales, and record-keeping. *Opening New Doors: Alternative Careers for Librarians*, edited by Ellis Mount (Washington, DC: Special Libraries Association, 1993) provides profiles of librarians who are working outside libraries. *Extending the Librarian's Domain: A Survey of Emerging Occupation Opportunities for Librarians and Information Professionals* by Forest Woody Horton, Jr. (Washington, DC: Special Libraries Association, 1994) explores information job components in a variety of sectors.

Guide to Careers in Abstracting and Indexing by Wendy Wicks and Ann Marie Cunningham (1992, 126 pp.), is available for $35 from the National Federation of Abstracting & Information Services, 1518 Walnut St., Philadelphia, PA 19102, 215-893-1561. The American Society of Indexers, Box 48267, Seattle, WA 98148-0267, 206-241-9196, has a number of publications that would be useful for individuals who are interested in indexing careers. Check out the Web page, http://www.well.com/user/asi for membership and publication information.

Temporary/Part-Time Positions

Working as a substitute librarian or in temporary positions may be considered to be an alternative career path as well as an interim step while looking for a regular job. This type of work can provide valuable contacts and experience. Organizations that hire library workers for part-time or temporary jobs include Advanced Information Management, 444 Castro St., Suite 320, Mountain View, CA 94041 (415-965-7799), or 900 Wilshire Blvd., Suite 1424, Los Angeles, CA 90017 (213-243-9236); C. Berger and Company, 327 E. Gundersen Dr., Carol Stream, IL 60188 (630-653-1115 or 800-382-4222); Gossage Regan Associates, Inc., 25 W. 43rd St., New York, NY 10036 (212-869-3348) and Wontawk Gossge Associates, 304 Newbury St., Suite 304, Boston, MA 02115 (617-867-9209); Information Management Division, 1160 Veirs Mill Rd., Suite 414, Wheaton, MD 20902 (301-949-4097); The Library Co-Op, Inc., 3840 Park Ave., Suite 107, Edison, NJ 08820 (908-906-1777 or 800-654-6275); Library Management Systems, Corporate Pointe, Suite 755, Culver City, CA 90230 (310-216-6436; 800-567-4669) and Three Bethesda Metro Center, Suite 700, Bethesda, MD 20814 (301-961-1984); Pro Libra Associates, Inc., 6 Inwood Place, Maplewood, NJ 07040 (201-762-0070).

Part-time jobs are not always advertised, but often found by canvasing local libraries and leaving applications.

Job Hunting in General

Wherever information needs to be organized and presented to patrons in an effective, efficient, and service-oriented fashion, the skills of librarians can be applied, whether or not they are in traditional library settings. However, it will take considerable investment of time, energy, imagination, and money on the part of an individual before a satisfying position is created or obtained, in a conventional library or another type of information service. Usually, no one method or source of job-hunting can be used alone. *Library Services for Career Planning, Job Searching, and Employment Opportunities*, edited by Byron Anderson, Haworth Press, New York, 183 p., 1992, is a timely source and it includes bibliographical references.

Public and school library certification requirements often vary from state to state; contact the state library agency for such information in a particular state. Certification requirements are summarized in *Certification of Public Librarians in the United States*, 4th ed., 1991, from the ALA Office for Library Personnel Resources. A summary of school library/media certification requirements by state is found in *Requirements for Certification of Teachers, Counselors, Librarians and Administrators for Elementary and Secondary Schools*, published annually by the University of Chicago Press. "School Library Media Certification Requirements: 1994 Update" by Patsy H. Perritt also provides a compilation in *School Library Journal*, June 1994, pp. 32–49. State supervisors of school library media services may also be contacted for information on specific states.

Civil service requirements either on a local, county, or state level often add another layer of procedures to the job search. Some civil service jurisdictions require written and/or oral examinations; others assign a ranking based on a review of credentials. Jobs are usually filled from the top candidates on a qualified list of applicants. Since the exams are held only at certain time periods and a variety of jobs can be filled from a single list of applicants (e.g., all Librarian I positions regardless of type of function), it is important to check whether a library in which one is interested falls under civil service procedures.

If one wishes a position in a specific subject area or in a particular geographical location, remember those reference skills to ferret information from directories and other tools regarding local industries, schools, subject collections, etc. Directories such as the *American Library Directory*, *Subject Collections*, *Directory of Special Libraries and Information Centers*, and *Directory of Federal Libraries*, as well as state directories or directories of other special subject areas can provide a wealth of information for job seekers. "The Job Hunter's Search for Company Information" by Robert Favini (*RQ*, Winter 1991, pp. 155–161) lists general reference business sources that might be useful for librarians seeking employment in companies. Some state employment offices will include library listings as part of their Job Services department. In some cases, students have pooled resources to hire a clipping service for a specific time period in order to get classified librarian ads for a particular geographical area. Other Internet access not mentioned elsewhere: Association of Research Libraries (http://arl.cni.org/careers/vacancy.html) and LibJobs (http://www.nicnbc.ca/cgi-bin/ifla-lwgate/LIBJOBS/archives/).

For information on other job-hunting and personnel matters, request a checklist of personnel materials available from the ALA Office for Library Personnel Resources, 50 E. Huron St., Chicago, IL 60611.

Placements and Salaries, 1995: Beginner's Luck—A Growing Job Market

C. Herbert Carson
Associate Professor, Graduate School of Library and Information Studies, University of Rhode Island, Kingston

If you are a woman whose first library job is a "nontraditional" one like Web developer, you're likely to be earning 4.5 percent more than your first-year counterpart in a more "traditional" job in, say, acquisitions or collection development. *Library Journal*'s 45th annual placement and salaries survey confirms that those entering nontraditional fields tend to do better financially than those in traditional areas. Moreover, if you're a man entering the profession, you're likely to be earning on average 5.3 percent more than your female counterpart, whatever your job title. The disparity between women's and men's starting salaries appears to be creeping up, after years of hovering in the 1–2 percent range.

The mean starting salary for women in nontraditional fields is $29,800, or $1,286 more than for women in traditional fields ($28,514). Men in nontraditional positions earn 12.3 percent more ($32,705) than men in traditional jobs ($29,132); and for both men and women, the nontraditional salary ($30,595) is 6.9 percent greater than the traditional one ($28,627). Men accounted for 16.4 percent of those in nontraditional fields as opposed to 11.9 percent men in the traditional areas. This higher proportion may contribute to the higher salaries in the nontraditional areas, as well as the increasing inequity in women's and men's salaries.

More in Professional Posts

The good news from *LJ*'s 45th annual placements and salaries survey is that more than half of the 4,222 graduates of library and information science programs appear to be finding professional positions, and ones with greater purchasing power. The average beginning salary for a full-time professional has increased by 7.5 percent as compared to the 1982–1984 base period. (Salary index divided by CPI, see Table 8).

Both the mean and the median salaries of graduates in full-time professional positions have risen. The average salary for women rose from $28,065 in 1994 to $28,616 in 1995 for a 2 percent increase. The men's salary went from $28,182 to $30,029 for a 6.5 percent increase. The combined permanent/full-time placements average salary edged up from $28,086 to $28,997, or 3.2 percent. However, minority salaries increased by only $382, from $28,512 to $28,894, or 1.3 percent.

Note: Adapted from *Library Journal*, October 15, 1996

(text continues on page 366)

Table 1 / Status of 1995 U.S. Graduates, Spring 1996

Region	Number of Schools Reporting	Number of Graduates Total	Not in Lib. Positions Women	Not in Lib. Positions Men	Not in Lib. Positions Total	Employment Unknown Women	Employment Unknown Men	Employment Unknown Total	Perm. Prof. Positions Women	Perm. Prof. Positions Men	Perm. Prof. Positions Total	Temp. Prof. Positions* Women	Temp. Prof. Positions* Men	Temp. Prof. Positions* Total	Nonprof. Lib. Positions** Women	Nonprof. Lib. Positions** Men	Nonprof. Lib. Positions** Total	Total in Lib. Positions*** Women	Total in Lib. Positions*** Men	Total in Lib. Positions*** Total
Northeast	13	1288	100	60	160	386	112	498	406	100	508	61	14	75	43	9	52	510	123	635
Southeast	10	871	21	5	26	127	36	163	248	55	305	15	6	21	28	10	38	291	71	364
Midwest	10	1229	72	17	89	308	90	398	422	105	528	37	12	49	63	12	75	522	129	652
Southwest	5	448	42	13	55	84	15	99	192	43	236	28	4	32	16	1	17	236	48	285
West	4	386	14	4	18	145	39	184	99	31	130	28	13	41	13	6	19	140	50	190
All schools	42	4222	249	99	348	1050	292	1342	1406	354	1766	172	51	223	175	39	214	1753	444	2203

Note: Tables do not always add up, individually or collectively, because schools omitted data in some cases.
*30 positions filled in foreign jurisdictions and 29 did not report job location.
**1 position filled in foreign jurisdiction and 4 did not report job location.
***2 positions filled in foreign jurisdictions and 11 did not report job location.

Table 2 / Placements and Full-Time Salaries of 1995 U.S. Graduates: Summary by Region

Region	Total Placements	Number of Reported Salaries Women	Number of Reported Salaries Men	Number of Reported Salaries Total	Low Salary Women	Low Salary Men	High Salary Women	High Salary Men	Average Salary Women	Average Salary Men	Average Salary Total	Median Salary Women	Median Salary Men	Median Salary Total
Northeast	584	335	84	419	$15,000	$20,000	$62,500	$85,000	$30,039	$32,276	$30,488	$28,500	$30,000	$28,800
Southeast	328	227	51	278	11,000	14,000	60,000	57,000	26,790	27,971	27,007	26,000	26,736	26,000
Midwest	577	331	98	429	10,000	17,000	65,000	48,000	28,235	28,985	28,406	27,000	28,000	27,500
Southwest	269	193	39	232	15,000	10,000	55,000	87,100	27,311	29,101	27,596	26,269	27,000	26,500
West	172	88	34	122	20,100	18,885	90,000	50,000	31,788	32,133	31,877	30,000	31,200	30,000
Combined	1997*	1188	314	1480	10,000	10,000	90,000	87,100	28,616	30,029	28,997	28,000	28,550	28,000

*Includes 32 placements in foreign jurisdictions and 35 placements with unknown job location.

Table 3 / Full-Time Salaries of Traditional vs. Nontraditional Graduates

Region	Number of Placements	Number of Reported Salaries Women	Number of Reported Salaries Men	Number of Reported Salaries Total	Low Women	Low Men	High Women	High Men	Average Women	Average Men	Average Total	Median Women	Median Men	Median Total
Traditional	1721	915	204	1119	$10,000	$10,000	$65,000	$85,000	$28,514	$29,132	$28,627	$27,800	$28,000	$28,000
Nontraditional	482	209	79	288	10,000	17,400	90,000	87,100	29,800	32,705	30,595	28,142	30,000	29,000
Combined	2203	1188	314	1480	10,000	10,000	90,000	87,100	28,616	30,029	28,997	28,000	28,550	28,000

Table 4 / Placements by Type of Library

School	Public Women	Public Men	Public Total	Elementary & Secondary Women	Elementary & Secondary Men	Elementary & Secondary Total	College & University Women	College & University Men	College & University Total	Special Women	Special Men	Special Total	Other Women	Other Men	Other Total	Total Women	Total Men	Total Total
Alabama	6	2	8	5	0	5	7	1	8	5	0	5	4	1	5	27	4	34
Arizona	17	2	19	17	0	17	8	3	11	3	1	4	4	0	4	49	6	57
California (L.A.)	3	0	3	0	0	0	4	4	8	5	1	6	1	0	1	13	5	20
Catholic	6	0	6	6	0	6	4	0	4	15	4	19	6	5	11	37	9	49
Clarion	4	4	8	2	0	2	0	3	3	1	0	1	1	0	1	8	7	18
Drexel	3	3	6	12	2	14	6	2	8	4	1	5	2	0	2	27	8	44
Emporia	14	2	16	12	2	14	6	3	9	8	0	9	4	1	5	44	8	60
Florida State	—	—	—	—	—	—	—	—	—	—	—	—	—	—	—	—	—	—
Hawaii	1	1	2	14	1	15	6	1	7	4	1	5	6	3	9	31	7	43
Indiana	23	4	27	12	2	14	9	7	16	7	1	8	17	6	23	68	20	93
Iowa	5	1	6	2	0	2	3	4	7	1	1	2	5	2	7	16	8	26
Kent State	19	6	25	14	0	14	6	5	11	11	1	12	2	2	4	52	14	79

School																
Kentucky	16	—	—	—	—	—	—	—	—	—	—	—	—	—	—	—
Long Island	16	1	17	6	2	8	4	1	5	2	0	2	3	1	4	5	38
Louisiana State	15	1	16	4	0	4	8	6	14	7	1	8	4	2	6	10	49
Maryland	0	0	0	1	1	2	3	1	4	6	0	6	5	0	5	2	25
Michigan	13	1	14	4	1	5	8	6	14	0	0	0	14	8	22	16	58
Missouri	3	3	6	6	3	9	7	1	8	3	0	3	4	0	4	7	30
North Carolina Central	3	0	3	4	0	4	1	—	2	1	1	—	2	1	3	2	14
North Carolina Chapel Hill	1	1	2	0	0	0	1	—	2	—	1	—	0	0	0	4	8
North Carolina Greensboro	10	3	13	13	1	14	8	2	10	3	2	5	0	3	8	11	55
North Texas	17	7	24	7	0	7	8	6	14	5	2	7	5	1	10	16	72
Oklahoma	8	3	11	10	1	11	4	1	5	1	0	1	9	0	9	5	33
Pittsburgh	16	3	19	10	1	11	3	4	8	7	1	8	1	0	2	9	55
Pratt	14	3	17	1	0	1	1	0	1	7	1	8	2	5	8	9	37
Queens	11	1	12	8	0	8	1	1	2	2	—	2	4	0	3	4	36
Rhode Island	9	3	12	12	0	12	2	—	3	2	2	—	3	1	1	6	44
Rosary	25	11	36	19	0	19	11	9	20	15	7	22	0	2	5	29	121
San Jose	5	2	7	2	1	3	3	0	3	4	3	7	3	2	6	8	34
Simmons	23	3	26	7	0	7	17	9	26	19	1	20	4	2	30	25	124
South Carolina	20	4	25	18	0	18	19	0	19	9	0	9	18	12	2	4	79
South Florida	9	5	14	16	1	17	6	2	8	2	0	2	2	0	3	9	44
SUNY-Albany	12	1	13	14	0	14	7	2	9	5	3	8	2	1	3	5	52
SUNY-Buffalo	4	4	8	14	2	17	7	—	9	3	1	4	5	0	5	9	57
Syracuse	2	1	3	5	1	5	6	1	7	2	0	2	1	0	—	2	25
Tennessee	4	1	5	4	1	5	3	—	4	—	0	—	0	1	1	4	18
Texas (Austin)	22	8	30	18	3	21	21	10	31	21	5	26	20	9	29	35	141
Texas Woman's	5	0	5	13	0	13	5	1	6	1	—	1	3	0	3	1	32
Washington	3	5	8	8	0	8	11	4	15	7	3	10	2	0	2	12	59
Wayne State	9	3	12	12	1	13	8	1	9	11	3	14	1	4	5	12	56
Wisconsin (Madison)	10	3	13	2	0	2	8	2	10	4	0	4	8	1	9	6	48
Wisconsin (Milwaukee)	12	4	16	11	2	13	12	4	16	13	4	17	4	1	5	15	72
Total	402	110	513	345	28	374	262	113	377	229	52	282	182	75	257	378	1798

363

Table 5 / Placements and Full-Time Salaries of 1995 U.S. Graduates

School	Total Placements	Salaries Women	Salaries Men	Salaries Total	Low Salary Women	Low Salary Men	High Salary Women	High Salary Men	Average Salary Women	Average Salary Men	Average Salary Total	Median Salary Women	Median Salary Men	Median Salary Total
Alabama	34	21	2	23	$18,000	$17,400	$39,000	$29,000	$26,512	$23,200	$26,224	$25,000	$23,200	$25,000
Arizona	55	37	3	40	15,000	21,000	49,000	36,000	28,213	29,833	28,355	27,000	32,500	27,150
California (L.A.)	20	12	5	17	23,000	30,300	44,000	36,109	32,800	33,282	32,942	31,625	34,000	32,000
Catholic	50	36	9	45	23,500	15,800	41,000	37,000	30,654	28,767	30,276	29,500	30,000	30,000
Clarion	19	9	7	16	18,000	17,000	38,000	28,162	25,609	24,919	25,307	25,092	26,000	25,546
Drexel	44	20	7	27	24,000	27,000	44,000	35,395	30,396	31,618	30,725	29,700	32,000	30,246
Emporia	61	42	8	50	17,000	10,000	48,000	32,000	27,963	25,475	27,565	27,250	26,900	27,250
Florida State	49	—	—	—	—	—	—	—	—	—	—	—	—	—
Hawaii	38	21	4	25	22,000	30,000	38,200	35,417	29,409	32,604	29,920	28,800	32,500	29,000
Indiana	84	54	18	72	18,000	24,000	50,000	48,000	27,779	30,167	28,376	26,625	29,000	27,000
Iowa	32	10	4	14	22,500	24,000	32,000	37,000	28,294	31,150	29,110	27,750	31,800	29,100
Kent State	91	38	10	48	21,000	19,500	44,775	36,000	29,067	27,030	28,689	28,331	26,900	28,000
Kentucky	—	—	—	—	—	—	—	—	—	—	—	—	—	—
Long Island	38	25	4	29	18,000	23,500	55,000	40,000	29,814	31,167	29,959	28,162	30,000	28,581
Louisiana State	49	36	8	44	18,000	23,200	50,000	32,000	26,388	27,679	26,623	25,820	26,868	26,000
Maryland	24	13	2	15	26,000	28,500	50,000	32,000	33,498	30,250	33,065	31,000	30,250	31,000
Michigan	58	38	14	52	17,500	18,720	57,333	62,500	29,643	31,208	30,056	28,000	29,400	28,000
Missouri	30	19	7	26	18,500	20,000	50,000	38,000	26,307	27,000	26,493	25,000	26,000	25,646
N. C. Central	12	7	2	9	23,000	22,000	33,500	30,000	27,071	26,000	26,833	25,000	26,000	25,000

364

N. C., Chapel Hill	8	4	3	7	21,000	26,000	32,000	85,000	26,500	46,000	34,857	26,500	27,000	27,000
N. C., Greensboro	49	31	9	40	18,000	20,000	37,000	57,000	24,759	29,444	25,813	24,900	28,000	24,950
North Texas	66	40	15	55	16,000	19,000	39,000	42,000	26,249	28,767	27,009	25,709	29,000	26,000
Oklahoma	34	21	5	26	21,000	22,380	31,000	40,000	25,330	27,876	25,820	25,000	25,000	25,000
Pittsburgh	67	36	9	45	17,000	22,500	40,000	40,000	27,776	28,500	27,914	26,834	28,000	27,000
Pratt	37	25	7	32	26,300	28,000	62,500	52,000	33,920	38,553	34,934	28,500	38,000	29,469
Queens	36	24	4	28	24,177	25,000	55,850	38,000	33,314	31,916	33,115	31,499	32,331	31,499
Rhode Island	41	21	8	29	20,000	22,000	38,000	32,000	26,621	24,755	26,061	26,000	26,000	26,000
Rosary	120	49	26	75	20,000	22,000	49,000	42,000	30,139	29,648	29,969	28,188	28,250	28,188
San Jose	34	13	7	20	25,000	27,300	35,500	50,000	30,054	38,414	32,980	30,000	38,500	31,450
Simmons	116	54	13	67	18,000	20,000	54,000	63,000	29,112	29,171	29,123	28,000	27,000	28,000
South Carolina	77	62	4	66	11,000	23,500	60,000	28,800	27,759	26,325	27,672	26,163	26,500	26,163
South Florida	45	36	9	45	18,000	14,000	36,000	48,000	26,811	28,833	27,215	26,000	25,800	26,000
SUNY-Albany	52	35	4	39	20,000	21,000	45,000	33,000	30,688	27,160	30,247	30,000	28,000	29,754
SUNY-Buffalo	58	31	8	39	16,600	20,000	48,000	50,000	27,663	30,603	28,266	27,500	29,487	28,000
Syracuse	25	13	0	13	19,200	—	39,000	—	26,938	—	26,938	27,000	—	27,000
Tennessee	17	10	4	14	23,226	24,000	40,000	30,000	29,707	27,041	28,945	28,600	27,081	28,181
Texas Austin	141	100	34	134	10,000	18,000	90,000	87,100	28,190	32,507	29,285	27,550	29,400	28,000
Texas Woman's	30	25	1	26	21,000	24,000	45,000	24,000	29,111	24,000	28,914	29,200	29,100	29,100
Washington	59	28	10	38	23,000	21,000	65,000	35,000	35,481	28,448	33,630	33,200	30,000	31,500
Wayne State	54	29	10	39	10,000	17,000	46,374	40,000	26,268	28,823	26,923	25,500	27,514	26,800
Wis. (Madison)	63	30	6	36	20,088	23,226	34,620	32,000	26,378	27,724	26,602	27,000	27,750	27,250
Wis. (Milwaukee)	70	27	5	32	20,259	18,000	40,000	48,000	28,932	32,420	29,477	29,000	29,500	29,000

(continued from page 360)

Temp/Part-time Jobs Still Rising

The bad news from *LJ*'s survey is that more graduates are being placed in temporary or part-time positions. Unfortunately, this method of cutting costs is adversely affecting library and information-related fields.

Temporary positions account for 223 (10.1 percent) of 1995's 2,203 professional positions, as compared with 156 in 1994 and 267 in 1993. Of those in permanent professional positions, 196 (9 percent) are part-time. The number of graduates working in either temporary or part-time positions amounted to 461, or 21 percent of those reporting positions in libraries. This is up about 5 percent over last year.

Library Schools Stable

The first half of this decade has been a turbulent time for library schools and their graduates. Brigham Young, Columbia, and Northern Illinois are among the schools that have shut their doors since the early 1990s. The 50 library and information science programs in operation today will, one hopes, provide a stable pool of graduates as we move toward the next century.

Forty-two of the 50 library and information science programs submitted data for this survey (Table 1). Females (3,314) accounted for 78.5 percent of the pool and the 908 males represented 21.5 percent. The total number of graduates, 4,222, is down somewhat from the total number in 1994 (4,363), but fewer schools reported. Complete or partial information was received from all programs except Clark Atlanta, University of California at Berkeley, Illinois, Puerto Rico, Rutgers, St. John's, Southern Connecticut, and Southern Mississippi. Due to the temporary suspension of admissions at the School of Library and Information Systems at University of California at Berkeley, there was no class of 1995. Florida State and Kentucky submitted information on total placements but no placement or demographic detail. Arizona provided demographic and individual graduate placements but no information on total placements.

Return to Traditional Jobs

Library and information science programs have been changing dramatically during the first half of this decade as well. They are finding new roles within their institutions, and their curricula are focusing on the need for library and information specialists to meet the challenges of the Information Age. The surveys of 1993 and 1994 graduates showed a decline in traditional library and information-related jobs while areas considered nontraditional increased dramatically.

This trend appears to have reversed as the 1995 graduates found jobs in the more traditional library positions. Of the 2,203 graduates in library positions, 1,721 (78.1 percent) are in "traditional" fields (42 percent of 1994 graduates were in traditional jobs, 53 percent of 1993 graduates). Although a universally accepted definition of traditional library fields may not currently exist, for the

Table 6 / Special Placements

	Women	Men	Total
Government Jurisdictions (U.S.)			
National libraries	0	0	0
Armed services libraries (domestic)	1	0	1
State & provincial libraries	8	1	9
Overseas agencies (incl. armed services libs. abroad)	0	0	0
Other government agencies (except USVA hospitals)	5	2	7
Library Science			
Post-MLS studies or advanced academic studies	7	2	9
Teaching library & information studies	0	0	0
Other			
Architecture	1	0	1
Art and/or museum library	5	0	5
Audiovisual & media centers	27	6	33
Bibliographic instruction	8	1	9
Retail and/or wholesale book trade sales	1	0	1
Commercial enterprises (finance, mfg., insurance, etc.)	17	2	19
Correctional institutions (federal, state, adult, youth)	3	1	4
Database publishing & services	3	0	3
Freelance consultants & information brokers	2	0	2
Genealogical libraries & services	0	0	0
Government documents	2	0	2
Historical societies, agencies, & archives	4	3	7
Hospitals (incl. USVA hospital libraries)	4	2	6
Indexing & abstracting	1	1	2
Information services in a nonlibrary setting	7	2	9
International relations, area studies, & nongovernmental international agencies	0	0	0
Law libraries (incl. academic, bar assn., etc.)	28	5	33
Library services to the handicapped	0	0	0
Map library services	0	1	1
Medical & allied health libraries	8	4	12
Music, theater, motion picture, dance	0	1	1
Library consortia, bibl., utilities & automated networks	2	0	2
Outreach services to underserved populations	4	0	4
Pharmaceutical	1	0	1
Professional associations	1	0	1
Rare books, manuscripts, archives	16	5	21
Records management	0	3	3
Seminary & theology school libraries	1	0	1
Science & technology (incl. R&D)	4	1	5
Social sciences	0	0	0
Spanish-speaking centers	0	0	0
Lib. automation, systems, & automation vendors	10	2	12
Library suppliers & vendors other than automation	1	0	1
Technical writing & documentation	2	0	2
Youth/young adult services	214	4	218
Total Special Placements	**398**	**49**	**447**

purpose of this study, any respondent was considered to be working in a "traditional" field who indicated that he or she works in an academic, public, school, or special library *and* works in acquisitions, cataloging, collection development, media, administration/supervision, adult services, reference, or youth services.

If the respondent indicated that he or she works in some other type of library, in an information industry, or any other type or organization, he or she

Table 7 / Salaries of Minority Placements by Type of Library

Library Type	Number	Percent of Total	Low Salary	Average Salary	High Salary
Academic	45	30.41	$16,640	$28,342	$40,000
Public	42	28.38	17,000	27,286	43,000
School	25	16.89	22,000	32,507	43,000
Special	14	9.46	18,000	30,791	65,000
Other	22	14.86	10,000	29,889	50,000
Total	148	100	10,000	28,894	65,000

Table 8 / Average Salary Index Starting Library Positions, 1985–1995*

	Library Schools	Average Beginning Salary	Dollar Increase in Average Salary	Salary Index	BLS-CPI
1985	58	$19,753	$962	111.64	109.3
1986	54	20,874	1,121	117.98	110.5
1987	55	22,247	1,373	125.74	115.4
1988	51	23,491	1,244	132.77	120.5
1989	43	24,581	1,090	138.93	124.0
1990	38	25,306	725	143.03	130.7
1991	46	25,583	277	144.59	136.2
1992	41	26,666	1,083	150.71	140.5
1993	50	27,116	450	153.26	144.4
1994	43	28,086	970	158.74	148.4
1995	41	28,997	911	163.89	152.5

* The U.S. Bureau of Labor Statistics' present Consumer Price Index is based on the average price data from 1982–1984 as equaling 100. The average beginning professional salary from the period was $17,693 and is used as the equivalent base of 100 for salary data.

was designated as "nontraditional." Respondents were also included in the nontraditional pool if they worked in a "traditional" library but did not work in a traditional area such as acquisitions, cataloging, etc. Titles such as Internet reference, Web developer, Web page designer, Web master, systems manager, and World Wide Web consultant were used to describe some of the positions held by these respondents. Of this year's respondents, 482 (21.9 percent) are in "nontraditional" positions.

Placement Trends

Seventeen out of the 42 institutions reported an increase in positions listed in their placement services. The University of Texas at Austin nearly quadrupled its placement listings because it has been exploring new placement sources, including the Internet and subscription services. It is too soon yet to say what the impact of these new sources will be. Four institutions had about the same number of positions listed this year, and seven saw a decrease in their listings.

(text continues on page 371)

Table 9 / 1995 Graduates, Placement by Location

Library School Location	Number of Graduates Placed	Placed in Same State (as library school)	Placed in Same Region (as library school)	Northeast	Southeast	Midwest	Southwest	West	Foreign Jurisdiction
Alabama	34	25	7	1	—	1	0	0	0
Arizona	55	28	1	4	3	7	—	11	0
California	54	47	0	3	1	2	1	—	0
District of Columbia	49	16	14	—	18	0	0	0	0
Florida	47	38	5	2	—	0	—	—	1
Hawaii	42	23	4	3	1	1	1	1	4
Illinois	120	89	22	2	0	—	0	0	1
Indiana	84	41	19	5	9	—	5	4	1
Iowa	26	9	10	3	2	—	0	2	0
Kansas	61	20	5	1	0	—	32	2	0
Louisiana	48	35	3	2	—	4	4	0	0
Maryland	24	8	12	—	3	0	0	0	0
Massachusetts	116	73	24	—	3	1	1	2	9
Michigan	113	89	7	7	3	—	1	3	0
Missouri	30	22	4	0	1	—	0	—	0
New York	246	195	24	—	4	8	4	3	3
North Carolina	69	39	18	3	—	2	5	0	0
Ohio	78	63	3	5	4	—	1	0	0
Oklahoma	32	23	5	0	2	1	—	1	0
Pennsylvania	120	65	29	—	3	13	—	5	2
Rhode Island	42	18	23	—	1	1	0	0	0
South Carolina	77	27	43	2	—	3	0	1	0
Tennessee	17	9	3	2	—	2	0	1	0
Texas	237	172	6	17	10	11	—	15	5
Washington	59	40	5	7	2	3	1	—	1
Wisconsin	116	56	27	12	6	—	6	2	7
Totals	1996	1270	323	81	76	60	63	54	34
Percentages	—	64%	16%	4%	4%	3%	3%	3%	2%

Table 10 / Comparison of Salaries by Type of Library, 1995

	Total Placements	Salaries Women	Salaries Men	Salaries Total	Low Salary Women	Low Salary Men	High Salary Women	High Salary Men	Average Salary Women	Average Salary Men	Average Salary Total	Median Salary Women	Median Salary Men	Median Salary Total
Public Libraries														
Northeast	187	115	24	139	$17,000	$22,500	$37,500	$52,000	$27,099	$29,308	$27,480	$28,000	$28,162	$28,000
Southeast	96	65	16	81	13,000	14,000	60,000	43,000	25,038	27,345	25,493	24,900	25,900	25,000
Midwest	204	103	36	139	10,000	17,000	41,000	40,000	25,413	26,675	25,740	25,025	26,300	25,000
Southwest	77	52	11	63	15,000	10,000	38,700	30,000	25,756	22,918	25,261	25,025	24,700	25,000
West	49	20	7	27	20,100	19,000	37,440	46,000	29,621	30,786	29,923	30,050	32,000	30,100
All Public	614	356	96	452	10,000	10,000	60,000	52,000	26,173	27,264	26,405	26,000	26,668	26,000
School Libraries														
Northeast	109	76	5	81	15,000	31,450	60,000	50,000	32,234	37,769	32,576	30,496	35,395	31,000
Southeast	74	64	4	68	18,000	23,000	40,000	35,000	27,364	27,750	27,387	26,650	26,500	26,650
Midwest	116	86	8	94	16,000	25,000	56,680	43,000	31,780	33,500	31,927	30,000	33,000	30,000
Southwest	58	49	4	53	20,000	23,000	49,000	32,200	28,146	27,425	28,092	26,400	27,250	26,500
West	22	21	1	22	24,000	27,300	45,000	27,300	32,438	27,300	32,205	28,000	27,300	28,000
All School	395	281	23	304	15,000	23,000	60,000	50,000	30,757	32,776	30,910	29,000	31,450	29,100
College/University Libraries														
Northeast	122	52	30	82	16,000	20,000	44,332	85,000	30,220	32,119	30,915	29,669	30,000	30,000
Southeast	86	53	20	73	11,000	17,400	49,000	44,000	26,163	27,284	26,470	26,000	26,750	26,000
Midwest	123	62	30	92	16,000	20,000	40,000	48,000	27,207	29,817	28,058	27,125	28,000	27,500
Southwest	49	34	10	44	16,000	23,476	32,500	35,000	26,041	27,188	26,302	26,000	26,500	26,000
West	40	18	11	29	24,000	20,460	44,000	36,109	29,808	30,355	30,009	29,004	30,300	29,391
All Academic	434	224	101	320	11,000	17,400	49,000	85,000	27,797	29,721	28,399	27,100	28,000	27,500
Special Libraries														
Northeast	94	56	12	68	18,900	21,000	50,000	38,000	32,031	29,594	31,601	30,000	30,500	30,000
Southeast	45	30	4	34	18,000	20,000	50,000	57,000	29,511	35,500	30,215	28,500	32,500	29,250
Midwest	89	60	14	74	18,000	18,000	65,000	37,336	29,097	29,392	29,162	28,094	29,000	28,094
Southwest	42	31	5	36	20,000	29,000	39,600	35,000	28,615	32,220	29,115	28,000	34,000	29,000
West	37	22	9	31	20,500	22,000	41,500	42,100	30,836	32,611	31,256	30,000	31,400	31,000
All Special	322	189	45	248	18,000	18,000	65,000	57,000	30,012	30,760	30,156	29,898	31,000	30,000
Other Libraries														
Northeast	64	38	13	51	18,000	21,840	62,500	63,000	31,376	38,476	33,186	28,121	37,000	30,000
Southeast	27	15	7	22	20,000	15,800	40,000	34,000	28,712	26,686	28,067	26,000	28,000	27,000
Midwest	52	30	10	40	17,500	18,700	43,000	40,000	28,446	30,622	31,062	28,000	35,000	28,900
Southwest	39	27	9	36	18,000	25,000	55,000	87,100	28,890	37,400	31,017	28,500	30,000	29,000
West	17	8	7	15	30,000	18,885	90,000	50,000	44,473	37,050	41,292	34,050	35,709	35,259
All Other	241	122	47	163	10,000	15,800	90,000	87,100	30,493	34,449	31,593	38,331	32,000	30,000

2,006 total placements were reported for this section; only 1,487 included region, type of library, and salary.

370

(continued from page 368)

Only two institutions (both from the western United States) reported having difficulty placing their graduates. Thirty-three said they had no difficulty placing graduates, and two of these stated that it was even easier placing them than in 1994.

Of those graduates finding positions, a greater percentage are staying closer to home than in the past. In this year's survey, 64 percent of graduates found placements in the same state as their library school, and 16 percent found placements in the same region (Table 9). In the 1994 survey, the figures were 45 percent and 11 percent, respectively.

Demand for academic librarians was down, according to five institutions. While the data give few clues, it is likely that the effects of outsourcing are being felt. Three reported a decreased demand for school library media specialists, not surprising given the continued cuts to school libraries.

As has been true for many years, graduates with backgrounds in mathematics, the sciences, and computers continue to be in demand to fill positions. Several institutions also recognize the need for graduates to have coursework in advanced cataloging and information technology-related areas such as networking, systems administration, and automation.

Where We Go From Here

There still is a demand for positions in traditional areas. However, professionals with skills and knowledge in the new information technologies in both traditional and nontraditional fields are in demand and will continue to be needed.

Accredited Master's Programs in Library and Information Studies

This list of graduate programs accredited by the American Library Association was issued in January 1997. The list of accredited programs is issued annually at the start of each calendar year and is available from the ALA Office for Accreditation. A list of more than 200 institutions offering both accredited and non-accredited programs in librarianship appears in the 49th edition of the *American Library Directory* (R. R. Bowker, 1996).

Northeast: Conn., D.C., Md., Mass., N.J., N.Y., Pa., R.I.

Catholic University of America, School of Lib. and Info. Science, Washington, DC 20064. Elizabeth S. Aversa, Dean. 202-319-5085. aversa@cua.edu.

Clarion University of Pennsylvania, Dept. of Lib. Science, 166 Carlson, Clarion, PA 16214-1232. James T. Maccaferri, Chair. 814-226-2271. mccafer@vaxa.clarion.edu.

Drexel University, College of Info. Science and Technology, Philadelphia, PA 19104-2875. Richard H. Lytle, Dean. 215-895-2474. tannerab@duvm.ocs.drexel.edu. World Wide Web http://www.cis.drexel.edu.

Long Island University, Palmer School of Lib. and Info. Science, Brookville, NY 11548-1300. Anne Woodsworth, Dean. 516-299-2866. palmer@aurora.liunet.edu.

Pratt Institute, School of Info. and Lib. Science, Brooklyn, NY 11205. S. M. Matta, Dean. 718-636-3702. matta@sils.pratt.edu. World Wide Web http://sils.pratt.edu.

Queens College, City University of New York, Grad. School of Lib. and Info. Studies, Flushing, NY 11367. Marianne Cooper, Dir. 718-997-3797.

Rutgers University, School of Communication, Info., and Lib. Studies, New Brunswick, NJ 08903-1071. Richard W. Budd, Dean. 908-932-7500. carr-dcarr@sclis.rutgers.edu.

Saint John's University, Div. of Lib. and Info. Science, Jamaica, NY 11439. James A. Benson, Dir. 718-990-6200. libis@sjumisic.stjohns.edu.

Simmons College, Grad. School of Lib. and Info. Science, Boston, MA 02115-5898. James M. Matarazzo, Dean. 617-521-2800. jbeals@vmsvax.simmons.edu.

Southern Connecticut State University, School of Communication, Info., and Lib. Science, New Haven, CT 06515. Edward C. Harris, Dean. 203-392-5781. libsciit@scsu.ctstateu.edu.

State University of New York at Albany, School of Info. Science and Policy, Albany, NY 12222. Philip B. Eppard, Interim Dean. 518-442-5110. infosci@cnsvax.albany.edu.

State University of New York at Buffalo, School of Info. and Lib. Studies, Buffalo, NY 14260. George S. Bobinski, Dean. 716-645-2412. sils@ubvms.cc.bufalo.edu. World Wide Web http://www.sils.buffalo.edu.

Syracuse University, School of Info. Studies, Syracuse, NY 13244-4100. Raymond F. von Dran, Dean. 315-443-2911. vondran@syr.edu. World Wide Web http://istweb.svr.edu.

University of Maryland, College of Lib. and Info. Services, College Park, MD 20742-4345. Ann E. Prentice, Dean. 301-405-2033. dbarlow@deans.umd.edu.

University of Pittsburgh, School of Lib. and Info. Science, Pittsburgh, PA 15260. Toni Carbo, Dean. 412-624-5230. nk@sis.pitt.edu. World Wide Web http://www.sis.pitt.edu.

University of Rhode Island, Grad. School of Lib. and Info. Studies, Kingston, RI 02881. Jonathan S. Tryon, Dir. 401-792-2947. chcarson@uriacc.uri.edu.

Southeast: Ala., Fla., Ga., Ky., La., Miss., N.C., S.C., Tenn., P.R.

Clark Atlanta University, School of Lib. and Info. Studies, Atlanta, GA 30314. Arthur

C. Gunn, Acting Dean. 404-880-8695. agunn@cau.edu.

Florida State University, School of Lib. and Info. Studies, Tallahassee, FL 32306-2048. Jane B. Robbins, Dean. 904-644-5775. logan@lis.fsu.edu. World Wide Web http://www.fsu.edu/~lis

Louisiana State University, School of Lib. and Info. Science, Baton Rouge, LA 70803. Bert R. Boyce, Dean. 504-388-3158. lsslis@lsuvm.sncc.lsu.edu.

North Carolina Central University, School of Lib. and Info. Sciences, Durham, NC 27707. Benjamin F. Speller, Jr., Dean. 919-560-6485. duaneb@nccu.edu.

University of Alabama, School of Lib. and Info. Studies, Tuscaloosa, AL 35487-0252. Charles Osburn, Interim Dean. 205-348-4610.

University of Kentucky, School of Lib. and Info. Science, Lexington, KY 40506-0039. Donald O. Case, Dir. 606-257-8876. gmccowa@pop.uky.edu. World Wide Web http://www.uky.edu/CommInfoStudies/SLIS.

University of North Carolina, School of Info. and Lib. Science, Chapel Hill, NC 27599-3360. Barbara B. Moran, Dean. 919-962-8366. kompst.ils@mhs.unc.edu.

University of North Carolina, Dept. of Lib. and Info. Studies, Greensboro, NC 27412-5001. Marilyn Shontz, Interim Chair. 910-334-3477. kovacsb@iris.uncg.edu. World Wide Web http://www.uncg.edu/lis.

University of Puerto Rico, Graduate School of Lib. and Info. Science (Escuela Graduada de Bibliotecologia y Ciencia de la Información), San Juan, PR 00931-1906. Mariano A. Maura, Dir. 809-763-6199. m_davila@rrpad.upr.clu.edu.

University of South Carolina, College of Lib. and Info. Science, Columbia, SC 29208. Fred W. Roper, Dean. 803-777-3858. nbeitz@sc.edu. World Wide Web http://www.libsci.scarolina.edu.

University of South Florida, School of Lib. and Info. Science, Tampa, FL 33620-7800. Kathleen de la Peña McCook, Dir. 813-974-3520. swohlmut@cis01.cis.usf.edu. World Wide Web http://www.cas.usf.edu/lis/index.html.

University of Southern Mississippi, School of Lib. and Info. Science, Hattiesburg, MS 39406-5146. Joy M. Greiner, Dir. 601-266-4228.

University of Tennessee, School of Info. Sciences, Knoxville, TN 37996-4330. W. David Penniman, Interim Dir. 423-974-2148. hoemann@utk.edu. World Wide Web http://www.pepper.lis.utk.edu.

Midwest: Ill., Ind., Iowa, Kan., Mich., Mo., Ohio, Wis.

Emporia State University, School of Lib. and Info. Management, Emporia, KS 66801. Faye Vowell, Dean. 316-341-5203. andersoj@esumail.emporia.edu.

Indiana University, School of Lib. and Info. Science, Bloomington, IN 47405-1801. Blaise Cronin, Dean. 812-855-2018. krutulis@indiana.edu.

Kent State University, School of Lib. and Info. Science, Kent, OH 44242-0001. Danny P. Wallace, Dir. 216-672-2782. mhayden@slis.kent.edu.

Rosary College, Grad. School of Lib. and Info. Science, River Forest, IL 60305. Peggy Sullivan, Dean. 708-524-6845. sullivan@email.rosary.edu.

University of Illinois, Grad. School of Lib. and Info. Science, Champaign, IL 61820. Leigh S. Estabrook, Dean. 217-333-3280. devoss@alexia.lis.uiuc.edu. World Wide Web http://alexia.lis.uiuc.edu.

University of Iowa, School of Lib. and Info. Science, Iowa City, IA 52242-1420. Padmini Srinivasan, Dir. 319-335-5707. ethel-bloesch@uiowa.edu. World Wide Web http://www.uiowa.edu/~libsci.

University of Michigan, School of Info., Ann Arbor, MI 48109-1092. Daniel E. Atkins, Dean. 313-763-2285. si.admissions@umich.edu. World Wide Web http://www.si.umich.edu.

University of Missouri–Columbia, School of Lib. and Info. Science, Columbia, MO 65211. Richard Andrews, Interim Dir. 573-882-4546. jruth@tiger.coe.missouri.edu. World Wide Web http://www.phlab.missouri.edu/~slis.

University of Wisconsin, School of Lib. and Info. Studies, Madison, WI 53706. James

Krikelas, Interim Dir. 608-263-2900. bjarnold@facstaff.wisc.edu.
University of Wisconsin, School of Lib. and Info. Science, Milwaukee, WI 53211. Mohammed M. Aman, Dean. 414-229-4707. robin@csd.uwm.edu.
Wayne State University, Lib. and Info. Science Program, Detroit, MI 48202. Robert P. Holley, Dir. 313-577-1825. rholley@lisp.purdy.wayne.edu. World Wide Web http://www.wayne.edu.

Southwest: Ariz., Okla., Tex.

Texas Woman's University, School of Lib. and Info. Studies, Denton, TX 76204-5438. Keith Swigger, Dean. 817-898-2602. a_swigger@twu.edu. World Wide Web http://www.twu.edu/slis/lishome/lishome.htm.
University of Arizona, School of Lib. Science, Tucson, AZ 85719. Charlie D. Hurt, Dir. 520-621-3566. ualibsci@ccit.arizona.edu; cpa@ccit.arizona.edu. World Wide Web http://www.sir.arizona.edu.
University of North Texas, School of Lib. and Info. Sciences, Denton, TX 76203. Philip M. Turner, Dean. 817-565-2445. totten@lis.unt.edu. World Wide Web http://www-lan/slis.
University of Oklahoma, School of Lib. and Info. Studies, Norman, OK 73019-0528. June Lester, Dir. 405-325-3921. slisinfo@ou.edu. World Wide Web http://www.uoknor.edu/cas/slis.
University of Texas at Austin, Grad. School of Lib. and Info. Science, Austin, TX 78712-1276. Brooke E. Sheldon, Dean. 512-471-3821. immroth@uts.cc.utexas.edu. World Wide Web http://fiat.gslis.utexas.edu.

West: Calif., Hawaii, Wash.

San Jose State University, School of Lib. and Info. Science, San Jose, CA 95192-0029. William Fisher, Interim Dir. 408-924-2490. office@wahoo.sjsu.edu, fielder@sjsuvm1.sjsu.edu.

University of California at Los Angeles, Grad. School of Education and Info. Studies, Los Angeles, CA 90095-1521. Christine L. Borgman, Chair. 310-825-8799. cborgman@ucla.edu. World Wide Web http://www.gslis.ucla.edu/LIS.
University of Hawaii, School of Lib. and Info. Studies, Honolulu, HI 96822. Larry N. Osborne, Interim Dean. 808-956-7321. osborne@hawaii.edu, teshima@hawaii.edu.
University of Washington, Grad. School of Lib. and Info. Science, Seattle, WA 98195-2930. Edward P. Bassett, Acting Dir. 206-543-1794. dpotter@u.washington.edu.

Canada

Dalhousie University, School of Lib. and Info. Studies, Halifax, NS B3H 3J5. Bertrum H. MacDonald, Dir. 902-494-3656. shanna@is.dal.ca. World Wide Web http://www.mgmt.dal.ca/slis.
McGill University, Grad. School of Lib. and Info. Studies, Montreal, PQ H3A 1Y1. J. Andrew Large, Dir. 514-398-4204. ad27@musica.mcgill.ca. World Wide Web http://www.gslis.mcgill.ca.
Université de Montréal, Ecole de Bibliothèconomie et des Sciences de l'Information, Montreal, PQ H3C 3J7. Gilles Deschâtelets, Dir. 514-343-6044. mayerdi@daa.umontreal.ca. World Wide Web http://tornado.ere.umontreal.ca/~carmellu/ebsi.
University of Alberta, School of Lib. and Info. Studies, Edmonton, AB T6G 2J4. Alvin Schrader, Dir. 403-492-4578. office@slis.ualberta.ca.
University of British Columbia, School of Lib., Archival, and Info. Studies, Vancouver, BC V6T 1Z1. Ken Haycock, Dir. 604-822-2404. admit@slais.ubc.ca. World Wide Web http://www.slais.ubc.ca.
University of Toronto, Faculty of Info. Studies, Toronto, ON M5S 1A1. Lynne C. Howarth, Dean. 416-978-8589. muia@fis.utoronto.ca.
University of Western Ontario, Grad. School of Lib. and Info. Science, London, ON N6G 1H1. B. P. Frohmann, Acting Dean. 519-661-3542. dineen@julian.uwo.ca.

Library Scholarship Sources

For a more complete list of scholarships, fellowships, and assistantships offered for library study, see *Financial Assistance for Library and Information Studies*, published annually by the American Library Association.

American Association of Law Libraries. (1) A varying number of scholarships of a minimum of $1,000 for graduates of an accredited law school who are degree candidates in an ALA-accredited library school; (2) a varying number of scholarships of varying amounts for library school graduates working on a law degree, non-law graduates enrolled in an ALA-accredited library school, and law librarians taking a course related to law librarianship; (3) the George A. Strait Minority Stipend of $3,500 for an experienced minority librarian working toward an advanced degree to further a law library career. For information, write to: Scholarship Committee, AALL, 53 W. Jackson Blvd., Suite 940, Chicago, IL 60604.

American Library Association. (1) The Marshall Cavendish Scholarship of $3,000 for a varying number of students who have been admitted to an ALA-accredited library school. For information, write to Staff Liaison, Cavendish Scholarship Jury, ALA, 50 E. Huron St., Chicago, IL 60611; (2) The David H. Clift Scholarship of $3,000 for a varying number of students who have been admitted to an ALA-accredited library school. For information, write to: Staff Liaison, Clift Scholarship Jury, ALA, 50 E. Huron St., Chicago, IL 60611; (3) the Shirley Crawford Minority Scholarship of $3,000 for a varying number of minority students who have been admitted to an ALA-accredited library school. For information, write to: Staff Liaison, Crawford Scholarship Jury, ALA, 50 E. Huron St., Chicago, IL 60611; (4) the Tom and Roberta Drewes Scholarship of $3,000 for a varying number of library support staff. For information, write to: Staff Liaison, Drewes Scholarship Jury, ALA, 50 E. Huron St., Chicago, IL 60611; (5) the Mary V. Gaver Scholarship of $3,000 to a varying number of individuals specializing in youth services. For information, write to: Staff Liaison, Gaver Scholarship Jury, ALA, 50 E. Huron St., Chicago, IL 60611; (6) the Louise Giles Minority Scholarship of $3,000 for a varying number of minority students who have been admitted to an ALA-accredited library school. For information, write to: Staff Liaison, Giles Minority Scholarship Jury, ALA, 50 E. Huron St., Chicago, IL 60611; (7) the Miriam L. Hornback Scholarship of $3,000 for a varying number of ALA or library support staff. For information, write to: Staff Liaison, Hornback Scholarship Jury, ALA, 50 E. Huron St., Chicago, IL 60611; (8) the Christopher J. Hoy/ERT Scholarship of $3,000 for a varying number of students who have been admitted to an ALA-accredited library school. For information, write to: Staff Liaison, Hoy/ERT Scholarship Jury, ALA, 50 E. Huron St., Chicago, IL 60611; (9) the Tony B. Leisner Scholarship of $3,000 for a varying number of library support staff. For information, write to: Staff Liaison, Leisner Scholarship Jury, ALA, 50 E. Huron St., Chicago, IL 60611.

ALA/American Association of School Librarians. The AASL School Librarians Workshop Scholarship of $2,500 for a candidate admitted to a full-time ALA-accredited MLS or school library media program. For information, write to: AASL/ALA, 50 E. Huron St., Chicago, IL 60611.

ALA/Association for Library Service to Children. (1) The Bound to Stay Bound Books Scholarship of $6,000 each for two students who are U.S. or Canadian citizens, who have been admitted to an ALA-accredited program, and who will work with children in a library for one year after graduation; (2) the Frederic G. Melcher Scholarship of $6,000 each for two U.S. or Canadian citizens admitted to an ALA-accredited library school who will work with children in school or public libraries for one year after graduation. For information, write to: Executive Director, ALSC/ALA, 50 E. Huron St., Chicago, IL 60611.

ALA/Association of College and Research Libraries and the Institute for Scientific Information. (1) The ACRL Doctoral Dissertation Fellowship of $1,000 for a student who has completed all coursework and submitted a dissertation proposal that has been accepted, in the area of academic librarianship; (2) the Samuel Lazerow Fellowship of $1,000 for research in acquisitions or technical services in an academic or research library; (3) the ACRL and Martinus Nijhoff International West European Specialist Study Grant, which pays travel expenses, room, and board for a ten-day trip to the Netherlands and two other European countries for an ALA member (selection is based on proposal outlining purpose of trip). For information, write to: Althea Jenkins, ACRL/ALA, 50 E. Huron St., Chicago, IL 60611.

ALA/Government Documents Round Table. The David Rozkuszka Scholarship of $3,000 for a student currently working in a library who has been accepted to an ALA-accredited program and is committed to government documents. For information, write to: Susan Tulis, Law Library, University of Virginia, 580 Massie Rd., Charlottesville, VA 22901.

ALA/International Relations Committee. The Bogle International Library Travel Fund grant of $500 for a varying number of ALA members to attend a first international conference. For information, write to: Carol Erickson, ALA, 50 E. Huron St., Chicago, IL 60611.

ALA/Library and Information Technology Association. Three LITA Scholarships in library and information technology of $2,500 each for students (two of whom are minority students) who have been admitted to an ALA-accredited program in library automation and information science. For information, write to: LITA/ALA, 50 E. Huron St., Chicago, IL 60611.

ALA/New Members Round Table. EBSCO/NMRT Scholarship of $1,000 for a U.S. or Canadian citizen who is a member of the ALA New Members Round Table. Based on financial need, professional goals, and admission to an ALA-accredited program. For information, write to: Pamela Padley, Mail Code 1-32, California Technical Library System, California Institute of Technical Libraries, Pasadena, CA 91125.

ALA/Public Library Association. The New Leaders Travel Grant Study Award of up to $1,500 for a varying number of PLA members with five years or less experience. For information, write to: PLA/ALA, 50 E. Huron St., Chicago, IL 60611.

American-Scandinavian Foundation. Fellowships and grants for 25 to 30 students, in amounts from $3,000 to $15,000, for advanced study in Denmark, Finland, Iceland, Norway, or Sweden. For information, write to: Exchange Division, American-Scandinavian Foundation, 725 Park Ave., New York, NY 10021.

Association for Library and Information Science Education. A varying number of research grants of up to $2,500 each for members of ALISE. For information, write to: Association for Library and Information Science Education, Rm. 304 West Hall, 550 E. University Ave., Ann Arbor MI 48109-1092.

Association of Jewish Libraries. The May K. Simon Memorial Scholarship Fund offers a varying number of scholarships of at least $500 each for MLS students who plan to work as Judaica librarians. For information, write to: Sharona R. Wachs, Association of Jewish Libraries, 1000 Washington Ave., Albany, NY 12203.

Association of Seventh-Day Adventist Librarians. The D. Glenn Hilts Scholarship of $1,000 to a member of the Seventh-Day Adventist Church in a graduate library program. For information, write to: Ms. Wisel, Association of Seventh-Day Adventist Librarians, Columbia Union College, Takoma Park, MD 20912.

Beta Phi Mu. (1) The Sarah Rebecca Reed Scholarship of $1,500 for a person accepted in an ALA-accredited library program; (2) the Frank B. Sessa Scholarship of $750 for a Beta Phi Mu member for continuing education; (3) the Harold Lancour Scholarship of $1,000 for study in a foreign country related to the applicant's work or schooling. For information, write to: F. William Summers, Executive Secretary, Beta Phi Mu, Florida State University, SLIS, Tallahassee, FL 32306-2048.

Canadian Association of Law Libraries. The Diana M. Priestly Scholarship of $2,000 for a student with previous law experience or for entry to an approved Canadian law school or accredited Canadian library school. For information, write to: John Davis, Law Library, University of Victoria, Box 2300, Victoria, BC V8W 3B1, Canada.

Canadian Federation of University Women. The Alice E. Wilson Award of $1,000 for three Canadian citizens or permanent residents with a BA degree or equivalent accepted into a program of specialized study. For information, write to: Canadian Federation of University Women, 297 Dupuis St., Suite 308, Ottawa, ON K1L 7H8, Canada.

Canadian Health Libraries Association. The Student Paper Prize, a scholarship of $300 to a student or recent MLIS graduate or library technician; topic of paper must be in health or information science. For information, write to: Student Paper Prize, Canadian Health Libraries Association/ABSC, Box 94038, 3332 Yonge St., Toronto, ON M4N 3R1, Canada.

Canadian Library Association. (1) The Howard V. Phalin World Book Graduate Scholarship in Library Science of $2,500; (2) the CLA Dafoe Scholarship of $1,750; and (3) the H. W. Wilson Scholarship of $2,000. Each scholarship is given to a Canadian citizen or landed immigrant to attend an accredited Canadian library school; the Phalin scholarship can also be used for an ALA-accredited U.S. school; (4) the Library Research and Development Grant of $1,000 for a member of the Canadian Library Association, in support of theoretical and applied research in library and information science. For information, write to: CLA Membership Services Department, Scholarships and Awards Committee, 200 Elgin St., Suite 602, Ottawa, ON K2P 1L5, Canada.

Catholic Library Association. The World Book, Inc., Grant of $1,500 is divided among no more than three CLA members for workshops, institutes, etc. For information, write to: Jean R. Bostley, SSJ, Scholarship Committee, St. Joseph Central High School Library, 22 Maplewood Ave., Pittsfield, MA 01201-4780.

Chinese American Librarians Association. (1) The Sheila Suen Lai Scholarship; (2) the CALA Scholarship; (3) the C. C. Seetoo/CALA Conference Travel Scholarship. Each scholarship offers $500 to a Chinese descendant who has been accepted in an ALA-accredited program. For information, write to: Clara Chu, UCLA Department of Library Science, 210 GSEIS Bldg., Box 951520, Los Angeles, CA 90095-1520.

Church and Synagogue Library Association. The Muriel Fuller Memorial Scholarship of $115 plus cost of texts for a correspondence course offered by the University of Utah Continuing Education Division. Open to CSLA members only. For information, write to: CSLA, Box 19357, Portland, OR 97280-0357.

Massachusetts Black Librarians' Network. Two scholarships of at least $500 and $1,000 for a minority student entering an ALA-accredited master's program in library science, with no more than 12 semester hours toward a degree. For information, write to: Pearl Mosley, Chair, Massachusetts Black Librarians' Network, 27 Beech Glen St., Roxbury, MA 02119.

Medical Library Association. (1) A scholarship of $2,000 for a person entering an ALA-accredited library program, with no more than one-half of the program yet to be completed; (2) a scholarship of $2,000 for a minority student for graduate study; (3) a varying number of Research, Development and Demonstration Project Grants of $100 to $1,000 for U.S. or Canadian citizens who are MLA members; (4) Continuing Education Grants of $100 to $500 for U.S. or Canadian citizens who are MLA members; (5) the Cunningham Memorial International Fellowship of $3,000 plus travel expenses for a foreign student for postgraduate study in the United States;

(6) the MLA Doctoral Fellowship of $1,000 for postgraduate work in medical librarianship or information science. For information, write to: Professional Service Area, Medical Library Association, 6 N. Michigan Ave., Suite 300, Chicago, IL 60602.

Mountain Plains Library Association. (1) A varying number of grants of up to $600 each and (2) a varying number of grants of up to $150 each for MPLA members with at least two years of membership for continuing education. For information, write to: Joseph R. Edelen, Jr., MPLA Executive Secretary, I. D. Weeks Library, University of South Dakota, Vermillion, SD 57069.

REFORMA, the National Association to Promote Library Services to the Spanish-Speaking. A varying number of scholarships of $1,000 each to attend an ALA-accredited school. For information, write to: Yolanda Marino, 2407 Ridgeway Ave., Evanston, IL 60201.

Society of American Archivists. The Colonial Dames Awards, two grants of $1,200 each for specific types of repositories and collections. For information, write to: Debra Mills, Society of American Archivists, 600 S. Federal St., Suite 504, Chicago, IL 60605.

Southern Regional Education Board. For residents of Arkansas, Georgia, Louisiana, Mississippi, Oklahoma, South Carolina, Tennessee, Virginia, and West Virginia, a varying number of grants of varying amounts to cover in-state tuition for graduate or postgraduate study in an ALA-accredited library school. For information, write to: Academic Common Market, c/o Southern Regional Education Board, 592 Tenth St. N.W., Atlanta, GA 30318-5790.

Special Libraries Association. (1) Two $6,000 scholarships for students interested in special-library work; (2) the Plenum Scholarship of $1,000, and (3) the ISI Scholarship of $1,000, each also for students interested in special-library work; (4) two Affirmative Action Scholarships of $6,000 each for minority students interested in special-library work; and (5) two Pharmaceutical Division Stipend Awards of $750 and $250 for students with an undergraduate degree in chemistry, life sciences, or pharmacy entering or enrolled in an ALA-accredited program. For information on the first four scholarships, write to: Scholarship Committee, Special Libraries Association, 1700 18th St. N.W., Washington, DC 20009-2508; for information on the Pharmaceutical Stipend, write to: Susan E. Katz, Awards Chair, Knoll Pharmaceuticals Science Information Center, 30 N. Jefferson St., Whippany, NJ 07981.

Library Scholarship and Award Recipients, 1996

Library awards are listed by organization. An index listing awards alphabetically by title follows this section.

American Association of Law Libraries (AALL)

AALL Scholarships. Offered by: AALL; Matthew Bender & Company; Lexis-Nexis; Thomson Professional Publishing; West Publishing Company. *Winners*: (Library Degree for Law School Graduates) Denise Carpenter, Kristine Buchanan, Kimberley Clarke; (Library School Graduates Attending Law School) Herbert Somers; (Library Degree for Non-Law School Graduates) Jennifer Calfa, Elizabeth J. Tabor, Jana Apergis, Michele Habian, Catherine Clukey, Joshua Kantor; (John Johnson Lexis-Nexis Memorial Scholarship) James Gernert, Philip Bohl, Melissa Harter, Suzanne Mucklow; (George A. Strait Minority Stipend) Jose Aleman, Deborah Kenney, Rahim Naseem.

Special Course in Law Librarianship. *Winners*: Roger Skalbeck, Linda Baltrusch.

American Library Association (ALA)

ALA/Information Today Library of the Future Award ($2,000). For a library, consortium, group of librarians, or support organization for innovative planning for, applications of or development of patron training programs about information technology in a library setting. *Donor*: Information Today, Inc. *Winner*: The Public Library of Charlotte and Mecklenburg County, NC.

Hugh C. Atkinson Memorial Award ($2,000). For outstanding achievement (including risk-taking) by academic librarians that has contributed significantly to improvements in library automation, management, and/or development or research. Offered by: ACRL, ALCTS, LAMA, and LITA divisions. *Winner*: Thomas Shaughnessy.

Carroll Preston Baber Research Grant ($7,500). For innovative research that could lead to an improvement in library services to any specified group(s) of people. *Donor*: Eric R. Baber. *Winners*: Gloria J. Leckie, Anne Fullerton.

Beta Phi Mu Award ($500). For distinguished service in library education. *Donor*: Beta Phi Mu International Library Science Honorary Society. *Winner*: Robert N. Broadus.

Bogle International Library Travel Fund Award ($500). To ALA member(s) to attend their first international conference. *Donor*: Bogle Memorial Fund. *Winner*: Dianne Stalker.

William Boyd Military Novel Award ($10,000). To an author for a military novel that honors the service of American veterans. *Donor*: William Young Boyd. *Winner*: Not awarded in 1996.

Marshall Cavendish Scholarship ($3,000). To a worthy U.S. or Canadian citizen to begin an MLS degree in an ALA-accredited program. *Winner*: Mary Prendegast Murphy.

David H. Clift Scholarship ($3,000). To a worthy U.S. or Canadian citizen to begin an MLS degree in an ALA-accredited program. *Winner*: Eileen Ball.

Shirley Crawford Minority Scholarship ($3,000). To a worthy U.S. or Canadian citizen to begin an MLS degree in an ALA-accredited program. *Donor*: Reed Reference Publishing. *Winner*: Iva Ashe.

Robert B. Downs Intellectual Freedom Award. *Winner*: Sanford Berman.

Tom C. Drewes Scholarship ($3,000). To a library support staff person pursuing a master's degree. *Winner*: Lars Leon.

EBSCO ALA Conference Sponsorships (up to $1,000). To allow librarians to attend ALA's Annual Conferences. *Donor*: EBSCO Subscription Services. *Winners*: May Anstee, Cheryl Anthony, Rebekah Azen, Barbara Hauer, Patricia Henderson

William Kehler, Sarah Killoran, Nancy Moore, Lillie Peterson, Betty Lee Roayne Equality Award ($500). To an individual or group for an outstanding contribution that promotes equality of women and men in the library profession. *Donor*: Scarecrow Press. *Winner*: Michele Leber.

Freedom to Read Foundation Roll of Honor Award. *Winner*: Gordon M. Conable.

Loleta D. Fyan Public Library Research Grant (up to $10,000). For projects in public library development. *Winner*: Plainsboro (NJ) Public Library.

Gale Research Company Financial Development Award ($2,500). To a library organization for a financial development project to secure new funding resources for a public or academic library. *Donor*: Gale Research Company. *Winner*: Friends of the Town of Pelham (NY) Public Library.

Mary V. Gaver Scholarship ($3,000). To a library support staff specializing in youth services. *Winner*: Anne Johnson.

Louise Giles Minority Scholarship ($3,000). To a worthy U.S. or Canadian minority student to begin an MLS degree in an ALA-accredited program. *Winner*: Debra Quarles.

Grolier Foundation Award ($1,000). For stimulation and guidance of reading by children and young people. *Donor*: Grolier Education Corporation, Inc. *Winner*: Patricia S. Siegfried.

Grolier National Library Week Grant ($2,000). To libraries or library associations of all types for a public awareness campaign in connection with National Library Week in the year the grant is awarded. *Donor*: Grolier Educational Corporation. *Winner*: Danville (IL) Public Library.

G. K. Hall Award for Library Literature ($500). For outstanding contribution to library literature issued during the three years preceding presentation. *Donor*: G. K. Hall & Company. *Winner*: Karen Patricia Smith for *African-American Voices in Young Adult Literature: Tradition, Transition, Transformation*.

Mirian L. Hornback Scholarship ($3,000). To an ALA or library support staff person pursuing a master's degree in library science. *Winner*: Margaret Lewis.

Paul Howard Award for Courage ($1,000). To a librarian, library board, library group, or an individual who has exhibited unusual courage for the benefit of library programs or services. *Donor*: Paul Howard. *Winner*: Not awarded in 1996.

John Ames Humphry/OCLC/Forest Press Award ($1,000). To an individual for significant contributions to international librarianship. *Donor*: OCLC/Forest Press. *Winner*: Ching-chih Chen.

Tony B. Leisner Scholarship ($3,000). To a library support staff member pursuing a master's degree program. *Winner*: Susan Scheiberg.

Joseph W. Lippincott Award ($1,000). To a librarian for distinguished service to the profession. *Donor*: Joseph W. Lippincott, Jr. *Winner*: F. William Summers.

Bessie Boehm Moore Award ($1,000). Presented to a public library that has developed an outstanding and creative program for public library services to the aging. *Donor*: Bessie Boehm Moore. *Winner*: East Brunswick (NJ) Public Library.

H. W. Wilson Library Staff Development Grant ($3,500). To a library organization for a program to further its staff development goals and objectives. *Donor*: The H. W. Wilson Company. *Winner*: Rocky River (OH) Public Library.

World Book–ALA Goal Grant (up to $10,000). To ALA units for the advancement of public, academic, or school library service and librarianship through support of programs that implement the goals and priorities of ALA. *Donor*: World Book, Inc. *Winners*: ALA Public Awareness Committee, Chapter Relations Committee, Committee on Legislation.

American Association of School Librarians (AASL)

AASL ABC/CLIO Leadership Grant (up to $1,750). For planning and implementing leadership programs at state, regional, or local levels to be given to school library associations that are affiliates of AASL. *Donor*: ABC/CLIO. *Winner*: Massachusetts School Library Media Association and Massachusetts Library Association Children's Issues Section.

AASL/Highsmith Research Grant (up to $5,000). To conduct innovative research aimed at measuring and evaluating the impact of school library media programs on learning and education. *Donor*: The Highsmith Company. *Winner*: Kansas Association of School Librarians Research Committee.

AASL Information Plus Continuing Education Scholarship ($500). To a school library media specialist, supervisor, or educator to attend an ALA or AASL continuing education event. *Donor*: Information Plus. *Winner*: Candace Jensen.

AASL President's Crystal Apple Award. *Winners*: Elliot and Eleanor Goldstein.

AASL School Librarian's Workshop Scholarship ($2,500). To a full-time student preparing to become a school library media specialist at the preschool, elementary, or secondary level. *Donor*: Jay W. Toor, President, Library Learning Resources. *Winner*: Laura Michelle Mench.

Distinguished School Administrators Award ($2,000). For expanding the role of the library in elementary and/or secondary school education. *Donor*: Social Issues Resources Series, Inc. *Winner*: Faye Kimsey.

Distinguished Service Award, AASL/Baker & Taylor ($3,000). For outstanding contributions to librarianship and school library development. *Donor*: Baker & Taylor Books. *Winner*: Ken Haycock.

Frances Henne Award ($1,250). To a school library media specialist with five or fewer years in the profession to attend an AASL regional conference or ALA Annual Conference for the first time. *Donor*: R. R. Bowker Company. *Winner*: Jane Baldwin.

Intellectual Freedom Award ($2,000, plus $1,000 to media center of recipient's choice). To a school library media specialist who has upheld the principles of intellectual freedom. *Donor*: Social Issues Resources Series, Inc. *Winner*: Ann K. Symons.

Microcomputer in the Media Center Award ($1,000 to the specialist and $500 to the library). To library media specialists for innovative approaches to microcomputer applications in the school library media center. *Donor*: Follett Software Company. *Winners*: Elementary, Marsha L. West; Secondary, Cynthia Montoya.

National School Library Media Program of the Year Award ($3,000). To school districts and a single school for excellence and innovation in outstanding library media programs. *Donor*: AASL and Encyclopaedia Britannica Companies. *Winner*: Maine Township High School West, Des Plaines, IL.

American Library Trustee Association (ALTA)

ALTA/Gale Outstanding Trustee Conference Grant Award ($750). *Donor*: Gale Research Company. *Winners*: Sylvia McGill, Pina T. Riccobono.

ALTA Literacy Award (citation). To a library trustee or an individual who, in a volunteer capacity, has made a significant contribution to addressing the illiteracy problem in the United States. *Winner*: Joe Augustine.

ALTA Major Benefactors Honor Award (citation). To individual(s), families, or corporate bodies that have made major benefactions to public libraries. *Winner*: Maynard Sauder.

Trustee Citations. To recognize public library trustees for individual service to library development on the local, state, regional, or national level. *Winners*: Ann L. Donoghue, Judith B. Nudelman.

Armed Forces Libraries Round Table

Armed Forces Library Certificate of Merit. To librarians or "friends" who are members of AFLRT who provide an exemplary program to an Armed Forces library. *Winner*: Not awarded in 1996.

Armed Forces Libraries Round Table Achievement Citation. For contributions toward development of interest in libraries and reading in armed forces library service and organizations. Candidates must be members of the Armed Forces Libraries Round Table. *Winner*: Annette Gohlke.

Armed Forces Libraries Round Table NewsBank Scholarship ($1,000 to the school of the recipient's choice). To members of the Armed Forces Libraries Round Table who have given exemplary service in the area of library support for off-duty education programs in the armed forces. *Donor*: NewsBank, Inc. *Winner*: Mary Rogerson.

Association for Library Collections and Technical Services (ALCTS)

Hugh C. Atkinson Memorial Award. See under American Library Association.

Best of LRTS Award (citation). To the author(s) of the best paper published each year in the division's official journal. *Winners*: Samuel G. Demas, Peter McDonald, Gregory W. Lawrence.

Blackwell North America Scholarship Award ($2,000 scholarship to the U.S. or Canadian library school of the recipient's choice). To honor the author(s) of the year's outstanding monograph, article, or original paper in the field of acquisitions, collection development, and related areas of resource development in libraries. *Donor*: Blackwell/North America: *Winner*: Samuel G. Demas.

Bowker/Ulrich's Serials Librarianship Award ($1,500). For demonstrated leadership in serials-related activities through participation in professional associations and/or library education programs, contributions to the body of serials literature, research in the area of serials, or development of tools or methods to enhance access to or management of serials. *Donor*: R. R. Bowker Company/Ulrich's. *Winner*: Jean Hirons.

First Step Award (Wiley Professional Development Grant) ($1,500). For librarians new to the serials field to attend ALA's Annual Conference. *Donor*: John Wiley & Sons. *Winner*: Corinne C. Jacox.

Leadership in Library Acquisitions Award ($1,500). For significant contributions by an outstanding leader in the field of library acquisitions. *Donor*: Harrassowitz. *Winner*: Joseph W. Barker.

Margaret Mann Citation. To a cataloger or classifier for achievement in the areas of cataloging or classification. *Winner*: Arlene G. Taylor.

Esther J. Piercy Award ($1,500). To a librarian with fewer than ten years experience for contributions and leadership in the field of library collections and technical services. *Donor*: Yankee Book Peddler. *Winner*: Not awarded in 1996.

Association for Library Service to Children (ALSC)

ALSC/Book Wholesalers Summer Reading Program Grant ($3,000). To an ALSC member for implementation of an outstanding public library summer reading program for children. *Donor*: Book Wholesalers, Inc. *Winner*: Clark County Public Library, Winchester, KY.

ALSC/Econo-Clad Literature Program Award ($1,000). To an ALSC member who has developed and implemented an outstanding library program for children involving reading and the use of literature, to attend an ALA conference. *Donor*: Econo-Clad Books. *Winner*: Kathy Costa.

ALSC/REFORMA Pura Belpre Award. *Winners*: Judith Ortiz Coffer for narrative *An Island Like You: Stories of the Barrio*, Susan Guevara for illustration *Chato's Kitchen*.

May Hill Arbuthnot Honor Lecturer 1997. To invite an individual of distinction to prepare and present a paper that will be a significant contribution to the field of children's literature and that will subsequently be published in *Journal of Youth Services in Libraries*. *Winner*: Katherine Paterson.

Mildred L. Batchelder Award (citation). To an American publisher of an English-language translation of a children's book originally published in a foreign language in a foreign country. *Winner*: Houghton Mifflin for *The Lady with the Hat* by Uri Orlev.

Batchelder Honor Books. *Winners*: Walker and Company for *Star of Fear, Star of Hope* by Jo Hoestlandt; Henry Holt and Company for *Damned Strong Love: The True Story of Willi G. and Stephen K.* by Lutz van Dijk.

Louise Seaman Bechtel Fellowship ($3,750). For librarians with 12 or more years of professional level work in children's library collections, to read and study at the Baldwin Library/George Smathers Libraries, University of Florida (must be an ALSC member with an MLS from an

ALA-accredited program). *Donor*: Bechtel Fund. *Winner*: Jan Watkins.

Bound to Stay Bound Books Scholarship ($5,000). Two awards for study in the field of library service to children toward the MLS or beyond in an ALA-accredited program. *Donor*: Bound to Stay Bound Books. *Winners*: Debra Snyder, Kay Evey.

Caldecott Medal. *See* "Literary Prizes, 1996" by Gary Ink.

Andrew Carnegie Medal. To U.S. producer of the most distinguished video for children in the previous year. *Donor*: Carnegie Corporation of New York. *Winner*: Paul R. Gagne, Weston Woods Studios, for *Owen*, based on Kevin Henkes's Caldecott Honor Book.

Distinguished Service to ALSC Award ($1,000). To recognize significant contributions to, and an impact on, library services to children and/or ALSC. *Winner*: Ginny Moore Kruse.

Frederic G. Melcher Scholarship ($5,000). To students entering the field of library service to children for graduate work in an ALA-accredited program. *Winners*: Kathleen Kelly, Mara Beverwyk.

John Newbery Medal. *See* "Literary Prizes, 1996" by Gary Ink.

Putnam and Grosset Group Awards ($600). To children's librarians in school or public libraries with ten or fewer years of experience to attend ALA Annual Conference for the first time. Must be a member of ALSC. *Donor*: Putnam and Grosset Book Group. *Winners*: Meaghan M. Battle, Diane M. Lafrenaye, Judi Moreillon.

Laura Ingalls Wilder Medal. To an author or illustrator whose works have made a lasting contribution to children's literature. *Winner*: Not awarded in 1996.

Association of College and Research Libraries (ACRL)

ACRL Academic or Research Librarian of the Year Award ($3,000). For outstanding contribution to academic and research librarianship and library development. *Donor*: Baker & Taylor. *Winner*: Ralph E. Russell.

ACRL EBSS Distinguished Education and Behavioral Sciences Librarian Award (citation). To an academic librarian who has made an outstanding contribution as an education and/or behavioral sciences librarian through accomplishments and service to the profession. *Winner*: Not awarded in 1996.

ACRL Doctoral Dissertation Fellowship ($1,500). To a doctoral student in the field of academic librarianship whose research has potential significance in the field. *Winner*: Nongyao Premkamolnetr.

Hugh C. Atkinson Memorial Award. *See under* American Library Association.

Miriam Dudley Bibliographic Instruction Librarian Award ($1,000). For contribution to the advancement of bibliographic instruction in a college or research institution. *Donor*: Mountainside Publishing. *Winner*: Barbara MacAdam.

EBSCO Community College Leadership Award ($500). *Donor*: EBSCO Subscription Services. *Winner*: Margaret A. Holleman.

EBSCO Community College Learning Resources Award. *Donor*: EBSCO Subscription Services. *Winner*: Southwestern College Library, Chula Vista, CA.

Education Behavioral Sciences Section Librarian Award. *Winner*: Donald V. Osler.

Instruction Section Innovation in Instruction Award (citation). Recognizes and honors librarians who have developed and implemented innovative approaches to instruction within their institution in the preceding two years. *Winner*: Patricia Carroll-Mathes.

Instruction Section Publication of the Year Award (citation). Recognizes an outstanding publication related to instruction in a library environment published in the preceding two years. *Winner*: *Faculty Culture and Bibliographic Instruction: An Exploratory Analysis* by Larry Hardesty.

Marta Lange/*CQ* Award ($1,000). Recognizes an academic or law librarian for contributions to bibliography and information service in law or political science. *Donor*: Congressional Quarterly. *Winner*: Robert Goehlert

Samuel Lazerow Fellowship for Research in Acquisitions or Technical Services ($1,000).

To foster advances in acquisitions or technical services by providing librarians a fellowship for travel or writing in those fields. Sponsor: Institute for Scientific Information (ISI). *Winners*: Jimmie Lundgren, Betsy Simpson.

Katharine Kyes Leab and Daniel J. Leab American Book Prices Current Exhibition Catalog Awards (citations). For the three best catalogs published by American or Canadian institutions in conjunction with exhibitions of books and/or manuscripts. *Winners*: (First Division) *Sendak at the Rosenbach*, Rosenbach Museum and Library, Philadelphia; (Second Division) *In Praise of Aldus Manutius*, Pierpont Morgan Library, New York. (Third Division) *Garbage! The History and Politics of Trash in New York City*, New York Public Library.

Martinus Nijhoff International West European Specialist Study Grant (travel funding for up to 14 days research in Europe). Supports research pertaining to West European studies, librarianship, or the book trade. Sponsor: Martinus Nijhoff International. *Winner*: Eleanor O. Hofstetter.

Oberly Award for Bibliography in the Agricultural Sciences. Biennially, for the best English-language bibliography in the field of agriculture or a related science in the preceding two-year period. *Donor*: Eunice R. Oberly Fund. *Winner*: Not awarded in 1996.

Rare Books & Manuscripts Librarianship Award ($1,000). For articles of superior quality published in the ACRL journal *Rare Books & Manuscripts Librarianship*. *Donor*: Christie, Manson & Woods. *Winner*: Not awarded in 1996.

K. G. Saur Award for Best College and Research Libraries Article ($500). To author(s) to recognize the most outstanding article published in *College and Research Libraries* during the preceding year. *Donor*: K. G. Saur. *Winner*: Peter S. Graham.

Association of Specialized and Cooperative Library Agencies (ASCLA)

ASCLA Leadership Achievement Award. To recognize leadership and achievement in the areas of consulting, multitype library cooperation, and state library development. *Winners*: Millie Fry, Jacqueline Mundell.

ASCLA/National Organization on Disability Award for Library Service to People with Disabilities ($1,000). To institutions or organizations that have made the library's total service more accessible through changing physical and/or additional barriers. *Donor*: National Organization on Disability, funded by J. C. Penney. *Winner*: Loudoun Public Library, Leesburg, VA.

ASCLA Professional Achievement Award (citation). For professional achievement within the areas of consulting, networking, statewide services, and programs. *Winner*: Sandra Nelson.

ASCLA Research Grant ($500). To stimulate researchers to look at state library services, interlibrary cooperation, networking, and services to special populations as valid areas of research interest. *Donor*: Auto-Graphics, Inc. *Winner*: Not awarded in 1996.

ASCLA Service Award (citation). For outstanding service and leadership to the division. *Winner*: Barbara L. Perkis.

Francis Joseph Campbell Citation. For a contribution of recognized importance to library service for the blind and physically handicapped. *Winner*: Miriam Pace.

Exhibits Round Table

Accessibility for Attendees with Disabilities Award (citation). *Winner*: Highsmith Company, Inc.

Friendly Booth Award (citation). Cosponsor: New Members Round Table. *Winners*: First place, Pan Asian Publishing, Inc.; second place, Gingerbread Fun for Everyone; third place, ME Sharpe, Inc.

Kohlstedt Exhibit Award (citation). To companies or organizations for the best single, multiple, and island booth displays at the ALA Annual Conference. Citation. *Winners*: Storey/Garden Way Publishing, Highsmith Company, Inc., and H. W. Wilson Company.

Federal Librarians Round Table (FLRT)

Adelaide del Frate Conference Sponsor Award. To encourage library school students to become familiar with federal librarianship and ultimately seek work in federal libraries; for attendance at ALA Annual Conference and activities of the Federal Librarians Round Table. *Winner*: Emily Mandelbaum.

Distinguished Service Award (citation). To honor a FLRT member for outstanding and sustained contributions to the association and to federal librarianship. *Winner*: Arlene Leong.

Federal Librarians Achievement Award (citation). For leadership or achievement in the promotion of library and information science in the federal community. *Winner*: Not awarded in 1996.

Government Documents Round Table (GODORT)

James Bennett Childs Award. To a librarian or other individual for distinguished lifetime contributions to documents librarianship. *Winner*: Julia F. Wallace.

CIS/GODORT/ALA Documents to the People Award ($2,000). To an individual, library, organization, or noncommercial group that most effectively encourages or enhances the use of government documents in library services. *Donor*: Congressional Information Service, Inc. (CIS). *Winner*: Jack Sulzer.

Bernadine Abbott Hoduski Founders Award (plaque). To recognize documents librarians who may not be known at the national level but who have made significant contributions to the field of state, international, local, or federal documents. *Winner*: Not awarded in 1996.

Readex/GODORT/ALA Catharine J. Reynolds Award ($2,000). Grants to documents librarians for travel and/or study in the field of documents librarianship or area of study benefitting performance as documents librarians. *Donor*: Readex Corporation. *Winners*: Susan M. Ryan, George D. Barnum.

David Rozkuszka Scholarship ($3,000). To provide financial assistance to an individual who is currently working with government documents in a library while completing a master's program in library science. *Winner*: Linda Chia.

Intellectual Freedom Round Table (IFRT)

John Phillip Immroth Memorial Award for Intellectual Freedom ($500). For notable contribution to intellectual freedom fueled by personal courage. *Winner*: The Plaintiffs of *Stevena Case et al v. Unified School District*.

Eli M. Oboler Memorial Award ($1,500). Biennially, to an author of a published work in English or in English translation dealing with issues, events, questions, or controversies in the area of intellectual freedom. *Donor*: Providence Associates, Inc. *Winner*: Edward J. Cleary for *Beyond the Burning Cross: The First Amendment and the Landmark R.A.V. Case*.

State and Regional Achievement Award ($1,000). To the intellectual freedom committee of a state library state library media association, or a state/regional coalition for the most successful and creative project during the calendar year. *Donor*: Social Issues Resource Series, Inc. (SIRS). *Winner*: Long Island Coalition Against Censorship.

Library Administration and Management Association (LAMA)

Hugh C. Atkinson Memorial Award. *See under* American Library Association.

Certificate of Appreciation: *Winner*: Diane J. Graves.

John Cotton Dana Library Public Relations Awards. To libraries or library organizations of all types for public relations programs or special projects ended during the preceding year. *Donor*: H. W. Wilson Company. *Winners*: Association of Public Library Administrators of South Carolina, Sumter; Sterling C. Evans Library, Texas A&M University, College Station; Oklahoma Department of Libraries, Oklahoma City; Cherry Creek High School Library,

Englewood, CO; Birmingham (AL) Public Library; Denver (CO) Public Library; King County Library System, Seattle; New York Public Library; San Antonio (TX) Public Library; Westminster Public Library, Colorado.

Library Buildings Award (citation). A biannual award given to all types of libraries for excellence in architectural design and planning by an American architect. *Donor*: American Institute of Architects and LAMA. *Winner*: Not awarded in 1996.

Library and Information Technology Association (LITA)

Hugh C. Atkinson Memorial Award. *See under* American Library Association.

LITA/GEAC-CLSI Scholarship in Library and Information Technology ($3,000). For work toward an MLS in an ALA-accredited program with emphasis on library automation. *Donor*: CLSI, Inc. *Winner*: Angela Hodge.

LITA/Library Hi Tech Award ($1,000). To an individual or institution for a work that shows outstanding communication for continuing education in library and information technology. *Donor*: Pierian Press. *Winner*: University of Wisconsin, Madison Continuing Education Services Program.

LITA/LSSI Minority Scholarship in Library and Information Science ($3,000). To encourage a qualified member of a principal minority group, with a strong commitment to the use of automation in libraries, to enter library automation. *Donor*: Library Systems & Services, Inc. *Winner*: Maurice Okereke.

LITA/OCLC Minority Scholarship in Library and Information Technology ($3,000). To encourage a qualified member of a principal minority group, with a strong commitment to the use of automation in libraries, to enter library automation. *Donor*: OCLC. *Winner*: Yin-Fen Pao.

LITA Technology Achievement Award. *Winners*: Paul Sybrowsky, D. Keith Wilson.

Library History Round Table (LHRT)

Phyllis Dain Library History Dissertation Award ($500). To the author of a dissertation treating the history of books, libraries, librarianship, or information science. *Winner*: Not awarded in 1996.

Justin Winsor Prize Essay ($500). To an author of an outstanding essay embodying original historical research on a significant subject of library history. *Winner*: Wayne A. Wiegand for "The Amherst Method: The Origins of the Dewey Decimal Classification Scheme."

Library Research Round Table (LRRT)

Jesse H. Shera Award for Research ($500). For an outstanding and original paper reporting the results of research related to libraries. *Winner*: Not awarded in 1996.

Map and Geography Round Table (MAGERT)

MAGERT Honors Award (citation and cash award). To recognize outstanding contributions by a MAGERT personal member to map librarianship, MAGERT, and/or a specific MAGERT project. *Winner*: Robert W. Karrow, Jr.

New Members Round Table (NMRT)

NMRT/EBSCO Scholarship ($1,000). To a U.S. or Canadian citizen to begin an MLS degree in an ALA-accredited program. Candidates must be members of NMRT. *Donor*: EBSCO Subscription Services. *Winner*: Melissa Haraughty.

Shirley Olofson Memorial Award. Cash award for individuals to attend their second ALA Annual Conference. *Winner*: Antoinette Nelson.

3M/NMRT Professional Development Grant. To NMRT members to encourage professional development and participation in national ALA and NMRT activities. *Donor*: 3M. *Winners*: Susan Benjamin, Holly Nardini, S. Denise Sisco.

Public Library Association (PLA)

Advancement of Literacy Award (plaque). To a publisher, bookseller, hardware and/or software dealer, foundation or similar group that has made a significant contribution to the advancement of adult literacy. *Donor*: Library Journal. *Winner*: The Office of the Illinois Secretary of State.

Excellence in Small and/or Rural Public Service Award ($1,000). Honors a library serving a population of 10,000 or less that demonstrates excellence of service to its community as exemplified by an overall service program or a special program of significant accomplishment. *Donor*: EBSCO Subscription Services. *Winner*: Franklin County Public Library, Eastpoint, FL.

Allie Beth Martin Award ($3,000). Honors a librarian who, in a public library setting, has demonstrated extraordinary range and depth of knowledge about books or other library materials and has distinguished ability to share that knowledge. *Donor*: Baker & Taylor Books. *Winner*: William (Ted) Balcom.

New Leaders Travel Grant (up to $1,500 each). To enhance the professional development and improve the expertise of public librarians by making their attendance at major professional development activities possible. *Donor*: GEAC, Inc. *Winners:* Thomas Larry Bush, Susan L. Hauer, Barbara Kesel, Sandra Rosenfield.

Publishing Committee

Carnegie Reading List Awards (amount varies). To ALA units for preparation and publication of reading lists, indexes, and other bibliographical and library aids useful in U.S. circulating libraries. *Donor*: Andrew Carnegie Fund. *Winner*: ALSC Task Force for "Extending Your Museum Visit" ($4,080).

Whitney-Carnegie Awards ($5,000 maximum). For the preparation of bibliographic aids for research, with scholarly intent and general applicability. *Donor*: James Lyman Whitney and Andrew Carnegie Funds. *Winners:* John Waiblinger for *Guide to Lesbian Resources in Community Archives and Oral History Collections on the West Coast of the United States* ($5,000); Joanna Kruckenberg for *Pioneering Women Practitioners of Psychology: A Proposal for a Bibliographic Source Book* ($3,750).

Reference and Adult Services Division (RASD) (now Reference and User Services Association)

Dartmouth Medal. For creating current reference works of outstanding quality and significance. *Donor*: Dartmouth College, Hanover, New Hampshire. *Winners*: Macmillan Library Reference for *Civilizations of the Ancient Near East* edited by Jack M. Sasson, (honorable mention) Macmillan for *Encyclopedia of Bioethics* edited by Warren T. Reich, Yale University Press for *Encyclopedia of New York City*, edited by Kenneth T. Jackson.

Denali Press Award ($500). For creating reference works of outstanding quality and significance that provide information specifically about ethnic and minority groups in the United States. *Donor*: Denali Press. *Winners:* Nicolas Kanellos, Claudio Esteva-Fabregat.

Disclosure Student Travel Award (BRASS) ($1,000). To enable a student in an ALA-accredited master's program interested in a career as a business librarian to attend an ALA Annual Conference. *Donor*: Disclosure, Inc. *Winner*: Deborah Lynn Harrington.

Facts on File Grant ($2,000). To a library for imaginative programming that would make current affairs more meaningful to an adult audience. *Donor*: Facts on File, Inc. *Winner*: Beth Israel Learning Center at Beth Israel Hospital, Boston.

Gale Research Award for Excellence in Business Librarianship (BRASS) ($1,000). To an individual for distinguished activities in the field of business librarianship. *Donor*: Gale Research Co. *Winner*: Ruth A. Pagell.

Gale Research Award for Excellence in Reference and Adult Services. To a library or library system for developing an imaginative and unique library resource to meet patrons' reference needs ($1,000). *Donor*: Gale Research Co. *Winner*: Rochester Hills Public Library, Michigan.

Genealogical Publishing Company/History Section Award ($1,000). To encourage and commend professional achievement in historical reference and research librarianship. *Donor*: The Genealogical Publishing Company. *Winner*: Gunther Erich Pohl.

Margaret E. Monroe Library Adult Services Award (citation). To a librarian for impact on library service to adults. *Winner*: Connie Van Fleet.

Isadore Gilbert Mudge–R. R. Bowker Award ($1,500). For distinguished contributions to reference librarianship. *Winner*: Joe Morehead.

Reference Service Press Award ($1,000). To the author of the most outstanding article published in *RQ* during the preceding two volume years. *Donor*: Reference Service Press, Inc. *Winners*: Patricia Dewdney, Catherine Sheldrick Ross.

John Sessions Memorial Award (plaque). To a library or library system in recognition of work with the labor community. *Donor*: AFL/CIO. *Winner*: Metropolitan Detroit Professionals Library, UAW Local 2200.

Louis Shores Oryx Press Award ($1,000). To an individual, team, or organization to recognize excellence in reviewing of books and other materials for libraries. *Donor*: Oryx Press. *Winner*: Cheryl M. LaGuardia.

Social Responsibilities Round Table (SRRT)

Jackie Eubanks Memorial Award ($500). To honor outstanding achievement in promoting the acquisition and use of alternative media in libraries. *Donor*: AIP Task Force. *Winner*: Chris Dodge.

Coretta Scott King Awards. See "Literary Prizes, 1996" by Gary Ink.

SRRT Gay, Lesbian, and Bisexual Book Awards. To authors of fiction and non-fiction books of exceptional merit relating to the gay/lesbian experience. *Donor*: SRRT Gay Book Award Committee. *Winners*: Jim Grimsley for *Dream Boy* (fiction), Urvashi Vaid for *Virtual Equality: The Mainstreaming of Gay and Lesbian Liberation* (nonfiction).

Young Adult Library Services Association (YALSA)

Baker & Taylor Conference Grants ($1,000). To young adult librarians in public or school libraries to attend an ALA Annual Conference for the first time. Candidates must be members of YALSA and have one to ten years of library experience. *Donor*: Baker & Taylor Books. *Winners*: Jennifer Baltes, Linda B. Gray.

Book Wholesalers, Inc./YALSA Collection Development Grant ($1,000). To YALSA members who represent a public library and work directly with young adults, for collection development materials for young adults. *Winners*: Alison Kastner, Jean A. Wipf.

Econo-Clad/YALSA Literature Program Award ($1,000). To a YALSA member for development and implementation of an outstanding program for young adults, ages 12–18, involving reading and the use of literature. *Donor*: Econo-Clad Books. *Winner*: Not awarded in 1996.

Margaret A. Edwards Award ($1,000). To an author whose book or books have provided young adults with a window through which they can view their world and which will help them to grow and to understand themselves and their role in society. *Donor*: School Library Journal. *Winner*: Judy Blume.

Frances Henne/YALSA/VOYA Research Grant ($500 minimum). To provide seed money to an individual, institution, or group for a project to encourage research on library service to young adults. *Donor*: Voice of Youth Advocates. *Winners*: Evie Wilson-Lingbloom, Carol Doll, Barbara Carmody.

American Society for Information Science (ASIS)

ASIS Award of Merit. For an outstanding contribution to the field of information science. *Winner*: Jean Tague-Sutcliffe.

ASIS Best Information Science Book. *Winner*: Jean Tague-Sutcliffe for *Measuring Information: An Information Science Perspective Approach.*

ASIS Doctoral Dissertation Scholarship ($1,000). *Winner*: Abby Goodrum for *Evaluation of Text-Based and Image-Based Representations for Moving Image Documents.*

ASIS Doctoral Forum Award (travel reimbursement to ASIS annual meeting, up to $250). *Winner*: Howard Rosenbaum for *Managers and Information in Organizations: Towards a Structural Concept of the Information Use Environment of Managers.*

ASIS Outstanding Information Science Teacher Award ($500). *Winner*: Stephanie Haas, University of North Carolina.

ASIS Research Award. For a systematic program of research in a single area at a level beyond the single study, recognizing contributions in the field of information science. *Winner*: Gary Marchionini.

ASIS Special Award. To recognize long-term contributions to the advancement of information science and technology and enhancement of public access to information and discovery of mechanisms for improved transfer and utilization of knowledge. *Winner*: Douglas Engelbart.

Cretsos Leadership Award. *Winners:* Kristen Liberman, Lotus Notes.

JASIS Paper Award. *Winners:* Christine L. Borgman, Sandra G. Hirsch Virginia A. Walter, Andrea L. Gallagher for *Children's Searching Behavior on Browsing and Keyword Online Catalogs: The Science Library Catalog Project.*

Pratt Severn Student Research Award. *Winner:* Mark Spasser for *The Enacted Fate of Undiscovered Public Knowledge.*

Art Libraries Society of North America (ARLIS/NA)

Chadwyck-Healey Professional Development Award ($500). To encourage contribution to the society by participating as a moderator, panelist, or presenter of a paper at the ARLIS/NA annual conference. *Winner*: Not awarded in 1996.

Florence DaLuiso Award. *Winner*: Not awarded in 1996.

Jim and Anna Emmett Travel Award ($600). To assist information professionals who are physically challenged to participate in the ARLIS/NA annual conference. *Winner*: Not awarded in 1996.

G. K. Hall Conference Attendance Award ($400). To encourage attendance at the annual conference by ARLIS/NA committee members, chapter officers, and moderators. *Winner*: Madelyn Cook.

Howard Karno Travel Award ($1,000). To provide financial assistance to a professional art librarian from Mexico or Latin America to attend the ARLIS/NA annual conference. Cosponsor: Howard Karno Books. *Winner*: Nelva Quevedo Pacheco.

Léonce Laget Travel Award ($1,000). To provide financial assistance for an art information professional from outside North America to attend the ARLIS/NA annual conference. Cosponsor: Librairie Léonce Laget. *Winner*: Mireille Etignard.

Nancy Pohlmann McCauley Travel Award. *Winner*: Not awarded in 1996.

Fraiser McConnell Travel Award ($500). For members of an ethnic or cultural group under-represented within ARLIS/NA. *Winner*: Not awarded in 1996.

David Mirvish Books/Books on Art Travel Award ($500 Canadian). To encourage art librarianship in Canada. *Winner*: Linda Bren.

Norman Ross Travel Award. To encourage professional development through attendance at the ARLIS/NA annual conference. *Winner*: Not awarded in 1996.

Association for Library and Information Science Education (ALISE)

ALISE Doctoral Student Dissertation Awards ($400). To promote the exchange of research ideas between doctoral students and established researchers. *Winner*: Danuta A. Nitecki.

ALISE Methodology Paper Competition ($250). To stimulate the communication of research methodology *Winner*: Ronald Day.

ALISE Research Award ($2,500). For a project that reflects ALISE goals and objectives. *Winner*: Ronald Day.

ALISE Research Paper Competition ($500). For a research paper concerning any aspect

of librarianship or information studies by a member of ALISE. *Winner*: Paul Solomon.
Jane Anne Hannigan Research Award ($500). *Winner*: Not awarded in 1996.

Association of Jewish Libraries (AJL)

AJL Bibliography Book Award. *Winner*: Ann R. Shapiro, Sara R. Horowitz, Ellen Schiff, Miriyam Glazer, for *Jewish American Women Writers: A Bio-Bibliographical and Critical Sourcebook.*
AJL Reference Book Award. *Winner:* Benjamin Richler, for *Guide to Hebrew Manuscript Collections.*
Special Body of Work Citation. *Winner:* Nathan M. Kaganoff for *Judaica Americana*, an annotated bibliography of publications from 1960 to 1990. (Awarded posthumously).
Sydney Taylor Children's Book Award. *Winners*: Jo Hoestlandt, Johanna Kang (illus.), for *Star of Fear, Star of Hope.*
Sydney Taylor Manuscript Award. *Winner*: Donna Brown Agins for *Passover Promise.*
Sydney Taylor Older Children's Book Award. *Winner*: Ida Vos for *Dancing on the Bridge of Avignon.*

Beta Phi Mu

Beta Phi Mu Award. *See under* American Library Association.
Harold Lancour Scholarship for Foreign Study ($1,000). For graduate study in a foreign country related to the applicant's work or schooling. *Winner*: Lois C. Rogers.
Sarah Rebecca Reed Scholarship ($1,500). For study at an ALA-accredited library school. *Winner*: Barbara D'Angelo.
Frank B. Sessa Scholarship for Continuing Professional Education ($750). For continuing education for a Beta Phi Mu member. *Winner*: Jennifer Frankel.

Canadian Library Association (CLA)

CLA Award for Achievement in Technical Services. *Winner*: Not awarded in 1996.
CLA Award for the Advancement of Intellectual Freedom in Canada. *Winner*: Burlington Public Library, Burlington, ON.
CLA/Information Today Award for Innovative Technology. *Donor*: Information Today Inc. *Winner*: Richmond Public Library, Richmond, BC.
CLA Outstanding Service to Librarianship Award. *Donor*: Reed Reference Publishing/R. R. Bowker. *Winner*: Diane Macquarrie.
CLA Research and Development Grant ($1,000). *Winner*: Eileen Daniel.
CLA Student Article Award. *Winner*: Rebecca Hunt.

Canadian Association of College and University Libraries (CACUL)

CACUL Award for Outstanding Academic Librarian. *Winner*: Frances Groen.
CACUL Innovation Achievement Award ($1,500). *Winner*: Electronic Library Network, Burnaby, BC.
CACUL/CTCL Award of Merit. *Winners*: To be announced.

Canadian Association of Public Libraries (CAPL)

CAPL Outstanding Public Library Service Award. *Winner*: Gladys Watson.
CAPL/Faxon Marketing Award. *Winner*: Not awarded in 1996.

Canadian Association of Special Libraries and Information Services (CASLIS)

CASLIS Award for Special Librarianship in Canada. *Winner*: Marie DeYoung.

Canadian Library Trustees Association (CLTA)

CLTA Achievement in Literacy Award. For an innovative literacy program by a public library board. *Donor*: ABC Canada. *Winner*: Not awarded in 1996.
CLTA Merit Award for Distinguished Service as a Public Library Trustee. For outstanding leadership in the advancement of public library trusteeship and public library service in Canada. *Winner*: Elizabeth Hoffman.

Canadian School Library Association (CSLA)

National Book Service Teacher-Librarian of the Year Award. *Winner*: Judith Dueck, Winnipeg School Division No. 1 School Board.

Margaret B. Scott Award of Merit. For the development of school libraries in Canada. *Winner*: Victoria Pennell, Avalon Consolidated School Board.

Chinese-American Librarians Association (CALA)

Sheila Suen Lai Scholarship ($500). To a student of Chinese nationality or descent pursuing full-time graduate studies for a master's degree or Ph.D. degree in an ALA-accredited library school. *Winners*: Adrian Ho, Xiaotian Chen.

C. C. Seetoo/CALA Conference Travel Scholarship ($500). For a student to attend the ALA Annual Conference and CALKA program. *Winner*: Pui-Ching Ho.

Church and Synagogue Library Association (CSLA)

CSLA Award for Outstanding Congregational Librarian. For distinguished service to the congregation and/or community through devotion to the congregational library. *Winner*: Sheila Liu.

CSLA Award for Outstanding Congregational Library. For responding in creative and innovative ways to the library's mission of reaching and serving the congregation and/or the wider community. *Winner*: Moses I. Polowin Memorial Library in the Saint John Jewish Historical Museum, Saint John, New Brunswick, Canada.

CSLA Award for Outstanding Contribution to Congregational Libraries. For providing inspiration, guidance, leadership, or resources to enrich the field of church or synagogue librarianship. *Winner*: Lois Ward.

Helen Keating Ott Award for Outstanding Contribution to Congregational Libraries. *Winner*: Marjorie Ainsborough Decker.

Pat Tabler Memorial Scholarship Award. *Winner*: Lena Coffman.

Muriel Fuller Scholarship Award. *Winner*: Wilma Preissler.

Council on Library Resources, Commission on Preservation and Access (CLR/CPA)

Grants. For a partial list of the recipients of grants, see the report from the Council on Library Resources/Commission on Preservation and Access in Part 1.

Gale Research Company

ALTA/Gale Outstanding Trustee Conference Grant Award. *See under* American Library Association, American Library Trustee Association.

Gale Research Award for Excellence in Business Librarianship; and Gale Research Award for Excellence in Reference and Adult Services. *See under* American Library Association, Reference and Adult Services Division.

Gale Research Financial Development Award. *See under* American Library Association.

Medical Library Association (MLA)

Estelle Brodman Award for the Academic Medical Librarian of the Year. To honor significant achievement, potential for leadership, and continuing excellence at mid-career in the area of academic health sciences librarianship. *Winner*: Gale G. Hannigan.

Cunningham Memorial International Fellowship ($3,000). A six-month grant and travel expenses in the United States and Canada for a foreign librarian. *Winner*: W. R. G. deSilva.

Louise Darling Medal. For distinguished achievement in collection development in the health sciences. *Winner*: National Library of Medicine Preservation Program for Biomedical Literature.

Janet Doe Lectureship ($250). *Winner*: Robert M. Brande.
EBSCO/MLA Annual Meeting Grant ($1,000). *Winners*: Kathryn Chmiel, Carol Swank.
Ida and George Eliot Prize ($200). For an essay published in any journal in the preceding calendar year that has been judged most effective in furthering medical librarianship. *Donor*: Login Brothers Books. *Winners*: Deborah L. Adams, Carole M. Gilbert, Michele S. Klein, Faith V. Ross.
Murray Gottlieb Prize ($100). For the best unpublished essay submitted by a medical librarian on the history of some aspect of health sciences or a detailed description of a library exhibit. *Donor*: Ralph and Jo Grimes. *Winner*: Stephen J. Greenberg.
Joseph Leiter NLM/MLA Lectureship. *Winner*: Larry Smarr.
MLA Award for Distinguished Public Service. *Winners*: Nancy Kassebaum, John Porter.
MLA Award for Excellence and Achievement in Hospital Librarianship ($500). To a member of the MLA who has made significant contributions to the profession in the area of overall distinction or leadership in hospital librarianship. *Winner*: Michele S. Klein.
MLA Doctoral Fellowship ($1,000). *Donor*: Institute for Scientific Information (ISI). *Winner*: Gale G. Hannigan.
MLA Scholarship ($2,000). For graduate study in medical librarianship at an ALA-accredited library school. *Winner*: Sally K. Fessler.
MLA Scholarship for Minority Students ($2,000). *Winner*: Jean Chung.
John P. McGovern Award Lectureships ($500). *Winners*: Michael P. D'Allesandro, Jeffrey R. Galvin.
Marcia C. Noyes Award. For an outstanding contribution to medical librarianship. The award is the highest professional distinction of MLA. *Winner*: Lucretia W. McClure.
Rittenhouse Award ($500). For the best unpublished paper on medical librarianship submitted by a student enrolled in, or having been enrolled in, a course for credit in an ALA-accredited library school or a trainee in an internship program in medical librarianship. *Donor*: Rittenhouse Medical Bookstore. *Winner*: Jennifer K. Lloyd.
Frank Bradway Rogers Information Advancement Award ($500). For an outstanding contribution to knowledge of health science information delivery. *Donor*: Institute for Scientific Information (ISI). *Winner*: Julie McGowan.

K. G. Saur (Munich, Germany)

Hans-Peter Geh Grant. To enable a librarian from the former Soviet Union to attend a conference in Germany or elsewhere. *Winner*: Elena B. Artem'eva, State Public Scientific Library for Scientific and Technological Literature, Novosibirsk.
Gustav Hofmann Study Grant. To allow a librarian in a country where librarianship is a newly developing profession to study an issue in one or more countries of Western Europe. *Winner*: Kejing Liu (China).
K. G. Saur Award for Best College and Research Libraries Article. *See under* American Library Association, Association of College and Research Libraries.

Society of American Archivists (SAA)

Philip M. Hamer–Elizabeth Hamer Kegan Award. For individuals and/or institutions that have increased public awareness of a specific body of documents. *Winners*: Julie Daniels, Judy Hohmann, Jean West, New York State Archives and Records Administration, for *Consider the Source: Historical Records in the Classroom*.
J. Franklin Jameson Award for Archival Advocacy. *Winner*: Richard Benson.
Sister M. Claude Lane Award. For a significant contribution to the field of religious archives. *Winner*: Sister Blaithin Sullivan, archivist, Sisters of St. Joseph, Boston.
Waldo Gifford Leland Prize. For writing of superior excellence and usefulness in the field of archival history, theory, or practice. *Winner*: Charles H. Lesser for *South Carolina Begins: The Records of a Proprietary Colony, 1663–1721*.

Minority Student Award. Encourages minority students to consider careers in the archival profession and promotes minority participation in the Society of American Archivists with complimentary registration to the annual meeting. *Winner*: Letha Johnson.

Theodore Calvin Pease Award. For superior writing achievements by students enrolled in archival administration classes or engaged in formal archival internship programs. *Winner*: Shauna McRanor.

Preservation Publication Award. Recognizes the author of an outstanding work published in North America that advances the theory or the practice of preservation in archival institutions. *Winner*: Anne R. Kenney, Stephen Chapman, for *Tutorial—Digital Resolution Requirements for Replacing Text Based Material: Methods for Benchmarking Image Quality.*

SAA Fellows. Highest individual distinction awarded to a limited number of members for their outstanding contribution to the archival profession. *Honored:* Thomas Elton Brown, National Archives and Records Administration; Elaine Engst, Cornell University; Mary Janzen, Newberry Library; Leon Stout, Pennsylvania State University.

Special Libraries Association (SLA)

Mary Adeline Connor Professional Development Scholarship ($6,000). *Winner*: Not awarded in 1996.

John Cotton Dana Award. For exceptional support and encouragement of special librarianship. *Winners*: Not awarded in 1996.

Steven I. Goldspiel Research Grant. Sponsor: Disclosure, Inc. *Winners*: F. W. Lancaster, Linda C. Smith.

Hall of Fame Award. To a member of the association at or near the end of an active professional career for an extended and sustained period of distinguished service to the association. *Winners*: Muriel Regan, Catherine Scott.

SLA Affirmative Action Scholarship ($6,000). *Winner*: Colleen Trollinger.

SLA Fellows. *Winners*: Monica Ertel, Guy St. Clair, Ruth Seidman.

SLA Information Today Award for Innovations in Technology. *Winner*: George Schlukbier.

SLA President's Award. *Winner*: Not awarded in 1996.

SLA Professional Award. *Winner*: Ann W. Talcott.

SLA Student Scholarships ($6,000). For students with financial need who show potential for special librarianship. *Winners*: Sandy Oelschlegel, Karen Dominique Hallett, Andrea Wilson.

SLA H. W. Wilson Company Award. For the most outstanding article in the past year's *Special Libraries*. *Donor*: H. W. Wilson Company. *Winner*: Not awarded in 1996.

Alphabetical List of Award Names

Individual award names are followed by a colon and the name of the awarding body; e.g., the Bound to Stay Bound Books Scholarship is given by ALA/Association for Library Service to Children. Consult the preceding list of Library Scholarship and Award Recipients, 1996, which is alphabetically arranged by organization, to locate recipients and further information. Awards named for individuals are listed by surname.

AALL Scholarships: American Association of Law Libraries

AASL ABC/Clio Leadership Grant: ALA/American Association of School Librarians

AASL/Highsmith Research Grant: ALA/American Association of School Librarians

AASL Information Plus Continuing Education Scholarship: ALA/American Association of School Librarians

AASL President's Crystal Apple Award: ALA/American Association of School Librarians

AASL School Librarians Workshop Scholarship: ALA/American Association of School Librarians

ACRL Academic or Research Librarian of the Year Award: ALA/Association of College and Research Libraries

ACRL/EBSS Distinguished Education and Behavioral Sciences Librarian Award: ALA/Association of College and Research Libraries

ACRL Doctoral Dissertation Fellowship: ALA/Association of College and Research Libraries

AJL Bibliography Book Award: Association of Jewish Libraries

AJL Reference Book Award: Association of Jewish Libraries

ALA/Information Today Library of the Future Award: ALA

ALISE Doctoral Student Dissertation Awards: Association for Library and Information Science Education

ALISE Methodology Paper Competition: Association for Library and Information Science Education

ALISE Research Award: Association for Library and Information Science Education

ALISE Research Paper Competition: Association for Library and Information Science Education

ALSC/Book Wholesalers Summer Reading Program Grant: ALA/Association for Library Service to Children

ALSC/Econo-Clad Literature Program Award: ALA/Association for Library Service to Children

ALSC/REFORMA Pura Belpre Award: ALA/Association for Library Service to Children

ALTA/Gale Outstanding Trustee Conference Grant Award: ALA/American Library Trustee Association
ALTA Literacy Award: ALA/American Library Trustee Association
ALTA Major Benefactors Honor Awards: ALA/American Library Trustee Association
ASCLA Leadership Achievement Award: ALA/Association of Specialized and Cooperative Library Agencies
ASCLA/National Organization on Disability Award: ALA/Association of Specialized and Cooperative Library Agencies
ASCLA Professional Achievement Award: ALA/Association of Specialized and Cooperative Library Agencies
ASCLA Research Award: ALA/Association of Specialized and Cooperative Library Agencies
ASCLA Service Award: ALA/Association of Specialized and Cooperative Library Agencies
ASIS Award of Merit: American Society for Information Science
ASIS Best Information Science Book: American Society for Information Science
ASIS Doctoral Forum Award: American Society for Information Science
ASIS Doctoral Dissertation Scholarship: American Society for Information Science
ASIS Outstanding Information Science Teacher Award: American Society for Information Science
ASIS Research Award: American Society for Information Science
ASIS Special Award: American Society for Information Science
Accessibility for Attendees with Disabilities Award: ALA/Exhibits Round Table
Advancement of Literacy Award: ALA/Public Library Association
May Hill Arbuthnot Honor Lecturer: ALA/Association for Library Service to Children
Armed Forces Library Certificate of Merit: ALA/Armed Forces Libraries Round Table
Armed Forces Libraries Round Table Newsbank Scholarship Award: ALA/Armed Forces Libraries Round Table
Armed Forces Libraries Round Table Achievement Citation: ALA/Armed Forces Libraries Round Table
Hugh C. Atkinson Memorial Award: ALA
Award for the Advancement of Intellectual Freedom in Canada: Canadian Library Association
Carroll Preston Baber Research Grant: ALA
Baker & Taylor Conference Grants: ALA/Young Adult Library Services Association
Mildred L. Batchelder Award: ALA/Association for Library Service to Children
Batchelder Honor Books: ALA/Association for Library Service to Children

Louise Seaman Bechtel Fellowship: ALA/Association for Library Service to Children
Best of LRTS Award: ALA/Association for Library Collections and Technical Services
Beta Phi Mu Award: ALA
Blackwell/North America Scholarship Award: ALA/Association for Library Collections and Technical Services
Bogle International Travel Fund Award: ALA
Book Wholesalers, Inc. Collection Development Grant: ALA/Young Adult Library Services Association
Bound to Stay Bound Books Scholarship: ALA/Association for Library Service to Children
Bowker/Ulrich's Serials Librarianship Award: ALA/Association for Library Collections and Technical Services, Serials Section
William Boyd Military Novel Award: ALA
Estelle Brodman Award for the Academic Medical Librarian of the Year: Medical Library Association
CACUL Award for Outstanding Academic Librarian: Canadian Association of College and University Libraries
CACUL Innovation Achievement Award: Canadian Association of College and University Libraries
CACUL/CTCL Award of Merit: Canadian Association of College and University Libraries
CAPL Outstanding Public Library Service Award: Canadian Association of Public Libraries
CAPL/Faxon Marketing Award: Canadian Association of Public Libraries
CASLIS Award for Special Librarianship in Canada: Canadian Association of Special Libraries and Information Services
CIS/GODORT/ALA Documents to the People Award: ALA/Government Documents Round Table
CLA Award for Achievement in Technical Services: Canadian Library Association
CLA Award for the Advancement of Intellectual Freedom in Canada: Canadian Library Association
CLA/Information Today Award for Innovative Technology: Canadian Library Association
CLA Outstanding Service to Librarianship Award: Canadian Library Association
CLA Research and Development Grants: Canadian Library Association
CLA Student Article Award: Canadian Library Association
CLTA Achievement in Literacy Award: Canadian Library Trustees Association
CLTA Merit Award for Distinguished Service as a Public Library Trustee: Canadian Library Trustees Association

CSLA Award for Outstanding Congregational Librarian: Church and Synagogue Library Association
CSLA Award for Outstanding Congregational Library: Church and Synagogue Library Association
CSLA Award for Outstanding Contribution to Congregational Libraries: Church and Synagogue Library Association
Francis Joseph Campbell Citation: ALA/Association of Specialized and Cooperative Library Agencies
Andrew Carnegie Medal: ALA/Association for Library Service to Children
Carnegie Reading List Awards: ALA/Publishing Committee
Marshall Cavendish Scholarship: ALA
Certificate of Appreciation: ALA/Library Administration and Management Association
Chadwyck-Healey Professional Development Award: Art Libraries Society of North America
James Bennett Childs Award: ALA/Government Documents Round Table
David H. Clift Scholarship: ALA
Mary Adeline Connor Professional Development Scholarship: Special Libraries Association
Shirley Crawford Minority Scholarship: ALA
Cretsos Leadership Award: American Society for Information Science
Cunningham Memorial International Fellowship: Medical Library Association
Phyllis Dain Library History Dissertation Award: ALA/Library History Round Table
Florence DaLuiso Award: Art Libraries Society of North America
John Cotton Dana Award: Special Libraries Association
John Cotton Dana Library Public Relations Award: ALA/Library Administration and Management Association
Louise Darling Medal: Medical Library Association
Dartmouth Medal: ALA/Reference and Adult Services Division
Adelaide del Frate Conference Sponsor Award: ALA/Federal Librarians Round Table
Denali Press Award: ALA/Reference and Adult Services Division
Disclosure Student Travel Award (BRASS): ALA/Reference and Adult Services Division
Distinguished School Administrators Award: ALA/American Association of School Librarians
Distinguished Service Award: ALA/Federal Librarians Round Table
Distinguished Service Award, AASL/Baker & Taylor: ALA/American Association of School Librarians
Distinguished Service to ALSC Award: ALA/Association for Library Service to Children

Janet Doe Lectureship: Medical Library Association
Tom C. Drewes Scholarship: ALA
Miriam Dudley Bibliographic Instruction Librarian of the Year: ALA/ Association of College and Research Libraries
EBSCO ALA Conference Sponsorships: ALA
EBSCO Community College Leadership Resources Achievement Awards: ALA/Association of College and Research Libraries
EBSCO Community College Learning Resources Award: ALA/Association of College and Research Libraries
EBSCO/MLA Annual Meeting Grant: Medical Library Association
Econo-Clad/YALSA Literature Program Award: ALA/Young Adult Library Services Association
Margaret A. Edwards Award: ALA/Young Adult Library Services Association
Education Behavioral Sciences Section Library Award: ALA/Association of College and Research Libraries
Ida and George Eliot Prize: Medical Library Association
Jim and Anna Emmett Travel Award: Art Libraries Society of North America
Equality Award: ALA
Jackie Eubanks Memorial Award: ALA/Social Responsibilities Round Table
Excellence in Small and/or Rural Public Service Award: ALA/Public Library Association
Facts on File Grant: ALA/Reference and Adult Services Division
Federal Librarians Achievement Award: ALA/Federal Librarians Round Table
First Step Award, Serials Section/Wiley Professional Development Grant: ALA/Association for Library Collections and Technical Services
Freedom to Read Foundation Roll of Honor Awards: ALA
Friendly Booth Award: ALA/Exhibits Round Table
Loleta D. Fyan Award: ALA
Gale Research Award for Excellence in Business Librarianship (BRASS): ALA/Reference and Adult Services Division
Gale Research Award for Excellence in Reference and Adult Services: ALA/Reference and Adult Services Division
Gale Research Financial Development Award: ALA
Mary V. Gaver Scholarship: ALA
Hans-Peter Geh Grant: K. G. Saur
Genealogical Publishing Company/History Section Award: ALA/Reference and Adult Services Division
Louise Giles Minority Scholarship: ALA
Steven I. Goldspiel Research Grant: Special Libraries Association
Murray Gottlieb Prize: Medical Library Association
Grolier Foundation Award: ALA
Grolier National Library Week Grant: ALA

G. K. Hall Award for Library Literature: ALA
G. K. Hall Conference Attendance Award: Art Libraries Society of North America
Hall of Fame Award: Special Libraries Association
Philip M. Hamer–Elizabeth Hamer Kegan Award: Society of American Archivists
Jane Anne Hannigan Research Award: Association for Library and Information Science Education
Frances Henne Award: ALA/American Association of School Librarians
Frances Henne/YALSA/VOYA Reserach Grant: ALA/Young Adult Library Services Association
Bernadine Abbott Hoduski Founders Award: ALA/Government Documents Round Table
Gustav Hoffmann Study Grant: K. G. Saur
Miriam L. Hornback Scholarship: ALA
Paul Howard Award for Courage: ALA
John Ames Humphry/OCLC/Forest Press Award: ALA
John Phillip Immroth Memorial Award for Intellectual Freedom: ALA/Intellectual Freedom Round Table
Instruction Section Innovation in Instruction Award: ALA/Association of College and Research Libraries
Instruction Section Publication of the Year Award: ALA/Association of College and Research Libraries
J. Franklin Jameson Award for Archival Advocacy: Society of American Archivists
JASIS Paper Award: American Society for Information Science
Howard Karno Travel Award: Art Libraries Society of North America
Kohlstedt Exhibit Award: ALA/Exhibits Round Table
LITA/GEAC-CLSI Scholarship in Library and Information Technology: ALA/Library and Information Technology Association
LITA/Library Hi Tech Award: ALA/Library and Information Technology Association
LITA/LSSI Minority Scholarship in Library and Information Science: ALA/Library and Information Technology Association
LITA/OCLC Minority Scholarship in Library and Information Technology: ALA/Library and Information Technology Association
LITA Technology Achievement Award: ALA/Library and Information Technology Association
Léonce Laget Travel Award: Art Libraries Society of North America
Sheila Suen Lai Scholarship: Chinese-American Librarians Association
Harold Lancour Scholarship for Foreign Study: Beta Phi Mu
Marta Lange/*CQ* Award: ALA/Association of College and Research Libraries

Sister M. Claude Lane Award: Society of American Archivists
Samuel Lazerow Fellowship for Research in Acquisitions or Technical Services: ALA/Association of College and Research Libraries
Katharine Kyes Leab and Daniel J. Leab American Book Prices Current Exhibition Catalogue Awards: ALA/Association of College and Research Libraries
Leadership in Library Acquisitions Award: ALA/Association for Library Collections and Technical Services
Tony B. Leisner Scholarship: ALA
Joseph Leiter NLM/MLA Lectureship: Medical Library Association
Waldo Gifford Leland Prize: Society of American Archivists
Library Buildings Award: ALA/Library Administration and Management Association
Joseph W. Lippincott Award: ALA
MAGERT Honors Award: ALA/Map and Geography Round Table
MLA Award for Distinguished Public Service: Medical Library Association
MLA Award for Excellence and Achievement in Hospital Librarianship: Medical Library Association
MLA Doctoral Fellowship: Medical Library Association
MLA Scholarship: Medical Library Association
MLA Scholarship for Minority Students: Medical Library Association
Nancy Pohlmann McCauley Travel Award: Art Libraries Society of North America
Fraiser McConnell Travel Award: Art Libraries Society of North America
John P. McGovern Award Lectureships: Medical Library Association
Margaret Mann Citation: ALA/Association for Library Collections and Technical Services
Marshall Cavendish Scholarship: ALA
Allie Beth Martin Award: ALA/Public Library Association
Frederic G. Melcher Scholarship: ALA/Association for Library Service to Children
Microcomputer in the Media Center Award: ALA/American Association of School Librarians
Minority Student Award: Society of American Archivists
David Mirvish Books/Books on Art Travel Award: Art Libraries Society of North America
Margaret E. Monroe Library Adult Services Award: ALA/Reference and Adult Services Division
Bessie Boehm Moore Award: ALA
Isadore Gilbert Mudge–R. R. Bowker Award: ALA/Reference and Adult Services Division
NMRT/EBSCO Scholarship: ALA/New Members Round Table
NMRT/3M Professional Development Grant: ALA/New Members Round Table

National Book Service Teacher-Librarian of the Year Award: Canadian School Library Association
National School Library Media Program of the Year Award: ALA/American Association of School Librarians
New Leaders Travel Grant: ALA/Public Library Association
Martinus Nijhoff International West European Specialist Study Grant: ALA/Association of College and Research Libraries
Marcia C. Noyes Award: Medical Library Association
Oberly Award for Bibliography in the Agricultural Sciences: ALA/Association of College and Research Libraries
Eli M. Oboler Memorial Award: ALA/Intellectual Freedom Round Table
Shirley Olofson Memorial Award: ALA/New Members Round Table
Helen Keating Ott Award for Outstanding Contribution to Congregational Libraries: Church and Synagogue Library Association
Theodore Calvin Pease Award: Society of American Archivists
Esther J. Piercy Award: ALA/Association for Library Collections and Technical Services
Preservation Publication Award: Society of American Archivists
Pratt Severn Student Research Award: American Society for Information Science
Putnam and Grosset Book Group Awards: ALA/Association for Library Service to Children
Rare Books & Manuscripts Librarianship Award: ALA/Association of College and Research Libraries
Readex/GODORT/ALA Catharine J. Reynolds Award: ALA/Government Documents Round Table
Sarah Rebecca Reed Scholarship: Beta Phi Mu
Reference Service Press Award: ALA/Reference and Adult Services Division
Rittenhouse Award: Medical Library Association
Frank Bradway Rogers Information Advancement Award: Medical Library Association
Norman Ross Travel Award: Art Libraries Society of North America
David Rozkuszka Scholarship: ALA/Government Documents Round Table
SAA Fellows: Society of American Archivists
SLA Affirmative Action Scholarship: Special Libraries Association
SLA Fellows: Special Libraries Association
SLA Information Today Award for Innovations in Technology: Special Libraries Association
SLA President's Award: Special Libraries Association
SLA Professional Award: Special Libraries Association
SLA Student Scholarships: Special Libraries Association
SLA H. W. Wilson Award: Special Libraries Association

SRRT/Gay and Lesbian Task Force, Gay, Lesbian, and Bisexual Book Awards: ALA/Social Responsibilities Round Table
K. G. Saur Award for Best College and Research Libraries Article: ALA/Association of College and Research Libraries
Margaret B. Scott Award of Merit: Canadian School Library Association
C. C. Seetoo/CALA Conference Travel Scholarship: Chinese-American Librarians Association
Frank B. Sessa Scholarship for Continuing Professional Education: Beta Phi Mu
John Sessions Memorial Award: ALA/Reference and Adult Services Division
Jesse H. Shera Award for Research: ALA/Library Research Round Table
Louis Shores Oryx Press Award: ALA/Reference and Adult Services Division
Special Body of Work Citation: Association of Jewish Libraries
State and Regional Achievement Award–Freedom to Read Foundation: ALA/Intellectual Freedom Round Table
Pat Tabler Memorial Scholarship: Church and Synagogue Library Association
Sydney Taylor Children's Book Award: Association of Jewish Libraries
Sydney Taylor Manuscript Award: Association of Jewish Libraries
Sydney Taylor Older Children's Book Award: Association of Jewish Libraries
Trustee Citations: ALA/American Library Trustee Association
Whitney-Carnegie Awards: ALA/Publishing Committee
Laura Ingalls Wilder Award: ALA/Association for Library Service to Children
H. W. Wilson Library Staff Development Grant: ALA
Justin Winsor Prize Essay: ALA/Library History Round Table
World Book ALA Goal Grants: ALA

Part 4
Research and Statistics

Library Research and Statistics

Research on Libraries and Librarianship in 1996

Mary Jo Lynch
Director, Office for Research and Statistics, American Library Association

The most important research event of the year occurred on November 1 and 2 in Tallahassee, Florida. ALA's Library and Research Round Table (LRRT) sponsored Library Research Seminar I, titled "Partners and Paradigms: Library and Research in the Information Age." This first national Library Research Seminar met at Florida State University's Graduate School of Library and Information Studies with 115 educators, researchers, practitioners, and doctoral students attending. This seminar was designed to further the development of research-based knowledge for the library and information profession to explore interdisciplinary views and new methodological approaches and to encourage collaborative research by practicing professionals and educators. Sponsors of the event were the Council on Library Resources (CLR), the Online Computer Library Center (OCLC), Ablex, the Library History Round Table (LHRT), the Library Research Round Table (LRRT), and Beta Phi Mu.

Speakers from 20 U.S. states and from Canada and Sweden presented 36 papers in concurrent sessions. A sampling of paper titles indicates the variety of topics and methodologies presented. Doris Fidishur of Penn State described "Using Symbolic Interaction in Library Research." Tom Peters of Northern Illinois University spoke about "Web Server Logs as Data Sources for Library and Information Science Research." Mark Kinnacan of the University of Western Ontario and Mark Ferguson of the University of Toronto presented the paper "Public Opinion Toward User Fees in Public Libraries." Shirley Fitzgibbons of Indiana University described "A Multiple-Operational Approach to Assessing the Factors that Motivate Youth to Read and Enjoy Reading."

Participants also heard three invited papers: Clifford A. Lynch of the Division of Library Automation at the University of California spoke on "Networked Information Community and Technology"; Theresa Sullivan, vice-president and dean of graduate studies at the University of Texas at Austin, talked about "The Cashier Complex and the Transformation of American Work"; and Carl F. Kaestle of the Department of Education at the University of Chicago presented "Literacy and Print Culture."

Arthur Young of Northern Illinois University chaired the planning committee, made up of eight distinguished library practitioners and educators from LRRT. On the last day, Young announced that the first research seminar was dedicated to Mary Jo Lynch, director of the ALA Office for Research and

Statistics, for serving as the "national conscience" of library and information science research for almost two decades.

Another important research event occurred on December 16, when the Office for Education Research and Improvement (OERI) released its national plan for education research, *Building Knowledge for a Nation of Learners*, which described needed research on education. This report resulted from several years of work by the staff of OERI Office of Research, which was reorganized in 1995 into five "institutes," one of which is the Postsecondary Education, Libraries, and Lifelong Learning Institute (PLLI). The five institutes are advised by a National Education Research Board appointed by President Clinton. In the report released on December 16, the board announced seven priorities for research in the next two years:

- Improving learning and development in early childhood so that all children can enter kindergarten prepared to learn and succeed in elementary and secondary schools
- Improving curriculum, instruction, assessment, and student learning at all levels of education to promote high academic achievement, problem-solving abilities, creativity, and the motivation for further learning
- Ensuring effective teaching by expanding the supply of potential teachers, improving teacher preparation, and promoting career-long professional development at all levels of education
- Strengthening schools, particularly middle and high schools, as institutions capable of engaging young people as active and responsible learners
- Supporting schools to effectively prepare diverse populations to meet high standards for knowledge, skills, and productivity, and to participate fully in American economic, cultural, social, and civil life
- Promoting learning in informal and formal settings, and building the connections that cause out-of-school experiences to contribute to in-school achievement
- Understanding the changing requirements for adult competence in civic, work, and social contexts and how these requirements affect learning and the futures of individuals in the nation

Libraries are not mentioned prominently in this report, but it does present a very broad agenda that recognizes the importance of factors outside the classroom in creating a "nation of learners."

Public Libraries

The W. K. Kellogg Foundation (Battle Creek, Michigan) has long supported projects that help people to help themselves. Realizing the increasing importance of information in all aspects of life today, the foundation started a program several years ago to improve the people and agencies that provide access to information. That program was named Human Resources for Information Systems Management (HRISM). The grantees spanned the library and information science world: library schools, large public library systems, university libraries, the

Library of Congress, the American Library Association, the Council on Library Resources, Libraries for the Future, the Urban Libraries Council, community networks, video producers, and other key information providers.

Recently, the Kellogg Foundation decided to help its grantees develop a public message about American libraries that reflected both library leaders' visions and the American people's expectations. To accomplish this, the foundation funded a report prepared by the Benton Foundation, an agency that works to realize the social benefits of communication. This report, published late in 1996, is titled *Buildings, Books, and Bytes; Libraries and Communities in the Digital Age*.

This report on the public's opinion of library leaders' visions for the future bases its conclusions on several sources:

- Vision statements by the 19 grantees, supplemented by telephone interviews with the authors of the statements
- Public opinion surveys, especially a new one conducted for this report, and a single focus group of library users
- Public policy issues currently under discussion: universal service, copyright, intellectual property, funding

Our interest here is in the new public opinion data.

In spring 1996 the Benton Foundation commissioned a national survey to test public support for libraries in the digital age. The poll was conducted for Lake Research and the Tarrance Group between April 18 and April 21, 1996, by the Opinion Research Corporation (Princeton, New Jersey). Telephone interviews were conducted by paid, trained, and professionally supervised interviewers using a stratified random-digit replicate sample. A total of 1,015 interviews were completed, and respondents were limited to adults (at least 18 years old) living in private households in the United States. Interviews were weighted by age, sex, geographic region, and race to ensure that the sample accurately reflects the total adult population.

Building on earlier research conducted by George D'Elia and by Leigh Estabrook, the Benton survey asked 29 questions. Results summarized in Chapter 2 of the Kellogg/Benton report are generally favorable, as is evident in the subheadings in the text:

- Americans support digital library collections, access, and services.
- Americans are evenly divided over whether libraries in the future should be a place for books or digital information.
- Americans want libraries to provide digital information—and they are willing to spend tax dollars to make this happen.
- Families with children are much more likely to have home computers and use libraries.
- Americans are uncertain about librarians' roles as trainer and navigator for the Information Superhighway.
- Americans look to libraries to provide computer services to individuals who don't have their own computers.
- Library buildings score high.
- Americans are mixed in their support for libraries as community centers.

The bad news is that the youngest group surveyed—ages 18–24—registered weak support for the public library's digital activities, and nonusers were not enthusiastic about paying more taxes to support libraries. The entire report will be the topic of essays in a forthcoming issue of *Library Trends*.

A related report, also published in late 1996, included results of case study research. *Public Libraries, Communities, and Technology: Twelve Case Studies* contains site-visit reports from 12 public libraries, an analytical essay, and a selected list of resources on how public libraries are serving their communities. This report from the Council on Library Resources (CLR) was funded by the Kellogg Foundation as part of the HRISM program described above.

The case study sites were selected by CLR's Kellogg Program Advisory Committee from among 293 responses to a call for participation. Initial responses came from individual public libraries and from state libraries and regional networks. In selecting the sites, the CLR Advisory Committee looked for examples of small and large libraries in rural, urban, and suburban locations and for operational programs with community impact. Other factors included technological sophistication, collaboration with community organizations, and encouragement of diversity.

The publication describes each library's approach to technology implementation, taking into account its organizational and local community context. Each case study explores the accomplishments and challenges of the library's development and use of new technologies. The case studies also focus on the role of the library within its community and on the place of partnerships in new technology and community-based services.

New national data on the use of network technology became available in 1996. The *1996 National Survey of Public Libraries and the Internet: Progress and Issues* builds upon and expands a 1994 report with a similar title also issued by the National Commission on Libraries and Information Science. Researchers John Bertot, Charles McClure, and Douglas Zweizig state that the purpose of the study was to:

- Provide policy makers, researchers, and library professionals with longitudinal data that measure changes in public library Internet involvement since the first *Public Libraries and the Internet* study (McClure, Bertot, and Zweizig, 1994)
- Identify costs for public library Internet services
- Identify issues and inform the policy debate concerning public library roles in the electronic networked environment.

Data were collected between January and March 1996 using a mailed questionnaire and sample similar to those used in the 1994 study. Among the key findings are these:

- Between 1994 and 1996, public library Internet connectivity increased 113 percent (overall from 20.9 percent to 44.6 percent).
- Public library use of the Internet varies with the size of the population served.

- Nearly 40 percent of public libraries without Internet have no plans to connect in the next 12 months.

For many years public library leaders have talked about the need for evidence that an investment in a public library is good for the economy of an area. At the March 1996 Public Library Association (PLA) National Conference in Portland, Oregon, Glen Holt, director of the Saint Louis Public Library, presented a paper describing a methodology for gathering that evidence. An article in *The Bottom Line* (Vol. 9, No. 4) described his plan.

The abstract of Holt's article, "A Framework for Evaluating Public Investment in Urban Libraries," reads:

> Along with most public institutions, public libraries are under attack for being socially unresponsive and economically unworthy of public funds. [This article] looks at how urban libraries can defend their case by considering three main points: selecting appropriate methodology; building a framework for benefit-cost analysis; and assessing necessary research. [The article] concludes that continued research is very important as library resources are always changing [and] proposes a pilot project to estimate direct and external benefits from public investment in library resources in one sector of library operations.

PLA has already given $10,000 to support the pilot project, which holds promise for beginning an important series of studies that break new ground for public library development.

Government Libraries

During 1996 the National Center for Education Statistics (NCES) issued two reports of descriptive statistics on libraries that serve government agencies. *Federal Libraries and Information Centers in the United States: 1994* was issued in July. It was prepared for NCES by the Census Bureau, Governments Division, with the active cooperation of the Federal Library and Information Center Committee (FLICC).

For the purposes of this survey, a library is defined as "an organization that includes among its functions the following: selection, acquisition, organization, preservation, retrieval, and provision of access to information resources." An information center is defined as "an organization that performs the function of linking requestors with appropriate information resources through established mechanisms, such as database searching, providing referrals, answering specific questions, or by other means."

Facilities were included in the survey that (1) are either a library or information center as defined above (not a public affairs office, an agency locator service, a records management facility, a publications distribution facility, or a computer center), (2) are staffed with at least one paid part-time or full-time librarian, technical information specialist, library technician, archivist, or other trained person whose principal function is to assist people in meeting their information needs, (3) are considered to be a federal government operation or receiving at least half of its funding from federal appropriations, and (4) support the information needs of a federal agency or supply information as part of the agency's mission.

From a universe of 1,234 federal library and information centers identified for the survey, 1,161 (94 percent) were respondents. The tables in this publication summarize staffing, collections, service per typical week, automation, technology, and preservation for federal libraries and information centers in the 50 states and the District of Columbia, excluding elementary and secondary school libraries. This survey updates the federal library statistics last collected in 1978.

Another report of government libraries, this one focused on the state level, also updates a report from the late 1970s. *State Library Agencies, Financial Survey 1994* is the first in a series of annual statistical reports produced with the cooperation of the 50 chief officers of state library agencies. The report defines a state library agency as "the official agency of a State charged by the law of that State with the extension and development of public library services throughout the State, which has adequate authority under law of the State to administer State plans in accordance with the provisions of the Library Services and Construction act (LSCA)." [See the article "State Library Agencies: What Do the Numbers Tell Us?"—*Ed.*]

Academic Libraries

Last year this article noted that ALA would conduct a survey of electronic services offered by college and university libraries in spring 1996. The project was a joint effort between the ALA Office for Research and Statistics (ORS) and the Association of College and Research Libraries (ACRL), with financial support from Ameritech Library Services. It was designed to provide timely and reliable data regarding the extent to which specific electronic services are offered by libraries in the various sectors of the higher education community.

The following topics were covered: electronic public catalogs, electronic reference databases, electronic journals, electronic reserves, Internet services, computer hardware and software, technology for the disabled, electronic document delivery services, digitization, cooperative practices, instruction, and future plans. Survey results were published in late 1996 by ALA in *Electronic Services in Academic Libraries*. An Executive Summary may be found on the ALA Web site at http://www.ala.org/alaorg/ors/exsummary.html. These results show that electronic services are now widespread in academic libraries and that those libraries anticipate increased spending in this area over the next three years.

Another research report released in 1996 provides an in-depth look at the difficulties involved in providing electronic journals. The TULIP Final Report (http:www.elsevier.nl:80/homepage/about/resproj/trmenu.htm#ExecSummary) describes The University Licensing Program (TULIP), which started in early 1991 and concluded at the end of 1995. Participants in this collaborative project were Elsevier Science and nine leading universities in the United States: Carnegie Mellon University, Cornell University, Georgia Institute of Technology, Massachusetts Institute of Technology, University of California (all campuses), University of Michigan, University of Tennessee, University of Washington, and Virginia Polytechnic Institute and State University.

The goal of the project was to jointly test systems for networked delivery to, and use of journals at, the user's desktop. In the TULIP project, the scanned page plus bibliographic data and unedited, OCR-generated *raw* ASCII full text, of 43

Elsevier and Pergamon materials science and engineering journals were provided by Elsevier Science to the universities, which developed or adapted systems to deliver these journals in electronic form to the desktops of their end users. The focus of the research was on technical issues, user behavior, and organizational and economic questions. When this project started, there were very few institutions willing or able to bring up large-scale implementations aimed at bringing primary information to the desktop on their entire campuses. Many of the participants did just that and learned many lessons about technology along the way.

The objective of the user behavior research was to obtain specific feedback about TULIP from end users, in order to guide future development of the delivery of journal information from the desktop and to acquire insights on the requirements for electronic services to be attractive and valuable, from both the content provider's and infrastructure provider's side.

Two types of research were done: quantitative and qualitative. The quantitative research consisted mainly of analysis of the logfiles, i.e., records of user action. The qualitative research—which consisted mainly of focus groups and one-on-one interviews, using basically the same interview guides for each site—was aimed at answering the questions raised by the quantitative research. For instance, What gets (and keeps) users interested in electronic products? Which requirements should electronic products meet to be attractive and valuable? How should we bring electronic (full-text) information to the desktop? The organizational and economic issues were explored through a series of interviews with key players at the universities.

The final report provides details on what was done and what was learned. Six chapters on this project as a whole are followed by 14 appendices, including one for each of the nine participants. The Executive Summary that begins the report contains several key conclusions for libraries:

- TULIP proved to its participants that building digital libraries will be a costly and lengthy process.
- All see the role of libraries increasing instead of decreasing, fulfilling the following functions: finding, selecting, and providing the information needed by the community, leading people to the right information, and protecting holdings.
- A common view of all TULIP participants is that the transition to a digital library will go slower than they had expected before starting the project.

Awards that Support Research
Association for Library and Information Science Education (ALISE)

The first award that supports the conduct of library and information science research is presented each year at the annual meeting of ALISE, which precedes the ALA Midwinter Meeting. In 1996 ALISE met in January in San Antonio. The ALISE Research Grant ($2,500) was awarded to Ruth Palmquist (Texas) for her study "Cognitive Strategies in a Hyper-Linked Environment: An Exploration of Tools and Techniques."

American Library Association (ALA)

Gloria J. Leckie and Anne A. Fullerton were the 1996 recipients of the ALA Carroll Preston Baber Research Grant ($7,500). This grant supports innovative research that could lead to an improvement in library services to any specific group of people. The winning project, "Information Literacy in Science and Engineering: Faculty Attitudes and Pedagogical Practices," will investigate faculty perceptions of, attitudes toward, and pedagogical practices in teaching information literacy skills in science and engineering. The study will be conducted within the faculties of science and engineering at two Canadian sites: the University of Waterloo and the University of Western Ontario. The research will build upon and extend a 1992 study carried out at York University, which considered faculty perceptions, expectations, and practices for teaching information literacy in the social sciences, arts, and humanities.

Association of College and Research Libraries (ACRL)

The $1,000 Samuel Lazerow Fellowship for Research in Acquisitions or Technical Service was donated to ACRL by the Institute for Scientific Information (ISI) to foster advances in acquisitions or technical services. The 1996 winners were Jimmie Lundgren, instructor librarian, and Betsy Simpson, social sciences monograph cataloger and psychology collection manager, at the University of Florida in Gainesville. Their project is the second phase of a two-part study on the needs of catalog users in the University of Florida Library. Part one surveyed 1,900 nonmedical University of Florida instruction faculty. Part two will survey a portion of the university's graduate school population.

Nongyao Premkamolnetr, a student at the School of Information and Library Studies at Curtin University in Western Australia, is the 1996 recipient of the Doctoral Dissertation Fellowship ($1,000) presented by the Association of College and Research Libraries. The fellowship and a plaque donated by the Institute for Scientific Information are given to a doctoral student in academic librarianship whose research has potential significance in the field. Premkamolnetr's dissertation is titled "A Model for a University Library Which Provides Services to Tenant Companies in a Technology Park: The Australian Experience."

American Association of School Librarians (AASL)/Highsmith

Robert Grover, Jacqueline Lakin, Sheila Blume, and Carol Fox, representing the Kansas Association of School Librarians Research Committee, were the recipients of the 1996 American Association of School Librarians/Highsmith Research Grant for their project "Testing an Interdisciplinary Assessment Model." The $5,000 grant, sponsored by AASL, a division of ALA, and the Highsmith Company, Inc., is given to one or more school library media specialists, library educators, or library information science or education professors to conduct innovative research aimed at measuring and evaluating the impact of school library media programs on learning and education. The grant allows the researchers the opportunity to continue their work with the Kansas State Board of Education, with which they have developed an interdisciplinary assessment model for measuring the teaching and learning of information skills as part of an integrated curriculum.

Frances Henne/YALSA/Voya Research Grant

The winners of this grant were Evie Wilson-Lingbloom, managing librarian, Mill Creek (Washington) Library, Sno-Isle Regional Library System; Carol Doll, associate professor, School of Library and Information Sciences, University of Washington; and Barbara Carmondy, librarian, Henry M. Jackson High School in Mill Creek. Their project, "Storytelling Teenage Folklore," an experiment in building self-esteem with American oral tradition, links library programming with learning objectives established by the Washington State Commission on Student Learning.

Special Libraries Association (SLA)

SLA's Stephen I. Goldspiel Memorial Research Grant for 1996 (up to $20,000) was awarded to F. W. Lancaster and Linda G. Smith for a project examining the applicability of artificial intelligence/expert system (AI/ES) technologies to current and future special library operations. They plan to comprehensively review the literature in all relevant disciplines, identify applications in both library and nonlibrary environments that are relevant to special library operations and services, determine the success or failure of relevant applications, and document the determinants of success or failure. Findings will provide guidance to information professionals on the appropriateness and utility of developing an AI/ES-based system and on the most promising approach to the development and implementation of AI/ES technologies. Results will be presented at the 1997 SLA Annual Conference in Seattle and published in early 1998.

Documentation Abstracts, Inc.

In December 1996 the board of directors of Documentation Abstracts, Inc. (DAI) announced that it will award Information Science Abstracts (ISA) Research Grants of $1,000 to each of the following applicants: Ruben Urbizagástegul Alvarado, associate librarian, University of California at Riverside, for his project "Selecting Literature on Bibliometrics Through Bradford's Law" and Berenika M. Winclawska, librarian, Nicholas Copernicus University, Torun, Poland, for her project "Creation of Local Citation Indices for Polish Sociology Citation Index (PSCI)."

American Association of Law Libraries (AALL)

In March 1996 AALL announced the first winner of the AALL/Little Brown and Company Research Grant, an award program conducted by the AALL Research Agenda Committee to fund projects of practical value to professionals who create, disseminate, or use legal and law-related information. Bert J. Dempsey and Robert Vreeland of the University of North Carolina at Chapel Hill, School of Information and Library Science, will receive $25,000 to create the first legal information search engine for the Internet. The hypothesis behind the search engine is that knowledge of the specialized needs of the legal researcher and innovative use of emerging World Wide Web technologies (e.g., the new Java language) can be used to produce a superior Internet searching tool. To evaluate the effectiveness and degree of user acceptance for the search engine software, this project will include extensive user studies in conjunction with the Katherine R. Everett Law Library at the University of North Carolina at Chapel Hill.

Medical Library Association (MLA)

Gale Hannigan was the 1996 winner of the MLA Doctoral Fellowship ($1,000). Hannigan will study "Self-Directed Learning in a Primary Care Preceptorship." Alexandra Dimitroff was the 1996 winner of the MLA Research, Development, and Demonstration Project Grant. Dimitroff's project was "The Use of Problem Based Learning in a Health Sciences Librarianship Course."

Awards that Recognize Research

Association for Library and Information Science Education (ALISE)

The first 1996 awards for research well done were made at the January 1996 ALISE conference in San Antonio. The ALISE Doctoral Dissertation Competition went to Danuta Nitecki (University of Maryland) for "An Assessment of the Applicability of SERVQUAL Dimensions . . . for Evaluating Quality of Service in an Academic Library." She received $400 to defray travel expenses plus conference registration and personal membership in ALISE for 1996–1997.

The 1996 ALISE Research Paper Competition award ($500) went to Paul Solomon (University of North Carolina at Chapel Hill) for "Discovering Sense Making in Information Behavior: An Ethnography of Communication at Work." The 1996 ALISE Methodology Paper Award ($250) went to Ron Day (Laney College and the College Preparatory School) for "LIS, Method, and Postmodern Science."

American Library Association (ALA)

ALA usually announces winners of two awards during the Joint Research Awards program at its Annual Conference: The Library Research Round Table (LRRT) Jesse H. Shera Award for Research and the Library History Round Table (LHRT) Justin Winsor Prize. The Shera Award was not given this year. The 1996 Justin Winsor Prize was given to Wayne A. Wiegand, professor at the University of Wisconsin at Madison, School of Library and Information Studies. Wiegand won the prize for his essay "The Amherst Method: The Origins of the Dewey Decimal Classification System." This essay presents a detailed study of the origins of the decimal classification that incorporates new evidence and places it within the context of 19th-century American intellectual life and the influences of the Amherst community.

American Society for Information Science (ASIS)

In October 1996, at its annual meeting in Baltimore, ASIS announced awards to several researchers. The ASIS Research Award, which honors a systematic program of research in a single area at a level beyond the single study and recognizes outstanding research contributions in the field of information science, was presented to Gary Marchionini, professor at the University of Maryland at College Park, College of Library and Information Services, for his research in the design of information retrieval systems and in the human use of such systems, providing new insights on information seeking in electronic environments. The award has been presented to only seven individuals in the society's 57-year history.

The Best JASIS Paper Award went to Christine Borgman and Virginia Walter of UCLA and Sandra Hirsh of the University of Arizona for their paper "Children's Searching Behavior on Browsing and Keyword Online Catalogs: The Science Library Catalog Project." The paper addresses the results of research as an outgrowth of Project SEED (Science for Early Educational Development). The research attempts to understand children's information searching abilities to improve public school education in high-technology areas and to link them to the "Information Superhighway." The reported results have general implications for the design of information retrieval systems for children.

The winner of the ASIS Doctoral Forum Award, presented for outstanding doctoral research in the information field, is Howard Rosenbaum of Indiana University for his paper "Managers and Information in Organization: Towards a Structural Concept of the Information Use Environment of Managers." This research proposes a novel conceptual framework, the structurally informed value-added approach, with which to investigate information seeking and use in organizational settings; and it demonstrates its utility in the study of the information use environment of managers in a public sector organization.

The 1996 Information Science Doctoral Dissertation Scholarship, sponsored by the Institute for Scientific Information, went to Abby Goodrum, a doctoral student in the interdisciplinary information science Ph.D. program at the University of North Texas, for her dissertation proposal "Evaluation of Text-Based and Image-Based Representations for Moving Image Documents." In citing Goodrum, the jury noted that "She has a good handle on the problem of the efficacy with which record knowledge is transmitted from one social cohort to another. Her dissertation indicates that she will incorporate what we already know about the problem of image choice and use methodologies which originated in the field but have not been directly connected since the early 1970s Systems Development Corporation studies."

A new research award was announced by ASIS. With a bequest of $55,000 to Pratt Institute School of Information and Library Science (SILS) from alumnus David Severn (1921–1992), the school will fund an annual national award for best student research in information science. The annual Pratt-Severn Best Student Research Award in Information Science ($500) will be presented to a master's degree student selected by ASIS. Mark Spasser, a doctoral student at the University of Illinois, was the 1996 winner of the Pratt-Severn Student Research Award for his paper "The Enacted Fate of Undiscovered Public Knowledge." This paper reports on the results from a citation context analysis of the ways in which Don Swanson's ideas about knowledge fragmentation have been incorporated into the work of subsequent authors. He was commended for his efficient use of citation index analysis in bringing forward new findings of interest to the information science community.

Major Funding Agencies

Funding for research in library and information sciences has never been abundant, but three agencies have consistently supported research in the field: the

U.S. Department of Education, the Council on Library Resources, and the Online Computer Library Center. All three provided support in 1996.

The U.S. Department of Education Office for Education Research and Improvement (OERI), National Institute on Postsecondary Education, Libraries, and Lifelong Learning conducted a competition last year for field-initiated studies. Six awards were made in amounts from $381,431 to $895,505. The following two awards involve public libraries:

- $422,559 to Christine M. Koontz, Florida State University, to conduct research on, demonstrate, and validate the combined use of marketing principles and information technology to inventory and evaluate lifelong-learning needs for areas served by public libraries. The study will develop a national baseline on adult educational needs in low-income areas and a low-cost replicable methodology that will assist public librarians in evaluating educational needs in their communities. (The project's duration is 2½ years.)
- $895,505 to Cynthia Johnston, Central Piedmont Community College, Charlotte, North Carolina, to determine the effectiveness of providing basic-skills instruction through community networks and through the Internet to adults who need a high school credential. She will work with the Public Library of Charlotte and Mecklenburg County, North Carolina, Johnston C. Smith University, the Charlotte Housing Authority, Charlotte-Mecklenburg Schools, and TRO Learning, Inc. to examine how community-based institutions can use new, low-cost technologies to expand opportunities for adult lifelong learners. (The project's duration is three years).

No research was funded by HEA Title II-B managed by OERI's Library Programs Office in fiscal year (FY) 1996, but it seems likely that funds will be available from that source in FY 1997—the transition year between federal funding for libraries through the Department of Education and funding through the Institute for Libraries and Museum Services. The act that mandated that change, the Library Services and Technology Act (LSTA), became law in September 1996. Most of the money ($91 million in FY 1997) goes to libraries through state library agencies, but 5 percent is reserved for "national leadership grants." Four possibilities are stipulated for that 5 percent; one of them is "Research and demonstration projects related to the improvement of libraries, education in library and information science, enhancement of library services through effective and efficient use of new technologies, and dissemination of information derived from such projects."

Council on Library Resources

The Council on Library Resources awarded eight grants in its Economic of Information Small Grants Program, funded by the Andrew Mellon Foundation. The grants are made for studies that will broaden an understanding of the cost benefits and efficiency of using electronic technology to deliver information in libraries.

The recipients of the grants were:

- The University of California at Berkeley: "Performance Measures for Research Library Collection and Information Services" ($25,000). This pilot project will develop a set of qualitative and quantitative measures for evaluating the performance and costs of research library collections and related information services.
- Association of Research Libraries: "The Character and Nature of Research Library Investment in Electronic Resources" ($11,800). This study will examine data on expenditures for electronic resources that ARL has been collecting for several years but that suffer from variations in reporting that in the past have made analysis and comparison difficult. The project will refine definitions or develop new categories to facilitate constructive use of the existing database.
- Johns Hopkins University: "Comprehensive Access to Print Materials" ($7,920). This is a continuing project to develop a system that permits scholars and students to have access to print materials stored in off-site locations by using a combination of new technologies, including robotics, digital cameras, scanners, and high-speed communications.
- University of Michigan: "Pricing Electronic Information: A Research Collaboration" ($25,000). This project will study the design of pricing systems and their influence on usage of an electronic journal access system. Through a partnership with Elsevier, a commercial information provider, the University of Michigan will implement a large-scale field experiment on innovative price schemes and customer usage of electronic distribution of traditional print-on-paper scholarly journals. Economists, professional librarians, and a computer systems professional will collaborate on the study.
- Iowa State University: "A Decision Model for Serial Access Choices" ($18,650). This project is aimed toward building an economic model that will assist librarians in making purchases to maximize user access to serial information. The model will enable librarians to avoid making purchase decisions on the basis of rough estimates of demand or time-consuming usage studies of particular titles. The purpose of the study will be to demonstrate that the application of usage data to a decision model will allow the library to expend its funds more efficiently.
- Rutgers University: "Exploration of Variable Pricing for Online Services at Research Libraries" ($24,954). The project will address the question of whether pricing can adapt in real time to variations in demand for different publications so that revenue to publishers and providers is increased. This is an important question in the context of Internet access, as the excess of such revenues over costs provides the most reliable source for fair and equal access to the digital library of the future. The goal of the study is to determine, by simulation, whether prices can adapt to variations in consumer demand in such a way as to generate an excess of income over costs. The study will lay the foundation for potential real experiments using Web sites.

- Rutgers University: "The Efficiency of Research Libraries: A New Analytical Tool and Pilot Study Using 1995 ARL Data" ($24,973). This study will assess the applicability of certain new analytical techniques for the analysis of multiproduct firms, not unlike the "products" that libraries routinely offer their patrons. In developing a cost model, statistics collected by the Association of Research Libraries will be used; and by means of a technique called data envelopment analysis the project will attempt to "score" the performance of various library operations.
- Virginia Commonwealth University: "Using the Contingent Valuation Method to Measure Patron Benefits of Reference Desk Service in an Academic Library" ($20,003). This project will apply a survey technique called the contingent valuation method to estimate economic value that patrons attach to reference desk service in an academic library. The contingent valuation method has been used in environmental economics for the past 30 years to determine values of environmental amenities, such as pollution abatement and recreational areas, where no explicit market transactions take place. The study will provide the basis for a cost-benefit analysis of reference desk services.

The projects receiving grants were chosen from proposals submitted during the grant program's first and second cycles by an advisory committee comprised of academic librarians, economists, and information specialists.

Online Computer Library Center (OCLC)

OCLC has a staff of 25 in its Office of Research and Special Projects. They carry out an impressive program of research on questions central to progress in our field and also support research by others. During 1996 OCLC Library and Information Science Research Grants of up to $10,000 each were made to the following projects:

- Myke Gluck, assistant professor, Florida State University, "A Descriptive Study of the Usability of Geospatial Metadata." This study will investigate the usability and usefulness of geospatial metadata for a range of users. Ten participants in each of the three phases of the study will be videotaped while exploring geospatial metadata online providing talk-aloud protocols and screen image sequences. Dr. Gluck's overall goal is to describe metadata usability precisely enough so that user needs for geospatial metadata may be incorporated into either metadata standards or geographic information retrieval systems.
- Gregory H. Leazer, assistant professor, University of California at Los Angeles, "A Demonstration System for the Explicit Control of Bibliographic Works and Relationships." Dr. Leazer will help develop a robust prototype system for the control of bibliographic works and relationships. The prototype system consists of separate descriptive records for works and items and uses hypertext links to express bibliographic relationships. The prototype system will be automatically derived from a sample of USMARC records drawn from the OCLC Online Union Catalog.

- Charles R. McClure, professor, Syracuse University, "Quality Criteria for Evaluating Information Resources and Services Available from Federal Web Sites Based on User Feedback." Dr. McClure's research will focus attention on a unique opportunity to design and implement carefully evaluated elements into this potentially valuable communications medium before too much effort is wasted on ill-conceived Web pages. The research may save considerable effort, anxiety, and taxpayer dollars while pointing the way toward reaching the Web page stakeholders in an optimal fashion. Additionally, the distributed feedback concept is a powerful means of evolving open network systems.

Work currently under way in the OCLC Office of Research was summarized in the September/October issue of the *OCLC Newsletter*:

- Cataloging and Classifying the World Wide Web: a project designed to determine how best to bring the benefits of cataloging and classification knowledge and skills to the World Wide Web.
- National Language Processing (NLP) Research: to enhance Dewey terminology via a number of methods, including the use of NLP techniques.
- Classification Research: a series of linked efforts, including, but not limited to, the Cataloging and Classifying the World Wide Web and NLP Research activities mentioned previously, which aim to understand the what, how, and why of classification schemes, specifically Dewey, in the networked environment of the Internet in general and the World Wide Web in particular.
- Uniform Titles: a project with the goal of algorithmically assigning consistent titles to works in WorldCat, the OCLC Online Union Catalog.
- Interlibrary Loan (ILL) Research: a series of studies aimed at gaining a deeper understanding of ILL characteristics. Current work is looking at the extent to which commercial suppliers are or can be involved in ILL request fulfillment and attributes that can be used to predict availability of sought items.
- Metadata Workshops: a series of workshops sponsored by the Office of Research, aimed at defining core data elements and a framework in which they can work for data stored on the Internet and World Wide Web. Current effort is directed toward determining how best to take advantage of the work done to date.
- FirstSearch in the Future: a project aimed at prototyping a next-generation software system for the FirstSearch Service. Significant work has been done since the last RAC report in getting a first cut of the server and search systems working, as well as exploration of several possible user interface designs.

State Library Agencies: What Do the Numbers Tell Us?

Mary Jo Lynch
Director, Office for Research and Statistics, American Library Association

Keith Curry Lance
Director, Library Research Service, Colorado State Library

When is a library more than a library? When it's a state library agency!

Even with today's emphasis on electronic access, a library is usually defined in terms of a collection of materials and a set of services to a specific group of people in a particular place or agency. Most state library agencies could be defined this way, but all of them fit the definition of a state library agency used in the report this article describes (*State Library Agencies: Fiscal Year 1994*, National Center for Education Statistics, U.S. Department of Education):

> A state library agency is the official agency of a state charged by the law of that state with the extension and development of public library services throughout the state, which has adequate authority under the law of the state to administer state plans in accordance with the provisions of the Library Services and Construction Act (LSCA).

Under this definition, the focus is on developing other libraries and administering state plans. Clearly, this agency is different from other libraries, but what do we know about the 50 state library agencies? How do they fit into state government? Where do they get their income, and what do they spend it on? How many people are employed in state library agencies, and what services do they deliver? Do these libraries have collections? Do people use them directly or only through other libraries? All of these questions and many more can now be answered with current statistics.

The National Center for Education Statistics (NCES) published the 167-page statistical report—the first in what will be an annual series—in June 1996. It contains 28 numbered tables, some of them subdivided so that the total number of tables is 51. All have one line summarizing results for all 50 states followed by data for each state individually.[1]

Most of the tables cover topics common to all NCES library surveys: hours and outlets, collections, service transactions, staff, income, and expenditures. Topics unique to state library agencies are also covered: place in state government, services to libraries, and electronic network functions.

Background

NCES sponsored an earlier statistical report on this topic: *Survey of State Library Agencies, 1977* by Barratt Wilkins, State Librarian, State Library of Florida, was published for NCES as No. 142 in the University of Illinois Graduate School of Library Science Occasional Paper series. It contained 17 numbered tables, several subdivided so that the total number was 21 tables—less than half the number of tables (51) in the report described in this article.

The 1977 survey was never repeated and statistics about state library agencies have been scarce since 1977. The Association of Specialized and Cooperative Library Agencies (ASCLA)—a division of the American Library Association (ALA)—in cooperation with the Chief Officers of State Library Agencies (COSLA) published the biennial report *State Library Agencies* from 1973 through 1991. This report had several statistical tables in an appendix. Before COSLA was organized, Joe Shubert, then State Librarian of Ohio, collected fiscal and salary data and distributed it to other state library agencies. This became a COSLA project in 1973 and continued through 1993. Statistics from both of these sources were used by William G. Asp to describe "The State of State Library Agencies" in a compilation of essays, *State Library Services and Issues*, edited by Charles R. McClure (Ablex, 1986). Several of the essays in this monograph mention an important reality about state library agencies: they vary greatly from state to state. The 1994 NCES report confirms this fact for the 1990s.

Position in State Government

State library agencies vary in terms of where they are located in state government and how they are governed, but 48 of them are located in the executive branch. In only two states, Arizona and Michigan, the state library agency reports to the legislature. Within the executive branch, 18 are independent agencies, 16 are a part of a department of education, and 14 are part of some other department (Tables 1a and 1b).

Services to Libraries

All state library agencies distribute federal LSCA Title I and II grants to public libraries[2] and almost all state governments also provide financial assistance to individual public libraries and public library systems. In 1994 the 50 state library agencies gave the following amounts to individual public libraries and public library systems: $43.1 million in LSCA Title I grants (Table 25b), $14.3 million in LSCA Title II grants (Table 25c), and $409.2 million in state aid (Table 19). In addition, the 20 services shown in Figure 1 are offered to public libraries in from as few as ten states to as many as 50 states. In all states, the state library agency administers LSCA Title III grants to academic, school, and special libraries and to library systems (a total of $10.8 million to all four categories in 1994), but additional services to libraries other than public libraries vary (Tables 4a–4e, 25d). This is what is done in a majority of states:

- For academic libraries (Table 4b): interlibrary loan referral and developing union lists in over two-thirds of the states; continuing education and reference referral in three-fifths of the states

- For school library media centers (Table 4c): interlibrary loan referral in over two-thirds of the states; continuing education and reference referral in over one-half
- For special libraries (Table 4d): continuing education, interlibrary loan, and reference referral in at least two-thirds of the states; union list development and consulting services in at least one-half
- For systems (Table 4e): consulting services, continuing education, interlibrary loan referral services, library legislation preparation or review, and library planning, evaluation, and research in three-fifths of the states

(Figures from Hawaii are not included in the sections "Direct Service to People," "Collections," "Where Does the Money Come from, Where Does It Go?" and "How Many Staff and What Are They Doing?" because the Hawaii State Library manages a public library system comparable to that of a large city on the mainland. It is not comparable to other states. Therefore, many of the figures in these sections will not match those in the report.)

Direct Service to People

Service Outlets

The state library agencies operate 158 outlets. These outlets vary in terms of the primary clientele they are designed to serve (Table 5).

- More than two-thirds of the agency outlets serve the general public.
- Two-thirds of the outlets serve state government employees.
- Two-fifths serve residents of state institutions.
- More than one-third serve the blind and physically handicapped.

The overwhelming majority of state library agencies—46 out of 50—operate outlets that are open to the general public on a walk-in basis (Table 6). Three state agencies (Massachusetts, Mississippi, and Wisconsin) operate outlets that are open to the general public on a referral basis only.

Hours

Public service hours of state agency outlets are restricted to regular office hours in most states. Only 11 state agencies have outlets that are open on Saturday or Sunday. Only seven state agencies have outlets that are open on weekday evenings (Monday–Friday, after 5:00 P.M.) (Table 6).

Service Transactions

Various figures indicate that state library agencies provide substantial amounts of direct library service to individuals (Table 9). During 1994 outlets of state library agencies received almost 1.4 million visits, circulated 2.9 million items, and received 1.7 million reference questions. In addition, these state library outlets participated in interlibrary loan by providing more than 780,000 items to other libraries and receiving more than 212,000 items from other libraries and commercial document delivery services.

Electronic Networking

In recent years state library agencies have assumed substantial leadership roles in electronic networking. Evidence of that came recently in a special double issue of *Library High Tech* (Vol. 14, Nos. 2–3, 1996). Thirty-nine of the 46 "State of the State Reports: Statewide Library Automation, Connectivity, Resource Access Initiatives" were written by state library personnel, and almost all of the others included a section on the state library agency.

Table 3 in the NCES report covers nine electronic networking functions. The most frequent function performed by state library agencies as of 1994 is electronic network planning or monitoring (48 states), followed by the development of bibliographic databases (45), and electronic network operation (41). Almost half (21) develop full-text databases.

State agencies also provide significant support to library access to the Internet. Almost all of them (48) train library staff to use Internet resources or consult with libraries that are establishing access to the Internet. The vast majority of state agencies (45) are also involved in facilitating library access to the Internet in one or more of the following ways: providing a subsidy for Internet participation; providing equipment needed to access the Internet; managing gophers, file servers, bulletin boards, or listservs; or mounting directories, databases, or online catalogs.

Collections

State library agencies vary greatly in the size of their collections (Table 7). Six have over one million books and serial volumes (Arizona, Illinois, Michigan, New Jersey, New York, Oregon); but 10 have less than 50,000 (Colorado, Delaware, Georgia, Kansas, Maryland, Massachusetts, Minnesota, Rhode Island, Utah, Wyoming). Maryland has no collection but contracts with the Enoch Pratt Free Library in Baltimore to provide statewide service. Thirteen other state library agencies also contract with libraries in the state to supplement their resources (Alaska, California, Colorado, Maine, Massachusetts, Minnesota, Missouri, Montana, Oregon, Pennsylvania, Rhode Island, Vermont, Wisconsin) (Table 2). All but five states have collections of state documents, and all but six are federal documents depositories (Table 7).

Allied Operations

Laws in some states have designated state library agencies to perform what the report calls allied operations (Table 2). Nine state library agencies manage both the state archives and the state records management service (Alaska, Arizona, Connecticut, Florida, Nevada, Kentucky, Oklahoma, Texas, Virginia). In Tennessee the agency manages only the state archives, and in Vermont the agency manages only the state records management service. Nine state library agencies operate a state legislative reference/research service, and three agencies manage a state history museum/art gallery.

Where Does the Money Come from, Where Does It Go?

In 1994 state library agencies spent $689.6 million (Table 17). Most of that amount (66.2 percent) was spent on financial assistance to libraries (Table 22), including individual public libraries (55 percent), other individual libraries (2.1 percent), public library systems (17.9 percent), multitype library systems (10.9 percent), single libraries providing statewide services (5.8 percent), and library construction (8.1 percent) (Table 24b).

Operating expenditures consume 30.8 percent of the budget of state library agencies (Table 22), with most of that amount spent for staff (63.7 percent) (Table 23). State governments provided 82.6 percent, the federal government provided 16.5 percent, and 0.9 percent came from other sources. Overall, the expenditure on state library agencies is $1.73 per capita, ranging from a low of 87 cents per capita in Louisiana to a high of $7.33 in Alaska (Table 17).

How Many Staff and What Are They Doing?

In 1994 the 50 state library agencies had a total of 3,578 full-time employees (Table 11a). Thirty-one percent were librarians, 15 percent were other professionals, and 55 percent were other paid staff. Distribution of staff by function (Table 11b) was as follows:

Library Services	64.8 percent
Library Development	12.7 percent
Administration	12.0 percent
Other	10.5 percent

These staffing figures seem to contradict the definition of a state library agency used in the report because few staff are devoted to library development. In fact, the definition is useful only as a tool for describing the common denominator that makes state library agencies alike. They are actually quite different from one another, as this report demonstrates.

Conclusion

This report is a mine of information that was previously unavailable. It will provide a useful benchmark as state library agencies change in response to the transformations now under way in library services and in federal and state funding.

Notes

1. Washington, D.C., is shown as a state in the report because the District of Columbia Public Library performs some functions of a state library agency. However, this article covers only the 50 states; therefore, many of the figures here will not match those in the report unless the figure for the District of Columbia is removed.
2. At the time of the 1994 survey, LSCA Titles I, II, and III could be described as follows: Title I—Extension and improvement of public library services; Title II—Public library construction and technology enhancement; Title III—Interlibrary cooperation and resource sharing.

Figure 1 / State Library Agencies: Services to Libraries

(Number shows how many agencies offer the service to public libraries)

Accreditation of libraries	12
Administration of LSCA grants	50
Administration of state aid	41
Certification of librarians	26
Collection of library statistics	50
Consulting services	50
Continuing education programs	50
Cooperative purchasing	10
Interlibrary loan referral services	44
Library legislation preparation/review	45
Library planning/evaluation/research	50
Literacy program support	48
OCLC Group Access Capability	32
Preservation/conservation services	19
Reference referral services	40
Retrospective conversion	16
State standards/guidelines	42
Statewide library promotion campaigns	38
Summer reading programs support	42
Union list development	39

Source: *State Library Agencies: Fiscal Year 1994.*

Number of Libraries in the United States, Canada, and Mexico

Statistics are from the 49th edition of the *American Library Directory 1996–97 (ALD)* (R. R. Bowker, 1996). Data are exclusive of elementary and secondary school libraries.

Libraries in the United States

Public Libraries	15,370 *
Public libraries, excluding branches	9,165 †
Main public libraries that have branches	1,254
Public library branches	6,205
Academic Libraries	4,730 *
Junior college	1,262
Departmental	102
Medical	6
Religious	3
University and college	3,468
Departmental	1,491
Law	175
Medical	210
Religious	106
Armed Forces Libraries	409 *
Air Force	108
Medical	13
Army	168
Law	1
Medical	35
Navy	133
Law	1
Medical	15
Government Libraries	1,875 *
Law	423
Medical	221
Special Libraries (excluding public, academic, armed forces, and government)	10,282 *
Law	1,155
Medical	1,982
Religious	1,04
Total Special Libraries (including public, academic, armed forces, and government)	11,340
Total law	1,764
Total medical	2,487
Total religious	1,152
Total Libraries Counted(*)	32,666

Libraries in Regions Administered by the United States

Public Libraries	28	*
Public libraries, excluding branches	12	†
Main public libraries that have branches	2	
Public library branches	16	
Academic Libraries	54	*
Junior college	7	
University and college	47	
Departmental	21	
Law	2	
Medical	1	
Armed Forces Libraries	3	*
Air Force	1	
Army	1	
Navy	1	
Government Libraries	8	*
Law	1	
Medical	2	
Special Libraries (excluding public, academic, armed forces, and government)	17	*
Law	4	
Medical	5	
Religious	1	
Total Special Libraries (including public, academic, armed forces, and government)	19	
Total law	7	
Total medical	8	
Total religious	1	
Total Libraries Counted(*)	110	

Libraries in Canada

Public Libraries	1,735	*
Public libraries, excluding branches	792	†
Main public libraries that have branches	132	
Public library branches	943	
Academic Libraries	497	*
Junior college	134	
Departmental	39	
Medical	0	
Religious	3	
University and college	363	
Departmental	164	
Law	16	
Medical	15	
Religious	17	

Government Libraries	402 *
Law	21
Medical	6
Special Libraries (excluding public, academic, armed forces, and government)	1,454 *
Law	122
Medical	276
Religious	60
Total Special Libraries (including public, academic, and government)	1,554
Total law	162
Total medical	301
Total religious	108
Total Libraries Counted(*)	4,088

Libraries in Mexico

Public Libraries	25 *
Public libraries, excluding branches	25 †
Main public libraries that have branches	0
Public library branches	0
Academic Libraries	326 *
Junior college	0
Departmental	0
Medical	0
Religious	0
University and college	326
Departmental	255
Law	0
Medical	2
Religious	0
Government Libraries	10 *
Law	0
Medical	1
Special Libraries (excluding public, academic, armed forces, and government)	33 *
Law	0
Medical	10
Religious	0
Total Special Libraries (including public, academic, and government)	41
Total law	0
Total medical	14
Total religious	0
Total Libraries Counted(*)	394

Summary

Total U.S. Libraries	32,666
Total Libraries Administered by the United States	110
Total Canadian Libraries	4,088
Total Mexican Libraries	394
Grand Total of Libraries Listed	37,258

Note: Numbers followed by an asterisk are added to find "Total libraries counted" for each of the four geographic areas (United States, U.S.-administered regions, Canada, and Mexico). The sum of the four totals is the "Grand total of libraries listed" in *ALD*. For details on the count of libraries, see the preface to the 49th edition of *ALD—Ed.*

† Federal, state, and other statistical sources use this figure (libraries *excluding* branches) as the total for public libraries.

Highlights of NCES Surveys

Public Libraries

The following are highlights from *E.D. TABS Public Libraries in the United States: 1993* released in June 1995.

Number of Public Libraries and Their Service Outlets and Governance

- 8,929 public libraries (administrative entities) were reported in the 50 states and the District of Columbia in 1993.
- Fewer than 11 percent of the public libraries serve over 71 percent of the population of legally served areas in the United States. Each of these public libraries has a legal service area population of 50,000 or more.
- 1,454 public libraries (over 16 percent) reported one or more branch library outlets, with a total of 7,017. The total number of central library outlets reported was 8,887. The total number of stationary outlets reported (central library outlets and branch library outlets) was 15,904. Nearly 10 percent of reporting public library outlets had one or more bookmobile outlets, with a total of 1,035.
- Nearly 56 percent of public libraries were part of a municipal government; 12 percent were part of a county/parish; nearly 7 percent had multijurisdictional governance under an intergovernmental agreement; nearly 10 percent were non-profit association or agency libraries in a given state; nearly 4 percent were part of a school district; and nearly 6 percent were separate government units known as library districts. Less than 1 percent were combinations of academic/public libraries or school/public libraries. Over 5 percent did not report or reported a form of governance not mentioned here.
- Over 80 percent of public libraries had only one direct service outlet.

Income, Expenditures, and Staffing

- Public libraries reported that 78 percent of total operating income of over $5.0 billion came from local sources, nearly 13 percent from the state, about 1 percent from federal sources, and over 8 percent from other sources, such as gifts and donations, service fees, and fines.
- Per capita operating income from local sources was under $3 for nearly 14 percent of public libraries, $3 to $14.99 for over 52 percent, and $15 or more for 34 percent of public libraries. Per capita income from local sources varies considerably, with a percentage distribution of about 10 percent in each of 10 categories reported.
- Total operating expenditures for public libraries were over $4.7 billion in 1993. Of this, over 65 percent was for paid FTE staff and 15 percent for the library collection. The average U.S. per capita operating expenditure was $19.16. The highest average per capita operating expenditure in the 50 states was $31.66 and the lowest was $7.85.

- Nearly 41 percent of public libraries reported operating expenditures of less than $50,000 in 1993. Just over 38 percent expended between $50,000 and $399,999, and just over 21 percent exceeded $400,000.

Staffing and Collections

- Public libraries reported a total of nearly 111,945 paid full-time equivalent (FTE) staff.
- Nationwide, public libraries reported over 656 million books and serial volumes in their collections or 2.7 volumes per capita. By state, the number of volumes per capita ranged from 1.6 to 4.9.
- Nationwide, public libraries reported collections of over 22 million audio materials, 535,000 films, and nearly 7.9 million video materials.

Circulation and Interlibrary Loans

- Total nationwide circulation of library materials was nearly 1.6 billion or 6.5 per capita. Highest statewide circulation per capita was 11.9 and lowest was 3.2.
- Nationwide, nearly 7.6 million library materials were loaned by public libraries to other libraries.

Children's Services

- Nationwide circulation of children's materials was nearly 462.9 million or over 29 percent of total circulation. Attendance at children's programs was nearly 35.6 million. Information on public library service to children is included in the E.D. TABS for the first time.

Per capita figures in these highlights are based on the total unduplicated population of legal service areas in the states, not on the total population of the states. Population of legal service area means the population of those areas in the state or nation where public library service is available. It does not include the population of unserved areas.

Academic Libraries

The following are highlights from the *E.D. TABS Academic Libraries: 1992*, released in November 1994.

- In 1992, total operating expenditures for libraries at the 3,274 institutions of higher education totaled $3.6 billion.
- The three largest individual expenditure items for all academic libraries were salaries and wages, $1.9 billion (51.8 percent); current serial subscription expenditures, $639 million (17.5 percent); and print material expenditures, $421 million (11.5 percent).

- The libraries of the 500 doctoral-granting institutions (15.3 percent of the total institutions) accounted for $2.3 billion, or 62 percent of the total operating expenditure dollars at all college and university libraries. This included $1.1 billion for salaries and wages, $467 million current serial subscription expenditures, and $253 million print material expenditures.
- The number of volumes held at all academic libraries at the end of FY 1992 totaled about 749 million.
- Libraries at institutions granting doctoral degrees held about 471 million volumes, or 63 percent of the total volumes held.
- The total number of full-time-equivalent (FTE) staff members in college and university libraries equaled 96,000, including about 26,000 librarians and other professional staff, 40,000 other paid staff, 29,000 student assistants, and 404 staff who contributed their services.
- Libraries at institutions granting doctoral degrees accounted for 52,000, or half of all, FTE staff at all academic libraries. This included about 14,000 librarians and other professional staff, 24,000 other paid staff, 14,000 student assistants, and 128 staff who contributed their services.
- Academic libraries had 229 million circulation transactions; 78.8 percent from general collections, and 21.2 percent from reserve collections.
- Libraries at institutions granting doctoral degrees accounted for more than half of this total circulation with 129 million circulation transactions.

School Library Media Centers

In 1991 a small amount of data on school libraries was collected as embedded items from a sample of public and private elementary and secondary schools as part of the NCES 1990–1991 Schools and Staffing Survey (SASS). Data collected included number of students served, number of professional staff and aides, number of full-time equivalent librarians/media specialists, number of vacant positions, number of positions abolished, number of approved positions, and amount of librarian input in establishing curriculum. NCES released a short report on these data in November 1994.

The following are highlights from the report *Survey Report School Library Media Centers in the United States 1990–1991,* released in November 1994.

Historical Overview

- In 1958 only 50 percent of public elementary and secondary schools in the United States had a library or library media center. As of 1990–1991, 96 percent of public and 87 percent of U.S. private elementary and secondary schools had a library or library media center.
- From 1960 to 1980 the number of public school librarians/media specialists in the United States nearly tripled, from 17,363 to 48,018, outstripping increases in student enrollments. Since 1980, expansion in the number of public school librarians/media specialists substantially slowed, and in the early 1990s school library media center staffing levels did not keep pace with increases in student enrollments.

Availability of School Library Media Centers

- In the public sector, small schools (those with fewer than 300 students) and combined schools (those jointly offering both elementary and secondary levels) were the least likely to be equipped with library media centers in 1990–1991. Ten percent of small public schools and 15 percent of combined public schools did not have library media centers.
- In the private sector, small schools, elementary schools, combined schools, and non-Catholic private schools, both religious and nonsectarian, were the least likely to be equipped with library media centers in 1990–1991. The percentages of schools in these groups without library media centers ranged from 14 to 23 percent.

Staffing Levels of School Library Media Centers

- In the public sector, 8 percent of schools with library media centers did not employ some kind of library media center staff, neither a professional librarian/media specialist nor a library aide, in 1990–1991. Four percent of public school students attended such schools. Elementary schools, combined schools, and small public schools were the most likely to have employed no library staff. One third of small public schools had no librarian/media specialist, and one-fifth of those same schools had neither a librarian/media specialist nor an aide.
- The proportion of private schools with unstaffed library media centers was far greater than for public schools in 1990–1991. Over half of smaller, elementary, and non-Catholic religious private schools employed neither a librarian/media specialist nor a library aide. Overall, a quarter of all private school students were enrolled in schools with no employed library media center staff.

Role of School Library Media Specialists

- Teachers in public schools were slightly more likely than teachers in private schools to strongly agree that the materials in their school library media centers were supportive of their instructional objectives.
- Few school principals (16 percent) reported that school librarians/media specialists had a great deal of influence over decisions concerned with establishing the curriculum in their schools. Librarians/media specialists in private schools were more frequently reported to have a great deal of influence over curricular decisions than in public schools.

Surveys on Children, Young Adults

The following are highlights from the report *Services and Resources for Children and Young Adults in Public Libraries (1995).*

- Sixty percent of the 18 million people entering public libraries during a typical week in fall 1993 were youth—children and young adults.

- The percentage of libraries with children's and young adult librarians has not changed since the late 1980s. Thirty-nine percent of libraries employ a children's librarian, 11 percent have a young adult librarian, and 24 percent have a youth services specialist on staff.
- Librarians report that ethnic diversity of children and young adult patrons has increased in over 40 percent of U.S. public libraries over the last five years. Seventy-six percent of public libraries currently have children's materials and 64 percent have young adult materials in languages other than English.
- Although computer technologies are among the most heavily used children's and young adult resources in public libraries, they are also among the most scarce. Only 30 percent of public libraries reported the availability of personal computers for use by children and young adults. However, 75 percent of libraries having this resource report moderate to heavy use by children, and 71 percent report moderate to heavy use by young adults.
- Less than half of all public libraries (40 percent) offer group programs for infants and toddlers. These programs are more prevalent now than in 1988, when only 29 percent of libraries offered group programs for infants to two-year-olds. Eighty-six percent of libraries offer group programs, such as story times, booktalks, puppetry, and crafts, for preschool and kindergarten age children; 79 percent of libraries offer group programs for school-age children.
- Seventy-six percent of public libraries report working with schools; 66 percent work with preschools and 56 percent with day care centers.
- While almost all libraries provide reference assistance, only about 1 in 7 libraries offer homework assistance programs for children or young adults. However, fairly large percentages of libraries with homework assistance programs report moderate to heavy use by children and young adults. Sixty-four percent report moderate to heavy use by children and 58 percent report moderate to heavy use by young adults.
- Librarians report that insufficient library staff is a leading barrier to increasing services and resources for both children and young adults. Sixty-five percent of librarians consider this a moderate or major barrier to increasing services for children, and 58 percent consider lack of staff a barrier to increasing services for young adults.

For further information about statistics collected by the National Center for Education Statistics, see the article in Part 1—*Ed.*

Library Acquisition Expenditures, 1995–1996: U.S. Public, Academic, Special, and Government Libraries

The information in these tables is taken from the 49th edition of the *American Library Directory (ALD)* (1996–1997), published by R. R. Bowker. The tables report acquisition expenditures by public, academic, special, and government libraries.

The total number of U.S. libraries listed in the 49th edition of *ALD* is 32,666, including 15,370 public libraries, 4,730 academic libraries, 10,282 special libraries, and 1,875 government libraries.

Understanding the Tables

Number of libraries includes only those U.S. libraries in *ALD* that reported annual acquisition expenditures (4,636 public libraries, 1,976 academic libraries, 1,590 special libraries, 404 government libraries). Libraries that reported annual income but not expenditures are not included in the count. Academic libraries include university, college, and junior college libraries. Special academic libraries, such as law and medical libraries, that reported acquisition expenditures separately from the institution's main library are counted as independent libraries.

The amount in the *total acquisition expenditures* column for a given state is generally greater than the sum of the categories of expenditures. This is because the total acquisition expenditures amount also includes the expenditures of libraries that did not itemize by category.

Figures in *categories of expenditure* columns represent only those libraries that itemized expenditures. Libraries that reported a total acquisition expenditure amount but did not itemize are only represented in the total acquisition expenditures column.

Unspecified includes monies reported as not specifically for books, periodicals, audiovisual materials and equipment, microform, preservation, other print materials, manuscripts and archives, machine-readable materials, or database fees (e.g., library materials). This column also includes monies reported for categories in combination—for example, audiovisual *and* microform. When libraries report only total acquisition expenditures without itemizing by category, the total amount is not reflected as unspecified.

Table 1 / Public Library Acquisition Expenditures

Categories of Expenditure

State	Number of Libraries	Total Acquisition Expenditures	Books	Other Print Materials	Periodicals	Manuscripts & Archives	AV Materials	AV Equipment	Microform	Machine Readable Materials	Preservation	Database Fees	Unspecified
Alabama	60	6,168,054	3,434,533	249,718	783,605	—	542,498	5,059	343,940	68,406	27,945	13,044	294,617
Alaska	19	1,771,026	737,325	111,095	531,006	—	58,363	40,925	15,544	28,236	5,690	1,550	754
Arizona	46	11,600,453	6,959,211	67,907	1,590,152	—	554,917	80,600	304,709	693,080	133,773	69,662	16,004
Arkansas	25	2,459,614	1,297,349	2,215	168,489	—	65,082	1,425	36,262	3,500	26,170	43,400	32,527
California	151	62,288,092	28,479,531	815,766	7,205,594	90,514	2,881,813	8,812	3,800,382	736,158	322,064	1,079,923	1,592,368
Colorado	86	11,260,661	6,119,880	259,984	1,175,126	10,715	597,989	22,000	97,672	204,435	24,428	234,969	203,769
Connecticut	124	12,913,209	6,017,960	630,880	828,480	1,750	608,804	30,140	239,464	131,141	46,072	408,638	116,848
Delaware	16	2,171,707	713,506	498	89,963	—	44,937	—	31,647	20,273	—	33,746	—
District of Columbia	3	10,746,000	30,000	—	5,000	—	5,000	—	—	—	—	—	5,000
Florida	90	35,982,342	17,605,223	128,950	4,646,295	—	2,165,490	111,558	645,106	922,606	173,298	408,421	322,188
Georgia	50	13,349,756	4,850,614	46,962	384,931	6,687	618,304	19,060	142,813	192,566	32,381	19,587	6,926
Hawaii	1	3,280,658	—	—	—	—	—	—	—	—	—	—	—
Idaho	55	2,067,292	1,100,884	2,300	139,973	—	121,473	8,000	12,029	23,086	4,336	109,257	11,375
Illinois	331	52,552,818	28,227,954	553,819	3,808,981	3,010	2,804,370	516,927	537,630	871,114	161,317	746,222	376,207
Indiana	121	23,978,294	13,655,934	29,624	1,790,855	5,500	2,704,555	125,382	507,007	446,218	151,341	203,665	510,024
Iowa	225	7,856,389	4,532,414	158,453	714,505	—	454,790	56,307	46,805	71,657	6,054	121,054	773,696
Kansas	129	6,398,775	2,851,690	52,780	429,501	—	292,200	14,593	38,057	93,565	22,204	146,675	135,359
Kentucky	66	7,272,159	3,918,935	43,809	480,200	3,358	302,738	166,651	64,085	139,294	2,703	305,826	138,562
Louisiana	41	9,764,824	4,640,830	58,331	871,041	—	364,864	24,815	107,704	7,856	41,725	116,410	5,000
Maine	84	2,188,064	1,044,373	2,244	178,576	698	70,034	6,200	5,700	5,276	7,071	44,764	5,709
Maryland	22	20,012,378	10,663,131	40,000	943,895	—	2,053,060	1,612	70,898	1,182,660	1,829	93,590	70,000
Massachusetts	221	12,956,483	7,513,404	30,171	1,135,771	—	650,932	43,318	207,281	222,309	18,466	230,257	88,057
Michigan	194	26,071,023	10,865,219	87,997	1,699,548	2,950	1,898,151	44,811	245,771	690,841	34,126	245,916	179,973
Minnesota	83	15,400,817	8,117,532	183,766	1,192,285	—	960,873	16,027	62,067	614,065	39,466	435,131	708,105
Mississippi	28	3,690,315	2,354,060	8,700	358,627	—	152,309	10,775	82,601	131,628	5,892	26,724	1,954

Missouri	80	12,704,866	7,928,658	84,435	1,163,459	219	1,133,278	40,200	534,784	258,522	10,183	108,913	243,904
Montana	43	1,507,246	736,707	1,120	158,803	—	30,206	787	2,356	14,595	6,620	105,817	50,509
Nebraska	75	3,141,927	1,397,343	8,650	188,945	200	106,515	2,230	26,584	22,916	14,850	77,528	35,292
Nevada	17	6,211,856	845,445	2,000	332,630	—	33,506	6,704	21,294	19,000	4,596	51,512	17,566
New Hampshire	109	2,538,915	1,152,034	11,583	142,346	—	89,880	9,000	68,233	20,402	11,258	8,974	10,012
New Jersey	166	23,094,494	12,482,787	62,782	2,310,970	1,750	1,318,932	147,021	432,939	650,334	63,967	500,469	615,976
New Mexico	31	3,618,438	926,279	15,000	88,240	—	36,073	7,000	4,310	10,050	6,178	11,750	15,000
New York	321	52,906,717	27,000,201	1,105,763	6,564,546	29,519	3,187,050	395,329	758,022	621,862	164,005	387,674	157,653
North Carolina	89	16,279,012	10,590,410	46,425	1,577,085	4,459	1,059,980	164,205	219,461	313,637	61,023	282,677	72,353
North Dakota	23	905,735	545,954	20,000	134,412	—	54,108	5,920	16,600	6,000	3,350	5,000	2,591
Ohio	149	53,958,653	30,803,497	847,678	6,419,749	332	6,477,751	62,379	852,819	945,786	943,657	1,366,518	358,300
Oklahoma	59	6,820,722	3,130,406	3,290	792,742	—	360,465	38,508	44,170	9,755	25,794	161,582	311,138
Oregon	80	27,328,853	4,509,294	79,925	1,134,421	—	762,704	250	27,457	181,813	52,855	32,795	25,290
Pennsylvania	270	19,678,805	7,247,222	79,866	1,562,220	800	881,186	50,859	190,195	179,927	149,623	276,090	332,892
Rhode Island	33	2,012,626	1,175,513	545	215,577	21,129	122,156	22,034	26,168	108,758	31,896	105,741	1,020
South Carolina	36	8,923,060	5,263,438	1,500	617,227	3,000	413,642	17,578	138,627	181,281	49,327	214,888	104,584
South Dakota	34	1,761,320	805,917	1,940	176,562	—	106,365	8,427	27,057	3,686	1,400	339,622	11,793
Tennessee	70	9,520,785	4,956,180	18,293	875,685	250	697,928	43,200	281,761	20,710	61,618	115,353	1,953,108
Texas	220	28,930,356	14,359,822	136,877	2,687,642	1,575	1,511,812	219,006	294,175	333,538	188,612	364,233	228,365
Utah	34	6,370,832	4,352,911	12,002	504,197	—	712,106	21,900	39,955	186,202	12,015	43,665	23,586
Vermont	66	1,363,327	865,341	3,500	148,293	—	29,455	1,200	21,002	1,600	300	2,800	2,000
Virginia	76	20,860,184	13,171,826	29,976	2,336,778	3,826	1,076,147	38,983	349,032	315,669	78,921	293,225	159,726
Washington	41	18,409,212	7,030,395	142,098	1,192,147	100	799,770	32,692	219,574	185,717	41,692	440,785	129,020
West Virginia	45	3,106,044	1,464,355	4,050	150,446	500	223,821	12,185	6,784	26,012	14,974	12,816	75,621
Wisconsin	179	13,359,092	6,957,807	84,195	1,700,472	—	960,407	76,032	111,582	172,658	32,372	147,910	703,944
Wyoming	17	1,249,081	582,387	525	76,886	—	92,065	3,450	39,670	7,014	8,819	37,411	15,850
Puerto Rico	2	364,134	309,184	2,250	12,000	—	—	—	—	—	32,700	—	8,000
Total	4,636	711,127,497	346,322,805	6,372,237	64,416,879	192,841	43,250,854	2,782,076	12,399,785	12,297,414	3,360,956	10,634,179	11,260,115
Estimated % of Acquisition Expenditure			67.47	1.24	12.55	0.04	8.43	0.54	2.42	2.40	0.65	2.07	2.19

Table 2 / Academic Library Acquisition Expenditures

Categories of Expenditure

State	Number of Libraries	Total Acquisition Expenditures	Books	Other Print Materials	Periodicals	Manuscripts & Archives	AV Materials	AV Equipment	Microform	Machine Readable Materials	Preservation	Database Fees	Unspecified
Alabama	30	5,290,391	1,849,230	119,770	2,191,709	3,500	72,583	123,652	88,653	88,607	96,863	34,244	321,648
Alaska	4	1,188,202	79,833	5,801	29,982	—	143	—	1,600	5,307	1,780	3,600	8,200
Arizona	18	18,781,475	6,758,211	2,900	7,284,467	—	146,787	37,700	423,525	138,460	278,931	313,586	381,606
Arkansas	20	4,363,669	1,524,086	10,062	1,886,554	2,594	82,723	25,689	242,987	165,779	86,718	145,879	14,891
California	153	84,802,919	23,362,645	1,507,093	35,262,183	4,463	670,860	365,034	1,463,048	1,567,446	3,092,304	1,310,353	1,331,492
Colorado	28	11,553,711	3,268,678	137,862	5,440,361	—	185,585	41,434	330,589	232,506	291,496	293,337	108,019
Connecticut	32	28,027,032	8,291,877	70,411	11,400,532	1,066,000	196,355	84,159	1,357,161	680,226	882,297	235,278	635,729
Delaware	6	5,231,384	2,303,928	33,580	2,653,344	45	25,554	2,910	26,582	14,346	2,910	37,250	130,315
District of Columbia	12	14,558,798	2,533,529	5,528	5,843,560	10,000	51,450	16,000	116,649	92,736	100,358	236,632	1,551,416
Florida	59	31,234,035	5,920,026	63,420	11,208,855	1,866	606,352	216,526	1,212,806	1,428,418	371,836	409,134	242,597
Georgia	48	19,811,307	5,464,342	78,755	7,158,954	—	218,615	167,909	1,007,075	253,946	159,111	683,222	642,024
Hawaii	15	6,664,043	2,330,134	400	2,578,497	—	89,919	16,320	293,271	191,589	274,786	139,790	145,905
Idaho	9	5,877,692	1,623,107	72,590	3,036,151	500	71,725	8,500	75,096	25,636	183,341	89,876	595,012
Illinois	82	45,940,594	13,216,112	515,957	18,041,323	5,200	698,193	417,703	682,150	861,812	450,046	557,535	627,868
Indiana	44	30,259,467	9,275,304	163,198	15,294,139	7,944	310,389	171,457	147,658	355,436	776,289	147,713	453,753
Iowa	37	18,899,661	3,399,124	171,758	4,837,178	200	155,265	126,648	208,506	104,938	287,722	100,876	277,099
Kansas	34	12,588,516	4,405,662	171,010	6,485,987	48,198	101,893	78,183	114,716	178,075	608,687	138,923	53,598
Kentucky	34	16,478,075	4,548,749	264,344	9,027,546	25,900	157,626	48,954	341,532	303,831	314,791	245,341	663,451
Louisiana	23	14,279,603	3,972,155	101,607	7,933,910	29,939	74,124	205,117	260,166	138,378	227,453	77,258	149,556
Maine	23	7,529,461	2,521,725	244,297	3,519,004	9,000	75,219	76,040	228,851	167,403	130,286	81,526	69,368
Maryland	36	14,429,721	4,747,450	70,987	6,033,714	—	194,183	138,664	530,911	633,191	383,419	195,271	1,028,200
Massachusetts	73	41,518,006	11,228,124	829,720	18,256,262	31,032	487,834	178,541	613,739	835,200	1,310,990	1,459,073	1,368,390
Michigan	56	34,193,219	5,664,142	338,462	9,230,309	11,473	326,497	101,427	616,278	454,656	523,781	894,956	623,587
Minnesota	37	19,251,600	5,950,530	985,936	9,302,124	—	224,629	123,837	190,602	309,717	755,137	220,748	203,963
Mississippi	25	10,096,024	1,885,113	—	6,147,382	21,250	282,943	62,023	359,805	278,394	223,256	214,981	244,871

Missouri	47	22,892,281	5,180,644	26,806	10,253,832	2,158	483,294	165,843	656,737	1,143,083	512,361	795,134	317,460
Montana	15	2,548,998	553,635	3,908	1,537,265	—	25,203	8,850	30,351	15,662	7,098	16,817	29,890
Nebraska	19	5,520,419	1,530,251	128,158	2,434,848	—	69,569	60,469	96,661	59,161	100,264	129,486	490,561
Nevada	7	5,506,324	886,326	1,359	1,513,929	—	73,845	9,046	56,337	166,741	133,003	47,624	16,276
New Hampshire	16	2,322,279	829,805	37,000	654,409	—	25,311	48,689	94,959	113,940	71,381	60,679	34,600
New Jersey	34	24,406,737	7,922,920	1,096,842	9,296,567	200,472	309,884	132,420	825,317	665,450	103,466	363,654	1,088,766
New Mexico	17	7,288,517	2,205,205	8,182	4,172,542	—	49,756	48,600	367,284	151,904	153,510	73,786	36,526
New York	146	91,490,692	21,312,588	1,510,304	37,173,923	15,225	1,018,960	357,925	1,831,325	2,386,883	1,778,789	1,861,628	5,956,105
North Carolina	76	37,069,572	9,553,113	23,431	11,367,398	5,588	721,258	565,433	887,797	886,729	322,773	432,237	497,885
North Dakota	8	1,952,371	508,018	20,357	1,144,232	—	35,771	27,382	59,833	4,352	4,168	64,792	9,300
Ohio	72	38,201,360	10,696,062	507,472	16,176,283	882	489,922	168,175	1,280,111	1,209,134	884,618	377,505	1,099,569
Oklahoma	33	12,166,390	2,083,032	130,132	4,496,516	2,900	48,146	47,705	198,156	242,828	194,402	116,966	112,747
Oregon	30	11,504,124	3,572,562	1,783	5,459,845	500	198,125	50,477	201,555	245,302	251,774	165,327	240,126
Pennsylvania	113	54,247,638	14,340,691	821,452	21,393,157	15,750	732,617	329,737	1,193,637	1,169,226	1,460,695	739,194	990,339
Rhode Island	11	3,903,989	877,246	68,000	2,143,515	4,822	53,977	39,536	139,391	132,364	86,632	38,065	2,767
South Carolina	36	12,743,860	3,917,957	99,931	6,337,667	790	194,909	24,551	217,449	349,213	374,946	128,019	97,235
South Dakota	11	4,324,867	1,103,612	132,888	1,964,178	—	34,222	135,529	40,583	51,802	91,186	86,156	432,604
Tennessee	43	21,897,520	5,503,970	310,907	10,619,606	1,050	210,801	123,957	382,974	368,257	272,640	206,219	1,928,490
Texas	102	58,939,529	14,451,887	470,767	24,300,519	30,701	1,414,220	371,474	1,625,932	2,184,295	974,550	1,886,806	1,937,653
Utah	6	3,808,670	818,925	—	2,019,110	—	94,304	86,024	44,548	161,943	137,717	148,312	72,514
Vermont	19	6,546,253	2,159,665	500	2,061,798	200	57,350	70,970	323,690	217,878	122,191	181,898	1,106,706
Virginia	53	34,966,143	10,388,744	679,258	14,773,496	2,000	536,073	402,845	1,142,603	1,670,523	446,641	342,739	1,347,456
Washington	34	23,628,280	6,534,326	179,995	13,251,835	2,300	316,160	187,415	293,016	268,776	231,483	488,186	78,432
West Virginia	21	6,660,014	1,907,917	35,465	3,366,801	—	48,559	77,699	111,798	84,510	98,759	82,878	640,609
Wisconsin	50	21,254,818	3,744,782	8,727	6,183,774	800	410,006	271,914	470,876	536,873	261,586	341,488	1,420,131
Wyoming	5	2,792,877	267,695	5,465	2,019,586	—	27,607	13,044	6,800	17,000	72,569	24,376	322,685
Pacific Islands	3	300,136	38,687	—	182,281	—	6,143	—	41,570	15,156	—	4,799	—
Puerto Rico	10	3,580,127	1,270,895	1,100	1,947,775	500	115,000	47,300	713	26,640	71,995	59,385	37,250
Virgin Islands	1	56,300	28,000	—	23,000	—	—	—	5,000	—	—	300	—
Total	1,976	1,025,369,690	270,312,976	12,275,637	428,353,714	1,565,742	13,308,438	6,707,436	23,560,959	24,051,658	21,035,785	17,530,837	32,217,240
Estimated % of Acquisition Expenditure			31.77	1.44	50.34	0.18	1.56	0.79	2.77	2.83	2.47	2.06	3.79

Table 3 / Special Library Acquisition Expenditures

State	Number of Libraries	Total Acquisition Expenditures	Books	Other Print Materials	Periodicals	Manuscripts & Archives	AV Materials	AV Equipment	Microform	Machine Readable Materials	Preservation	Database Fees	Unspecified
Alabama	7	233,296	37,400	1,000	86,577	1,000	—	—	3,000	30,000	1,500	10,500	—
Alaska	5	24,271	12,535	—	5,500	300	86	—	—	1,600	200	—	—
Arizona	36	1,031,153	154,301	6,500	182,540	700	13,130	14,000	10,300	9,095	11,230	61,952	12,970
Arkansas	4	46,853	28,300	1,003	15,750	100	—	—	200	—	500	—	—
California	168	10,882,981	1,446,682	81,031	2,626,468	81,200	113,770	66,252	142,602	265,790	102,744	1,901,531	99,947
Colorado	29	2,458,642	447,884	41,000	771,055	33,820	15,530	—	25,000	97,400	3,840	397,050	22,000
Connecticut	34	2,730,948	576,230	131,299	841,414	77,269	39,395	7,500	35,570	64,175	182,825	210,409	20,600
Delaware	7	1,142,455	189,395	—	158,500	—	3,750	3,000	4,935	—	12,200	76,260	568,000
District of Columbia	43	10,739,236	1,656,643	286,250	1,774,160	—	3,750	700	21,700	64,500	74,650	205,235	3,100
Florida	46	1,761,403	260,755	3,550	417,926	10,000	33,402	18,615	28,700	59,015	29,025	326,400	31,525
Georgia	28	1,451,204	121,192	3,300	317,742	—	18,150	7,500	17,500	92,504	21,800	158,282	3,706
Hawaii	5	267,661	47,702	—	125,992	—	—	—	—	6,200	1,208	19,880	—
Idaho	7	124,713	17,700	—	40,535	—	—	—	—	—	178	11,000	—
Illinois	97	5,381,590	1,516,040	32,048	1,322,953	81,025	54,936	26,800	78,008	95,262	46,924	191,337	10,068
Indiana	32	906,441	142,573	4,100	299,772	—	22,022	11,000	30,500	79,500	1,625	246,489	—
Iowa	23	877,181	423,995	17,389	314,465	—	14,194	1,000	900	5,500	10,110	23,357	6,000
Kansas	10	166,424	46,679	4,500	86,790	—	—	5,550	12,700	—	2,850	5,855	—
Kentucky	14	597,195	133,775	—	164,607	—	12,200	5,000	23,500	—	2,400	2,525	—
Louisiana	6	151,726	31,800	2,425	64,200	2,000	6,251	—	—	5,000	3,000	50	—
Maine	18	582,602	137,594	2,418	62,009	200	5,725	4,680	40,000	1,168	53,540	22,250	326
Maryland	49	3,265,433	747,342	68,005	1,404,763	7,550	22,280	30,834	85,810	25,900	47,441	333,656	50,300
Massachusetts	72	8,251,473	1,040,290	18,610	1,652,436	1,350	45,986	22,570	12,679	40,030	47,916	396,268	96,726
Michigan	47	2,902,137	566,968	2,223	1,128,707	2,800	41,558	6,210	16,676	125,054	14,927	203,775	44,959
Minnesota	35	374,493,576	111,430,005	200,040,200	62,697,766	2,500	14,950	10,000	15,391	71,599	3,100	68,700	610
Mississippi	4	58,053	125	25	55,165	—	2,200	100	238	—	200	—	—

Missouri	34	4,178,379	560,697	75,739	2,098,560	1,650	3,805	34,725	8,125	143,967	65,352	380,444
Montana	10	208,468	24,078	1,030	34,104	115,000	468	—	11,751	700	736	—
Nebraska	13	291,927	27,904	200	52,295	2,000	2,007	—	39,102	1,250	3,395	10,071
Nevada	3	80,100	15,000	—	30,500	—	—	—	—	2,600	2,105	—
New Hampshire	19	1,246,206	289,408	4,000	529,520	5,000	3,100	15,631	2,210	26,500	28,149	10,000
New Jersey	49	3,522,162	909,580	8,775	1,419,296	3,525	29,359	30,068	56,020	88,550	396,044	20,576
New Mexico	20	281,005	92,520	1,300	77,934	—	2,750	100	750	200	2,000	600
New York	141	11,672,903	2,161,180	91,425	2,036,547	42,800	36,663	42,295	49,015	215,837	501,458	173,553
North Carolina	27	1,009,607	269,002	9,250	417,798	65	19,800	12,500	20,288	1,700	52,800	200
North Dakota	3	112,541	22,046	—	30,498	—	1,430	7,355	—	25,801	—	3,136
Ohio	64	5,851,490	710,091	357,244	757,720	17,959	21,172	5,250	23,790	35,817	192,522	34,654
Oklahoma	9	251,550	34,000	2,000	155,000	—	2,500	4,000	6,000	—	1,550	—
Oregon	17	540,254	85,559	3,640	176,746	—	8,255	700	4,125	1,049	26,400	—
Pennsylvania	99	6,844,349	868,965	63,660	1,689,943	219,815	46,176	28,870	122,353	94,596	490,178	70,616
Rhode Island	9	50,706	23,564	300	12,534	—	1,742	—	100	9,232	—	1,838
South Carolina	9	367,053	44,500	165	45,413	3,500	10,000	5,000	16,000	5,900	10,544	9,400
South Dakota	3	124,139	46,120	—	55,500	—	—	—	—	—	15,919	—
Tennessee	17	397,327	94,717	2,718	121,407	2,030	15,073	40	5,100	7,272	11,218	1,164
Texas	58	5,954,937	914,251	10,340	1,807,440	14,300	36,353	2,164	21,248	29,805	271,550	64,844
Utah	6	331,850	221,035	—	12,515	—	5,000	—	50,000	40,000	—	—
Vermont	11	159,793	23,791	100	14,612	1,595	280	—	—	5,071	6,630	—
Virginia	57	2,223,686	471,050	17,469	554,705	73,565	17,349	30,625	145,279	29,104	76,179	8,990
Washington	27	1,643,364	166,807	3,887	632,049	12,350	1,813	6,275	900	9,996	148,350	—
West Virginia	8	578,947	92,000	1,900	420,400	—	7,500	11,375	10,500	2,300	12,400	590
Wisconsin	41	1,826,054	558,736	46,465	445,645	4,200	50,100	16,000	8,050	11,200	121,325	46,290
Wyoming	7	33,805	3,050	150	350	100	500	100	200	250	600	285
Puerto Rico	3	183,116	60,212	—	100,545	—	12,105	—	—	6,254	—	3,500
Total	1,590	480,494,365	130,003,768	201,448,633	90,347,418	821,268	818,565	494,384	1,206,815	1,470,884	7,310,165	1,811,588
Estimated % of Acquisition Expenditure			29.68	45.98	20.62	0.19	0.19	0.11	0.28	0.53	0.34	1.67	0.41

Table 4 / Government Library Acquisition Expenditures

Categories of Expenditure

State	Number of Libraries	Total Acquisition Expenditures	Books	Other Print Materials	Periodicals	Manuscripts & Archives	AV Materials	AV Equipment	Microform	Machine Readable Materials	Preservation	Database Fees	Unspecified
Alabama	6	408,664	155,212	3,000	99,189	—	14,200	—	5,672	11,096	—	97,675	5,450
Alaska	10	135,650	24,450	2,050	80,350	—	500	—	—	1,350	—	16,250	500
Arizona	12	533,078	309,714	—	19,001	—	4,100	100	—	13,546	3,553	3,046	37,269
Arkansas	1	59,259	10,082	2,183	30,200	—	5,832	—	4,270	—	—	5,214	1,478
California	37	7,047,185	1,461,044	327,396	2,640,883	—	22,440	34,616	87,213	53,843	96,800	87,505	79,257
Colorado	16	1,012,653	111,171	400	184,694	300	8,578	7,600	33,950	21,500	500	62,827	—
Connecticut	6	188,865	13,275	2,000	33,600	1,000	3,075	3,000	—	10,000	—	10,225	—
Delaware	2	172,623	170,673	—	1,000	—	—	—	—	—	950	—	—
District of Columbia	19	3,525,200	429,800	44,700	677,300	3,400	40,500	10,500	229,000	133,000	13,750	1,417,750	34,000
Florida	23	2,313,453	486,831	17,000	657,440	1,000	51,858	2,175	22,629	25,876	1,500	30,417	4,323
Georgia	4	160,000	26,000	—	36,100	—	—	—	5,000	7,500	900	—	—
Hawaii	1	840,572	254,754	557,805	—	—	—	—	2,496	—	—	—	25,517
Idaho	2	337,400	11,000	—	37,000	—	800	—	—	7,400	—	2,400	—
Illinois	13	4,452,710	1,100,485	—	226,245	—	7,200	1,000	50,458	700	83,000	7,000	—
Indiana	6	274,700	35,000	—	2,000	—	—	1,260	—	—	11,457	—	—
Iowa	2	19,669	6,700	500	8,250	20	400	400	—	2,000	—	700	—
Kansas	5	736,857	271,224	192,509	219,751	700	5,200	6,300	4,800	5,000	16,132	14,941	—
Kentucky	3	474,600	376,500	12,000	8,500	—	—	—	9,895	—	2,700	7,700	8,863
Louisiana	4	2,717,040	6,000	200	58,000	—	600	—	—	3,500	300	12,340	1,000
Maine	2	227,999	11,280	—	172,976	—	—	—	2,387	—	1,314	30,542	—
Maryland	8	5,842,250	1,004,450	2,000	3,071,400	25,000	155,500	20,100	10,000	37,000	1,077,000	176,500	1,700
Massachusetts	15	2,756,228	2,096,452	—	97,823	1,000	4,000	1,050	8,746	550	2,235	—	—
Michigan	9	667,014	116,158	3,350	228,538	—	21,110	100	7,899	14,100	120	22,029	4,680
Minnesota	6	579,896	39,833	212,650	203,098	—	5,421	3,400	13,000	22,480	10,500	50,689	5,675
Mississippi	3	306,090	19,500	—	85,000	—	3,892	—	—	—	—	1,168	—

Missouri	10	354,195	33,618	300	80,177	—	11,400	—	—	—	21,800	—
Montana	4	287,376	8,430	1,539	19,874	—	—	—	3,565	264	2,500	1,507
Nebraska	5	95,750	12,507	—	21,647	—	54,142	—	—	—	1,322	4,000
Nevada	4	673,664	474,043	2,000	83,072	—	5,000	5,520	3,304	5,375	64,331	—
New Hampshire	4	96,500	37,500	5,000	20,500	—	1,000	—	29,500	50	—	—
New Jersey	6	385,000	95,547	5,000	107,553	—	—	—	—	442	89,000	7,000
New Mexico	6	472,400	27,000	164,250	69,450	—	6,000	2,500	2,000	5,252	61,800	4,500
New York	30	2,715,971	1,041,628	31,050	579,256	—	68,552	3,097	40,869	—	27,983	17,083
North Carolina	8	1,016,779	451,946	3,050	486,567	—	4,000	—	25,716	500	6,020	4,050
North Dakota	2	53,300	5,400	—	15,950	—	50	—	—	12,000	5,430	2,370
Ohio	11	810,506	597,555	61,000	69,081	—	11,000	2,000	4,285	18,100	14,795	4,805
Oklahoma	8	272,495	21,184	132	158,010	—	267	1,000	—	16,185	10,895	1,021
Oregon	6	540,563	104,024	—	194,900	—	—	—	4,200	300	10,939	—
Pennsylvania	13	1,927,557	574,001	40,000	4,500	—	—	—	12,150	2,500	14,500	—
Rhode Island	3	122,687	37,969	—	63,349	—	2,040	—	3,895	1,539	1,000	—
South Carolina	3	106,273	500	—	100	—	500	—	14,333	—	54,355	—
South Dakota	5	89,343	14,882	—	50,094	—	3,342	3,141	2,425	4,600	600	—
Tennessee	3	30,491	16,646	—	7,845	—	—	—	6,000	—	—	11,822
Texas	10	155,024	40,909	1,387	57,551	117	6,496	4,400	8,000	—	682	4,700
Utah	4	817,870	6,000	—	24,500	—	12,700	10,000	60,000	4,478	25,000	—
Vermont	1	30,158	1,000	1,500	100	—	—	—	3,000	4,830	200	—
Virginia	11	853,770	110,150	24,000	195,820	22,000	300	—	7,000	5,000	134,000	130,300
Washington	12	1,656,934	60,123	—	277,093	—	14,608	—	3,000	3,500	14,471	30,564
West Virginia	4	590,300	366,500	2,900	89,500	400	4,780	300	16,500	10,736	32,055	31,665
Wisconsin	10	770,857	109,313	10,000	187,119	600	5,515	4,000	4,828	6,000	59,555	802
Wyoming	4	239,430	176,230	3,000	30,100	—	2,500	10,000	4,900	4,700	2,000	—
Puerto Rico	2	426,471	142,344	—	273,127	—	—	500	10,000	—	—	4,500
Total	404	51,378,319	13,114,537	1,735,851	12,045,173	55,537	569,398	138,059	756,885	1,418,495	2,712,421	470,401
Estimated % of Acquisition Expenditure			38.89	5.15	35.71	0.16	1.69	0.41	2.24	2.10	4.21	8.04	1.39

Price Indexes for Public and Academic Libraries

Research Associates of Washington, 2605 Klingle Rd. N.W., Washington DC 20008
202-966-3326

Kent Halstead

A rise in prices with the gradual loss of the dollar's value has been a continuing phenomenon in the U.S. economy. This article reports price indexes measuring this inflation for public libraries, college and university academic libraries, and school libraries. (Current data for these indexes are published annually by Research Associates of Washington. See *Inflation Measures for Schools, Colleges and Libraries, 1996 Update*.) Price indexes report the year-to-year price level of what is purchased. Dividing past expenditures per user unit by index values determines if purchasing power has been maintained. Future funding requirements to offset expected inflation may be estimated by projecting the indexes.

A price index compares the aggregate price level of a fixed market basket of goods and services in a given year with the price in the base year. To measure price change accurately, the *quality* and *quantity* of the items purchased must remain constant as defined in the base year. Weights attached to the importance of each item in the budget are changed infrequently—only when the relative *amount* of the various items purchased clearly shifts or when new items are introduced.

Public Library Price Index

The Public Library Price Index (PLPI) is designed for a hypothetical *average* public library. The index together with its various subcomponents are reported in Tables 2 through 6. The PLPI reflects the relative year-to-year price level of the goods and services purchased by public libraries for their current operations. The budget mix shown in Table 1 is based on national and state average expenditure patterns. Individual libraries may need to tailor the weighting scheme to match their own budget compositions.

The Public Library Price Index components are described below together with sources of the price series employed.

Personnel Compensation

PL1.0 Salaries and Wages

PL1.1 *Professional libraries*—Average salary of professional librarians at medium and large size libraries. Six positions are reported: director, deputy/associate/assistant director, department head/branch head, reference/information librarian, cataloger and/or classifier and children's and/or young adult services librarian. Source: Mary Jo Lynch, Margaret Myers, and Jeniece Guy, *ALA Survey of Librarian Salaries, 1994* Office for Research and Statistics, American Library Association, Chicago, IL, 1994.

(text continues on page 449)

Table 1 / Taxonomy of Public Library Current Operations Expenditures by Object Category, 1991–1992 estimate

Category	Mean	Percent	Distribution
Personnel Compensation			64.7
PL1.0 Salaries and Wages		81.8	
PL1.1 Professional librarians	44		
PL1.2 Other professional and managerial staff	6		
PL1.3 Technical staff (copy cataloging, circulation, binding, etc.)	43		
PL1.4 Support staff (clerical, custodial, guard, etc.)	7		
	100		
PL2.0 Fringe Benefits		18.2	
		100.0	
Acquisitions			15.2
PL3.0 Books and Serials		74.0	
PL3.1 Books printed	82		
PL3.1a Hardcover			
PL3.1b Trade paper			
PL3.1c Mass market paper			
PL3.2 Periodicals (U.S. and foreign titles)	16		
PL3.2a U.S. titles			
PL3.2b Foreign titles			
PL3.3 Other serials (newspapers, annuals, proceedings, etc.)	2		
	100		
PL4.0 Other Printed Materials		2.0	
PL5.0 Non-Print Media		22.0	
PL5.1 Microforms (microfiche and microfilm)	21		
PL5.2 Audio recordings (primarily instructional and children's content)	17		
PL5.2a Tape cassette			
PL5.2b Compact disk			
PL5.3 Video (TV) recordings (primarily books & children's content)	58		
PL5.3a VHS Cassette			
PL5.3b Laser disk			
PL5.4 Graphic image individual item use	2		
PL5.5 Computer files (CD-Rom, floppy disks, and tape)	2		
	100		
PL6.0 Electronic Services		2.0	
		100.0	
Operating Expenses			20.1
PL7.0 Office Operations		27.0	
PL7.1 Office expenses	20		
PL7.2 Supplies and materials	80		
	100		
PL8.0 Contracted Services		38.0	
PL9.0 Non-capital Equipment		1.0	
PL10.0 Utilities		34.0	
		100.0	100.0

Table 2 / Public Library Price Index and Major Component Subindexes, FY 1992 to 1995

1992=100 Fiscal year	Personnel Compensation — Salaries and wages (PL1.0)	Personnel Compensation — Fringe benefits (PL2.0)	Acquisitions — Books and serials (PL3.0)	Acquisitions — Other printed materials (PL4.0)	Acquisitions — Non-print media (PL5.0)	Acquisitions — On-line services (PL6.0)	Operating Expenses — Office operations (PL7.0)	Operating Expenses — Contracted services (PL8.0)	Operating Expenses — Non-capital Equipment (PL9.0)	Operating Expenses — Utilities (PL10.0)	Public Library Price Index^ PLPI
1992	100	100	100	100	100	100	100	100	100	100	100
1993	102.5	104.8	101.7	102.9	75.3	101.6	99.2	102.6	101.8	101.5	101.5
1994	105.8	107.9	103.8	105.5	65.8	103.3	100.8	105.1	103.6	105.8	104.2
1995	110.5	110.6	105.1	107.7	64.8	104.9	102.6	107.7	105.7	103.8	107.2
1993	2.50%	4.80%	1.70%	2.90%	-24.71%	1.60%	-.80%	2.60%	1.80%	1.50%	1.50%
1994	3.20%	3.00%	2.10%	2.50%	-12.61%	1.70%	1.60%	2.40%	1.70%	4.20%	2.60%
1995	4.40%	2.50%	1.20%	2.10%	-1.41%	1.50%	1.70%	2.50%	2.10%	-1.90%	2.90%

^ PLPI weightings: See text.
Sources: See text.

Table 3 / Public Library Price Index, Personnel Compensation, FY 1992 to 1995

1992=100 Fiscal year	Professional librarians — Medium size lib~	Professional librarians — Large size lib~	Professional librarians — Index^ (PL1.1)	Other professional & managerial (PL1.2)	Technical staff (PL1.3)	Support staff (PL1.4)	Salaries & wages index* (PL1.0)	Fringe benefits index (PL2.0)
1992	100.0	100.0	100.0	100.0	100.0	100.0	100.0	100.0
1993	105.0	99.5	102.3	102.8	102.7	102.8	102.5	104.8
1994	109.2	102.7	106.0	105.7	105.7	106.0	105.8	107.9
1995	115.5	106.9	111.2	109.5	110.1	109.1	110.5	110.6
1993	5.0	-0.5%	2.3%	2.8%	2.7%	2.8%	2.5%	4.8%
1994	4.0%	3.2%	3.6%	2.8%	2.9%	3.1%	3.2%	3.0%
1995	5.8%	4.1%	5.0%	3.6%	4.2%	2.9%	4.4%	2.5%

~ medium size libraries have service areas from 25,000 to 99,999 population; large libraries, 100,000 or more.
^ Professional librarian salary weights: 50% medium libraries + 50% large libraries.
* Salaries and wages index weights: 44% professional librarians + 6% other professional + 43% technical staff + 7% support staff.
Sources: See text.

Table 4 / Public Library Price Index, Books and Serials, FY 1992 to 1995

Books and Serials

1992=100	Hardcover		Trade paper		Mass market		Books printed index* (PL3.1)	Periodicals United States		Periodicals Foreign			Other serials (newspapers)		Books & Serials index (PL3.0)	Other printed materials index (PL4.0)
Fiscal year	Price^	Index (PL3.1a)	Price^	Index (PL3.1b)	Price^	Index (PL3.1c)		Price^	Index (PL3.2a)	Price^	Index (PL3.2b)	Periodicals index~ (PL3.2)	Price	Index (PL3.3)		
1992	$12.85	100	$7.24	100	$2.71	100	100	$45.18	100.0	$117.71	100.0	100	$222.68	100	100	100
1993	12.98	101.0	7.40	102.2	2.79	103.0	101.2	46.97	104.0	123.76	105.1	104.1	229.92	103.3	101.7	102.9
1994	13.16	102.4	7.59	104.8	2.85	105.2	102.7	48.61	107.6	128.90	109.5	107.8	261.91	117.6	103.8	105.5
1995	13.19	102.6	7.75	107.0	2.98	110.0	103.2	50.67	112.2	139.08	118.2	112.9	270.22	121.3	105.1	107.7
1993		1.00%		2.20%		3.00%	1.20%		4.00%		5.10%	4.10%		3.30%	1.70%	2.90%
1994		1.40%		2.60%		2.20%	1.50%		3.50%		4.20%	3.60%		13.90%	2.10%	2.50%
1995		0.20%		2.10%		4.60%	0.50%		4.20%		7.90%	4.70%		3.20%	1.20%	2.10%

^ Book and periodical prices are for calendar year. *Books printed index weights: 89.5% hardcover + 8.2% trade paper + 2.3% mass market.
~ Periodical index weights: 87.9% U.S.titles + 12.1% foreign titles. Shaded cell data estimated by Research Associates of Washington. Sources: See text.
^ Other serials prices are for calendar year. ^ Books & serials index weights: 82% books + 16% periodicals + 2% other serials. Sources: See text.

Table 5 / Public Library Price Index, Non-Print Media and On-Line Services, FY 1992 to 1995

Non-Print Media

Fiscal year 1992=100	Microforms (microfilm) Index (PL5.1)	Audio recordings Tape cassette Price^	Index (PL5.2a)	Compact disk Price^	Index (PL5.2b)	Audio recordings* index (PL5.2)	Video VHS cassette Price^	Index (PL5.3a)	Laser disk Price^	Index (PL5.3b)	Video index (PL5.3)	Graphic image (PL5.4)	Computer files (CD-ROM) Price^	Index (PL5.5)	Non-print media index* (PL5.0)	On-line services index (PL6.0)
1992	100.0	$12.18	100	NA		100	$199.67	100	NA	NA	100	100	$1,601	100	100	100
1993	104.3	11.73	96.3	NA		96.3	112.92	56.6	NA	NA	56.6	97.3	1,793	112.0	75.3	101.6
1994	107.9	8.20	67.3	13.36	67.3	67.3	93.22	46.7	NA	NA	46.7	108.4	1,945	121.5	65.8	103.3
1995	110.6	8.82	72.4	14.80	74.6	73.5	84.19	42.2	NA	NA	42.2	111.3	1,986	122.5	64.8	104.9
1993	4.30%		-3.70%			-3.70%		-43.40%			-43.40%	-2.70%		12.0%	-24.70%	1.60%
1994	3.50%		-30.10%			-30.10%		-17.40%			-17.40%	11.40%		8.50%	-12.60%	1.70%
1995	2.50%		7.60%		10.80%	9.20%		-9.70%			-9.70%	2.70%		0.80%	-1.40%	1.50%

^ Prices are for immediate preceding calendar year, e.g., CY 1993 prices are reported for FY 1994.
* Audio recordings index weights: 50% tape cassette + 50% compact disk. Non-print media index weights: 21% microforms + 17% audio recordings + 58% video + 2% graphic image + 2% computer files.
Sources: See text

Table 6 / Public Library Price Index, Operating Expenses, FY 1992 to 1995

1992=100

Fiscal year	Office Operations — Office expenses (PL7.1)	Supplies and materials (PL7.2)	Office Operations index^ (PL7.0)	Contracted services index (PL8.0)	Noncapital equipment index (PL9.0)	Utilities index (PL10.0)
1992	100	100	100	100	100	100
1993	103.1	98.3	99.2	102.6	101.8	101.5
1994	107.3	99.2	100.8	105.1	103.6	105.8
1995	111.1	100.4	102.6	107.7	105.7	103.8
1993	3.10%	-1.70%	-.80%	2.60%	1.80%	1.50%
1994	4.10%	1.0%	1.50%	2.40%	1.70%	4.20%
1995	3.50%	1.20%	1.70%	2.50%	2.10%	-1.90%

^ Office operations index weights: 20% office expenses + 80% supplies and materials.
Sources: See text.

(text continued from page 444)

PL1.2 *Other professional and managerial staff* (systems analyst, business manager, public relations, personnel, etc.)—Employment Cost Index (ECI) for wages and salaries for state and local government workers employed in "Executive, administrative, and managerial" occupations, *Employment Cost Index*, Bureau of Labor Statistics, U.S. Department of Labor, Washington, DC.

PL1.3 *Technical staff* (copy cataloging, circulation, binding, etc.)—ECI as above for government employees in "Service" occupations.

PL1.4 *Support staff* (clerical, custodial, guard, etc.)—ECI as above for government employees in "Administrative support, including clerical" occupations.

PL2.0 Fringe Benefits

ECI as above for state and local government worker "Benefits."

Acquisitions

PL3.0 Books and Serials

PL3.1 *Books printed*—Weighted average of sale prices (including jobber's discount) of hardcover (PL3.1a), trade paper (PL3.1b), and mass market paperback books (PL3.1c) sold to public libraries. Excludes university press publications and reference works. Source: Frank Daly, Baker & Taylor Books, Bridgewater, NJ.

PL3.2 *Periodicals*—Publisher's prices of sales of approximately 2,400 U.S. serial titles (PL3.2a) and 115 foreign serials (PL3.2b) sold to public libraries. Source: *Serials Prices 1991–1995*, EBSCO Subscription Services, Birmingham, AL.

PL3.3 *Other serials* (newspapers, annuals, proceedings, etc.)—Average prices of approximately 170 U.S. daily newspapers. Source: Genevieve S. Owens, University of Missouri, St. Louis, and Wilba Swearingen, Louisiana State

University Medical Center. Reported by Adrian W. Alexander, "Prices of U.S. and Foreign Published Materials," in *The Bowker Annual*, R. R. Bowker, New Providence, NJ.

PL4.0 Other Printed Materials (manuscripts, documents, pamphlets, sheet music, printed material for the handicapped, etc.)

No direct price series exists for this category. The proxy price series used is the Producer Price Index for publishing pamphlets and catalogs and directories, Bureau of Labor Statistics.

PL5.0 Non-Print Media

PL5.1 *Microforms*—Producer Price Index for micropublishing in microform, including original and republished material, Bureau of Labor Statistics.

PL5.2 *Audio recordings*

PL5.2a *Tape cassette*—Cost per cassette of sound recording. Source: Dana Alessi, Baker & Taylor Books, Bridgewater, NJ. Reported by Alexander in *The Bowker Annual*, R. R. Bowker, New Providence, NJ.

PL5.2b *Compact disk*—Cost per compact disk. Source: See Alessi above.

PL5.3 *Video (TV) recordings*

PL5.3a. *VHS cassette*—Cost per video. Source: See Alessi above.

PL5.3b. *Laser disk*—No price series currently available.

PL5.4 *Graphic image* (individual use of such items as maps, photos, art work, single slides, etc.). The following proxy is used. Average median weekly earnings for the following two occupational groups: painters, sculptors, craft artists, and artist printmakers; and photographers. Source: *Employment and Earnings Series*, U.S. Bureau of Labor Statistics

PL5.5 *Computer files* (CD-ROM, floppy disks, and tape). Average price of CD-ROM disks. Source: Martha Kellogg and Theodore Kellogg, University of Rhode Island. Reported by Alexander in *The Bowker Annual*, R. R. Bowker, New Providence, NJ.

PL6.0 Electronic Services

Average price for selected digital electronic computer and telecommunications networking available to libraries. Source: This source has requested anonymity.

Operating Expenses

PL7.0 Office Operations

PL7.1 *Office expenses* (telephone, postage and freight, publicity and printing, travel, professional fees, automobile operating cost, etc.)—The price series used for office expenses consists of the subindex for printed materials (PL4.0) described above; Consumer Price Index values for telephone and postage; CPI values for public transportation; the IRS allowance for individual business travel as reported by Runzheimer International; and CPI values for college tuition as a proxy for professional fees.

PL7.2 *Supplies and materials*—Producer Price Index price series for office supplies, writing papers, and pens and pencils. Source: U.S. Bureau of Labor Statistics.

PL8.0 Contracted Services (outside contracts for cleaning, building and grounds maintenance, equipment rental and repair, acquisition processing, binding, auditing, legal, payroll, etc.)

Prices used for contracted services include ECI wages paid material handlers, equipment cleaners, helpers, and laborers; average weekly earnings of production or non-supervisory workers in the printing and publishing industry, and the price of printing paper, as a proxy for binding costs; ECI salaries of attorneys, directors of personnel, and accountant, for contracted consulting fees; and ECI wages of precision production, craft, and repair occupations for the costs of equipment rental and repair.

PL9.0 Non-Capital Equipment

The type of equipment generally purchased as part of current library operations is usually small and easily movable. To be classified as "equipment" rather than as "expendable utensils" or "supplies," an item generally must cost $50 or more and have a useful life of at least three years. Examples may be hand calculators, small TVs, simple cameras, tape recorders, pagers, fans, desk lamps, books, etc. Equipment purchased as an operating expenditure is usually not depreciated. Items priced for this category include PPI commodity price series for machinery and equipment, office and store machines/equipment, hand tools, cutting tools and accessories, scales and balances, electrical measuring instruments, television receivers, musical instruments, photographic equipment, sporting and athletic goods, and books and periodicals.

PL10.0 Utilities

This subindex is a composite of the Producer Price Index series for natural gas, residual fuels, and commercial electric power, and the Consumer Price Index series for water and sewerage services. Source: U.S. Bureau of Labor Statistics.

Academic Library Price Indexes

The two academic library price indexes—the University Library Price Index (ULPI) and the College Library Price Index (CLPI)—together with their various subcomponents are reported for 1992–1995 in Tables 8–12A. The two indexes report the relative year-to-year price level of the staff salaries, acquisitions, and other goods and services purchased by university and college libraries respectively for their current operations. Universities are the 500 institutions with doctorate programs responding to the National Center for Education Statistics, U.S. Department of Education, *Academic Library Survey, 1992*. Colleges are the 1,472 responding institutions with master's and baccalaureate programs.

The composition of the library budgets involved, defined for pricing purposes, and the 1992 estimated national weighting structure are presented in Table 7.

The priced components are organized in three major divisions: personnel compensation; acquisitions; and contracted services, supplies, and equipment.

The various components of the University and College Library Price Indexes are described in this section. Different weightings for components are designated in the tables "UL" for university libraries, "CL" for college libraries, and "AL" common for both types. Source citations for the acquisitions price series are listed.

UL1.0 and CL1.0 Salaries and Wages

AL1.1 *Administrators* consists of the chief, deputy associate, and assistant librarian, e.g., important staff members having administrative responsibilities for management of the library. Administrators are priced by the head librarian salary series reported by the College and University Personnel Association (CUPA).

AL1.2 *Librarians* are all other professional library staff. Librarians are priced by the average of the median salaries for circulation/catalog, acquisition, technical service, and public service librarians reported by CUPA.

AL1.3 *Other professionals* are personnel who are not librarians in positions normally requiring at least a bachelor's degree. This group includes curators, archivists, computer specialists, budget officers, information and system specialists, subject bibliographers, and media specialists. Priced by the Higher Education Price Index (HEPI) faculty salary price series (H1.1) as a proxy.

AL1.4 *Nonprofessional staff* includes technical assistants, secretaries, and clerical, shipping, and storage personnel who are specifically assigned to the library and covered by the library budget. This category excludes general custodial and maintenance workers and student employees. This staff category is dominated by office-type workers and is priced by the HEPI clerical workers price series (H2.3) reported by the BLS Employment Cost Index.

AL1.5 *Students* are usually employed part-time for near minimum hourly wages. In some instances these wages are set by work-study program requirements of the institution's student financial aid office. The proxy price series used for student wages is the Employment Cost Index series for non-farm laborers, U.S. Bureau of Labor Statistics.

AL2.0 Fringe Benefits

The fringe benefits price series for faculty used in the HEPI is employed in pricing fringe benefits for library personnel.

UL3.0 and CL3.0 Books and Serials

UL3.1a *Books printed, universities.* Book acquisitions for university libraries are priced by the North American Academic Books price series reporting the average list price of approximately 60,000 titles sold to college and university libraries by four of the largest book vendors. Compiled by Stephen Bosch, University of Arizona.

CL3.1a *Books printed, colleges*. Book acquisitions for college libraries are priced by the price series for U.S. College Books representing approximately 6,300 titles compiled from book reviews appearing in *Choice* during the calendar year. Compiled by Donna Alsbury, Florida Center for Library Automation.

AL3.1b *Foreign Books*. Books with foreign titles *and* published in foreign countries are priced using U.S. book imports data. William S. Lofquist, U.S. Department of Commerce.

AL3.2a *Periodicals, U.S. titles*. U.S. periodicals are priced by the average subscription price of approximately 2,100 U.S. serial titles purchased by college and university libraries reported by EBSCO Subscription Services, Birmingham, AL.

AL3.2b *Periodicals, Foreign*. Foreign periodicals are priced by the average subscription price of approximately 600 foreign serial titles purchased by college and university libraries reported by EBSCO Subscription Services.

AL3.3 *Other Serials* (newspapers, annuals, proceedings, etc.). Average prices of approximately 170 U.S. daily newspapers. Source: Genevieve S. Owens, University of Missouri, St. Louis, and Wilba Swearingen, Louisiana State University Medical Center. Reported by Adrian W. Alexander, "Prices of U.S. and Foreign Published Materials," in *The Bowker Annual*, R. R. Bowker, New Providence, NJ.

Other Printed Materials

These acquisitions include manuscripts, documents, pamphlets, sheet music, printed material for the handicapped, and so forth. No direct price series exists for this category. The proxy price series used is the Producer Price Index (PPI) for publishing pamphlets (PC 2731-9) and catalogs and directors (PC 2741-1), Bureau of Labor Statistics, U.S. Department of Labor.

AL5.0 Non-Print Media

AL5.1 *Microforms*. Producer Price Index for micropublishing in microform, including original and republished material (PC 2741-597), Bureau of Labor Statistics.

AL5.2 *Audio recordings*
  AL5.2a *Tape cassette*—Cost per cassette of sound recording. Source: Dana Alessi, Baker & Taylor Books, Bridgewater, NJ. Reported by Alexander in *The Bowker Annual*, R. R. Bowker, New Providence, NJ.
  AL5.2b *Compact Disk*—Cost per compact disk. Source: See Alessi above.

AL5.3 *Video (TV) recordings*
  PL5.3a *VHS cassette*—cost per video. Source: See Alessi above.

AL5.4 *Graphic image* (individual use of such items as maps, photos, art work, single slides, etc.). No direct price series exists for graphic image materials. Average median weekly earnings for two related occupational groups (painters, sculptors, craft artists; artist printmakers; and photographers) is used as a proxy. these earnings series are reported in *Employment and Earnings Series*, U.S. bureau of Labor Statistics.

AL5.5 *Computer files* (CD-ROM floppy disks, and tape). Average price of CD-ROM disks; primarily bibliographic, abstracts, and other databases of interest to academic libraries. Source: Developed from *Faxon Guide to CD-ROM* by Martha Kellogg and Theodore Kellogg, University of Rhode Island. Reported by Alexander in *The Bowker Annual*, R. R. Bowker, New Providence, NJ.

AL6.0 Electronic Services

Average price for selected digital electronic computer and telecommunications networking available to libraries. The source of this price series has requested anonymity.

AL7.0 Binding/Preservation

In-house maintenance of the specialized skills required for binding is increasingly being replaced by contracting out this service at all but the largest libraries. No wage series exists exclusively for binding. As a proxy, the Producer Price Index (PPI) for bookbinding and related work (PC 2789) is used. Source: Bureau of Labor Statistics, U.S. Department of Labor.

AL8.0 Contracted Services

Services contracted by libraries include such generic categories as communications, postal service, data processing, and printing and duplication. The HEPI contracted services subcomponent (H4.0), which reports these items, is used as the price series. (In this instance the data processing component of H4.0 generally represents the library's payment for use of a central campus computer service.) However, libraries may also contract out certain specialized activities such as ongoing public access cataloging (OPAC) that are not distinctively priced in this AL8.0 component.

AL9.0 Supplies and Materials

Office supplies, writing papers, and pens and pencils constitute the bulk of library supplies and materials and are priced by these BLS categories for the Producer Price Index, Bureau of Labor Statistics, U.S. Department of Labor.

AL10.0 Equipment

This category is limited to small, easily movable, relatively inexpensive and short-lived items that are not carried on the books as depreciable capital equipment. Examples can include personal computers, hand calculators, projectors, fans, cameras, tape recorders, small TVs, etc. The HEPI equipment price series (H6.0) has been used for pricing.

Table 7 / Budget Composition of University Library and College Library Current Operations by Object Category, FY 1992 Estimate

Category	University Libraries Percent Distribution		College Libraries Percent Distribution
Personnel Compensation			
1.0 Salaries and wages		43.4	47.2
1.1 Administrators (head librarian)	10		25
1.2 Librarians	20		15
1.3 Other professionals^	10		5
1.4 Nonprofessional staff	50		40
1.5 Students hourly employed	10		15
	100		100
2.0 Fringe benefits		10.6	11.5
Acquisitions			
3.0 Books and Serials		28.5	24.8
3.1 Books printed	35		47
3.1a U.S. titles	80		95
3.1b Foreign titles	20		5
3.2 Periodicals	60		48
3.2a U.S. titles	80		95
3.2b Foreign titles	20		5
3.3 Other serials (newspapers, annuals, proceedings, etc.)	5		5
	100		100
4.0 Other Printed Materials*		1.2	0.7
5.0 Non-Print Media		1.6	3.3
5.1 Microforms (microfiche and microfilm)	45		45
5.2 Audio recordings	5		5
5.2a Tape cassette			
5.2b Compact disc (CDs)			
5.3 Video (TV) VHS recordings	15		15
5.4 Graphic image individual item use~	5		5
5.5 Computer materials (CD-ROM, floppy disks, and tape)	30		30
	100		100
6.0. Electronic Services^^		4.0	3.5
Contracted Services, Supplies, Equipment			
7.0 Binding/preservation		1.3	0.8
8.0 Services**		4.4	3.1
9.0 Supplies and materials		3.1	2.6
10.0 Equipment (non-capital)#		1.9	2.5
		100	100

^ Other professional and managerial staff includes systems analyst, business manager, public relations, personnel, etc.
* Other printed materials includes manuscripts, documents, pamphlets, sheet music, printed material for the handicapped, etc.
~ Graphic image individual item use includes maps, photos, art work, single slides, etc.
^^Electronic services includes software license fees, network intra-structure costs, terminal access to the Internet, desktop computer operating budget, and subscription services.
**Contracted services includes outside contracts for communications, postal service, data processing, printing and duplication, equipment rental and repair, acquisition processing, etc.
Relatively inexpensive items not carried on the books as depreciable capital equipment. Examples include microform and audiovisual equipment, personal computers, hand calculators, projectors, fans, cameras, tape recorders, and small TVs.
Source: Derived, in part, from data published in *Academic Libraries: 1992*, National Center for Education Statistics, USDE.

Table 8 / University Library Price Index and Major Component Subindexes, FY 1992 to 1996

| 1992=100 Fiscal year | Personnel Compensation ||| Acquisitions ||||| Operating Expenses ||| University Library Price Index^ ULPI |
	Salaries and wages (UL1.0)	Fringe benefits (AL2.0)	Books and serials (UL3.0)	Other printed materials (AL4.0)	Non-print media (AL5.0)	Electronic services (AL6.0)	Binding/preservation (AL7.0)	Contracted services (AL8.0)	Supplies and material (AL9.0)	Equipment (AL10.0)	
1992	100.0	100.0	100.0	100.0	100.0	100.0	100.0	100.0	100.0	100.0	100.0
1993	103.2	105.4	105.7	102.9	98.7	101.6	100.5	102.9	98.3	101.8	103.8
1994	106.3	110.5	111.6	105.5	100.8	103.3	101.2	105.9	99.2	103.6	107.7
1995	110	114.2	120.5	107.7	102.1	104.9	102.9	108.4	100.4	105.7	112.5

^ ULPI weights: See table 3-A.
Sources: See text.

Table 9 / College Library Price Index and Major Component Subindexes, FY 1992 to 1996

| 1992=100 Fiscal year | Personnel Compensation ||| Acquisitions ||||| Operating Expenses ||| College Library Price Index^ CLPI |
	Salaries and wages (CL1.0)	Fringe benefits (AL2.0)	Books and serials (CL3.0)	Other printed materials (AL4.0)	Non-print media (AL5.0)	Electronic services (AL6.0)	Binding/preservation (AL7.0)	Contracted services (AL8.0)	Supplies and material (AL9.0)	Equipment (AL10.0)	
1992	100.0	100.0	100.0	100.0	100.0	100.0	100.0	100.0	100.0	100.0	100.0
1993	103.5	105.4	107.2	102.9	98.7	101.6	100.5	102.9	98.3	101.8	104.2
1994	106.5	110.5	113.1	105.5	100.8	103.3	101.2	105.9	99.2	103.6	107.9
1995	110.0	114.2	118.6	107.7	102.1	104.9	102.9	108.4	100.4	105.7	111.7

^ CLPI weights: See table 3-A
Sources: See text.

Table 10 / Academic Library Price Indexes, Personnel Compensation, FY 1992 to 1996

1992=100 Fiscal year	Administrators (head librarian) (AL1.1)	Librarians (AL1.2)	Other professional (AL1.3)	Non-professional (AL1.4)	Students hourly employed (AL1.5)	Salaries and wages indexes Universities* (UL1.0)	Colleges^ (CL1.0)	Fringe benefits index (AL2.0)
1992	100.0	100.0	100.0	100.0	100.0	100.0	100.0	100.0
1993	105.0	102.6	102.5	103.2	102.7	103.2	103.5	105.4
1994	107.3	106.0	105.6	106.6	105.4	106.3	106.5	110.5
1995	110.6	110.2	109.3	110.1	108.5	110.0	110.0	114.2

* University library salaries and wages index weights: 10 percent administrators, 20 percent librarians, 10 percent other professionals, 50 percent nonprofessional staff, and 10 percent students.
^ College library salaries and wages index weights: 25 percent administrators, 15 percent librarians, 5 percent other professionals, 40 percent nonprofessional staff, and 15 percent students.
Sources: See text.

Table 11 / Academic Library Price Indexes, Books and Serials, FY 1992 to 1996

1992=100 Fiscal year	North American Price~	Index (UL3.1a)	Books printed U.S. college Price~	Index (CL3.1a)	Foreign books Price	Index (AL3.1b)	Book indexes University* (UL3.1)	College^ (CL3.1)
1992	$45.84	100.0	$44.55	100.0	NA	100.0	100.0	100.0
1993	$45.91	100.2	$47.48	106.6		98.9	99.9	106.2
1994	$47.17	102.9	$48.92	109.8		96.7	101.7	109.2
1995	$48.16	105.1	$47.93	107.6		105.0	105.0	107.5

~ Prices are for previous calendar year, e.g., CY 1993 prices are reported for FY 1994.
* University library books printed index weights: 80 percent U.S. titles, 20 percent foreign titles.
^ College Library books printed index weights: 95 percent U.S. titles, 5 percent foreign titles.
Sources: See text.
NA Not Available

Table 11A / Academic Library Price Indexes, Books and Serials, FY 1992 to 1996

1992=100	Periodicals						Other serials (newspapers)		Books and serials indexes			Other printed materials index (AL4.0)
	US titles		Foreign		Periodical indexes							
Fiscal year	Price~	Index (AL3.2a)	Price~	Index (AL3.2b)	University* (UL3.2)	College^ (CL3.2)	Price~	Index (AL3.3)	University** (UL3.0)	College^^ (CL3.0)	
1992	$125.86	100.0	$341.02	100.0	100.0	100.0	$222.68	100.0	100.0	100.0	100.0
1993	$136.47	108.4	$384.16	112.7	109.3	108.6	$229.92	103.3	105.7	107.2	102.9
1994	$146.32	116.3	$408.04	119.7	116.9	116.4	$261.91	117.6	111.6	113.1	105.5
1995	$162.50	129.1	$445.81	130.7	129.4	129.2	$270.22	121.3	120.5	118.6	107.7

~ Prices are for previous calendar year, e.g., CY 1993 prices are reported for FY 1994.
* University library periodicals index weights: 80 percent U.S. titles, 20 percent foreign titles.
^ College library periodicals index weights: 95 percent U.S. titles, 5 percent foreign titles.
** University library books and serials index weights: 35 percent books, 60 percent periodicals, 5 percent other serials.
^^College library books and serials index weights: 47 percent books, 48 percent periodicals, 5 percent other serials.
Sources: See text.

Table 12 / Academic Library Price Indexes, Non-Print Media and Electronic Services, FY 1992 to 1996

1992=100	Microforms (microfilm)	Audio recordings					Audio recordings index* (AL5.2)	Video			
		Tape cassette		Compact disc				VHS cassette		Video index (AL5.3)
Fiscal year	Index (AL5.1)	Price~	Index (AL5.2a)	Price~	Index (AL5.2b)			Price~	Index (AL5.3a)	
1992	100.0	$12.18	100.0	NA			100.0	$199.67	100.0	100.0
1993	104.3	$11.73	96.3	NA			96.3	$112.92	56.6	56.6
1994	107.9	$8.20	67.3	$13.36	67.3		67.3	$93.22	46.7	46.7
1995	110.6	$8.82	72.4	$14.80	74.6		73.5	$84.19	42.2	42.2

~ Prices are for previous calendar year, e.g., CY 1993 prices are reported for FY 1994.
* Audio recordings index weights: 50 percent tape cassette, 50 percent compact disc.
Sources: See text.
NA Not Available

Table 12A / Academic Library Price Indexes, Non-Print Media and Electronic Services, FY 1992 to 1996

1992=100 Fiscal year	Non-print Med Graphic image (AL5.4)	Computer files (CD-ROM) Price~	Index (AL5.5)	Non-print media index# (AL5.0)	Electronic services index (AL6.0)	Total Acquisitions Indexes Univ*	College^	All Institutions**
1992	100.0	$1,601	100.0	100.0	100.0	100.0	100.0	100.0
1993	97.3	$1,793	112.0	98.7	101.6	104.8	105.7	105.0
1994	108.4	$1,945	121.5	100.8	103.3	110.0	110.6	110.2
1995	111.3	$1,961	122.5	102.1	104.9	117.5	115.2	116.8

~ Prices are for immediate preceding calendar year, e.g., CY 1993 prices are reported for FY 1994.
# Non-print media index weights: 45 percent microforms, 5 percent audio recordings, 15 percent video, 5 percent graphic image, 30 percent computer materials.
* University total acquisitions 1992 weights: 81 percent books, 3 percent other printed material, 5 percent non-print media, and 11 percent electronic services.
^ College total acquisitions 1992 weights: 77 percent books, 2 percent other printed material, 10 percent non-print media, and 11 percent electronic services.
** All institutions total acquisitions weights: 72 percent university acquisitions, 28 percent college acquisitions.
Sources: See text.

State Rankings of Selected Public Library Data, 1995

State	Circulation Transactions per capita*	Reference Transactions per capita	Book and Serials Vols. per capita	ALA-MLS Librarians per 25,000	Operating Expenditures per capita	Local Income per capita
Alabama	48	41	44	42	43	43
Alaska	32	29	24	17	7	6
Arizona	28	21	43	25	27	22
Arkansas	47	45	37	48	49	47
California	40	10	46	23	32	27
Colorado	12	6	32	16	11	11
Connecticut	19	16	14	4	9	9
Delaware	42	40	40	44	38	36
Dist. of Columbia	50	1	6	2	2	1
Florida	35	2	49	22	30	28
Georgia	41	35	47	24	37	42
Hawaii	n.a.†	n.a.	n.a.	n.a.	n.a.	n.a.
Idaho	17	25	22	43	33	31
Illinois	18	5	18	10	6	2
Indiana	2	14	10	9	5	8
Iowa	10	32	13	29	29	30
Kansas	6	7	5	18	12	15
Kentucky	34	46	39	50	44	41
Louisiana	43	32	34	34	35	32
Maine	20	39	1	27	28	34
Maryland	7	9	30	1	10	17
Massachusetts	23	27	3	6	14	16
Michigan	35	23	27	12	21	23
Minnesota	5	4	25	19	13	14
Mississippi	49	44	45	45	50	49
Missouri	15	20	9	39	23	20
Montana	29	26	23	46	42	33
Nebraska	14	47	15	31	20	18
Nevada	37	28	38	38	31	7
New Hampshire	24	37	12	15	24	29
New Jersey	31	18	15	5	4	5
New Mexico	25	43	20	21	25	26
New York	22	3	8	3	1	3
North Carolina	33	22	40	32	39	38
North Dakota	16	32	18	49	46	45
Ohio	1	48	17	8	2	48
Oklahoma	26	30	35	36	40	35
Oregon	4	31	33	20	17	10
Pennsylvania	39	36	36	25	36	44
Rhode Island	30	50	11	7	18	24
South Carolina	45	11	48	28	41	40
South Dakota	11	24	4	39	26	19
Tennessee	46	14	50	41	48	46
Texas	43	13	42	30	45	39
Utah	8	37	29	33	22	25
Vermont	26	42	7	34	34	37
Washington	3	17	26	11	8	4
West Virginia	38	49	28	46	47	50
Wisconsin	9	8	21	13	16	13
Wyoming	13	19	2	37	15	12

These preliminary rankings were compiled by the Library Research Service of the Colorado State Library and University of Denver. They are also based on data submitted in 1996 to NCES through the Federal State Cooperative System (FSCS) for public library data. The raw data are available on the Early Release File posted to the NCES Web site. A full report of these data will eventually be published as *Public Libraries in the U.S.: 1995*.

The District of Columbia contributes to FSCS as do the 50 states and is therefore shown in the rankings. The reader is cautioned, however, that this library is probably more appropriately compared to libraries serving large urban areas rather than to states.

Source: *Preliminary State Rankings of Public Library Statistics: 1995*. Denver: Library Research Service, Colorado Department of Education, 1997.

* Per capita calculations are based on libraries that reported the specific item and a nonzero value for population of legal service areas.

† n.a.=Not applicable.

Library Buildings 1996: Beating the High Cost of Libraries

Bette-Lee Fox

Managing Editor, *Library Journal*

Erin Cassin

Intern, *Library Journal*

As many single big-city dwellers come to realize, moving to an apartment often means sharing living space in order to cut costs and perhaps ensure a level of security. Roommates can range from awesome to abominable, but sharing expenses often makes up for a good many problems.

A number of library projects listed this year illustrate the wisdom of finding "housemates," chief among them senior centers, government offices, police stations, schools, and in one case, a city hall. The library data for the Spearfish Public Library, South Dakota could not be separated out from the $4.5 million municipal building with which it shares space.

To reiterate our observations from last year, the number of new buildings completed between July 1, 1995, and June 30, 1996, (100) is again outdistanced by the number of addition and renovation projects (145), but together they account for the third largest building boom since 1985.

Costs for the 1996 buildings have reached an all-time high ($723 million), thanks in part to the New York Public Library renovation of B. Altman's department store for its new Science, Industry and Business Library ($100 million) and the New Main of the San Francisco Public Library ($165 million). Along with these multimillion-dollar projects, there are others simply upgrading facilities for Americans with Disabilities Act compliance.

Funding levels have increased across the board, with gift funds accounting for 21 percent of total funding and at $154 million, coming in at more than three times higher than 1995 figures.

After a significant drop in the number of academic buildings in 1995, we seem back on track in 1996 with 40 new projects. Perhaps we've turned the corner in the academic building slump. Will academic libraries find "shacking up" on campus the answer for them as well? We'll keep you posted.

Note: Adapted from the December 1996 issue of *Library Journal*, which also lists architects' addresses.

Table 1 / New Public Library Buildings, 1996

Community	Pop. ('000)	Code	Project Cost	Const. Cost	Gross Sq.Ft.	Sq.Ft. Cost	Equip. Cost	Site Cost	Other Costs	Volumes	Federal Funds	State Funds	Local Funds	Gift Funds	Architect
Alabama															
Birmingham	15	B	$1,253,601	$937,290	8,000	$117.17	$184,667	Owned	$131,644	45,000	0	0	$1,253,601	0	CLJ & Assocs.
Arkansas															
De Queen	15	M	242,032	224,392	4,860	46.17	2,415	Owned	15,225	20,000	55,811	0	111,653	74,568	Arnold & Stacks
Lake City	5	B	223,458	165,315	2,000	82.66	23,243	20,000	14,900	13,000	22,401	0	181,057	20,000	Brackett Krennerich
Little Rock	50	B	2,177,854	1,629,046	13,500	120.67	171,972	213,308	163,528	70,000	0	0	2,177,854	0	AMR Architects
Maumelle	9	B	1,434,480	1,052,860	8,500	123.87	140,903	150,000	90,717	30,000	0	0	1,433,480	1,000	Fennell Purifoy
Arizona															
Chandler	140	M	8,018,742	5,958,054	64,000	93.09	1,151,832	Owned	908,856	300,000	0	0	6,018,742	2,000,000	ADP Fluor Daniel
California															
Cathedral City	40	B	5,385,619	3,050,304	20,000	152.51	283,000	1,100,000	952,315	90,690	0	4,200,642	1,184,977	0	Thirtieth Street
Eureka	46	M	11,142,000	7,835,087	63,395	123.59	599,157	624,959	2,082,797	243,840	0	6,147,238	3,908,813	1,085,949	Robert J. Gianelli
North Hills	53	BS	5,760,183	5,036,361	27,981	179.99	293,276	Owned	430,546	100,000	0	4,998,462	761,721	0	Killefer, Flammang...
Palm Desert	47	B	8,500,000	6,380,000	41,600	153.37	302,380	Owned	1,817,620	180,000	0	0	8,500,000	0	IBI Group
Paso Robles	23	M	6,200,000	5,365,000	28,800	186.28	393,000	Owned	442,000	50,000	0	960,000	4,980,000	260,000	Charles Walton
Pine Valley	2	B	144,695	114,000	2,000	57.00	21,695	Owned	9,000	5,792	0	0	137,909	6,786	San Diego Cty.
Redwood City	25	B	690,000	558,661	3,200	174.58	80,000	Leased	51,339	20,000	0	0	680,000	10,000	Van Housen
Rio Vista	4	B	853,732	680,516	5,288	128.69	130,000	Owned	43,216	40,000	325,000	0	528,732	0	B. Michael Wahl
San Andreas	39	MS	2,677,390	1,847,760	14,848	124.45	539,090	150,000	140,540	65,680	0	1,574,442	1,102,948	0	Oshima & Vee
San Diego	34	B	6,012,583	2,619,573	22,950	114.14	455,000	1,325,000	1,613,010	87,000	3,618,795	0	2,123,588	270,200	Brandon de Arakal
San Diego	39	B	7,256,916	4,681,950	26,042	179.78	500,252	560,000	1,514,714	59,650	2,966,943	0	4,290,000	0	Manuel Oncina
San Francisco	700	MS	164,953,000	110,000,000	381,000	288.71	34,000,000	253,000	20,700,000	n/a	0	0	134,953,000	30,000,000	James Ingo Freed
Stockton	13	B	2,727,000	1,943,443	10,500	185.09	384,981	95,000	303,576	53,000	775,972	0	1,951,028	0	Tom Bowe
Tujunga	48	B	2,253,723	1,932,392	10,500	184.04	79,077	Owned	242,254	40,000	0	0	2,253,723	0	Widom, Wein, Cohen
Venice	42	B	3,382,854	3,066,202	10,500	292.02	87,981	Owned	228,671	40,000	2,174,344	0	1,208,510	0	Ernest P. Howard
Watts	50	B	2,684,114	2,254,995	12,500	180.40	156,642	Owned	272,477	48,000	0	0	2,684,114	0	James C. Moore

Symbol Code: B—Branch Library; BS—Branch & System Headquarters; M—Main Library; MS—Main & System Headquarters; S—System Headquarters; n/a—not available

Table 1 / New Public Library Buildings, 1996 (cont.)

Community	Pop. ('000)	Code	Project Cost	Const. Cost	Gross Sq.Ft.	Sq.Ft. Cost	Equip. Cost	Site Cost	Other Costs	Volumes	Federal Funds	State Funds	Local Funds	Gift Funds	Architect
Colorado															
Breckenridge	6	B	721,000	364,016	3,473	104.81	44,500	250,000	62,484	20,000	73,759	0	397,509	249,732	Baker Hogan Houx
Denver	503	B	1,182,871	690,580	5,000	138.12	40,000	135,000	317,291	40,000	0	0	1,182,871	0	Bertram A. Bruton
Denver	503	B	1,371,113	700,564	5,000	140.11	45,000	103,000	522,549	40,000	0	0	1,371,113	0	Architecture Denver
Connecticut															
Bridgeport	40	B	3,358,000	2,064,000	20,000	103.20	350,000	490,000	454,000	59,000	0	3,358,000	0	0	Galliher Baier & Best
Florida															
Beverly Hills	33	MS	1,773,000	1,323,000	20,000	66.15	350,000	Owned	100,000	50,000	400,000	0	1,373,000	0	Harvard, Jolly, Clees...
Bradenton	67	B	1,417,119	1,038,145	13,000	79.86	107,000	231,245	40,729	75,000	0	0	1,360,119	57,000	Jerry N. Zoller
Deltona	70	B	3,141,750	2,307,049	25,000	92.28	775,906	Owned	58,795	100,000	0	400,000	2,741,750	0	Jack J. Rood
Mount Dora	26	M	1,800,000	1,438,213	15,000	95.88	60,500	Owned	301,287	75,000	0	400,000	600,000	800,000	Morris Architects
Port Orange	60	M	2,737,055	2,061,206	25,000	82.45	621,360	Owned	54,489	100,000	0	400,000	2,337,055	0	Jack J. Rood
Trenton	11	M	176,745	110,708	5,193	21.32	0	61,237	4,800	16,500	0	67,693	110,708	0	Eugene Russell Davis
Georgia															
Hiram	53	B	681,179	504,769	5,000	100.95	131,429	Owned	44,981	15,388	0	523,071	158,108	0	Sterling Pettefer
Jasper	17	B	1,302,354	965,122	11,000	87.74	189,422	45,000	102,810	46,000	0	943,841	313,513	45,000	Sterling Pettefer
Illinois															
Chicago	25	B	$3,658,986	$2,744,478	13,000	$211.11	n/a	$202,647	$711,861	67,530	0	$3,642,396	$16,590	0	Restrepo Group
Forest Park	15	M	3,295,000	2,401,500	26,400	90.97	650,000	Owned	243,500	n/a	0	250,000	2,695,000	350,000	Wendt Cedarholm...
Glen Ellyn	26	B	6,905,350	4,954,000	52,000	95.27	634,000	834,100	483,250	190,000	0	250,000	6,551,350	104,000	Cordogan, Clark...
Mendon	4	M	221,702	168,177	2,700	62.29	20,706	Leased	32,819	10,000	0	76,300	131,677	13,725	Architechnics, Inc.
Morrison	4	M	1,828,576	1,642,027	16,400	100.12	71,905	Owned	114,644	n/a	250,000	0	1,570,576	8,000	Williams & Elliott
Western Springs	12	M	3,744,988	2,923,629	24,000	121.82	250,557	302,741	268,061	70,000	250,000	0	3,494,988	0	Frye, Gillan, Molinaro
Indiana															
Albion	19	M	1,740,096	1,379,240	25,000	55.17	190,938	32,000	137,918	80,000	1,285,000	0	156,678	298,418	D. Eric Leedy
Kouts	4	B	2,211,629	1,481,474	11,875	124.75	138,547	97,000	494,608	60,000	0	0	2,104,629	107,000	InterDesign Group
No. Manchester	6	M	2,865,000	2,279,750	21,000	108.56	290,667	Owned	294,583	60,000	0	0	0	2,865,000	Moake Park Group

Symbol Code: B—Branch Library; BS—Branch & System Headquarters; M—Main Library; MS—Main & System Headquarters; S—System Headquarters; n/a—not available

Table 1 / New Public Library Buildings, 1996 *(cont.)*

Community	Pop. ('000)	Code	Project Cost	Const. Cost	Gross Sq.Ft.	Sq.Ft. Cost	Equip. Cost	Site Cost	Other Costs	Volumes	Federal Funds	State Funds	Local Funds	Gift Funds	Architect
Valparaiso	12	B	2,211,699	1,541,272	13,250	116.32	145,750	30,000	494,677	80,000	0	0	2,211,699	0	InterDesign Group
Iowa															
Marion	24	M	4,380,132	2,613,075	24,500	106.66	583,000	783,000	401,057	96,942	25,000	0	2,020,432	2,334,700	Brown Healey Stone...
Osage	5	M	1,582,115	1,170,860	11,000	106.44	141,855	140,000	129,400	55,000	165,000	0	0	1,435,315	Schute-Larson
West Des Moines	40	M	6,950,000	4,952,150	51,400	96.35	706,586	Owned	1,291,264	125,000	0	0	6,950,000	0	Meyer, Scherer...
Louisiana															
Boyce	5	B	n/a	n/a	1,800	n/a	15,000	Leased	0	14,000	0	0	15,000	0	not reported
Michigan															
Brighton	20	M	4,319,108	3,197,482	23,070	138.60	300,000	501,000	320,626	70,000	0	0	4,289,625	29,483	TMP Assocs.
Escanaba	38	M	3,405,000	2,160,000	17,000	127.06	575,000	400,000	270,000	70,000	1,700,000	0	1,705,000	0	Koster & Assocs.
Kingsford	129	M	378,577	289,077	4,250	68.02	5,000	22,500	62,000	50,000	0	0	378,577	0	Blomquist & Assocs.
Zeeland	11	M	4,700,725	4,162,950	44,000	94.61	229,475	Owned	308,300	50,000	0	0	2,402,000	2,298,725	GMB Architects
Minnesota															
Blaine	18	B	1,172,500	994,800	7,500	132.64	96,800	Owned	80,900	35,000	0	0	1,169,500	3,000	Boarman, Kroops...
Plymouth	57	B	3,165,245	1,888,535	16,087	117.40	254,000	Owned	1,022,710	n/a	0	0	3,165,245	0	Jeff Sweitzer
Missouri															
Brookfield	5	M	530,000	426,000	6,000	71.00	30,000	Owned	74,000	45,000	0	0	11,900	62,625	George Esser
Claycomo	7	B	733,890	527,288	9,733	54.18	65,000	115,326	26,276	82,600	455,475	0	733,890	0	Tognascioli & Assocs.
Kansas City	27	B	2,386,657	1,800,743	15,000	120.05	177,671	288,567	119,676	58,000	0	0	2,386,657	0	Devine deFlon Yaeger
O'Fallon	55	B	1,210,764	956,928	19,200	49.84	160,000	82,386	11,450	120,000	0	0	380,764	830,000	Rataj Architects
O'Fallon	20	B	887,807	687,363	11,880	57.86	110,000	80,469	9,975	80,000	0	0	857,807	30,000	Rataj Architects
Nebraska															
Auburn	7	M	645,800	510,000	6,000	85.00	88,000	Owned	47,800	25,000	0	60,000	0	585,800	David Littrell
Elkhorn	5	M	1,542,284	756,284	8,100	93.36	105,000	600,000	81,000	35,000	50,000	0	781,284	711,000	Don Peters & Assocs.
Nevada															
Las Vegas	25	B	4,558,250	3,130,646	26,062	120.12	546,198	575,325	306,081	95,000	0	0	4,558,250	0	Domingo Cambiero

Symbol Code: B—Branch Library; BS—Branch & System Headquarters; M—Main Library; MS—Main & System Headquarters; S—System Headquarters; n/a—not available

Table 1 / **New Public Library Buildings, 1996** *(cont.)*

Community	Pop. ('000)	Code	Project Cost	Const. Cost	Gross Sq.Ft.	Sq.Ft. Cost	Equip. Cost	Site Cost	Other Costs	Volumes	Federal Funds	State Funds	Local Funds	Gift Funds	Architect
New Hampshire															
Bedford	16	M	2,700,000	1,847,536	20,000	92.38	532,464	100,000	220,000	90,000	0	0	2,200,000	500,000	Dennis Mires
New Jersey															
Logan Twp.	9	B	1,199,050	788,709	9,660	81.65	99,500	141,500	169,341	40,000	0	0	1,199,050	0	Garrison Architects
Long Valley	16	M	2,010,597	1,170,694	12,000	97.56	260,000	321,403	258,500	55,000	66,865	0	1,906,732	37,000	Faridy Thorne Fraytak
Palisades Park	15	M	2,030,000	1,800,000	13,000	138.46	100,000	Leased	130,000	40,000	130,000	268,000	1,612,000	20,000	Design Group
New York															
Baldwinsville	30	M	3,700,000	2,887,126	34,500	83.68	194,352	330,000	288,522	65,000	0	16,695	3,583,305	100,000	Bruce King
Cheektowaga	34	BS	2,449,281	2,229,042	20,000	111.45	89,067	Owned	131,172	50,000	152,355	45,729	2,211,197	40,000	Foit-Albert Assocs.
Saratoga Springs	41	M	7,861,347	6,419,547	58,626	109.50	735,000	312,800	394,000	156,600	0	0	7,861,347	0	Architecture+
Victor	15	M	1,078,000	800,000	9,000	88.89	128,000	150,000	n/a	40,000	0	0	800,000	278,000	Labella Assocs.
North Carolina															
Apex	85	B	3,629,026	2,820,016	23,000	122.60	575,253	Owned	233,757	100,000	0	0	129,924	3,499,102	Cherry Huffman
Charlotte	30	B	2,074,947	1,683,447	12,500	134.68	272,500	Owned	119,000	55,000	0	0	2,074,947	0	Clark-Nexsen
King	16	B	1,371,872	1,014,782	12,500	81.18	198,436	75,000	83,654	50,000	150,000	0	991,006	230,866	Thomas H. Hughes
Lakelure	15	B	591,483	404,076	4,185	96.55	45,000	25,000	117,407	12,900	0	0	472,626	118,857	William Burgin
Southern Pines	10	M	2,002,790	1,469,549	14,750	99.63	243,835	114,321	175,085	56,000	15,000	0	1,893,052	94,738	Hayes/Howell
Williamston	13	B	930,453	732,380	9,331	78.49	106,804	45,000	46,269	38,100	0	75,000	2,015	853,438	Wilson Architecture
Ohio															
Archbold	7	M	$1,768,143	$983,008	11,568	$84.98	$290,554	$255,385	$239,196	40,000	0	0	$192,298	$1,575,845	Munger Munger
Columbus	32	B	3,178,188	1,908,666	20,065	95.12	370,400	351,900	547,222	130,900	0	1,589,094	1,589,094	0	Schooley Caldwell
Hilliard	46	B	3,466,016	2,273,654	20,005	113.65	318,668	609,582	264,112	98,300	0	1,733,008	1,733,008	0	Design Group
Oklahoma															
Fairview	8	M	362,402	277,965	4,368	63.04	39,524	32,375	12,538	18,932	0	0	322,878	39,524	Ken Corbin
Wilburton	10	B	500,000	450,000	10,000	45.00	20,000	13,500	16,500	20,000	0	0	0	500,127	Tim Wynn
Oregon															
Monmouth	11	M	1,681,070	1,085,194	14,654	74.05	203,267	214,390	178,219	65,500	125,000	0	1,448,971	107,099	Richard P. Turi

Symbol Code: B—Branch Library; BS—Branch & System Headquarters; M—Main Library; MS—Main & System Headquarters; S—System Headquarters; n/a—not available

Table 1 / New Public Library Buildings, 1996 (cont.)

Community	Pop. ('000)	Code	Project Cost	Const. Cost	Gross Sq.Ft.	Sq.Ft. Cost	Equip. Cost	Site Cost	Other Costs	Volumes	Federal Funds	State Funds	Local Funds	Gift Funds	Architect
Pennsylvania															
Corry	15	M	854,296	669,446	10,800	61.99	107,324	40,000	37,526	67,696	300,000	10,000	135,000	419,296	D.A. Johnson
Eagleville	19	M	1,710,000	1,446,000	11,760	122.96	112,000	Owned	152,000	37,000	100,000	100,000	1,510,000	0	Diseroad Wolfe...
South Carolina															
Conway	5	B	n/a	n/a	3,000	n/a	n/a	Owned	n/a	12,000	0	0	n/a	0	not reported
Greer	36	B	1,699,483	1,115,915	10,864	102.72	237,854	221,000	124,714	43,700	100,000	0	1,218,534	380,949	Tarleton-Tankersley
Little River	11	B	n/a	n/a	4,000	n/a	n/a	Owned	n/a	20,000	0	0	n/a	0	Wilkins, Wood, Goforth
Surfside Beach	17	B	822,379	497,841	7,150	69.63	74,000	125,000	125,538	n/a	75,000	0	622,379	125,000	Steven Goggans
South Dakota															
Spearfish*	12	B	4,557,202	3,491,404	40,000	87.29	217,330	511,500	336,968	70,200	125,000	0	4,332,202	100,000	Arch. by Thurston
Texas															
Denton	11	B	1,024,947	777,080	10,000	77.71	128,754	Owned	119,113	40,000	97,133	0	882,511	45,303	Hidell Assocs.
El Paso	48	B	1,654,640	1,018,000	12,000	84.83	350,000	180,000	106,640	70,000	868,000	0	786,640	0	Mario Lopez
El Paso	51	B	1,166,037	896,400	10,000	89.64	200,000	Owned	69,637	55,000	696,400	0	469,637	0	Jorge Mora
Euless	42	M	5,532,546	3,572,527	40,510	88.19	263,671	122,766	1,573,582	90,000	0	0	5,532,546	0	Phillips Swager
Houston	38	B	3,304,903	1,801,586	16,000	112.59	480,000	483,000	540,317	90,000	0	0	3,304,903	0	Farrell Sudin Partners
Washington															
Spokane	36	B	2,669,548	1,597,000	15,000	106.47	454,060	468,004	150,484	74,799	0	0	2,669,548	0	Integrus Architecture
Spokane	18	B	1,013,066	750,000	6,394	117.30	189,645	Owned	73,421	35,000	0	0	1,013,066	0	Tan Heyamoto
Stellacoom	7	B	968,348	626,005	4,040	154.95	70,566	159,512	112,265	25,000	0	0	963,348	5,000	Cardwell/Thomas
Wisconsin															
Mukwonago	12	M	1,780,270	1,397,141	12,200	114.52	168,043	Owned	215,086	45,000	0	0	793,270	987,000	Engberg Anderson
Spring Green	2	M	680,062	511,825	8,800	58.16	28,548	95,000	44,689	17,500	125,000	0	181,762	373,300	Taliesin Assocs.
Stratford	6	B	348,569	287,457	3,000	95.82	40,281	Owned	20,831	14,000	0	0	247,569	101,000	Tharen Gorski

*Part of a $4.5 million municipal building

Symbol Code: B—Branch Library; BS—Branch & System Headquarters; M—Main Library; MS—Main & System Headquarters; S—System Headquarters; n/a—not available

Table 2 / Public Library Buildings: Additions and Renovations, 1996

Community	Pop. ('000)	Code	Project Cost	Const. Cost	Gross Sq.Ft.	Sq.Ft. Cost	Equip. Cost	Site Cost	Other Costs	Volumes	Federal Funds	State Funds	Local Funds	Gift Funds	Architect
Alabama															
Birmingham	6	B	$455,408	$377,653	5,308	$71.15	$32,053	Owned	$45,702	20,000	0	0	$455,408	0	Khafra Engineering
Decatur	30	B	50,206	3,675	2,294	1.60	23,345	Leased	23,186	15,000	0	0	41,250	8,956	none
Orange Beach	3	M	90,000	50,000	3,500	14.28	35,000	Owned	5,000	16,000	0	0	90,000	0	not reported
Arizona															
Buckeye	9	M	185,000	155,000	2,419	64.08	20,000	Owned	10,000	25,000	85,000	0	0	100,000	Rex Hinshaw
California															
Beaumont	22	M	154,000	122,525	350	350.07	0	Owned	31,475	n/a	39,280	0	114,720	0	Interactive Design
Davis	59	B	5,193,100	3,755,690	30,000	125.19	439,497	Leased	997,913	163,251	0	2,722,200	2,465,361	5,539	Alan Oshima
Elk Grove	47	B	236,430	171,168	7,767	22.04	31,430	Leased	33,832	41,173	0	0	236,430	0	Jerry Schroder
Escondido	121	B	6,764,854	2,546,219	39,917	63.79	161,509	3,725,000	332,126	46,225	0	0	6,764,854	0	Don Iler
Fresno	70	B	n/a	n/a	9,929	n/a	0	Leased	n/a	39,733	0	0	n/a	0	Associated Designs
Huron	6	B	202,197	200,537	2,824	17.01	0	Owned	1,660	13,000	0	0	202,197	0	Tri-City Engineering
Los Angeles	30	B	2,451,080	2,109,931	12,912	163.41	131,453	Owned	209,696	48,000	648,861	0	1,802,219	0	City of Los Angeles
Los Angeles	25	B	2,324,182	1,405,174	7,361	190.89	87,483	619,060	212,465	33,750	0	0	2,324,182	0	M2A Milofsky,...
Los Angeles	58	B	2,827,986	1,916,139	10,942	175.12	152,340	524,198	235,309	45,000	1,245,000	0	1,582,986	0	Artec, Inc.
Los Angeles	28	B	1,298,122	1,064,424	5,243	203.02	52,621	Owned	181,077	30,000	1,003,000	0	295,122	0	Froehlich, Kow...
Los Angeles	33	B	2,611,408	2,170,736	8,736	248.48	97,435	Owned	343,237	37,500	0	0	2,611,408	0	Shimazu Partnership
Moorpark	30	B	371,225	283,082	2,717	104.19	0	Owned	88,143	40,000	0	0	325,000	46,225	Robert Tveit
Palm Springs	43	M	770,000	700,000	33,000	21.21	30,000	Owned	40,000	170,000	0	0	0	770,000	Revel Young
Ramona	32	B	58,817	42,600	666	63.96	11,017	Owned	5,200	5,064	0	0	22,000	16,017	San Diego Orange
Rancho Mirage	11	M	2,972,999	1,258,726	10,887	115.62	538,845	837,201	338,227	40,000	35,000	0	2,646,261	0	Thirtieth St. Architects
Rolling Hills Ests.	69	MS	20,168,779	14,817,305	81,125	182.65	1,926,411	Owned	3,425,063	300,000	326,738	0	20,057,832	110,947	Jeff Murray
San Francisco	43	B	9,491,000	9,141,000	17,340	n/a	350,000	Owned	n/a	n/a	0	2,597,000	6,544,000	350,000	Cty. of San Francisco
Colorado															
Fruita	12	B	158,505	95,976	1,800	53.32	22,637	18,511	21,381	10,532	66,899	0	83,906	7,700	Vanderwood Assocs.
Golden	21	B	1,800,000	1,170,000	14,000	83.57	320,000	Owned	310,000	70,000	30,000	0	1,770,000	0	Andrews & Anderson
Loveland	56	M	421,264	365,125	3,425	106.61	25,139	Owned	31,000	6,833	0	0	436,074	0	Architecture I
Parker	30	B	1,665,004	592,210	20,000	29.61	99,360	932,750	40,684	70,000	0	0	1,595,740	69,264	Humphries Poli
Connecticut															
Groton	45	M	2,730,000	2,328,000	13,700	169.93	100,000	Owned	302,000	150,000	0	350,000	2,380,000	0	King & Tuthill

Symbol Code: B—Branch Library; BS—Branch & System Headquarters; M—Main Library; MS—Main & System Headquarters; S—System Headquarters; n/a—not available

Table 2 / Public Library Buildings: Additions and Renovations, 1996 (cont.)

Community	Pop. ('000)	Code	Project Cost	Const. Cost	Gross Sq.Ft.	Sq.Ft. Cost	Equip. Cost	Site Cost	Other Costs	Volumes	Federal Funds	State Funds	Local Funds	Gift Funds	Architect
New London	29	M	85,000	70,000	8,000	8.75	0	Owned	15,000	120,000	70,000	0	0	15,000	John Walsh
Old Lyme	7	M	2,534,971	2,071,358	11,980	172.90	162,701	105,193	195,719	40,000	100,000	350,000	1,476,309	608,662	Kenneth Best
Delaware															
Dover	666	M	610,200	530,200	16,600	31.93	15,000	Owned	65,000	85,000	225,000	385,200	0	0	Becker Morgan
Florida															
Clermont	31	M	437,705	328,908	4,882	67.37	70,296	Owned	38,501	20,104	0	0	0	437,705	Robert J. Zahradnik
Gulf Breeze	20	B	648,950	485,000	11,540	42.03	130,000	Owned	33,950	28,500	0	324,475	249,475	75,000	Caldwell Assocs.
North Fort Myers	38	B	1,213,449	934,760	8,994	103.93	175,000	Owned	103,689	51,000	0	0	1,213,449	0	Avalon Engineering
Waldo	2	B	120,478	82,771	1,370	60.42	28,307	Leased	9,400	10,500	0	0	120,478	0	Paul W. Portal
Winter Park	24	M	1,560,000	1,342,000	30,000	44.73	60,000	Leased	158,000	180,000	0	400,000	1,100,000	60,000	C.T. Hsu & Assocs.
Illinois															
Bartlett	27	M	3,894,914	3,092,027	33,000	93.70	441,896	Owned	360,991	100,000	0	250,000	3,639,849	5,065	LaRoi Architects
Bartonville	24	M	1,867,946	1,460,997	21,500	67.95	211,916	Owned	195,033	100,000	0	250,000	1,616,946	1,000	Frye Gillan Molinaro
Blue Island	21	M	10,578	10,578	n/a	n/a	0	Owned	0	n/a	0	5,000	5,578	0	none
Carlinville	5	M	725,000	384,841	8,292	46.41	91,885	187,500	60,774	40,000	0	250,000	0	475,000	Gatewood, Hance
Carol Stream	37	M	761,646	436,666	26,597	16.42	259,627	Owned	65,353	130,000	65,000	0	686,556	10,090	Wendt, Cedarholm...
Chicago	67	B	3,356,000	2,670,000	7,211	370.27	n/a	131,000	555,000	40,000	1,500,000	346,000	1,510,000	0	McClier/UBM
East Alton	15	M	632,095	556,653	17,001	32.74	29,988	Owned	45,454	70,000	0	238,100	393,495	500	M. Thomas Hall
Effingham	12	M	236,819	186,710	3,115	59.94	33,601	Owned	16,508	65,000	0	73,670	88,149	75,000	Gatewood & Hance
Galva	4	M	48,432	41,050	100	410.50	0	Owned	7,382	n/a	0	0	21,632	2,000	Metzger Johnson
Golconda	1	M	135,668	133,293	1,700	78.41	2,375	Owned	0	3,360	24,800	54,400	27,375	53,893	Walker/Baker
Hazel Crest	29	M	$6,176	n/a	n/a	n/a	n/a	Owned	0	n/a	$3,088	0	$3,088	0	none
Jacksonville	19	M	2,773,121	2,141,282	21,960	97.51	161,834	Owned	470,005	90,000	0	500,000	1,557,752	715,369	Frye Gillan Molinaro
Johnsburg	11	M	1,600,745	1,177,626	10,000	117.76	85,000	129,000	209,119	40,590	250,000	0	1,300,445	50,300	Lieberbach & Graham
Lake Bluff	5	M	21,000	18,100	139	130.22	300	Owned	2,600	n/a	0	10,000	11,000	0	Charles Adams
St. Charles	37	M	53,840	47,989	500	95.98	1,490	Owned	4,361	350	0	450	12,616	40,774	Wendt, Cedarholm...
Warrensburg	6	M	273,660	204,000	2,500	81.60	34,660	7,000	28,000	32,000	0	100,000	167,000	6,660	Michael A. Cardinal
Western Springs	12	M	3,744,988	2,923,629	24,000	121.82	250,557	302,741	268,061	70,000	0	0	3,494,988	0	Frye Gillan Molinaro
Indiana															
Auburn	15	M	2,020,700	1,632,200	15,440	105.71	230,000	Owned	158,500	85,000	143,000	0	229,000	1,587,700	Morrison Kattman...
Flora	4	M	1,570,037	1,013,591	9,796	103.47	228,615	72,300	255,531	43,920	0	0	1,500,000	70,037	H.L. Mohler & Assocs.

Symbol Code: B—Branch Library; BS—Branch & System Headquarters; M—Main Library; MS—Main & System Headquarters; S—System Headquarters; n/a—not available

Table 2 / Public Library Buildings: Additions and Renovations, 1996 (cont.)

Community	Pop. ('000)	Code	Project Cost	Const. Cost	Gross Sq.Ft.	Sq.Ft. Cost	Equip. Cost	Site Cost	Other Costs	Volumes	Federal Funds	State Funds	Local Funds	Gift Funds	Architect
Hebron	7	B	2,285,936	1,566,989	12,800	122.42	147,753	80,500	490,694	75,000	0	0	2,285,936	0	InterDesign Group
Mitchell	10	M	2,202,000	1,404,481	12,800	109.73	334,655	35,000	427,864	70,000	167,000	0	2,035,000	0	Scott Veazey
Portage	36	B	3,968,486	3,086,158	33,560	91.96	295,848	Owned	586,480	175,000	0	0	3,968,486	0	InterDesign Group
Sullivan	18	MS	554,801	503,980	7,500	67.20	13,843	Owned	36,978	50,000	0	0	554,801	0	Architectural Alliance
Valparaiso	60	MS	5,364,618	4,061,605	55,945	72.60	335,754	99,000	868,259	250,000	0	0	5,364,618	0	InterDesign Group
Iowa															
Estherville	10	M	1,493,594	1,260,449	13,300	94.77	124,954	Owned	108,191	76,200	0	0	900,000	593,594	Brown Healey Stone...
Rockwell	1	M	97,118	53,598	2,700	19.85	6,404	37,116	0	n/a	0	0	29,500	71,820	none
Kansas															
McPherson	13	M	395,000	241,900	13,189	18.35	126,300	Owned	26,800	76,000	0	0	395,000	0	Architectural Design
Overland Park	329	MS	12,568,221	7,693,736	90,500	85.01	1,372,925	2,371,984	1,129,576	300,000	0	0	12,568,221	0	Gould Evans...
Kentucky															
Cumberland	8	B	n/a	n/a	7,425	n/a	n/a	10,000	n/a	25,816	0	0	n/a	0	Richardson Assocs.
Harlan	28	MS	841,715	663,559	15,866	41.82	101,150	10,000	67,006	36,086	298,627	0	356,188	186,900	Richardson Assocs.
Louisiana															
Gonzales	36	B	592,993	526,500	4,500	117.00	15,861	Owned	50,632	45,000	0	0	592,993	0	Henry Chauvin
Lafayette	178	MS	289,416	60,575	63,000	00.96	223,165	Owned	5,676	n/a	0	0	289,416	0	Associated Design
Luling	45	M	975,000	825,000	8,000	103.13	75,000	Owned	75,000	30,000	0	0	975,000	0	Caserta/Carroll
Natchitoches	38	M	206,000	186,000	6,000	31.00	0	Owned	20,000	6,000	0	0	206,000	0	Slack, Alost, Miremont
Maine															
Falmouth	8	M	1,240,000	950,000	10,040	94.62	145,000	Owned	145,000	45,000	0	0	500,000	740,000	WBRC/Steve Rich
Winslow	8	M	415,000	160,000	10,500	15.24	60,000	175,000	20,000	50,000	5,500	0	350,000	54,000	A.E. Hodsdon
Massachusetts															
Arlington	45	M	6,750,909	5,100,039	51,000	100.00	565,062	Owned	1,085,808	200,000	0	3,312,681	2,856,676	581,552	Wallace, Floyd
Dover	6	M	1,465,614	1,191,703	12,000	99.31	40,457	Owned	233,454	55,000	106,131	200,000	844,869	314,614	Anthony Tappe
Michigan															
Burton	29	B	189,844	155,929	2,000	77.96	0	Owned	33,915	n/a	85,429	0	104,415	0	Wade-Trim
Coopesville	11	M	322,850	247,940	4,000	61.99	58,430	Owned	16,480	35,000	103,000	0	219,850	0	GMB
Dexter	12	M	414,542	142,077	4,300	33.04	46,907	193,000	32,558	22,000	0	0	392,542	22,000	Cornerstone Design
East Jordan	6	M	178,000	78,000	5,000	15.60	95,000	Owned	5,000	40,000	0	0	178,000	0	Tim Fekete

Symbol Code: B—Branch Library; BS—Branch & System Headquarters; M—Main Library; MS—Main & System Headquarters; S—System Headquarters; n/a—not available

Table 2 / Public Library Buildings: Additions and Renovations, 1996 (cont.)

Community	Pop. ('000)	Code	Project Cost	Const. Cost	Gross Sq.Ft.	Sq.Ft. Cost	Equip. Cost	Site Cost	Other Costs	Volumes	Federal Funds	State Funds	Local Funds	Gift Funds	Architect
Grand Rapids	5	B	1,885,947	1,508,780	20,170	74.80	243,336	Owned	133,831	80,000	80,659	0	1,781,868	23,420	Van Wienen
Kalamazoo	119	B	331,975	177,410	4,000	44.35	52,788	Leased	101,777	31,385	0	0	331,975	0	David Milling
Kent City	4	B	119,600	104,000	1,002	103.80	15,000	Owned	600	n/a	61,700	0	42,400	15,500	Isaac Norris
Portage	42	M	3,599,504	3,030,650	46,778	64.79	388,854	Owned	180,000	170,000	0	0	3,599,504	0	Frye Gillan Molinaro
St. Ignace	4	M	40,000	28,000	200	140.00	12,000	Owned	0	15,000	0	0	40,000	0	R. Scott & Assocs.
Suttons Bay	5	M	206,719	169,030	2,032	83.18	16,448	Leased	21,241	20,000	83,925	0	101,777	21,017	Larry Graves
Minnesota															
Eden Prairie	44	B	1,245,790	907,139	5,080	178.57	50,000	Owned	288,651	8,715	0	0	1,245,790	0	Marc Partridge
Maple Grove	44	B	1,149,600	788,013	5,000	157.60	86,718	Owned	274,869	17,080	0	0	1,149,600	0	Bernard Jacob
Minneapolis	71	B	1,280,000	1,100,000	16,000	68.75	40,000	Owned	140,000	70,000	0	0	1,280,000	0	Leonard Parker
St. Michael	10	B	26,000	20,000	1,150	17.39	6,000	Leased	0	30,000	0	0	0	26,000	not reported
Missouri															
Buckner	3	B	101,169	92,547	1,163	79.58	0	Owned	8,622	60,000	0	0	0	101,169	Tagnascioli & Assocs.
Independence	112	B	928,045	741,249	12,061	61.46	142,321	Owned	44,475	142,500	0	0	928,045	0	Tagnascioli & Assocs.
Joplin	41	M	677,246	583,678	6,500	89.80	47,792	Owned	45,776	35,000	0	0	404,546	272,700	Vivian McLain Baker
Portageville	18	BS	314,966	270,188	5,000	54.04	34,178	Owned	10,600	20,000	0	0	308,896	6,070	John Colton Sargent
St. Louis	n/a	B	1,298,087	871,391	11,276	77.28	268,150	Owned	158,546	30,000	0	0	1,298,087	0	John Koch & Assocs.
Wentzville	16	B	419,883	235,034	4,500	52.23	60,000	121,049	3,800	20,000	0	0	389,883	30,000	Adams Architectural
Montana															
Deer Lodge	7	M	413,530	361,731	8,500	42.56	5,277	Owned	46,522	30,000	100,989	10,285	24,350	277,906	Rick Schlenker
New Hampshire															
Rochester	28	M	2,145,000	1,632,225	25,000	65.29	250,000	180,000	82,775	100,000	170,000	0	1,725,000	250,000	Dennis Mires
New York															
Bronx	31	B	2,036,000	1,659,000	15,591	106.41	126,000	Owned	251,000	47,185	0	294,000	1,242,000	500,000	Castro Blanco...
Cazenovia	9	M	1,044,955	916,551	10,120	90.57	33,327	Owned	95,077	40,000	0	0	0	1,044,955	Teitsch-Kent
Clinton	10	M	575,000	494,000	9,500	52.00	25,000	Owned	56,000	35,000	13,000	20,000	20,000	522,000	Alesia & Crewell
Geneseo	9	M	547,444	430,494	2,442	176.29	18,613	Owned	98,337	30,000	0	0	538,294	9,150	Handler, Grosso...
Johnstown	9	M	751,640	594,614	3,900	152.47	17,926	108,000	31,100	3,360	50,000	65,050	513,634	122,956	Architecture+
New York	3070	B	100,000,000	40,000,000	250,000	160.00	5,000,000	23,000,000	32,000,000	1,500,000	4,000,000	7,500,000	13,000,000	75,500,000	Gwathmey Siegel
New York	68	B	2,687,000	2,106,000	13,126	160.45	204,000	Owned	377,000	60,530	0	269,000	1,918,000	500,000	Gruzen Samton
New York	29	B	2,324,034	2,139,101	14,703	145.49	118,500	Owned	66,433	58,000	315,977	35,038	1,539,452	433,567	Rothzeid, Kaizerman...

Symbol Code: B—Branch Library; BS—Branch & System Headquarters; M—Main Library; MS—Main & System Headquarters; S—System Headquarters; n/a—not available

Table 2 / Public Library Buildings: Additions and Renovations, 1996 *(cont.)*

Community	Pop. ('000)	Code	Project Cost	Const. Cost	Gross Sq.Ft.	Sq.Ft. Cost	Equip. Cost	Site Cost	Other Costs	Volumes	Federal Funds	State Funds	Local Funds	Gift Funds	Architect
Shirley	44	M	3,999,334	2,699,468	23,000	117.37	625,000	Owned	674,866	400,000	0	15,275	3,984,059	0	Bentel & Bentel
North Carolina															
Newland	15	M	361,547	286,523	4,780	54.95	53,721	Owned	21,303	20,000	118,856	0	40,485	202,206	John P. Stevens
Ohio															
Coshocton	35	M	339,693	143,488	6,310	22.74	170,713	Owned	25,492	81,700	0	0	339,693	0	Pamela Maxfield-Ontko
East Cleveland	40	B	100,000	20,000	3,000	6.67	75,000	Owned	5,000	0	0	0	0	100,000	David Holzheimer
Eastlake	18	B	1,284,983	911,973	15,301	59.60	173,491	Owned	199,519	n/a	0	0	1,284,983	0	David Holzheimer
Eaton	41	S	431,000	25,000	6,500	3.85	5,000	400,000	1,000	45,000	0	0	431,000	0	Thomas Kline
North Canton	32	M	109,303	24,507	2,845	8.61	75,871	Owned	8,925	31,050	0	0	106,803	2,500	Library Design Assn.
Plain City	10	M	801,472	578,492	4,200	137.74	69,748	Owned	103,232	13,000	0	0	417,749	383,723	McDonald, Cassell...
Springfield	140	MS	1,402,890	1,126,325	9,400	119.82	153,675	Owned	122,890	17,500	0	0	1,299,890	103,000	Stephen L. Sharp
Vermilion	11	M	1,678,693	1,141,707	19,689	57.99	225,699	Owned	311,287	n/a	0	0	1,678,693	0	David Holzheimer
Willoughby	22	B	1,577,906	1,092,519	18,789	58.15	213,040	Owned	272,347	n/a	0	0	1,577,906	0	David Holzheimer
Willowick	28	MS	2,022,162	1,497,270	24,079	62.18	273,021	Owned	251,871	n/a	0	0	2,022,162	0	David Holzheimer
Youngstown	265	MS	3,663,758	3,337,192	74,633	44.71	143,934	Owned	182,632	31,542	0	0	3,402,642	261,116	Ricciuti Balog
Oklahoma															
Stroud	3	M	360,586	335,998	7,624	44.07	17,688	Owned	6,900	17,000	0	55,000	305,586	0	Quinn & Assocs.
South Carolina															
Columbia	n/a	B	175,333	59,893	18,000	3.33	23,948	Owned	91,492	n/a	0	0	175,333	0	not reported
Eastover	n/a	B	32,030	9,362	2,583	3.62	3,909	Owned	18,759	n/a	0	0	32,030	0	not reported
South Dakota															
Madison	11	M	1,255,413	1,097,913	12,750	86.11	92,500	Owned	65,000	70,000	50,000	150,000	995,000	60,413	Steven Jastram
Tennessee															
Chattanooga	286	B	100,000	100,000	9,084	11.01	0	Leased	0	50,000	0	0	0	100,000	not reported
Columbia	64	M	352,227	295,900	6,000	49.32	35,327	Owned	21,000	100,000	0	0	116,000	136,227	Davis, Stokes, Chilton
Erin	7	M	325,000	145,000	1,600	90.63	10,000	Owned	170,000	16,000	100,000	70,000	255,000	0	Rufus Johnson
Humboldt	13	M	9,008	8,654	1,272	6.80	354	Owned	0	5,000	0	0	0	9,008	not reported
Nashville	15	B	272,315	207,873	1,332	156.06	42,079	Owned	22,363	16,230	225,000	0	47,315	0	Matchett & Assocs.
Texas															
Austin	500	MS	877,258	729,096	110,000	6.63	42,318	Owned	105,844	350,000	0	0	877,258	0	Gordon Bartram
Austin	500	B	1,800,468	1,164,171	76,176	15.29	114,980	Owned	521,317	2,054,435	0	0	1,800,468	0	David Hoffman

Symbol Code: B—Branch Library; BS—Branch & System Headquarters; M—Main Library; MS—Main & System Headquarters; S—System Headquarters; n/a—not available

Table 2 / Public Library Buildings: Additions and Renovations, 1996 (cont.)

Community	Pop. ('000)	Code	Project Cost	Const. Cost	Gross Sq.Ft.	Sq.Ft. Cost	Equip. Cost	Site Cost	Other Costs	Volumes	Federal Funds	State Funds	Local Funds	Gift Funds	Architect
Baytown	68	M	2,090,678	1,505,138	50,500	29.80	321,935	Owned	263,605	300,000	90,920	0	1,937,164	62,594	Bill Burge
Houston	152	B	2,298,492	1,640,492	18,000	91.13	100,000	58,000	500,000	102,449	1,232,492	0	1,066,000	0	Lo & Assocs.
Plano	76	B	1,385,000	1,074,673	20,000	53.73	180,427	Owned	129,900	58,852	0	0	1,385,000	0	Phillips Swager
San Antonio	41	B	276,937	231,750	9,000	25.75	15,000	Owned	30,187	43,000	0	0	276,937	0	Delara Architects
San Antonio Oppelt	34	B	215,486	160,026	1,000	160.02	37,800	Owned	17,660	50,000	0	0	215,486	0	O'Neill Conrad
San Antonio	100	B	709,768	617,557	4,000	154.39	40,355	Owned	51,856	125,000	0	0	669,768	40,000	Debra J. Dockery
San Antonio	51	B	662,277	554,297	3,000	184.77	51,213	Owned	56,767	95,000	0	0	662,277	0	Kinneson & Assocs.
San Antonio	26	B	211,648	150,000	9,000	16.66	36,648	Owned	25,000	48,811	0	0	211,648	0	Alamo Architects
Virginia															
Alexandria	116	MS	3,732,309	2,765,000	25,000	110.60	365,000	Owned	602,309	109,000	0	0	3,732,309	0	Lukmire Partnership
Kenbridge	6	B	226,055	137,942	8,000	17.24	22,681	65,432	56,767	n/a	0	0	15,000	211,055	Richard P. Ballou
Midlothian	30	B	1,910,000	1,388,000	15,000	92.53	107,900	104,800	309,300	90,000	0	0	1,780,200	129,800	Richard J. Fitts
Victoria	6	B	80,200	70,000	5,000	14.00	10,200	Leased	0	13,000	0	0	30,000	59,000	Aubrey Arvin
Washington															
Sumner	21	B	1,454,807	909,747	10,600	85.83	152,000	235,000	158,060	55,000	76,612	0	1,378,195	0	Boyle-Wagoner
Wisconsin															
Hudson	19	M	663,313	266,890	11,000	24.26	96,423	300,000	0	43,428	0	0	425,685	237,628	none
Janesville	79	M	8,225,000	5,790,000	65,000	89.08	1,340,000	325,000	770,000	238,000	0	0	1,590,000	6,635,000	Meyer, Scherer...
Mosinee	8	B	292,895	230,880	5,940	38.87	36,873	Owned	25,142	16,300	0	0	292,895	0	Tharen Gorski
Random Lake	5	M	624,277	519,777	8,000	64.97	55,000	Owned	49,500	30,000	125,000	0	285,000	214,277	Linde Jensen...
Wyoming															
Casper	63	M	439,346	301,639	2,688	112.22	102,003	Owned	35,704	40,000	0	9,716	355,067	74,563	Therkildsen & Amend
Granger	1	B	4,000	4,000	750	5.33	0	Owned	0	198	0	0	2,000	2,000	not reported

Symbol Code: B—Branch Library; BS—Branch & System Headquarters; M—Main Library; MS—Main & System Headquarters; S—System Headquarters; n/a—not available

Table 3 / Public Library Buildings: Six-Year Cost Summary, 1991–1996

	Fiscal 1991	Fiscal 1992	Fiscal 1993	Fiscal 1994	Fiscal 1995	Fiscal 1996
Number of new buildings	120	118	113	108	99	100
Number of ARRs[1]	108	115	105	127	124	145
Sq. ft. new buildings	1,520,121	1,935,111	1,896,197	1,818,522	2,102,851	2,002,067
Sq. ft. ARRs	1,689,484	1,819,787	1,878,628	2,163,909	2,469,345	2,315,523
New Buildings						
Construction cost	$121,884,749	$188,143,273	$183,978,065	$176,678,555	$232,050,462	$286,141,319
Equipment cost	18,603,687	27,234,207	22,651,001	27,617,314	28,239,712	57,222,035
Site cost	14,504,740	21,011,768	28,353,201	34,696,765	31,406,749	16,391,748
Other cost	18,521,472	31,315,471	32,275,926	30,114,637	42,946,629	49,498,901
Total—Project cost	176,127,088	267,704,719	267,770,932	271,051,271	334,643,552	409,254,003
ARRs—Project cost	141,262,919	205,103,863	160,825,726	345,135,792	281,750,499	314,191,342
New and ARR project cost	$317,390,007	$472,808,582	$428,596,658	$616,187,063	$616,394,051	$723,445,345
Fund sources						
Federal, new buildings	$8,139,146	$9,851,065	$4,320,934	$4,483,792	$10,532,079	$17,719,253
Federal, ARRs	6,533,719	7,413,576	3,646,307	6,188,756	3,292,272	13,771,483
Federal, total	$14,672,865	$17,264,641	$7,967,241	$10,672,548	$13,824,351	$31,490,736
State, new buildings	$14,349,412	$10,753,499	$26,376,138	$45,559,588	$31,051,654	$32,089,611
State, ARRs	11,439,866	43,002,552	10,841,063	10,361,213	28,482,199	21,212,540
State, total	$25,789,278	$53,756,051	$37,217,201	$55,920,801	$59,533,853	$53,302,151
Local, new buildings	$138,176,957	$230,815,119	$208,363,930	$203,676,929	$268,609,523	$301,996,679
Local, ARRs	111,788,933	139,135,045	141,961,411	302,050,882	227,108,845	182,163,428
Local, total	$249,965,890	$369,950,164	$350,325,341	$505,727,811	$495,718,368	$484,160,107
Gift, new buildings	$15,810,151	$16,487,880	$28,878,559	$17,663,214	$25,433,205	$57,478,470
Gift, ARRs	11,561,261	15,849,230	4,389,236	26,614,547	23,951,472	97,019,403
Gift, total	$27,371,412	$32,337,110	$33,267,795	$44,277,761	$49,384,677	$154,497,873
Total Funds Used	$317,799,445	$473,307,966	$428,777,578	$616,598,921	$618,461,249	$723,450,867

[1] Additions, remodelings, and renovations.

Table 4 / New Academic Library Buildings, 1996

Institution	Project Cost	Gross Sq.Ft.	Sq.Ft. Cost	Construction Cost	Equipment Cost	Book Capacity	Seating Capacity	Architect
George W. Johnson Lib., George Mason Univ., Fairfax, Va.	$30,000,000	323,960	$71.30	$23,100,000	$2,734,753	100,000	1,900	Shepley, Bulfinch...; Marcellus, Wright...; Studios Architecture
Law Lib., Univ. of Connecticut, Hartford	22,739,835	127,000	167.37	21,256,424	1,483,411	925,605	797	Stecker, LaBau, Arneill...
Frances Willson Thompson Lib., Univ. of Michigan–Flint	21,315,000	112,000	133.04	14,900,000	n/a	350,000	700	Gunnar Birkerts & Assocs.
Science and Technology Lib., Utah State Univ., Logan	16,281,800	111,000	105.38	11,697,100	3,800,000	1,000,000	957	JHCH Architects
Southern Utah Univ. Lib., Cedar City	10,404,400	80,500	113.53	9,139,100	1,265,300	260,000	1,210	FFKR
Thomas J. Dodd Research Ctr., Univ. of Connecticut, Storrs	10,363,486	55,000	145.05	7,977,807	860,000	n/a	50	Fletcher Thompson
Quinnipiac College School of Law Lib., Hamden, Ct.	9,645,000	51,000	142.00	7,242,000	1,605,000	300,000	400	Riley & Childress
North Hall Lib., Mansfield Univ., Pa.	9,400,000	150,000	54.00	8,100,000	900,000	325,000	475	Eckles Company
Oklahoma City Community College Lib.	9,000,000	108,757	68.96	7,500,000	1,500,000	100,000	500	Walt Joyce, RGDC
St. Ambrose Univ. Lib., Davenport, Iowa	8,500,000	58,500	113.73	6,653,127	900,000	250,000	400	Woolen Molzan & Partners
Warren County Community College Lib., Washington, N.J.	7,500,000	50,000	120.00	6,000,000	750,000	15,000	90	The Hillier Group
Bishop Lib., Lebanon Valley College, Annville, Pa.	7,355,314	43,500	120.92	5,259,918	771,419	174,900	250	Breslin Ridyard Fadero
Main Campus Lib., Trident Technical College, North Charleston, S.C.	5,135,442	50,000	95.88	4,793,810	341,632	80,000	500	Cummings & McCrady
Patrick Info. Technology Ctr., Augusta Technical Institute, Ga.	4,805,000	40,000	106.88	4,275,000	530,000	130,000	210	Gossens/Bachman
Veterinary Med. Lib., Biomedical Info. Ctr., Purdue Univ., W. Lafayette, Ind.	4,106,748	23,602	136.00	3,209,872	169,000	70,000	107	Scholer Corp.
Robson Lib., Univ. of the Ozarks, Clarksville, Ark.	n/a	37,833	88.52	3,349,000	n/a	95,000	156	BCCGBN Architects
Lib. & Admin. Bldg., St. Vincent de Paul Regional Seminary, Boynton Beach, Fla.	2,900,000	30,000	83.33	2,500,000	400,000	100,000	120	Spillis, Candela & Partners
Health Professions Division Lib., NOVA Southeastern Univ., Davie, Fla.	2,000,000	25,000	70.00	1,750,000	n/a	70,000	240	ACAI Assocs.

Table 5 / Academic Library Buildings: Additions and Renovations, 1996

Institution	Status	Project Cost	Gross Sq.Ft.	Sq.Ft. Cost	Construction Cost	Equipment Cost	Book Capacity	Seating Capacity	Architect
Malcolm Love Lib., San Diego State Univ.	Total	$25,915,000	271,500	$78.88	$21,415,000	$4,500,000	569,720	2,072	Mosher Drew Watson...
	New	n/a	201,000	99.58	20,015,000	n/a	381,368	1,282	DWL Archs. & Planners
	Renovated	n/a	70,500	19.86	1,400,000	n/a	188,352	790	
Tisch Lib., Tufts Univ., Medford, Mass.	Total	19,820,000	184,000	84.00	15,456,000	101,000	1,000,000	1,325	Shepley Bulfinch...
	New	n/a	84,000	138.00	11,592,000	n/a	n/a	n/a	
	Renovated	n/a	100,000	38.60	3,864,000	n/a	n/a	n/a	
Kuhn Lib. & Gallery, Univ. of Maryland, Baltimore County	Total	18,240,000	133,000	117.44	15,620,000	2,400,000	920,000	1,155	Shepley Bulfinch...
	New	n/a	n/a	n/a	n/a	n/a	580,000	850	Cho Wilks & Benn
	Renovated	n/a	n/a	n/a	n/a	n/a	340,000	305	
Mitchell Memorial Lib., Mississippi State Univ.	Total	17,800,000	229,500	60.56	13,899,490	3,299,000	1,570,000	2,200	Foil-Wyatt Architects
	New	14,700,000	108,500	102.30	11,099,550	2,998,940	650,000	1,250	
	Renovated	3,100,000	121,000	23.14	2,799,940	300,060	920,000	950	
Broward Community College, Florida Atlantic Univ., Davie	Total	14,500,000	153,183	76.78	11,761,430	633,872	433,448	1,432	The Russell Partnership
	New	11,106,394	98,124	91.81	9,008,764	485,520	n/a	n/a	
	Renovated	3,393,606	55,059	49.99	2,752,666	148,352	n/a	n/a	
D. Hiden Ramsey Lib., Univ. of North Carolina at Asheville	Total	11,300,000	110,000	81.95	9,015,000	1,050,000	450,000	900	Boney Architects
	New	6,800,000	60,000	86.42	5,185,000	841,000	n/a	n/a	
	Renovated	4,500,000	50,000	76.60	3,830,000	209,000	n/a	n/a	
Info. Technology Ctr., Buena Vista Univ., Storm Lake, Iowa	Total	9,731,634	79,054	103.58	8,188,114	1,543,520	300,000	366	Leonard Lampert Architects
	New	n/a	50,611	n/a	n/a	1,543,520	95,000	245	
	Renovated	n/a	28,443	n/a	n/a	0	205,000	121	

Table 5 / Academic Library Buildings: Additions and Renovations, 1996 *(cont.)*

Institution	Status	Project Cost	Gross Sq.Ft.	Sq.Ft. Cost	Construction Cost	Equipment Cost	Book Capacity	Seating Capacity	Architect
College of Wooster Libs., Ohio	Total	7,210,227	132,000	53.33	7,039,814	170,413	488,900	682	Perry, Dean, Rogers
	New	n/a	32,000	n/a	n/a	n/a	n/a	n/a	
	Renovated	n/a	100,000	n/a	n/a	n/a	n/a	n/a	
Rod Lib., Univ. of Northern Iowa, Cedar Falls	Total	n/a	238,836	29.48	7,040,403	797,206	1,000,000	2,165	Herbert Lewis Kruse Blunck
	New	n/a	61,239	n/a	n/a	n/a	n/a	790	
	Renovated	n/a	177,597	n/a	n/a	n/a	n/a	1,375	
Nancy Thompson Lib., Kean College of New Jersey, Union	Total	5,625,000	73,910	66.87	4,943,000	n/a	n/a	1,250	Kehri Shatken Sharon
	New	n/a	14,000	n/a	n/a	n/a	n/a	n/a	
	Renovated	n/a	59,910	n/a	n/a	n/a	n/a	n/a	
Beulah Williams Lib., Northern State Univ., Aberdeen, S.D.	Total	4,500,000	62,097	61.20	3,800,000	340,000	480,000	400	Koch Hazard Baltzer Ltd.
	New	n/a	41,687	n/a	n/a	n/a	n/a	n/a	
	Renovated	n/a	20,410	n/a	n/a	n/a	n/a	n/a	
Schuler LRC, Thaddeus Stevens State School of Technology, Lancaster, Pa.	Total	4,000,000	30,000	106.67	3,200,000	100,000	40,000	120	Atkin, Olshin, Lawson-Bell
	New	n/a	21,000	124.52	2,615,000	n/a	40,000	n/a	
	Renovated	n/a	9,000	65.00	585,000	n/a	0	n/a	
Reeves Lib./Hazel Wing, Westminster College, Fulton, Mo.	Total	3,834,613	37,100	74.29	2,756,000	816,163	107,000	342	Peckham, Guyton, Albers...
	New	2,275,945	15,704	103.16	1,620,000	524,720	0	161	
	Renovated	1,558,668	21,396	53.09	1,136,000	291,443	107,000	181	

Table 6 / Academic Library Buildings: Renovations Only, 1996

Institution	Project Cost	Gross Area	Sq.Ft. Cost	Construction Cost	Equipment Cost	Book Capacity	Seating Capacity	Architect
Galter Health Sciences Lib., Northwestern Univ., Chicago	$10,000,000	57,000	$131.58	$7,500,000	$1,500,000	30,000	500	James W. Baird
Russell D. Cole Lib., Cornell College, Mt. Vernon, Iowa	3,400,000	39,100	69.05	2,700,000	96,872	226,250	500	Herbert Lewis Kruse Blunck
Mabee-Simpson Library, Lyon College, Batesville, Ark.	1,000,000	10,000	100.00	1,000,000	0	150,000	250	Cromwell Architects
Firestone Lib., Microforms Service, Princeton Univ., N.J.	788,000	5,000	132.00	660,000	32,000	n/a	45	Kehrt Shatken Sharon
Kellenberger Lib., Northwest Christian College, Eugene, Ore.	650,000	20,890	27.76	580,000	70,000	70,000	100	William A. Randall
Greenawalt Lib., Northwestern College of Chiropractic, Bloomington, Minn.	600,000	12,000	37.50	450,000	150,000	10,000	2	David Constable
Mary L. Williams Curriculum Materials Lib., Oklahoma State Univ., Stillwater	486,936	5,278	79.23	418,200	68,736	65,000	73	H.T.B., Inc.
Med. Ctr. Lib., Louisiana State Univ. School of Medicine, Shreveport	149,900	2,060	38.35	79,000	70,000	0	70	Harry Wyatt
Moellering Lib., Valparaiso Univ., Ind.	53,016	1,878	28.23	53,016	0	370	10	not reported

Book Trade Research and Statistics

Prices of U.S. and Foreign Published Materials

Gay N. Dannelly
Chair, ALA ALCTS Library Materials Price Index Committee

The Library Materials Price Index Committee (LMPIC) continues to monitor library prices for a variety of library materials and sources. As seen below, prices for library materials in general continued to increase in 1995 at a rate much higher than the general U.S. Consumer Price Index.

Index	1993	Percent Change 1994	1995	1996/97
Consumer price index (1996)	1.3	2.7	2.9	3.3
Periodicals	5.5	5.5	10.8	9.9*
Serial services	4.8	5.0	6.6	3.9*
Hardcover books	-22.3	22.7	5.6	n.a.
Academic books	2.8	2.1	-0.1	n.a.
College books	3.0	-2.0	4.7	n.a.
Mass market paperbacks	11.5	-1.4	15.4	n.a.
Trade paperbacks	2.2	-2.5	5.4	n.a.

*Payments made in 1996 for 1997 receipt

U.S. Published Materials

Tables 1 through 10 consist of average prices and price indexes for library materials published primarily in the United States. These indexes include periodicals (Table 1), serial services (Table 2), U.S. hardcover books (Table 3), North American academic books (Table 4), college books (Table 5), mass market paperback books (Table 6), trade paperback books (Table 7), daily newspapers (Table 8), nonprint media (Table 9), and CD-ROMs (Table 10).

Periodical and Serial Prices

The LMPI Committee and the Faxon Company jointly produce the U.S. periodical price index (Table 1). The subscription prices shown are publishers' list prices, excluding publisher discounts or vendor service charges. This report

(text continues on p. 490)

Table 1 / U.S. Periodicals: Average Prices and Price Indexes, 1995–1997
(Index Base: 1977 = 100)

Subject Area	1977 Average Price	1995 Average Price	1995 Index	1996 Average Price	1996 Index	1997 Average Price	1997 Index
U.S. periodicals excluding Russian translations*	$24.59	$149.46	607.8	$165.61	673.5	$181.98	740.1
U.S. periodicals including Russian translations	33.42	196.57	588.2	215.37	644.4	237.14	709.6
Agriculture	11.58	62.07	536.0	67.12	579.6	72.40	625.2
Business and economics	18.62	94.37	506.8	102.69	551.5	114.18	613.2
Chemistry and physics	93.76	767.96	819.1	867.00	924.7	957.36	1,021.1
Children's periodicals	5.82	21.31	366.2	21.65	372.0	23.08	396.6
Education	17.54	80.87	451.1	86.90	495.4	95.34	543.5
Engineering	35.77	216.23	604.5	247.72	692.6	273.31	764.1
Fine and applied arts	13.72	46.74	340.7	48.24	351.6	50.02	364.6
General interest periodicals	16.19	38.45	237.5	39.37	243.2	40.58	250.7
History	12.64	47.83	378.4	50.76	401.6	54.47	430.9
Home economics	18.73	86.32	460.9	92.44	493.6	98.88	527.9
Industrial arts	14.37	82.49	574.0	87.57	609.4	93.79	652.7

Journalism and communications	16.97	86.06	507.1	91.31	538.1	98.16	578.4
Labor and industrial relations	11.24	81.59	725.9	85.80	763.3	92.28	821.0
Law	17.36	78.26	450.8	82.48	475.1	85.57	492.9
Library and information sciences	16.97	67.98	400.6	72.50	427.2	78.00	459.6
Literature and language	11.82	41.80	353.6	44.16	373.6	46.72	395.3
Mathematics, botany, geology, general science	47.13	308.79	655.2	342.07	725.8	379.84	805.9
Medicine	51.31	362.52	706.5	410.66	800.4	461.60	899.6
Philosophy and religion	10.89	42.86	393.6	45.71	419.8	48.84	448.5
Physical education and recreation	10.00	41.59	415.9	43.73	437.3	45.65	456.5
Political science	14.83	77.99	525.9	86.02	560.1	91.82	619.1
Psychology	31.74	190.58	600.4	211.72	667.0	233.90	736.9
Russian translations	175.41	1,033.65	589.3	1,099.42	626.8	1,216.51	693.5
Sociology and anthropology	19.68	115.77	588.3	125.77	644.1	137.54	698.9
Zoology	33.69	266.72	791.7	299.84	890.0	338.31	1,004.2
Total number of periodicals							
Excluding Russian translations	3,218	3,731		3,731		3,729	
Including Russian translations	3,418	3,941		3,941		3,939	

For further comments, see *American Libraries*, May 1993, May 1994, May 1995, and May 1996 issues.

Compiled by Adrian W. Alexander and Kathryn Hammell Carpenter.

*The category Russian translations was added in 1986.

Table 2 / U.S. Serial Services: Average Prices and Price Indexes, 1995–1997
(Index Base: 1977 = 100)

Subject Area	1977 Average Price	1995 Average Price	1995 Index	1996 Average Price	1996 Percent Increase	1996 Index	1997 Average Price	1997 Percent Increase	1997 Index
U.S. serial services*	$142.27	$522.01	366.9	$556.58	6.6	391.2	$578.22	3.9	406.4
Business	216.28	695.88	321.7	737.14	5.9	340.8	751.99	2.0	347.7
General and humanities	90.44	381.8	422.2	410.75	7.6	454.2	429.12	4.5	474.5
Law	126.74	542.73	428.2	593.81	9.4	468.5	592.84	-0.2	467.8
Science and technology	141.16	640.14	453.5	675.82	5.6	478.8	716.95	6.1	507.9
Social sciences	145.50	487.16	334.8	513.08	5.3	352.6	536.85	4.6	369.0
U.S. documents	62.88	121.28	192.9	129.37	6.7	205.7	151.38	17.0	240.7
Wilson Index	87.51	304.05	347.4	333.87	9.8	381.5	392.09	15.7	448.1
Total number of services	1,432		1,280		1,280			1,281	

Compiled by Nancy J. Chaffin, Arizona State University (West) from data supplied by the Faxon Company, publishers' list prices, and library acquisition records. For further comments, see *American Libraries*, May 1997, Serials Services 1997, by Nancy J. Chaffin.

The definition of a serial service has been taken from *American National Standard for Library and Information Services and Related Publishing Practices—Library Materials—Criteria for Price Indexes* (ANSI Z39.20—1983).

* Excludes Wilson Index; excludes Russian Translations as of 1988.

Table 3 / U.S. Hardcover Books: Average Prices and Price Indexes, 1993–1996
(Index Base: 1977 = 100)

Subject Area	1977 Average Price	Volumes	1993 Average Price	Index	Volumes	1994 Average Price	Index	Volumes	1995 Final Average Price	Index	Volumes	1996 Preliminary Average Price	Index
Agriculture	$16.24	269	$41.84	257.6	284	$58.10	357.8	392	$49.00	301.7	322	$45.54	280.4
Art	21.24	812	39.99	188.3	864	39.97	188.2	1,116	41.22	194.1	892	54.98	258.9
Biography	15.34	1,290	28.37	198.0	1,320	30.43	198.4	1,596	30.01	195.6	1,649	31.01	202.2
Business	18.00	791	37.95	210.8	854	42.72	237.3	972	46.89	260.5	984	51.40	285.6
Education	12.95	574	38.60	298.1	536	47.98	370.5	610	42.99	331.9	634	47.83	369.3
Fiction	10.09	2,093	19.50	193.3	2,221	20.95	207.6	2,345	21.47	212.8	2,586	23.46	232.5
General works	30.99	882	45.41	146.5	952	60.41	194.9	1,209	54.10	174.6	1,004	67.87	219.0
History	17.12	1,429	40.78	238.2	1,457	40.20	234.8	1,691	42.18	246.4	1,722	43.11	251.8
Home economics	11.16	422	20.55	184.1	482	20.49	183.6	651	22.53	201.9	558	23.78	213.1
Juvenile	6.65	3,599	13.87	208.6	3,414	14.59	218.0	3,649	14.55	218.8	3,420	16.42	246.9
Language	14.96	308	34.02	227.4	293	52.09	348.2	320	54.88	366.8	362	58.37	390.2
Law	25.04	560	53.94	215.4	681	72.32	288.8	716	73.09	291.9	682	71.96	287.4
Literature	15.78	1,289	35.30	223.7	1,227	37.77	239.4	1,302	38.48	243.9	1,482	43.91	278.3
Medicine	24.00	1,360	49.78	207.4	1,761	76.30	317.9	2,035	75.80	315.8	2,268	78.38	326.6
Music	20.13	198	41.44	205.9	179	39.27	195.1	251	43.27	214.9	225	41.63	206.8
Philosophy and psychology	14.43	912	39.44	273.3	843	44.71	309.8	1,001	45.25	313.6	1,091	48.32	334.9
Poetry and drama	13.63	500	31.06	227.9	505	31.56	231.6	567	34.95	256.4	525	35.21	258.3
Religion	12.26	1,204	29.16	237.8	1,169	30.73	250.7	1,364	34.27	279.5	1,302	36.45	297.3
Science	24.88	1,261	52.71	211.9	1,712	90.12	362.2	2,095	93.51	375.8	2,046	87.26	350.8
Sociology and economics	29.88	4,300	41.32	138.3	4,303	50.24	168.1	5,145	55.51	185.8	5,451	54.20	181.4
Sports and recreation	12.28	462	32.28	262.9	435	33.39	271.9	517	32.14	261.7	530	34.32	279.5
Technology	23.61	981	56.31	238.5	1,041	81.03	343.2	1,454	88.27	373.9	1,324	85.99	364.2
Travel	18.44	159	26.22	142.2	181	32.13	174.2	199	38.30	207.7	145	34.34	186.2
Total	$19.22	25,665	$35.00	182.0	26,714	$44.65	232.3	31,197	$47.15	245.3	31,204	$48.72	253.5

Compiled by Gay N. Dannelly, Ohio State University, from data supplied by the R. R. Bowker Company. Price indexes on Tables 3 and 7 are based on books recorded in the R. R. Bowker Company's *Weekly Record* (cumulated in *American Book Publishing Record*). The 1996 preliminary figures include items listed during 1996 with an imprint date of 1996. Final data for previous years include items listed between January and June of the following year with an imprint date of the specified year.

483

Table 4 / North American Academic Books: Average Prices and Price Indexes 1993–1995
(Index Base: 1989 = 100)

Subject Area	LC Class	1989 No. of Titles	1989 Average Price	1993 No. of Titles	1993 Average Price	1994 No. of Titles	1994 Average Price	1995 No. of Titles	1995 Average Price	1995 % Change 1994–1995	Index
Agriculture	S	897	$45.13	682	$53.33	985	$56.74	1,230	$67.41	18.8	149.4
Anthropology	GN	406	32.81	463	36.75	537	41.84	514	35.51	-15.1	108.2
Botany	QK	251	69.02	234	97.92	207	97.80	204	82.05	-16.1	118.9
Business and economics	H	5,979	41.67	5,779	45.95	6,576	48.91	6,294	48.65	-0.5	116.8
Chemistry	QD	577	110.61	544	127.3	536	145.53	506	153.12	5.2	138.4
Education	L	1,685	29.61	1,844	37.62	2,083	37.77	2,200	35.10	-7.1	118.5
Engineering and technology	T	4,569	64.94	4,659	76.48	4,864	77.81	5,076	74.82	-3.8	115.2
Fine and applied arts	M-N	3,040	40.72	2,984	44.37	3,119	42.91	4,444	48.85	13.8	120.0
General works	A	333	134.65	90	47.29	178	111.05	481	45.16	-59.3	33.5
Geography	G	396	47.34	548	50.64	588	55.79	626	50.78	-9.0	107.3
Geology	QE	303	63.49	251	78.72	193	71.90	207	86.69	20.6	136.5
History	C-D-E-F	5,549	31.34	5,662	34.05	5,741	34.16	6,279	33.28	-2.6	106.2
Home economics	TX	535	27.10	614	29.60	665	26.68	781	27.62	3.5	101.9
Industrial arts	TT	175	23.89	173	22.68	240	22.88	251	22.97	0.4	96.1

Subject	LC Class									
Law	K	1,252	51.10	1,555	62.04	1,494	58.83	1,455	59.49	1.1	116.4
Library and information science	Z	857	44.51	686	40.99	641	48.53	764	49.95	2.9	112.2
Literature and language	P	10,812	24.99	11,066	27.83	11,316	27.95	12,285	29.58	5.8	118.4
Mathematics and computer science	QA	2,707	44.68	3,010	53.53	3,084	55.75	3,109	57.13	2.5	127.9
Medicine	R	5,028	58.38	4,889	67.01	5,350	66.22	5,707	66.14	-0.1	113.3
Military and naval science	U-V	715	33.57	412	39.88	466	44.18	387	39.10	-11.5	116.5
Physical education and recreation	GV	814	20.38	777	22.61	802	22.72	1,106	31.70	39.5	155.5
Philosophy and religion	B	3,518	29.06	3,734	34.22	3,985	35.52	4,537	36.14	1.7	124.4
Physics and astronomy	QB	1,219	64.59	1,180	87.75	1,175	86.33	1,161	91.73	6.3	142.0
Political science	J	1,650	36.76	1,524	43.03	1,592	37.59	1,681	47.83	0.5	130.1
Psychology	BF	890	31.97	813	39.03	968	37.38	1,046	38.71	3.6	121.1
Science (general)	Q	433	56.10	359	64.04	427	70.02	360	73.06	4.3	130.2
Sociology	HM	2,742	29.36	2,997	35.19	3,402	38.40	3,692	37.36	-2.7	127.2
Zoology	QH,L,P,R	1,967	71.28	1,853	82.43	1,823	79.40	1,924	79.87	0.6	112.1
Average for all subjects		59,299	$41.69	59,382	$47.17	63,037	$48.16	68,307	$48.11	-0.1	115.4

Compiled by Stephen Bosch, University of Arizona, from electronic data provided by Baker and Taylor, Blackwell/North America, Coutts Library Services, and Yankee Book Peddler. This table covers titles published or distributed in the United States and Canada during the calendar years listed. This index does include paperback editions. The overall average price of materials is lower than if the index consisted of only hardbound editions.

485

Table 5 / U.S. College Books: **Average Prices and Price Indexes, 1978, 1994, 1995, 1996**
(Index Base for all years: 1978 = 100. 1995 also indexed to 1994; 1996 also indexed to 1995)

Subject Area	1978 Number of Titles	1978 Average Price per Title	1994 Number of Titles	1994 Average Price per Title	1994 Prices Indexed to 1978	1995 Number of Titles	1995 Average Price per Title	1995 Prices Indexed to 1978	1995 Prices Indexed to 1994	1996 Preliminary Number of Titles	1996 Preliminary Average Price per Title	1996 Preliminary Prices Indexed to 1978	1996 Preliminary Prices Indexed to 1995
General	47	$15.25	8	$47.16	309.3	14	$46.90	307.5	99.4	32	$43.65	286.3	93.1
Humanities	92	16.14	18	39.46	244.5	29	50.96	315.7	129.1	29	44.04	272.9	86.4
Art and architecture	315	26.60	311	60.03	225.7	278	54.61	205.3	91.0	269	58.36	219.4	106.9
Communication	71	14.03	73	39.17	279.2	76	43.15	307.6	110.2	77	42.06	299.8	97.5
Language and literature	97	13.38	83	42.84	320.2	117	41.45	309.8	96.8	128	45.56	340.5	109.9
African and Middle Eastern[5]	—	—	—	—	—	9	32.36	—	—	22	40.47	—	125.1
Asian and Oceanian[5]	—	—	—	—	—	12	36.03	—	—	31	38.66	—	107.3
Classical[7]	—	—	—	—	—	—	—	—	—	14	53.26	—	—
English and American	834	12.42	488	38.33	308.6	567	37.05	298.3	96.7	562	37.91	305.2	102.3
Germanic	51	12.35	44	35.57	288.0	37	42.87	347.1	120.5	36	47.64	385.7	111.1
Romance	101	12.27	124	33.16	270.2	103	35.48	289.2	107.0	126	37.66	307.0	106.2
Slavic	46	13.22	36	41.31	312.5	31	43.56	329.5	105.5	32	36.23	274.1	83.2
Non-European[4]	67	13.03	35	37.41	287.1	33	31.92	245.0	85.3	—	—	—	—
Performing arts	16	15.07	23	35.10	232.9	9	40.41	268.2	115.1	4	34.60	229.6	85.6
Film	80	15.70	104	38.47	245.0	74	41.61	265.0	108.2	83	42.51	270.7	102.2
Music	138	15.10	166	40.18	266.1	148	41.52	275.0	103.3	113	43.33	287.0	104.4
Theater and dance[6]	55	13.50	68	44.38	328.7	62	40.63	301.0	91.6	68	46.85	347.1	115.3
Philosophy	197	14.21	221	41.91	294.9	163	45.00	316.7	107.4	163	46.20	325.1	102.7
Religion	300	11.98	179	36.66	306.0	219	41.23	344.2	112.5	197	42.58	355.4	103.3
Total humanities[3]	2,500	$14.86	1,973	$42.22	284.1	1,967	$42.01	282.7	99.5	1,954	$43.74	294.4	104.1
Science and technology	102	$21.31	118	$40.76	191.3	106	$41.00	192.4	100.6	81	$46.46	218.0	113.3
History of science/technology	85	17.37	42	41.02	236.2	71	43.00	247.6	104.8	81	46.70	268.8	108.6
Astronautics/astronomy	22	23.78	38	35.51	149.3	42	56.23	263.5	158.4	51	48.42	203.6	86.1
Biology	231	23.67	107	54.22	229.1	128	49.53	209.3	91.3	130	50.66	214.0	102.3
Botany[1]	—	—	75	51.88	—	66	57.96	—	111.7	78	53.07	—	91.6
Zoology[1]	—	—	60	53.69	—	77	54.05	—	100.7	84	50.70	—	93.8
Chemistry	95	28.59	64	74.81	261.7	86	73.83	258.2	98.8	68	87.63	306.5	118.7
Earth science	84	29.99	48	65.90	219.8	53	65.08	217.0	98.8	57	58.81	196.1	90.4
Engineering	241	25.75	120	72.34	280.9	126	76.00	295.1	105.1	138	76.50	297.1	100.7
Health sciences	92	14.88	164	42.10	283.0	132	41.79	280.8	99.3	169	42.83	287.8	102.5
Information/computer science	53	20.37	78	45.56	223.7	69	51.05	250.6	112.1	62	43.87	215.4	85.9

Subject									
Sports and physical education	73	10.32		297.8	46	39.08	378.7	127.2	41	39.04	378.3	99.9
Total sciences	1,195	$22.77	1,091	30.74	1,153	$53.37	234.4	104.1	1,197	$54.39	238.9	101.9
Social/behavioral sciences	156	$16.37	38	$51.26	44	$42.18	257.7	104.9	48	$41.20	251.7	97.7
Anthropology	102	16.97	141	$40.21	118	45.55	268.4	103.1	143	46.47	273.9	102.0
				44.17								
Business, management, labor	136	14.36	147	36.63	145	44.46	309.6	121.4	146	44.36	308.9	99.8
Economics	242	17.65	303	44.78	273	50.09	283.8	111.9	275	54.43	308.4	108.7
Education	129	12.48	114	40.10	122	40.88	327.6	101.9	124	43.38	347.6	106.1
History/geography/area studies	116	16.26	47	42.61	46	37.67	231.7	88.4	58	48.27	296.9	128.1
Africa	38	16.34	44	46.68	44	48.12	294.5	103.1	37	48.87	299.1	101.6
Ancient History[7]									9	67.94		
Asia and Oceania	78	19.03	79	53.50	65	47.29	248.5	88.4	74	43.54	228.8	92.1
Europe	308	16.52	276	47.64	377	48.54	293.8	101.9	364	49.94	302.3	102.9
Latin America and Caribbean	47	15.82	58	43.35	48	45.63	288.4	105.3	56	46.85	296.1	102.7
Middle East and North Africa	40	16.80	56	45.16	52	50.74	302.0	112.4	26	52.56	312.9	103.6
North America	275	16.08	371	36.99	382	37.08	230.6	100.2	402	37.28	231.8	100.5
Political science	281	14.74	18	40.73	8	39.93	270.9	98.0	52	44.23	300.1	110.8
Comparative politics[2]			202	44.81	229	43.42		96.9	183	50.64		116.6
International relations[2]			138	43.24	118	43.03		99.5	142	46.53		108.1
Political theory[2]			72	40.31	80	42.49		105.4	105	43.75		103.0
U.S. politics[2]			164	38.51	164	39.29		102.0	177	40.88		104.1
Psychology	142	15.39	149	39.33	159	39.25	255.0	99.8	172	42.22	274.3	107.6
Sociology	280	14.69	201	41.16	231	44.74	304.6	108.7	218	45.33	308.5	101.3
Total social/behavioral sciences	2,437	$15.98	2,618	$42.24	2,705	$43.74	273.7	103.6	2,811	$45.60	285.4	104.3
Total (excluding reference)[3]	6,179	$16.83	5,690	$43.97	5,839	$45.07	267.8	102.5	5,994	$46.74	277.7	103.7
Reference	453	$34.15	683	$80.91	668	$75.30	220.5	93.1	648	$84.60	247.7	112.4
Grand total (with reference)[3]	6,632	$18.02	6,373	$47.93	6,507	$48.17	267.3	100.5	6,642	$50.44	279.9	104.7

Compiled by Donna Alsbury, Florida Center for Library Automation, from book reviews appearing in *Choice* during the calendar year indicated. The cooperation of the *Choice* editorial staff is gratefully acknowledged. Additional information about these data appears in the April issue of *Choice*.

1 Began appearing as a separate section in September 1983.
2 Began appearing as a separate section in March 1988.
3 1978 totals include Linguistics (incorporated into Language and Literature in December 1985) and Classical Language and Literature and Ancient History (incorporated into Classical Studies in 1985).
4 Replaced Other in 1994. Replaced by African and Middle Eastern and Asian and Oceanian in September 1995.
5 Began appearing as a separate section in September 1995.
6 Separate sections for Theater and Dance combined in September 1995.
7 Began appearing as a separate section in September 1996.

Table 6 / U.S. Mass Market Paperback Books: Average Prices and Price Indexes, 1993–1996
(Index Base: 1981 = 100)

Subject Area	1981 Average Price	1993 Volumes	1993 Average Price	1993 Index	1994 Volumes	1994 Average Price	1994 Index	1995 Final Volumes	1995 Final Average Price	1995 Final Index	1996 Preliminary Volumes	1996 Preliminary Average Price	1996 Preliminary Index
Agriculture	$2.54	23	$6.48	255.1	7	$8.25	324.8	10	$9.13	359.4	10	$10.07	396.5
Art	5.49	14	14.47	263.6	10	11.04	201.1	12	11.24	204.7	8	11.99	218.4
Biography	3.82	89	6.23	163.1	36	7.76	203.1	39	8.08	211.5	36	9.80	256.5
Business	4.63	22	10.89	235.2	17	11.76	253.9	18	10.81	233.5	17	11.86	256.2
Education	3.96	45	4.55	114.9	17	13.08	330.3	29	12.40	313.1	29	11.17	282.1
Fiction	2.47	2,298	4.79	193.9	1,944	4.75	192.3	3,680	5.51	223.1	3,569	6.25	253.0
General works	3.63	61	12.79	352.3	42	9.26	255.1	29	19.37	533.6	34	9.31	256.5
History	3.53	17	8.79	249.0	10	10.94	309.9	24	10.06	285.0	17	10.91	309.1
Home economics	4.35	83	7.91	181.8	57	8.02	184.4	43	8.70	200.0	35	8.67	199.3
Juvenile	1.79	450	3.54	197.8	230	3.71	207.3	396	3.99	222.9	288	4.25	237.4
Language	3.42	9	8.32	243.3	3	14.30	418.1	8	9.60	280.7	7	7.27	212.6
Law	3.09	0	—	—	3	6.66	215.5	5	9.79	316.8	5	10.39	336.2
Literature	3.42	26	6.99	204.4	16	6.42	187.7	47	8.73	255.3	70	9.20	269.0
Medicine	3.66	25	10.23	279.5	7	8.49	231.9	10	8.38	229.0	16	8.42	230.1
Music	5.68	2	7.75	136.4	2	17.50	308.1	3	24.98	439.8	5	20.57	362.1
Philosophy and psychology	2.84	89	6.40	225.4	37	9.17	322.9	103	4.83	170.1	102	18.19	640.5
Poetry and drama	3.22	6	6.99	217.1	8	8.80	273.3	32	9.70	301.2	28	10.88	337.9
Religion	2.70	14	2.92	108.1	11	8.31	307.7	16	9.39	347.8	16	8.93	330.7
Science	4.45	10	7.30	164.0	10	11.67	262.2	8	11.28	243.5	9	12.15	273.0
Sociology and economics	3.43	55	8.83	257.4	40	9.15	266.8	42	9.60	279.9	34	9.91	288.9
Sports and recreation	3.05	144	7.93	260.0	102	9.03	296.1	82	8.28	271.5	75	8.75	286.9
Technology	4.20	73	30.47	725.5	39	25.20	600.0	22	11.62	276.7	19	10.30	245.2
Travel	3.23	9	10.1	312.7	5	13.57	420.1	3	13.96	432.2	10	9.63	298.1
Total	$2.65	3,564	$5.82	219.6	2,653	$5.70	215.1	4,661	$5.85	220.8	4,439	$6.53	246.4

Compiled by Gay N. Dannelly, Ohio State University, from data supplied by the R. R. Bowker Company. Average prices of mass market paperbacks are based on listings of mass market titles in *Paperbound Books in Print*.

Table 7 / U.S. Trade (Higher Priced) Paperback Books: Average Prices and Price Indexes, 1993–1996
(Index Base: 1977 = 100)

Subject Area	1977 Average Price	1977 Volumes	1993 Average Price	1993 Volumes	1993 Index	1994 Volumes	1994 Average Price	1994 Index	1995 Final Volumes	1995 Final Average Price	1995 Final Index	1996 Preliminary Volumes	1996 Preliminary Average Price	1996 Preliminary Index
Agriculture	$5.01	186	$18.32	365.7	173	$18.26	364.5	218	$26.96	538.1	191	$21.20	423.2
Art	6.27	596	19.98	318.7	572	20.99	334.8	874	20.57	328.1	690	21.47	342.4
Biography	4.91	555	15.75	320.8	605	15.65	318.7	813	16.59	337.9	751	17.06	347.5
Business	7.09	472	25.18	355.1	471	23.94	337.7	709	24.23	341.5	608	24.67	348.0
Education	5.72	502	23.06	403.1	508	21.47	375.3	738	22.96	401.4	760	23.98	419.2
Fiction	4.20	877	13.56	322.9	953	14.94	355.7	1,275	12.71	302.6	1,405	12.60	300.0
General works	6.18	693	31.19	504.7	851	33.81	547.1	1,375	32.98	533.7	1,305	33.35	539.6
History	5.81	730	21.2	364.9	756	20.15	346.8	1,041	18.47	317.9	1,050	20.82	358.3
Home economics	4.77	344	14.47	303.4	376	14.72	308.6	629	14.87	311.7	603	15.37	322.2
Juvenile	2.68	1,059	7.73	288.4	1,030	6.83	254.8	990	15.74	587.3	856	8.24	307.5
Language	7.79	279	42.93	551.1	269	23.82	305.8	304	15.74	277.0	335	21.59	277.2
Law	10.66	316	28.86	270.7	328	30.57	286.6	415	30.26	283.9	331	27.45	257.5
Literature	5.18	724	17.38	335.5	756	18.21	351.5	945	16.54	319.3	1,113	17.71	341.9
Medicine	7.63	842	29.66	388.7	756	25.15	329.6	1,092	27.91	365.8	1,344	28.09	368.2
Music	6.36	142	21.64	340.3	127	19.48	306.3	174	19.81	311.5	150	18.82	295.9
Philosophy and psychology	5.57	614	18.23	327.3	621	18.19	326.6	800	19.91	557.5	885	19.45	349.2
Poetry and drama	4.71	436	13.29	282.2	444	13.25	280.3	712	15.69	333.1	628	12.72	270.1
Religion	3.68	1,275	13.67	371.5	1,303	14.69	399.2	1,723	14.59	396.5	1,726	15.03	408.4
Science	8.81	602	31.79	360.8	672	35.71	405.3	874	33.41	379.2	948	32.04	363.7
Sociology and economics	6.03	2,508	22.42	371.8	2,615	23.19	384.6	3,321	23.68	392.7	3,452	23.27	385.9
Sports and recreation	4.87	504	15.82	324.8	513	16.39	336.6	900	16.53	339.4	818	16.27	334.1
Technology	7.97	557	30.04	376.9	582	29.50	370.1	827	38.75	486.2	615	33.29	417.7
Travel	5.21	297	15.90	305.2	334	15.54	298.3	480	16.37	314.2	400	16.80	322.5
Total	$5.93	15,110	$20.56	346.7	15,615	$20.56	346.7	21,229	$21.70	365.9	20,964	$21.14	356.5

Compiled by Gay N. Dannelly, Ohio State University, from data supplied by the R. R. Bowker Company. Price Indexes on Tables 3 and 7 are based on books recorded in R. R. Bowker Company's *Weekly Record* (cumulated in *American Book Publishing Record*). The 1996 preliminary figures include items listed during 1996 with an imprint date of 1996. Final data for previous years include items listed between January of that year and June of the following year with an imprint date of the specified year.

Table 8 / U.S. Daily Newspapers, 1990–1997
(Index Base: 1990 = 100)

Year	No. Titles	Average Price	Percent Increase	Index
1990	165	$189.58	—	100
1991	166	198.13	4.5	104.5
1992	167	222.68	12.4	117.5
1993	171	229.92	3.3	121.3
1994	171	261.91	13.9	138.2
1995	172	270.22	3.2	142.5
1996	166	300.21	11.1	158.4
1997	165	$311.77	3.9	164.5

Compiled by Genevieve S. Owens, Williamsburg Regional Library, and Wilba Swearingen, Louisiana State University Medical Center, from data supplied by EBSCO Subscription Services. The compilers are grateful to Kathleen Born and Mary Beth Vanderpoorten of EBSCO for their assistance with this project.

Table 9 / U.S. Nonprint Media: Average Prices and Price Indexes, 1995–1996
(Index Base: 1980 = 100)

Category	1980 Average Price	1995 Average Price	1995 Index	1996 Average Price	1996 Index
Videocassettes					
Rental cost per minute	$1.41*	$1.96	139.0	$1.97	140.0
Purchase cost per minute	7.59	2.15	28.4	2.03	26.8
Cost per video	271.93	83.48	30.7	82.10	30.2
Length per video (min.)		38.83		40.40	
Sound recordings					
Cost per cassette	$9.34	$7.96	85.2	$8.13	87.0
Cost per compact disc**	13.36	14.86	112.2	16.43	123.0

Compiled by Dana Alessi, Baker & Taylor, from data in *Booklist, Library Journal,* and *School Library Journal.*
* Rental cost per minute for 16 mm films.
** Base year for compact discs = 1983.
Note: The 16 mm film and filmstrip categories were discontinued due to the small number of reviews of these products.

includes 1995, 1996, and 1997 indexed to the base year of 1977. A more extensive report, including subject breakdowns, LC-class comparisons, and rankings by rate of increase and average price, was published annually in the April 15 issue of *Library Journal* through 1992 and is now published in the May issue of *American Libraries.*

Compiled by Adrian Alexander, U.S. periodical prices increased by 9.9 percent from 1996 to 1997, excluding Russian translations. This figure represents a decrease in the rate of inflation of almost an entire percentage point from the 10.8 percent figure of 1996. With the Russian translations category included, the single-year increase was only slightly higher, at 10.1 percent. This figure is 0.5 percent higher than the increase of 9.6 percent for this group in 1995. While Zoology and Medicine led the various subject categories in rate of increase in

Table 10 / CD-ROM Price Inventory 1994–1996: Average Costs by Subject Classification

Classification	LC Class	Number of Titles 1994	Number of Titles 1995	Number of Titles 1996	Average Price per Title 1994	Average Price per Title 1995	Average Price per Title 1996	Percent Change 1994–1995	Percent Change 1995–1996
General works	A	131	134	128	$1,694	$1,603	$1,805	-5	13
Philosophy, psychology, and religion	B	22	24	22	1,256	1,170	1,153	-7	-1
History: general & Old World	D	7	7	7	868	788	786	-9	0
History: America	E-F	19	20	20	523	632	641	21	1
Geography, anthropology, and recreation	G	37	37	35	1,700	1,767	1,884	4	7
Social sciences	H	77	91	101	1,962	2,317	2,196	18	-5
Business	HB-HJ	87	109	118	3,825	3,855	3,700	1	-4
Political science	J	23	18	19	1,376	1,272	1,297		
Law	K	25	27	27	2,149	2,095	2,074	-3	-1
Education	L	24	23	30	969	936	921	-3	-2
Music	M	13	14	12	890	822	974	-8	18
Fine arts	N	34	36	36	1,712	1,227	1,278	-28	4
Language & literature	P	47	45	44	2,864	2,956	2,983	3	1
Science	Q	153	171	172	1,665	1,931	2,045	16	6
Medicine	R	128	177	188	1,524	1,458	1,404	-4	-4
Agriculture	S	38	34	32	2,888	3,836	4,139	33	8
Technology	T	58	67	72	2,373	2,248	2,208	-5	-2
Military science	U-V	25	24	25	1,229	1,252	1,094	2	-13
Bibliography, library science	Z	75	73	72	1,388	1,388	1,430	0	3
Totals		1,023	1,131	1,160	$1,913	$1,988	$2,012	4	1

Compiled by Martha Kellogg and Theodore Kellogg, University of Rhode Island.

Note: In 1995, 176 titles were added and 68 removed. In 1996, 103 titles were added and 74 removed.

1997 with 12.8 percent and 12.4 percent, respectively, double-digit inflation was not limited to the sciences this year. Business and Economics jumped from 8.8 percent in 1996 to 11.2 percent in 1997, and Psychology posted an increase of 10.5 percent in 1997 for its third consecutive year above 10 percent. The Russian Translations category, meanwhile, showed a 10.7 percent increase in 1997 after only a 6.4 rise in 1996.

U.S. serial services, compiled by Nancy Chaffin based on data from the Faxon Company, required the replacement of several titles as publications ceased. The replacements reflected the same subject areas, but prices were, overall, somewhat lower. Some of these changes reflected the movement from paper publication to solely electronic publications. A more detailed article on this topic will also be published in the May 1997 *American Libraries*.

U.S. serial services (Table 2), excluding "Wilson Index" titles and Russian translations, increased an overall 3.9 percent, reflecting the lowest price increase since 1990. All areas exhibited increases with the exception of Law, which reflects the varying amount published, particularly in the reporters and case-law publications, and is reflected in the varying annual price rate charged. Science and Technology continues to increase at a rate higher than the other subject areas. U.S. government documents have increased by 17 percent, reflecting both the erosion in the number of titles published by the government and the inclusion of two expensive titles not previously identified in the selection of titles that make up the index pool. "Wilson Index" titles increased 15.74 percent. Deborah Loeding, Wilson Director of Product Management, reports that the change reflects service-based pricing, i.e. customers are paying a higher average price for print index subscriptions because they have increased their journal holdings or because Wilson has added coverage of more titles owned by the subscribing libraries.

Book Prices

U.S. hardcover books (Table 3) encompasses four years: 1993, 1994, final figures for 1995, and preliminary figures for 1996. American book title costs continued to rise in 1995 to an average price of $47.15 in a modest increase of 5.6 percent in contrast to the 27.6 percent increase in 1994. This index is compiled from information published in Bowker's *Weekly Record*.

North American Academic Books (Table 4) decreased a minimal 0.1 percent in contrast to the preceding year, which showed a modest increase in pricing. The data used for this index comprises titles treated by Baker and Taylor, Blackwell North American, Coutts, and Yankee Book Peddler in their approval plans during the calendar years listed. It does not include paperback editions as provided by the vendors and the recent increase in the number of these editions as part of the approval plans has clearly influenced the prices reflected in the index figures. Paperbacks continue to be included in this index, as they are in the approval plan data used for the index. Thus the inflation variance (hardback versus paperback editions) is much less clear than it has been in previous years. Price changes vary, as always, among subject areas, with double-digit increases in agriculture, fine and applied arts, geology, and physical education and recreation.

U.S. college books (Table 5) is compiled by Donna Alsbury from reviews appearing in *Choice* during the calendar year. Hardcover prices were used when available. The table includes the past three years (1994, 1995, and 1996) and the base index year (1978). The 2.0 percent increase between 1995 and 1996 represents a continuing modest increase following the 5.0 percent increase in 1994. Note that a secondary index, based on the immediate preceding year, is now a feature of this index. The sciences continue to have the largest price increases, while publications in Africana and Middle Eastern studies also show a significant increase in costs.

U.S. mass market paperbacks (Table 6) and U.S. trade paperbacks (Table 7) are compiled from data supplied by Bowker's *Paperbound Books in Print*. Mass market paperback prices showed a slight increase, rising from $5.70 in 1994 to $5.85 in 1995 for a 2.6 percent increase. U.S. trade paperbacks also increased in price from $20.56 in 1994 to $21.70 in 1995 for an increase of 5.5 percent.

Newspaper Prices

U.S. daily newspapers (Table 8) includes one fewer title than the previous year's index, reflecting the ongoing hard times of the newspaper industry as titles merge or cease altogether. Compilers Genevieve Owens and Wilba Swearingen observe that U.S. newspaper pricing continues to reflect a different dynamic than that of books or serials. Pricing data suggests that increases occur on an 18- or 24-month cycle rather than the more usual annual cycle that librarians see in other segments of the publishing industry. The increase in pricing for titles to be delivered in 1997 is 3.9 percent, confirming a consistent pattern of high/low price increases demonstrated since 1991.

Prices of Other Media

Data for the U.S. nonprint media index (Table 9) including videocassettes and sound recordings is compiled by Dana Alessi from titles reviewed in *Booklist, Library Journal,* and *School Library Journal*. Since there are so few 16 mm films and filmstrips produced or reviewed each year, both these indexes have been discontinued. As has been the trend over the past several years, the cost of a video has continued to decline. There seem to be two primary reasons for this: the increasing numbers of videos reviewed that are directed at the consumer market, especially in the areas of instructional and self-help material; and as reported by Alessi, "the recognition by several of the former 16 mm suppliers that the lower-priced video is dominating the market" and the price decreases from these suppliers as they replace 16 mm with video products. Cassettes increased by 2.0 percent in average cost per title. Alessi notes: "This may be attributed to the increased numbers of cassettes reviewed, especially children's music cassettes and a slight reduction in the number of recorded books reviewed." Again, many of these are targeted at the individual consumer market, with the result of lower prices for libraries. Compact disc sound recordings increased significantly in price from $14.86 to $16.43, or 10.6 percent.

Data for the CD-ROM price inventory (Table 10) was compiled by Martha Kellogg and Theodore Kellogg from the *Faxon Guide to CD-ROMs* and *CD-ROMs in Print*, supplemented by selected publishers catalogs. All prices used are for single user (non-networked) workstations at the most complete level of service, including all archival discs. Only those titles with current year price information are included in the index. The Kelloggs have found that there are fewer numbers of new CD-ROM titles of interest to libraries. There are a smaller number of database suppliers as a few major players are coming to dominate the market. Prices remain steady with a very modest 1.0 percent increase. Subject areas reflect wide fluctuations. These tend to be the result of the small number of titles within some categories, the way in which supplementary discs are included one year, but not the next, and the inclusion of new and more expensive titles in the title mix. The index includes both monograph and serial titles.

Foreign Prices

U.S. Purchasing Power Abroad

The U.S. dollar had made consistent gains against the major currencies at the close of 1996. The gradual strengthening of the dollar is expected to continue in 1997. The following chart reports rates in currency per U.S. dollar based on quotations in the *Wall Street Journal*. Readers interested in quotations for earlier years should refer to previous volumes of the *Bowker Annual* or directly to the *Wall Street Journal*.

	6/30/94	12/30/94	6/30/95	12/31/95	12/31/96
Canada	1.3835	1.4088	1.3724	1.3644	1.3705
France	5.4260	5.3640	4.8405	4.9050	5.1900
U.K.	0.6468	0.6412	0.6272	0.6439	0.5839
Germany	1.5845	1.5525	1.3820	1.4365	1.5400
Japan	98.69	99.65	84.71	103.43	115.85
Netherlands	1.7769	1.7391	1.5477	1.6080	1.7410

Indexes are included for British academic books (Table 11), German academic books (Table 12), German academic periodicals (Table 13), Dutch English-language periodicals (Table 14), and Latin American Books (Table 15).

British Prices

Prices for British academic books (Table 11) are compiled by Curt Holleman from data supplied by B. H. Blackwell. The average price was £37.50 in 1996, which reflects an increase of 4.2 percent over the 1995 average of £36.00. Holleman notes that "inflation in price (4.2 percent) combined with an increase in output of British academic books in 1995 (15.2 percent) to increase the cost of keeping up with British academic publications significantly. Including the average daily strengthening of the dollar in relation to the pound in 1996 (1.1 percent), we find that the cost for U.S. academic libraries of maintaining a proportional collection of British books rose 18.7 percent in 1996." Note that the total number of titles exceeds the sum of the subject areas, since some titles included in the data are not classified by subject.

(text continues on p. 498)

Table 11 / British Academic Books: Average Prices and Price Indexes, 1994–1996
(Index Base: 1985 = 100; prices listed are pounds sterling)

Subject Area	1985 No. of Titles	1985 Average Price	1994 No. of Titles	1994 Average Price	1994 Index	1995 No. of Titles	1995 Average Price	1995 Index	1996 No. of Titles	1996 Average Price	1996 Index
General works	29	£30.54	51	£42.75	140.0	29	£40.72	133.3	38	£66.88	219.0
Fine arts	329	21.70	408	30.99	142.8	407	35.82	165.1	472	32.16	148.2
Architecture	97	20.68	145	33.48	161.9	159	31.81	153.8	203	32.17	155.6
Music	136	17.01	123	25.86	152.0	164	29.79	175.1	132	28.89	169.8
Performing arts except music	110	13.30	118	24.44	183.8	130	24.98	187.8	178	26.43	198.7
Archaeology	146	18.80	126	33.28	177.0	159	33.86	180.1	192	33.57	178.6
Geography	60	22.74	56	37.21	163.6	60	35.68	156.9	63	40.65	178.8
History	1,123	16.92	1,361	32.37	191.3	1,352	32.80	193.9	1,505	34.51	204.0
Philosophy	127	18.41	156	39.20	212.9	180	35.70	193.9	233	42.07	228.5
Religion	328	10.40	362	24.62	236.7	452	24.08	231.5	486	25.68	246.9
Language	135	19.37	154	35.35	182.5	157	36.64	189.2	218	41.06	212.0
Miscellaneous humanities	59	21.71	63	29.59	136.3	61	28.73	132.3	64	30.39	140.0
Literary texts (excluding fiction)	570	9.31	493	14.91	160.2	522	16.15	173.5	581	18.64	200.2
Literary criticism	438	14.82	520	29.26	197.4	492	37.02	249.8	579	36.22	244.4
Law	188	24.64	298	45.72	185.6	317	47.38	192.3	364	46.26	187.7
Library science and book trade	78	18.69	83	36.04	192.8	67	37.46	200.4	78	54.39	291.0
Mass communications	38	14.20	84	24.68	173.8	96	29.94	210.8	109	30.78	216.8
Anthropology and ethnology	42	20.71	57	42.21	203.8	80	37.05	178.9	90	39.77	192.0
Sociology	136	15.24	187	42.19	276.8	174	38.60	253.3	229	45.55	298.9

Table 11 / British Academic Books: Average Prices and Price Indexes, 1994–1996 *(cont.)*
(Index Base: 1985 = 100; prices listed are pounds sterling)

	1985		1994			1995			1996		
Subject Area	No. of Titles	Average Price	No. of Titles	Average Price	Index	No. of Titles	Average Price	Index	No. of Titles	Average Price	Index
Psychology	107	19.25	128	33.66	174.9	157	32.72	170.0	146	36.60	190.1
Economics	334	20.48	505	51.80	252.9	540	51.06	249.3	525	49.67	242.5
Political science, international relations	314	15.54	458	30.87	198.6	423	34.58	222.5	549	37.06	238.5
Miscellaneous social sciences	20	26.84	15	33.50	124.8	14	33.84	126.1	23	42.75	159.3
Military science	83	17.69	54	31.03	175.4	38	36.57	206.7	59	32.92	186.1
Sports and recreation	44	11.23	64	21.66	192.9	61	20.06	178.6	82	19.97	177.8
Social service	56	12.17	351	24.57	201.9	90	28.76	236.3	106	28.45	233.8
Education	295	12.22	536	26.50	216.9	333	28.46	232.9	423	28.51	233.3
Management and business administration	427	19.55	536	37.04	189.5	504	36.10	184.7	594	44.11	225.6
Miscellaneous applied social sciences	13	9.58	20	23.89	249.4	17	23.04	240.5	28	31.58	329.6
Criminology	45	11.45	62	35.83	312.9	66	31.51	275.2	69	36.29	316.9
Applied interdisciplinary social sciences	254	14.17	435	32.60	230.1	515	33.02	233.0	601	33.50	236.4
General science	43	13.73	42	39.29	286.2	36	59.32	432.0	40	37.11	270.3
Botany	55	30.54	36	63.06	206.5	37	43.99	144.0	57	46.58	152.5
Zoology	85	25.67	73	46.13	179.7	67	44.70	174.1	80	41.48	161.6
Human biology	35	28.91	36	45.21	156.4	28	55.60	192.3	32	46.57	161.1
Biochemistry	26	33.57	36	54.97	163.7	35	44.76	133.3	43	54.39	162.0
Miscellaneous biological sciences	152	26.64	160	41.92	157.4	131	43.44	163.1	158	43.20	162.2
Chemistry	109	48.84	124	66.53	136.2	93	76.30	156.2	100	75.81	155.2

Earth sciences	87	28.94	93	55.13	190.5	91	55.59	192.1	117	59.55	205.8
Astronomy	43	20.36	46	34.45	169.2	37	42.79	210.2	50	35.33	173.5
Physics	76	26.58	84	54.37	204.6	103	65.67	247.1	97	65.99	248.3
Mathematics	123	20.20	147	34.71	171.8	167	35.70	176.7	170	37.21	184.2
Computer sciences	150	20.14	211	31.11	154.5	213	36.64	181.9	227	38.12	189.3
Interdisciplinary technical fields	38	26.14	63	39.86	152.5	63	43.36	165.9	68	42.45	162.4
Civil engineering	134	28.68	150	50.39	175.7	120	52.77	184.0	155	58.66	204.5
Mechanical engineering	27	31.73	39	61.65	194.3	32	59.19	186.5	45	57.42	181.0
Electrical and electronic engineering	100	33.12	111	53.01	160.1	86	46.06	139.1	112	52.56	159.0
Materials science	54	37.93	98	78.88	208.0	69	77.45	204.2	99	95.89	252.8
Chemical engineering	24	40.48	32	78.48	193.9	34	73.53	181.6	37	69.22	171.0
Miscellaneous technology	217	36.33	219	51.30	141.2	210	52.57	144.7	248	52.58	144.7
Food and domestic science	38	23.75	56	57.41	241.7	41	45.08	189.8	40	54.27	228.5
Non-clinical medicine	97	18.19	134	28.45	156.4	137	31.55	173.4	177	29.02	159.5
General medicine	73	21.03	64	34.31	163.1	67	39.70	188.8	68	44.43	211.3
Internal medicine	163	27.30	194	44.76	164.0	168	46.99	172.1	179	45.29	165.9
Psychiatry and mental disorders	71	17.97	106	29.94	166.6	130	33.52	186.5	132	32.00	178.1
Surgery	50	29.37	63	70.14	238.8	55	62.94	214.3	62	64.60	220.0
Miscellaneous medicine	292	22.08	284	43.05	195.0	278	41.39	187.5	301	39.16	177.4
Dentistry	20	19.39	20	36.98	190.7	21	44.65	230.3	22	50.22	259.0
Nursing	71	8.00	90	15.64	195.5	86	17.46	218.2	99	17.96	224.5
Agriculture and forestry	78	23.69	78	45.42	191.7	69	41.94	177.0	69	45.65	192.7
Animal husbandry and veterinary medicine	34	20.92	52	42.70	204.1	46	45.08	215.5	46	37.69	180.2
Natural resources and conservation	58	22.88	40	45.24	197.7	39	34.73	151.8	42	40.82	178.4
Total, all books	9,049	£19.07	10,893	£35.44	185.8	10,605	£36.00	188.8	12,622	£37.50	196.6

Compiled by Curt Holleman, Southern Methodist University, from data supplied by B.H. Blackwell and the Library and Information Statistics Unit at Loughborough University.

German Prices

German academic books (Table 12) is based on data supplied by Otto Harrassowitz. This year the index includes all German publications made available for purchase to U.S. libraries during the calendar year. It also includes some CD-ROMs and other audiovisual materials. Both mixed media and stand-alone CD prices are included in the data. Compiler John Haar notes that "these media form only a very small portion of the index" and because mixed media are implicitly reflected in book indexes he does not see the inclusion of such data as invalidating the index.

This data shows that following an overall increase in 1995 of 7.6 percent (in DM), prices decreased in 1996 by 0.8 percent. Double-digit price increases occurred in anthropology, literature and language, military and naval science, physiology, and zoology. Significant decreases occurred in general works, geography, geology, and library and information science. Harrassowitz attributes the decrease in prices to a reduction in the number of multivolume sets published in 1996.

German academic periodicals (Table 13) compiled by Steven Thompson and also based on data from Otto Harrassowitz, exhibits an increase of 15 percent, in contrast to the preceding year's lower rise of 9.6 percent. Double-digit DM inflation occurred in several subject areas, unlike the preceding year when such inflation was limited to two areas: math and computer science. Preliminary data for 1997 projects a much more modest rise, with only chemistry expected to see major cost increases.

Dutch Prices

Dutch English language periodicals (Table 14) is compiled by Fred Lynden based on data supplied by Martinus Nijhoff International. In past years, the data provided has varied in the number of titles included. This has been changed effective with 1997 prices, shown as usual in DFL (Dutch guilders). The 1997 overall price increase of 11.2 percent shows an increase over 1996's rise of 7.43 percent with double-digit inflation in the majority of subject areas.

Lynden notes that there are two important issues to be considered for the future recording of these prices: "The first is that it is harder and harder to distinguish the country of origin for Dutch publishers since Elsevier has offices in many countries. The second is that the price for most Dutch publishers is not being stated in dollars. As a result it is necessary . . . to convert the price back to guilders. This adds a currency factor into the price which should not be there. Nevertheless, the companies producing the periodicals are located in Holland, therefore it seems eminently reasonable to state a Dutch price."

A further potential complication for all European Community member countries is the potential for the adoption of a single Euro currency. This is not yet a settled issue and the committee will monitor the situation as it pertains to library materials pricing.

(text continues on p. 502)

Table 12 / German Academic Books: Average Prices and Price Index, 1994–1996
(Index Base: 1989 = 100)

Subject Area	LC Class	1989 No. of Titles	1989 Average Price	1994 No. of Titles	1994 Average Price	1994 Index	1995 No. of Titles	1995 Average Price	1995 Percent Increase	1995 Index	1996 No. of Titles	1996 Average Price	1996 Percent Increase	1996 Index
Agriculture	S	251	DM74.99	392	DM67.35	89.8	376	DM69.53	3.2	92.7	335	DM72.62	4.4	96.8
Anthropology	GN-GT	129	70.88	154	70.47	99.4	164	68.03	-3.5	96.0	187	75.81	11.4	107.0
Botany	QK	83	109.94	88	96.18	87.5	108	106.87	11.1	97.2	94	115.01	7.6	104.6
Business and economics	H-HJ	1,308	86.82	2,624	67.14	77.3	2,240	70.12	4.4	80.8	2,560	74.54	6.3	85.9
Chemistry	QD	87	116.50	258	112.74	96.8	231	136.09	20.7	116.8	214	125.86	-7.5	108.0
Education	L	426	41.64	618	47.74	114.7	490	46.06	-3.5	110.6	679	49.83	8.2	119.7
Engineering and technology	T	906	79.49	1,170	90.17	113.4	1,221	90.10	-0.1	113.4	994	91.60	1.7	115.2
Fine and applied arts	M-N	1,766	55.57	2,312	69.02	124.2	1,963	77.07	11.7	138.7	2,515	70.08	-9.1	126.1
General works	A	43	59.63	42	69.96	117.3	47	301.69	331.2	505.9	58	166.11	-44.9	278.5
Geography	G-GF	202	48.96	151	67.84	138.6	126	97.76	44.1	199.7	150	76.68	-21.6	156.6
Geology	QE	46	77.10	82	88.95	115.4	83	121.90	37.0	158.1	76	79.18	-35.0	102.7
History	C,D,E,F	1,064	62.93	1,853	62.20	98.8	2,332	60.60	-2.6	96.3	2,194	67.92	12.1	107.9
Law	K	1,006	11.52	1,576	79.59	79.2	1,771	90.85	14.1	90.4	1,889	87.72	-3.5	87.3
Library and information science	Z	118	94.71	166	181.44	191.6	183	333.33	83.7	352.0	165	151.38	-54.6	159.8
Literature and language	P	2,395	52.10	3,380	56.33	108.1	3,797	56.41	0.2	108.3	3,689	62.59	11.0	120.1
Mathematics and computer science	QA	367	68.16	762	82.07	120.4	717	85.39	4.0	125.3	779	80.89	-5.3	118.7
Medicine	R	1,410	82.67	1,541	89.69	108.5	1,628	96.34	7.4	116.5	1,849	93.01	-3.5	112.5
Military and naval science	U-V	67	70.43	51	78.70	111.7	49	78.39	-0.4	111.3	52	90.15	15.0	128.0
Natural history	QH	78	85.23	155	91.83	107.7	230	97.24	5.9	114.1	185	102.95	5.9	120.8
Philosophy and religion	B	918	56.91	1,456	70.45	123.8	1,510	73.58	4.4	129.3	1,638	73.46	-0.2	129.1
Physical education and recreation	GV	110	35.65	137	36.60	102.7	134	43.52	18.9	122.1	149	39.82	-8.5	111.7
Physics and astronomy	QB-QC	192	85.12	310	91.71	107.7	317	86.84	-5.3	102.0	347	91.61	5.5	107.6
Physiology	QM-QR	163	124.67	179	116.98	93.8	210	113.55	-2.9	91.1	168	128.73	13.4	103.3
Political science	J	482	50.38	592	53.76	106.7	651	56.46	5.0	112.1	615	59.63	5.6	118.4
Psychology	BF	116	54.95	187	57.88	105.3	205	55.88	-3.5	101.7	220	58.85	5.3	107.1
Science (general)	Q	100	115.90	109	87.27	75.3	94	79.36	-9.1	68.5	86	80.19	1.0	69.2
Sociology	HM-HX	722	41.52	1,094	42.41	102.2	1,013	45.62	7.6	109.9	1,034	49.75	9.0	119.8
Zoology	QL	49	82.74	85	87.09	105.3	98	85.03	-2.4	102.8	91	100.07	17.7	120.9
Total		14,604	DM67.84	21,524	DM70.11	103.3	21,988	DM75.41	7.6	111.2	23,012	DM74.81	-0.8	110.3

Compiled by John Haar, Vanderbilt University, from approval plan data supplied by Otto Harrassowitz. Data represent a selection of materials relevant to research and documentation published in Germany (see text for more information regarding the nature of the data).
Unclassified material as well as titles in home economics and industrial arts have been excluded.
The index is not adjusted for high-priced titles.

Table 13 / German Academic Periodical Price Index, 1995–1997
(Index Base: 1990 = 100)

Subject Area	LC Class	1990 Average Price	1995 No. of Titles	1995 Average Price	1995 Percent Increase	1995 Index	1996 No. of Titles	1996 Average Price	1996 Percent Increase	1996 Index	1997 Preliminary No. of Titles	1997 Preliminary Average Price	1997 Preliminary Percent Increase	1997 Preliminary Index
Agriculture	S	DM235.11	171	DM296.59	5.7	126.1	118	DM331.64	11.8	141.1	122	DM342.71	3.3	145.8
Anthropology	GN	112.88	11	366.92	116.8	325.1	15	152.75	-58.4	135.3	15	161.35	5.6	142.9
Botany	QK	498.79	18	727.15	14.8	145.8	16	821.19	12.9	164.6	8	745.84	-9.2	149.5
Business and economics	H-HJ	153.48	284	206.23	5.1	134.4	278	218.06	5.7	142.1	295	223.61	2.5	145.7
Chemistry	QD	553.06	47	1,041.02	30.1	188.2	46	1,448.40	39.1	261.9	48	1,931.86	33.4	349.3
Education	L	70.86	60	82.05	-2.6	115.8	54	85.65	4.4	120.9	55	89.89	5.0	126.9
Engineering and technology	T-TS	239.40	363	267.05	1.1	111.5	359	319.29	19.6	133.4	378	347.08	8.7	145.0
Fine and applied arts	M-N	84.15	166	101.07	2.3	120.1	172	101.50	0.4	120.6	177	103.55	2.0	123.1
General works	A	349.37	78	423.10	4.1	121.1	84	457.56	8.1	131.0	87	452.91	-1.0	129.6
Geography	G	90.42	16	128.30	-12.5	141.9	19	136.87	6.7	151.4	21	152.30	11.3	168.4
Geology	QE	261.30	39	368.88	9.6	141.2	39	454.72	23.3	174.0	39	470.81	3.5	180.2
History	C,D,E,F	66.09	146	89.87	2.9	136.0	151	92.73	3.2	140.3	152	94.34	1.7	142.7
Law	K	193.88	155	267.46	3.6	138.0	156	301.15	12.6	155.3	156	309.87	2.9	159.8
Library and information science	Z	317.50	58	580.88	15.4	183.0	59	609.72	5.0	192.0	61	601.99	-1.3	189.6
Literature and language	P	102.69	167	126.15	4.9	122.8	176	137.93	9.3	134.3	182	141.49	2.6	137.8
Mathematics and computer science	QA	1,064.62	39	1,202.40	6.4	112.9	40	1,663.11	38.3	156.2	42	1,640.90	-1.3	154.1
Medicine	R	320.62	362	513.13	32.1	160.0	368	630.78	22.9	196.7	390	638.77	1.3	199.2
Military and naval science	U-V	86.38	19	80.75	-16.8	93.5	20	100.65	24.6	116.5	22	99.39	-1.3	115.1
Natural history	QH	728.36	55	1,015.36	5.3	139.4	52	1,361.30	34.1	186.9	53	1,465.78	7.7	201.2
Philosophy and religion	B	65.00	194	101.12	2.4	155.6	197	104.53	3.4	160.8	199	106.23	1.6	163.4
Physical education and recreation	GV	81.96	47	98.75	3.4	120.5	46	96.77	-2.0	118.1	46	97.42	0.7	118.9
Physics and astronomy	QB-QC	684.40	50	1,044.70	13.8	152.6	48	1,378.60	32.0	201.4	51	1,517.24	10.1	221.7
Physiology	QM-QR	962.83	11	2,000.60	45.0	207.8	11	2,763.69	38.1	287.0	12	2,535.17	-8.3	263.3
Political science	J	80.67	142	100.85	8.0	125.0	137	104.03	3.2	129.0	140	105.63	1.3	130.7
Psychology	BF	94.10	34	131.28	17.0	139.5	36	144.41	10.0	153.5	36	147.43	2.1	156.7
Science (general)	Q	310.54	34	351.51	-13.5	113.2	33	429.52	22.2	138.3	36	433.74	1.0	139.7
Sociology	HM-HX	109.61	68	123.57	-6.2	112.7	59	143.32	16.0	130.8	59	149.25	4.1	136.2
Zoology	QL	161.02	27	258.63	5.0	160.6	29	264.53	2.3	164.3	31	267.31	1.0	166.0
Total		DM228.40	2,861	DM309.83	9.5	135.7	2,818	DM356.26	15.0	156.0	2,923	DM367.35	3.1	160.8

Data, supplied by Otto Harrassowitz, represent periodical and newspaper titles published in Germany; prices listed in marks. Price information for 1997 is preliminary; price data are 87% complete. Index is compiled by Steven E. Thompson, Brown University Library.

Table 14 / Dutch (English Language) Periodicals Price Index, 1994–1997
(Index Base: 1994 = 100; currency Units: DFL)

Subject Area	LC Class	1994 No. of Titles	1994 Average Price	1995 No. of Titles	1995 Average Price	1995 Index	1996 No. of Titles	1996 Average Price	1996 Index	1997 No. of Titles	1997 Average Price	1997 Index
Agriculture	S	39	DFL912.67	35	DFL1,109.06	121.5	36	DFL1,215.10	133.1	37	DFL1,335.84	146.4
Botany	QK	10	1,350.60	10	1,470.30	108.9	10	1,654.90	122.5	10	1,899.60	140.6
Business and economics	H-HJ	79	600.62	82	678.94	113.0	86	721.95	120.2	92	766.85	127.7
Chemistry	QD	32	3,761.88	35	3,836.81	102.0	32	4,258.83	113.2	32	4,886.74	129.9
Education	L	7	382.43	6	386.00	100.9	6	411.67	107.6	6	483.83	126.5
Engineering and technology	T-TS	70	1,332.74	71	1,458.27	109.4	77	1,526.30	114.5	78	1,725.26	129.5
Fine and applied arts	M-N	5	205.58	4	249.34	121.3	3	326.67	158.9	2	444.50	216.2
Geography	G	8	1,173.00	7	1,429.57	121.9	8	1,425.88	121.6	8	1,563.38	133.3
Geology	QE	24	1,275.41	24	1,433.07	112.4	25	1,587.60	124.5	26	1,764.78	138.4
History	C,D,E,F	11	225.73	9	236.25	104.7	9	257.00	113.9	9	290.06	128.5
Law	K	11	427.55	13	452.46	105.8	14	494.21	115.6	14	531.50	124.3
Library and information science	Z	6	243.17	6	254.33	104.6	6	262.67	108.0	6	281.83	115.9
Literature and language	P	35	309.83	33	336.55	108.6	35	348.26	112.4	34	380.32	122.8
Mathematics and computer science	QA	52	1,316.73	55	1,367.23	103.8	56	1,473.25	111.9	56	1,664.64	126.4
Medicine	R	54	1,142.24	60	1,214.67	106.3	62	1,357.47	118.8	63	1,577.76	138.1
Military and naval science	U-V	2	190.00	2	200.00	105.3	1	295.00	155.3	1	278.00	146.3
Natural history	QH	31	1,869.05	30	2,070.96	110.8	33	2,226.92	119.1	39	2,196.41	117.5
Philosophy and religion	B,BL,BP	34	398.10	31	384.29	96.5	33	407.21	102.3	34	436.97	109.8
Physics and astronomy	QB-QC	42	3,613.01	44	3,847.54	106.5	43	4,329.47	119.8	44	4,694.05	129.9
Physiology	QM-QR	17	2,675.41	16	3,149.88	117.7	16	3,568.00	133.4	16	7,904.67	295.5
Political science	J	2	483.00	3	467.67	96.8	4	428.25	88.7	4	508.25	105.2
Psychology	BF	n.a.	n.a.	4	810.25	0.0	4	925.50	0.0	5	977.00	0.0
Science (general)	Q	10	889.78	11	921.30	103.5	12	1,071.98	120.5	12	1,203.92	135.3
Sociology	HM-HX	5	378.00	6	365.67	96.7	6	377.33	99.8	5	448.60	118.7
Zoology	QL	11	608.16	10	712.80	117.2	11	776.21	127.6	10	992.60	163.2
Total		597	DFL1,325.10	607	DFL1,452.52	109.6	628	DFL1,560.44	117.8	643	DFL1,734.69	130.9

No data exist for Anthropology, General Works, and Physical Education.

Source: Martinus Nijhoff International. Compiled by Bas Guijt and Frederick C. Lynden.

Latin American Prices

Costs of Latin American books for 1995–1996 are reported in Table 15. The continued inclusion of Central American and Other Caribbean categories is an attempt to capture an aggregate consistent with past years, despite having lost the capacity to track receipts from individual countries.

Compiler David Block reports that "the seven research libraries reported almost exactly the same expenditures in FY 1996 as they had for the past year, an increase of less than $700 on an aggregate of over $800,000. Over the same period, the average cost of a Latin American volume increased at a relatively modest 7.4 percent. However, statistical anomalies inherent in the survey mitigate against using the aggregate as an indicator of trends in Latin American book prices between 1995 and 1996." The differences in inflation by country do not always follow a consistent pattern and therefore the individual country figures may be more appropriate to a specific library collection's experience. A most complete report can be accessed at http://ino.lib.cornell.edu/salalmmono96.html.

Latin American periodicals (Table 16), compiled by Scott Van Jacob, provides an analysis of prices quoted by the Faxon Company, Library of Congress's Rio field office, and the University of Texas at Austin. Weighted mean prices by subject grouping continue to follow a consistent trend. Humanities journals remain the least expensive, while science journals are slightly more expensive than social science titles. The prices, indexed to 1992, provide data both including and excluding newspapers, recognizing that foreign newspapers have a significant influence on average price figures.

Using the Price Indexes

Librarians are encouraged to monitor both trends in the publishing industry and changes in economic conditions when preparing budget projections. The ALA ALCTS Library Materials Price Index Committee endeavors to make information on publishing trends readily available by sponsoring the annual compilation and publication of the price data contained in Tables 1–16. The indexes cover newly published library materials and document prices and rates of price changes at the national level. They are useful benchmarks against which local costs may be compared, but because they reflect retail prices in the aggregate, they are not a substitute for cost data that reflects the collecting patterns of individual libraries and they are not a substitute for specific cost studies.

In part, differences arise because the national indexes exclude discounts, service charges, shipping and handling fees, or other costs that the library may bear. Discrepancies may also be related to subject focus, mix of current and retrospective materials, and the portion of total library acquisitions composed of foreign imprints. Such variables can affect the average price paid by a particular library although the library's rate of price increase may not significantly differ from national price indexes. LMPIC is interested in pursuing studies correlating a particular library's costs with national prices and would appreciate being informed of any planned or ongoing studies. The committee welcomes interested parties to its meetings at the ALA annual and midwinter conferences.

Table 15 / Number of Copies and Average Cost of Latin American Books Purchased by Seven Selected U.S. Libraries in FY 1995–1996

	Number of Books	Average Cost
Argentina	6,405	$20.10
Bolivia	1,879	13.74
Brazil	5,735	27.43
Central America	1,028	21.62
Chile	1,014	30.37
Colombia	2,607	23.83
Costa Rica	467	16.77
Cuba	135	16.91
Dominican Republic	416	31.44
Ecuador	1,882	14.17
El Salvador	361	13.30
Guatemala	287	13.63
Guyana	3	48.33
Haiti	103	21.06
Honduras	187	9.70
Jamaica	0	—
Mexico	9,515	22.45
Nicaragua	221	19.58
Panama	80	18.36
Paraguay	430	17.73
Peru	1,559	24.40
Puerto Rico	192	34.31
Suriname	0	—
Trinidad and Tobago	0	—
Uruguay	897	28.31
Venezuela	1,897	13.71
Other Caribbean	897	21.73
Total	38,197	$21.79

Compiled by David Block from data supplied by the Library of Congress, the New York Public Library, and the university libraries of Arizona, Cornell, Illinois at Champaign/Urbana, Texas at Austin, and Wisconsin at Madison.

In addition to the tables included, you may wish to consult a new publication on the costs of law materials: *Price Index for Legal Publications, 1996*, prepared by Margaret Mae Axtmann and published by the American Association of Law Libraries. In addition, Yale University Libraries has established a very useful web site under the leadership of Martha Brogan: "Price and Title Output Reports for Collection Management" at http://www.library.yale.edu/colldev/.

Current members of the Library Materials Price Index Committee are Gay N. Dannelly (chair), Steven Bosch, Penny Schroeder, Wanda Dole, Amy Dykeman, Marifran Bustion, Virginia Gilbert, Brenda Dingley, and Rita Echt. They are joined by consultants Dana Alessi, Adrian W. Alexander, Donna D. Alsbury, Catherine Barr, David Block, Dave Bogart, Nancy Chaffin, John Haar, Curt Holleman, Martha Kellogg, Fred Lynden, Genevieve Owens, Wilba Swearingen, Steve Thompson, and Scott Van Jacob.

Table 16 / Latin American Periodicals, 1995–1996
(Index Base: 1992 = 100)

	Number of Titles	Average Price*	Index	Weighted Average Price*	Index
Argentina	123	$94.00	92.98	$80.45	96.58
Bolivia	5	64.76	200.74	69.11	211.67
Brazil	182	73.67	119.44	67.92	124.21
Caribbean	27	45.26	110.39	44.36	107.77
Chile	61	81.78	117.31	81.74	152.76
Colombia	53	60.82	119.75	64.37	119.16
Costa Rica	25	56.68	149.34	49.16	124.36
Cuba	6	48.79	174.25	49.99	172.92
Ecuador	13	39.12	107.38	39.22	110.63
El Salvador	n.a.	n.a.	n.a.	n.a.	n.a.
Guatemala	10	124.82	140.40	160.62	168.07
Honduras	n.a.	n.a.	n.a.	n.a.	n.a.
Jamaica	17	38.02	105.85	58.51	163.89
Mexico	154	65.27	96.74	62.52	100.84
Nicaragua	5	35.60	103.01	39.63	108.13
Panama	n.a.	n.a.	n.a.	n.a.	n.a.
Paraguay	6	25.50	137.10	33.03	116.06
Peru	34	97.30	99.79	105.97	99.32
Uruguay	10	61.48	122.20	40.03	95.29
Venezuela	31	63.69	56.46	52.56	87.60
Region					
Caribbean	48	45.02	116.33	50.79	133.52
Central America	36	75.42	168.69	78.25	155.13
South America	510	76.73	102.79	72.96	113.05
Mexico	154	65.27	100.84	62.52	100.84
Latin America	748	73.43	106.93	71.10	120.90
Subjects					
Social sciences		$82.18	115.05	$70.52	130.74
Humanities		51.37	127.98	49.11	135.18
Science/technology		64.62	109.54	66.17	117.59
General		77.96	89.20	90.27	97.83
Law		93.29	90.57	86.36	116.77
Newspapers		464.36	114.66	437.16	107.67
Totals w/o newspapers		73.43	106.93	71.10	122.63
Totals with newspapers		96.63	110.42	96.63	150.30

Compiled by Scott Van Jacob, Notre Dame University, from data supplied by the Library of Congress field office in Rio de Janeiro, the Faxon Company, and the University of Texas at Austin. Index based on 1992 LAPPI mean prices. Totals based on all subscription titles for Latin America.
* Without newspapers.
n.a.=fewer than five subscriptions were found

Book Title Output and Average Prices: 1995 Final and 1996 Preliminary Figures

Gary Ink
Research Librarian, *Publishers Weekly*

American book title production soared in 1995, reaching a total of 62,039 titles. This is the highest American title output figure ever recorded, exceeding the previous high of 56,027 titles recorded in 1987. The final 1995 data, compiled by R. R. Bowker, shows that title output increased by an astounding 10,176 titles over the 1994 final figure of 51,863 titles. This is the largest year-to-year increase recorded since 1982–1983. It is also the largest year-to-year increase recorded in the post-World War II era. It is now clear that the decline in title output that began in 1988 has ended. In fact, the 1996 preliminary figure of 58,465, 13,608 units ahead of the preliminary figures for 1995, suggests a surge in title output.

Output by Format and by Category

Title output for 1995 increased for all formats and in all categories, with the largest increase occurring for trade paperbacks. Hardcover output increased by 4,483 titles, trade paperback output increased by 5,614 titles, and mass market output increased by 2,008 titles. The unexpected decline in mass market output recorded in 1994 appears to have been an anomaly that has been corrected by the current data.

Overall category totals (Table 1) indicate that all areas experienced growth in 1995. Categories showing significant growth include: fiction with an increase of 2,190 titles; sociology and economics with an increase of 1,324 titles; and religion with an increase of 594 titles. The small declines in fiction and children's books (Juveniles) that occurred in 1994 have been reversed. The major growth in both of these categories resulted from increased mass market output. This growth in children's book publishing may be an indication that the two-year slowdown in this category is ending.

Mass market output (Table 3), which recorded a large decline in 1994, has shown a dramatic recovery in 1995. Total output for 1995 stands at 4,686 titles, an increase of 2,028 titles over the 1994 final figure. As noted above, much of this growth is due to the large title output increases that reversed the previously recorded declines in fiction and children's books. Fiction has recorded an increase of 1,757 titles over the 1994 final figure, and children's books (Juveniles) has recorded an increase of 168 titles over 1994. While most categories showed at least a small increase over 1994, several categories did record a slight decrease in title output in 1995. The most significant declines were recorded in technology with a decrease of 17 titles, sports and recreation with a decrease of 20 titles, and home economics with a decrease of 15 titles. At least some of this year's increase in mass market title output must be attributed to the introduction by Bowker of improved methodology for collecting the necessary data.

(text continues on p. 507)

Table 1 / American Book Title Production, 1994–1996

Category	1994 All Hard and Paper*	1995 Final Hard and Trade Paper Books	1995 Final Hard and Trade Paper Editions	1995 Final Total	1995 Final All Hard and Paper*	1996 Preliminary Hard and Trade Paper Books	1996 Preliminary Hard and Trade Paper Editions	1996 Preliminary Total	1996 Preliminary All Hard and Paper*
Agriculture	532	539	124	663	673	443	78	521	531
Art	1,621	1,958	198	2,156	2,168	1,511	132	1,643	1,651
Biography	2,197	2,287	332	2,619	2,658	2,238	274	2,512	2,548
Business	1,616	1,467	358	1,825	1,843	1,266	365	1,631	1,648
Education	1,310	1,281	216	1,497	1,526	1,215	229	1,444	1,473
Fiction	5,415	3,676	228	3,904	7,605	3,919	230	4,149	7,718
General Works	2,208	2,331	389	2,720	2,751	2,061	309	2,370	2,404
History	2,507	2,601	374	2,975	2,999	2,466	398	2,864	2,881
Home Economics	1,004	1,185	167	1,352	1,395	1,027	153	1,180	1,215
Juveniles	5,321	5,032	248	5,280	5,678	4,291	155	4,446	4,734
Language	700	583	141	724	732	592	150	742	749
Law	1,168	845	380	1,225	1,230	764	294	1,058	1,063
Literature	2,356	2,212	266	2,478	2,525	2,412	285	2,697	2,767
Medicine	3,147	2,813	687	3,500	3,510	2,866	841	3,707	3,723
Music	364	370	106	476	479	322	63	385	390
Philosophy, Psychology	1,741	1,673	292	1,965	2,068	1,749	296	2,045	2,147
Poetry, Drama	1,065	1,328	47	1,375	1,407	1,119	73	1,192	1,220
Religion	2,730	2,914	394	3,308	3,324	2,725	389	3,114	3,130
Science	3,021	2,786	529	3,315	3,323	2,576	548	3,124	3,133
Sociology, Economics	8,038	8,241	1,079	9,320	9,362	8,180	1,106	9,286	9,320
Sports, Recreation	1,161	1,314	195	1,509	1,591	1,198	173	1,371	1,446
Technology	2,085	2,027	421	2,448	2,470	1,572	420	1,992	2,011
Travel	556	505	214	719	722	386	167	553	563
Totals	51,863	49,968	7,385	57,353	62,039	46,898	7,128	54,026	58,465

* Includes mass market paperbacks (see Table 3).

Note: Figures for mass market paperbound book production are based on entries in R. R. Bowker's *Paperbound Books in Print*. Other figures are from the *Weekly Record* (American Book Publishing Record) database. Figures under "Books" and "Editions" designate new books and new editions.

Table 2 / Paperbacks (Excluding Mass Market), 1994–1996

Category	1994 Totals	1995 Final Books	Editions	Totals	1996 Preliminary Books	Editions	Totals
Fiction	516	594	154	748	485	147	632
Nonfiction	16,560	18,222	3,699	21,921	17,789	3,749	21,538
Total	17,076	18,816	3,853	22,669	18,274	3,896	22,170

Table 3 / Mass Market Paperbacks, 1994–1996

Category	1993	1994	1995 Final	1996 Preliminary
Agriculture	23	7	10	10
Art	14	10	12	8
Biography	89	40	39	36
Business	22	17	18	17
Education	45	17	29	29
Fiction	2,298	1,944	3,701	3,569
General Works	61	42	31	34
History	17	10	24	17
Home Economics	83	58	43	35
Juveniles	450	230	398	288
Language	9	3	8	7
Law	0	3	5	5
Literature	26	16	47	70
Medicine	25	7	10	16
Music	2	2	3	5
Philosophy, Psychology	89	37	103	102
Poetry, Drama	6	8	32	28
Religion	14	11	16	16
Science	10	10	8	9
Sociology, Economics	55	40	42	34
Sports, Recreation	144	102	82	75
Technology	73	39	22	19
Travel	9	5	3	10
Total	3,564	2,658	4,686	4,439

Price Data Shows Rise

Average book prices in 1995, taken as a whole, rose significantly. The overall average price for hardcover books (Table A) increased by $2.50 between 1994 and 1995; the overall average price for trade paperbacks (Table C) increased by $1.15 in the same period; however, the overall average price for mass market paperbacks (Table C) increased by only 15 cents between 1994 and 1995. The small price increase for mass market paperbacks in 1995, may be due to a perception on the part of book publishers of a psychological price barrier beyond

(text continues on p. 509)

Table 4 / Imported Titles, 1994–1996
(Hard and Trade Paper Only)

Category	1994 Totals	1995 Final Books	1995 Final Editions	1995 Final Totals	1996 Preliminary Books	1996 Preliminary Editions	1996 Preliminary Totals
Agriculture	87	76	21	97	32	9	41
Art	205	259	14	273	108	7	115
Biography	144	124	18	142	99	21	120
Business	276	238	30	268	132	32	164
Education	287	267	18	285	204	17	221
Fiction	247	239	12	251	158	28	186
General works	331	341	26	367	236	23	259
History	447	413	49	462	284	40	324
Home economics	31	38	3	41	9	0	9
Juveniles	45	61	2	63	15	0	15
Language	199	232	31	263	201	32	233
Law	261	182	33	215	133	15	148
Literature	326	289	19	308	286	25	311
Medicine	605	525	86	611	456	103	559
Music	49	70	3	73	44	6	50
Philosophy, psychology	379	312	34	346	268	25	293
Poetry, drama	226	199	7	206	113	12	125
Religion	225	215	20	235	173	19	192
Science	997	916	152	1068	651	105	756
Sociology, economics	2,121	2,025	173	2,198	1,542	149	1691
Sports, recreation	106	104	14	118	71	5	76
Technology	465	404	83	487	273	55	328
Travel	113	109	53	162	31	27	58
Total	8,172	7,638	901	8,539	5,519	755	6,274

Table 5 / Translations into English, 1991–1996

	1991	1992	1993	1994	1995 Final	1996 Prelim.
Arabic	24	26	23	17	36	22
Chinese	35	49	50	55	63	40
Danish	20	25	14	21	15	10
Dutch	30	30	35	39	50	44
Finnish	1	42	4	4	4	2
French	365	383	339	374	438	388
German	402	337	353	362	477	438
Hebrew	45	47	40	35	54	54
Italian	87	91	87	132	118	101
Japanese	83	70	59	50	58	64
Latin	49	10	55	46	72	58
Norwegian	8	62	2	5	9	12
Russian	168	146	133	137	100	111
Spanish	125	122	135	120	119	173
Swedish	25	25	27	13	20	24
Turkish	0	0	1	2	0	2
Yiddish	13	4	3	6	6	12
Total	1,480	1,469	1,360	1,418	1,639	1,555

Note: Total covers only the languages listed here.

Table A / Hardcover Average Per-Volume Prices, 1993–1996

Category	1993 Prices	1994 Prices	Vols.	1995 Final $ Total	Prices	Vols.	1996 Preliminary $ Total	Prices
Agriculture	$41.84	$58.10	392	$19,208.76	$49.00	322	$14,666.88	$45.55
Art	39.99	39.97	1,116	46,008.18	41.23	892	49,045.04	54.99
Biography	28.37	30.43	1,596	47,899.42	30.01	1,649	51,141.70	31.01
Business	37.95	42.72	972	45,585.30	46.90	984	50,586.49	51.41
Education	38.60	47.98	610	26,229.70	43.00	634	30,326.36	47.83
Fiction	19.50	20.95	2,345	50,354.20	21.47	2,586	60,690.49	23.47
General Works	45.41	60.41	1,209	65,414.99	54.11	1,004	68,150.37	67.88
History	40.78	40.20	1,691	71,342.81	42.19	1,722	74,248.66	43.12
Home Economics	20.55	20.49	651	14,670.02	22.53	558	13,270.72	23.78
Juveniles	13.87	14.60	3,649	53,110.10	14.55	3,420	56,166.44	16.42
Language	34.02	52.09	320	17,564.64	54.89	362	21,129.97	58.37
Law	53.94	72.32	716	52,333.57	73.09	682	49,082.39	71.97
Literature	35.30	37.77	1,302	50,107.71	38.49	1,482	65,084.62	43.92
Medicine	49.78	76.30	2,035	154,261.48	75.80	2,268	177,787.88	78.39
Music	41.44	39.27	251	10,860.94	43.27	225	9,368.79	41.64
Philosophy, Psychology	39.44	44.71	1,001	45,302.80	45.26	1,091	52,779.10	48.38
Poetry, Drama	31.06	31.56	567	19,822.08	34.96	525	18,489.15	35.21
Religion	29.16	30.73	1,364	46,748.96	34.27	1,302	47,462.17	36.45
Science	52.71	90.12	2,095	195,914.22	93.52	2,046	178,576.17	87.28
Sociology, Economics	41.32	50.24	5,145	285,607.93	55.51	5,451	295,458.85	54.20
Sports, Recreation	32.28	33.39	517	16,617.58	32.14	530	18,191.67	34.32
Technology	56.31	81.03	1,454	128,354.74	88.28	1,324	113,862.11	86.00
Travel	26.22	32.13	199	7,622.59	38.30	145	4,979.53	34.34
Total	$34.98	$44.65	31,197	$1,470,942.82	$47.15	31,204	$1,520,485.55	$48.73

which consumers will not pass. However, 1996 preliminary figures show a jump to $6.53.

Hardcover books recorded price increases in most categories in 1995. Fiction continued to rise above the $20 mark, with an increase of 52 cents to $21.47. The largest increases were recorded in technology with an increase of $7.25, travel with an increase of $6.17, and sociology and economics with an increase of $5.27. The closely watched children's books (Juveniles) category recorded a slight decrease of 5 cents in 1995. Mass market paperbacks also saw a price increase for fiction of 76 cents, and a price increase for children's books of 29 cents. Figures shown here are derived from R. R. Bowker databases—*American Book Publishing Record* for hardcovers and trade paperbacks, and *Paperbound Books in Print* for mass market paperbacks (Tables A–C).

(text continues on p. 511)

Table A1 / Hardcover Average Per-Volume Prices—Less Than $81, 1993–1996

Category	1993 Prices	1994 Prices	1995 Final Vols.	1995 Final $ Total	1995 Final Prices	1996 Preliminary Vols.	1996 Preliminary $ Total	1996 Preliminary Prices
Agriculture	$36.54	$30.67	332	10,209.76	30.75	274	8,429.13	30.76
Art	37.93	36.20	1,053	38,011.58	36.10	814	31,048.64	38.14
Biography	27.90	27.53	1,552	42,612.32	27.46	1,589	44,229.15	27.83
Business	36.39	37.74	898	34,396.60	38.30	899	37,044.47	41.21
Education	38.23	38.76	573	22,335.60	38.98	591	25,432.55	43.03
Fiction	19.39	20.35	2,333	48,948.85	20.98	2,570	55,717.64	21.68
General works	43.33	41.02	1,031	42,923.49	41.63	825	36,874.87	44.70
History	37.36	37.18	1,614	60,136.41	37.26	1,622	62,581.16	38.58
Home economics	20.55	20.35	647	14,236.02	22.00	556	13,055.72	23.48
Juveniles	13.87	13.91	3,644	52,221.15	14.33	3,408	51,476.64	15.10
Language	32.91	38.57	265	10,867.04	41.01	295	12,408.09	42.06
Law	43.39	44.20	515	23,218.37	45.08	516	24,243.49	46.98
Literature	35.12	35.07	1,244	45,088.36	36.24	1,395	53,826.92	38.59
Medicine	41.64	40.66	1,329	54,373.23	40.91	1,398	58,953.13	42.17
Music	37.49	38.26	239	9,617.84	40.24	206	8,041.89	39.04
Philosophy, psychology	37.70	37.89	935	36,364.80	38.89	1,009	41,725.90	41.35
Poetry, drama	31.06	29.49	549	16,669.38	30.36	504	16,345.45	32.43
Religion	28.73	28.68	1,267	36,643.22	28.92	1,205	37,273.40	30.93
Science	45.90	46.79	1,189	56,895.01	47.85	1,338	63,178.67	47.22
Sociology, economics	40.68	41.90	4,755	196,537.39	41.33	5,035	221,498.24	43.99
Sports, recreation	32.15	31.67	514	16,033.68	31.19	517	16,737.42	32.37
Technology	45.87	48.16	873	43,046.49	49.31	807	39,848.92	49.38
Travel	26.22	28.60	185	5,357.39	28.96	138	4,087.52	29.62
Total	$32.68	$32.65	27,536	$916,743.98	$33.29	27,511	$964,059.01	$35.04

Table B / Mass Market Paperbacks Average Per-Volume Prices, 1994–1996

Category	1994 Prices	1995 Final Vols.	1995 Final $ Total	1995 Final Prices	1996 Preliminary Vols.	1996 Preliminary $ Total	1996 Preliminary Prices
Agriculture	$8.25	10	$91.33	$9.13	10	$100.78	$10.08
Art	11.04	12	134.91	11.24	8	95.99	12.00
Biography	7.76	39	315.38	8.09	36	352.95	9.80
Business	11.76	18	194.72	10.81	17	201.76	11.87
Education	13.08	29	359.64	12.40	29	324.08	11.18
Fiction	4.75	3,680	20,287.34	5.51	3,569	22,317.73	6.25
General Works	9.26	29	562.00	19.38	34	316.66	9.31
History	10.94	24	241.54	10.06	17	185.63	10.92
Home Economics	8.02	43	374.52	8.71	35	303.55	8.67
Juveniles	3.71	396	1,582.88	4.00	288	1,224.20	4.25
Language	14.30	8	76.86	9.61	7	50.94	7.28
Law	6.66	5	48.97	9.79	5	51.97	10.39
Literature	6.42	47	410.31	8.73	70	644.29	9.20
Medicine	8.49	10	83.89	8.39	16	134.80	8.42
Music	17.50	3	74.95	24.98	5	102.85	20.57
Philosophy, Psychology	9.17	103	498.04	4.84	102	718.36	7.04
Poetry, Drama	8.80	32	310.68	9.71	28	304.75	10.88
Religion	8.31	16	150.27	9.39	16	142.90	8.93
Science	11.67	8	90.29	11.29	9	109.40	12.16
Sociology, Economics	9.15	42	403.30	9.60	34	337.01	9.91
Sports, Recreation	9.03	82	679.28	8.28	75	659.47	8.79
Technology	25.20	22	255.73	11.62	19	195.82	10.31
Travel	13.57	3	41.90	13.97	10	96.34	9.63
Total	$5.70	4,661	$27,268.73	$5.85	4,439	$28,972.23	$6.53

Table C / Trade Paperbacks Average Per-Volume Prices, 1993–1996

Category	1993 Prices	1994 Prices	1995 Final Vols.	1995 Final $ Total	1995 Final Prices	1996 Preliminary Vols.	1996 Preliminary $ Total	1996 Preliminary Prices
Agriculture	$18.32	$18.26	218	$5,878.84	$26.97	191	$4,049.99	$21.20
Art	19.98	20.99	874	17,984.67	20.58	690	14,815.65	21.47
Biography	15.75	15.65	813	13,487.73	16.59	751	12,817.37	17.07
Business	25.18	23.94	709	17,182.83	24.24	608	15,000.90	24.67
Education	23.06	21.47	738	16,945.30	22.96	760	18,232.32	23.99
Fiction	13.56	14.94	1,275	16,206.68	12.71	1,405	17,713.03	12.61
General Works	31.19	33.81	1,375	45,355.33	32.99	1,305	43,528.41	33.36
History	21.20	20.15	1,041	19,237.56	18.48	1,050	21,869.54	20.83
Home Economics	14.47	14.72	629	9,354.00	14.87	603	9,272.28	15.38
Juveniles	7.73	6.83	990	15,589.51	15.75	856	7,055.42	8.24
Language	42.93	23.82	304	6,561.12	21.58	335	7,234.30	21.59
Law	28.86	30.57	415	12,558.30	30.26	331	9,088.04	27.46
Literature	17.38	18.21	945	15,631.20	16.54	1,113	19,721.76	17.72
Medicine	29.66	25.15	1,092	30,483.04	27.91	1,344	37,758.90	28.09
Music	21.64	19.48	174	3,447.88	19.81	150	2,823.85	18.83
Philosophy, Psychology	18.23	18.19	800	15,932.52	19.92	885	17,214.44	19.45
Poetry, Drama	13.29	13.25	712	11,174.27	15.69	628	7,989.24	12.72
Religion	13.67	14.69	1,723	25,150.06	14.60	1,726	25,952.49	15.04
Science	31.79	35.71	874	29,206.97	33.42	948	30,378.36	32.04
Sociology, Economics	22.42	23.19	3,321	78,673.18	23.69	3,452	80,351.36	23.28
Sports, Recreation	15.82	16.39	900	14,880.92	16.53	818	13,310.71	16.27
Technology	30.04	29.50	827	32,047.04	38.75	615	20,473.92	33.29
Travel	15.90	15.54	480	7,861.20	16.38	400	6,722.35	16.81
Total	$20.56	$20.56	21,229	$460,830.15	$21.71	20,964	$443,374.83	$21.15

Subject Groups

Each of the 23 standard subject groups used here represents one or more specific Dewey Decimal Classification numbers, as follows: Agriculture, 630–639, 712–719; Art, 700–711, 720–779; Biography, 920–929; Business, 650–659; Education, 370–379; Fiction; General Works, 000–099; History, 900–909, 930–999; Home Economics, 640–649; Juveniles; Language, 400–499; Law, 340–349; Literature, 800–810, 813–820, 823–899; Medicine, 610–619; Music, 780–789; Philosophy, Psychology, 100–199; Poetry, Drama, 811, 812, 821, 822; Religion, 200–299; Science, 500–599; Sociology, Economics, 300–339, 350–369, 380–389; Sports, Recreation, 790–799; Technology, 600–609, 620–629, 660–699; Travel, 910–919.

Book Sales Statistics, 1996: AAP Preliminary Estimates

Association of American Publishers

The industry estimates shown in the following table are based on the U.S. Census of Manufactures. This census is conducted every fifth year—the most recent being the 1992 census.

Between censuses, the Association of American Publishers (AAP) estimates are "pushed forward" by the percentage changes that are reported to the AAP statistics program, and by other industry data that are available. Some AAP data are collected in a monthly statistics program, and it is largely this material that is shown in this preliminary estimate table. More detailed data are available from, and additional publishers report to, the AAP annual statistics program, and this additional data will be incorporated into Table S1 that will be published in the AAP 1996 Industry Statistics.

Readers comparing the estimated data with census reports should recall that the U.S. Census of Manufactures does not include data on many university presses or on other institutionally sponsored and not-for-profit publishing activities, or (under SIC 2731: Book Publishing) for the audiovisual and some other media materials that are included in this table. On the other hand, AAP estimates have traditionally excluded some "Sunday School" materials and certain pamphlets that are included in the census data.

As in prior reports, the estimates reflect the impact of industry expansion created by new establishments entering the field, as well as nontraditional forms of book publishing, in addition to incorporating the sales increases and decreases of established firms.

It should also be noted that the "Other Sales" category includes only incidental book sales, such as music, sheet sales (both domestic and export, except those to prebinders), and miscellaneous merchandise sales.

Estimates include domestic sales and export sales of U.S. product and do not cover indigenous activities of publishers' foreign subsidiaries.

Non-rack-size Mass Market Publishing is included in Trade—Paperbound. Prior to the 1988 AAP Annual Statistics, this was treated as Adult Trade Paperbound. It is recognized that part of this is Juvenile (1987 estimate: 20 percent), and adjustments have been made in this respect. AAP also notes that this area includes sales through traditional "mass market paperback channels" by publishers not generally recognized as being "mass market paperback."

Table 1 / Estimated Book Publishing Industry Sales 1987, 1992, 1994–1996
(Millions of Dollars)

	1987 $	1992 $	1994 $	1995 $	% Change from 1994	1996 $	% Change from 1995	Compound Growth Rate (%) 1987–1996	1992–1996
Trade (total)	2,712.8	4,661.6	5,540.6	5,560.8	0.4	5,626.0	1.2	8.4	4.8
Adult hardbound	1,350.6	2,222.5	2,803.9	2,646.9	-5.6	2,530.4	-4.4	7.2	3.3
Adult paperbound	727.1	1,261.7	1,520.3	1,587.2	4.4	1,616.4	1.8	9.3	6.4
Juvenile hardbound	478.5	850.8	823.4	836.6	1.6	909.1	8.7	7.4	1.7
Juvenile paperbound	156.6	326.6	393.0	490.1	24.7	570.1	16.3	15.4	14.9
Religious (total)	638.8	907.1	979.4	1,036.9	5.9	1,104.2	6.5	6.3	5.0
Bibles, testaments, hymnals, etc.	177.6	260.1	275.6	293.0	6.3	298.2	1.8	5.9	3.5
Other religious	461.2	647.0	703.8	743.9	5.7	806.0	8.3	6.4	5.6
Professional (total)	2,207.3	3,106.7	3,606.1	3,869.3	7.3	3,994.6	3.2	6.8	6.5
Business	388.8	490.3	560.0	617.6	10.3	—	—	—	—
Law	780.0	1,128.1	1,299.0	1,400.4	7.8	—	—	—	—
Medical	406.5	622.7	754.1	809.3	7.3	—	—	—	—
Technical, scientific, other prof'l	632.0	865.6	993.0	1,042.0	4.9	—	—	—	—
Book clubs	678.7	742.3	873.9	976.1	11.7	1,091.8	11.9	5.4	10.1
Mail order publications	657.6	630.2	557.3	559.5	0.4	579.5	3.6	-1.4	-2.1
Mass market paperback, rack-sized	913.7	1,263.8	1,392.4	1,499.6	7.7	1,533.3	2.2	5.9	5.0
University presses	170.9	280.1	325.7	339.7	4.3	349.3	2.8	8.3	5.7
Elementary and secondary text	1,695.6	2,080.9	2,155.8	2,466.2	14.4	2,607.6	5.7	4.9	5.8
College text	1,549.5	2,084.1	2,176.8	2,324.8	6.8	2,485.8	6.9	5.4	4.5
Standardized tests	104.0	140.4	156.5	167.3	6.9	178.7	6.8	6.2	6.3
Subscription reference	437.6	572.3	641.3	670.8	4.6	706.1	5.3	5.5	5.4
Other sales (incl. AV)	423.8	449.0	452.9	476.0	5.1	493.2	3.6	1.7	2.4
Total	12,190.3	16,918.5	18,858.7	19,947.0	5.8	20,750.1	4.0	6.1	5.2

Source: Association of American Publishers.

United States Trade in Books: 1996

William S. Lofquist
Senior Analyst, U.S. Department of Commerce

Recent estimates place global sales of books at approximately $85–90 billion. Perhaps 10 percent of this value represents trade across borders. Germany, the United Kingdom, and the United States are the world's leading book exporters, with each country's foreign sales in the range of $1.5–2.0 billion annually.

Factors influencing international trade in books include market demand, copyright protection, currency exchange rates and market efficiency, a synthesis reflecting literacy levels, educational attainment, and upscale occupations. Although the world's developed and developing economies show marked improvements in copyright protection and market efficiency, global book demand has not kept pace with overall economic growth.

U.S. Book Exports

For most of the 1990s, the level of U.S. book exports recorded minimal rates of growth. This ended in 1996, with exports of U.S. books receding to $1.76 billion, a decline of 0.6 percent from the 1995 value of $1.77 billion. This represented the first decline in U.S. book exports since 1985. The drop in U.S. export sales in 1996 was subtle but widespread. As shown in Table 2, two-thirds of the 30 leading foreign markets for U.S. books recorded a fall off in the number of U.S.

Table 1 / U.S. Exports of Books: 1996

Category	Value (millions of current $)	Percent change, 1996-95	Units (millions of copies)	Percent change, 1996-95
Dictionaries and thesauruses	$5.4	-26.2%	1.4	-12.3%
Encyclopedias	38.4	-7.3	5.6	-17.9
Textbooks	316.9	8.7	49.9	11.1
Religious books	51.8	5.6	41.1	10.9
Technical, scientific, and professional books	506.5	-4.8	79.6	-15.2
Art and pictorial books	12.1	-29.0	14.8	-21.5
Hardcover books, n.e.s	184.6	12.5	55.8	3.0
Mass market paperbound books	208.1	0.7	103.0	-6.3
Children's picture and coloring books	17.1	-9.2	21.6	-17.4
Music books	15.9	-27.4	2.5	-25.3
Atlases	2.9	18.5	0.5	22.4
All other books	395.9	-4.2	452.0	-7.5
Total, all books	$1,755.6	-0.6%	827.8	-6.5%

Notes: n.e.s.=Not elsewhere specified. Individual shipments are excluded from the foreign trade data if valued under $2,500. Data for individual categories may not add to totals due to statistical rounding.

Source: U.S. Department of Commerce, Bureau of the Census.

books purchased in 1996 compared to 1995. These declines resulted from a combination of weak market demand and the deleterious effect of a strengthened U.S. dollar. As the U.S. dollar grows in value against most major currencies, the purchasing power of the affected currencies declines, thus weakening foreign demand for U.S. exports.

The classification of U.S. book exports by subject category appears in Table 1. Of the five largest book categories (those with at least $100 million in ship-

Table 2 / U.S. Book Exports to Principal Countries: 1996

Country	Value (millions of current $)	Percent change, 1996-95	Units (millions of copies)	Percent change, 1996-95
Canada	$737.0	-2.4%	409.5	-6.1%
United Kingdom	225.6	7.8	87.8	-6.1
Japan	128.5	2.3	39.5	-5.6
Australia	116.4	-4.6	54.1	-14.3
Mexico	55.1	35.6	37.9	48.4
Germany	41.9	-16.1	16.3	-7.4
Singapore	35.9	-10.3	19.6	3.6
Korea, Republic of	33.6	19.7	13.1	8.5
Brazil	29.0	17.2	13.0	40.6
Netherlands	27.1	-1.8	7.4	-34.8
Philippines	26.6	16.0	10.6	11.6
Taiwan	26.3	-1.6	9.5	-2.6
Hong Kong	21.6	-2.6	6.2	-11.5
South Africa, Republic of	17.7	-12.5	8.2	-8.3
France	17.1	-18.9	5.7	-16.4
Denmark	16.3	7.2	3.8	56.5
New Zealand	14.6	-2.9	8.5	13.5
India	14.5	-11.7	6.8	-29.2
Switzerland	11.4	11.9	2.9	-17.0
Italy	11.0	60.0	2.6	-16.8
Israel	9.9	110.3	7.6	442.5
Colombia	9.3	62.9	4.1	50.7
Belgium	8.1	-1.6	2.0	12.9
Argentina	8.1	-22.1	4.1	-58.4
Thailand	7.8	3.3	2.9	-7.1
Spain	7.8	-16.8	2.4	-26.2
Saudi Arabia	7.4	14.4	1.9	-4.3
Ireland	6.7	-38.2	1.5	-56.3
Malaysia	5.6	5.8	2.1	-1.2
Sweden	5.4	-26.4	1.3	-54.7
Total, all countries	$1,765.6	-0.6%	827.8	-6.5%

Notes: Individual shipments are excluded from the foreign trade data if valued under $2,500.
Source: U.S. Department of Commerce, Bureau of the Census.

Table 3 / U.S. Imports of Books: 1996

Category	Value (millions of current $)	Percent change, 1996-95	Units (millions of copies)	Percent change, 1996-95
Dictionaries and thesauruses	$7.0	-30.7%	2.1	-21.6%
Encyclopedias	6.6	-9.7	1.3	0.2
Textbooks	118.7	20.9	26.8	12.8
Religious books	52.2	-4.5	38.7	8.6
Technical, scientific, and professional books	165.7	5.4	32.4	3.0
Art and pictorial books, valued under $5	15.2	-19.0	8.8	-9.0
Art and pictorial books, valued at $5 or more	20.9	-11.1	1.9	-10.5
Hardcover books, n.e.s	450.8	1.2	132.5	-7.0
Mass market paperbound books	41.2	-17.6	27.2	-15.4
Children's picture and coloring books	151.6	1.5	133.6	-2.1
Music books	3.3	0.6	0.9	4.3
Atlases	4.3	19.2	1.3	19.8
All other books	261.9	13.4	151.8	36.8
Total, all books	$1,299.6	3.8%	559.2	5.4%

Notes: n.e.s.=Not elsewhere specified. Individual shipments are excluded from the foreign trade data if valued under $1,250. Data for individual categories may not add to totals due to statistical rounding.
Source: U.S. Department of Commerce, Bureau of the Census.

ments), only two categories—textbooks, and hardcover books, n.e.s. (not elsewhere specified)—showed gains in both dollar value and in number of units shipped. Sales of U.S. textbooks to the United Kingdom and Australia rose by 22 percent and 48 percent, respectively, in 1996, although textbook exports to Canada declined by 3 percent. Perhaps most disturbing is the receding global market for U.S. publishers of technical, scientific, and professional books. United States prowess in this sector is unsurpassed, yet foreign demand for U.S. technical, scientific, and technical books in 1996 fell by 5 percent in dollar terms and 15 percent in number of copies shipped, compared to 1995.

As earlier noted, Table 2 presents a listing of the 30 largest markets for U.S. books. One can view this listing from several perspectives. From a country standpoint, combined U.S. book exports to just four countries—Canada, the United Kingdom, Japan and Australia—represent 69 percent of the export total. Regionally, combined U.S. book exports to North America (Canada), Europe, and the Pacific Rim represent 88 percent of the export total. Despite the decline of U.S. book exports to Argentina, 1996 book demand from Brazil, Colombia, and—especially—Mexico helped increase the percentage of U.S. book volume destined for Latin America.

U.S. Book Imports

Steady growth in the U.S. economy plus the stronger purchasing power of the U.S. dollar increased the level of U.S. book imports in 1996. As shown in Table 3, total U.S. imports rose to $1.3 billion, an increase of 3.8 percent over 1995.

Table 4 / U.S. Book Imports from Principal Countries: 1996

Country	Value (millions of current $)	Percent change, 1996-95	Units (millions of copies)	Percent change, 1996-95
United Kingdom	$279.8	3.8%	63.8	0.0%
Hong Kong	226.5	5.3	111.1	12.3
Canada	122.9	21.4	115.1	20.5
Singapore	113.9	7.0	50.1	-0.6
Italy	99.0	-2.9	44.3	-1.4
China	74.8	14.8	42.6	4.2
Japan	60.4	-18.6	12.2	-32.1
Germany	53.3	11.4	8.2	20.4
Mexico	49.0	2.0	29.8	36.9
France	33.5	0.6	7.6	6.6
Spain	32.3	-4.6	11.1	2.1
Korea, Republic of	20.4	-6.8	8.8	-10.9
Belgium	16.4	-21.7	7.8	-10.6
Netherlands	13.6	-10.8	1.2	-11.9
Taiwan	11.5	35.0	6.8	24.7
Colombia	11.3	-4.9	7.1	-16.5
Thailand	10.8	6.0	8.5	-8.4
Australia	9.2	-5.5	2.8	-12.8
Israel	8.4	7.4	1.9	-3.2
Switzerland	7.7	9.4	0.9	-19.4
Sweden	5.8	24.5	2.2	47.4
New Zealand	5.7	187.4	1.1	-4.0
Malaysia	3.7	-22.8	1.4	-16.5
Portugal	3.5	9.5	1.4	-9.7
Ecuador	2.8	-18.1	1.1	-31.9
India	2.4	-10.0	2.0	-63.5
Slovenia	2.3	21.7	0.5	-5.6
United Arab Emirates	2.1	239.6	0.6	156.4
Denmark	1.5	-46.3	0.3	-78.5
Dominican Republic	1.1	56.6	0.7	100.3
Total, all countries	$1,299.6	3.8%	559.2	5.4%

Notes: Individual shipments are excluded from the foreign trade data if valued under $1,250.
Source: U.S. Department of Commerce, Bureau of the Census.

The number of books imported in 1996 reached 559 million, up 5.4 percent from 1995.

United States imports of books are statistically classified in categories similar to U.S. book exports. Import/export comparability, however, is clouded by the fact that unlike the majority of U.S. book exports, the U.S. importation of books is as much a factor of purchasing foreign printing and binding as it is a factor of appreciating foreign editorial content. Certain countries—Italy and Spain, in Europe; Colombia, in Latin America; and China, Hong Kong, Korea, Singapore,

Table 5 / U.S. Trade in Books: 1970–1995
(in millions of current dollars)

Year	U.S. Book Exports	U.S. Book Imports	Ratio, U.S. Book Exports/Imports
1996	$1,755.6	$1,299.6	1.35
1995	1,765.7	1,252.5	1.41
1990	1,428.0	845.1	1.69
1985	591.2	564.2	1.05
1980	518.9	306.5	1.69
1975	269.3	147.6	1.82
1970	174.9	92.0	1.90

Source: U.S. Department of Commerce, Bureau of the Census.

Table 6 / U.S. Book Industry Shipments Compared to U.S. Book Exports: 1970–1996
(in millions of current dollars)

Year	Total Shipments, U.S. Book Industry	U.S. Book Exports	Exports as a Percent of Total Shipments
1996	$21,480.0[1]	$1,755.6	8.2
1995	20,603.6	1,765.7	8.6
1990	15,317.9	1,428.0	9.3
1985	10,196.2	591.2	5.8
1980	6,114.4	518.9	8.5
1975	3,536.5	269.3	7.6
1970	2,434.2	174.9	7.2

1 Estimated by International Trade Administration, U.S. Department of Commerce.
Source: U.S. Department of Commerce, Bureau of the Census.

and Taiwan, in Asia—are renowned as providers of economical printing and binding. As regards Table 3, certain book categories represent products imported primarily for their lower manufacturing costs: art and pictorial books, and children's picture and coloring books. Both of these categories experienced declines in the number of units shipped to the U.S. in 1996. Other books—including textbooks, and technical, scientific and professional books—are imported for their editorial content. Both of these imported book categories recorded gains in dollar value and in units shipped in 1996.

Table 4 offers a listing of the 30 major suppliers of books to the United States. It appears that U.S. book demand and the strong U.S. dollar have an uneven effect among those countries known primarily for their printing and binding capabilities. While the number of books imported from Hong Kong, China, Spain, and Taiwan increased in 1996, the volume of imports from other printing/binding countries—Singapore, Italy, Japan, Korea, and Colombia—declined in 1996. Countries regarded as content providers—Canada, Germany, France, and Sweden—witnessed a rise in U.S. demand for their products in 1996. Other countries similarly regarded faired less well: the United Kingdom, Belgium, the Netherlands, Australia, Israel, and Switzerland all showed either no improvement or a decline in the number of books shipped to the U.S. in 1996.

Foreign/Domestic Book Trade

A combination of factors is closing the gap between U.S. book exports and book imports. As noted in Table 5, the export/import ratio is influenced most significantly by changes in currency exchange rates. The strong U.S. dollar nearly equalized book exports and imports in the mid-1980s, and the trend through the 1990s is again leaning in that direction. As the millennium draws closer, factors beyond exchange rates and market demand are also at work as regards book exports. Growth in global communications and international copyright protection enables U.S. publishers to reach foreign markets through aggressive rights and translation activities, rather than direct exports. Rising levels of U.S. book imports, however, are largely determined by exchange rates. A strong U.S. dollar expands the purchasing power of U.S. libraries and institutions. It also aids those U.S. publishers seeking to stretch out their expenditures for printing and binding.

Table 6 depicts the relationship between the U.S. book industry's total shipments vs. the industry's exports. Although U.S. book exports grew at a more rapid annual rate than industry shipments over the period 1970–1996 (9.3 percent vs. 8.7 percent, respectively), since 1990 industry shipments have clearly outpaced exports (5.8 percent vs. 3.5 percent). But focusing exclusively on book exports is an insufficient measure of the influence U.S. publishers have on the global marketplace. Growth in U.S. exports of electronically published products supports and enhances the importance of U.S. printed products as a conveyor of knowledge and information.

International Book Title Output: 1990–1994

William S. Lofquist
Senior Analyst, U.S. Department of Commerce

Each year the United Nations Educational, Scientific, and Cultural Organization (UNESCO) surveys its member countries to determine international book title output. The information is released in UNESCO's annual yearbook, the most recent dated 1996. Of the world's 200+ countries, responses covering book title output for the period 1990–1994 were received from 104 UNESCO-member countries (it must be phrased this way, since one major "country"—Taiwan—is not a UNESCO member and thus not included in the compilation).

The number of new titles or new editions released by the world's publishers for any given year probably exceeds one million. For the most recent year (1994) UNESCO records book title output at approximately 800,000. Data on some countries (e.g., Taiwan) are missing, and title output by some entities (governments, educational institutions) may not be shown. Statistics on book title output by the United States, for example, exclude school textbooks, government publications, and university theses—titles that may well be included in the recorded data of other countries.

The accompanying table shows international book title output from the world's leading publishing countries. Listed is the title output of those 36 countries publishing at least 5,000 new titles or new editions in at least one of the years covering the period 1990–1994. All the major publishing countries are shown, although the reporting of title data is frequently erratic: (1) Australia and Japan show data for only one of the five years; (2) Belgium, Indonesia, Japan, and Thailand last reported title output in 1992. In addition to lack of recent data, some countries report recent title output at levels inconsistent with previous disclosures. The Netherlands reported 1993 title output at 34,067—although title output over the period 1990–1992 was at the level of 11,000–16,000.

The UNESCO data indicate that 1994 was a very strong year for the world's publishers. Of those 24 major countries reporting title output for 1993 and 1994, a comparison of aggregate book title output shows an increase of 8.9 percent in the number of titles published in 1994 over title output in 1993. Only three countries (India, Romania, and Turkey) reported fewer titles published in 1994 than in 1993. For some countries—such as Canada—the growth book title output in 1994 compared to 1993 borders on unbelievable (22,208 titles in 1994 vs. 9,764 titles in 1993). But such anomalies were the exception. Most countries showed title growth consistent with trends in previous years.

The world's largest publishing countries—with annual title output exceeding 50,000 titles per year—are China, the United Kingdom, Germany, and the United States. However, none of these countries recorded 1994–1993 growth rates equal to or greater than the 8.9 percent rate of growth averaged by the 24 major publishing countries over this period.

International Book Title Output: 1990–1994

Country	1990	1991	1992	1993	1994
China	73,923	90,156	n.a.	92,972	100,951
United Kingdom	n.a.	n.a.	86,573	n.a.	95,015
Germany	61,015	67,890	67,277	67,206	70,643
United States	46,743	48,146	49,276	49,757	51,863
France	41,720	43,682	45,379	41,234	45,311
Spain	36,239	39,082	41,816	40,758	44,261
Korea, Republic of	39,330	29,432	27,889	30,861	34,204
Japan	n.a.	n.a.	35,496	n.a.	n.a.
Netherlands	13,691	11,613	15,997	34,067	n.a.
Russia	n.a.	34,050	28,716	29,017	30,390
Italy	25,068	27,751	29,351	30,110	32,673
Brazil	n.a.	n.a.	27,557	20,141	21,574
Canada	8,291	8,722	9,056	9,764	22,208
India	13,937	14,438	15,778	12,768	11,460
Switzerland	13,839	14,886	14,663	14,870	15,378
Belgium	12,157	13,913	n.a.	n.a.	n.a.
Sweden	12,034	11,866	12,813	12,895	13,822
Finland	10,153	11,208	11,033	11,785	12,539
Denmark	11,082	10,198	11,761	11,492	11,973
Poland	10,242	10,688	10,727	9,788	10,874
Australia	n.a.	n.a.	n.a.	n.a.	10,835
Iran	n.a.	5,018	6,822	n.a.	10,753
Hungary	8,322	8,133	8,536	9,170	10,108
Serbia[1]	9,797	4,049	2,618	n.a.	n.a.
Czech Republic[2]	8,585	9,362	6,743	8,203	9,309
Argentina	4,915	6,092	5,628	n.a.	9,065
Austria	3,740	6,505	4,986	5,628	7,987
Thailand	7,783	7,676	7,626	n.a.	n.a.
Ukraine	7,046	5,857	4,410	5,002	n.a.
Norway	3,712	3,884	4,881	4,943	6,946
Portugal	6,150	6,430	6,462	6,089	6,667
Turkey	6,291	6,365	6,549	5,978	4,473
Indonesia	1,518	1,774	6,303	n.a.	n.a.
Romania	2,178	2,914	3,662	6,130	4,074
Bulgaria	3,412	3,260	4,773	5,771	5,925
Vietnam	n.a.	n.a.	4,707	n.a.	5,581

Notes: n.a.=Not available.
1 Title output for 1990 refers to the former Yugoslavia.
2 Title output for 1990 and 1991 refer to the former Czechoslovakia.
Source: UNESCO Statistical Yearbook, 1996.

Number of Book Outlets in the United States and Canada

The *American Book Trade Directory* has been published by R. R. Bowker since 1915. Revised annually, it features lists of booksellers, wholesalers, periodicals, reference tools, and other information about the U.S. and Canadian book markets. The data shown in Table 1, the most current available, are from the 1996–1997 edition of the directory.

Table 1 / Bookstores in the United States and Canada, 1996

Category	United States	Canada
Antiquarian General	1,495	88
Antiquarian Mail Order	623	11
Antiquarian Specialized	284	11
Art Supply Store	74	1
College General	3,430	171
College Specialized	151	12
Comics	331	30
Computer Software	469	0
Cooking	186	6
Department Store	2,316	86
Educational*	253	77
Federal Sites†	280	1
Foreign Language*	136	32
General	7,090	979
Gift Shop	373	22
Juvenile*	442	44
Mail Order General	417	18
Mail Order Specialized	892	23
Metaphysics, New Age, and Occult	305	23
Museum Store and Art Gallery	582	34
Nature and Natural History	172	9
Newsdealer	134	7
Office Supply	56	15
Other§	2,275	240
Paperback‡	424	18
Religious*	4,012	239
Self Help/Development	68	15
Stationer	46	24
Toy Store	122	9
Used*	842	96
Totals	28,280	2,341

* Includes Mail Order Shops for this topic, which are not counted elsewhere in this survey.

† National Historic Sites, National Monuments, and National Parks.

‡ Includes Mail Order. Excludes used paperback bookstores, stationers, drugstores, or wholesalers handling paperbacks.

§ Stores specializing in subjects or services other than those covered in this survey.

The 30,621 stores of various types shown are located throughout the United States, Canada, and regions administered by the United States. "General" bookstores stock trade books and children's books in a general variety of subjects. "College" stores carry college-level textbooks. "Educational" outlets handle school textbooks up to and including the high school level. "Mail order" outlets sell general trade books by mail and are not book clubs; all others operating by mail are classified according to the kinds of books carried. "Antiquarian" dealers sell old and rare books. Stores handling secondhand books are classified as "used." "Paperback" stores have more than 80 percent of their stock in paperbound books. Stores with paperback departments are listed under the appropriate major classification ("general," "department store," "stationer," etc.). Bookstores with at least 50 percent of their stock on a particular subject are classified by subject.

Book Review Media Statistics

Compiled by the staff of *The Bowker Annual*

Number of Books Reviewed by Major Book-Reviewing Publications, 1995–1996

	Adult 1995	Adult 1996	Juvenile 1995	Juvenile 1996	Young Adult 1995	Young Adult 1996	Total 1995	Total 1996
Booklist [1]	4,172	4,080	2,540	2,397	825	712	7,537	7,189
Bulletin of the Center for Children's Books [2]	—	—	810	800	—	—	810	800
Chicago Tribune	640	650	—	—	—	—	640	650
Choice [3]	6,563	6,728	—	—	—	—	6,563	6,728
Horn Book Magazine [4]	—	8	500	410	—	71	500	489
Horn Book Guide	—	—	3,202	3,000	424	500	3,626	3,500
Kirkus Reviews [4]	3,091	3,085	1,087	1,225	—	—	4,178	4,310
Library Journal [5]	5,472	5,553	—	—	—	—	5,472	5,553
Los Angeles Times	1,650	1,760	100	110	—	—	1,750	1,870
New York Review of Books	428	408	—	—	—	—	428	408
New York Times Sunday Book Review [4]	1,963	1,800	297	285	—	—	2,260	2,085
Publishers Weekly	5,512	6,300	1,600	1,600	—	—	7,110	7,900
Rapport (formerly West Coast Review of Books)	900	520	—	—	—	—	900	520
School Library Journal [6]	305	253	2,454	3,278	—	—	3,580	3,531
Washington Post Book World	1,856	1,941	103	58	43	59	2,002	2,058

1 All figures are for a 12-month period from September 1 to August 31; 1996 figures are for September 1, 1995–August 31, 1996 (vol. 92). Some YA books are included in the juvenile total, and the YA total includes reviews of adult books that are appropriate for young adults.
2 All figures are for 12-month period beginning September and ending July/August.
3 All books reviewed in *Choice* are scholarly publications intended for undergraduate libraries.
4 Juvenile figures include young adult titles.
5 In addition, LJ reviewed 62 magazines, 356 audio books, 375 videos, 675 books in "Prepub Alert," 349 books in "Collection Development," 65 Web sites, and 100 CD-ROMs.
6 1996 adult figure includes young adult titles; juvenile figure includes 1,500 books for preschool-primary readers, 1,122 for grades 3–6, and 656 junior high titles.

Part 5
Reference Information

Bibliographies

The Librarian's Bookshelf

Sandy Whiteley, MSLS
Editor, *Chase's Calendar of Events*, NTC/Contemporary Publishing Co.

Since the last bibliography of professional reading was published here nearly a decade ago, the library profession has undergone radical changes. Topics scarcely found on earlier lists dominate this one: CD-ROM, online, and other electronic tools; fund-raising; customer service; the Internet; document delivery and resource sharing; the "electronic library." Most of the books on this list have been published since 1990; a few titles from the 1980s are retained because of their continuing importance.

General Works

Alternative Library Literature, 1994/1995: A Biennial Anthology. Ed. by Sanford Berman and James P. Danky. McFarland, 1996. Paper $35.

American Library Directory, 1997–98. 2v. Bowker, 1997. $259.95. Also available online as file number 460 on Knight-Ridder's DIALOG and on CD-ROM as *Publishing Market Place Reference PLUS* (see below).

The Bowker Annual Library and Book Trade Almanac, 1997. Bowker, 1997. $175.

CALL: Current Awareness—Library Literature. Goldstein Associates. Monthly. $25.

Concise Dictionary of Library and Information Science. By Stella Keenan. Bowker-Saur, 1996. $50.

Dictionary of Bibliometrics. By Virgil Diodato. Haworth Press, 1995. $34.95.

Directory of Library and Information Science Professionals. 2v. Gale, 1988. $365.

Encyclopedia of Library and Information Science. 59v. to date. Marcel Dekker, 1968–. $115/v.

The International Encyclopedia of Information and Library Science. Ed. by John Feather and Paul Sturges. Routledge, 1997. $130.

The Librarian's Companion: A Handbook of Thousands of Facts on Libraries/Librarians, Books/Newspapers, Publishers/Booksellers. 2d ed. By Vladimir F. Wertsman. Greenwood Press, 1996. $65.

Librarians' Thesaurus: A Concise Guide to Library and Information Terms. By Mary Ellen Soper and others. American Library Association, 1990. Paper $25.

Library Literature. H. W. Wilson, 1921. Also available online and on CD-ROM, 1984–. Indexes periodicals in librarianship.

Library Reference Center. http://www.epnet.com. Indexes 30 periodicals in librarianship for the past five years.

Library Technology Reports. American Library Association, 1965–. Bi-monthly. $215.

Publishing Market Place Reference PLUS. CD-ROM. Bowker, annual. $895. Formerly titled *Library Reference PLUS*. Contains several Bowker titles, including *American Library Directory* and *Literary Market Place*.

The Whole Library Handbook: Current Data, Professional Advice, and Curiosa about

Libraries and Library Services. 2d ed. Comp. by George Eberhart. American Library Association, 1995. Paper $30.

World Encyclopedia of Library and Information Services. 3d ed. Ed. by Robert Wedgeworth. American Library Association, 1993. $200.

Academic Libraries

ACRL University Library Statistics, 1994–1995. Association of College and Research Libraries/American Library Association, 1996. $79.95.

ARL Statistics. Association of Research Libraries. Annual. 1964–. $65.

Academic Libraries: The Dimensions of Their Effectiveness. By Joseph A. McDonald and Lynda Basney Micikas. Greenwood Press, 1994. $52.95.

Academic Libraries: Their Rationale and Role in American Higher Education. Ed. by Gerard B. McCabe and Ruth J. Person. Greenwood Press, 1995. $55.

Administering the Community College Learning Resources Program. By Wanda K. Johnston. G. K. Hall, 1994. $38.50.

The Challenge and Practice of Academic Accreditation: A Sourcebook for Library Administrators. Ed. by Edward G. Garten. Greenwood Press, 1995. $65.

CLIP (College Library Information Packet) *Notes.* Association of College and Research Libraries/American Library Association, 1980–. Most recent volume is No. 24, 1996. $31.95.

Community College Libraries: Centers for Lifelong Learning. Ed. by Rosanne Kalick. Scarecrow, 1992. $27.50.

Electronic Services in Academic Libraries. Ed. by Mary Jo Lynch. American Library Association, 1996. Paper $6. A statistical survey.

Measuring Academic Library Performance: A Practical Approach. By Nancy Van House, Beth Weil, and Charles McClure. American Library Association, 1990. Paper $36. Accompanying diskette with data collection and analysis forms. $60.

Planning in the University Library. By Stanton F. Biddle. Greenwood Press, 1992. $49.95.

Preparing for Accreditation: A Handbook for Academic Librarians. By Patricia Ann Sacks and Sara Lou Whildin. American Library Association, 1993. Paper $18.

SPEC Kits. Association of Research Libraries. 1973–. 10/yr. $280.

The State and the Academic Library. Ed. by Vicki L. Gregory. Greenwood Press, 1993. $55.

Tenure and Promotion for Academic Librarians: A Guidebook with Advice and Vignettes. By Carol W. Cubberly. McFarland, 1996. $32.50.

Administration and Personnel

Avoiding Liability Risk: An Attorney's Advice to Library Trustees and Others. By Renee Rubin. American Library Association, 1994. Paper $10.

Budgeting and the Political Process in Libraries: Simulation Games. By Peter Hamon and others. Libraries Unlimited, 1992. Paper $20.

Budgeting for Information Access: Resource Management for Connected Libraries. By Murray Martin and Milton Wolf. American Library Association, 1996. Paper $30.

Creating a Financial Plan: A How-to-Do-It Manual for Librarians. By Betty J. Turock and Andrea Pedolsky. Neal-Schuman, 1992. Paper $42.50.

Keeping the Books: Public Library Financial Practices. Ed. by Jane B. Robbins and Douglas L. Zweizig. Highsmith Press, 1992. $39.

Library and Information Center Management. 4th ed. By Robert D. Stueart and Barbara B. Moran. Libraries Unlimited, 1993. Cloth $50; paper $35.

Library Personnel Administration. By Lowell Martin. Scarecrow, 1995. $29.50.

Managing Student Library Employees PLUS: A Workshop for Supervisors. By Michael and Jane Kathman. Library Solutions Press, 1995. Paper $45. An accompanying diskette contains presentation slides.

Multiculturalism in Libraries. By Rosemary Ruhig DuMont, Lois Buttlar, and William Caynon. Greenwood Press, 1994. $55. Discusses the recruitment of a diverse staff and education for multicultural librarianship.

Performance Analysis and Appraisal: A How-to-Do-It Manual for Librarians. By Robert D. Stueart and Maureen Sullivan. Neal-Schuman, 1991. Paper $42.50.
The Personnel Manual: An Outline for Libraries. Rev. ed. Ed. by Valerie Anna Platz and Charles E. Kratz. American Library Association, 1993. Paper $18.
Practical Help for New Supervisors. 3d ed. Ed. by Joan Giesecke. American Library Association, 1997. Paper $22.
Successful Staff Development: A How-to-Do-It Manual. By Marcia Trotta. Neal-Schuman, 1995. Paper $39.95.
Total Quality Management in Libraries: A Sourcebook. Ed. by Rosanna M. O'Neil. Libraries Unlimited, 1994. $25.
Using Consultants in Libraries and Information Centers: A Management Handbook. Ed. by Edward D. Garten. Greenwood Press, 1992. $55.

Bibliographic Instruction

Evaluating Library Instruction: Sample Questions, Forms, and Strategies for Practical Use. Ed. by Diana Shonrock. American Library Association, 1995. Paper $32.
Information for a New Age: Redefining the Librarian. Libraries Unlimited, 1995. Paper $26.50. Papers from a program in honor of ALA's Library Instruction Round Table.
Teaching Library Skills in Grades K through 6: A How-to-Do-It Manual. By Catharyn Roach and JoAnne Moore. Neal-Schuman, 1993. Paper $35.
Teaching Library Skills in Middle and High School: A How-to-Do-It Manual. By Linda J. Garrett and JoAnne Moore. Neal-Schuman, 1993. Paper $35.
Teaching the New Library: A How-to-Do-It Manual. By Michael Blake and others from the Electronic Teaching Center for the Harvard College Libraries. Neal-Schuman, 1996. Paper $39.95.
The Upside of Downsizing: Using Library Instruction to Cope. By Cheryl LaGuardia. Neal-Schuman, 1995. Paper $39.95.

Cataloging and Classification

A Beginner's Guide to Copy Cataloging on OCLC/PRISM. By Lois Massengale Schultz. Libraries Unlimited, 1995. $35.
Cooperative Cataloging: Past, Present and Future. Haworth, 1994. $49.95.
Immroth's Guide to the Library of Congress Classification. 4th ed. By Lois Mai Chan. Libraries Unlimited, 1990. $32.50.
Introduction to Cataloging and Classification. 6th ed. By Mildred Harlow Downing and David H. Downing. McFarland, 1992. $36.50.
Introduction to Cataloging and Classification. 8th ed. By Arlene G. Taylor. Libraries Unlimited, 1991. Cloth $47.50; paper $37.50.
Library of Congress Subject Headings: Principles and Application. 3d ed. By Lois Mai Chan. Libraries Unlimited, 1995. $35.
MARC Manual: Understanding and Using MARC Records. By Deborah J. Byrne. Libraries Unlimited, 1991. Paper $29.50.
Standard Cataloging for School and Public Libraries. 2d ed. By Sheila S. Intner and Jean Weihs. Libraries Unlimited, 1996. $32.50.
SUPERLCSS on CD-ROM. Gale, 1996. $3,200. The text of the Library of Congress classification schedules integrated with all changes through December 1994.

CD-ROM

CD-ROM for Library Users: A Guide to Managing and Maintaining User Access. Ed. by Pat Ensor and Paul Nicholls. Information Today, 1995. $39.50.
The CD-ROM Primer: The ABCs of CD-ROM. By Cheryl LaGuardia. Neal-Schuman, 1994. Paper $45.
CD-ROM Software, Dataware, and Hardware: Evaluation, Selection, and Installation. By Peter Jacso. Libraries Unlimited, 1991. $35.
Networking CD-ROMs: The Decision Maker's Guide to Local Area Network Solutions. By Ahmed M. Elshami. American Library Association, 1996. Paper $50.

Children's and Young Adult Services and Materials

African-American Voices in Young Adult Literature: Tradition, Transition, Transformation. By Karen Patricia Smith. Scarecrow, 1994. $45.

Against Borders: Promoting Books for a Multicultural World. By Hazel Rochman. Booklist/American Library Association, 1993. Paper $25.

The Center for the Study of Books in Spanish for Children and Adolescents at California State University, San Marcos Web site: http://www.csusm.edu/campus_centers/csb. Lists recommended books in Spanish for youth published worldwide.

Connecting Young Adults and Libraries: A How-to-Do-It Manual. By Patrick Jones. Neal-Schuman, 1992. Paper $42.50.

The Frugal Youth Cybrarian: Bargain Computing for Kids. By Calvin Ross. American Library Association, 1997. Paper $28.

Inviting Children's Authors and Illustrators: A How-to-Do-It Manual for School and Public Librarians. By Kathy East. Neal-Schuman, 1995. Paper $32.50.

Managing Children's Services in the Public Library. By Adele M. Fasick. Libraries Unlimited, 1991. $25.

Output Measures and More: Planning and Evaluating Public Library Services for Young Adults. By Virginia A. Walter. American Library Association, 1995. Paper $28.

Output Measures for Public Library Service to Children: A Manual of Standardized Procedures. By Virginia A. Walter. American Library Association, 1992. Paper $25.

Youth Services Librarians as Managers: A How-to Guide from Budgeting to Personnel. Comp. by Kathleen Staerkel, Mary Fellows, and Sue McCleaf. American Library Association, 1995. Paper $30.

Collection Development

Collection Development & Finance: A Guide to Strategic Library-Materials Budgeting. By Murray S. Martin. American Library Association, 1995. Paper $30.

Cooperative Collection Management: The Conspectus Approach. Ed. by Georgine N. Olson and Barbara Allen. Neal-Schuman, 1994. Paper $29.95.

Developing Library and Information Center Collections. 3d ed. By G. Edward Evans. Libraries Unlimited, 1995. Cloth $65; paper $42.

Guide for Training Collection Development Librarians. Ed. by Susan Fales. American Library Association, 1996. Paper $15.

Guide to Cooperative Collection Development. Ed. by Bart Harloe. American Library Association, 1994. Paper $15.

Guides for Written Collection Policy Statements. 2d ed. Ed. by Joanne S. Anderson. American Library Association, 1996. Paper $15.

Recruiting, Educating, and Training Librarians for Collection Development. Ed. by Peggy Johnson and Sheila S. Intner. Greenwood Press, 1994. $55.

Selection and Evaluation of Electronic Resources. By Gail K. Dickinson. Libraries Unlimited, 1994. $21.

Copyright

The Copyright Primer for Librarians and Educators. 2d ed. By Janis H. Bruwelheide. American Library Association, 1995. Paper $25.

Does Your Project Have a Copyright Problem? A Decision-Making Guide for Librarians. By Mary Brandt-Jensen. McFarland, 1996. Paper $25.

Libraries and Copyright: A Guide to Copyright Law in the Nineties. By Laura N. Gasaway and Sarah K. Wiant. Special Libraries Association, 1994. Paper $50.

Customer Service

Customer Service: A How-to-Do-It Manual for Librarians. By Suzanne Walters. Neal-Schuman, 1994. Paper $39.95.

Customer Service and Innovation in Libraries. By Glenn Miller. Highsmith Press, 1996. Paper $12.

Customer Service Excellence: A Concise Guide for Librarians. By Darlene E.

Weingand. American Library Association, 1997. Paper $27.
Serving the Difficult Customer: A How-to-Do-It Manual for Library Staff. By Kitty Smith. Neal-Schuman, 1994. Paper $39.95.

Education for Librarianship

The Closing of American Library Schools: Problems and Opportunities. By Larry J. Ostler, Therrin C. Dahlin, and J. D. Willardson. Greenwood Press, 1995. $49.95.
Education for the Library/Information Profession: Strategies for the Mid-1990s. Ed. by Patricia Reeling. McFarland, 1993. Paper $18.95.

The Electronic Library

"Books, Bricks and Bytes." *Daedalus,* vol. 125, no. 4, Fall, 1996. $7.95. Prominent librarians write about the future of the library in this issue of *Daedalus* totally devoted to the topic.
Buildings, Books, and Bytes: Libraries and Communities in the Digital Age. The Benton Foundation, 1996. http://www.benton.org. Interviews with the public about their views of libraries show that they have trouble figuring out where libraries fit in the new digital world.
Future Libraries: Dreams, Madness, and Reality. By Walt Crawford and Michael Gorman. American Library Association, 1995. Paper $25. Deflates the overblown "virtual" library concept.
A Nation of Opportunity: Realizing the Promise of the Information Superhighway. By the National Information Infrastructure Advisory Council. The Benton Foundation, 1996. http://www.benton.org/KickStart
The National Electronic Library: A Guide to the Future for Library Managers. Ed. by Gary M. Pitkin. Greenwood Press, 1996. $55.
Scholarly Journals at the Crossroads: A Subversive Proposal for Electronic Publishing. Ed. by Ann Okerson and James J. O'Donnell. Association of Research Libraries, 1995. Paper $20.

"State of the State Reports: Statewide Library Automation, Connectivity, and Resource Access Initiatives." *Library Hi-Tech,* vol. 14, numbers 2–3, 1996. $44. Reports from 46 states.

Evaluation of Library Services

Brief Tests of Collection Strength: A Methodology for All Types of Libraries. By Howard D. White. Greenwood Press, 1995. $55.
The TELL IT! Manual: The Complete Program for Evaluating Library Performance. By Douglas Zweizig, Debra Wilcox Johnson, and Jane Robbins. American Library Association, 1996. Paper $30.

Fund-Raising

Becoming a Fundraiser: The Principles and Practice of Library Development. By Victoria Steele and Stephen D. Elder. American Library Association, 1992. Paper $27.
The Big Book of Library Grant Money 1996–1997: Profiles of Private and Corporate Foundations and Direct Corporate Givers Receptive to Library Grant Proposals. By the Taft Group. American Library Association, 1996. Paper $225. Also available on CD-ROM as *The Searchable Big Book of Library Grant Money.* American Library Association, 1997. DOS $450.
Friends of Libraries Sourcebook. 3rd ed. Ed. by Sandy Dolnick. American Library Association, 1996. Paper $32.
Getting Your Grant: A How-to-Do-It Manual for Librarians. By Peggy Barber and Linda Crowe. Neal-Schuman, 1992. Paper $45.
Library Fundraising: Models for Success. Ed. by Dwight Burlingame. American Library Association, 1995. Paper $25.
Organizing Friends Groups: A How-to-Do-It Manual for Librarians. By Mark Y. Herring. Neal-Schuman, 1992. Paper $39.95.

Government Documents

Introduction to United States Government Information Sources. 5th ed. By Joe More-

head. Libraries Unlimited, 1996. Cloth $55; paper $40.
Management of Government Information Resources in Libraries. Ed. by Diane H. Smith. Libraries Unlimited, 1993. $40.
Subject Guide to U.S. Government Reference Sources. 2d ed. By Gayle J. Hardy and Judith Schiek Robinson. Libraries Unlimited, 1996. $45.

Intellectual Freedom

Banned Books Resource Guide. Office for Intellectual Freedom/American Library Association, 1997. Paper $20.
Banned in the U.S.A.: A Reference Guide to Book Censorship in Schools and Public Libraries. By Herbert N. Foerstel. Greenwood Press, 1994. $45.
Censorship of Expression in the 1980s: A Statistical Survey. By John B. Harer and Steven R. Harris. Greenwood Press, 1995. $49.95.
Hit List: Frequently Challenged Books for Young Adults. American Library Association, 1996. $22.
Hit List: Frequently Challenged Books for Children. By Donna Reidy Pistolis. American Library Association, 1996. $22.
Intellectual Freedom Manual. 5th ed. ALA Office for Intellectual Freedom. American Library Association, 1996. Paper $35.
Protecting the Right to Read: A How-to-Do-It Manual for School and Public Librarians. By Ann K. Symons and Charles Harmon. Neal-Schuman, 1995. Paper $39.95.

Interlibrary Loan, Document Delivery, and Resource Sharing

Document Delivery Services: Issues and Answers. By Eleanor Mitchell and Sheila Walters. Information Today, 1995. $42.50.
The Economics of Access versus Ownership. Ed. by Bruce R. Kingma. Haworth Press, 1996. $19.95.
The Future of Resource Sharing. Ed. by Shirley K. Baker and Mary E. Jackson. Haworth Press, 1995. $34.95.

Interlibrary Loan: Theory and Management. By Lois C. Gilmer. Libraries Unlimited, 1994. $37.50.
Interlibrary Loan Policies Directory. 5th ed. Ed. by Leslie R. Morris. Neal-Schuman, 1995. Paper $119.95.
Interlibrary Loan Practices Handbook. 2d ed. By Virginia Boucher. American Library Association, 1996. Paper $45.

The Internet

Building the Service-Based Web Site: A Step-by-Step Guide to Design and Options. By Kristen L. Garlock and Sherry Piontek. American Library Association, 1996. Paper $25.
The Cybrarian's Manual. Ed. by Pat Ensor. American Library Association, 1997. Paper $42. Excerpts from this book are on the Web at http://www.ala.org/editions/cyberlib.net.
Internet Access Cookbook: A Librarian's Commonsense Guide to Low-Cost Connections. By Karen G. Schneider. Neal-Schuman, 1996. Paper $24.95.
Internet Costs and Cost Models for Public Libraries. By Charles R. McClure, John Carlo Bertot, and John C. Beachboard. National Commission on Libraries and Information Science, 1995. Free.
The Internet Initiative: Libraries Providing Internet Services and How They Pay, Plan, and Manage. Edward R. Valauskas and Nancy R. John. American Library Association, 1995. Paper $27.
The Internet Resource Directory for K–12 Teachers and Librarians, 96/97 Edition. By Elizabeth B. Miller. Libraries Unlimited, 1996. $25.
The Internet Troubleshooter: Help for the Logged-On and Lost. By Nancy R. John and Edward J. Valauskas. American Library Association, 1994. Spiral $27.
Libraries and the Internet/NREN: Perspectives, Issues, and Challenges. By Charles R. McClure, Bill Moen, and Joe Ryan. Mecklermedia, 1994. Paper $35.
The 1996 National Survey of Public Libraries and the Internet: Progress and Issues. By John Carlo Bertot, Charles R. McClure, and Douglas L. Zweizig. Governmen

Printing Office, 1996. $7. A statistical report issued by the National Commission on Libraries and Information Science.
Using the World Wide Web and Creating Home Pages: A How-to-Do-It Manual for Librarians. By Ray E. Metz and Gail Junion-Metz. Neal-Schuman, 1996. Paper $49.95.

Librarians and Librarianship

The Age Demographics of Academic Libraries: A Profession Apart. By Stanley J. Wilder. Association of Research Libraries, 1996. Paper $30. Shows that 32 percent of librarians in large university libraries will retire by 2005.
The ALA Survey of Librarian Salaries 1996. Ed. by Mary Jo Lynch. American Library Association, 1996. Paper $50.
ARL Annual Salary Survey, 1995–96. Association of Research Libraries, 1995. Paper $65.
The Black Librarian in America Revisited. Scarecrow, 1994. $42.50.
Discovering Librarians: Profiles of a Profession. Ed. by Mary Jane Scherdin. Association of College & Research Libraries/ American Library Association, 1995. Paper $35.95.
The Manley Art of Librarianship. By Will Manley. McFarland, 1993. $23.95. Other humorous books by Manley include *The Truth About Reference Librarians* and *The Truth About Catalogers.*
Professional Ethics in Librarianship: A Real Life Casebook. By Fay Zipkowitz. McFarland, 1996. $29.50.

Library Automation

Advances in Library Automation and Networking. Annual. JAI Press. $73.25.
Automating Small Libraries. By James Swan. Highsmith Press, 1996. Paper $15.
Automation for School Libraries: How to Do It from Those Who Have Done It. By Teresa Thurman Day, Bruce Flanders, and Gregory Zuck. American Library Association, 1994. Paper $22.

Directory of Library Automation Software, Systems, and Services. Comp. by Pamela Cibbarelli. Information Today, 1996. Paper $79. Published biannially.
From A to Z39.50: A Networking Primer. Ed. by James J. Michael and Mark Hinnebusch. Mecklermedia, 1995. Paper $35.
Implementing an Automated Circulation System: A How-to-Do-It Manual. By Kathleen G. Fouty. Neal-Schuman, 1994. Paper $39.95.
Insider's Guide to Library Automation: Essays of Practical Experience. Ed. by John W. Head and Gerard B. McCabe. Greenwood Press, 1993. $55.
Integrated Library Systems for PCs & PC Networks. By Marshall Breeding. Information Today, 1996. $42.50.
Introducing and Managing Library Automation Projects. Ed. by John W. Head and Gerard B. McCabe. Greenwood Press, 1996. $59.95.
Introduction to Automation for Librarians. 3d ed. By William Saffady. American Library Association, 1994. $49.

Library Buildings and Space Planning

Academic Libraries as High-Tech Gateways: A Guide to Design and Space Decisions. By Richard J. Bazillion and Connie Braun. American Library Association, 1995. Paper $40.
Administrators' Guide to Library Building Maintenance. By Dianne Lueder and Sally Webb. American Library Association, 1992. Paper $45.
Designing and Renovating School Library Media Centers. By Jane P. Klasing. American Library Association, 1991. Paper $25.
Determining Your Public Library's Future Size: A Needs Assessment and Planning Model. By Lee B. Brawner and Donald K. Beck, Jr. American Library Association, 1996. $30.
Financing Public Library Buildings. By Richard B. Hall. Neal-Schuman, 1994. Paper $55.

Library Building Projects: Tips for Survival. By Susan B. Hagloch. Libraries Unlimited, 1994. $27.50.

Library Buildings, Equipment, and the ADA: Compliance Issues and Solutions. By Susan E. Cirilolo and Robert E. Danford. American Library Association, 1996. Paper $25.

Planning Additions to Academic Libraries: A Seamless Approach. Ed. by Pat Hawthorne and Ron G. Martin. American Library Association, 1995. Spiral $25.

Planning Library Interiors: The Selection of Furnishings for the 21st Century. By Carol Brown. Oryx Press, 1995. Paper $29.95.

Library History

Censorship and the American Library: The American Library Association's Response to Threats to Intellectual Freedom, 1939–1969. By Louise Robbins. Greenwood Press, 1996. $59.95.

History of Libraries in the Western World. 4th ed. By Michael H. Harris. Scarecrow, 1995. $39.50.

Irrepressible Reformer: A Biography of Melvil Dewey. By Wayne A. Wiegand. American Library Association, 1996. Paper $35.

Louis Shores: Defining Educational Librarianship. By Lee Shiflett. Scarecrow, 1996. $36.

The Nation's Great Library: Herbert Putnam and the Library of Congress, 1899–1939. By Jane A. Rosenberg. University of Illinois Press, 1993. $39.95.

Zoia! Memoirs of Zoia Horn, Battler for the People's Right to Know. By Zoia Horn. McFarland, 1995. $25.

Nonprint Materials

Audio Book Breakthrough: A Guide to Selection and Use in Public Libraries and Education. By Preston Hoffman and Carol H. Osteyee. Greenwood Press, 1993. $39.95.

Developing and Managing Video Collections: A How-to-Do-It Manual for Public Libraries. By Sally Mason-Robinson. Neal-Schuman, 1996. Paper $39.95.

A Library Manager's Guide to the Physical Processing of Nonprint Materials. By Karen C. Driessen and Sheila A. Smyth. Greenwood Press, 1995. $59.95.

Video Acquisitions and Cataloging: A Handbook. By James C. Scholtz. Greenwood Press, 1995. $55.

Video Collection Development in Multi-Type Libraries: A Handbook. Ed. by Gary P. Handman. Greenwood Press, 1994. $75.

Online Searching

Cases in Online Search Strategy. By Bruce A. Shuman. Libraries Unlimited, 1993. $30.

The Online Deskbook. By Mary Ellen Bates. Pemberton Press, 1996. Paper $29.95.

Online Retrieval: A Dialogue of Theory and Practice. By Geraldene Walker and Joseph Janes. Libraries Unlimited, 1993. $35.

Secrets of the Super Net Searchers. By Reva Basch. Pemberton Press, 1996. Paper $29.95.

Secrets of the Super Searchers. By Reva Basch. Pemberton Press, 1993. Paper $39.95.

Preservation

Advances in Preservation and Access. v.2. Ed. by Barbra Buckner Higginbotham. Information Today, 1995. $49.50.

Book Repair: A How-to-Do-It Manual for Librarians. By Kenneth Lavender and Scott Stockton. Neal-Schuman, 1992. Paper $39.95.

Digital Imaging Technology for Preservation. Ed. by Nancy E. Elkington. Research Libraries Group, 1995. Paper $20.

New Tools for Preservation: Assessing Long-Term Environmental Effects on Library and Archives Conditions. By James M. Reilly, Douglas W. Nishimura, and Edward Zinn. Commission on Preservation and Access, 1996. Paper $10.

Managing Preservation: A Guidebook. The State Library of Ohio, 1995. Free.

Preservation Microfilming: A Guide for Librarians and Archivists. 2d ed. By Lisa

L. Fox. American Library Association, 1996. $70.
Preserving Digital Information. By Donald Waters and John Garrett. Commission on Preservation and Access, 1996. Paper $15.

Public Libraries

Achieving School Readiness: Public Libraries and National Education Goal 1. Ed. by Barbara Froling Immroth and Viki Ash-Geisler. American Library Association, 1995. $30.
Administration of the Small Public Library. 3d ed. By Darlene E. Weingand. American Library Association, 1992. Paper $30.
Collecting and Using Public Library Statistics. By Mark L. Smith. Neal-Schuman, 1996. Paper $39.95.
Innovation and the Library: The Adoption of New Ideas in Public Libraries. By Verna L. Pungitore. Greenwood Press, 1995. $49.95.
The Library Trustee: A Practical Guidebook. 5th ed. By Virginia G. Young. American Library Association, 1995. $37.
Long-Range Planning: A How-to-Do-It Manual for Public Libraries. By Suzanne W. Bremer. Neal-Schuman, 1994. Paper $39.95
Managing Today's Public Library: Blueprint for Change. By Darlene E. Weingand. Libraries Unlimited, 1994. $30.
Output Measures for Public Libraries: A Manual of Standardized Procedures. 2d ed. By Nancy A. Van House and others. American Library Association, 1987. Paper $25
Public Libraries, Communities, and Technology: Twelve Case Studies. Council on Library Resources, 1996. Paper $15
Public Library Data Service Statistical Report. Public Library Association/ALA, 1996. Paper $75.
The Public Library Effectiveness Study: The Complete Report. By Nancy A. Van House and Thomas A. Childers. American Library Association, 1993. Paper $25.
Public Library Planning: Case Studies for Management. By Brett Sutton. Greenwood Press, 1995. $65.

Research Issues in Public Librarianship: Trends for the Future. Ed. by Joy M. Greiner. Greenwood Press, 1994. $59.95.
The Responsive Public Library: How to Develop and Market It. By Sharon L. Baker. Libraries Unlimited, 1993. $45.
Selecting a Library Director: Workbook for Members of a Selection Committee. By Jack Cole and Suzanne Mahmoodi. Friends of the Minnesota Office of Library Development and Services, 1996. Paper $17.
Strategic Management for Public Libraries: A Handbook. By Robert M. Hayes and Virginia A. Walter. Greenwood Press, 1996. $59.
What's Good? Describing Your Public Library's Effectiveness. By Thomas A. Childers and Nancy A. Van House. American Library Association, 1993. Paper $25.
Why Adults Use the Public Library: A Research Perspective. By Maurice P. Marchant. Libraries Unlimited, 1994. Paper $24.
Winning Library Referenda Campaigns: A How-to-Do-It Manual. By Richard B. Hall. Neal-Schuman, 1995. Paper $39.95.

Public Services

Circulation Services in a Small Academic Library. By Connie Battaile. Greenwood Press, 1992. $47.95.
Introduction to Library Public Services. 5th ed. By G. Edward Evans, Anthony J. Amodeo, and Thomas L. Carter. Libraries Unlimited, 1992. Cloth $47.50; paper $35.

Reference and Readers' Advisory

Automation in Library Reference Services: A Handbook. By Robert J. Carande. Greenwood, 1992. $55.
Developing Readers' Advisory Services: Concepts and Commitments. Ed. by Kathleen de la Peña and others. Neal-Schuman, 1993. Paper $29.95.
Introduction to Reference Work. 7th ed. 2v. By William A. Katz. McGraw-Hill, 1997. $57.75.

Knowledge-Based Systems for General Reference Work. By John V. Richardson. Academic Press, 1995. $49.95

Reference and Information Services: An Introduction. 2d ed. Ed. by Richard E. Bopp and Linda C. Smith. Libraries Unlimited, 1995. $35.

The Reference Assessment Manual. Comp. by the Evaluation of Reference & Adult Services Committee of RASD/ALA. Pierian Press, 1995. Paper $35. A disk with copies of assessment instruments is also available for $15.

Reference Services Planning in the 90s. Ed. by Gail Z. Eckwright and Lori M. Keenan. Haworth Press, 1995. $29.95.

Rethinking Reference in Academic Libraries. Ed. by Anne G. Lipow. Library Solutions Press, 1993. Paper $32.

School Libraries/Media Centers

Achieving a Curriculum-Based Library Media Center: The Middle School Model for Change. By Jane Bandy Smith. American Library Association, 1995. Paper $25.

Collection Analysis in the School Library Media Center: A Practical Approach. By Carol A. Doll and Pamela Petrick Barron. American Library Association, 1991. Paper $17.

The Collection Program in Schools: Concepts, Practices, and Information Sources. 2d ed. By Phyllis J. Van Orden. Libraries Unlimited, 1995. Cloth $42.50; paper $32.50.

Developing a Vision: Strategic Planning and the Library Media Specialist. By John D. Crowley. Greenwood Press, 1995. $35.

Helpful Hints for the School Library: Ideas for Organization, Time Management and Bulletin Boards. By Carol Smallwood. McFarland, 1993. Paper $22.95.

Helping Teachers Teach: A School Library Media Specialist's Role. 2d ed. By Philip M. Turner. Libraries Unlimited, 1993. Paper $26.50.

Ideas for Promoting Your School Library Media Center. Comp. by Ann Wasman. American Library Association, 1996. Looseleaf $30.

Information Power: Guidelines for School Library Media Programs. American Library Association, 1988. Paper $20.

The Impact of School Library Media Centers on Academic Achievement. By Keith Lance and others. Hi Willow, 1993. Paper $25.

POWER Teaching: A Primary Role of the School Library Media Specialist. By Kay E. Vandergrift. American Library Association, 1993. Paper $25.

Public School Library Media Centers in 12 States: Report of the NCLIS/ALA Survey. The National Commission on Library and Information Science, 1994. Free.

School Library Media Centers in the 21st Century. By Kathleen W. Craver. Greenwood Press, 1995. $35.

The School Library Media Manager. By Blanche Woolls. Libraries Unlimited, 1994. Cloth $38.50; paper $31.50.

School Library Reference Services in the '90s: Where We Are, Where We're Heading. Ed. by Carol Truett. Haworth Press, 1994. $39.95.

Serving Linguistically and Culturally Diverse Students: Strategies for the School Library Media Specialist. By Melvina A. Dame. Neal-Schuman, 1993. Paper $29.95.

The Virtual School Library: Gateways to the Information Superhighway. Ed. by Carol Collier Kuhlthau. Libraries Unlimited, 1996. Paper $24.

Serials

Buying Serials: A How-to-Do-It Manual for Librarians. By N. Bernard Basch and Judy McQueen. Neal-Schuman, 1991. Paper $42.50.

International Subscription Agents. 6th ed. By Lenore Rae Wilkas. American Library Association, 1993. Paper $35.

Serials Management: A Practical Guide. By Chiou-sen Dora Chen. American Library Association, 1995. Paper $35.

Services for Special Groups

Choosing and Using Books with Adult New Readers. By Marguerite Crowley Weibel. Neal-Schuman, 1996. Paper $29.95.

Disabilities, Children, and Libraries: Mainstreaming Services in Public Libraries and School Library Media Centers. By Linda Lucas Walling and Marilyn H. Karrenbrock. Libraries Unlimited, 1993. $35.

A Guide to Homeschooling for Librarians. By David C. Brostrom. Highsmith Press, 1995. Paper $15.

Information Services for People with Developmental Disabilities: The Library Manager's Handbook. Ed. by Linda Lucas Walling and Marilyn M. Irwin. Greenwood Press, 1995. $65.

Libraries Inside: A Practical Guide for Prison Librarians. Ed. by Rhea Joyce Rubin and Daniel Suvak. McFarland, 1995. $41.50.

Preparing Staff to Serve Patrons with Disabilities: A How-to-Do-It Manual for Librarians. By Courtney Deines-Jones and Connie Van Fleet. Neal-Schuman, 1995. Paper $39.95.

Serving Older Adults in Libraries: Strategies and Solutions. Ed. by Virginia H. Mathews. Neal-Schuman, 1996. Paper $29.95.

Serving Print Disabled Library Patrons: A Textbook. Ed. by Bruce Edward Massis. McFarland, 1996. $42.50.

Special Libraries

The Best of OPL II. Ed. by Andrew Berner and Guy St. Clair. Special Libraries Association, 1996. $43.50. An anthology of articles published 1989–1994 in The One-Person Library.

Internet Tools of the Profession: A Guide for Special Librarians. Ed. by Hope N. Tillman. Special Libraries Association, 1995. Paper $37.50.

Special Libraries in Action: Cases and Crises. By Esther Green Bierbaum. Libraries Unlimited, 1993. $25.

Technical Services

Guide to Technical Services Resources. Ed. by Peggy Johnson. American Library Association, 1994. $65.

Introduction to Technical Services. 6th ed. By G. Edward Evans and Sandra M. Heft. Libraries Unlimited, 1993. $30.

New Directions in Technical Services: Trends and Sources (1993–1995). Ed. by Peggy Johnson. American Library Association, 1997. Paper $35. Continues "Year's Work in Technical Services," which used to appear in Library Resources and Technical Services.

Outsourcing Library Technical Services: A How-to-Do-It Manual for Librarians. By Arnold Hirshon and Barbara Winters. Neal-Schuman, 1996. $49.95. (Sample RFPs are available on diskette for $20 via Outsourcing Technical Services: Ready-to-Import RFP Specifications Disk.)

Planning and Implementing Technical Services Workstations. Ed. by Michael Kaplan. American Library Association, 1996. Paper $30.

Technical Services in the Medium-Sized Library. By Sheila S. Intner and Josephine R. Fang. Shoe String, 1991. $35.

Volunteers

Library Volunteers—Worth the Effort! A Program Manager's Guide. By Sally Gardner Reed. McFarland, 1994. Paper $27.50.

Recruiting and Managing Volunteers in Libraries: A How-to-Do-It Manual for Librarians. By Bonnie F. McCune and Charleszine "Terry" Nelson. Neal-Schuman, 1995. Paper $39.95.

Periodicals and Periodical Indexes

Acquisitions Librarian
Advanced Technology Libraries
Against the Grain
American Libraries
American Society for Information Science Journal
Behavioral and Social Sciences Librarian
Book Links
Book Report: Journal for Junior and Senior High School Librarians
Booklist
The Bottom Line

Cataloging and Classification Quarterly
CD-ROM World
CHOICE
College and Research Libraries
Collection Management
Community and Junior College Libraries
Computers in Libraries
The Electronic Library: The International Journal for Minicomputer, Microcomputer and Software Applications in Libraries
Government Information Quarterly
Internet Reference Services Quarterly
Journal of Academic Librarianship
Journal of Information Ethics
Journal of Interlibrary Loan, Document Delivery and Information Supply
Journal of Library Administration
Journal of Youth Services in Libraries
Law Library Journal
Legal Reference Services Quarterly
Libraries & Culture
Library Administration and Management
Library and Information Science Research
Library Issues: Briefings for Faculty and Academic Administrators (also on the Web by subscription at http://www.netpubsintl.com/LI.html)
Library Hi-Tech
Library Journal
The Library Quarterly
Library Resources and Technical Services
Library Talk: The Magazine for Elementary School Librarians
Library Trends
Medical Reference Services Quarterly
MLS: Marketing Library Services
MultiCultural Review
MultiMedia Schools
Music Library Association Notes
Music Reference Services Quarterly
The One-Person Library
Online & CD-ROM Review
Online–Offline: Themes and Resources
Public and Access Services Quarterly
Public Libraries
Public Library Quarterly
Rare Books and Manuscripts Librarianship
Reference Librarian
Reference Services Review
Resource Sharing & Information Networks
RQ
Rural Libraries
School Library Journal
School Library Quarterly
Science & Technology Libraries
Serials Librarian
Serials Review
Searcher: The Magazine for Database Professionals
Special Libraries
Technical Services Quarterly
Technicalities
Video Librarian
VOYA

Ready Reference

Publishers' Toll-Free Telephone Numbers

Publishers' toll-free numbers continue to play an important role in ordering, verification, and customer service. This year's list comes from *Literary Market Place* (R. R. Bowker) and includes distributors and regional toll-free numbers, where applicable. The list is not comprehensive, and toll-free numbers are subject to change. Readers may want to call for toll-free directory assistance (800-555-1212).

Publisher/Distributor	Toll-Free No.
Abbeville Publishing Group, New York, NY	800-ART-BOOK
ABC-CLIO, Santa Barbara, CA	800-422-2546; 800-368-6868
Abdo & Daughters Publishing, Minneapolis, MN	800-458-8399
Aberdeen Group, Addison, IL	800-837-0870
Abingdon Press, Nashville, TN	800-251-3320
Harry N Abrams Inc., New York, NY	800-345-1359
Academic Press, San Diego, CA	(cust serv) 800-321-5068
Academic Therapy Publications, Novato, CA	800-422-7249
Academy Chicago Publishers, Chicago, IL	800-248-READ
Acres USA, Metairie, LA	800-355-5313
ACS Publications, San Diego, CA	(orders only) 800-888-9983
ACTA Publications, Chicago, IL	800-397-2282
Active Parenting Publishers Inc., Marietta, GA	800-825-0060
ACU Press, Abilene, TX	800-444-4228
Adams-Blake Publishing, Fair Oaks, CA	800-368-ADAM
Adams Media Corp., Holbrook, MA	800-872-5627
Addison-Wesley Longman Publishing Co., Reading, MA (orders only)	
	(school serv team) 800-552-2259
	(college serv team) 800-322-1377
	(college sales) 800-552-2499
	(trade & agency) 800-358-4566
	(corporate & professional) 800-822-6339
Adi, Gaia, Esalen Publications Inc., Los Angeles, CA	800-652-8574
	(order fulfillment) 800-263-1991
	(fax order fulfillment) 800-458-0025
Adventure Publications, Cambridge, MN	800-678-7006
Aegean Park Press, Laguna Hills, CA	800-736-3587
Aegis Publishing Group Ltd, Newport, RI	800-828-6961

540 / Ready Reference

Publisher/Distributor	Toll-Free No.
The AEI Press, Washington, DC	800-223-2336
African American Images, Chicago, IL	800-552-1991
Ages Publications, Thornhill, ON	(fulfillment) 800-263-1991
Aglow Communications, Edmonds, WA	800-755-2456
Agora Inc., Baltimore, MD	800-433-1528
Ahsahta Press, Boise, ID	800-992-TEXT
AIHA Publications of America (ALPHA Publications of America Inc.), Tucson, AZ	800-528-3494
Airmont Publishing Co. Inc., New York, NY	800-223-5251
Alamo Publishing Co., Pleasanton, CA	800-732-6066
Alba House, Staten Island, NY	800-343-ALBA
Alban Institute Inc., Bethesda, MD	800-436-1318
Alexander Books, Alexander, NC	800-472-0438
Alfred Publishing Co. Inc., Van Nuys, CA	800-292-6122
ALI-ABA Committee on Continuing Professional Education, Philadelphia, PA	800-CLE-NEWS
Allied Health Publications, National City, CA	800-221-7374
Allworth Communications Inc., New York, NY	800-247-6553
Allyn & Bacon (Simon & Schuster Higher Education Division), Needham Heights, MA	800-223-1360
AlphaBooks, Inc., Topanga, CA	800-957-3529
Alpine Publications Inc., Loveland, CO	(orders only) 800-777-7257
AMACOM Books, New York, NY	(orders) 800-538-4761
Frank Amato Publications Inc., Portland, OR	800-541-9498
Amber Press, South Burlington, VT	(voice & fax) 800-892-5484
Amboy Associates, San Diego, CA	800-448-4023
American Academy of Orthopaedic Surgeons, Rosemont, IL	800-626-6726
American Academy of Pediatrics, Elk Grove Village, IL	800-433-9016
American & World Geographic Publishing, Helena, MT	800-654-1105
American Association for Vocational Instructional Materials (AAVIM), Winterville, GA	800-228-4689
American Association of Cereal Chemists, St Paul, MN	800-328-7560
American Association of Community Colleges (AACC), Washington, DC	800-250-6557
American Association of Engineering Societies, Washington, DC	800-658-8897
American Bible Society, New York, NY	800-543-8000
American Brain Tumor Association, Des Plaines, IL	800-886-2282
American Business Directories, Omaha, NE	800-555-6124
American Chemical Society, Washington, DC	800-227-9919
American College of Physician Executives, Tampa, FL	800-562-8088
American Correctional Association, Lanham, MD	800-825-2665
American Counseling Association, Alexandria, VA	800-422-2648
American Diabetes Association, Alexandria, VA	800-232-3472
American Eagle Publications Inc., Show Low, AZ	800-719-4957
The American Federation of Arts, New York, NY	800-AFA-0270
American Foundation for the Blind, New York, NY	800-232-3044
American Geophysical Union, Washington, DC	800-966-2481

Publisher/Distributor	Toll-Free No.
American Guidance Service Inc., Circle Pines, MN	800-328-2560
American Health Publishing Co., Dallas, TX	800-736-7323
American Institute of Aeronautics & Astronautics, Reston, VA	800-639-2422
The American Institute of Architects Press, Washington, DC	(orders) 800-365-ARCH
American Institute of Certified Public Accountants, Jersey City, NJ	800-862-4272
American Institute of Chemical Engineers, New York, NY	800-242-4363
American Law Institute, Philadelphia, PA	800-CLE-NEWS
American Library Association (ALA), Chicago, IL	800-545-2433
American Map Corp., Maspeth, NY	800-432-MAPS
American Marketing Association, Chicago, IL	800-262-1150
American Mathematical Society, Providence, RI	800-321-4267
American Nurses Publishing, Washington, DC	800-637-0323
American Occupational Therapy Association Inc., Bethesda, MD	(TDD) 800-377-8555
American Phytopathological Society, St Paul, MN	800-328-7560
American Printing House for the Blind Inc., Louisville, KY	(cust serv) 800-223-1839
	(sales & marketing) 800-572-0844
American Psychiatric Press Inc., Washington, DC	800-368-5777
American Showcase Inc., New York, NY	800-894-7469
American Society for Nondestructive Testing, Columbus, OH	800-222-2768
American Society of Civil Engineers, New York, NY	800-548-2723;
	(NY) 628-0041
American Society of Mechanical Engineers (ASME), New York, NY	800-843-2763
American Technical Publishers Inc., Homewood, IL	800-323-3471
Amsco School Publications Inc., New York, NY	800-969-8398
The Analytic Press, Hillsdale, NJ	(orders only) 800-926-6579
Ancestry Inc., Salt Lake City, UT	800-531-1790
Anderson Publishing Co., Cincinnati, OH	800-582-7295
Andrews & McMeel, Kansas City, MO	800-826-4216
Andrews University Press, Berrien Springs, MI	(Visa & Mastercard) 800-467-6369
Angelus Press, Kansas City, MO	800-966-7337
Annabooks, San Diego, CA	800-462-1042
Annual Reviews Inc., Palo Alto, CA	800-523-8635
Another Language Press, Cincinnati, OH	800-733-2067
ANR Publications University of California, Oakland, CA	800-994-8849
Antique Collectors Club Ltd, Wappingers Falls, NY	800-252-5231
Antique Publications, Marietta, OH	800-533-3433
AOCS Press, Champaign, IL	800-336-AOCS
Aperture, New York, NY	800-929-2323
The Apex Press, New York, NY	800-316-2739
Appleton & Lange, Stamford, CT	800-423-1359
Aqua Quest Publications Inc., Locust Valley, NY	800-933-8989
A-R Editions Inc., Madison, WI	800-736-0070
Archival Services Inc., Shreveport, LA	800-484-8274, ext. 8900
Ardis Publishers, Dana Pt, CA	(orders) 800-877-7133
ARE Press, Virginia Beach, VA	800-723-1112
Ariel Press, Alpharetta, GA	800-336-7769

Publisher/Distributor	Toll-Free No.
Armenian Reference Books Co., Glendale, CA	800-587-2361
Jason Aronson Inc., Northvale, NJ	800-782-0015
Arrow Map Inc., Bridgewater, MA	800-343-7500
Artabras Inc., New York, NY	800-ART-BOOK
Arte Publico Press, Houston, TX	800-633-ARTE
Artech House Inc., Norwood, MA	800-225-9977
ASCP Press, Chicago, IL	800-621-4142
Ashgate Publishing Co., Brookfield, VT	800-535-9544
Aslan Publishing, Santa Rosa, CA	800-275-2606
ASM International, Materials Park, OH	800-336-5152
Aspen Publishers Inc., Gaithersburg, MD	(orders) 800-638-8437
Association for the Advancement of Medical Instrumentation, Arlington, VA	800-332-2264
Astor Books, New York, NY	800-762-2328
Astronomical Society of the Pacific, San Francisco, CA	(orders only) 800-335-2624
ATL Press, Shrewsbury, MA	800-835-7543
Augsburg Fortress Publishers Publishing House of the Evangelical Lutheran Church in America, Minneapolis, MN	800-328-4648
August House Publishers Inc., Little Rock, AR	800-284-8784
Austin & Winfield Publishers Inc., Bethesda, MD	800-99-AUSTIN
Ave Maria Press, Notre Dame, IN	800-282-1865
Avery Publishing Group Inc., Wayne, NJ	800-548-5757
Avon Books, New York, NY	800-238-0658
Back to the Bible, Lincoln, NE	800-759-2425
Baio & Co. USA Inc., Edison, NJ	800-568-2246
Baker Books, Grand Rapids, MI	800-877-2665
Ballantine/Del Rey/Fawcett/House of Collectibles/Ivy/One World, New York, NY	800-638-6460
Banks-Baldwin Law Publishing Co., Cleveland, OH	800-362-4500
Bantam Books, New York, NY	800-223-6834
Bantam Doubleday Dell Books for Young Readers, New York, NY	800-223-6834
Bantam Doubleday Dell Publishing Group Inc., New York, NY	800-223-6834
Baptist Spanish Publishing House, El Paso, TX	(cust serv & orders) 800-755-5958
Barbour & Co. Inc., Uhrichsville, OH	(orders) 800-852-8010
Barcelona Publishers, Gilsum, NH	800-345-6665
Barnes & Noble Books (Imports & Reprints), Lanham, MD	800-462-6420
Barney Publishing, Allen, TX	800-418-2371
Barron's Educational Series Inc., Hauppauge, NY	800-645-3476
Battelle Press, Columbus, OH	800-451-3543
Bawn Publishers Inc., Cincinnati, OH	800-761-8646
Bayhampton Publications, Marrietta, GA	800-360-7467
Baywood Publishing Co. Inc., Amityville, NY	800-638-7819
Beacham Publishing Inc., Osprey, FL	800-466-9644
Beacon Hill Press of Kansas City, Kansas City, MO	800-877-0700
Bear & Co. Inc., Santa Fe, NM	800-932-3277
Beautiful America Publishing Co., Wilsonville, OR	800-874-1233

Publisher/Distributor	Toll-Free No.
Peter Bedrick Books Inc., New York, NY	800-788-3123
Thomas T Beeler Publisher, Hampton Falls, NH	800-251-8726
Beginning Press, Seattle, WA	800-831-4088
Behavioral Sciences Research Press Inc., Dallas, TX	800-323-4659
Frederic C Beil Publisher Inc., Savannah, GA	800-829-8406
Bellerophon Books, Santa Barbara, CA	800-253-9943
R Bemis Publishing Ltd, Marietta, GA	800-497-6663
Matthew Bender & Co. Inc., New York, NY	800-422-2022
	(outside NY) 800-223-1940
Benjamin Co. Inc., White Plains, NY	800-735-2473
John Benjamins Publishing Co., Erdenheim, PA	800-562-5666
Robert Bentley Publishers, Cambridge, MA	800-423-4595
Benziger Publishing Co., Mission Hills, CA	800-423-9534
Berg Publishers, Herndon, VA	800-546-9326
Berkley Publishing Group, New York, NY	800-223-0510
Berkshire House Publishers, Lee, MA	800-321-8526
Berlitz Publishing Co. Inc., Princeton, NJ	800-923-7548
Bernan Associates, Lanham, MD	(US) 800-274-4447
Bess Press, Honolulu, HI	800-910-2377
Best Publishing Co., Flagstaff, AZ	800-468-1055
Bethany House Publishers, Minneapolis, MN	800-328-6109
Bethel Publishing Co., Elkhart, IN	800-348-7657
Bethlehem Books, Minto, ND	800-757-6831
Beverage Marketing Corp/, Mingo Junction, OH	800-332-6222
Beverly Publishing Co., Houston, TX	800-955-2665
Beyond Words Publishing Inc., Hillsboro, OR	800-284-9673
Bhaktivedanta Book Publishing Inc., Los Angeles, CA	800-927-4152
Biblical Archaeology Society, Washington, DC	800-221-4644
Biblo & Tannen Booksellers & Publishers Inc., Cheshire, CT	(voice & fax) 800-272-8778
Bicycle Books Inc., San Francisco, CA	800-468-8233
Birkhauser Boston, Cambridge, MA	800-777-4643
George T Bisel Co., Philadelphia, PA	800-247-3526
Bisk Publishing Co., Tampa, FL	800-874-7877
Black Belt Press, Montgomery, AL	800-959-3245
Black Diamond Book Publishing, Los Angeles, CA	800-444-2524
Blackbirch Press Inc., Woodbridge, CT	800-831-9183
John F Blair, Publisher, Winston-Salem, NC	800-222-9796
Bloomberg Press, Princeton, NJ	800-388-2749
Blue Dolphin Publishing Inc., Nevada City, CA	800-643-0765
Blue Dove Press, San Diego, CA	800-691-1008
Blue Moon Books Inc., New York, NY	800-535-0007
Blue Mountain Press Inc., Boulder, CO	800-525-0642
Blue Note Publications, Cape Canaveral, FL	800-624-0401
Blue Poppy Press Inc., Boulder, CO	800-487-9296
Bluestar Communication Corp., Woodside, CA	800-625-8378

Publisher/Distributor	Toll-Free No.
Bluestocking Press, Placerville, CA	800-959-8586
Blushing Rose Publishing, San Anselmo, CA	800-898-2263
BNA Books, Washington, DC	800-960-1220
Bob Jones University Press, Greenville, SC	800-845-5731
Bold Strummer Ltd, Westport, CT	800-375-3786
Bonus Books Inc., Chicago, IL	800-225-3775
Book Peddlers, Deephaven, MN	800-255-3379
Book Publishing Co., Summertown, TN	800-695-2241
Book Sales Inc., Edison, NJ	800-526-7257
Books Americana Inc., Florence, AL	800-726-9966
Books Beyond Borders LLC, Boulder, CO	800-347-6440
BookWorld Press Inc., Sarasota, FL	800-444-2524
Thomas Bouregy & Co. Inc., New York, NY	800-223-5251
R R Bowker, New Providence, NJ	(sales) 800-521-8110
R R Bowker Direct Sales Group, New Providence, NJ	800-521-8110, ext. 2830
Boyd & Fraser Publishing Co., Danvers, MA	800-225-3782
Boyds Mills Press, Honesdale, PA	800-949-7777
Boynton/Cook Publishers Inc., Portsmouth, NH	(orders) 800-541-2086
Boys Town Press, Boys Town, NE	800-282-6657
Branden Publishing Co. Inc., Brookline Village, MA (Visa & Mastercard only)	800-537-7335
Breakthrough Publications, Ossining, NY	800-824-5000
Brethren Press, Elgin, IL	800-323-8039
Brick House Publishing Co., Amherst, NH	(orders only) 800-446-8642
Bridge Learning Systems Inc., American Canyon, CA	800-487-9868
Bridge Publications Inc., Los Angeles, CA	800-722-1733
	(CA) 800-843-7389
E J Brill USA Inc., Kinderhook, NY	800-962-4406
Bristol Publishing Enterprises Inc., San Leandro, CA	800-346-4889
Broadman & Holman Publishers, Nashville, TN	800-251-3225
Broadway Books, New York, NY	800-290-2929
Broadway Press, Shelter Island, NY	800-869-6372
Paul H Brookes Publishing Co., Baltimore, MD	800-638-3775
The Brookings Institution, Washington, DC	800-275-1447
Brookline Books Inc., Cambridge, MA	800-666-2665
Brooks/Cole Publishing Co., Pacific Grove, CA	800-354-9706
Brown & Benchmark Publishers (Times Mirror), Madison, WI	800-527-8198
Brunner/Mazel Inc., New York, NY	800-825-3089
Stephen Bruno Publishing Inc., Redmond, WA	800-881-4008
Building News, Needham, MA	800-873-6397
Bull Publishing Co., Palo Alto, CA	800-676-2855
Burrelle's Information Services, Livingston, NJ	800-876-3342
Business & Legal Reports Inc., Madison, CT	800-727-5257
Business Research Services Inc., Washington, DC	800-845-8420
Butterworth-Heinemann, Newton, MA	(orders & cust serv) 800-366-2665
C & T Publishing, Lafayette, CA	800-284-1114

Publisher/Distributor	Toll-Free No.
Cambridge Educational, Charleston, WV	800-468-4227
Cambridge University Press, New York, NY	800-221-4512
Camden House Inc., Columbia, SC	(orders only) 800-723-9455
Cameron & Co., San Francisco, CA	800-779-5582
Career Press Inc., Franklin Lakes, NJ	800-CAREER-1
Career Publishing Inc., Orange, CA	800-854-4014
William Carey Library, Pasadena, CA	800-647-7466
Carlson Publishing Inc., Brooklyn, NY	800-336-7460
Carlton Press Inc., New York, NY	800-BOOKS-08 (266-5708)
Carolrhoda Books Inc.	800-328-4929
Carroll Press, New York, NY	800-366-7086
CarTech Inc., North Branch, MN	800-551-4754
CAS, Columbus, OH	800-848-6538
Castle Books Inc., Edison, NJ	(orders) 800-526-7257
Catbird Press, North Haven, CT	800-360-2391
Catholic News Publishing Co. Inc., New Rochelle, NY	800-433-7771
Caxton Printers Ltd, Caldwell, ID	800-657-6465
CCH Inc., Riverwoods, IL	800-835-5224
Cedar Fort Inc./C F T Distribution, Springville, UT	800-759-2665
CEDCO Publishing Co., San Rafael, CA	800-227-6162
CEF Press, Warrenton, MO	800-748-7710
Celestial Arts, Berkeley, CA	800-841-BOOK
Central Conference of American Rabbis/CCAR Press, New York, NY	800-935-CCAR
Chadwyck-Healey Inc., Alexandria, VA	800-752-0515
Chalice Press, St Louis, MO	800-366-3383
Richard Chang Associates Inc., Irvine, CA	800-756-8096
Chapman & Hall Inc., New York, NY	(cust serv) 800-842-3636
Chariot Publishing, Inc., Montrose, PA	800-628-8244
Chariot Victor Publishing, Colorado Springs, CO	800-437-4337
CharismaLife Publishers, Lake Mary, FL	800-451-4598
Chartwell Books Inc., Edison, NJ	(orders) 800-526-7257
Chatelaine Press, Burke, VA	800-249-9527
Chelsea Green Publishing Co., White River Junction, VT	800-639-4099
Chelsea House Publishers, Broomall, PA	800-848-BOOK
Chemical Publishing Co. Inc., New York, NY	800-786-3659
Cherokee Publishing Co., Marietta, GA	800-653-3952
Chess Combination Inc., Bridgeport, CT	800-354-4083
Chicago Review Press Inc., Chicago, IL	800-888-4741
Chicago Spectrum Press, Evanston, IL	800-594-5190
Child's Play, Auburn, ME	800-639-6404
Chilton Enterprises, Radnor, PA	800-695-1214
Chivers North America Inc., Hampton, NH	800-621-0182
Chosen Books, Grand Rapids, MI	800-877-2665
Christendom Press, Front Royal, VA	800-877-5456
Christian Classics, Allen, TX	800-527-5030
Christian Literature Crusade Inc., Fort Washington, PA	800-659-1240

Publisher/Distributor	Toll-Free No.
Christian Publications Inc., Camp Hill, PA	800-233-4443
Christian Schools International, Grand Rapids, MI	800-635-8288
Christopher Gordon Publishers Inc., Norwood, MA	800-934-8322
Chronicle Books, San Francisco, CA	(orders) 800-722-6657
Chronicle Guidance Publications Inc., Moravia, NY	800-622-7284
Chronimed Publishing, Minnetonka, MN	800-444-5951
Churchill Livingstone, New York, NY	800-553-5426
Clarity Press Inc., Atlanta, GA (COD & credit card orders only)	800-247-6553
Classics International Entertainment Inc., Chicago, IL	800-569-2434
Clear Light Publishers, Santa Fe, NM	800-253-2747
Cliffs Notes Inc., Lincoln, NE	800-228-4078
ClockWorks Press, Shingle Springs, CA	800-276-0701
Close Up Publishing, Alexandria, VA	800-765-3131
Clymer Publications, Overland Park, KS	800-262-1954
Cold Spring Harbor Laboratory Press, Cold Spring Harbor, NY	800-843-4388
Cole Publishing Group Inc., Santa Rosa, CA	800-959-2717
Collector Books, Paducah, KY	800-626-5420
College Press Publishing Co., Joplin, MO	800-289-3300
Colorado Railroad Museum, Golden, CO	800-365-6263
Colorado School of Mines Press, Golden, CO	800-446-9488
Columba Publishing Co., Akron, OH	800-999-7491
Columbia University Press, New York, NY	800-944-8648
Commune-A-Key Publishing Inc., Salt Lake City, UT	800-983-0600
Communication Publications & Resources, Alexandria, VA	800-888-4402
Communication Skill Builders, Tucson, AZ	800-763-2306
Commuter's Library, Falls Church, VA	800-643-0295
Compact Books, Hollywood, FL	800-771-3355
Competency Press, White Plains, NY	800-603-3779
Comprehensive Health Education Foundation (CHEF), Seattle, WA	800-323-2433
Conari Press, Berkeley, CA	800-685-9595
Conciliar Press, Ben Lomond, CA	800-967-7377
Concordia Publishing House, St Louis, MO	800-325-3040
Congressional Information Service Inc., Bethesda, MD	800-638-8380
Congressional Quarterly Books, Washington, DC	800-638-1710
Contemporary Books Inc., Chicago, IL	800-540-9440
The Continuum Publishing Group, New York, NY	800-937-5557
Conway Greene Publishing Co., Cleveland, OH	800-977-2665
Cool Hand Communications Inc., Boca Raton, FL	800-428-0578
Copley Publishing Group, Acton, MA	800-562-2147
Cornell Maritime Press Inc., Centreville, MD	800-638-7641
CorpTech (Corporate Technology Information Services Inc.), Woburn, MA	800-333-8036
Cortina Learning International Inc., Wilton, CT	800-245-2145
Cottonwood Press Inc., Fort Collins, CO	800-864-4297
Council for Exceptional Children, Reston, VA	800-232-7323
Council Oak Publishing Co. Inc., Tulsa, OK	800-247-8850

Publisher/Distributor	Toll-Free No.
Council of State Governments, Lexington, KY	800-800-1910
Country Roads Press Inc., Oaks, PA	800-462-6420
The Countryman Press, Woodstock, VT	800-245-4151
Countrysport Press, Traverse City, MI	800-367-4114
Course Technology Inc., Cambridge, MA	800-648-7450
Covered Bridge Press, North Attleboro, MA	(New England only) 800-752-3769
Cowley Publications, Boston, MA	800-225-1534
CQ Staff Directories Ltd, Alexandria, VA	800-252-1722
Crabtree Publishing Co., New York, NY	800-387-7650
Beverly Cracom Publications, Maryland Heights, MO	800-341-0880
Craftsman Book Co., Carlsbad, CA	800-829-8123
Crane Hill Publishers, Birmingham, AL	800-841-2682
CRC Publications, Grand Rapids, MI	800-333-8300
Creative Arts Book Co., Berkeley, CA	800-848-7789
The Creative Co., Mankato, MN	800-445-6209
Creative Homeowner Press, Upper Saddle River, NJ	800-631-7795
Creative Teaching Press/Youngheart Music, Cypress, CA	800-444-4287
Crisp Publications Inc., Menlo Park, CA	800-442-7477
Cross Cultural Publications Inc., South Bend, IN	800-273-6526
Crossing Press, Freedom, CA	800-777-1048
Crossroad Publishing Co. Inc., New York, NY	800-937-5557
Crossway Books, Wheaton, IL	800-323-3890
Crystal Clarity Publishers, Nevada City, CA	800-424-1055
Crystal Productions, Glenview, IL	800-255-8629
CT Publishing Co., Redding, CA	800-767-0511
Cummings & Hathaway Publishers, East Rockaway, NY	800-344-7579
Current Clinical Strategies Publishing, Laguna Hills, CA	800-331-8227
Current Medicine, Philadelphia, PA	800-427-1796
Da Capo Press Inc., New York, NY	800-221-9369
Dandy Lion Publications, San Luis Obispo, CA	800-776-8032
John Daniel & Co., Publishers, Santa Barbara, CA	800-662-8351
Dartnell Books, Chicago, IL	800-621-5463
DATA Business Publishing, Englewood, CO	800-447-4666
Data Research Inc., Eagan, MN	800-365-4900
Data Trace Publishing Co., Towson, MD	(orders only) 800-342-0454
Databooks, Worcester, MA	800-642-6657
Davies-Black Publishing, Palo Alto, CA	800-624-1765
F A Davis Co., Philadelphia, PA	800-523-4049
Davis Publications Inc. (MA), Worcester, MA	800-533-2847
DAW Books Inc., New York, NY	800-526-0275
Dawbert Press, Duxbury, MA	800-93-DAWBERT
The Dawn Horse Press, Middletown, CA	800-524-4941
Dawn Publications, Nevada City, CA	800-545-7475
Dawn Sign Press, San Diego, CA	800-549-5350
DBI Books, Northbrook, IL	800-767-6310
DDC Publishing, New York, NY	800-528-3897

Publisher/Distributor	Toll-Free No.
DDL Books Inc., Miami, FL	800-635-4276
Cy De Cosse Inc., Minnetonka, MN	800-328-0590
De Vorss & Co. Inc., Marina del Rey, CA	800-843-5743
	(CA) 800-331-4719
Ivan R Dee Inc., Chicago, IL	(orders) 800-634-0226
Marcel Dekker Inc., New York, NY	(outside NY) 800-228-1160
Dell Publishing, New York, NY	800-223-6834
Delmar Publishers, Albany, NY	(NY) 800-347-7707
Delta Books	(outside NY) 800-223-6834
Delta Systems Co. Inc., McHenry, IL	800-323-8270
Demibach Editions, Stockton, CA	800-366-8577
Demos Vermande, New York, NY	800-532-8663
T S Denison & Co. Inc., Minneapolis, MN	800-328-3831
Depth Charge, Evanston, IL	888-DepthCh
Derrydale Press Inc., Lyon, MS	800-443-6753
Deseret Book Co., Salt Lake City, UT	800-453-3876
Destiny Image, Shippensburg, PA	(orders only) 800-722-6774
Developmental Studies Center, Oakland, CA	800-666-7270
Devyn Press, Louisville, KY	800-274-2221
Dharma Publishing, Berkeley, CA	800-873-4276
Diablo Press Inc., Emeryville, CA	800-488-2665
Diamond Communications Inc., South Bend, IN	800-480-3717
Diamond Farm Book Publishers, Alexandria Bay, NY	800-481-1353
Digital Wisdom Inc., Tappahannock, VA	800-800-8560
Dimensions for Living, Nashville, TN	800-281-3320
Discipleship Publications International (DPI), Woburn, MA	800-727-8273
Discipleship Resources, Nashville, TN	800-814-7833
	(orders) 800-685-4370
Discovery Enterprises Ltd, Carlisle, MA	800-729-1720
Discovery House Publishers, Grand Rapids, MI	800-653-8333
Distributed Art Publishers (DAP), New York, NY	800-338-2665
Dominie Press Inc., Carlsbad, CA	800-232-4570
Donning Co./Publishers, Virginia Beach, VA	800-296-8572
Doral Publishing, Wilsonville, OR	(orders) 800-633-5385
Dorset House Publishing Co. Inc., New York, NY	800-DHBOOKS
Doubleday, New York, NY	800-223-6834
Douglas Charles Press, North Attleboro, MA	(New England only) 800-752-3769
Dover Publications Inc., Mineola, NY	(orders) 800-223-3130
Down East Books, Camden, ME	800-766-1670
The Dramatic Publishing Co., Woodstock, IL	800-448-7469
The Dryden Press, Fort Worth, TX	800-323-7437
Dual Dolphin Publishing Inc., Wrentham, MA	800-336-5746
Duke Communications International, Loveland, CO	800-621-1544
Dun & Bradstreet Information Services, Murray Hill, NJ	800-526-0651
Duquesne University Press, Pittsburgh, PA	800-666-2211
Durkin Hayes Publishing, Niagara Falls, NY	800-962-5200

Publisher/Distributor	Toll-Free No.
Dushkin Publishing Group (Times Mirror), Guilford, CT	800-243-6532
Dustbooks, Paradise, CA	800-477-6110
Eagle's View Publishing, Liberty, UT	(orders over $100) 800-547-3364
East View Publications, Minneapolis, MN	800-477-1005
Eastland Press, Vista, CA	(US & Canada only) 800-241-3329; 800-4453-3278
EDC Publishing, Tulsa, OK	800-475-4522
Nellie Edge Resources Inc., Salem, OR	800-523-4594
Editorial Caribe, Miami, FL	800-322-7423
Editorial Unilit, Miami, FL	800-767-7726
Educational Impressions Inc., Hawthorne, NJ	800-451-7450
Educational Insights Inc., Carson, CA	800-933-3277
Educational Ministries Inc., Prescott, AZ	800-221-0910
Educational Press, Baltimore, MD	800-645-6564
Educational Technology Publications, Englewood Cliffs, NJ	(US & Canada only, orders) 800-952-BOOK
Educators Publishing Service Inc., Cambridge, MA	800-225-5750
Edupress, San Juan Capistrano, CA	800-835-7978
Wm B Eerdmans Publishing Co., Grand Rapids, MI	800-253-7521
Elysium Growth Press, Los Angeles, CA	800-350-2020
E M Press Inc., Manassas, VA	800-727-4630
Emanuel Law Outlines Inc., Larchmont, NY	800-362-6835
E M C Corp., St Paul, MN	800-328-1452
Emerald Books, Lynnwood, WA	800-922-2143
Encore Performance Publishing, Orem, UT	800-927-1605
Encyclopaedia Britannica Educational Corp.	800-554-9862
Encyclopaedia Britannica Inc., Chicago, IL	800-323-1229
Energeia Publishing Inc., Salem, OR	800-639-6048
Engineering Information Inc. (Ei), Hoboken, NJ	800-221-1044
EPM Publications Inc., McLean, VA	800-289-2339
ERIC Clearinghouse on Reading, English & Communication, Bloomington, IN	800-759-4723
Essential Medical Information Systems Inc., Durant, OK	800-225-0694
ETC Publications, Palm Springs, CA	800-382-7869
ETR Associates, Santa Cruz, CA	800-321-4407
Evan-Moor Educational Publishers, Monterey, CA	800-777-4362
Evangel Publishing House, Nappanee, IN	800-253-9315
Evanston Publishing Inc., Evanston, IL	800-594-5190
Everglory Publishing Co., Newburyport, MA	800-270-1127
Everyday Learning Corp., Chicago, IL	800-382-7670
Exley Giftbooks, New York, NY	800-423-9539
Explorers Guide Publishing, Rhinelander, WI	800-497-6029
Faber & Faber Inc., Winchester, MA	(outside NY) 800-666-2211
	(NY, CUP services orders) 607-666-2211
Factor Press, Mobile, AL	(orders only) 800-304-0077
Facts & Comparisons Inc., St Louis, MO	800-223-0554
Facts On File Inc., New York, NY	800-322-8755

Publisher/Distributor	Toll-Free No.
Fairchild Books & Visuals, New York, NY	800-247-6622
Fairview Press, Minneapolis, MN	800-544-8207; 800-888-KEESHAN
Faith & Life Press, Newton, KS	800-743-2484
Faith Publishing Co., Milford, OH	800-576-6477
Falcon Press Publishing Co. Inc., Helena, MT	800-582-2665
Fantagraphics Books, Seattle, WA	800-657-1100
Favorite Recipes Press, Nashville, TN	800-358-0560
Faxon Co., Westwood, MA	800-999-3594, ext. 292
F C & A Publishing, Peachtree City, GA	800-226-8024
Fearon Teacher Aids, Columbus, OH	800-321-3106
Federal Publications Inc., Washington, DC	800-922-4330
Philipp Feldheim Inc., Nanuet, NY	800-237-7149
Fell Publishers, Hollywood, FL	800-771-FELL
Finley-Greene Publications Inc., Island Park, NY	800-431-1131
Fire Engineering Books & Videos, Saddle Brook, NJ	800-752-9768
Firebird Publications Inc., Rockville, MD	800-854-9595
Fisher Books, Tucson, AZ	800-324-3791
Fisherman Library, Point Pleasant, NJ	800-553-4745
Fitzroy Dearborn Publishers, Chicago, IL	800-850-8102
J Flores Publications Inc. Action Direct, Miami, FL	800-472-2388
Flower Valley Press Inc., Gaithersburg, MD	800-735-5197
Focus Information Group Inc., Newburyport, MA	(orders) 800-848-7236
Focus on the Family Publishing, Colorado Springs, CO	800-232-6459
Focus Publishing, Bemidji, MN	800-913-6287
Fodor's Travel Publications Inc., New York, NY	800-733-3000; 800-533-6478
Foghorn Press, San Francisco, CA	800-FOGHORN
Fondo de Cultura Economica USA Inc., San Diego, CA	800-532-3872
Fordham University Press, Bronx, NY	800-247-6553
Forest House Publishing Co. Inc., Lake Forest, IL	800-394-READ
Forward Movement Publications, Cincinnati, OH	800-543-1813
Foundation Center, New York, NY	800-424-9836
Foundation for Economic Education Inc., Irvington-on-Hudson, NY	800-452-3518
Franciscan University Press, Steubenville, OH	800-783-6357
Fraser Publishing Co., Burlington, VT	800-253-0900
Free Spirit Publishing Inc., Minneapolis, MN	800-735-7323
Friends United Press, Richmond, IN	800-537-8839
Front Row Experience, Byron, CA	(voice & fax) 800-524-9091
Fulcrum Publishing Inc., Golden, CO	800-992-2908
Fulton-Hall Publishing Co., San Francisco, CA	800-FULTON5
Futura Publishing Co. Inc., Armonk, NY	800-877-8761
Future Horizons Inc., Arlington, TX	800-489-0727
P Gaines Co., Oak Park, IL	800-578-3853
Gale, Detroit, MI	(cust serv) 800-877-GALE (edit) 800-347-GALE
Gallaudet University Press, Washington, DC	800-451-1073
Gallopade Publishing Group, Atlanta, GA	800-536-2GET

Publisher/Distributor	Toll-Free No.
Gardner Press Inc., Lake Worth, FL	800-756-8534
Gareth Stevens Inc., Milwaukee, WI	800-341-3569
Garrett Educational Corp., Ada, OK	800-654-9366
Garrett Publishing Inc., Deerfield Beach, FL	800-638-7571
Gateway Books, Oakland, CA	(credit card orders only) 800-669-0773
Gaunt Inc., Holmes Beach, FL	800-942-8683
Gayot/Gault Millau Inc., Los Angeles, CA	800-LE BEST 1
Gefen Books, Hewlett, NY	800-477-5257
GemStone Press, Woodstock, VT	800-962-4544
Genealogical Publishing Co. Inc., Baltimore, MD	800-296-6687
General Publications Group, Boston, MA	800-228-7090
Geological Society of America (GSA), Boulder, CO	800-472-1988
George Washington University, School of Education & Human Development, Washington, DC	800-773-ERIC
Georgetown University Press, Washington, DC	800-246-9606
Gessler Publishing Co. Inc., Roanoke, VA	800-456-5825
C R Gibson Co., Norwalk, CT	800-243-6004
Giga Information Group, Norwell, MA	800-874-9980
Gleim Publications Inc., Gainesville, FL	800-87-GLEIM
Glenbridge Publishing Ltd, Lakewood, CO	800-986-4135
Glencoe/McGraw-Hill, Westerville, OH	800-848-1567
Peter Glenn Publications Ltd, New York, NY	800-223-1254
Global Professional Publications, Englewood, CO	800-854-7179
Global Travel Publishers Inc., Pompano Beach, FL	800-882-9453
Globe Pequot Press Inc., Old Saybrook, CT	800-243-0495
David R Godine Publisher Inc., Lincoln, MA	800-344-4771
The Gold Book, Atlanta, GA	800-842-6848
Gold Horse Publishing Inc., Annapolis, MD	800-966-DOLL
Golden Aura Publishing, Philadelphia, PA	800-979-8642
Golden Books Publishing Co. Inc., New York, NY	(ordering & shipping info) 800-558-5972
Golden Educational Center, Redding, CA	800-800-1791
Golf Gifts & Gallery Inc., Lombard, IL	800-552-4430
Good Books, Intercourse, PA	800-762-7171
Goodheart-Willcox Co., Tinley Park, IL	800-687-5068
Goofy Foot Press, West Hollywood, CA	800-310-PLAY
Goosefoot Acres Press, Cleveland Heights, OH	800-697-4858
Gospel Publishing House, Springfield, MO	800-641-4310
Gould Publications Inc., Longwood, FL	800-847-6502
Government Research Service, Topeka, KS	800-346-6898
Donald M Grant Publisher Inc., Hampton Falls, NH	800-476-0510
Grapevine Publications Inc., Corvallis, OR	800-338-4331
Graphic Arts Center Publishing Co., Portland, OR	800-452-3032
Graphic Arts Technical Foundation, Pittsburgh, PA	800-910-GATF
Graphic Learning, Waterbury, CT	800-874-0029
Grayson Bernard Publishers, Bloomington, IN	800-925-7853

Publisher/Distributor	Toll-Free No.
Great Quotations Inc., Glendale Heights, IL	800-354-4889
Warren H Green Inc., St Louis, MO	800-537-0655
Greenhaven Press Inc., San Diego, CA	800-231-5163
Greenwillow Books, New York, NY	800-631-1199
Greenwood Publishing Group Inc., Westport, CT	(orders) 800-225-5800
Grey House Publishing Inc., Lakeville, CT	800-562-2139
Grolier Educational Corp., Danbury, CT	800-243-7256
Group Publishing Inc., Loveland, CO	800-447-1070
Grove's Dictionaries Inc., New York, NY	800-221-2123
Grove/Atlantic Inc., New York, NY	800-521-0178
Gryphon Editions, New York, NY	800-633-8911
Gryphon House Inc., Beltsville, MD	800-638-0928
The Guild, Madison, WI	800-969-1556
Guilford Press, New York, NY	(orders) 800-365-7006
Gulf Publishing Co., Book Division, Houston, TX	(TX) 800-392-4390
	(all other except AK, HI) 800-231-6275
G W Medical Publishing Inc., St Louis, MO	800-600-0330
Hachai Publications Inc., Brooklyn, NY	800-50-HACHAI
Hagstrom Map Co. Inc., Maspeth, NY	800-432-MAPS
Hal Leonard Corp., Milwaukee, WI	800-524-4425
Half Halt Press Inc., Boonsboro, MD	800-822-9635
George D Hall Co., Boston, MA	800-446-1215
Hambleton Hill Publishing Inc., Nashville, TN	800-327-5113
Alexander Hamilton Institute, Ramsey, NJ	800-879-2441
Hammond Inc., Maplewood, NJ	800-526-4953
Hampton Press Inc., Cresskill, NJ	800-894-8955
Hampton Roads Publishing Co. Inc., Charlottesville, VA	800-766-8009
Hampton-Brown Co. Inc., Carmel, CA	800-933-3510
Hanley & Belfus Inc., Philadelphia, PA	800-962-1892
Hannibal Books, Hannibal, MO	800-747-0738
Hanser Gardner Publications, Cincinnati, OH	800-950-8977
Harcourt Brace & Co., Orlando, FL	(cust serv) 800-225-5425
Harcourt Brace College Publishers, Fort Worth, TX	(cust serv) 800-782-4479
Harcourt Brace Legal & Professional Publications, Chicago, IL	800-787-8717
Harcourt Brace Professional Publishing, San Diego, CA	800-831-7799
Harmonie Park Press, Warren, MI	800-886-3080
HarperCollins Publishers, New York, NY	800-242-7737
	(PA) 800-982-4377
Harris InfoSource, Twinsburg, OH	800-888-5900
Harris Media/Newspower, Northfield, MA	800-346-8330
Harrison House Publishers, Tulsa, OK	800-888-4126
Hartley & Marks Publishers Inc., Point Roberts, WA	800-277-5887
Harvard Business School Press, Boston, MA	800-545-7685
Harvard University Press, Cambridge, MA	(orders, US & Canada) 800-448-2242
Harvest House Publishers Inc., Eugene, OR	800-547-8979
Hatherleigh Press, New York, NY	800-367-2550

Publisher/Distributor	Toll-Free No.
Haworth Press Inc., Binghamton, NY	800-342-9678
Hay House Inc., Carlsbad, CA	(orders) 800-654-5126
Haynes Publications Inc., Newbury Park, CA	800-442-9637
Hazelden Publishing & Education, Center City, MN	800-328-9000
HB School Department	(cust serv) 800-225-5425
HB Trade Division, San Diego, CA	(cust serv) 800-543-1918
H C I A Inc., Baltimore, MD	800-568-3282
H D I Publishers, Houston, TX	800-321-7037
Health Communications Inc., Deerfield Beach, FL	(cust serv) 800-851-9100
Health for Life, Marina del Rey, CA	800-874-5339
Health Leadership Associates Inc., Potomac, MD	800-435-4775
Health Press, Santa Fe, NM	800-643-BOOK
Health Science, Santa Barbara, CA	800-446-1990
Healthcare Management Group McGraw-Hill, New York, NY	800-544-8168
Heartland Samplers Inc., Edina, MN	800-999-2233
Hearts & Tummies Cookbook Co., Fort Madison, IA	800-571-BOOK
William S Hein & Co. Inc., Buffalo, NY	800-828-7571
Heinemann, Portsmouth, NH	800-541-2086
Heinle & Heinle Publishers, Boston, MA	800-237-0053
Hemingway Western Studies Series, Boise, ID	800-992-TEXT
Hendrickson Publishers Inc., Peabody, MA	800-358-3111
Virgil Hensley Publishing, Tulsa, OK	800-288-8520
Herald House, Independence, MO	800-767-8181
Herald Press, Scottdale, PA	800-245-7894
Heritage Books Inc., Bowie, MD	800-398-7709
Heritage House, Indianapolis, IN	800-419-0200
Hi-Time Publishing Corp., Milwaukee, WI	800-558-2292
High Mountain Press, Santa Fe, NM	800-4-ONWORD; 800-466-9693
Highsmith Press LLC, Fort Atkinson, WI	800-558-2110
Hill & Wang, New York, NY	(orders, cust serv) 800-631-8571
Hillsdale College Press, Hillsdale, MI	800-437-2268
Hogrefe & Huber Publishers, Kirkland, WA	800-228-3749
Hohm Press, Prescott, AZ	800-381-2700
Holbrook & Kellogg, Vienna, VA	800-506-4450
Holmes & Meier Publishers Inc., New York, NY	(orders only) 800-698-7781
Henry Holt & Co. Inc., New York, NY	800-488-5233
Holt, Rinehart & Winston, Inc., Austin, TX	(cust serv) 800-782-4479
Home Builder Press, Washington, DC	800-223-2665
Home Planners Inc., Tucson, AZ	800-322-6797
Homestyles Publishing & Marketing Inc., Minneapolis, MN	800-547-5570
HomeTech Information Systems, Bethesda, MD	800-638-8292
Hope Publishing Co., Carol Stream, IL	800-323-1049
Horizon Books, Camp Hill, PA	800-233-4443
Horizon Publishers & Distributors Inc., Bountiful, UT	800-453-0812
Houghton Mifflin Co., Boston, MA	(trade books) 800-225-3362
	(textbooks) 800-257-9107

Publisher/Distributor	Toll-Free No.
Houghton Mifflin Co., Boston, MA (cont.)	(college texts) 800-225-1464
Howard Publishing, West Monroe, LA	800-858-4109
Howell Book House Inc., New York, NY	800-428-5331
Howell Press Inc., Charlottesville, VA	800-868-4512
Human Kinetics Inc., Champaign, IL	800-747-4457
Human Resource Development Press, Amherst, MA	800-822-2801
Humanics Publishing Group, Atlanta, GA	800-874-8844
Hunter House Inc., Publishers, Alameda, CA	800-266-5592
Huntington House Publishers, Lafayette, LA	800-749-4009
Hyperion, New York, NY	(orders) 800-343-9204
I Do Publishing Co. Inc., Wauconda, IL	800-392-9039
IBC USA (Publications) Inc., Ashland, MA	800-343-5412
Iconografix Inc., Osceola, WI	(orders only) 800-289-3504
ICS Books Inc., Merrillville, IN	800-541-7323
ICS Press, San Francisco, CA	800-326-0263
IDG Books Worldwide Inc., Foster City, CA	800-762-2974
IEEE Computer Society Press, Los Alamitos, CA	800-272-6657
Igaku-Shoin Medical Publishers Inc., New York, NY	800-765-0800
Ignatius Press, San Francisco, CA	(orders only) 800-651-1531
Illuminated Way Publishing Inc., Golden Valley, MN	800-509-5556
IllumiNet Press, Lilburn, GA	800-236-INET
Imaginart Press, Bisbee, AZ	800-828-1376
Incentive Publications Inc., Nashville, TN	800-421-2830
Index Publishing Group Inc., San Diego, CA	800-546-6707
Indiana Historical Society, Indianapolis, IN	(orders only) 800-447-1830
Indiana University Press, Bloomington, IN	(orders only) 800-842-6796
InfoBooks, Santa Monica, CA	800-669-0409
Information Guides, Hermosa Beach, CA	800-347-3257
Information Plus, Wylie, TX	800-463-6757
Inner Traditions International Ltd, Rochester, VT	800-246-8648
Innovanna Corp., Sugar Land, TX	800-577-9810
Institute for International Economics, Washington, DC	800-229-3266
Institute for Language Study, Wilton, CT	800-245-2145
Institute for Palestine Studies, Washington, DC	800-874-3614
Institute for Research & Education, Minneapolis, MN	800-372-7775
Inter Trade Corp., Norcross, GA	800-653-7363
Interarts Ltd, Cambridge, MA	800-626-4655
The International Center for Creative Thinking, Larchmont, NY	800-328-4465
International Chess Enterprises (I C E), Seattle, WA	800-26-CHESS
International Foundation of Employee Benefit Plans, Brookfield, WI	800-466-2366
International Law Library-Book Publishers Inc., Arlington, VA	800-876-0226
International Linguistics Corp., Kansas City, MO	800-237-1830
International Risk Management Institute Inc., Dallas, TX	800-827-4242
International Scholars Publications, Bethesda, MD	800-55-PUBLISH
International Society for Technology in Education, Eugene, OR	(orders only) 800-336-5191

Publisher/Distributor	Toll-Free No.
International Specialized Book Services, Portland, OR	800-944-6190
International Wealth Success, Merrick, NY	800-323-0548
Interstate Publishers Inc., Danville, IL	800-843-4774
Intertec Publishing Corp., Overland Park, KS	800-262-1954
InterVarsity Press, Downers Grove, IL	800-843-7225
Interweave Press, Loveland, CO	800-272-2193
I O P Publishing Inc., Philadelphia, PA	800-358-4677
Iowa State University Press, Ames, IA	(orders only) 800-862-6657
IPS Publishing Inc., Vancouver, WA	800-933-8378
IRI/Skylight Training & Publishing Inc., Arlington Heights, IL	800-348-4474
Irwin Professional Publishing, Burr Ridge, IL	800-634-3963
Richard D Irwin (Times Mirror), Burr Ridge, IL	(orders only) 800-634-3961
Ishiyaku EuroAmerica Inc., St Louis, MO	800-633-1921
Island Press, Washington, DC	800-828-1302
J & B Editions Inc., Richmond, VA	800-266-5480
Jalmar Press, Torrance, CA	800-662-9662
Jameson Books Inc., Ottawa, IL	800-426-1357
Jane's Information Group, Alexandria, VA	800-243-3852
Janson Publications Inc., Dedham, MA	800-322-MATH
January Productions Inc., Hawthorne, NJ	800-451-7450
Jewish Lights Publishing, Woodstock, VT	800-962-4544
Jewish Publication Society, Philadelphia, PA	800-234-3151
JIST Works Inc., Indianapolis, IN	800-648-5478
	(fax) 800-547-8329
Johns Hopkins University Press, Baltimore, MD	800-537-5487
Johnson Institute, Minneapolis, MN	800-231-5165
Jones & Bartlett Publishers Inc., Sudbury, MA	800-832-0034
Jones Publishing Inc., Iola, WI	800-331-0038
Joy Publishing, Fountain Valley, CA	800-783-6265
Judson Press, Valley Forge, PA	800-331-1053
Kaleidoscope Press, Puyallup, WA	800-977-7323
Kalmbach Books, Waukesha, WI	800-533-6644
Kalmbach Publishing Co., Waukesha, WI	800-558-1544
Kar-Ben Copies Inc., Rockville, MD	800-4-KARBEN
Kaye Wood Publishing, West Branch, MI	800-248-KAYE
KC Publications Inc., Las Vegas, NV	800-626-9673
Keats Publishing Inc., New Canaan, CT	800-858-7014
Kendall/Hunt Publishing Co., Dubuque, IA	(orders only) 800-228-0810
Kennedy Publications, Fitzwilliam, NH	800-531-0007
Kent State University Press, Kent, OH	(orders) 800-247-6553
Key Curriculum Press, Berkeley, CA	800-338-7638
Kidsbooks Inc., Chicago, IL	800-515-KIDS
Kirkbride Bible Co. Inc., Indianapolis, IN	800-428-4385
Neil A Kjos Music Co., San Diego, CA	800-854-1592
Kluwer Law International (KLI), Cambridge, MA	800-577-8118
Alfred A Knopf Inc., New York, NY	800-638-6460

Publisher/Distributor	Toll-Free No.
Knopf Publishing Group, New York, NY	800-638-6460
Knowledge Ideas & Trends Inc., Manchester, CT	800-826-0529
Kodansha America Inc., New York, NY	800-788-6262
Krause Publications, Iola, WI	800-258-0929
Kregel Publications, Grand Rapids, MI	(orders) 800-733-2607
Kumarian Press Inc., West Hartford, CT	(orders only) 800-289-2664
Lakewood Publications, Minneapolis, MN	800-328-4329
Langenscheidt Publishers Inc., Maspeth, NY	800-432-MAPS
LangMarc Publishing, San Antonio, TX	800-864-1648
Laredo Publishing Co. Inc., Beverly Hills, CA	800-547-5113
Larousse Kingfisher Chambers Inc., New York, NY	800-497-1657
Larson Publications, Burdett, NY	800-828-2197
Laureate Press, Milbridge, ME	800-946-2727
Lawrence Erlbaum Associates Inc., Mahwah, NJ	(orders only) 800-9-BOOKS-9
Lawyers Cooperative Publishing, Rochester, NY	800-527-0430
LDA Publishers, Bayside, NY	800-784-0300
Leadership Publishers Inc., Des Moines, IA	800-814-3757
Leading Edge Reports, Commack, NY	800-866-4648
The Learning Connection, Frostproof, FL	800-338-2282
Learning Links Inc., New Hyde Park, NY	800-724-2616
Learning Publications Inc., Holmes Beach, FL	(orders) 800-222-1525
Learning Resources Network (LERN), Manhattan, KS	(orders only) 800-678-5376
The Learning Works Inc., Santa Barbara, CA	800-235-5767
Lectorum Publications Inc., New York, NY	800-345-5946
Legacy Publishing Group, Clinton, MA	800-322-3866
Leisure Arts Inc., Little Rock, AR	800-643-8030
Leisure Books, New York, NY	(orders) 800-481-9191
Lerner Publications Co., Minneapolis, MN	800-328-4929
Liberty Fund Inc., Indianapolis, IN	800-955-8335
Libraries Unlimited Inc., Englewood, CO	800-237-6124
Mary Ann Liebert Inc., Larchmont, NY	800-MLIEBERT
Lifetime Books Inc., Hollywood, FL	800-771-3355
Liguori Publications, Liguori, MO	800-464-2555
Lincoln Institute of Land Policy, Cambridge, MA	800-LAND-USE
LinguiSystems Inc., East Moline, IL	800-PRO-IDEA
Linton Day Publishing Co., Stone Mountain, GA	800-927-0409
Lippincott-Raven Publishers, Philadelphia, PA	(MD) 800-638-3030
Little, Brown and Company Inc., Boston, MA	800-343-9204
Little Tiger Press, Wauwatosa, WI	800-541-2205
Littlefield, Adams Quality Paperbacks, Lanham, MD	800-462-6420
Liturgical Press, Collegeville, MN	800-858-5450
Liturgy Training Publications, Chicago, IL	800-933-1800
Llewellyn Publications, St Paul, MN	800-843-6666
L L P Inc., New York, NY	800-955-6937
Loizeaux Brothers Inc., Neptune, NJ	800-526-2796
Lone Eagle Publishing Co., Los Angeles, CA	800-345-6257

Publisher/Distributor	Toll-Free No.
Lonely Planet Publications, Oakland, CA	(orders) 800-275-8555
Longstreet Press, Marietta, GA	800-927-1488
Loompanics Unlimited, Port Townsend, WA	800-380-2230
Lothrop, Lee & Shepard Books, New York, NY	800-843-9389
Lotus Light Publications, Twin Lakes, WI	(orders only) 800-824-6396
Loyola Press, Chicago, IL	800-621-1008
Lucent Books Inc., San Diego, CA	800-231-5163
LuraMedia Inc., San Diego, CA	800-367-5872
M & H Publishing Co. Inc., LaGrange, TX	800-521-9950
Macalester Park Publishing Co., Minneapolis, MN	800-407-9078
The McDonald & Woodward Publishing Co., Fort Pierce, FL	800-233-8787
Madison Books Inc., Lanham, MD	800-462-6420
Madison House Publishers, Madison, WI	800-604-1776
Mage Publishers Inc., Washington, DC	800-962-0922
Magna Publications Inc., Madison, WI	800-433-0499
Maharishi International University Press, Fairfield, IA	800-831-6523
Mancorp Publishing Inc., Tampa, FL	800-853-3888
Many Cultures Publishing, San Francisco, CA	800-484-4173, ext. 1073
MAR CO Products Inc., Warminster, PA	800-448-2197
MARC Publications, Monrovia, CA	(US only) 800-777-7752
Mariposa Publishing Co., St Paul, MN	800-442-1419
Market Data Retrieval Inc., Shelton, CT	800-333-8802
Markowski International Publishers, Hummelstown, PA	800-566-0534
Marlor Press Inc., St Paul, MN	800-669-4908
MarshMedia, Kansas City, MO	800-821-3303
Marsilio Publishers Corp., New York, NY	800-992-9685
The Massachusetts Medical Society, Waltham, MA	800-322-2303
MasterMedia Ltd, New York, NY	800-334-8232
Masters Press, Indianapolis, IN	800-9-SPORTS
Mathematical Association of America, Washington, DC	(orders) 800-331-1622
Maval Publishing Inc., Denver, CO	800-746-3088
Maverick Publications Inc., Bend, OR	800-800-4831
Mayfair Games Inc., Niles, IL	800-432-4376
Mayfield Publishing Co., Mountain View, CA	800-433-1279
McClanahan Publishing House Inc., Kuttawa, KY	800-544-6959
McCormack's Guides, Martinez, CA	800-222-3602
McCutchan Publishing Corp., Berkeley, CA	800-227-1540
McFarland & Co. Inc., Publishers, Jefferson, NC	(orders only) 800-253-2187
McGraw-Hill School Systems, Monterey, CA	(orders) 800-663-0544
McGuinn & McGuire Publishing Inc., Bradenton, FL	800-690-7779
McPherson & Co., Kingston, NY	800-613-8219
Meadowbrook Press Inc., Deephaven, MN	800-338-2232
R S Means Co. Inc., Kingston, MA	800-448-8182
Mecklermedia, Westport, CT	800-632-5537
Medbooks, Dallas, TX	800-443-7397
Media Associates, Wilton, CA	(orders) 800-373-1897

Publisher/Distributor	Toll-Free No.
Media & Methods, Philadelphia, PA	800-523-4540
Medical Physics Publishing Corp., Madison, WI	800-442-5778
Medicode Publications, Salt Lake City, UT	800-999-4600
Russell Meerdink Co. Ltd, Neenah, WI	800-635-6499
Mel Bay Publications Inc., Pacific, MO	800-863-5229
Menasha Ridge Press Inc., Birmingham, AL	800-247-9437
Mercer University Press, Macon, GA	(outside GA) 800-637-2378, ext. 2880
	(GA) 800-342-0841, ext. 2880
Meriwether Publishing Ltd/Contemporary Drama Service, Colorado Springs, CO	800-937-5297
Merlyn's Pen: Stories by American Students, East Greenwich, RI	800-247-2027
Merriam-Webster Inc., Springfield, MA	800-201-5029
	(orders & cust serv) 800-828-1880
Merrill-West Publishing, Carmel, CA	800-676-1256
Merritt Publishing, Santa Monica, CA	800-638-7597
Merryant Publishers Inc., Vashon, WA	800-228-8958
Mesorah Publications Ltd, Brooklyn, NY	800-637-6724
Metal Bulletin Inc., New York, NY	800-METAL-25
Metamorphous Press, Portland, OR	800-937-7771
Michelin Travel Publications, Greenville, SC	800-423-0485; 800-223-0987
Michie Butterworth, Charlottesville, VA	800-446-3410
MicroMash, Englewood, CO	800-272-7277
Microsoft Press, Redmond, WA	800-MSPRESS
MidWest Plan Service, Ames, IA	800-562-3618
Midwest Traditions Inc., Mount Horeb, WI	800-736-9189
Milady Publishing Co., Albany, NY	800-836-5239
Milkweed Editions, Minneapolis, MN	800-520-6455
Millbrook Press Inc., Brookfield, CT	800-462-4703
Miller Freeman Inc., San Francisco, CA	(orders only) 800-848-5594
Milliken Publishing Co., St Louis, MO	800-325-4136
Minerals, Metals & Materials Society (TMS), Warrendale, PA	800-759-4867
Ministry Publications, Scottsdale, AZ	800-573-4105
Minnesota Historical Society Press, St Paul, MN	800-647-7827
MIT Press, Cambridge, MA	(orders only) 800-356-0343
Mitchell Lane Publishers, Elkton, MD	800-814-5484
MMB Music Inc., St Louis, MO	800-543-3771
Modern Learning Press/Programs for Education, Rosemont, NJ	800-627-5867
Momentum Books Ltd, Troy, MI	800-758-1870
Monday Morning Books Inc., Palo Alto, CA	800-255-6048
Mondo Publishing, Greenvale, NY	800-242-3650
Money Market Directories Inc., Charlottesville, VA	800-446-2810
Monthly Review Press, New York, NY	800-670-9499
Moody Press, Chicago, IL	800-678-8912
Moon Publications Inc., Chico, CA	800-345-5473
More Than a Card Inc., New Orleans, LA	800-635-9672
Morehouse Publishing Co., Ridgefield, CT	(cust serv) 800-877-0012

Publisher/Distributor	Toll-Free No.
Morgan Kaufmann Publishers Inc., San Francisco, CA	800-745-7323
Morgan Quitno Corp., Lawrence, KS	800-457-0742
Morgan-Rand Inc., Huntingdon Valley, PA	800-677-3839
Morningside Bookshop, Dayton, OH	800-648-9710
Morrow Junior Books, New York, NY	800-843-9389
William Morrow & Co. Inc., New York, NY	800-843-9389
Morton Publishing Co., Englewood, CO	800-384-3777
Mosaic Press, Buffalo, NY	800-387-8992
Mosaic Press, Cincinnati, OH	800-932-4044
Mosby, St Louis, MO	800-325-4177
Motorbooks International Publishers & Wholesalers Inc., Osceola, WI	800-458-0454
Mountain n' Air Books, Tujunga, CA	800-446-9696
Mountain Press Publishing Co., Missoula, MT	800-234-5308
Mountaineers Books, Seattle, WA	800-553-4453
Andrew Mowbray Inc. Publishers, Lincoln, RI	800-999-4697
Moznaim Publishing Corp., Brooklyn, NY	800-364-5118
Mulberry Paperback Books, New York, NY	800-843-9389
Multnomah Books, Sisters, OR	800-929-0910
Municipal Analysis Services Inc., Austin, TX	800-488-3932
Mike Murach & Associates Inc., Fresno, CA	800-221-5528
MUSA Video Publishing, Carrolton, TX	800-933-6872
Music Sales Corp., New York, NY	800-431-7187
Mustang Publishing Co. Inc., Memphis, TN	800-250-8713
NADJA Publishing, Lake Forest, CA	800-795-9750
NAFSA: Association of International Educators, Washington, DC	800-836-4994
Naiad Press Inc., Tallahassee, FL	(orders only) 800-533-1973
NAPSAC Reproductions, Marble Hill, MO	800-758-8629
Narwhal Press Inc., Charleston, SC	800-981-1943
National Academy Press, Washington, DC	800-624-6242
National Archives & Records Administration, Washington, DC	(orders) 800-234-8861
National Association of Broadcasters, Washington, DC	800-368-5644
National Association of Secondary School Principals, Reston, VA	800-253-7746
National Association of Social Workers (NASW), Washington, DC	800-638-8799
National Council of Teachers of English (NCTE), Urbana, IL	800-369-6283
National Council on Radiation Protection & Measurements, Bethesda, MD	800-229-2652
National Geographic Society, Washington, DC	800-638-4077
National Golf Foundation, Jupiter, FL	800-733-6006
National Information Center for Educational Media, Albuquerque, NM	800-926-8328
National Institute for Trial Advocacy, Notre Dame, IN	800-225-6482
National Learning Corp., Syosset, NY	800-645-6337
National Museum of Women in the Arts, Washington, DC	800-222-7270
National Science Teachers Association (NSTA), Arlington, VA	(sales) 800-722-NSTA
National Textbook Co. (NTC), Lincolnwood, IL	(orders only) 800-323-4900
National Underwriter Co., Cincinnati, OH	800-543-0874
Naturegraph Publishers Inc., Happy Camp, CA	800-390-5353
Naval Institute Press, Annapolis, MD	800-233-8764

Publisher/Distributor	Toll-Free No.
NavPress Publishing Group, Colorado Springs, CO	800-366-7788
NBM Publishing Inc., New York, NY	800-886-1223
Neibauer Press, Warminster, PA	800-322-6277
Nelson Publications, Port Chester, NY	800-333-6357
Thomas Nelson Inc., Nashville, TN	800-251-4000
NelsonWord Childrens Publication Group, Nashville, TN	800-251-4000
New Amsterdam Books, Franklin, NY	800-944-4040
New City Press, Hyde Park, NY	(orders only) 800-462-5980
New Dimensions in Education, Waterbury, CT	800-227-9120
New Directions Publishing Corp., New York, NY	(PA) 800-233-4830
New Editions International Ltd, Sedona, AZ	800-777-4751
New Harbinger Publications Inc., Oakland, CA	(orders only) 800-748-6273
New Horizon Press, Far Hills, NJ	(orders only) 800-533-7978
New Leaf Press Inc., Green Forest, AR	800-643-9535
The New Press, New York, NY	(orders) 800-233-4830
New Readers Press, Syracuse, NY	800-448-8878
New Victoria Publishers, Norwich, VT	800-326-5297
New World Library, Novato, CA	(retail orders) 800-227-3900
New York Academy of Sciences, New York, NY	800-843-6927
New York University Press, New York, NY	(orders) 800-996-6987
Newcastle Publishing Co. Inc., North Hollywood, CA	800-932-4809
NewLife Publications, Orlando, FL	800-235-7255
Newmarket Press, New York, NY	800-669-3903
Nightingale-Conant, Niles, IL	800-572-2770
Nightshade Press, Troy, ME	(book orders only) 800-497-9258
Nilgiri Press, Tomales, CA	800-475-2369
Nolo Press, Berkeley, CA	800-992-6656
Norman Publishing, San Francisco, CA	800-544-9359
North Country Press, Unity, ME	800-722-2169
North River Press Inc., Great Barrington, MA	800-486-2665
North-South Books Inc., New York, NY	800-282-8257
Northland Publishing Co., Flagstaff, AZ	800-346-3257
Northmont Publishing Co., West Bloomfield, MI	800-472-3485
NorthWord Press Inc., Minocqua, WI	(orders only) 800-336-6398
Jeffrey Norton Publishers Inc., Guilford, CT	800-243-1234
W W Norton & Company Inc., New York, NY	(orders & cust serv) 800-233-4830
Nova Press, Los Angeles, CA	800-949-6175
NTC Publishing Group, Lincolnwood, IL	800-323-4900
Nystrom, Chicago, IL	800-621-8086
Oasis Press, Grants Pass, OR	800-228-2275
Ocean View Books, Denver, CO	800-848-6222
Offender Preparation & Education Network Inc. (OPEN), Dallas, TX	800-966-1966
Official Airline Guides, Oak Brook, IL	800-323-3537
Ohara Publications Inc., Valencia, CA	800-423-2874
Ohio University Press, Athens, OH	800-621-2736
Oldbuck Press Inc., Conway, AR	800-884-8184

Publisher/Distributor	Toll-Free No.
Oliver Press Inc., Minneapolis, MN	800-8-OLIVER
OM SAI Publications, Arcadia, CA	800-900-9917
Omnibus Press, New York, NY	800-431-7187
Omnigraphics Inc., Detroit, MI	800-234-1340
One-Off CD Shop Washington Inc., White Plains, MD	800-678-8760
OneOnOne Computer Training, Addison, IL	800-424-8668
Online Press Inc/Quick Course(R) Books, Bellevue, WA	800-854-3344
Open Horizons Publishing Co., Fairfield, IA	800-796-6130
Optical Society of America (OSA), Washington, DC	800-582-0416
Orbis Books, Maryknoll, NY	(orders) 800-258-5838
Orca Book Publishers, Custer, WA	800-210-5277
Orchard Books, New York, NY	800-433-3411
Oregon Catholic Press, Portland, OR	800-548-8749
O'Reilly & Associates Inc., Sebastopol, CA	800-998-9938
Organization for Economic Cooperation & Development, Washington, DC	800-456-6323
Orion Research Corp., Scottsdale, AZ	800-844-0759
Oryx Press, Phoenix, AZ	800-279-6799
Osborne/McGraw-Hill, Berkeley, CA	800-227-0900
Otter Creek Publishing Co., Mulvane, KS	(voice & fax) 800-447-9099
Our Sunday Visitor Publishing, Huntington, IN	(orders) 800-348-2440
Overmountain Press, Johnson City, TN	800-992-2691
Richard C Owen Publishers Inc., Katonah, NY	800-336-5588
Oxbridge Communications Inc., New York, NY	800-955-0231
Oxford University Press, Inc., New York, NY	(orders) 800-451-7556
Oxmoor House Inc., Birmingham, AL	800-366-4712
Ozark Publishing Inc., Prairie Grove, AR	800-321-5671
P & R Publishing Co., Phillipsburg, NJ	800-631-0094
Pacific Press Publishing Association, Nampa, ID	800-447-7377
Paladin Press, Boulder, CO	800-392-2400
Palm Island Press, Key West, FL	800-763-4345
Panoptic Enterprises, Burke, VA	800-594-4766
Pantheon Books/Schocken Books, New York, NY	800-638-6460
Papier-Mache Press, Watsonville, CA	800-776-1956
PAR Publishers, Burr Ridge, IL	800-634-3963
Para Publishing Co., Santa Barbara, CA	800-PARAPUB
Paraclete Press, Orleans, MA	800-451-5006
Paradigm Publications, Brookline, MA	800-873-3946
Paradise Cay Publications, Middletown, CA	800-736-4509
Paragon House, New York, NY	800-937-5557
Parenting Press Inc., Seattle, WA	800-99-BOOKS
Parker Publications Division, Michie Butterworth, Carlsbad, CA	800-452-9873
Parlay International, Emeryville, CA	800-457-2752
Parthenon Publishing Group Inc., Pearl River, NY	800-735-4744
Passage Press, Sandy, UT	800-873-0075
Passport Books, Lincolnwood, IL	(orders only) 800-323-4900
Path Press Inc., Chicago, IL	800-548-2600

Publisher/Distributor	Toll-Free No.
Patrice Press, Tucson, AZ	800-367-9242
Pauline Books & Media, Boston, MA	800-876-4463
Paulist Press, Mahwah, NJ	(fax orders only) 800-836-3161
PBC International Inc., Glen Cove, NY	800-527-2826
Peachpit Press, Berkeley, CA	800-283-9444
Peachtree Publishers Ltd, Atlanta, GA	800-241-0113
T H Peek Publisher, Palo Alto, CA	800-962-9245
Pelican Publishing Co. Inc., Gretna, LA	800-843-1724
Pencil Point Press Inc., Fairfield, NJ	800-356-1299
Penfield Press, Iowa City, IA	800-728-9998
The Pennsylvania State University Press, University Park, PA	800-326-9180
PennWell Books, Tulsa, OK	800-752-9764
Pentrex Pub, Pasadena, CA	(continental US only) 800-950-9333
Per Annum Inc., New York, NY	800-548-1108
Peradam Press, Santa Barbara, CA	800-241-8689
Perfection Learning Corp., Des Moines, IA	800-762-2999
Peter Pauper Press Inc., White Plains, NY	800-833-2311
Peterson's, Princeton, NJ	800-338-3282
Petroleum Extension Service Petex, Austin, TX	800-687-4132
Pfeifer-Hamilton Publishers, Duluth, MN	800-247-6789
Pfeiffer & Co., San Francisco, CA	800-274-4434
Phi Delta Kappa Educational Foundation, Bloomington, IN	800-766-1156
Philosophy Documentation Center, Bowling Green, OH	800-444-2419
Phoenix Learning Resources, New York, NY	800-221-1274
Phoenix Publishing, Lansing, MI	800-345-0325
Picton Press, Rockport, ME	(credit card orders only) 800-742-8667
Pictorial Histories Publishing Co. Inc., Missoula, MT	800-638-6873
Picture Me Books, Akron, OH	800-762-6775
Pierian Press, Ann Arbor, MI	800-678-2435
Pilgrim Press/United Church Press, Cleveland, OH	800-537-3394
The Pilgrim's Path, Ojai, CA	800-284-5864, ext. H
Pineapple Press Inc., Sarasota, FL	(orders) 800-746-3275
Pinon Press, Colorado Springs, CO	800-746-6624
Pitspopany Press, Cedarhurst, NY	800-232-2931
PJS Publications Inc., Peoria, IL	800-521-2885
Planetary Publications, Boulder Creek, CA	800-372-3100
Planning/Communications, River Forest, IL	888-366-5200
Pleasant Co. Publications Inc., Middleton, WI	800-845-0005
Plenum Publishing Corp., New York, NY	800-221-9369
Plough Publishing House, Farmington, PA	800-521-8011
Pomegranate Artbooks Inc., Rohnert Park, CA	800-227-1428
Popular Culture Ink, Ann Arbor, MI	800-678-8828
Clarkson Potter Publishers, New York, NY	800-526-4264
Powersource Press, Maui, HI	800-646-0415
P P I Publishing, Kettering, OH	800-668-7325
Prakken Publications Inc., Ann Arbor, MI	(orders only) 800-530-9673

Publisher/Distributor	Toll-Free No.
Praxis Music Publications Inc., Bedford, TX	800-814-0107
P R B Productions, Albany, CA	800-772-0780
Precept Press, Chicago, IL	800-225-3775
Prehistory Press, Madison, WI	800-809-6960
PREP Publishing, Fayetteville, NC	800-533-2814
Prescott Publishing Co., Maryville, MO	800-528-5197
Preservation Press, Washington, DC	800-766-6847
Preservation Press Inc., Swedesboro, NJ	800-264-5422
Presidio Press, Novato, CA	800-966-5179
Princeton Architectural Press, New York, NY	800-458-1131
Princeton Book Co. Publishers, Pennington, NJ	800-220-7149
Princeton University Press, Princeton, NJ	800-777-4726
The Printers Shopper, Chula Vista, CA	800-854-2911
Pro Lingua Associates, Brattleboro, VT	800-366-4775
Productivity Press Inc., Portland, OR	800-394-6868
Professional & Technical Publishing, New York, NY	800-735-8655
The Professional Education Group Inc., Minnetonka, MN	800-229-2531
Professional Publications Inc., Belmont, CA	800-426-1178
Professional Publishing, Burr Ridge, IL	800-634-3966
Professional Resource Exchange Inc., Sarasota, FL	800-443-3364
Professional Tax & Business Publications, Columbia, SC	800-829-8087
Prometheus Books, Amherst, NY	800-421-0351
Pruett Publishing Co., Boulder, CO	800-247-8224
Prufrock Press, Waco, TX	800-998-2208
Psychological Assessment Resources Inc. (PAR), Lutz, FL	800-331-8378
The Psychological Corp., San Antonio, TX	(cust serv) 800-228-0752
Public Utilities Reports Inc., Vienna, VA	800-368-5001
Purdue University Press, West Lafayette, IN	800-933-9637
Purple Mountain Press Ltd, Fleischmanns, NY	800-325-2665
Putnam Berkley Group Inc., New York, NY	800-631-8571
QED Press, Fort Bragg, CA	800-773-7782
Quail Ridge Press, Brandon, MS	800-343-1583
Quality Education Data, Denver, CO	800-525-5811
Quality Medical Publishing Inc., St Louis, MO	800-423-6865
Quality Press, Milwaukee, WI	800-248-1946
Quality Resources, New York, NY	800-247-8519
Queenship Publishing Co., Santa Barbara, CA	800-647-9882
Quintessence Publishing Co. Inc., Carol Stream, IL	800-621-0387
Quixote Press, Fort Madison, IA	800-571-BOOK
Rainbow Books Inc., Highland City, FL	(book orders) 800-356-9315
Rainbow Publishers, La Jolla, CA	800-323-7337
Raintree/Steck-Vaughn Publishers, Austin, TX	800-531-5015
Rand McNally, Skokie, IL	800-333-0136
Random House Inc., New York, NY	800-726-0600
Ransom Hill Press, Ramona, CA	800-423-0620
Rayve Productions Inc., Windsor, CA	800-852-4890

Publisher/Distributor	Toll-Free No.
Reader's Digest Association Inc., Pleasantville, NY	800-431-1726
Reader's Digest USA, Pleasantville, NY	800-431-1726
Reader's Digest USA Condensed Books, Pleasantville, NY	800-431-1726
Red Crane Books Inc., Santa Fe, NM	800-922-3392
Redleaf Press, St Paul, MN	800-423-8309
Thomas Reed Publications Inc., Boston, MA	800-995-4995
Reference Press Inc., Austin, TX	(orders only) 800-486-8666
Regal Books, Ventura, CA	800-235-3415
Regnery Publishing Inc., Washington, DC	800-462-6420
Regular Baptist Press, Schaumburg, IL	(orders only) 800-727-4440
Rei America Inc., Miami, FL	800-726-5337
Research Periodicals & Books Publishing House, Houston, TX	800-521-0061
Research Press, Champaign, IL	800-519-2707
Resurrection Press Ltd, Williston Park, NY	800-892-6657
Retail Reporting Corp., New York, NY	800-251-4545
Fleming H Revell, Grand Rapids, MI	800-877-2665
Review & Herald Publishing Association, Hagerstown, MD	800-234-7630
Rip Off Press Inc., Auburn, CA	800-468-2669
Rising Sun Publishing, Marietta, GA	800-524-2813
Riverside Publishing Co., Itasca, IL	800-656-8420
	(orders) 800-767-3378
Rizzoli International Publications Inc., New York, NY	(orders & cust serv) 800-221-7945
Roberts Rinehart Publishing Group, Boulder, CO	800-352-1985
Rockbridge Publishing Co., Berryville, VA	800-473-3943
Rock Hill Press, Bala Cynwyd, PA	888-ROCKHILL
Rockwell Publishing, Bellvue, WA	800-221-9347
Rocky River Publishers, Shepherdstown, WV	800-343-0686
Rodale Press Inc., Emmaus, PA	800-848-4735
Rosen Publishing Group Inc., New York, NY	800-237-9932
Ross Books, Berkeley, CA	800-367-0930
Norman Ross Publishing Inc., New York, NY	800-648-8850
Roth Publishing Inc., Great Neck, NY	800-899-ROTH
Fred B Rothman & Co., Littleton, CO	800-457-1986
Rowman & Littlefield Publishers Inc., Lanham, MD	800-462-6420
Royal House Publishing Co. Inc., Beverly Hills, CA	800-277-5533
RPI Publishing Inc., Julian, CA	800-873-8384
Rudi Publishing, San Francisco, CA	(orders only) 800-999-6901
Rudra Press, Portland, OR	800-876-7798
Running Press Book Publishers, Philadelphia, PA	(orders) 800-345-5359
Russell Sage Foundation, New York, NY	800-666-2211
Rutgers University Press, New Brunswick, NJ	(orders only) 800-446-9323
Rutledge Books Inc., Bethel, CT	800-278-8533
Rutledge Hill Press, Nashville, TN	800-234-4234
William H Sadlier Inc., New York, NY	800-221-5175
Sagamore Publishing Inc., Champaign, IL	(orders) 800-327-5557
St Anthony Messenger Press, Cincinnati, OH	800-488-0488

Publisher/Distributor	Toll-Free No.
Saint Anthony Publishing Inc., Reston, VA	800-632-0123
St Bede's Publications, Petersham, MA	(orders) 800-247-6553
St Martin's Press Inc., New York, NY	800-221-7945
St Martin's Press Inc. College Division (New York), New York, NY	800-470-4767
St Martin's Press Inc. Scholarly & Reference Division, New York, NY	800-817-2525
Saint Mary's Press, Winona, MN	800-533-8095
Saint Nectarios Press, Seattle, WA	800-643-4233
Salem Press Inc., Englewood Cliffs, NJ	800-221-1592
San Francisco Study Center, San Francisco, CA	800-484-4173
J S Sanders & Co. Inc., Nashville, TN	800-350-1101
Sandlapper Publishing Inc., Orangeburg, SC	800-849-7263
Santa Monica Press, Santa Monica, CA	800-784-9553
Santillana Publishing Co. Inc., Miami, FL	800-245-8584
Sarpedon, New York, NY	800-207-8045
Sasquatch Books, Seattle, WA	800-775-0817
W B Saunders Company, Philadelphia, PA	(cust serv) 800-545-2522
K G Saur, New Providence, NJ	(orders only) 800-521-8110
Savage Press, Superior, WI	800-732-3867
Scarborough House, Lanham, MD	800-462-6420
Scepter Publishers, Princeton, NJ	800-322-8773
Schaffer Frank Publications Inc., Torrance, CA	800-421-5565
Scholarly Resources Inc., Wilmington, DE	800-772-8937
Scholars Press, Atlanta, GA	(cust serv) 800-437-6692
Scholastic Inc., New York, NY	800-392-2179
Schonfeld & Associates Inc., Lincolnshire, IL	800-205-0030
School Zone Publishing Co., Grand Haven, MI	800-253-0564
Arthur Schwartz & Co. Inc., Woodstock, NY	800-669-9080
Scott & Daughters Publishing Inc., Los Angeles, CA	800-547-2688
Scott Publications, Livonia, MI	800-458-8237
Search Resources, Houston, TX	800-460-4673
The SeedSowers, Sargent, GA	800-228-2665
Self-Counsel Press Inc., Bellingham, WA	800-663-3007
Seven Locks Press Inc., Santa Ana, CA	800-354-5348
Severn House Publishers Inc., New York, NY	800-830-3044
M E Sharpe Inc., Armonk, NY	800-541-6563
Harold Shaw Publishers, Wheaton, IL	800-SHAW-PUB
Sheed & Ward, Kansas City, MO	(cust serv) 800-333-7373
	800-444-8910
Sheep Meadow Press, Bronx, NY	800-972-4491
Sherman Asher Publishing, Santa Fe, NM	(orders) 800-474-1543
Shooting Star Press, New York, NY	800-364-5403
Signature Books Inc., Salt Lake City, UT	800-356-5687
Sigo Press, Salem, MA	800-338-0446
SIGS Books & Multimedia, New York, NY	(orders only) 800-871-7447
Silver Pixel Press, Rochester, NY	800-394-3686
Simon & Schuster, New York, NY	(cust serv) 800-223-2348

Publisher/Distributor	Toll-Free No.
Simon & Schuster, New York, NY (cont.)	(orders) 800-223-2336
Simon & Schuster Education Group, Adult Education Division: Invest Learning, San Diego, CA	800-927-9997
Simon & Schuster Trade Division, New York, NY	(orders) 800-223-2336
	(cust serv) 800-223-2348
Singular Publishing Group Inc., San Diego, CA	800-521-8545
SIRS Inc., Boca Raton, FL	800-232-7477
Skidmore-Roth Publishing Inc., Aurora, CO	800-825-3150
Skillpath Publications, Mission, KS	800-873-7545
Sky Publishing Corp., Cambridge, MA	800-253-0245
Slack Incorporated, Thorofare, NJ	800-257-8290
Smith & Kraus Inc. Publishers, Lyme, NH	800-895-4331
Gibbs Smith Publisher, Layton, UT	800-748-5439
M Lee Smith Publishers & Printers LLC, Nashville, TN	800-274-6774
Smithmark Publishers, New York, NY	800-645-9990
Smithsonian Institution Press, Washington, DC	800-782-4612
Smyth & Helwys Publishing Inc., Macon, GA	800-747-3016; 568-1248
Snow Lion Publications Inc., Ithaca, NY	800-950-0313
Society for Industrial & Applied Mathematics, Philadelphia, PA	800-447-SIAM
Society for Mining, Metallurgy & Exploration Inc., Littleton, CO	800-763-3132
Society of Manufacturing Engineers, Dearborn, MI	800-733-4SME
Solitaire Publishing, Tampa, FL	800-226-0286
Sophia Institute Press, Manchester, NH	800-888-9344
Sopris West Inc., Longmont, CO	800-547-6747
Soundprints, Norwalk, CT	800-228-7839
Source Books, Trabuco Canyon, CA	800-695-4237
South Carolina Bar, Columbia, SC	(SC only) 800-768-7787
South-Western Educational Publishing, Cincinnati, OH	800-543-0487
Southern Illinois University Press, Carbondale, IL	800-346-2680
Southern Institute Press, Indian Rocks Beach, FL	800-633-4891
Space Link Books, New York, NY	800-444-2524
Specialty Press Publishers & Wholesalers, North Branch, MN	800-895-4585
Sphinx Publishing, Clearwater, FL	800-226-5291
Spinsters Ink, Duluth, MN	800-301-6860
SPIRAL Books, Manchester, NH	800-SPIRALL
Spizzirri Publishing Inc., Rapid City, SD	800-325-9819
Spoken Arts Inc., New Rochelle, NY	800-726-4090
Springer-Verlag New York Inc., New York, NY	800-SPRINGER
Springhouse Corp., Springhouse, PA	800-346-7844
Squarebooks Inc., Santa Rosa, CA	800-345-6699
ST Publications Book Division, Cincinnati, OH	800-925-1110
STA-Kris Inc., Marshalltown, IA	800-369-5676
Stackpole Books, Mechanicsburg, PA	800-732-3669
Stalsby-Wilson Press, Houston, TX	800-642-3228
Standard Publishing Co., Cincinnati, OH	800-543-1301
Standard Publishing Corp., Boston, MA	800-682-5959

Publisher/Distributor	Toll-Free No.
Starlite Inc., St Petersburg, FL	800-577-2929
State House Press, Austin, TX	800-421-3378
State University of New York Press, Albany, NY	800-666-2211
Steck-Vaughn Co., Austin, TX	800-531-5015
Stenhouse Publishers, York, ME	(sales) 800-988-9812
Sterling Publishing Co. Inc., New York, NY	800-367-9692
Stillpoint Publishing, Walpole, NH	800-847-4014
Stockton Press, New York, NY	800-221-2123
Stoeger Publishing Co., Wayne, NJ	800-631-0722
Stone Bridge Press, Berkeley, CA	800-947-7271
Storey Publishing/Garden Way Publishing, Pownal, VT	800-359-7436
Storm Peak Press, Seattle, WA	800-499-0162
Strang Communications Co./Creation House, Lake Mary, FL	800-451-4598
Studio Press, Soulsbyville, CA	800-445-7160
Success Advertising & Publishing, Warsaw, NY	800-330-4643
Sulzburger & Graham Publishing Co. Ltd, New York, NY	800-366-7086
Summit Publications, Indianapolis, IN	800-419-0200
Summit Publishing Group, Arlington, TX	800-875-3346
Summit University Press, Livingston, MT	800-245-5445
Summy-Birchard Inc., Miami, FL	800-327-7643
Sunbelt Books, El Cajon, CA	800-626-6579
Sundance Publishing LP, Littleton, MA	800-245-3388
Sunset Books, Menlo Park, CA	800-227-7346
	(CA) 800-321-0372
Sunstar Publishing Ltd, Fairfield, IA	800-532-4734
SuperPuppy Press, Escondido, CA	800-342-7877
Surrey Books Inc., Chicago, IL	800-326-4430
Swedenborg Foundation Inc., West Chester, PA	(cust serv) 800-355-3222
SYBEX Inc., Alameda, CA	800-227-2346
Syracuse University Press, Syracuse, NY	(orders only) 800-365-8929
The Taft Group, Rockville, MD	800-877-8238
Tapestry Press Ltd, Acton, MA	800-535-2007
Taunton Press Inc., Newtown, CT	800-283-7252
	(orders) 800-888-8286
Taylor & Francis Publishers Inc., Bristol, PA	800-821-8312
Taylor Publishing Co., Dallas, TX	(voice & fax) 800-677-2800
te Neues Publishing Co., New York, NY	800-352-0305
TEACH Services, Brushton, NY	800-367-1844
Teacher Created Materials Inc., Westminster, CA	800-662-4321
Teacher Ideas Press, Englewood, CO	800-237-6124
Teachers Friend Publications Inc., Riverside, CA	800-343-9680
Teaching Strategies, Washington, DC	800-637-3652
Technical Association of the Pulp & Paper Industry (TAPPI), Atlanta, GA	800-332-8686
Technology Training Systems Inc., Aurora, CO	800-676-8871
Technomic Publishing Co. Inc., Lancaster, PA	800-233-9936
Techware Corp., Altamonte Springs, FL	800-TECHWARE

Publisher/Distributor	Toll-Free No.
Telecom Library Inc., New York, NY	800-542-7279
Temple University Press, Philadelphia, PA	800-447-1656
Templegate Publishers, Springfield, IL	800-367-4844
Ten Speed Press, Berkeley, CA	800-841-BOOK
Tesla Book Co., Chula Vista, CA	800-398-2056
Tetra Press, Blacksburg, VA	800-526-0650
Texas A & M University Press, College Station, TX	(orders) 800-826-8911
Texas Instruments Data Book Marketing, Dallas, TX	800-336-5236
Texas Tech University Press, Lubbock, TX	800-832-4042
Texas Western Press, El Paso, TX	800-488-3789 (4UTEP-TWP)
TFH Publications Inc., Neptune, NJ	800-631-2188
Thames and Hudson Inc., New York, NY	800-233-4830
That Patchwork Place Inc., Bothell, WA	800-426-3126
Theosophical Publishing House, Wheaton, IL	800-669-9425
Theta Corp., Rocky Hill, CT	800-995-1550
Thieme Medical Publishers Inc., New York, NY	800-782-3488
Thinkers Press, Davenport, IA	800-397-7117
Thinking Publications, Eau Claire, WI	800-225-4769
Third Story Books, Wichita, KS	800-334-6018
Charles C Thomas Publisher Ltd, Springfield, IL	800-258-8980
Thomas More, Allen, TX	800-527-5030
Thomasson-Grant Publishers, Charlottesville, VA	800-999-1780
Thomson Financial Publishing, Skokie, IL	800-444-0064
Thorndike Press (Macmillan Publishing USA, Div. of Simon & Schuster Inc.), Thorndike, ME	800-223-6121
Tiare Publications, Lake Geneva, WI	800-420-0579
Tidewater Publishers, Centreville, MD	800-638-7641
Timber Press Inc., Portland, OR	800-327-5680
Time Being Books-Poetry in Sight & Sound, St Louis, MO	800-331-6605
Time Life Inc., Alexandria, VA	800-621-7026
Times Books, New York, NY	800-733-3000
Times Mirror Higher Education Group, Dubuque, IA	800-338-5578
T L C Genealogy, Miami Beach, FL	800-858-8558
Todd Publications, West Nyack, NY	800-747-1056
TODTRI Productions Ltd, New York, NY	800-241-4477
Tor Books, New York, NY	(cust serv) 800-221-7945
Torah Aura Productions, Los Angeles, CA	800-238-6724
Tower Publishing Co., Standish, ME	800-969-8693
J N Townsend Publishing, Exeter, NH	800-333-9883
Traders Press Inc., Greenville, SC	800-927-8222
Tradery House, Memphis, TN	800-727-1034
Trafton Publishing, Cary, NC	800-356-9315
Trails Illustrated, Evergreen, CO	800-962-1643
Trakker Maps Inc., Miami, FL	800-432-1730
Transnational Publishers Inc., Irvington-on-Hudson, NY	(orders) 800-914-8186
Transportation Technical Service Inc., Fredericksburg, VA	800-666-4TTS

Publisher/Distributor	Toll-Free No.
Travelers' Tales Inc., Sebastopol, CA	800-998-9938
Treasure Publishing, Fort Collins, CO	800-284-0158
Tree of Life Publications, Joshua Tree, CA	800-200-2046
Treehaus Communications Inc., Loveland, OH	(orders) 800-638-4287
Tricycle Press, Berkeley, CA	800-841-2665
Trinity Press International, Valley Forge, PA	800-421-8874
TripBuilder Inc., New York, NY	800-525-9745
TriQuarterly Books, Evanston, IL	(orders only) 800-621-2736
Troll Communications, Mahwah, NJ	800-526-5289
Turtle Point Press, Chappaqua, NY	800-453-2992
Charles E Tuttle Co. Inc., Boston, MA	(cust serv) 800-526-2778
Twenty-Third Publications Inc., Mystic, CT	800-321-0411
Twin Sisters Productions Inc., Akron, OH	800-248-8946
Two Roads Publishing, Santa Barbara, CA	800-438-7444
2 13 61 Publications Inc., Los Angeles, CA	800-992-1361
Tyndale House Publishers Inc., Wheaton, IL	800-323-9400
Type & Temperament Inc., Gladwyne, PA	800-IHS-TYPE
ULI-The Urban Land Institute, Washington, DC	800-462-1254
Ulysses Press, Berkeley, CA	800-377-2542
UMI, Ann Arbor, MI	800-521-0600
	(Canada) 800-343-5299
UMI Publications Inc., Charlotte, NC	800-462-5831
Unarius Academy of Science Publications, El Cajon, CA	800-475-7062
Unicor Medical Inc., Montgomery, AL	800-825-7421
Unique Publications Books & Videos, Burbank, CA	800-332-3330
United Methodist Publishing House, Nashville, TN	800-251-3320
United Nations Publications, New York, NY	800-253-9646
United States Holocaust Memorial Museum, Washington, DC	(orders) 800-259-9998
United States Institute of Peace, Washington, DC	(cust serv) 800-868-8064
United States Pharmacopoeial Convention Inc., Rockville, MD	800-227-8772
United States Tennis Association, White Plains, NY	800-223-0456
Universal Reference Publications, Boca Raton, FL	800-377-7551
University Museum of Archaeology & Anthropology, Philadelphia, PA	800-306-1941
University of Alabama Press, Tuscaloosa, AL	(orders only) 800-825-9980
The University of Arizona Press, Tucson, AZ	(orders) 800-426-3797
University of Arkansas Press, Fayetteville, AR	800-626-0090
University of California Press, Berkeley, CA	800-822-6657
University of Chicago Press, Chicago, IL	(orders) 800-621-2736
University of Denver Center for Teaching International Relations Publications, Denver, CO	800-967-2847
University of Georgia Press, Athens, GA	(orders only) 800-266-5842
University of Hawaii Press, Honolulu, HI	800-956-2840
University of Idaho Press, Moscow, ID	800-847-7377
University of Illinois Press, Champaign, IL	(orders) 800-545-4703
University of Iowa Press, Iowa City, IA	(orders only) 800-235-2665
University of Minnesota Press, Minneapolis, MN	800-388-3863

Publisher/Distributor	Toll-Free No.
University of Missouri Press, Columbia, MO	800-828-1894
University of Nebraska Press, Lincoln, NE	(orders) 800-755-1105
University of New Mexico Press, Albuquerque, NM	(orders only) 800-249-7737
The University of North Carolina Press, Chapel Hill, NC	(orders only) 800-848-6224
University of Notre Dame Press, Notre Dame, IN	(orders) 800-621-2736
University of Oklahoma Press, Norman, OK	(orders) 800-627-7377
University of Oregon ERIC Clearinghouse on Educational Management, Eugene, OR	800-438-8841
University of Pennsylvania Press, Philadelphia, PA	(orders & cust serv only) 800-445-9880
University of Pittsburgh Press, Pittsburgh, PA	800-666-2211
University of Tennessee Press, Knoxville, TN	(warehouse, continental US except IL) 800-621-2736
University of the South Press, Sewanee, TN	800-367-1179
University of Utah Press, Salt Lake City, UT	800-773-6672
University of Washington Press, Seattle, WA	800-441-4115
University of Wisconsin Press, Madison, WI	800-829-9559
University Press of America Inc., Lanham, MD	800-462-6420
University Press of Florida, Gainesville, FL	(sales only) 800-226-3822
The University Press of Kentucky, Lexington, KY	800-666-2211
University Press of Mississippi, Jackson, MS	800-737-7788
University Press of New England, Hanover, NH	(orders only) 800-421-1561
University Publications of America, Bethesda, MD	800-692-6300
University Publishing Group, Frederick, MD	800-654-8188
Upper Room Books, Nashville, TN	800-972-0433
U S A Gymnastics, Indianapolis, IN	800-4-USAGYM
US Catholic Conference, Washington, DC	800-235-8722
US Games Systems Inc., Stamford, CT	800-544-2637, 800-54GAMES
Utah State University Press, Logan, UT	800-239-9974
VanDam Inc., New York, NY	800-UNFOLDS
Vanderbilt University Press, Nashville, TN	(orders only) 800-937-5557
VCH Publishers Inc., New York, NY	800-367-8249
Ventana Communications Group Inc., Chapel Hill, NC	(orders only) 800-743-5369
Vernon Publications Inc., Bellevue, WA	800-726-4707
Vestal Press Ltd, Vestal, NY	800-292-4738
VGM Career Horizons, Lincolnwood, IL	(orders only) 800-323-4900
Visible Ink Press, Detroit, MI	800-776-6265
Vision Books International, Santa Rosa, CA	800-377-3431
Vista Publishing Inc., Long Branch, NJ	800-634-2498
Visual Education Association, Springfield, OH	(US) 800-243-7070
Volcano Press Inc., Volcano, CA	800-879-9636
Voyageur Press, Stillwater, MN	800-888-9653
W D Farmer Residence Designer Inc., Atlanta, GA	800-225-7526 (GA) 800-221-7526
Wadsworth Publishing Co	800-354-9706
George Wahr Publishing Co., Ann Arbor, MI	800-805-2497

Publisher/Distributor	Toll-Free No.
Waite Group Press, Corte Madera, CA	800-368-9369
J Weston Walch Publisher, Portland, ME	800-558-2846
Walker & Co., New York, NY	800-AT-WALKER
Walker's Research LLC, San Mateo, CA	800-258-5737
Wallace Homestead Book Co., Radnor, PA	800-695-1214
Walnut Creek CDROM, Walnut, CA	800-786-9907
Walter Foster Publishing Inc., Laguna Hills, CA	800-426-0099
Warren, Gorham & Lamont, New York, NY	800-922-0066
Warren Publishing House, Everett, WA	800-421-5565
Washington State University Press, Pullman, WA	800-354-7360
Waterfront Books, Burlington, VT	(orders) 800-639-6063
Watson-Guptill Publications, New York, NY	800-451-1741
Weatherhill Inc., New York, NY	800-788-7323
Weil Publishing Co. Inc., Augusta, ME	800-877-WEIL
Samuel Weiser Inc., York Beach, ME	800-423-7087
Weka Publishing Inc., Shelton, CT	800-222-9352
Wellspring, York, PA	800-533-3561
Wesleyan University Press, Middletown, CT	800-421-1561
West Publishing Co., St Paul, MN	(orders only) 800-328-9352
	(credit card only) 800-340-9378
Westcliffe Publishers Inc., Englewood, CO	800-523-3692
Western Psychological Services, Los Angeles, CA	(US & Canada) 800-648-8857
The Westminster Press/John Knox Press, Louisville, KY	800-395-7234
WH&O International, Wellesley, MA	800-553-6678
Wheatherstone Press, Portland, OR	800-980-0077
Whispering Coyote Press, Dallas, TX	800-929-6104
Whitaker House, Springdale, PA	800-444-4484
Whitehorse Press, North Conway, NH	800-531-1133
Albert Whitman & Co., Morton Grove, IL	800-255-7675
Whole Person Associates Inc., Duluth, MN	800-247-6789
Wichita Eagle & Beacon Publishing Co., Wichita, KS	800-825-6397
Wide World of Maps Inc., Phoenix, AZ	800-279-7654
Wilderness Adventures Press, Gallatin Gateway, MT	800-925-3339
Wilderness Press, Berkeley, CA	800-443-7227
John Wiley & Sons Inc., New York, NY	(orders only) 800-CALL WILEY
Wiley-QED Publishing, Somerset, NJ	800-225-5945
William K Bradford Publishing Co. Inc., Acton, MA	800-421-2009
Williams & Wilkins, Baltimore, MD	800-638-0672
Williamson Publishing Co., Charlotte, VT	800-234-8791
Willow Creek Press, Minocqua, WI	800-850-9453
H W Wilson Co., Bronx, NY	800-367-6770
The Wimmer Companies/Cook Book Distribution, Memphis, TN	800-727-1034
Win Publications!, Tulsa, OK	800-749-4597
Windhorse Publications, Newmarket, NH	800-303-5728
Windward Publishing Inc., Miami, FL	800-330-6232
The Wine Appreciation Guild Ltd, San Francisco, CA	800-231-9463

Publisher/Distributor	Toll-Free No.
Winston-Derek Publishers Group Inc., Nashville, TN	800-826-1888
Wintergreen/Orchard House Inc., New Orleans, LA	800-321-9479
WJ Fantasy Inc., Bridgeport, CT	800-ABC-PLAY
Woodbine House, Bethesda, MD	800-843-7323
Woodbridge Press Publishing Co., Santa Barbara, CA	800-237-6053
Woodland Books, Pleasant Grove, UT	800-777-2665
Word Publishing, Dallas, TX	800-933-9673
Wordware Publishing Inc., Plano, TX	800-229-4949
Workman Publishing Co., New York, NY	800-722-7202
World Bible Publishers Inc., Iowa Falls, IA	800-247-5111
World Book Direct Marketing, Chicago, IL	(cust serv) 800-621-8202
World Book Educational Products, Chicago, IL	(cust serv) 800-621-2802
World Book Inc., Chicago, IL	(cust serv) 800-621-8202
World Book Publishing, Chicago, IL	800-255-1750
World Citizens, Mill Valley, CA	(orders only) 800-247-6553
World Eagle Inc., Littleton, MA	800-854-8273
World Information Technologies Inc., Northport, NY	800-WORLD-INFO
World Resources Institute, Washington, DC	800-822-0504
World Scientific Publishing Co. Inc., River Edge, NJ	800-227-7562
Worldtariff, San Francisco, CA	800-556-9334
The Wright Group, Bothell, WA	(training dept) 800-523-2371
	800-345-6073
Writer's Digest Books, Cincinnati, OH	800-289-0963
Writer's Press, Boise, ID	800-574-1715
Wrox Press Inc., Chicago, IL	800-814-4527
WRS Publishing, Waco, TX	800-299-3366, ext. 616
Wyrick & Co., Charleston, SC	800-227-5898
Yardbird Books, Airville, PA	(sales) 800-622-6044
YMAA Publication Center, Jamaica Plain, MA	800-669-8892
York Press Inc., Timonium, MD	800-962-2763
Young Discovery Library, Ossining, NY	800-343-7854
Young People's Press Inc. (YPPI), San Diego, CA	800-231-9774
Yucca Tree Press, Las Cruces, NM	800-383-6183
Zagat Survey, New York, NY	800-333-3421
Zaner-Bloser Inc., Columbus, OH	800-421-3018
Zebra Books, New York, NY	800-221-2647
Ziff-Davis Press, Emeryville, CA	800-428-5331
Zondervan Publishing House, Grand Rapids, MI	(cust serv) 800-727-1309

How to Obtain an ISBN

Emery Koltay
Director
United States ISBN Agency

The International Standard Book Numbering (ISBN) system was introduced into the United Kingdom by J. Whitaker & Sons Ltd., in 1967 and into the United States in 1968 by the R. R. Bowker Company. The Technical Committee on Documentation of the International Organization for Standardization (ISO TC 46) defines the scope of the standard as follows:

... the purpose of this standard is to coordinate and standardize the use of identifying numbers so that each ISBN is unique to a title, edition of a book, or monographic publication published, or produced, by a specific publisher, or producer. Also, the standard specifies the construction of the ISBN and the location of the printing on the publication.
Books and other monographic publications may include printed books and pamphlets (in various bindings), mixed media publications, other similar media including educational films/videos and transparencies, books on cassettes, microcomputer software, electronic publications, microform publications, braille publications and maps. Serial publications and music sound recordings are specifically excluded, as they are covered by other identification systems. [ISO Standard 2108]

The ISBN is used by publishers, distributors, wholesalers, bookstores, and libraries, among others, in 90 countries to expedite such operations as order fulfillment, electronic point-of-sale checkout, inventory control, returns processing, circulation/location control, file maintenance and update, library union lists, and royalty payments.

Construction of an ISBN

An ISBN consists of 10 digits separated into the following parts:

1 Group identifier: national, geographic, language, or other convenient group
2 Publisher or producer identifier
3 Title identifier
4 Check digit

When an ISBN is written or printed, it should be preceded by the letters *ISBN,* and each part should be separated by a space or hyphen. In the United States, the hyphen is used for separation, as in the following example: ISBN 1-879500-01-9. In this example, 1 is the group identifier, 879500 is the publisher identifier, 01 is the title identifier, and 9 is the check digit. The group of English-speaking countries, which includes the United States, Australia, Canada, New Zealand, and the United Kingdom, uses the group identifiers 0 and 1.

The ISBN Organization

The administration of the ISBN system is carried out at three levels—through the International ISBN Agency in Berlin, Germany; the national agencies; and the publishing houses themselves. Responsible for assigning country prefixes and for coordinating the worldwide implementation of the system, the International ISBN Agency in Berlin has an advisory panel that represents the International Organization for Standardization (ISO), publishers, and libraries. The International ISBN Agency publishes the *Publishers International ISBN Directory,* which is distributed in the United States by R. R. Bowker. As the publisher of *Books in Print,* with its extensive and varied database of publishers' addresses, R. R. Bowker was the obvious place to initiate the ISBN system and to provide the service to the U.S. publishing industry. To date, the U.S. ISBN Agency has entered more than 87,000 publishers into the system.

ISBN Assignment Procedure

Assignment of ISBNs is a shared endeavor between the U.S. ISBN Agency and the publisher. The publisher is provided with an application form, an Advance Book Information (ABI) form, and an instruction sheet. After an application is received and verified by the agency, an ISBN publisher prefix is assigned, along with a computer-generated block of ISBNs. The publisher then has the responsibility to assign an ISBN to each title, to keep an accurate record of the numbers assigned by entering each title in the ISBN Log Book, and to report each title to the *Books in Print* database. One of the responsibilities of the ISBN Agency is to validate assigned ISBNs and to retain a record of all ISBNs in circulation.

ISBN implementation is very much market-driven. Wholesalers and distributors, such as Baker & Taylor, Brodart, and Ingram, as well as such large retail chains as Waldenbooks and B. Dalton recognize and enforce the ISBN system by requiring all new publishers to register with the ISBN Agency before accepting their books for sale. Also, the ISBN is a mandatory bibliographic element in the International Standard Bibliographical Description (ISBD). The Library of Congress Cataloging in Publication (CIP) Division directs publishers to the agency to obtain their ISBN prefixes.

Location and Display of the ISBN

On books, pamphlets, and other printed material, the ISBN shall be on the verso of the title leaf or, if this is not possible, at the foot of the title leaf itself. It should also appear at the foot of the outside back cover if practicable and at the foot of the back of the jacket if the book has one (the lower right-hand corner is recommended). If neither of these alternatives is possible, then the number shall be printed in some other prominent position on the outside. The ISBN shall also appear on any accompanying promotional materials following the provisions for location according to the format of the material.

On other monographic publications, the ISBN shall appear on the title or credit frames and any labels permanently affixed to the publication. If the publication is issued in a container that is an integral part of the publication, the ISBN shall be displayed on the label. If it is not possible to place the ISBN on the item or its label, then the number should be displayed on the bottom or the back of the container, box, sleeve, or frame. It should also appear on any accompanying material, including each component of a multitype publication.

Printing of ISBN in Machine-Readable Coding

In the last few years, much work has been done on machine-readable representations of the ISBN, and now all books should carry ISBNs in bar code. The rapid worldwide extension of bar code scanning has brought into prominence the 1980 agreement between the International Article Numbering, formerly the European Article Numbering (EAN), Association and the International ISBN Agency that translates the ISBN into an ISBN Bookland EAN bar code.

All ISBN Bookland EAN bar codes start with a national identifier (00–09 representing the United States), *except* those on books and periodicals. The agreement replaces the usual national identifier with a special "ISBN Bookland" identifier represented by the digits 978 for books (see Figure 1) and 977 for periodicals. The 978 ISBN Bookland/EAN prefix is followed by the first nine digits of the ISBN. The check digit of the ISBN is dropped and replaced by a check digit calculated according to the EAN rules.

Figure 1 / Printing the ISBN in Bookland/EAN Symbology

ISBN 1 - 879500 - 01 - 9

9 781879 500013

The following is an example of the conversion of the ISBN to ISBN Bookland/EAN:

ISBN	1-879500-01-9
ISBN without check digit	1-879500-01
Adding EAN flag	978187950001
EAN with EAN check digit	9781879500013

Five-Digit Add-On Code

In the United States, a five-digit add-on code is used for additional information. In the publishing industry, this code can be used for price information or some other specific coding. The lead digit of the five-digit add-on has been designated a currency identifier, when the add-on is used for price. Number 5 is the code for the U.S. dollar; 6 denotes the Canadian dollar; 1 the British pound; 3 the Australian dollar; and 4 the New Zealand dollar. Publishers that do not want to indicate price in the add-on should print the code 90000 (see Figure 2).

Figure 2 / Printing the ISBN Bookland/EAN Number in Bar Code with the Five-Digit Add-On Code

978 = ISBN Bookland/EAN prefix
5 + Code for U.S. $
0995 = $9.95

90000 means no information in the add-on code

Reporting the Title and the ISBN

After the publisher reports a title to the ISBN Agency, the number is validated and the title is listed in the many R. R. Bowker hard-copy and electronic publications, including *Books in Print, Forthcoming Books, Paperbound Books in Print, Books in Print Supplement, Books Out of Print, Books in Print Online, Books in Print Plus-CD ROM, Children's Books in Print, Subject Guide to Children's Books in Print, On Cassette: A Comprehensive Bibliography of Spoken Word Audiocassettes, Variety's Complete Home Video Directory, Software Encyclopedia, Software for Schools,* and other specialized publications.

For an ISBN application form and additional information, write to United States ISBN Agency, R. R. Bowker Company, 121 Chanlon Rd., New Providence, NJ 07974, or call 908-665-6770.

How to Obtain an ISSN

National Serials Data Program
Library of Congress

Two decades ago, the rapid increase in the production and dissemination of information and an intensified desire to exchange information about serials in computerized form among different systems and organizations made it increasingly clear that a means to identify serial publications at an international level was needed. The International Standard Serial Number (ISSN) was developed and has become the internationally accepted code for identifying serial publications. The number itself has no significance other than as a brief, unique, and unambiguous identifier. It is an international standard, ISO 3297, as well as a U.S. standard, ANSI/NISO Z39.9. The ISSN consists of eight digits in arabic numerals 0 to 9, except for the last, or check, digit, which can be an X. The numbers appear as two groups of four digits separated by a hyphen and preceded by the letters ISSN—for example, ISSN 1234-5679.

The ISSN is not self-assigned by publishers. Administration of the ISSN is coordinated through the ISSN Network, an intergovernmental organization within the UNESCO/UNISIST program. The network consists of national and regional centers, coordinated by the ISSN International Centre. Centers have the responsibility to register serials published in their respective countries.

Because serials are generally known and cited by title, assignment of the ISSN is inseparably linked to the key title, a standardized form of the title derived from information in the serial issue. Only one ISSN can be assigned to a title; if the title changes, a new ISSN must be assigned. Centers responsible for assigning ISSNs also construct the key title and create an associated bibliographic record.

The ISSN International Centre handles ISSN assignments for international organizations and for countries that do not have a national center. It also maintains and distributes the collective ISSN database that contains bibliographic records corresponding to each ISSN assignment as reported by the rest of the network. The database contains more than 750,000 ISSNs.

In the United States, the National Serials Data Program at the Library of Congress is responsible for assigning and maintaining the ISSNs for all U.S. serial titles. Publishers wishing to have an ISSN assigned can either request an application form from or send a current issue of the publication to the program and ask for an assignment. Assignment of the ISSN is free, and there is no charge for its use.

The ISSN is used all over the world by serial publishers to distinguish similar titles from each other. It is used by subscription services and libraries to manage files for orders, claims, and back issues. It is used in automated check-in systems by libraries that wish to process receipts more quickly. Copyright centers use the ISSN as a means to collect and disseminate royalties. It is also used as an identification code by postal services and legal deposit services. The ISSN is included as a verification element in interlibrary lending activities and for union catalogs as a collocating device. In recent years, the ISSN has been incorporated into bar codes for optical recognition of serial publications and into the standards for the identification of issues and articles in serial publications.

For further information about the ISSN or the ISSN Network, U.S. libraries and publishers should contact the National Serials Data Program, Library of Congress, Washington, DC 20540-4160 (202-707-6452; fax 202-707-6333; e-mail issn@loc.gov). Non-U.S. parties should contact the ISSN International Centre, 20 rue Bachaumont, 75002 Paris, France (telephone: (33 1) 44-88-22-20; fax (33 1) 40-26-32-43; e-mail issnic@issn.org).

ISSN application forms and instructions for obtaining an ISSN are also available via the Library of Congress World Wide Web Site, http://lcweb.loc.gov/issn, and from the Library of Congress Internet gopher site, LC MARVEL; point your gopher client to marvel.loc.gov (use port 70), or telnet to marvel.loc.gov and log in as marvel).

How to Obtain an SAN

Emery Koltay
Director,
United States ISBN/SAN Agency

SAN stands for Standard Address Number. It is a unique identification code for addresses of organizations that are involved in or served by the book industry, and that engage in repeated transactions with other members within this group. For purposes of this standard, the book industry includes book publishers, book wholesalers, book distributors, book retailers, college bookstores, libraries, library binders, and serial vendors. Schools, school systems, technical institutes, colleges, and universities are not members of this industry, but are served by it and therefore included in the SAN system.

The purpose of SAN is to facilitate communications among these organizations, of which there are several hundreds of thousands, that engage in a large volume of separate transactions with one another. These transactions include purchases of books by book dealers, wholesalers, schools, colleges, and libraries from publishers and wholesalers; payments for all such purchases; and other communications between participants. The objective of this standard is to establish an identification code system by assigning each address within the industry a discrete code to be used for positive identification for all book and serial buying and selling transactions.

Many organizations have similar names and multiple addresses, making identification of the correct contact point difficult and subject to error. In many cases, the physical movement of materials takes place between addresses that differ from the addresses to be used for the financial transactions. In such instances, there is ample opportunity for confusion and errors. Without identification by SAN, a complex record-keeping system would have to be instituted to avoid introducing errors. In addition, it is expected that problems with the current numbering system such as errors in billing, shipping, payments, and returns, will be significantly reduced by using the SAN system. SAN will also eliminate one step in the order fulfillment process: the "look-up procedure" used to assign account numbers. Previously a store or library dealing with 50 different publishers was assigned a different account number by each of the suppliers. SAN solved this problem. If a publisher indicates its SAN on its stationery and ordering documents, vendors to whom it sends transactions do not have to look up the account number, but can proceed immediately to process orders by SAN.

Libraries are involved in many of the same transactions as are book dealers, such as ordering and paying for books, charging and paying for various services to other libraries. Keeping records of transactions, whether these involve buying, selling, lending, or donations, entails similar operations that require a SAN. Having the SAN on all stationery will speed up order fulfillment and eliminate errors in shipping, billing, and crediting; this, in turn, means savings in both time and money.

History

Development of the Standard Address Number began in 1968 when Russell Reynolds, general manager of the National Association of College Stores (NACS), approached the R. R. Bowker Company and suggested that a "Standard Account Number" system be implemented in the book industry. The first draft of a standard was prepared by an American National Standards Institute (ANSI) Committee Z39 subcommittee, which was co-chaired by Russell Reynolds and Emery Koltay. After Z39 members proposed changes, the current version of the standard was approved by NACS on December 17, 1979.

The chairperson of the ANSI Z39 Subcommittee 30, which developed the approved standard, was Herbert W. Bell, former senior vice president of McGraw-Hill Book Company. The subcommittee comprised the following representatives from publishing companies, distributors, wholesalers, libraries, national cooperative online systems, schools, and school systems: Herbert W. Bell (chair), McGraw-Hill Book Company; Richard E. Bates, Holt, Rinehart and Winston; Thomas G. Brady, The Baker & Taylor Companies, Paul J. Fasana, New York Public Library; Emery I. Koltay, R. R. Bowker Company; Joan McGreevey, New York University Book Centers; Pauline F. Micciche, OCLC, Inc.; Sandra K. Paul, SKP Associates; David Gray Remington, Library of Congress; Frank Sanders, Hammond Public School System; and Peter P. Chirimbes (alternate), Stamford Board of Education.

Format

SAN consists of six digits plus a seventh *Modulus 11* check digit; a hyphen follows the third digit (XXX-XXXX) to facilitate transcription. The hyphen is to be used in print form, but need not be entered or retained in computer systems. Printed on documents, the Standard Address Number should be preceded by the identifier "SAN" to avoid confusion with other numerical codes (SAN XXX-XXXX).

Check Digit Calculation

The check digit is based on *Modulus 11*, and can be derived as follows:

1. Write the digits of the basic number. 2 3 4 5 6 7
2. Write the constant weighting factors associated with each position by the basic number. 7 6 5 4 3 2
3. Multiply each digit by its associated weighting factor. 14 18 20 20 18 14
4. Add the products of the multiplications. 14 + 18 + 20 + 20 + 18 + 14 =104
5. Divide the sum by *Modulus 11* to find the remainder. 104 ÷ 11 = 9 plus a remainder of 5
6. Subtract the remainder from the *Modulus 11* to generate the required check digit. If there is no remainder, generate a check digit of zero. If the check digit is 10,

generate a check digit of X to represent 10,
since the use of 10 would require an extra digit. $\quad$ 11 - 5 = 6
7. Append the check digit to create the standard
seven-digit Standard Address Number. $\quad$ SAN 234-5676

SAN Assignment

The R. R. Bowker Company accepted responsibility for being the central administrative agency for SAN, and in that capacity assigns SANs to identify uniquely the addresses of organizations. No SANs can be reassigned; in the event that an organization should cease to exist, for example, its SAN would cease to be in circulation entirely. If an organization using SAN should move or change its name with no change in ownership, its SAN would remain the same, and only the name or address would be updated to reflect the change.

SAN should be used in all transactions; it is recommended that the SAN be imprinted on stationery, letterheads, order and invoice forms, checks, and all other documents used in executing various book transactions. The SAN should always be printed on a separate line above the name and address of the organization, preferably in the upper left-hand corner of the stationery to avoid confusion with other numerical codes pertaining to the organization, such as telephone number, zip code, and the like.

SAN Functions and Suffixes

The SAN is strictly a Standard Address Number, becoming functional only in applications determined by the user; these may include activities such as purchasing, billing, shipping, receiving, paying, crediting, and refunding. Every department that has an independent function within an organization could have a SAN for its own identification. Users may choose to assign a suffix (a separate field) to its own SAN strictly for internal use. Faculty members ordering books through a library acquisitions department, for example, may not have their own separate SAN, but may be assigned a suffix by the library. There is no standardized provision for placement of suffixes. Existing numbering systems do not have suffixes to take care of the "subset" type addresses. The SAN does not standardize this part of the address. For the implementation of SAN, it is suggested that wherever applicable the four-position suffix be used. This four-position suffix makes available 10,000 numbers, ranging from 0000 to 9999, and will accommodate all existing subset numbering presently in use.

For example, there are various ways to incorporate SAN in an order fulfillment system. Firms just beginning to assign account numbers to their customers will have no conversion problems and will simply use SAN as the numbering system. Firms that already have an existing number system can convert either on a step-by-step basis by adopting SANs whenever orders or payments are processed on the account, or by converting the whole file by using the SAN listing provided by the SAN Agency. Using the step-by-step conversion, firms may adopt SANs as customers provide them on their forms, orders, payments, and returns.

For additional information or suggestions, please write to Diana Fumando, SAN Coordinator, ISBN/SAN Agency, R. R. Bowker Company, Reed Reference Publishing, 121 Chanlon Rd., New Providence, NJ 07974, call 908-771-7755, or fax 908-665-2895.

Distinguished Books

Best Books of 1996

This is the 50th year in which the American Library Association's Notable Books Council has issued its list of "Notable Books" for adults.

Fiction

Atkinson, Kate. *Behind the Scenes at the Museum*. St. Martin's Press.
Barrett, Andrea. *Ship Fever: Stories*. W. W. Norton.
Diaz, Junot. *Drown*. Riverhead Books.
Doyle, Roddy. *The Woman Who Walked into Doors*. Viking.
Iida, Deborah. *Middle Son*. Algonquin.
Mistry, Rohinton. *A Fine Balance*. Knopf.
Robinson, Roxana. *Asking for Love and Other Stories*. Random House.
Selvadurai, Shyam. *Funny Boy*. William Morrow.
Swift, Graham. *Last Orders*. Knopf.
Trevor, William. *After Rain*. Viking.
Wolff, Tobias. *The Night in Question*. Knopf.

Poetry

Heaney, Seamus. *The Spirit Level*. Farrar, Straus & Giroux.
Hicok, Bob. *The Legend of Light*. University of Wisconsin Press.
Kenyon, Jane. *Otherwise*. Graywolf Press.

Nonfiction

Ambrose, Stephen E. *Undaunted Courage*. Simon & Schuster.
Denby, David. *Great Books*. Simon & Schuster.
D'Orso, Michael. *Like Judgment Day*. Putnam.
Luker, Kristin. *Dubious Conceptions*. Harvard University Press.
McBride, James. *The Color of Water*. Riverhead Books.
McCourt, Frank. *Angela's Ashes*. Scribner.
Manguel, Alberto. *A History of Reading*. Viking.
Miller, Judith. *God Has Ninety-Nine Names*. Simon and Schuster.
Page, Clarence. *Showing My Color*. HarperCollins.
Painter, Nell Irvin. *Sojourner Truth*. W. W. Norton.
Quammen, David. *The Song of the Dodo*. Scribner.
Sobol, Dava. *Longitude*. Walker.

Best Young Adult Books

In January each year a committee of the Young Adult Library Services Association of the American Library Association compiles a list of best books published for young adults in the last 16 months, selected for their proven or potential appeal to the personal reading taste of the young adult.

Atkin, S. Beth. *Voices from the Streets: Young Former Gang Members Tell Their Stories*. Little, Brown.
Avi. *Beyond the Western Sea, Book One: The Escape from Home*. Orchard Books.
Barron, T.A. *Lost Years of Merlin*. Philomel.
Berry, Liz. *The China Garden*. Farrar, Straus & Giroux.
Blum, Joshua, and Bob Holman and Mark Pellington. *The United States of Poetry*. Harry N. Abrams.
Bode, Janet, and Stan Mack. *Hard Time: A Real Life Look at Juvenile Crime*. Delacorte Press.
Card, Orson Scott. *Pastwatch: The Redemption of Christopher Columbus*. Tor Books.
Cart, Michael. *My Father's Scar*. Simon & Schuster Books for Young Readers.
Chambers, Veronica. *Mama's Girl*. Riverhead Books.
Coles, Jr., William. *Another Kind of Monday*. Atheneum.
Conly, Jane Leslie. *Trout Summer*. Henry Holt.
Cooney, Caroline B. *The Voice on the Radio*. Delacorte Press.
Dash, Joan. *We Shall Not Be Moved*. Scholastic Press.
Denenberg, Barry. *An American Hero: The True Story of Charles A. Lindbergh*. Scholastic Press.
Dessen, Sarah. *That Summer*. Orchard Books.
DeVries, Anke. *Bruises*. Front Street.
Farmer, Nancy. *A Girl Named Disaster*. Orchard Books.
Fleischman, Paul. *Dateline: Troy*. Candlewick Press.
Fleischman, Sid. *The Abracadabra Kid: A Writer's Life*. Greenwillow Books.
Freedman, Russell. *The Life and Death of Crazy Horse*. Holiday House.
Freeman, Suzanne. *Cuckoo's Child*. Greenwillow Books.
Gilstrap, John. *Nathan's Run*. HarperCollins.

Glenn, Mel. *Who Killed Mr. Chippendale? A Mystery in Poems*. Lodestar Books.
Gould, Steven. *Wildside*. Tor Books.
Haddix, Margaret Peterson. *Don't You Dare Read This, Mrs. Dunphrey*. Simon & Schuster Books for Young Readers.
Haddix, Margaret Peterson. *Running Out of Time*. Simon & Schuster Books for Young Readers.
Hanauer, Cathi. *My Sister's Bones*. Delacorte Press.
Hautman, Pete. *Mr. Was*. Simon & Schuster Books for Young Readers.
Hesse, Karen. *The Music of Dolphins*. Scholastic Press.
Hobbs, Will. *Far North*. Morrow Junior Books.
Huth, Angela. *Land Girls*. St. Martin's.
Ingold, Jeanette. *The Window*. Harcourt Brace.
Keillor, Garrison, and Jenny Lind Nilson. *The Sandy Bottom Orchestra*. Hyperion.
Klass, David. *Danger Zone*. Scholastic Press.
Kozol, Jonathan. *Amazing Grace*. Crown.
Krakauer, Jon. *Into the Wild*. Villard.
Lane, Dakota. *Johnny Voodoo*. Delacorte Press.
Levy, Marilyn. *Run for Your Life*. Houghton Mifflin.
McKissack, Patricia C., and Fredrick L. McKissack. *Rebels Against Slavery: American Slave Revolts*. Scholastic Press.
Macy, Sue. *Winning Ways: A Photohistory of American Women in Sports*. Henry Holt.
Matas, Carol. *After the War*. Simon & Schuster Books for Young Readers.
Mead, Alice. *Adem's Cross*. Farrar, Straus & Giroux.
Meyer, Carolyn. *Gideon's People*. Harcourt Brace.
Myers, Walter Dean. *One More River to Cross: An African American Photograph Album*. Harcourt Brace.
Myers, Walter Dean, *Slam!* Harcourt Brace.

Napoli, Donna Jo. *Song of the Magdalene.* Scholastic Press.

Nix, Garth. *Sabriel.* HarperCollins.

Nye, Naomi Shihab, and Paul Janeczko. *I Feel a Little Jumpy Around You.* Simon & Schuster Books for Young Readers.

Paschen, Elise, and Molly Peacock and Neil Neches (editors). *Poetry in Motion: One Hundred Poems from the Subways and Buses.* W. W. Norton.

Paterson, Katherine. *Jip, His Story.* Lodestar Books.

Paulsen, Gary. *Puppies, Dogs, and Blue Northers: Reflections on Being Raised by a Pack of Sled Dogs.* Harcourt Brace.

Pausewang, Gudrun. *The Final Journey.* Viking.

Pennebaker, Ruth. *Don't Think Twice.* Henry Holt.

Pullman, Philip. *The Golden Compass.* Alfred A. Knopf.

Rinaldi, Ann. *Hang a Thousand Trees with Ribbons: The Story of Phillis Wheatley.* Harcourt Brace.

Salzman, Mark. *Lost in Place.* Random House.

Savage, Candace. *Cowgirls.* Ten Speed Press.

Schmidt, Gary D. *The Sin Eater.* Lodestar Books.

Shevelev, Raphael, and Karine Schomer. *Liberating the Ghosts: Photographs and Text from the March of the Living.* LensWork Publishing.

Southgate, Martha. *Another Way to Dance.* Delacorte Press.

Spinelli, Jerry. *Crash.* Alfred A. Knopf.

Staples, Suzanne Fisher. *Dangerous Skies.* Farrar, Straus & Giroux/Frances Foster Books.

Thesman, Jean. *The Ornament Tree.* Houghton Mifflin.

Thomas, Rob. *Rats Saw God.* Simon & Schuster Books for Young Readers.

Turner, Megan Whalen. *The Thief.* Greenwillow Books.

Wallace, Rich. *Wrestling Sturbridge.* Alfred A. Knopf.

Welter, John. *I Want to Buy a Vowel.* Algonquin.

Westall, Robert. *Gulf.* Scholastic Press.

White, Ruth. *Belle Prater's Boy.* Farrar, Straus & Giroux.

Wilkomirski, Binjamin. *Fragments.* Schocken Books.

Best Children's Books

A list of notable children's books is selected each year by the Notable Children's Books Committee of the Association for Library Service to Children of the American Library Association. Recommended titles are selected by children's librarians and educators based on originality, creativity, and suitability for children. [See "Literary Prizes, 1996" later in Part 5 for Caldecott, Newbery, and other award winners.—*Ed.*]

For Younger Readers

Bannerman, Helen. *The Story of Little Babaji.* HarperCollins/Michael di Capua.
Buehner, Caralyn. *Fanny's Dream.* Dial.
Byars, Betsy. *My Brother, Ant.* Viking.
Dyer, Jane. *Animal Crackers: A Delectable Collection of Pictures, Poems, and Lullabies for the Very Young.* Little, Brown.
Fleming, Denise. *Where Once There Was a Wood.* Henry Holt.
Henkes, Kevin. *Lilly's Purple Plastic Purse.* Greenwillow.
Ho, Minfong. *Hush! A Thai Lullaby.* Orchard.
Lester, Julius. *Sam and the Tigers.* Dial.
McMillan, Bruce. *Jelly Beans for Sale.* Scholastic.
Opie, Iona, ed. *My Very First Mother Goose.* Candlewick.
Pilkey, Dav. *The Paperboy.* Orchard.
Schaefer, Carole Lexa. *The Squiggle.* Crown.
Sisulu, Elinor Batezat. *The Day Gogo Went to Vote: South Africa April 1994.* Little, Brown.

For Middle Readers

Bartoletti, Susan Campbell. *Growing Up in Coal Country.* Houghton.
Brewster, Hugh. *Anastasia's Album.* Hyperion/Madison Press.
Bunting, Eve. *Train to Somewhere.* Clarion.
Conrad, Pam. *The Rooster's Gift.* HarperCollins/Laura Geringer.
Cooney, Barbara. *Eleanor.* Viking.
DeFelice, Cynthia. *The Apprenticeship of Lucas Whitaker.* Farrar.
Jackson, Donna M. *The Bone Detectives: How Forensic Anthropologists Solve Crimes and Uncover Mysteries of the Dead.* Little, Brown.
Kehret, Peg. *Small Steps: The Year I Got Polio.* Whitman.
Krull, Kathleen. *Wilma Unlimited: How Wilma Rudolph Became the World's Fastest Woman.* Harcourt.
Warren, Andrea. *Orphan Train Rider: One Boy's True Story.* Houghton.
Wisniewski, David. *Golem.* Clarion.
Yumoto, Kazumi. *The Friends.* Farrar.

For Older Readers

Aiken, Joan. *Cold Shoulder Road.* Delacorte.
Bawden, Nina. *Granny the Pag.* Clarion.
Farmer, Nancy. *A Girl Named Disaster.* Orchard/Richard Jackson.
Fleischman, Sid. *The Abracadabra Kid: A Writer's Life.* Greenwillow.
Freedman, Russell. *The Life and Death of Crazy Horse.* Holiday.
Konigsburg, E. L. *The View from Saturday.* Atheneum.
McGraw, Eloise. *The Moorchild.* Simon & Schuster/Margaret K. McElderry.
Macy, Sue. *Winning Ways: A Photohistory of American Women in Sports.* Henry Holt.
Martin, Rafe. *Mysterious Tales of Japan.* Putnam.
Myers, Walter Dean. *Toussaint L'Ouverture: The Fight for Haiti's Freedom.* Simon & Schuster.
Nix, Garth. *Sabriel.* HarperCollins.
Onyefulu, Ifeoma. *Ogbo: Sharing Life in an African Village.* Harcourt/Gulliver.
Paterson, Katherine. *Jip: His Story.* Dutton/Lodestar.

Perl, Lila, and Marion Blumenthal Lazen. *Four Perfect Pebbles: A Holocaust Story.* Greenwillow.
Pinkney, Andrea D. *Bill Pickett: Rodeo-Ridin' Cowboy.* Harcourt/Gulliver.
Rael, Elsa. *What Zeesie Saw on Delancey Street.* Simon & Schuster.
Schroeder, Alan. *Minty: A Story of Young Harriet Tubman.* Dial.
Sis, Peter. *Starry Messenger: A Book Depicting the Life of a Famous Scientist, Mathematician, Astronomer, Philosopher, Physicist, Galileo Galilei.* Farrar/Frances Foster.
Stanley, Diane. *Leonardo Da Vinci.* Morrow.
Warren, Andrea. *Orphan Train Rider: One Boy's True Story.* Houghton.
Wisniewski, David. *Golem.* Clarion.
Yumoto, Kazumi. *The Friends.* Farrar.

Notable Recordings for Children

This list of notable recordings for children has been released by the Association for Library Service to Children (ALSC), a division of the American Library Association. Recommended titles are chosen by children's librarians and educators on the basis of their originality, creativity, and suitability.

"Adventures at Catfish Pond." Music for Little People.
"An Awfully Big Adventure: The Best of Peter Pan 1904–1996." Delos International Inc.
"Bibbidi Bobbidi Bach." Delos International Inc.
"Big Blues." Music for Little People.
"Blanket Full of Dreams." Rounder Records.
"Bridge to Terebithia." Recorded Books, Inc.
"Brown Honey in Broom Wheat Tea." Spoken Arts.
"Cada Niño/Every Child." Rounder Records.
"Castle in the Attic." Listening Library.
"Celebrate! Jack Grunsky Live." Youngheart Music.
"Child's Celebration of Folk Music." Music for Little People.
"Daughters of Ishi-Shin." Black Cricket Press.
"Ear, the Eye and the Arm." Recorded Books.
"Giant and the Rabbit." High Haven Music.
"Halloween Howls." Music for Little People.
"Ironman." Recorded Books.
"Jeremiah Was A Bullfrog." Youngheart Music.
"Jill Gill Makes It Noisy in Boise, Idaho." Jim Gill Music, Inc.
"I am Livina Cumming." Recorded Books.
"Lessons From the Animal People." Yellow Moon Press.
"Lullabies and Long Songs." DreamSong Recordings.
"Little Princess." Recorded Books.
"Mark Twain and the Laughing River." Woodside Ave. Music Productions.
"Monday's Troll." Listening Library.
"Noah and the Ark." Rabbit Ears, dist. by Simon & Schuster Children's Publishing Division
"Old Turtle." Pfeifer-Hamilton Publishers.
"Penguin Parade." Music for Little People.
"Planet With One Mind." One Step Records.
"Quiet Time." Pearcy Co.
"Rifle." Recorded Books.
"Sleeping With the Fishes." Baby Music Boom.
"Songs for Singing Children." Revels Records.
"Stellaluna." High Windy Audio.
"Three Terrible Trins." Listening Library.
"Tom Chapin." Sony Wonder.
"When I Was a Child." Good Moos Productions.
"Wolf Under the Bed." Old Coyote Music.
"World's Gonna Listen." JHO Music

Notable Children's Films and Videos

This list of notable children's films and videos has been released by the Association for Library Service to Children (ALSC), a division of the American Library Association. Recommended titles are selected by children's librarians and educators on the basis of their originality, creativity, and suitability.

Brown Honey in Broomwheat Tea. Distributed by Spoken Arts, Inc.

Children Remember the Holocaust. Dist. by Society for Visual Education.

How Dinosaurs Learned to Fly—Not a True Story. Dist. by Bullfrog Films.

The Maestro Plays. Dist. by SRA. Notes Alive!

On the Day You Were Born. Dist. by Minnesota Orchestra.

Reading Rainbow. Dist. by GPN (Great Plains National ITV Library).

Sousa to Satchmo. Dist. by Columbia Music Video.

Why Toes Tap. Dist. by Columbia Music Video.

Notable Children's Software

Eyewitness Virtual Reality Dinosaur Hunter. DK, 1996. CD-ROM. Mac/Windows.

Discovering Origami. Geode, 1996. CD-ROM. Mac/Windows hybrid.

Nickelodeon 3-D Movie Maker. Microsoft, 1996. CD-ROM. Windows 95 only.

Creative Writer. Microsoft, 1996. CD-ROM. Windows 95 only.

Quick Picks for Reluctant Young Adult Readers

The Young Adult Library Services Association of the American Library Association selects these titles as suitable for reluctant young adult readers.

Amend, Bill. *At Least This Place Sells T-Shirts*. Andrews & McMeel.
Athkins, D. E. *The Bride*. Scholastic.
Atkin, S. Beth. *Voices from the Streets: Young Former Gang Members Tell Their Stories*. Little, Brown.
Base, Graeme. *The Discovery of Dragons*. Harry N. Abrams.
Bjarkman, Peter. *Top 10 Basketball Slam Dunkers 1995*. Enslow.
Block, Francesca Lia. *Girl Goddess #9*. HarperCollins.
Bode, Janet, and Stan Mack. *Hard Time: A Real Life Look at Juvenile Crime and Violence*. Delacorte.
Branzei, Sylvia. *Planet Dexter's Grossology*. Addison-Wesley.
Brewster, Hugh. *Anastasia's Album*. Hyperion.
Bruce-Mitford, Miranda. *The Illustrated Book of Signs & Symbols*. Dorling Kindersley.
Cohen, Daniel. *Dangerous Ghosts*. Putnam.
Coville, Bruce. *William Shakespeare's A Midsummer Night's Dream*. Dial.
Crowther, Robert. *Pop-Up Olympics: Amazing Facts and Record Breakers*. Candlewick.
Dangerous Animals (The Nature Company Discovery Libraries.) Time-Life.
De Vries, Anke. *Bruises*. Front Street.
Doyle, Larry. *Huh Huh for Hollywood*. MTV Books/Pocket.
Ewing, Lynne. *Drive-By*. HarperCollins.
Fletcher, Ralph. *Buried Alive: The Elements of Love*. Atheneum.
Freedman, Russell. *The Life and Death of Crazy Horse*. Holiday House.
Ganeri, Anita. *Inside the Body*. Dorling Kindersley.
Glenn, Mel. *Who Killed Mr. Chippendale?* Dutton/Lodestar.
Gorog, Judith. *When Nobody's Home: Fifteen Baby-Sitting Tales of Terror*. Scholastic.
Haddix, Margaret Peterson. *Don't You Dare Read This, Mrs. Dunphrey*. Simon & Schuster.

Hill, Grant. *Change the Game: One Athlete's Thoughts on Sports, Dreams, and Growing Up*. Warner.
Hobbs, Will. *Far North*. Morrow Junior Books.
Hoffman, Charles. *Bruce Lee, Brandon Lee, and the Dragon's Curse*. Random House.
Jackson, Donna M. *The Bone Detectives: How Forensic Anthropologists Solve Crimes and Uncover Mysteries of the Dead*. Little, Brown.
Jarrow, Gail, and Paul Sherman. *Naked Mole Rats*. Lerner/Carolrhoda.
Jones, Charlotte Foltz. *Accidents May Happen: Fifty Inventions Discovered by Mistake*. Delacorte.
Jukes, Mavis. *It's a Girl Thing: How to Stay Healthy, Safe, and In Charge*. Knopf.
Kehret, Peg. *Small Steps: The Year I Got Polio*. Albert Whitman.
Kite, Patricia L. *Blood-Feeding Bugs and Beasts*. Millbrook.
Lauber, Patricia. *Hurricanes: Earth's Mightiest Storms*. Scholastic.
Letterman, David. *David Letterman's Book of Top Ten Lists & Zesty Lo-Cal Chicken Recipes*. Bantam.
Lorbiecki, Marybeth. *Just One Flick of a Finger*. Dial.
Lurie, Jon. *Fundamental Snowboarding*. Lerner.
Maizels, Jennie, and Kate Petty. *The Amazing Pop-Up Grammar Book*. Dutton.
Martin, Les. *Humbug (The X Files)*. Harper Trophy.
Matas, Carol. *After the War*. Simon & Schuster.
Melton, H. Keith. *The Ultimate Spy Book*. Dorling Kindersley.
Meltzer, Milton. *Weapons & Warfare: From the Stone Age to the Space Age*. HarperCollins.
Merriam, Eve. *The Inner City Mother Goose* (New ed.). Simon & Schuster.
Montpetit, Charles, ed. *The First Time: True Stories. Vol. 2*. Orca.

Morpurgo, Michael. *Robin of Sherwood*. Harcourt Brace.
Mowry, Jess. *Ghost Train*. Henry Holt.
Myers, Walter Dean. *Slam!* Scholastic.
Nance, John. *Pandora's Clock*. Doubleday.
Osofsky, Audrey. *Free to Dream: The Making of a Poet: Langston Hughes*. Lothrop, Lee & Shepard.
Ousseimi, Maria. *Caught in the Crossfire: Growing Up in a War Zone*. Walker.
Paulsen, Gary. *Brian's Winter*. Delacorte.
Paulsen, Gary. *Puppies, Dogs and Blue Northers: Reflections on Being Raised By a Pack of Sled Dogs*. Harcourt Brace.
Perl, Lila, and Marion Blumenthal Lazan. *Four Perfect Pebbles: A Holocaust Story*. Greenwillow.
Platt, Richard. *Stephen Biesty's Incredible Explosions*. Dorling Kindersley.
Reid, Lori. *The Art of Hand Reading*. Dorling Kindersley.
Reybold, Laura. *Everything You Need to Know about the Dangers of Tattooing and Body Piercing*. Rosen.
Reynolds, Marilyn. *Telling*. Morning Glory Press.
Rossiter, Sean. *Hockey the NHL Way: The Basics*. Greystone.
Sanderson, Peter. *Marvel Universe*. Harry N. Abrams.
Shusterman, Neal. *Mindquakes: Stories to Shatter Your Brain*. Tor.
Silverstein, Shel. *Falling Up*. HarperCollins.
Smith, Miranda. *Living Earth*. Dorling Kindersley.
Snedden, Robert. *Yuck! A Big Book of Little Horrors*. Simon & Schuster.
Solin, Sabrina. *Seventeen Guide to Sex and Your Body*. Simon & Schuster.
Steiber, Ellen. *Shapes (The X Files)*. Harper Trophy.
Steiber, Ellen. *Squeeze (The X Files)*. Harper Trophy.
Sturgis, Alexander. *Optical Illusions in Art*. Sterling.
Sullivan, George. *Glovemen: Twenty-Seven of Baseball's Greatest*. Atheneum.
Sweeney, Joyce. *Free Fall*. Delacorte.
Tanaka, Shelley. *On Board the Titanic*. Hyperion.
Thomas, Rob. *Rats Saw God*. Simon & Schuster.
Vancil, Mark. *NBA Basketball Offense Basics*. Sterling.
Wallace, Rich. *Wrestling Sturbridge*. Knopf.
Willey, Margaret. *Facing the Music*. Delacorte.
Willson, Quentin. *The Ultimate Classic Car Book*. Dorling Kindersley.
Windsor, Patricia. *The Blooding*. Scholastic.

Bestsellers of 1996

Hardcover Bestsellers: How High Can You Go?

Daisy Maryles
Executive Editor, *Publishers Weekly*

Each year the analysis of these end-of-the-year bestseller charts contains two basic facts. The first is that the "shipped and billed" figures are higher than in the previous years. The second is that almost all the bestselling novels are by veteran authors, and bestselling nonfiction is usually about a person or issue with a high media profile.

Both those points can once again be made about the 1996 roster of high rollers. And in fact there were more books with reported sales of 100,000 or more last year than in any previous year. Fiction's tally was 93, the same all-time high figure set in both 1995 and 1993. Nonfiction's tally of 109 books is a new record. And while the number of titles with sales over the one-million mark—11 in total for hardcover fiction and nonfiction—is the same as the 1995 tally (the record still intact is 17, set in 1994), there were more books with sales of 300,000-plus in 1996 than in any previous year. The No. 15 fiction bestseller, *The Celestine Prophecy*, sold about 718,000 copies in 1996 (total sales: nearly four million); that's the highest figure ever for the bottom of the list. The nonfiction record for No. 15, set in 1994 by *The Bubba Gump Shrimp Co. Cookbook* (Oxmoor House/Leisure Arts), still holds, with reported sales of about 650,000.

Considering that the big news in the first half of 1996 was the enormous returns that were shaking up publishers' bottom lines, this crop of top sellers doesn't bode well for the bottom line, either. That is because of yet another new record set by the 1996 group of big books: there are more titles than ever before that did not even place once on *Publishers Weekly*'s weekly charts. A total of 18 novels and 39 nonfiction titles didn't even make a single appearance; this is considerably higher than the 13 fiction and 30 nonfiction no-shows in the 1995 group. Even among the top-15 nonfiction, there was one book that has not made an appearance on *PW*'s weekly charts: Pope John Paul II's *Gift & Mystery* from Doubleday. The "shipped and billed" figure could be greatly reduced by final net if the book does not have a strong life as an Easter title.

Oprah, front-page rave reviews, a media blitz can make a difference for the chosen few, but there are at least eight to ten fiction spots sewn up each year by a core group of authors who manage to write one and sometimes more blockbusters on a bankable annual schedule. Consider that Stephen King has not missed a spot on these lists since 1979, except for a brief one-year hiatus in 1988 when he decided not to publish any new hardcovers. Back in 1979, *The Dead Zone* landed in the No. 7 slot with about 175,000 copies. In 1996, *The Regulators*—written by King alter ego Richard Bachman—needed about 1.2 million in sales for the same position. Danielle Steel, another longtime resident of these year-end lists, has not missed a year since 1982, when sales of about 198,000

Note: Adapted from *Publishers Weekly*, April 7, 1997.

copies of *Crossings* were enough for the 13th ranking. Since then Steel has had at least two books in the top 15 seven times, and in 1994 took the No. 4, No. 7, and No. 8 spots with *The Gift*, *Wings*, and *Accident*; each sold more than one million copies. John Grisham has not missed a performance on these annual lists since 1991, when *The Firm* landed in the No. 7 slot with sales of about 544,000. For the last three years, he has commandeered the No. 1 position, beginning in 1994 when *The Chamber* had reported sales of more than three million copies. It's no wonder there are so many lawyer/Grisham wannabes. Mary Higgins Clark, too, has not missed a beat on these lists since 1991 and also sometime takes two slots.

The list of top-15 fiction includes the usual suspects: Grisham, Clancy, and Crichton, plus Steel, King, and Clark with two apiece. James Redfield is back, with his 1995 mega-bestseller, *The Celestine Prophecy*, as well as with his second book, *The Tenth Insight*; and two other regulars, Cornwell and McMillan, also land top slots. What's left are two first novels—*Primary Colors* by Anonymous (aka Joe Klein) and Jacquelyn Mitchard's *The Deep End of the Ocean*. And while it's no small feat to land a first fiction in the top 15, the factors that did it for these two books are unique and unlikely to recur. A media frenzy over the anonymous author of *Primary Colors* certainly helped keep this realistic political novel high on the bestseller charts. For Mitchard, being picked by Oprah as the first book for her on-air reading club made all the difference between being a well-published and modestly successful first novel and being a mega blockbuster.

Looking at the Blockbusters

Nonfiction, too, saw the usual suspects—thespians, sports figures, and media personalities—along with what has become almost a nonfiction top-15 fixture, John Gray's *Men Are from Mars, Women Are from Venus* making its fourth annual appearance and reaching six million in hardcover sales. With re-engineering and downsizing as part of the general corporate zeitgeist, business cartoonist Scott Adams (he's syndicated in 1,200 newspapers nationwide) successfully offered Dilbert and Dogbert for the "little people." The ever-popular how-to category has two new players among the top 15. Landing in the No. 5 slot is Barry Sears's *The Zone*, with information on diet and exercise that makes for peak physical and mental performance. Even higher is a feel-good book by Sarah Ban Breathnach, *Simple Abundance: A Daybook of Comfort and Joy*, an excellent example of Warner's very effective marketing acumen in getting books on the list and keeping them there for a long time (and yes, it helped that Breathnach was one of three guests on an Oprah spring show entitled "People I'd Like to Have Dinner With").

There are also some new publishing players on these year-end hardcover charts. Broadway Books debuted in 1996, and two of its four titles made it onto the charts. Also on the charts are two titles from Riverhead, a relatively new player whose first list appeared about two years ago.

Publishers Weekly 1996 Bestsellers

FICTION

1. **The Runaway Jury** by John Grisham. Doubleday (5/96) **2,775,000
2. **Executive Orders** by Tom Clancy. Putnam (8/96) 2,371,602
3. **Desperation** by Stephen King. Viking (9/96) 1,542,077
4. **Airframe** by Michael Crichton. Knopf (12/96) 1,487,494
5. **The Regulators** by Richard Bachman. Dutton (9/96) 1,200,000
6. **Malice** by Danielle Steel. Delacorte (5/96) **1,150,000
7. **Silent Honor** by Danielle Steel. Delacorte (12/96) **1,150,000
8. **Primary Colors** by Anonymous. Random House (2/96) 972,385
9. **Cause of Death** by Patricia Cornwell. Putnam (7/96) 920,403
10. **The Tenth Insight: Holding the Vision** by James Redfield. Warner (4/96) 892,687
11. **The Deep End of the Ocean** by Jacquelyn Mitchard. Viking (6/96) 840,263
12. **How Stella Got Her Groove Back** by Terry McMillan. Viking (4/96) 782,699
13. **Moonlight Becomes You** by Mary Higgins Clark. Simon & Schuster (4/96) **775,000
14. **My Gal Sunday** by Mary Higgins Clark. Simon & Schuster (10/96) **750,000
15. **The Celestine Prophecy** by James Redfield. Warner (3/94) **718,000

NONFICTION

1. **Make the Connection: Ten Steps to a Better Body and a Better Life** by Oprah Winfrey and Bob Greene. Hyperion (9/96) 2,302,697
2. **Men Are From Mars Women Are From Venus** by John Gray. HarperCollins(4/93) 1,458,089
3. **The Dilbert Principle** by Scott Adams. HarperBusiness (3/96) 1,319,507
4. **Simple Abundance: A Daybook of Comfort and Joy** by Sarah Ban Breathnach.Warner (11/95) 1,087,149
5. **The Zone** by Barry Sears with Bill Lawren. ReganBooks (5/95) 930,311
6. **Bad as I Wanna Be** by Dennis Rodman. Delacorte (6/96) **800,000
7. **In Contempt** by Christopher Darden. ReganBooks (3/96) 752,648
8. **A Reporter's Life** by Walter Cronkite. Knopf (12/96) 673,591
9. **Dogbert's Top Secret Management Handbook** by Scott Adams. HarperBusiness (9/96) 652,085
10. **My Sergei: A Love Story** by Ekaterina Gordeeva with E. M. Swift. Warner (11/95) 563,567
11. **Gift & Mystery** by Pope John Paul II. Doubleday 523,000*
12. **I'm Not Really Here** by Tim Allen. Hyperion 508,015
13. **Rush Limbaugh is a Big Fat Idiot and Other Observations** by Al Franken.Delacorte (2/96) **500,000
14. **James Herriot's Favorite Dog Stories** by James Herriot. St. Martin's (9/96)**500,000
15. **My Story** by The Duchess of York. Simon & Schuster (11/96) **450,000

Note: Rankings are determined by sales figures provided by publishers; the numbers generally reflect reports of copies "shipped and billed" in calendar year 1996, and publishers were instructed to adjust sales figures to include returns through February 24, 1997. Publishers did not at that time know what their total returns would be—indeed, the majority of returns occur later in the year—so not all of these figures should be regarded as final net sales.

(Dates in parentheses indicate month and year of publication.)

*Sales figures only reflect books sold in calendar year 1996.

**Sales figures were submitted to *PW* in confidence, for use in placing titles on the lists. Numbers shown are rounded down to the nearest 25,000 to indicate relationship to sales figures of other titles.

Checking Out Religion

Last year was the first in five years that we combined hardcover religion best-sellers with general titles. Maintaining separate lists had become unwieldy, especially since many titles placed on both. This year, religion and spiritual titles accounted for six of the top 30 nonfiction titles; in fiction, those categories accounted for five of the top 30. A careful perusal of the lists offers many more titles, including four books from Word.

The Long Road from Gross to Net Sales

As in previous years, all our calculations are based on shipped and billed figures supplied by publishers in 1996 and 1995 (a few books published earlier that continued their long tenure on the year's bestseller charts are also included). These figures reflect only 1996 trade sales—publishers were instructed not to include book club and overseas transactions. And this year we asked publishers to take into account returns through February 24 (previously we asked publishers to adjust for returns through the end of January, so the higher numbers are even more telling). Even with the extra time, the sales figures—more accurately described as books "shipped and billed"—are not to be considered net. For many books, especially those published in the latter half of the year, returns are still to be calculated.

Also telling is the comparison of *PW*'s top 15 annual bestsellers to the top sellers at selected national and independent accounts. We also added a column for Amazon.com's list of top-100 1996 bestsellers. One might ask: If a top bestseller has a low profile at all the retail outlets listed, especially at the national chains and the warehouse clubs, where are these "shipped & billed" figures coming from? Consider that for the No. 1 fiction title, *Runaway Jury*, the three national chains accounted for about 22 percent of total sales. For *Primary Colors*, it was about 35 percent. For *My Sergei*, it was nearly 33 percent. For Dennis Rodman's *Bad as I Wanna Be*, the three national chains accounted for a little more than 40 percent. Clearly, to be a contender for these top slots on the annual list, a serious quantity of books has to move in the national chains.

The Fiction Runners-Up

The patterns for the 1996 group of runners-up were similar to the 1995 group, when we noted that this was the first time that books with such high sales figures still could not place on the top-15 list. But the majority of last year's group had double-digit runs on *PW*'s weekly charts. This year there were eight books with weekly runs of eight weeks or less, with titles by Judith McNaught, Barbara Taylor Bradford, and Julie Salamon on the charts for three weeks or less. While Salamon's book was one of the many Christmas stories trying to replicate the huge success of *The Christmas Box* (hers was one of the few that did land on the weekly charts), she and debut novelist Nicholas Sparks are the only new names on this runner-up list. In fact, in previous years, a number of these veteran authors were able to score a top-15 slot with smaller unit sales.

16. *The Christmas Box* by Richard Paul Evans (Simon & Schuster, **700,000)
17. *The Laws of Our Fathers* by Scott Turow (Farrar, Straus & Giroux, 605,000)
18. *Servant of the Bones* by Anne Rice (Knopf, 599,384)
19. *M Is for Malice* by Sue Grafton (Holt/Marion Wood, 526,000)
20. *The Notebook* by Nicholas Sparks (Warner, 512,254)
21. *Shock Wave* by Clive Cussler (Simon & Schuster, **475,000)
22. *Timepiece* by Richard Paul Evans (Simon & Schuster, **425,000)
23. *The Last Don* by Mario Puzo (Random House, 416,537)
24. *The Third Twin* by Ken Follett (Crown, 399,379)
25. *Jack and Jill* by James Patterson (Little, Brown, 389,334)
26. *A Crown of Swords* by Robert Jordan (Tor, 343,907)
27. *The Fallen Man* by Tony Hillerman (HarperCollins, 340,436)
28. *That Camden Summer* by LaVyrle Spencer (Putnam, 336,193)
29. *The Christmas Tree* by Julie Salamon (Random House, 334,475)
30. *Contagion* by Robin Cook (Putnam, 323,796)

Lower Ranks for Higher Numbers

This year there were three books with sales over the 300,000 mark that did not even make a top-30 list: *Secret Affair* by Barbara Taylor Bradford (HarperCollins), *Remember When* by Judith McNaught (Pocket), and *The Tailor of Panama* by John le Carré (Knopf).

At the 200,000-plus level, only Kensington's *The Special Guest* did not have at least one appearance on the weekly charts.

In ranked order, the 18 novels with sales of 200,000 and more are: *Sudden Prey* by John Sandford (Putnam), *Intensity* by Dean Koontz (Knopf), *Absolute Power* by David Baldacci (Warner), *To the Hilt* by Dick Francis (Putnam), *Say You Love Me* by Johanna Lindsey (Morrow), *Exclusive* by Sandra Brown (Warner), *The Horse Whisperer* by Nicholas Evans (Delacorte), *Gods and Generals* by Jeff Shaara (Ballantine), *The Wedding* by Julie Garwood (Pocket), *Montana Sky* by Nevada Barr (Pocket), *Legend* by Jude Deveraux (Pocket), *The Law of Love* by Laura Esquivel (Crown), *Icon* by Frederick Forsyth (Bantam), *The Special Guest* by Lee and Donna Allen (Kensington), *The Cat Who Said Cheese* by Lilian Jackson Braun (Putnam), *McNally's Puzzle* by Lawrence Sanders (Putnam), *Drink with the Devil* by Jack Higgins (Putnam), and *Blood and Honor* by W. E. B. Griffin (Putnam).

At the 150,000-Plus Level

There were 15 works of fiction with sales of 150,000-plus that did not make it on the year's top 30, the same number as in 1995. Books by James Patterson (his golfing inspiration fable), Kristine K. Rusch, Belva Plain, and a *Star Trek* title did not achieve even a one-week run on the 1996 charts. Books by Jonathan

Kellerman, Jeffrey Archer, Jane Mendelsohn, Susan Isaacs, and Margaret Atwood all enjoyed double-digit tenure on the weekly charts.

In ranked order, books with sales of 150,000-plus are: *The Web* by Jonathan Kellerman (Bantam), *Her Own Rules* by Barbara Taylor Bradford (Harper Collins), *Miracle on the 17th Green* by James Patterson and Peter De Jonge (Little, Brown), *The Fourth Estate* by Jeffrey Archer (HarperCollins), *Shadows of the Empire* by Steve Perry (Bantam), *First King of Shannara* by Terry Brooks (Del Rey), *I Was Amelia Earhart* by Jane Mendelsohn (Knopf), *The New Rebellion* by Kristine K. Rusch (Bantam), *Promises* by Belva Plain (Delacorte), *Star Trek: First Contact* by J. M. Dillard (Pocket), *Lily White* by Susan Isaacs (HarperCollins), *And This Too Shall Pass* by E. Lynn Harris (Doubleday), *The Burning Man* by Philip Margolin (Doubleday), *Spring Collection* by Judith Krantz (Crown), and *Alias Grace* by Margaret Atwood (Doubleday/Nan A. Talese).

The 125,000-Plus Group

There were 11 books with reported sales of 125,000 copies or more that did not make our top-30 chart, one less than in 1995. About half did not appear on any of *PW*'s weekly charts in the course of 1996.

The group that did make it onto the weekly charts included two novels that had a run of at least two months. They are *Guilty as Sin* by Tami Hoag (Bantam) and *Neanderthal* by John Darnton (Random House). Other books with appearances on weekly charts are: *Floaters* by Joseph Wambaugh (Bantam), *Shadows of Steel* by Dale Brown (Putnam), and *Chance* by Robert B. Parker (Putnam). *The Book of God: The Bible as a Novel* by Walter Wangerin, Jr. (Zondervan) was a regular on *PW*'s 1996 monthly religion lists.

The five that did not make an appearance on the weekly lists are: *Rosehaven* by Catherine Coulter (Putnam), *The X-Files Ground Zero* by Kevin J. Anderson (HarperPaperbacks), *A Magical Christmas* by Heather Graham (Topaz), *Winter Fire* by Elizabeth Lowell (Avon), and *Breakfast in Bed* by Sandra Brown (Bantam).

Fiction's 100,000-Plus Group

Last year 16 novels sold more than 100,000 copies, one more than in 1995. Half of these books never made it on our weekly charts. And of the eight that did, the two by Elizabeth George and Elmore Leonard were on for eight and seven weeks, respectively.

The 100,000-plus titles that did make it onto the weekly charts are: *In the Presence of the Enemy* by Elizabeth George (Bantam), *Dirt* by Stuart Woods (HarperCollins), *The Yellow Admiral* by Patrick O'Brian (Norton), *Rogue Warrior: Task Force Blue* by Richard Marcinko and John Weisman (Pocket), *A Little Yellow Dog* by Walter Mosley (Norton), *Cadillac Jukebox* by James Lee Burke (Hyperion), *The Return* by William Shatner (Pocket), and *Out of Sight* by Elmore Leonard (Delacorte).

The eight no-shows are: *Certain Poor Shepherds: A Christmas Tale* by Elizabeth Marshall Thomas (Simon & Schuster), *The X-Files Ruins* by Kevin J.

Anderson (HarperPaperbacks), *Critical Judgment* by Michael Palmer (Bantam), *Mischief* by Amanda Quick (Bantam), *Black Light* by Steven Hunter (Doubleday), *Harvest* by Tess Gerritsen (Pocket), *The Hand I Fan With* by Tina McElroy Ansa (Doubleday), and *West of Dodge* by Louis L'Amour (Bantam).

Nonfiction Runners-Up

Almost all of the books on the runner-up list enjoyed long stays on the weekly charts, and a number are still selling in quantities large enough to remain on those charts. Only books by Erma Bombeck and Anne Geddes did not make it to a double-digit tenure. But considering that neither book was published by one of the major publishing conglomerates, a bestseller run of almost two months for each title is very good.

16. *How Could You Do That?!* by Laura Schlessinger (HarperCollins, 410,491)
17. *Forever, Erma* by Erma Bombeck (Andrews & McMeel, 401,123)
18. *The Seven Spiritual Laws of Success* by Deepak Chopra (New World Library/Amber Allen, 389,278; 1,600,000 total since December 1994)
19. *Unlimited Access: An FBI Agent Inside the Clinton White House* by Gary Aldrich (Regnery, 387,365)
20. *Undaunted Courage: Meriwether Lewis, Thomas Jefferson, and the Opening of the American West* by Stephen Ambrose (Simon & Schuster)
21. *Down in the Garden* by Anne Geddes (Cedco, 385,188)
22. *Conversations with God, Book 1* by Neale Donald Walsch (Putnam, 384,648)
23. *Angela's Ashes* by Frank McCourt (Scribner, 377,718)
24. *It Takes a Village: And Other Lessons Children Teach Us* by Hillary Rodham Clinton (Simon & Schuster)
25. *The Soul's Code: In Search of Character and Calling* by James Hillman (Random House, 366,654)
26. *Outrage: The Five Reasons Why O.J. Simpson Got Away with Murder* by Vincent Bugliosi (Norton, 360,000)
27. *Midnight in the Garden of Good and Evil* by John Berendt (Random House, 359,320; more than one million in sales since publication in January 1994)
28. *Blood Sport: The President and His Adversaries* by James B. Stewart (Simon & Schuster)
29. *Path to Love* by Deepak Chopra (Harmony, 319,252)
30. *Living Faith* by President Jimmy Carter (Times Books, 317,677)

A First for the 300,000-Plus Level

This was the first time ever that books with reported sales of more than 300,000 copies did not make our top-30 list. There were three such performers, although one, *Emotional Intelligence* by Daniel Goleman (Bantam), was enjoying its second year on these annual charts; in 1995 it placed at No. 14, with sales of more than 400,000 copies. The two other titles with sales of 300,000-plus are *The Awakening Heart* by Betty Eadie (Pocket) and *Don't Block the Blessings* by Patti LaBelle with Laura Randolph (Riverhead).

The 200,000-Plus Players

This level, too, set a record, with 19 books that did not place on our top-30 annual list. While the majority of titles in this group did make it onto the weekly charts—among them books by Adele Puhn and Robert Bork that enjoyed impressive runs of 14 and 13 weeks, respectively—there were a handful of no-shows on *PW*'s weekly charts, including books by Jay Leno, Johnnie Cochran, Clive Cussler, John Gray, and a cookbook by Dorie Greenspan.

In ranked order, the books with sales of 200,000 copies or more are: *Cindy Crawford's Basic Face: A Makeup Workbook by Cindy Crawford* (Broadway), *Leading with My Chin* by Jay Leno (HarperCollins), *Love, Lucy* by Lucille Ball with Betty Hannah (Putnam), *The 5-Day Miracle Diet* by Adele Puhn (Ballantine), *Slouching Towards Gomorrah* by Robert Bork (ReganBooks), *Journey to Justice* by Johnnie L. Cochran, Jr. (Ballantine/One World), *Everyone Is Entitled to My Opinion* by David Brinkley (Knopf), *Letterman's New Top 10* by David Letterman (Bantam), *In the Grip of Grace* by Max Lucado (Word), *How Good Do We Have to Be: A New Understanding of Guilt and Forgiveness* by Rabbi Harold Kushner (Little, Brown), *The Sea Hunters: True Adventures with Famous Shipwrecks* by Clive Cussler and Craig Dirgo (Simon & Schuster), *The Choice* by Bob Woodward (Simon & Schuster), *No Shirt, No Shoes, No Problem* by Jeff Foxworthy (Hyperion), *100 Years, 100 Stories* by George Burns (Putnam), *Baking with Julia* by Dorie Greenspan (Morrow), *The Children's Book of Virtues* by William J. Bennett (Simon & Schuster), *Mars & Venus in Love* by John Gray (HarperCollins), *American Tragedy: The Uncensored Story of the Simpson Defense* by Lawrence Schiller and James Willwerth (Random House), and *Joan Lunden's Healthy Cooking* by Joan Lunden and Laura Morton (Little, Brown).

A Smaller 150,000-Plus Group

This year only eight books with sales over 150,000 did not make the top 30 list, considerably fewer than the 17 titles in 1995 and the record 20 in 1994. Perhaps this is a sign of some print sensibility, with publishers watching this level more carefully.

Only two books in this group never made it onto *PW*'s weekly charts: *Making Love Last Forever* by Gary Smalley (Word) and *The Making of a Country Lawyer* by Gerry Spence (St. Martin's). And while *Genesis* by Bill Moyers (Doubleday) didn't make it onto the weekly lists, it did make a few appearances on the monthly religion list.

The books in this group that did enjoy a run on the charts are: *The Run of His Life: The People v. O. J. Simpson* by Jeffrey Toobin (Random House), *Way of the Wizard* by Deepak Chopra (Harmony), *The Beardstown Ladies Stitch-in-Time Guide to Growing Your Nest Egg: Step-by-Step Planning for a Comfortable*

Financial Future by Robin Dellabough (Hyperion), *Bare Knuckles and Back Rooms, My Life in American Politics* by Ed Rollins with Tom DeFrank (Broadway), and *Practical Intuition: How to Harness the Power of Your Instinct and Make It Work for You* by Laura Day (Villard).

Nonfiction's 125,000 Group

Here, too, the gross sales did not seem to match bestseller chart performance. A record 18 books, compared with 15 in 1995, did not make *PW*'s annual top-30 list; nine of these still have not seen a slot on the magazine's weekly list.

The books at this level that did land on the weekly charts during the year did so for very short stays. The best performer was *All Too Human* by Edward Klein (Pocket), which had a five-week run; second best was *The Search for Justice: A Defense Attorney's Brief on the O. J. Simpson Case* by Robert Shapiro (Warner). *God's Inspirational Promises* by J. Countryman (Word) appeared several times on *PW*'s monthly religion charts.

The titles that did have a one-, two- or three-week run are: *Between Hope and History: Meeting America's Challenges for the 21st Century* by President Bill Clinton (Times Books), *His Holiness* by Carl Bernstein and Marco Politi (Doubleday), *I Lived to Tell It All* by George Jones with Tom Carter (Villard), *The Rants* by Dennis Miller (Doubleday), *Enter Whining* by Fran Drescher (ReganBooks), and *Partners in Power: The Clintons and Their America* by Roger Morris (Holt).

The nine that did not make a weekly *PW* slot are: *Slaying the Dragon* by Michael Johnson (ReganBooks), *The Wall Street Money Machine* by Wade B. Cook (Lighthouse Publishing), *Dave Barry in Cyberspace* by Dave Barry (Crown), *All Madden* by John Madden (HarperCollins), *The Glory of Christmas* by J. Countryman (Word), *Protein Power* by Drs. Michael and Mary Dan Eades (Bantam), *Home Cookin' with Dave's Mom* by Dave's Mom, Dorothy, with Jess Cagle (Pocket), *The Playmate Book: Five Decades of Centerfolds* by Gretchen Edgren (General Publishing Group), and *Fitonics for Life* by Marilyn Diamond and Dr. Donald Burton Schnell (Avon).

A Crowded 100,000-Plus List

This group set a new record for number of books "shipped and billed" that did not make *PW*'s top-30 annual list. A total of 31 books fell into this category.

Another dismal record was set in this group's performance on *PW*'s weekly charts. Only eight books showed enough sales muscle to get a slot. The best performer was *Hitler's Willing Executioners: Ordinary Germans and the Holocaust* by Daniel Goldhagen (Knopf), which enjoyed an impressive eight-week run in the course of 1996. Three other bestsellers were regulars on *PW*'s monthly religion charts: *The Jesus I Never Knew* by Philip Yancey (Zondervan), *Cloister Walk* by Kathleen Norris (Riverhead), and *Meditations from a Simple Path* by Mother Teresa (Ballantine).

Four that had a one- or two-week run are: *Downsize This!* by Michael Moore (Crown), *Knee Deep in Paradise* by Brett Butler (Hyperion), *Everyday Cooking* with *Dr. Dean Ornish* by Dean Ornish (HarperCollins), and *Drinking: A Love Story* by Caroline Knapp (Dial).

The 23 that did not show on the weekly charts are: *Christmas Joy: A Keepsake Book from the Heart of the Home* by Susan Branch (Little, Brown), *The Game for a Lifetime* by Harvey Penick with Bud Shrake (Simon & Schuster), *The West: An Illustrated History* by Geoffrey Ward (Little, Brown), *True Love* by Robert Fulghum (HarperCollins), *Living the Simple Life* by Elaine St. James (Hyperion), *Vein of Gold* by Julia Cameron (Putnam), *The Motley Fool Investment Guide: How the Fool Beats Wall Street's Wise Men and How You Can Too* by David and Tom Gardner (Simon & Schuster), *Shelter of Each Other* by Mary Pipher (Grosset/Putnam), *Pillsbury: Best of the Bakeoff Cookbook* by Pillsbury (Clarkson Potter), *IF2: 500 New Questions for the Game of Life* by Evelyn McFarlane & James Saywell (Villard), *The Doctor's Book of Home Remedies for Dogs and Cats* by the editors of Prevention Magazine Health Books (Rodale), *IF: Questions for the Game of Life* by Evelyn McFarlane & James Saywell (Villard), *The Young and the Restless Most Memorable Moments* by Barbara Irwin and Mary Cassata (General Publishing Group), *Tiger Woods: The Making of a Champion* by Sports Illustrated (Simon & Schuster), *Only the Paranoid Survive* by Andrew S. Grove (Doubleday/Currency), *Comic Relief* by Todd Gold (Avon), *The Demon-Haunted World: Science as a Candle in the Dark* by Carl Sagan (Random House), *Mayo Clinic Family Health Book, Revised* by David E. Larson (Morrow), *Telling It Like It Isn't* by Scott Adams (Andrews & McMeel), *Mary Engelbreit: The Art and the Artist* by Mary Engelbreit & Patrick Regan (Andrews & McMeel), *The Physics of Star Trek* by Lawrence M. Krauss (Basic Books), *All You Need Is a Friend* by Mary Engelbreit (Andrews & McMeel), and *The Purpose Driven Church: Growth Without Compromising Your Message and Mission* by Rick Warren (Zondervan).

Hardcover Misses: They Shall Return

Judy Quinn
Editor, Book News, *Publishers Weekly*

In just two days in early December 1996, almost 15,000 copies of President Clinton's *Between Hope and History* were returned to its publisher, Times Books. And that amount, the entire print run for many a first novel, is just a fraction of the hit the book took. According to publicity director Mary Beth Roche, the publisher sold only a quarter of its 400,000-plus printing—sales made possible only through additional discounting and promotion.

"This was one of the biggest disasters for me; I sold 26, returned 147," said Karen Pennington, buyer for Kepler's Books & Magazines in Menlo Park, California. "It was a standing president and no one cared."

Between Hope and History is just one of the worst examples of the overall returns that plagued publishers last year. According to the Association of American Publishers, the average return rate of a book rose 8.9 percentage points, to 35 percent, last year, with many books, like Clinton's, returning at double that rate.

What are the reasons? Many pointed to the continuing pressures of attracting consumer attention in the expanded outlets of warehouse and price clubs and superstores as a key factor in over-shipping. "The biggest returns issue is setting up the big displays and then having them come back," said Lou Aronica, president and publisher of Avon Books. "But it's a risk you have to take, and it's a reality of the business."

"With 100,000-plus titles in the typical superstore, you have to do what you can to get noticed," said Warner CEO Larry Kirshbaum.

"There are certainly more choices, more channels of distribution, than ever before," said Bantam CEO Irwyn Applebaum. "There is a bigger chance for a hardcover success—and failure. There are a lot of carcasses at the side of the road."

Earning out the big advances for perceived "big" books also pushes up the heat to increase a print run. "This was a book every publisher was hot for—every publisher was chasing this book, and bookseller orders were based on the success of her last book," said Pocket Books publisher Gina Centrello about Betty Eadie's *The Awakening Heart*, 1996's follow-up to *Embraced by the Light*. Centrello reportedly paid a seven-figure advance for it, but *The Awakening Heart* sold only 300,000 of a 650,000-copy shipment, a scaleback of an originally announced first printing. And Ballantine paid a reported $3.5 million for Johnnie Cochran's *Journey to Justice*, and sold only half its 500,000 first printing. "We simply shipped too much," admitted publisher Linda Grey.

Beyond overpaying and overprinting, there's simply William Goldman's golden rule: "No one knows anything." Consumers just may or may not be in sync with publishers'—and/or booksellers'—great expectations. "I think the public was definitely distracted by the election and the Olympics this year," said Simon & Schuster publisher Carolyn Reidy—a distraction that did not necessarily lead consumers to related books.

Not All O. J. Books Have Juice

The public has certainly been distracted by the "Trial of the Century," and Barnes & Noble's director of merchandising, Bob Wietrak, said that no discussion of 1996 bookselling would be complete without acknowledging the success of many O. J.-related books in what is an ever-growing, not-so-mini genre. But while Cochran's *Journey to Justice* and Robert Shapiro's *The Search for Justice* (Warner) sold what would be decent numbers for most books—250,000 and 100,000, respectively, according to their publishers—they both had seven-figure advances, and about 50 percent returns on their initial print run.

"Shapiro sold very well out of the box and then it sputtered," said Kirshbaum. "In retrospect, we would have put out less. And we're not going to do a paperback."

Kevan Lyon, vice-president/merchandising for Advanced Marketing Services, a San Diego-based supplier to warehouse and price clubs, had a 40 percent return on Shapiro's book, and a 21 percent return on Cochran's. Ingram buyer Susie Russenberger "did not sell all our initial order" on Cochran, "and we didn't order nearly as many as the publisher would have liked." Surprisingly, however, Russenberger said that Shapiro's book, which had the advantage of being one of the first out on the case, "was the perfect fit for us—we sold more than we ordered and ultimately four times more than we did of Cochran."

Karen Pennington, at Kepler's Books & Magazines, said, "In our community, Cochran didn't work. It was the biggest fiasco. I advanced 100 copies and sold 15. I think it was his personality."

Pennington's comment points to the extreme emotional fervor about the case, which reflected which books sold. "My gosh, when we had Chris Darden here, he was practically thrown rose petals!" said Margaret Maupin, buyer for Denver's Tattered Cover. "We had Cochran here and ordered a lot of books, but we didn't get a big crowd." The arising conventional wisdom: Defense books don't fare too well in the O. J. stakes. "If you look to the bestseller list, you could reach that conclusion," said Grey, who plans to reissue Cochran's book—"a complete autobiography, not just a book about the trial"— in mass market.

And even those O. J. books that were more impartial or more prosecution-oriented weren't always sure things. A mere blip on the radar for most booksellers was *A Problem of Evidence*, a Morrow book by Joseph Bosco, one of the four reporters who had permanent seats at the trial. Pennington ordered 10, returned seven. Michael Kindness, buyer for Boston-based Waterstone's Booksellers, ordered 12 and sold only one. AMS's Lyon did a test ship and "it did not perform." At Ingram, Russenberger said, the Bosco book "fell through the cracks." And although her earlier Nicole Brown Simpson was a bestseller, many booksellers didn't even order Faye Resnick's *Shattered* (Dove), proving that there's just so much fascination for certain players in the case.

It's Not Politics as Usual

Pennington was "really quite depressed" by the performance of Bob Woodward's *The Choice*. Based on Woodward's track record for his previous book, *The Agenda*, Pennington ordered 85 books—but returned 58.

"We thought it was going to be the book for the election," she said. "But I don't think it has anything to do with the book or the marketing of it. In June, when the book came out, it was starting to become clear how torpid the public reaction to the election would be."

Not that the public was entirely indifferent to political books; Wietrak counts the fiction *Primary Colors* and the nonfiction *Unlimited Access*, *Blood Sport*, *Slouching to Gomorrah*, *It Takes a Village,* and *Rush Limbaugh Is a Big Fat Idiot* as winners for Barnes & Noble last year. But some books too closely tied to the campaign lost.

"It turned out people didn't care about Dole," said S&S's Reidy. The book sold more than 200,000 on a 600,000 first printing. Additionally, Woodward's book, originally entitled *The Race*, was to reflect the drama of Republican contenders battling it out; that fizzled when Dole took an early lead.

Reidy said S&S will issue *The Choice* in trade paperback (Woodward's previous books have all gone right to mass market). "It's an important historical record," she said.

Even though it experienced dismal sales on the Bill Clinton book, Ingram still sold 10 times more copies of it than the later *Trusting the People*, the Dole/Kemp manifesto HarperCollins rushed out with a six-figure first printing.

Barbara Morrow, owner of the Northshire Bookstore in Manchester Center, Vermont, was shipped 25 copies and only sold one. "Our buyer says everyone but the diehards knew they were going to lose," said Ingram's Russenberger.

Still, booksellers felt pressured to at least stock the book. "You didn't want to be stuck not having them," said Tom Allen, buyer for Davis-Kidd Booksellers in Nashville, Tennessee.

Perhaps because its conservative author went surprisingly easy on the First Lady, David Brock's *The Seduction of Hillary Rodham* didn't seduce as many readers as expected. AMS's Lyon did a "fairly aggressive buy," but three-quarters of them came back. Tom Allen ordered 50 and sold only nine. "It seems like the Anita Hill book he did was more of a controversy," said Waterstone's Kindness. Ingram's Russenberger said she was "very bold on this," but experienced only a 12 percent sell-through.

Booksellers also got stuck with books they thought were worthy but perhaps suffered because of the general political malaise. A leading example of this is former Planned Parenthood leader Faye Wattleton's *Life on the Line*, which Ballantine promoted heavily with author appearances at bookstores and bookseller conventions. "We had an extensive laydown on this, but abortion rights never became a talking point in the campaign," said Grey, who will reissue the book in trade paper. Books such as Candace Gingrich's *The Accidental Activist* (Scribner), David Mixner's *Stranger Among Friends* (Bantam), and Andrew Young's *An Easy Burden* (HarperCollins) experienced similar deflation, booksellers reported.

The Pope—and PBS—Are Not Infallible

Ingram's Russenberger didn't even want to share how low the sell-through was for *Gift & Mystery*, the book by Pope John Paul II that Doubleday rushed to stores in December. "It's one of the biggest disappointments. They really loaded the stores with this one," she said.

"The Pope went over well once, that was plenty," said Pennington, referring to the Pope's *Crossing the Threshold of Hope*, a bestseller for Knopf in 1994. She sold 14 copies of *Gift & Mystery*, returning 36. Kindness was not kind either, noting that people are "more interested in the Pope's inspirational sayings than his life." He ordered 100 copies of the book but sold only 27. Politics & Prose's Barbara Meade ordered 22 and sold four. "He didn't go on Oprah—big mistake," half-joked Dan Wilson of The Bookshop in Boise, Idaho, which ordered only 10 copies and still has seven.

Doubleday publisher Arlene Friedman pointed out that the book remains a religion bestseller but admitted there was a big "scheduling problem" with it. "We originally planned to release it for Easter, with plenty of time for promotion, but the Vatican wanted the book to come out quickly because it was already out in Europe," she said. "I'm not sure that the book was even unpacked in some cases."

Friedman, who reportedly paid a fraction of the $6 million Knopf had paid, said that she has received 130,000 returns so far on a 750,000-copy announced first printing that became a scaled-back shipping of 650,000. But the publisher was making a promotional push for Easter, and many booksellers and AMS vice-president Lyon held on to copies to put out again for that season.

Another chance to push a 1996 book once more may be reruns of the PBS series "Genesis" in the next few months. Many booksellers had expected big sales on Bill Moyers's tie-in book of the same name published by Doubleday.

That turned out to be the problem, said Friedman. "The media picked it up as a trend story, not a book story. This was the first time Bill had at least a half-dozen other books on the same topic come out. They cannibalized each other."

Based on publisher expectations expressed at last year's American Booksellers Association (ABA) Convention, Lyon took 37,000 copies of Genesis—and returned just under half. Ingram's Russenberger said that Genesis was "a disappointment, but not disastrous. We eventually sold 70 percent, but it took forever to sell."

"There are just far too many PBS tie-in books," claimed Isabella Reitzel, a former buyer at Chicago-based Barbara's Bookstores. "If you were a person who watched PBS and liked to read the tie-in book, you could have been reading one every day."

Another PBS tie-in last year was *The West*, a Little, Brown title that is one of only two 1996 disappointments that Barnes & Noble's Wietrak would admit to. Ingram sold only 15 percent of its buy, and Little, Brown publicity director Beth Davey acknowledged the house was "disappointed in the sell-through. The accounts were as convinced of this one as we were, but the media really didn't cover the series." Davey said Little, Brown will redistribute the book at a lower price point this fall and noted that "we still sold 150,000 copies of a $60 book."

Comedy's Not Pretty

Jay Leno may be gaining on David Letterman in the ratings—but not in the book race. Wietrak's second disappointment was Leno's autobiography *Leading with My Chin*, which had a $4 million-plus advance and an announced one million-copy printing. But the book sold considerably less.

Booksellers felt that the book wasn't funny enough. "He's a bit of a milquetoast," said Pennington. Ingram's Russenberger said they ordered more on Leno than she did for Brett Butler's *Knee Deep in Paradise* (Hyperion) and sold about the same—which is not saying much. "It was a real tough year for celebrity books and this [the Butler book] was a comic writing about dysfunction," said Russenberger, who sold only a third of her Butler buy. Even discounting didn't help, said Pennington. "Customers didn't beat a path to buy. And I didn't even claim the credit offered—not worth the paperwork."

Hyperion publisher Bob Miller said that Butler's book "was a few degrees away from what her TV audience expected," a TV audience that informed his decision for a 300,000 first printing. For him, the 120,000-plus sell-through "is good, but not compared to our expectations."

"At this point we're not expecting anything with comedian books; it peaked with Seinfeld," said Kindness, who referred to Kelsey Grammer's *So Far* (Viking) as another comic fiasco last year. "We'll see what happens with [upcoming books by] Sinbad [Bantam], Drew Carey [Hyperion], and Whoopi [Morrow/Rob Weisbach]."

Sports Figures Don't Always Make Book

Dennis Rodman may have strutted with *Bad as I Wanna Be* (Dell) last year, but other sports books rebounded back to publishers. A lead title in Avon's new hardcover line, tennis coach Nick Bolletierri's *My Aces, My Faults*, "definitely didn't work," admitted publisher Lou Aronica. "We published it during the U.S. Open—it seemed like the right strategy. But the media never picked up on his controversial opinions; they were often respectful!"

"There was a good coauthor [Dick Schaap] but it just didn't work," said Russenberger, who saw only a 20 percent sell-through. Kindness ordered four copies and didn't sell any. For Morrow, Bolletierri wasn't quite famous enough. "If people are interested in tennis, it wouldn't be from him," she said.

Even the more high-profile Monica Seles, signed up for a rumored $1 million advance from HarperCollins, didn't score. "I think this one would have done better as a mass-market for kids," said Morrow. Ingram's Russenberger ended up having only a 20 percent sell-through on a very "conservative order."

And finally, ReganBooks paid a reported $1 million advance for Olympic track star Michael Johnson's *Slaying the Dragon*, which was rushed to stores soon after the Games but didn't break any selling records. AMS's Lyon took a moderate order and took back a third. "A previous photo book of Johnson was a better seller for me," said Karen Pennington.

The First Fiction Gamble

Perhaps nowhere is hardcover roulette more in play than launching first fiction. Warner's Kirshbaum perhaps justifiably boasted that "we are the best at marketing first novels." But for every *Notebook*, one could be filled with a list of failed or disappointing launches. Random House paid a rumored seven figures for TV writer Karen Hall's *Dark Debts*, but Ingram's Russenberger was only able to sell about 40 percent of her order. "The ads were everywhere but, personally, I didn't like the cover because it didn't give you a sense of what the book was about," said Kindness, who sold six copies of an initial order of 15. Lyon did a "light roll" and took back half.

Said Reitzel, late of Barbara's Bookstores: "It's an excellent book, but I guess it didn't catch on. I think it will do well in paperback."

Paperback is indeed the saving grace for first fiction, as Bantam's Applebaum full well knows. His big stand for John Ramsey Miller's *The Last Family* (he even featured himself in ads for the book) didn't "materialize into the bestseller" he hoped for, although he expects eventual sell-through of the 100,000 first printing. Said AMS's Lyon, "We took a big stand, supported it with an order of 40,000, but we took 65 percent back." Said Russenberger, "It had a promising start, but it didn't last."

For the mass market paperback of the book, Applebaum is shooting for a one-million-copy bestseller and has revised the book jacket so there is more "sell copy," as well as a cover image that "gets across the terror better. It's the advantage of being a hardcover and paperback publisher to learn from the hardcover and build." Best of all, he noted, "we didn't pay a huge advance on this one."

That wasn't the case for *Almost Adam* (Morrow), a first novel by Petru Popescu for which the house reportedly paid and shipped big. The problem was it was competing against a similar-themed book, *Neanderthal*, which turned out to be the bestseller. (A comparable Dell title, *Ember from the Sun*, also got muscled by the Random title.)

Whatever the pressures on Morrow (which would not comment on the book), booksellers got mad that the heat was applied to them.

"*Almost Adam* shipped so quickly that I don't think our rep even read it," said Reitzel. "It was definitely sold to us as the next big hit."

"I got into a bit of a wrestling match with my rep on this one," said Pennington. "He compared it to Grisham!"

"*Almost Adam* was a joke. I remember our Morrow rep begging us to take a bunch. I ordered 24 and sold two," said Morrow at the Northshire Bookstore.

Lyon said that "the publisher asked us for a high level of support. We responded and took back three-quarters."

Almost Adam has already come out in mass market without the head-to-head competition of *Neanderthal*, and it briefly hit the *New York Times* list.

Change-of-Pace Is Chancy

Martin Cruz Smith's *Rose* was more historical in flavor than his typical thriller, and Ingram's Russenberger sold only half of a "fairly aggressive buy" while AMS's Lyon sold the same percentage of her order. For independent booksellers Meade and Morrow, however, it sold well via handselling, and Ballantine will be reissuing the book first in trade paper in July with a 50,000 first printing, possibly followed by a mass market (particularly if the movie plans progress) a year later.

Although Davis-Kidd's Allen said E. Annie Proulx's *Accordion Crimes* handsold fine in his stores, Barbara Morrow found the book, more episodic than her bestselling *The Shipping News*, tough going: "The word of mouth was not good. It was hard to sell even to her ardent fans."

"We didn't have a conservative buy on this one, but we certainly didn't buy to the level of *Shipping News* either," said Russenberger. "We sold a bit better than half, but it turned out to be not the same kind of book."

Similarly, Laura Esquivel's *The Law of Love* (Crown) wasn't nearly as loved as her previous blockbuster. Doubleday, publisher of her bestselling *Like Water for Chocolate*, passed on doing this book, believing the color illustrations throughout and an attached CD made the book too expensive a proposition. Plus, "it was too offbeat," said Russenberger of the New Age bent to the book. Russenberger had only a 15 percent sell-through on her order, which was fairly aggressive.

"It was a New Age topic; a lot of her fans weren't expecting it. We ordered 50 and sold 33, but I bet a lot of people ended up not really reading the book," said Morrow. Commented Kindness, "It has a beautiful cover, but perhaps that was part of the problem: it looked too slick after the down-home charm of *Like Water for Chocolate*." Reitzel, too, worried that *The Law of Love* was too gimmicky, "but it worked well for us." Said Lyon, "We all wanted it to work." She got a 15 percent return on her order—not bad, but a quarter of the sell-through she saw on Esquivel's earlier book.

And just to prove that no one is immune to the fickleness of the market, booksellers even experienced returns for Anne Rice's 1996 novel *Servant of the Bones* (Knopf) because, booksellers said, it did not focus on fans' favorite topic, vampires. "I sold 125 copies, but I expected twice that," said Reitzel. "I think the reviews hurt the book," said Kindness. "We sold 70 percent, which sounds good, but usually Rice sells 100 percent," said Russenberger. "I think Rice has built her audience as far as it can go," said Richard Howorth, owner of Square Books in Oxford, Mississippi, who was glad to have some leeway in ordering for this blockbuster author. "Ah, returns; they are the problem—and delight—of the business," he said, somewhat ghoulishly.

Paperback Bestsellers: King Is King—Or at Least Crown Prince

While the trade paperback bestseller list continues to reflect a steady stream of chicken soup, cedars, comics, and computers, the big news was in mass market sales.

As in the past four years, John Grisham clings to the top slot, with *The Rainmaker* garnering sales of 5,110,613. It may not be as big as big a year for the attorney/author as 1993, when he held three of the top five slots (the other two going to Michael Crichton) with 10,232,480 for *The Pelican Brief*, 6,175,800 for *The Firm*, and 3,933,900 for *A Time to Kill*. But as Francis Ford Coppola's movie of *Rainmaker* is due from Paramount in November, look for Grisham and his *Rainmaker* at the top again next year.

Danielle Steel is holding steady (as she has for over a decade) with figures in the three million-plus range, and other stalwarts like Crichton and Mary Higgins Clark and Tom Clancy are putting in appearances at two million-plus, but the real news is Stephen King, who holds six of the top seven slots.

King has yet to gain the top prize—even in 1980 when the movie tie-in edition of *The Shining* did spectacularly well (4,450,000), it was beat out by two other monstrously successful movie tie-ins—James Clavell's *Shogun* (6,600,000) and Judith Krantz's *Scruples* (4,800,000). And if the numbers for individual King titles are not as high as past years' top sellers (the figures range from 3,865,447 to 3,475,036), they're still impressive. Add up the number of copies sold of each installment of *The Green Mile*, and King outsold the closest competitor by 100 percent with 22 million copies. Add the 2,330,508 copies of *Rose Madder* and the figure climbs to over 24 million. Signet is clearly thrilled that King's *Mile* indeed came up green, and Ballantine has decided to follow suit with John Saul's serialization, *The Blackstone Chronicles*, which, if it continues to grow as it has, may capture its own segment of the list next year.

Both trade paperback and mass market figures reflect originals, reprints, or dual editions published in 1995 or 1996 for which publishers have billed and shipped at least 50,000 (for trade paperbacks) or one million (for mass markets) in 1996. They do not always reflect net sales. Titles released in 1995 are marked by an asterisk.

Paperback listings compiled by Ingrid Chevannes and Dermot McEvoy.

Trade Paperbacks

100,000+

A 3rd Serving of Chicken Soup for the Soul. Jack Canfield and Mark Victor Hansen. Orig. Health Communications (1,602, 439)

*Snow Falling on Cedars. David Guterson. Rep. Vintage (1,490,590)

It's a Magical World: A Calvin and Hobbes Collection. Bill Watterson. Orig. Andrews & McMeel (1,250,000)

There's Treasure Everywhere: A Calvin and Hobbes Collection. Bill Watterson. Orig. Andrews & McMeel (1,100,000)

Chicken Soup for the Woman's Soul. Jack Canfield, Mark Victor Hansen, Jennifer Read Hawthorne, and Marci Shimoff. Orig. Health Communications (1,069,402)

A Journal of Daily Renewal: The Companion to Make the Connection. Bob Greene and Oprah Winfrey. Orig. Hyperion (1,034, 160)

*Windows 95 for Dummies. Andy Rathbone. Orig. IDG (1,000,000)

Fugitive from the Cubicle Police: A Dilbert Book. Scott Adams. Orig. Andrews & McMeel (663,123)

The Last Chapter and Worse: A Far Side Collection. Gary Larson. Orig. Andrews & McMeel (605,000)

The English Patient (movie tie-in). Michael Ondaatje. Rep. Vintage (575,630)

*Reviving Ophelia. Mary Pipher. Rep. Ballantine (556,347)

*Microsoft Windows 95 Resource Kit. Microsoft. Rep. Microsoft (468,337)

Still Pumped From Using the Mouse: A Dilbert Book. Scott Adams. Orig. Andrews & McMeel (451,023)

SSN: A Strategy Guide to Submarine Warfare. Tom Clancy. Orig. Berkley (450,000)

*Dr. Atkin's New Diet Revolution. Robert C. Atkins, M.D. Rep. M. Evans (427,148)

Dianetics. L. Ron Hubbard. Reprint. Bridge Pub. (423,512)

Prescription for Nutritional Healing. James Balch, M.D., and Phyllis Balch. Orig. Avery (400,000)

*Internet for Dummies, 3rd Ed. John Levine, Carol Baroudi, and Margaret Levine Young. Orig. IDG (400,000)

*Ten Stupid Things Women Do to Mess Up Their Lives. Laura Schlessinger. Rep. HarperCollins (394,330)

*The Great Gatsby. F. Scott Fitzgerald. Rep. Scribners (370,000)

C'mon America Let's Eat! Susan's Favorite Low-Fat Recipes to Fit Your Lifestyle. Susan Powter. Orig. Fireside (335,000)

Mars and Venus Together Forever. John Gray. Rep. HarperPerennial (334,664)

The Beardstown Ladies' Stitch-in-Time Guide to Growing Your Nest Egg: Step-by-Step Planning for a Comfortable Financial Future. The Beardstown Ladies' Investment Club with Robin Dellabough. Rep. Hyperion (334,481)

Ladder of Years. Anne Tyler. Rep. Fawcett (316,577)

Dead Man Walking (movie tie-in). Sister Helen Prejean. Rep. Vintage (311,500)

The Liar's Club. Mary Karr. Rep. Penguin (290,000)

Beginning of the End: The Assassination of Yitzhak Rabin and Coming Antichrist. John Hagee. Orig. Nelson (287,085)

MTV's Beavis and Butthead: Huh-Huh! For Hollywood. Larry Doyle. Orig. MTV/Pocket (277,383)

The Road Ahead. Bill Gates. Reprint/Revised. Penguin (275,000)

A Civil Action. Jonathan Harr. Rep. Vintage (269,600)

The Code: Time-Tested Secrets for Getting What You Want from Women Without Marrying Them! Nathaniel Penn and Lawrence LaRose. Rep. Fireside (265,000)

Moo. Jane Smiley. Rep. Fawcett (261,495)

Marine: A Guided Tour of a Marine Expeditionary Unit. Tom Clancy. Orig. Berkley (260,000)

Drums of Change. Janette Oke. Orig. Bethany (258,444)

Windows 3.11 for Dummies, 3rd Ed. Andy Rathbone. Orig. IDG (250,000)

We're Right, They're Wrong. James Carville. Orig. Random (249,402)

Chicken Soup for the Soul at Work. Jack Canfield, Mark Victor Hansen, Martin Rutte, Maida Rogerson, and Tim Klauss. Orig. Health Communications (248,282)

Spontaneous Healing. Andrew Weil, M.D. Rep. Fawcett (242,656)

Memnoch the Devil. Anne Rice. Rep. Ballantine (240,270)
Learn to Earn: A Beginner's Guide to the Basics of Investing and Business. Peter Lynch. Rep. Fireside (240,000)
**Secrets of Fat-Free Cooking.* Sandra Woodruff. Orig. Avery (240,000)
A Cup of Chicken Soup for the Soul. Jack Canfield, Mark Victor Hansen, and Barry Spilchuk. Orig. Health Communications (239,282)
Condensed Chicken Soup for the Soul. Jack Canfield, Mark Victor Hansen, and Patty Hansen. Orig. Health Communciations (219,330)
Independence Day. Richard Ford. Rep. Vintage (215,300)
Western Garden Book. Sunset Editors. Rev. Sunset (207,272)
New Passages. Gail Sheehy. Rep. Ballantine (206,868)
A Good Walk Spoiled: Days and Nights on the PGA Tour. John Feinstein. Rep. Little, Brown (203,209)
PC's for Dummies, 4th Ed. Dan Gookin. Orig. IDG (200,000)
Windows 95 for Dummies. Andy Rathbone. Orig. IDG (200,000)
Gold for Dummies. Gary McCord with John Huggan. Orig. IDG (200,000)
Kelley's Blue Book: Consumer Edition. Orig. Kelley Blue Book (187,894)
The 20 Gram Diet. Gabe Mirkin, M.D. Orig. Linx Corp. (186,799)
Return to Harmony. Janette Oke and T. Davis Bunn. Orig. Bethany (182,635)
Book of Virtues: A Treasure of the World's Great Moral Stories. William Bennett. Rep. Touchstone (180,000)
Mars and Venus in the Bedroom. John Gray. Rep. HarperCollins (176,011)
More So Far, Low Fat, No Fat: Recipes for Family and Friends That Cut the Fat But Not the Flavor! Betty Rohde. Orig. Fireside (170,000)
**The Old Man and the Sea.* Ernest Hemingway. Rep. Scribners (170,000)
**America's Dumbest Criminals.* Daniel Butler, Alan Ray, and Leland Gregory. Orig. Rutledge Hill (169,151)
DHEA: A Practical Guide. Ray Sahelian, M.D. Orig. Avery (167,000)

High Tide in Tucson. Barbara Kingsolver. Rep. HarperPerennial (164,213)
Being Digital. Nicholas Negroponte. Rep. Vintage (162,500)
Dragons of Summer Flame. Margaret Weis and Tracy Hickman. Reprint. TSR (158,440)
Ishmael. Daniel Quinn. Rep. Bantam (158,000)
God: A Biography. Jack Miles. Rep. Vintage (157,300)
Better Homes and Gardens New Cook Book, 11th edition. Editors of Better Homes and Gardens. Revised. Meredith (155,399)
It Takes a Village: And Other Lessons Children Teach Us. Hillary Rodham Clinton. Orig. Touchstone (155,000)
Twister. Michael Crichton. Orig. Ballantine (154,973)
How to Decorate. Editors of Martha Stewart Living. Orig. Crown (153,189)
**Inner Simplicity: 100 Ways to Regain Peace & Nourish Your Soul.* Elaine St. James. Orig. Hyperion (151,269)
The Real World Diaries. MTV. Orig. MTV/Pocket (151,007)
Trust No One: The Official Guide to the X-Files. Brian Lowry. Orig. HarperPrism (150,212)
How to Argue and Win Every Time. Gerry Spence. Rep. St. Martin's/Griffin (150,165)
**Windows 95 Simplified.* Ruth Maran. Orig. CPG/IDG (150,000)
Longitude: The True Story of a Lone Genius Who Solved the Greatest Scientific Problem of His Time. Dava Sobel. Rep. Penguin (150,000)
Investing for Dummies. Eric Tyson. Orig. IDG (150,000)
Macs for Dummies. Orig. IDG (150,000)
Taxes for Dummies. Eric Tyson and David J. Silverman. Orig. IDG (150,000)
Chicken Soup for the Surviving Soul. Jack Canfield, Mark Victor Hansen, Patty Aubrey, and Nancy Mitchell. Orig. Health Communications (147,095)
The Tenth Insight: Holding the Vision: An Experimental Guide. James Redfield and Carol Adrienne. Orig. Warner (143,539)
**Karate for Kids.* J. Allen Queen. Rep. Sterling (141,087)
Java in a Nutshell. David Flanagan. Orig. O'Reilly & Associates (140,986)

When Elephants Weep. Jeffrey. Masson and Susan McCarthy. Rep. Delta (140,951)
*Joslin's Guide to Diabetes. Richard S. Beaser. Orig. Fireside (140,000)
Get a Financial Life: Personal Finance in Your 20s and 30s. Beth Kobliner. Orig. Fireside (140,000)
*Driven to Distraction: Recognizing and Coping with Attention Deficit Disorder from Childhood Through Adulthood. Edward M. Hallowell, M.D., and John J. Ratey, M.D. Rep. Touchstone (140,000)
Patrick's Notebook: Words of Love from One Life to Live. Patrick Thornhart. Orig. Hyperion (139,458)
Garfield Tons of Fun (#29). Jim Davis. Orig. Ballantine (139,307)
I'm So Glad You Told Me What I Didn't Wanna Hear. Barbara Johnson. Orig. Word (137,575)
Paula. Isabel Allende. Rep. HarperPerennial (136,979)
Martha Stuart's Better Than You at Entertaining. Tom Connor. Orig. HarperPerennial (134,508)
Christmas Ideals. Ideals Editors. Orig. Ideals (133,900)
Aunt Bee's Delightful Desserts. Jim Clark and Ken Beck. Orig. Rutledge Hill (130,875)
MTV's Road Rules: Road Trips. Genevieve Field. Orig. MTV/Pocket(127,425)
*Girlfriends: Invisible Bonds, Enduring Ties. Carmen Renee Berry and Tamara Traeder. Orig. Wildcat Canyon Press, Circulus Publishing Group (126,372)
*Running Microsoft Windows 95. Craig Stinson. Rep. Microsoft (125,165)
Faith in the Valley: Lessons for Women on the Journey to Peace. Iyanla Vanzant. Rep. Fireside (125,000)
Practical Guide to Practically Everything, Vol. 2. Peter Bernstein and Christopher Ma. Orig. Random (124,282)
The Return of Merlin. Deepak Chopra. Rep. Fawcett (123,591)
An Anthropologist on Mars: Seven Paradoxical Tales. Oliver Sacks. Rep. Vintage (123,200)
*Your Pregnancy Week-by-Week. Glade Curtis. Orig. Fisher (121,438)

The Only Investment Guide You'll Ever Need. Andrew Tobias. Orig. Harcourt Brace/Harvest (121,132)
Mary's Message to the World. Annie Kirkwood. Rep. Perigee (120,000)
Dave Barry's Complete Guide to Guys. Dave Barry. Rep. Fawcett (119,698)
*Wherever You Go, There You Are: Mindfulness Meditation in Everyday Life. Jon Kabat-Zinn. Rep. Hyperion (118,266)
Trainspotting. Irvine Welsh. Orig. Norton (115,973)
The Very Best Baby Name Book in the Whole Wide World. Bruce Lansky. Orig. Meadowbrook (115,317)
Blueprints: Star Wars. Rick Sternbach. Orig. Pocket (113,148)
Jesus CEO: Using Ancient Wisdom for Visionary Leadership. Laurie Beth Jones. Rep. Hyperion (113,091)
The Oath. Frank Peretti. Rep. Word (111, 065)
*Stone Diaries. Carol Shields. Rep. Penguin (108,000)
Sleeping at the Starlight Motel. Bailey White. Rep. Vintage (107,000)
*Life's Little Instruction Book, Vol. 3. H. Jackson Brown, Jr. Orig. Rutledge Hill (106,448)
Garfield Bigger and Better (#30). Jim Davis. Orig. Ballantine (104,499)
*Girlfriend's Guide to Pregnancy. Vicki Iovine. Reissue. Pocket (104,224)
Wanted! Dumb or Alive. Daniel Butler and Alan Ray. Orig. Rutledge Hill (104,141)
*The Truth Is Out There: The Official Third Season Guide to the X-Files. Brian Lowry. Orig. HarperPrism (102,610)
*T-Factor Fat Gram Counter. Jamie Pope and Martin Katahn. Orig. Norton (102, 309)
*35,000 Baby Names. Bruce Lansky. Orig. Meadowbrook (100,969)
Moosewood Restaurant Low-Fat Favorites. The Moosewood Collective. Orig. Crown (100,683)
Where the Wild Rose Blooms. Lori Wick. Orig. Harvest House (100,112)
Star Trek Federation Passport. J. M. Dillard. Orig. Pocket (100,088)
Wine for Dummies. Mary Ewing-Mulligan and Ed McCarthy. Orig. IDG (100,000)

*Notes from a Friend. Tony Robbins. Orig. Fireside (100,000)
Lincoln. David Herbert Donald. Rep. Touchstone (100,000)

75,000+

Great American Wreaths. Editors of Martha Stewart Living. Orig. Crown (98,362)
David Brinkley: A Memoir. David Brinkley. Rep. Ballantine (96,858)
Growing Up With Dick and Jane. Carole Kismaric and Marvin Heiferman. Orig. HarperCollins (96,762)
The Death of Common Sense: How Law Is Suffocating America. Philip K. Howard. Rep. Warner (96,526)
*Dr. Atkin's New Diet Cookbook. Robert C. Atkins, M.D. Rep. M. Evans (96,463)
The Stokes Field Guide to Birds: Eastern Region. Donald and Lillian Stokes. Rep. Little, Brown (96,322)
Fresh Start. Julee Rosso. Orig. Crown (95,662)
The Alchemist. Paulo Coelho. Rep. HarperSanFrancisco (95,599)
At Home in Mitford. Jan Karon. Rep. Penguin (93,000)
*Celestine Prophecy: An Experimental Guide. James Redfield and Carol Adrienne. Orig. Warner (92,864)
Amazing Grace. Jonathan Kozol. Rep. Harper Perennial (91,717)
Star Wars: The Essential Guide to Vehicles and Vessels. Bill Smith. Rep. Ballantine (91,168)
*Ageless Body, Timeless Mind. Deepak Chopra. Rep. Crown (90,888)
Frazier. Jefferson Graham. Orig. Pocket (90,454)
*The Little Mac Book, 4th Edition. Robin Williams. Orig. Peachpit (88,884)
A Dog's Life. Peter Mayle. Rep. Vintage (88,600)
Grow Old Along With Me: The Best Is Yet to Be. Sandra Haldeman Martz. Orig. Papier-Mache (88,436)
Stop Aging Now. Jean Carper. Rep. HarperPerennial (87,681)
The Microscope Book. Shar Levine. Rep. Sterling (86,553)
*Women Who Run with the Wolves. Clarissa Estes. Rep. Ballantine (86,221)
Whispers of Moonlight. Lori Wick. Orig. Harvest House (85,000)
*Farewell to Arms. Ernest Hemingway. Rep. Scribners (85,000)
Journey to the Heart. Melodie Beattie. Orig. HarperSanFrancisco (84,107)
What to Have for Dinner. Editors of Martha Stewart Living. Orig. Crown (83,756)
My Old Man and the Sea. David Hays. Rep. HarperPerennial (83,655)
*The Sun Also Rises. Ernest Hemingway. Rep. Scribners (83,000)
3rd Rock From the Sun. Bonnie and Terry Turner. Orig. HarperPerennial (82,868)
*Stones from the River. Ursula Hegi. Rep. Scribners (82,000)
Joshua. Joseph P. Girzone. Rep. Scribners (82,000)
In Retrospect: The Tragedy and Lessons of Vietnam. Robert McNamara. Rep. Vintage (81,800)
Hellion. Bertrice Small. Rep. Ballantine (81,147)
The Island of the Day Before. Umberto Eco. Rep. Penguin (81,000)
*Live and Learn and Pass It On, Vol. 2. H. Jackson Brown, Jr. Orig. Rutledge Hill (80,721)
A Hero in Every Heart. H. Jackson Brown, Jr. and Robyn Spizman. Orig. Nelson (80,557)
At Least This Place Sells T-Shirts: A FoxTrot Collection. Bill Amend. Orig. Andrews & McMeel (80,000)
Ship Fever. Andrea Barrett. Rep. Norton (79,629)
Dawning of a New Age. Jean Rabe. Orig. TSR (79,370)
Schoolhouse Rock: The Official Guide. Tom Yohe and George Newall. Orig. Hyperion (78,768)
*Field Guide to Microsoft Windows 95. Craig Stinson. Rep. Microsoft (78,528)
*Secrets of Fat-Free Cooking: Over 150 Fat-Free and Low-Fat Recipes, from Breakfast to Dinner—Appetizers to Desserts. Sandra Woodruff. Orig. Avery (77,623)
You Know You're Anonymous in Washington When... Anonymous. Orig. St. Martin's (76,786)

1001 Ways to Be Romantic, 5th Anniversary Edtion. Gregory J. P. Godek. Rep. Sourcebooks (76,689)

What to Expect When You're Expecting Pregnancy Organizer. Arlene Eisenberg, Heidi Murkoff, and Sandee Hathaway. Orig. Workman (76,615)

Dilbert: A Book of Postcards. Scott Adams. Orig. Andrews & McMeel (76,219)

The Physics of Star Trek. Lawrence M. Krauss. Rep. HarperPerennial (76,129)

Sacred Hoops: Spiritual Lessons of a Hardwood Warrior. Phil Jackson and Hugh Delehanty. Rep. Hyperion (75,780)

The Return of the Lone Iguana: A FoxTrot Collection. Bill Amend. Orig. Andrews & McMeel (75,123)

Cooking for Dummies. Bryan Miller and Marie Rama. Orig. IDG (75,000)

Crockery Cookery. Maple Hoffman. Orig. Perigee (75,000)

Earl Mindell's Anti-Aging Bible. Earl Mindell. Rep. Fireside (75,000)

Follow the Wind. Bo Links. Rep. Scribners (75,000)

50,000+

Lord Only You Can Change Me. Kay Arthur. Orig. Multnomah (74,000)

Dragons at War. Margaret Weis and Tracy Hickman. Orig. TSR (72,160)

Programming Windows 95. Charles Petzold. Rep. Microsoft (72,158)

The Secrets of Star Wars: Shadows of the Empire. Mark Cotta Vaz. Orig. Ballantine (70,722)

Doctor, What Should I Eat? Nutritional Prescriptions for Ailments in Which Diet Can Really Make a Difference. Isadore Rosenfeld, M.D. Rep. Warner (70,390)

Brand Name Fat-Fighter's Cookbook. Sandra Woodruff. Orig. Avery (70,000)

The Wall Street Journal Guide to Planning Your Financial Future. Kenneth M. Morris and Alan M. Siegel. Orig. Fireside (70,000)

Mountain Mazes. Roger Moreau. Orig. Sterling (69,675)

The Paperboy. Pete Dexter. Rep. Delta (69,673)

Klingon Book of Virtues. Okrand. Orig. Pocket (69,507)

Patient's Guide to Prostate Cancer. Marc Garnick. Orig. Plume (69,340)

Prescription for Nutritional Healing, 2nd Ed. James and Phyllis Balch. Orig. Avery (69,103)

Knight in Rusty Armor. Robert Fisher. Rep. Wilshire (68,972)

Do What You Are: Discover the Perfect Career for You Through the Secrets of Personality. Paul Teiger and Barbara Barron-Teiger. Orig. Little, Brown (68,962)

Meditations for Women Who Do Too Much. Anne Wilson Schaef. Rep. HarperSanFrancisco (68,014)

Breaking the Rules: Last-Ditch Tactics for Landing the Man of Your Dreams. Laura Banks and Janette Barber. Orig. Career (67,272)

Divine Sex. Caroline Alred. Orig. HarperSanFrancisco. (66,561)

Feng Shui: Arranging Your Home to Change Your Life. Kirsten M. Lagatree. Orig. Villard (65,292)

Basic Wiring. Sunset Editors. Rev. Sunset (65,229)

Remembering Farley: A Tribute to the Life of Our Favorite Cartoon Dog—A For Better or For Worse Special Collection. Lynn Johnston. Orig. Andrews & McMeel (65,123)

No Ordinary Time: Franklin and Eleanor Roosevelt: The Home Front in World War II. Doris Kearns Goodwin. Rep. Touchstone (65,000)

New Our Bodies, Our Selves: A Book By and For Women. The Boston Women's Health Book Collective. Rep. Touchstone (65,000)

You Mean I'm Not Lazy, Stupid, or Crazy: A Self Help Book for Adults with Attention Deficit Disorder. Kate Kelly and Peggy Ramundo. Rep. Fireside (65,000)

Dare to Win. Jack Canfield and Mark Victor Hansen. Rep. Berkley (65,000)

God's Vitamin "C" for the Spirit: "Tug at-Heart" Stories to Fortify and Enrich Your Life. Compiled by Kathy Collard Miller and D. Larry Miller. Orig. Starburst (65,000)

Days of Our Lives. Lorra Zenka. Orig. HarperPerennial (64,602)

The Official Beckett Pride Guide to Baseball Cards, 16th Edition. James Beckett. Orig. House of Collectibles (63,990)

Stories for the Heart. Compiled by Alice Gray. Orig. Multnomah (63,000)
Paint Your House with Powdered Milk: And Hundreds More Offbeat Uses for Brand-Name Products. Joey Green. Orig. Hyperion (62,987)
The Quotable Star Wars. Stephen J. Sansweet. Orig. Ballantine (62,736)
*Programming Perl, 2nd Ed.*Larry Wall, Randall Schwartz, and Tom Christiansen. Orig. O'Reilly & Associates (62,521)
Lies My Teacher Told Me: Everything Your American History Textbook Got Wrong. James W. Loewen. Rep. Touchstone (62,000)
The Commodore. Patrick O'Brian. Rep. Norton (61,781)
**Resumes that Knock 'Em Dead.* Martin Yate. Orig. Adams (61,553)
The Ultimate Windows 95 Book, 2nd Ed. Eric Stroosic. Rep. Microsoft (61,486)
How to Study, 4th Edition. Ron Fry. Orig. Career (61,380)
The Verbally Abusive Relationship. Patricia Evans. Orig. Adams (60,782)
**Microsoft Windows 95 Step By Step.* Catapult Inc. Rep. Microsoft (60,733)
Don't Go to the Cosmetics Counter Without Me, 3rd Ed. Paula Begoun. Orig. Beginning Press (60,666)
Baby Signs: How to Talk to Your Baby Before Your Baby Can Talk. Linda Acredolo and Susan Goodwyn. Orig. Contemporary (60,662)
An Angel to Watch Over Me. Joan Wester Anderson. Rep. Ballantine (60,117)
Gardening for Dummies. Michael MacCaskey and the National Gardening Assoc. Orig. IDG (60,000)
Nick at Nite Classic TV Companion. Tom Hill. Orig. Fireside (60,000)
High Fidelity: A Novel. Nick Hornsby. Rep. Riverhead (60,000)
Native Speaker. Chang-rae Lee. Rep. Riverhead (60,000)
Marino. Edited by Mark Vancil. Orig. HarperCollins (59,658)
The Unofficial X-Files Companion II. N. E. Genge. Orig. Avon (59,563)
Toward the Sunrising. Gilbert Morris. Orig. Bethany (59,383)

Realm of the Underdark. J. Robert King. Orig. TSR (59,090)
Exit to Eden. Anne Rice. Rep. Ballantine (59,011)
Follow Your Heart. Susanna Tamaro. Rep. Dell (58,719)
The Flat Tax. Richard Armey. Orig. Fawcett (58,339)
MTV Singled Out Guide to Dating. J. D. Heiman with Lynn Harris. MTV/Pocket (58,007)
Heart at Work: Stories and Strategies for Building Self-Esteem and Rewakening the Soul at Work. Jack Canfield and Jacqueline Miller. Orig. McGraw-Hill (58,000)
**View With a Grain of Sand: Selected Poems.* Wislawa Szymborska. Rep. Harcourt Brace/Harvest (57,439)
**Six Hours One Friday.* Max Lucado. Rep. Multnomah (57,000)
**365 Days of Creative Play.* Sheila Ellison and Judith Gray. Rep. Sourcebooks (56,860)
Meditations for People Who (May) Worry Too Much. Anne Wilson Schaef. Orig. Ballantine (56,348)
HTML: The Definitive Guide. Chuck Musiano and Bill Kennedy. Orig. O'Reilly & Associates. (56,246)
**Fuzzy Memories.* Jack Handey. Orig. Andrews & McMeel (56,154)
The Science Explorer: The Best Family Activities and Experiments from the World's Favorite Hands-on Science Museum. Pat Murphy, Ellen Klages, and the Staff of the Exploratorium. Orig. Holt (56,000)
The Fourth Millennium. Paul Meier and Robert Wise. Orig. Nelson (55,217)
Beer Lover's Rating Guide. Bob Klein. Orig. Workman (55,213)
**The Aladdin Factor.* Jack Canfield and Mark Victor Hansen. Orig. Berkley (55,000)
**20 Teachable Virtues: Practical Ways to Pass on Lessons of Virtue.* Barbara C. Unell and Jerry L. Wyckoff. Orig. Perigee (55,000)
Elegant Stitches. Judith Baker Montano. Orig. C&T Publishing (54,029)
Silver Shadows. Elaine Cunningham. Orig. TSR (53,990)
**101 Great Answers to the Toughest Interview Questions.* Ron Fry. Orig. Career (53,775)

Angel Letters. Sophy Burnham. Rep. Ballantine (53,474)
*Upgrading to Microsoft Windows 95. Catapult Inc. Rep. Microsoft (53,444)
*HTML for the World Wide Web: Visual QuickStar Guide. Elizabeth Castro. (53,430)
Daughter of the Draw. Elaine Cunningham. Rep. TSR (53,370)
America: Who Stole the Dream. Donald L. Barlett and James B. Steele. Orig. Andrews & McMeel (53,123)
Star Trek Chronology. Mike and Denise Okuda. Reissue. Pocket 53,088)
Where No One Has Gone Before. J. M. Dillard. Reprint. Pocket (53,057)
*Low-Fat Cooking for Good Health. Gloria Rose. Rep. Avery (53,000)
Lord I'm Torn Between Two Masters. Kay Arthur. Orig. Multnomah (53,000)
Land of the Minotaurs. Richard A. Knaak. Orig. TSR (52,990)
Your Pregnancy After 30. Glade Curtis. Orig. Fisher (52,937)
Northwest Best Places. Stephanie Irving and David Brewster. Rep. Sasquatch (52,779)
*Essential System Administration, 2nd Ed. A. Frisch. Orig. O'Reilly & Associates (52,649)
Internet for Busy People. Christian Crumlish. Orig. Osborne/McGraw-Hill (51,724)
Absolut Book. The Story of the Absolut Vodka Advertising Campaign. Richard W. Lewis. Orig. Journey/Tuttle (51,643)
People's Pharmacy. Joe Graedon and Teresa Graedon. Rep. St. Martin's/Griffin (51,545)
*Microsoft Windows NT 3.51 Resource Kit 3.51. Microsoft. Rep. Microsoft (51,513)
Breaking the Surface. Greg Louganis. Rep. Plume (51,500)
Adams Streetwise Small Business Start-up. Bob Adams. Orig. Adams (51,436)
Child of the Dawn: A Magical Journey of Awakening. Gautama Chopra. Orig. Amber Allen (51,387)
The Western Guide to Feng Shui: Creating Balance, Harmony, and Prosperity in Your Environment. Terah Kathryn Collins. Orig. Hay House (51,247)
The Hunchback of Notre Dame: An Animated Flip Book. Walt Disney's Feature Animation Department Animators. Orig. Hyperion (51,239)

Cathy's Twentieth Anniversary Collection. Cathy Guisewite. Orig. Andrews & McMeel (51,150)
A Random Walk Down Wall Street. Burton G. Malkiel. Norton (51,134)
Five Rituals of Wealth. Todd Barnhart. Rep. HarperPerennial (51,086)
*Bread Machine Gourmet. Shea MacKenzie. Rep. Avery (51,000)
A Return to Love. Marianne Williamson. Rep. HarperPerennial (50,919)
*Beckett's Great Sports Heroes: Michael Jordan. James Beckett. Orig. House of Collectibles (50,629)
The Discipline of Market Leaders. Michael Treary and Fred Wiersema. Rep. Addison-Wesley (50,500)
Montana 1948. Larry Watson. Rep. Pocket (50,491)
RL's Dream. Walter Mosley. Rep. Pocket (50,294)
Secrets of Fat-Free Italian Cooking. Sandra Woodruff, RD. Orig. Avery (50,000)
Value in the Valley: A Black Woman's Guide Through Life's Dilemmas. Iyanla Vanzant. Orig. Fireside (50,000)
Tell Newt to Shut Up! David Maraniss and Michael Weisskopf. Orig. Touchstone (50,000)

Almanacs, Atlases & Annuals

The World Almanac and Book of Facts, 1997. Edited by Robert Famighetti. Orig. World Almanac (1,812,877)
The Universal Almanac, 1997 Edition. Edited by John Wright. Orig. Andrews & McMeel (536,154)
The World Almanac for Kids, 1997. Edited by Judith Levey. Orig. World Almanac (327,506)
*What Color Is Your Parachute 1996. Richard Nelson Bolles. Orig. Ten Speed (320,000)
*The World Almanac and Book of Facts, 1996. Edited by Robert Famighetti. Orig. World Almanac (271,318)
Old Farmer's Almanac. Editors of Old Farmer's Almanac. Orig. Random (189,538)
Birnbaum's Walt Disney World: The Official 1997 Guide. Alice Garrard. Orig. Hyperion (184,660)

Birnbaum's Walt Disney World: The Official 1996 Guide. Alice Garrard. Orig. Hyperion (123,479)
1997 Sports Illustrated Almanac. The Editors of Sports Illustrated. Orig. Little, Brown (115,893)
*Let's Go Europe 1996. Harvard Student Agencies. Orig. St. Martin's/Griffin (109,433)
*H&R Block 1996 Income Tax Guide. H&R Block. Orig. Fireside (100,000)
H&R Block 1997 Income Tax Guide. H&R Block. Orig. Fireside (100,000)
Harley Hahn's Internet and Web Yellow Pages, 1997 Edition. Harley Hahn. Rep. Osborne/McGraw-Hill (94,626)
Nursing '97 Drug Handbook. Orig. Springhouse (87,459)
Unbelievably Good Deals and Great Adventures That You Absolutely Can't Get Unless You're Over 50, 8th Edition. Joan Rattner Heilman. Orig. Contemporary (81,844)
*The Internet Yellow Pages, 3rd Edition. Harley Hahn. Rep. Osborne/McGraw-Hill (78,228)
Peterson's Guide to Four-Year Colleges '97. Orig. Peterson's (75,249)
The Essential Guide to Prescription Drugs 1996. James Rybacki and James Long. HarperReference (75,090)
The Complete Guide to Prescription/NonPrescription Drugs 1997. H. Winter Griffith, M.D. Orig. Perigee (75,000)
Kovels' Antiques & Collectibles Price List, 29th Edition. Ralph and Terry Kovel. Orig. Crown (68,970)
*Knock 'Em Dead 1996. Martin Yate. Orig. Adams Media (64,724)
*Let's Go USA 1996. Harvard Student Agencies. Orig. St. Martin's/Griffin (61,911)
The 1997 Blackbook OPG of U.S. Coins. Thomas E. Hudgeons, Jr. Orig. House of Collectibles (59,031)
*The Nursing Mother's Companion, 3rd Revised Edition. Kathleen Huggin. Harvard Common (52,101)
Knock 'Em Dead 1997. Martin Yate. Orig. Adams Media (51,686)
Peterson's SAT Success '97. Joan Carris with Michael R. Crystal. Orig. Peterson's (51,381)

Let's Go Britain and Ireland 1996. Harvard Student Agencies. Orig. St. Martin's/Griffin (50,000)

Mass Market

2 Million Up

The Green Mile, Part 1: The Two Dead Girls. Stephen King. Orig. Signet (3,865,447)
The Green Mile, Part 2: The Mouse on the Mile. Stephen King. Orig. Signet (3,655,547)
The Green Mile, Part 3: Coffey's Hands. Stephen King. Orig. Signet (3,515,141)
The Green Mile, Part 5: Night Journey. Stephen King. Orig. Signet (3,480,382)
The Green Mile, Part 4: The Bad Death of Eduard Delacroix. Stephen King. Orig. Signet (3,475,145)
The Green Mile, Part 6: Coffey on the Mile. Stephen King. Orig. Signet (3,475,036)
The Gift. Danielle Steel. Rep. Dell (3,093,781)
Lightning. Danielle Steel. Rep. Dell (3,092,532)
The Lost World. Michael Crichton. Rep. Ballantine (2,738,561)
Let Me Call You Sweetheart. Mary Higgins Clark. Rep. Pocket (2,526,987)
The Horse Whisperer. Nicholas Evans. Reprint. Dell (2,384,141)
Rose Madder. Stephen King. Rep. Signet (2,330,508)
Tom Clancy's Op-Center (III): Games of State. Tom Clancy and Steve Pieczenik. Orig. Berkley (2,300,000)
From Potter's Field. Patricia Cornwell. Rep. Berkley (2,200,000)
Silent Night. Mary Higgins Clark. Rep. Pocket (2,118,442)

1 Million+

Morning, Noon & Night. Sidney Sheldon. Rep. Warner Vision (1,907,097)
The Eyes of Darkness. Dean Koontz. Rep. Berkley (1,900,000)
Sleepers. Lorenzo Carcaterra. Rep. Ballantine (1,842,832)
Intensity. Dean Koontz. Rep. Ballantine (1,756,792)
Beach Music. Pat Conroy. Rep. Bantam (1,683,000)

Tarnished Gold. V. C. Andrews. Orig. Pocket (1,681,515)
Melody. V. C. Andrews. Orig. Pocket (1,649,344)
The Cry of the Halidon. Robert Ludlum. Rep. Bantam (1,624,000)
Strange Highways. Dean Koontz. Rep. Warner Vision (1,603,003)
The Carousel. Belva Plain. Rep. Dell (1,575,121)
Coming Home. Rosamunde Pilcher. Rep. St. Martin's (1,551,608)
Home Song. LaVyrle Spencer. Rep. Jove (1,500,000)
Hide & Seek. James Patterson. Rep. Warner (1,498,446)
Love Me Forever. Johanna Lindsey. Rep. Avon (1,450,065)
The Witness. Sandra Brown. Rep. Warner Vision (1,416,095)
A Place Called Freedom. Ken Follett. Rep. Fawcett (1,411,815)
L Is for Lawless. Sue Grafton. Rep. Fawcett (1,402,661)
Contagion. Robin Cook. Rep. Berkley (1,400,000)
Mind Prey. John Sandford. Rep. Berkley (1,400,000)
Absolute Power. David Baldacci. Rep. Warner (1,375,261)
Shock Wave. Clive Cussler. Rep. Pocket (1,330,604)
The Glass Lake. Maeve Binchy. Rep. Dell (1,324,849)
The Cove. Catherine Coulter. Orig. Jove (1,300,000)
The Judge. Steve Martini. Rep. Jove (1,300,000)
Taltos. Anne Rice. Rep. Ballantine (1,269,428)
The Rules. Ellen Fein and Sherrie Schneider. Rep. Warner (1,259,339)
The Apocalypse Watch. Robert Ludlum. Rep. Bantam (1,228,000)

Night Sins. Tami Hoag. Rep. Bantam (1,215,000)
For the Roses. Julie Garwood. Rep. Pocket (1,192,930)
Black Lightning. John Saul. Rep. Fawcett (1,183,595)
Primary Colors. Anonymous. Rep. Warner (1,177,509)
The Web. Jonathan Kellerman. Rep. Bantam (1,164,000)
Dead Man's Walk. Larry McMurtry. Rep. Pocket (1,123,968)
Trial by Fire. Nancy Taylor Rosenberg. Rep. Signet (1,120,399)
Silent Treatment. Michael Palmer. Rep. Bantam (1,117,000)
The Heir. Catherine Coulter. Orig. Topaz (1,100,061)
Daring to Dream. Nora Roberts. Orig. Jove (1,100,000)
True Betrayals. Nora Roberts. Rep. Jove (1,100,000)
The Valentine Legacy. Catherine Coulter. Rep. Jove (1,100,000)
The Hundred Secret Senses. Amy Tan. Reprint. Ivy (1,086,476)
The Fourth Procedure. Stanley Pottinger. Rep. Ballantine (1,080,077)
Dead By Sunset. Ann Rule. Rep.. Pocket (1,067,345)
Border Music. Robert James Waller. Rep. Warner (1,058,996)
Love in Another Town. Barbara Taylor Bradford. Rep. HarperPaperbacks (1,052, 049)
My American Journey. Colin Powell. Rep. Ballantine (1,040,874)
The Relic. Douglas Preston and Lincoln Child. Rep. Tor (1,024,453)
From the Heart. Nora Roberts. Orig. Jove (1,010,000)
Dangerous Man. Rosemary Rogers. Orig. Avon (1,001,599)
Wish List. Fern Michaels. Orig. Zebra (1,000,000)

Children's Bestsellers: Big Names Top the Charts

The sales picture in children's books is encouraging, with frontlist hardcovers racking up bigger numbers last year than in the previous year—24 new hardcover titles sold more than 200,000 copies in 1996, while only 15 did so in 1995. At the top of the list, selling over one million copies, was a book of poetry—Shel Silverstein's, his first in 15 years. In addition, some of booksellers' favorite books to handsell made the charts—*Lilly's Purple Plastic Purse, A Pizza the Size of the Sun,* and *My Many Colored Days.*

Board-book versions of favorite picture books appear in full force on this year's lists; titles like *Goodnight Moon, Guess How Much I Love You, The Mitten, Goodnight, Gorilla,* and *The Rainbow Fish*—all backlist staples—are now racking up even stronger sales in the younger format.

Characters from Disney movies, in various book formats, are still extremely popular, and movie and TV tie-in titles, with their built-in audience, are almost guaranteed bestsellers; witness the number of books on the lists based on *The Hunchback of Notre Dame, 101 Dalmatians, Barney, Sesame Street, Star Wars,* and *Animorphs.*

The story in paperbacks mirrors last year's results, with R. L. Stine's Goosebumps filling the majority of slots with both frontlist and backlist titles. There were a total of 31 new Goosebumps titles on the list; the top 18 of these accounted for sales of 22,689,000 units. Last year, there were a total of 18 new Goosebumps titles on the list, adding up to 19,125,700 copies. It seems that only books with award clout, movie tie-in status, or classic appeal (Laura Ingalls Wilder, Roald Dahl, or Beverly Cleary, for example) are drawing sales big enough to approach Stine's success.

For this roundup, publishers were asked to supply trade figures only, reflecting returns as of February 1, 1997. Since figures do not include total returns, they consequently do not necessarily represent net sales. Some books appear on our lists without sales figures; these figures were supplied in confidence, for use in ranking the titles only.

Hardcover Frontlist

200,000+

1. *Falling Up.* Shel Silverstein. HarperCollins (1,268,728)
2. *The Hunchback of Notre Dame (Classic).* Disney/Mouse Works (1,204,600)
3. *Disney's Hunchback of Notre Dame.* Adapted by Justine Korman, illus. by Don Williams. Golden (603,600)
4. *My Many Colored Days.* Dr. Seuss, illus. by Steve Johnson and Lou Fancher. Knopf (496,833)
5. *Disney's Hunchback of Notre Dame: Quasimodo the Hero.* Barbara Bazaldua, illus. by Don Williams. Golden (485,100)
6. *Disney's 101 Dalmatians: Snow Puppies.* Barbara Bazaldua, illus. by Don Williams. Golden (455,555)

7. *Disney's Winnie the Pooh: The Sweetest Christmas.* Ann Braybrooks, illus. by Josie Yee. Golden (441,200)
8. *Guess How Much I Love You (board book).* Sam McBratney, illus. by Anita Jeram. Candlewick (434,018)
9. *The Hunchback of Notre Dame (Little Library).* Disney/Mouse Works (315,200)
10. *Djali's Jolly Day (Squeeze Me).* Disney/Mouse Works (305,100)
11. *Forever Free (Sturdy Tab Book).* Disney/Mouse Works (296,600)
12. *Muppets Treasure Island.* Ellen Weiss, illus. by Tom Brannon. Golden (287,400)
13. *Sesame Street: Elmo's Twelve Days of Christmas.* Sarah Albee, illus. by Maggie Swanson. Golden (253,600)
14. *The Rainbow Fish (board book).* Marcus Pfister. North-South (250,781)
15. *Dr. Seuss's ABC (board book).* Random House (241,412)
16. *Mr. Brown Can Moo, Can You?* Dr. Seuss. Random House (231,272)
17. *The Foot Book.* Dr. Seuss. Random House (230,439)
18. *Scholastic Children's Dictionary.* Scholastic (228,000)
19. *There's a Wocket in My Pocket.* Dr. Seuss. Random House (226,693)
20. *Barney's Number Friends.* Adapted by Mark Bernthal, illus. by Darren McKee. Lyrick/Barney (217,556)
21. *Brown Bear, Brown Bear, What Do You See? (board book).* Bill Martin, Jr., illus. by Eric Carle. Holt (216,477)
22. *Disney's Lion King: The Cave Monster.* Justine Korman, illus. by Don Williams. Golden (214,300)
23. *Topsy Turvy Day (Pop Up Pal).* Disney/Mouse Works (212,800)
24. *Bedtime for Baby Bop.* Donna Cooner, illus. by Bill Alger. Lyrick/Barney (211,837)

100,000+

25. *The Twelve Days of Christmas: A Pop-Up Celebration.* Robert Sabuda. Little Simon (199,334)
26. *Disney's Winnie the Pooh: Thank You, Pooh!* Ronne Randall, illus. by Rigol. Golden (197,000)
27. *Disney's Mickey Mouse Christmas Carol.* Golden (193,500)
28. *The Small One.* Alex Walsh, illus. by Jesse Clay. Disney (188,562)
29. *My Very First Mother Goose.* Edited by Iona Opie, illus. by Rosemary Wells. Candlewick (171,994)
30. *Disney's 101 Dalmatians: Puppy Roundup!* Margo Lundell, illus. by Josie Yee. Golden (171,300)
31. *Disney's Lion King: Way to Go, Simba!* Ann Braybrooks, illus. by Serrat. Golden (161,000)
32. *Sesame Street: Zip! Pop! Hop!* Michaela Muntean, illus. by David Prebenna. Golden (160,000)

33. *Barney: Sharing Is Caring.* Mark Bernthal, illus. by June Valentine. Golden (155,200)
34. *Elmo's Lift and Peek Around the Corner.* Anna Ross. Random House (153,237)
35. *Comet's Nine Lives.* Jan Brett. Putnam (152,199)
36. *Barney Plays Nose to Toes.* Mary Ann Dudko and Margie Larsen, photos by Dennis Full. Lyrick/Barney (150,156)
37. *I Spy Spooky Night.* Jean Marzollo, photos by Walter Wick. Cartwheel (150,000)
38. *The Complete Tales of Winnie the Pooh.* A. A. Milne, illus. by Ernest H. Shepard. Dutton (148,598)
39. *Disney's Hunchback of Notre Dame (Big Golden Book).* Justine Korman, illus. by Don Williams. Golden (147,600)
40. *The Hunchback of Notre Dame: Meet the Characters.* Disney/Mouse Works (147,500)
41. *Disney's Hunchback of Notre Dame City Sounds.* Mary Packard, illus. by Darrell Baker. Golden (146,900)
42. *My First Book of Sounds.* Melanie Bellah, illus. by Kathy Wilburn. Golden (144,600)
43. *Good Night, Gorilla (board book).* Peggy Rathmann. Putnam (139,430)
44. *Toy Story Movie Storybook.* Disney/Mouse Works (139,100)
45. *The Mitten (board book).* Jan Brett. Putnam (138,566)
46. *Baby's First Bible.* Illus. by Colin and Moira Maclean. Reader's Digest. (136,536)
47. *The Little Bunny (Fluffy Tales).* Stewart Cowley, illus. by Susi Adams. Reader's Digest (135,483)
48. *The Magnificent Seven.* N. H. Kleinbaum. Bantam (134,453)
49. *Bugs That Go Bump in the Night.* David A. Carter. Little Simon (133,339)
50. *Santa's Littlest Helper (Fluffy Tales Christmas).* Stewart Cowley, illus. by Susi Adams. Reader's Digest (131,058)
51. *Special Stocking (Fluffy Tales Christmas).* Stewart Cowley, illus. by Susi Adams. Reader's Digest (129,718)
52. *The Little Chick (Fluffy Tales).* Stewart Cowley, illus. by Susi Adams. Reader's Digest (126,529)
53. *Song of the Zubble Wump.* Dr. Seuss. Random House (125,953)
54. *Toy Story (Classic).* Disney/Mouse Works (124,500)
55. *Baby's Christmas.* Eloise Wilkin, illus. by Barbara Lanza. Golden (122,800)
56. *Santa's Twin.* Dean Koontz, illus. by Phil Parks. HarperPrism (119,678)
57. *Mattel: Barbie and the Scavenger Hunt.* Mary Packard. Golden (117,000)
58. *Barney & BJ's Treehouse.* Donna Cooner, illus. by June Valentine-Ruppe. Lyrick/Barney (115,770)

59. *Owl Babies (board book)*. Martin Waddell, illus. by Patrick Benson. Candlewick (114,665)
60. *The Kind Snowman (Little Christmas Window Books)*. Jane Walker, illus. by Kate Davies. Reader's Digest (105,713)
61. *Santa's Hat (Little Christmas Window Books)*. Jane Walker, illus. by Kate Davies. Reader's Digest (104,696)
62. *The Star (Little Christmas Window Books)*. Jane Walker, illus. by Kate Davies. Reader's Digest (100,165)
63. *Lilly's Purple Plastic Purse*. Kevin Henkes. Greenwillow (100,000)

75,000+

64. *Please, Can I Help? (Little Christmas Window Books)*. Jane Walker, illus. by Kate Davies. Reader's Digest (98,912)
65. *Who's Coming to Stay? (Little Christmas Windows Books)*. Jane Walker, illus. by Kate Davies. Reader's Digest (97,214)
66. *I Spy School Days*. Jean Marzollo, photos by Walter Wick. Scholastic/Cartwheel (97,000)
67. *Where's My Stocking? (Little Christmas Windows Books)*. Jane Walker, illus. by Kate Davies. Reader's Digest (96,772)
68. *A Pizza the Size of the Sun*. Jack Prelutsky, illus. by James Stevenson. Greenwillow (95,000)
69. *Sam's Pizza*. David Pelham. Dutton (89,454)
70. *Dominique Moceanu: An American Champion*. Dominique Moceanu, as told to Steve Woodward. Bantam (81,059)
71. *The Magic School Bus Inside a Beehive*. Joanna Cole, illus. by Bruce Degen. Scholastic (80,000)
72. *Tell Me Again About the Night I Was Born*. Jamie Lee Curtis, illus. by Laura Cornell. HarperCollins/Cotler(79,965)
73. *Merry Christmas, Baby*. Joan Walsh Anglund. Golden (79,700)
74. *Toy Story Pop-Up Book*. Disney (79,644)
75. *Stephen Biesty's Incredible Explosions*. Richard Platt, illus. by Stephen Biesty. DK (77,573)
76. *The Discovery of Dragons*. Graeme Base. Abrams (76,500)
77. *Winnie the Pooh's Stories for Christmas*. Bruce Talkington, illus. by John Kurtz. Disney (76,354)
78. *1, 2, 3 to the Zoo*. Eric Carle. Philomel (76,226)
79. *Hurry Up, Timmy Toot! (Squeak and Go Books)*. Illus. by Carolyn Bracken. Reader's Digest (75,663)
80. *Good Dog Carl*. Alexandra Day. Little Simon (75,505)

Hardcover Backlist

300,000+

1. *Oh, the Places You'll Go!* Dr. Seuss. Random House, 1990 (395,594)
2. *Guess How Much I Love You.* Sam McBratney, illus. by Anita Jeram. Candlewick, 1995 (384,016)
3. *Barney's Farm Animals.* Kimberly Kearns and Marie O'Brien, illus. by Karen Malzeke-McDonald. Lyrick/Barney, 1993 (383,603)
4. *Green Eggs and Ham.* Dr. Seuss. Random House, 1966 (373,484)
5. *Disney's Winnie the Pooh: Grand and Wonderful Day.* Mary Packard, illus. by Darrell Baker. Golden, 1995 (371,100)
6. *Disney's 101 Dalmatians.* Adapted by Justine Korman, illus. by Bill Langley and Ron Dias. Golden, 1988 (365,300)
7. *Goodnight Moon (board book).* Margaret Wise Brown, illus. by Clement Hurd. HarperFestival, 1991 (360,753)
8. *The Giving Tree.* Shel Silverstein. HarperCollins, 1964 (347,487)
9. *The Very Hungry Caterpillar (board book).* Eric Carle. Philomel, 1994 (335,811)
10. *Baby Animals on the Farm.* James Shooter, illus. by J. Ellen Dolee. Golden, 1990 (335,700)
11. *A Day with Barney.* Mary Ann Dudko and Margie Larsen, illus. by Larry Daste. Lyrick/Barney, 1994 (317,197)
12. *Winnie the Pooh (Classic).* Disney/Mouse Works, 1994 (306,300)
13. *Disney's Winnie the Pooh: Eeyore, Be Happy.* Don Ferguson. Golden, 1991 (300,800)

200,000+

14. *Disney's Pocahontas: Into the Forest.* Mary Packard, illus. by Darrell Baker. Golden, 1995 (297,100)
15. *Disney's Baby Mickey's Book of Shapes.* Golden, 1986 (292,600)
16. *One Fish, Two Fish, Red Fish, Blue Fish.* Dr. Seuss. Random House, 1966 (291,500)
17. *Barney Goes to the Zoo.* Linda Cress Dowdy, illus. by Karen Malzeke-McDonald. Lyrick/Barney, 1993 (284,825)
18. *Disney's Pocahontas.* Adapted by Justine Korman, illus. by Don Williams. Golden, 1995 (273,600)
19. *The Cat in the Hat.* Dr. Seuss. Random House, 1966 (266,219)
20. *Where the Sidewalk Ends.* Shel Silverstein. HarperCollins, 1974 (263,622)
21. *Disney's The Lion King.* Adapted by Justine Korman, illus. by Don Williams and H. R. Russell. Golden, 1994 (260,400)
22. *Disney's Pocahontas: Voice of the Wind.* Justine Korman, illus. by Peter Emslie and Don Williams. Golden, 1995 (255,000)
23. *The Three Bears.* Carol North, illus. by Lisa McCue. Golden, 1983 (254,800)

24. *The Rainbow Fish.* Marcus Pfister. North-South, 1992 (253,438)
25. *The Wheels on the Bus.* Illus. by R. W. Alley. Golden, 1992 (247,900)
26. *Dr. Seuss's ABC.* Dr. Seuss. Random House, 1966 (242,062)
27. *Barney's Book of Opposites.* Mary Ann Dudko and Margie Larsen, photos by Dennis Full. Lyrick/Barney, 1994 (228,308)
28. *Muppet Babies: Be Nice.* Bonnie Worth, illus. by David Prebenna. Golden, 1993 (225,300)
29. *My Little Golden Book About God.* Jane Werner Watson, illus. by Eloise Wilkin. Golden, 1994 (224,900)
30. *Barney's Color Surprise.* Mary Ann Dudko and Margie Larsen, photos by Dennis Full. Lyrick/Barney, 1993 (215,723)
31. *Baby Bop's Foods.* Mary Ann Dudko and Margie Larsen, photos by Dennis Full. Lyrick/Barney, 1994 (210,309)
32. *101 Dalmatians (Classic).* Disney/Mouse Works, 1994 (204,400)

100,000+

33. *Hop on Pop.* Dr. Seuss. Random House, 1966 (198,374)
34. *The Littlest Angel.* Charles Tazewell, illus. by Paul Micich. Ideals, 1991 (196,663)
35. *Dumbo's Book of Colors.* Golden, 1988 (195,800)
36. *The Very Busy Spider (board book).* Eric Carle. Philomel, 1995 (191,076)
37. *Barney & Baby Bop Follow That Cat.* Stephen White, illus. by June Valentine-Ruppe. Lyrick/Barney, 1994 (188,218)
38. *Are You My Mother?* P. D. Eastman. Random House, 1960 (183,264)
39. *Pat the Bunny.* Dorothy Kunhardt. Golden, 1940 (183,200)
40. *Disney's The Lion King: No Worries.* Justine Korman, illus. by Don Williams and H. R. Russell. Golden, 1995 (179,300)
41. *Prayers for Children.* Illus. by Eloise Wilkin. Golden, 1942 (177,000)
42. *How the Grinch Stole Christmas.* Dr. Seuss. Random House, 1966 (176,498)
43. *A Light in the Attic.* Shel Silverstein. HarperCollins, 1981 (171,341)
44. *Fuzzy Duckling.* Jane Werner, illus. by Alice and Martin Provensen. Golden, 1994 (171,300)
45. *Disney's Lion King: Best Friends.* Mary Packard, illus. by Darrell Baker. Golden, 1994 (170,800)
46. *Go, Dog. Go!* P. D. Eastman. Random House, 1966 (170,550)
47. *Baby Bop's Toys.* Kimberly Kearns and Marie O'Brien, photos by Dennis Full. Lyrick/Barney, 1993 (169,296)
48. *Sesame Street: Big Bird's Busy Day.* Jessie Smith, illus. by Ellen Appleby. Golden, 1987 (168,900)
49. *Math Curse.* Jon Scieszka, illus. by Lane Smith. Viking, 1995 (167,353)

50. *Disney's Cinderella.* Illus. by Ron Dias and Bill Lorencz. Golden, 1986 (164,900)
51. *Disney's I Am Winnie the Pooh.* Betty Birney, illus. by Darrell Baker. Golden, 1994 (163,000)
52. *The Polar Express.* Chris Van Allsburg. Houghton Mifflin, 1985 (161,810)
53. *The Going to Bed Book.* Sandra Boynton. Little Simon, 1982 (161,238)
54. *Baby Bop's Counting Book.* Mary Ann Dudko and Margie Larsen, photos by Dennis Full. Lyrick/Barney, 1993 (160,244)
55. *The Christmas Miracle of Jonathan Toomey.* Susan Wojciechowski, illus. by P. J. Lynch. Candlewick, 1995 (156,625)
56. *Fox in Socks.* Dr. Seuss. Random House, 1966 (153,346)
57. *Disney's Snow White & the Seven Dwarfs.* Golden, 1994 (146,400)
58. *Stellaluna.* Janell Cannon. Harcourt Brace, 1993(146,097)
59. *The Very Lonely Firefly.* Eric Carle. Philomel, 1995 (145,735)
60. *Chicka Chicka ABC.* Bill Martin Jr. and John Archambault, illus. by Lois Ehlert. Little Simon, 1993 (144,438)
61. *I See the Sun.* Disney/Mouse Works, 1995 (144,000)
62. *Disney's Peter Pan.* Adapted by Eugene Bradley Coco, illus. by Ron Dias. Golden, 1989 (142,000)
63. *Goosebumps Monster Edition.* R. L. Stine. Scholastic, 1995 (139,000)
64. *The Poky Little Puppy.* Jeanette Sebring Lowrey, illus. by Gustaf Tenggren. Golden, 1942 (133,200)
65. *Officer Buckle and Gloria.* Peggy Rathmann. Putnam, 1995 (132,672)
66. *Disney's Winnie the Pooh: All Year Long.* Golden, 1991 (129,800)
67. *Disney's Babies Nursery Rhymes.* Illus. by Darrell Baker. Golden, 1988 (129,300)
68. *Snuggle Up—Squeeze Me.* Disney/Mouse Works, 1994 (129,000)
69. *Fuzzy Yellow Ducklings.* Matthew Van Fleet. Dial, 1995 (128,611)
70. *Pages & Pockets.* Illus. by Merle Nacht. Pleasant Co., 1995 (126,939)
71. *The Night Before Christmas.* Clement C. Moore, illus. by Kathy Wilburn. Golden, 1985 (125,100)
72. *Disney's Sleeping Beauty.* Illus. by Ron Dias. Golden, 1986 (123,400)
73. *The Lion King (Classic).* Disney/Mouse Works, 1994 (121,400)
74. *My First Counting Book.* Lillian Moore, illus. by Garth Williams. Golden, 1957 (120,900)
75. *The Little Engine That Could.* Watty Piper. Grosset & Dunlap, 1930 (120,730)
76. *A Friend Is . . . (Toy Story Storybook).* Disney/Mouse Works, 1995 (120,600)
77. *The Color Kittens.* Margaret Wise Brown, illus. by Kathy Ember. Golden, 1994 (120,500)

78. *I Spy: A Book of Picture Riddles.* Jean Marzollo, illus. by Walter Wick. Cartwheel, 1992 (119,000)
79. *Put Me in the Zoo.* Robert Lopshire. Random House, 1960 (117,925)
80. *Disney's Aladdin.* Adapted by Karen Kreider, illus. by Darrell Baker. Golden, 1992 (117,300)
81. *Little Golden Picture Dictionary.* Illus. by Marie DeJohn. Golden, 1994 (114,500)
82. *Love You Forever.* Robert Munsch, illus. by Sheila McGraw. Firefly, 1986 (112,949)
83. *Precious Moments: Put on a Happy Face.* Debbie Wiersma, illus. by Samuel Butcher. Golden, 1992 (111,600)
84. *Where's Piglet? Peek-a-Pooh.* Disney/Mouse Works, 1995 (111,100)
85. *Disney's Beauty and the Beast: Chip the Tea Cup.* Betty Birney, illus. by Edward Gutierrez and Mones. Golden, 1992 (110,600)
86. *Disney's the Little Mermaid: Flounder to the Rescue.* Jean Lewis, illus. by Cardona. Golden, 1995 (110,400)
87. *The Jester Has Lost His Jingle.* David Saltzman. The Jester Co., 1995 (110,000)
88. *The Aristocats (Classic).* Disney/Mouse Works, 1994 (109,800)
89. *Cinderella (Classic).* Disney/Mouse Works, 1994 (109,600)
90. *Animal Sounds.* Illus. by Aurelius Battaglia. Golden, 1991 (109,300)
91. *BJ Makes Music.* Margie Larsen and Mary Ann Dudko, photos by Dennis Full. Lyrick/Barney, 1995 (109,052)
92. *Miss Spider's Tea Party.* David Kirk. Calloway, 1994 (108,000)
93. *I Spy Christmas.* Jean Marzollo, illus. by Walter Wick. Cartwheel, 1992 (108,000)
94. *Oh, the Thinks You Can Think!* Dr. Seuss. Random House, 1975 (107,886)
95. *The Very Hungry Caterpillar.* Eric Carle. Philomel, 1981 (104,519)
96. *Christmas Carols.* Compiled by Carol North. Golden, 1981 (102,300)
97. *The Little Engine That Could (board book).* Watty Piper. Grosset & Dunlap, 1991 (101,692)
98. *The Children's Illustrated Bible.* Retold by Selina Hastings, illus. by Eric Thomas. DK, 1994 (101,216)
99. *The Twelve Dancing Princesses.* Diane Muldrow, illus. by Fred Marvin. Golden, 1995 (100,400)
100. *If You Give a Mouse a Cookie.* Laura Numeroff, illus. by Felicia Bond. HarperCollins, 1985 (100,170)

Paperback Frontlist
500,000+

1. *Say Cheese and Die . . . Again* (Goosebumps #44). R. L. Stine. Scholastic/Apple (2,140,000)

2. *Ghost Camp (GB #45)*. R. L. Stine. Scholastic/Apple (1,741,000)
3. *How to Kill a Monster (GB #46)*. R. L. Stine. Scholastic/Apple (1,734,000)
4. *Night of the Living Dummy III (GB #40)*. R. L. Stine. Scholastic/Apple (1,633,000)
5. *Egg Monsters from Mars (GB #42)*. R. L. Stine. Scholastic/Apple (1,631,000)
6. *Bad Hare Day (GB #41)*. R. L. Stine. Scholastic/Apple (1,579,000)
7. *Legend of the Lost Legend (GB #47)*. R. L. Stine. Scholastic/Apple (1,466,000)
8. *The Beast from the East (GB #43)*. R. L. Stine. Scholastic/Apple (1,460,000)
9. *Attack of the Jack-o'-Lanterns (GB #48)*. R. L. Stine. Scholastic/Apple (1,418,000)
10. *Vampire Breath (GB #49)*. R. L. Stine. Scholastic/Apple (1,070,000)
11. *Beware of the Purple Peanut Butter (Give Yourself Goosebumps #6)*. R. L. Stine. Scholastic/Apple (1,049,000)
12. *Calling All Creeps! (GB #50)*. R. L. Stine. Scholastic/Apple (1,008,000)
13. *Night in Werewolf Woods (GYGB #5)*. R. L. Stine. Scholastic/Apple (843,000)
14. *The Deadly Experiments of Dr. Eeek (GYGB #8)*. R. L. Stine. Scholastic/Apple (826,000)
15. *The Curse of the Creeping Coffin (GYGB #8)*. R. L. Stine. Scholastic/Apple (800,000)
16. *How I Got My Shrunken Head (GB #39)*. R. L. Stine. Scholastic/Apple (792,000)
17. *Under the Magician's Spell (GYGB #7)*. R. L. Stine. Scholastic/Apple (788,000)
18. *James and the Giant Peach*. Roald Dahl, illus. by Lane Smith. Puffin (748,684)
19. *The Abominable Snowman of Pasadena (GB #38)*. R. L. Stine. Scholastic/Apple (711,000)
20. *The Headless Ghost (GB #37)*. R. L. Stine. Scholastic/Apple (689,000)
21. *The Knight in Screaming Armor (GYGB #9)*. R. L. Stine. Scholastic/Apple (649,000)

200,000+

22. *Disney's Hunchback of Notre Dame: Esmeralda's Lucky Charm*. Margo Lundell, illus. by Cardona Studio. Golden (480,800)
23. *Deep in the Jungle of Doom (GYGB #11)*. R. L. Stine. Scholastic/Apple (444,000)
24. *The Cuckoo Clock of Doom (Goosebumps Presents 2)*. R. L. Stine. Scholastic/Apple (408,000)
25. *Welcome to the Wicked Wax Museum (GYGB #12)*. R. L. Stine. Scholastic/Apple (400,000)

26. *The Girl Who Cried Monster (Goosebumps Presents #1)*. R. L. Stine. Scholastic/Apple (360,000)
27. *Barney & Baby Bop Go to the Doctor*. Margie Larsen, photos by Dennis Full. Lyrick/Barney (346,118)
28. *Disney's 101 Dalmatians*. Mary J. Fulton, illus. by Don Williams. Golden (338,000)
29. *Matilda (movie tie-in)*. Roald Dahl. Puffin (326,383)
30. *Barney & BJ Go to the Fire Station*. Mark Bernthal, photos by Dennis Full. Lyrick/Barney (314,183)
31. *Tick Tock, You're Dead! (GYGB #2)*. R. L. Stine. Scholastic/Apple (313,000)
32. *Barney & Baby Bop Go to School*. Mark Bernthal, photos by Dennis Full. Lyrick/Barney (295,940)
33. *Welcome to Camp Nightmare (Goosebumps Presents #3)*. R. L. Stine. Scholastic/Apple (290,000)
34. *Space Jam (Digest)*. Francine Hughes. Scholastic (285,000)
35. *The Bellmaker*. Brian Jacques. Berkley/Ace (250,000)
36. *Lightsabers (Star Wars: Young Jedi Knights #4)*. Kevin J. Anderson and Rebecca Moesta. Berkley/Boulevard (250,000)
37. *Space Jam Deluxe Movie Storybook*. Adapted by Nancy E. Krulik. Scholastic (238,000)
38. *Trapped in Bat Wing Hall (GYGB #3)*. R. L. Stine. Scholastic/Apple (238,000)
39. *Return of the Mummy (Goosebumps Presents #4)*. R. L. Stine. Scholastic/Apple (232,000)
40. *How I Saved the World: Bugs Bunny's Space Jam Scrapbook*. James Preller. Scholastic (218,000)
41. *Jedi Under Siege (Star Wars: Young Jedi Knights #6)*. Kevin J. Anderson and Rebecca Moesta. Berkley/Boulevard (200,000)
42. *Darkest Knight (Star Wars: Young Jedi Knights #5)*. Kevin J. Anderson and Rebecca Moesta. Berkley/Boulevard (200,000)

125,000+

43. *Silent Night #3 (Fear Street Super Chiller)*. R. L. Stine. Pocket/Archway (185,093)
44. *Goosebumps Monster Edition #2*. R. L. Stine. Scholastic/Apple (182,000)
45. *Jingle All the Way (novelization)*. David Cody Weiss and Bobbi Weiss. Pocket/Minstrel (180,948)
46. *Barney's Beginnings—Colors Activity Workbooks*. Lyrick/Barney (179,079)
47. *Barney's Beginnings—Numbers Activity Workbooks*. Lyrick/Barney (174,540)
48. *Barney's Christmas Surprise*. Mark Bernthal, illus. by Bill Alger. Lyrick/Barney (173,092)

49. *The First Scream (Fear Street: Fear Park #1)*. R. L. Stine. Pocket/Archway (172,420)
50. *Barney's Beginnings—Shapes Activity Workbooks*. Lyrick/Barney (170,528)
51. *Night Games (Fear Street)*. R. L. Stine. Pocket/Archway(168,872)
52. *A New Fear (Fear Street Sagas #1)*. R. L. Stine. Pocket/Archway(167,355)
53. *Space Jam*. Adapted by James Preller. Scholastic (167,000)
54. *Barney's Beginnings—Same/Different Activity Workbooks*. Lyrick/Barney (163,860)
55. *How to Be a Vampire (Ghosts of Fear Street #13)*. R. L. Stine. Pocket/Minstrel (163,736)
56. *The Visitor (Animorphs #2)*. K. A. Applegate. Scholastic (163,000)
57. *The Invasion (Animorphs #1)*. K. A. Applegate. Scholastic (163,000)
58. *Winnie the Pooh: Just Be Nice to Your Little Friends*. Caroline Kenneth, illus. by Phil Ortiz and Josie Yee. Golden (160,100)
59. *The Face (Fear Street)*. R. L. Stine. Pocket/Archway(158,977)
60. *The Last Scream (Fear Street: Fear Park #3)*. R. L. Stine. Pocket/Archway (158,523)
61. *Wayside School Gets a Little Stranger*. Louis Sachar, illus. by Joel Schick. Avon/Camelot (158,429)
62. *The Sign of Fear (Fear Street Sagas #4)*. R. L. Stine. Pocket/Archway (157,916)
63. *Stay Away from the Tree House (Ghosts of Fear Street #5)*. R. L. Stine. Pocket/Minstrel (156,427)
64. *Toy Story (Junior Novelization)*. Cathy East Dubowski. Disney (153,588)
65. *The Ooze (Ghosts of Fear Street #8)*. R. L. Stine. Pocket/Minstrel(153,524)
66. *Toy Story Joke Book*. Barbara Bazaldua. Golden (152,400)
67. *The Berenstain Bears Count Their Blessings*. Stan and Jan Berenstain. Random House (151,973)
68. *The Loudest Scream (Fear Street: Fear Park #2)*. R. L. Stine. Pocket/Archway (151,753)
69. *The Perfect Date (Fear Street)*. R. L. Stine. Pocket/Archway (151,029)
70. *Fright Knight (Ghosts of Fear Street #7)*. R. L. Stine. Pocket/Minstrel (150,328)
71. *House of Whispers (Fear Street Sagas #2)*. R. L. Stine. Pocket/Archway (149,907)
72. *Revenge of the Shadow People (Ghosts of Fear Street #9)*. R. L. Stine. Pocket/Minstrel (149,736)
73. *The Secret Admirer (Fear Street)*. R. L. Stine. Pocket/Archway (149,678)
74. *No Howling in the House*. Mercer Mayer. Random House (149,531)
75. *The Boy Who Ate Fear Street (Ghosts of Fear Street #11)*. R. L. Stine. Pocket/Minstrel (148,224)
76. *Winnie the Pooh: Just Be Nice . . . and Not Too Rough*. Eleanor Fremont, illus. by Darrell Baker. Golden (148,000)

77. *Night of the Werecat (Ghosts of Fear Street #12)*. R. L. Stine. Pocket/Minstrel (147,709)
78. *The Bugman Lives (Ghosts of Fear Street #10)*. R. L. Stine. Pocket/Minstrel (146,751)
79. *Forbidden Secrets (Fear Street Sagas #3)*. R. L. Stine. Pocket/Archway (146,616)
80. *Goodnight Kiss 2 (Fear Street Super Chiller)*. R. L. Stine. Pocket/Archway (145,583)
81. *The Boy Next Door (Fear Street)*. R. L. Stine. Pocket/Archway (145,514)
82. *Eye of the Fortuneteller (Ghosts of Fear Street #6)*. R. L. Stine. Pocket/Minstrel (144,937)
83. *101 Dalmatians (Junior Novelization)*. Adapted by Anne Mazer. Disney (142,893)
84. *Big Black Bear*. Wong Herbert Yee. Houghton Mifflin (141,600)
85. *Pirate Soup*. Mercer Mayer. Random House (141,095)
86. *The Confession (Fear Street)*. R. L. Stine. Pocket/Archway (135,144)
87. *Fright Christmas (Ghosts of Fear Street #15)*. R. L. Stine. Pocket/Minstrel (134,420)
88. *Purple Pickle Juice*. Mercer Mayer. Random House (133,873)
89. *Arthur's Reading Race*. Marc Brown. Random House (132,876)
90. *Fear Street Sagas Collector's Edition*. R. L. Stine. Pocket/Archway (131,402)
91. *Martha Calling*. Susan Meddaugh. Houghton Mifflin/Lorraine (130,800)
92. *Stacey McGill, Super Sitter (Baby-sitters Club #94)*. Ann M. Martin. Scholastic/Apple (130,000)
93. *My Hairiest Day (Goosebumps Presents #6)*. R. L. Stine. Scholastic/Apple (130,000)
94. *Phantom (Last Vampire #4)*. Christopher Pike. Pocket/Archway (129,775)
95. *Body Switchers from Outer Space (Ghosts of Fear Street #14)*. R. L. Stine. Pocket/Minstrel (129,609)
96. *Creatures of Forever (The Last Vampire #6)*. Christopher Pike. Pocket/Archway (129,488)
97. *Evil Thirst (The Last Vampire #5)*. Christopher Pike. Pocket/Archway (128,299)
98. *The Headless Ghost (Goosebumps Presents #7)*. R. L. Stine. Scholastic/Apple (127,000)
99. *Glasses for D. W.* Marc Brown. Random House (126,715)
100. *Night of the Living Dummy II (Goosebumps Presents #5)*. R. L. Stine. Scholastic/Apple (126,000)
101. *Walk Two Moons*. Sharon Creech. HarperTrophy (125,179)
102. *The Care and Keeping of Friends*. Illus. by Nadine Bernard Westcott. Pleasant Co. (125,027)
103. *Kristy's Worst Idea (BSC #100)*. Ann M. Martin. Scholastic/Apple (125,000)

Literary Prizes, 1996

Gary Ink
Research Librarian, *Publishers Weekly*

ABBY Awards. To honor titles that members have most enjoyed handselling in the past year. *Offered by*: American Booksellers Association. *Winners*: (adult) David Guterson for *Snow Falling on Cedars* (Harcourt Brace); (children's) Sue McBratney for *Guess How Much I Love You*, illus. by Anita Jeram (Candlewick).

J. R. Ackerley Award (United Kingdom). For autobiography. *Offered by*: PEN (UK). *Winner*: Eric Lomax for *The Railway Man* (Cape).

Jane Addams Children's Book Award. For a book promoting the cause of peace, social justice, and world community. *Offered by*: Women's International League for Peace and Freedom and the Jane Addams Peace Association. *Winner*: Mildred Taylor for *The Well: David's Story* (Dial).

Martha Albrand Award for Nonfiction. For a distinguished first book of nonfiction. *Offered by*: PEN American Center. *Winner*: Mary Karr for *The Liars' Club* (Viking).

American Academy of Arts and Letters Award for Distinguished Service to the Arts. *Offered by*: American Academy of Arts and Letters. *Winner*: Ethylyn Chase.

American Academy of Arts and Letters Awards in Literature. *Offered by:* American Academy of Arts and Letters. *Winners:* (fiction) Whitney Balliett, Carol Brightman, Robert Fagles, Robert Hughes, Larry Kramer, David Quammen; (poetry) Arthur Kleinzahler, Paul Muldoon.

American Academy of Arts and Letters Gold Medal for History. *Offered by:* American Academy of Arts and Letters. *Winner:* Peter Gay.

Hans Christian Andersen Awards. *Offered by:* International Board on Books for Young People (IBBY). *Winners*: (author) Uri Orlov (Israel); (illustrator) Klaus Ensikat (Germany).

Mildred L. Batchelder Award. For an American publisher of a children's book originally published in a foreign language in a foreign country, and subsequently published in English in the United States. *Offered by:* American Library Association, Association for Library Service to Children. *Winner:* Houghton Mifflin for *The Lady with the Hat* by Uri Orlov.

Before Columbus Foundation American Book Awards. For literary achievement by people of various ethnic backgrounds. *Offered by:* Before Columbus Foundation. *Winners*: Sherman Alexie for *Reservation Blues* (Atlantic Monthly Press); Stephanie Cowell for *The Physician of London* (Norton); Chita Banerjee Divakaruni for *Arranged Marriage* (Anchor Books); Maria Espinosa for *Longing* (Arte Publico); William Gass for *The Tunnel* (Knopf); Kimiko Hahn for *The Unbearable Heart* (Kaya); E. J. Miller Laino for *Girl Hurt* (Alice James); Chang-rae Lee for *Native Speaker* (Riverhead); James W. Loewen for *Lies My Teacher Told Me* (New Press); Glenn C. Loury for *One by One from the Inside Out* (Free Press); Agate Nesaule for *Woman in Amber* (Soho Press); Joe Sacco for *Palestine* (Fantagraphics); Ron Sakolsky & Fred Wei-Han Ho, eds., for *Sounding Off! Music as Subversion/Resistance/Revolution* (Autonomedia); Arthur Sze for *Archipelago* (Copper Canyon); Robert Viscusi for *Astoria* (Guernica Editions); (children's book award) Paul Owen Lewis for *Storm Boy* (Beyond Words); (lifetime achievement award) Janice Mirikitani.

Curtis Benjamin Award for Creative Publishing. *Offered by:* Association of American Publishers. *Winner:* Robert Bernstein.

Bingham Poetry Prize. For the best work of poetry. *Offered by:* Boston Book Review. *Winner:* Mark Doty for *Atlantis* (HarperPerennial).

James Tait Black Memorial Prizes (United Kingdom). For the best biography and the best novel of the year. *Offered by:* University of Edinburgh. *Winners*: (biography) Gitta Sereny for *Albert Speer: His Battle* with *Truth* (Macmillan); (fiction) Christopher Priest for *The Prestige* (Simon & Schuster).

Rebekah Johnson Bobbitt National Prize for Poetry. *Offered by:* Library of Congress. *Winner:* Kenneth Koch for *One Train* (Knopf).

Booker Prize for Fiction (United Kingdom). *Offered by:* Book Trust and Booker PLC. *Winner:* Graham Swift for *Last Orders* (Picador).

Boston Globe/Horn Book Awards. For excellence in text and illustration. *Winners*: (fiction) Avi for *Poppy*, illus. by Brian Floca (Orchard/Jackson); (nonfiction) Andrea Warren for *Orphan Train Rider* (Houghton Mifflin); (picture book) Amy Hest for *Baby Duck*, illus. by Jill Barton (Candlewick).

Witter Bynner Prize for Poetry. To support the work of young poets. *Offered by:* American Academy of Arts and Letters. *Winner:* Lucie Brock-Broido.

Caldecott Medal. For the artist of the most distinguished picture book. *Offered by:* R. R. Bowker Company. *Winner:* Peggy Rathmann for *Officer Buckle and Gloria* (Putnam).

John W. Campbell Memorial Award. For outstanding science fiction writing. *Offered by:* Center for the Study of Science Fiction. *Winner:* Stephen Baxter.

Truman Capote Lifetime Achievement Award for Literary Criticism. *Offered by:* Truman Capote Foundation. *Winner:* Alfred Kazin.

Carnegie Medal (United Kingdom). For the outstanding children's book of the year. *Offered by:* The Library Association. *Winner:* Philip Pullman for *His Dark Materials: Book I, Northern Lights* (Scholastic).

Cholmondeley Awards (United Kingdom). For contributions to poetry. *Offered by:* Society of Authors. *Winners*: Elizabeth Bartlett; Dorothy Nimmo; Peter Scupham; Iain Crichton Smith.

Arthur C. Clarke Award (United Kingdom). For the best science fiction novel of the year. *Offered by:* British Science Fiction Association. *Winner:* Paul J. McAuley for *Fairyland* (Gollancz).

Commonwealth Writers Prize (United Kingdom). *Offered by:* Commonwealth Institute. *Winners*: Rohinton Mistry for *A Fine Balance* (Faber); (first work) Vikram Chandra for *Red Earth and Pouring Rain* (Faber).

Thomas Cook Travel Book Award (United Kingdom). *Offered by:* Book Trust. *Winner:* Stanley Stewart for *Frontiers of Heaven* (Murray/Flamingo).

Alice Fay Di Castagnola Award. For a work in progress to recognize a poet at a critical stage of his or her work. *Offered by:* Poetry Society of America. *Winner:* Stephanie Strickland for *True North* (work in progress).

Philip K. Dick Award. For a distinguished paperback original published in the United States. *Offered by:* Norwescon. *Winner:* Bruce Bethke for *Headcrash* (Warner Books).

T. S. Eliot Prize (United Kingdom). For poetry. *Offered by:* Poetry Book Society. *Winner:* Mark Doty for *My Alexandria* (Cape).

Encore Award (United Kingdom). For a second novel. *Offered by:* Society of Authors. *Winner:* A. L. Kennedy for *So I Am Glad* (Cape).

Esquire/Apple/Waterstone's Non-Fiction Award (United Kingdom). To give a greater prominence to good general nonfiction. *Winner:* Peter Godwin for *Mukiwa* (Picador).

Norma Faber First Book Award. For a first book of poetry. *Offered by:* Poetry Society of America. *Winner:* Barbara Hamby for *Delirium* (Univ. of North Texas).

Faulkner Award for Fiction. To honor the best work of fiction published by an American. *Offered by:* PEN American Center. *Winner:* Richard Ford for *Independence Day* (Knopf).

Fisk Fiction Prize. For the best work of fiction. *Offered by:* Boston Book Review. *Winner:* Joyce Carol Oates for *Zombie* (Dutton).

E. M. Forster Award in Literature. To a young writer from England, Ireland, Scotland, or Wales for a stay in the United States. *Offered by:* American Academy of Arts and Letters. *Winner:* Jim Crace.

Forward Poetry Prize (United Kingdom). For best poetry published in the United Kingdom or the Republic of Ireland. *Offered by*: The *Forward*. *Winners*: (best collection) Sean O'Brien for *Ghost Train*

(Oxford); (best first collection) Jane Duran for *Breathe Now, Breathe* (Enitharmon); (best individual poem) Jenny Joseph for "In Honour of Love."

Frost Medal for Distinguished Achievement. To recognize achievement in poetry over a lifetime. *Offered by:* Poetry Society of America. *Winner:* Richard Wilbur.

Ralph J. Gleason Music Book Awards. To honor outstanding books about music and musicians in all areas of popular music. *Offered by:* Rolling Stone, BMI, and New York University. *Winners:* (first prize) Daniel Wolff and others for *You Send Me: The Life and Times of Sam Cooke* (William Morrow); (second prize) Etta James and David Ritz for *Rage to Survive* (Villard); (third prize) Daniel Cooper for *Lefty Frizzell* (Little, Brown).

Golden Kite Awards. For outstanding children's books. *Offered by:* Society of Children's Book Writers and Illustrators. *Winners:* (fiction) Christopher Paul Curtis for *The Watsons Go to Birmingham—1963* (Delacorte); (nonfiction) Natalie Bober for *Abigail Adams* (Simon & Schuster); (illustration) Dennis Nolan and Lauren Mills for *Fairy Wings* (Little, Brown).

Kate Greenaway Medal (United Kingdom). For children's book illustration. *Offered by:* The Library Association. *Winner:* P. J. Lynch for *The Christmas Miracle of Jonathan Toomey* by Susan Wojciechowski (Walker Books).

Eric Gregory Trust Awards (United Kingdom). For poets under the age of 30. *Offered by:* Society of Authors. *Winners:* Sue Butler; Cathy Cullis; Jane Griffiths; Jane Holland; Chris Jones; Sinead Morrissey; Kate Thomas.

Guardian Fiction Prize (United Kingdom). For recognition of a novel by a British or Commonwealth writer. *Offered by:* The *Guardian*. *Winner:* Seamus Deane for *Reading in the Dark* (Cape).

Drue Heinz Literature Prize. To recognize and encourage writing of short fiction. *Offered by:* Drue Heinz Foundation and University of Pittsburgh. *Winner:* Edith Pearlman for *Vaquita and Other Stories* (Univ. of Pittsburgh).

Ernest Hemingway Foundation Award. For a work of first fiction by an American. *Offered by:* PEN American Center. *Winner:* Chang-rae Lee for *Native Speaker* (Riverhead).

David Higham Prize for Fiction (United Kingdom). For recognition of a first novel or book of short stories written in English. *Offered by:* Book Trust. *Winner:* Linda Grant for *The Cast Iron Shore* (Picador).

IMPAC Dublin Literary Award (Ireland). For a book of high literary merit written in English, or translated into English. *Offered by:* IMPAC Corp. and the City of Dublin. *Winner:* David Malouf for *Remembering Babylon* (Chatto).

Sue Kaufman Prize for First Fiction. *Offered by:* American Academy of Arts and Letters. *Winner:* Peter Landesman for *The Raven* (Baskerville).

Robert F. Kennedy Book Award. To recognize authors whose books faithfully reflect Robert Kennedy's concerns: justice and equality for the poor, the minorities, and the young; and the responsible examination of major social issues. *Offered by:* Robert F. Kennedy Memorial. *Winner:* Dan Carter for *The Politics of Rage* (Simon & Schuster).

Sir Peter Kent Conservation Book Prize (United Kingdom). For books that most imaginatively promote nature conservation. *Offered by:* Book Trust. *Winner:* Colin Tudge for *The Day Before Yesterday* (Cape).

Coretta Scott King Awards. For works that promote the cause of peace and brotherhood. *Offered by:* American Library Association Social Responsibilities Round Table. *Winners:* (author award) Virginia Hamilton for *Her Stories* (Scholastic); (illustrator award) Tom Feelings for *Middle Passage* (Dial).

Kiriyama Pacific Rim Book Prize. To promote books that contribute to greater understanding and increased cooperation among the peoples of the nations of the Pacific Rim. *Offered by:* Kiriyama Pacific Rim Foundation and the University of San Francisco. *Winner:* Alan Brown for *Audrey Hepburn's Neck* (Pocket Books).

Gregory Kolovakos Award. For a sustained contribution over time to Hispanic literature in English translation. *Offered by:* PEN American Center. *Winners*: Suzanne Jill Levine; Jean Franco.

Harold Morton Landon Translation Award. For a book of verse translated into English by a single translator. *Offered by:* Academy of American Poets. *Winner:* Guy Davenport for *7 Greeks* (New Directions).

Lannan Literary Awards. *Offered by:* Lannan Foundation. *Winners*: (poetry) Anne Carson, Lucille Clifton, Donald Justice; (fiction) Howard Norman, Tim Pears, William Trevor; (nonfiction) David Abram, Charles Bowden; (life achievement award for poetry) R. S. Thomas.

James Laughlin Award. To support the publication of a second book of poetry. *Offered by:* Academy of American Poets. *Winner:* David Rivard for *Wise Poison* (Graywolf).

Ruth Lilly Poetry Prize. To a United States poet whose accomplishments warrant extraordinary recognition. *Offered by:* Modern Poetry Association. *Winner:* Gerald Stern.

Locus Awards. For science fiction writing. *Offered by:* Locus Publications. *Winners*: (science fiction novel) Neal Stephenson for *The Diamond Age* (Bantam); (fantasy novel) Orson Scott Card for *Alvin Journeyman* (Tor); (dark fantasy/horror novel) Tim Powers for *Expiration Date* (Tor); (first novel) Linda Nagata for *The Bohr Maker* (Bantam); (nonfiction) John Clute for *Science Fiction: The Illustrated Encyclopedia* (Dorling Kindersley); (art book) Cathy Burnett & Arnie Fenner, eds., for *Spectrum II: The Best in Contemporary Fantasy Art* (Underwood); (collection) Ursula K. LeGuin for *Four Ways to Forgiveness* (HarperPrism); (anthology) Gardner Dozois, ed., for *The Year's Best Science Fiction: Twelfth Annual Collection* (St. Martin's).

Amy Lowell Poetry Travelling Scholarship. For a U.S.-born poet to spend one year outside North America in a country the recipient feels will most advance his or her work. *Offered by:* Amy Lowell Poetry Scholarship. *Winner:* Craig Arnold.

McKitterick Prize (United Kingdom). For a first novel by a writer over the age of 40. *Offered by:* Society of Authors. *Winner:* Stephen Blanchard for *Gagarin and I* (Chatto).

McVitie's Prize (United Kingdom). For the Scottish writer of the year. *Offered by:* City of Glasgow. *Winner:* Alan Spence for *Stone Garden and Other Stories* (Phoenix House).

Kurt Maschler Award (United Kingdom). For a children's book in which text and illustrations are both excellent and perfectly harmonious. *Offered by:* Book Trust. *Winner:* Babette Cole for *Drop Dead* (Cape).

Somerset Maugham Awards (United Kingdom). For young British writers to gain experience in foreign countries. *Offered by:* Society of Authors. *Winners*: Katherine Pierpont for *Truffle Beds* (Faber); Alan Warner for *Morven Caller* (Cape).

National Arts Club Medal of Honor for Literature. *Offered by:* National Arts Club. *Winner:* E. L. Doctorow.

National Book Awards. *Offered by:* National Book Foundation. *Winners*: (fiction) Andrea Barrett for *Ship Fever and Other Stories* (Norton); (nonfiction) James Carroll for *An American Requiem* (Houghton Mifflin); (poetry) Hayden Carruth for *Scrambled Eggs and Whiskey* (Copper Canyon); (children's) Victor Martinez for *Parrot in the Oven: Mi Vida* (HarperCollins).

National Book Critics Circle Awards. *Offered by:* National Book Critics Circle. *Winners*: (fiction) Stanley Elkin for *Mrs. Ted Bliss* (Hyperion); (general nonfiction) Jonathan Harr for *A Civil Action* (Random House); (biography/autobiography) Robert Polito for *Savage Art: A Biography of Jim Thompson* (Knopf); (poetry) William Matthews for *Time & Money* (Houghton Mifflin); (criticism) Robert Darnton for *The Forbidden Bestsellers of Pre-Revolutionary France* (Norton).

National Book Foundation Medal for Distinguished Contribution to American Letters. *Offered by:* National Book Foundation. *Winner:* Toni Morrison.

NCR Book Award (United Kingdom). For the best nonfiction book of the year. *Offered by:* NCR Corp. *Winner:* Eric Lomax for *The Railway Man* (Cape).

Nebula Awards. For the best science fiction writing. *Offered by:* Science Fiction Writers of America. *Winners*: (best novel) Robert J. Sawyer for *Hobson's Choice/The Terminal Experiment* (HarperPrism); (Grand Master) A. E. van Vogt.

Neustadt International Prize for Literature. *Offered by:* World Literature Today and the University of Oklahoma. *Winner:* Assia Djebar.

John Newbery Medal. For the most distinguished contribution to literature for children. *Donor:* American Library Association, Association for Library Service to Children. *Medal Contributed by:* Daniel Melcher. *Winner:* Karen Cushman for *The Midwife's Apprentice* (Clarion).

Nobel Prize in Literature. For the total literary output of a distinguished writer. *Offered by:* Swedish Academy. *Winner:* Wislawa Szymborska.

Noma Award (Japan). For Japanese literature in translation published in Africa. *Winner:* Kitia Toure for *Destins Paralleles* (Nouvelles Editions Ivoiriennes).

Flannery O'Connor Awards for Short Fiction. *Offered by:* PEN American Center. *Winners*: Harvey Grossinger for *The Quarry* (Univ. of Georgia); Paul Rawlins for *No Lie Like Love* (Univ. of Georgia).

Scott O'Dell Award for Historical Fiction. *Offered by: Bulletin of the Center for Children's Books*, University of Chicago. *Winner:* Theodore Taylor for *The Bomb* (Harcourt Brace).

Orange Prize for Fiction (United Kingdom). For the best novel written by a woman and published in the United Kingdom. *Offered by:* Orange. *Winner:* Helen Dunmore for *A Spell of Winter* (Viking).

PEN Award for Poetry in Translation. *Offered by:* PEN American Center. *Winner:* Guy Davenport for *7 Greeks* (New Directions).

PEN/Book-of-the-Month Club Translation Prize. *Offered by:* PEN American Center. *Winner:* Wislawa Szymborska for *View With A Grain of Sand* (Harcourt Brace).

PEN/Newman's Own First Amendment Award. To recognize extraordinary actions in defense of freedom of expression. *Offered by:* PEN American Center and Newman's Own. *Winner:* Cissy Lacks.

Edgar Allan Poe Awards. For outstanding mystery, crime, and suspense writing. *Offered by:* Mystery Writers of America. *Winners*: (novel) Dick Francis for *Come to Grief* (Putnam); (first novel) David Housewright for *Penance* (Foul Play/Countryman); (original paperback) William Heffernan for *Tarnished Angel* (Onyx); (fact crime) Pete Earley for *Circumstantial Evidence* (Bantam); (critical/biographical) Robert Polito for *Savage Art: A Biography of Jim Thompson* (Knopf); (young adult) Rob MacGregor for *Prophecy Rock* (Simon & Schuster); (juvenile) Nancy Springer for *Looking for Jamie Bridger* (Dial); (Grand Master) Dick Francis.

Renato Poggioli Translation Award. To assist a translator of Italian whose work in progress is especially outstanding. *Offered by:* PEN American Center. *Winner:* Louise Rozier for *Little Jesus of Sicily* by Fortunato Paqualino (work in progress).

Prix Goncourt (France). For a work of imagination, preferably a novel, exemplifying youth, originality, esprit, and form. *Winner:* Pascale Roze for *Le Chasseur Zero* (Albin Michel).

Pulitzer Prizes in Letters. To honor distinguished work by American writers, dealing preferably with American themes. *Offered by:* Columbia University, Graduate School of Journalism. *Winners*: (fiction) Richard Ford for *Independence Day* (Knopf); (history) Alan Taylor for *William Cooper's Town* (Knopf); (biography) Jack Miles for *God: A Biography* (Knopf); (poetry) Jorie Graham for *The Dream of the Unified Field* (Ecco Press); (general nonfiction) Tina Rosenberg for *The Haunted Land: Facing Europe's Ghosts after Communism* (Random House).

QPB New Voice Award. For the most distinctive and promising work of fiction offered by the Quality Paperback Book Club. *Winner:* Chang-rae Lee for *Native Speaker* (Riverhead).

Rea Award for the Short Story. To honor a living writer who has made a significant contribution to the short story as a art form. *Offered by:* Dungannon Foundation. *Winner:* Andre Dubus.

John Llewellyn Rhys Memorial Award (United Kingdom). *Offered by:* The *Mail on Sunday*. *Winner:* Melanie McGrath for *Motel Nirvana* (Flamingo).

Romance Writers of America RITA Awards. For excellence in the romance genre. *Offered by:* Romance Writers of America. Winners: (favorite book of the year) Nora Roberts for *Born in Ice* (Berkley); (short contemporary) Jennifer Greene for *Single Dad* (Silhouette); (long contemporary) Justine Davis for *The Morning Side of Dawn* (Silhouette); (contemporary single) Nora Roberts for *Born in Ice* (Berkley); (traditional) Elizabeth Sites for *Stranger in Her Arms* (Silhouette); (short historical) Loretta Chase for *Lord of Scoundrels* (Avon); (long historical) Pamela Morsi for *Something Shady* (Berkley); (Regency) Lynn Kerstan and Alicia Rasley for *Gwen's Christmas Ghost* (Zebra); (romantic suspense/Gothic) Anne Stuart for *Winter's Edge* (Harlequin); (paranormal/fantasy/time travel) Modean Moon for *The Covenant* (Harper); (young adult) Cheryl Zach for *Runaway* (Berkley); (inspirational) Francine Rivers for *As Sure as the Dawn* (Tyndale House); (best first book) Elizabeth Elliott for *The Warlord* (Bantam).

Rome Fellowship in Literature. For a one-year residence at the American Academy in Rome. *Offered by:* American Academy of Arts and Letters and Philip Morris Companies. *Winner:* Randall Kenan.

Richard and Hinda Rosenthal Foundation Award. For a work of fiction that is a considerable literary achievement though not necessarily a commercial success. *Offered by:* American Academy of Arts and Letters. *Winner:* David Long for *Blue Spruce* (Simon & Schuster).

Juan Rulfo International Latin American and Caribbean Prize for Literature (Mexico). To a writer of noteworthy poetry, novels, drama, short stories, or essays who is a native of Latin America or the Caribbean and who is writing in Spanish, Portuguese, or English. *Offered by:* Juan Rulfo International Latin American and Caribbean Prize for Literature Award Committee. *Winner:* Augusto Monterroso.

Sagittarius Prize (United Kingdom). For a first novel by a writer over the age of 40. *Offered by:* Society of Authors. *Winner:* Samuel Lock for *As Luck Would Have It* (Cape).

Delmore Schwartz Memorial Poetry Award. To a young poet of exceptional promise or a more mature poet who has received insufficient national acclaim. *Offered by:* New York University. *Winner:* Grace Schulman.

Shelley Memorial Award. To a poet living in the United States who is chosen on the basis of genius and need. *Offered by:* Poetry Society of America. *Winner:* Robert Pinsky.

Smarties Book Prizes (United Kingdom). To encourage high standards and to stimulate interest in books for children. *Offered by:* Book Trust and Nestle Rowntree. *Winners:* (ages 9–11) Philip Pullman for *The Firework-Maker's Daughter* (Corgi); (ages 6–8) Michael Morpurgo for *The Butterfly Lion* (Collins); (ages 0–5) Colin McNaughton for *Oops!* (Andersen Press).

W. H. Smith Literary Award (United Kingdom). For a significant contribution to literature. *Offered by:* W. H. Smith. *Winner:* Simon Scharma for *Landscape and Memory* (HarperCollins).

Tanning Prize. To recognize outstanding and proven mastery in the art of poetry. *Offered by:* Academy of American Poets. *Winner:* Adrienne Rich.

Templeton Prize for Progress in Religion. *Offered by:* Templeton Foundation. *Winner:* Bill Bright.

Betty Trask Awards (United Kingdom). For works of a romantic or traditional nature by writers under the age of 35. *Offered by:* Society of Authors. *Winners:* John Lanchester for *The Debt to Pleasure* (Picador); Meera Syal for *Anita and Me* (Flamingo); Rhidian Brook for *The Testimony of Taliesin Jones* (Flamingo); Louis Caron Buss for *The Luxury of Exile* (Cape).

Kingsley Tufts Poetry Award. *Offered by:* Claremont Graduate School. *Winner:* Deborah Digges for *Rough Music* (Knopf).

Voelcker Award for Poetry. For a U.S. poet whose body of work represents a notable and accomplished presence in American literature. *Offered by:* PEN American Center. *Winner:* Franz Wright.

Harold D. Vursell Memorial Award in Literature. *Offered by:* American Academy of Arts and Letters. *Winner:* A. J. Verdelle.

Lila Wallace-Reader's Digest Fund Writer's Awards. *Offered by:* Lila Wallace Foundation. *Winners*: (poetry) Lorna Dee Cervantes; Robert Creeley; James Galvin; Adrian C. Louis; Heather McHugh; Susan Stewart; (fiction) Don DeLillo; Mona Simpson.

Whitbread Book of the Year (United Kingdom). *Offered by:* Booksellers Association of Great Britain. *Winner:* Kate Atkinson for *Behind the Scenes at the Museum* (Doubleday).

William Allen White Children's Book Award. *Offered by:* Emporia State University. *Winner:* Lois Lowry for *The Giver* (Houghton Mifflin).

Whiting Writers Awards. For outstanding talent and promise. *Offered by:* Mrs. Giles Whiting Foundation. *Winners*: Anderson Ferrell; Cristina Garcia; Molly Gloss; Brigit Pegeen Kelly; Brian Kitely; Chris Offutt; Elizabeth Spires; Patricia Storace; Judy Troy; A. J. Verdelle.

Walt Whitman Award. For poetry. *Offered by:* Academy of American Poets. *Winner:* Joshua Clover for *Madonna Anno Domini* (Louisiana State University).

William Carlos Williams Award. For the best book of poetry published by a small, non-profit, or university press. *Offered by:* Poetry Society of America. *Winner:* Josephine Jacobsen for *In the Crevice of Time* (Johns Hopkins).

Robert H. Winner Memorial Award. For a poem or sequence of poems characterized by a delight in language and the possibilities of ordinary life. *Offered by:* Poetry Society of America. *Winner:* Daniel Rifenberg.

L. L. Winship/PEN Award. To an author who has written the best book with a connection to New England. *Offered by:* Boston Globe and PEN New England. *Winner:* Jane Brox for *Here and Nowhere Else* (Beacon Press).

Owen Wister Award. For a lifetime contribution to the literature of the American West. *Offered by:* Western Writers of America. *Winner:* David S. Lavender.

World Fantasy Convention Awards. For outstanding fantasy writing. *Offered by:* World Fantasy Convention. *Winners*: (novel) Christopher Priest for *The Prestige* (St. Martin's); (anthology) A. Susan Williams and Richard Glyn Jones, eds., *The Penguin Book of Modern Fantasy by Women* (Viking Penguin); (collection) Gwyneth Jones for *Seven Tales and a Fable* (Edgewood Press); (lifetime achievement) Gene Wolfe.

World Science Fiction Convention Hugo Awards. For outstanding science fiction writing. *Offered by:* World Science Fiction Convention. *Winners*: (best novel) Neal Stephenson for *The Diamond Age* (Bantam); (best nonfiction book) John Clue for *Science Fiction: The Illustrated Encyclopedia* (Dorling Kindersley).

Morton Dauwen Zabel Award in Poetry. *Offered by:* American Academy of Arts and Letters. *Winner:* J. D. Landis.

Part 6
Directory of Organizations

Directory of Library and Related Organizations

Networks, Consortia, and Other Cooperative Library Organizations

This list is taken from the 1996–1997 edition of *American Library Directory* (R. R. Bowker), which includes additional information on member libraries and primary functions of each organization.

United States

Alabama

Alabama Health Libraries Association, Inc. (ALHeLa), Cary Veterinary Medical Lib., James E. Green Hall, Rm. 101, Auburn 36849-5606. SAN 372-8218. Tel. 334-844-1750, fax 334-844-1758. *Pres.* Tamera Lee; *V.P.* Kay Hogan.

Jefferson County Hospital Librarians Association, Brookwood Medical Center, 2010 Brookwood Medical Center Dr., Birmingham 35209. SAN 371-2168. Tel. 205-877-1131, fax 205-877-1189. *Coord.* Lucy Moor.

Library Management Network, Inc. 915 Monroe St., Box 443, Huntsville 35804. SAN 322-3906. Tel. 205-532-5963, fax 205-536-1772. *System Coord.* Charlotte Moncrief.

Marine Environmental Sciences Consortium, Dauphin Island Sea Lab, Box 369-370, Dauphin Island 36528. SAN 322-0001. Tel. 334-861-2141, fax 334-861-4646. *Dir.* George Crozier; *Libn.* Connie Mallon.

Network of Alabama Academic Libraries, c/o Alabama Commission on Higher Education, Box 302000, Montgomery 36130-2000. SAN 322-4570. Tel. 334-242-2211, fax 334-242-0270. *Dir.* Sue O. Medina.

Alaska

Alaska Library Network (ALN), 344 W. Third Ave., Suite 125, Anchorage 99501. SAN 371-0688. Tel. 907-269-6570, fax 907-269-6580, e-mail ASLANC@MUSKOX.Alaska.Edu. *Coord.* Judy Monroe; *Automation* Susan Elliott.

Arizona

Central Arizona Biomedical Librarians (CABL), c/o Health Sciences Lib., Desert Samaritan Medical Center, 1400 S. Dobson Rd., Mesa 85202. SAN 370-7598. Tel. 602-835-3024, fax 602-835-8796. *Pres.* Kathy Bilko; *Program Chair and Pres.-Elect.* Dawn Murray Humay.

Maricopa County Community College District, 2411 W. 14 St., Tempe 85281-6941. SAN 322-0060. Tel. 602-731-8776, fax 602-731-8787, e-mail lynch@maricopa. *Coord. Acquisitions* Randi Sher; *Coord. Tech. Services* Lori Roberts.

Arkansas

Arkansas Area Health Education Center Consortium (AHEC), Sparks Regional Medical Center, 1311 South I St., Box 17006, Fort Smith 72917-7006. SAN 329-3734. Tel. 501-441-5337, fax 501-441-5339, e-mail

639

grace@sparks.org. *Regional Health Sciences Libn.* Grace Anderson.

Independent College Fund of Arkansas, 1 Riverfront Place, Suite 610, North Little Rock 72114. SAN 322-0079. Tel. 501-378-0843, fax 501-374-1523. *Pres.* E. Kearney Dietz.

Northeast Arkansas Hospital Library Consortium, 223 E. Jackson, Jonesboro 72401. SAN 329-529X. Tel. 501-972-1290, fax 501-931-0839. *Dir.* Peggy Blair.

South Arkansas Film Coop, 202 E. Third St., Malvern 72104. SAN 321-5938. Tel. 501-332-5442, fax 501-332-6679. *Coord.* Tammy Lackey; *Project Dir.* Mary Cheatham.

California

Area Wide Library Network (AWLNET), 2420 Mariposa St., Fresno 93721. SAN 322-0087. Tel. 209-488-3229. *Dir. Info. Services* Sharon Vandercook.

Bay Area Library and Information Network (BAYNET), 405 14th St., Suite 211, Oakland 94612. SAN 371-0610. Tel. 415-353-0421, fax 415-561-0307. *Pres.* Rose Falanga; *Treas.* Sara O'Keefe.

Central Association of Libraries (CAL), 605 N. El Dorado St., Stockton 95202. SAN 322-0125. Tel. 209-937-8698, fax 209-937-8292. *Supervising Libn.* Deborah Westler.

Chiropractic Library Consortium (CLIBCON), Cleveland Chiropractic College, 590 N. Vermont Ave., Los Angeles 90004-2196. SAN 328-8218. Tel. 213-660-6166, fax 213-665-1931. *Chair* Cheryl Duggan.

Consortium for Distance Learning, 2595 Capitol Oaks Dr., Sacramento 95833. SAN 329-4412. Tel. 916-565-0188, fax 916-565-0189. *Exec. Dir.* Jerome Thompson; *Operations Mgr.* Sandra Scott-Smith.

Consumer Health Information Program and Services (CHIPS), County of Los Angeles Public Lib., 151 E. Carson St., Carson 90745. SAN 372-8110. Tel. 310-830-0909, fax 310-834-4097. *Libn.* Scott A. Willis; *Aide* Mona Porotesano.

Cooperating Libraries In Claremont (CLIC), c/o Honnold Lib., 800 Dartmouth Ave., Claremont Colleges, Claremont 91711. SAN 322-3949. Tel. 909-621-8045, fax 909-621-8681. *Dir.* Bonnie J. Clemens; *Assoc. Dir.* Alberta Walker.

Hewlett-Packard Library Information Network 1501 Page Mill Rd., Palo Alto 94304. SAN 375-0019. Tel. 415-857-3091. *Chair* Eugenie Prime.

Inland Empire Academic Libraries Cooperative, California State Univ., Psau Lib., 5500 University Pkwy., San Bernardino 92407. SAN 322-015X. Tel. 909-593-6251, fax 909-880-5906, 880-5111. *Coord.* Les Kong.

Inland Empire Medical Library Cooperative (IEMLC), c/o Kaiser Permanente Medical Center, 10800 Magnolia Ave., Riverside 92505. SAN 371-8980. Tel. 909-353-3658, fax 909-353-3262. *Chair* Ilga Pubulis.

Kaiser Permanente Library System, Southern California Region (KPLS), Health Sciences Lib., 4647 Zion Ave., San Diego 92120. SAN 372-8153. Tel. 619-528-7323, fax 619-528-3444. *Dir.* Sheila Latus.

Knight-Ridder Information, Inc., 2440 El Camino Real, Mountain View 94040. SAN 322-0176. Tel. 415-254-7000, fax 415-254-8093. *Pres.* Patrick Tierney.

Learning Resources Cooperative, c/o County Office of Education, 6401 Linda Vista Rd., San Diego 92111. SAN 371-0785. Tel. 619-292-3608, fax 619-467-1549. *Dir.* Marvin Barbula.

Learning Resources Cooperative, Southwestern College, 900 Otay Lakes Rd., Chula Vista 91910. SAN 375-006X. Tel. 619-421-6700, fax 619-482-6413. *Pres.* Joseph Conte.

Los Angeles County Health Sciences Library Consortium, c/o Rancho Los Amigos Medical Center, Health Sciences Lib., 7601 E. Imperial Hwy., Downey 90242. SAN 322-4317. Tel. 310-940-7696. *Coord.* Evelyn Marks.

Metropolitan Cooperative Library System (MCLS), 3675 E. Huntington Dr., Suite 100, Pasadena 91107. SAN 371-3865. Tel. 818-683-8244, fax 818-683-8097. *Exec. Dir.* Linda Katsouleas.

National Network of Libraries of Medicine–Pacific Southwest Region (PSRML), Louise Darling Biomedical Lib., 10833 Leconte Ave., Los Angeles 90095. SAN 372-8234. Tel. 310-825-1200, fax 310-

825-5389. *Dir.* Alison Bunting; *Assoc. Dir.* Beryl Glitz.
Northern California and Nevada Medical Library Group, 2140 Shattuck Ave., Box 2105, Berkeley 94704. SAN 329-4617. Tel. 916-734-3529. *Pres.* Rochelle Perrine Schmalz.
Northern California Association of Law Libraries (NOCALL), 1800 Market St., Box 109, San Francisco 94102. SAN 323-5777. Tel. 415-576-3066, fax 415-576-3099. *Pres.* Donna Purvis; *Public Relations* Jenny Wu.
Northern California Consortium of Psychology Libraries (NCCPL), California School of Professional Psychology, 1005 Atlantic, Alameda 94501. SAN 371-9006. Tel. 510-523-2300, ext. 185, fax 510-523-5943, e-mail pgsp@itsa.uscf.edu. *Chair* Deanna Gaige.
OCLC Pacific, 9227 Haven Ave., Suite 260, Rancho Cucamonga 91730. SAN 370-0747. Tel. 909-941-4220, fax 909-948-9803. *Dir.* Mary Ann Nash.
Peninsula Libraries Automated Network (PLAN), 25 Tower Rd., San Mateo 94402-4000. SAN 371-5035. Tel. 415-358-6704, fax 415-358-6706. *Database Mgr.* Susan Yasar.
Performing Arts Libraries Network of Southern California (PALNET), Univ. Southern California Cinema-Television Lib., University Park, Los Angeles 90089. SAN 371-3997. Tel. 213-740-3994. *Chair* Steve Hanson; *V. Chair and Chair-Elect.* Sharon Johnson.
Research Libraries Group, Inc. (RLG), 1200 Villa St., Mountain View 94041-1100. SAN 322-0206. Tel. 800-537-7546, fax 415-964-0943, e-mail bl.ric@rlg.stanford.edu. *Pres.* James Michalko.
Sacramento Area Health Sciences Librarians, Sutter Resource Lib., 2800 L St., Sacramento 95816. SAN 322-4007. Tel. 916-733-3880, fax 916-733-3879. *Pres.* K. D. Proffit.
San Bernardino, Inyo, Riverside Counties United Library Services (SIRCULS), 3581 Mission Inn Ave., Box 468, Riverside 92502. SAN 322-0222. Tel. 909-369-7995, fax 909-784-1158. *Exec. Dir.* Kathleen F. Aaron; *Reference Libn.* Linda Taylor.

San Francisco Biomedical Library Network (SFBLN), c/o California College of Podiatric Medicine, 1210 Scott St., San Francisco 94115. SAN 371-2125. Tel. 415-292-0409, fax 415-292-0467. *Pres.* Douglas Varner.
Santa Clarita Interlibrary Network (SCIL-NET), 24700 McBean Pwky., Santa Clarita 91355. SAN 371-8964. Tel. 805-253-7885, fax 805-254-4561. *Pres.* Judith Hist; *Recorder* Judy Trapenberg.
Serra Cooperative Library System, 5555 Overland Ave., Bldg. 15, San Diego 92123. SAN 372-8129. Tel. 619-694-3600, fax 619-495-5905. *Systems Coord.* Susan Swisher.
The SMERC Library, 101 Twin Dolphin Dr., Redwood City 94065-1064. SAN 322-0265. Tel. 415-802-5655, fax 415-802-5665. *Educ. Services Mgr.* Karol Thomas; *Electronic Reference Services Coord.* Carol Quigley.
SOUTHNET, c/o South Bay Cooperative Lib. System, 180 W. San Carlos St., San Jose 95113. SAN 322-4260. Tel. 408-294-2345, fax 408-295-7388. *Asst. Systems Dir.* Susan Holmer.
Substance Abuse Librarians and Information Specialists (SALIS), Box 9513, Berkeley 94709-0513. SAN 372-4042. Tel. 510-642-5208, fax 510-642-7175. *Chair* Sharon Crockett.
Total Interlibrary Exchange (TIE), 5755 Valentine Rd., Suite 210, Ventura 93003-7441. SAN 322-0311. Tel. 805-650-7732, fax 805-642-9095, e-mail jsegel@eis.calstate.edu. *Pres.* Ed Tennen.

Colorado

Arkansas Valley Regional Library Service System (AVRLSS), 635 W. Corona, Suite 113, Pueblo 81004. SAN 371-5094. Tel. 719-542-2156, fax 719-542- 3155. *Dir.* Donna Jones Morris; *Chair* Sharon Johnson.
Bibliographical Center for Research, Rocky Mountain Region, Inc., 14394 E. Evans Ave., Aurora 80014-1478. SAN 322-0338. Tel. 303-751-6277, fax 303-751-9787. *Exec. Dir.* David H. Brunell.
Central Colorado Library System (CCLS), 4350 Wadsworth, Suite 340, Wheat Ridge 80033-4638. SAN 371-3970. Tel. 303-

422-1150, fax 303-431-9752. *Dir.* Gordon C. Barhydt; *Asst. Dir.* Judy Zelenski.
Colorado Alliance of Research Libraries (CARL), 3801 E. Florida Ave., Suite 370, Denver 80210. SAN 322-3760. Tel. 303-758-3030. *Exec. Dir.* Alan Charnes.
Colorado Association of Law Libraries, Box 13363, Denver 80201. SAN 322-4325. Tel. 303-871-6016, fax 303-871-6999. *Pres.* Cathy Pabich.
Colorado Council of Medical Librarians (CCML), Jefferson Center for Mental Health, 9808 W. Cedar Ave., Lakewood 80226. SAN 370-0755. Tel. 303-425-0300, fax 303-234-0117. *Pres.* Linda Van Wert.
Colorado Resource Sharing Network, c/o Colorado State Lib., 201 E. Colfax, Denver 80203-1799. SAN 322-3868. Tel. 303-866-6900, fax 303-866-6940. *Coord.* Susan Fayad.
High Plains Regional Library Service System, 800 Eighth Ave., Suite 341, Greeley 80631. SAN 371-0505. Tel. 970-356-4357, fax 970-353-4355, e-mail nknepel@csn.org. *Dir.* Nancy Knepel; *Chair* Sharrel Walter.
Irving Library Network, c/o Jefferson County Public Lib., 10200 W. 20 Ave., Lakewood 80215. SAN 325-321X. Tel. 303-232-7114, fax 303-467-6978. *Network Mgr.* John Zacrep.
Peaks & Valleys Library Consortium, c/o Arkansas Valley Regional Lib. Service System, 635 W. Corona Ave., Suite 113, Pueblo 81004. SAN 328-8684. Tel. 719-542-2156, fax 719-546-4484. *Secy.* Carol Ann Smith.
Pueblo Library System Software Users Group, 300 N. Adams, Loveland 80537. SAN 322-4635. Tel. 970-962-2665, fax 970-962-2905. *Pres.* Ted Schmidt; *Treas.* Charles E. Bates.
Southwest Regional Library Service System (SWRLSS), P.O. Drawer B, Durango 81302-1090. SAN 371-0815. Tel. 970-247-4782, fax 970-247-5087. *Dir.* S. Jane Ulrich.

Connecticut

Capitol Area Health Consortium, 183 E. Cedar St., Newington 06111. SAN 322-0370. Tel. 860-666-3304, fax 860-666-8110. *Pres.* Robert Boardman.

Capitol Region Library Council, 599 Matianuck Ave., Windsor 06095-3567. SAN 322-0389. Tel. 860-298-5319, fax 860-298-5328. *Exec. Dir.* Dency Sargent.
Connecticut Association of Health Sciences Libraries (CAHSL), Manchester Memorial Hospital Medical Lib., 71 Haynes St., Manchester 06040. SAN 322-0397. Tel. 860-647-6853, fax 860-647-6443. *Pres.* Jeannine Syr Gluck; *V.P.* Janice Swiatek.
Council of State Library Agencies in the Northeast (COSLINE), Connecticut State Lib., 231 Capitol Ave., Hartford 06106. SAN 322-0451. Tel. 860-566-4301, 207-287-5600 (Maine), fax 860-566-8940. *Pres.* Gary Nichols.
CTW Library Consortium, Olin Memorial Lib., Wesleyan Univ., Middletown 06457-6065. SAN 329-4587. Tel. 860-685-3889, fax 860-685-2661, e-mail ahagyard@wesleyan. *Dir.* Alan E. Hagyard; *Applications Programmer* Mary Wilson.
Eastern Connecticut Libraries (ECL), 74 W. Main St., Norwich 06360-5654. SAN 322-0478. Tel. 860-885-2760, fax 860-885-2757, e-mail pholloway@ecl.org. *Dirs.* Patricia Holloway, Marietta Johnson.
Hartford Consortium for Higher Education, 260 Girard Ave., Hartford 06105. SAN 322-0443. Tel. 860-236-1203, fax 860-233-9723. *Exec. Dir.* Kimberly Burris.
LEAP (Library Exchange Aids Patrons), 110 Washington Ave., North Haven 06473. SAN 322-4082. Tel. 203-239-1411, fax 203-234-6398. *Exec. Dir.* Richard J. Dionne; *Chair* Lois Baldini.
Libraries Online, Inc. (LION), 123 Broad St., Middletown 06457. SAN 322-3922. Tel. 860-347-1704, fax 860-346-3707. *Pres.* Edward Murray; *Exec. Dir.* William F. Edge, Jr.
National Network of Libraries of Medicine, New England Region (NN-LM NE Region), Univ. of Connecticut Health Center, 263 Farmington Ave., Farmington 06030-5370. SAN 372-5448. Tel. 860-679-4500, fax 860-679-1305. *Dir.* Ralph D. Arcari; *Assoc. Dir.* John Stey.
Northwestern Connecticut Health Science Libraries, Charlotte Hungerford Hospital, Torrington 06790. SAN 329-5257. Tel. 203-496-6689, fax 203-496-6631. *Coord.* Jackie Rorke.

Southern Connecticut Library Council, 2405 Whitney Ave., Suite 3, Hamden 06518. SAN 322-0486. Tel. 203-288-5757, fax 203-287-0757, e-mail mgolrick@sclc.org. *Dir.* Michael Golrick; *Project Dir.* Kate Oser.

Western Connecticut Library Council, Inc. 530 Middlebury Rd., Suite 210B, Box 1284, Middlebury 06762. SAN 322-0494. Tel. 203-577-4010, fax 203-577-4015, e-mail abarney@wclc.org. *Exec. Dir.* Anita R. Barney.

Delaware

Central Delaware Library Consortium, Dover Public Lib., 45 S. State St., Dover 19901. SAN 329-3696. Tel. 302-736-7030, fax 302-736-5087. *Pres.* Robert S. Wetherall.

Delaware Library Consortium (DLC), Delaware Academy of Medicine, 1925 Lovering Ave., Wilmington 19806. SAN 329-3718. Tel. 302-656-6398, fax 302-656-0470. *Pres.* Gail P. Gill.

Kent Library Network, Robert W. O'Brien Bldg., Rm. 209, 414 Federal St., Dover 19901. SAN 371-2214. Tel. 302-736-2265, fax 302-736-2262. *Pres.* Richard Krueger.

Libraries in the New Castle County System (LINCS), Hockessin Public Lib., Hockessin 19707. SAN 329-4889. Tel. 302-239-5160, fax 302-239-1519. *Pres.* Louise Tabasso.

Sussex Help Organization for Resources Exchange (SHORE), 109 E. Laurel, Georgetown 19947-1442. SAN 322-4333. Tel. 302-855-7890, fax 302-855-7895.

Wilmington Area Biomedical Library Consortium (WABLC), Delaware Academy of Medicine, 1925 Lovering Ave., Wilmington 19806. SAN 322-0508. Tel. 302-656-6398, fax 302-656-0470. *Pres.* Gail P. Gill.

District of Columbia

American Zoo and Aquarium Association (AZA-LSIG), National Zoological Park, Washington 20008. SAN 373-0891. Tel. 673-4771, fax 202-673-4900. *Chair* Kay Kenyon; *Ed.* Suzanne Braun.

CAPCON Library Network, 1320 19th St. N.W., Suite 400, Washington 20036. SAN 321-5954. Tel. 202-331-5771, fax 202-797-7719, e-mail capcon@capcon.net. *Pres.* Dennis Reynolds.

Cluster of Independent Theological Schools, 721 Lawrence St. N.E., Washington 20017. SAN 322-0532. Tel. 202-269-9412, fax 202-526-2720. *Chair* William Ruhl.

Coalition for Christian Colleges and Universities, 329 Eighth St. N.E., Washington 20002. SAN 322-0524. Tel. 202-546-8713, fax 202-546-8913. *Pres.* Robert C. Andringa.

District of Columbia Health Sciences Information Network (DOCHSIN), Himmelfarb Lib., George Washington Univ. Medical Center, Washington 20037. SAN 323-9918. Tel. 202-994-2963. *Pres.* Mary Ryan.

Educational Resources Information Center (ERIC), U.S. Dept. of Education, Office of Educational Research and Improvement, 555 New Jersey Ave. N.W., Washington 20208-5720. SAN 322-0567. Tel. 202-219-2289, fax 202-219-1817, e-mail eric@inet.ed.gov.

EDUCOM, c/o 1112 16th St. N.W., Suite 600, Washington 20036. SAN 371-487X. Tel. 202-872-4200, fax 202-872-4318. *Pres.* Robert Heterick, Jr.; *Publications Mgr.* John Gehl.

FEDLINK (Federal Library and Information Network), c/o Federal Lib. and Info. Center Committee, Lib. of Congress, Washington 20540-5110. SAN 322-0761. Tel. 202-707-4800, fax 202-707-4818. *Dir.* Susan M. Tarr; *Network Coord.* Milton Megee.

NASA Library Network ARIN (Aerospace Research Information Network), NASA Headquarters, Code JT, Washington 20546-0001. SAN 322-0788. Tel. 202-358-4485, fax 202-358-3063. *Project Dir.* Roland Ridgeway.

National Education Medical School Consortium, c/o Dahlgren Memorial Lib., Georgetown Univ. Medical Center, 3900 Reservoir Rd. N.W., Washington 20007. SAN 371-067X. Tel. 202-687-1176, fax 202-687-1862. *Libn.* Naomi C. Broering.

National Library Service for the Blind and Physically Handicapped, Lib. of Congress (NLS), 1291 Taylor St. N.W., Washington 20542. SAN 370-5870. Tel. 202-707-5100, fax 202-707-0712. *Dir.* Frank Kurt Cylke; *Asst. to the Dir.* Marvine R. Wanamaker.

Transportation Research Information Services (TRIS), 2101 Constitution Ave.

N.W., TRB, 2133-307, Washington 20418. SAN 370-582X. Tel. 202-334-3250, fax 202-334-3495. *Dir.* Jerome T. Maddock.

Veterans Affairs Library Network (VALNET), Lib. Division Programs Office, 810 Vermont Ave. N.W., Washington 20420. SAN 322-0834. Tel. 202-535-7521, fax 202-565-7539. *Dir. Lib. Programs* Wendy N. Carter.

Washington Theological Consortium, 487 Michigan Ave. N.E., Washington 20017-1585. SAN 322-0842. Tel. 202-832-2675, fax 202-526-0818. *Exec. Dir.* Richard Abbott.

Florida

Central Florida Library Consortium (CFLC), 431 E. Horatio Ave., Suite 230, Maitland 32751. SAN 371-9014. Tel. 407-644-9050, fax 407-644-7023. *Exec. Dir.* Marta Westall.

Florida Library Information Network, c/o Bureau of Lib. and Network Services, State Lib. of Florida, R. A. Gray Bldg., Tallahassee 32399-0250. SAN 322-0869. Tel. 904-487-2651, fax 904-922-3678. *Chief, Lib. and Network Services Bureau* Linda Tepp Fuchs.

Miami Health Sciences Library Consortium (MHSLC), c/o Jackson Memorial Hospital, School of Nursing Lib., 1500 N.W. 12 Ave., Miami 33136. SAN 371-0734. Tel. 305-585-6873, fax 305-326-7982. *Chair* Lynn McAuley.

Palm Beach Health Sciences Library Consortium (PBHSLC), c/o Good Samaritan Medical Center Medical Lib., Box 3166, West Palm Beach 33402. SAN 370-0380. Tel. 407-650-6315, fax 407-650-6417. *Chair* Linda Kressal.

Panhandle Library Access Network (PLAN), 5 Miracle Strip Loop, Suite 2, Panama City Beach 32407. SAN 370-047X. Tel. 904-233-9051, fax 904-235-2286, e-mail jaskows@firnvx.firn.edu. *Dir.* William P. Conniff; *Consortium Asst.* Carol A. DeMent.

Southeast Florida Library Information Network, Inc. (SEFLIN), 100 S. Andrews Ave., Fort Lauderdale 33301. SAN 370-0666. Tel. 954-357-7318, fax 954-357-6998. *Exec. Dir.* Elizabeth Curry; *Pres.* Douglas K. Lehman.

Tampa Bay Library Consortium, Inc., 10002 Princess Palm Ave., Suite 124, Tampa 33619. SAN 322-371X. Tel. 352-622-8252, fax 352-628-4425. *Exec. Dir.* Diane Solomon; *Pres.* Jonnie Sprimont.

Tampa Bay Medical Library Network (TABAMLN), Box 4117, Bay Pines 33504. SAN 322-0885. Tel. 813-586-7103, fax 813-585-7205. *Pres.* Dorothy Kelly.

Georgia

Atlanta Health Science Libraries Consortium, Georgia Baptist College of Nursing Lib., 274 Blvd. N.E., Atlanta 30312. SAN 322-0893. Tel. 404-265-4020, fax 404-265-3811. *Pres.* Sharon Lee Cann.

Emory Medical Television Network, 1440 Clifton Rd. N.E., Rm. 110, Atlanta 30322. SAN 322-0931. Tel. 404-727-9797, fax 404-727-9798. *Dir.* Leonard Vilchez; *Mgr.* Dirk Olson.

Georgia Health Sciences Library Association (GHSLA), Solvay Pharmaceuticals, 901 Sawyer Rd., Marietta 30062. SAN 372-8307. Tel. 770-578-5648, fax 770-578-5634. *Pres.* Ellen Cooper.

Georgia Interactive Network for Medical Information (GaIN), c/o Medical Lib., School of Medicine, Mercer Univ., 1550 College St., Macon 31207. SAN 370-0577. Tel. 912-752-2515, fax 912-752-2051. *Dir.* Jocelyn A. Rankin.

Georgia Online Database (GOLD), c/o Public Lib. Services, 156 Trinity Ave. S.W., 1st fl., Atlanta 30303-3692. SAN 322-094X. Tel. 404-657-6220, fax 404-656-7297. *Dir.* Tom Ploeg; *Coord.* Jo Ellen Ostendorf.

Health Science Libraries of Central Georgia (HSLCG), c/o J. Rankin Medical Lib., School of Medicine, Mercer Univ., 1550 College St., Macon 31207. SAN 371-5051. Tel. 912-752-2515, fax 912-752-2051. *In Charge* Michael Shadix.

South Georgia Associated Libraries, 208 Gloucester St., Brunswick 31523-0901. SAN 322-0966. Tel. 912-267-1212, fax 912-267-9597. *Pres.* Susan Roberts; *Secy-Treas.* Jim Darby.

SOLINET (Southeastern Library Network), 1438 W. Peachtree St. N.W., Suite 200, Atlanta 30309-2955. SAN 322-0974. Tel. 404-892-0943, fax 404-892-7879, e-mail mrichard@mail.solinet.net. *Exec. Dir.* Kate Nevins.

Southwest Georgia Health Science Library Consortium (SWGHSLC), Colquitt Regional Medical Center, Health Sciences Lib., Moultrie 31776. SAN 372-8072. Tel. 912-890-3460, fax 912-891-9345. *Medical Libn.* Susan Staton.

University Center in Georgia, Inc., 50 Hurt Plaza, Suite 465, Atlanta 30303-2923. SAN 322-0990. Tel. 404-651-2668, fax 404-651-1797. *Exec. Dir.* Charles B. Bedford.

Hawaii

Hawaii-Pacific Chapter of the Medical Library Association (HIPAC-MLA), 1221 Punchbowl St., Honolulu 96813. SAN 371-3946. Tel. 808-536-9302, fax 808-524-6956. *Chair* Suzanne Clark.

Idaho

Boise Valley Health Sciences Library Consortium (BVHSLC), Health Sciences Lib., St. Alphonsus Regional Medical Center, Boise 83706. SAN 371-0807. Tel. 208-378-2271, fax 208-378-2702. *Contact* Judy Balcerzak.

Canyon Owyhee Library Group, c/o Homedale Junior-Senior High School, 203 E. Idaho, Homedale 83628. SAN 375-006X. Tel. 208-337-4613, fax 208-337-4933. *Contact* Ned Stokes.

Catalyst, c/o Boise State Univ. Lib., Box 46, Boise 83707-0046. SAN 375-0078. Tel. 208-385-4024, fax 208-385-1394. *Contact* Tim Brown.

Cooperative Information Network (CIN), 8385 N. Government Way, Hayden Lake 83835-9280. SAN 323-7656. Tel. 208-772-5612, fax 208-772-2498. *Contact* John Hartung.

Eastern Idaho Library System, 457 Broadway, Idaho Falls 83402. SAN 323-7699. Tel. 208-529-1450, fax 208-529-1467. *Contact* Paul Holland.

Gooding County Library Consortium, c/o Gooding High School, 1050 Seventh Ave. W., Gooding 83330. SAN 375-0094. Tel. 208-934-4831, fax 208-934-4403. *Contact* Cora Caldwell.

Grangeville Cooperative Network, c/o Grangeville Centennial Lib., 215 W. North St., Grangeville 83530-1729. SAN 375-0108. Tel. 208-983-0951, fax 208-983-2336. *Contact* Linda Ruthruff.

Idaho Health Information Association (IHIA), c/o Idaho Health Sciences Lib., Idaho State Univ., Campus Box 8089, Pocatello 83209. SAN 371-5078. Tel. 208-236-4686, fax 208-236-4687. *Pres.* Marcy Horner.

Lynx, c/o Boise Public Lib., 715 Capitol Blvd., Boise 83702-7122. SAN 375-0086. Tel. 208-384-4237, fax 208-384-4025. *Contact* Lynn Melton.

Palouse Area Library Information Services (PALIS), c/o Latah County Free Lib. District, 110 S. Jefferson, Moscow 83843-2833. SAN 375-0132. Tel. 208-882-3925, fax 208-882-5098. *Contact* Lori Keenan.

Southeast Idaho Document Delivery Network, c/o American Falls District Lib., 308 Roosevelt St., American Falls 83211-1219. SAN 375-0140. Tel. 208-226-2335, fax 208-226-2303. *Contact* Margaret McNamara.

VALNET, Lewis Clark State College Lib., 500 Eighth Ave., Lewiston 83501. SAN 323-7672. Tel. 208-799-2227, fax 208-799-2831. *Contact* Paul Krause.

Illinois

Alliance Library System, 845 Brenkman Dr., Pekin 61554. SAN 371-0637. Tel. 309-353-4110, fax 309-353-8281. *Exec. Dir.* Valerie J. Wilford.

American Theological Library Association (ATLA), 820 Church St., Suite 300, Evanston 60201-5613. SAN 371-9022. Tel. 708-869-7788, fax 708-869-8513. *Dir. Member Services* Melody S. Chartier.

Areawide Hospital Library Consortium of Southwestern Illinois (AHLC), c/o St. Elizabeth Hospital Health Sciences Lib., 211 S. Third St., Belleville 62222. SAN 322-1016. Tel. 618-234-1181, fax 618-234-0408, e-mail campese@apci.net. *Coord.* Michael Campese.

Association of Chicago Theological Schools (ACTS), c/o Garrett-Evangelical Theological Seminary, 2121 Sheridan Rd., Evanston

60201. SAN 370-0658. Tel. 847-866-3900, fax 847-866-3957. *Pres.* Neil Fisher.

Capital Area Consortium, Prevention Resource Center, Prevention First, 2800 Montvale Dr., Springfield 62704. SAN 322-1024. Tel. 217-793-7353, fax 217-793-7354. *Coord.* Pat Ruestman.

Center for Research Libraries, 6050 S. Kenwood, Chicago 60637-2804. SAN 322-1032. Tel. 312-955-4545, fax 312-955-4339, e-mail simpson@uhuru.uchicago.edu. *Pres.* Donald B. Simpson.

Chicago and South Consortium, Saint Joseph Medical Center, Joliet 60435. SAN 322-1067. Tel. 815-725-7133, ext. 3530, fax 815-725-9459. *Coord.* Virginia Gale.

Chicago Library System (CLS), 224 S. Michigan, Suite 400, Chicago 60604. SAN 372-8188. Tel. 312-341-8500, fax 312-341-1985. *Exec. Dir.* Alice Calabrese.

Consortium of Museum Libraries in the Chicago Area, c/o John G. Shedd Aquarium, Info. Services and Technology, 1200 S. Lake Shore Dr., Chicago 60605. SAN 371-392X. Tel. 312-986-2289, fax 312-939-2216. *Chair* Michael T. Stieber; *Secy.* Laura Jenkins.

Council of Directors of State University Libraries of Illinois (CODSULI), Illinois State Univ., Campus Box 8900, Normal 61709-8900. SAN 322-1083. Tel. 309-438-3481, fax 309-438-3676, e-mail snyderca@siucvmb.siu.edu. *Chair* Fred Peterson.

East Central Illinois Consortium, Carle Foundation Hospital Lib., 611 W. Park St., Urbana 61801. SAN 322-1040. Tel. 217-383-3011, fax 217-383-3452. *Coord.* Anita Johnson.

Fox Valley Health Science Library Consortium, Delnor-Community Hospital, 300 Randall Rd., Geneva 60134. SAN 329-3831. Tel. 708-208-4299, fax 708-208-3479. *Coord.* Marie Krula.

Heart of Illinois Library Consortium, College of Nursing Lib., Saint Francis Medical Center, 211 Greenleaf St., Peoria 61603. SAN 322-1113. Tel. 309-655-2180, fax 309-655-3648. *Dir.* Joyce Hexdall.

Illinois Department of Mental Health and Developmental Disabilities Library Services Network (LISN), Elgin Mental Health Center, 750 S. State St., Elgin 60123. SAN 322-1121. Tel. 847-742-1040, ext. 2660, fax 847-742-1063. *Chair* Jennifer Ford.

Illinois Health Libraries Consortium, c/o Meat Industry Info. Center, National Cattleman's Beef Assn., 444 N. Michigan Ave., Chicago 60611. SAN 322-113X. Tel. 312-467-5520, ext. 272, fax 312-467-9729. *Coord.* William D. Siarny, Jr.

Illinois Library and Information Network (ILLINET), c/o Illinois State Lib., 300 S. Second St., Springfield 62701-1796. SAN 322-1148. Tel. 217-782-2994, fax 217-785-4326. *Dir.* Bridget L. Lamont; *Asst. Dir. for Lib. Development* Patricia Norris.

Illinois Library Computer Systems Office (ILCSO), Univ. of Illinois, 205 Johnstowne Centre, 502 E. John St., Champaign 61820. SAN 322-3736. Tel. 217-244-7593, fax 217-244-7596, e-mail khammer@uiuc.edu. *Dir.* Kristine Hammerstrand; *Lib. Systems Coord.* Mary Ellen Farrell.

Illinois State Curriculum Center–East Central Network (ISCC), Univ. of Illinois at Springfield, K-80, Springfield 62794-9423. SAN 371-5108. Tel. 217-786-6375, fax 217-786-6036. *Dir.* Rebecca Woodhull; *Libn.* Susie Shackleton.

Judaica Library Network of Metropolitan Chicago (JLNMC), 145 Laurel Ave., Highland Park 60035. SAN 370-0615. Tel. 708-433-2006, fax 708-433-2106, e-mail WOLFECG&INTERACCESS.COM. *Pres.* Nira Wolfe.

Libras, Inc., North Park College, Chicago 60625. SAN 322-1172. Tel. 312-244-5586, fax 312-244-4891. *Pres.* Ann Briody.

Metropolitan Consortium of Chicago Northwest Community Hospital, 800 W. Central Rd., Arlington Heights 60005. SAN 322-1180. Tel. 847-259-1000, ext. 5071, fax 847-577-4049. *Coord.* Joy Kennedy.

National Network of Libraries of Medicine, c/o Lib. of the Health Sciences, Univ. of Illinois at Chicago, 1750 W. Polk St., Chicago 60612-7223. SAN 322-1202. Tel. 312-996-2464, fax 312-996-2226. *Dir.* Elaine Martin; *Assoc. Dir.* Linda Walton.

Northern Illinois Learning Resources Cooperative (NILRC), 80 Main St., Suite 1A, Box 509, Sugar Grove 60554-0509. SAN 329-5583. Tel. 708-466-4848, fax 708-466-4895. *Exec. Dir.* Donald E. Drake.

Private Academic Libraries of Illinois (PALI), c/o North Park College Lib., 3225 W. Foster Ave., Chicago 60625. SAN 370-050X. Tel. 312-244-5582, fax 312-244-4891. *Pres.* Dorothy-Ellen Gross.

Quad Cities Libraries in Cooperation (QUADLINC), 220 W. 23 Ave., Coal Valley 61240. SAN 373-093X. Tel. 309-799-3155, fax 309-799-7916. *Dir.* Robert McKay; *Asst. Dir.* Mary Anne Stewart.

Quad City Area Biomedical Consortium, Perlmutter Lib., 855 Hospital Rd., Silvis 61282. SAN 322-435X. Tel. 309-792-4360, fax 309-792-4362. *Coord.* Barbara Tharp.

River Bend Library System (RBLS), Box 125, Coal Valley 61240. SAN 371-0653. Tel. 309-799-3155, fax 309-799-7916. *Coord.* Nancy Buikema.

Sangamon Valley Academic Library Consortium, c/o Illinois College, Schewe Lib., 1101 W. College Ave., Jacksonville 62650. SAN 322-4406. Tel. 217-245-3020, fax 217-243-2520. *Chair* Martin Gallas; *Secy.-Treas.* W. Michael Westbrook.

Shabbona Consortium, c/o Illinois Valley Community Hospital, 925 West St., Peru 61354. SAN 329-5133. Tel. 815-223-3300, ext. 494, fax 815-223-3394. *Dir. and Medical Staff Services Dir.* Linda Maciejewski.

Upstate Consortium, Highland Community College, 2998 W. Pearl St., Freeport 61032. SAN 329-3793. Tel. 815-235-6121, ext. 338, fax 815-235-1366. *Coord.* Eric Welch.

USA Toy Library Association, 2530 Crawford Ave., Suite 111, Evanston 60201. SAN 371-215X. Tel. 847-864-3330, fax 847-864-3331. *Exec. Dir.* Judith Q. Iacuzzi.

Indiana

Association of Visual Science Librarians (AVSL), Indiana Univ., Optometry Lib., Bloomington 47405. SAN 370-0569. Tel. 812-855-8629, fax 812-855-6616. *Chair* Douglas Freeman.

Central Indiana Health Science Libraries Consortium, Methodist Hospital Lib., I 65 at 21 St., Box 1367, Indianapolis 46206. SAN 322-1245. Tel. 317-929-8021, fax 317-929-8397. *Coord.* Christine Bockrath.

Collegiate Consortium Western Indiana, c/o Cunningham Memorial Lib., Indiana State Univ., Terre Haute 47809. SAN 329-4439. Tel. 812-237-3700, fax 812-237-2567. *Dean* Ronald G. Leach.

Evansville Area Library Consortium, 3700 Washington Ave., Evansville 47750. SAN 322-1261. Tel. 812-479-4151, fax 812-473-7564. *Coord.* E. Jane Saltzman.

Indiana Cooperative Library Services Authority (INCOLSA), 6202 Morenci Trail, Indianapolis 46268-2536. SAN 322-1296. Tel. 317-298-6570, fax 317-328-2380. *Exec. Dir.* Millard Johnson; *Asst. Exec. Dir.* Jan Cox.

Indiana State Data Center, Indiana State Lib., 140 N. Senate Ave., Indianapolis 46204-2296. SAN 322-1318. Tel. 317-232-3733, fax 317-232-3728. *Acting Dir.* Cynthia St. Martin.

Northeast Indiana Health Science Libraries Consortium (NEIHSL), Lutheran Center for Health Services, Health Sciences Lib., 3024 Fairfield Ave., Fort Wayne 46807. SAN 373-1383. Tel. 219-458-2277, fax 219-458-3077. *Provisional Coord.* Lauralee Aven.

Northwest Indiana Health Science Library Consortium, c/o NW Center for Medical Educ., Indiana Univ. School of Medicine, 3400 Broadway, Gary 46408-1197. SAN 322-1350. Tel. 219-980-6852, fax 219-980-6566. *Coord.* Rachel Feldman.

Society of Indiana Archivists, c/o The Conner Prairie Museum, Rudell Lib., 13400 Alisonville Rd., Fishers 46038. SAN 329-5508. Tel. 317-776-6000, fax 317-776-6014. *Pres.* Tim Crumrin; *Secy.-Treas.* Joan Cunningham.

Wabash Valley Health Science Library Consortium, Indiana State Univ., Cunningham Memorial Lib., Terre Haute 47809. SAN 371-3903. Tel. 812-237-2540, fax 812-237-8028, e-mail LIBBIRK@cml.indstate. edu. *Medical Libn./Consortium Coord.* Evelyn J. Birkey.

Iowa

Bi-State Academic Libraries (BI-SAL), c/o Teikyo Marycrest Univ., Davenport 52804. SAN 322-1393. Tel. 319-326-9255. *Chair* Sister Joan Sheil.

Consortium of College and University Media Centers, Iowa State Univ., 121 Pearson Hall, Ames 50011-2203. SAN 322-1091. Tel. 515-294-1811, fax 515-294-8089, e-mail e1dar@isuvax.bitnet. *Exec. Dir.* Don A. Rieck.

Dubuque Area Library Information Consortium, 360 W. 11 St., Dubuque 52001-4697. SAN 322-1407. Tel. 319-589-4225, fax 319-589-4217. *Pres.* Deb Seiffert.

Iowa Private Academic Library Consortium (IPAL), c/o William Penn College, Wilcox Lib., 201 Trueblood Ave., Oskaloosa 52577. SAN 329-5311. Tel. 515-673-1096, fax 515-673-1098. *Chair* Julie E. Hansen.

Iowa Resource and Information Sharing (IRIS), State Lib. of Iowa, E. 12 and Grand, Des Moines 50319. SAN 322-1415. Tel. 515-281-4105, fax 515-281-6191. *State Libn.* Sharman B. Smith.

Linn County Library Consortium, Kirkwood Community College Lib., 6301 Kirkwood Blvd. S.W., Cedar Rapids 52406. SAN 322-4597. Tel. 319-398-5553, fax 319-398-4908. *Pres.* Jill Miller; *V.P.* Margaret White.

Polk County Biomedical Consortium, c/o State Lib. of Iowa, E. 12 and Grand, Des Moines 50319. SAN 322-1431. *Coord.* Pam Rees.

Sioux City Library Cooperative (SCLC), c/o Sioux City Public Lib., 529 Pierce St., Sioux City 51101-1203. SAN 329-4722. Tel. 712-252-5669. *Agent* Betsy J. Thompson.

Tri-College Cooperative Effort, Wahlert Memorial Lib., Loras College, 1450 Alta Vista, Dubuque 52004-0178. SAN 322-1466. Tel. 319-588-7125, fax 319-588-7292. *Dir.* Robert Klein.

Kansas

Associated Colleges of Central Kansas, 105 E. Kansas, McPherson 67460. SAN 322-1474. Tel. 316-241-5150, fax 316-241-5153. *Libn.* Donna Zerger.

Dodge City Library Consortium, 905 Central, Dodge City 67801. SAN 322-4368. Tel. 316-227-6532. *Chair* Marlene Trenkle.

Kansas Library Network Board, State Capital, Rm. 343N, 300 S.W. Tenth, Topeka 66612-1593. SAN 329-5621. Tel. 913-296-3296, fax 913-296-6650. *Exec. Dir.* Michael Piper.

Kentucky

Association of Independent Kentucky Colleges and Universities, Box 46, Danville 40423-0046. SAN 322-1490. Tel. 606-236-3533, fax 606-236-3534. *Pres.* M. Fred Mullinax.

Bluegrass Medical Librarians (BML), 1740 Nicholasville Rd., Lexington 40503. SAN 371-3881. Tel. 606-275-6297, fax 606-275-6442. *Pres.* David Holt; *Secy.-Treas.* Gloria Lester.

Eastern Kentucky Health Science Information Network (EKHSIN), c/o Camden-Carroll Lib., Morehead State Univ., Morehead 40351. SAN 370-0631. Tel. 606-783-2610, fax 606-783-5311. *Coord.* William J. DeBord.

Kentuckiana Metroversity, Inc., 3113 Lexington Rd., Louisville 40206. SAN 322-1504. Tel. 502-897-3374, fax 502-895-1647. *Exec. Dir.* Open.

Kentucky Health Science Libraries Consortium, Western Baptist Hospital, 2501 Kentucky Ave., Paducah 42003-3200. SAN 370-0623. Tel. 502-575-2725, fax 502-575-2164. *Pres.* Stephanie Young.

Kentucky Library Information Center (KLIC), Kentucky Dept. for Libs. and Archives, 300 Coffee Tree Rd., Box 537, Frankfort 40602. SAN 322-1512. Tel. 502-745-6118, 875-7000, fax 502-745-5943. *Pres.* Cindy Brown.

Kentucky Library Network, Inc., 300 Coffee Tree Rd., Box 537, Frankfort 40602. SAN 371-2184. Tel. 502-564-8300, fax 502-564-5773. *Pres.* Cindy Brown.

State Assisted Academic Library Council of Kentucky (SAALCK), c/o Steely Lib., Northern Kentucky Univ., Highland Heights 41099. SAN 371-2222. Tel. 606-572-5483, fax 606-572-5390. *Chair and Pres.* Marian C. Winner.

Theological Education Association of Mid America (TEAM-A), c/o Southern Baptist Theological Seminary, 2825 Lexington Rd., Louisville 40280-0294. SAN 322-1547. Tel. 502-897-4807, fax 502-897-4600. *Dir.* Ronald F. Deering.

Louisiana

Baton Rouge Hospital Library Consortium, Earl K. Long Hospital, 5825 Airline Hwy., Baton Rouge 70805. SAN 329-4714. Tel. 504-387-7012, 358-1089, fax 504-336-2914, 342-5983. *Pres.* Eileen Stanley.

Health Sciences Library Association of Louisiana, c/o LSU School of Medicine, Shreveport 71301. SAN 375-0035. Tel. 318-473-0010, fax 318-473-9491. *Chair* David Duggar.

Lasernet, State Lib. of Louisiana, Box 131, Baton Rouge 70821. SAN 371-6880. Tel. 504-342-4923, 342-4922, fax 504-342-3547. *Dep. Asst. Libn.* Michael R. McKann; *Automation Consultant* Sara Taffae.

Louisiana Government Information Network (LaGIN), c/o State Lib. of Louisiana, Box 131, Baton Rouge 70821. SAN 329-5036. Tel. 504-342-4920, fax 504-342-3547. *Coord. User Services* Blanche Cretini.

New Orleans Educational Telecommunications Consortium, 2929 S. Carrollton Ave., New Orleans 70118. SAN 329-5214. Tel. 504-861-3028, fax 504-861-3014. *Chair* Gregory O'Brien; *Exec. Dir.* Robert J. Lucas.

Maine

Health Science Library Information Consortium (HSLIC), Penobscot Bay Medical Center, 6 Glen Cove Dr., Rockport 04856. SAN 322-1601. Tel. 207-596-8223, fax 207-596-5294. *Dir.* Patricia Kahn.

Maryland

American Library Association VideoLibrary Video Network (ALA Video-LVN), 320 York Rd., Towson 21204. SAN 375-5320. Tel. 410-887-2082, e-mail INLIB@mail.bcpl.lib.md.us. *Production Mgr.* Jeff Lifton; *Program Mgr.* Kathy Coster.

Cooperating Libraries of Central Maryland (CLCM), 5 Harry S. Truman Pkwy., Annapolis 21601. SAN 322-3914. Tel. 410-222-7288, fax 410-222-7188. *Exec. Dir.* Cecy Keller.

Educational Resources Information Center (ERIC) Processing and Reference Facility, 1301 Piccard Dr., Suite 300, Rockville 20850-4305. SAN 322-161X. Tel. 301-258-5500, fax 301-948-3695, e-mail ericfac@inet.ed.gov. *Dir.* Ted Brandhorst.

Interlibrary Users Association (IUA), c/o COMSAT Corp, 22300 COMSAT Dr., Clarksburg 20871. SAN 322-1628. Tel. 301-428-4512, fax 301-428-7747. *Pres.* Merilee J. Worsey; *V.P.* Herb Foerstel.

Maryland Interlibrary Organization (MILO), c/o Enoch Pratt Free Lib., 400 Cathedral St., Baltimore 21201-4484. SAN 343-8600. Tel. 410-396-5498, fax 410-396-5837. *Administrator* Patricia E. Wallace.

National Clearinghouse for Alcohol and Drug Information (NCADI), Box 2345, Rockville 20847-2345. SAN 371-9162. Tel. 301-468-2600, fax 301-468-6433. *Project Dir.* John Noble; *Deputy Dir.* Roe Wilson.

National Library of Medicine, Medical Literature Analysis and Retrieval System (MEDLARS), 8600 Rockville Pike, Bethesda 20894. SAN 322-1652. Fax 301-496-0822, e-mail mms@nlm.nih.gov. *Head MEDLARS Management Section* Carolyn Tilley.

National Network of Libraries of Medicine (NN-LM), National Lib. of Medicine, 8600 Rockville Pike, Rm. B1E03, Bethesda 20894. SAN 373-0905. Tel. 301-496-4777, fax 301-480-1467. *Head* Becky Lyon.

National Network of Libraries of Medicine, Univ. of Maryland Health Sciences Lib., 111 S. Greene St., Baltimore 21201-1583. SAN 322-1644. Tel. 410-706-2855, fax 410-706-0099, e-mail fmeakin@umab.umd.edu. *Exec. Dir.* Janice Kelly; *RML Dir.* Frieda Weise.

Washington Research Library Consortium (WRLC), 901 Commerce Dr., Upper Marlboro 20772. SAN 373-0883. Tel. 301-390-2000, fax 301-390-2020. *Exec. Dir.* Lizanne Payne; *Dir. Computing and Telecommunications* Carl Whitman.

Massachusetts

Boston Area Music Libraries (BAML), Music Lib., Music Bldg., Harvard Univ., Cambridge 02138. SAN 322-4392. Tel. 617-495-2794, fax 617-496-4636. *Coord.* Millard Irion.

Boston Biomedical Library Consortium (BBLC), Dana-Farber Cancer Institute, 44 Binney St., Boston 02115. SAN 322-1725.

Tel. 617-632-2489, fax 617-632-2488. *Chair* Chris Fleuriel.

Boston Library Consortium, 666 Boylston St., Rm. 317, Boston 02117. SAN 322-1733. Tel. 617-262-0380, fax 617-262-0163, e-mail hstevens@bpl.org. *Exec. Dir.* Hannah M. Stevens.

Boston Theological Institute Library Program, 45 Francis Ave., Cambridge 02138. SAN 322-1741. Tel. 617-495-5780, 527-4880, fax 617-495-9489, e-mail putney@harvarda.harvard.edu. *Lib. Coord.* Clifford Putney.

Cape Libraries Automated Materials Sharing (CLAMS), 270 Communication Way, Unit 4E-4F, Hyannis 02601. SAN 370-579X. Tel. 508-790-4399, fax 508-771-4533, e-mail defoe@clams.lib.ma.us. *Pres.* Helen DeFoe; *Network Administrator* Monica Grace.

Catholic Library Association, St. Joseph Central High School Lib., 22 Maplewood Ave., Pittsfield 01201-4780. SAN 329-1030. Tel. 413-443-2252. *Contact* Jean R. Bostley.

Central Massachusetts Consortium of Health Related Libraries (CMCHRL), c/o Lamar Soutter Medical Lib., Univ. of Massachusetts Medical Center, 55 Lake Ave N., Worcester 01655. SAN 371-2133. Tel. 508-856-6857, fax 508-856-5899. *Pres.* Annanaomi Sams.

Consortium for Information Resources, Emerson Hospital, Old Road to Nine Acre Corner, Concord 01742. SAN 322-4503. Tel. 508-369-1400, fax 508-369-7655. *Pres.* Nancy Caloander.

Cooperating Libraries of Greater Springfield (CLGS), 263 Alden St., Springfield 01109. SAN 322-1768. Tel. 413-256-8316, 549-4600, fax 413-748-3631. *Dir.* Gerald Davis.

Corporate Library Group (CLG), 30 Porter Rd., LJ02/I4, Littleton 01460-1446. SAN 370-0534. Tel. 508-486-2300, fax 508-486-2944. *Mgr.* Mary Lee Kennedy.

C W Mars (Central/Western Massachusetts Automated Resource Sharing), 1 Sunset Lane, Paxton 01612-1197. SAN 322-3973. Tel. 508-755-3323, fax 508-755-3721. *Mgr.* David T. Sheehan; *Supv. User Services* Gale E. Eckerson.

Essex County Cooperating Libraries, Peabody Institute Lib., 82 Main St., Peabody 01960. SAN 322-1776. Tel. 508-921-6062, 531-0100, fax 508-922-8329, 532-1797. *Pres.* Helena Minton.

Fenway Libraries Online (FLO), Wentworth Institute of Technology, 550 Huntington Ave., Boston 02115. SAN 373-9112. Tel. 617-442-2384, fax 617-442-1519. *Network Dir.* Jamie Ingram.

Fenway Library Consortium, New England Conservatory, 33 Gainsborough St., Boston 02115. SAN 327-9766. Tel. 617-262-1120, ext. 305, fax 617-262-0500. *Coord.* Jean Morrow.

HILC, Inc. (Hampshire Interlibrary Center), 97 Spring St., Amherst 01002. SAN 322-1806. Tel. 413-256-8316, 549-4600, fax 413-256-0249. *Administrative Asst.* Dora Tudryn; *Mgr.* Jean Stabell.

Merrimac Interlibrary Cooperative, c/o J. V. Fletcher Lib., 50 Main St., Westford 01886. SAN 329-4234. Tel. 508-692-5555, fax 508-692-0287. *Chairs* Sue Jefferson, Nanette Eichell.

Merrimack Valley Library Consortium, c/o Memorial Hall Lib., Elm Square, Andover 01810. SAN 322-4384. *Pres.* Elisabeth Desmarais; *Network Administrator* Evelyn Kuo.

Minuteman Library Network, 4 California Ave., 5th fl., Framingham 01701. SAN 322-4252. Tel. 508-879-8575, fax 508-879-5470. *Exec. Dir.* Joan Kuklinski.

NELINET, Inc., 2 Newton Executive Park, Newton 02162. SAN 322-1822. Tel. 617-969-0400, fax 617-332-9634, e-mail admin@nelinet.org, nelinet@bcvms.bitnet. *Exec. Dir.* Marshall Keys.

New England Law Library Consortium, Inc., Harvard Law School Lib., Langdell Hall, Cambridge 02138. SAN 322-4244. Tel. 617-495-9918, 495-3100, fax 617-495-4449, e-mail crane@hulaw1.harvard.edu. *Exec. Dir.* Diane Klaiber.

Northeastern Consortium for Health Information (NECHI), c/o Salem Hospital, 81 Highland Ave., Salem 02143. SAN 322-1857. Tel. 508-741-1200, ext. 4951, fax 508-744-9110. *Pres.* Nancy Fazzone.

Northeast Consortium of Colleges and Universities in Massachusetts (NECCUM), c/o Gordon College, 255 Grapevine Rd.,

Wenham 01984. SAN 371-0602. Tel. 508-927-2300, fax 508-524-3708. *Coord.* Stephen MacLeod.
North of Boston Library Exchange, Inc. (NOBLE), 26 Cherry Hill Dr., Danvers 01923. SAN 322-4023. Tel. 508-777-8844, fax 508-750-8472. *Exec. Dir.* Ronald A. Gagnon; *Member Services Mgr.* Elizabeth B. Thomsen.
Southeastern Automated Libraries, Inc. (SEAL), 547 W. Grove St., Box 4, Middleboro 02346. SAN 371-5000. Tel. 508-946-8605, fax 508-946-8605. *Exec. Dir.* Deborah K. Conrad; *Coord. User Services* Barbara Bonville.
Southeastern Massachusetts Consortium of Health Science Libraries (SEMCO), Shattuck Hospital, 170 Morton St., Jamaica Plain 02130. SAN 322-1873. Tel. 617-522-8110, ext. 307, fax 617-524-9779. *Pres.* Bonnie Shu.
Southeastern Massachusetts Cooperating Libraries (SMCL), c/o Stonehill College, Cushing-Martin Lib., North Easton 02357-4015. SAN 322-1865. Tel. 508-230-1111, fax 508-230-1424. *Chair* Edward Hynes.
Western Massachusetts Health Information Consortium, Baystate Medical Center, 759 Chestnut St., Springfield 01199. SAN 329-4579. Tel. 413-784-3549. *Chair* Mark Kennedy.
West of Boston Network (WEBNET), Horn Lib., Babson College, Babson Park 02157. SAN 371-5019. Tel. 617-239-4308, fax 617-239-5226. *System Administrator* Orley J. Jones; *Network Pres.* Elizabeth Keenan.
Worcester Area Cooperating Libraries, c/o Worcester State College Learning Resources Center, Rm. 221, 486 Chandler St., Worcester 01602-2597. SAN 322-1881. Tel. 508-754-3964, 793-8000, ext. 8544, fax 508-793-8198, e-mail gwood @mecn.mass.edu. *Coord.* Gladys Wood.

Michigan

Berrien Library Consortium, Andrews Univ. Campus, Berrien Springs 49104. SAN 322-4678. Tel. 616-926-6139, fax 616-982-3710. *Pres.* Bob Nichols; *Treas.* Harvey Brenneise.
Capital Area Library Network Inc. (CALNET), 706 Curtis St., Mason 48854. SAN 370-5927. Tel. 517-676-8445, fax 517-676-9646. *Contact* Kathleen M. Vera; *Chair* Susan Schwartz.
Cloverland Processing Center, c/o Bay de Noc Community College LRC, 2001 N. Lincoln Rd., Escanaba 49829-2511. SAN 322-189X. Tel. 906-786-5802, ext. 122, fax 906-786-5802. *Dean* Christian Holmes.
Council on Resource Development (CORD), Alumni Memorial Lib., St. Mary's College, 3535 Indian Trail, Orchard Lake 48324. SAN 374-6119. Tel. 810-683-0524. *Chair* Nancy Ward; *V. Chair* Clara Bohrer.
Detroit Area Consortium of Catholic Colleges, c/o Sacred Heart Seminary, 2701 Chicago Blvd., Detroit 48206. SAN 329-482X. Tel. 313-883-8500, fax 313-868-6440. *Rector and Pres.* Allen H. Vigneron.
Detroit Associated Libraries Region of Cooperation (DALROC), Detroit Public Lib., 5201 Woodward Ave., Detroit 48202. SAN 371-0831. Tel. 313-833-4036, fax 313-832-0877. *Board Chair* Patrice Merritt; *Regional Contact* James Lawrence.
Eastern Regional Health Science Libraries Association, c/o Mercy Hospital Medical Lib., 2601 Electric Ave., Port Huron 48060. SAN 329-4757. Tel. 810-985-1378, fax 810-985-1508. *Pres.* Bonnie Swegles.
Kalamazoo Consortium for Higher Education (KCHE), Kalamazoo College, 1200 Academy St., Kalamazoo 49006. SAN 329-4994. Tel. 616-337-7220, fax 616-337-7305. *Pres.* Lawrence Bryan; *Administrative Coord.* Margie Flynn.
Lakeland Area Library Network (LAKENET), 60 Library Plaza N.E., Grand Rapids 49503. SAN 371-0696. Tel. 616-454-0272, fax 616-454-4517. *Coord.* Harriet Field.
Library Cooperative of Macomb (LCM), Macomb County Lib., 16480 Hall Rd., Clinton Township 48038. SAN 373-9082. Tel. 810-286-6660, fax 810-228-8530. *Dir.* Susan Hill.
The Library Network, 33030 Van Born Rd., Wayne 48184. SAN 370-596X. Tel. 313-326-8910, fax 313-326-3035, 326-5140. *Dir.* Harry Courtright.
Michigan Association of Consumer Health Information Specialists (MACHIS), Battle Creek Health System Professional Lib., 300 North Ave., Battle Creek 49016. SAN

375-0043. Tel. 616-966-8331, fax 616-966-8322. *Chair* Robin Alanen-Mosher.

Michigan Health Sciences Libraries Association (MHSLA), c/o Butterworth Hospital, 100 Michigan Ave. N.E., Grand Rapids 49503. SAN 323-987X. Tel. 616-774-1655, fax 616-732-3527. *Pres.* Melba Moss.

Michigan Library Consortium (MLC), 6810 S. Cedar St., Suite 8, Lansing 48911. SAN 322-192X. Tel. 517-694-4242, fax 517-694-9303. *Exec. Dir.* Randy Dykhuis.

Northland Interlibrary System (NILS), 316 E. Chisholm St., Alpena 49707. SAN 329-4773. Tel. 517-356-1622, fax 517-354-3939, e-mail cawleyr@northand.lib.mi.us. *Dir.* Rebecca E. Cawley.

Sault Area International Library Association, c/o Lake Superior State Univ. Lib., Sault Sainte Marie 49783. SAN 322-1946. Tel. 906-635-2402, fax 906-635-2193. *Chair* Ruth Neveu.

Southeastern Michigan League of Libraries (SEMLOL), c/o Mardigian Lib., Univ. of Michigan–Dearborn, 4901 Evergreen, Dearborn 48128. SAN 322-4481. Tel. 313-593-5614, fax 313-593-5561. *Chair* Barbara Kriigel.

Southern Michigan Region of Cooperation (SMROC), 415 S. Superior, Suite A, Albion 49224-2135. SAN 371-3857. Tel. 517-629-9469, fax 517-628-3812. *Fiscal Agent* James C. Seidl.

Southwest Michigan Library Cooperative (SMLC), 305 Oak St., Paw Paw 49079. SAN 371-5027. Tel. 616-657-4698, fax 616-657-4494. *Dir.* Alida L. Geppert.

Upper Peninsula of Michigan Health Science Library Consortium, c/o Marquette General Hospital, 420 W. Magnetic, Marquette 49855. SAN 329-4803. Tel. 906-225-3429, fax 906-225-3524. *Chair* Kenneth Nelson.

Upper Peninsula Region Library Cooperation, Inc., 1615 Presque Isle Ave., Marquette 49855. SAN 329-5540. Tel. 906-228-7697, fax 906-228-5627. *Pres.* Mary June; *Treas.* Suzanne Dees.

Minnesota

Capital Area Library Consortium (CALCO), c/o Minnesota Dept. of Human Services, 444 Lafayette Rd., Saint Paul 55155. SAN 374-6127. Tel. 612-297-8708, fax 612-282-5340. *Pres.* Kale Nelson.

Central Minnesota Libraries Exchange (CMLE), c/o Learning Resources, Rm. 61, Saint Cloud State Univ., Saint Cloud 56301-4498. SAN 322-3779. Tel. 612-255-2950, fax 612-654-5131. *Dir.* Patricia E. Peterson.

Community Health Science Library, c/o Saint Francis Medical Center, 415 Oak St., Breckenridge 56520. SAN 370-0585. Tel. 218-643-7507, fax 218-643-7487. *Dir.* Geralyn Mategcek.

Cooperating Libraries in Consortium (CLIC), 1619 Dayton Ave., Suite 204A, Saint Paul 55104. SAN 322-1970. Tel. 612-644-3878, fax 612-644-6258. *Exec. Dir.* Chris Olson; *Computer Systems Specialist* Steve Waage.

METRONET, 2324 University Ave. W., Suite 116, Saint Paul 55114. SAN 322-1989. Tel. 612-646-0475, fax 612-646-0657. *Dir.* Mary Treacy.

Metropolitan Library Service Agency (MELSA), 570 Asbury St., Suite 201, Saint Paul 55104-1849. SAN 371-5124. Tel. 612-645-5731, fax 612-649-3169, e-mail melsa@gopher.melsa.lib.mn.us. *Exec. Dir.* William M. Duncan-O'Neal; *Assoc. Dir.* Tzvee Morris.

Minitex Library Information Network, c/o S-33 Wilson Lib., Univ. of Minnesota, 309 19th Ave. S., Minneapolis 55455-0414. SAN 322-1997. Tel. 612-624-4002, fax 612-624-4508. *Dir.* William DeJohn; *Administrative Dir.* Anne Stagg.

Minnesota Department of Human Services Library Consortium, DHS Lib. and Resource Center, 444 Lafayette, Saint Paul 55155-3821. SAN 371-0750. Tel. 612-297-8708, fax 612-282-5340. *Dir./Coord.* Kate Nelson.

Minnesota Theological Library Association, c/o Luther Theological Seminary Lib., 2375 Como Ave., Saint Paul 55108. SAN 322-1962. Tel. 612-641-3202, fax 612-641-3280. *Database Administrator* Mark Heutmaker.

North Country Library Cooperative, Olcott Plaza, Suite 110, 820 Ninth St. N., Virginia 55792-2298. SAN 322-3795. Tel.

218-741-1907, fax 218-741-1907. *Bookkeeper* Pam Johnson; *Secy.* Joyce Malterud.
Northern Lights Library Network, 318 17th Ave. E., Box 845, Alexandria 56308-0845. SAN 322-2004. Tel. 612-762-1032, fax 612-762-1032. *Dir.* Joan B. Larson.
SMILE (Southcentral Minnesota Inter-Library Exchange), Box 3031, Mankato 56002-3031. SAN 321-3358. Tel. 507-389-5108, fax 507-625-4049. *Dir.* Lucy Lowry; *Smiline I&R Dir.* Kate Tohal.
Southeast Library System (SELS), 107 W. Frontage Rd., Hwy. 52 N., Rochester 55901. SAN 322-3981. Tel. 507-288-5513, fax 507-288-8697. *Multitype Libn.* Roger M. Leachman.
Southwest Area Multi-County Multi-Type Interlibrary Exchange (SAMMIE), Southwest State Univ. Lib., Marshall 56258. SAN 322-2039. Tel. 507-532-9013, fax 507-532-2039. *Coord.* Robin Chaney.
Twin Cities Biomedical Consortium, c/o Saint Mary's Campus, College of Saint Catherine's Lib., 2500 S. Sixth St., Minneapolis 55454. SAN 322-2055. Tel. 612-690-7780, fax 612-690-7849. *Chair* Rocky Ralebipi.
Waseca Interlibrary Resource Exchange (WIRE), Janesville-Waldorf-Pemberton Public Schools, 110 E. Third St., Box 389, Janesville 56048-0389. SAN 370-0593. Tel. 507-234-5181, fax 507-234-5796. *Dir.* Pauline Fenelon.
Westlaw, 620 Opperman Dr., Box 64779, Saint Paul 55164-0779. SAN 322-4031. Tel. 612-687-7000, fax 612-687-5614. *V.P.* Thomas Mcleod.

Mississippi

Central Mississippi Consortium of Medical Libraries (CMCML), Medical Center, U.S. Dept. of Veterans Affairs, 1500 E. Woodrow Wilson Dr., Jackson 39216. SAN 372-8099. Tel. 601-362-4471, ext. 1703. *Chair* Rose Anne Tucker; *V. Chair* Wanda King.
Central Mississippi Library Council (CMLC), c/o McLendon Lib., Hinds Community College, Raymond 39154. SAN 372-8250. Tel. 601-857-3378, fax 601-857-3293. *Chair* Wayne Woodward; *V. Chair* Charles Brenner.

Mississippi Biomedical Library Consortium, c/o Magnolia Regional Medical Center, 611 Alcorn Dr., Corinth 38834. SAN 371-070X. Tel. 601-286-6961, ext. 1240, fax 601-286-4272. *Pres.* Marcia W. Elisson.

Missouri

Kansas City Library Network, Inc., Univ. of Missouri Dental Lib., 650 E. 25 St., Kansas City 64108. SAN 322-2098. Tel. 816-235-2030, fax 816-235-2157.
Kansas City Metropolitan Library Network, 15624 E. 24 Hwy., Independence 64050. SAN 322-2101. Tel. 816-521-7257, fax 816-521-7253. *Office Mgr.* Susan Burton.
Kansas City Regional Council for Higher Education Park College, Box 40, 8700 N.W. River Park Dr., Parkville 64152-3795. SAN 322-211X. Tel. 816-741-2000, ext. 6435, fax 816-741-1296. *Pres.* Ron Doering.
Missouri Libraries Film Cooperative (MLFC), 15616 E. Hwy. 24, Independence 64050. SAN 371-4993. Tel. 816-836-5200, fax 816-521-7253. *Administrator* Billy F. Windes; *Board Pres.* John Mertens.
Missouri Library Network Corporation, 10332 Old Olive St. Rd., Saint Louis 63141. SAN 322-466X. Tel. 314-567-3799, fax 314-567-3798. *Dir.* Susan Singleton.
Municipal Library Cooperative, 140 E. Jefferson, Kirkwood 63122. SAN 322-2152. Tel. 314-966-5568, fax 314-822-3755. *ILL* Gayle Camarda.
PHILSOM-PHILNET-BACS Network, c/o Washington Univ. Medical Lib. and Biomedical Communications Center, 660 S. Euclid Ave., Saint Louis 63110. SAN 322-2187. Tel. 314-362-2788, fax 314-367-9547. *Dir.* Loretta Stucki.
Saint Louis Medical Librarians Consortia, St. Mary's Health Center, 6420 Clayton Rd., Saint Louis 63117. SAN 375-0027. Tel. 314-768-8112, fax 314-768-8974. *Chair* Candy Thayer.
Saint Louis Regional Library Network, 9425 Big Bend, Saint Louis 63119. SAN 322-2209. Tel. 314-965-1305, fax 314-965-4443. *Administrator* Bernyce Christiansen.

Montana

Helena Area Health Science Libraries Consortium (HAHSLC), Corette Lib., Carroll College, Helena 59625. SAN 371-2192. Tel. 406-447-4341, fax 406-447-4525. *Chair* Lois Fitzpatrick.

Nebraska

Eastern Library System (ELS), 11929 Elm St., Suite 12, Omaha 68144. SAN 371-506X. Tel. 402-330-7884, fax 402-330-1859, e-mail ktooker@nde.unl.edu. *Administrator* Kathleen Tooker; *Board Pres.* Nina Little.
Lincoln Health Sciences Library Group (LHSLG), Southeast Community College, Learning Resource Center, 8800 O St., Lincoln 68520. SAN 329-5001. Tel. 402-437-2588, fax 402-437-2404. *Chair* Susan M. Dunn.
Meridian Library System, 3423 Second Ave., Suite 301, Kearney 68847. SAN 325-3554. Tel. 308-234-2087, fax 308-234-4040. *Pres.* Carol Reed; *Administrator* Sharon Osenga.
Metro Omaha Health Information Consortium (ICON), McGoogan Lib. of Medicine, 600 S. 42 St., Omaha 68198-6705. SAN 372-8102. Tel. 402-398-6092, fax 402-398-6923. *Pres.* Ken Oyer.
Mid-America Law School Library Consortium (MALSLC), c/o Schmid Law Lib., Univ. of Nebraska, College of Law, Lincoln 68583-0902. SAN 371-6813. Tel. 402-472-5737, fax 402-472-8260. *Chair* Sally H. Wise.
National Network of Libraries of Medicine-Midcontinental Region (NN-LM MR), c/o McGoogan Lib. of Medicine, Univ. of Nebraska Medical Center, 600 S. 42 St., Box 686706, Omaha 68198-6706. SAN 322-225X. Tel. 402-559-4326, fax 402-559-5482, e-mail nwoelfl@unmcvm.unmc. edu; pmullaly@unmcvm. unmc.edu. *Dir.* Nancy N. Woelfl; *Assoc. Dir.* Peggy Mullaly-Quijas.
NEBASE, c/o Nebraska Lib. Commission, 1200 N St., Suite 120, Lincoln 68508-2023. SAN 322-2268. Tel. 402-471-2045, fax 402-471-2083. *Dir.* Jo Budler; *Network Services Staff Asst.* Jeanette Powell.

Northeast Library System, 2813 13th St., Columbus 68601. SAN 329-5524. Tel. 402-564-1586. *Administrator* Carol Speicher.
Southeast Nebraska Library System, Union College Lib., 3800 S. 48 St., Lincoln 68506. SAN 322-4732. Tel. 402-486-2555, fax 402-486-2557. *Administrator* Kate Marek; *Administrative Asst.* Sara Schott.

Nevada

Information Nevada, Interlibrary Loan Dept., Nevada State Lib. and Archives, Capitol Complex, Carson City 89710-0001. SAN 322-2276. Tel. 702-687-8325, fax 702-687-8330. *Dir.* Joan Kerschner.
Nevada Cooperative Medical Library, 2040 W. Charleston Blvd., Suite 500, Las Vegas 89102. SAN 321-5962. Tel. 702-383-2368, fax 702-383-2369. *Dir. Lib. Services* Aldona Jonynas.
Nevada Medical Library Group (NMLG), c/o Dept. of Veterans Affairs Medical Center, Lib. Service, 1000 Locust St., Reno 89520. SAN 370-0445. Tel. 702-328-1470, fax 702-328-1732. *Chair* Christine Simpson.
Western Council of State Libraries, Inc., Nevada State Lib., Capitol Complex, Carson City 89710. SAN 322-2314. Tel. 702-687-8315, fax 702-687-8311. *Pres.* Nancy Bolt Colorado.

New Hampshire

Carroll County Library Cooperative, Box 240, Madison 03849. SAN 371-8999. Tel. 603-367-8545. *Secy.* Carolyn Busell.
Hillstown Cooperative, 3 Meetinghouse Rd., Bedford 03110. SAN 371-3873. Tel. 603-472-2300, fax 603-472-2978. *Chair* Frances M. Wiggin; *Secy.* Sarah Chapman.
Librarians of the Upper Valley Coop. (LUV), Enfield Public Lib., Main St., Box 1030, Enfield 03748-1030. SAN 371-6856. Tel. 603-632-7145. *Secy.* Marjorie Carr; *Treas.* Patricia Hand.
Merri-Hill-Rock Library Cooperative, Box 382, Raymond 03077. SAN 329-5338. *Chair* Sherry Brox.
New Hampshire College and University Council Libraries Committee, 116S River Rd., D4, Bedford 03110. SAN 322-2322.

Tel. 603-669-3432, fax 603-623-8182. *Exec. Dir.* Thomas R. Horgan.

North Country Consortium (NCC), Gale Medical Lib., Littleton Regional Hospital, 262 Cottage St., Littleton 03561. SAN 370-0410. Tel. 603-444-7731, ext. 164, fax 603-444-0443. *Coord.* Linda L. Ford.

Nubanusit Library Cooperative, c/o Peterborough Town Lib., Two Concord, Peterborough 03458. SAN 322-4600. Tel. 603-924-6401, fax 603-924-0037. *Contact* Ann Geisel.

Scrooge & Marley Cooperative, 310 Central St., Franklin 03235. SAN 329-515X. Tel. 603-934-2911. *Chair* Randy Brough.

Seacoast Coop. Libraries, North Hampton Public Lib., 235 Atlantic Ave., North Hampton 03862. SAN 322-4619. Tel. 603-964-6326, fax 603-964-1107. *Contact* Pam Schwatzer.

New Jersey

AT&T Information Services Network, 600 Mountain Ave., Rm. 6A-311, Murray Hill 07974. SAN 329-5400. Tel. 908-582-6880, fax 908-582-2255, e-mail ATTMAIL! RPSCHREIBER. *Managing Dir.* Nancy J. Miller.

Bergen County Cooperative Library System, 810 Main St., Hackensack 07601. SAN 322-4546. Tel. 201-489-1904, fax 201-489-4215. *Exec. Dir.* Robert W. White; *Mgr. Computer Services* Brian DeSantis.

Bergen-Passaic Health Sciences Library Consortium, c/o Englewood Hospital and Medical Center, 350 Engle St., Englewood 07631. SAN 371-0904. Tel. 201-894-3069, fax 201-894-9049. *Pres.* Lia Sabbagh.

Central Jersey Health Science Libraries Association, Saint Francis Medical Center Medical Lib., 601 Hamilton Ave., Trenton 08629. SAN 370-0712. Tel. 609-599-5068, fax 609-599-5773. *Dir.* Donna Barlow; *Tech. Info. Specialist* Eileen Monroe.

Central Jersey Regional Library Cooperative–Region V, 4400 Rte. 9 S., Freehold 07728-2942. SAN 370-5102. Tel. 908-409-6484, fax 908-409-6492. *Interim Dir.* Leslie Burger.

Cosmopolitan Biomedical Library Consortium, William Pierson Medical Lib., Hospital Center at Orange, 188 S. Essex Ave., Orange 07201. SAN 322-4414. Tel. 201-266-2067. *Pres.* Barbara Reich.

Dow Jones News Retrieval, Box 300, Princeton 08543-0300. SAN 322-404X. Tel. 609-452-1511, fax 609-520-4775. *Customer Service* Maggie Landis.

Health Sciences Library Association of New Jersey (HSLANJ), Rutgers Univ. Lib. of Science and Medicine, Box 1029, Piscataway 08855-1029. SAN 370-0488. Tel. 908-445-2890, fax 908-445-3208. *Pres.* Jackie Mardikian.

Highlands Regional Library Cooperative, 31 Fairmount Ave., Box 486, Chester 07930. SAN 329-4609. Tel. 908-879-2442, fax 908-879-8812. *Interim Exec. Dir.* Joyce L. Wemer; *Acting Prog. Coord.* Barbara A. Carroll.

Infolink Eastern New Jersey Regional Library Cooperative, Inc., 44 Stelton Rd., Suite 330, Piscataway 08854. SAN 371-5116. Tel. 908-752-7720, fax 908-752-7785, e-mail infolink@llnj.ll.pbs.org. *Exec. Dir.* Gail L. Rosenberg; *Prog. and Services Coord.* Cheryl O'Connor.

LMX Automation Consortium, 1030 Saint George, Suite 203, Avenel 07001. SAN 329-448X. Tel. 908-750-2525, fax 908-750-9392. *Exec. Dir.* Ellen Parravano.

Monmouth-Ocean Biomedical Information Consortium (MOBIC), Community Medical Center, 99 Hwy. 37 W., Toms River 08755. SAN 329-5389. Tel. 908-240-8117, fax 908-240-8354. *Dir.* Reina Reisler.

Morris Automated Information Network (MAIN), Box 900, Morristown 07963-0900. SAN 322-4058. Tel. 201-989-6112, fax 201-285-6886, e-mail sleeter@main.morris.org. *Network Administrator and Dir.* Ellen Sleeter.

Morris-Union Federation, 214 Main St., Chatham 07928. SAN 310-2629. Tel. 201-635-0603. *Treas.* Diane O'Brien.

New Jersey Academic Library Network, c/o Kean College Lib., Nancy Thompson Lib., Union 07083. SAN 329-4927. Tel. 908-527-2017, fax 908-527-2365. *Chair* Mary Biggs.

New Jersey Health Sciences Library Network (NJHSN), Mountainside Hospital, Health Sciences Lib., Montclair 07042. SAN 371-4829. Tel. 201-429-6240, fax 201-680-7850. *Chair* Patricia Regenberg.

New Jersey Library Network Library Development Bureau, 185 W. State St., CN-520, Trenton 08625-0520. SAN 372-8161. Tel. 609-984-3293. *Service Coord.* Marilyn R. Veldof.

Pinelands Consortium for Health Information, c/o Kennedy Memorial Hospital, Washington Township Division, Medical Lib., 435 Huffville-Cross Keys Rd., Turnersville 08012. SAN 370-4874. Tel. 609-582-2675, fax 609-582-3190. *Coord.* William Dobkowski.

Society for Cooperative Healthcare and Related Education (SCHARE), 1776 Raritan Rd., Scotch Plains 07076. SAN 371-0718. Tel. 908-889-6410. *Chair* Geri Farina; *Coord.* Anne Calhoun.

South Jersey Regional Library Cooperative, Paint Works Corporate Center, 10 Foster Ave., Suite F-3, Gibbsboro 08026. SAN 329-4625. Tel. 609-346-1222, fax 609-346-2839. *Exec. Dir.* Karen Hyman; *Program Development Coord.* Katherine Schalk-Greene.

New Mexico

New Mexico Consortium of Academic Libraries, New Mexico State Univ. Lib., Box 30006, Dept. 3475, Las Cruces 88003. SAN 371-6872. Tel. 505-646-1508, fax 505-646-6940, e-mail ctownley@lib.nmsu.edu. *Pres.* Charles Townley.

New Mexico Consortium of Biomedical and Hospital Libraries, c/o Lovelace Medical Lib., 5400 Gibson Blvd. SE, Albuquerque 87108. SAN 322-449X. Tel. 505-262-7158, fax 505-262-7897. *Permanent Contact* Sarah Morley.

New York

Academic Libraries of Brooklyn, 175 Willoughby St., Suite 15C, Brooklyn 11201. SAN 322-2411. Tel. 718-260-3626, fax 718-260-3756, e-mail chick@pratt.bitnet. *Dir.* Jana Richman.

Associated Colleges of the Saint Lawrence Valley, Merritt Hall, State Univ. of New York at Potsdam, Potsdam 13676-2299. SAN 322-242X. Tel. 315-267-3331, fax 315-267-2389. *Exec. Dir.* Anneke J. Larrance.

Brooklyn-Queens-Staten Island Health Sciences Librarians (BQSI), Brookdale Hospital, Rockaway Pkwy. and Linden Blvd., Brooklyn 11212. SAN 370-0828. Tel. 718-240-5302, fax 718-240-5030. *Pres.* Carol Cave-Davis; *V.P.* Kalpana Desai.

Capital District Library Council for Reference and Research Resources, 28 Essex St., Albany 12206. SAN 322-2446. Tel. 518-438-2500, fax 518-438-2872. *Exec. Dir.* Charles D. Custer; *Administrative Sec.* Carol Houlihan.

Central New York Library Resources Council (CLRC), 3049 E. Genesee St., Syracuse 13224-1690. SAN 322-2454. Tel. 315-446-5446, fax 315-446-5590, e-mail clrc1@transit.nyser.net. *Exec. Dir.* Keith E. Washburn; *Asst. Dir.* Jeannette Smithee.

Consortium of Foundation Libraries, c/o UNICEF Lib., H-12G, 3 UN Plaza, New York 10017. SAN 322-2462. Tel. 212-326-7065, fax 212-303-7989. *Chair* Jean Ando.

Council of Archives and Research Libraries in Jewish Studies (CARLJS), 330 Seventh Ave., 21st fl., New York 10001. SAN 371-053X. Tel. 212-629-0500, fax 212-629-0508. *Pres.* Michael Grunberger; *Dir. Cultural Services* Joseph Lowin.

Educational Film Library Association, c/o AV Resource Center, Cornell Univ., Business and Technology Park, Ithaca 14850. SAN 371-0874. Tel. 607-255-2090, fax 607-255-9946. *AV Coord.* Rich Gray; *AV Sales* Liz Powers.

Health Information Libraries of Westchester (HILOW), New York Medical College, Medical Science Lib., Basic Sciences Bldg., Valhalla 10595. SAN 371-0823. Tel. 914-993-4204. *Pres.* Charlene Sikorski.

Library Consortium of Health Institutions in Buffalo, Office of the Consortium, Health Sciences Lib., Univ. at Buffalo, Buffalo 14214. SAN 329-367X. Tel. 716-829-3402, fax 716-835-4891. *Dir. Health Sciences* Gary Byrd.

Long Island Library Resources Council, Melville Lib. Bldg., Suite E5310, Stony Brook 11794-3399. SAN 322-2489. Tel. 516-632-6650, fax 516-632-6662, e-mail hbiblo@ccmail.sunysb.edu. *Dir.* Herbert Biblo; *Asst. Dir.* Judith Neufeld.

Manhattan-Bronx Health Sciences Libraries Group, c/o KPR Medical Lib., 333 E. 38 St., New York 10016. SAN 322-4465. Tel. 212-856-8721, fax 212-856-8884. *Pres.* Penny Klein.

Medical and Scientific Libraries of Long Island (MEDLI), c/o Palmer School of Lib. and Info. Science, C. W. Post Campus, Long Island Univ., Brookville 11548. SAN 322-4309. Tel. 516-299-2866, fax 516-299-4168. *Pres.* William Casey.

Medical Library Center of New York, 5 E. 102 St., 7th fl., New York 10029. SAN 322-3957. Tel. 212-427-1630, fax 212-860-3496, 876-6697. *Dir.* Lois Weinstein.

Middle Atlantic Region, National Network of Libraries of Medicine, New York Academy of Medicine, 1216 Fifth Ave., New York 10029-5293. SAN 322-2497. Tel. 212-876-8763, fax 212-534-7042. *Dir.* Arthur Downing; *Assoc. Dir.* Mary Mylenki.

New York Metropolitan Reference and Research Library Agency (METRO), 57 E. 11 St., New York 10003. SAN 322-2500. Tel. 212-228-2320, fax 212-228-2598. *Dir.* Dottie Hiebing.

New York State Interlibrary Loan Network (NYSILL), c/o New York State Lib., Albany 12230. SAN 322-2519. Tel. 518-474-5129, fax 518-474-5786, e-mail ny6002@mail.nysen.net. *State Libn.* Joseph F. Shubert; *Dir.* Jerome Yavarkovsky.

North Country Reference and Research Resources Council, 7 Commerce La., Canton 13617. SAN 322-2527. Tel. 315-386-4569, fax 315-379-9553, e-mail staff@nc3r.org. *Exec. Dir.* John J. Hammond; *Head, Bibliographical Services* Tom Blauvelt.

Northeast Foreign Law Cooperative Group, Fordham Univ., 127 Wall St., New York 10023. SAN 375-0000. Tel. 212-636-6913, fax 212-977-2662, e-mail vessien@law.fordham.edu. *Chair* Victor Essien.

Research Library Association of South Manhattan, Bobst Lib., New York Univ., 70 Washington Sq. S., New York 10012. SAN 372-8080. Tel. 212-998-2566, fax 212-995-4583. *Coord.* Joan Grant.

Rochester Regional Library Council (RRLC), 390 Packetts Landing, Box 66160, Fairport 14450. SAN 322-2535. Tel. 716-223-7570, fax 716-223-7712, e-mail rrlcwml@ritvax.isc.rit.edu. *Dir.* Janet M. Welch.

South Central Research Library Council, 215 N. Cayuga St., Ithaca 14850. SAN 322-2543. Tel. 607-273-9106, fax 607-272-0740, e-mail jcurrie@lakenet.org. *Exec. Dir.* Jean Currie.

Southeastern New York Library Resources Council, 220 Rte. 299, Box 879, Highland 12528. SAN 322-2551. Tel. 914-691-2734, fax 914-691-6987. *Exec. Dir.* John L. Shaloiko; *Asst. Dir.* Ron Covisier.

State University of New York–OCLC Library Network (SUNY-OCLC), System Administration, State Univ. Plaza, Albany 12246. SAN 322-256X. Tel. 518-443-5444, fax 518-432-4346, e-mail (Bitnet) sunyoclc@snycenvm. *Interim Dir.* Liz Lane.

Western New York Library Resources Council, 4455 Genesee St., Box 400, Buffalo 14225-0400. SAN 322-2578. Tel. 716-633-0705, fax 716-633-1736. *Exec. Dir.* Betsy Sywetz.

North Carolina

Association of Southeastern Research Libraries, Reynolds Lib., Wake Forest Univ., Box 7777, Winston-Salem 27109-7777. SAN 322-1555. Tel. 910-759-5480, fax 910-759-9831, e-mail channing@lib.wfu.edu. *Chair* Rhoda K. Channing.

Cape Fear Health Sciences Information Consortium, c/o Robeson Community College, Lumberton 28359. SAN 322-3930. Tel. 910-738-7101, ext. 231, fax 910-671-4143. *Dir.* Marilyn Locklear-Hunt.

Microcomputer Users Group for Libraries in North Carolina, Perkins Lib., Duke Univ., Durham 27708-0177. SAN 322-4449. Tel. 919-660-5850, fax 919-684-2855. *Pres.* John Little; *Treas.* Barbara Thompson.

Mid-Carolina Academic Library Network (MID-CAL), Campbell Univ., Carrie Rich Lib., Box 98, Bules Creek 27506. SAN 371-3989. Tel. 910-893-1460, fax 910-893-1470, e-mail Gregory@ecsvax.uncecs.edu. *Chair* Ronnie Faulkner.

NC Area Health Education Centers Health Sciences Library, CB 7585, Univ. of North Carolina, Chapel Hill 27599-7585. SAN 323-9950. Tel. 919-962-0700, fax 919-966-5592. *Network Coord.* Diana C. McDuffee.

North Carolina Department of Community Colleges, Institutional Services, 200 W. Jones St., Raleigh 27603-1879. SAN 322-2594. Tel. 919-733-7051, ext. 634, fax 919-733-0680. *Dir.* Major Boyd; *Coord. of Lib. Tech. Assistance* Pamela B. Doyle.

North Carolina Information Network, 109 E. Jones St., Raleigh 27601-2807. SAN 329-3092. Tel. 919-733-2570, fax 919-733-8748. *Dir.* Gary Harden.

Northwest AHEC Library at Salisbury, c/o Rowan Regional Medical Center, 612 Mocksville Ave., Salisbury 28144. SAN 322-4589. Tel. 704-638-1081, fax 704-636-5050. *Coord. Lib. Info. Services* Connie Schardt.

Northwest AHEC Library Information Network, Northwest Area Health Education Center, Bowman Gray School of Medicine, Medical Center Blvd., Winston-Salem 27157-1060. SAN 322-4716. Tel. 910-716-9210, fax 910-716-9199. *Coord.* Connie Schardt.

Resources for Health Information Consortium (REHI), c/o Wake Medical Center Medical Lib., 3024 Newbern Ave., Suite 601, Raleigh 27610. SAN 329-3777. Tel. 919-250-8529, fax 919-250-8836. *Assoc. Dir.* Beverly Richardson.

Triangle Research Libraries Network, Wilson Lib., CB No. 3940, Chapel Hill 27599. SAN 329-5362. Tel. 919-962-8022, fax 919-962-4452, e-mail DAVID-Carlson@UNC.EDU; *Exec. Dir.* Open.

Unifour Consortium of Health Care and Educational Institutions, c/o Northwest AHEC Lib. at Hickory, Catawba Memorial Hospital, 810 Fair Grove Church, Hickory 28602. SAN 322-4708. Tel. 704-326-3662, fax 704-326-7164. *Dir.* Karen Martines; *Assoc. Dir.* Donna Bancroft.

North Dakota

American Indian Higher Education Consortium (AIHEC), c/o UTTC, 3315 University Dr., Bismarck 58501. SAN 329-4056. Tel. 701-255-3285, fax 701-255-1844. *Pres.* David Gipp.

Central Dakota Cooperating Libraries (CDCL), 515 N. Fifth St., Bismarck 58501. SAN 373-1391. Tel. 701-222-6410, fax 701-221-6854. *Chair* Thomas T. Jones; *Secy.-Treas.* Cheryl Bailey.

North Dakota Network for Knowledge, c/o North Dakota State Lib., Liberty Memorial Bldg., Capitol Grounds, 604 E. Blvd. Ave., Bismarck 58505-0800. SAN 322-2616. Tel. 701-328-2492, fax 701-328-2040. *Acting State Libn.* Joseph Linnertz.

Tri-College University Libraries Consortium, 209 Engineering Technology, North Dakota State Univ., Fargo 58105. SAN 322-2047. Tel. 701-231-8170, fax 701-231-7205. *Coord.* John W. Beecher; *Provost, Tri-College Univ.* Jean Strandness.

Valley Medical Network, c/o North Dakota State Univ. Lib., Fargo 58105. SAN 329-4730. Tel. 701-231-8885, fax 701-231-7138. *Pres.* Deb Fayler.

Ohio

Central Ohio Hospital Library Consortium, Medical Lib., Riverside Methodist Hospital, 3535 Olentangy River Rd., Columbus 43214. SAN 371-084X. Tel. 614-566-5230, fax 614-265-2437. *Archivist* Jo Yeoh.

Cleveland Area Metropolitan Library System (CAMLS), 20600 Chagrin Blvd., Suite 500, Shaker Heights 44122-5334. SAN 322-2632. Tel. 216-921-3900, fax 216-921-7220. *Dir.* Jacqueline Mundell.

Columbus Area Library and Information Council of Ohio (CALICO), c/o Westerville Public Lib., 126 S. State St., Westerville 43081. SAN 371-683X. Tel. 614-882-7277, fax 614-882-5369. *Treas.* Norman Ekleberry.

Consortium of Popular Culture Collections in the Midwest (CPCCM), c/o Popular Culture Lib., Bowling Green State Univ., Bowling Green 43403-0600. SAN 370-5811. Tel. 419-372-2450, fax 419-372-7996, e-mail bmccall@epic.bgsu.edu.

Greater Cincinnati Library Consortium, 3333 Vine St., Suite 605, Cincinnati 45220-2214. SAN 322-2675. Tel. 513-751-4422, fax 513-751-0463. *Exec. Dir.* Martha J. McDonald.

Miami Valley Libraries (MVL), c/o Flesh Public Lib., 124 W. Green St., Piqua 45356-2399. SAN 322-2691. Tel. 513-773-6753, fax 513-773-5981. *Exec. Dir.* Mark Kister.

MOLO Regional Library System, 1260 Monroe Ave., New Philadelphia 44663-4147. SAN 322-2705. Tel. 216-364-8537, fax

216-364-8537. *Exec. Dir.* Dave Simmons; *PGM Coord.* Shirley G. Rembert.
NEOUCOM Council of Associated Hospital Librarians, Ocasek Regional Medical Info. Center, Box 95, Rootstown 44272-0095. SAN 370-0526. Tel. 216-325-2511, ext. 542, fax 216-325-0522. *Chair* Jean Williams Sayre.
Northeastern Ohio Major Academic and Research Libraries (NEOMARL), Oberlin College Lib., Oberlin 44074. SAN 322-4236. Tel. 216-775-8285, fax 216-775-8739. *Chair* Ray English.
NOLA Regional Library System, 4445 Mahoning Ave. N.W., Warren 44483. SAN 322-2713. Tel. 216-847-7744, fax 216-847-7704. *Dir.* Holly C. Carroll; *ILL Coord.* Debbie Huberman.
Northwest Library District (NORWELD), 251 N. Main St., Bowling Green 43402. SAN 322-273X. Tel. 419-352-2903, fax 419-354-0405. *Dir.* Allan Gray; *Consultant* Susan Hill.
OCLC (Online Computer Library Center), Inc., 6565 Frantz Rd., Dublin 43017-3395. SAN 322-2748. Tel. 614-764-6000, fax 614-764-6096. *Pres.* K. Wayne Smith.
Ohio-Kentucky Cooperative Libraries, Box 647, Cedarville, 45314. SAN 325-3570. Tel. 513-766-7842, 766-2955, fax 513-766-2337. *Eds.* Janice Bosma, Kelly Hellwig.
Ohio Library and Information Network (OhioLINK), 2455 North Star Rd., Columbus 43221. SAN 374-8014. Tel. 614-728-3600, fax 614-728-3610. *Exec. Dir.* Thomas J. Sanville; *Dir. Lib. Systems* Anita I. Cook.
OHIONET, 1500 W. Lane Ave., Columbus 43221-3975. SAN 322-2764. Tel. 614-486-2966, fax 614-486-1527. *Exec. Dir.* Michael P. Butler; *Manager Computer Services* Robert Busick.
Ohio Network of American History Research Centers, Ohio Historical Society Archives/Library, 1982 Velma Ave., Columbus 43211-2497. SAN 323-9624. Tel. 614-297-2550, fax 614-297-2546. *Archivist* George Parkinson.
Ohio Regional Consortium of Law Libraries (ORCLL), Univ. of Akron School of Law Lib., 150 University Blvd., Akron 44325-2902. SAN 371-3954. Tel. 216-972-7330, fax 216-972-4948. *Dir.* Paul Richert.
Ohio Valley Area Libraries (OVAL), 252 W. 13 St., Wellston 45692-2299. SAN 322-2756. Tel. 614-384-2103, fax 614-384-2106, e-mail ovaorls@winslo.ohio.gov. *Dir.* Eric S. Anderson; *Consultant* Gail Zachariah.
Southwestern Ohio Council for Higher Education, 3171 Research Blvd., Suite 141, Dayton 45420-4014. SAN 322-2659. Tel. 513-259-1370, fax 513-259-1380. *Dir.* Tamara Yeager; *Chair Lib. Div.* Jean Mulhern.
The Sworl Group, 505 Kathryn Dr., Wilmington 45177-2274. SAN 322-2780. Tel. 513-382-2503, fax 513-382-2504. *Dir.* Corinne Johnson.

Oklahoma

Greater Oklahoma Area Health Sciences Library Consortium, St. Anthony's Hospital, 1000 N. Lee, Oklahoma City 73102. SAN 329-3858. Tel. 405-272-6285, fax 405-272-7075. *Pres.* Sharon Jorski.
Midwest Curriculum Coordination Center, 1500 W. Seventh Ave., Stillwater 74074-4364. SAN 329-3874. Tel. 405-377-2000, fax 405-743-5142. *Dir.* Julie G. Willcut.
Metropolitan Libraries Network of Central Oklahoma, Inc. (MetroNetwork), Box 250, Oklahoma City 73101-0250. SAN 372-8137. Tel. 405-231-8602, fax 405-236-5219. *Chair* Cheryl Suttles.
Oklahoma Health Sciences Library Association (OHSLA), Dean A. McGee Institute Medical Lib., 608 Stanton L. Young Blvd., Oklahoma City 73104. SAN 375-0051. Tel. 405-271-6085. *Pres.* Sheri Greenwood.
Tulsa Area Library Cooperative, 400 Civic Center, Tulsa 74103. SAN 321-6489. Tel. 918-491-2037, fax 918-596-7895. *Coord.* James Henry Davis.

Oregon

Chemeketa Cooperative Regional Library Service, c/o Chemeketa Community College, 4000 Lancaster Dr. N.E., Salem 97309-7070. SAN 322-2837. Tel. 503-399-5105, fax 503-399-5214. *Coord.* Linda Cochrane.
Coos County Library Service District, Extended Service Office, Tioga 107, 1988 Newmark, Coos Bay 97420. SAN 322-4279. Tel. 541-888-7260, fax 541-888-

7285. *Extension Services Coord.* Mary Jane Fisher.
Library Information Network of Clackamas County, 16239 S.E. McLoughlin Blvd., Suite 208, Oak Grove 97267. SAN 322-2845. Tel. 503-655-8550, fax 503-655-8555. *Network Administrator* Joanna Rood; *Systems Libn.* Wayne Hay.
Northwest Association of Private Colleges and Universities (NAPCU), c/o Shoen Lib., Maryhurst College, Maryhurst 97036. SAN 375-5312. Tel. 503-636-8141, ext. 374. *Pres.* Larry Oberg.
Oregon Health Sciences Libraries Association (OHSLA), c/o Mid-Columbia Medical Center, Planetree Health Center, 200 E. Fourth St., The Dalles 97058. SAN 371-2176. Tel. 503-296-8444, fax 503-296-6054. *Chair* Michele Johns.
Portland Area Health Sciences Librarians, Portland VA Medical Center Lib., 3710 S.W. U.S. Veterans Hospital Rd., Portland 97207. SAN 371-0912. Tel. 503-220-8262, ext. 5955, fax 503-721-7816. *Chief Lib. Services* Mara R. Wilhelm.
Southern Oregon Library Federation, c/o Jackson County Public Lib. System, Medford Lib. Branch, 413 W. Main St., Medford 97501. SAN 322-2861. Tel. 541-776-7281, fax 541-776-7290. *Pres.* Gary Sharp.
Washington County Cooperative Library Services, 17880 S.W. Blanton St., Box 5129, Aloha 97006. SAN 322-287X. Tel. 503-642-1544, fax 503-591-0445. *Mgr.* Peggy Forcier; *Automation Specialist* Eva Calcagno.

Pennsylvania

Associated College Libraries of Central Pennsylvania, c/o Lebanon Valley College, Annville 17003. SAN 322-2888. Tel. 717-867-6122, fax 717-867-6124. *Pres.* Robert Paustain; *Treas.* Scott Anderson.
Basic Health Sciences Library Network, c/o Consortium for Health Information, 1 Medical Center Blvd., Upland 19013. SAN 371-4888. Tel. 610-447-6163, fax 610-447-6164. *Chair* Stephanie Schneider.
Berks County Library Association (BCLA), RD 1, Box 1343, Hamburg 19526. SAN 371-0866. Tel. 610-655-6355. *Treas.* Pamela Hehr.
Berks County Public Libraries (BCPLS), Agricultural Center, Box 520, Leesport 19533. SAN 371-8972. Tel. 610-378-5260, fax 610-378-1525. *Administrator* Julie Rinehart; *Extension Services Libn.* Susan Harvard.
Central Pennsylvania Consortium, c/o Franklin & Marshall College, Box 3003, Lancaster 17604-3003. SAN 322-2896. Tel. 717-291-3919, fax 717-399-4455. *Dir.* Marigrace Bellart.
Central Pennsylvania Health Science Library Association (CPHSLA), 503 N. 21 St., Camp Hill 17011. SAN 375-5290. Tel. 717-763-2664, fax 717-763-2136. *Pres.* Edie Asbury; *V.P.-Pres.-Elect.* Susan Robishaw.
Confederation of State and State Related Institutions, Somerset State Hospital Staff Lib., Box 631, Somerset 15501. SAN 323-9829. Tel. 814-443-0216, 443-0231, 443-0319, fax 814-443-0217. *Dir. Lib. Services* Eve Kline; *Asst. Libn.* Kathy Plaso.
Consortium for Health Information and Library Services, 1 Medical Center Blvd., Upland 19013-3995. SAN 322-290X. Tel. 610-447-6163, fax 610-447-6164, e-mail ch1@hslc.org. *Exec. Dir.* Stephanie Schneider.
Cooperating Hospital Libraries of the Lehigh Valley Area, Easton Hospital Medical Lib., 250 S. 21 St., Easton 18042. SAN 371-0858. Tel. 610-250-4130, fax 610-250-4905. *Libn.* Kristine Petre.
Delaware Valley Information Consortium, Abington Memorial Hospital, 1200 York Rd., Abington 19001. SAN 329-3912. Tel. 215-576-2096. *Coord.* Marion Chayes.
Eastern Mennonite Associated Libraries and Archives (EMALA), 2215 Millstream Rd., Lancaster 17602. SAN 372-8226. Tel. 717-393-9745. *Chair* Ray K. Hacker; *Secy.* Lloyd Zeager.
Erie Area Health Information Library Cooperative (EAHILC), DuBois Regional Medical Center, Box 447, DuBois 15801. SAN 371-0564. Tel. 814-375-3575, fax 814-375-3576. *Chair* Kathy Scott.
Greater Philadelphia Law Library Association (GPLLA), Duane Morris & Heckscher, 1 Liberty Pl., Philadelphia 19103. SAN 373-1375. Tel. Tel 215-979-1722, fax 215-979-1020. *Pres.* David Falk; *V.P.* Michelle Ayres.

Health Information Library Network of Northeastern Pennsylvania, c/o Wyoming Valley Health Care System, Inc., Lib. Services, Wilkes-Barre 18764. SAN 322-2934.Tel. 717-820-2180. *Chair* Rosemarie Taylor.

Health Sciences Libraries Consortium, 3600 Market St., Suite 550, Philadelphia 19104-2646. SAN 323-9780. Tel. 215-222-1532, fax 215-222-0416. *Exec. Dir.* Joseph C. Scorza; *Assoc. Dir.* Alan C. Simon.

Interlibrary Delivery Service of Pennsylvania, 471 Park Lane, State College 16803-3208. SAN 322-2942. Tel. 814-238-0254, fax 814-238-9686. *Administrative Dir.* Janet C. Phillips.

Laurel Highlands Health Sciences Library Consortium, Owen Lib., Rm. 209, Univ. of Pittsburgh, Johnstown 15904. SAN 322-2950. Tel. 814-269-7280, fax 814-266-8230. *Dir.* Heather W. Brice.

Lehigh Valley Association of Independent Colleges, Inc., 119 W. Greenwich St., Bethlehem 18018-2307. SAN 322-2969. Tel. 601-882-5275, fax 601-882-5515. *Dir.* Galen C. Godbey.

Lower Providence Township Library, 2765 Egypt Rd., Audubon 19403-2252. SAN 375-3115. Tel. 610-666-6640, fax 610-666-5109.

Mid-Atlantic Law Library Cooperative (MALLCO), c/o Allegheny County Law Lib., 921 City/County Bldg., Pittsburgh 15219. SAN 371-0645. Tel. 412-350-5353, fax 412-350-5889. *Dir.* Joel Fishman; *Coord.* Frank Liu.

NEIU Consortium, 1300 Old Plank Rd., Mayfield 18433. SAN 372-817X. Tel. 717-282-9268, fax 717-963-9436. *IMS Dir.* Robert Carpenter; *Program Coord.* Rose Bennett.

Northeastern Pennsylvania Bibliographic Center, c/o Learning Resources Center, Marywood College, Scranton 18509-1598. SAN 322-2993. Tel. 717-348-6260, fax 717-348-1817. *Dir.* Catherine H. Schappert.

Northwest Interlibrary Cooperative of Pennsylvania (NICOP), c/o Mercyhurst College, Hammermill Lib., 501 E. 38 St., Erie 16546. SAN 370-5862. Tel. 814-824-2231, fax 814-824-2219. *Chair* Roy Strausbaugh.

Oakland Library Consortium (OLC), Univ. of Pittsburgh Lib., 271 Hillman Lib., Pittsburgh 15260. SAN 370-5803. Tel. 412-648-7753, fax 412-648-7887, e-mail sf0v @andrew.cmu.edu. *Board Pres.* Rush Miller; *Secy.* Staci Quackenbush.

PALINET and Union Library Catalogue of Pennsylvania (PALINET), 3401 Market St., Suite 262, Philadelphia 19104. SAN 322-3000. Tel. 215-382-7031, fax 215-382-0022, e-mail palinet@shrsys.hslc.org. *Exec. Dir.* James E. Rush; *Mgr. OCLC and Info. Services* Meryl Cinnamon.

Pennsylvania Citizens for Better Libraries (PCBL), 806 West St., Homestead 15120. SAN 372-8285. Tel. 412-461-1322, fax 412-461-1250. *Chief Exec. Officer* Sharon A. Alberts.

Pennsylvania Community College Library Consortium, c/o Bucks County Community College, Swamp Rd., Newtown 18940. SAN 329-3939. Tel. 215-968-8004, fax 215-968-8005. *Pres.* James Linksz.

Pennsylvania Library Association, 1919 N. Front St., Harrisburg 17102. SAN 372-8145. Tel. 717-233-3113, fax 717-233-3121. *Exec. Dir.* Glenn R. Miller; *Pres.* Mary Anne Fedrick.

Philadelphia Area Consortium of Special Collections Libraries (PACSCL), College of Physicians of Philadelphia, 19 S. 22 St., Philadelphia 19103. SAN 370-7504. Tel. 215-563-3737, ext. 246, fax 215-561-6477. *Chair Exec. Committee* Thomas Horrocks.

Pittsburgh Council on Higher Education (PCHE), 3814 Forbes Ave., Pittsburgh 15213-3506. SAN 322-3019. Tel. 412-683-7905, fax 412-648-1492. *Exec. Dir.* Betty K. Hunter.

Pittsburgh-East Hospital Library Cooperative, Harmarville Rehabilitation Center, Guys Run Rd., Box 11460, Pittsburgh 15238. SAN 322-3027. Tel. 412-826-2741. *Pres.* Valerie Gross.

Southeastern Pennsylvania Theological Library Association (SEPTLA), c/o Saint Charles Borromeo Seminary, Ryan Memorial Lib., 100 E. Wynnewood Rd., Wynnewood 19096-3012. SAN 371-0793. Tel. 610-667-3394, ext. 274, fax 610-664-7913. *Pres.* Lorena Boylan.

State System of Higher Education Libraries Council (SSHELCO), c/o Louis L. Manderind Lib., California Univ. of Pennsylvania, California 15419-1394. SAN 322-2918. Tel. 412-938-4096, fax 412-938-5901. *Chair* William L. Beck.

Susquehanna Library Cooperative, c/o Susquehanna Univ., 415 University Ave., Selingrove 17870-1050. SAN 322-3051. Tel. 717-372-4320, e-mail gunning@einstein.susqu.edu. *Pres.* Kathleen Gunning; *Treas.* Brian Bunnett.

Tri-State College Library Cooperative (TCLC), c/o Rosemont College Lib., 1400 Montgomery Ave., Rosemont 19010-1699. SAN 322-3078. Tel. 610-525-0796, fax 610-525-1939. *Coord.* Ellen Gasiewski.

Rhode Island

Association of Rhode Island Health Sciences Librarians (ARIHSL), Health Sciences Lib., Memorial Hospital, 111 Brewster St., Pawtucket 02860. SAN 371-0742. Tel. 401-729-2211, fax 401-729-3383. *Pres.* Carolyn Mills.

Consortium of Rhode Island Academic and Research Libraries (CRIARL), Box 40041, Providence 02940-0041. SAN 322-3086. Tel. 401-865-2244, fax 401-865-2823, e-mail amaxwell@acad.bryant.edu. *Pres.* Edgar C. Bailey, Jr.

Cooperating Libraries Automated Network (CLAN), c/o Providence Public Lib., 225 Washington St., Providence 02903. SAN 329-4560. Tel. 401-455-8044, 455-8085, 732-7687, fax 401-455-8080. *Chair* Donna Dufault; *V. Chair* Mary Ellen Hardiman.

North Atlantic Health Sciences Libraries, Inc. (NAHSL), Sciences Lib., Box I, Brown Univ., Providence 02912. SAN 371-0599. Tel. 401-863-3334, fax 401-863-2753. *Chair* Tovach Reis; *Chair-Elect* Laurie Fornes.

Rhode Island Library Network (RHILINET), 300 Richmond St., Providence 02903-4222. SAN 371-6821. Tel. 401-277-2726, fax 401-831-1131. *Dir.* Barbara Weaver; *Deputy Dir.* Dorothy Frechette.

South Carolina

Catawba-Wateree Area Health Education Consortium, 1228 Colonial Commons, Box 2049, Lancaster 29721. SAN 329-3971. Tel. 803-286-4121, fax 803-286-4165. *Libn.* Martha Williams.

Columbia Area Medical Librarians' Association (CAMLA), Professional Lib., Box 202, Columbia 29202. SAN 372-9400. Tel. 803-734-7136, fax 803-734-7087. *Coord.* Neeta N. Shah.

South Carolina AHEC Consortium, 171 Ashley Ave., Charleston 29425. SAN 329-3998. Tel. 803-792-4431, fax 803-792-4430. *Exec. Dir.* G. Dean Claghorn.

South Carolina Library Network, South Carolina State Lib., 1500 Senate St., Box 11469, Columbia 29211-1469. SAN 322-4198. Tel. 803-734-8666, fax 803-734-8676. *State Libn.* James B. Johnson, Jr.; *Dir. Network Services* Lea Walsh.

Upper Savannah AHEC Medical Library, Self Memorial Hospital, 1325 Spring St., Greenwood 29646. SAN 329-4110. Tel. 864-227-4851, fax 864-227-4838. *Libn.* Thomas Hill.

South Dakota

South Dakota Library Network (SDLN), Univ. Sta., Box 9672, Spearfish 57799-9672. SAN 371-2117. Tel. 605-642-6835, fax 605-642-6298. *Operations Dir.* Gary Johnson.

Tennessee

Association of Memphis Area Health Science Libraries (AMAHSL), c/o Health Sciences Lib., Le Bonheur Children's Medical Center, 50 N. Dunlap Ave., Memphis 38103. SAN 323-9802. Tel. 901-572-3167, fax 901-572-5203. *Pres.* Kerry Palmertree; *Asst. Dir.* Deborah Heath.

Consortium of Southern Biomedical Libraries (CONBLS), Meharry Medical College, 1005 Dr. D. B. Todd Blvd., Nashville 37208. SAN 370-7717. Tel. 615-327-6728, fax 615-321-2932. *Treas.* Cheryl Hamburg.

Knoxville Area Health Sciences Library Consortium (KAHSLC), ORAU Medical Lib., Box 117, Oakridge 37831. SAN 371-0556. Tel. 423-576-3070, fax 423-576-3194. *Pres.* Rana Dole.

Mid-Tennessee Health Science Librarians Consortium, Saint Thomas Hospital, Box 380, Nashville 37202. SAN 329-5028. Tel.

615-222-6658, fax 615-222-6765. *Pres.* Alice Lovvorn.
Tennessee Health Science Library Association (THeSLA), St. Jude's Children's Research Hospital, Biomed Lib., 332 N. Lauderdale, Memphis 38105-2794. SAN 371-0726. Tel. 901-495-3388, fax 901-495-3117, e-mail FORBESEH@CTRVAX. vanderbilt.edu. *Pres.* Cindy Suter.
Tri-Cities Area Health Sciences Libraries Consortium, East Tennessee State Univ., James H. Quillen College of Medicine, Medical Lib., Box 70693, Johnson City 37614-0693. SAN 329-4099. Tel. 423-929-6252, fax 423-461-7025. *Dir.* Janet S. Fisher.
West Tennessee Academic Library Consortium, c/o Jackson State Community College Lib., 2046 N. Pkwy., Jackson 38301. SAN 322-3175. Tel. 901-425-2615, fax 901-425-2647. *Chair* Scott Cohen.

Texas

Abilene Library Consortium, ACU Sta., Box 8177, Abilene 79699-8177. SAN 322-4694. Tel. 915-674-6525, fax 915-674-2202, e-mail gillette@alcon.acu.edu. *System Mgr.* Robert Gillette.
Alliance for Higher Education Alliance, Suite 250, LB 107, 17103 Preston Rd., Dallas 75248-1373. SAN 322-3337. Tel. 214-713-8170, fax 214-713-8209. *Pres.* Allan Watson.
AMIGOS Bibliographic Council, Inc., 12200 Park Central Dr., Suite 500, Dallas 75251. SAN 322-3191. Tel. 214-851-8000, fax 214-991-6061. *Exec. Dir.* Bonnie Juergens.
APLIC International Census Network, c/o Population Research Center, 1800 Main Bldg., Univ. of Texas, Austin 78713. SAN 370-0690. Tel. 512-471-8335, fax 512-471-4886. *Dir.* Gera Draaijer; *Libn.* Diane Fisher.
Council of Research and Academic Libraries (CORAL), Box 290236, San Antonio 78280-1636. SAN 322-3213. Tel. 210-341-1366, fax 210-341-4519. *Pres.* Cliff Dawdy.
Del Norte Biosciences Library Consortium, c/o Reference Dept., Lib., Univ. of Texas at El Paso, 500 W. Univ., El Paso 79968-0582. SAN 322-3302. Tel. 915-747-6714, fax 915-747-5327, e-mail emoreno@mail. uted.edu. *Pres.* Esperanza A. Moreno.

Forest Trail Library Consortium, Inc. (FTLC), 222 W. Cotton St., Longview 75601. SAN 374-6283. Tel. 903-237-1340. *Pres.* Ron Heezen; *V.P.-Pres.-Elect* Brenda Russell.
Harrington Library Consortium, Box 447, Amarillo 79178. SAN 329-546X. Tel. 806-371-5135, fax 803-345-5678. *Exec. Dir.* Roseann Perez.
Health Library Information Network, Saint Paul Medical Center CB, Sacher Lib., 5909 Harry Hines Blvd., Dallas 75235. SAN 322-3299. Tel. 214-879-2390, fax 214-879-3154. *Chair* Brenda Mahar.
Health Oriented Libraries of San Antonio (HOLSA), Briscoe Lib., Univ. of Texas Health Sciences Center, 7703 Floyd Curl Dr., San Antonio 78284. SAN 373-5907. Tel. 210-567-2425, fax 210-567-2490. *Pres.* Dorothy Jobe.
Houston Area Research Library Consortium (HARLiC), c/o Moody Medical Lib., Univ. Texas Medical Branch, Galveston 77555-1035. SAN 322-3329. Tel. 409-772-2371, fax 409-762-9782. *Pres.* Brett Kirkpatrick.
National Network of Libraries of Medicine–South Central Region, c/o HAM-TMC Lib., 1133 M. D. Anderson Blvd., Houston 77030-2809. SAN 322-3353. Tel. 713-790-7053, fax 713-790-7030, e-mail nnlm.library.tmc.edu. *Contact* Mary Ryan.
Northeast Texas Library System (NETLS), 625 Austin, Garland 75040-6365. SAN 370-5943. Tel. 214-205-2566, fax 214-205-2523. *Dir.* Claire Bausch; *Coord.* Dale Fleeger.
Piasano Consortium, Victoria College, Univ. of Houston at Victoria, 2602 N. Ben Jordan, Victoria 77901-5699. SAN 329-4943. Tel. 512-573-3291, 576-3151, fax 512-788-6227. *Coord.* Joe F. Dahlstrom.
South Central Academic Medical Libraries Consortium (SCAMEL), Univ. of North Texas Health Science Center, Gibson D. Lewis Health Science Lib., 3500 Camp Bowie Blvd., Fort Worth 76107. SAN 372-8269. Tel. 817-735-2380, fax 817-735-5158. *Chair* Janet Minnerath; *Chair-Elect* Audrey Newcomer.
Texas Council of State University Librarians, Texas Tech Univ. Lib., Lubbock 79409-

0002. SAN 322-337X. Tel. 806-742-2261, fax 806-742-0737. *Pres.* Dale Cluff.

TEXNET, Box 12927, Austin 78711. SAN 322-3396. Tel. 512-463-5465, fax 512-463-5436. *Mgr.* Rebecca Linton.

USDA Southwest Regional Document Delivery System, c/o ILS, Texas A&M Univ. Lib., College Station 77843-5000. SAN 322-340X. Tel. 409-862-1842, fax 409-862-1841, e-mail raschke@tamu.edu or raschke@tamvm1.bitnet. *ILL Head* Kathy M. Jackson; *Document Delivery* Linda Deason.

Utah

FS-INFO, Intermountain Research Sta., 324 25th St., Ogden 84401. SAN 322-032X. Tel. 801-625-5445, fax 801-625-5129. *Coord.* Carol A. Ayer.

Utah Academic Library Consortium (UALC), Stewart Lib., Weber State Univ., Ogden 84408. SAN 322-3418. Tel. 801-626-6403, fax 801-626-7045. *Chair* Joan Hubbard.

Utah Health Sciences Library Consortium, c/o Eccles Health Science Lib., Univ. of Utah, Salt Lake City 84112. SAN 376-2246. Tel. 581-8771, fax 801-581-3632. *Chair* Joan Stoddart.

Vermont

Vermont Resource Sharing Network, c/o Vermont Dept. of Libraries, 109 State St., Montpelier 05609-0601. SAN 322-3426. Tel. 802-828-3261, fax 802-828-2199. *Contact* Marjorie Zunder.

Virginia

American Gas Association–Library Services (AGA-LSC), 1515 Wilson Blvd., Arlington 22209. SAN 371-0890. Tel. 703-841-8400, fax 703-841-8406. *Dir.* Steven Dorner.

Defense Technical Information Center, 8725 John J. Kingman Rd., Fort Belvoir 22060-6218. SAN 322-3442. Tel. 703-767-8274, fax 703-767-9070. *Administrator* Kurt N. Molholm.

Huntington Health Science Library Consortium, Marshall Univ. Health Science Libraries, Huntington 25755-9210. SAN 322-4295. Tel. 304-696-3170, fax 304-696-6740. *Chair* Edward Dzierzak.

Lynchburg Area Library Cooperative, Lynchburg College, Knight-Capron Lib., 1501 Lakeside Dr., Lynchburg 24501. SAN 322-3450. Tel. 804-544-8441, fax 804-544-8499. *Chair* Virginia Dunn; *Secy.* Allyson Williams.

Lynchburg Information Online Network, c/o Knight-Capron Lib., Lynchburg College, Lynchburg 24501. SAN 374-6097. Tel. 804-544-8398, fax 804-544-8499. *Project Dir.* John G. Jaffe; *System Administrator* Marjorie Freeman.

Metropolitan Area Collection Development Consortium (MCDAC), c/o Arlington County Dept. of Libs., 1015 N. Quincy St., Arlington 22201. SAN 323-9748. Tel. 703-358-5981, fax 703-358-5998. *Chief Materials Mgt. Div.* Eleanor K. Pourron.

Questel Orbit, Inc., 8000 Westpark Dr., McLean 22102. SAN 322-2438. Tel. 703-556-7401, fax 703-893-4632. *Pres.* John Jenkins.

Richmond Academic Library Consortium (RALC), Virginia State Univ., Box 9406, Petersburg 23806. SAN 371-3938. Tel. 804-524-5040, fax 804-524-5482, e-mail estephens@vsu.edu. *Dean Lib. and Tech. Services* Elsie Stephens.

Richmond Area Film-Video Cooperative, c/o Union Theological Seminary, 3401 Brook Rd., Richmond 23227. SAN 322-3469. Tel. 804-278-4324, fax 804-355-3919. *Pres.* Ann Knox.

Richmond Area Libraries Cooperative, c/o J. Sargeant Reynolds Community College, Box 85622, Richmond 23285. SAN 375-8729. Tel. 804-371-3220.

Southside Virginia Library Network (SVLN), Longwood College, 201 High St., Farmville 23909-1897. SAN 372-8242. Tel. 804-395-2433, fax 804-395-2453. *Dir.* Calvin J. Boyer; *Head Tech. Services* Rebecca R. Laine.

Southwestern Virginia Health Information Librarians (SWVAHILI), c/o Southwestern Virginia Mental Health Institute, Marion 24354. SAN 323-9527. Tel. 540-783-1200, ext. 161, fax 540-783-9712. *Chair* Alice Hurlebaus; *Secy.-Treas.* Mary Horner.

United States Army Training and Doctrine Command (TRADOC) Library and Information Network (TRALINET) Center, ATBO-N, Bldg. 5, Rm. A203, Fort Monroe 23651-5000. SAN 322-418X. Tel. 804-727-4491, fax 804-727-2750. *Systems Libn.* Edwin Burgess; *Dir.* Janet Scheitle.
Virginia Library and Information Network (VLIN), c/o The Lib. of Virginia, 11 St. at Capitol Sq., Richmond 23219-3491. SAN 373-0921. Tel. 804-786-2320, fax 804-225-4608. *State Libn.* Nolan T. Yelich.
Virginia Private College Libraries, c/o Mary Helen Cochran Lib., Sweet Briar College, Sweet Briar 24595. SAN 374-6089. Tel. 804-381-6139, fax 804-381-6173. *Convener* John G. Jaffe.
Virginia Tidewater Consortium for Higher Education, 5215 Hampton Blvd., Health Science Bldg., Rm. 129, Norfolk 23529-0293. SAN 329-5486. Tel. 804-683-3183, fax 804-683-4515. *Pres.* Lawrence G. Dotolo.

Washington

Consortium for Automated Library Services (CALS), Evergreen State College Lib. L2300, Olympia 98505. SAN 329-4528. Tel. 360-866-6000, ext. 6260, fax 360-866-6790, e-mail metcalfs@milton.u.washington.edu. *Systems Mgr.* Steven A. Metcalf.
Council on Botanical Horticultural Libraries, Lawrence Pierce Lib., Rhododendron Species Federation, 2525 S. 336 St., Box 3798, Federal Way 98063-3798. SAN 371-0521. Tel. 206-927-6960, fax 206-838-4686. *Chair* Mrs. George Harrison.
Inland Northwest Health Sciences Libraries (INWHSL), Box 10283, Spokane 99209-0283. SAN 370-5099. Tel. 509-324-7344, fax 509-324-7349, e-mail pringle@wsuvmi.csc.wsu.edu. *Chair* Kathy Schwanz.
Inland Northwest Library Automation Network (INLAN), Foley Center, Gonzaga Univ., Spokane 99258. SAN 375-0124. Tel. 509-328-4220, ext. 3132, fax 509-484-2804. *Contact* Robert Burr.
National Network of Libraries of Medicine–Pacific Northwest Region (NN-LM PNR), Univ. of Washington, Box 357155, Seattle 98195-7155. SAN 322-3485. Tel. 206-543-8262, fax 206-543-2469, e-mail nnlm@u.washington.edu. *Dir.* Sherrilynne S. Fuller.
Spokane Cooperative Library Information System (SCOLIS), E12004 Main, Spokane 99206-5193. SAN 322-3892. Tel. 509-922-1371, fax 509-926-7139. *Mgr.* Linda Dunham.
WLN, Box 3888, Lacey 98509-3888. SAN 322-3507. Tel. 360-923-4000, fax 360-923-4009, e-mail info@wln.com. *Acting Pres.* Paul McCarthy; *Acting Mgr. Customer Service* David Forsythe.

West Virginia

Consortium of South Eastern Law Libraries (COSELL), c/o West Virginia Univ. College of Law Lib., Center Dr., Box 6135, Morgantown 26506-6135. SAN 372-8277. Tel. 304-293-7641, fax 304-293-6020. *Chair* Camille Riley; *Pres.* Thomas Steele.
East Central Colleges, c/o Bethany College, Box AJ, Bethany 26032-1434. SAN 322-2667. Tel. 304-829-7812, fax 304-829-7546. *Exec. Dir.* Dennis Landon.
Mountain States Consortium, c/o Alderson Broaddus College, Philippi 26416. SAN 329-4765. Tel. 304-457-1700. *Treas.* Leonard Lobello.
Southern West Virginia Library Automation Corporation, 221 N. Kanawha St., Box 1876, Beckley 25802. SAN 322-421X. Tel. 304-255-0511, fax 304-255-9161. *Pres.* Tom Brown; *Systems Mgr.* John McPeak.

Wisconsin

Arrowhead Health Sciences Library Network, WITC-Superior/District LRC, 600 N. 21 St., Superior 54880. SAN 322-1954. Tel. 715-394-6677, fax 715-394-3771. *Coord.* Judy Lyons.
Council of Wisconsin Libraries, Inc. (COWL), 728 State St., Rm. 464, Madison 53706-1494. SAN 322-3523. Tel. 608-263-4962, fax 608-263-3684, e-mail schneid@macc.wisc.edu. *Dir.* Kathryn Schneider Michaelis.
Fox River Valley Area Library Consortium, Holy Family Memorial Medical Center, Box 1450, Manitowoc 54221-1450. SAN

322-3531. Tel. 414-684- 2011, ext. 260, fax 414-684-2522. *Coord.* Dan Eckert.

Fox Valley Library Council (FVLC), c/o Outagamie/Wayaaca Lib. System, 225 N. Oneida St., Appleton 54911. SAN 323-9640. Tel. 414-832-6190, fax 414-832-6422. *Pres.* Karen Probst.

Library Council of Metropolitan Milwaukee, Inc., 814 W. Wisconsin Ave., Milwaukee 53233. SAN 322-354X. Tel. 414-271-8470, fax 414-286-2794, e-mail ricec@vms.csd.mu.edu. *Exec. Dir.* Corliss Rice.

North East Wisconsin Intertype Libraries, Inc. (NEWIL), c/o Nicolet Federated Lib. System, 515 Pine St., Green Bay 54301. SAN 322-3574. Tel. 414-448-4412, fax 414-448-4420, e-mail howet@uwgb.edu. *Coord.* Terrie Howe.

South Central Wisconsin Health Science Library Cooperative, Department of Surgery Lib., 600 Highland Ave., G5/316, Madison 53792. SAN 322-4686. Tel. 608-263-7309. *Coord.* Bronte Moran.

Southeastern Wisconsin Health Science Library Consortium, c/o Sinai-Samaritan Medical Center, Hurwitz Memorial Lib., Box 0342, Milwaukee 53201-0342. SAN 322-3582. Tel. 414-283-6710. *Contact* Mary Jo Baertschy.

Southeastern Wisconsin Information Technology Exchange, Inc. (SWITCH), 6801 N. Yates Rd., Milwaukee 53217-3985. SAN 371-3962. Tel. 414-351-2423, fax 414-352-6062. *Exec. Dir.* David Weinberg-Kinsey.

Wisconsin Area Research Center Network ARC Network, 816 State St., Madison 53706. SAN 373-0875. Tel. 608-264-6480, fax 608-264-6486. *State Archivist* Peter Gottlieb.

Wisconsin Interlibrary Services (WILS), 728 State St., Rm. 464, Madison 53706-1494. SAN 322-3612. Tel. 608-263-4962, fax 608-263-3684, e-mail schneid@macc.wisc.edu. *Dir.* Kathryn Schneider Michaelis; *Asst. Dir.* Mary Williamson.

Wisconsin Valley Library Service (WVLS), 300 N. First St., Wausau 54403. SAN 371-3911. Tel. 715-847-5549, fax 715-845-4270. *Dir.* Heather Ann Eldred; *Administrator* Fay Maas.

Wyoming

Health Sciences Information Network (HSIN), Univ. of Wyoming, 205 Coe Lib., Box 3334, Laramie 82071-3334. SAN 371-4861. Tel. 307-766-6537, fax 307-766-3062. *Coord.* Janice Gahagan.

Northeastern Wyoming Medical Library Consortium, Campbell County Memorial Hospital, Box 3011, Gillette 82716. SAN 370-484X. Tel. 307-682-8811, ext. 183, fax 307-687-5182. *Chair* Dorothy O'Brien.

WYLD Network, c/o Wyoming State Lib., Supreme Court and State Lib. Bldg., Cheyenne 82002. SAN 371-0661. Tel. 307-777-7281, fax 307-777-6289. *State Libn.* Helen Meadors Maul.

Virgin Islands

VILINET (Virgin Islands Library and Information Network), c/o Division of Libs., Museums and Archives, 23 Dronningens Gade, Saint Thomas 00802. SAN 322-3639. Tel. 809-774-3407 (DLMAS), 774-3725, fax 809-775-1887. *Chair* Jeanette Allis Bastian.

Canada

Alberta

Alberta Association of College Librarians (AACL), Grant MacEwan Community College, Box 1796, Edmonton T5J 2P2. SAN 370-0763. Tel. 403-497-5894, fax 403-497-5895, e-mail lloydp@admin.gmcc.ab.ca. *Chair* Patricia Lloyd.

Alberta Government Libraries Council (AGLC), c/o Alberta Public Safety Service Lib., 10320 146th St., Edmonton T5N 3A2. SAN 370-0372. Tel. 403-451-7178, fax 403-451-7199. *Chair* Teresa Richey.

Northern Alberta Health Libraries Association (NAHLA), c/o Lib. Services, Alberta Health, 10025 Jasper Ave., Box 2222, Edmonton T5J 2P4. SAN 370-5951. Tel. 403-427-8720, fax 403-427-1643. *Pres.* Peggy Yeh.

British Columbia

British Columbia College and Institute Library Services, Vancouver Community College, Langara Campus Lib., 100 W. 49 Ave., Vancouver V5Y 2Z6. SAN 329-6970. Tel. 604-323-5237, fax 604-323-5544. *Contact* Phyllis Mason.

Central Vancouver Librarian Group (CVLG), Univ. of British Columbia Lib., Centre-Serials, Box 2119, Vancouver V6V 3T5. SAN 323-9543. Tel. 604-822-4578, fax 604-822-3201. *Chair* Kat McGrath.

Media Exchange Cooperative (MEC), Langara College, 100 W. 49 Ave., Vancouver V5Y 2Z6. SAN 329-6954. Tel. 604-323-5459, fax 604-323-5577. *Pres.* Linda Prince.

Manitoba

Manitoba Government Libraries Council (MGLC), 200-401 York Ave., Winnipeg R3C 0P8. SAN 371-6848. Tel. 204-945-0580, fax 204-945-4556. *Chair* Jean Van Walleghem.

Manitoba Library Consortium, Inc. (MLCI), c/o Aikins, MacAulay & Thorvaldson, Commodity Exchange Tower, 360 Main St., Winnipeg R3C 4G1. SAN 372-820X. Tel. 204-632-2232. *V. Chair* Iris Loewen.

New Brunswick

Maritimes Health Libraries Association (MHLA/ABSM), Dr. Everett Chalmers Hospital, Box 9000, Fredrickton E3B 5N5. SAN 370-0836. Tel. 506-452-5432, fax 506-452-5571. *Pres.* Paul Clark.

Nova Scotia

Council of Metropolitan University Librarians (COMUL), Technical Univ. of Nova Scotia, Box 1000, Halifax B3J 2X4. SAN 370-0704. Tel. 902-420-7500, fax 902-420-7551. *Chair* Donna Richardson.

Novanet, 1379 Seymour St., Halifax B3H 3J5. SAN 372-4050. Tel. 902-494-1785, fax 902-494-1536, e-mail novanet@ac.dal.ca. *System Supervisor* Scott W. Nickerson.

Ontario

Bibliocentre, 80 Cowdray Ct., Scarborough M1S 4N1. SAN 322-3663. Tel. 416-289-5151, fax 416-299-0902, e-mail admw@cenvmc.cencol.on.ca. *Dir.* Annetta Protain.

Canadian Association of Research Libraries (CARL/ABRC), Univ. of Ottawa, Morisset Hall, Rm. 602, 65 University St., Ottawa K1N 9A5. SAN 323-9721. Tel. 613-562-5800, ext. 3652, fax 613-562-5195, e-mail Internet: carl-acadvm1.uottawa.ca. *Interim Exec. Dir.* Timothy Mark.

Canadian Health Libraries Association (CHLA-ABSC), Office of Secretariat, 3332 Yonge St., Box 94038, Toronto M4N 3R1. SAN 370-0720. Tel. 416-485-0377, fax 416-485-0377. *Pres.* Lea Starr.

Canadian Heritage Information Network (CHIN), Dept. of Canadian Heritage, Journal Tower S., 365 Laurier Ave. W., 14th fl., Ottawa K1A 0C8. SAN 329-3076. Tel. Tel 613-992-3333, fax 613-952-2318, e-mail service@chin.gc.ca. *Dir. Gen.* Lyn Elliot Sherwood; *Dir. Info. Services* Bruce Williams.

County and Regional Municipal Library (CARML), c/o Lennox and Addington County Lib., 97 Thomas St. E., Napanee K7R 3S9. SAN 323-9705. Tel. 613-354-2585, fax 613-354-3112. *Chair* Beth Ross; *Secy.* Mary Anne Evans.

Disability Resource Library Network (DRLN), c/o North York Public Lib., 5120 Yonge St., North York M2N 5N9. SAN 323-9837. Tel. 416-395-5581, fax 416-395-5669. *Chair* Joan McCathy.

Education Libraries Sharing of Resources–A Network (ELSOR), 45 York Mills Rd., Willowdale M2P 1B6. SAN 370-0399. Tel. 416-397-2523, fax 416-397-2640. *Chair* Catherine Spiridanov.

Hamilton and District Health Library Network, c/o Health Sciences Lib., McMaster Univ., Hamilton L8N 3Z5. SAN 370-5846. Tel. 905-525-9140, ext. 22322, fax 905-528-3733. *Network Coord.* Linda Panton.

Health Science Information Consortium of Toronto, Univ. of Toronto, 7 King's College Circle, Toronto M5S 1A5. SAN 370-5080. Tel. 416-978-6359, fax 416-971-

2637, e-mail leishman@vax.library.utoronto.ca. *Exec. Dir.* Joan L. Leishman.

Hi-Tech Libraries Network, c/o Cal Corp, 1050 Morrison Dr., Ottawa K2H 8K7. SAN 323-9586. Tel. 613-820-8280, fax 613-820-8314. *Contact* Sandra Spence.

Information Network for Ontario, Ministry of Culture, Tourism and Recreation, Libs. and Community Information Branch, 77 Bloor St. W., 3rd fl., Toronto M7A 2R9. SAN 329-5605. Tel. 416-314-7611, fax 416-314-7635. *Dir.* Barbara Clubb.

Kingston Area Health Libraries Association (KAHLA), c/o Staff Lib., Kingston Psychiatric Hospital, Bag 603, Kingston K7L 4X3. SAN 370-0674. Tel. 613-546-1101, ext. 5745, fax 613-548-5588. *Pres.* Karen Gagnon.

Ontario Council of University Libraries (OCUL), Univ. of Ottawa, 65 University St., Ottawa K1N 9A5. SAN 371-9413. Tel. 613-562-5883, fax 613-562-5195. *Chair* Richard Greene.

Ontario Hospital Libraries Association (OHLA), c/o Ottawa General Hospital Medical Lib., 501 Smyth Rd., Ottawa K1H 8L6. SAN 370-0739. Tel. 613-737-8529, fax 416-429-1363. *Pres.* Jesse McGowan.

QL Systems Limited, 1 Gore St., Box 2080, Kingston K7L 5J8. SAN 322-368X. Tel. 613-549-4611, fax 613-548-4260. *Pres.* Hugh Lawford.

Shared Library Services (SLS), South Huron Hospital, Shared Lib. Services, 24 Huron St. W., Exeter N0M 1S2. SAN 323-9500. Tel. 519-235-2700, ext. 249, fax 519-235-3405. *Dir.* Linda Wilcox.

Sheridan Park Association Library and Information Science Committee (SPA-LISC), 2275 Speakman Dr., Mississauga L5K 1B1. SAN 370-0437. Tel. 905-823-6160, fax 905-823-6160. *Chair* Carolyne Sidey.

Southern Ontario Library Service–Richmond Hill (SOLS), 55 W. Beaver Creek, Unit 50, Richmond Hill L4E 1K5. SAN 371-0629. Tel. 905-771-1522. *Dir.* L. Irvine.

Toronto Health Libraries Association (THLA), Box 94056, Toronto M4N 3R1. SAN 323-9853. Tel. 416-978-2872. *Pres.* Elaine Wright.

Toronto School of Theology, c/o Wycliffe College, 5 Hoskin Ave., Toronto M5S 1H7. SAN 322-452X. Tel. 416-979-2870, fax 416-979-0471. *Secy. Lib. Committee* Cindy Derrenbacker.

Wellington Waterloo Dufferin (WWD) Health Library Network, c/o William Howitt Memorial Lib., Guelph General Hospital, 115 Delhi St., Guelph N1E 4S4. SAN 370-0496. Tel. 519-822-5350, ext. 215. *Coord.* Brenda Vegso.

Quebec

Association des Bibliothèques de la Santé Affiliées à l'Université de Montréal (ABSAUM), c/o Health Lib., Univ. of Montreal, Montreal H3C 3J7. SAN 370-5838. Tel. 514-343-6826, fax 514-343-2350. *Secy.* Danielle Tardif.

Center for Information Technology Innovation (CITI), 1575 Blvd., Chomedy, Laval H7V 2X2. SAN 327-9111. Tel. 514-973-5700, fax 514-682-3400.

McGill Medical and Health Libraries Association (MMAHLA), c/o Saint Mary's Hospital Health Sciences Lib., 3830 Lacombe Ave., Rm. 1501, Montreal H3T 1M5. SAN 374-6100. Tel. 514-345-3317, fax 514-345-3695. *Co-Chairs* Jeannine Lawlor, Elizabeth Lamont.

Montreal Health Libraries Association (MHLA), Univ. of Montreal, Box 6128, Montreal H3C 3J7. SAN 323-9608. Tel. 514-343-6180. *Pres.* Johanne Hopper.

Montreal Medical Online Users Group (MMOUG), McGill Health Sciences Lib., 3655 Drummond St., Montreal H3G 1Y6. SAN 370-0771. Tel. 514-398-4757, fax 514-398-3890. *Coord.* Angella Lambrou.

Saskatchewan

Saskatchewan Government Libraries Council (SGLC), c/o Saskatchewan Agriculture and Food Lib., 3085 Albert St., Regina S4S 0B1. SAN 323-956X. Tel. 306-787-5151, fax 306-787-0216, e-mail ENVOY 100SK.AG. LIB. *Chair* Helene Stewart.

National Library and Information-Industry Associations, United States and Canada

American Association of Law Libraries

Executive Director, Roger Parent
53 W. Jackson Blvd., Suite 940, Chicago, IL 60604
312-939-4764, fax 312-431-1097
e-mail aallhq@aol.com

Object

The American Association of Law Libraries (AALL) is established for educational and scientific purposes. It shall be conducted as a nonprofit corporation to promote and enhance the value of law libraries to the public, the legal community, and the world; to foster the profession of law librarianship; to provide leadership in the field of legal information; and to foster a spirit of cooperation among the members of the profession. Established 1906.

Membership

Memb. 5,000. Persons officially connected with a law library or with a law section of a state or general library, separately maintained. Associate membership available for others. Dues (Indiv., Indiv. Assoc., and Inst.) $126; (Inst. Assoc.) $242 times the number of members; (Retired) $32.50; (Student) $28; (SIS Memb.) $12 each per year. Year. July 1 to June 30.

Officers

Pres. Frank G. Houdek, School of Law Lib., Southern Illinois Univ., Mail Code 6803, Lesar Law Bldg., Carbondale, IL 62901-6803. Tel. 618-453-8788, fax 618-453-8728, e-mail houdek@siu.edu; *V.P./Pres.-Elect* Judith Meadows, State Law Lib. of Montana, Justice Bldg., 215 N. Sanders, Helena, MT 59620-3004. Tel. 406-444-3660, fax 406-444-3603, e-mail jmeadows@mt.gov; *Past Pres.* Patrick E. Kehoe, Washington College of Law Lib., American Univ., 4801 Massachusetts Ave. N.W., Washington, DC 20016-8182. Tel. 202-274-4374, fax 202-274-4365, e-mail pkehoe@american.edu; *Secy.* Susan P. Siebers, Katten Muchin and Zavis, 525 W. Monroe St., Suite 1600, Chicago, IL 60661-3693. Tel. 312-902-5675, fax 312-902-1626, e-mail ssiebers@kmz.com; *Treas.* Anne W. Grande, Hennepin County Law Lib., C-2451 Government Center, Minneapolis, MN 55487. Tel. 612-348-7977, fax 612-348-4230, e-mail anne.grande@co.hennepin.mn.us.

Executive Board

Shelley L. Dowling (1998), e-mail annex@capcon.net; Nancy P. Johnson (1999), e-mail lawnpj@gsusgi2.gsu.edu; Kathleen S. Martin (1999), e-mail mart7131@mlb.com; Carol Avery Nicholson (1998), e-mail carol_nicholson@unc.edu; Patricia G. Strougal (1997), e-mail pstrouga@ix.netcom.com; Victoria K. Trotta (1997), e-mail victoria.trotta@asu.edu.

Committee Chairpersons

Annual Meeting Program Selection. Donald Jack Dunn.
Awards. D. R. Jones.
Bylaws. Alvin M. Podboy, Jr.
Call for Papers. Katharine Ewing.
Chapter Relations (Ad Hoc Advisory Group). Sarah Holterhoff.
Citation Format. Marcia J. Koslov.
Copyright. James S. Heller.
Diversity. Cossette T. Sun.
Government Relations. Susan E. Tulis.
Grants. John D. Edwards.
Index to Foreign Legal Periodicals (Advisory). Milagros Rush.

Indexing Periodical Literature (Advisory). Daniel L. May.
Information Technology and Implementation (Ad Hoc Working Group). Timothy L. Coggins.
Law Library Journal and AALL Spectrum (Advisory). Joe K. Stephens.
Local Arrangements (Advisory). Emily R. Greenberg.
Mentoring and Retention. Karen M. Moss.
Nominations. Rita R. Dermody.
Placement. Joyce Manna Janto.
Preservation. Willis C. Meredith.
Professional Development. Kay Moller Todd.
Professional Education Series (Advisory). Roy M. Mersky; Bob Willard.
Public Relations. Michelle Schmidt.
Publications Policy. Mary Ann Nelson.
Publications Review. Marsha Baum.
Recruitment. Madison Mosley, Jr.
Relations with Information Vendors. Janeen M. Heath.
Research. Mary B. Jensen.
Scholarships. Patricia Wellinger.
Statistics. Helena W. Lai.

Special-Interest Section Chairpersons

Academic Law Libraries. Sara Robbins.
Computing Services. James Milles.
Foreign, Comparative, and International Law. Margareta Horiba.
Government Documents. David Gay.
Legal History and Rare Books. Gretchen Feltes.
Legal Information Services to the Public. David McFadden.
Micrographics and Audiovisual. Laura Ray.
Online Bibliographic Services. Sally H. Wambold.
Private Law Libraries. Michael Saint-Onge.
Research Instruction and Patron Services. Duane A. Strojny.
SIS Council. Anne K. Myers.
Social Responsibility. D. Prano Amjadi.
State Court and County Law Libraries. Frank Alan Herch.
Technical Services. James A. Mumm.

American Library Association

Executive Director, Elizabeth Martinez
50 E. Huron St., Chicago, IL 60611
800-545-2433, 312-280-3215, fax 312-944-3897
World Wide Web http://www.ala.org

Object

The mission of the American Library Association (ALA) is to provide leadership for the development, promotion, and improvement of library and information services and the profession of librarianship in order to enhance learning and ensure access to information for all. Founded 1876.

Membership

Memb. (Indiv.) 53,961; (Inst.) 2,742; (Total) 56,703. Any person, library, or other organization interested in library service and librarians. Dues (Indiv.) 1st year, $48; 2nd year, $71, 3rd year and later, $95; (Trustee and Assoc. Memb.) $43; (Student) $24; (Foreign Indiv.) $57; (Other) $33; (Inst.) $70 and up, depending on operating expenses of institution.

Officers (1996–1997)

Pres. Mary R. Somerville, Dir., Miami-Dade Public Lib. System, 101 W. Flagler St., Miami, FL 33130-1523. Tel. 305-375-5026, fax 305-375-5545, e-mail mspres@dcfreenet.seflin.lib.fl.us; *Pres.-Elect* Barbara J. Ford, Exec. Dir., Univ. Lib. Services, Virginia Commonwealth Univ., 901 Park Ave., Box 842033, Richmond, VA 23284-2033. Tel. 804-828-1107, fax 804-828-0151, e-mail bjford@gems.vcu.edu; *Immediate Past Pres.* Betty J. Turock, Professor, Lib. and Info. Studies, Rutgers SCILS, 4 Huntington St., New Brunswick, NJ 08903. Tel. 908-632-3836, fax 908-932-1134, e-mail bturock@scils.rutgers.edu; *Treas.* Bruce E. Daniels, Onondaga County Public Lib. at the Galleries, 447 S. Salina St., Syracuse, NY 13202-2494. Tel. 315-435-1800, fax 315-435-8533, e-mail ocplbed@transit.nyser.net; *Exec. Dir.* Elizabeth Martinez, ALA Headquarters, 50 E. Huron St., Chicago, IL 60611. Tel. 312-280-3215, fax 312-944-3897, e-mail emartinez@ala.org.

Executive Board

Charles E. Beard (1997); Charles M. Brown (1999); Martin J. Gomez (1997); Nancy C. Kranich (1998); James G. Neal (2000); Robert R. Newlen (2000); Patricia H. Smith (1999); Evie Wilson-Lingbloom (1998).

Endowment Trustees

Gerald Garbacz (1997); one member to be elected; *Exec. Board Liaison* Ann K. Symons; *Staff Liaison* Elizabeth Martinez.

Divisions

See the separate entries that follow: American Assn. of School Libns.; American Lib. Trustee Assn.; Assn. for Lib. Collections and Technical Services; Assn. for Lib. Service to Children; Assn. of College and Research Libs.; Assn. of Specialized and Cooperative Lib. Agencies; Lib. Admin. and Management Assn.; Lib. and Info. Technology Assn.; Public Lib. Assn.; Reference and User Services Assn.; Young Adult Lib. Services Assn.

Publications

ALA Handbook of Organization and Membership Directory 1996–1997 (ann.).
American Libraries (11 per year; membs.; organizations $60; foreign $70; single copy $6).
Book Links (6 per year; U.S. $20; foreign $22; single copy $3.50).
Booklist (22 per year; U.S. and possessions $65; foreign $85; single copy $4.50).
Choice (11 per year; U.S. $165; foreign $187; single copy $20).

Round Table Chairpersons

(ALA staff liaison is given in parentheses.)
Armed Forces Libraries. Lydia Rives (Patricia A. Muir).
Continuing Library Education Network and Exchange. Amy Bernath (Coleen Sullivan).
Ethnic Materials and Information Exchange. Francesca Hary (Patricia Muir).
Exhibits. John Ison (Diedre Ross).
Federal Librarians. Jane T. Sessa (Patricia A. Muir).
Government Documents. Andrea L. Sevetson (Patricia A. Muir).
Independent Librarians Exchange. Linda Cooper (Coleen Sullivan).
Intellectual Freedom. Frederick J. Stielow (Deborah Liebow).
International Relations. Opritsa Popa (Carol Erickson).
Library History. Nancy Becker Johnson (Mary Jo Lynch).
Library Instruction. Kari M. Lucas (Coleen Sullivan).
Library Research. Ron Powell (Mary Jo Lynch).
Map and Geography. Melissa Lamont (Danielle Alderson).
New Members. Laura Sill (Gerald Hodges).
Social Responsibilities. Wendy Thomas (Satia Orange).
Staff Organizations. Yvonne J. Beever (Coleen Sullivan).
Support Staff Interests. James L. Hill (Coleen Sullivan).
Video. Paula Murphy (Irene Wood).

Committee Chairpersons

Accreditation (Standing). Carla D. Hayden (Prudence W. Dalrymple).
American Libraries Advisory (Standing). Betsy Baker (Leonard Kniffel).

Appointments (Standing). Barbara J. Ford (Emily Melton).
Awards (Standing). Susan S. DiMattia (Daphne Whitehead).
Budget Analysis and Review (Standing). Molly Raphael (Gregory Calloway).
Chapter Relations (Standing). Margaret L. Crist (Gerald Hodges).
Committee on Committees (Elected Council Committee). Barbara J. Ford (Emily Melton).
Conference Comittee. Susan S. Goldberg-Kent (Mary W. Ghikas).
Conference Program (Special). Fred E. Goodman (Mary W. Ghikas).
Constitution and Bylaws (Standing). Pamela Gay Bonnell (Sylvia Kraft-Walker).
Council Orientation. Kathie L. Meizner (Lois Ann Gregory-Wood).
Education. Ling H. Jeng (Coleen Sullivan).
Election. Terri C. Jacobs (Ernest Martin).
Information Technology. Robert Wedgeworth (Andrew Magpantay).
Intellectual Freedom. Ann K. Symons (Judith F. Krug).
International Relations. E. J. Josey (Carol Erickson).
Legislation. Patricia Glass Schuman (Carol C. Henderson).
Library of Congress (Special, advisory). Ann E. Prentice (Carol C. Henderson).
Library Records Retention (ad hoc). Deanna B. Marcum (To be appointed).
Literacy and Outreach. Kathleen de la Pe$a McCook (To be appointed).
Membership. Loretta R. O'Brien (Gerald Hodges).
Minority Concerns and Cultural Diversity. Gloria J. Leonard (To be appointed).
Nominating—1997 Election. Andrew A. Venable, Jr. (Emily I. Melton).
Organization. Marva L. DeLoach (Lois Ann Gregory-Wood).
Pay Equity. Carol K. DiPrete (Coleen Sullvan).
Policy Monitoring. Donald J. Sager (Lois Ann Gregory-Wood).
Professional Ethics. To be appointed (Judith F. Krug).
Public Awareness. Diane Gordon Kadanoff (Linda K. Wallace).
Publishing. Betty-Carol Sellen (Donald Chatham).
Research and Statistics. Marianne Burke (Mary Jo Lynch).
Resolutions. Sally G. Reed (Filippa A. Genovese).
Standards. Irene M. Padilla (Mary Jo Lynch).
Structure Revision (Special). Sarah M. Pritchard (Emily I. Melton).
Status of Women in Librarianship. Naomi Caldwell-Wood (Coleen Sullivan).
User Instruction for Information Literacy. Marcellus Turner (Coleen Sullivan).

Joint Committee Chairpersons

American Association of Law Libraries/American Correctional Association–ASCLA Committee on Institution Libraries (joint). Thea B. Chesley (ACA); To be appointed (ASCLA).
American Federation of Labor/Congress of Industrial Organizations–ALA, Library Service to Labor Groups, RASD. Mary F. Hicks (ALA); To be appointed (AFL/CIO).
Anglo-American Cataloguing Rules Fund. Elizabeth Martinez (ALA); Karen S. Adams (Canadian Lib. Assn.); Ross Shimmon (Library Assn.).
Anglo-American Cataloguing Rules, Joint Steering Committee for Revision of. Brian Schottlaender (ALA), Ralph W. Manning (Canadian Commission on Cataloguing), Margaret Stewart (National Lib. of Canada), Ann Huthwaite (Australian Commission on Cataloguing), Sally Strutt (British Lib.), Barbara B. Tillett (Lib. of Congress).
Association for Educational Communications and Technology–AASL. Daniel D. Barron (AASL), Annette C. Lamb (AECT).
Association of American Publishers–ALA. Mary R. Somerville (ALA); To be appointed (AAP).
Association of American Publishers–ALCTS. Jana L. Longberger (ALCTS); Linda Parise (AAP).
Children's Book Council–ALA. R. Randall Enos (ALA); To be appointed (CBC).
Society of American Archivists–ALA (Joint Committee on Library-Archives Relationships). George Arnold (ALA); William E. Brown, Jr. (SAA).

American Library Association
American Association of School Librarians

Interim Executive Director, Don Adcock
50 E. Huron St., Chicago, IL 60611
312-280-4381, 800-545-2433 ext. 4381, fax 312-664-7459

Object

The American Association of School Librarians (AASL) is interested in the general improvement and extension of library media services for children and young people. AASL has specific responsibility for planning a program of study and service for the improvement and extension of library media services in elementary and secondary schools as a means of strengthening the educational program; evaluation, selection, interpretation, and utilization of media as they are used in the context of the school program; stimulation of continuous study and research in the library field and establishing criteria of evaluation; synthesis of the activities of all units of the American Library Association in areas of mutual concern; representation and interpretation of the need for the function of school libraries to other educational and lay groups; stimulation of professional growth, improvement of the status of school librarians, and encouragement of participation by members in appropriate type-of-activity divisions; conducting activities and projects for improvement and extension of service in the school library when such projects are beyond the scope of type-of-activity divisions, after specific approval by the ALA Council. Established in 1951 as a separate division of ALA.

Membership

Memb. 7,715. Open to all libraries, school library media specialists, interested individuals, and business firms with requisite membership in ALA.

Officers (1996–1997)

Pres. Barbara Stripling, Public Education Foundation, 100 E. Tenth St., Suite 500, Chattanooga, TN 37402. Tel. 423-265-9403, fax 423-265-9832, e-mail bstripli@cecasun.utc.edu; *Pres.-Elect* Ken Haycock, 5118 Meadfield Rd., West Vancouver, BC V7W 3G2, Canada. Tel. 604-822-4991, fax 604-822-6006, e-mail haycock@unixg.ubc.ca; *Treas./Financial Officer* Nancy Zimmerman, School of Lib. and Info. Science, SUNY at Buffalo, 381 Baldy Hall, Buffalo, NY 14051. Tel. 716-645-6474, fax 716-645-3775, e-mail liszimme@ubvms.cc.buffalo.edu; *Secy.* Joie Taylor, Columbus Public School, Box 947, Columbus, NE 68602. Tel. 402-563-7000, fax 402-564-8049, e-mail jtaylor@gilligan.esu7.k12.ne.us; *Past Pres.* David V. Loertscher, School of Lib. and Info. Science, 1 Washington Sq., San Jose, CA 95192. Tel. 408-924-2501, fax 408-924-2476, e-mail davidl@csn.net.

Board of Directors

Officers; Judy Arteaga; Augie Beasley; Susan M. Bryan; Gail Dickinson; Su Eckhardt; Marybeth Green; Ken Haycock; Phyllis Heroy; Judith M. King; Carol Kroll; David Loertscher; Vivian Melton; Drucilla Raines; Jackie Ridings; Barbara Stripling; Joie Taylor; Jean Van Deusen; Barbara Weathers; Ann C. Weeks.

Publications

AASL Presidential Hotline/CONNECTIONS (q.; memb.; not available by subscription).
School Library Media Quarterly (q.; memb.; nonmemb. $40). *Ed.* Mary Kay Biagini, School of Lib. and Info. Sciences, Univ. of Pittsburgh, 135 N. Bellefield Ave., Pittsburgh, PA 15260.

Committee Chairpersons

AASL/Highsmith Research Grant. Jean van Deusen.
ABC-CLIO Leadership Grant. Susan Bryan.
Access Through Technology. Drucie Raines.
Advocacy Task Force. Pam Chesky.
American Univ. Press. Antoinette Negro.
Annual Conference, San Francisco. Dagmar Finkle.
Awards. Bettie Day.
Bylaws. Judy King.
Count on Reading Task Force. Bettie Estes-Rickner.
Distinguished School Administrator's Award. Bernice (Bunny) Yesner.
Distinguished Service Award. Connie Champlin.
Education for School Library Media Specialists. Pauletta Bracy, Selvin Royal.
ELMSS. William Pichette.
Executive Committee. Barbara Stripling.
Frances Henne Award. Jeanie McNamara.
General Conference, Portland, 1997. John McGinnis.
ICONnect Task Force. Pam Berger.
Information Plus Continuing Education Scholarship. Barbara Nemer.
Intellectual Freedom Award. Pat Scales.
Intellectual Freedom Committee. Gail Richmond.
ISS. Kathleen Wilson.
Learning Through the Library. Violet Harada.
Legislation. Blanche Woolls.
Membership Task Force. Gail Dickinson.
Mentoring the Profession Task Force. Joseph Mattie.
Microcomputer in the Media Center Award. Stephen Matthews.
National School Library Media Program of the Year. Sheila Salmon.
National Guidelines: Implementation. Barbara Jeffus.
National Guidelines: Vision. Betty Marcoux.
Nominating Committee, 1997. Marjorie Pappas.
Publications. Frances Bradburn.
Research/Statistics. June Kahler Berry.
Restructuring: Continuing Education. Phyllis Heroy.
Restructuring: Governance. Barbara Weathers.
Retired Members Interest Group. Diane Biesel.
School Librarians' Workshop Scholarship. Anne Hird.
SPVS. Donna Peterson.

American Library Association
American Library Trustee Association

Executive Director, Susan Roman
50 E. Huron St., Chicago, IL 60611-2795
312-280-2161, 800-545-2433 ext. 2161, fax 312-280-3257

Object

The American Library Trustee Association (ALTA) is interested in the development of effective library service for all people in all types of communities and in all types of libraries; it follows that its members are concerned, as policymakers, with organizational patterns of service, with the development of competent personnel, the provision of adequate financing, the passage of suitable legislation, and the encouragement of citizen support for libraries. ALTA recognizes that responsibility for professional action in these fields has been assigned to other divisions of ALA; its specific responsibilities as a division, therefore, are

1. A continuing and comprehensive educational program to enable library trustees to discharge their grave responsibilities in a manner best fitted to benefit the public and the libraries they represent.
2. Continuous study and review of the activities of library trustees.
3. Cooperation with other units within ALA concerning their activities relating to trustees.
4. Encouraging participation of trustees in other appropriate divisions of ALA.

5. Representation and interpretation of the activities of library trustees in contacts outside the library profession, particularly with national organizations and governmental agencies.
6. Promotion of strong state and regional trustee organizations.
7. Efforts to secure and support adequate library funding.
8. Promulgation and dissemination of recommended library policy.
9. Assuring equal access of information to all segments of the population.
10. Encouraging participation of trustees in trustee/library activities, at local, state, regional, and national levels.

Organized 1890. Became an ALA division in 1961.

Membership

Memb. 1,566. Open to all interested persons and organizations. For dues and membership year, see ALA entry.

Officers (1996–1997)

Pres. Virginia M. McCurdy; *1st V.P./Pres.-Elect* Clifford Dittrich; *Past Pres.* Wayne Coco; *Councillor* Judith Baker.

Board of Directors

Officers; *Trustee Voice Ed.* Tari Marshall Sliz (1999); *Regional V.P.s* To be appointed; *Ex officio* Susan Roman.

Staff

Exec. Dir. Susan Roman; *Deputy Exec. Dir.* Lorelle R. Swader; *Admin. Secy.* Dollester Thorp.

Publication

Trustee Voice (q.; memb.). Ed. Tari Marshall Sliz.

American Library Association
Association for Library Collections and Technical Services

Executive Director, Karen Muller
50 E. Huron St., Chicago, IL 60611
800-545-2433 ext. 5031, fax 312-280-3257
e-mail kmuller@ala.org

Object

The Association for Library Collections and Technical Services (ALCTS) is responsible for the following activities: acquisition, identification, cataloging, classification, and preservation of library materials; the development and coordination of the country's library resources; and those areas of selection and evaluation involved in the acquisition of library materials and pertinent to the development of library resources. ALCTS has specific responsibility for:

1. Continuous study and review of the activities assigned to the division.
2. Conduct of activities and projects within its area of responsibility.
3. Syntheses of activities of all units within ALA that have a bearing on the type of activity represented.
4. Representation and interpretation of its type of activity in contacts outside the profession.
5. Stimulation of the development of librarians engaged in its type of activity, and stimulation of participation by members in appropriate type-of-library divisions.
6. Planning and development of programs of study and research for the type of activity for the total profession.

ALCTS will provide its members, other ALA divisions and members, and the library and information community with leadership and a program for action on the access to, and identification, acquisition, description, organization, preservation, and dissemination of information resources in a dynamic collaborative environment. In addition, ALCTS provides forums for discussion, research, and development and opportunities for learning in all of these areas. To achieve this mission, ALCTS has the following organizational goals:

1. To promote the role of the library and information science in an information society.
2. To provide its members with opportunities for information exchange.
3. To promote innovative and effective library education and training, to foster the recruitment of individuals with diverse qualities to library work, and to provide continuing education for librarians and library practitioners.
4. To develop, support, review, and promote standards to meet library and information needs.
5. To provide opportunities for members to participate through research and publications and professional growth.
6. To manage the association effectively and efficiently.

Established 1957; renamed 1988.

Membership

Memb. 5,265. Any member of the American Library Association may elect membership in this division according to the provisions of the bylaws.

Officers (July 1996–July 1997)

Pres. Carol E. Chamberlain, Northeastern Univ., Boston, MA 02115; *V.P./Pres.-Elect* Janet Swan Hill, 450 Oakwood Place, Boulder, CO 80304-1046. Tel. 303-492-1702, fax 303-492-0494, e-mail hilljs@colorado.edu;

Past Pres. David Farrell, 1285 Brighton Ave., Albany, CA 94706.

Address correspondence to the executive director.

Directors

Officers; *Exec. Dir.* Karen Muller; *Past Pres.* David Farrell; *Dirs.-at-Large* Alice J. Allen, Peggy Johnson, Barbara B. Tillett; *ALCTS Councillor* Alexander Bloss; *CRG Rep.* Mary Helen Faust; *Dirs.* Pamela M. Bluh, Thomas F. R. Clareson, Bruce Chr. Johnson, Joseph W. Raker, Edward Shreeves; *Ex-officio* Barry B. Baker, Brian E. Schottlaender, Dale S. Swenson.

Publications

ALCTS Network News (irreg.; free). *Ed.* Karen Whittlesey. Subscribe via listproc@ala.org "subscribe an2 [yourname]."

ALCTS Newsletter (6 per year; memb.; nonmemb. $25). *Ed.* Dale S. Swensen, Lee Lib., Brigham Young Univ., Provo, UT 84602.

Library Resources and Technical Services (q.; memb.; nonmemb. $55). *Ed.* Jennifer A. Younger, Ohio State Univ. Libs., Columbus, OH 43210. Tel. 614-292-6151.

Section Chairpersons

Acquisitions. Joseph Raker.
Cataloging and Classification. Bruce Johnson.
Collection Management and Development. Edward Shreeves.
Preservation and Reformatting. Thomas F. R. Clareson.
Serials. Pamela M. Bluh.

Committee Chairpersons

Association of American Publishers/ALCTS Joint Committee. Jana L. Lonberger, Linda Parise.
Audiovisual. Mary Beth Fecko.
Best of *LRTS*. Paula A. De Stefano.

Blackwell North America Scholarship Award. Karen A. Schmidt.
Budget and Finance. Brian E. Schottlaender.
Catalog Form and Function. Arlene G. Taylor.
Commercial Technical Services. Roxanne J. Sellberg.
Digital Resources. Ann Sandberg-Fox.
Duplicates Exchange Union. Lydia A. Morrow.
Education. Barbara L. Spivey.
International Relations. Sheryl J. Nichin.
Legislation. Derry C. Juneja.
Library Materials Price Index. Gay N. Dannelly.
LRTS Editorial Board. Sally W. Somers.
MARBI. Jacquelene W. Riley.
Membership. Robert McDonald.
Nominating. Sharon C. Bonk.
Organization and Bylaws. David Farrell.
Esther J. Piercy Award Jury. Deana L. Astle.
Planning. Barry B. Baker.
Publications. Bonita Bryant.
Publisher/Vendor Library Relations. Trisha L. Davis.
Research and Statistics. Ruth C. Carter.

Discussion Groups

Authority Control in the Online Environment. James T. Maccaferri.
Automated Acquisitions/In-Process Control Systems. Michele J. Crump.
Cataloging Norms. James D. Le Blanc.
Chief Collection Development Officers of Large Research Libraries. Ross W. Atkinson.
CMDS/PARS. Patricia E. Palmer.
Collection Development Librarians of Academic Lilbraries. John M. Haar, III.
Collection Management and Development in Public Libraries. Sarah C. Duffel, Dorothy E. Pittman.
Cooperative Preservation Programs. Virgilia I. Rawneley.
Creative Ideas in Technical Services. Judy L. Johnson, Margaret Mering.
Gifts and Exchange. Catherine Denning.
Library Binding. Brian G. Baird.
MARC Formats, LITA/ALCTS. Mary Ann E. Van Cura.
Microcomputer Support of Technical Services, LITA/ALCTS. Matthew L. Beacom.
Micropublishers. John R. Brunswick.
Newspaper. Clay G. Dixon.
Out of Print. Bill G. Slater.
PARS. Ann Olszewski, Steven D. Smith.
Physical Quality and Treatment of Library Materials. Julian J. Stam.
Pre-Order and Pre-Catalog Searching. Barbara L. Albee.
Preservation Administration. Wesley L. Boomgaarden, Veronica Colley Cunningham, Julian Stam.
Preservation Course and Workshop Instructors. Shannon Zachary.
Preservation Education and Outreach. Margit G. Smith.
Preservation Issues in Small to Mid-Sized Libraries. Anita F. Shaughnessy.
Research Libraries. Sandra M. Heft.
Retrospective Conversion, LITA/ALCTS. Deborah A. Fritz, Vicki L. Smith.
Role of the Professional in Academic Research Technical Services Departments. Marilyn Myers.
Serials Automation Interest Group, LITA/ALCTS. Carol L. Jones.
Technical Services Administrators of Medium-Sized Research Libraries. Patricia Kantner.
Technical Services Directors of Large Research Libraries. John Lubans, Jr.
Technical Services in Public Libraries. To be appointed.

American Library Association
Association for Library Service to Children

Executive Director, Susan Roman
50 E. Huron St., Chicago, IL 60611
312-280-2163, 800-545-2433
e-mail sroman@ala.org

Object

Interested in the improvement and extension of library services to children in all types of libraries. Responsible for the evaluation and selection of book and nonbook materials for, and the improvement of techniques of, library services to children from preschool through the eighth grade or junior high school age, when such materials or techniques are intended for use in more than one type of library. Founded 1901.

Membership

Memb. 3,609. Open to anyone interested in library services to children. For information on dues, see ALA entry.

Officers

Pres. Steven Herb. E-mail slh@psulias.psu.edu; *Pres.-Elect* Elizabeth Watson. E-mail ewatson@site.cwmars.org; *Past Pres.* Therese G. Bigelow. E-mail therese@kcpl.lib.mo.us.

Address correspondence to the executive director.

Directors

Oralia Garza Cortes, Margery Cuyler, Eliza Dresang, Carol D. Fiore, Barbara Genco, Virginia McKee, Cynthia K. Richey, Anita Steele, Kathy Toon; *Councillor* Eliza Dresang; *Staff Liaison* Susan Roman.

Publications

ALSC Newsletter (q.; memb.). *Ed.* Anitra T. Steele.

Journal of Youth Services in Libraries (q.; memb.; nonmemb. $40; foreign $50). *Eds.* Donald J. Kenney, Virginia Polytechnic Institute, Box 90001, Blacksburg, VA 24062-9001; Linda J. Wilson, Dept. of Educational Studies, 206A Russell Hall, Radford Univ., Radford, VA 24142.

Committee Chairpersons
Priority Group I: Child Advocacy

Consultant. Cynthia K. Richey.
National Children and Youth Membership Organizations Outreach.
Legislation.
Liaison with Mass Media.
Liaison with National Organizations Serving Children and Youth.

Priority Group II: Evaluation of Media

Consultant. Judith Davie.
Computer Software Evaluation.
Film and Video Evaluation.
Notable Children's Books.
Recording Evaluation.
Selection of Children's Books from Various Cultures.

Priority Group III: Professional Development

Consultant. Leslie Edmonds Holt.
Arbuthnot Honor Lecture.
Louise Seaman Bechtel Fellowship.
Distinguished Service Award.
Econo-Clad Literature Program Award.
Education.
Managing Children's Services (Committee and Discussion Group).
Putnam and Grosset Group Awards.
Scholarships: Melcher and Bound to Stay Bound.

Teachers of Children's Literature (Discussion Group).

Priority Group IV: Social Responsibilities

Consultant. Gretchen Wronka.
Intellectual Freedom.
International Relations.
Library Service to Children with Special Needs.
Preschool Services (Discussion Group).
Preschool Services and Parent Education.
Social Issues (Discussion Group).
Social Issues in Relation to Materials and Services for Children.

Priority Group V: Planning and Research

Consultant. Kate McClelland.
Caldecott Medal Calendar.
Collections of Children's Books for Adult Research (Discussion Group).

Local Arrangements.
Membership.
National Planning of Special Collections.
National Reading Program.
Nominating.
Oral Record Project (Advisory Committee).
Organization and Bylaws.
Planning and Budget.
Preconference Planning.
Publications.
Research and Development.
Storytelling (Discussion Group).

Priority Group VI: Award Committees

Consultant. Rita Auerbach.
Mildred L. Batchelder Award Selection.
Pura Belpr Award.
Caldecott Award.
Carnegie Award.
Newbery Award.
Wilder Award.

American Library Association
Association of College and Research Libraries

Executive Director, Althea H. Jenkins
50 E. Huron St., Chicago, IL 60611-2795
312-280-3248, 800-545-2433 ext. 2521, fax 312-280-2520
e-mail ajenkins@ala.org

Object

The Association of College and Research Libraries (ACRL) provides leadership for development, promotion, and improvement of academic and research library resources and services to facilitate learning, research, and the scholarly communication process. ACRL promotes the highest level of professional excellence for librarians and library personnel in order to serve the users of academic and research libraries. Founded 1938.

Membership

Memb. 10,846. For information on dues, see ALA entry.

Officers

Pres. William Miller, Dir. of Libs., S. E. Wimberly Lib., Florida Atlantic Univ., Box 3092, Boca Raton, FL 33431-0992. Tel. 561-367-3717, fax 561-338-3863; *Pres.-Elect* W. Lee Hisle, Assoc. V.P. for Learning Resource Services, Austin Community College, 1212 Rio Grande Ave., Austin, TX 78701. Tel. 512-223-3069, fax 512-495-7431; *Past Pres.* Patricia Senn Breivik, Dean of Libs., Wayne State Univ., Purdy/Kresge Lib., 5265 Cass Ave., Detroit, MI 48202-3939. Tel. 313-577-4048, fax 313-577-5525; *Budget and Finance Chair* Ray English, Dir. of Libs., Oberlin College Lib., 148 W. College St., Oberlin, OH 44074. Tel. 216-775-8285 Ext. 231, fax 216-775-8739; *ACRL Councillor* Maxine H. Reneker, 740 Dry Creek Rd., Monterey, CA

93940-4208. Tel. 408-656-2341, fax 408-656-2842.

Board of Directors

Officers; Jill B. Fatzer, Bernard Fradkin, Frances J. Maloy, Victoria A. Montavon, Linda S. Muroi, Carol M. Pfeiffer, Mary Reichel.

Publications

ACRL Publications in Librarianship (formerly ACRL Monograph Series) (irreg.). *Ed.* Stephen E. Wiberly, Jr., Univ. of Illinois at Chicago, Chicago, IL 60680.

Choice (11 per year; $185; foreign $210).

Choice Reviews-on-Cards ($293; foreign $315). *Ed.* Irving Rockwood, 100 Riverview Center, Middletown, CT 06457-3401.

College and Research Libraries (6 per year; memb.; nonmemb. $55). *Ed.* Donald E. Riggs, Univ. of Michigan, 818 Hatcher Grad. Lib., Ann Arbor, MI 48109.

College and Research Libraries News (11 per year; memb.; nonmemb. $35). *Ed.* Mary Ellen Kyger Davis, ACRL, ALA, 50 E. Huron St., Chicago, IL 60611-2795.

Rare Books and Manuscripts Librarianship (2 per year; $35). *Ed.* Sidney E. Berger, Special Collections, Univ. of California, Riverside, CA 92517-5900.

List of other publications available through the ACRL office, ALA, 50 E. Huron St., Chicago, IL 60611-2795; or call 312-280-2517.

Committee and Task Force Chairpersons

Academic Library Outcomes Assessment (Task Force). Jill B. Fatzer.
Academic or Research Librarian of the Year Award. Ann E. Prentice.
Academic Status. Rush Miller.
ACRL Publications in Librarianship Editorial Board. Stephen E. Wiberley, Jr.
Appointments (1996) and Nominations (1997). Betsy Baker.
Appointments (1997). Helen H. Spalding.
Hugh C. Atkinson Memorial Award. Maureen Sullivan.
Budget and Finance. Ray English.
Chapters/ACRL Relations Task Force. John Collins, Ray English.
Choice Editorial Board. Victoria L. Hanawalt.
Colleagues. Joseph A. Boisse.
College and Research Libraries Editorial Board. Donald E. Riggs.
College and Research Libraries News Editorial Board. Pamela Snelson.
Community Information Organizations. John A. Shuler.
Conference Program Planning, San Francisco (1997). William Miller.
Constitution and Bylaws. Nancy Magnuson.
Copyright. Erika C. Linke.
Council of Liaisons. Althea H. Jenkins.
Doctoral Dissertation Fellowship. Johnny L. Johnson.
Equal Access to Software Information Advisory Committee. Tom McNulty.
Government Relations. Susan Kay Phillips.
Institutional Priorities and Faculty Reward Task Force. W. Bede Mitchell.
Intellectual Freedom. Susana Hinojosa.
International Relations. Patricia Wand.
Samuel Lazerow Fellowship. Nicholas E. Gaymon.
Leadership Center (Advisory Committee). Elaine K. Didier.
Media Resources. Rick E. Provine.
Membership. Ray E. Metz.
National Conference Executive Committee, Nashville, 1997. Carla J. Stoffle.
New Publications (Advisory Board). Cynthia S. Faries.
Nominations (1998). Susan M. Anderson.
Orientation. Patricia Breivik.
President's Program Planning (1997). Natalie Pelster.
Professional Education. Laurene E. Zaporozhetz.
Professional Enhancement. Anne K. Beaubien.
Publications. Ann C. Schaffner.
Racial and Ethnic Diversity. Alma Dawson.
Rare Books and Manuscripts Librarianship Editorial Board. Sidney E. Berger.
Research. Marilyn Martin.
K. G. Saur Award for Best *College and Research Libraries* Article. Caroline M. Coughlin.

Section Funding (Task Force). Frances Maloy.
Standards and Accreditation. Virginia S. O'Herron.
Statistics. Patricia M. Kelley.

Popular Culture and Libraries. Sandra S. Ballasch.
Public Relations in Academic Libraries. Margaret Gordon.
Research. Darrell L. Jenkins.
Undergraduate Librarians. David C. Taylor.

Discussion Group Chairpersons

Alliances for New Directions in Teaching/Learning. Timothy Richards.
Australian Studies. Noelene P. Martin.
Canadian Studies. Pamela M. Hays.
Electronic Library Development in Academic Libraries. Todd Kelley.
Electronic Reserves. Joan Arlene Reyes.
Electronic Text Centers. Mark Day.
Exhibits and Displays. Michael M. Miller.
Fee-Based Information Service Centers in Academic Libraries. Sue Ward.
Fund-Raising and Development. Eva Sartori.
Heads of Public/Readers Services. Allan W. Bosch
Home Economics/Human Ecology Librarians. Linda Lawrence Stein.
Librarians of Library Science Collections. Cathy Rentschler.
Medium-Sized Libraries. Jeanne G. Sohn.
MLA International Bibliography in Academic Libraries. Catherine S. Palmer.
Personnel Administrators and Staff Development Officers of Large Research Libraries. Julie A. Brewer, Janice D. Simmons-Welburn.
Philosophical, Religious, and Theological Studies. Barbara L. Berman.

Section Chairpersons

Afro-American Studies Librarians. Rochelle R. Ballard.
Anthropology and Sociology. Fred J. Hay.
Arts. Nancy L. Stokes.
Asian, African and Middle Eastern. David L. Easterbrook.
College Libraries. Pamela Snelson.
Community and Junior College Libraries. Douglas K. Lehman.
Educational and Behavioral Sciences. Mary Beth Minick.
English and American Literature. Charles Perry Willett.
Extended Campus Library Services. Thomas E. Abbott.
Instruction. Loanne L. Snavely.
Law and Political Science. Catherine F. Doyle.
Rare Books and Manuscripts. Susan M. Allen.
Science and Technology. Amy L. Paster.
Slavic and East European. Cathy M. Zeljak.
University Libraries. Donald G. Frank.
Western European Specialists. Diana Chlebek.
Women's Studies. Bonnie J. Cox.

American Library Association
Association of Specialized and Cooperative Library Agencies

Executive Director, Cathleen Bourdon
50 E. Huron St., Chicago, IL 60611
312-280-4395, 800-545-2433 ext. 4396, fax 312-944-8085

Object

To represent state library agencies, specialized library agencies, and multitype library cooperatives. Within the interest of these types of library organizations, the Association of Specialized and Cooperative Library Agencies (ASCLA) has specific responsibility for

1. Development and evaluation of goals and plans for state library agencies, specialized library agencies, and multitype library cooperatives to facilitate the implementation, improvement, and extension of library activities designed to foster improved user services, coordinating such activities with other appropriate ALA units.
2. Representation and interpretation of the role, functions, and services of state library agencies, specialized library agencies, and multitype library cooperatives within and outside the profession, including contact with national organizations and government agencies.
3. Development of policies, studies, and activities in matters affecting state library agencies, specialized library agencies, and multitype library cooperatives relating to (a) state and local library legislation, (b) state grants-in-aid and appropriations, and (c) relationships among state, federal, regional, and local governments, coordinating such activities with other appropriate ALA units.
4. Establishment, evaluation, and promotion of standards and service guidelines relating to the concerns of this association.
5. Identifying the interests and needs of all persons, encouraging the creation of services to meet these needs within the areas of concern of the association, and promoting the use of these services provided by state library agencies, specialized library agencies, and multitype library cooperatives.
6. Stimulating the professional growth and promoting the specialized training and continuing education of library personnel at all levels of concern of this association* and encouraging membership participation in appropriate type-of-activity divisions within ALA.
7. Assisting in the coordination of activities of other units within ALA that have a bearing on the concerns of this association.
8. Granting recognition for outstanding library service within the areas of concern of this association.
9. Acting as a clearinghouse for the exchange of information and encouraging the development of materials, publications, and research within the areas of concern of this association.

Membership

Memb. 1,420.

Board of Directors (1996–1997)

Pres. Kate Nevins, Exec. Dir., SOLINET, 1438 W. Peachtree St. N.W., Suite 200, Atlanta, GA 30309-2955. Tel. 404-892-0943, 800-999-8558, fax 404-892-7879, e-mail kate_nevins@solinet.net; *Pres.-Elect* Nancy M. Bolt, Deputy State Libn., Colorado State Lib., Dept. of Educ., 201 E. Colfax Ave., Denver, CO 80203-1704. Tel. 303-866-6732, fax 303-866-6940, e-mail nbolt@csn.org; *Past Pres.* Leslie B. Burger, Lib. Development Solutions, 64 Princeton-Hightstown Rd., Princeton Junction, NJ 08550-1103. Tel. 609-275-4821, fax 609-275-4784, e-mail lburger951@aol.com.; *Dirs.-at-Large* John Day, Keith Michael Fiels, Martha McDonald, Patricia L. Owens; *Div. Councillor* Lorraine S. Summers; *Section Reps.* Steven A. Baughman, Elizabeth A. Funk, Edwin S. Gleaves, H. Neil Kelley; *Interface Ed. (ex officio)* Frederick Duda (1997); *Organization and Bylaws Committee Chair (ex officio)* Clarence Walters (1997).

Executive Staff

Exec. Dir. Cathleen Bourdon; *Deputy Exec. Dir.* Lillian Lewis.

Publications

Interface (q.; memb.; nonmemb. $20). *Ed.* Frederick Duda, Talking Book Service, 4884 Kestral Park Circle, Sarasota, FL 34231-3369. Tel. 941-742-5914, fax 941-751-7098.

Committee Chairpersons

American Correctional Association/ASCLA Joint Committee on Institution Libraries. Thea Chesley, Tim Brown.
Awards. Barbara T. Mates.
Budget and Finance. To be appointed.
Conference Program Coordination. Diane Solomon.
Guidelines for Library Service for People with Developmental Disabilities, Marilyn Irwin.
Legislation. Barbara Will.
Library Personnel and Education. Amy Kellerstrass.
Membership Promotion. Marjorie MacKenzie.
Organization and Bylaws. Rod Wagner.
Planning. Nancy Bolt.
Publications. Tina Roose.
Research. Ruth Kowal.
Standards Review. Ethel Himmell.

American Library Association
Library Administration and Management Association

Executive Director, Karen Muller
50 E. Huron St., Chicago, IL 60611
312-280-5031, 800-545-2433 ext. 5031, fax 312-280-3257
e-mail kmuller@ala.org

Object

The Library Administration and Management Association (LAMA) provides an organizational framework for encouraging the study of administrative theory, for improving the practice of administration in libraries, and for identifying and fostering administrative skill. Toward these ends, the division is responsible for all elements of general administration that are common to more than one type of library. These may include organizational structure, financial administration, personnel management and training, buildings and equipment, and public relations. LAMA meets this responsibility in the following ways:

1. Study and review of activities assigned to the division with due regard for changing developments in these activities.
2. Initiating and overseeing activities and projects appropriate to the division, including activities involving bibliography compilation, publication, study, and review of professional literature within the scope of the division.
3. Synthesis of those activities of other ALA units that have a bearing upon the responsibilities or work of the division.
4. Representation and interpretation of library administrative activities in contacts outside the library profession.

5. Aiding the professional development of librarians engaged in administration and encouragement of their participation in appropriate type-of-library divisions.
6. Planning and development of those programs of study and research in library administrative problems that are most needed by the profession.

Established 1957.

Membership

Memb. 5,064.

Officers (1996–1997)

Pres. William Sannwald, Dir., San Diego Public Lib., 820 E St., San Diego, CA 92101-6416. Tel 619-236-5871, fax 619-236-5878, e-mail wws@citymgr.sannet.gov; *Pres.-Elect* Charles E. Kratz, Jr., Dir., Harry and Jeanette Weinberg Memorial Lib., Univ. of Scranton, Scranton, PA 18510-4700. Tel. 717-941-4008, fax 717-941-7817, e-mail kratzc1@lion.uofs.edu; *Past Pres.* John J. Vasi, UCSB Lib., Univ. of California, Santa Barbara, CA 93106-9010. Tel. 805-893-2674, fax 805-893-7010, e-mail vasi@library.ucsb.edu.; *Councillor* Malcolm K. Hill, Dir., Mid-York Lib. System, 463 Ernst Rd., Clinton, NY 13323. Tel. 315-735-8328, fax 315-735-0943, e-mail hill@midyork.lib.ny.us; *Exec. Dir.* Karen Muller, 50 E. Huron St., Chicago, IL 60611. Tel. 312-280-5031, fax 312-280-3257, e-mail kmuller@ala.org.

Address correspondence to the executive director.

Board of Directors

Dirs. Charles E. Kratz, William Sannwald, John J. Vasi; *Div. Councillor* Judith A. Adams; *Dirs.-at-Large* Susan F. Gregory, Joyce C. Wright; *Section Chairs* Paul Anderson, Paula C. Banks, Melissa Carr, Gail M. Dow, Andrea Lapsley, Deborah J. Leather, Andrea A. Michaels; *Ex officio* Jack F. Bulow, Susanne Henderson, Rodney M. Hersberger, Eddy Hogan, Patricia M. Larsen, Louise S. McAulay, Caroline M. Oyama, Marion T. Reid; *Ed.* Barbara G. Preece; *Assoc. Ed.* Maria Otero-Boisvert; *Exec. Dir.* Karen Muller.

Publication

Library Administration and Management (q.; memb.; nonmemb. $50; foreign $60). *Ed.* Joan R. Giesecke, Univ. of Nebraska–Lincoln, 106 Live Lib., Lincoln NE 68588-0410. Tel. 402-472-2426, fax 402-472-5131, e-mail joang@unllib.unl.edu.

Committee Chairpersons

Budget and Finance. Rodney M. Hersberger.
Cultural Diversity. Joan S. Howland.
Education. Gloria J. Stockton.
Governmental Affairs. Doria Beachell Grimes.
Membership. Robert A. Daugherty.
Organization. Susanne Henderson.
Orientation. Thomas L. Wilding.
Program. Curtis L. Kendrick.
Publications. John Lubans, Jr.
Recognition of Achievement. Carol L. Anderson.
Small Libraries Publications Series. Anders C. Dahlgren.
Special Conferences and Programs. Rod Henshaw.

Section Chairpersons

Buildings and Equipment. Andrea A. Michaels.
Fund-Raising and Financial Development. Andrea Lapsley.
Library Organization and Management. Deborah J. Leather.
Personnel Administration. Melissa Carr.
Public Relations. Paula C. Banks.
Statistics. Gail M. Dow.
Systems and Services. Paul M. Anderson.

American Library Association
Library and Information Technology Association

Executive Director, Jacqueline Mundell
50 E. Huron St., Chicago, IL 60611
312-280-4270, 800-545-2433

Object

The Library and Information Technology Association (LITA) envisions a world in which the complete spectrum of information technology is available to everyone. People in all their diversity will have access to a wealth of information technology in libraries, at work, and at home. In this world, everybody can realize their full potential with the help of information technology. The very boundaries of human relations will expand beyond the limitations of time and space we experience today. The outer limits are still unknown; what is known is that the exploration will be challenging.

LITA provides its members, other ALA divisions and members, and the library and information science field as a whole with a forum for discussion, an environment for learning, and a program for action on the design, development, and implementation of automated and technological systems in the library and information science field.

LITA is concerned with the planning, development, design, application, and integration of technologies within the library and information environment, with the impact of emerging technologies on library service, and with the effect of automated technologies on people. Its major focus is on the interdisciplinary issues and emerging technologies. LITA disseminates information, provides educational opportunities for learning about information technologies and forums for the discussion of common concerns, monitors new technologies with potential applications in information science, encourages and fosters research, promotes the development of technical standards, and examines the effects of library systems and networks.

LITA's strategic planning goals are to provide opportunities for professional growth and performance in areas of information technology; to influence national- and international-level initiatives relating to information and access; to promote, participate in, and influence the development of technical standards related to the storage, dissemination, and delivery of information; and to strengthen the association and assure its continued success.

Membership

Memb. 5,310.

Officers (1996–1997)

Pres. Thomas W. Leonhardt (1998); *V.P. and Pres.-Elect* Linda D. Miller (1999); *Past Pres.* Michele Newberry (1997).

Directors

Officers; Pamela Q. J. Andre (1997); Barbra B. Higginbotham (1997); Elizabeth Lane Lawley (1997); Pamela R. Mason (1998); Edward J. Valauskas (1998); Kathleen A. Wakefield (1999); Florence Wilson (1999); *Councillor* Carol A. Parkhurst (1997); *Bylaws and Organization* Sara L. Randall (1998); *Exec. Dir.* Jacqueline Mundell.

Publications

Information Technology and Libraries (q.; memb.; nonmemb. $50; single copy $15). *Ed.* James J. Kopp. For information or to send manuscripts, contact the editor.

LITA Newsletter (q.; memb.; nonmemb. $25; single copy $8). *Ed.* Gail Junion-Metz.

Committee Chairpersons

Hugh C. Atkinson Memorial Award. Maureen Sullivan, e-mail maureen@chi.org.
Budget Review. Michele Newberry, e-mail fclmin@nervm.nerdc.ufl.edu.
Bylaws and Organization. Sara L. Randall, e-mail srandall@mcs.net.
Education. Xiao-Yan Shen, e-mail xshen@scuacc.scu.edu.
Executive. Thomas W. Leonhardt, e-mail tleonhardt@libsy2.uoknor.edu.
Information Technology and Libraries (ITAL) Editorial Board. James J. Kopp, e-mail kopp@uofport.edu.
International Relations. John R. James, e-mail John.R.James@Dartmouth.edu.
Internet Room Steering. Gail P. Clement.
Leadership Development. Mary Ann Sheble, e-mail sheblema@udmercy.edu.
Legislation and Regulation. Marilyn Lutz, e-mail lutz@maine.maine.edu.
LISAN Steering. Nancy K. Roderer, e-mail roderer@biomed.med.yale.edu.
LITA/Gaylord Award. Sandra E. Swanson.
LITA/Geac Scholarship (Subcommittee). Marianne Burke, e-mail mburke@warren.med.harvard.edu.
LITA/*Library Hi Tech* Award. Robert P. Burrows, e-mail burrows@als.ameritech.com.
LITA Newsletter (Subcommittee). Gail Junion-Metz, e-mail gail@iage.com.
LITA/OCLC and LITA/LSSI Minority Scholarship (Subcommittee). Maurice J. Freedman, e-mail freedman@wls.lib.ny.us.
Machine-Readable Form of Bibliographic Information (MARBI) (ALCTS/LITA/RUSA). Jacquelene W. Riley, e-mail jacquelene.riley@uc.edu.
Membership. Linda J. Robinson, e-mail robinsol@oclc.org.
National Conference 1996 Evaluation (LITA/LAMA). Charles E. Kratz.
National Conference 1996 Fundraising (Advisory) (LITA/LAMA). Sherrie Schmidt, e-mail idsxs@asuvm.inre.asu.edu.
National Conference 1996 Local Arrangements (LITA/LAMA). Susan Webreck Alman, e-mail swa@icarus.lis.pitt.edu.
National Conference 1996 Networking/Technology (LITA/LAMA). Gretchen Whitney, e-mail gwhitney@utkvx.utk.edu.
National Conference 1996 Program Planning (LITA/LAMA). Marcia K. Deddens, e-mail marcia.deddens@uc.edu.
National Conference 1996 Steering (LITA/LAMA). Dennis J. Reynolds (LITA), Terri Tomchyshyn (LAMA).
Nominating. Nancy K. Roderer, e-mail roderer@biomed.med.yale.edu.
Program Planning. Janet C. Woody, e-mail jwoody@pen.k12.va.us.
Publications. George S. Machovec, e-mail gmachove@colliance.org.
Regional Institutes. Mark A. Beatty, e-mail mbeatty@wils.wisc.edu.
Research. Don L. Bosseau, e-mail bosseau@sdsu.edu.
Technical Standards for Library Automation (TESLA). Corrie V. Marsh, e-mail cmarsh@ovid.com.
Technology and Access. Charles W. Husbands, e-mail charles_husbands@harvard.edu.
Telecommunications Electronic Reviews (TER) Board. Thomas C. Wilson, e-mail twilson@uh.edu.

Interest Group Chairpersons

Interest Group Coordinator. Mary Ann Van Cura, e-mail vancuram@mlc.lib.mi.us.
Adaptive Technologies. Dennis Norlin, e-mail dnorlin@atla.com.
Artificial Intelligence/Expert Systems (AI/ES). Stephen R. Westman, e-mail swestman@coyote.utsa.edu.
Authority Control in the Online Environment (LITA/ALCTS). Sherry Kelley, e-mail skelley@sil.si.edu.
Customized Applications for Library Microcomputers (CALM). Andy D. Boze, e-mail Boze.1@nd.edu.
Desktop Publishing. John Maxymuk.
Distributed Systems and Networks. Beth Helsel, bard@clemson.edu.
Electronic Mail/Electronic Bulletin Boards. Ray E. Metz.
Emerging Technologies. Joseph B. Ford, e-mail fordjb@win.com.
Geographic Information Systems (GIS). Denise Stephens, e-mail cds2m@virginia.edu.

Human/Machine Interface. Tona Henderson, e-mail tah@psulias.psu.edu.
Imagineering. Diane C. Kachmar, e-mail kachmar@acc.fau.edu.
Internet Resources. Abbie Basile, e-mail basila@rpi.edu.
Library Consortia/Automated Systems. Anne G. Flint, e-mail anne@ohiolink.edu.
MARC Formats (LITA/ALCTS). Kathleen Bales, e-mail bl.kob@rig.org.
Microcomputer Support of Technical Services (LITA/ALCTS). David Williamson, e-mail dawi@loc.gov.
Microcomputer Users. Robert B. McGeachin, e-mail r-mcgeachin@tamu.edu.
Online Catalogs. Ellen Crosby, e-mail ecrosby@statelib.lib.in.us.
Optical Information Systems. Stuart Glogoff, e-mail sglogoff@bird.library.arizona.edu.
Programmer/Analyst. Kurt W. Kopp, e-mail Koppk@ext.missouri.edu.
Retrospective Conversion (LITA/ALCTS). Karl Fattig, e-mail kfattig@polar.bowdoin.edu.
Secure Systems and Services. Thomas P. Dowling, e-mail tdowling@ohiolink.edu.
Serials Automation (LITA/ALCTS). Mahnaz Moshfegh, e-mail moshfeg@hamlet.ucs.indiana.edu.
Small Integrated Library Systems. Carl E. Bengston, e-mail bengston@dominican.edu.
Technology and the Arts. Belinda Dunford Urquiza, e-mail burq@loc.gov.
Telecommunications. Scott Muir, e-mail smuir@gorgas.lib.ua.edu.
Vendor/User. Virginia M. Allen, e-mail allen@library.lamar.edu.

American Library Association
Public Library Association

Executive Director, Greta K. Southard
50 E. Huron St., Chicago, IL 60611
312-280-5026, 800-545-2433 ext. 5025, fax 312-280-5029
e-mail gsouthard@ala.org

Object

The Public Library Association (PLA) will advance the development and effectiveness of public library service and public librarians. The PLA has specific responsibility for

1. Conducting and sponsoring research about how the public library can respond to changing social needs and technical developments.
2. Developing and disseminating materials useful to public libraries in interpreting public library services and needs.
3. Conducting continuing education for public librarians by programming at national and regional conferences, by publications such as the newsletter, and by other delivery means.
4. Establishing, evaluating, and promoting goals, guidelines, and standards for public libraries.
5. Maintaining liaison with relevant national agencies and organizations engaged in public administration and human services, such as the National Association of Counties, the Municipal League, and the Commission on Post-Secondary Education.
6. Maintaining liaison with other divisions and units of ALA and other library organizations, such as the Association of American Library Schools and the Urban Libraries Council.
7. Defining the role of the public library in service to a wide range of user and potential user groups.
8. Promoting and interpreting the public library to a changing society through legislative programs and other appropriate means.
9. Identifying legislation to improve and to equalize support of public libraries.

PLA exists to provide a diverse program of communication, publication, advocacy, and continuing education. The program priorities are determined by PLA members and may include some areas or concerns also identified as priorities by ALA. The primary staff program responsibility is to facilitate members' activities and initiatives by providing coordination and support.

As a division, we are effective when we

1. Provide leadership for the improvement of public libraries.
2. Provide an effective forum for discussing issues of concern to public librarians.
3. Provide relevant, high-quality continuing education through publications, workshops, and programs.
4. Provide opportunities for developing and enhancing individual professional networks.
5. Develop and disseminate policy statements on matters affecting public libraries.
6. Communicate effectively with the nonlibrary world about matters impacting public library service.
7. Maintain a stable membership and financial base.

PLA's priority concerns are adequate funding for public libraries; improved management of public libraries; recognition of the importance of all library staff in providing quality public service; recruitment, education, training, and compensation of public librarians; effective use of technology; intellectual freedom; improved access to library resources; and effective communication with the nonlibrary world. Organized 1944.

Membership

Memb. 8,500+. Open to all ALA members interested in the improvement and expansion of public library services to all ages in various types of communities.

Officers (1996–1997)

Pres. Linda Mielke, Carroll County Public Lib., 115 Airport Dr., Westminster, MD 21157. Tel. 410-876-6008, fax 410-876-3002, e-mail lmielke@ccpl.carr.lib.md.us; *V.P./Pres.-Elect* Ginnie Cooper, Multnomah County Lib., Lib. Assn. of Portland, 205 N.E. Russell St., Portland, OR 97212. Tel. 503-248-5203, fax 503-248-5441, e-mail ginniec@nethost.multnomah.lib.or.us; *Past Pres.* LaDonna T. Kienitz, Newport Beach Public Lib., 3300 Newport Blvd., Newport Beach, CA 92658-9815. Tel. 714-644-3157, fax 714-644-3155, e-mail nbplijk@class.org.

Board of Directors

Officers; *Dirs.-at-Large* Marilyn H. Bora (1997), Donna Joy Burke (PLSS, 1997), Jane S. Eickhoff (PPPLS, 1999), Luis Herrera (1999), Anthony B. Leisner (MPLSS, 1997), Rosemary S. Martin (PLMES, 1997), Annette M. Milliron (SMLS, 1997), Caryl Jean E. Mobley (ALLS, 1997), Catherine A. O'Connell (1998), Stephen Russo (CIS, 1997), Carol Starr (1997), Nancy Tessman (1999), Jerry A. Thrasher (1998), K. Lynn Wheeler (MLS, 1997); *Div. Councillor* Jo Ann Pinder (1998); *Ex officio/Nonvoting Members: Exec. Dir.* Greta K. Southard (1997), *PLA Budget and Finance Rep.* Fran C. Freimarck (1997).

Publication

Public Libraries (bi-m.; memb.; nonmemb. $50; foreign $60; single copy $10). *Feature Ed. (Interim)* Helene S. Woodhams, 6211 N. Camino Esquina, Tucson, AZ 85718; *Managing Ed.* Kathleen Hughes, PLA, 50 E. Huron St., Chicago, IL 60611.

Section Presidents

Adult Lifelong Learning (ALLS). Vera A. Green.
Community Information (CIS). Trish Skaptason.
Marketing of Public Library Services (MPLSS). Carol G. Walters.

Metropolitan Libraries (MLS). K. Lynn Wheeler.
Planning, Measurement, and Evaluation (PLMES). June Garcia.
Public Library Systems (PLSS). Donna Joy Burke.
Public Policy for Public Libraries (PPPLS). Claudia B. Sumler.
Small and Medium-Sized Libraries (SMLS). Stephen A. Kershner.

Committee Chairpersons

Audiovisual. James E. Massey, Harford County Lib., 1221-A Brass Mill Rd., Belcamp, MD 21017.
Awards. Robert Smith, Medina County Dist. Lib., 210 S. Broadway, Medina, OH 44256.
Budget and Finance. Fran C. Freimarck, Box 437, Manquin, VA 23106.
Bylaws and Organization. Harriet Henderson, Louisville Free Public Lib., 301 York St., Louisville, KY 40203.
Cataloging Needs of Public Libraries. Karen Cook, SIRSI, Inc., 689 Discovery Dr., Huntsville, AL 35806.
Conference Program Coordinating (1997). Clara N. Bohrer, West Bloomfield Township Public Lib., 4600 Walnut Lake Rd., West Bloomfield, MI 48323.
Conference Program Coordinating (1998). Annette M. Milliron, North Bay Coop. Lib. System, 55 E St., Santa Rosa, CA 95404; Kelley Glancy-Grabowski, Detroit Public Lib., 5201 Woodward Ave., Detroit, MI 48202-4007.
Demco Creative Merchandising Grant Jury. John Brooks-Barr, Upper Arlington Public Lib., 2800 Tremont Rd., Upper Arlington, OH 43221-3199.
Highsmith Library Innovation Award Jury. Michael Madden, Schaumburg Township Dist. Lib., 32 W. Library Lane, Schaumburg, IL 60194-3421.
Intellectual Freedom. Charles Parker, State Lib. of Florida, R. A. Gray Bldg., Tallahassee, FL 32399-0250.
Leadership Development (1997). Margaret P. Stillman, Chesapeake Public Lib., 298 Cedar Rd., Chesapeake, VA 23320.
Leadership Development (1998). Sandra Nelson, Tennessee State Lib., 403 Seventh Ave. N., Nashville, TN 37243-0312.
Legislation. Roberta A. E. Cairns, East Providence Public Lib., 41 Grove Ave., East Providence, RI 02914-4504.
LSCA Ad Hoc (Special). Sarah A. Long, N. Suburban Lib. System, 200 W. Dundee Rd., Wheeling, IL 60090.
Allie Beth Martin Award. Ann Barnett Hutton, SELCO, 107 W. Frontage Rd., Hwy. 52 N., Rochester, MN 55901.
Membership. Christine L. Hage, Rochester Hills Public Lib., 500 Olde Towne Rd., Rochester, MI 48307.
National Conference (1998). Sarah A. Long, N. Suburban Lib. System, 200 W. Dundee Rd., Wheeling, IL 60090.
National Conference (1998) Exhibitors Advisory. Joe K. Weed, EBSCO Subscriptions Services, Box 1943, Birmingham, AL 35201.
National Conference (1998) Local Arrangements. Daniel J. Bradbury, Kansas City Public Lib., 311 E. 12 St., Kansas City, MO 64106.
National Conference (1998) Program. Clara N. Bohrer, West Bloomfield Township Public Lib., 4600 Walnut Lake Rd., West Bloomfield, MI 48323.
New Leaders Travel Grant Jury. Sarah Kelley, Bluegrass Regional Lib., 305 Wapping St., Frankfort, KY 40601.
Nominating (1997). Patrick O'Brien, Alexandria Lib., 717 Queen St., Alexandria, VA 22314-2420.
Nominating (1998). Judith A. Drescher, Memphis–Shelby County Public Lib., 1850 Peabody Ave., Memphis, TN 38104.
NTC Career Materials Resource Grant Jury. Anthony Leisner, 1350 Riverside Ave., Tarpon Springs, FL 34689-6614.
PLA Partners. Kay K. Runge, Davenport Public Lib., 321 Main St., Davenport, IA 52801.
President's Events (1997). K. Lynn Wheeler, Baltimore County Public Lib., 320 York Rd., Towson, MD 21204-5179.
President's Events (1998). Kay K. Runge, Davenport Public Lib., 321 Main St., Davenport, IA 52801.

Public Libraries Advisory. Jane S. Eickhoff, 11 Timber Way Ct., Reisterstown, MD 21136.
Publications. Barbara Webb, Chester County Lib., 400 Exton Sq. Pkwy., Exton, PA 19341.
Research and Statistics. Barbara G. Smith, Montgomery County Public Libs., 99 Maryland Ave., Rockville, MD 20850.
Services to Business. Don W. Barlow, Westerville Public Lib., 126 S. State St., Westerville, OH 43081-2095.
Services to Children. Fran Ware, 5032 Rushlight Path, Columbia, MD 21044.
Statistical Report Advisory. Donna Mancini, Public Lib. of Nashville and Davidson County, 225 Polk Ave., Nashville, TN 37203-3585.
Technology in Public Libraries. William H. Ptacek, King County Lib. System, 300 Eighth Ave. N., Seattle, WA 98109-5116.
Leonard Wertheimer Award. Mary L. Lawson, Minneapolis Public Lib., 300 Nicollet Mall, Minneapolis, MN 55401.

American Library Association Reference and User Services Association

Executive Director, Cathleen Bourdon
50 E. Huron St., Chicago, IL 60611
312-944-6780, 800-545-2433 ext. 4398, fax 312-944-8085

Object

The Reference and User Services Association (RUSA)—formerly the Reference and Adult Services Division (RASD)—is responsible for stimulating and supporting in every type of library the delivery of reference/information services to all groups, regardless of age, and of general library services and materials to adults. This involves facilitating the development and conduct of direct service to library users, the development of programs and guidelines for service to meet the needs of these users, and assisting libraries in reaching potential users.

The specific responsibilities of RUSA are

1. Conduct of activities and projects within the division's areas of responsibility.
2. Encouragement of the development of librarians engaged in these activities and stimulation of participation by members of appropriate type-of-library divisions.
3. Synthesis of the activities of all units within the American Library Association that have a bearing on the type of activities represented by the division.
4. Representation and interpretation of the division's activities in contacts outside the profession.
5. Planning and development of programs of study and research in these areas for the total profession.
6. Continuous study and review of the division's activities.

Membership

Memb. 5,382. For information on dues, see ALA entry.

Officers (June 1996–June 1997)

Pres. Kathleen Kluegel; *Pres.-Elect* Caroline Long; *Secy.* Rebecca J. Whitaker.

Directors and Other Members

Nancy B. Crane, Eva Greenberg, Karen Liston Newsome, Bernard F. Pasqualini, Margaret Ann Reinert, Carol Tobin, Beth S. Woodard; *Councillor* Pam Sieving; *Past Pres.* Marilu Goodyear; *Ed., RUSA Update*

Edward Erazo; *Eds., RQ* Connie Van Fleet, Danny Wallace; *RQ Ed.-Designate* Gail Schlachter; *Exec. Dir.* Cathleen Bourdon. Address correspondence to the executive director.

Publications

RUSA Update (q.; memb.; nonmemb. $20). *Ed.* Edward Erazo.
RQ (q.; memb; nonmemb. $50). *Eds.* Connie Van Fleet, Danny Wallace.

Section Chairpersons

Business Reference and Services. Susan G. Neuman.
Collection Development and Evaluation. Cindy Kaag.
History. Charles D. King.
Machine-Assisted Reference. E. Paige Weston.
Management and Operation of Public Services. Carolyn M. Mulac.

Committee Chairpersons

Access to Information. James P. Niessen.
AFL/CIO Joint Committee on Library Services to Labor Groups. Mary Hicks.
Awards Coordinating. Elaine R. Lyon.
Conference Program. Kathleen Kluegel.
Conference Program Coordinating. Janice Simons-Welburn.
Dartmouth Medal. Richard Bleiler.
Denali Press Award. Deborah Hollis.
Facts on File Grant. Christine Bulson.
Gale Research Award for Excellence in Reference and Adult Services. Marcelle Elaine Hughes.
Membership. Mary M. Mintz.
Margaret E. Monroe Library Adult Services Award. Joyce M. Voss.
Isadore Gilbert Mudge/R. R. Bowker Award. Louise S. Sherby.
Nominating. Julia M. Rholes.
Organization. Laryne J. Dallas.
Planning and Finance. Marilu Goodyear.
Publications. Nancy Huling.
Reference Services Press Award. David Null.
RQ Editorial Advisory Board. Connie Van Fleet, Danny Wallace.
John Sessions Memorial Award. Carol H. Krismann.
Louis Shores/Oryx Press Award. Joyce C. Wright.
Standards and Guidelines. George S. Porter.

American Library Association
Young Adult Library Services Association

Interim Executive Director, Linda Waddle
50 E. Huron St., Chicago, IL 60611
312-280-4390, 800-545-2433 ext. 4390, fax 312-664-7459
e-mail yalsa@ala.org

Object

In every library in the nation, quality library service to young adults is provided by a staff that understands and respects the unique informational, educational, and recreational needs of teenagers. Equal access to information, services, and materials is recognized as a right, not a privilege. Young adults are actively involved in the library decision-making process. The library staff collaborates and cooperates with other youth-serving agencies to provide a holistic, community-wide network of activities and services that support healthy youth development. To ensure that this vision becomes a reality, the Young Adult Library Services Association (YALSA), a division of the American Library Association (ALA)

1. Advocates extensive and developmentally appropriate library and information services for young adults, ages 12 to 18.
2. Promotes reading and supports the literacy movement.
3. Advocates the use of information and communications technologies to provide effective library service.
4. Supports equality of access to the full range of library materials and services, including existing and emerging information and communications technologies, for young adults.
5. Provides education and professional development to enable its members to serve as effective advocates for young people.
6. Fosters collaboration and partnerships among its individual members with the library community and other groups involved in providing library and information services to young adults.
7. Influences public policy by demonstrating the importance of providing library and information services that meet the unique needs and interests of young adults.
8. Encourages research and is in the vanguard of new thinking concerning the provision of library and information services for youth.

Membership

Memb. 2,200. Open to anyone interested in library services and materials for young adults. For information on dues, see ALA entry.

Officers (July 1996–July 1997)

Pres. Deborah Taylor, Enoch Pratt Free Lib., 400 Cathedral St., Baltimore, MD 21201. Tel. 410-396-5356, fax 410-396-1095, e-mail dtaylor@epfl2.epflbalto.org; *V.P./Pres.-Elect* Michael Cart, 4220 Arch Dr., Apt. 10, Studio City, CA 91604. Tel. 818-769-1278, fax 818-769-0729, e-mail mrmcart@aol.com; *Past Pres.* Patricia Mueller, 14425 Coachway Dr., Centreville, VA 22020. Tel. 703-358-5951, fax 703-358-7697, e-mail pmuller@leo.vsla.edu; *Councillor* Pamela Spencer, 9101 Patton Blvd., Alexandria, VA 22309. Tel. 703-503-7414, fax 703-978-3001, e-mail pspencer@pen.k12.va.us.

Directors

Officers; Mary Arnold (1999), Kate Birdseye (1997), Susan Farber (1998), Phyllis Fisher (1999), Judy Sasges (1998), Joel Shoemaker (1997); *Ex officio Chair, Budget and Finance* Jack Forman; *Ex officio Chair, Long-Range Planning* Jana Fine; *Ex officio Chair, Organization and Bylaws* Melanie Lightbody.

Publications

Journal of Youth Services in Libraries (q.; memb.; nonmemb. $40; foreign $50). *Eds.* Donald J. Kenney, Director's Office, Virginia Polytechnic Institute, Box 90001, Blacksburg, VA 24062-9001. Tel. 703-231-5595, fax 703-231-9263; Linda J. Wilson, Dept. of Educational Studies, Radford Univ., 206A Russell Hall, Radford, VA 24142. Tel. 703-831-5344, fax 703-831-5302.

Voices: Newsletter of the Young Adult Services Association (s. ann.; memb.). *Ed.* Jana Fine, Clearwater Public Lib., 100 N. Osceola Ave., Clearwater, FL 34615. Tel. 813-462-6800 ext. 252, fax 813-462-6420, e-mail finej@mail.firn.edu.

Committee Chairpersons

AASL/ALSC/YALSA White House Conference on Library and Information Services Resolution Implementation (Task Force). Virginia Matthews.
ALSC/YALSA JOYS Editorial (Advisory). Donald Kenny, Linda J. Wilson.
Best Books for Young Adults (1997). Chapple Langemack.
Budget and Finance. Jack Forman.
Division Promotion. Ayo Dayo.
Education. Elizabeth Rosen.
Margaret A. Edwards Award (1997). Helen Vandersluis.
Margaret A. Edwards Award (1998). Jeri Baker.
Intellectual Freedom. Barbara Balbirer.
Legislation. Judy Flum.
Library Service to Young Adults with Special Needs. Stella Baker.
Local Arrangements (1997). Lesley S. J. Farmer.
Long-Range Planning. Jana Fine.
Media Selection and Usage. Robin Whitten.
Membership. Jennia Dilger-Hill.
National Organizations Serving the Young Adult (Liaison). Nora Jane Natke.
Nominating (1997). Constance Lawson.
Organization and Bylaws. Melanie Lightbody.
Outreach. Karen Morgan.
Oversight. Jana Fine.
Popular Reading. Mary Huebscher.
President's Program (1997). Caryn Sipos.
Program Planning Clearinghouse and Evaluation. Elizabeth Acerra.
Publications. JoAnn Mondowney.
Publishers' Liaison. Ann Theis.
Quick Picks for Reluctant Young Adult Readers (1997). Naomi Angler.
Research. Gloria Waity.
Selected Films and Videos for Young Adults (1997). Mary Flournoy.
Technology for Young Adults. Kate Birdseye.
Youth Participation. Constance Lawson.

American Merchant Marine Library Association

(An affiliate of United Seamen's Service)
Executive Director, Roger T. Korner
One World Trade Center, Suite 2161, New York, NY 10048
212-775-1038

Object

Provides ship and shore library service for American-flag merchant vessels, the Military Sealift Command, the U.S. Coast Guard, and other waterborne operations of the U.S. government. Established 1921.

Officers (1996–1997)

Honorary Chair Adm. Albert J. Herberger; *Pres.* Talmage E. Simpkins; *Chair, Exec. Committee* Arthur W. Friedberg; *V.P.s* John M. Bowers, Capt. Timothy E. Brown, James Capo, Ernest Corrado, Remo DiFiore, John Halas, George E. Murphy, S. Nakanishi, Capt. Gregorio Oca, Louis Parise, Michael Sacco, John J. Sweeney; *Secy.* Lillian Rabins; *Treas.* William D. Potts; *Exec. Dir.* Roger T. Korner.

American Society for Information Science

Executive Director, Richard B. Hill
8720 Georgia Ave., Suite 501, Silver Spring, MD 20910
301-495-0900, fax 301-495-0810, e-mail ASIS@asis.org

Object

The American Society for Information Science (ASIS) provides a forum for the discussion, publication, and critical analysis of work dealing with the design, management, and use of information, information systems, and information technology.

Membership

Memb. (Indiv.) 3,700; (Student) 600; (Inst.) 200. Dues (Indiv.) $95; (Student) $25; (Inst.) $350 and $550.

Officers

Pres. Debora Shaw, Indiana Univ.; *Pres.-Elect* Michael Buckland, Univ. of California, Berkeley; *Treas.* Ernest DiMattia, Ferguson Lib.; *Past Pres.* Clifford Lynch, Univ. of California.

Address correspondence to the executive director.

Board of Directors

Dirs.-at-Large Steve Hardin, Samantha Kelly Hastings, Julie M. Hurd, Barbara H. Kwasnik, Merri Beth Lavagnino, Bonnie Lawlor, Ellen L. Sleeter, Carol Tenopir; *Deputy Dirs.* Janet M. Arth, Myke H. Gluck; *Exec. Dir.* Richard B. Hill.

Publications

Advances in Classification Research, Vols. 1–5. *Eds.* Barbara Kwasnik and Raya Fidel. Available from Information Today, 143 Old Marlton Pike, Medford, NJ 08055.

Annual Review of Information Science and Technology. Available from Information Today, 143 Old Marlton Pike, Medford, NJ 08055.

ASIS Thesaurus of Information Science and Librarianship. Available from Information Today, 143 Old Marlton Pike, Medford, NJ 08055.

Bulletin of the American Society for Information Science. Available from ASIS.

Challenges in Indexing Electronic Texts and Images. Eds. Raya Fidel, Trudi Bellardo (Hahn), Edie M. Rasmussen, and Philip J. Smith. Available from Information Today, 143 Old Marlton Pike, Medford, NJ 08055.

Entertainment Technology and the Information Business. Thomas E. Kinney. Available from ASIS.

From Print to Electronic: The Transformation of Scientific Communication. Susan Y. Crawford, Julie M. Hurd, and Ann C. Weller. Available from Information Today, 143 Old Marlton Pike, Medford, NJ 08055.

Information Management for the Intelligent Organization: The Art of Environmental Scanning. Chun Wei Choo. Available from ASIS.

Interfaces for Information Retrieval and Online Systems: The State of the Art. Ed. Martin Dillon. Available from Greenwood Press, 88 Post Rd. W., Westport, CT 06881.

Journal of the American Society for Information Science. Available from John Wiley and Sons, 605 Third Ave., New York, NY 10016.

Networking, Telecommunications and the Networked Information Revolution. Proceedings of the 1992 ASIS Mid-Year Meeting. Available from ASIS.

Proceedings of the ASIS Annual Meetings. Available from Information Today, 143 Old Marlton Pike, Medford, NJ 08055.

Scholarly Publishing: The Electronic Frontier. Eds. Robin P. Peek and Gregory B. Newby. Available from MIT Press, Cambridge, Massachusetts.

Studies in Multimedia. Eds. Susan Stone and Michael Buckland. Based on the Proceedings of the 1991 ASIS Mid-Year Meeting. Available from Information Today, 143 Old Marlton Pike, Medford, NJ 08055.

Committee Chairpersons

Awards and Honors. Paula Galbraith.
Budget and Finance. Ernest DiMattia.
Constitution and Bylaws. Nancy Blase.
Continuing Education. Mark Rorvig.
Education. Beth Logan.
Membership. Robert Greschover.
Standards. Kurt Kopp.

American Theological Library Association

820 Church St., Suite 400, Evanston, IL 60201-5613
708-869-7788, fax 708-869-8513

Object

To bring its members into close working relationships with each other, to support theological and religious librarianship, to improve theological libraries, and to interpret the role of such libraries in theological education, developing and implementing standards of library service, promoting research and experimental projects, encouraging cooperative programs that make resources more available, publishing and disseminating literature and research tools and aids, cooperating with organizations having similar aims, and otherwise supporting and aiding theological education. Founded 1946.

Membership

Memb. (Inst.) 200; (Indiv.) 600. Membership is open to persons engaged in professional library or bibliographical work in theological or religious fields and others who are interested in the work of theological librarianship. Dues (Inst.) $75 to $500, based on total library expenditure; (Indiv.) $15 to $100, based on salary scale. Year. Sept. 1–Aug. 31.

Officers (July 1996–June 1997)

Pres. M. Patrick Graham, Pitts Theology Lib., Emory Univ., Atlanta, GA 30322. Tel. 404-727-4165, fax 404-727-2915, e-mail libmpg@emory.edu; *V.P.* Lorena A. Boylan, Ryan Memorial Lib., Saint Charles Borromeo Seminary, 1000 E. Wynnewood Rd., Wynnewood, PA 19096. Tel. 610-667-3394, fax 610-664-7913, e-mail lboylan@hslc.org; *Secy.* Christopher Brennan, Ambrose Swasey Lib., Colgate Rochester Divinity School, 1100 S. Goodman St., Rochester, NY 14520. Tel. 716-271-1320, fax 716-271-2166, e-mail crbn@uhura.cc.rochester.edu.

Board of Directors

Officers; Richard R. Berg, David Bundy, Linda Corman, William Hook, Alan D. Krieger, Roger L. Loyd, Paul Stuehrenberg, Sharon A. Taylor, Dorothy G. Thomason; *Exec. Dir.* Dennis A. Norlin; *Dir. of Finance* Patricia Adamek; *Dir. of Development* John Bollier; *Dir. of Member Services* Melody S. Chartier.

Publications

ATLA Indexes in MARC Format (semi-ann.).
ATLA Religion database on CD-ROM, 1949– (Mar./Sept.).
Biblical Studies on CD-ROM (ann.).
Catholic Periodical and Literature Index on CD-ROM (ann.).
Index to Book Reviews in Religion (ann.).
Newsletter (q.; memb.; nonmemb. $10). *Ed.* Melody Chartier.
Old Testament Abstracts on CD-ROM (ann.).
Proceedings (ann.; memb.; nonmemb. $20). *Ed.* Melody Chartier.
Religion Index One: Periodicals (semi-ann.).
Religion Index Two: Multi-Author Works (ann.).
Religion Indexes: RIO/RIT/IBRR 1975–on CD-ROM.
Research in Ministry: An Index to Doctor of Ministry Project Reports (ann.).
South African Theological Bibliography on CD-ROM (ann.).

Committee Chairpersons and Other Officials

Annual Conference. Christine Wenderoth.
Archivist. Boyd Reese.
Collection Evaluation and Development. Martha Smalley.
College and University. Elizabeth Leahy.
Education. Roberta Schaafsma.
NISO Representative. Myron Chace.
Nominating. David Bundy.
OCLC Theological User Group. Linda Umoh.
Online Reference Resource. Charles Willard.
Oral History. Alice Kendrick.
Preservation. Myron Chace.
Public Services. Alva Caldwell.
Publication. William Miller.
Special Collections. Steve Crocco.
Technical Services. Christine Schone.
Technology. William Hook.

Archivists and Librarians in the History of the Health Sciences

(formerly the Association of Librarians in the History of the Health Sciences)
President, Elizabeth Borst White
Houston Academy of Medicine–Texas Medical Center Library
1133 M. D. Anderson Blvd., Houston, TX 77030
713-799-7139

Object

This association is established exclusively for educational purposes to serve the professional interests of librarians, archivists, and other specialists actively engaged in the librarianship of the history of the health sciences by promoting the exchange of information and by improving the standards of service.

Membership

Memb. (Voting) 200. Dues $10, membs.; outside U.S. and Canada $16.

Officers (May 1996–May 1998)

Pres. Elizabeth Borst White, HAM-TMC Lib., 1133 M. D. Anderson Blvd., Houston, TX 77030. Tel. 713-795-4200, e-mail ewhite@library.tmc.edu; *Secy.-Treas.* Elizabeth Ihrig, Bakken Lib. of Electricity, 3537 Zenith Ave. S., Minneapolis, MN 55416. Tel. 612-927-6508, e-mail eihrig@aol.com; *Eds.* Jodi Koste, Special Collections and Archives, Medical College of Virginia, MCV Box 582, Richmond, VA 23113-0582. E-mail jkoste@gems.vcu.edu; Joan Echtenkamp Klein, Historical Collections, Univ. of Virginia Health Sciences Center, Box 234, Charlottesville, VA 22908. E-mail jre@virginia.edu.

Steering Committee

Officers; Billie Broaddus, Historical, Archival and Museum Services, Univ. of Cincinnati, 231 Bethesda Ave., Cincinnati, OH 45267-0574; Suzanne Porter, Medical Center Lib., Duke Univ., DUMC 3702, Durham, NC 27710.

Committees

Archives. Thomas A. Horrocks, College of Physicians of Philadelphia, 19 S. 22 St., Philadelphia, PA 19103.
Awards. Philip Tiegen, Historical Medical Div., National Lib. of Medicine, 8600 Rockville Pike, Bethesda, MD 20894.
Nominating. Elaine Challacombe, Wangensteen Historical Lib., Bio-Medical Lib., Diehl Hall, 505 Essex St. S.E., Minneapolis, MN 55455.
Membership. Jonathon Erlen, 123 Northview Dr., Pittsburgh, PA 15261.

Publication

Watermark (q.; memb.; nonmem. $16). *Eds.* Jodi Koste, Special Collections and Archives, Medical College of Virginia, MCV Box 582, Richmond, VA 23113-0582. E-mail jkoste@gems.vcu.edu; Joan Echtenkamp Klein, Historical Collections, Univ. of Virginia, Health Sciences Center, Box 234, Charlottesville, VA 22908. E-mail jre@virginia.edu.

ARMA International
(Association of Records Managers and Administrators)

Executive Director, James P. Souders
4200 Somerset Dr., Suite 215, Prairie Village, KS 66208
800-422-2762, 913-341-3808, fax 913-341-3742
e-mail 76015.3151@compuserve.com

Object

To advance the practice of records and information management as a discipline and a profession; to organize and promote programs of research, education, training, and networking within that profession; to support the enhancement of professionalism of the membership; and to promote cooperative endeavors with related professional groups.

Membership

Membership application is available through ARMA headquarters. Annual dues are $100 for international affiliation. Chapter dues vary from city to city. Membership categories are chapter member ($100 plus chapter dues), student member ($15), and unaffiliated member.

Officers (1996–1997)

Pres. Kenneth L. Hopkins, TeamWorks Personnel, 4915 W. Cypress St., Suite 130, Tampa, FL 33607. Tel. 813-286-2830, fax 813-286-2737; *Immediate Past Pres. and Chair of the Board* Richard Weinholdt, National Archives, 1700 Inskster Blvd., Winnipeg, MB R2X 2T1, Canada. Tel. 204-983-8845, fax 204-983-4649; *Pres.-Elect* Robert Nawrucki, 10287 Cedar Ridge Dr., Manassas, VA 22110. Tel. 703-361-3879, fax 703-257-5459; *Secy.-Treas.* Kristi K. Woods, Document Bank, 20815 N.E. 16 Ave., B-23, North Miami, FL 33179. Tel. 305-770-9933, fax 305-770-4375; *Region V.P.s: Region I* H. Larry Eiring; *Region II* Timothy W. Hughes; *Region III* Jack R. Ingle; *Region IV* Wayne Duncan; *Region V* Tad Howington; *Region VI* Linda L. Masquefa; *Region VII* Anne Taylor-Butler; *Region VIII* Susan A. Dalati; *Region IX* Rosalie C. Stremple; *Region X* Carole Guy Blowers; *Region XI* Phyllis W. Parker; *Region XII* Christine M. Ardern.

Publication

Records Management Quarterly. Ed. Ira Penn, 310 Appomattox Dr., Brentwood, TN 37027. Tel. 615-376-2732, e-mail rmqeditor@aol.com.

Committee Chairpersons

Awards. Kenneth L. Hopkins, TeamWorks Personnel, 4915 W. Cypress St., Suite 130, Tampa, FL 33607. Tel. 813-286-2830, fax 813-286-2737.

Canadian Legislative and Regulatory Affairs (CLARA). Raphael Thierrin, 4515 45th St. S.W., Calgary, AB T3E 6K7. Tel. 403-686-3310, fax 403-686-0075.

Education Development. Deborah J. Marshall, Wilkes Artis Hedrick and Lane, 1666 K St. N.W., Suite 1100, Washington, DC 20000-2866. Tel. 202-457-7869, fax 202-457-7814.

Financial Planning/Management Audit. Kristi K. Woods, Document Bank, 20815 N.E. 16 Ave., Suite B-23, North Miami, FL 33179. Tel. 305-770-9933, fax 305-770-4375.

Industry Action. Timothy W. Hughes, Madison Gas and Electric Co., Box 1231, Madison, WI 53701-1231. Tel. 608-252-4799, fax 608-252-7098.

Industry Specific Program. Lee G. Webster, School Dist. of Philadelphia, 734 Schuylkill Ave., Rm. 234, Philadelphia, PA 19146-2397. Tel. 215-875-3938, fax 215-875-5780.

Industry Specific Program Assistants. Nyoakee B. Salway, Occidental Petroleum

Corp., 10889 Wilshire Blvd., Suite 920, Los Angeles, CA 90024. Tel. 310-443-6219, fax 310-443-6340; Kate Brass, Rhone Poulenc Rorer Pharmaceuticals, 500 Arcola Rd. H-11, Collegeville, PA 19426. Tel. 610-454-3028, fax 610-454-5299; Joyce W. Ellis, Whitehall-Robins, Box 9113, Richmond, VA 23227. Tel. 804-257-2794, fax 804-329-6721; Donald J. Prososki, Hallmark Cards, Box 419580, Kansas City, MO 64141-6580. Tel. 816-274-4559, fax 816-274-4323.
Information Technology. John T. Phillips, 1803 Nantasket Rd., Knoxville, TN 37922. Tel./fax 615-966-9413.
Marketing (Advisory). Stuart Dunkel, 4901 Angelia, Jefferson City, MO 65109. Tel. 573-893-3027.
Nominating. Richard Weinholdt, National Archives, 1700 Inskster Blvd., Winnipeg, MB R2X 2T1, Canada. Tel. 204-983-8845, fax 204-983-4649.
Professional Issues. David O. Stephens, Zasio, Box 2674, Smithfield, NC 27577. Tel. 919-989-1106, fax 919-989-6453.
Publications Coordination. Jean K. Brown, Univ. Archives, Univ. of Delaware, 002 Pearson Hall, Newark, DE 19716. Tel. 302-831-2750, fax 302-831-6903.
Standards Advisory and Development (Subcommittee). Marti Fischer, First American Records Management, 559 Charcot Ave., San Jose, CA 95131. Tel. 408-435-8141, fax 408-435-0701.
U.S. Government Relations. Andrea D. Lentz, Info. Mgt. Section, Ohio Dept. of Human Services, 2098 Integrity Dr. N., Columbus, OH 43209. Tel. 614-443-5800, fax 614-443-2822.

Art Libraries Society of North America

Executive Director, Penney De Pas
4101 Lake Boone Trail, Suite 201
Raleigh, NC 27607
919-787-5181, fax 919-787-4916
e-mail 74517.3400@compuserve.com, World Wide Web http://www.uflib.ufl.edu/arlis

Object

To foster excellence in art librarianship and visual resources curatorship for the advancement of the visual arts. Established 1972.

Membership

Memb. 1,325. Dues (Inst.) $80; (Indiv.) $65; (Business Affiliate) $100; (Student/Retired/Unemployed) $40; (Sustaining) $200; (Sponsor) $500; (Overseas) $80. Year. Jan. 1–Dec. 31. Membership is open and encouraged for all those interested in visual librarianship, whether they be professional librarians, students, library assistants, art book publishers, art book dealers, art historians, archivists, architects, slide and photograph curators, or retired associates in these fields.

Officers (1996–1997)

Pres. Jack Robertson, Kimball Fine Arts Lib., Univ. of Virginia, Bayly Dr., Charlottesville, VA 22903. Tel. 804-924-6601, fax 804-982-2678, e-mail jsr8s@virginia.edu; *V.P./Pres.-Elect* Roger Lawson, National Gallery of Art Lib., Sixth St. and Constitution Ave. N.W., Washington, DC 20565. Tel. 202-842-6529, fax 202-408-8530, e-mail r-lawson@nga.gov; *Past Pres.* Edward Teague, Architecture and Fine Arts Lib., Univ. of Florida, Box 115800, Gainesville, FL 32611. Tel. 352-392-0222, fax 352-846-2747, e-mail edteag@nervm.nerdc.ufl.edu; *Secy.* Maryly Snow, Architecture Slide Lib., Univ. of California at Berkeley, 232 Wurster Hall, Berkeley, CA 94720-1800. Tel. 510-642-3439, fax 510-643-5607, e-mail slides@ced.berkeley.edu; *Treas.* Ross Day, Robert Goldwater Lib., Metropolitan Museum of Art, 1000 Fifth

Ave., New York, NY 10028-0198. Tel. 212-570-3707, fax 212-570-3879, e-mail rglib2@metgate.metro.org.

Address correspondence to the executive director.

Executive Board

Officers; *Regional Reps.* (Northeast) Elizabeth Peck Learned, (South) Janine Henri, (Midwest) Stephanie Sigala, (West) Deborah Barlow Smedstad, (Canada) Jane Devine.

Publications

ARLIS/NA Update (bi-m.; memb.).
Art Documentation (semi-ann.; memb.).
Handbook and List of Members (ann.; memb.).
Occasional Papers (price varies).
Miscellaneous others (request current list from headquarters).

Committees

AAT (Advisory).
Awards.
Cataloging (Advisory).
Collection Development.
Conference.
Development.
Diversity.
Finance.
International Relations.
Membership.
Gerd Muehsam Award.
Nominating.
North American Relations.
Professional Development.
Public Policy.
Publications.
Research.
Standards.
Technology Education.
Technology Relations.
Travel.
George Wittenborn Award.

Chapters

Arizona; Central Plains; D.C.-Maryland-Virginia; Delaware Valley; Michigan; Midstates; Montreal-Ottawa-Quebec; New England; New Jersey; New York; Northern California; Northwest; Ohio Valley; Ontario; Southeast; Southern California; Texas; Twin Cities; Western New York.

Asian/Pacific American Librarians Association

President, Kenneth A. Yamashita
Library Division Manager, Central Library and Technical Services
Stockton–San Joaquin County Public Library, 605 N. El Dorado St., Stockton, CA 95202
209-937-8467, fax 209-937-8683, e-mail yamask04@stockton.lib.ca.us

Object

To provide a forum for discussing problems and concerns of Asian/Pacific American librarians; to provide a forum for the exchange of ideas by Asian/Pacific American librarians and other librarians; to support and encourage library services to Asian/Pacific American communities; to recruit and support Asian/Pacific American librarians in the library/information science professions; to seek funding for scholarships in library/information science schools for Asian/Pacific Americans; and to provide a vehicle whereby Asian/Pacific American librarians can cooperate with other associations and organizations having similar or allied interests. Founded 1980; incorporated 1981; affiliated with the American Library Association 1982.

Membership

Open to all librarians and information specialists of Asian/Pacific descent working in U.S. libraries and information centers and other related organizations and to others who support the goals and purposes of APALA.

Asian/Pacific Americans are defined as those who consider themselves Asian/Pacific Americans. They may be Americans of Asian/Pacific descent, Asian/Pacific people with the status of permanent residency, or Asian/Pacific people living in the United States. Dues (Inst.) $25; (Indiv.) $10; (Students/Unemployed Librarians) $5.

Officers (July 1996–June 1997)

Pres. Kenneth A. Yamashita, Lib. Div. Mgr., Central Lib. and Technical Services, Stockton–San Joaquin County Public Lib., 605 N. El Dorado St., Stockton, CA 95202. Tel. 209-937-8467, fax 209-937-8683, e-mail yamask04@stockton.lib.ca.us; *V.P./Pres.-Elect* Abulfazal M. F. Kabir, School of Lib. and Info. Studies, Clark Atlanta Univ., 223 James P. Brawley Dr. S.W., Atlanta, GA 30314. Tel. 404-880-8701, fax 404-880-8222; *Secy.* Fenghua Wang, Libn., SUNY College at Purchase Lib., 735 Anderson Hill Rd., Purchase, NY 10577. Tel. 914-251-6435, fax 914-251-6437, e-mail fwang@brick.purchase.edu; *Treas.* Julita C. Awkard, Head Libn., School of Nursing/Allied Health Sciences Lib., Florida A&M Univ., 5605 Maple Forest Dr., Tallahassee, FL 32303. Tel. 904-599-3872, fax 904-599-3900.

Advisory Committee

Officers; immediate past president; Sharad Karkhanis; Suzine Har-Nicolescu.

Publication

APALA Newsletter. Ed. Sandra Yamate, Polychrome Publishing Corp., 4509 N. Francisco Ave., Chicago, IL 60625. Tel. 773-478-4455, fax 773-478-0786.

Committee Chairpersons

Awards. Suzine Har-Nicolescu.
Constitution and Bylaws. Lourdes Collantes, Patricia Wong.
Finance. To be appointed.
Membership. Rama Vishwanatham.
Newsletter and Publications. Sandra Yamate.
Nominations. Amy Seetoo.
Program. Patricia Wong.
Publicity. To be appointed.
Recruitment and Scholarship. Rochelle Amores.

Association for Information and Image Management

President, John F. Mancini
1100 Wayne Ave., Suite 1100, Silver Spring, MD 20910
301-587-8202, fax 301-587-2711
e-mail aiim@aiim.org, World Wide Web http://www.aiim.org

Object

The mission of the Association for Information and Image Management is to be the leading global association bringing together the users of document technologies with the providers of that technology. Our focus is on helping corporate and institutional users understand these technologies and how they can be applied to improve critical business processes.

Officers

Chair Thornton A. May, Cambridge Technology Partners, 304 Vassar St., Cambridge, MA 02139; *V. Chair* Barry N. Lurie, Unisys Corp., Box 500, MS B230, Blue Bell, PA 19424; *Treas.* William N. Stratigos, Wang Software, 622 Third Ave., 30th fl., New York, NY 10017.

Publication

INFORM (10 per year; memb.). *Ed.* Robert Head.

Association for Library and Information Science Education

Executive Director, Sharon Rogers
Box 7640, Arlington, VA 22207
703-522-1899, e-mail srogers@gwis2.circ.gwu.edu
World Wide Web http://www.si.umich.edu/ALISE

Object

The Association for Library and Information Science Education (ALISE) is an association devoted to the advancement of knowledge and learning in the interdisciplinary field of information studies. Established 1915.

Membership

Memb. 690. Dues (Inst.) for ALA-accredited programs $250; all others $150; (International Affiliate Inst.) $75; (Indiv.) $25 or $60. Year. Sept.–Aug. Any library/information science school with a program accredited by the ALA Committee on Accreditation may become an institutional member. Any school that offers a graduate degree in librarianship or a cognate field but whose program is not accredited by the ALA Committee on Accreditation may become an institutional member at the lower rate. Any school outside the United States and Canada offering a program comparable to that of institutional membership may become an international affiliate institutional member. Any faculty member, administrator, librarian, researcher, or other individual employed full time may become a personal member. Any retired or part-time faculty member, student, or other individual employed less than full time may become a personal member at the lower rate.

Officers (1996–1997)

Pres. Joan C. Durrance, Univ. of Michigan. E-mail durrance@umich.edu; *V.P./Pres.-Elect* Toni Carbo, Univ. of Pittsburgh. E-mail carbo@lis.pitt.edu; *Past Pres.* June Lester, Univ. of Oklahoma. E-mail jlester@slis.lib.uoknor.edu; *Secy.-Treas.* Carl Orgren, Univ. of Iowa. E-mail carl-orgren@uiowa.edu.

Directors

Officers; Elfreda Chatman, Univ. of North Carolina (1998). E-mail Chatman@ils.unc.edu; Carol Kuhlthau, Rutgers Univ. (2000). E-mail kuhlthau@scils.rutgers.edu; Dan O'Connor, Rutgers Univ. (1999). E-mail oconnor@scils.rutgers.edu; *Co-Eds.* Joseph Mika (1999), Wayne State Univ. E-mail jmika@cms.cc.wayne.edu; Ronald W. Powell (1999), Wayne State Univ. E-mail rpowell@cms.cc.wayne.edu; *Exec. Dir.* Emily Lenhart. E-mail elenhart@umich.edu; *Parliamentarians* Charles A. Bunge, Norman Horrocks.

Publications

ALISE Library and Information Science Education Statistical Report (ann.; $54, foreign $56).
Journal of Education for Library and Information Science (4 per year; $60; foreign $70).
Membership Directory (ann.; $50).

Committee Chairpersons

Awards and Honors. Shirley Fitzgibbons, Indiana Univ.
Communications and Public Relations. Connie Van Fleet.
Conference Planning. Joan C. Durrance, Univ. of Michigan.
Editorial Board. Danny Wallace, Kent State Univ.
Government Relations. Ron Doctor, Univ. of Alabama.
International Relations. Terry Crowley, San Jose State Univ.
LIS Education Statistical Report Project. Evelyn Daniel and Jerry Saye, Univ. of North Carolina.

Membership. Jose-Marie Griffiths, Univ. of Michigan.
Nominating. Ken Haycock, Univ. of British Columbia.
Organization and Bylaws. Ken Shearer, North Carolina Central Univ.
Recruitment. Kathleen McCook, Univ. of South Florida.
Research. Bob Williams, Univ. of South Carolina.
Resolutions. Marianne Cooper, Queens College.
Tellers. Margaret Taylor, Univ. of Michigan.

Association of Academic Health Sciences Libraries

2033 Sixth Ave., Suite 804, Seattle, WA 98121
206-441-6020, fax 206-441-8262
e-mail sbinc@halcyon.com

Object

To promote—in cooperation with educational institutions, other educational associations, government agencies, and other nonprofit organizations—the common interests of academic health sciences libraries located in the United States and elsewhere, through publications, research, and discussion of problems of mutual interest and concern, and to advance the efficient and effective operation of academic health sciences libraries for the benefit of faculty, students, administrators, and practitioners.

Membership

Dues (Inst.) $500; (Assoc. Inst.) $200. Regular membership is available to nonprofit educational institutions operating a school of health sciences that has full or provisional accreditation by the Association of American Medical Colleges. Regular members shall be represented by the chief administrative officer of the member institution's health sciences library. Associate membership (and nonvoting representation) is available to organizations having an interest in the purposes and activities of the association.

Association of Jewish Libraries

15 E. 26 St., Rm. 1034, New York, NY 10010
212-678-8093, fax 212-678-8998

Object

To promote the improvement of library services and professional standards in all Jewish libraries and collections of Judaica; to serve as a center of dissemination of Jewish library information and guidance; to encourage the establishment of Jewish libraries and collections of Judaica; to promote publication of literature that will be of assistance to Jewish librarianship; and to encourage people to enter the field of librarianship. Organized in 1965 from the merger of the Jewish Librarians Association and the Jewish Library Association.

Membership

Memb. 1,100. Dues $35; (Student/Retired) $18. Year. July 1–June 30.

Officers (June 1996–June 1998)

Pres. Esther Nussbaum, Ramaz Upper School Lib., 60 E. 78 St., New York, NY 10021; *V.P./Pres.-Elect* David Gilner, Hebrew Union College–J.I.R., Lib., 3101 Clifton Ave., Cincinnati, OH 45220; *Past Pres.* Zachary Baker, Lib., YIVO Inst. for Jewish Research, 555 W. 57 St., New York, NY 10019; *V.P., Memb.* Shoshanah Seidman, Univ. of Chicago, 1100 E. 57 St., Chicago, IL 60637; *Treas.* Nira Wolfe, Hebrew Theological College, 7135 Carpenter Rd., Skokie, IL 60077; *Rec. Secy.* Frances Wolf, Congregation Beth Shalom, 9400 Wornall Rd., Kansas City, MO 64114; *Corresponding Secy.* Sarah Spiegel, Lib., Jewish Theological Seminary of America, 3080 Broadway, New York, NY 10027; *Publications V.P.* Beverly Newman, 11808 High Dr., Leawood, KS 66211.

Address correspondence to the association.

Publications

AJL Newsletter (q.). *Eds.* Irene Levin-Wixman, 5494 Palm Springs Lane, Boynton Beach, FL 33437; Hazel Karp, 880 Somerset Dr. N.W., Atlanta, GA 30327.

Judaica Librarianship (irreg.). *Ed.* Bella Hass Weinberg, Div. of Lib. and Info. Science, Saint John's Univ., 8000 Utopia Pkwy., Jamaica, NY 11439.

Division Presidents

Research and Special Library. Aviva Astrinsky.

Synagogue, School, and Center Libraries. Fred Isaac.

Association of Research Libraries

Executive Director, Duane E. Webster
21 Dupont Circle N.W., Suite 800, Washington, DC 20036
202-296-2296, fax 202-872-0884
e-mail arlhq@cni.org, World Wide Web http://www.arl.cni.org/

Object

The mission of the Association of Research Libraries (ARL) is to shape and influence forces affecting the future of research libraries in the process of scholarly communication. ARL's programs and services promote equitable access to and effective use of recorded knowledge in support of teaching, research, scholarship, and community service. The association articulates the concerns of research libraries and their institutions, forges coalitions, influences information policy development, and supports innovation and improvement in research library operations. ARL is a not-for-profit membership organization comprising the libraries of North American research institutions and operates as a forum for the exchange of ideas and as an agent for collective action.

Membership

Memb. 120. Membership is institutional. Dues $14,450. Year. Jan.–Dec.

Officers (Oct. 1996–Oct. 1997)

Pres. Gloria Werner, Univ. Libn., UCLA; *Pres.-Elect* James Neal, Dir. of Libs., Johns Hopkins Univ.; *Past Pres.* Nancy Cline, Libn. of Harvard College, Harvard Univ.

Board of Directors

Shirley K. Baker, Washington Univ. (Saint Louis); Betty L. Bengtson, Univ. of Washington; Nancy Cline, Harvard Univ.; William J. Crowe, Univ. of Kansas; Nancy L. Eaton, Univ. of Iowa; Kenneth Frazier, Univ. of Wisconsin; Carole Moore, Univ. of Toronto;

James G. Neal, Johns Hopkins Univ.; William G. Potter, Univ. of Georgia; Barbara von Wahlde, SUNY Buffalo; Gloria Werner, UCLA.

Publications

ARL: A Bimonthly Newsletter of Research Libraries Issues and Actions (bi-m.; memb. $25; nonmemb. $50).
ARL Academic Law and Medical Library Statistics (ann.; memb. $35; nonmemb. $65).
ARL Annual Salary Survey (ann.; memb. $35; nonmemb. $65).
ARL Preservation Statistics (ann.; memb. $35; nonmemb. $65).
ARL Statistics (ann.; memb. $35; nonmemb. $65).
Developing Indicators for Academic Library Performance: Ratios from the ARL Statistics 1993–94 and 1994–95 (ann.; memb. $25; nonmemb. $50).
Directory of Electronic Journals, Newsletters, and Academic Discussion Lists. (ann.; memb. $55; nonmemb. $79).
Proceedings of the ARL Membership Meetings (2 per yr.; memb. $45; nonmemb. $70).
Systems and Procedures Exchange Center (SPEC): Kits and Flyers (10 per year; kits: memb. $185, nonmemb. $280; flyers $50).

Committee and Work Group Chairpersons

Access to Information Resources. Shirley K. Baker, Washington Univ., Saint Louis.
Copyright Issues (Working Group). James G. Neal, Johns Hopkins Univ.
Diversity. Nancy Baker, Washington State Univ.
Information Policy. Nancy Cline, Harvard Univ.
Management of Research Library Resources. Paul Kobulnicky, Univ. of Connecticut.
Preservation of Research Library Materials. Meredith Butler, SUNY Albany.
Research Collections. Joe A. Hewitt, Univ. of North Carolina at Chapel Hill.
Scholarly Communication. Elaine F. Sloan, Columbia Univ.
Scientific and Technical Information (Working Group). Marilyn Sharrow. Univ. of California at Davis.
Statistics and Measurement. William J. Studer, Ohio State Univ.

Units

Coalition for Networked Information. Formed by ARL, CAUSE, and EDUCOM in March 1990 to advance scholarship and intellectual productivity by promoting the provision of information resources on existing and future telecommunications networks, and the linkage of research libraries to these networks and to their respective constituencies.
Office of Management Services. Provides consulting, training, and publishing services on the management of human and material resources in libraries.
Office of Research and Development. Pursues the ARL research agenda through the identification and development of projects in support of the research library community's mission.
Office of Scholarly Communication. Established in 1990 to identify and influence the forces affecting the production, dissemination, and use of scholarly and scientific information.

ARL Membership

Nonuniversity Libraries

Boston Public Lib., Canada Inst. for Scientific and Technical Info., Center for Research Libs., Linda Hall Lib., Lib. of Congress, National Agricultural Lib., National Lib. of Canada, National Lib. of Medicine, New York Public Lib., New York State Lib., Smithsonian Institution Libs.

University Libraries

Alabama, Alberta, Arizona, Arizona State, Auburn, Boston, Brigham Young, British Columbia, Brown, California (Berkeley), California (Davis), California (Irvine), California (Los Angeles), California (Riverside), California (San Diego), California (Santa

Barbara), Case Western Reserve, Chicago, Cincinnati, Colorado, Colorado State, Columbia, Connecticut, Cornell, Dartmouth, Delaware, Duke, Emory, Florida, Florida State, Georgetown, Georgia, Georgia Inst. of Technology, Guelph, Harvard, Hawaii, Houston, Howard, Illinois (Chicago), Illinois (Urbana), Indiana, Iowa, Iowa State, Johns Hopkins, Kansas, Kent State, Kentucky, Laval, Louisiana State, McGill, McMaster, Manitoba, Maryland, Massachusetts, Massachusetts Inst. of Technology, Miami (Fla.), Michigan, Michigan State, Minnesota, Missouri, Nebraska (Lincoln), New Mexico, New York, North Carolina, North Carolina State, Northwestern, Notre Dame, Ohio, Ohio State, Oklahoma, Oklahoma State, Oregon, Pennsylvania, Pennsylvania State, Pittsburgh, Princeton, Purdue, Queen's (Kingston, Canada), Rice, Rochester, Rutgers, Saskatchewan, South Carolina, Southern California, Southern Illinois, Stanford, SUNY (Albany), SUNY (Buffalo), SUNY (Stony Brook), Syracuse, Temple, Tennessee, Texas, Texas A&M, Toronto, Tulane, Utah, Vanderbilt, Virginia, Virginia Polytechnic, Washington, Washington (Saint Louis, Mo.), Washington State, Waterloo, Wayne State, Western Ontario, Wisconsin, Yale, York.

Association of Vision Science Librarians

Chair, Douglas Freeman, Optometry Library, Indiana University, Bloomington, IN 47405
812-855-8629, fax 812-855-6616
e-mail freeman@indiana.edu

Object

To foster collective and individual acquisition and dissemination of vision science information, to improve services for all persons seeking such information, and to develop standards for libraries to which members are attached. Founded 1968.

Membership

Memb. (U.S.) 55; (Foreign) 9.

Publications

Guidelines for Vision Science Libraries.
Opening Day Book Collection—Visual Science.
PhD Theses in Physiological Optics (irreg.).
Standards for Vision Science Libraries.
Union List of Vision-Related Serials (irreg.).

Meetings

Annual meeting held in December in connection with the American Academy of Optometry; midyear mini-meeting with the Medical Library Association.

Beta Phi Mu
(International Library and Information Science Honor Society)

Executive Secretary, F. William Summers
School of Library and Information Studies, Florida State University,
Tallahassee, FL 32306-2048
904-644-3907, fax 904-644-6253
e-mail beta_phi_mu@lis.fsu.edu

Object

To recognize high scholarship in the study of librarianship and to sponsor appropriate professional and scholarly projects. Founded at the University of Illinois in 1948.

Membership

Memb. 23,000. Open to graduates of library school programs accredited by the American Library Association who fulfill the following requirements: complete the course requirements leading to a fifth year or other advanced degree in librarianship with a scholastic average of 3.75 where A equals 4 points (this provision shall also apply to planned programs of advanced study beyond the fifth year that do not culminate in a degree but that require full-time study for one or more academic years) and in the top 25 percent of their class; receive a letter of recommendation from their respective library schools attesting to their demonstrated fitness for successful professional careers.

Officers

Pres. Mary Biggs, West Lib., Trenton State College, Hillwood Lakes, CN 4700, Trenton, NJ 08650-4700; *V.P./Pres.-Elect* Marion T. Reid, Dean of Lib. Services, California State Univ. at San Marcos, 820 Los Vallecitos Blvd., San Marcos, CA 92096-0001; *Past Pres.* Elfreda A. Chatman, School of Lib. and Info. Science, Univ. of North Carolina, Chapel Hill, NC 27599-3360; *Treas.* Sondra Taylor-Furbee, State Lib. of Florida, 500 S. Bronough St., Tallahassee, FL 32399; *Exec. Secy.* F. William Summers, School of Lib. and Info. Studies, Florida State Univ., Tallahassee, FL 32306-2048.

Directors

Arthur C. Gunn (1997), W. Michael Havener (1997), Rhonda Marker (1996), Zary M. Shafa (1996), Darlene E. Weingand (1998); *Dirs.-at-Large* Susan Webreck Alman, Nancy P. Zimmerman.

Publications

Beta Phi Mu Monograph Series. Book-length scholarly works based on original research in subjects of interest to library and information professionals. Available from Greenwood Press, 88 Post Rd. W., Box 5007, Westport, CT 06881-9990.

Chapbook Series. Limited editions on topics of interest to information professionals. Call Beta Phi Mu for availability.

Newsletter. Ed. William Scheeren.

Chapters

Alpha. Univ. of Illinois, Grad. School of Lib. and Info. Science, Urbana, IL 61801; *Beta.* (Inactive). Univ. of Southern California, School of Lib. Science, Univ. Park, Los Angeles, CA 90007; *Gamma.* Florida State Univ., School of Lib. and Info. Studies, Tallahassee, FL 32306; *Delta* (Inactive). Loughborough College of Further Education, School of Libnshp., Loughborough, England; *Epsilon.* Univ. of North Carolina, School of Lib. Science, Chapel Hill, NC 27599; *Zeta.* Atlanta Univ., School of Lib. and Info. Studies, Atlanta, GA 30314; *Theta.* Pratt Inst., Grad. School of Lib. and Info. Science, Brooklyn,

NY 11205; *Iota.* Catholic Univ. of America, School of Lib. and Info. Science, Washington, DC 20064; Univ. of Maryland, College of Lib. and Info. Services, College Park, MD 20742; *Kappa.* (Inactive). Western Michigan Univ., School of Libnshp., Kalamazoo, MI 49008; *Lambda.* Univ. of Oklahoma, School of Lib. Science, Norman, OK 73019; *Mu.* Univ. of Michigan, School of Lib. Science, Ann Arbor, MI 48109; *Nu* (Inactive); *Xi.* Univ. of Hawaii, Grad. School of Lib. Studies, Honolulu, HI 96822; *Omicron.* Rutgers Univ., Grad. School of Lib. and Info. Studies, New Brunswick, NJ 08903; *Pi.* Univ. of Pittsburgh, School of Lib. and Info. Science, Pittsburgh, PA 15260; *Rho.* Kent State Univ., School of Lib. Science, Kent, OH 44242; *Sigma.* Drexel Univ., School of Lib. and Info. Science, Philadelphia, PA 19104; *Tau* (Inactive). State Univ. of New York at Geneseo, School of Lib. and Info. Science, Geneseo, NY 14454; *Upsilon.* (Inactive). Univ. of Kentucky, College of Lib. Science, Lexington, KY 40506; *Phi* Univ. of Denver, Grad. School of Libnshp. and Info. Mgt., Denver, CO 80208; *Chi.* Indiana Univ., School of Lib. and Info. Science, Bloomington, IN 47401; *Psi.* Univ. of Missouri at Columbia, School of Lib. and Info. Sciences, Columbia, MO 65211; *Omega* (Inactive). San Jose State Univ., Div. of Lib. Science, San Jose, CA 95192; *Beta Alpha.* Queens College, City College of New York, Grad. School of Lib. and Info. Studies, Flushing, NY 11367; *Beta Beta.* Simmons College, Grad. School of Lib. and Info. Science, Boston, MA 02115; *Beta Delta.* State Univ. of New York at Buffalo, School of Info. and Lib. Studies, Buffalo, NY 14260; *Beta Epsilon.* Emporia State Univ., School of Lib. Science, Emporia, KS 66801; *Beta Zeta.* Louisiana State Univ., Grad. School of Lib. Science, Baton Rouge, LA 70803; *Beta Eta.* Univ. of Texas at Austin, Grad. School of Lib. and Info. Science, Austin, TX 78712; *Beta Theta.* (Inactive). Brigham Young Univ., School of Lib. and Info. Science, Provo, UT 84602; *Beta Iota.* Univ. of Rhode Island, Grad. Lib. School, Kingston, RI 02881; *Beta Kappa.* Univ. of Alabama, Grad. School of Lib. Service, University, AL 35486; *Beta Lambda.* North Texas State Univ., School of Lib. and Info. Science, Denton, TX 76203; Texas Woman's Univ., School of Lib. Science, Denton, TX 76204; *Beta Mu.* Long Island Univ., Palmer Grad. Lib. School, C. W. Post Center, Greenvale, NY 11548; *Beta Nu.* Saint John's Univ., Div. of Lib. and Info. Science, Jamaica, NY 11439. *Beta Xi.* North Carolina Central Univ., School of Lib. Science, Durham, NC 27707; *Beta Omicron.* (Inactive). Univ. of Tennessee at Knoxville, Grad. School of Lib. and Info. Science, Knoxville, TN 37916; *Beta Pi.* Univ. of Arizona, Grad. Lib. School, Tucson, AZ 85721; *Beta Rho.* Univ. of Wisconsin at Milwaukee, School of Lib. Science, Milwaukee, WI 53201; *Beta Sigma.* (Inactive). Clarion State College, School of Lib. Science, Clarion, PA 16214; *Beta Tau.* Wayne State Univ., Div. of Lib. Science, Detroit, MI 48202; *Beta Upsilon* (Inactive). Alabama A & M Univ., School of Lib. Media, Normal, AL 35762; *Beta Phi.* Univ. of South Florida, Grad. Dept. of Lib., Media, and Info. Studies, Tampa, FL 33647; *Beta Psi.* Univ. of Southern Mississippi, School of Lib. Service, Hattiesburg, MS 39406; *Beta Omega.* Univ. of South Carolina, College of Libnshp., Columbia, SC 29208; *Beta Beta Alpha.* Univ. of California at Los Angeles, Grad. School of Lib. and Info. Science, Los Angeles, CA 90024; *Beta Beta Gamma.* Rosary College, Grad. School of Lib. and Info. Science, River Forest, IL 60305; *Beta Beta Delta.* Univ. of Cologne, Germany; *Beta Beta Epsilon.* Univ. of Wisconsin at Madison, Lib. School, Madison, WI 53706; *Beta Beta Zeta.* Univ. of North Carolina at Greensboro, Dept. of Lib. Science and Educational Technology, Greensboro, NC 27412; *Beta Beta Theta.* Univ. of Iowa, School of Lib. and Info. Science, Iowa City, IA 52242; *Beta Beta Iota.* State Univ. of New York, Univ. at Albany, School of Info. Science and Policy, Albany, NY 12222; *Pi Lambda Sigma.* Syracuse Univ., School of Info. Studies, Syracuse, NY 13210.

Bibliographical Society of America

Executive Secretary, Marjory Zaik
Box 397, Grand Central Station, New York, NY 10163
212-647-9171

Object

To promote bibliographical research and to issue bibliographical publications. Organized 1904.

Membership

Memb. 1,200. Dues $50. Year. Jan.–Dec.

Officers (Jan. 1997–Jan. 1998)

Pres. Roger E. Stoddard; *V.P.* Katharine Kyes Leab; *Treas.* R. Dyke Benjamin; *Secy.* Hope Mayo.

Council

T. Kimball Brooker (1997), Peter S. Graham (1998), James N. Green (1999), Trevor Howard-Hill (1997), Katharine Kyes Leab (1997), Leslie Morris (1999), Paul Needham (1997), Fred Schreiber (1998), Alice Schreyer (1998), William P. Stoneman (1998), Michael Winship (1999), David S. Zeidberg (1999).

Publication

Papers (q.; memb.). *Ed.* Trevor Howard-Hill, Dept. of English, Univ. of South Carolina, Columbia, SC 29208.

Committee Chairpersons

Bibliographical Projects. Michael Winship.
Delegate to American Council of Learned Societies. Marcus McCorison.
Fellowship Program. Richard Landon.
Finance. Paul Gouray.
Publications. Katharine Kyes Leab.

Canadian Association for Information Science
(Association Canadienne des Sciences de l'Information)

140 Saint George St., Toronto, ON M5S 1A1, Canada
416-978-8876

Object

To bring together individuals and organizations concerned with the production, manipulation, storage, retrieval, and dissemination of information, with emphasis on the application of modern technologies in these areas. The Canadian Association for Information Science (CAIS) is dedicated to enhancing the activity of the information transfer process; utilizing the vehicles of research, development, application, and education; and serving as a forum for dialogue and exchange of ideas concerned with the theory and practice of all factors involved in the communication of information.

Membership

Institutions and individuals interested in information science and involved in the gathering, organization, and dissemination of information (computer scientists, documentalists, information scientists, librarians, journalists, sociologists, psychologists, linguists, administrators, etc.) can become members of CAIS. Dues (Inst.) $165; (Personal) $75; (Student) $40.

Chapters

CAIS West. Jocelyn Godolphin.
Ottawa. Pat Johnston.

Publication

Canadian Journal of Information and Library Science (q.; $95; outside Canada $110).

Canadian Library Association

Executive Director, Karen Adams
200 Elgin St., Ottawa, ON K2P 1L5, Canada
613-232-9625, fax 613-563-9895
e-mail aim77@freenet.carleton.ca

Object

To provide leadership in the promotion, development, and support of library and information services in Canada for the benefit of association members, the profession, and Canadian society. Offers library school scholarship and book awards; carries on international liaison with other library associations; makes representation to government and official commissions; offers professional development programs; and supports intellectual freedom. Founded in 1946, CLA is a nonprofit voluntary organization governed by an elected executive council.

Membership

Memb. (Indiv.) 4,000; (Inst.) 1,000. Open to individuals, institutions, and groups interested in librarianship and in library and information services. Dues (Indiv.) $55 to $175, depending on salary; (Inst.) from $175 up, graduated on budget basis. Year. Anniversary date renewal.

Officers (1996–1997)

Pres. Karen Harrison, Chief Libn., Thunder Bay Public Lib., 285 Red River Rd., Thunder Bay, ON P7B 1A9. Tel. 807-344-3585, fax 807-345-8727, e-mail kharriso@flash.lakeheadu.ca; *V.P./Pres.-Elect* Paul Whitney, Chief Libn., Burnaby Public Lib., 6100 Willingdon Ave., Burnaby, BC V5H 4N5. Tel. 604-436-5431, fax 604-436-2961, e-mail pwhitnea@sfu.ca; *Treas.* Rowena Lunn, Dir., Marigold Lib. System, Strathmore, AB T1P 1G4. Tel. 403-934-5334, fax 403-934-5331, e-mail rlunn@freenet.calgary.ab.ca; *Past Pres.* Penelope J. Marshall, Univ. Libn., Univ. College of Cape Breton, Sydney, NS B1P 6L2. Tel. 902-563-1388, fax 902-563-1177, e-mail pmarshall@caper2.uccb.ns.ca.

Executive Council

Table officers, divisional presidents, and councillors-at-large.

Publication

Feliciter (10 per year; newsletter).

Division Representatives

Canadian Association of College and University Libraries. Frank Winter, Dir. of Libs., Univ. of Saskatchewan, 811 Nesslin Ct., Saskatoon, SK S7N 0W0. Tel. 306-966-5942, fax 306-966-5932, e-mail winter@sklib.usask.ca.

Canadian Association of Public Libraries (CAPL). Beth Hovius, Marketing Mgr., Hamilton Public Lib., Box 2700, Sta. LCD 1, Hamilton, ON L8N 4E4. Tel. 905-546-3285, fax 905-546-3282.

Canadian Association of Special Libraries and Information Services (CASLIS). Mary-Lu Brennan, 3 Greystone Walk Dr., PH 29, Scarborough, ON M1K 5J4. Tel. 416-261-1263.

Canadian Library Trustees' Association (CLTA). Barrie Lynch, 1261 Nestor St., Coquitlam, BC V3E 1H4. Tel. 604-430-9626, fax 604-576-9474, e-mail aa072@freenet.victoria.bc.ca.

Canadian School Library Association (CSLA). Judith A. Kootte, Consultant, Richmond School Board, 7811 Granville Ave., Richmond, BC V6Y 3E3. Tel. 604-668-6056, fax 604-668-6191, e-mail jkootte@cln.etc.bc.ca.

Catholic Library Association

Past President, Jean R. Bostley, SSJ, St. Joseph Central High School, 22 Maplewood Ave., Pittsfield, MA 01201-4780.

Object

The promotion and encouragement of Catholic literature and library work through cooperation, publications, education, and information. Founded 1921.

Membership

Memb. 1,300. Dues $45–$500. Year. July–June.

Officers (1997–1999)

Past Pres. Jean R. Bostley, SSJ, Saint Joseph Central High School, 22 Maplewood Ave., Pittsfield, MA 01201-4780. Tel. 413-443-2252, fax 413-443-7020; *V.P.* Rev. Bonaventure Hayes, OFM, Christ the King Seminary, 711 Knox Rd., East Aurora, NY 14052-0607

Address correspondence to the past president or vice-president.

Executive Board

Officers; Mary Agnes Casey, SSJ, Marist High School, 1241 Kennedy Blvd., Bayonne, NJ 07002; Mary K. Dobbs, Ocean County College, Box 2001, Toms River, NJ 08754-2001; Nicholas Falco, 1256 Pelham Pkwy.,

Bronx, NY 10461; Mary E. Gallagher, SSJ, College of Our Lady of the Elms, 291 Springfield St., Chicopee, MA 01013; Julanne M. Good, 5005 Jamieson Ave., Saint Louis, MO 63109; Barbara Anne Kilpatrick, RSM, Saint Bernard Academy, 2020 24th Ave. S., Nashville, TN 37212-4202.

Publications

Catholic Library World (q.; memb.; nonmemb. $60). *Ed.* Allen Gruenke.
Catholic Periodical and Literature Index (q.) *Ed.* Barry C. Hopkins.

Section Chairpersons

Academic Libraries/Library Education. William Brace.
Archives. Rev. Bonaventure Hayes, OFM.
Children's Libraries. Sister Rose Marie Anthony, OP.
High School Libraries. Sister Patricia Ann Berger, IHM.
Parish/Community Libraries. Phyllis Petre.

Round Table Chairpersons

Cataloging and Classification. Tina-Karen Forman.

Committee Chairpersons

Catholic Library World Editorial. Mary E. Gallagher, SSJ.
Catholic Periodical and Literature Index. Brother Paul J. Ostendorf, FSC.
Elections. Bert Thompson.
Finance. Rev. Bonaventure Hayes, OFM.
Membership Development. Julanne M. Good.
Nominations. Brother Paul J. Ostendorf, FSC.
Scholarship. Jean R. Bostley, SSJ.

Special Appointments

American Friends of the Vatican Library Board. Jean R. Bostley, SSJ.
Convention Program Coordinator. Tina-Karen Forman.
Parliamentarian. Rev. Joseph P. Browne.

Chief Officers of State Library Agencies

167 W. Main Street, Suite 600, Lexington, KY 40507
606-231-1925, fax 606-231-1928

Object

To provide a means of cooperative action among its state and territorial members to strengthen the work of the respective state and territorial agencies, and to provide a continuing mechanism for dealing with the problems faced by the heads of these agencies, which are responsible for state and territorial library development.

Membership

The Chief Officers of State Library Agencies (COSLA) is an independent organization of the men and women who head the state and territorial agencies responsible for library development. Its membership consists solely of the top library officers of the 50 states, the District of Columbia, and the territories, variously designated as state librarian, director, commissioner, or executive secretary.

Officers (1996–1998)

Pres. Sara Parker, State Libn., Missouri State Lib., 600 W. Main, Box 387, Jefferson City, MO 65102-0387. Tel. 573-751-2751, fax 573-751-3612, e-mail sparker@mail.sos.state.mo.us; *V.P./Pres.-Elect* C. Ray Ewick, Dir., State Lib., 140 N. Senate Ave., Indianapolis, IN 46204. Tel. 317-232-3692, fax 317-232-3728, e-mail ewick@statelib.lib.in.us; *Secy.* Kendall F. Wiggin, State Libn., 20

Park St., Concord, NH 03301-6314. Tel. 603-271-2397, fax 603-271-6826, e-mail wiggin@lilac.nhsl.lib.nh.us; *Treas.* Nancy Bolt, Deputy State Libn., Dept. of Educ., 201 E. Colfax Ave., Denver, CO 80203. Tel. 303-866-6733, fax 303-866-6940, e-mail nbolt@csn.net.

Directors

Officers; *Immediate Past Pres.* J. Maurice Travillian, Asst. State Superintendent for Libs., Div. of Lib. Development and Services, Dept. of Educ., 200 W. Baltimore St., Baltimore, MD 21201-2595. Tel. 410-767-0435, fax 410-333-2507, e-mail maurice@charm.net; *Dirs.* Keith Fiels, Dir., Bd. of Lib. Commissioners, 648 Beacon St., Boston, MA 02215. Tel. 617-267-9400, fax 617-421-9833, e-mail kfiels@state.ma.us; Edwin S. Gleaves, State Libn. and Archivist, 403 Seventh Ave. N., Nashville, TN 37243-0312. Tel. 615-741-7996, fax 615-741-6471, e-mail egleaves@mail.state.tn.us.

Chinese-American Librarians Association

Executive Director, Sheila S. Lai
c/o California State University, Sacramento
University Library, Room 2053, 2000 Jed Smith Drive E., Sacramento, CA 95819-6039
916-278-6201, fax 916-363-0868
e-mail SheilaLai@csus.edu

Object

To enhance communications among Chinese-American librarians as well as between Chinese-American librarians and other librarians; to serve as a forum for discussion of mutual problems and professional concerns among Chinese-American librarians; to promote Sino-American librarianship and library services; and to provide a vehicle whereby Chinese-American librarians may cooperate with other associations and organizations having similar or allied interest.

Membership

Memb. 770. Open to everyone who is interested in the association's goals and activities. Dues (Regular) $15; (Student/Nonsalaried) $7.50; (Inst.) $45; (Permanent) $200.

Officers (July 1996–June 1997)

Pres. Mengxiong Liu; *V.P./Pres.-Elect* Harriet Ying; *Exec. Dir.* Sheila S. Lai; *Treas.* Janet C. Nguyen.

Publications

Journal of Library and Information Science (2 per year; memb.; nonmemb. $15).
Membership Directory (memb.).
Newsletter (3 per year; memb.; nonmemb. $10).

Committee Chairpersons

Awards. Susana Liu.
Books to China. Dora Ho, Julia Tung.
Constitution and Bylaws. Peiling Wu.
Finance. Ming Li.
International Relations. Sha Li Zhang.
Membership. Diana Wu, Leslie Yi.
Public Relations/Fund-Raising. Linna Yu.
Publications. Liana Zhou.
Scholarship. Ingrid Hsieh-Yee.

Chapter Presidents

California. Grace Liu.
Greater Mid-Atlantic. Ernestine Wang.
Midwest. Liana Zhou.
Northeast. Diana Shih.
Southwest. William Wan.

Journal Officers

Newsletter Eds. Philip Ng, Center for Research Libs., 6050 S. Kenwood Ave., Chicago, IL 60637. Tel. 312-955-4545 ext. 327, fax 312-955-4339, e-mail ng@cr/mail.uchicago.edu; Lan Yang, Sterling C. Evans Lib., Texas A&M Univ., College Station, TX 77843-5000. Tel. 409-862-1904, fax 409-862-4575, e-mail qyang@tamu.edu.

Church and Synagogue Library Association

Box 19357, Portland, OR 97280-0357
503-244-6919, e-mail CSLA@worldaccess.com

Object

To act as a unifying core for the many existing church and synagogue libraries; to provide the opportunity for a mutual sharing of practices and problems; to inspire and encourage a sense of purpose and mission among church and synagogue librarians; to study and guide the development of church and synagogue librarianship toward recognition as a formal branch of the library profession. Founded 1967.

Membership

Memb. 1,900. Dues (Inst.) $125; (Affiliated) $60; (Church/Synagogue) $35; (Indiv.) $20. Year. July–June.

Officers (July 1996–June 1997)

Pres. Dottie Lewis, 1245 Sam Lions Trail, Martinsville, VA 24112; *1st V.P.* Lois Ward, 502 North St., Box 368, Prospect, OH 43302; *2nd V.P.* Russell Newburn, 9493 Moulin Ave., Alliance, OH 44601; *Treas.* Marilyn Demeter, 3145 Corydon Rd., Cleveland Heights, OH 44118; *Exec. Secy.* Judith Janzen; *Financial Asst.* J. Robert Waggoner, 413 Robindale Ave., Dearborn, MI 48128; *Publications Ed.* Karen Bota; *Book Review Ed.* Charles Snyder.

Executive Board

Officers; committee chairpersons.

Publications

Bibliographies (1–6; price varies).
Church and Synagogue Libraries (bi-mo.; memb.; nonmemb. $25; Canada $35). *Ed.* Karen Bota.
CSLA Guides (1–16; price varies).

Committee Chairpersons

Awards. Alrene Hall.
Chapters. Gail Waggoner.
Conference. Joyce White.
Continuing Education. Dianne Oswald.
Finance and Fund-raising. J. Robert Waggoner.
Library Services. Jane Parke.
Nominations and Elections. Donna McLaughlin-Schuereb.
Personnel. Joyce Allen.
Publications. Carol Campbell.

Council of Planning Librarians

114 N. Aberdeen St., Chicago, IL 60607-2004
312-409-3349

Object

To provide a special interest group in the field of city and regional planning for libraries and librarians, faculty, professional planners, university, government, and private planning organizations; to provide an opportunity for exchange among those interested in problems of library organization and research and in the dissemination of information about city and regional planning; to sponsor programs of service to the planning profession and librarianship; to advise on library organization for new planning programs; and to aid and support administrators, faculty, and librarians in their efforts to educate the public and their appointed or elected representatives to the necessity for strong library programs in support of planning. Founded 1960.

Membership

Memb. 242. Open to any individual or institution that supports the purpose of the council, upon written application and payment of dues to the treasurer. Dues (Inst.) $45; (Indiv.) $35; Year. July 1–June 30.

Officers and Board (1996–1997)

Pres. Linda S. Drake, Chapin Planning Lib., CB 3140, Univ. of North Carolina, Chapel Hill, NC 27599-3140. Tel. 919-962-4770; *V.P./Pres.-Elect* Julia M. Gelfand, Univ. Lib., Univ. of California at Irvine, Box 19557, Irvine, CA 92713. Tel. 714-824-4971; *Past Pres.* Debbie Fowler, City of Toronto Planning and Devt. Dept., City Hall, 19th fl., Toronto, ON M5H 2N2. Tel. 416-392-1526; *Treas.* Barbara Sykes-Austin, Avery Architectural and Fine Arts Lib., Columbia Univ., New York, NY 10027. Tel. 212-854-8907; *Secy.* Deborah Sommer, Environmental Design Lib., 210 Wurster Hall, Univ. of California, Berkeley, CA 94720. Tel. 510-642-4819; *Member-at-Large* Jan Horah, Jack Brause Lib., Real Estate Inst., New York Univ., 11 W. 42 St., Suite 510, New York, NY 10036-8002. Tel. 212-790-1325; *Ed., CPL Newsletter* Thelma Helyar, Inst. for Public Policy and Business Research, 607 Blake Hall, Univ. of Kansas, Lawrence, KS 56045-2960. Tel. 913-864-3701.

Publications

CPL Newsletter. (bi-m.; memb.)
CPLFYI-L. Electronic Discussion List. Contact Marilyn Myers at iadmxm@asuvm.inre.asu.edu.

Council on Library Resources/Commission on Preservation and Access

1400 16th St. N.W., Suite 715, Washington, DC 20036-2217
202-939-3400, fax 202-939-3407
World Wide Web: http://www-clr.stanford.edu/clr.html or http://www-cpa.stanford.edu/cpa.html

Object

In 1995–1996 the Council on Library Resources (CLR) and the Commission on Preservation and Access (CPA) moved toward a merged organization by integrating their programs and operating under a single president. The mission of the council and commission is to identify and define the key emerging issues related to the welfare of libraries and the constituencies they serve, convene the leaders who can influence change, and promote collaboration among the institutions and organizations that can achieve change. The council and commission's interests embrace the entire range of information resources and services from traditional library and archival materials to emerging digital formats. It assumes a particular interest in helping institutions cope with the accelerating pace of change associated with the transition into the digital environment. The council and commission pursue this mission out of the conviction that information is a public good and has great social utility.

The term *library* is construed to embrace its traditional meanings and purposes and to encompass any and all information agencies and organizations that are involved in gathering, cataloging, storing, preserving, and distributing information and in helping users meet their information requirements.

While maintaining appropriate collaboration and liaison with other institutions and organizations, the council and commission operate independently of any particular institutional or vested interests. Through the composition of its board, the affiliated organization brings the broadest possible perspective to bear upon defining and establishing the priority of the issues with which it is concerned.

Membership

The council and commission's membership and board of directors are limited to 25.

Officers

Chair Stanley Chodorow; *V. Chair* Marilyn Gell Mason; *Pres.* Deanna B. Marcum. E-mail dmarcum@cpa.org; *V.P.* James Morris; *Secy.* David B. Gracy, II; *Treas.* Dan Tonkery.

Address correspondence to headquarters.

Publications

Annual Report.
Various program publications.

Federal Library and Information Center Committee

Executive Director, Susan M. Tarr
Library of Congress, Washington, DC 20540-4920
202-707-4800
World Wide Web http://lcweb.loc.gov/flicc

Object

The committee makes recommendations on federal library and information policies, programs, and procedures to federal agencies and to others concerned with libraries and information centers. The committee coordinates cooperative activities and services among federal libraries and information centers and serves as a forum to consider issues and policies that affect federal libraries and information centers, needs and priorities in providing information services to the government and to the nation at large, and efficient and cost-effective use of federal library and information resources and services. Furthermore, the committee promotes improved access to information, continued development and use of the Federal Library and Information Network (FEDLINK), research and development in the application of new technologies to federal libraries and information centers, improvements in the management of federal libraries and information centers, and relevant education opportunities. Founded 1965.

Membership

Libn. of Congress, Dir. of the National Agricultural Lib., Dir. of the National Lib. of Medicine, Dir. of the National Lib. of Education, representatives from each of the other executive departments, and representatives from each of the following agencies: National Aeronautics and Space Admin., National Science Foundation, Smithsonian Institution, U.S. Supreme Court, U.S. Info. Agency, National Archives and Records Admin., Admin. Offices of the U.S. Courts, Defense Technical Info. Center, Government Printing Office, National Technical Info. Service, and Office of Scientific and Technical Info. (Dept. of Energy), Exec. Office of the President, Dept. of the Army, Dept. of the Navy, Dept. of the Air Force, and chairperson of the FEDLINK Advisory Council. Fifteen additional voting member agencies shall be selected on a rotating basis by the voting members of FEDLINK and nine rotating members through selection by the permanent members of the committee. These rotating members will serve three terms. One representative from each of the following agencies is invited as an observer to committee meetings: General Accounting Office, General Services Admin., Joint Committee on Printing, National Commission on Libs. and Info. Science, Office of Mgt. and Budget, Office of Personnel Mgt., and Lib. of Congress Financial Services Directorate.

Officers

Chair James H. Billington, Libn. of Congress; *Chair Designate* Winston Tabb, Assoc. Libn. for Lib. Services, Lib. of Congress; *Exec. Dir.* Susan M. Tarr, Federal Lib. and Info. Center Committee, Lib. of Congress, Washington, DC 20540-4930.

Address correspondence to the executive director.

Publications

Annual FLICC Forum on Federal Information Policies (summary and papers).
FEDLINK Technical Notes (m.).
FLICC Newsletter (q.).

Federal Publishers Committee

Chairperson, John Weiner
Energy Information Administration, EI-23, Mail Sta. BG-057,
1000 Independence Ave. S.W., Washington, DC 20585
202-586-6537, fax 202-586-0114
e-mail jweiner@eia.doe.gov

Object

To foster and promote effective management of data development and dissemination in the federal government through exchange of information, and to act as a focal point for federal agency publishing.

Membership

Memb. 700. Membership is available to persons involved in publishing and dissemination in federal government departments, agencies, and corporations, as well as independent organizations concerned with federal government publishing and dissemination. Some key federal government organizations represented are the Joint Committee on Printing, Government Printing Office, National Technical Info. Service, National Commission on Libs. and Info. Science, and the Lib. of Congress. Meetings are held monthly during business hours.

Officers

Chair John Weiner; *V.-Chair, Programs* Sandra Smith; *V.-Chair, Roundtables* June Malina; *Secy.* Marilyn Marbrook.

Roundtable Leaders

Marketing and Promotion. John Ward.
Subscriptions and Periodicals. Nancy Nicoletti.

Information Industry Association

1625 Massachusetts Ave. N.W., Suite 700, Washington, DC 20036
202-986-0280, fax 202-638-4403
e-mail info@infoindustry.org

Membership

Memb. 500+ companies. Open to companies involved in the creation, distribution, and use of information products, services, and technologies. For details on membership and dues, write to the association headquarters.

Staff

Pres. Ronald G. Dunn; *V.P.* Emily Pilk; *V.P., Government Relations* Dan Duncan; *Dir., Finance* John Dragovich; *Staff Advisor, Divisions and Councils* Irene Hughes; *Acting Dir., Membership* Sheri R. Robey; *Exec. Asst.* Virginia Nelson; *Ed./Publisher* Serge I. Obolensky.

Board of Directors

Chair Patrick J. Tierney; *Past Chair* Barbara A. Munder, Sr. V.P., McGraw-Hill Cos.; *Treas.* James E. Coane, Telebase Systems; *Secy.* Paul N. Wojcik, Bureau of National Affairs; *V. Chairs* Robert Aber, NASDAQ Stock Market Trade Dissemination Services; Herbert R. Brinberg, Parnassus Associates International; Jerrell Shelton, Thomson Business Info.; Audrey Y. Weil, America Online; *Membs.* Kathleen Bingham, Exec. V.P.,

FIND/SVP; Julie Chapman, Pres., InfoWorks Group; Erik K. Grimmelmann, Service Integration and Realization V.P., AT&T WorldNet Service; Robert L. (Jay) Jordan, Jr., Pres., Software, Consumer and Print Products, IHS Group; Patrick J. Marshall, Pres., New Media Services, GTE Directories Corp.; Pamela Maythenyi, Pres., Source Maythenyi; Gerry Mueller, Pres. and General Mgr., Prodigy Network, Prodigy Services Co.; Vance K. Opperman, Bd. of Dirs., Thomson Corp.; Hank Riner, Pres./CEO, UMI; Paul T. Sheils, V.P., Business Info. Services, Dow Jones and Co.; Peter Simon, Exec. V.P., Business Development and Database Publishing, Reed Reference Publishing; Margaret (Peg) B. Smith, Marketing V.P., Experian Info. Solutions; William Whitehurst, Dir., Data Security Programs, IBM Corp.; Hugh J. Yarrington, Pres./CEO, CCH.

Financial Information Services. Richard Carleton, Asst. General Counsel, Dir. of Legal Services, Toronto Stock Exchange.

Council Chairpersons

Board Committee on Dues Structure. Oakleigh Thorne, Pres./CEO, TBG Info. Investors.
Emerging Business. Jeremy Grayzel, CEO, Grayfire Info. Services.
Global Issues. Alison Meersschaert, Dir., New Ventures Corporate Devt., McGraw-Hill Cos.
Marketing and Business Development Council. David B. Boelio, Exec. V.P., CD-MAX.
Public Policy and Government Relations. To be appointed.
Small and Emerging Business. H. Donald Wilson, Conquest Software.

Division Chairpersons

Directory. Russell Perkins, Perkins Group.
Electronic Information Services. Huw Morgan, Southam Info. and Technology Group.

Publication

Information Sources (ann.; memb. $45; nonmemb. $125).

Lutheran Church Library Association

Executive Director, Leanna D. Kloempken
122 W. Franklin Ave., No. 604, Minneapolis, MN 55404
612-870-3623, fax 612-870-3623
e-mail lclahq@aol.com

Object

To promote the growth of church libraries by publishing a quarterly journal, *Lutheran Libraries*; furnishing booklists; assisting member libraries with technical problems; and providing workshops and meetings for mutual encouragement, guidance, and exchange of ideas among members. Founded 1958.

Membership

Memb. 1,800. Dues $25, $37.50, $50, $75, $100, $500, $1,000. Year. Jan.–Jan.

Officers (1995–1997)

Pres. Vernita Kennen; *V.P.* Willis Erickson; *Secy.* Patti Yount; *Treas.* Ruby Forlan.
Address correspondence to the executive director.

Directors

Judy Casserberg, Robert King, Jan Koski, Henrietta Pruissen, Charlotte Sawyer, Karen Trageser.

Publication

Lutheran Libraries (q.; memb.; nonmemb. $25).

Board Chairpersons

Advisory. Rolf Aaseng.
Finance. L. Edwin Wang.
Library Services. Betty Le Dell.
Publications. Rod Olson.
Telecommunications. Chuck Mann.

Medical Library Association

Executive Director, Carla Funk
6 N. Michigan Ave., Suite 300, Chicago, IL 60602
312-419-9094, fax 312-419-8950

Object

The major purposes of the Medical Library Association (MLA) are to foster medical and allied scientific libraries, to promote the educational and professional growth of health science librarians, and to exchange medical literature among the members. Through its programs and publications, MLA encourages professional development of its membership, whose foremost concern is dissemination of health sciences information for those in research, education, and patient care. Founded 1898; incorporated 1934.

Membership

Memb. (Inst.) 1,300; (Indiv.) 3,700. Institutional members are medical and allied scientific libraries. Individual members are people who are (or were at the time membership was established) engaged in professional library or bibliographic work in medical and allied scientific libraries or people who are interested in medical or allied scientific libraries. Dues (Student) $25; (Emeritus) $40; (Intro.) $75; (Indiv.) $110; (Sustaining) $345; and (Inst.) $175–$410, based on the number of the library's periodical subscriptions. Members may be affiliated with one or more of MLA's 23 special-interest sections and 14 regional chapters.

Officers

Pres. Naomi C. Broering, Dahgren Memorial Lib., Georgetown Univ. Medical Center, 3900 Reservoir Rd. N.W., Washington, DC 20007; *Pres.-Elect* Rachael K. Anderson, Arizona H.S. Lib., 1501 N. Campbell Ave., Tucson, AZ 85724; *Past Pres.* Jana Bradley, School of Lib. and Info. Science, Indiana Univ. at Indianapolis, 755 W. Michigan St., UL1110D, Indianapolis, IN 46202-5195.

Directors

Shelley A. Bader (1998), Dottie Eakin (1997), Cynthia H. Goldstein (1998), Joanne G. Marshall (1997), Elaine Russo Martin (1999), James Shedlock (1999), Patricia L. Thibodeau (1999), Linda A. Watson (1999), Kay E. Wellik (1998).

Publications

Bulletin of the Medical Library Association (q.; $136).
Directory of the Medical Library Association, 1992/93 ($150).
MLA News (10 per year; $48.50).
Miscellaneous (request current list from association headquarters).

Committee Chairpersons

Awards. Pamela Arpen Neumann.
Books (Panel). Michel Atlas.
Bulletin Editorial Board. J. Michael Homan.
Bylaws. Mary Mylenki.
Continuing Education. Marla Graber.
Credentialing. B. J. Schorre.
Exchange (Advisory). Virginia A. Lingle.
Governmental Relations. Roger Guard.
Grants and Scholarships. Linda Jeanne Walton.
Health Sciences Library Technicians. Esther E. Carrigan.
Joseph Leiter NLM/MLA Lectureship. Sheldon Kotzin.
Membership. Patricia W. Martin.
National Program (1997). Kathryn J. Hoffman.
National Program (1998). Frieda O. Weise.
National Program (1999). Mark E. Funk.
Professional Recognition (Review Panel). Alan Carr.
Publications. Janet M. Coggan.
Publishing and Information Industries Relations. Melissa M. Nasea.
Status and Economic Interests. Susan Kroll.

Ad Hoc Committee Chairpersons

Centennial Coordinating. June H. Fulton.
Executive. Naomi C. Broering.
Government (Task Force). Fred W. Roper.
Joint MLA/AAHSLD Legislative (Task Force). Marianne Puckett.
MLANET (Task Force). Nancy K. Roderer.
Research Policy Implementation. Joanne G. Marshall.
Section/Chapter Compliance (Task Force). Cynthia H. Goldstein.

Music Library Association

Box 487, Canton, MA 02021
617-828-8450, fax 617-828-8915
e-mail adadsvc@aol.com

Object

To promote the establishment, growth, and use of music libraries; to encourage the collection of music and musical literature in libraries; to further studies in musical bibliography; to increase efficiency in music library service and administration; and to promote the profession of music librarianship. Founded 1931.

Membership

Memb. 2,000. Dues (Inst.) $90; (Indiv.) $75; (Retired) $45; (Student) $35. Year. Sept. 1–Aug. 31.

Officers

Pres. Diane Parr Walker, 1437 Rugby Ave., Charlottesville, VA 22903. Tel. 804-924-4606, e-mail dpw@poe.acc.virginia.edu; *Rec. Secy.* Laura Snyder, 132 Amsterdam Rd., Rochester, NY 14601-10008. Tel. 716-654-6412, e-mail sydr@uhura.cc.rochester.edu; *Treas.* James P. Cassaro, 550 Warren Rd., Ithaca, NY 14850-1853. Tel. 607-255-7046, fax 607-254-2877, e-mail jpc3@cornell.edu; *Exec. Secy.* Bonna J. Boettcher, Music Lib. and Sound Recording Archives, Jerome Lib., 3rd fl., Bowling Green State Univ., Bowling Green, OH 43403-0179. Tel. 419-372-2307, fax 419-372-7996, e-mail bboettc@bgnet.bgsu.edu; *Past Pres.* Jane Gottlieb, Juilliard School, 60 Lincoln Center Plaza, New York, NY 10023-6588. Tel. 212-799-5000 ext. 265, fax 212-724-0263, e-mail gottlieb@panix.com.

Members-at-Large

Deborah Campana, Northwestern Univ.; Michael Colby, Univ. of California–Davis; Calvin Elliker, Univ. of Michigan; Marjorie Hassen, Univ. of Pennsylvania; Mimi Tashiro, Stanford Univ.; Daniel Zager, Oberlin College.

Special Officers

Advertising Mgr. Susan Dearborn, 1572 Massachusetts Ave., No. 57, Cambridge, MA 02138. Tel. 617-876-0934; *Convention Mgr.* Susan H. Hitchens, 8214B Wooster Pike, Cincinnati, OH 45227. Tel. 513-561-7157, e-mail hitchens@fuse.net; *Asst. Convention Mgr.* Edwin A. Quist, Arthur Friedheim Lib., Peabody Conservatory of Music, 1 E. Mount Vernon Place, Baltimore, MD 21202. Tel. 410-659-8256, e-mail quist@peabody.jhu.edu; *Placement* Elizabeth Rebman, Music Lib., Morrison Hall, Univ. of California, Berkeley, CA 94720. Tel. 510-643-5198, e-mail arebman@library.berkeley.edu; *Publicity* Leslie Bennett, Knight Lib., Music Services, Univ. of Oregon, Eugene, OR 97103. Tel. 503-346-1930, e-mail lbennett@oregon.uoregon.edu.

Publications

MLA Index and Bibliography Series (irreg.; price varies).
MLA Newsletter (q.; memb.).
MLA Technical Reports (irreg.; price varies).
Music Cataloging Bulletin (mo.; $25).
Notes (q.; indiv. $70; inst. $80).

Committee and Roundtable Chairpersons

Administration. Deborah Pierce, Univ. of Washington. Tel. 206-543-1159, e-mail dpierce@u.washington.edu.
American Music (Roundtable). George Boziwick, New York Public Lib. Tel. 212-870-1652, e-mail 5726471@mcimail.com.
Archives (Roundtable). Patricia Elliott, San Jose State Univ. Tel. 408-924-4590, e-mail elliott@sjsuvml.sjsu.edu.
Bibliographic Control. Linda Barnhart, Univ. of California–San Diego. Tel. 619-534-6759, e-mail lbarnhart@ucsd.edu.
Bibliography (Roundtable). Calvin Elliker, Univ. of Michigan. Tel. 313-764-2512, e-mail celliker@umich.edu.
Black Music Collections (Roundtable). Suzanne Flandreau, Center for Black Music Research, Columbia College. Tel. 312-663-1600, e-mail suzanne.flandreau@mail.colum.edu.
Conservatories (Roundtable). Pamela Bristah, Manhattan School of Music. Tel. 212-749-2802, e-mail msoml@metgate.metro.org.
Contemporary Music (Roundtable). Ralph Hartsock, Univ. of North Texas. E-mail rhartsoc@library.unt.edu; Dan Cherubin, New York Public Lib.
Development. Linda Solow Blotner, Univ. of Hartford. Tel. 203-768-4492, e-mail blotner@uhavax.hartford.edu.
Education. Roberta Chodacki, East Carolina Univ. Tel. 919-757-6250, e-mail lmchodac@ecuvm.cis.ecu.edu.
Film Music (Roundtable). Robert Kosovsky, New York Public Lib. Tel. 212-870-1677, e-mail kos@cunyvmsl.gc.cuny.edu.
Finance. Mark McKnight, Univ. of North Texas. Tel. 817-565-2859, e-mail mmcknigh@library.unt.edu.
Jazz and Popular Music (Roundtable). Vincent Pelote, Rutgers Univ. Tel. 201-648-5595, e-mail pelote@andromeda.rutgers.edu.
Jewish Music (Roundtable). Marion H. Stein. Tel. 718-858-9626, e-mail marions@panix.com.
Large Research Libraries (Roundtable). Paula Morgan, Princeton Univ. Tel. 609-258-3230, Bitnet: PMMORGAN@PUCC.
Legislation. Lenore Coral, Cornell Univ. Tel. 607-255-7126, e-mail lfcl@cornell.edu.
New Members (Roundtable). Sarah B. Dorsey, Univ. of North Carolina–Greensboro. E-mail sbdorsey@iris.uncg.edu.
Organ Music (Roundtable). Myron Patterson, Univ. of Utah. Tel. 801-581-8104, e-mail mpatters@alexandria.lib.utah.edu.
Preservation. Brenda Nelson-Strauss, Chicago Symphony Orchestra. Tel. 312-435-8129, e-mail strauss@chicagosymph.org.
Program. Laura Gayle Green, Univ. of Missouri–Kansas City. Tel. 816-235-1679, e-mail greenl@smtpgate.umkc.edu.

Public Libraries. Jeannette Casey, Chicago Public Lib. Tel. 312-747-4835, e-mail mucpl@mcs.com.
Publications. Susan T. Sommer, New York Public Lib. Tel. 212-870-1620, e-mail ssomer@nypl.org.
Reference and Public Service. Ruthann McTyre, Baylor Univ. Tel. 817-755-2160, e-mail ruthann_mctyre@baylor.edu.
Research in Music Librarianship (Roundtable). Sherry L. Vellucci, Saint John's Univ. Tel. 718-990-6200, e-mail 4652928@mcimail.com.
Resource Sharing and Collection Development. Brad Short, Washington Univ. Tel. 314-935-5529, e-mail brad-short@library.wustl.edu.
Sheet Music (Roundtable). Lois Schultz, Duke Univ. Tel. 919-684-5896, e-mail lois@acpub.duke.edu.
Small Academic Libraries (Roundtable). Dorothy Bognar, Univ. of Connecticut. Tel. 203-486-0519, e-mail hbladm22@uconnvm.uconn.edu.
Social Responsibilities (Roundtable). Donald Brown, El Camino College. Tel. 310-660-3722, e-mail dib95@ix.netcom.com.
Technical Services (Roundtable). Grace Fitzgerald, Univ. of Iowa. Tel. 319-335-5889, e-mail grace-fitzgerald@uiowa.edu.
Video (Roundtable). Ian Fairclough, Univ. of Wyoming. Tel. 307-755-1947, e-mail ifairclo@uwyo.edu.
Women in Music (Roundtable). Candice Feldt, Tufts Univ. Tel. 617-628-5000, e-mail cfeldt@pearl.tufts.edu.
World Music (Roundtable). Philip Vandermeer, Univ. of Maryland. Tel. 301-405-9221, e-mail pv12@umail.umd.edu.

National Association of Government Archives and Records Administrators

Executive Director, Bruce W. Dearstyne
48 Howard St., Albany, NY 12207
518-463-8644, fax 518-463-8656
e-mail nagara@caphill.com

Object

Founded in 1984, the association is successor to the National Association of State Archives and Records Administrators, which had been established in 1974. NAGARA is a growing nationwide association of local, state, and federal archivists and records administrators, and others interested in improved care and management of government records. NAGARA promotes public awareness of government records and archives management programs, encourages interchange of information among government archives and records management agencies, develops and implements professional standards of government records and archival administration, and encourages study and research into records management problems and issues.

Membership

Most NAGARA members are federal, state, and local archival and records management agencies.

Officers

Pres. Kathryn Hammond Baker, Pres., Archives of the Commonwealth of Massachusetts; *V.P.* Marie B. Allen, National Archives and Records Admin.; *Secy.* Gerald G. Newborg, State Historical Society of North Dakota; *Treas.* Jim Berberich, Florida Bureau of Archives and Records Management.

Directors

Lynn Bellardo, National Archives and Records Admin.; David H. Hoober, Arizona Dept. of

Lib., Archives and Public Records; Laura McGee, City of Dallas, Texas; Michael Miller, U.S. Environmental Protection Agency; Peter Schinkel, Georgia Dept. of Archives and History; Roy Turnbaugh, Oregon State Archives; David M. Weinberg, City of Philadelphia (Pa.) Dept. of Records.

Publications

Clearinghouse (q.; memb.).
Crosswords.
Government Records Issues (series).
Preservation Needs in State Archives (report).
Program Reporting Guidelines for Government Records Programs.

National Federation of Abstracting and Information Services

Executive Director, Richard T. Kaser
1518 Walnut St., Philadelphia, PA 19102
215-893-1561, fax 215-893-1564
e-mail nfais@hslc.org

Object

NFAIS is an international, not-for-profit membership organization comprising leading information producers, distributors, and corporate users of secondary information. Its purpose is to serve the information community through education, research, and publication. Founded 1958.

Membership

Memb. 60+. Full membership (regular and government) is open to organizations that, as a substantial part of their activity, produce secondary information services for external use. Secondary information products are compilations containing printed or electronic summaries of, or references to, multiple sources of publicly available information. For example, organizations that assemble bibliographic citations, abstracts, indexes, and data are all secondary information services.

Associate membership is available to organizations that operate or manage online information services, networks, in-house information centers, and libraries; conduct research or development work in information science or systems; are otherwise involved in the generation, promotion, or distribution of secondary information products under contract; or publish primary information sources. Members pay dues annually based on the fiscal year of July 1–June 30. Dues are assessed based on the member's revenue derived from information-related activities.

Officers (1996–1997)

Pres. Taissa Kusma; *Past Pres.* Dennis Auld; *Pres.-Elect* John Anderson; *Secy.* Gladys Cotter; *Treas.* Sheldon Kotzin.

Directors

Phyllis Franklin, George Lewicky, James Lohr, Kurt Molholm, Barbara Preschel, Brian Sweet, Ralph Ubico.

Staff

Exec. Dir. Richard T. Kaser; *Asst. Dir.* Marian H. Gloninger; *Office Mgr.* Wendy Carter; *Customer Service* Margaret Manson.

Publications

Automated Support to Indexing (1992; memb. $50; nonmemb. $75).
Beyond Boolean (1996; memb. $50; nonmemb. $75).
Changing Roles in Information Distribution (1994; memb. $50; nonmemb. $75).
Developing New Markets for Information Products (1993; memb. $50; nonmemb. $75).
Document Delivery in an Electronic Age (1995; memb. $50; nonmemb. $75).
Flexible Workstyles in the Information Industry (1993; memb. $50; nonmemb. $75).
Government Information and Policy: Chang-

ing Roles in a New Administration (1994; memb. $50; nonmemb. $75).
Guide to Careers in Abstracting and Indexing (1992; memb. $25; nonmemb. $35).
Guide to Database Distribution, 2nd ed., (1994; memb. $100; nonmemb. $175).
Impacts of Changing Production Technologies (1995; memb. $50; nonmemb. $75).

NFAIS Member Directory and Guide to Leading Information Companies (1996; memb. $25, nonmemb. $35).
NFAIS Newsletter (mo.; North America $120; elsewhere $135).
Partnering in the Information Industry (1996; memb. $50, nonmemb. $75).

National Information Standards Organization

Executive Director, Patricia R. Harris
4733 Bethesda Ave., Suite 300, Bethesda, MD 20814
301-654-2512, fax 301-654-1721
e-mail nisohq@cni.org

Object

To develop technical standards used in libraries, publishing, and information services. Experts from the information field volunteer to lend their expertise in the development and writing of NISO standards. The standards are approved by the consensus of NISO's voting membership, which consists of 69 voting members representing libraries, government, associations, and private businesses and organizations. NISO is supported by its membership and corporate grants. Formerly a committee of the American National Standards Institute (ANSI), NISO, formed in 1939, was incorporated in 1983 as a nonprofit educational organization. NISO is accredited by ANSI and serves as the U.S. Technical Advisory Group to ISO/TC 46.

Membership

Memb. 69. Open to any organization, association, government agency, or company—national in scope—willing to participate in and having substantial concern for the development of NISO standards.

Officers

Chair Michael J. McGill, Chief Info. Officer, Univ. of Michigan Medical Center, 1500 E. Medical Center Dr., TCB 1240-0308, Ann Arbor, MI 48019-0308; *Past Chair* Michael Mellinger, Pres., Data Research Assocs., 1276 N. Warson Rd., Saint Louis, MO 63132-1806; *V. Chair/Chair-Elect* Joel H. Baron, Group Dir., Dawson, PLC, 15 Southwest Park, Westwood, MA 02090; *Exec. Dir./Secy.* Patricia R. Harris, NISO, 4733 Bethesda Ave., Suite 300, Bethesda, MD 20814; *Dirs.* Robert C. Badger, Springer Verlag, New York, NY; Marjorie Hlava, Access Innovations, Albuquerque, NM; Beverly P. Lynch, UCLA; Donald J. Muccino, OCLC, Dublin, OH; Clifford Lynch, Univ. of California, Oakland, CA; Nolan F. Pope, Univ. of Wisconsin–Madison; Lennie Stovel, Research Lib. Group, Mountain View, CA; Vinod Chachra, VTLS, Inc., Blacksburg, VA; Elizabeth Bole Eddison, Inmagic, Woburn, MA; Howard Turtle, West Publishing, Eagan, MN 55123.

Publications

Information Standards Quarterly (q.; $75; foreign $105).
NISO published standards are available from NISO Press Fulfillment, Box 338, Oxon Hill, MD 20750-0338. Tel. 301-567-9522, 800-282-6476, fax 301-567-9553, e-mail nisohq@cni.org.
NISO Press catalogs and the *NISO Annual Report* are available on request.

REFORMA
(National Association to Promote Library Services to the Spanish Speaking)

President, Edward Erazo, New Mexico State University
Box 30006, Dept. 3475, Las Cruces, NM 88003-8006
505-646-6930, fax 505-646-6940
e-mail ederazo@lib.nmsu.edu

Object

Celebrating 25 years of promoting library services to the Spanish-speaking, REFORMA, an ALA affiliate, works in a number of areas: to promote the development of library collections to include Spanish-language and Hispanic-oriented materials; the recruitment of more bilingual and bicultural professionals and support staff; the development of library services and programs that meet the needs of the Hispanic community; the establishment of a national network among individuals who share our goals; the education of the U.S. Hispanic population in regard to the availability and types of library services; and lobbying efforts to preserve existing library resource centers serving the interest of Hispanics.

Membership

Memb. 900. Any person who is supportive of the goals and objectives of REFORMA.

Officers

Pres. Edward Erazo, REFORMA, New Mexico State Univ., Box 30006, Dept. 3475, Las Cruces, NM 88003-8006. Tel. 505-646-6930, fax 505-646-6940, e-mail ederazo@lib.nmsu.edu; *Pres.-Elect* Sandra Balderrama; *Past Pres.* Judith Castiano, San Diego Public Lib., Tierra Santa Branch, 4985 La Cuenta Dr., San Diego, CA 92124. Tel. 619-573-1385, fax 619-236-5878, e-mail $ts_m@library.sannet.gov. *Treas.* Rene Amaya, 1750 Coolidge Ave., Altadena, CA 91001; *Secy.* Christine Gonzalez; *Newsletter Ed.* Ramiro Gonzalez; *Archivist/Historian* Salvador Guerena.

Publications

REFORMA Membership Directory. Eds. Al Milo, Dir., Fullerton Public Lib., 353 W. Commonwealth Ave., Fullerton, CA 92632; Edward Erazo, REFORMA, New Mexico State Univ., Box 30006, Dept. 3475, Las Cruces, NM 88003-8006. Tel. 505-646-6930, fax 505-646-6940, e-mail ederazo@lib.nmsu.edu.

REFORMA Newsletter (q.; memb.). *Ed.* Ramiro Gonzalez, San Diego Public Lib., James P. Beckworth Branch, 721 Pasqual, San Diego, CA 92113. Tel. 619-527-3408, fax 619-236-5878, e-mail r4g@library.sannet.gov.

Committees

Children's Services/Book Awards. Oralia Garza de Cortez.
Nominations. Ramiro Salazar.
Organizational Development. To be appointed.
Public Relations. Edward Erazo.
Scholarship. Luis Chaparro.
Librarian-of-the-Year Award. To be appointed.

Meetings

General membership and board meetings take place at the American Library Association's Midwinter Meeting and Annual Conference.

Research Libraries Group, Inc.

Director of Corporate Communications, Jennifer Hartzell
1200 Villa St., Mountain View, CA 94041-1100
415-691-2207, fax 415-964-0943
e-mail bl.jlh@rlg.org, World Wide Web http://www.rlg.org

Object

The Research Libraries Group, Inc. (RLG) is a not-for-profit membership corporation of over 150 universities, archives, historical societies, national libraries, and other institutions devoted to improving access to information that supports research and learning. RLG exists to support its members in containing costs, improving local services, and contributing to the nation's collective access to scholarly materials. For its members, RLG develops and operates cooperative programs to manage, preserve, and extend access to research library, museum, and archival holdings. For both its members and for nonmember institutions and individuals worldwide, RLG develops and operates databases and software to serve an array of information access and management needs. Ariel, CitaDel, Diogenes, Eureka, RLIN, and Zephyr are trademarks of the Research Libraries Group, Inc.

Membership

Memb. 150+. Membership is open to any nonprofit institution with an educational, cultural, or scientific mission. There are two membership categories: general and special. General members are institutions that serve a clientele of more than 5,000 faculty, academic staff, research staff, professional staff, students, fellows, or members. Special members serve a similar clientele of 5,000 or fewer.

Directors

RLG has a 19-member board of directors, comprising 12 directors elected from and by RLG's member institutions, six at-large directors elected by the board itself, and the president. Theirs is the overall responsibility for the organization's governance and for ensuring that it faithfully fulfills its purpose and goals. Annual board elections are held in the spring. In 1997 the board's chair is Martin Runkle, Director, University of Chicago Library. For a current list of directors, contact RLG.

Staff

Pres. James Michalko; *V.P., Planning and Research Resources* John W. Haeger; *Dir., Member Services* Linda West; *Dir., Lib. and Bibliographic Services* Karen Smith-Yoshimura; *Dir., Access Services* Wayne Davison; *Dir., Customer and Operations Support* Jack Grantham; *Dir., Computer Devt.* David Richards; *Dir., Finance and Administration* Molly Singer; *Dir., Sales and Marketing* Kristin Tague; *Dir., Corporate Communications* Jennifer Hartzell.

Publications

Digital Imaging Technology for Preservation (symposium proceedings).
Electronic Access to Information: A New Service Paradigm (symposium proceedings).
Research Libraries Group News (3 per year; 16-page news magazine).
RLG Archives Microfilming Manual (RLG-developed guidelines and practice).
RLG Digital Image Access Project (final workshop proceedings).
RLG Preservation Microfilming Handbook (RLG-developed guidelines and practice).
RLIN Focus (bi-m.; eight-page user services newsletter).
Scholarship in the New Information Environment (symposium proceedings).
Selecting Library and Archive Collections for Digital Reformatting (symposium proceedings).
Contact RLG for other informational and user publications available.

Society for Scholarly Publishing

Executive Director, Francine Butler
10200 W. 44 Ave., Suite 304, Wheat Ridge, CO 80033
303-422-3914, fax 303-422-8894
e-mail 5686814@mcimail.com

Object

To draw together individuals involved in the process of scholarly publishing. This process requires successful interaction of the many functions performed within the scholarly community. The Society for Scholarly Publishing (SSP) provides the leadership for such interaction by creating opportunities for the exchange of information and opinions among scholars, editors, publishers, librarians, printers, booksellers, and all others engaged in scholarly publishing.

Membership

Memb. 950. Open to all with an interest in the scholarly publishing process and dissemination of information. There are four categories of membership: individual ($60), contributing ($500), sustaining ($1,000), and sponsoring ($1,500). Year. Jan. 1–Dec. 31.

Executive Committee (July 1996–June 1997)

Pres. Margaret Foti, American Assn. for Cancer Research, Public Ledger Bldg., Suite 816, 150 S. Independence Mall W., Philadelphia, PA 19106-3485; *Pres.-Elect* Jan Fleming, Cadmus Journal Services, 940 Elkridge Landing Rd., Linthicum, MD 21090-2908; *Secy.-Treas.* Patricia Sabosik, AOL/GNN, 75 Second Ave., Suite 710, Needham, MA 02194; *Past Pres.* Christine Lamb, SilverPlatter Info., 100 River Ridge Dr., Norwood, MA 02062; *Board Memb.* Robert Bovenschulte, *New England Journal of Medicine*, 1440 Main St., Waltham, MA 02154-1649.

Directors

Ed Barnas, Cambridge Univ. Press, 40 W. 20 St., New York, NY 10011-4211; *Assoc. Exec. Dir.* Jerry Bowman, 10200 W. 44 Ave., Suite 304, Wheat Ridge, CO 80033; *Exec. Dir.* Francine Butler, 10200 W. 44 Ave., Suite 304, Wheat Ridge, CO 80033; Nancy Hammerman, Sage Publications, 2455 Teller Rd., Thousand Oaks, CA 91320; Maria Lebron, American Physical Society, 1 Physics Ellipse, College Park, MD 20740; Beth Luey, ASU Scholarly Publishing Program, Arizona State Univ., Tempe, AZ 85287-2501; Virginia Martin, Transparent Language, 22 Proctor Hill Rd., Hollis, NH 03049; Patricia Scarry, 5720 S. Woodlawn Ave., Chicago, IL 60637; Marcia Tuttle, Lib., Univ. of North Carolina, 215 Flemington Rd., Chapel Hill, NC 27514; Sandra Whisler, Electronic Publishing and Journals, Univ. of California Press, 2120 Berkeley Way, Berkeley, CA 94720.

Meetings

An annual meeting is conducted in either May or June. The location changes each year. Additionally, SSP conducts several seminars throughout the year.

Publications

Scholarly Publishing Today (bi-m.; memb., nonmemb. $70)

Society of American Archivists

Executive Director, Susan E. Fox
600 S. Federal St., Suite 504, Chicago, IL 60605
312-922-0140, fax 312-347-1452

Object

To promote sound principles of archival economy and to facilitate cooperation among archivists and archival agencies. Founded 1936.

Membership

Memb. 4,800. Dues (Indiv.) $65–$170, graduated according to salary; (Assoc.) $65, domestic; (Student) $40, with a two-year maximum on membership; (Inst.) $210; (Sustaining) $410.

Officers (1996–1997)

Pres. Nicholas Burckel; *V.P.* William Maher; *Treas.* Lee Stout.

Council

Valerie Browne, Bruce Bruemmer, Susan Davis, Anne Gilliland-Swetland, Lori Hefner, Steve Hensen, Peter Hirtle, Sharon Thibodeau, Sharron Uhler.

Staff

Exec. Dir. Susan E. Fox; *Meetings/Memb. Coord.* Bernice E. Brack; *Publications Dir.* Teresa Brinati; *Publications Asst.* Troy Sturdivant; *Bookkeeper* Carroll Dendler; *Assistant Exec. Dir.* Debra Mills; *Educ. Dir.* Joan Sander.

Publications

American Archivist (q.; $75; foreign $90). *Ed.* Philip Eppard; *Managing Ed.* Teresa Brinati. Books for review and related correspondence should be addressed to the managing editor.

Archival Outlook (bi-m.; memb.). *Ed.* Teresa Brinati.

Special Libraries Association

Executive Director, David R. Bender
1700 18 St. N.W., Washington, DC 20009-2508
202-234-4700, fax 202-265-9317
e-mail slal@sla.org

Object

To advance the leadership role of special librarians in putting knowledge to work in the information society.

Membership

Memb. 14,500. Dues (Sustaining) $400; (Indiv.) $105; (Student) $30. Year. Jan.–Dec. or July–June.

Officers (July 1996–June 1997)

Pres. Sylvia E. A. Piggott, InfoPLUS, 5230 Trenholme, Montreal, PQ H4V 1Y5, Canada. Tel. 514-486-0305, fax 514-486-9809, e-mail spiggott@accent.net; *Pres.-Elect* Judith Field, Lib. Science Program, Wayne State Univ., 106 Kresge Lib., Detroit, MI 48202. Tel. 313-577-8539, fax 313-577-7563, e-mail jfield@lisp.purdy.wayne.edu; *Past Pres.* Jane Dysart, Dysart & Jones Assocs., 47 Rose Park Dr., Toronto, ON M4T 1R2, Canada. Tel. 416-484-6129, fax 416-484-7063, e-mail dysart@inforamp.net; *Treas.* Donna W. Scheeder, Lib. of Congress, Congressional Reference Div., Rm. LM 219, I and Independence Aves. S.E., Washington, DC 20504. Tel. 202-707-8939, fax 202-707-1833, e-mail dscheeder@crs.loc.gov; *Chapter Cabinet Chair* G. Lynn Tinsley, Engineering Science Lib., Carnegie Mellon Univ., Wean Hall, Pittsburgh, PA 15213-3890. Tel. 412-268-2428, fax 412-681-1998, e-mail ltinsley@andrew.cmu.edu; *Chapter Cabinet Chair-Elect* Peter Moon, Hartford Steam Boiler Inspection and Insurance Co., 1 State St., 9th fl., Hartford, CT 06102-3199. Tel. 203-722-5486, fax 203-722-5530, e-mail peter_moon@hsb.com; *Div. Cabinet Chair* Dorothy McGarry, UCLA Science and Engineering Lib., 8251 Boelter Hall, Los Angeles, CA 90095-1598. Tel. 310-825-3438, fax 310-206-3908, e-mail dmcgarry@library.ucla.edu; *Div. Chapter Chair-Elect* Rebecca Vargha, SAS Institute, Lib. RA347, SAS Campus Dr., Cary, NC 27513. Tel. 919-677-8000 Ext. 6293, fax 919-677-8224, e-mail vargha@aol.com.

Directors

Officers; Stephen Abram (1999), Charlene Baldwin (1997), Bruce Hubbard (1998), Sharyn Ladner (1999), Julia Peterson (1998), Hope Tillman (1997).

Publications

Special Libraries (q.) and *SpeciaList* (mo.). Cannot be ordered separately ($60 for both; foreign $65). *Ed.* Gail Repsher.

Committee Chairpersons

Affirmative Action. Rosalind Lett.
Association Office Operations. Sylvia E. A. Piggott.
Awards and Honors. Didi Pancake.
Bylaws. Eleanor MacLean.
Cataloging. Amy L. Paster.
Committees. James B. Tchobanoff.
Conference Program, Indianapolis (1998). Gloria Zamora.
Conference Program, Seattle (1997). Corinne Campbell.
Consultation Service. Janice Suter.
Copyright. Lawrence Guthrie.
Finance. Donna W. Scheeder.
Government Relations. Joan Gervino.
Information Today Award. Anne C. Gregg.
International Relations. Mary Lee Kennedy.
Networking. Sandra Spurlock.

Nominating, 1997 Elections. Janice C. Anderson.
Nominating, 1998 Elections. Terry Dean.
Professional Development. Mary E. Dickerson.
Public Relations. Ann Talcott.
Publisher Relations. Connie Kelley.
Research. Laura N. Gasaway.
SLA Scholarship. Bill Fisher.
Special Programs Fund. Elizabeth Eddison.
Strategic Planning. Julie Peterson.
Student and Academic Relations. Larry L. Wright.
Technical Standards. Marjorie Hlava.
Tellers. Marilyn Bromley.
H. W. Wilson Award. Barbara Semonche.

Theatre Library Association

New York Public Library for the Performing Arts
111 Amsterdam Ave., New York, NY 10023-7498
212-870-1644, 212-870-1670

Object

To further the interests of collecting, preserving, and using theater, cinema, and performing-arts materials in libraries, museums, and private collections. Founded 1937.

Membership

Memb. 500. Dues (Indiv.) $20; (Inst.) $25. Year. Jan. 1–Dec. 31.

Officers (1997)

Pres. Geraldine Duclow, Free Lib. of Philadelphia; *V.P.* Susan Brady, Yale Univ.; *Exec. Secy.* Maryann Chach, Shubert Archive; *Treas.* Jane Suda, New York Public Lib. for the Performing Arts.

Executive Board

Lauren Bufferd, Nena Couch, Rosemary Cullen, Annette Fern, B. Donald Grose, Mary Ann Jensen, Martha S. LoMonaco, Lois Erickson McDonald, Paul Newman, Louis A. Rachow, Anne G. Schlosser, Kevin Winkler; *Ex officio* Madeleine Nichols, Barbara Naomi Cohen-Stratyner, Maryann Chach; *Honorary* Paul Myers; *Historian* Louis A. Rachow.

Publications

Broadside (q.; memb.). *Ed.* Maryann Chach.
Performing Arts Resources (ann.; memb.). *Ed.* Publications Committee.

Committee Chairpersons

Awards. Richard Wall.
Membership. Geraldine Duclow.
Nominations. Martha S. LoMonaco.
Program and Special Events. Richard M. Buck, Bob Taylor.
Publications. Maryann Chach, Catherine Johnson.

Urban Libraries Council

President, Eleanor Jo (Joey) Rodger
1603 Orrington Ave., Suite 1080, Evanston, IL 60201
847-866-9999, fax 847-866-9989
e-mail ejr@gpl.glenview.lib.il.us; World Wide Web http://www.clpgh.org/ulc/

Object

To identify and make known the problems relating to urban libraries serving cities of 50,000 or more individuals, located in a Standard Metropolitan Statistical Area; to provide information on state and federal legislation affecting urban library programs and systems; to facilitate the exchange of ideas and programs of member libraries and other libraries; to develop programs that enable libraries to act as a focus of community development and to supply the informational needs of the new urban populations; to conduct research and educational programs that will benefit urban libraries and to solicit and accept grants, contributions, and donations essential to their implementation.

ULC currently receives most of its funding from membership dues. Future projects will involve the solicitation of grant funding. ULC is a 501(c)(3) not-for-profit corporation based in the state of Illinois.

Membership

Membership is open to public libraries and library systems serving populations of 50,000 or more located in a Standard Metropolitan Statistical Area and to corporations specializing in library-related materials and services. Dues are based on the size of the organization's operating budget, according to the following schedule: under $2 million, $700; $2 million to $5 million, $1,000; $5 million to $10 million, $1,250; $10 million to $15 million, $1,500; over $15 million, $2,000. In addition, ULC member libraries may choose Sustaining or Contributing status (Sustaining, $10,000; Contributing, $5,000).

Officers (1996–1997)

Chair Michael A. Schott, 9901 I.H. 10 W., Suite 900, San Antonio, TX 78230. Tel. 210-696-5177, fax 210-696-0567; *V. Chair/Chair Elect* Robert B. Croneberger, Carnegie Lib. of Pittsburgh, 4400 Forbes Ave., Pittsburgh, PA 15213. Tel. 412-622-3100, fax 412-622-6278, e-mail croneberger@clpgh.org; *Secy.* Sally Freeman Frasier, 7204 Sleepy Hollow Dr., Tulsa, OK 74136. Tel. 918-492-5627, fax 918-492-6423, e-mail sfra5354@aol.com; *Treas.* Susan Goldberg Kent, Los Angeles Public Lib., 630 W. Fifth St., Los Angeles, CA 90071. Tel. 213-228-7516, fax 213-228-7519, e-mail skent@lapl.org.

Officers and members of the executive board serve two-year terms. New officers are elected and take office at the summer annual meeting of the council.

Executive Board

Andrew Blau. E-mail blau@benton.org; Steven A. Coulter. E-mail coult@pacbell.net; Mary Doty. Tel. 612-332-7853; Harriet Henderson. E-mail harriet.henderson@louky.iglou.com; Frances Hunter. E-mail fran@cua3.csuohio.edu; G. Victor Johnson. E-mail Vic-Johnson@Checkers-LLP.COM; Roslyn Kurland. Tel. 305-468-2783; Esther W. Lopato. Tel. 718-253-9595; Eleanor Jo

Rodger. E-mail ejr@gpl.glenview.lib.il.us; Elliot L. Shelkrot. E-mail shelkrot@hslc.org; Edward M. Szynaka. E-mail eds@imcpl.lib.in.us.

Key Staff

Pres. Eleanor Jo Rodger; *V.P., Admin. and Program* Bridget A. Bradley; *Project Dir.* Marybeth Schroeder.

Publications

Frequent Fast Facts Surveys: *Fees Survey Results* (1993); *Fund Raising and Financial Development Survey Results* (1993); *Staffing Survey Results* (1993); *Collection Development Survey Results* (1994); *Library Security Survey Results* (1994); *Public Libraries and Private Fund Raising: Opportunities and Issues* (1994); *Off Site Survey Results* (1995).

Urban Libraries Exchange (mo.; memb.).

State, Provincial, and Regional Library Associations

The associations in this section are organized under three headings: United States, Canada, and Regional. Both the United States and Canada are represented under Regional associations.

United States

Alabama

Memb. 1,200. Term of Office. Apr. 1996–Apr. 1997. Publication. *The Alabama Librarian* (q.).

Pres. Nancy Simms Donahoo, North Shelby County Lib.; *Secy.* Jane Garrett, 3533 Honeysuckle Rd., Montgomery 36109; *Treas.* Donna Fitch, 2917 Dublin Dr., Helena 35080; *Exec. Dir.* Barbara Black, 400 S. Union St., Suite 255, Montgomery 36104. Tel. 334-262-5210, fax 334-834-6398.

Address correspondence to the executive director.

Alaska

Memb. 359. Term of Office. Mar. 1996–Mar. 1997. Publication. *Newspoke* (bi-mo.).

Pres. Mary Ellen Emmons, Wasilla Public Lib., 391 N. Main St., Wasilla 99654-7085. Tel. 907-376-5913, e-mail marye@muskox. alaska.edu; *Secy.* CharlotteGlover, Ketchikan Public Lib., 629 Dock St., Ketchikan 99901. Tel. 907-225-0370, fax 907-225-0153, e-mail charg@muskox.alaska.edu; *Treas.* Peg Thompson, Anchorage Municipal Lib., 9651 Birch Rd., Anchorage 99516. Tel. 907-343-2891, fax 907-562-1244, e-mail pegt@muskox. alaska.edu.

Address correspondence to the secretary.

Arizona

Memb. 1,241. Term of Office. Dec. 1996–Nov. 1997. Publication. *AzLA Newsletter* (mo.). Articles for the newsletter should be sent to the attention of the newsletter editor.

Pres. David Gunckel, Sierra Vista Public Lib., 2950 E. Tacoma St., Sierra Vista 85635. Tel. 520-458-4239, fax 520-458-5377, e-mail dgunckl\@>primenet.com; *Treas.* Bill Pillow, Scottsdale Public Lib., 3839 Civic Center Blvd., Scottsdale 85251. Tel. 602-994-2474; *Exec. Secy.* Jean Johnson, 14449 N. 73 St., Scottsdale 85260-3133. Tel. 602-998-1954, fax 602-998-7838, e-mail meetmore@aol. com. Address correspondence to the executive secretary.

Arkansas

Memb. 625. Term of Office. Jan–Dec. 1997. Publication. *Arkansas Libraries* (bi-mo.).

Pres. Mary Farris, Dir., Lib., Garland County Community College, 101 College Dr., Hot Springs 71913; *Exec. Dir.* Jennifer Coleman, Arkansas Lib. Assn., 9 Shackleford Plaza, Little Rock 72211. Tel. 501-661-1127, fax 501-228-5535.

Address correspondence to the executive director.

California

Memb. 2,500. Term of Office. Nov. 1996–Nov. 1997. Publication. *California Libraries*.

Pres. Gregg Atkins, San Mateo Community College; *V.P./Pres.-Elect* Anne Marie Gold; *Exec. Dir.* Mary Sue Ferrell, California Lib. Assn., 717 K St., Sacramento 95814. Tel. 916-447-8541, fax 916-447-8394, e-mail cmember@netcom.com.

Address correspondence to the executive director.

Colorado

Memb. 863. Term of Office. Aug. 1996–Aug. 1997. Publication. *Colorado Libraries* (q.). *Ed.* Nancy Carter, Univ. of Colorado, Campus Box 184, Boulder 80309.

Pres. Gail M. Dow, Denver Public Lib., 10 W. 14 Ave. Pkwy., Denver 80204. Tel. 303-640-6121, fax 303-604-6142, e-mail gdow@ denver.lib.co.us; *V.P./Pres.-Elect* William Knott; *Treas.* George Jaramillo, Univ. of Northern Colorado, Greeley 80634; *Exec. Secy.* Ruth Jarles.

Address correspondence to the executive secretary at the association, Box 140355,

Edgewater 80214. Tel. 303-205-9284, fax 303-205-9285.

Connecticut

Memb. 1,100. Term of Office. July 1996–June 1997. Publication. *Connecticut Libraries* (11 per year). *Ed.* David Kapp, 4 Llynwood Dr., Bolton 06040. Tel. 203-647-0697.
Pres. Barbara Gibson, Farmington Lib., Farmington 06034. Tel. 860-673-6791; *V.P./Pres.-Elect* Robert Gallucci, Brookfield Lib., Brookfield 06804; *Treas.* Sherry Hupp, Hamden Lib., Hamden 06518. Tel. 203-287-2686; *Administrator* Karen Zoller, Connecticut Lib. Assn., Box 1046, Norwich 06360-1046. Tel. 860-885-2758.
Address correspondence to the administrator.

Delaware

Memb. 300. Term of Office. Apr. 1996–Apr. 1997. Publication. *DLA Bulletin* (3 per year).
Pres. Thomas C. Melvin, Morris Lib., Univ. of Delaware, Newark 19717. Tel. 302-831-1730, fax 302-831-1046; *V.P./Pres.-Elect* Dave Burdash, Wilmington Institute Lib., Wilmington. Tel. 302-571-7400. *Secy.-Treas.* John Brunswick, Morris Lib., Univ. of Delaware, Newark 19717. Tel. 302-831-2965, fax 302-831-1046.
Address correspondence to the association, Box 816, Dover 19903-0816.

District of Columbia

Memb. 600. Term of Office. Aug. 1996–Aug. 1997. Publication. *INTERCOM* (mo.).
Pres. Patricia Wand, Univ. Lib., American Univ., 4400 Massachusetts Ave. N.W., Washington 20016-8046. Tel. 202-885-3237, fax 202-885-3226, e-mail patwand@american. edu; *V.P./Pres.-Elect* Dennis Reynolds, Exec. Dir., CAPCON, 1320 19th St. N.W., Suite 400, Washington 20036-1679. Tel. 202-331-5771, fax 202-797-7719, e-mail dreynold@ capcon.net; *Secy.* Blanche Anderson, Arlington County Public Lib., 1015 N. Quincy St., Arlington, VA 22201. Tel. 703-358-6334, fax 703-358-7720, e-mail banderso@leo.vsla. edu; *Treas.* Mary A. Martin, Sugar Assn., 1101 15th St. N.W., Suite 600, Washington 20005. Tel. 202-785-1122, fax 202-785-5019.

Address correspondence to the association, Box 14177, Benjamin Franklin Sta., Washington 20044.

Florida

Memb. (Indiv.) 1,506; (In-state Inst.) 93. Term of Office. July 1996–June 1997. Publication. *Florida Libraries* (bi-mo.).
Pres. Eileen Cobb, Broward County Main Lib., 100 S. Andrews Ave., Fort Lauderdale 33301. Tel. 954-357-7379, fax 954-357-5681, e-mail cobbe@mail.bcl.lib.fl.us; *V.P./ Pres.-Elect* Patricia De Salvo Young, Seminole Community College Lib., 100 Weldon Blvd., Sanford 32773. Tel. 407-328-4722, fax 407-328-2233, e-mail youngpscl@lincc. ccla.lib.fl.us; *Secy.* Laurie Linsley, Seminole Community College Lib., 100 Weldon Blvd., Sanford 32773. Tel. 407-328-4722 ext. 3335, fax 407-328-2233, e-mail llinsley@ipo. seminole.cc.fl.us; *Treas.* Kathleen de la Pena McCook, Univ. of South Florida, Box 1027, Ruskin 33570. Tel. 813-974-3520, fax 813-974-6840, e-mail kmccook@cis01.cis.usf. edu; *Exec. Secy.* Marjorie Stealey, Florida Lib. Assn., 1133 W. Morse Blvd., Suite 201, Winter Park 32789. Tel. 407-647-8839, fax 407-629-2502.
Address correspondence to the executive secretary.

Georgia

Memb. 1,100. Term of Office. Oct. 1996–Oct. 1997. Publication. *Georgia Librarian*. *Ed.* Susan Cooley, Sara Hightower Regional Lib., 203 Riverside Pkwy., Rome 30161. Tel. 706-236-4621.
Pres. Richard Leach, East Central Regional Lib., 902 Greene St., Augusta 30901. Tel. 706-821-2600; *1st V.P./Pres.-Elect* Alan Kaye, Roddenbery Memorial Lib., 320 N. Broad St., Cairo 31728. Tel. 912-377-3632; *2nd V.P.* James Cooper, West Georgia Regional Lib., 710 Rome St., Carrollton 30117. Tel. 706-836-6711; *Secy.* Elizabeth Bagley, South Georgia College, 100 W. College Park Dr., Douglas 31533. Tel. 912-383-4233; *Treas.* Tom Budlong, Atlanta Fulton Public Lib., 269 Buckhead Ave., Atlanta 30305. Tel. 404-814-3502.
Address correspondence to the president.

Hawaii

Memb. 450. Term of Office. Apr. 1996–Apr. 1997. Publications. *HLA Newsletter* (q.); *HLA Journal* (ann.); *HLA Membership Directory* (ann.).

Pres. Helen Wong Smith, Box 82, Papaikou 96781. Tel. 808-933-3678, e-mail smith@Hawaii.edu.

Address correspondence to the association, Box 4441, Honolulu 96812-4441.

Idaho

Memb. 500. Term of Office. Oct. 1995–Oct. 1996. Publication. *Idaho Librarian* (q.). *Ed.* Mary Bolin, Univ. of Idaho Lib., Moscow 83844-2363. Tel. 208-885-7737, e-mail mbolin@uidaho.edu.

Pres. Vivian Wells, 3219 E. 3600 N., Kimberly 83341. Tel. 208-733-6551, fax 208-733-8192; *1st V.P.* Mary Carr, North Idaho College Lib., 1000 W. Garden Ave., Coeur d'Alene 83814. Tel. 208-769-3215, fax 208-769-3428, e-mail carr@nidc.edu; *2nd V.P.* Susannah Price, Boise Public Lib., 715 S. Capitol Blvd., Boise 83702-7122. Tel. 208-384-4026, fax 208-384-4065; *Treas.* Tim Brown, Albertsons Lib., Boise State Univ., 1910 Univ. Dr., Boise 83725. Tel. 208-385-1234, fax 208-385-1885, e-mail tbrown@bsu.idbsu.edu; *Secy.* Annie-Laurie Burton, Twin Falls Public Lib., 434 Second St. E., Twin Falls 83301. Tel. 208-733-2964, fax 208-733-2965; *Conference Exhibits Chair* Pat Stewart, 1424 Four Mile Rd., Viola 83872. Tel. 208-882-3577, fax 208-883-4440.

Address conference exhibits correspondence to the exhibits chairperson. Address all other correspondence to the president.

Illinois

Memb. 3,000. Term of Office. July 1996–June 1997. Publication. *ILA Reporter* (bi-mo.).

Pres. Ruth Faklis, Prairie Trails Public Lib. Dist., 8449 S. Moody, Burbank 60459; *V.P./Pres.-Elect* Kathleen M. Balcom, Arlington Heights Memorial Public Lib., 500 N. Dunton Ave., Arlington Heights 60004-5910; *Treas.* Robert Harris, Helen M. Plum Memorial Lib., 110 W. Maple St., Lombard 60148-2514; *Exec. Dir.* Robert P. Doyle, 33 W. Grand Ave., Suite 301, Chicago 60610. Tel. 312-644-1896, fax 312-644-1899.

Address correspondence to the executive director.

Indiana

Memb. (Indiv.) 3,000; (Inst.) 300. Term of Office. May 1997–May 1998. Publications. *Focus on Indiana Libraries* (11 per year), *Indiana Libraries* (s. ann.). *Ed.* Patricia Plascac.

Pres. Steven Schmidt, 50 S. Butler Ave., Indianapolis 46219. Tel. 317-274-0470, fax 317-274-0492, e-mail schmidt@library.iupui.edu; *1st V.P.* Charr Skirvin, Plainfield Public Lib., 1120 Stafford Rd., Plainfield 46168. Tel 317-839-6602, fax 317-839-4044, e-mail cskirvin.plpl@incolsa.palni.edu; *Secy.* Shirleen Martens, 20321 Kenilworth Rd., Argos 46501. Tel. 219-255-9095, fax 219-255-8489 e-mail s.martens@gomail.sjcpl.lib.in; *Treas.* Connie Patsiner, IVAN, 6201 LaPaz Trail, Suite 280, Indianapolis 46268. Tel./fax 317-329-9163; *Past Pres.* Sally Otte, 5251 N. Delaware St., Indianapolis 46220. Tel. 317-257-5800.

Address correspondence to the Indiana Lib. Federation, 6408 Carrollton Ave., Indianapolis 46220. Tel. 317-257-2040, fax 317-257-1393.

Iowa

Memb. 1,700. Term of Office. Jan.–Dec. 1997. Publication. *The Catalyst* (bi-mo.). *Ed.* Naomi Stovall.

Pres. Nancy Kraft, State Historical Society, 402 Iowa Ave., Iowa City 52240. Tel. 319-335-3922; *V.P.* Susan K. Ling, Marion Public Lib.

Address correspondence to the association, 505 Fifth Ave., Suite 823, Des Moines 50309. Tel. 515-243-2172, fax 515-243-0614, e-mail ialib@acad.drake.edu.

Kansas

Memb. 1,100. Term of Office. July 1996–June 1997. Publications. *KLA Newsletter* (q.); *KLA Membership Directory* (ann.).

Exec. Secy. Leroy Gattin, South Central Kansas Lib. System, 901 N. Main St., Hutchinson 67501. Tel. 316-663-5441 ext. 110, fax 316-663-1215, e-mail lgatt@class.org; *Secy.* Marianne Eichelberger, Newton Public Lib., 720 N. Oak, Newton 67114. Tel. 316-283-2890, fax 316-283-2916; *Treas.* Marcella Ratzlaff, Hutchinson Public Lib., 901 N. Main St., Hutchinson 67501. Tel. 316-663-5441.

Address correspondence to the executive secretary.

Kentucky

Memb. 1,900. Term of Office. Oct. 1996–Oct. 1997. Publication. *Kentucky Libraries* (q.).

Pres. Elaine Steinberg. Tel. 502-637-4712 ext. 152; *V.P./Pres.-Elect* Sally Livingston. Tel. 502-485-3091; *Secy.* Carolyn Tassie. Tel. 606-233-8225; *Exec. Secy.* Tom Underwood, 1501 Twilight Trail, Frankfort 40601. Tel. 502-223-5322.

Address correspondence to the executive secretary.

Loui siana

Memb. (Indiv.) 1,500; (Inst.) 60. Term of Office. July1996–June 1997. Publication. *LLA Bulletin* (q.). *Ed.* Mary Cosper Le Boeuf, 424 Roussell St., Houma 70360. Tel. 504-876-5861, fax 504-876-5864, e-mail ter@pelican.state.lib.la.us.

Pres. Elizabeth Vandersteen, 3299 Hwy. 457, Alexandria 71302. Tel. 318-445-6376, fax 318-445-6478; *1st V.P./Pres.-Elect* Carol Billings, 12 Swallow St., New Orleans 70124. Tel. 504-568-5706, fax 504-568-5069; *2nd V.P.* Gloria Spooner, 312 Margaret St., Baton Rouge 70802-7038. Tel. 504-342-4931, fax 504-342-3547, e-mail gspooner@pelican.state.lib.la.us; *Secy.* Joyce Lilly, Box 730, Gibsland 71028-0730. Tel. 318-263-7410, e-mail bvlib1@bienville.lib.la.us; *Parliamentarian* Sona Dombourian, Box 5404, Lafayette 70502. Tel. 318-261-5775, fax 318-261-5782, e-mail SONAD@aol.com; *Past Pres.* Marvene Dearman, 1471 Chevelle Dr., Baton Rouge 70806. Tel. 504-357-6464, fax 504-357-0610; *ALA Councillor* Joy Lowe, Box 3161, Tech Sta., Ruston 71272. Tel. 318-257-3430, e-mail joylowe@vm.cc.latech.edu; *SELA Rep.* Sybil Boudreaux, 860 Hidalgo St., New Orleans 70124. Tel. 504-286-6625, e-mail SABLS@uno.edu; *Admin.*

Officer Carol McMahan, Box 3058, Baton Rouge 70821-3058. Tel. 504-342-4928, fax 504-342-3547, e-mail LLA@pelican.state. lib.la.us.

Address correspondence to the association, Box 3058, Baton Rouge 70821. Tel. 504-342-4928, fax 504-342-3547, e-mail lla@pelican. state.lib.la.us.

Maine

Memb. 900. Term of Office. (Pres., V.P.) spring 1996–spring 1998. Publications. *Maine Entry* (q.); *Maine Memo* (mo.).

Pres. Karen Reilly, Lib., Eastern Maine Technical College, Bangor 04401; *V.P.* Elizabeth Moran, Camden Public Lib., Camden 04843; *Secy.* Leanne Pander, Hawthorne-Longfellow Lib., Bowdoin College, Brunswick 04011; *Treas.* Robert Filgate, McArthur Public Lib., Biddeford 04005.

Address correspondence to the association, 60 Community Dr., Augusta 04330. Tel. 207-623-8428, fax 207-626-5947.

Maryland

Memb. 1,300. Term of Office. July 1996–June 1997. Publication. *The Crab.*

Pres. Cathy Butler, Anne Arundel County Public Lib., 5 Harry S. Truman Pkwy., Annapolis 31401. Tel. 410-222-7371; *V.P./ Pres.-Elect* Sharan Marshall, Southern Maryland Regional Lib. Assn., Box 459, Charlotte Hall 20622-0459. Tel. 301-934-9442, fax 301-884-0438; *2nd V.P.* Sandra E. Owen, Harford County Lib., 1221-A Brass Mill Road, Belcamp 21017. Tel. 410-273-5600 ext. 249, fax 410-273-5606, e-mail owen@vax1.harf.lib.md.us; *Secy.* Debra Sambuco, Essex Community College, 7201 Rossville Bldvd., Baltimore 21237. Tel. 410-780-6423, fax 410-391-2642, e-mail dsambuco@mail. bcpl.lib.md.us; *Treas.* Audra Caplan, Harford County Lib., 1221-A Brass Mill Rd., Belcamp 21017. Tel. 410-273-5600 ext 246, fax 410-273-5606, e-mail caplan@vax1.harf.lib. mid.us; *Exec. Dir.* Nicole Cernigliaro.

Address correspondence to the association, 400 Cathedral St., Baltimore 21201-4401. Tel. 410-727-7422, fax 410-625-9594, e-mail mla@epfl1.epflbalto.org.

Massachusetts

Memb. (Indiv.) 950; (Inst.) 100. Term of Office. July1996–June 1997. Publication. *Bay State Librarian* (10 per year).

Pres. Bonnie Isman, Jones Lib., 43 Amity St., Amherst 01002. Tel. 413-256-4090, fax 413-256-4096; *V.P.* Marjorie Judd, Middleborough Public Lib., 102 N. Main St., Middleborough 02346. Tel. 508-946-2470, e-mail middpl@ultranet.com; *Secy.* Katherine Ogle, Worcester Public Lib., 3 Salem Sq., Worcester 01608. Tel. 508-799-1701, fax 508-799-1713; *Treas.* Gerald Davis, Springfield College Lib., 263 Alden St., Springfield 01109. Tel. 413-748-3309, fax 413-748-3631; *Exec. Secy.* Barry Blaisdell, Massachusetts Lib. Assn., Countryside Offices, 707 Turnpike St., North Andover 01845. Tel. 508-686-8543, e-mail masslib@world.std.com.

Address correspondence to the executive secretary.

Michigan

Memb. (Indiv.) 2,200; (Inst.) 375. Term of Office. July 1996–June 1997. Publication. *Michigan Librarian Newsletter* (10 per year).

Pres. Beverly Papai, Farmington Community Lib., 32737 W. Twelve Mile Rd., Farmington Hills 48334; *Treas.* Tom Genson, Grand Rapids Public Lib., 60 Library Plaza N.E., Grand Rapids 49503; *Exec. Dir.* Marianne Hartzell, Michigan Lib. Assn., 6810 S. Cedar St., Suite 6, Lansing 48911. Tel. 517-694-6615.

Address correspondence to the executive director.

Minnesota

Memb. 1,079. Term of Office. (Pres., Pres.-Elect) Jan.–Dec. 1997; (Treas.) Jan. 1996–Dec. 1997; (Secy.) Jan. 1996–Dec. 1997. Publication. *MLA Newsletter* (10 per year).

Pres. Barbara Jauquet-Kalinowski, N.W. Regional Lib., 101 E. First St., Thief River Falls 56701; *Pres.-Elect* Mary E. Martin, Univ. of Saint Thomas, 2115 Summit Ave., Saint Paul 55105; *ALA Chapter Councillor* Gretchen Marie Wronka, Hennepin County Lib., 12601 Ridgedale Dr., Minnetonka 55343; *Secy.* Janet Urbanowicz, Minneapolis Public Lib., 300 Nicollet Mall, Minneapolis 55401; *Treas.* Mary Parker, MINITEX, Univ. of Minnesota, S-33 Wilson Lib., 309 19th Ave. S., Minneapolis 55455; *Exec. Dir.* Deborah K. Sales, Minnesota Lib. Assn., 1315 Lowry Ave. N., Minneapolis 55411. Tel. 612-521-1735, fax 612-529-5503.

Address correspondence to the executive director.

Mississippi

Memb. 1,100. Term of Office. Jan.–Dec. 1997. Publication. *Mississippi Libraries* (q.).

Pres. Glenda Segars; *Treas.* Carol Cubberley; *Secy.* Pat Matthes; *Exec. Secy.* Mary Julia Anderson.

Address correspondence to the executive secretary, Box 20448, Jackson 39289-1448. Tel. 601-352-3917.

Missouri

Memb. 1,000. Term of Office. Oct. 1996–Oct. 1997. Publication. *MO INFO* (bi-mo.). *Ed.* Jean Ann McCartney.

Pres. Judy Siebert Pallardy, Head, Science Libs., W2001 Engineering Bldg. E., Univ. of Missouri, Columbia 65211. Tel. 573-882-2715, fax 573-884-4499, e-mail engjudy@mizzou1.missouri.edu; *V.P./Pres.-Elect* Elizabeth Ader, Dir., Cape Girardeau Public Lib., 711 N. Clark, Cape Girardeau 63701. Tel. 573-334-5279, fax 573-334-8334, e-mail sct@mail.more.net; *Secy.* Nancy Ogg, Asst. Libn., Missouri Supreme Court Lib., Box 448, Jefferson City 65102. Tel. 573-751-7331, fax 573-751-2636, e-mail nogg01@mail.state.mo.us; *Treas.* Robert A. Almony, Jr., Asst. Dir. of Libs., Univ. of Missouri, 104 Ellis Lib., Columbia 65201-5149. Tel. 573-882-4701, fax 573-882-8044, e-mail ellisbob@mizzou1.missouri.edu; *ALA Councillor* June De Weese, Head of Access Services, Ellis Lib., Univ. of Missouri, Columbia 65201-5149. Tel. 573-882-7315, fax 573-882-8044, e-mail elsjune@mizzou1.missouri.edu; *Exec. Dir.* Jean Ann McCartney, Missouri Lib. Assn., 1306 Business 63 S., Suite B, Columbia 65201. Tel. 314-449-4627, fax 314-449-4655, e-mail jmccartney@mail.more.net, or mla001@mail.more.net.

Address correspondence to the executive director.

Montana

Memb. 700. Term of Office. July 1996–June 1997. Publication. *Montana Library Focus* (bi-mo.). *Ed.* David Pauli, Missoula Public Lib., 301 E. Main St., Missoula 59802. Tel. 406-721-2665, e-mail dpauli@mtlib.org.

Pres. Jim Heckel, Great Falls Public Lib., 301 Second Ave. N., Great Falls 59401-2593. Tel. 406-453-9706, fax 406-453-1081, e-mail jheckel@orion.mtgr.mtlib.org; *V.P./Pres.-Elect* Darlene Staffeldt, Montana State Lib., Box 201800, Helena 59620-1800. Tel. 406-444-5381, fax 406-444-5612, e-mail dmstaff@win.com; *Secy./Treas.* Bonnie Williamson, Havre-Hill County Lib., 402 Third St., Havre 59501. Tel. 406-265-2123, e-mail bwilliam@mtlib.org; *Admin. Asst.* John Thomas, Box 505, Helena 59624-0505. Tel. 406-442-9446.

Address correspondence to the administrative assistant.

Nebraska

Memb. 1,000. Term of Office. Oct. 1996–Oct. 1997. Publication. *NLA Quarterly* (q.).

Pres. Sharon Mason, Calvin T. Ryan Lib., Univ. of Nebraska at Kearney, 905 W. 25 St., Box 76, Kearney 68849-7000. Tel. 308-865-8582, e-mail mason@platte.unk.edu; *Exec. Dir.* Burns Davis, 425 S. 30 St., Lincoln 68510-1424. Tel. 402-476-6111, fax 402-476-6779, e-mail docbiz@aol.com.

Address correspondence to the executive director.

Nevada

Memb. 400. Term of Office. Jan.–Dec. 1997. Publication. *Highroller* (q.).

Pres. Sally Kinsey; *Treas.* Delsie Stayner; *Exec. Secy.* Judy Soper.

Address correspondence to the executive secretary, Washoe County Lib., Reno. Tel. 702-785-4190.

New Hampshire

Memb. 700. Publication. *NHLA Newsletter* (bi-mo.).

Pres. Michael Sullivan, Wiggin Memorial Lib., Stratham 03885-2403. Tel. 603-772-4346, e-mail msullivan@lilac.nh.lib.us.

Address correspondence to the association, Box 2332, Concord 03302-2332.

New Jersey

Memb. 1,700. Term of Office. May 1996–Apr. 1997. Publications. *New Jersey Libraries* (q.); *New Jersey Libraries Newsletter* (mo.).

Pres. Lynn Randall, Jennings Lib., Caldwell College, 9 Ryerson Ave., Caldwell 07006. Tel. 201-228-4424, ext. 314; *V.P./Pres.-Elect* Alex Boyd, Newark Public Lib., Box 630, Newark 07101; *Treas.* James Hecht, Somerset County Lib., Box 6700, Bridgewater 08807; *Exec. Dir.* Patricia Tumulty, New Jersey Lib. Assn., 4 W. Lafayette St., Trenton 08608. Tel. 609-394-8032.

Address correspondence to the executive director, Box 1534, Trenton 08607.

New Mexico

Memb. 550. Term of Office. Apr. 1997–Apr. 1998. Publication. *New Mexico Library Association Newsletter* (q.). *Co-Eds.* Jackie Shane. Tel. 505-277-5410, e-mail jshane@unm.edu; Nora Stoecker. Tel. 505-234-0049, e-mail nksinfo@caverns.com.

Pres. Jennifer Minter, 1090 Crossley, Las Cruces 88005. Tel. 505-527-7556, fax 505-527-7515, e-mail jminter@lib.nmsu.edu; *1st V.P.* Betty Long, Roswell Public Lib., 301 N. Pennsylvania, Roswell 88201. Tel. 505-622-3400, fax 505-622-7107.

Address correspondence to the association, El Dorado Sq., 11200 Montgomery N.E., Suite 8, Albuquerque 87111.

New York

Memb. 3,000. Term of Office. Oct. 1996–Nov. 1997. Publication. *NYLA Bulletin* (10 per year). *Ed.* Paul Girsdansky.

Pres. Ristiina Wigg, Mid-Hudson Lib. System, 103 Market St., Poughkeepsie 12601. Tel. 914-471-6060; *V.P./Pres.-Elect* Paul Crumlish, Warren/Hunting/Smith Lib., Hobart and William Smith College, Geneva 14456-3398. E-mail crumlish@hws.edu; *Treas.* J. Robert Verbesey, Mastic Moriches-Shirley Community Lib., William Floyd Pkwy., Shirley 11967. Tel. 516-399-1511 ext. 200; *Exec. Dir.* Susan Lehman Keitel, New York

Lib. Assn., 252 Hudson Ave., Albany 12210. Tel. 518-432-6952.

Address correspondence to the executive director.

North Carolina

Memb. 2,200. Term of Office. Oct. 1995–Oct. 1997. Publication. *North Carolina Libraries* (q.). Ed. Frances Bradburn, Media and Technology, N.C. Dept. of Public Instruction, 301 N. Wilmington St., Raleigh 27601-2825.

Pres. David Fergusson, Forsyth County Public Lib., 660 W. Fifth St., Winston-Salem 27101. Tel. 910-727-2556, fax 910-727-2549; *V.P./Pres.-Elect* Beverley Gass, Guilford Technical Community College, Box 309, Jamestown 27282-0309. Tel. 910-334-4822 ext. 2434, fax 910-841-4350; *Secy.* Steven Sumerford, Glenwood Branch Lib., 1901 W. Florida St., Greensboro 27403. Tel. 910-297-5002, fax 910-297-5004; *Treas.* Wanda Brown, Reynolds Lib., Wake Forest Univ., Box 7777, Reynolda Sta., Winston-Salem 27109-7777. Tel. 910-759-5094, fax 910-759-9831.

Address correspondence to the secretary.

North Dakota

Memb. (Indiv.) 367; (Inst.) 18. Term of Office. Oct. 1996–Sept. 1997. Publication. *The Good Stuff* (q.). Ed. Kelly Steckler, Mandan Public Lib., 108 First St. N.W., Mandan 58554.

Pres. Lillian Sorenson, Stoxen Lib., Dickinson State Univ., 291 Campus Dr., Dickinson 58601. Tel. 701-227-2561; *V.P./Pres.-Elect* Ellen Kotrba, UND Box 7085, Grand Forks 58202-7085. Tel. 701-777-6346; *Secy.* Phyllis Bratton, Raugust Lib., 6070 College La., Jamestown 58405-0002. Tel. 701-252-3467; *Treas.* Donna Maston, Bismarck Public Lib., 515 N. Fifth St., Bismarck 58501. Tel. 701-222-6414.

Address correspondence to the president.

Ohio

Memb. 3,090. Term of Office. Jan.–Dec. 1997. Publications. *Access* (mo.); *Ohio Libraries* (q.).

Chair Elaine Paulette, Wood County Dist. Lib., 251 N. Main St., Bowling Green 43402. Tel. 419-352-5104; *V. Chair* Terry Casey, 249 Overbrook Dr., Columbus 43214; *Secy.* Jack Carlson, 2904 Green Vista Dr., Fairborn 45324; *Treas.* Jim Switzer, 891 Elmore Ave., Akron 44302-1238.

Address correspondence to the association, 35 E. Gay St., Suite 305, Columbus 43215. Tel. 614-221-9057.

Oklahoma

Memb. (Indiv.) 1,050; (Inst.) 60. Term of Office. July 1996–June 1997. Publication. *Oklahoma Librarian* (bi-mo.).

Pres. Clinton Thompson, Jr.; *Secy.* Karen Marriott; *Treas.* Jeanette McQuitty; *Exec. Dir.* Kay Boies, 300 Hardy Dr., Edmond 73013. Tel./fax 405-348-0506, e-mail kboies@ionet.net.

Address correspondence to the executive director.

Oregon

Memb. (Indiv.) 1,000. Term of Office. Sept. 1996–Aug. 1997. Publications. *OLA Hotline* (bi-w.), *OLA Quarterly*.

Pres. Ed House, Albany Public Lib., 1390 Waverly Dr. S.E., Albany 97321. Tel. 503-967-4307; *Secy.* Anne Van Sickle, McMinnville Public Lib., 225 N. Adams St., McMinnville 97128. Tel. 503-434-7433; *Treas.* Donetta Sheffold, Kerr Lib., Oregon State Univ., Corvallis 97331. Tel. 503-737-7297.

Address correspondence to the secretary.

Pennsylvania

Memb. 1,500. Term of Office. Jan.–Dec. 1997. Publication. *PaLA Bulletin* (mo.).

Pres. Karl Helicher, Upper Merion Twp. Lib., 175 W. Valley Forge Rd., King of Prussia 19406. Tel. 610-265-1196, e-mail umerpublib@shrsys.hslc.org; *1st V.P.* Sally Felix, Lackawanna County Lib. System, 520 Vine St., Scranton 18509. Tel. 717-348-3003, e-mail sfelix19@soho.ios.com; *Exec. Dir.* Glenn R. Miller, Pennsylvania Lib. Assn., 1919 N. Front St., Harrisburg 17102. Tel. 717-233-3113, e-mail plassn@hslc.org.

Address correspondence to the executive director.

Rhode Island

Memb. (Indiv.) 341; (Inst.) 59. Term of Office. Nov. 1996–Nov. 1997. Publication. *Rhode Island Library Association Bulletin*. Ed. To be appointed.

Pres. Susan L. Reed, Pawtucket Public Lib., 13 Summer St., Pawtucket 02860. Tel. 401-725-3714 ext. 202, fax 401-782-2710, e-mail susanrd@dsl.rhilinet.gov; *V.P./Pres.-Elect* Kathy Ellen Bullard, Woonsocket Harris Public Lib., 303 Clinton St., Woonsocket 02895. Tel. 401-769-9044, fax 401-767-4140, e-mail kathybd@dsl.rhilinet. gov; *Secy.* James A. Barrett, Univ. Lib., Univ. of Rhode Island, 15 Lippitt Rd., Kingston 02881. Tel. 401-874-2662, fax 401-874-4608, e-mail barrett@uriacc.uri.edu; *Treas.* Ann Morgan Dodge, John Hay Lib., Brown Univ., Providence 02912. Tel. 401-863-1502, fax 401-863-2093, e-mail AP201078@ brownvm.brown.edu; *Membs.-at-Large* David Macksam, Cranston Public Lib.; Karen Quinn, R.I. State Law Lib.; *ALA Councillor* Frank Iacono, Dept. of State Lib. Services, 300 Richmond St., Providence 02903. Tel. 401-277-2726 ext. 116, fax 401-831-1131, e-mail frankio@dsl.rhilinet.gov; *NELA Councillor* Fran Farrell-Bergeron, West Warwick Public Lib., 1043 Main St., West Warwick 02893. Tel. 401-828-3750, fax 401-828-8493.

Address correspondence to the secretary.

South Carolina

Memb. 700. Term of Office. Jan.–Dec. 1997. Publication. *News and Views*.

Pres. Tom Sutherland, Westinghouse Savannah River Site. Tel. 803-725-1316, fax 803-725-1169, e-mail tom.sutherland@srs.gov; *V.P./Pres.-Elect* Faith Line, Sumter County Lib., Sumter. Tel. 803-773-7273, fax 803-773-4875, e-mail fline@ftc-i-net; *2nd V.P.* Betsey Carter, The Citadel, Charleston. Tel. 803-953-6844, fax 803-953-5190, e-mail cartere@citadel.edu; *Secy.* Terry Barksdale, Greenville County Lib., Greenville. Tel. 864-242-5000 ext. 222, fax 864-235-8375, e-mail tbarksdale@infoave.net; *Treas.* Chris Rogers, Spartanburg County Lib., Spartanburg. Tel. 864-596-3505, fax 864-596-3518, e-mail chrisr@spart.spartanburg.lib.sc.us; *Exec. Secy.* Drucie Raines, South Carolina Lib. Assn., Box 219, Goose Creek 29445. Tel. 803-764-3668, fax 803-824-2690, e-mail Rainesd@citadel.edu.

Address correspondence to the executive secretary.

South Dakota

Memb. (Indiv.) 451; (Inst.) 61. Term of Office. Oct. 1996–Oct. 1997. Publication. *Book Marks* (bi-mo.).

Pres. Jane Larson, Vermillion Public Lib., 18 Church St., Vermillion 57069. Tel. 605-677-7060; *V.P./Pres.-Elect* Ris Smith, Karl E. Mundt Lib., Dakota State Univ., Madison 57042. Tel. 605-256-7128; *Secy.* Jane Goettsch, Siouxland Libs., Ronning Branch, 3100 E. 49 St., Sioux Falls 57103. Tel. 605-367-4607; *Treas.* Cathy R. Enlow, Brookings Public Lib., 515 Third St., Brookings 57006-2077. Tel. 605-692-9407, fax 605-692-9386; *ALA Councillor* Ethelle Bean, Karl E. Mundt Lib., Dakota State Univ., Madison 57042; *MPLA Rep.* Colleen Kirby, E. Y. Berry Lib., Black Hills State Univ., Spearfish 57783. Tel. 605-642-6361.

Address correspondence to Ann Smith, Exec. Secy., SDLA, c/o Mikkelsen Lib., Augustana College, Sioux Falls 57197. E-mail asmith@inst.augie.edu.

Tennessee

Memb. 1,050. Term of Office. July 1996–July 1997. Publications. *Tennessee Librarian* (q.), *TLA Newsletter* (bi-mo.).

Pres. Annelle Huggins, Univ. of Memphis Lib., Memphis 38152. Tel. 901-678-4482, fax 901-678-8218; *V.P./Pres.-Elect* Martha Earl, ETSU Medical Lib., Johnson City 37614. Tel. 423929-6254, fax 423-462-7025; *Treas.* Deborah Fetch, APSU, Clarksville 37044. Tel. 615-648-7617, fax 615-648-5986; *Exec. Secy.* Betty Nance, Box 158417, Nashville 37215-8417. Tel. 615-297-8316, fax 615-269-1807.

Address correspondence to the executive secretary.

Texas

Memb. 6,400. Term of Office. Apr. 1996–Apr. 1997. Publications. *Texas Library Journal* (q.); *TLAcast* (9 per year).

Pres. Barbara Immroth; *Exec. Dir.* Patricia Smith, TLA, 3355 Bee Cave Rd., Suite 401, Austin 78746-6763. Tel. 512-328-1518, fax 512-328-8852, e-mail pats@txla.org.

Address correspondence to the executive director.

Utah

Memb. 650. Term of Office. May 1997–May 1998. Publication. *UTAH Libraries News* (bimo.).

Pres. Ranae Pierce; *V.P./Pres.-Elect* Warren Babcock; *Treas./Exec. Secy.* Chris Anderson. Tel. 801-581-8771.

Address correspondence to the executive secretary, Box 711789, Salt Lake City 84171-8789.

Vermont

Memb. 450. Term of Office. May 1996–May 1997. Publication. *VLA News* (10 per year).

Pres. Patricia Hazlehurst, Cobleigh Public Lib., Box 147, Lyndonville 05851. E-mail cobleigh@dol.vt.state.us; *V.P./Pres.-Elect Secy.* Katherine Ludwig, Norman Williams Public Lib., 10 S. Park St., Woodstock 05091. Tel. 802-457-2295; *Treas.* Pamela Murphy, Hartness Lib., Vermont Technical College, Randoph Center 05061. Tel. 802-728-1236; *ALA Councillor* Melissa Malcolm, Mount Abraham Union H.S., 7 Airport Dr., Bristol 05443. Tel. 802-453-2333; *NELA Rep.* Laurel Stanley, Samuel Reed Hall Lib., Lyndon State College, Lyndonville 05851. Tel. 802-626-9371.

Address correspondence to the president.

Virginia

Memb. 1,500+. Term of Office. Jan.–Dec. 1997. Publication. *Virginia Libraries* (q.), *Ed.* Cy Dillon; *VLA Newsletter* (10 per year). *Ed.* Sue Trask, College of William and Mary, Williamsburg 23187.

Pres. Liz Chabot, Mary Baldwin Lib., Staunton 24401; *V.P./Pres.-Elect* Thomas Hehman, Bedford Public Lib.; *2nd V.P.* Carolyn Barkley, Virginia Beach Public Lib. System, 4100 Virginia Beach Blvd., Virginia Beach 23452. Tel. 804-431-3071; *Secy.* Patricia Howe, Longwood College Lib.; *Past Pres.* Caroline Parr, Central Rappahannock Regional Lib.; *Treas.* Linda Hahne, Norfolk Public Lib., 301 E. City Hall Ave., Norfolk 23510. Tel. 804-441-2889; *Exec. Dir.* Deborah M. Trocchi, Virginia Lib. Assn., 669 S. Washington St., Alexandria 22314. Tel. 703-519-7853, fax 703-519-7732.

Address correspondence to the executive director.

Washington

Memb. 1,350. Term of Office. Aug. 1995–July 1997. Publications. *ALKI* (3 per year); *WLA Link* (5 per year).

Pres. Joan Weber, Dir., LMC, Yakima Valley Community College, Box 1647, Yakima 98907-1647. Tel. 509-574-4984.

Address correspondence to the association, 4016 First Ave. N.E., Seattle 98105-6502. Tel. 206-545-1529, fax 206-545-1543, e-mail washla@wln.com.

West Virginia

Memb. 650. Term of Office. Dec. 1996–Nov. 1997. Publication. *West Virginia Libraries* (q.). *Eds.* Karen Goff, West Virginia Lib. Commission, and Marjorie Price, West Virginia Supreme Court of Appeals Law Lib.

Pres. Marjorie Price, West Virginia Supreme Court of Appeals Law Lib., Bldg. 1-E404, 1900 Kanawha Blvd. E., Charleston 25305. Tel. 304-558-2607, fax 304-558-3815, e-mail mprice@wvlv.wvnet.edu; *Past Pres.* Jo Ann Calzonetti, Evansdale Lib., Box 6105, West Virginia Univ., Morgantown 26506-6105. Tel. 304-293-4695 ext. 5112, fax 304-293-7330, e-mail JCALZONE@wvu.edu; *1st V.P./Pres.-Elect* Judy Duncan, Saint Albans Public Lib., 602 Fourth St., Saint Albans 25177-2820. Tel. 304-722-4244, fax 304-722-4245, e-mail Duncanj@wvlc.wvnet.edu; *2nd V.P.* Betty Gunnoe, Martinsburg Public Lib., 101 W. King St., Martinsburg 25401. Tel. 304-267-8933, fax 304-267-9720; *Treas.* R. David Childers, West Virginia Lib. Commission, Cultural Center, 1900 Kanawha Blvd. E., Charleston

25305. Tel. 304-558-2041, fax 304-558-2044; *Secy.* Myra Ziegler, Summers County Public Lib., 201 Temple St., Hinton 25951. Tel. 304-466-4490, fax 304-466-5260, e-mail zieglerm@wvlc.wvnet.edu; *ALA Councillor* Joseph W. Barnes, Scarborough Lib., Shepherd College, Shepherdstown 25443. Tel. 304-876-5312, fax 304-876-0731, e-mail jbarnes@scvax.wvnet.edu.

Address correspondence to the president.

Wisconsin

Memb. 2,100. Term of Office. Jan.–Dec. 1997. Publication. *WLA Newsletter* (bi-mo.).

Pres. Alice A. Sturzl. Tel. 715-674-4751; *Pres.-Elect* Paul E. Nelson. Tel. 608-835-5131; *Exec. Dir.* Larry J. Martin, 4785 Hayes Rd., Madison 53704-7364. Tel. 608-242-2040, fax 608-242-2050.

Address correspondence to the executive director.

Wyoming

Memb. (Indiv.) 450; (Inst.) 21; (Subscribers) 24. Term of Office. Oct. 1996–Oct. 1997.

Pres. Crystal Havely-Stratton, LCCC, 1400 E. College Dr., Cheyenne 82001. Tel. 307-778-1210; *Past Pres.* Lucie Osborn; *V.P./Pres.-Elect* Mary Jayne Jordan; *Exec. Secy.* Laura Grott, Box 1387, Cheyenne 82003. Tel. 307-632-7622, fax 307-638-3469.

Address correspondence to the executive secretary.

Guam

Memb. 75. Publication. *Guam Library Association News* (mo. during school year).

Pres. Katherine Moser Kelly, Andersen Air Force Base Lib., Yigo 96929. Tel. 671-366-4294, e-mail kath@kuentos.guam.net, or kellyk@emh.andersen.af.mil; *V.P., Programs* Rick Castro, RFK Lib., Univ. of Guam, Mangilao 96923. Tel. 671-735-2341, e-mail rcastro@uog.edu; *V.P., Memb.* Harry Uyehara, Guam Community College Lib., Mangilao 96923; *Treas.* Olivia Grande, Guam Community College Lib., Mangilao 96923; *Secy.* Alice Hadley, Naval Hospital Guam Lib., Agana Heights.

Address correspondence to the association, Box 20981 GMF, Guam 96921.

Canada

Alberta

Memb. 700. Term of Office. May 1996–Apr. 1997. Publication. *Letter of the LAA* (5 per year).

Pres. Peg Hofmann, Calgary Public Lib., 616 Macleod Terr. S.E., Calgary T2G 2M2. Tel. 403-260-2635, fax 403-234-8763; *Exec. Dir.* Christine Sheppard, 80 Baker Crescent N.W., Calgary T2L 1R4. Tel. 403-284-5832, fax 403-262-6646.

Address correspondence to the executive director.

British Columbia

Memb. 750. Term of Office. Apr. 1996–May 1997. Publication. *BCLA Reporter.* Ed. Ted Benson.

Pres. Ron Clancy; *V.P./Pres.-Elect* Frieda Wiebe.

Address correspondence to the association, 110-6545 Bonsor Ave., Burnaby V5H 1H3. Tel. 604-430-9633, fax 604-430-8595, e-mail bcla@unixg.ubc.ca.

Manitoba

Memb. 494. Term of Office. May 1996–May 1997. Publication. *Newsline* (mo.).

Pres. Ganga Dakshinamurti; *V.P.* Karen Hunt; *Office Mgr.* Jeannette Dankewych.

Address correspondence to the association, 208-100 Arthur St., Winnipeg R3B 1H3. Tel. 204-943-4567, fax 204-942-1555.

Ontario

Memb. 3,800+. Term of Office. Jan. 1997–Jan. 1998. Publications. *Access* (q.); *The Teaching Librarian* (q.); *Inside OLA* (electronic; mo.).

Pres. Greg Haylon, Cambridge Public Lib.; *Treas.* June Wilson, Ministry of Transportation Lib. Tel. 905-477-5733.

Address correspondence to the association, 100 Lombard St., Suite 303, Toronto M5C

1M3. Tel. 416-363-3388, fax 416-941-9581, e-mail ola@interlog.com.

Quebec

Memb. (Indiv.) 170; (Inst.) 42; (Commercial) 7. Term of Office. June 1996–May 1997. Publications. *ABQ/QLA Bulletin* (3 per year); *QASL Newsletter* (3 per year).

Pres. Beverley Gilbertson, Kirkland Municipal Lib., 171000 Hymus Blvd., Kirkland H9J 2W2; *Exec. Secy.* Mary Ciampini, Quebec Lib. Assn., Box 1095, Pointe Claire H9S 4H9. Tel./fax 514-630-4875.

Address correspondence to the executive secretary.

Saskatchewan

Memb. 350. Term of Office. July 1996–June 1997. Publication. *Forum* (5 per year).

Pres. Audrey Mark; *Exec. Dir.* Andrea Wagner, Box 3388, Regina S4P 3H1. Tel. 306-780-9413, fax 306-780-9447, e-mail sla@pleis.lib.sk.ca.

Address correspondence to the executive director.

Regional

Atlantic Provinces: N.B., Nfld., N.S., P.E.I.

Memb. (Indiv.) 272; (Inst.) 33. Term of Office. May 1996–May 1997. Publications. *APLA Bulletin* (bi-mo.), *Ed.* Suzanne Sexty; *Membership Directory and Handbook* (ann.).

Pres. Sara Lochhead; *V.P./Pres.-Elect* John Teskey; *V.P., Nova Scotia* Faye Hopkins; *V.P., Prince Edward Island* Norine Hanus; *V.P., New Brunswick* Marilynn Rudi; *V.P., Newfoundland* Beverley Neable; *V.P., Memb.* Elizabeth Browne; *Secy.* Anita Cannon. Tel. 506-364-2572; *Treas.* Rashid Tayyeb.

Address correspondence to Atlantic Provinces Lib. Assn., c/o School of Lib. and Info. Studies, Dalhousie Univ., Halifax, NS B3H 4H8.

Midwest: Ill., Ind., Minn., Ohio

Pres. Patricia Llerandi, Schaumburg Township Lib., 32 W. Library Lane, Schaumburg, IL 60194. Tel. 708-885-3373 ext. 150; *V.P./Pres.-Elect* Kathy East. Tel. 419-352-5104; *Secys.* Diane Bever. Tel. 317-455-9265; Linda Kolb. Tel. 317-257-2040.

Address correspondence to the president, Midwest Federation of Lib. Assns.

Mountain Plains: Ariz., Colo., Kans., Mont., Neb., Nev., N.Dak., Okla., S.Dak., Utah, Wyo.

Memb. 920. Term of Office. One year. Publication. *MPLA Newsletter* (bi-mo.), *Ed. and Adv. Mgr.* Heidi M. Nickisch, I. D. Weeks Lib., Univ. of South Dakota, Vermillion, SD 57069. Tel. 605-677-6088, e-mail nickisch@sunbird.usd.edu; *Membership Directory* (ann.).

Pres. Judy Zelenski, Central Colorado Lib. Systems, Wheat Ridge, CO 80033. Tel. 303-422-1150; *V.P./Pres.-Elect* Carol J. Connor, Lincoln City Libs., 136 S. 14 St., Lincoln, NE 68502. Tel. 402-441-8510, e-mail cjc@rand.lcl.lib.ne.us; *Exec. Secy.* Joe Edelen, I. D. Weeks Lib., Univ. of South Dakota, Vermillion, SD 57069. Tel. 605-677-6082, e-mail jedelen@sunbird.usd.edu.

Address correspondence to the executive secretary, Mountain Plains Lib. Assn.

New England: Conn., Maine, Mass., N.H., R.I., Vt.

Memb. (Indiv.) 1,200; (Inst.) 100. Term of Office. One year (Treas., Dirs., two years). Publication. *New England Libraries* (bi-mo.). *Ed.* Cara Barlow, Massachusetts Board of Libs. Commission, 648 Beacon St., Boston, MA 02115. Tel. 617-267-9400.

Pres. George Parks, Libn., Univ. of Southern Maine, 314 Forest Ave., Box 9301, Portland, ME 04104-9301. Tel. 207-780-4276, e-mail gparks@usm.maine.edu; *Secy.* Leslie Markey; *Treas.* Lucy Gangone; *Exec. Secy.* Barry Blaisdell, New England Lib. Assn., 707 Turnpike St., North Andover, MA 01845.

Tel. 508-685-5966, e-mail nela@world.std. com.

Address correspondence to the executive secretary.

Pacific Northwest: Alaska, Idaho, Mont., Oreg., Wash., Alberta, B.C.

Memb. (Active) 554; (Subscribers) 112. Term of Office. Oct. 1995–Sept. 1997. Publication. *PNLA Quarterly. Ed.* Sue Samson, Mansfield Lib., Univ. of Montana, Missoula, MT 59812-1195. Tel. 406-243-4335, fax 406-243-2060, e-mail ss@selway.umt.edu. *Pres.* Karen A. Hatcher, Mansfield Lib., Univ. of Montana, Missoula, MT 59812-1195. Tel. 406-243-6800, fax 406-243-2060, e-mail hatcher@selway.umt.edu; *1st V.P./Pres.-Elect* Gordon Ray, Public Lib. Inter-LINK, 110-6545 Bonsor Ave., Burnaby, BC V5H 1H3. Tel. 604-437-8441, fax 604-430-8595, e-mail bcla@unixg.ubc.ca; *2nd V.P./Memb.* Barry Brown, Mansfield Lib., Univ. of Montana, Missoula, MT 59812. Tel. 406-243-6811, fax 406-243-2060, e-mail barry@selway.umt.edu; *Past Pres.* Bette Ammon, Missoula Public Lib., 301 E. Main St., Missoula, MT 59802. Tel. 406-721-2005, fax 406-728-5900, e-mail bammon@mtlib. org; *Secy.* Marg Anderson, Lib. and Info. Technology Program, SAIT, 1301 16 Ave. N.W., Calgary, AB T3H 1K2. Tel. 403-284-7016, fax 403-284-7121, e-mail marg.anderson@sait.ab.ca; *Treas.* Monica Weyhe, State Dept. of Transportation and Public Facilities, 118 Troy Ave., Juneau, AK 99801. Tel. 907-465-6989, fax 907-465-2665, e-mail Monica_Weyhe@dot.state.ak.us.

Address correspondence to the president, Pacific Northwest Lib. Assn.

Southeastern: Ala., Ark., Fla., Ga., Ky., La., Miss., N.C., S.C., Tenn., Va., W. Va.

Memb. 1,350. Term of Office. Oct. 1996–Oct. 1998. Publication. *The Southeastern Librarian* (q.).

Pres. Lorraine D. Summers, State Lib. of Florida, R. A. Gray Bldg., Tallahassee, FL 32399-0250; *V.P./Pres.-Elect* Frances N. Coleman, 2403 Maple Dr., Starkville, MS 39759; *Secy.* Carolyn T. Wilson, Crisman Memorial Lib., David Lipscomb Univ., Nashville, TN 37204; *Treas.* Billy Pennington, 397 Cambo Lane, Birmingham, AL 35226.

Address correspondence to the president or executive secretary, SELA Headquarters, Box 987, Tucker, GA 30085-0987. Tel./fax 770-939-5080.

State and Provincial Library Agencies

The state library administrative agency in each of the U.S. states will have the latest information on its state plan for the use of federal funds under the Library Services and Technology Act. The directors and addresses of these state agencies are listed below.

Alabama

Patricia L. Harris, Dir., Alabama Public Lib. Service, 6030 Monticello Dr., Montgomery 36130-2001. Tel. 334-213-3900, fax 334-213-3993, e-mail p_l_harris@solinet.net.

Alaska

Karen Crane, Dir., Div. of Libs., Archives, and Museums, Alaska Dept. of Educ., Box 110571, Juneau 99811-0571. Tel. 907-465-2910, fax 907-465-2151, e-mail karenc@muskox.alaska.edu.

Arizona

Mary Johnson, Acting Dir., Dept. of Lib.,Archives, and Public Records, State Capitol, 1700 W. Washington, Suite 200, Phoenix 85007-2896. Tel. 602-542-4035, fax 602-542-4972, e-mail mjohnso@dlapr.lib.az.us.

Arkansas

John A. (Pat) Murphey, Jr., State Libn., Arkansas State Lib., One Capitol Mall, Little Rock 72201-1081. Tel. 501-682-1526, fax 501-682-1529, e-mail jmurphey@comp.uark.edu.

California

Kevin Starr, State Libn., California State Lib., Box 942837, Sacramento 94237-0001. Tel. 916-654-0174, fax 916-654-0064, e-mail kstarr@library.ca.gov.

Colorado

Nancy M. Bolt, Asst. Commissioner, Colorado State Lib., 201 E. Colfax Ave., Rm. 309, Denver 80203. Tel. 303-866-6900, fax 303-866-6940, e-mail nbolt@csn.org.

Connecticut

Richard G. Akeroyd, Jr., State Libn., Connecticut State Lib., 231 Capitol Ave., Hartford 06106. Tel. 203-566-4301, fax 203-566-8940, e-mail rakeroyd@csunet.ctstateu.edu.

Delaware

Tom Sloan, State Libn. and Div. Dir., Div. of Libs., 43 S. DuPont Hwy., Dover 19901. Tel. 302-739-4748, fax 302-739-6787, e-mail tsloan@kentnet.dtcc.edu.

District of Columbia

Mary E. Raphael, Acting Dir., Dist. of Columbia Public Lib., 901 G St. N.W., Suite 400, Washington 20001. Tel. 202-727-1101, fax 202-727-1129.

Florida

Barratt Wilkins, State Libn., State Lib. of Florida, R. A. Gray Bldg., Tallahassee 32399-0250. Tel. 904-487-2651, fax 904-488-2746, e-mail bwilkins@dlis.state.fl.us.

Georgia

Thomas A. Ploeg, Dir., Div. of Public Lib. Services, 156 Trinity Ave. S.W., Atlanta 30303-3692. Tel. 404-657-6241, fax 404-656-7297, e-mail tploeg@mail.gpls.public.lib.ga.us.

Hawaii

Bartholomew A. Kane, State Libn., Hawaii State Public Lib. System, 465 S. King St., Rm. B1, Honolulu 96813. Tel. 808-586-3704, fax 808-586-3715.

Idaho

Charles A. Bolles, State Libn., Idaho State Lib., 325 W. State St., Boise 83702-6072.

Tel. 208-334-2150, fax 208-334-4016, e-mail cbolles@isl.state.id.us.

Illinois

Bridget L. Lamont, Dir., Illinois State Lib., 300 S. Second St., Springfield 62701-1796. Tel. 217-782-2994, fax 217-785-4326, e-mail blamont@library.sos.state.il.us.

Indiana

C. Ray Ewick, Dir., Indiana State Lib., 140 N. Senate Ave., Indianapolis 46204-2296. Tel. 317-232-3692, fax 317-232-0002, e-mail ewick@statelib.lib.in.us.

Iowa

Sharman B. Smith, State Libn., State Lib. of Iowa, E. 12 and Grand, Des Moines 50319. Tel. 515-281-4105, fax 515-281-6191, e-mail ssmith@mail.lib.state.ia.us.

Kansas

Duane F. Johnson, State Libn., Kansas State Lib., 300 S.W. Tenth Ave., Rm. 343, Topeka 66612-1593. Tel. 913-296-3296, fax 913-296-6650, e-mail duanej@ink.org.

Kentucky

James A. Nelson, State Libn./Commissioner, Kentucky Dept. for Libs. and Archives, 300 Coffee Tree Rd., Box 537, Frankfort 40602-0537. Tel. 502-875-7000, fax 502-564-5773, e-mail jnelson@usctr.kdla.state.ky.

Louisiana

Thomas F. Jaques, State Libn., State Lib. of Louisiana, Box 131, Baton Rouge 70821-0131. Tel. 504-342-4923, fax 504-342-3547, e-mail tjaques@pelican.state.lib.la.us.

Maine

J. Gary Nichols, State Libn., Maine State Lib., LMA Bldg., 64 State House Sta., Augusta 04333-0064. Tel. 207-287-5600, fax 207-287-5615, e-mail gary.nichols@state.me.us.

Maryland

J. Maurice Travillian, Asst. State Superintendent for Libs., Div. of Lib. Development and Services, Maryland State Dept. of Educ., 200 W. Baltimore St., Baltimore 21201-2595. Tel. 410-767-0435, fax 410-333-2507, e-mail mj54@umail.umd.ed.

Massachusetts

Keith M. Fiels, Dir., Massachusetts Board of Lib. Commissioners, 648 Beacon St., Boston 02215. Tel. 617-267-9400, fax 617-421-9833, e-mail kfiels@mecn.mass.edu.

Michigan

George M. Needham, State Libn., Lib. of Michigan, 717 Allegan St., Box 30007, Lansing 48909-9945. Tel. 517-373-1580, fax 517-373-4480, e-mail gneedham@libomich.lib.mi.us.

Minnesota

Joyce C. Swanger, Dir., Office of Lib. Development and Service, Minnesota Dept. of Educ., 440 Capitol Sq. Bldg., 550 Cedar St., Saint Paul 55101. Tel. 612-296-2821, fax 612-296-5418, e-mail joyce.swanger@state.mn.us.

Mississippi

Jane Smith, Acting Exec. Dir., Mississippi Lib. Commission, 1221 Ellis Ave., Box 10700, Jackson 39289-0700. Tel. 601-359-1036, fax 601-354-4181.

Missouri

Sara Parker, State Libn., Missouri State Lib., 600 W. Main, Box 387, Jefferson City 65102-0387. Tel. 573-751-2751, fax 573-751-3612, e-mail sparker@mail.sos.state.mo.us.

Montana

Karen Strege, State Libn., Montana State Lib., 1515 E. Sixth Ave., Helena 59620-1800. Tel. 406-444-3116, fax 406-444-5612, e-mail kstrege@msl.mt.gov.

Nebraska

Rod Wagner, Dir., Nebraska Lib. Commission, The Atrium, 1200 N St., Suite 120, Lincoln 68508-2023. Tel. 402-471-2045, fax 402-471-2083, e-mail rwagner@neon.nlc.state.ne.us.

Nevada

Joan Kerschner, Dir., Museums, Lib. and Arts, Nevada State Lib. and Archives, Capitol Complex, Carson City 89710. Tel. 702-687-8315, fax 702-687-8311, e-mail joangk@unr.edu.

New Hampshire

Kendall F. Wiggin, State Libn., New Hampshire State Lib., 20 Park St., Concord 03301-6314. Tel. 603-271-2397, fax 603-271-6826, e-mail wiggin@lilac.nhsl.lib.nh.us.

New Jersey

John H. Livingstone, Jr., Acting State Libn., New Jersey State Lib., 185 W. State St., CN520, Trenton 08625-0520. Tel. 609-292-6200, fax 609-292-2746, e-mail jaliving@pilot.njin.net.

New Mexico

State Libn., New Mexico State Lib., 325 Don Gaspar Ave., Santa Fe 87501-2777. Tel. 505-827-3804, fax 505-827-3888.

New York

State Libn./Asst. Commissioner for Libs., New York State Lib., C.E.C., Rm. 10C34, Empire State Plaza, Albany 12230. Tel. 518-474-5930, fax 518-474-2718.

North Carolina

Sandra M. Cooper, Dir./State Libn., State Lib. of North Carolina, Dept. of Cultural Resources, 109 E. Jones St., Raleigh 27601-2807. Tel. 919-733-2570, fax 919-733-8784, e-mail scooper@hal.dcr.state.nc.us.

North Dakota

Mike Jaugstetter, Acting Dir., North Dakota State Lib., Capitol Grounds, 604 E. Boulevard Ave., Bismarck 58505-0800. Tel. 701-328-2492, fax 701-328-2040, e-mail msmail.mjaugster@ranch.state.nd.us.

Ohio

Michael Lucas, State Libn., State Lib. of Ohio, 65 S. Front St., Columbus 43215-4163. Tel. 614-644-6845, fax 614-466-3584, e-mail mlucas@mail.slonet.ohio.gov.

Oklahoma

Robert L. Clark, Jr., State Libn., Oklahoma Dept. of Libs., 200 N.E. 18 St., Oklahoma City 73105-3298. Tel. 405-521-2502, fax 405-525-7804, e-mail rclark@oltn.odl.state.ok.us.

Oregon

Jim Scheppke, State Libn., Oregon State Lib., State Lib. Bldg., Salem 97310-0640. Tel. 503-378-4367, fax 503-588-7119, e-mail jim.b.scheppke@state.or.us.

Pennsylvania

Gary D. Wolfe, Deputy Secy. of Educ. for Commonwealth Libs., Box 1601, Harrisburg 17105. Tel. 717-787-2646, fax 717-772-3265, e-mail wolfe@hslc.org.

Rhode Island

Barbara Weaver, Dir., Rhode Island Dept. of State Lib. Services, 300 Richmond St., Providence 02903-4222. Tel. 401-277-2726, fax 401-831-1131, e-mail barbarawr@dsl.rhilinet.gov.

South Carolina

James B. Johnson, Dir., South Carolina State Lib., 1500 Senate St., Box 11469, Columbia 29211. Tel. 803-734-8666, fax 803-734-8676, e-mail jim@leo.scsl.state.sc.us.

South Dakota

Jane Kolbe, State Libn., South Dakota State Lib., 800 Governors Dr., Pierre 57501-

2294. Tel. 605-773-3131, fax 605-773-4950, e-mail janeK@stlib.state.sd.us.

Tennessee

Edwin Gleaves, State Libn./Archivist Tennessee State Lib. and Archives, 403 Seventh Ave. N., Nashville 37243-0312. Tel. 615-741-7996, fax 615-741-6471, e-mail egleaves@mail.state.tn.us.

Texas

Robert S. Martin, Dir./State Libn., Texas State Lib., 1201 Brazos St., Box 12927, Austin 78711-2927. Tel. 512-463-5460, fax 512-463-5436, e-mail rmartin@tsl.state.tx.us.

Utah

Amy Owen, Dir., State Lib. Div., 2150 S. 300 W., Suite 16, Salt Lake City 84115-2579. Tel. 801-466-5888, fax 801-533-4657, e-mail aowen@inter.state.lib.ut.us.

Vermont

Patricia E. Klinck, State Libn., Vermont Dept. of Libs., 109 State St., Montpelier 05609-0601. Tel. 802-828-3265, fax 802-828-2199, e-mail pklinck@dol.state.vt.us.

Virginia

Nolan T. Yelich, State Libn., Lib. of Virginia, 11 St. at Capitol Sq., Richmond 23219-3491. Tel. 804-786-2332, fax 804-786-5855, e-mail nyelich@leo.vsla.edu.

Washington

Nancy L. Zussy, State Libn., Washington State Lib., Box 42460, Olympia 98504-2460. Tel. 360-753-2915, fax 360-586-7575, e-mail nzussy@wln.com.

West Virginia

R. David Childers, Acting Dir., West Virginia Lib. Commission, Cultural Center, Charleston 25305. Tel. 304-558-2041, fax 304-558-2044, e-mail childers@wvlc.wvnet.edu.

Wisconsin

William J. Wilson, Asst. Superintendent, Div. for Libs. and Community Learning, Dept. of Public Instruction, 125 S. Webster St., Box 7841, Madison 53707-7841. Tel. 608-266-2205, fax 608-267-1052, e-mail wilson@milkyway.wils.wisc.edu.

Wyoming

Helen Meadors Maul, State Libn., Wyoming State Lib., Supreme Court and State Lib. Bldg., Cheyenne 82002-0060. Tel. 307-777-7281, fax 307-777-6289, e-mail hmeado@windy.state.wy.us.

American Samoa

Emma C. Penn, Program Dir., Office of Lib. Services, Box 1329, Pago Pago 96799. Tel. LD Operator 633-1181 or 1182.

Guam

Christine K. Scott-Smith, Dir./Territorial Libn., Guam Public Lib., 254 Martyr St., Agana 96910-0254. Tel. 671-477-6913, 472-1389, fax 671-477-9777, e-mail csctsmth@kuentos.guam.net.

Northern Mariana Islands

Paul Steere, Dir., Joeten-Kiyu Public Lib., Box 1092, Commonwealth of the Northern Mariana Islands, Saipan 96950. Tel. 670-235-7322, fax 670-235-7550, e-mail psteere@saipan.com; William Matson, Federal Programs Coordinator, Dept. of Educ., Commonwealth of the Northern Mariana Islands, Saipan 96950. Tel. 670-322-6405, fax 670-322-4056.

Palau (Republic of)

Masa-Aki N. Emeschiol, Federal Grants Coord., Ministry of Educ., Box 189, Koror 96940. Tel. 680-488-2570, ext. 1003, fax 680-488-2830, e-mail emesiocm@prel.hawaii.edu.; Fermina Salvador, Libn., Palau Public Lib., Box 189, Koror 96940. Tel. 680-488-2973, fax 680-488-3310.

Puerto Rico

Victor Fajardo, Secy., Dept. of Educ., Apartado 190759, San Juan 00919-0759. Tel. 809-754-5972, fax 809-754-0843.

Virgin Islands

Jeannette Allis Bastian, Dir. and Territorial Libn., Div. of Libs., Archives and Museums, 23 Dronningens Gade, Saint Thomas 00802. Tel. 809-774-3407, fax 809-775-1887, e-mail jbastian@icarus.lis.pitt.edu.

Canada

Alberta

Punch Jackson, Mgr. Libs. Section, Arts, Recreation & Libs. Branch, Alberta Community Development, 3rd fl., 10158 103rd St., Edmonton T5J 0X6. Tel. 403-427-2556, fax 403-422-9132.

British Columbia

Barbara Greeniaus, Dir., Lib. Services Branch, Ministry of Municipal Affairs and Housing, Box 9490 Stn. Prov. Govt., Victoria V8W 9N7. Tel. 250-356-1791, fax 250-387-4048, e-mail bgreeniaus@hq.marh.gov.bc.ca.

Manitoba

Sylvia Nicholson, Dir., Manitoba Culture, Heritage, and Citizenship, Public Lib. Services, Unit 200, 1525 First St., Brandon R7A 7A1. Tel. 204-726-6864, fax 204-726-6868.

New Brunswick

Jocelyne LeBel, Dir., New Brunswick Lib. Service, Box 6000, Fredericton E3B 5H1. Tel. 506-453-2354, fax 506-453-2416, e-mail jlebel@gov.nb.ca.

Newfoundland

David Gale, Provincial Dir., Public Libs. Service, Arts and Culture Centre, Allandale Rd., St. John's A1B 3A3. Tel. 709-737-3964, fax 709-737-3009.

Northwest Territories

Suliang Feng, Territorial Libn., Northwest Territories Lib. Services, Rm. 207, 2nd fl., Wright Centre, 62 Woodland Dr., Hay River X0E 1G1. Tel. 403-874-6531, fax 403-874-3321, e-mail suliang@gov.nt.ca.

Nova Scotia

Marion L. Pape, Provincial Libn., Nova Scotia Provincial Lib., 3770 Kempt Rd., Halifax B3K 4X8. Tel. 902-424-2456, fax 902-424-0633, e-mail mpape@nshpl.library.ns.ca.

Ontario

Michael Langford, Dir., Cultural Partnerships Branch, Ontario Government Ministry of Citizenship, Culture, and Recreation, 77 Bloor St. W., 3rd fl., Toronto M7A 2R9. Tel. 416-314-7342, fax 416-314-7635.

Prince Edward Island

Harry Holman, Dir., P.E.I. Provincial Lib., Red Head Rd., Box 7500, Morell C0A 1S0. Tel. 902-961-7320, fax 902-961-7322, e-mail plshq@gov.pe.ca.ca.

Quebec

Denis Delangie, Dir., Direction des arts et de la culture, 225 Grande Allée Est, Bloc A, 2e étage, Quebec G1R 5G5. Tel. 418-644-0485, fax 418-644-0380, e-mail jacques.morrier@mccq.gouv.qc.ca.

Saskatchewan

Maureen Woods, Provincial Libn., Saskatchewan Provincial Lib., 1352 Winnipeg St., Regina S4P 3V7. Tel. 306-787-2976, fax 306-787-2029.

Yukon Territory

Linda R. Johnson, Dir., Dept. of Educ., Libs., and Archives, Box 2703, Whitehorse Y1A 2C6. Tel. 403-667-5309, fax 403-393-6253, e-mail ljohnson@gov.yk.ca.

State School Library Media Associations

Alabama

Children's and School Libns. Div., Alabama Lib. Assn. Memb. 450. Publication. *The Alabama Librarian* (q.).

Exec. Dir. Barbara Black, 400 S. Union St., Suite 255, Montgomery 36104.

Address correspondence to the executive director.

Arizona

School Lib. Media Div., Arizona Lib. Assn. Memb. 500. Term of Office. Dec. 1996-Nov. 1997. Publication. *ASLA Newsletter*.

Pres. Annie Weissman, Sevilla Elementary School, 3801 W. Missouri Ave., Phoenix 85019. Tel. 602-246-5008, fax 602-336-3043; *Pres.-Elect* Gail Scheck. Tel. 602-232-4240.

Address correspondence to the president.

Arkansas

Arkansas Assn. of School Libns. and Media Educators. Term of Office. Jan.-Dec. 1997.

Chair Karen Richardson. Jessieville H.S., Box 4, Jessieville 71949. Tel. 501-984-5624; *Secy.-Treas.* Rachel Shankles, Lakeside H.S., 202 Stonehenge Ct., Hot Springs 71901. Tel. 501-624-7138.

Address correspondence to the chairperson.

California

California School Lib. Assn. Memb. 1,500. Term of Office. June 1996-May 1997. Publication. *Journal of the CSLA*. (mo.) *Ed.* John Archer. Job Hotline 415-697-8832; *Good Ideas!* (ann.); *TLC's (Together: Libraries + Classrooms)*.

Pres. Susan Choi, Santa Clara County Office of Education, 1290 Ridder Park Dr., Suite 232, San Jose 95131-2304. Tel. 408-453-6670; *Pres.-Elect* Janet Minami, L.A. Unified School Dist., 1320 W. Third St., Rm. 140, Los Angeles 90017. Tel. 213-625-6971; *Secy.* Cynthia Wong, Pacoima Middle School, 9919 Laurel Canyon Blvd., Pacoima 91331. Tel. 818-899-5291; *Treas.* Betty D. Silva, Fairfield H.S., 205 E. Atlantic, Fairfield 94533. Tel. 707-422-8672 ext. 32; *Business Office Secy.* Nancy D. Kohn, CSLA, 1499 Old Bayshore Hwy., Suite 142, Burlingame 94010. Tel. 415-692-2350.

Address correspondence to the business office secretary.

Colorado

Colorado Educational Media Assn. Memb. 600. Term of Office. Feb. 1996-Feb. 1997.

Pres. Lorena Mitchell. Tel. 303-777-9122; *Pres.-Elect* Beth Hager; *Secy.* Debra Phillips; *Exec. Secy.* Mary Anne Strasser.

Address correspondence to the executive secretary, Box 22814, Wellshire Sta., Denver 80222. Tel. 303-777-9122.

Connecticut

Connecticut Educational Media Assn. Term of Office. May 1996-May 1997. Publications. *CEMA Update Quarterly*; *CEMA Gram Monthly*; CEMA videotape *The School Library Media Specialist—A Continuing Story* ($35); *Resource Guide* ($14).

Pres. Judy Savage, 15 Evergreen Rd., Northford 06472. Tel. 860-346-7735; *V.P.* Janet Marchand, 87 Birch Lane, Greenwich 06830. Tel. 203-625-8026; *Secy.* Jane Preston, 320 Wheeler Rd., Monroe 06468. Tel. 203-268-5403; *Treas.* Carole Braunschweig, 2 Althea Lane, Darien 06820. Tel. 203-655-8417; *Admin. Secy.* Anne Weimann, 25 Elmwood Ave., Trumbull 06611. Tel. 203-372-2260.

Address correspondence to the administrative secretary.

Delaware

Delaware School Lib. Media Assn., Div. of Delaware Lib. Assn. Memb. 115. Term of Office. Apr. 1996-Apr. 1997. Publications. *DSLMA Newsletter* (irreg.); column in *DLA Bulletin* (3 per year).

Pres. Susan Cushwa, Middletown H.S. Appoquinimink, 504 S. Broad St., Middle-

town. Tel. 302-378-5000, e-mail scushwa@dpi1.k12.state.de.us.
Address correspondence to the president.

District of Columbia

District of Columbia Assn. of School Libns. Memb. 93. Term of Office. Jan. 1997–Jan. 1998.
Publication. *Newsletter* (4 per year).
Pres. Lydia Jenkins; *Rec. Secy.* Olivia Hardison; *Treas.* Mary Minnis; *Financial Secy.* Connie Lawson; *Corres. Secy.* Sharon Sorrels, Banneker H.S., 800 Euclid St. N.W., Washington 20001.

Florida

Florida Assn. for Media in Education. Memb. 1,450. Term of Office. Oct. 1996–Oct. 1997.
Publication. *Florida Media Quarterly. Ed.* Nancy Teger, 2560 Bass Way, Cooper City 33026. Tel. 305-691-8324, fax 305-693-9463.
Pres. Pat Evans, 2905 Albatross Dr., Cooper City 33026. Tel. 305-995-2421, fax 305-995-2251, e-mail Evanspl@mail.firn.edu; *Pres.-Elect* Chuck St. Louis, 16808 Waterline Rd., Bradenton 34202. Tel. 941-741-3470 ext. 204, fax 941-741-3480, e-mail Louisc@firnvx.firn.edu;
V.P. Sherie Bargar, 907 Citrus Isle, Fort Lauderdale 33315. Tel. 954-765-6153, fax 954-765-6773, e-mail Bargars@mail.firn.edu; *Secy.* Alison Rials, 10811 S.W. 51 Ct., Fort Lauderdale 33328. Tel. 305-926-0800 ext. 239; *Treas.* Donna Heald, 1941 N.E. 51 St., Suite 48, Fort Lauderdale 33308. Tel. 954-572-1336, fax 954-572-1344, e-mail DHealdfl@aol.com; *FAME Office Correspondent* Mary Margaret Rogers, Box 13119, Tallahassee 32317. Tel./fax 904-668-7606.
Address correspondence to the office correspondent.

Georgia

School Lib. Media Div., Georgia Lib. Assn. Memb. 217. Term of Office. Oct. 1996 Oct. 1997.
Chair Anne Maish, Hephzibah Elementary School, Hephzibah 30815. Tel./fax 706-592-3703, e-mail hcz@mindspring.com.

Hawaii

Hawaii Assn. of School Libns. Memb. 299. Term of Office. June 1996–May 1997. Publications. *HASL Newsletter* (1 per semester); *Golden Key Journal* (1 every 5 years).
Pres. Faith Ishihara; *1st V.P.* Myles Furubayashi; *2nd V.P.* Derri-lynn Slavens; *Rec. Secy.* Laura Kwock, Kris Nakakura; *Corres. Secy./P.R.* Maddie Oshiro; *Treas.* Grace Omura; *Dirs.* Dori Seatriz, Mike Lee.
Address correspondence to the association, Box 235019, Honolulu 96823.

Idaho

Educational Media Div., Idaho Lib. Assn. Memb. 125. Term of Office. Oct. 1996–Oct. 1997. Publication. Column in *The Idaho Librarian* (q.).
Chair Barbara Barrett, Hillside Jr. H.S., 6806 Fernwood, Boise 83709. Tel. 208-376-7180; *Secy.* Sue Crafts, 33 Purdue Ave., Pocatello 83204.
Address correspondence to the chairperson.

Illinois

Illinois School Lib. Media Assn. Memb. 1,000. Term of Office. July 1996–July 1997. Publications. *ISLMA News* (5 per year), *ISLMA Membership Directory* (ann.).
Pres. Jane Yoder, 2226 Alta Vista, Waukegan 60087. Tel. 847-244-0631, e-mail wkgnhs@nslsilus.org; *Pres.-Elect* Joan Herron, 505 S. Henry, Eureka 61530. Tel. 309-467-6004, e-mail joherron@isbe.state.il.us; *Exec. Secy.* Kay Maynard, Box 598, Canton 61520. Tel. 309-649-0911, fax 309-647-0140, e-mail kaym830175@aol.com.
Address correspondence to the executive secretary.

Indiana

Assn. for Indiana Media Educators. Memb. 825. Term of Office. May 1996–Apr. 1997.
Publications. *AIME News* (mo.); *Indiana Media Journal* (q.).
Pres. Anne M. Mallett, Gary Community School/Corp., 620 E. Tenth Place, Gary 46402. Tel. 219-881-5462, fax 219-886-6432; *Pres.-Elect* Nancy McGriff, South Central Schools, 9808 S. 600 W., Union

Mills 46382. Tel. 219-767-2263, fax 219-767-2260; *Assn. Mgt. Consultant* Karen G. Burch, 1908 E. 64 St., South Dr., Indianapolis 46220. Tel. 317-257-8558, fax 317-259-4191.

Address correspondence to the association management consultant.

Iowa

Iowa Educational Media Assn. Memb. 500. Term of Office. Mar. 1996–Mar. 1997. Publication. *Iowa Media Message* (5 per year). *Ed.* Linda Macrae, 1206 Second Ave. N., Northwood 50459.

Pres. Sharon Smaldino; *Pres.-Elect* MaryJo Langhorne; *Secy.* Loretta Moon; *Treas.* Rick Valley; *Exec. Secy.* Paula Behrendt, 2306 Sixth, Harlan 51537. Tel./fax 712-755-5918, e-mail paulab@netins.net.

Address correspondence to the executive secretary.

Kansas

Kansas Assn. of School Libns. Memb. 700. Term of Office. Aug. 1996–July 1997. Publication. *KASL Newsletter* (s. ann.).

Pres. Joanne Proctor, 3725 S.W. Tenth, Topeka 66604-1907. Tel. 913-273-1186; *V.P./Pres.-Elect* Janice Ostrom, 675 Georgetown, Salina 67401-3795. Tel. 913-825-9041; *Exec. Secy.* Dannette Schmidt, 2092 Norton, Salina 67401. Tel. 913-827-4018.

Address correspondence to the executive secretary.

Kentucky

Kentucky School Media Assn. Memb. 695. Term of Office. Oct. 1996–Oct. 1997. Publication. *KSMA Newsletter* (q.).

Pres. Margarette Morris, Belfry H.S., Box 457, Belfry 41514. Tel. 606-353-9093, fax 606-353-0530, e-mail mmorris@msmail.bhs.pike.k12.ky.us; *Pres.-Elect* Terri Gipson, Heath H.S., 4330 Metropolis Lake Rd., West Paducah 42086. Tel. 502-488-3126, fax 502-488-3732, e-mail tgg.bson@vci.net; *Secy.* Shirley Wathen, Bend Gate Elementary School, 920 Bend Gate Rd., Henderson 42420. Tel. 502-831-5040, fax 502-831-5043, e-mail swathen@henderson.k12.ky.us; *Treas.*

Lisa Hughes, Ballard Memorial H.S., 3561 Paducah Rd., Barlow 42024. Tel. 502-665-5151, fax 502-665-5312, e-mail lhughes@msmail.bmhs.ballard.k12.ky.us.

Address correspondence to the president.

Louisiana

Louisiana Assn. of School Libns. Memb. 500. Term of Office. July 1996–June 1997.

Pres. Andrea Laborde, 508 E. Charles St., Hammond 70401. Tel. 504-549-2206, e-mail alaborde@selu.edu; *1st V.P./Pres.-Elect* Penny Lee Johnson, 6531 Burke, Shreveport 71108. Tel. 318-635-9633; *2nd V.P.* Catherine Brooks, 6123 Hagerstown Dr., Baton Rouge 70817. Tel. 504-775-5924; *Secy.* Debra Rollins, 107 Rock Pointe E., Pineville 71360. Tel. 318-776-9371.

Address correspondence to the association, c/o Louisiana Lib. Assn., Box 3058, Baton Rouge 70821.

Maine

Maine Educational Media Assn. Memb. 350. Term of Office. May 1995–May 1997. Publication. *Maine Entry* (with the Maine Lib. Assn.; q.).

Pres. Linda Lord, Maine State Lib., 64 State House Sta., Augusta 04333. Tel. 207-287-5620, fax 207-287-5624, e-mail sllord@state.me.us; *1st V.P.* Sylvia Norton, Freeport H.S. Lib., Holbrook St., Freeport 04032; *2nd V.P.* Jodi Breau, Messalonskee H.S., 62 Oak St., Oakland 04963; *Secy.* Nancy Grant, Penquis Valley H.S., 37 W. Main St., Milo 04463; *Treas.* Donna Chale, Warsaw Middle School, School St., Pittsfield 04967.

Address correspondence to the president.

Maryland

Maryland Educational Media Organization. Term of Office. July 1996–June 1997. Publication. *MEMORANDOM*.

Pres. Carole Working, 7223 Harbor Lane, Columbia 21045; *Pres.-Elect* Linda Williams; *Secy.* Jayne Moore, 25943 Fox Grape Rd., Greensboro 21639; *Treas.* Patrick L. Miller, 7731 River Rock Ct., Williamsport 21795.

Address correspondence to the association, Box 21127, Baltimore 21228.

Massachusetts

Massachusetts School Lib. Media Assn. Memb. 800. Term of Office. June 1996–May 1997. Publication. *Media Forum* (q.).

Pres. Margaret Hallisey. Tel. 617-270-1878; *Secy.* Sheila Callahan. Tel. 508-363-5507; *Admin. Asst.* Sue Rebello, MSLMA, 18 Sasur St., Three Rivers 01080-1031. Tel./fax 413-283-6675.

Address correspondence to the administrative assistant.

Michigan

Michigan Assn. for Media in Education. Memb. 1,400. Term of Office. Jan.–Dec. 1997. Publications. *Media Spectrum* (4 per year); *MAME Newsletter* (5 per year).

Pres. Elaine Woods, Livonia Public Schools, 32401 Pembroke, Livonia 48152; *Pres.-Elect* Ruth Lumpkins, Grand Rapids Public Schools, 1440 Davis N.W., Grand Rapids 49504. Tel. 616-771-2595; *V.P. for Regions/Special Interest Groups* Diane Nye, Saint Joseph Public Schools, 2214 S. State St., Saint Joseph 49085; *Secy.* Kathleen Nist, Algonac Community Schools, 5200 Taft Rd., Algonac 48001. Tel. 810-794-4911; *Treas.* Susan Luse Thornton, Napoleon Community Schools, Box 308, Napoleon 49261. Tel. 517-536-8667. *Exec. Dir.* Burton H. Brooks, 6810 S. Cedar St., Suite 8, Lansing 48911. Tel. 517-699-1717, fax 616-842-9195, e-mail bhbrooks@aol.com.

Address correspondence to the executive director.

Minnesota

Minnesota Educational Media Organization. Memb. 750. Term of Office. (Pres.) Aug. 1996–Aug. 1997 (other offices, 2 years in alternating years). Publications. *Minnesota Media* (3 per year); *ImMEDIAte*; *MEMOrandom* (mo.).

Pres. Donna Winder, HCR 78, Box 101, Pine River 56474. Tel. 218-587-2752, e-mail Winder@uslink.net; *Secy.* Mary Childs, 8612 Vincent Ave. S., Bloomington 55431. Tel. 612-888-7746, e-mail 0271hel@informns. k12.mn.us; *Treas.* Sybil Solting, 502 Second Ave. S.E., Box 154, Mapleton 56065. Tel. 507-524-3917, e-mail 2135mrhs@informns. k12.mn.us; *Admin. Asst.* Fran Laske, R.R. 1, Box 120C, Nevis 56467. Tel. 518-652-2449, e-mail flaske@nevis.cfa.org.

Mississippi

School Section, Mississippi Lib. Assn. Memb. 1,300.

Chair Florence Box; *Secy.* Robert McKay.

Address correspondence to the association, c/o Mississippi Lib. Assn., Box 20448, Jackson 39289-1448.

Missouri

Missouri Assn. of School Libns. Memb. 985. Term of Office. June 1996–May 1997. *Media Horizons* (ann.).

Pres. Sharon Early, Lee's Summit Dist. Coord., Lee's Summit 64063. Tel. 816-524-0297; *1st V.P./Pres.-Elect* Sara Stubbins; *2nd V.P.* Kay Rebstock; *Secy.* Debbie Thompson; *Treas.* Ann Bartlett.

Address correspondence to the association, 8049 Hwy. E., Bonne Terre 63628-3771. Tel./fax 573-358-1053.

Montana

Montana School Lib. Media Div., Montana Lib. Assn. Memb. 175. Term of Office. July 1996–June 1997. Publication. *FOCUS* (published by Montana Lib. Assn.) (q.).

Chair Lynn Donvan, 1978 Crocus Dr., Sidney 59270. Tel. 406-482-2330; *Chair-Elect* Suzanne Goodman, Park H.S., 102 View Vista Dr., Livingston 59047. Tel. 406-222-9404; *Admin. Asst.* John Tomas, Box 505, Helena 59624-0505.

Address correspondence to the chairperson.

Nebraska

Nebraska Educational Media. Assn. Memb. 350. Term of Office. July 1996–June 1997. Publication. *NEMA News* (q.).

Pres. Roger Adkins, ESU 16, 314 W. First St., Agallah 69153. Tel. 308-284-8481, e-mail radkins@esu16.k12.ne.us; *Pres.-Elect* Joie Taylor, 2301 31 St., Columbus 68601. Tel.

402-563-7000, e-mail jtaylor@gilligan.esu7. k12.ne.us; *Secy.* Marilyn Scahill. E-mail mscahill@genie.esu10.k12.ne.us; *Treas.* Terry Zimmers. E-mail tzimmers@esu6.k12. ne.us; *Exec. Secy.* Phyllis Brunken, ESU 7, 2657 44 Ave., Columbus 68601. Tel. 402-564-5753, fax 402-563-1121, e-mail pbrunke@gilligan. esu7.k12.ne.us.

Address correspondence to the executive secretary.

Nevada

Nevada School and Children's Lib. Section, Nevada Lib. Assn. Memb. 120. Term of Office. One year.

Chair Sue Graf, North Las Vegas Lib., 2300 Civic Center Dr., North Las Vegas 89030. Tel. 702-649-2363, fax 702-649-2576; *Exec. Secy., Nevada Lib. Assn.* Judy Soper, Washoe County Lib., Reno. Tel. 702-785-4190.

New Hampshire

New Hampshire Educational Media Assn., Box 418, Concord 03302-0418. Memb. 265. Term of Office. June 1996–June 1997. Publications. *Online* (5 per year). *Ed.* Nancy J. Keane, Rundlett Jr. H.S., 144 South St., Concord 03301. Tel. 603-225-0862, fax 603-226-3288; Publication. *Taproot* (s. ann.).

Pres. Albert (Duke) Southard, Kennett Jr./Sr. H.S., Main St., Conway 03818. Tel. 603-447-6364, fax 603-447-6842; *V.P./Pres.-Elect* Kay Klein, Peter Woodbury Elementary School, 180 Country Rd., Bedford 03110. E-mail kay@kleins.mv.com; *Treas.* Jeffrey Kent, Broken Ground School, Portsmouth St., Concord 03301. Tel. 603-225-0825, fax 603-225-0869, e-mail jeff. kent@bg.concord.k12.nh.us; *Rec. Secy.* Mimi Crowley, Charlotte Ave. Elementary School, 48 Charlotte Ave., Nashua 03060. Tel. 603-594-4385, e-mail mimic@mv.mv.com; *Corres. Secy.* Barbara Thomas, Concord H.S., 170 Warren St., Concord 03301. Tel. 603-225-0800, fax 603-225-0826, e-mail barbara. thomas@chs.concord.k12.nh.us.

Address correspondence to the president.

New Jersey

Educational Media Assn. of New Jersey. Memb. 1,100. Term of Office. June 1996–June 1997. Publications. *Signal Tab* (mo.); *Emanations* (s. ann.).

Pres. Suzanne Manczuk, West Windsor Plainsboro Middle School, 55 Grover Mill Rd., Plainsboro 08536; *Pres.-Elect* Lois Wilkins, Sussex County Technical School, 105 N. Church Rd., Sparta 07871. Tel. 201-383-6700 ext. 257, e-mail lwilkins@intercall. com; *V.P.* Nina Kemps, Horace Mann Elementary School, 150 Walt Whitman Blvd., Cherry Hill 08003.

Address correspondence to the president or vice president.

New York

School Lib. Media Section, New York Lib. Assn., 252 Hudson St., Albany 12210. Tel. 518-432-6952, 800-252-6952. Memb. 950. Term of Office. Oct. 1997–Oct. 1998. Publications. *SLMSGram* (q.); participates in *NYLA Bulletin* (mo. except July and Aug.).

Pres. Eva Effron, Box 336, West Islip 11795-0336; *V.P./Pres.-Elect* Sue Norkelius, Box 98, Hyde Park 12538. Tel. 914-486-4880; *Past Pres.* Carolyn Giambra, Williamsville North H.S. Lib., 1595 Hopkins Rd., Williamsville 14221. Tel. 716-626-8025; *Secy.* Robert Brewster, 10-6 Loudon Dr., Fishkill 12524. Tel. 914-279-5051; *Treas.* Carol Brown, R.D. 1, Box 337, Fillmore 14735.

Address correspondence to the president or secretary.

North Carolina

North Carolina Assn. of School Libns. Memb. 800. Term of Office. Oct. 1995–Oct. 1997.

Chair Karen Perry, Griffin Middle School, E. Washington Dr., High Point 27260. Tel. 910-819-2870, e-mail kperry@guilford. k12.nc.us; *Chair-Elect* Melinda Ratchford, Gaston County Schools, 366 W. Garrison Blvd., Gastonia 28054. Tel. 704-866-6251, e-mail meleis@aol.com.

Address correspondence to the chairperson.

North Dakota

School Lib. and Youth Services Section, North Dakota Lib. Assn. Memb. 108. Term of Office. Sept. 1996–Sept. 1997. Publication. *The Good Stuff* (q).

Pres. Konnie Wightman, Lib. Media Office, Bismarck 58501. Tel. 701-221-3597, e-mail konda_wightman@mail.lmo.bismarck.k12.nd.us; *V.P./Pres.-Elect* Marira Boettcher, Bismarck Public Lib., 515 Fifth St. N., Bismarck 58501. Tel. 701-222-6412, fax 701-221-6854, e-mail m.boettcher@mail.cdln.lib.nd.us; *Secy.* Darlene Schwarz, Simle Middle School, 1215 N. 19 St., Bismarck 58501. Tel. 701-221-3579, e-mail SM_library@mail.lmo.bismarck.k12.nd.us.

Address correspondence to the president.

Ohio

Ohio Educational Lib. Media Assn. Memb. 1,300. Publication. *Ohio Media Spectrum*.

Exec. Dir. Ann Hanning, 1631 N.W. Professional Plaza, Columbus 43220. Tel. 614-326-1460, fax 614-459-2087, e-mail oelma@mec.ohio.gov.

Address correspondence to the executive director.

Oklahoma

Oklahoma Assn. of School Lib. Media Specialists. Memb. 3005. Term of Office. July 1996–June 1997. Publication. *Information Powerline*.

Chair Sue McAlister, Westmoore H.S., 12613 S. Western, Oklahoma City 73130. Tel. 405-691-8000, fax 405-692-5711, e-mail whsmedia@telepath.com; *Chair-Elect* Buffy Edwards, Jefferson Elementary School, 250 N. Cockerel, Norman 73071. Tel. 405-366-5889; *Secy.* Kay Neathery, Stillwater Middle School, 2200 S. Sangre Rd., Stillwater 74074. Tel. 405-743-6433; *Treas.* Carol Casey, Edmond North H.S., 215 W. Danforth, Edmond 73034. Tel. 405-340-2875, fax 405-340-2882; *AASL Delegate* Jonette Ellis, Enid Public Schools, 500 S. Independence, Enid 73701. Tel. 405-249-3558, fax 405-249-3565.

Address correspondence to the chairperson.

Oregon

Oregon Educational Media Assn. Memb. 600. Term of Office. Aug. 1996–July 1997. Publication. *INTERCHANGE*.

Pres. Mary McClintock; *Pres.-Elect* Tom Sprott; *Treas.* Patty Sorensen.

Address correspondence to officers at the association, Box 1759, Roseburg 97470. Tel. 541-839-6557, fax 541-440-4118, e-mail marymc@teleport.com.

Pennsylvania

Pennsylvania School Libns. Assn. Term of Office. July 1996–June 1998. Publication. *Learning and Media* (4 per year).

Pres. Peggy Benjamin, R.R. 6, Box 6362, Moscow 18444. Tel. 717-842-7201, fax 717-842-7026.

Address correspondence to the president.

Rhode Island

Rhode Island Educational Media Assn. Memb. 368. Term of Office. June 1996–May 1997. Publication. *RIEMA Newsletter* (8 per year). *Ed.* Dwight D. Barrett, 32 Glen Ave., Cranston 02905. Tel. 401-941-0094.

Pres. Donna Good, Moses Brown School, 250 Lloyd Ave., Providence 02906. Tel. 401-831-7350; *Pres.-Elect* Marykay Schnare, 11 Nelson St., Providence 02908. Tel. 401-331-2050; *V.P.* Margaret Bierden, Kevin Coleman School, 96 Second Ave., Woonsocket 02895. Tel. 401-767-4861; *Secy.* Patricia Menoche, Tiverton Middle School, 10 Quintal Dr., Tiverton 02878. Tel. 401-624-6668; *Treas.* Livia Giroux, West Warwick H.S., Webster Knight Dr., West Warwick 02893. Tel. 401-828-6596; *Memb. Chair* Michael Mello, 486 Water St., Portsmouth 02871. Tel. 401-683-4499, fax 401-683-5204, e-mail mellom@ride.ri.net.

Address correspondence to the association, Box 762, Portsmouth 02871.

South Carolina

South Carolina Assn. of School Libns. Memb. 1,100. Term of Office. June 1996–May 1997. Publication. *Media Center Messenger* (5 per year).

Pres. Jackie Ridings, Emerald H.S., 150 Bypass 225, Greenwood 29646. Tel. 864-941-5730, fax 864-942-9877; *Pres.-Elect* Betty Anne Smith, Royall Elementary School, 1400 Woods Rd., Florence 29501. Tel. 803-664-8167, fax 803-669-2860; *Secy.* Mary Jane Michaels, Hendrix Elementary School, 1084 Springfield Rd., Inman 29349. Tel. 864-578-1288; *Treas.* Betty Jo Hall, 200 Byrnes Ave., Abbeville 29620. Tel. 864-459-9589.

Address correspondence to the secretary.

South Dakota

South Dakota School Lib. Media Assn., Section of the South Dakota Lib. Assn. and South Dakota Education Assn. Memb. 146. Term of Office. Oct. 1996–Oct. 1997.

Pres. Marla Johnson, Deuel School; *Pres.-Elect* Janet Winkelman, Estelline H.S., Estelline 57234; *Secy.-Treas.* Rosalie Aslesen, Spearfish H.S., 525 E. Illinois, Spearfish 57783. Tel. 605-642-1212, fax 605-642-1211.

Address correspondence to the secretary-treasurer.

Tennessee

Tennessee Assn. of School Libns. (affiliated with the Tennessee Education Assn.). Memb. 450. Term of Office. Oct. 1996–Nov. 1997. Publication. *Footnotes* (q.).

Pres. Patty Willliams, 2601 Brighton Ct., Kingsport 37660. Tel. 423-378-2472, fax 423-378-2470, e-mail williamsp@TENNASH.ten.k12.tn.us; *V.P./Pres.-Elect* D. S. Thompson, 920 N. Highland St., Memphis 38122; *Secy.* Janis Perry, 44 Harts Bridge Rd., Jackson 38301; *Treas.* Brenda Moriarty, 4511 Timberlake Lane, Kingsport 37660.

Address correspondence to the president.

Texas

Texas Assn. of School Libns (Div. of Texas Lib. Assn.). Memb. 3,275. Term of Office. Apr. 1996–Apr. 1997. Publication. *Media Matters* (3 per year).

Chair Anne Morrison, 3400 Craigo Ave., El Paso 79904. Tel. 915-751-9952.

Address correspondence to the association, 3355 Bee Cave Rd., Suite 401, Austin 78746. Tel. 512-328-1518, fax 512-328-8852, e-mail havenwt@txla.org.

Utah

Utah Educational Lib. Media Assn. Memb. 327. Term of Office. Mar. 1996–Feb. 1997. Publication. *UELMA Newsletter* (4 per year).

Pres. Gary Temple, Fairfield Jr. H.S., 951 N. Fairfield Rd., Kaysville 84037. Tel. 801-546-7370, fax 801-546-7375, e-mail GaryT@Admin.Ffieldjr.Davis.k12.ut.us; *1st V.P.* Kathie Olsen, Ensign Elementary School, 775 12th Ave., Salt Lake City 84103. Tel. 801-578-8150, fax 801-578-8107; *2nd V.P.* Julie Bentley, Hawthorne Elementary School, 1675 S. 600 E., Salt Lake City 84105. Tel. 801-481-4824, fax 801-481-4927, e-mail julie.bentley@m.k12.ut.us; *Secy.* Gary Berensen, Mont Harmon Jr. H.S., 60 W. 400 N., Price 84501. Tel. 801-637-0510, fax 801-637-6074, e-mail berensen@mhjh.carbon.k12.ut.us; *Treas.* Annie Elsen, Box Elder Jr. H.S., 18 S. 500 E., Brigham City 84302. Tel. 801-734-4880, fax 801-734-4885; *Exec. Secy.* Larry Jeppesen, Cedar Ridge Middle School, 65 N. 200 W., Hyde Park 84318. Tel. 801-563-6229, fax 801-563-3915, e-mail larry.jeppesen@m.k12.ut.us.

Address correspondence to the executive secretary.

Vermont

Vermont Educational Media Assn. Memb. 203. Term of Office. May 1996–May 1997. Publication. *VEMA News* (q.).

Pres. Barbara Kieran, Mary Hogen Elementary School, Middlebury 05753. Tel. 802-388-4421; *Pres.-Elect* Harriette Phillips-Hamblett, Lake Region H.S., R.R. 1, Box 76, Orleans 05860; *Secy.* Dianne Wyllie, Teacher Learning Center, 7 Cherry St., Saint Johnsbury 05819. Tel 802-748-4569.

Address correspondence to the president.

Virginia

Virginia Educational Media Assn. Memb. 1,230. Term of Office. (Pres. and Pres.-Elect) Oct. 1996–Oct. 1997 (other offices 2 years in alternating years). Publications. *Mediagram* (q.).

Pres. Gerri Andrews, 112 Capital Ave., Chesapeake 23324. Tel. 804-547-0153, fax 804-547-0279; *Pres.-Elect* Melinda Younger, 152 Bon Ton Rd., Lynchburg 24503. Tel. 804-582-1120; *Exec. Secy.* Vickie Pearce. Tel 804-464-3834, fax 804-441-5871, e-mail vmpearce@pen.k12.va.us.

Address correspondence to the association, Box 5170, Virginia Beach 23455.

Washington

Washington Lib. Media Assn. Memb. 1,200. Term of Office. Oct. 1996–Oct. 1997. Publications. *The Medium* (3 per year); *The Message* (s.ann.). *Ed.* Mary Lou Gregory, 711 Spruce St., Hoquiam 98550. Tel. 206-533-4897.

Pres. Barbara L. Baker, 320 Baker Rd., Selah 98942. Tel. 509-697-4234, e-mail barbbk@aol.com; *V.P.* Paul Christensen, Box 50, Indianaola 98342. Tel. 360-297-2965; *Secy.* Jan Weber, 6622 W. Victoria Ave., Kennewick 99336. Tel. 509-783-3789, e-mail jweber@anchordoit.k12.wa.us; *Treas.* Barbara J. Baker, Box 1413, Bothell 98041. Tel. 206-823-0836, fax 206-821-5254.

Address correspondence to the president.

West Virginia

West Virginia Educational Media Assn. Memb. 150. Term of Office. Apr. 1996 Apr. 1997. Publication. *WVEMA Focus* (q.).

Pres. B. Darlene Milam, Horace Mann Jr. H.S., 1587 Lee St., Charleston 25311. Tel. 304-348-1971, fax 304-348-6591, e-mail bmilam@access.k12.wv.us; *Pres.-Elect.* Theresa Bruner, Follett Software, 309 Mackin St., Grafton 26354. Tel. 800-323-3397, fax 304-265-4731, e-mail tbruner@fsc.follett.com; *Secy.* June Geiger, John Marshall H.S., 1444 Sunset Lane, Glendale 26038. Tel. 304-843-4444, fax 304-843-4419, e-mail jgeiger@access.k12.wv.us; *Treas.* Lynn Bennett, RESA VII, 18 Meadow Lane, Bridgeport 26330. Tel. 800-427-3600, fax 304-366-4897, e-mail resa71b@wvnvms.wvnet.edu.

Address correspondence to the president.

Wisconsin

Wisconsin Educational Media Assn. Memb. 1,091. Term of Office. Apr. 1996–Apr. 1998. Publications. *Dispatch* (7 per year); *Wisconsin Ideas in Media* (ann.).

Pres. Helen Adams, Rosholt H.S., 346 W. Randolph St., Rosholt 54473. Tel. 715-677-4541, e-mail hadams@coredcs.com; *Pres.-Elect* Sherry Freiberg, Fond du Lac School Dist., 72 S. Portland St., Fond du Lac 54935. Tel. 414-929-2780, e-mail sherry_d._freiberg@fonddulac.k1.

Address correspondence to the president.

Wyoming

Section of School Library Media Personnel, Wyoming Lib. Assn. Memb. 80. Term of Office. Oct. 1996–Oct. 1997. Publication. *WLA Newsletter.*

Chair Leslie Davies, Dist. Lib. Dept. Head, 3600 Foothill Blvd., Box 1089, Rock Springs 82901. E-mail daviesl@rock.swl.k12.wy.us. *Chair-Elect* Vickie Hoff, Rawlins H.S., 1401 Colorado, Rawlins 82301. Tel. 307-328-9280 ext. 41, fax 307-328-9286.

Address correspondence to the chairperson.

International Library Associations

International Association of Agricultural Information Specialists

c/o J. van der Burg, President
Boeslaan 55, 6703 ER Wageningen, Netherlands
Tel./fax 31-317-422820

Object

The association shall, internationally and nationally, promote agricultural library science and documentation as well as the professional interest of agricultural librarians and documentalists. Founded 1955.

Membership

Memb. 600+. Dues (Inst.) $90; (Indiv.) $35

Officers

Pres. J. van der Burg, Boeslaan 55, 6703 ER Wageningen, Netherlands; *Secy.-Treas.* Margot Bellamy, c/o CAB International, Wallingford, Oxon, OX10 8DE, United Kingdom. Tel./fax 44-1491-833508.

Publications

Quarterly Bulletin of the IAALD (memb.).
World Directory of Agricultural Information Resource Centres.

International Association of Law Libraries

P.O. Box 5709, Washington, DC 20016-1309
804-924-3384, fax 804-924-7239

Object

IALL is a worldwide organization of librarians, libraries, and other persons or institutions concerned with the acquisition and use of legal information emanating from sources other than their jurisdictions, and from multinational and international organizations.

IALL's basic purpose is to facilitate the work of librarians who must acquire, process, organize, and provide access to foreign legal materials. IALL has no local chapters but maintains liaison with national law library associations in many countries and regions of the world.

Membership

Over 500 members in more than 50 countries on five continents.

Officers

Pres. Larry Wenger (USA); *1st V.P.* Roberta Shaffer (USA) *2nd V.P.* Fred Chapman (Switzerland); *Secy.* Britt S. M. Kjolstad (Switzerland); *Treas.* Gloria F. Chao (USA).

Board Members

Marie-Louise Bernal (USA); Jacqueline Elliott (Australia); Claire M. Germain (USA); Holger Knudsen (Germany); Ann Morrison (Canada); Harald Mueller (Germany); Josep Sort i Ticó (Spain); Jules Winterton (England).

Publications

International Journal of Legal Information (3 per year; US$55 for individuals; $80 for institutions).

Committee Chairpersons

Publications. Richard A. Danner (USA)

International Association of Music Libraries, Archives and Documentation Centres (IAML)

c/o Alison Hall, Secretary-General
Cataloging Dept., Carleton University Library
1125 Colonel By Drive, Ottawa, ON K1S 5B6, Canada
Fax 613-520-3583

Object

To promote the activities of music libraries, archives, and documentation centers and to strengthen the cooperation among them; to promote the availability of all publications and documents relating to music and further their bibliographical control; to encourage the development of standards in all areas that concern the association; and to support the protection and preservation of musical documents of the past and the present.

Membership

Memb. 1,900.

Board Members (1995–1998)

Pres. Veslemöy Heintz, Svenskt Musikhistoriskt Arkiv, Box 16326, S-103 26 Stockholm, Sweden; *Past Pres.* Don Roberts, Music Lib., Northwestern Univ., Evanston, IL 60208-2300; *V.P.s* Hugh Cobbe, Music Lib., British Lib., Great Russell St., London WC1B 3DG, England; John Roberts, Music Lib., 240 Morrison Hall, Univ. of California, Berkeley, Berkeley, CA 94720; Joachim Jaenecke, Staatsbibliothek zu Berlin, Preussischer Kulturbesitz, Tiergarten, Potsdamer Str. 33, D-10785, Berlin; Massimo Gentili-Tedeschi, Ufficio Ricerca Fondi Musicali, Via Conservatorio 12, I-20122 Milano; *Secy.-Gen.* Alison Hall, Cataloging Dept., Carleton Univ. Lib., 1125 Colonel By Dr., Ottawa ON K1S 5B6; *Treas.* Pam Thompson, Royal College of Music Lib., Prince Consort Rd., London SW7 2BS, England.

Publication

Fontes Artis Musicae (4 per year; memb.). *Ed.* Susan T. Sommer, New York Public Lib. for the Performing Arts, 111 Amsterdam Ave., New York, NY 10023-7498.

Professional Branches

Archives and Documentation Centres. Inger Enquist, Statens musikbibliotek, Box 16326, S-10326 Stockholm, Sweden.
Broadcasting and Orchestra Libraries. Kauko Karjalainen, Yleisradio Oy, Box 76, FIN-00024 Yleisradio, Finland.
Libraries in Music Teaching Institutions. Federica Riva, Conservatorio di Musica G. Verdi, Via del Conservatorio 12, I-20122 Milano, Italy.
Public Libraries. Kirsten Voss-Eliassen, Herlev Bibliotek, Musikafdeling, Bygaden 70, DK-2730, Denmark.
Research Libraries. Ann Kersting, Music- und Theaterabteilung, Stadt- und Universitätsbibliothek, Bockenheimer Landstr. 134-138, D-60325 Frankfurt, Germany

International Association of School Librarianship

Ken Haycock, Executive Director
Box 34069, Dept. 300, Seattle, WA 98124-1069
604-925-0266, fax 604-925-0566, e-mail iasl@rockland.com

Object

To encourage the development of school libraries and library programs throughout all countries; to promote the professional preparation of school librarians; to bring about close collaboration among school libraries in all countries, including the loan and exchange of literature; to initiate and coordinate activities, conferences, and other projects in the field of school librarianship. Founded 1971.

Membership

Memb. (Indiv.) 800; (Assn.) 41.

Officers and Executive Board

Pres. Sigrun Klara Hannesdottir, Iceland; *V.P.* Gerald Brown, Canada; *Treas.* Donald Adcock, USA; *Dirs.* David Elaturoti, Nigeria; Anne Taylor, N. Ireland; Mieko Nagakura, Japan; Paul Lupton, Australia; Diljit Singh, Malaysia; Marvene Dearman, USA; Maril Jamil Fasheh, Israel; Faola V. Faundez Garcia, Chile; Charrell Shelley-Robinson, Jamaica.

Publications

Books and Borrowers. Connections: School Library Associations and Contact People Worldwide.
IASL Conference Proceedings (ann.). IASL Monograph Series.
School Libraries Worldwide (s-ann.).

U.S. Association Members

American Assn. of School Libns.; Illinois School Lib. Media Assn.; International Reading Assn.; Louisiana Assn. of School Libns.; Maryland Educational Media Organization; Michigan Assn. for Media in Education; Washington Lib. Media Assn.

International Association of Technological University Libraries

c/o President, Nancy Fjällbrant, Chalmers University of Technology Library,
412 96 Gothenburg, Sweden
46 31 7723754, fax 46 31 168494, e-mail nancyf@lib.chalmers.se

Object

To provide a forum where library directors can meet to exchange views on matters of current significance in the libraries of universities of science and technology. Research projects identified as being of sufficient interest may be followed through by working parties or study groups.

Membership

Ordinary, official observer, sustaining, and nonvoting associate. Membership fee is 550 kroner per year (1,450 kroner for three years, 2,300 kroner for five years). Memb. 187 (in 40 countries).

Officers and Executives

Pres. Nancy Fjällbrant, Chalmers University of Technology Library, 412 96 Gothenburg,

Sweden. Tel. 46 31 7723754, fax 46 31 168494, e-mail nancyf@lib.chalmers.se. *Secy.* Michael L. Breaks, Libn., Heriot-Watt Univ. Lib., Edinburgh EH14 4AS, Scotland. Tel. 44-131-451-3570, fax 44-131-451-3164, e-mail m.l.breaks@hw.ac.uk. *Treas.* Annette Winkel Schwarz, Technical Knowledge Centre & Lib. of Denmark, Box 777, Anker Engelunds Vej 1, DK-2800 Lyngby, Denmark. Tel. 45-4525-7320, fax 45-4588-8256, e-mail aws@dtv.dk; *Membs.* Tom Cochrane, Australia; Egbert D. Gerryts, South Africa; Sinikka Koskiala, Finland; *North American Regional Group Chair* Richard P. Widdicombe, USA; *Ed.* Nancy Fjällbrant, Sweden.

Publications

IATUL News (irreg.). *IATUL Proceedings* (ann.).

International Council on Archives

Charles Kecskeméti, Secretary General
60 Rue des Francs-Bourgeois, F-75003
Paris, France
33-1-4087-6306, fax 33-1-4278-2065, e-mail 100640.54@compuserve.com

Object

To establish, maintain, and strengthen relations among archivists of all lands, and among all professional and other agencies or institutions concerned with the custody, organization, or administration of archives, public or private, wherever located. Established 1948.

Membership

Memb. 1,487 (representing 156 countries and territories). Dues (Indiv.) $80 or $125; (Inst.) $125; (Archives Assns.) $125 or $275; (Central Archives Directorates) $275 or $150 minimum, computed on the basis of GNP and GNP per capita.

Officers

Secy.-Gen. Charles Kecskeméti. *Deputy Secy.-Gen.* George P. MacKenzie.

Publications

Archivum (ann.; memb. or subscription to K. G. Saur Verlag, Ortlerstr. 8, Postfach 70 16 20, W-8000 Munich 70, Germany).
Guide to the Sources of the History of Nations (Latin American Series, 12 vols. pub.; African Series, 16 vols. pub.; Asian Series, 15 vols. pub.). *ICA Bulletin* (s. ann.; memb.). *Janus* (s. ann.; memb.)

List of other publications available from the secretary general.

International Federation for Information and Documentation (FID)

Executive Director, Ben G. Goedegebuure
Box 90402, 2509 LK The Hague, Netherlands
3140671, fax 3140667, e-mail fid@python.konbib.nl

Object

To promote, through international cooperation, research in and development of information science, information management, and documentation, which includes inter alia the organization, storage, retrieval, repackaging, dissemination, value adding, and evaluation of information, however recorded, in the fields of science, technology, industry, social sciences, arts, and humanities.

Program

FID devotes much of its attention to corporate information; industrial, business, and finance information; information policy research; the application of information technology; information service management; the marketing of information systems and services; content analysis, for example, in the design of database systems; linking information and human resources; and the repackaging of information for specific user audiences. The following commissions, committees, and groups have been established to execute FID's program of activities: *Regional Commissions:* Commission for Western, Eastern and Southern Africa (FID/CAF), Commission for Asia and Oceania (FID/CAO), Commission for Latin America (FID/CLA), Commission for the Caribbean and North America (FID/CNA), Commission for Northern Africa and the Near East (FID/NANE), Regional Organization for Europe (FID/ROE); *Committees:* Classification Research for Knowledge Organization, Education and Training, Fundamental Theory of Information, Information for Industry, Information Policies and Programmes, Intellectual Property Issues, Social Sciences Documentation and Information; *Special Interest Groups:* Archives and Records Management; Banking, Finance, and Insurance Information; Environmental Information; Executive Information Systems; Information for Public Administration; Organizational Excellence; Roles, Careers, and Development of the Modern Information Professional; Safety Control and Risk Management.

Publications

FID Annual Report (ann.). *FID Directory* (bienn.). *FID News Bulletin* (mo.) with quarterly inserts
Document Delivery Survey and *ET Newsletter.*
FID Publications List (irreg.). *International Forum on Information and Documentation* (q.).
Newsletter on Education and Training Programmes for Information Personnel (q.).
Proceedings of congresses; directories; bibliographies on information science, documentation, education and training, and classification research.

International Federation of Film Archives (FIAF)

Secretariat, Rue Defacqz 1, 1000 Brussels, Belgium
(32-2) 538-3065, fax (32-2) 534-4774, e-mail fiaf@mail.interpac.be
World Wide Web http://www.cinema.ucla.edu/FIAF/fiaf.html

Object

To facilitate communication and cooperation between its members, and to promote the exchange of films and information; to maintain a code of archive practice calculated to satisfy all national film industries, and to encourage industries to assist in the work of the federation's members; to advise its members on all matters of interest to them, especially the preservation and study of films; to give every possible assistance and encouragement to new film archives and to those interested in creating them. Founded in Paris, 1938. Affiliates: 93 (in 60 countries).

Officers

Pres. Michelle Aubert, France; *V.P.s* Hoos Blotkamp, Netherlands; Vladimir Opela, Czech Republic; Ivan Trujillo Bolio, Mexico; *Secy.-Gen.* Roger Smither, UK; *Treas.* Mary Lea Bandy, USA.

Address correspondence to Christian Dimitriss, Senior Administrator, c/o the Secretariat.

Executive Committee

Officers; Hoos Blotkamp, Netherlands; Paolo Cherchi Usai, Steven Ricci, USA; Gabrielle Claes, Belgium; Robert Daudelin, Canada; Vladimir Opela, Czech Republic; Clyde Jeavons, UK; Jorge Nieto, Colombia; José Maria Prado, Spain; Ivan Trujillo Bolio, Mexico.

Publications

Annual Bibliography of FIAF Members Publications.

Bibliography of National Filmographies.

Evaluating Computer Cataloguing Systems by Roger Smither (a guide for film archivists).

FIAF Cataloguing Rules for Film Archives.

FIAF Journal of Film Preservation. Glossary of Filmographic Terms in English, French, German, Spanish, and Russian (a second version in 12 languages). *Handbook for Film Archives* (available in English or French).

International Directory to Film & TV Documentation Sources.

International Index to Film Periodicals (cumulative volumes).

International Index to Film and Television Periodicals (microfiche service and available on CD-ROM). *International Index to Television Periodicals* (cumulative volumes).

Study on the Usage of Computers for Film Cataloguing.

Technical Manual of the FIAF Preservation Commission.

International Federation of Library Associations and Institutions (IFLA)

c/o The Royal Library, Box 95312, 2509 CH The Hague, Netherlands

Object

To promote international understanding, cooperation, discussion, research, and development in all fields of library activity, including bibliography, information services, and the education of library personnel, and to provide a body through which librarianship can be represented in matters of international interest. Founded 1927.

Membership

Memb. (Lib. Assns.) 151; (Inst.) 1,069; (Aff.) 252; Sponsors: 28.

Officers and Executive Board

Pres. Robert Wedgeworth, Univ. of Illinois, Urbana-Champaign; *1st V.P.* Marta Terry, Biblioteca Nacional, Havana, Cuba; *Treas.* Warren Horton, National Lib. of Australia, Canberra, Australia; *Exec. Board* Ekaterina Genieva, Lib. for Foreign Literature, Moscow, Russia; Robert D. Stueart, GSLIS, Simmons College, Boston, Mass.; Sun Beixin, China Soc. of Lib. Science, Beijing, China; *Ex officio memb.* Sally McCallum, Library of Congress, Washington, D.C.; *Secy.-Gen.* Leo Voogt; *Coord. Professional Activities* Winston Roberts; *IFLA Office for Universal Bibliographic Control and International MARC Program Dir.* Kurt Nowak; *Program Officer* Marie-France Plassard, c/o Deutsche Bibliothek, Frankfurt/Main, Germany; *IFLA International Program for UAP Program Dir.* Graham Cornish, c/o British Lib. Document Supply Centre, Boston Spa, Wetherby, West Yorkshire, England; *IFLA Office for Preservation and Conservation Program Dir.* M. T. Varlamoff, c/o Bibliothèque Nationale de France, Paris; *IFLA Office for University Dataflow and Telecommunications Program Dir.* Leigh Swain, c/o National Lib. of Canada, Ottawa, Canada; *IFLA Office for the Advancement of Librarianship in the Third World Program Dir.* Birgitta Bergdahl, c/o Uppsala Univ. Lib., Uppsala, Sweden; *IFLA Office for International Lending Dir.* Graham Cornish.

Publications

IFLA Directory (bienn.). *IFLA Council Report 1995–1996 IFLA Journal* (q.).
IFLA Professional Reports. IFLA Publications Series. International Cataloguing and Bibliographic Control (q.).
PAC Newsletter. UAP Newsletter (s. ann.).
UDT Digest (electronic).

American Membership

American Assn. of Law Libs.; American Lib. Assn.; Art Libs. Society of North America; Assn. for Lib. and Info. Science Education; Assn. of Research Libs.; International Assn. of Law Libs.; International Assn. of School Libns.; Medical Lib. Assn.; Special Libs. Assn. *Institutional Membs.* There are 124 libraries and related institutions that are institutional members or consultative bodies and sponsors of IFLA in the United States (out of a total of 1,069), and 73 personal affiliates (out of a total of 252).

International Organization for Standardization (ISO)

ISO Central Secretariat, 1 rue de Varembé, Case Postale 56, CH-1211 Geneva 20, Switzerland
41-22-749-0111, fax 41-22-733-3430, e-mail central@isocs.iso.ch

Object

Worldwide federation of national standards bodies, founded in 1947, at present comprising 118 members, one in each country. The object of ISO is to promote the development of standardization and related activities in the world with a view to facilitating international exchange of goods and services, and to developing cooperation in the spheres of intellectual, scientific, technological, and economic activity. The scope of ISO covers international standardization in all fields except electrical and electronic engineering standardization, which is the responsibility of the International Electrotechnical Commission (IEC). The results of ISO technical work are published as *International Standards*.

Officers

Pres. Liew Mun Leong, Singapore; *V.P. (Policy)* H. Reihlen, Germany; *V.P. (Technical Management)* J. Kean, Canada; *Secy.-Gen.* L. D. Eicher.

Technical Work

The technical work of ISO is carried out by some 200 technical committees. These include:

ISO/TC 46—*Information and documentation* (Secretariat, Deutsches Institut für Normung, 10772 Berlin, Germany. Scope: Standardization of practices relating to libraries, documentation and information centers, indexing and abstracting services, archives, information science, and publishing.

ISO/TC 37—*Terminology (principles and coordination)* (Secretariat, Österreiches Normungsinstitut, Heinestr. 38, Postfach 130, A-1021 Vienna, Austria). Scope: Standardization of methods for creating, compiling, and coordinating terminologies.

ISO/IEC JTC 1—*Information technology* (Secretariat, American National Standards Institute, 11 W. 42 St., 13th fl., New York, NY 10036). Scope: Standardization in the field of information technology.

Publications

ISO Annual Report.
ISO Bulletin (mo.).
ISO Catalogue (ann.).
ISO International Standards.
ISO 9000 News (bi-mo.).
ISO Memento (ann.).
ISO Online information service on World Wide Web (http://www.iso.ch/).

Foreign Library Associations

The following list of regional and national library associations around the world is a selective one. A more complete list can be found in *International Literary Market Place* (R. R. Bowker).

Regional

Africa

Standing Conference of African Univ. Libs., c/o E. Bejide Bankole, Editor, African Journal of Academic Librarianship, Box 46, Univ. of Lagos, Akoka, Yaba, Lagos, Nigeria. Tel. 1-524968.

The Americas

Asociación de Bibliotecas Universitarias, de Investigación e Institucionales del Caribe (Assn. of Caribbean Univ., Research and Institutional Libs.), Box S, University Station, Rio Piedras 00931, Puerto Rico. Tel. 809-790-8054, fax 809-763-5685. *Exec. Secy.* Oneida R. Ortiz.

Seminar on the Acquisition of Latin American Lib. Materials, c/o *Exec. Secy.* Sharon Moynahan, General Lib., Univ. of New Mexico, Albuquerque, NM 87131-1466. Tel. 505-277-5102.

Asia

Congress of Southeast Asian Libns. IV (CONSAL IV), c/o Serafin D. Quiason, National Historic Institute of the Philippines, T. M. Kalaw St., 100 Ermita, Box 2926, Manila, Philippines. Tel./fax 2-590646.

The Commonwealth

Commonwealth Lib. Assn., c/o Hon. *Exec. Secy.* Norma Amenu-Kpodo, Box 144, Mona, Kingston 7, Jamaica. Tel. 809-927-2123, fax 809-927-1926. *Pres.* Michael Wooliscroft; *Exec. Secy.* Norma Amenu-Kpodo.

Standing Conference on Lib. Materials on Africa, Univ. of London, Institute of Commonwealth Studies, 27-28 Russell Sq., London WC1B 5DS, England. Tel. 171-580-5876. *Chair* J. Pinfold.

Europe

Ligue des Bibliothèques Européennes de Recherche (LIBER) (Assn. of European Research Libs.), c/o H.-A. Koch, Staats- und Universitätsbibliothek, Postfach 330440, 28334 Bremen, Germany. Tel. 421-218-3361. *Pres.* Esko Hkli.

National

Argentina

Asociación de Bibliotecarios Graduados de la República Argentina (Assn. of Graduate Libns. of Argentina), Corrientes 1642, 1° piso, Of. 22-2° cuerpo, 1042 Buenos Aires. Tel./fax 1-384-4821, 384-8095. *Pres.* Roberto Jorge Servidio; *Exec. Secy.* Ana María Peruchena Zimmermann.

Australia

Australian Council of Libs. and Info. Services, Box E202, Queen Victoria Terrace, Canberra, ACT 2600. Tel. 6-262-1244, fax 6-273-4493. *Pres.* Helen Hayes; *Exec. Officer* Gordon Bower.

Australian Lib. and Info. Assn., Box E441, Queen Victoria Terrace, Canberra, ACT 2600. Tel. 6-285-1877, fax 6-282-249.

Australian Society of Archivists, Box 83, O'Connor, ACT 2601. Tel. 9-291-7220, fax 9-291-8201, e-mail bsharman@biblio.curtin.edu.au. *Pres.* Chris Coggin; *Secy.* Jennifer Davidson.

Council of Australian State Libs., c/o State Lib. of Queensland, Queensland Cultural Centre, South Brisbane, Qld. Tel. 7-840-7666, fax 7-846-2421. *Chair* D. H. Stephens.

Austria

Österreichische Gesellschaft für Dokumentation und Information (Austrian Society for Documentation and Info.), c/o sterreichisches Normungsinstitut, Heinestrasse 38, A-1021 Vienna. Tel. 1-267535/310, fax 1-267552/2163272. *Pres.* H. Jobst.

Vereinigung Österreichischer Bibliothekare (Assn. of Austrian Libns.), Innrain 50, A-6010 Innsbruck. Tel. 512-507-2425, fax 512-507-2893, e-mail eva.ramminger@uibk.ac.at, or maria.seissl@uibk.ac.at. *Pres.* Walter Neuhauser; *Secy.* Mag Eva Ramminger.

Bangladesh

Lib. Assn. of Bangladesh, c/o Lib. Training Inst., Bangladesh Central Public Lib., Shahbagh, Ramna, Dacca 1000. Tel. 2-504-269. *Pres.* A. K. M. Abdur Nur; *Gen. Secy.* M. Shamsul Islam Khan.

Barbados

Lib. Assn. of Barbados, Box 827E, Bridgetown. *Pres.* Shirley Yearwood; *Secy.* Hazelyn Devonish.

Belgium

Archives et Bibliothèques de Belgique/ Archief- en Bibliotheekwezen in België (Archives and Libs. of Belgium), 4 Blvd. de l'Empereur, B-1000 Brussels. Tel. 2-519-5351, fax 2-519-5533. *Gen. Secy.* Tony Verschaffel.

Association Belge de Documentation/Belgische Vereniging voor Documentatie (Belgian Assn. for Documentation), Blvd. L. Schmidt-Laan 119, B3, B-1040 Brussels. Tel. 2-733-2663. *Pres.* Jean-Louis Janssens; *Secy.* Philippe Laurent.

Association Professionnelle des Bibliothécaires et Documentalistes, B.P. 31, B-1070 Brussels. *Pres.* Michel Gilles; *Secy.* Georges Lecocq.

Vlaamse Vereniging voor Bibliotheek-, Archief-, en Documentatiewezen (Flemish Assn. of Libns., Archivists, and Documentalists), Waterloostraat 11, 2600 Berchem, Antwerp. Tel.3-281-4457, fax 3-218-8077. *Pres.* J. Cooymans; *Exec. Dir.* Marc Storms.

Belize

Belize Lib. Assn., c/o Central Lib., Bliss Inst., Box 287, Belize City. Tel. 2-7267. *Pres.* H. W. Young; *Secy.* Robert Hulse.

Bolivia

Asociación Boliviana de Bibliotecarios (Bolivian Lib. Assn.), c/o Biblioteca y Archivo Nacional, Calle Bolivar, Sucre.

Bosnia and Herzegovina

Drustvo bibliotekara Bosne i Hercegovine (Libns. Society of Bosnia and Herzegovina), Obala v Stepe 42, 71000 Sarajevo. Tel. 71-283245. *Pres.* Neda Cukac.

Botswana

Botswana Lib. Assn., Box 1310, Gaborone. Tel. 31-351151, ext. 2297, fax 0267-356591. *Chair* Amos P. Thapisa; *Secy.* Edwin Qabose.

Brazil

Associação dos Arquivistas Brasileiros (Assn. of Brazilian Archivists), 9-sala 1004, Centro, Rio de Janeiro RJ 20091-020. Tel./fax 21-233-7142. *Pres.* Lia Temporal Malcher; *Secy.* Laura Regina Xavier.

Brunei

Persatuan Perpustakaan Kebangsaan Negara Brunei (National Lib. Assn. of Brunei), c/o Language and Literature Bureau Lib., Jalan Elizabeth I, Bandar Seri Begawan. Tel. 2-43511.

Bulgaria

Sâjuz na Bibliotechnite i Informazionnite Rabotnitzi (Union of Libns. and Info. Officers), Pl. Slavejkov 4, Rm. 609, Box 269, Sofia 1000. Tel. 2-864264. *Pres.* Maria Kapitanova-Iordandva.

Cameroon

Association des Bibliothécaires, Archivistes, Documentalistes et Muséographes du Cameroon (Assn. of Libns., Archivists,

Documentalists and Museum Curators of Cameroon), Université de Yaoundé, Bibliothèque Universitaire, B.P. 337, Yaounde Tel. 220744.

Canada

Bibliographical Society of Canada/La Société Bibliographique du Canada, Box 575, Postal Sta. P, Toronto, ON M5S 2T1. *Secy.* Anne Dondertman.

Canadian Assn. for Info. Science/Association Canadienne de Science de l'Information, Univ. of Toronto, 140 Saint George St., Toronto, ON M5S 1A1.

Canadian Council of Lib. Schools/Conseil Canadien des Ecoles de Bibliothéconomie, c/o Past Pres. Gilles Deschatelets, Ecole de Bibliothéconomie et des Sciences de l'Information, Université de Montréal, C.P. 6128, Succ. Centre-Ville, Montreal, PQ H3C 3J7.

Canadian Lib. Assn., c/o Exec. Dir. Karen Adams, 200 Elgin St., Suite 602, Ottawa, ON K2P 1L5. Tel. 613-232-9625, fax 613-563-9895. (For detailed information on the Canadian Lib. Assn. and its divisions, see "National Library and Information-Industry Associations, United States and Canada"; for information on the library associations of the provinces of Canada, see "State, Provincial, and Regional Library Associations.")

Chile

Colegio de Bibliotecarios de Chile AG (Chilean Lib. Assn.), Diagonal Paraguay 383, Depto 122 Torre 11, Santiago. Tel. 2-222-5652. *Pres.* Elfriede Herbstaedt Yañez; *Secy.* Sergio Rodriguez Quezada.

China

China Society for Lib. Science, 39 Bai Shi Qiao Rd., Beijing 100081. Tel. 10-684-15566 ext. 5563, fax 10-684-19271. *Secy.-Gen.* Liu Xiangsheng.

Colombia

Asociación Colombiana de Bibliotecarios (Colombian Lib. Assn.), Calle 10, No. 3-16, Apdo. Aéreo 30883, Bogotá.

Costa Rica

Asociación Costarricense de Bibliotecarios (Costa Rican Assn. of Libns.), Apdo. 3308, San José. *Secy.-Gen.* Nelly Kopper.

Croatia

Hrvatsko Bibliotekarsko Društvo (Croation Lib. Assn.), Ulica Hrvatske bratske zajednice b b, 10000 Zagreb. Tel. 616-4111, fax 611-64186. *Pres.* Aleksandra Horvat; *Secy.* Daniela Zivković.

Cuba

Lib. Assn. of Cuba, Biblioteca Nacional José Martí, Apdo 6881, Ave. de Independencia e/20 de Mayo y Aranguren, Plaza de la Revolución, Havana. Tel. 708-277. *Pres.* Marta Terry González.

Cyprus

Kypriakos Synthesmos Vivliothicarion (Lib. Assn. of Cyprus), Box 1039, Nicosia. *Pres.* Costas D. Stephanon; *Secy.* Paris G. Rossos.

Czech Republic

Svaz Knihovníkía Informačních Pracovníků-Ceské Republiky (Assn. of Lib. and Info. Professionals of the Czech Republic), Klementinum 190, c/o Národní Knihovna, 110 01 Prague 1. Tel. 2-2422-9500, 2422-9780, fax 2-2422-7726. *Pres.* Jarmila Burgetová.

Ústřední Knihovnická Rada CR (Central Lib. Council of the Czech Republic), Valdštejnské nám. 4, 11811 Prague 1. Tel. 2-531-225, fax 2-532-185. *Pres.* Jaroslav Vyčichlo; *Secy.* Adolf Knoll.

Denmark

Arkivforeningen (Archives Society), c/o Landsarkivet for Sjaelland, jagtvej 10, 2200 Copenhagen K. Tel. 3139-3520, fax 3315-3239. *Pres.* Tyge Krogh; *Secy.* Charlotte Steinmark.

Bibliotekarforbundet (Union of Libns.), Lindevangs All 2, DK-2000 Frederiksberg.

Tel. 3888-2233, fax 3888-3201. *Pres.* Anja Rasmussen; *V.P.* Flemming Faarup.

Danmarks Biblioteksforening (Danish Lib. Assn.), Telegrafvej 5, DK-2750 Ballerup. Tel. 4468-1466, fax 4468-1103. *Dir.* Jens Thorhauge.

Danmarks Forskningsbiblioteksforening (Danish Research Lib. Assn.), Danmarks Tekniske Bibliotek, Anker Engelundsvej 1, DK-2800 Lyngby. Tel. 4593-9979, fax 4288-3040. *Pres.* Lars Bjørnshauge; *Secy.* D. Skovgaard.

Danmarks Skolebiblioteksforening (Assn. of Danish School Libns.), Mariavej 1, Sdr Bjert, 6091 Bjert. Tel. 755-7101, fax 4239-4349. *Chair* Gert Larsen.

Dominican Republic

Asociación Dominicana de Bibliotecarios (Dominican Assn. of Libns.), c/o Biblioteca Nacional, Plaza de la Cultura, Cesar Nicolás Penson 91, Santo Domingo. Tel. 809-688-4086. *Pres.* Prospero J. Mella-Chavier; *Secy.-Gen.* V. Regús.

Ecuador

Asociación Ecuatoriana de Bibliotecarios (Ecuadoran Lib. Assn.), c/o Casa de la Cultura Ecuatoriana Benjamín Carrión, Apdo 67, Ave. 6 de Diciembre 794, Quito. Tel. 2-528-840, 02-263-474. *Pres.* Eulalia Galarza.

Egypt

Egyptian Assn. for Lib. and Info. Science, c/o Dept. of Archives, Librarianship and Info. Science, Faculty of Arts, Univ. of Cairo, Cairo. Tel. 2-728-211. *Pres.* M. El-Shenity; *Secy.* Hamed Diab.

El Salvador

Asociación de Bibliotecarios de El Salvador (El Salvador Lib. Assn.), c/o Biblioteca Nacional, 8A Avda. Norte y Calle Delgado, San Salvador. Tel. 216-312.

Asociación General de Archivistas de El Salvador (Assn. of Archivists of El Salvador), Archivo General de la Nación, Palacio Nacional, San Salvador. Tel. 229-418.

Ethiopia

Ye Ethiopia Betemetshaft Serategnoch Mahber (Ethiopian Lib. Assn.), Box 30530, Addis Ababa. Tel. 1-121-363, fax 1-552-544. *Pres.* Mulugeta Hunde; *Secy.* Girma Makonnen.

Fiji

Fiji Lib. Assn., Govt. Bldgs., Box 2292, Suva. *Secy.* E. Qica.

Finland

Suomen Kirjastoseura (Finnish Lib. Assn.), Kansakouluk 10 A 19, FIN-00100 Helsinki. Tel. 0-694-1858, fax 0-694-1859, e-mail fla@fla.fi. *Pres.* Mirja Ryyanen; *Secy.-Gen.* Tuula Haavisto.

Tietopalveluseura ry (Finnish Society for Info. Services), Harakantie 2, SF-02600 Espoo. Tel. 90-518-138, fax 90-518-167. *Secy.* H. Heikkinen.

France

Association des Archivistes Français (Assn. of French Archivists), 60 Rue des Francs-Bourgeois, F-75141 Paris cedex 3. Tel. 1-4027-6000. *Pres.* Jean-Luc Eichenlaub; *Secy.* Jean LePottier.

Association des Bibliothécaires Français (Assn. of French Libns.), 7 Rue des Lions-Saint-Paul, F-75004 Paris. Tel. 1-4887-9787, fax 4887-9713. *Pres.* F. Danset; *Gen. Secy.* Catherine Schmitt.

Association des Professionnels de l'Information et de la Documentation (French Assn. of Info. and Documentation Professionals), 25 Rue Claude Tillier, F-75012 Paris. Tel. 1-4372-2525, fax 1-4372-3041, e-mail adbs@adbs.fr. *Pres.* Jean Michel.

Germany

Arbeitsgemeinschaft der Spezialbibliotheken (Assn. of Special Libs.), c/o M. Schwarzer, Kekulé-Bibliothek, Bayer AG, 51368 Leverkusen-Bayerwerk. Tel. 214-307-819. *Chair* Wolfrudolf Laux; *Secretariat Dir.* Marianne Schwarzer.

Deutsche Gesellschaft für Dokumentation (German Society for Documentation), Ostbahnhofstr 13, 60314 Frankfurt-am-Main 1. Tel. 69-430-313, fax 69-490-9096. *Pres.* Arnoud de Kemp.

Deutscher Bibliotheksverband eV (German Lib. Assn.), Fehrbeliner Pl 3, 10707 Berlin. Tel. 30-3907-7274, fax 30-393-8011. *Pres.* Jochen Dieckmann.

Verein der Bibliothekare an Öffentlichen Bibliotheken (Assn. of Libns. at Public Libs.), Postfach 1324, 72703 Reutlingen. Tel. 7121-346999, fax 7121-300-433. *Pres.* Konrad Umlauf; *Secy.* Katharina Boulanger.

Verein der Diplom-Bibliothekare an Wissenschaftlichen Bibliotheken (Assn. of Certified Libns. at Academic Libs.), c/o *Chair* Marianne Saule, Universitätsbibliothek, Universitätsstr. 31, 93053 Regensburg. Tel. 941-943-3952, fax 941-943-3285.

Verein Deutscher Archivare (Assn. of German Archivists), Westphälisches Archivamt, 48133 Münster. Tel. 251-591-3886, fax 251-591-269. *Chair* Norbert Reimann.

Verein Deutscher Bibliothekare (Assn. of German Libns.), Jakob-Welder-Weg 6, 55128 Mainz. Tel. 6131-392-644, fax 6131-394-159. *Pres.* Andreas Anderhub; *Secy.* Monika Hagenmaier-Farnbauer.

Ghana

Ghana Lib. Assn., Box 4105, Accra. Tel. 2-668-731. *Pres.* E. S. Asiedo; *Secy.* A. W. K. Insaidoo.

Great Britain

See United Kingdom.

Greece

Enosis Hellinon Bibliothekarion (Greek Lib. Assn.), Skouleniou 4, 10561 Athens. Tel. 1-322-6625. *Pres.* K. Xatzopoulou; *Gen. Secy.* A. Solomou.

Guatemala

Asociación Bibliotecológica de Guatemala (Lib. Assn. of Guatemala), Apartdao Postal 2086, Guatemala City 01901. Tel. 711525. *Pres.* María Teresa Cuyún.

Guyana

Guyana Lib. Assn., c/o National Lib., Church St. & Ave. of the Republic, Georgetown. Tel. 2-62690, 2-62699. *Pres.* Hetty London; *Secy.* Dianand Indra.

Honduras

Asociación de Bibliotecarios y Archiveros de Honduras (Assn. of Libns. and Archivists of Honduras), 11a Calle, 1a y 2a Avdas. No. 105, Comayagüela DC, Tegucigalpa. *Pres.* Fransisca de Escoto Espinoza; *Secy.-Gen.* Juan Angel R. Ayes.

Hong Kong

Hong Kong Lib. Assn., GPO 10095, Hong Kong. E-mail sechkla@hk.super.net. *Pres.* Grace Cheng; *Hon. Secy.* Louisa Lam.

Hungary

Magyar Könyvtárosok Egyesülete (Assn. of Hungarian Libns.), Szabó Ervin tr 1, H-1088 Budapest. Tel./fax 1-118-2050. *Pres.* Tibor Horváth; *Secy.* István Papp.

Iceland

Bókavardafélag Islands (Icelandic Lib. Assn.), Box 1497, 121 Reykjavik. *Pres.* A. E. Bjarkadóttir; *Secy.* E. R. Gudmundsdóttir.

India

Indian Assn. of Special Libs. and Info. Centres, P-291, CIT Scheme 6M, Kankurgachi, Calcutta 700054. Tel. 33-349651.

Indian Lib. Assn., c/o Dr. Mukerjee Nagar, A/40-41, Flat 201, Ansal Bldg., Delhi 110009. Tel. 11-711-7743. *Pres.* P. S. G. Kumar.

Indonesia

Ikatan Pustakawan Indonesia (Indonesian Lib. Assn.), Jalan Merdeka Selatan No. 11, Box 274, Jakarta, Pusat. Tel. 21-375-718, fax 21-310-3554. *Pres.* S. Kartosdono.

Iraq

Iraqi Lib. Assn., c/o National Lib., Bab-el-Muaddum, Baghdad. Tel. 1-416-4190. *Dir.* Abdul Hameed Al-Alawchi.

Ireland

Cumann Leabharlann Na h-Eireann (Lib. Assn. of Ireland), 53 Upper Mount St., Dublin. Tel. 1-661-9000, fax 1-676-1628. *Pres.* L. Ronayne; *Hon. Secy.* Brendan Teeling.

Israel

Israel Lib. Assn., Box 303, Tel Aviv 61002. *Chair* Jacob Agmon; *Dir.* R. Eidelstein.
Israel Society of Special Libs. and Info. Centers, Atidim Scientific Park, 2 Dvora Haneviah St., Tel Aviv 61430. Tel. 3-492-064. *Chair* Liliane Frenkiel.

Italy

Associazione Italiana Biblioteche (Italian Lib. Assn.), C.P. 2461, I-00100 Rome A-D. Tel. 6-446-3532, fax 6-444-1139, e-mail aib.italia@agora.stm.it. *Chair* Rossella Caffo; *Secy.* Luca Bellingeri.

Ivory Coast (Côte d'Ivoire)

Association pour le Développement de la Documentation des Bibliothèques et Archives de la Côte d'Ivoire (Assn. for the Development of Documentation Libs. and Archives of the Ivory Coast), c/o Bibliothèque Nationale, B.P. V 180, Abidjan. *Dir.* Ambroise Agnero; *Secy.-Gen.* Cangah Guy.

Jamaica

Jamaica Lib. Assn., Box 58, Kingston 5. *Pres.* A. Jefferson; *Secy.* G. Greene.

Japan

Joho Kagaku Gijutsu Kyôkai (Info. Science and Technology Assn.), Sasaki Bldg., 5-7 Koisikawa 2, Bunkyo-ku, Tokyo. *Pres.* T. Gondoh; *Gen. Mgr.* Yukio Ichikawa.
Nihon Toshokan Kyôkai (Japan Lib. Assn.), c/o Secy.-Gen. Reiko Sakagawa, 1-10 Taishido, 1-chome, Setagaya-ku, Tokyo 154. Tel. 3-3410-6411, fax 3-3421-7588.
Senmon Toshokan Kyôgikai (Japan Special Libs. Assn.), c/o National Diet Lib., 10-1 Nagata-cho, 1-chome, Chiyoda-ku, Tokyo 100. Tel. 3-2581-2331. *Pres.* Rokuro Ishikawa; *Exec. Dir.* Naotake Ito.

Jordan

Jordan Lib. Assn., Box 6289, Amman. Tel. 6-629-412. *Pres.* Anwar Akroush; *Secy.* Yousra Abu Ajamieh.

Kenya

Kenya Lib. Assn., Box 46031, Nairobi. *Chair* Peter S. Weche; *Secy.* Damaris Ng'ang'a.

Korea (Democratic People's Republic of)

Lib. Assn. of the Democratic People's Republic of Korea, Grand People's Study House of the Democratic People's Republic of Korea, Pyongyang. Tel. 3-4066. *Exec. Secy.* Li Geug.

Korea (Republic of)

Korean Lib. Assn., c/o *Exec. Dir.* Dae Kwon Park, 60-1 Panpo 2 Dong, Box 2041, Seocho-ku, Seoul. *Pres.* Hyo-Soon Song.

Laos

Association des Bibliothécaires Laotiens (Assn. of Laotian Libns.), c/o Direction de la Bibliothèque Nationale, Ministry of Education, B.P. 704, Vientiane. *Dir.* Somthong.

Latvia

Lib. Assn. of Latvia, Latvian National Lib., Kr. Barona iela 14, 1423 Riga. Tel./fax 132-289-874. *Pres.* Aldis Abele.

Lebanon

Lebanese Lib. Assn., c/o American Univ. of Beirut, Univ. Lib./Gifts and Exchange, Box 113/5367, Beirut. Tel. 1-340740 ext. 2603. *Pres.* Rafi' Ma'rouf; *Exec. Secy..* Linda Sadaka.

Lesotho

Lesotho Lib. Assn., Private Bag A26, Maseru. *Chair* E. M. Nthunya; *Secy.* M. M. Moshoeshoe-Chadzingwa.

Malawi

Malawi Lib. Assn., Box 429, Zomba. Tel. 50-522-222, fax 50-523-225. *Chair* Joseph J. Uta; *Secy.* Vote D. Somba.

Malaysia

Persatuan Perpustakaan Malaysia (Lib. Assn. of Malaysia), Box 12545, 50782 Kuala Lumpur. Tel. 3-756-6516. *Pres.* Chew Wing Foong; *Secy.* Leni Abdul Latif.

Mali

Association Malienne des Bibliothécaires, Archivistes et Documentalistes (Mali Assn. of Libns., Archivists, and Documentalists), c/o Bibliothèque Nationale du Mali, Ave. Kasse Keita, B.P. 159, Bamako. Tel. 224963. *Dir.* Mamadou Konoba Keita.

Malta

Ghaqda Bibljotekarji/Lib. Assn. (Valletta), c/o Public Lib., Florianna. Tel. 243473. *Chair* Joe Grima; *Secy.* Joseph Debattista.

Mauritania

Association Mauritanienne des Bibliothécaires, Archivistes et Documentalistes (Mauritanian Assn. of Libns., Archivists, and Documentalists), c/o Bibliothèque Nationale, B.P. 20, Nouakchott. *Pres.* O. Diouwara; *Secy.* Sid'Ahmed Fall dit Dah.

Mauritius

Mauritius Lib. Assn., c/o The British Council, Royal Rd., Box 11, Rose Hill. Tel. 541-602, fax 549-553. *Pres.* K. Appadoo; *Secy.* S. Rughoo.

Mexico

Asociación Mexicana de Bibliotecarios (Mexican Assn. of Libns.), Apdo. 27-102, Admin. de Correos 27, México D.F. Tel. 5-550-1398, fax 5-550-7461. *Pres.* S. Peniche; *Secy.* Elías Cid Ramírez.

Nepal

Nepal Lib. Assn., c/o National Lib., Harihar Bhawan, Pulchowk Lib., Box 2773, Kathmandu. Tel. 521-132. *Libn.* Shusila Dwivedi.

The Netherlands

Nederlandse Vereniging van Bibliothecarissen, Documentalisten en Literatuur Onderzoekers (Netherlands Libns. Society), NVB-Verenigingsbureau, Plompetorengracht 11, NL-3512 CA Utrecht. Tel. 231-1263, fax 231-1830. *Pres.* C. T. Klys; *Secy.* A. C. G. M. Eyffinger.

UKB (Universiteitsbibliotheek Vriji Universiteit) (Assn. of the Univ. Libs., the Royal Lib., and the Lib. of the Royal Netherlands Academy of Arts and Sciences), De Boelelaan 1103, NL-1081 HV Amsterdam. Tel. 44-45140, fax 44-45259. *Pres.* N. P. van den Berg; *Libn.* J. H. de Swart.

New Zealand

New Zealand Lib. and Info. Assn., 86 Lambton Quay, Level 8, Wellington Mall, Box 12-212, Wellington. Tel. 4-473-5834, fax 4-499-1480, e-mail nzlia@netlink.co.nz. *Exec. Dir.* Lydia Klimovitch.

Nicaragua

Asociación Nicaraguense de Bibliotecarios y Profesionales a Fines (Nicaraguan Assn. of Libns.), Apdo. Postal 3257, Managua. *Exec. Secy.* Susana Morales Hernández.

Nigeria

Nigerian Lib. Assn., c/o National Lib. of Nigeria, 4 Wesley St., PMB 12626, Lagos. Tel. 1-634704, fax 1-616404. *Pres.* A. O. Banjo; *Secy.* L. I. Ehigiator.

Norway

Arkivarforeningen (Assn. of Archivists), c/o Riksarkivet, Folke Bernadottes Vei 21,

Postboks 10, N-0807 Oslo. Tel. 22-022-600, fax 22-237-489.

Norsk Bibliotekforening (Norwegian Lib. Assn.), Malerhaugveien 20, N-0661 Oslo. Tel. 2-268-8550, fax 2-267-2368. *Dir.* Berit Aaker.

Norsk Fagbibliotekforening (Norwegian Assn. of Special Libs.), c/o Technical Univ. Lib. of Norway, Chemistry Branch Lib., N-7034 Trondheim 6. Tel. 7-359-4188, fax 7-359-5103. *Chair* Else-Margrethe Bredland.

Pakistan

Pakistan Lib. Assn., c/o Pakistan Inst. of Development Economics, Univ. Campus, Box 1091, Islamabad. Tel. 824070/824080, fax 92-51-210886. *Pres.* Azmat Ullah Bhatti; *Secy.-Gen.* Hafiz Khubaib Ahmed.

Panama

Asociación Panameña de Bibliotecarios (Panama Lib. Assn.), c/o Biblioteca Interamericana Simón Bolívar, Estafeta Universitaría, Panama City. *Pres.* Bexie Rodríguez de León.

Paraguay

Asociación de Bibliotecarios del Paraguay (Assn. of Paraguayan Libns.), Casilla de Correo 1505, Asunción. *Secy.* Mafalda Cabrerar.

Peru

Asociación Peruana de Archiveros (Peruvian Assn. of Archivists), Archivo General de la Nación, Calle Manuel Cuadros s/n, Palacio de Justicia, Apdo. 3124, Lima.

Asociación Peruana de Bibliotecarios (Peruvian Assn. of Libns.), Bellavista 561 Miraflores, Apdo. 995, Lima 18. Tel. 14-474869. *Pres.* Martha Fernandez de Lopez; *Secy.* Luzmila Tello de Medina.

Philippines

Assn. of Special Libs. of the Philippines, Rm. 301, National Lib. Bldg., T. M. Kalaw St., Manila. Tel. 2-590177. *Pres.* Filamena C. Mercado; *Secy.* Edna P. Ortiz.

Bibliographical Society of the Philippines, National Lib. of the Philippines, T. M. Kalaw St., 1000 Ermita, Box 2926, Manila. Tel. 2-583252, fax 2-502329. *Secy.-Treas.* Leticia R. Maloles.

Philippine Libns. Assn., c/o National Lib. of the Philippines, Rm. 301, T. M. Kalaw St., Manila. Tel. 2-590177. *Pres.* Belen M. Vibar; *Secy.* Lisa LeGuiab.

Poland

Stowarzyszenie Bibliotekarzy Polskich (Polish Libns. Assn.), Ul. Konopczyńskiego 5/7, 00950 Warsaw. Tel. 22-275296. *Chair* Stanislaw Czajka; *Secy.-Gen.* Dariusz Kuzminski.

Portugal

Associação Portuguesa de Bibliotecários, Arquivistas e Documentalistas (Portuguese Assn. of Libns., Archivists, and Documentalists), R Morais Soares, 43C-1 DTD, 1900 Lisbon. Tel. 1-815-4479, fax 1-815-4508, e-mail badbn@telepac.pt. *Pres.* António Pina Falcão.

Puerto Rico

Sociedad de Bibliotecarios de Puerto Rico (Society of Libns. of Puerto Rico), Apdo. 22898, Universidad de Puerto Rico Sta., Rio Piedras 00931. Tel. 809-758-1125. *Pres.* Aura Jiménez de Panepinto; *Secy.* Olga L. Hernández.

Romania

Asociaţa Bibliotecarilor din Bibliotecile Publice-România (Assn. of Public Libns. of Romania), Strada Ion Ghica 4, Sector 3, 79900 Bucharest. Tel. 1-614-2434, fax 1-312-3381, e-mail bnr@ul.ici.ro. *Pres.* Gheorghe-Iosif Bercan; *Secy.* Georgeta Clinca.

Russia

Lib. Council, State V. I. Lenin Lib., Prospect Kalinina 3, Moscow 101000. Tel. 95-202-4656. *Exec. Secy.* G. A. Seminova.

Senegal

Association Sénégalaise des Bibliothécaires, Archivistes et Documentalistes (Senegalese Assn. of Libns., Archivists and Documentalists), B.P. 3252, Dakar. Tel. 246-981, fax 242-379. *Pres.* Mariétou Diongue Diop; *Secy.* Emmanuel Kabou.

Sierra Leone

Sierra Leone Assn. of Archivists, Libns., and Info. Scientists, c/o Sierra Leone Lib. Board, Box 326, Freetown. *Pres.* Deanna Thomas.

Singapore

Lib. Assn. of Singapore, c/o Branch Lib., Bukit Merah Central, Box 0693, Singapore 9115. *Hon. Secy.* Amarjeet Kaur.

Slovenia

Zveza Bibliotekarskih Drustev Slovenije (Lib. Assn. of Slovenia), Turjaska 1, 61000 Ljubljana. Tel. 61-150131, fax 61-213052. *Pres.* Ivan Kanic; *Secy.* Liljana Hubej.

South Africa

African Lib. Assn. of South Africa, c/o Lib., Univ. of the North, Private Bag X1106, Sovenga 0727. Tel. 1521-689111. *Secy. and Treas.* Mrs. A. N. Kambule.

Spain

Asociación Española de Archiveros, Bibliotecarios, Museólogos y Documentalistas (Spanish Assn. of Archivists, Libns., Curators and Documentalists), Recoletos 5, 28001 Madrid. Tel. 575-1727. *Pres.* Alonso Vicenta Cortés.

Sri Lanka

Sri Lanka Lib. Assn., Professional Center, 275/75 Bauddhaloka Mawatha, Colombo 7. Tel. 1-589103. *Pres.* P. Vidanapathirana; *Secy.* Nanda Fernando.

Swaziland

Swaziland Lib. Assn., Box 2309, Mbabane. Tel. 84011. *Chair* M. R. Mavuso; *Secy.* F. K. Tawete.

Sweden

Svenska Arkivsamfundet (Swedish Assn. of Archivists), c/o Riksarkivet, Fyrverkarbacken 13-17, Box 12541, S-102 29 Stockholm. Tel. 8-737-6350, fax 8-737-6474, e-mail en@ra.ra.se. *Pres.* Erik Norberg.

Sveriges Allmänna Biblioteksförening (Swedish Lib. Assn.), Box 3127, S-103 62 Stockholm. Tel. 8-241020/723-0082, fax 8-723-0083. *Secy.-Gen.* Christina Stenberg.

Swedish School of Library and Information Science Library, Box 874, S-50115 Borås. Tel. 33-164-000, fax 33-111-053. *Exec. Secy.* Staffan Lööf.

Switzerland

Association des Bibliothèques et Bibliothécaires Suisses/Vereinigung Schweizerischer Bibliothekare/Associazione dei Bibliotecari Svizzeri (Assn. of Swiss Libns.), Effingerstr. 35, CH-3008 Berne. Tel. 31-382-4240, fax 31-382-4648, e-mail bbss@bbs.ch, World Wide Web http://www.bbs.ch. *Secy.* Myriam Boussina Mercille.

Schweizerische Vereinigung für Dokumentation/Association Suisse de Documentation (Swiss Assn. of Documentation), Weinbergstr. 31, CH-8006 Zurich. Tel. 1-266-6474, fax 1-262-2996. *Pres.* E. Wyss; *Secy.* W. Bruderer.

Vereinigung Schweizerischer Archivare (Assn. of Swiss Archivists), Archivstr. 24, CH-3003 Berne. Tel. 31-618989. *Secy.* Bernard Truffer.

Taiwan

Lib. Assn. of China, c/o National Central Lib., 20 Chungshan S. Rd., Taipei. Tel. 2-331-2475, fax 2-382-0747. *Pres.* James S. C. Hu; *Secy.-Gen.* Teresa Wang Chang.

Tanzania

Tanzania Lib. Assn., Box 33433, Dar es Salaam. Tel. 51-402-6121. *Chair* T. E. Mlaki; *Secy.* A. Nkebukwa.

Thailand

Thai Lib. Assn., 273 Vibhavadee Rangsit Rd., Phayathai, Bangkok 10400. Tel. 2-271-2084. *Pres.* K. Gesmankit; *Secy.* Karnmanee Suckcharoen.

Trinidad and Tobago

Lib. Assn. of Trinidad and Tobago, Box 1275, Port of Spain. Tel. 809-623-2306. *Pres.* J. Blake; *Secy.* June Stewart.

Tunisia

Association Tunisienne des Documentalistes, Bibliothécaires et Archivistes (Tunisian Assn. of Documentalists, Libns., and Archivists), B.P. 380, 1015 Tunis. *Pres.* Ahmed Ksibi.

Turkey

Türk Küüphaneciler Dernegi (Turkish Libns. Assn.), Elgn Sok-8/8, 06440 Yenisehir, Ankara. Tel./fax 4-230-1325. *Pres.* S. Aslan; *Secy.* A. Kaygusuz.

Uganda

Uganda Lib. Assn., Box 5894, Kampala. Tel. 141-285001 ext. 4. *Chair* P. Birungi; *Secy.* L. M. Ssengero.

Ukraine

Ukrainian Library Assn., 14 Chyhorin St., Kyiv 252042, Ukraine. Tel. 380-44-268-2263, fax 380-44-295-8296. *Pres.* Valentyna S. Pashkova.

United Kingdom

ASLIB (The Assn. for Info. Management), Information House, 20-24 Old St., London EC1V 9AP, England. Tel. 171-253-4488, fax 171-430-0514. *Dir.* R. B. Bowes.

Bibliographical Society, c/o The National Art Lib., Victoria & Albert Museum, London SW7 2RL, England. Tel. 171-938-9655, fax171-938-8461, e-mail JM93@dial.pipex. com. *Hon. Secy.* David Pearson.

The Lib. Assn., 7 Ridgmount St., London WC1E 7AE, England. Tel. 171-636-7543, fax 171-436-7218. *Chief Exec.* Ross Shimmon.

School Lib. Assn., Liden Lib., Barrington Close, Liden, Swindon, Wiltshire SN3 6HF, England. Tel. 1793-617-838. *Pres.* Frank N. Hogg; *Exec. Secy.* Valerie Fea.

Scottish Lib. Assn., Motherwell Business Centre, Coursington Rd., Motherwell ML1 1PW, Scotland. Tel. 1698-252-526, fax 1698-252-057, e-mail sctlb@leapfrog. almac.co.uk. *Dir.* Robert Craig.

Society of Archivists, Information House, 20-24 Old St., London, EC1V 9AP, England. Tel. 171-253-5087, fax 171-253-3942. *Exec. Secy.* P. S. Cleary.

Standing Conference of National and Univ. Libs., 102 Euston St., London NW1 2HA, England. Tel. 171-387-0317, fax 171-383-3197. *Exec. Secy.* G. M. Pentelow.

Welsh Lib. Assn., c/o Publications Office, The Lib., Univ. of Wales, Swansea, West Glamorgan SA2 8PP, Wales. Tel. 1792-295-174, fax 1792-295-851, e-mail a.m.w. green@swansea.ac.uk. *Exec. Officer* Glyn Collins.

Uruguay

Agrupación Bibliotecológica del Uruguay (Uruguayan Lib. and Archive Science Assn.), Cerro Largo 1666, 11200 Montevideo. Tel. 2-405740. *Pres.* Luis Alberto Musso.

Asociación de Bibliocólogos del Uruguay, Eduardo V Haedo 2255, CC 1315, 11200 Montevideo. Tel. 2-499989.

Vatican City

Biblioteca Apostolica Vaticana, 00120 Vatican City, Rome. Tel. 6-698-83302, fax 6-698-84795, e-mail Libr@librsbk.Vatlib.it. *Prefect* Leonard E. Boyle.

Venezuela

Colegio de Bibliotecólogos y Archivólogos de Venezuela (Assn. of Venezuelan Libns. and Archivists), Apdo. 6283, Caracas. Tel. 2-781-3245. *Pres.* O. Ruiz LaScalea.

Vietnam

Hôi Thu-Viên Viet Nam (Vietnamese Lib. Assn.), National Lib. of Viet Nam, 31 Trang Thi, 10000 Hanoi. Tel. 4-52643.

Zaire

Association Zairoise des Archivistes, Bibliothécaires et Documentalistes (Zaire Assn. of Archivists, Librarians, and Documentalists), B.P. 805, Kinshasa X1. Tel. 12-30123/4. *Exec. Secy.* E. Kabeba-Bangasa.

Zambia

Zambia Lib. Assn., Box 32339, Lusaka. *Chair* C. Zulu; *Hon. Secy.* W. C. Mulalami.

Zimbabwe

Zimbabwe Lib. Assn., Box 3133, Harare. *Contact* A. L. Ngwenya; *Hon. Secy.* Driden Kunaka.

Directory of Book Trade and Related Organizations

Book Trade Associations, United States and Canada

For more extensive information on the associations listed in this section, see the annual edition of *Literary Market Place* (R. R. Bowker).

American Booksellers Assn. Inc., 828 S. Broadway, Tarrytown, NY 10591. Tel. 800-637-0037, 914-591-2665, fax 914-591-2720; *Pres.* Barbara Bonds Thomas, Toad Hall, Austin, TX 78705; *V.P.* Richard Howorth, Square Books, Oxford, MS 38665; *Secy.* Norman Laurila, A Different Light Bookstore, New York, NY 10011; *Treas.* Ned Densmore, Village Book Store Littleton, NH 03561; *Exec. Dir.* Bernie Rath.

American Institute of Graphic Arts, 164 Fifth Ave., New York, NY 10010. Tel. 212-807-1990, fax 212-807-1799, e-mail aiganatl@aol.com. *Exec. Dir.* Richard Grefe.

American Medical Publishers Assn., 14 Fort Hill Rd., Huntington, NY 11734. Tel./fax 516-423-0075. *Pres.* Eric Newman; *Pres.-elect* Dan Doody; *Exec. Dir.* Jill Rudansky.

American Printing History Assn., Box 4922, Grand Central Sta., New York, NY 10163-1005. *Pres.* Martin W. Hutner; *Exec. Secy.* Stephen Crook.

American Society of Indexers Inc., Box 48267, Seattle WA 98148. Tel. 206-241-9196, fax 206-727-6430, e-mail asi@well.com, World Wide Web http://www.well.com/user/asi. *Pres.* Carolyn McGovern; *Administrator* Linda K. Fetters.

American Society of Journalists and Authors, 1501 Broadway, Suite 302, New York, NY 10036. Tel. 212-997-0947, fax 212-768-7414, e-mail 75227.1650@compuserve.com. *Exec. Dir.* Alexandra Cantor Owens.

American Society of Media Photographers, 14 Washington Rd., Suite 502, Princeton Junction, NJ 08550-1033. Tel. 609-799-8300, fax 609-799-2233. *Pres.* Reagan Bradshaw; *Exec. Dir.* Richard Weisgrau.

American Society of Picture Professionals Inc., 2025 Pennsylvania Ave. N.W., Suite 226, Washington, DC 20006. Tel. 202-955-5578. *Exec. Dir.* Cathy Sachs; *National Pres.* Susan Soroko, Folio, Washington, DC. Tel. 202-965-2410.

American Translators Assn., 1800 Diagonal Rd., Suite 220, Alexandria, VA 22314-2840. Tel. 703-683-6100, fax 703-683-6122, e-mail 73564,2032@compuserve.com. *Pres.* Peter W. Krawutschke; *Pres.-Elect* Muriel Jerome-O'Keeffe; *Secy.* Betty Becker-Theye; *Treas.* Monique Paule Tubb; *Exec. Dir.* Walter W. Bacak, Jr.

Antiquarian Booksellers Assn. of America, 50 Rockefeller Plaza, New York, NY 10020. Tel. 212-757-9395, fax 212-459-0307. *Exec. Dir.* Liane Wood-Thomas.

Assn. of American Publishers, 71 Fifth Ave., New York, NY 10003. Tel. 212-255-0200. *Pres.* Nicholas Veliotes; *Exec. V.P.* Thomas D. McKee; *V.P.* Richard F. Blake; *Dir.* Barbara Meredith; *Washington Office* 1718 Connecticut Ave. N.W., Washington, DC 20009. Tel. 202-232-3335; *V.P.s* Allan Adler, Carol Risher; *Dir.* Judith Platt; *Chair* Richard Robinson, Scholastic; *V. Chair* Patrick A. Clifford, The Times Mirror Company; *Treas.* Thomas A. Paul,

International Thomson Publishing; *Secy.* Brian J. Knez, Harcourt Brace & Co.

Assn. of American Univ. Presses, 584 Broadway, Suite 410, New York, NY 10012. Tel. 212-941-6610. *Pres.* Kate Torrey, Univ. of North Carolina Press; *Exec. Dir.* Peter Grenquist; *Assoc. Exec. Dir.* Hollis Holmes. Address correspondence to the executive director.

Assn. of Authors' Representatives Inc., 10 Astor Place, 3rd fl., New York, NY 10003. Tel. 212-353-3709. *Pres.* Richard Curtis; *Admin. Secy.* Ginger Knowlton.

Assn. of Book Travelers, 100 Fifth ave., New York, NY 10011. Tel. 212-206-7102, fax 212-645-8487. *Pres.* Paul Gottlieb; *Treas.* Eileen O'Neil. Address correspondence to the president.

Assn. of Canadian Publishers, 2 Gloucester St., Suite 301, Toronto, ON M4Y 1L5, Canada. Tel. 416-413-4929, fax 416-413-4920. *Exec. Dir.* Paul Davidson. Address correspondence to the executive director.

Assn. of Jewish Book Publishers, c/o Jewish Lights Publishing, P.O. Box 237, Woodstock, VT 05091. Tel. 802-457-4000, fax 802-457-4004. *Pres.* Stuart M. Matlins. Address correspondence to the president.

Assn. of Graphic Communications, 330 Seventh Ave., New York, NY 10001. Tel. 212-279-2100, fax 212-279-5381, e-mail BDage@aol.com, World Wide Web http://www.agcomm.org. *Pres.* William A. Dirzulaitis; *Dir. Ed.* Pam Suett; *Dir. Exhibits* Carl Gessman.

Book Industry Study Group Inc., 160 Fifth Ave., New York, NY 10010. Tel. 212-929-1393, fax 212-989-7542. *Chair* Kent Freeman; *V.Chair* Robert Severud; *Treas.* Seymour Turk; *Secy.* Richard W. Hunt; *Managing Agent* SKP Assocs. Address correspondence to William Raggio.

Book Manufacturers Institute, 65 William St., Suite 300, Wellesley, MA 02181-4007. Tel. 617-239-0103. *Pres.* Charles Nason, Worzalla Publishing Co; *Exec. V.P.* Stephen P. Snyder. Address correspondence to the executive vice president.

Book Publicists of Southern California, 6464 Sunset Blvd., Suite 580, Hollywood, CA 90028. Tel. 213-461-3921, fax 213-461-0917. *Pres.* Barbara Gaughen; *V.P.* Ernest Weckbaugh; *Secy.* Joyce Schwarz; *Treas.* Lynn Walford.

Bookbinders Guild of New York, c/o *Secy.* Thomas P. Roche, Princeton Academic Press, 1527 Ninth St., Fort Lee, NJ 07024. Tel. 201-461-6491; *Pres.* Linda Palladino, William Morrow & Co., 1350 Ave. of the Americas, New York, NY 10019. Tel. 212-261-6675; *V.P.* Jim Arch, P. H. Glatfelter Co., 1085 Morris Ave., Union, NJ 07083; *Treas.* Irwin Wolf, Graphic Design Studio, 108 John St., North Massapequa, NY 11758; *Financial Secy.* Michelle Rothfarb, Worzalla Publishing Co., 43 Springbrook Rd., Livingston, NJ 07039.

Bookbuilders of Boston Inc., 1660 Soldiers Field Rd., Boston, MA 02135. Tel. 617-746-2902, fax 617-783-4375, e-mail bbboston@romnet.com. *Pres.* Richard Tonachel, Harvard Univ. Press; *1st V.P.* James Rigney, Addison Wesley Longman; *2nd V.P.* Talbot Goodyear, Acme Printing Co.; *Treas.* John Walsh, Harvard Univ. Press; *Auditor* Paula Lemay, Positions, Inc.; *Secy.* Elizabeth M. McMullen, Houghton Mifflin.

Bookbuilders West, Box 7046, San Francisco, CA 94120-9727. Tel. 415-273-5790, jobs bank 415-643-8600, World Wide Web http://www.booksatoz.com/bbwest.htm; *Pres.* Detta Penna; *Pres.-Elect* Arlene Cowan.

Canadian Booksellers Assn., 301 Donlands Ave., Toronto, ON M4J 3R8, Canada. Tel. 416-467-7883, fax 416-467-7886, e-mail enquiries@cbabook.org, World Wide Web http://www.cbabook.org. *Exec. Dir.* John J. Finlay; *Ed., Canadian Bookseller* Kim Laudrum; *Mgr., Conventions and Events* Lisa Shulist.

Catholic Book Publishers Assn. Inc., 2 Park Ave., Manhasset,, NY 11030. Tel. 516-869-0122, fax 516-627-1381; *Pres.* Peter Dwyer; *V.P.* John Thomas; *Exec. Dir.* Charles A. Roth.

Chicago Book Clinic, 11 S. LaSalle St., Suite 1400, Chicago, IL 60603-1210. Tel. 312-553-2200. *Exec. Dir.* Cindy Clark; *Pres.* James Ross.

Children's Book Council Inc., 568 Broadway, New York, NY 10012. Tel. 212-966-

1990, e-mail staff@CBCbooks.org; *Pres.* Paula Quint; *Asst. V.P.* Maria Juarez.
Christian Booksellers Assn., Box 200, Colorado Springs, CO 80901. Tel. 719-576-7880. *Pres.* William Anderson.
Educational Paperback Assn., c/o *Exec. Secy.* Marilyn Abel, Box 1399, East Hampton, NY 11937. Tel. 212-879-6850.
Evangelical Christian Publishers Assn., 1969 E. Broadway Rd., Suite 2, Tempe, AZ 85282. Tel. 602-966-3998, fax 602-966-1944. *Pres.* Doug Ross.
Graphic Artists Guild Inc., 11 W. 20 St., 8th fl., New York, NY 10011-3704. Tel. 212-463-7730, fax 212-463-8779, e-mail paulatgag@aol.com. *Exec. Dir.* Paul Basista. Address correspondence to the executive director.
Great Lakes Booksellers Assn., c/o *Exec. Dir.* Jim Dana, Box 901, 509 Lafayette, Grand Haven, MI 49417. Tel. 616-847-2460, fax 616-842-0051, e-mail glba@aol.com. *Pres.* Judy Betz, River City Books, 4191 Plainfield N.E., Grand Rapids MI 49505; *V.P.* Brad Eft, MicroCenter, 4119 Leap Road, Hilliard, OH 43026
Guild of Book Workers, 521 Fifth Ave., New York, NY 10175. Tel. 212-292-4444. *Pres.* Karen Crisalli. Tel. 908-264-0306, e-mail karenc5071@aol.com.
International Copyright Information Center, c/o Assn. of American Publishers, 1718 Connecticut Ave. N.W., 7th fl., Suite 700, Washington, DC 20009-1148. Tel. 202-232-3335 ext. 228, fax 202-745-0694, e-mail crisher@publishers.org. *Dir.* Carol Risher.
International Standard Book Numbering U.S. Agency, 121 Chanlon Rd., New Providence, NJ 07974. Tel. 908-665-6700, fax 908-665-2895. *Chair* Peter Simon; *Dir.* Albert Simmonds; *Dir. Emeritus* Emery I. Koltay; *Industrial Relations Mgr.* Don Riseborough; *ISBN Mgr.* Lynn Ann Sahner; *SAN Mgr.* Diana Fumando.
Jewish Book Council, 15 E. 26 St., New York, NY 10010. Tel. 212-532-4949 ext. 297, fax 212-481-4174. *Pres.* Arthur Kurzweil; *Exec. Dir.* Carolyn Starman Hessel.
Library Binding Institute, 7401 Metro Blvd., Suite 325, Edina, MN 55439. Tel. 612-835-4707, fax 612-835-4740, e-mail 71035.3504@compuserve.com. *Exec. Dir.* Sally Grauer.
Metropolitan Lithographers Assn., 950 Third Ave., Suite 1500, New York, NY 10022. Tel. 212-838-8480, fax 212-644-1936. *Pres.* Frank Stillo; *Secy.* Cynthia Luzon.
Mid-America Publishers Assn., c/o *Exec. Admin.* Doug Bandos, Box 376, Ada, MI 49301. Tel. 888-308-MAPA, 616-682-0470, fax 616-676-07592; *Pres.* Chris Roerden, Edit-It, 3225 Hill Crest Dr., Brookfield, WI 53045. Tel. 414-781-5412, fax 414-781-3348.
Mid-Atlantic Booksellers Assn., 108 S. 13 St., Philadelphia, PA 19107. Tel. 215-735-9598, fax 215-735-2670. *Exec. Dir.* Larry Robin.
Midwest Independent Publishers Assn., Box 581432, Minneapolis, MN 55458-1432. Tel. 612-646-0475, fax 612-646-0657, e-mail 733243.2012@compuserve.com, World Wide Web http://www.mipa.org; *Pres.* Paul Druckman.
Miniature Book Society Inc., c/o *Pres.* Doris Selmer, 55 E. Arthur Ave., Arcadia, CA 91006. Tel. 818-447-1411; *V.P.* Donn Sanford, 210 Swarthmore Court, Woodstock, IL 60098-7879. Tel. 815-337-2323; *Secy.* Michael A. Canoso, 22 Divinity Ave., Cambridge, MA 02138; *Treas.* Loretta Gentile, 10 Albert St., Waltham, MA 02154.
Minnesota Book Publishers Roundtable. *Pres.* Kathryn Grimes, Univ. of Minnesota Press, 111 Third Ave. S., Minneapolis, MN 55401; *V.P.* Lisa Bullard, Graywolf Press, 2402 University Ave. S., Suite 203, Saint Paul, MN 55114; *Secy.-Treas.* Brad Vogt, Liturgical Press, Collegeville, MN 56321. Tel. 612-363-2538. Address correspondence to the secretary-treasurer.
Mountains and Plains Booksellers Assn., 805 LaPorte Ave., Fort Collins, CO 80521. Tel. 970-484-5856, fax 970-407-1479, e-mail lknumpba@rmi.com. *Exec. Dir.* Lisa Knudsen; *Pres.* Patricia Nelson; *V.P.* Leslie Ryan; *Secy.* Brenda Allen. *Treas.* Molly Divine.
National Assn. of College Stores, 500 E. Lorain St., Oberlin, OH 44074-1294. Tel. 216-775-7777, fax 216-775-4769. *Pres./Treas.* Elroy Littlefield; *Pres.-Elect/Secy.* Jeff Mack; *Public Relations Dir.* Jerry L.

Buchs. Address correspondence to the public relations director.

New England Booksellers Assn., 847 Massachusetts Ave., Cambridge, MA 02139. Tel. 617-576-3070, fax 617-576-3091. *Pres.* Suzy Staubach; *V.P.* Donna Urey; *Treas.* Bruce MacMillan; *Exec. Dir.* Wayne Drugan.

New Mexico Book League, 8632 Horacio Place N.E., Albuquerque, NM 87111. Tel. 505-299-8940, fax 505-294-8032. *Editor, Book Talk* Carol A. Myers.

Northern California Independent Booksellers Assn., 5643 Paradise Dr., Suite 12, Corte Madera, CA 94925. Tel. 415-927-3937, fax 415-927-3971, e-mail nciba@aol.com. *Exec. Dir.* Ginie Thorp.

Pacific Northwest Booksellers Assn., 1510 Mill St., Eugene, OR 97401-4258. Tel. 541-683-4363, fax 541-683-3910. *Pres.* Patrick Moody, Snow Goose Bookstore, Box 939, Stanwood, WA 98292; *Exec. Dir.* Thom Chambliss.

Periodical and Book Assn. of America Inc., 120 E. 34 St., Suite 7K, New York, NY 10016. Tel. 212-689-4952, fax 212-545-8328. *Pres.* Mary C. McEvoy, MacDonald Communications; *V.P.s* Keith Furman; Will Michalopoulos, Consumer Reports; Gerald Cohen, Total Publisher Services; *Treas.* Edward Handi, LFP; *Secy.* Kathi Robold, Scientific American; *Exec. Dir.* Michael Morse; *Legal Counsel* Lee Feltman; *Advisers to the Pres.* Irwin Billman, Norman Jacobs, Adrian Lopez, Michael McCarthy.

Periodical Marketers of Canada, 1007-175 Bloor St. E., South Tower, Toronto, ON M4W 3R8, Canada. Tel. 416-968-7218, fax 416-968-6182. *Pres.* Paul Benjamin, Benjamin News, Inc., 9600 Jean-Milot St., Lasalle, PQ H8R 1X7, Canada. Tel. 514-364-1780, fax 514-364-7275; *Secy.-Treas.* Steve Shepherd, Ottawa Valley News Co., Box 157, Arnprior, ON K7S 3H4, Canada. Tel. 613-623-3197; *Asst. Exec. Dir.* Janette Hatcher. Tel. 416-968-7218.

Philadelphia Book Clinic, c/o *Secy.-Treas.* Thomas Colaiezzi, 136 Chester Ave., Yeadon, PA 19050-3831. Tel. 610-259-7022, fax 610-394-9886.

Publishers Advertising and Marketing Assn., The Crown Publishing Group, 201 E. 50 St., New York, NY 10022. Tel. 212-751-2600, fax 212-333-5374; *Pres.* Lee Wiggins; *Secy.* Cathy Collins; *Treas.* Stephanie Joel; *Contact* Lorie Shierman.

Religion Publishing Group, *Pres.* Elizabeth Gold, Guideposts Books, 16 E. 34 St., New York, NY 10016, Tel. 212-251-8130, fax 212-684-0689; *Secy.* Hargis Thomas; *Treas.* Theresa D'Orsogna.

Research and Engineering Council of the Graphic Arts Industry Inc., Box 639, Chadds Ford, PA 19317. Tel. 610-388-7394, fax 610-388-2708. *Pres.* Brian Chapman; *Exec. V.P./Secy.* James Henderson; *Exec. V.P./Treas.* Edmund Funk; *Managing Dir.* Fred Rogers.

Small Publishers Assn. of North America (SPAN), Box 1306, Buena Vista, CO 81211-1306. Tel. 719-395-4790, fax 719-395-8374, e-mail SPAN@span-assn.org. *Exec. Dir.* Marilyn Ross.

Technical Assn. of the Pulp and Paper Industry, Technology Pk./Atlanta, Box 105113, Atlanta, GA 30348-5113. Tel. 770-446-1400, fax 770-446-6947. *Pres.* Jack E. Chinn; *V.P.* Dale Dill.

West Coast Book People Assn., 27 McNear Dr., San Rafael, CA 94901. *Secy.* Frank G. Goodall. Tel. 415-459-1227, fax 415-459-1227.

Women's National Book Assn., 160 Fifth Ave., New York, NY 10010. Tel. 212-675-7805, fax 212-989-7542, e-mail 4164812 @mcimail.com; *Pres.* Donna Paz; *V.P.* Diane Ullius; *Secy.* Dorothy S. O'Connor; *Treas.* Margaret Auer; *Chapters in*: Atlanta, Binghamton, Boston, Dallas, Detroit, Los Angeles, Nashville, New York, San Francisco, Washington, D.C.

International and Foreign Book Trade Associations

For Canadian book trade associations, see the preceding section, "Book Trade Associations, United States and Canada." For a more extensive list of book trade organizations outside the United States and Canada, with more detailed information, consult *International Literary Market Place* (R. R. Bowker), which also provides extensive lists of major bookstores and publishers in each country.

International

Afro-Asian Book Council, 4835/24 Ansari Rd., Daryaganj, New Delhi 110-002, India. Tel. 11-326-1487, fax 11-326-7437. *Chair* Dato Jaji Jumaat; *Secy.-Gen.* Asang Machwe; *Dir.* Abul Hasan.

Centre Régional pour la Promotion du Livre en Afrique (Regional Center for Book Promotion in Africa), Box 1646, Yaoundé, Cameroon. Tel. 22-4782/2936. *Secy.* William Moutchia.

Centro Régional para el Fomento del Libro en América Latina y el Caribe (CERLALC) (Regional Center for Book Promotion in Latin America and the Caribbean), Calle 70, No. 9-52, Apdo. Aereó 57348, Santafé de Bogotá 2, Colombia. Tel. 1-249-5141, fax 1-255-4614. *Dir.* Carmen Barvo.

Federation of European Publishers, 92 Ave. de Tervuren, 1040 Brussels, Belgium. Tel. 2-736-3616, fax 2-736-1987. *Pres.* Volker Schwarz; *Secy. Gen.* Mechtild Von Alemann.

International Board on Books for Young People (IBBY), Nonnenweg 12, Postfach, CH-4003 Basel, Switzerland. Tel. 61-272-29-17, fax 61-272-27-57. *Dir.* Leena Maissen.

International Booksellers Federation, Boulevard Lambermont 140/1, 6000 B1030 Brussels, Belgium. Tel./fax 242-0957. *Pres.* John K. Hedgecock; *Gen. Secy.* Christiane Vuidar.

International League of Antiquarian Booksellers, Box 323, Victoria Sta., Montreal, PQ H3Z 2V8, Canada. Tel. 514-844-5344, fax 514-499-9274. *Pres.* Anton Gerits; *Secy.* Helen Kahn.

International Publishers Assn. (Union Internationale des Editeurs), Ave. Miremont 3, CH-1206 Geneva, Switzerland. Tel. 22-346-3018, fax 22-347-5717. *Pres.* Fernando Guedes; *Secy.-Gen.* J. Alexis Koutchoumow.

National

Argentina

Cámara Argentina de Publicaciones (Argentine Publications Assn.), Reconquesta 1011, piso 6° D, 1074 Buenos Aires. Tel. 01-311-6855. *Contact* Augustin dos Santos.

Cámara Argentina del Libro (Argentine Book Assn.), Avda. Belgrano 1580, 6° piso, 1093 Buenos Aires. Tel. 541-381-9277, fax 541-381-9253. *Dir.* Norberto J. Pou.

Australia

Australian and New Zealand Assn. of Antiquarian Booksellers, 161 Commercial Rd., South Yarra, Vic. 3141. Tel. 3-826-1779, fax 3-521-3412. *Secy.* Nicholas Dawes.

Australian Booksellers Assn., Box 1088, Carlton, Vic. 3053. Tel. 3-966-37-888, fax 3-966-37-557. *Pres.* Tim Peach; *Exec. Dir.* Celia Pollock.

Australian Publishers Assn., Suite 60, 89 Jones St., Ultimo, Sydney, N.S.W. 2007. Tel. 2-281-9788, fax 2-281-1073. *Dir.* Susan Blackwell.

National Book Council, Suite 3, 21 Drummond Pl., Carlton, Vic. 3053. Tel. 3-663-8655, fax 3-663-8658. *Pres.* Michael G. Zifcak; *Exec. Dir.* Thomas Shapcott.

Austria

Hauptverband des Österreichischen Buchhandels (Austrian Publishers and Booksellers Assn.), Grünangergasse 4, A-1010 Vienna.

Tel. 1-512-1535, fax 1-512-8482. *Pres. and Secy.* Otto Mang.

Österreichischer Buchhändlerverband (Austrian Booksellers Assn.), Grünangergasse 4, A-1010 Vienna. Tel. 1-512-1535, fax 1-512-8482. *Pres.* Michael Kernstock; *Secy.* Otto Mang.

Österreichischer Verlegerverband (Assn. of Austrian Publishers), Grünangergasse 4, A-1010 Vienna. Tel. 1-512-1535, fax 1-512-8482. *Secy.-Gen.* Otto Mang.

Verband der Antiquare Österreichs (Austrian Antiquarian Booksellers Assn.), Grünangergasse 4, A-1010 Vienna. Tel. 1-512-1535, fax 1-512-8482. *Pres.* Hansjörg Krug; *Secy.-Gen.* Otto Mang.

Belgium

Vereniging ter Bevordering van het Vlaamse Boekwezen (Assn. for the Promotion of Dutch Language Books/Books from Flanders), Hof ter Schrieeklaan 17, 2600 Berchem/Antwerp. Tel. 323-230-8923, fax 323-281-2240. *Pres.* Luc Demeester; *Gen. Secy.* Wim de Mont.

Vlaamse Boekverkopersbond (Flemish Booksellers Assn.), Hof ter Schrieeklaan 17, 2600 Berchem/Antwerp. Tel. 323-230-8923, fax 323-281-2240. *Pres.* Luc Vander Velpen; *Gen. Secy.* Carlo Van Baelen.

Bolivia

Cámara Boliviana del Libro (Bolivian Booksellers Assn.), Casilla 682, Edificio Las Palmas, Planta Baja, La Paz. Tel. 2-327-039, fax 2-391-817. *Pres.* Rolando S. Condori.

Brazil

Cámara Brasileira do Livro (Brazilian Book Assn.), Av. Ipiranga 1267, 10° andar, 01039-907 Sao Paulo. Tel. 11-225-8277, fax 11-229-7463. *Gen. Mgr.* Aloysio T. Costa.

Livraria Kosmos Editora Ltda (Brazilian Assn. of Antiquarian Booksellers), Rua do Rosario 155 Centro, 20041 Rio de Janeiro. Tel. 21-224-8616, fax 21-221-4582.

Sindicato Nacional dos Editores de Livros (Brazilian Book Publishers Assn.), Av. Rio Branco 37, 15° andar, Salas 1503/6e, 1510/12, 20090-003 Rio de Janeiro. Tel. 21-233-6481, fax 21-253-8502. *Pres.* Sérgio Abreu da Cruz Machado; *Exec. Secy.* Henrique Maltese.

Chile

Cámara Chilena del Libro AG (Chilean Assn. of Publishers, Distributors and Booksellers), Avda. Libertador Bernardo O'Higgins 1370, Of. 501, 13526 Santiago. Tel. 2-698-9519, fax 2-698-9226. *Exec. Secy.* Carlos Franz.

Colombia

Cámara Colombiana del Libro (Colombian Book Assn.), Carrera 17A, No. 37-27, Apdo. Aereo 8998, Santafé de Bogota. Tel. 1-245-1940, 232-7550, 288-6188, fax 1-287-3320.

Czech Republic

Svaz Český Nakladateluà Knihkupcù (Czech Publishers and Booksellers Assn.), Jana Masaryka 56, 120 00 Prague 2. Tel./fax 2-242-21-243, 242-14-6449.

Denmark

Danske Antikvarboghandlerforening (Danish Antiquarian Booksellers Assn.), Postboks 2028, DK-1012 Copenhagen K. Fax 33-125-494. *Chair* P. J. Poulsen.

Danske Forlaeggerforening (Danish Publishers Assn.), Købmagergade 11/13, DK-1150 Copenhagen K. Tel. 3-315-6688, fax 3-315-6588. *Dir.* Erik V. Krustrup.

Ecuador

Cámara Ecuatoriana del Libro, Guayaquil 1629, 4° piso, Casilla 17-01-3329, Quito. Tel. 2-322-1226, fax 2-325-66340. *Pres.* Fausto A. Coba.

Egypt

General Egyptian Book Organization, Box 1660, Corniche El-Nile, Boulac, Cairo. Tel. 2-77-549, 77-500, fax 2-93-932. *Pres.* Ezz El Dine Ismail.

Estonia

Estonian Publishers Assn., Parnu mnt 10, EE-0090 Tallinn. Tel. 142-691-828, fax 142-445-720. *Dir.* A. Tarvis.

Finland

Kirja-ja Paperikauppojen Liitto ry (Finnish Booksellers and Stationers Assn.), Eerikinkatu 15-17 D 43-44, 00100 Helsinki. Tel. 0-694-4899, fax 0-694-4900. *Chief Exec.* Olli Eräkivi.
Suomen Kustannusyhdistys ry (Finnish Book Publishers Assn.), SF 0015077, FIN-00121 Helsinki. Tel. 90-179185, fax 90-622-1143. *Dir.* Veikko Sonninen.

France

Cercle de la Librairie (Circle of Professionals of the Book Trade), 35 Rue Grégoire-de-Tours, F-75006 Paris. Tel. 1-44-41-28-00, fax 1-44-41-28-65. *Pres.* Marc Friedel.
Fédération Française des Syndicats de Libraires—FFSL (French Booksellers Assn.), 43 Rue de Châteaudun, F-75009 Paris. Tel. 1-42-82-00-03, fax 1-42-82-10-51. *Pres.* Jean-Luc Dewas.
France Edition, 35 Rue Grégoire-de-Tours, F-75006 Paris. Tel. 1-44-41-13-13, fax 1-46-34-63-83. *Chair* Bernard Foulon. *New York Branch* French Publishers Agency, 853 Broadway, New York, NY 10003-4703. Tel. 212-254-4520, fax 212-979-6229.
Syndicat National de la Librairie Ancienne et Moderne (National Assn. of Antiquarians and Modern Booksellers), 4 Rue Git-le-Coeur, F-75006 Paris. Tel. 1-43-29-46-38, fax 1-43-25-41-63. *Pres.* Jean-Etienne Huret.
Syndicat National de l'Edition (National Union of Publishers), 35 Rue Grégoire-de-Tours, F-75006 Paris. Tel. 1-44-41-28-00, fax 331-43-25-35-01. *Pres.* Serge Eyrolles; *Secy.* Jean Sarzana.
Union des Libraires de France, 40 Rue Grégoire-de-Tours, F-75006 Paris. Tel. 1-43-29-88-79, fax 1-46-33-65-27. *Pres.* Eric Hardin; *Gen. Delegate* Marie-Dominique Doumenc.

Germany

Börsenverein des Deutschen Buchhandels e.V. (Stock Exchange of German Booksellers), Postfach 100442, Grosser Hirschgraben 17-21, 60311 Frankfurt-am-Main. Tel. 69-130-6324, fax 69-130-6399; Gerichtsweg 26, 07010 Leipzig. Tel. 341-29-3851; Dahlmannstr. 20, 5300 Bonn 1. Tel. 228-22-1078. *Gen. Mgr.* Hans-Karl von Kupsch.
Bundesverband der Deutschen Versandbuchhändler e.V. (National Federation of German Mail-Order Booksellers), An der Ringkirche 6, 65197 Wiesbaden. Tel. 611-44-9091, fax 611-48451. *Mgrs.* Stefan Rutkowsky, Kornelia Wahl.
Verband Deutscher Antiquare e.V. (German Antiquarian Booksellers Assn.), Kreuzgasse 2-4, Postfach 18-01-80, 50504 Cologne. Tel. 221-92-54-82-82; *Pres.* Jochen Granier; *V.P.* Inge Utzt.

Ghana

Ghana Book Development Council, Box M430, Accra. Tel. 21-22-9178, fax 21-22-0271. *Deputy Exec. Dir.* Annor Nimako.

Great Britain

See United Kingdom

Greece

Hellenic Federation of Publishers and Booksellers, Themistocleous 73, 10683 Athens. Tel. 1-330-0924, fax 1-330-1617. *Pres.* Dimitris Pandeleskos.
Syllogos Ekdoton Bibliopolon Athinon (Publishers and Booksellers Assn. of Athens), Themistocleous 73, 10683 Athens. Tel. 1-383-0029, fax 1-382-3222. *Pres.* Thanasis Kastaniotis.

Hungary

Magyar Könyvkiadók és Könyvterjesztök Egyesülése (Assn. of Hungarian Publishers and Booksellers), Vörösmarty tér 1, 1051 Budapest (mail: PB 130, 1367 Budapest). Tel. 1-117-6222. *Pres.* István Bart; *Secy.-Gen.* Péter Zentai.

Iceland

Félag Islenskra Bókaútgefenda (Icelandic Publishers Assn.), Sudurlandsbraut 4A, 108 Reykjavik. Tel. 553-8020, fax 5-888-668. *Chair* Jóhann Páll Valdimarsson; *Gen. Mgr.* Vilborg Hardardóttir.

India

Federation of Indian Publishers, Federation House, 18/1-C Institutional Area, JNU Rd., Aruna Asaf Ali Marg, New Delhi 110067. Tel. 11-696-4847, 685-2263, fax 11-686-4054. *Pres.* Shri R. C. Govil; *Exec. Secy.* S. K. Ghai.

Indonesia

Ikatan Penerbit Indonesia (Assn. of Indonesian Book Publishers), Jl. Kalipasir 32, Jakarta 10330. Tel. 21-314-1907, fax 21-314-1433. *Pres.* Rozali Usman; *Secy. Gen.* Setia Dharma Majidd.

Ireland

Booksellers Assn. of Great Britain and Ireland (Irish Branch), 54 Middle Abbey St., Dublin 1. *Admin.* Cecily Golden.
CLÉ: The Irish Book Publishers' Assn., The Writers Centre, 19 Pannell Sq., Dublin 1. Tel. 1-872-9090, fax 1-872-2035. *Contact* Hilary Kennedy.

Israel

Book and Printing Center, Israel Export Institute, 29 Hamered St., Box 50084, Tel Aviv 68125. Tel. 3-514-2910, fax 3-514-2815. *Dir.* Corine Knafo.
Book Publishers Assn. of Israel, 29 Carlebach St., Box 20123, 61201, Tel Aviv 67132. Tel. 3-561-4121, fax 3-561-1996. *Managing Dir.* Amnon Ben-Shmuel.

Italy

Associazione Italiana Editori (Italian Publishers Assn.), Via delle Erbe 2, 20121 Milan. Tel. 2-86-46-3091, fax 2-89-01-0863.
Associazione Librai Antiquari d'Italia (Antiquarian Booksellers Assn. of Italy), Via Jacopo Nardi 6, I-50132 Florence. Tel./fax (055) 24-3253. *Pres.* Vittorio Soave.
Associazione Librai Italiani (Italian Booksellers Assn.), Corso Venezia 49, 20121 Milan. Tel. 2-775-0216, fax 2-775-0470.

Jamaica

Booksellers Assn. of Jamaica, c/o Novelty Training Co. Ltd., 53 Hanover St., Box 80, Kingston. Tel. 809-922-5883, fax 809-922-4743. *Pres.* Keith Shervington.

Japan

Japan Book Importers Assn., Chiyoda Kaikan 21-4, Nihonbashi 1-chome, Chuo-ku, Tokyo 103. Tel. 3-32-71-6901, fax 3-32-71-6920. *Secy.* Shunji Kanda.
Japan Book Publishers Assn., 6 Fukuromachi, Shinjuku-ku, Tokyo 162. Tel. 3-32-68-1301, fax 3-32-68-1196. *Pres.* Takio Watanabe; *Exec. Dir.* Toshikazu Gomi.

Kenya

Kenya Publishers Assn., c/o Phoenix Publishers Ltd., Box 18650, Nairobi. Tel. 2-22-2309, 22-3262, fax 2-33-9875. *Secy.* Stanley Irura.

Korea (Republic of)

Korean Publishers Assn., 105-2 Sagan-dong, Chongno-ku, Seoul 110-190. Tel. 2-7354-2701, fax 2-738-5414. *Pres.* Kim Nak-Joon; *Secy.-Gen.* Jong-Jin Jung.

Latvia

Latvian Book Publishers Assn., Aspazijas Bulvaris 24, 1050 Riga. Tel. 371-722-5843, fax 371-783-0518.

Lithuania

Lithuanian Publishers Assn., K. Sirvydo 6, 2600 Vilnius. Tel. 3702-628-945, fax 3702-619-696. *Pres.* Vincas Akelis.

Mexico

Cámara Nacional de la Industria Editorial Mexicana, Holanda No. 13, CP 04120

Mexico 21. Tel. 5-688-2221, fax 5-604-3147. *Secy.-Gen.* R. Servin.

The Netherlands

Koninklijke Nederlandse Uitgeversbond (Royal Dutch Publishers Assn.), Keizersgracht 391, 1016 EJ Amsterdam. Tel. 20-626-7736, fax 20-620-3859. *Pres.* Karel Leeflang; *Secy.* R. M. Vrij.

Koninklijke Vereeniging ter Bevordering van de Belangen des Boekhandels (Royal Dutch Book Trade Assn.), Postbus 15007, 1001 MA Amsterdam. Tel. 20-624-0212, fax 20-620-8871. *Secy.* M. van Vollenhoven-Nagel.

Nederlandsche Vereeniging van Antiquaren (Netherlands Assn. of Antiquarian Booksellers), Postbus 664, 1000 AR Amsterdam. Tel. 20-627-2285, fax 20-625-8970. *Pres.* F. W. Kuyper; *Secy.* A. Gerits.

Nederlandse Boekverkopersbond (Dutch Booksellers Assn.), Postbus 90731, 2509 LS The Hague. Tel. 70-324-4395, fax 70-324-4411. *Pres.* W. Karssen; *Exec. Secy.* A. C. Doeser.

New Zealand

Book Publishers Assn. of New Zealand, Box 36477, Auckland 1309. Tel. 9-480-2711, fax 9-480-1130. *Pres.* Tony Harkins.

Booksellers New Zealand, Box 11-377, Wellington. Tel. 4-472-8678, fax 4-472-8628. *Chair* Joan MacKenzie; *Pres.* Tony Harkins; *Chief Exec.* Jo Breese.

Nigeria

Nigerian Publishers Assn., 14 Awosika Ave., Off Oshunto Kun Ave., Old Bodija, GPO Box 3541, Dugbie, Ibadan. Tel. 22-411-557. *Pres.* A. O. Echebiri.

Norway

Norske Bokhandlerforening (Norwegian Booksellers Assn.), Ovre Vollgate 15, 0158 Oslo. Tel. 22-410-760, fax 22-333-269.

Norske Forleggerforening (Norwegian Publishers Assn.), Ovre Vollgate 15, 0158 Oslo 1. Tel. 22-421-355, fax 22-333-830. *Dir.* Paul Martens Røthe.

Pakistan

National Book Council of Pakistan, Block 14D, 1st fl., Al-Markaz F/8, Box 1610, Islamabad. Tel. 51-853-581. *Dir. Gen.* Rafiq Ahmad.

Paraguay

Cámara Paraguaya de Editores, Libreros y Asociados (Paraguayan Publishers Assn.), Caballero 270, Asunción. Tel. 21-496-991, fax 21-448-721. *Dir.* Alejandro Gatti.

Peru

Cámara Peruana del Libro (Peruvian Publishers Assn.), Ave. Cuba No. 427, Jesús María, Apdo Postal 10253, Lima 1. Tel./fax 1-472-9516. *Pres.* Julio César Flores Rodriguez; *Exec. Dir.* Guillermo Skinner Guzmán.

Philippines

Philippine Educational Publishers Assn., 84 P Florentino St., 3008 Quezon City. Tel. 2-968-316, fax 2-921-3788. *Pres.* D. D. Buhain.

Poland

Polskie Towarzystwo Wydawców Ksiazek (Polish Society of Book Editors), ul. Mazowiecka 2/4, 00-048 Warsaw. Tel./fax 22-260-735. *Pres.* Andrzej Karpowicz; *Gen. Secy.* Jan Miz.

Stowarzyszenie Ksiegarzy Polskich (Assn. of Polish Booksellers), ul. Mokotowska 4/6, 00-641 Warsaw. Tel. 22-252-874. *Pres.* Tadeusz Hussak.

Romania

Societa Ziaristilor din România (Journalists Society of Romania), Piata Presei Libere 1, 71341 Bucharest. Tel. 617-15-91, fax 312-82-66.

Russia

All-Union Book Chamber, Kremlevskaja nab 1/9, 121019 Moscow. Tel. 95-202-7172, fax 95-202-3992. *Dir.-Gen.* Yuri Torsuev.

Publishers Assn., 44B Hertsen Str., 121069 Moscow. Tel. 95-202-1174, fax 95-202-3989. *Contact* M. Shishigin.

Singapore

Singapore Book Publishers Assn., Block 86, Marine Parade Central, No. 03-213, Singapore 440086. Tel. 344-7801, fax 447-0897. *Pres.* K. P. Sivan; *Honorary Secy.* Wu Cheng Tan.

Slovenia

Zdruzenje Zaloznikov in Knjigotrzcev Slovenije Gospodarska Zbornica Slovenije (Assn. of Publishers and Booksellers of Slovenia), Dimičeva 9, 1504 Ljubljana. Tel./fax 61-342-398. *Contact* Joze Korinsek.

South Africa

Associated Booksellers of Southern Africa, Box 870, Bellville 7530. Tel. 21-951-6611, fax 21-951-4903. *Pres.* M. Hargraves; *Secy.* R. Stoltenkamp.
Publishers Assn. of South Africa, Box 1001, 7990 Kalk Bay. Tel. 21-788-6470, fax 21-788-6469. *Chair* Basil Van Rooyen.

Spain

Federación de Gremios de Editores de España (Federation of Spanish Publishers Assns.), Juan Ramón Jiménez, 45-9° Izda, 28036 Madrid. Tel. 1-350-9105, fax 1-345-4351. *Pres.* Pere Vincens; *Secy.* Ana Molto.
Gremio de Libreros de Barcelona (Booksellers Assn. of Barcelona and Catalonia), Mallorca 274, 08037 Barcelona. Tel. 3-215-4254.

Sri Lanka

Sri Lanka Assn. of Publishers, 112 S. Mahinda Mawatha, Colombo 10. Tel. 1-695-773, fax 1-696-653. *Pres.* Dayawansa Jayakody.

Sudan

Sudanese Publishers Assn., H. Q. Al Ikhwa Bldg., Flat 7, 7th fl., Box 2771, Khartoum. Tel. 249-11-75051, 79180.

Suriname

Publishers Assn. Suriname, Domineestr. 26, Box 1841, Paramaribo. Tel. 472-545, fax 410-563. *Mgr.* E. Hogenboom.

Sweden

Svenska Bokförläggareföreningen (Swedish Publishers Assn.), Drottninggatan 97, S-11360 Stockholm. Tel. 8-736-1940, fax 8-736-1944. *Dir.* Lena Westerberg.

Switzerland

Schweizerischer Buchhändler- und Verleger-Verband (Swiss German-Language Booksellers and Publishers Assn.), Baumackerstr. 42, Postfach 9045, 8050 Zurich. Tel. 1-312-5343. *Secy.* Egon Räz.
Societa Editori della Svizzera Italiana (Publishers Assn. for Italian-Speaking Switzerland), Via San Gottardo 50, 6900 Lugano. Tel. 91-232-271, fax 91-232-805. *Pres.* Alfonso Pezzati.
Société des Libraires et Editeurs de la Suisse Romande (Assn. of Swiss French-Language Booksellers and Publishers), 2 Ave. Agassiz, 1001 Lausanne. Tel. 21-319-7111, fax 21-319-7910. *Contact* Philippe Schibli.

Tanzania

Publishers Assn. of Tanzania, Box 1408, Dar es Salaam. Tel. 51-512-7608. *Dir.* A. Saiwaad.

Thailand

Publishers and Booksellers Assn. of Thailand, 320 Lat Phrao 94-aphat Pracha-u-thit Rd., Bangkok 10140. Tel. 2-662-559-3348, fax 2-662-538-1499.

United Kingdom

Antiquarian Booksellers Assn., Sackville House, 40 Piccadilly, London W1V 9PA, England. Tel. 171-439-3118, fax 171-439-3119. *Administrators* Philippa Gibson; Alexandra Bake-Sedgeick.

Assn. of Learned and Professional Society Publishers, 48 Kelsey Lane, Beckenham, Kent BR3 3NE, England. Tel. 181-658-0459. *Secy.-Gen.* B. T. Donovan.

Book Trust, 45 E. Hill, Wandsworth, London SW18 2QZ. Tel. 181-870-9055, fax 181-874-4790.

Book Trust Scotland, Scottish Book Centre, 137 Dundee St., Edinburgh EH11 1BG, Scotland. Tel. 131-229-3663, fax 131-228-4293. *Exec. Dir.* Lindsey Fraser.

Booksellers Assn. of Great Britain and Ireland, Minster House, 272 Vauxhall Bridge Rd., London SW1V 1BA, England. Tel. 171-834-5477, fax 171-834-8812. *Chief Exec.* Tim Godfray.

Educational Publishers Council, 19 Bedford Sq., London WC1B 3HJ, England. Tel. 171-580-6321, fax 171-636-5375. *Dir.* John R. M. Davies.

Publishers Assn., 19 Bedford Sq., London WC1B 3HJ, England. Tel. 171-580-6321, fax 171-636-5375. *Pres.* Simon Master; *Chief Exec.* Clive Bradley; *Secy.* Marian Donne.

Scottish Publishers Assn., Scottish Book Centre, 137 Dundee St., 1st fl., Edinburgh EH11 1BG, Scotland. Tel. 131-228-6866, fax 131-228-3220. *Dir.* Lorraine Fannin; *Chair* Mike Miller.

Welsh Books Council (Cyngor Llyfrau Cymraeg), Castell Brychan, Aberystwyth, Dyfed SY23 2JB, Wales. Tel. 1970-624-151, fax 1970-625-385. *Dir.* Gwerfyl Pierce Jones.

Uruguay

Cámara Uruguaya del Libro (Uruguayan Publishers Assn.), Juan D. Jackson 1118, 11200 Montevideo. Tel. 2-241-5732, fax 2-241-1860.

Venezuela

Cámara Venezolana del Libro (Venezuelan Publishers Assn.), Ave. Andrés Bello, Torre Oeste, 11° piso, Of. 112-0, Apdo. 51858, Caracas 1050-A. Tel. 2-793-1347, fax 2-793-1368. *Secy.* M. P. Vargas.

Zambia

Booksellers and Publishers Assn. of Zambia, Box 31838, Lusaka. Tel. 1-222-647, fax 1-225-195; *Exec. Dir.* Basil Mbewe.

Zimbabwe

Zimbabwe Book Publishers Assn., 12 Selous Ave., Harare. Tel. 4-739-681, fax 4-751-202.

National Information Standards Organization (NISO) Standards

Book Production and Publishing

Z39.5-1985*	Abbreviation of Titles of Publications
Z39.14-1997	Guidelines for Abstracts
Z39.22-1989	Proof Corrections
Z39.41-1997	Printed Information on Spines
Z39.43-1993	Standard Address Number (SAN) for the Publishing Industry
Z39.48-1992	Permanence of Paper for Publications and Documents in Libraries and Archives
Z39.66-1992	Durable Hard-Cover Binding for Books

Codes and Numbering Systems

Z39.9-1992	International Standard Serial Numbering (ISSN)
Z39.23-1997	Standard Technical Report Number
Z39.43-1993	Standard Address Number (SAN) for the Publishing Industry
Z39.47-1993	Extended Latin Alphabet Coded Character Set for Bibliographic Use (ANSEL)
Z39.53-1994	Codes for the Representation of Languages for Information Interchange
Z39.56-1996	Serial Item and Contribution Identifier
Z39.64-1989	East Asian Character Code for Bibliographic Use
Z39.76-1996	Data Elements for Binding Library Materials
NISO/ANSI/ISO 3166	Codes for the Representation of Names of Countries
NISO/ANSI/ISO 2108	International Standard Book Numbering (ISBN)

Indexes, Thesauri, and Database Development

Z39.19-1993	Guidelines for the Construction, Format, and Management of Monolingual Thesauri

Microforms

Z39.62-1993	Eye-Legible Information on Microfilm Leaders And Trailers and on Containers of Processed Microfilm on Open Reels
Z39.74-1996	Guides to Accompany Microform Sets
Z39.32-1996	Information on Microform Headers

Technical Writing

Z39.18-1995	Scientific and Technical Reports— Elements, Organization, and Design
Z39.23-1997	Standard Technical Report Number
Z39.19-1993	Guidelines for the Construction, Format, and Management of Monolingual Thesauri

Serial Publications

Z39.5-1985*	Abbreviation of Titles of Publications
Z39.9-1992	International Standard Serial Numbering (ISSN)
Z39.44-1986*	Serials Holding Statements
Z39.48-1992	Permanence of Paper for Printed Publications
Z39.56-1996	Serial Item and Contribution Identifiers

Automation and Electronic Publishing

Z39.2-1994	Information Interchange Format
Z39.44-1986*	Serials Holding Statements
Z39.47-1993	Extended Latin Alphabet Coded Character Set for Bibliographic Use (ANSEL)
Z39.50-1995	Information Retrieval (Z39.50) Application Service Definition and Protocol Specification
Z39.57-1989*	Holding Statements for Non-Serial Items
Z39.58-1992*	Common Command Language for Interactive Information Retrieval
Z39.63-1989*	Interlibrary Loan Data Elements
Z39.67-1993	Computer Software Description
NISO/ANSI/ISO 3166	Codes for the Representation of Names of Countries
NISO/ANSI/ISO 9660	Volume and File Structure of CD-ROM for Information Interchange
NISO/ANSI/ISO 12083	Electronic Manuscript Preparation and Markup

Library Equipment

Z39.73-1994	Single-Tier Steel Bracket Library Shelving

Standards Committees

SC MM	Environmental Conditions for the Exhibition of Library and Archival Materials
SC SS	Preservation Product Information
SC ZZ	Library Binding
SC OO	Revision of Z39.29-1977 Bibliographic References
SC YY	Revision of Z39.4-1989 Basic Criteria for Indexes
SC AJ	Standard Format for Downloading Records from Bibliographic and Abstracting Indexing Databases
SC AK	Sorting of Alphanumeric Characters and Other Symbols
SC AL	Holding Statements for Bibliographic Items
SC AO	Title Page Information for Conference Proceedings
SC AP	Book Item and Contribution Identifier (BICI)
SC AQ	The Digital Talking Book: A System for Audio Access to Printed Material

Other Standards in Development

Z39.20	Price Indexes for Print Library Materials
Z39.26	Advertising of Micropublications

*This standard is being reviewed by NISO's Standards Development Committee or is under revision. For further information, please contact NISO, 4733 Bethesda Ave., Suite 300, Bethesda, MD 20814. Tel. 301-654-2512, fax 301-654-1721, e-mail nisohq@cni.org, World Wide Web www.niso.org.

Calendar, 1997–2000

The list below contains information on association meetings or promotional events that are, for the most part, national or international in scope. State and regional library association meetings are also included. To confirm the starting or ending date of a meeting, which may change after the *Bowker Annual* has gone to press, contact the association directly. Addresses of library and book trade associations are listed in Part 6 of this volume. For information on additional book trade and promotional events, see the *Exhibits Directory*, published annually by the Association of American Publishers; *Chase's Annual Events*, published by Contemporary Books, 180 N. Michigan Ave., Chicago, IL 60601; *Literary Market Place* and *International Literary Market Place*, published by R. R. Bowker; and the "Calendar" section in each issue of *Publishers Weekly* and *Library Journal*.

1997

May

6-7	Florida Library Assn.	Daytona Beach, FL
8-10	British Columbia Library Assn.	Surrey, BC
8-10	Research and Engineering Council of the Graphic Arts Industry	Sea Island, GA
10-11	American Society of Journalists and Authors	New York, NY
14-15	Massachusetts School Library Media Assn.	Tyngsboro, MA
14-15	Vermont Library Conference	Burlington, VT
18-20	Main Libraries Conference	Orono, ME
22-24	Antiquarian Booksellers Assn.	Chicago, IL
23-29	Medical Library Assn.	Seattle, WA
27-30	Fifth European Conference on Archives	Barcelona, Spain
31-6/3	American Booksellers Assn.	Chicago, IL
31-6/2	Book Expo America (ABA)	Chicago, IL

June

2-4	American Society for Information Science	Scottsdale, AZ
4-6	Society for Scholarly Publishing	Washington, DC
7-12	Special Libraries Assn.	Seattle, WA

June 1997 *(cont.)*

8-10	Periodical and Book Assn. of America	Atlantic City, NJ
11-14	American Theological Library Assn.	Boston, MA
13-15	Periodical Marketers of Canada	St. Johns, NF
14-17	Assn. of American University Presses	Indianapolis, IN
18-22	Canadian Library Assn.	Ottawa, ON
21-25	Canadian Booksellers Assn.	Toronto, ON
25-26	Information Industry Investor Conference	New York, NY
26-7/3	American Library Assn.	San Francisco, CA
27	Chief Officers of State Library Agencies	San Francisco, CA
28-7/3	Chinese American Librarians Assn.	San Francisco, CA
30-7/4	International Assn. of Technological University Libraries	Trondheim, Norway

July

6-11	International Association of School Librarianship/Association of Teacher-Librarianship in Canada	Vancouver, BC
12-17	Christian Booksellers Assn.	Atlanta, GA
19-24	American Assn. of Law Libraries	Baltimore, MD
27-29	Church and Synagogue Library Assn.	Valley Forge, PA
30-8/4	National Conference of African American Librarians	Winston-Salem, NC
31-8/3	Black Caucus of the American Library Association	Winston-Salem, NC
*	National Assn. of Government Archives and Records Administrators	Sacramento, CA

August

6-9	Pacific Northwest Library Assn.	Seattle, WA
24-31	Society of American Archivists	Chicago, IL
29-9/1	Miniature Book Society Inc.	Bethlehem, PA
31-9/5	International Assn. of Music Libraries, Archives, and Documentation Centres	Geneva, Switzerland
31-9/5	International Federation of Library Associations and Institutions (IFLA)	Copenhagen, Denmark

September

3-7	Society of American Archivists	Chicago, IL
12-14	Pacific Northwest Booksellers Assn.	Portland, OR
14-18	International Association of Agricultural Information Specialists	Beijing, China
24-27	International Conference of the Roundtable on Archives	Edinburgh, Scotland
24-27	Pennsylvania Library Assn.	Philadelphia, PA
26-28	Mountains & Plains Booksellers Assn.	Denver, CO

* To be determined

26-28	Great Lakes Booksellers Association Trade Show	Indianapolis, IN
*	North Dakota Library Assn.	Minot, ND

October

1-3	Manitoba Public Library Services	Brandon, MB
1-3	Minnesota Library Assn.	Bloomington, MN
1-4	Idaho Library Assn.	Idaho Falls, ID
1-4	South Dakota Library Assn.	Huron, SD
2-4	Minnesota Educational Media Organization	Minneapolis, MN
3-5	Midatlantic Booksellers Assn.	Philadelphia, PA
3-5	New England Booksellers Assn.	Boston, MA
4-6	World Financial Information Conference	San Francisco, CA
5-8	Information Industry Assn.	San Francisco, CA
5-10	New England Library Assn.	Sturbridge, MA
8-10	Iowa Library Assn.	Sioux City, IA
8-10	Minnesota Library Assn.	Minneapolis/St. Paul, MN
8-10	Missouri Library Assn.	Lake Ozark, MO
9-13	Colorado Library Assn.	Copper Mountain, CO
13-16	ARMA International	Chicago, IL
15-19	Michigan Assn. for Media in Education	Lansing, MI
16-18	West Virginia Lib. Assn.	Flatwoods, WV
17-19	Virginia Educational Media Assn.	Roanoke, VA
19-20	Chief Officers of State Library Agencies	Boise, ID
23-25	Illinois School Library Media Assn.	Springfield, IL
23-25	Lutheran Church Library Assn.	Minneapolis, MN
25-28	Illinois Library Assn.	Springfield, IL
29-2/11	New York Library Assn.	Syracuse, NY
30-31	Nebraska Educational Media Assn.	Omaha, NE
30-31	Nebraska Library Assn.	Omaha, NE
*	ISBN International Agency Advisory Board	Stockholm, Sweden
*	Kentucky Library Assn.	Lexington, KY
*	Kentucky School Media Assn.	Lexington, KY
*	North Carolina Assn. of School Librarians	Raleigh, NC
*	Virginia Library Assn.	Arlington, VA

November

1-5	Evangelical Christian Publishers Assn.	Santa Fe, NM
2-5	American Society for Information Science	Washington, DC
3-4	Massachusetts School Library Media Assn.	Roxborough, MA
4-7	Wisconsin Library Assn.	Milwaukee, WI

* To be determined

November 1997 *(cont.)*

5-7	Michigan Library Assn.	Grand Rapids, MI
5-7	Ohio Educational Library Media Assn.	Columbus, OH
5-9	American Translators Assn.	San Francisco, CA
6-8	Arizona Library Assn.	Phoenix, AZ
6-8	Tennessee Assn. of School Librarians	Kingsport, TN
6-9	Colorado Educational Media Assn.	Beaver Creek, CO
9-12	Book Manufacturers Institute	Laguna Miguel, CA
10-15	Florida Assn. for Media Education	Fort Lauderdale, FL
13-15	Oregon Educational Media Assn.	Eugene, OR
15-18	California Library Assn.	Pasadena, CA
15-18	Periodical Marketers of Canada	Ottawa, ON
*	Virginia /D.C. Library Assns.	Arlington, VA

1998

January

6-9	Assn. for Library & Information Science Education (ALISE)	New Orleans, LA
9-15	American Library Assn.	New Orleans, LA

March

3-6	Louisiana Library Assn.	Shreveport, LA
4-8	Alaska Library Assn.	Anchorage, AK
5-13	ARLIS/NA	Philadelphia, PA
10-14	Public Library Assn.	Kansas City, MO
20-22	Michigan Assn. for Media in Education	Dearborn, MI

April

2-4	Association for Indiana Media Educators	Indianapolis, IN
14-17	Catholic Library Assn.	Los Angeles, CA
14-17	Washington Library Assn.	Wenatchee, WA
25-29	Evangelical Christian Publishers Assn.	Hilton Head, SC
29-5/2	Montana Library Assn.	Missoula, MT
29-5/2	Oklahoma Library Assn.	Tulsa, OK
*	FIAF–International Federation of Film Archives	Prague, Czech Republic

May

6-7	Archivists and Librarians in the History of the Health Sciences	Toronto, ON
22-28	Medical Libraries Assn.	Philadelphia, PA
28-6/1	Mountain Plains Library Assn.	Salt Lake City, UT
28-6/1	Utah Library Assn.	Salt Lake City, UT

* To be determined

June

3-5	Society for Scholarly Publishing	San Diego, CA
6-11	Special Libraries Assn.	Indianapolis, IN
17-20	American Theological Library Assn.	Philadelphia, PA
18-21	Canadian Library Assn.	Victoria, BC
25-7/2	American Library Assn.	Washington, DC
*	Colorado Educational Media Assn.	Greeley, CO

August

31-9/6	Society of American Archivists	Orlando, FL

September

2-6	Society of American Archivists	Orlando, FL
16-18	North Carolina Assn. of School Librarians	Raleigh, NC
29-10/3	Arkansas Library Assn.	Little Rock, AK
29-10/3	Southeastern Library Assn.	Little Rock, AK
30-10/3	South Dakota Library Assn.	Pierre, SD

October

3-5	New England Library Assn.	Providence, RI
7-9	Minnesota Library Assn.	Rochester, MN
13-15	Idaho Library Assn.	Sun Valley, ID
13-15	Pacific Northwest Library Assn.	Sun Valley, ID
14-16	Iowa Library Assn.	Waterloo, IA
18-21	ARMA International	Cincinnati, OH
21-23	Michigan Library Assn.	Grand Rapids, MI
24-28	Evangelical Christian Publishers Assn.	New Orleans, LA
*	ISBN International Agency Advisory Board	Berlin, Germany

November

4-6	Ohio Educational Library Media Assn.	Columbus, OH
4-7	Michigan Assn. for Media in Education	Acme, MI
5-7	Illinois School Library Media Assn.	Arlington Heights, IL
6-8	Oregon Educational Media Association	Sunriver, OR

1999

February

*	Colorado Educational Media Assn.	Colorado Springs, CO

March

4-6	Association for Indiana Media Educators	Indianapolis, IN

* To be determined

April

9-12	Assn. of College and Research Libraries	Detroit, MI
*	FIAF–International Federation of Film Archives	Madrid, Spain

June

13-16	Montana Library Assn.	Big Sky, MT
13-16	Mountain Plains Library Assn.	Big Sky, MT

August

23-29	Society of American Archivists	Pittsburgh, PA

September

26-28	New England Library Assn.	Manchester, NH
29-10/1	Minnesota Library Assn.	Duluth, MN

October

6-9	Idaho Library Assn.	Boise, ID
6-9	South Dakota Library Assn.	Watertown, SD
13-15	Iowa Library Assn.	Dubuque, IA
28-30	Illinois School Library Media Assn.	Decatur, IL

November

3-5	Ohio Educational Library Media Assn.	Columbus, OH

2000

March

9-11	Association for Indiana Media Educators	Indianapolis, IN

April

*	FIAF–International Federation of Film Archives	London, England

August

28-9/3	Society of American Archivists	Denver, CO

October

4-7	Idaho Library Assn.	Lewiston, ID
11-13	Minnesota Library Assn.	Minneapolis/Saint Paul, MN
24-28	Alabama Library Assn.	Mobile, AL
24-28	Southeastern Library Assn.	Mobile, AL

* To be determined

Acronyms

A

AALL. American Association of Law Libraries
AAP. Association of American Publishers
AASL. American Association of School Librarians
ABA. American Booksellers Association
ABFFE. American Booksellers Foundation for Free Expression
ACLIN. ACLIN (Access Colorado Library and Information Network)
ACRL. Association of College and Research Libraries
AFC. American Folklife Center
AgNIC. Agricultural Network Information Center
AJL. Association of Jewish Libraries
ALA. American Library Association
ALCTS. Association for Library Collections and Technical Services
ALF. National Agricultural Library, ALF (Agricultural Library Forum)
ALISE. Association for Library and Information Science Education
ALS. Academic Libraries Survey
ALSC. Association for Library Service to Children
ALTA. American Library Trustee Association
AMMLA. American Merchant Marine Library Association
AMS. Association Management System
APALA. Asian/Pacific American Librarians Association
ARL. Association of Research Libraries
ARLIS/NA. Art Libraries Society of North America
ARMA. Association of Records Managers and Administrators, *see* ARMA International
ASCLA. Association of Specialized and Cooperative Library Agencies
ASIS. American Society for Information Science
ATLA. American Theological Library Association
ATPA. American Technology Preeminence Act
AWIC. National Agricultural Library, Animal Welfare Information Center

B

BAM. Books-A-Million
BCR. Bibliographic Center for Research
BEA. BookExpo America
BOS. American Booksellers Association, Booksellers Order Service
BPI. Booksellers Publishing, Inc.

C

CACUL. Canadian Association of College and University Libraries
CAIFE. International Federation of Library Associations and Institutions, Committee on Access to Information and Freedom of Expression
CAIS. Canadian Association for Information Science
CALA. Chinese-American Librarians Association
CALS. Continuous Acquisition and Life-Cycle Support (CALS) Information Center
CAPL. Canadian Association of Public Libraries
CASLIS. Canadian Association of Special Libraries and Information Services
CBD. Commerce Business Daily (CBD)

CD-ROM. Compact Disc Read-Only Memory
CDA. Communications Decency Act
CIC. Creative Incentive Coalition
CIEC. Citizens Internet Empowerment Coalition
CIPS. National Archives and Records Administration, Centers Information Processing System
CLA. Canadian Library Association; Catholic Library Association
CLR. Council on Library Resources
CLTA. Canadian Library Trustees Association
CNI. Coalition for Networked Information
COPEARMS. International Federation of Library Associations and Institutions, Coordinating Project for an Electronic Authors' Right Management System
COPPUL. COPPUL (Council of Prairie and Pacific University Libraries)
CORDS. Library of Congress, CORDS (Copyright Office Electronic Registration, Recordation and Deposit System)
COSLA. Chief Officers of State Library Agencies
CPL. Council of Planning Librarians
CSLA. Canadian School Library Association; Church and Synagogue Library Association

D

DFC. Digital Future Coalition
DOE. Education, U.S. Department of

E

ECIP. Library of Congress, ECIP (Electronic Cataloging in Publication)
EDRS. Educational Resources Information Center, ERIC Document Reproduction Service
ELN. Electronic Library Network
ERIC. Educational Resources Information Center
EROMM. European Register of Microform Masters

F

FBB. Government Printing Office (GPO), GPO Access, Federal Bulletin Board
FBIS. Foreign Broadcast Information Service
FDLP. Government Printing Office, Federal Depository Library Program
FEDRIP. National Technical Information Service, FEDRIP (Federal Research in Progress Database)
FIAF. International Federation of Film Archives
FID. International Federation for Information and Documentation
FLICC. Federal Library and Information Center Committee
FLRT. American Library Association, Federal Librarians Round Table
FPC. Federal Publishers Committee
FSCS. Federal-State Cooperative System (FSCS) for Public Library Data
FTC. Federal Trade Commission

G

GIS. Geographic Information Systems
GLIN. Global Legal Information Network
GODORT. American Library Association, Government Documents Round Table
GPO. Government Printing Office

H

HEA. Higher Education Act

I

IALL. International Association of Law Libraries
IAML. International Association of Music Libraries, Archives and Documentation Centres
IASL. International Association of School Librarianship
IATUL. International Association of Technological University Libraries
ICSECA. International Contributions for Scientific, Educational and Cultural Activities

IFLA. International Federation of Library Associations and Institutions
IFRT. American Library Association, Intellectual Freedom Round Table
IIA. Information Industry Association
ILL. Interlibrary loan
IPA. International Publishers Association
IPEDS. Integrated Postsecondary Data System
IRC. Special Libraries Association, Information Resources Center
ISBN. International Standard Book Number
ISIS. ISIS (Integrated System for Information Services)
ISO. International Organization for Standardization
ISSN. International Standard Serial Number

J

JICPA. International Federation of Library Associations and Institutions, Joint Committee on Preservation in Africa

L

LAMA. Library Administration and Management Association
LHRT. American Library Association, Library History Round Table
LIS. Library of Congress, Legislative Information System
LIS. Library/information science
LITA. Library and Information Technology Association
LJ. Library Journal
LOCIS. Library of Congress, Library of Congress Information System
LPS. Government Printing Office (GPO), Library Programs Service
LRRT. American Library Association, Library Research Round Table
LSCA. Library Services and Construction Act
LSP. National Center for Education Statistics, Library Statistics Program
LSTA. Library Services and Technology Act

M

MAGERT. American Library Association, Map and Geography Round Table
Marvel. Library of Congress, Marvel (Machine- Assisted Realization of the Virtual Electronic Library)
MDC. Special Libraries Association, Management Document Collection
MLA. Medical Library Association; Music Library Association
MLC. Michigan Library Consortium

N

NAC. National Audiovisual Center
NAGARA. National Association of Government Archives and Records Administrators
NAILDD. North American Interlibrary Loan and Document Delivery (NAILDD) Project
NAL. National Agricultural Library
NALS. Literacy programs, National Adult Literacy Survey
NARA. National Archives and Records Administration
NAS. National Academy of Sciences
NATDP. National Agricultural Library, National Agricultural Text Digitizing Project
NCES. National Center for Education Statistics
NCLIS. National Commission on Libraries and Information Science
NDLF. National Digital Library Federation
NEH. National Endowment for the Humanities
NFAIS. National Federation of Abstracting and Information Services
NIBW. National Independent Bookstore Week
NII. National Information Infrastructure
NISO. National Information Standards Organization
NLC. National Library of Canada
NLE. National Library of Education
NLM. National Library of Medicine
NLS. National Library Service (NLS) for the Blind and Physically Handicapped

NMRT. American Library Association, New Members Round Table
NPIN. National Parent Information Network
NPR. National Performance Review
NRMM. National Register of Microform Masters (NRMM) RECON Project
NTIS. National Technical Information Service

O

OCLC. Online Computer Library Center
OERI. Education, U.S. Department of, Office of Educational Research and Improvement
OPLIN. Ohio PL information network

P

PBS. Public Broadcasting System
PDQ. United States Information Agency, library programs, Public Diplomacy Query (PDQ) database
PLA. Public Library Association
PRF. Government Printing Office (GPO), Publications Reference File
PSC. Preservation Science Council
PTW. Playing to Win
PW. Publishers Weekly

R

RASD. American Library Association, Reference and Adult Services Division. *See new name* Reference and User Services Association
RBOCs. Regional Bell Operating Companies
RLG. Research Libraries Group

S

SAA. Society of American Archivists
SAN. Standard Address Number
SLA. Special Libraries Association
SLC. Shared Legal Capability

SLED. Statewide Library Electronic Doorway
SLJ. School Library Journal
SRIM. Selected Research in Microfiche
SRKE. Snowe-Rockefeller-Kerry-Exon (SRKE) Amendment
SRRT. American Library Association, Social Responsibilities Round Table
SSP. Society for Scholarly Publishing
STM. Scientific, Technical and Medical Publishers

T

TIIAP. Telecommunications and Information Infrastructure Assistance Program
TLA. Theatre Library Association
TULIP. The University Licensing Program

U

ULC. Urban Libraries Council
UNESCO. United Nations Educational, Scientific, and Cultural Organization
USDA. Agriculture, U.S. Department of
USIA. United States Information Agency
USIS. United States Information Service, *overseas name for* United States Information Agency
USPS. Postal Service, U.S.

W

WINGS. WINGS (Web Interactive Network of Government Service)
WIPO. World Intellectual Property Organization
WNC. World News Connection
WTO. World Trade Organization
WWW. World Wide Web

Y

YALSA. Young Adult Library Services Association

Index of Organizations

Please note that this index includes cross-references to the Subject Index. Many additional organizations can be found in Part 6 under the following headings: Networks, Consortia, and Cooperative Library Organizations; National Library and Information-Industry Associations, United States and Canada; State, Provincial, and Regional Library Associations; State and Provincial Library Agencies; State School Library Media Associations; International Library Associations; Foreign Library Associations; Book Trade Associations, United States and Canada; International and Foreign Book Trade Associations.

A

ACLIN (Access Colorado Library and Information Network), 241
AGRICOLA (Agricultural OnLine Access), 102
Agricultural Network Information Center (AgNIC), 103
Agriculture, U.S. Department of, *see* ISIS; National Agricultural Library
AIDSLINE, 110, 114–115
American Association of Law Libraries (AALL), 669–670
  awards, 379
  intellectual property issues, 280, 281
  research and demonstration, 413–414
American Association of School Librarians (AASL), 673–674
  awards, 380–381
  Competencies for Prospective Teachers and Administrators, 255
  grants, 412
  ICONnect, 145
  Microsoft's Family Technology Nights and, 14
  school library media program guidelines, 253–254
  standards for students' learning, 250
American Booksellers Association (ABA), 163–172
  ABACUS Expanded, 168–169, 170
  American Bookseller, 169–170
  antitrust settlement terms, 27, 30–31, 163, 164
  awards, 166
  Book Buying Study, 163, 170–171
  Booksellers Order Service (BOS), 172
  bookstore promotion, 171–172
  convention and trade exhibit, 29–30, 165–167
  education and professional development, 167–168
  financial survey, 168–169, 170
  membership, 164–165
  publications, 168–170
    Manual on Bookselling..., 168
  research, 170–171
  surveys, 163–164, 170–171
  World Book Day, 172
  World Wide Web site, 164–165
American Booksellers Foundation for Free Expression (ABFFE), 167
American Folklife Center (AFC), 76, 276
American Library Association (ALA), 141–148, 670–672
  Armed Forces Libraries Round Table awards, 381–382
  awards, 142–144, 379–380, 414
  Banned Books Week, 143
  conferences, 405–406
  electronic services, college/university libraries; survey, 410–411

American Library Association (ALA), *(cont.)*
English Language Empowerment Act, opposition to, 276, 278
exhibits, 147
Exhibits Round Table awards, 384
Federal Librarians Round Table (FLRT) awards, 385
Goal 2000, 141, 144–145, 240
Government Documents Round Table (GODORT) awards, 385
grants, 146–147
Intellectual Freedom, Office for (OIF), 11, 143
Intellectual Freedom Round Table (IFRT) awards, 385
intellectual property issues, 281–282
Libraries Change Lives campaign, 146
Library History Round Table (LHRT) awards, 386
Library Research Round Table (LRRT), 386, 405–406
Map and Geography Round Table (MAGERT) awards, 386
MCI Telecommunications and, 145
Microsoft Corporation and, 144–145
National Library Week, 146
New Members Round Table (NMRT) awards, 386
notable books list, 583
online services, 145
personnel, 148
public awareness, 145–146
publishing highlights, 147–150
awards, 387
Reference and Adult Services Division (RASD), *see* Reference and User Services Association
research and demonstration, 412
Social Responsibilities Round Table (SRRT) awards, 388
special projects, 146–147
technology initiatives, *see* subhead Goal 2000
Washington report, 142–143
World Wide Web, 145
See also American Association of School Librarians; American Library Trustee Association; Association of College and Research Libraries; Association for Library Collections and Technical Services; Association for Library Service to Children; Association of Specialized and Cooperative Library Agencies; Library Administration and Management Association; Library and Information Technology Association; Young Adult Library Services Association
American Library Trustee Association (ALTA), 674–675
awards, 381
American Merchant Marine Library Association (AMMLA), 694
American National Standards Institute (ANSI), *see* National Information Standards Organization
American Society for Information Science (ASIS), 694–695
awards, 388–389, 414–415
American Theological Library Association (ATLA), 695–696
Andrews & McMeel, 34
Archivists and Librarians in the History of the Health Sciences, 697
ARMA International (Association of Records Managers and Administrators), 698–699
Art Libraries Society of North America (ARLIS/NA), 699–700
awards, 389
Asian/Pacific American Librarians Association (APALA), 700–701
Association of Academic Health Sciences Library Directors, 703
Association of American Publishers (AAP), 149–162
Administrative Committees, 162
antipiracy program, 157
Campus Copyright Education program, 156
Copyright Committee, 151–152, 156
Digital Committee, 152–153
education program, 153
Enabling Technologies, Committee on, 153–154
Freedom to Read Committee, 154–155
General Publishing Division
See also new name Trade Division
government affairs, 150–151
Higher Education Division, 155–156
highlights, 150
International Division, 156–157
International Freedom to Publish Committee, 157–159

Internet White Paper, 160
legislative activities, 284–291
New Media Committee, 159
NII activities, 152–153, 160
organizational changes, 149–150
Paperback Division, *see new name* Trade Division
Postal Committee, 159, 291
Professional and Scholarly Publishing Division, 159–160
public relations, 151
PUBNET, *see* PUBNET
School Division, 160–161
Trade Division, 161–162
See also Banned Books Week; Legislation affecting publishing
Association Canadienne des Sciences de l'Information, *see* Canadian Association for Information Science
Association of College and Research Libraries (ACRL), 410, 679–681
awards, 383–384, 412
Association for Information and Image Management, 701
Association of Jewish Libraries (AJL), 703–704
awards, 390
Association of Librarians in the History of the Health Sciences, *see new name* Archivists and Librarians in the History of the Health Sciences
Association for Library Collections and Technical Services (ALCTS), 675–677
awards, 382
Association of Library and Information Science Education (ALISE), 702–703
awards, 389–390, 411, 414
Association for Library Service to Children (ALSC), 678–679
awards, 144, 382–383
best books list, 586–587
best films/videos list, 588
best recordings list, 587
best software list, 588
Association Management System (AMS), 215
Association of Research Libraries (ARL), 173–184, 704–706
access and technology, 177
collection services program, 178–179

communications and external relations, 182–183
copyright education initiative, 182
Digital Future Coalition (DFC), 176
diversity, 179
federal relations and information policy program, 175
Global Resources program, 178
governance, 183–184
intellectual property and copyright issues, 176–177, 281–282
Internet access, 176–177
Japan Journal Access Project, 178
Latin American Demonstration Project, 178–179
Management Services, Office of, 180–181
membership activities, 183–184
networking and telecommunications activities, 175, 176–177
preservation activities, 178–179
Research and Development, Office of, 181–182
scholarly communication, 174–175
statistics program, 181
strategic objectives, 173–174
See also Coalition for Networked Information
Association of Specialized and Cooperative Library Agencies (ASCLA), 682–683
awards, 384
Association of Vision Science Librarians, 706

B

Bantam Doubleday Dell, 28
Barnes & Noble, 22, 23–24
Benton Foundation, 407–408
Beta Phi Mu, 707–708
awards, 390
Bibliographic Center for Research (BCR), 243
FirstSearch initiative, 243–244
Bibliographical Society of America, 709
Books-A-Million (BAM), 23, 24, 25
Booksellers Publishing, Inc. (BPI), 168–169
Borders Books & Music, 22, 23

C

CA*net, 222

Canadian Association of College and University Libraries (CACUL); awards, 390
Canadian Association for Information Science (CAIS), 710
Canadian Association of Law Libraries, 221
Canadian Association of Public Libraries (CAPL); awards, 390
Canadian Association of Special Libraries and Information Services (CASLIS), awards, 390
Canadian Library Association (CLA), 222, 710–711
  awards, 390
Canadian Library Trustees Association (CLTA); awards, 390
Canadian School Library Association (CSLA), awards, 391
CANCOPY, 223
CAPCON, 240
Catholic Library Association (CLA), 711–712
Center for the Book, 84–87
  events, 87
  highlights, 84
  outreach, 86–87
  projects, 86
  reading promotion partners, 85
  state centers, 85–86
  themes, 85
  World Wide Web site, 86–87
Center for Education Statistics, *see* National Center for Education Statistics
Chief Officers of State Library Agencies (COSLA), 712–713
Chinese-American Librarians Association (CALA), 713–714
  awards, 391
Church and Synagogue Library Association (CSLA), 714
  awards, 391
Citizens Internet Empowerment Coalition, 210
CLIO, 53
Coalition for Networked Information (CNI), 188
Combs & Combs, 24
Commission on Preservation and Access, *see* Council on Library Resources
Congress, U.S.
  CyberCongress, 265
  See also Legislation affecting information industry; Legislation affecting libraries; Legislation affecting publishing
Continuous Acquisition and Life-Cycle Support (CALS) Information Center, 50
COPPUL (Council of Prairie and Pacific University Libraries), 220, 226
Council on Library Resources (CLR), 185–194
  archiving of digital information, 186
  Brittle Books Program/Permanent Paper, 190
  College Libraries Committee, 192
  Commission on Preservation and Access, 185–194, 391, 716
  digital libraries, 186–187
  distance education, 190
  economics of information, 188–189
  education and training, 194
  grants and contracts, 416–418
  HighWire Press User Survey, 188
  international program, 192–194
  leadership, 189–190
  meetings, 189–190
  networked information, 188, 190
  overview, 185–186
  preservation activities, 190–192, 193–193
  public libraries and innovative technology, 189, 190
  research and development, 408, 416–418
  scanning projects, 187
  Vision 2010, 187
Council of Planning Librarians (CPL), 715
Creative Incentive Coalition (CIC), 284, 285
Crown Books, 23

D

DECPLUS, 62
Digital Future Coalition (DFC), 232, 237, 281
Disney movies, 617
Documentation Abstracts, Inc., 413

E

EdNet Wide Area Network, 224
Education, U.S. Department of (DOE)
  library programs, 302–334
  study of role of school/public libraries in education reform, 302–303

Office of Educational Research and
Improvement (OERI), 122
  online access, 138–140
  priorities, 406
  See also Educational Resources Information Center; Higher Education Act; Library Services and Construction Act
Educational Resources Information Center (ERIC), 116–124
  ACCESS ERIC, 119–120
  Annual Report, 116–117
  AskERIC, 120–121
  budget, FY 1997, 116
  on CD-ROM, 121–122
  database changes, 122
  ERIC Document Reproduction Service (EDRS), 118–119
    top documents ordered from (paper copies), 123–124(table)
  World Wide Web sites, 124
Electronic Library Network (ELN), 226
European Register of Microform Masters (EROMM), 192–193

F

Federal Communications Commission (FCC), 175, 273
  NII/SUPERNet devices, 13
  rule-making proceedings, 289–290
  telecommunications rates, discounted; implementation, 283
Federal Library and Information Center Committee (FLICC), 69, 88–101, 717
  budget and finance, 90
  education programs, 89–90
  FEDLINK, *see* FEDLINK
  highlights, 88
  information technology, 90
  membership/governance, 90
  membership meetings, 88–89
  nominating working group, 90–91
  personnel, 91
  policy working group, 91
  preservation/binding, 91
  publications, 92–93
  reference/public services, 91
  surveys, 92
  working groups, 89–93
Federal Publishers Committee (FPC), 718
Federal-State Cooperative System (FSCS) for Public Library Data, 60–64

Federal Trade Commission (FTC), 27
FEDLINK, 88, 93–99, 262
  accounts receivable, 97
  budget and revenue, 98
  education, 99–101
  executive summary, 99–101
  exhibits program, 95, 101
  financial management, 98
  fiscal operations, 96, 101
  Internet/technology program, 94–95
  member services, 97
  membership meeting, 100
  OCLC network activity, 93–94
  procurement program, 95, 96
  publications, 100
  strategic reviews, 99
  SYMIN system activities, 98–99
  training, 95
  transfer-pay accounts payable services, 97–98
  vendor services, 96
  working groups, 100
  World Wide Web site, 100
Fireside and Touchstone, 34
Foreign Broadcast Information Service (FBIS), 48–49
Fund for America's Libraries, 146

G

Gale Research Company; awards, 391
Geographic Information Systems (GIS), 78
Global Legal Information Network (GLIN), 78
Government Printing Office (GPO), 125–132
  background, 258
  bookstores, 128
  catalogs, 128–129
  challenges, 259, 261–264
  Commerce Business Daily (CBD), 131
  Congressional Record, online, 262, 264
  Electronic Information Access Enhancement Act, 262
  electronic information technology initiatives/studies, 264–265, 274, 278
  Federal Depository Library Program (FDLP), 126–127, 132, 266
    World Wide Web page, 132
  Federal Register, online, 262, 264
  GPO Access, 126–127, 130, 132, 262, 264
    Federal Bulletin Board (FBB), 131–132
    GPRA and, 260–261

Government Printing Office (GPO), *(cont.)*
  information access, 130–131
  Internet and, 130
  library programs, 125–126
  Library Programs Service (LPS), 127
  mission, 259
  NPR and, 259–260
  NTIS and, 262
  publications, 129–130
  Publications Reference File (PRF), 129
  recent changes, 258–268
  sales, 128
  standards, 40
  Superintendent of Documents, 125
  workforce, 260

H

HarperCollins, 28
Health Communications, 34
HealthSTAR, 110
Houghton Mifflin, 27, 30, 163

I

ICONnect, 145
IFLANET, 200
ILLINET, 244
INCOLSA, 243
Information Industry Association (IIA), 718–719
Institute of Museum and Library Services, 4, 37, 38, 142, 276, 303, 416
Integrated Postsecondary Data System (IPEDS), 64–65
International Association of Agricultural Information Specialists, 759
International Association of Law Libraries (IALL), 759
International Association of Music Libraries, Archives and Documentation Centres (IAML), 760
International Association of School Librarianship (IASL), 761
International Association of Technological University Libraries (IATUL), 761–762
International Contributions for Scientific, Educational and Cultural Activities (ICSECA), 41
International Council on Archives, 762

International Federation of Film Archives (FIAF), 764
International Federation for Information and Documentation (FID), 763
International Federation of Library Associations and Institutions (IFLA), 41, 197–203, 765
  awards and grants, 202
  Committee on Access to Information and Freedom of Expression (CAIFE), 198
  conferences, 197–198, 199, 202
  Coordinating Project for an Electronic Authors' Right Management System (COPEARMS), 198
  future prospects, 203
  Internet services, 200, 202–203
  Joint Committee on Preservation in Africa (JICPA), 198–199
  Medium Term Program, 203
  publications, 202–203
  World Wide Web, 198, 201(tables), 202
  See also IFLANET
International Organization for Standardization (ISO), 766
International Publishers Association (IPA), 219
Internet, 167
  AAP activities, 160
  ABA activities, 164, 165
  AIDS/HIV databases, 110, 114–115
  ARL and, 176–177
  bibliography for librarians, 532–533
  Braille access, 324
  in Canada, 221–222, 223
  copyright issues, 232–233
  FEDLINK program, 94–95
  government information, 130
  GPO Access, 132
  Grateful Med, 110–111
  IFLA and, 200, 202
  IFLANET, 200
  "Internet-worked Librarianship" initiative, 241
  KidsConnect, 145
  LC on, 76–77, 265
  library networking and cooperation, 239–245
  LJ news report, 3–8
  NARA and, 266
  NCES releases, 73
  NCLIS and, 39–40
  NLE, 138–140

Index of Organizations / 811

NLM programs, 111–112
NTIS, 47
OERI, 138–139
 as placement source, 337–338
 privacy legislation, 288–289
 public libraries and, 3–8, 408–409
 PW news report, 21
 regional networks and, 240–241
 security measures, 47
 SLA and, 212, 214–215
 SLED, 333
 TEKTRAN, 108
 See also Citizens Internet Empowerment Coalition
ISBN, *see* International Standard Book Number
ISIS (Integrated System for Information Services), 103

K

W.K. Kellogg Foundation, 406–408
Knopf, 34

L

Latin American Register of Microform Masters, 193
Hugh Lauter Levin Associates, 27, 30, 163
Library Administration and Management Association (LAMA), 683–684
 awards, 385–386
Library of Congress (LC), 74–83
 affirmative action, 82–83
 American Folklife Center (AFC), 76, 276
 arrearages, processing of, 75
 audit, 262–263
 background, 258
 bibliographic databases, 265
 budget, 258, 260
 Center for the Book, 84–87
 challenges, 259, 261–264
 Civilization magazine, 83
 collections, 78–79
 Copyright Office, 76, 263
 CORDS (Copyright Office Electronic Registration, Recordation and Deposit System), 78
 ECIP (Electronic Cataloging in Publication), 78
 electronic access, 76–77

 electronic information technology initiatives, 265–266
 exhibitions, 80–81
 films, 81
 Government Accounting Office and, 262–263
 GPRA and, 260–261
 human resources, 82–83
 Internet access, 76–77, 265
 Jefferson Building, 267
 Legislative Information System (LIS), 265
 Librarian of Congress, *see* Billington, James H.
 LOCIS (Library of Congress Information System), 76
 Marvel (Machine-Assisted Realization of the Virtual Electronic Library), 265
 mission, 259
 NPR and, 259–260
 Patent and Trademark Office and, 263
 preservation activities, 82
 publications, 79–80
 recent changes, 258–268
 restoration/renovation activities, 82
 security measures, 79
 services, 74–76
 telephone numbers, 83
 THOMAS, *see* THOMAS
 See also Center for the Book; National Digital Library Program
Library and Information Technology Association (LITA), 685–687
 awards, 386
LibraryNet, 221
Lutheran Church Library Association, 719–720

M

MAPLIN, 224
MCI Telecommunications Corporation
 ALA and, 145
Medical Library Association (MLA), 720–721
 awards, 391–392, 414
 intellectual property issues, 281–282
MEDLINE, 110, 111, 113, 115
Michigan Library Consortium (MLC), 240
Microsoft Canada, 221
Microsoft Corporation
 ALA and, 144–145, 241
 Family Technology Nights, 14

MONTICELLO, 243
Musicland, 25
Music Library Association (MLA), 721–723

N

National Academy of Sciences (NAS), 112
National Agricultural Library (NAL), 102–109
    ALF (Agricultural Library Forum) discontinued, 104–105
    Animal Welfare Information Center (AWIC), 106
    animals, laboratory, 107
    CALS (Current Awareness Literature Service), 104
    collections, 105
    computer training program, 109
    customer service, 106
    document delivery, 105, 106
    electronic media center, 107
    exhibits, 105
    Latin American project, 104
    National Agricultural Text Digitizing Project (NATDP), 104
    networks and networking, 103
    NIH and, 107
    nutrition project, 107
    preservation, 105–106
    publications, 107
    risk assessment, 107
    Soros intern program, 108
    terrestrial database, 108
    World Wide Web, 102
    See also AGRICOLA; Agricultural Network Information Center; ISIS
National Archives and Records Administration (NARA), 52–56
    administration, 56
    ARCHIVES II, 53, 266
    background, 258
    budget, 258, 260
    Centers Information Processing System (CIPS), 56
    challenges, 259, 261–264
    CLIO, 53
    customer service, 55–56
    electronic access, 55
    electronic information technology initiatives, 266
    Fax-on-Demand, 53
    Federal Register online, 54–55
    Government Accounting Office and, 263
    GPRA and, 260–261
    Internet access, 266
    mission, 259
    NPR and, 259–260
    presidential libraries, 54
    recent changes, 258–268
    strategic directions, 52–53, 264
    U.S. District Court and, 263–264
    the White House and, 264
National Assessment of Education Progress, 13
National Association of Government Archives and Records Administrators (NAGARA), 723–724
National Association of Secondary School Principals, 9
National Association to Promote Library Services to the Spanish Speaking, *see* REFORMA
National Audiovisual Center (NAC), 44–45
National Center for Education Statistics (NCES)
    academic library survey, *see* Academic Libraries Survey
    data files released on computer diskette, 73
    DECPLUS, 62
    electronic releases, 73
    government libraries, 409–410
    Internet and, 73
    Library Statistics Program (LSP), 40–41, 60–73
        academic libraries, 431–432
        children and young adults, surveys on, 67–68
        children's services, 63–64, 433–434
        collections, 63
        income/expenditures, 63
        interlibrary loan, 63
        library cooperatives, 69
        plans for, 70–71
        public library survey, 60–64, 430–434
        school library media centers, 65–66, 432–433
        staffing, 63
        state library agency survey, 69, 420–425
        young adults, 433–434
    publications, 71–73
National Commission on Libraries and Information Science (NCLIS), 37–42
    anniversary, 41–42
    highlights, 37–38

international activities, 41
legislative activities, 38–39
library statistics, 40–41
networked environment, 39–40
publications, 39
National Digital Library Federation (NDLF), 77, 186
 See also THOMAS
National Endowment for the Humanities (NEH), 293–301
 applications, 294–295
 challenge grants, 298
 education programs, 296
 enterprise, 298
 federal/state partnerships, 298–301
 fellowships and stipends, 297
 grantmaking programs, 295–296
 preservation and access, 295–296
 public programs, 295
 research programs, 296–297
 seminars and institutes, 297
National Federation of Abstracting and Information Services (NFAIS), 724–725
National Information Standards Organization (NISO), 725
 Z39 standards, 791–793
National Library of Canada (NLC), 198, 220
National Library of Education (NLE), 133–140
 activities, 135–136
 collections, 136–137
 functions, 134–135
 future plans, 136
 history, 133–134
 interlibrary loan, 137
 Internet access, 138–140
 mission, 133
 organizational structure, 133
 publications, 136
 Technology Resources Center, 137–138
 telephone numbers, 140
 themes and goals, 135
National Library of Medicine (NLM), 110–115
 AIDS/HIV online databases, 110, 114–115
 gene map, 112–113
 Grateful Med; Internet Grateful Med, 110–111
 Internet-based programs, 111–112
 National Center for Biotechnology Information, 112–113
 online network, 111

outreach program, 113–115
 statistics, selected, 113(table)
 telemedicine, 112
 Visible Human project, 112
 World Wide Web-based programs, 111–112
 See also MEDLINE
National Library Service (NLS) for the Blind and Physically Handicapped, 75–76
National Museum of Women in the Arts, 310–311
National Parent Information Network (NPIN), 121
National Performance Review (NPR), 259–260
National Register of Microform Masters (NRMM) RECON Project, 182
National Technical Information Service (NTIS), 43–51
 Alerts, 49
 contact numbers, 51
 customer services, 51
 database, 47–48
 Fax Direct, 50–51
 FEDRIP (Federal Research in Progress Database), 48
 FedWorld, 45
 government contributors, 44
 GPO and, 262
 National Audiovisual Center (NAC), 44–45
 Order Now Catalog on CD-ROM, 46–47
 Order Now online, 47
  security measures, 47
 published searches, 49–50
 World Wide Web, 46
 worldwide source contributors, 44
 See also Continuous Acquisition and Life-cycle Support (CALS) Information Center; World News Connection
North American Interlibrary Loan and Document Delivery (NAILDD) Project, 177

O

OCLC (Online Computer Library Center)
 equipment upgrade, 241
 FEDLINK involvement, 93–94
 research and demonstration, 418–419
 See also Internet
Ohio PL information network (OPLIN), 4
OhioLINK, 244, 247n26

OHIONET, 240
Online Computer Library Center, *see* OCLC

P

PALINET, 240
Penguin USA, 27, 31, 34, 163
PORTALS project, 311
Postal Service, U.S. (USPS), 159
  Kiosk Project, 279
  See also Association of American Publishers, Postal Committee
PreMEDLINE, 110
Preservation Science Council (PSC), 190–191
Public Broadcasting System (PBS) tie-in books, 604
Public Library Association (PLA), 687–690
  awards, 386–387
  conference, 409
PUBNET, 160, 164

R

Random House, 18–19, 27, 31, 34, 163
Reference and User Services Association, 690–691
  awards, 387–388
REFORMA, 726
Regional Bell Operating Companies (RBOCs), 289–290
Research Libraries Group Inc. (RLG), 727
Rutledge Hill Press, 27, 31, 163

S

K.G. Saur; awards, 392
Schoolnet, 221
Scientific, Technical and Medical (STM) Publishers, International Group, 219
Shared Legal Capability (SLC), 176
Simon & Schuster, 28, 34
Society of American Archivists (SAA), 729
  awards, 392–393
Society for Scholarly Publishing (SSP), 728
SOLINET, 240, 243, 244
Special Libraries Association (SLA), 205–215, 730–731
  awards, 393, 413
  computer services, 214–215
  conferences, 205, 206, 211–212, 213
  finance and administration, 213–214
  fund development, 212–213
  government relations, 209–210
  grants, 207–208
  Information Resources Center (IRC), 212
  intellectual property issues, 281–282
  Internet and, 212, 214–215
  Management Document Collection (MDC), 212
  membership development, 207–208, 209, 210–211
  professional development, 205–206
  public relations, 206–207, 211
  publications, 208–209
  research and grants, 207–208
  salary survey, 208
  World Wide Web site, 206–207
Statewide Library Electronic Doorway (SLED), 333
Stentor, 221, 222
St. Martin's Press, 27, 28, 31, 163

T

TEKTRAN, 108
Telecommunications and Information Infrastructure Assistance Program (TIIAP), 276
Theatre Library Association (TLA), 731
THOMAS, 77–78, 265
Time Warner, 34

U

United Nations Educational, Scientific, and Cultural Organization (UNESCO) survey, 520–521
United States Information Agency (USIA), 57–59
  book programs, 59
  current programs, 58
  library programs
    history of, 57–58
    Library Fellows program, 147
    Public Diplomacy Query (PDQ) database, 58
United States Information Service (USIS), *see* United States Information Agency
Urban Libraries Council (ULC), 732–733

W

WINGS (Web Interactive Network of Government Services), 279
WISCAT, 333–334
World Intellectual Property Organization (WIPO), 142, 199–200, 229–230, 236–237, 281, 285–286
World News Connection (WNC), 48–49
World Wide Web, 242–243
  ABA site, 164–165
  ALA site, 145
  in Canada, 220
  Center for the Book, 86–87
  DOE sites, 139–140
  ERIC sites, 124
  FEDLINK, 100
  GPO Federal Depository Library Program, 132
  IFLA and, 198, 200, 201(table), 202
  library service networks, 244(table)
  NAL site, 102
  NLM site, 111–112
  NTIS site, 46
  PORTALS project, 311
  regional networks and, 241, 245
  SLA site, 206–207
  THOMAS, 265
  WINGS, 279

Y

Young Adult Library Services Association (YALSA), 413, 692–693
  awards, 388
  best books list, 584–585
    for reluctant readers, 589–590

Subject Index

Please note that many cross-references refer to entries listed in the Index of Organizations

A

A Time to Kill (Grisham), 33
ABACUS Expanded, 168–169, 170
Absolute Power (Baldacci), 31
Academic books, prices and price indexes
  British averages, 495–497(table)
  German averages, 499(table)
  North American averages, 484–485(table)
  U.S. college books, averages, 486–487(table)
  See also Association of American Publishers, Professional and Scholarly Publishing Division; Society for Scholarly Publishing
Academic libraries, *see* Academic Libraries Survey; College and research libraries
Academic Libraries Survey (ALS), 64–65
ACLU v. *Reno*, 283
Acquisitions
  expenditures, 435–443
    academic libraries, 438–439(table)
    government libraries, 442–443(table)
    public libraries, 436–437(table)
    special libraries, 440–441(table)
  prices and price indexes for major components, 446(table), 456(table)
  See also Association of Research Libraries, collection services program *and* specific types of libraries, i.e., Public libraries
Adams, Scott, 592
Adults, services for
  bibliography for librarians, 536
  See also Literacy programs; Reference and User Services Association; Senior citizens, library services for
Affirmative action, 82–83
Africa, 198–199

Agencies, library, *see* Library associations and agencies
Agricultural libraries, *see* International Association of Agricultural Information Specialists; National Agricultural Library
AIDS/HIV information services, 45
  databases, 110, 114–115
Alabama
  networks and cooperative library organizations, 639
  school library media associations, 651
Alaska
  networks and cooperative library organizations, 639
  SLED, 333
Alliance for Community Media, 155
Almanacs, bestselling, 614–615
Almost Adam (Popescu), 605–606
"America Reads" program, 10
American Bookseller (AB), 169–170
American Booksellers Book of the Year (ABBY), 166
American Library Association v. *Department of Justice*, 283
American Technology Preeminence Act (ATPA), 44
Americana, 79
Anderson, Clyde, 25
Animal welfare, laboratory animals, 107–108
Antiterrorism Act of 1996, 287
Applebaum, Irwyn, 20, 21
Applebaum, Stuart, 28
Archives
  acquisition expenditures
    academic libraries, 438–439(table)
    government libraries, 442–443(table)
    public libraries, 437–438(table)
    special libraries, 440–441(table)

817

Archives, *(cont.)*
  digital, 186
  electronic records, 279
  preservation microfilming, 179
  See also Archivists and Librarians in the History of the Health Sciences; International Council on Archives; National Archives and Records Administration; National Association of Government Archives and Records Administrators; Society of American Archivists
Arizona
  networks and cooperative library organizations, 639
  school library media associations, 751
Arkansas
  networks and cooperative library organizations, 639–640
  school library media associations, 751
Armstrong et al. v. *Executive Office of the President*, 279
Aronica, Lou, 17, 19
Art libraries, 203
Associations, *see* Book trade, associations; Information industry, associations; Library associations and agencies; and names of specific associations
Atlases, bestselling, 614–615
Audiocassettes, prices and price indexes, 448(table), 493–494
  averages, 490(table)
Audiovisual materials
  acquisition expenditures
    academic libraries, 438–439(table)
    government libraries, 442–443(table)
    public libraries, 436–437(table)
    special libraries, 440–441(table)
  bibliography for librarians, 534
  prices and price indexes; sound recordings, 458(table)
  recordings for children, notable, 587
  See also Association of Visual Science Librarians; CD-ROM (Compact Disc Read-Only Memory), prices and price indexes; International Federation of Film Archives; National Audiovisual Center; Sound recordings; Theatre Library Association; Videocassettes, prices and price indexes
Authors
  electronic rights, 198

  monetary advances, 17–18
  online chats, 165
Automation, *see* Computers; Information technology; Networks and networking
The Awakening Heart (Eadie), 601
Awards
  AALL, 379
  AASL, 380–381
  ABA, 166
  ABBY, 166
  ACRL, 383–384, 412
  AJL, 390
  ALA, 142–144, 379–380, 381–382, 384, 387, 414, 583
  ALCTS, 382
  ALISE, 389–390, 411, 414
  alphabetical listing, 394–402
  ALSC, 144, 382–383
  ALTA, 381
  ARLIS/NA, 389
  ASCLA, 384
  ASIS, 388–389, 414–415
  Belpre, Pura, 144
  Beta Phi Mu, 390
  CACUL, 390
  CALA, 391
  CAPL, 390
  CASLIS, 390
  CLA, 390
  CLTA, 390
  CSLA, 391
  FLRT, 385
  Gale Research Company, 391
  GODORT, 385
  IFLA, 202
  IFRT, 385
  LAMA, 385–386
  Latino, 144
  LHRT, 386
  library scholarship and award recipients, 379–402
  LITA, 386
  literary, 629–635
  MAGERT, 386
  MLA, 391–392, 414
  NMRT, 386
  PLA, 386–387
  Reference and User Services Association, 387–388
  for research, 411–414
  SAA, 392–393
  K.G. Saur, 392

SLA, 393, 413
SRRT, 388
YALSA, 388
See also Books, best books; Grants *and* names of specific awards *or* organizations

B

Bad as I Wanna Be (Rodman), 33, 594, 605
Baldacci, David, 31
Banned Books Week, 143, 154–155, 167
Beijing International Book Fair, 216–217
Bestsellers, 591–628
 almanacs, atlases, annuals, 614–615
 children's books, 166, 617–628
  hardcover, 617–624
  paperbacks, 624–628
 fiction, 596–597, 605–606
  hardcover, 591–600
  mass market, 614–615
 nonfiction, 32, 592, 597
  paperback, 607, 608–614
 PW lists, 593, 595–600
 PW news report, 31–35
 religious, 594, 599
 sports, 605
Between Hope and History (Clinton), 600
Bibliographic databases, *see* CD-ROM; Educational Resources Information Center; OCLC
Bibliographic description, standards for, *see* National Information Standards Organization
Bibliographic instruction
 bibliography for librarians, 529
 See also Education for librarians and librarianship; Library/information science (LIS) education
Bibliographic utilities, *see* Networks and networking; OCLC; Research Libraries Group
Bibliography for librarians, 527–538
 academic libraries, 528
 bibliographic instruction, 529
 CD-ROM, 529
 children's/young adult services/materials, 530
 collection development, 530
 copyright, 530
 customer service, 530–531
 document delivery, 532

education for librarianship, 531
electronic libraries, 531
fund-raising, 531
general works, 527–528
government documents, 531–532
history of libraries, 534
intellectual freedom, 532
interlibrary loan, 532
Internet, 532–533
librarians and librarianship, 533
library automation, 533
library buildings/space planning, 533–534
nonprint materials, 534
online searching, 534
periodicals/periodical indexes, 537–538
preservation, 534–535
public librarians, 535
public services, 535
reference and readers' advisory, 535–536
school libraries/media centers, 536
serials, 536
services, evaluation of, 531
special groups, services for, 536–537
special libraries, 537
technical services, 537
Billington, James H., 199, 258
Blind, library services for the
 bibliography for librarians, 536–537
 Canadian, 221
 Internet access, braille, 324
 LSCA funding, 322, 323(table), 324
 See also National Library Service (NLS) for the Blind and Physically Handicapped
Blind, publishing for the; copyright exemption, 284
Bologna Children's Book Fair, 216
Book exports, *see* Books, exports and imports; United States, book exports
Book fairs, 216–219
 See also Book trade, calendar of events, *and* names of specific countries or fairs
Book imports, *see* Books, exports and imports; United States, book imports
Book review media statistics, 524(table)
The Book of Ruth (Hamilton), 18
Book sales, 163–164, 512–513
 AAP annual survey, statistics from, 512–513
 estimated book publishing industry sales, 513(table)

Book sales, *(cont.)*
  ABA studies, 170–171
  ABACUS Expanded, 168–169, 170
  bestsellers, *see* Bestsellers
  mall stores, 23
  Manual on Bookselling..., 168
  PW news report, 16–21
  U.S. trade, 514–519
  See also Acquisitions, expenditures; American Booksellers Association, Booksellers Order Service; Bestsellers; Books; Bookstores; Book trade; Frankfurt Book Fair; PUBNET
Book stores, *see* Bookstores
Book trade
  associations, 29, 779–782
    international and foreign, 783–789
  calendar of events, 795–800
  foreign/domestic, 519
  international, 216
  research and statistics, 479–504
  U.S., 514–519
  See also Bestsellers; Book sales; Books; Foreign book trade; Frankfurt Book Fair; Publishers and publishing *and* names of specific associations
BookExpo America (BEA), 29–30, 164, 165–167, 171
Books
  acquisition expenditures
    academic libraries, 438–439(table)
    government libraries, 442–443(table)
    public libraries, 436–437(table)
    special libraries, 440–441(table)
  banned, *see* Censorship
  best books
    adult, 583
    bestsellers, *see* Bestsellers
    children's, 586–587
    young adult, 584–585
  exports and imports
    U.S. book exports, 514(table)
    U.S. book exports to principal countries, 515(table)
    U.S. book imports, 508(table), 516(table), 516–518
    U.S. book imports from principal countries, 517(table)
    U.S. book industry shipments compared to exports, 518(table)
    U.S. book trade, 518(table)

    See also United States, book exports *or* book imports
  hardcover, *see* Hardcover books
  horror genre for children, 617
  imports, *see* subhead exports and imports; United States, book imports
  ISBN, *see* International Standard Book Number
  miniature, *see* Miniature Book Society, Inc.
  paperback, *see* Paperback books
  preservation and conservation, *see* Preservation
  prices and price indexes, 492–493, 507, 509
    academic books, *see* Academic books, prices and price indexes
    hardcover books, *see* Hardcover books, prices and price indexes
    library acquisitions, 457(table), 458(table)
    paperback books, *see* Paperback books, prices and price indexes
    See also names of specific countries, e.g., Germany
  scholarly, *see* Academic books, prices and price indexes; Association of American Publishers, Professional and Scholarly Publishing Division
  school library media centers
    expenditures, *see* School library media centers and services, expenditures for resources
  title output, 505–511
    American book title production, 506(table)
    by format/category, 505
    international, 520, 521(table)
  translation publishing
    translations into English, 508(table)
  See also American Booksellers Association; Awards; Book sales; Bookstores; Center for the Book, *and* names of specific countries, e.g., Great Britain
Booksellers and bookselling, *see* American Booksellers Association; Association of American Publishers; Book fairs; Book sales; Bookstores; Frankfurt Book Fair
Bookstores
  chain "superstores", 19–20, 22–27
  government, 128
  mall stores, 23

National Independent Bookstore Week
(NIBW), 171–172
PW news report, 19–20, 22–27
retail space versus sales growth, 22
U.S. and Canada, 522, 523(table)
See also Book Industry Systems Advisory Committee; Book sales; Multimedia; National Independent Bookstore Week
Bosco, Joseph, 602
Braille, online access in, 324
Brazil, 194
Breathnach, Sarah Ban, 592
Brown v. *Woodland Unified School District*
Budgets
 LC, 258, 260
 NARA, 258, 260
 public libraries and Internet costs, 3–8, 74
 See also Funding for libraries
Bush, George, 263–264
George Bush Presidential Library and Museum, 54
Butler, Brett, 32, 604

C

Caldecott Medal, 143
Calendar of events, 795–800
California
 Braille, online access in, 324
 LJ report, 4
 networks and cooperative library organizations, 640–641
 school library media services associations, 751
 SLJ news report, 12
Canada, 194, 220–228
 associations
  book trade, 779–782
  library, 743–745, 750
 bookstores, 522, 523(table)
 Depository Services Program, 222
 Goods and Services Tax, 222
 information access and rights, 221–222
 information technology, 220–221
 intellectual property, 222–223
 libraries
  academic, 225–226
  number of, 427–438
  public, 225
  school library resource centers, 227
  special, 226–227

trends, 228
networks and cooperative library organizations, 666–668
provincial outlook, 223–225
See also Canadian Association for Information Science; Canadian Library Association; Information Highway Advisory Council; National Library of Canada
CAREERS Act (Consolidated and Reformed Education, Employment, and Rehabilitation Systems Act)
Carlin, John W., 52
Andrew Carnegie Medal, 144
Cataloging and classification
 Electronic Cataloging in Publication (ECIP) project, 78
 See also Cooperative Cataloging Council; National Coordinated Cataloging Program
CD-ROM (Compact Disc Read-Only Memory)
 bibliography for librarians, 529
 NTIS Order Now catalog, 46–47
 prices and price indexes, 448(table), 493–494
  academic libraries, 458(table), 459(table)
  averages, 491(table)
 in publishing, 159, 221
 See also Electronics; Publishers and publishing, electronics
The Celestine Prophecy (Redfield), 591, 592
Censorship
 Banned Books Week, 143, 154–155, 167
 Canadian issues, 222
 on the Internet, 210
 Khawar v. *Globe International*, 155
 legislation, 286
 See also Association of American Publishers, Freedom to Read Committee *or* International Freedom to Publish Committee
Chambliss, 29–30
Child Pornography Prevention Act of 1996, 286
Children and young adults
 bibliography for librarians, 530
 book fairs, 216
 children's books, 586–587
  awards, 143–144, 166
  bestsellers, 617–628
 children's films/video, notable, 588

Children and young adults, *(cont.)*
  children's recordings, notable, 587
  children's software, notable, 588
  library services for
    NCES library statistics surveys, 63–64, 67–68, 431
    NCES survey, 433–434
    See also American Library Association, Young Adult Services Division; Association for Library Service for Children; Young Adult Library Services Association; Young adults, services for
  young adults
    notable books for, 584–585
    See also Young adults, services for
China, People's Republic of, 193
  Beijing conference, 197–198, 202
  See also Beijing International Book Fair
The Choice (Woodward), 602
Civic networks, 190
Civilization..., 83
Clark, Mary Higgins, 592
Clinton, Bill, 600
  See also Clinton-Gore administration
Clinton-Gore administration, 259–260
  "America Reads" program, 10
  encryption, 288
  funding for libraries, 275
  See also National Information Infrastructure
Cochran, Johnnie, 32, 601–602
Collection development
  ARL, 178–179
  bibliography for librarians, 530
  Library of Congress, 78–79
  NAL, 105
  NLE, 136–137
  NLM, 113
  public libraries; NCES library statistics survey, 63
  school library media programs, 251–252
  state library agencies, 423
College and research libraries, 203
  acquisition expenditures, 438–439(table)
  additions and renovations, *see* Library buildings
  bibliography for librarians, 528
  Canadian, 225–226
  CLR/CPA activities, 192
  construction, *see* Library buildings

electronic services, ALA survey of, 410–411
HEA grants, *see* College Library Resources Program; Improving Access to Research Library Resources; Strengthening Research Library Resources Program
NCES survey, 431–432
prices and price indexes, 451–459
  books and periodicals, 457(table), 458(table)
  budget composition of operations, 455(table)
  major components, 456(table)
  non-print media/electronic services, 459(table)
  personnel compensation, 457(table)
research on, 410–411
statistics, 41
See also Academic Libraries Survey; Association of College and Research Libraries; Association of Research Libraries; Council on Library Resources; Higher education
Colorado
  networks and cooperative library organizations, 641–642
  school library media associations, 751
  as TIIAP grant recipient, 276
Commerce Business Daily (CBD), 131
Communications Act, 273
Communications Decency Act of 1996 (CDA), 11–12, 143, 154, 273, 282–283
Computer software
  children's; notable, 588
Computers
  copyright and copyright law, *see* Copyright and copyright law, databases and software
  library automation; bibliography for librarians, 533
  software, *see* Computer software
  telecommunications and, 242–243
  See also Automation; CD-ROM; Computer software; High Performance Computing Act; Information technology; National Information Infrastructure; Networks and networking
Conferences and seminars
  AAP, 156–157, 160
  ALA, 161

ARL, 175, 183–184
Beijing, 197–198, 202
BookExpo America (BEA), 29–30, 164, 165–167, 171
Canadian, 220
CLR/CPA, 189–190
CONFU, 233–235
fair use, 200, 233–235, 286
FLICC, 100
LRRT, 405–406
NEH, 297
PLA, 409
SLA, 205, 206, 211, 213
Vologda, 199
WIPO, 199–200, 236–237, 285–286
See also as subhead, i.e., American Library Association, conferences
Congressional Record, online, 262, 264
Connecticut
  LJ report, 4
  networks and cooperative library organizations, 642–643
Conservation and preservation, *see* Preservation
Copyright and copyright law
  AAP activities, 151–152, 156
  anti-circumvention, 233
  ARL activities, 175, 176–177
  bibliography for librarians, 530
  blind, exemption for the, 284
  Canadian issues, 223
  clarifications legislation, 285
  copyright management information, 233
  coursepacks, 152
  digital material, 281
  distance education, 232
  education initiative, 182
  electronics issues, 199–200
  fair use, 176, 200, 232, 238n10, 274, 280–281, 286
    CONFU, 233–235
  GATT Uruguay Round Agreements Act, 76
  guidelines, proposed, 235–236
  IITF white paper, 234
  issues, in 1996, 229–238
  LC Copyright Office, 76, 78, 263
  legislation, 274
  online privacy, 289–290
  NII and, 177, 231–233, 284
  online service provider liability, 233
  piracy, 157
  term extension, 230–231, 284–285

WIPO activities, 199, 229–230
  See also Copyright Protection Act; Copyright Treaty; Generalized System of Preferences (GSP) trade program
Copyright Protection Act, 281
Copyright Treaty, 281
Coursepacks, 152
Customer service; bibliography for librarians, 531
Cyberspace
  intellectual property, 152–153
  users' rights, 145

D

Darden, Christopher, 32, 602
Database Treaty, 281
Databases
  acquisition expenditures
    academic libraries, 438–439(table)
    government libraries, 442–443(table)
    public libraries, 436–437(table)
    special libraries, 440–441(table)
  copyright issues, 235–236
  ERIC, 118, 122
  FEDRIP, 48
  fees, *see subhead* acquisition expenditures
  GenBank, 112–113
  HIV/AIDS-related, 114–115
  NTIS, 47–48
  PDQ, 58
  services, pricing for, 244
  TEKTRAN, 108
  terrestrial, 108–109
  THOMAS, 77–78
  See also Automation; Bibliographic databases; CD-ROM; Copyright and copyright law, databases and software; Database Treaty; Networks and networking *and* names of databases
Deacidification, 190
  See also Preservation
Deaf, library services to the, 324
The Deep End of the Ocean (Mitchard), 31, 32, 592
Delaware
  networks and cooperative library organizations, 643
  school library media associations, 751–752
Digital images, 235
Digital libraries, 186–187
  archiving, 186

Digital libraries, *(cont.)*
  IFLA, 203
  projects, 187
  research on, 407–408
  scanning, 187
  Vision 2010 project, 187
  See also Electronics; National Digital Library (NDL) Program; Text digitizing, NATDP
Disabled Americans
  services for; bibliography for librarians, 536–537
  See also Blind, library services for the; Blind, publishing for the; Handicapped, library services for the
Disney, Anthea, 17–18, 19, 20
Distance learning, 190, 205, 227–228, 232, 235
District of Columbia
  networks and cooperative library organizations, 643–644
  school library media associations, 752
  Services to the Deaf Community, 324
Document delivery, *see* Interlibrary loan (ILL)/document delivery
Duong Thu Huong, 158

E

Eadie, Betty, 601
Educate America Act, 141, 291
Education for booksellers, 167–168
Education for librarians and librarianship
  accredited master's programs, 373–374
  bibliography for librarians, 531
  Canadian, 227–228
  distance education, 190, 205, 227–228, 232
  HEA, 304–305
  honor society, *see* Beta Phi Mu
  IFLA's role, 203
  library media education institutions, 255
  library schools, 366
  qualifications for federal positions, 91
  SLA activities, 205–206, 212–212
  technical/support training, 243
    online, 246n9
  See also ARMA International; Association for Library and Information Science Education; Library Education and Human Resource Development Program; Library Research and Demonstration Program; Library/information science (LIS) education; Scholarships and fellowships; United States Information Agency
Education for publishers, 153
Education reform
  See also National Library of Education
Egen, Maureen, 16
The elderly, *see* Senior citizens, library services for
Electronic Freedom of Information Act Amendments, 279
Electronic Information Access Enhancement Act, *see* Government Printing Office, GPO Access
Electronic libraries
  bibliography for librarians, 531
  NAL electronic media center, 107
  See also Federal depository libraries
Electronic services; price indexes, academic libraries, 459(table)
Electronics
  fair use, 232, 238n10
  federal depository libraries, 126
  licensing considerations, 174
  publishing, 73, 153–154
  See also National Digital Library Program; Text digitizing, NATDP
Elementary and Secondary Education Act, 9, 290, 291
Emotional Intelligence (Goleman), 597–598
Employment opportunities, *see* International personnel exchanges for librarians; Placement
Encryption, 288
English Language Empowerment Act, 276, 278
Esquival, Laura, 606
Europe
  See also United States Information Agency, *and* names of specific countries, e.g., Germany
Exchange programs, *see* International personnel exchanges for librarians

F

Fair Pay Act, 278
Faxes
  ABA Fax-on-Demand, 165
  NARA Fax-on-Demand, 53
  NTIS Fax Direct, 50–51

Federal depository libraries, 40, 125–127, 132, 266
  Electronic Federal Depository Library Program (FDLP), 210, 265, 274, 278–279
Federal employment information sources, 351–353
Federal Library Survey, 68–69
Federal Register online, 54–55, 262, 264
Fedorko, Paul, 19, 20
Fein, Ellen, 32, 33
Feinstein, Dianne, 287
Feist v. *Rural Telephone Co.*, 235–236
Fellowships, *see* Scholarships and fellowships
Fiction, *see* Awards; Bestsellers; Books, best books
Film
  books turned into, 219
  children's; notable, 588
  LC collection, 81
  NAC collection, 45
  See also National Film Preservation Act
First amendment legislation, *see* Censorship
First sale doctrine, 232
Florida
  AAP activities, 161
  networks and cooperative library organizations, 644
  school library media associations, 752
Foreign book trade
  associations, 783–789
  foreign/domestic book trade, 479–504, 519
Foreign books; prices, 457(table), 458(table), 494, 498, 502
Foreign library associations, 767–777
  See also names of specific countries
France; Milia book fair, 218
Frankfurt Book Fair, 156–157, 216–219
  activities, 219
  American publishers, 218
  business picture, 217–218
  Irish theme of, 219
  variety at, 218
Freedom of Information Act electronic amendments, 287
Freedom of speech, *see* Intellectual freedom
Friedman, Arlene, 16, 18, 19–20
Fund-raising; bibliography for librarians, 531
Funding for education, *see* Higher Education Act
Funding for libraries, 146–147
  federal, 273, 275–276, 277(table)

LSTA, 4
  reauthorization, 4
  SLJ news report, 12–13
  See also Higher Education Act; Library Services and Construction Act; Library Services and Technology Act
fund-raising, 6, 212–213
ICSECA, 41
school library media programs, 250
  See also Grants; Library Services and Construction Act; Library Services and Technology Act

G

Galassi, Jonathan, 21
GATT Uruguay Round Agreements Act; Copyright Restoration Provision, 76
Gene Map, 112–113
Geography, 78, 79
Georgia
  networks and cooperative library organizations, 644–645
  school library media associations, 752
Germany
  prices and price indexes, 498
    academic books, 498, 499(table)
    academic periodicals, 498, 500(table)
  See also Frankfurt Book Fair
Gibson, Chip, 16–17
Gift & Mystery (John Paul II), 591, 603
Goal 2000, *see* Educate America Act
Goldhagen, Daniel, 599
Goleman, Daniel, 597–598
Gordeeva, Ekaterina, 594
Gore, Albert, *see* Clinton-Gore administration
Government documents; bibliography for librarians, 531–532
Government information, access to
  electronic records, 279
  See also Federal depository libraries
Government libraries
  acquisitions expenditures, 442–443(table)
  research, 409
Government Performance and Results Act (GPRA), 260–261
Government Printing Reform Act of 1996, 279
Grants, 6, 182, 241, 415–419
  ALA special projects, 146–147

Grants, *(cont.)*
  Carnegie Corporation, 187
  CLR, 416–418
  William and Flora Hewlitt Foundation, 190–191
  IFLA, 202
  W.K. Kellogg Foundation, 189, 406–408
  Library-Head Start Partnership Project, 86
  Andrew W. Mellon Foundation, 178–179, 188, 194
  NEH, 147, 182, 295–296, 298
  OCLC, 418–419
  "Parents as First Teachers", 10
  K.G. Saur, 392
  SLA, 207
  Lila Wallace-Reader's Digest Fund, 146–147
  See also American Library Association, special projects; Awards; Council on Library Resources; Higher Education Act; Library Education and Human Resource Development Program; Library Services and Construction Act; Library Services and Technology Act; Scholarships and fellowships
Gray, John, 592
Great Britain, 217–218
  book prices and price indexes, 494, 495–497(table)
The Green Mile (King), 33, 34
Greene, Bob, 32, 33
Grisham, John, 33, 592, 594
Guterson, David, 33

H

Hamilton, Jane, 18
Handicapped, library services for the
  bibliography for librarians, 536–537
  LSCA funding, 322, 323(table), 324
  See also National Library Service (NLS) for the Blind and Physically Handicapped
Hardcover books
  American book title production, 506(table)
  bestsellers, 591–600
  prices and price indexes
    averages, 483(table)
    averages per-volume, 509(table), 510(table)
  return rate, 600–601
Hatch, Orrin, 285

Hawaii
  networks and cooperative library organizations, 645
  school library media associations, 752
  services to natives under LSCA Title IV, 312
    basic grant awards, 313–315(table)
    special projects awards, 315–317(table)
  SLJ news report, 13–14
Health sciences libraries, *see* Association of Academic Health Sciences Library Directors; Archivists and Librarians in the History of the Health Sciences; Medical Library Association; National Library of Medicine
Higher Education Act (HEA), 303–312
  Title II-B, *see* Library Education and Human Resource Development Program; Library Research and Demonstration Program
  See also Library Services and Technology Act
Hillman, James, 32
History of libraries; bibliography for librarians, 534
Hitler's Willing Executioners... (Goldhagen), 599
HIV, *see* AIDS/HIV information sources
Holocaust survivor testimonies, 310
Homeschooling; bibliography for librarians, 536–537
Human Resources for Information Systems Management (HRISM), 406–407
Human rights issues, 157–159

I

Idaho
  networks and cooperative library organizations, 645
  school library media associations, 752
Illinois
  networks and cooperative library organizations, 241, 645–647
  school library media associations, 752
Improving America's Schools Act Title VI, 276
Imus, Don, 31
In Contempt (Darden), 32
In Search of Justice (Shapiro), 32

Indian tribes, library services to, *see* Native Americans, library and information services to
Indiana
  literacy projects, 321
  networks and cooperative library organizations, 241, 647
  school library media associations, 752–753
Infinite Jest (Wallace), 32
Information
  access to
    IFLA activities, 198
    services, importance of, 208
    See also Government information, access to
  Canadian policy, 221–222
  network infrastructure development, *see* National Information Infrastructure
  technology, *see* Information technology
  See also ARMA International; Association for Information and Image Management; Education for librarians and librarianship; Information industry; Information Industry Association; Library/information science (LIS) education; National Technical Information Service
Information highway, *see* National Information Infrastructure
Information industry
  associations, U.S. and Canadian, 669–733
  See also Federal Library and Information Center Committee; Information Industry Association; International Federation for Information and Documentation; Legislation affecting information industry; National Federation of Abstracting and Information Services; Placement
Information literacy, defined, 254
Information Outlook, 208–209
Information science, *see* American Society for Information Science; Association for Library and Information Science Education; Canadian Association for Information Science; National Commission on Libraries and Information Science
Information Superhighway, *see* National Information Infrastructure
Information technology
  in Canada, 220–221
  electronic
    GPO initiatives, 264–265
    LC initiatives, 265–266
    NARA initiatives, 266
  FLICC activities, 90
  library automation; bibliography for librarians, 533
  See also Library and Information Technology Association; National Commission on Libraries and Information Science; National Technical Information Science
Institutionalized, library services for the;
  LSCA funding, 326, 328(table), 329
Intellectual freedom
  AAP activities, 154–155
  ALA activities, 143
  See also American Library Association, Intellectual Freedom
  bibliography for librarians, 532
  See also Association of American Publishers, Freedom to Read Committee *and* International Freedom to Publish Committee; Censorship
Intellectual property, 274
  AAP activities, 152–153
  ALA activities, 281–282
  ARL activities, 175, 176–177
  Canadian issues, 222–223
  in cyberspace, 152–153, 199–200
  fair use, 176, 200, 238n10, 280–281
  legislation, 281–282, 284–286
Interlibrary cooperation, *see* Interlibrary loan (ILL)/document delivery; Internet; Networks and networking
Interlibrary loan (ILL)/document delivery
  ARL activities, 177
  bibliography for librarians, 532
  NAL activities, 106–107
  NCES library statistics survey, 63, 431
  NLE activities, 137
  See also Internet; Networks and networking; North American Interlibrary Loan and Document Delivery (NAILDD) Project
International book trade
  associations, 783–789
  title output, 520, 521(table)
International library activity
  associations, 759–766
  See also International personnel exchanges for librarians; Librarians and librarian-

International library activity, *(cont.)* ship; United States Information Agency
International personnel exchanges for librarians
  employment opportunities, 354–356
  overseas exchange programs, 356
International Standard Book Number (ISBN)
  assignment procedure, 574
  construction, 573
  five-digit add-on code, 575–576
  how to obtain, 573–576
  location and display of, 574–575
  machine-readable coding, 575
  organization of system, 574
  reporting the title and the ISBN, 576
International Standard Serial Number (ISSN), 577–578
Iowa
  networks and cooperative library organizations, 647–648
  school library media associations, 753
Ireland; as theme of Frankfurt Book Fair, 219
Italy, *see* Bologna Children's Book Fair

J

Japan; Journal Access Project, 178
Jazz, 79
Jobs, *see* Placement
John Paul II (Pope), 591, 603
Journey to Justice (Cochran), 32, 601–602

K

Kansas
  networks and cooperative library organizations, 648
  school library media associations, 753
  teacher certification requirements dropped, 10–11
  SLJ report, 10–11
Kentucky
  networks and cooperative library organizations, 648
  school library media associations, 753
Khawar v. *Globe International*, 155
Coretta Scott King Awards, 144
King, Stephen, 33, 34, 35, 591, 607
Klein, Joe, 31, 32, 592, 594
Knee Deep in Paradise (Butler), 604

Koster, Elaine, 16, 18, 19

L

The Last Family (Miller), 605
Latin America
  book prices and price indexes, 502
  number of copies and averages, as purchased by selected U.S. libraries, 503(table)
  Latin American Demonstration Project, 178–179
  Latin Americanist Research Resources Pilot Project, 104
  periodical prices and price indexes, 502, 504(table)
  Register of Microform Masters, 193
  See also Brazil; Mexico
Law libraries, *see* American Association of Law Libraries; International Association of Law Libraries
The Law of Love (Esquival), 606
Leading with My Chin (Leno), 604
Learning theory and information literacy, 250–251
Legislation affecting information industry
  Feist v. *Rural Telephone Co.*, 235–236
  See also Internet; National Information Infrastructure
Legislation affecting libraries, 261, 273–283
  ACLU v. *Reno*, 283
  American Library Association v. *Department of Justice*, 283
  Armstrong et al. v. *Executive Office of the President*, 279
  Communications Decency Act, 143, 282–283
  copyright issues
    See also subhead fair use
  electronic records, 279
  English as the official language, 276, 278
  Fair Pay Act, 278
  fair use, 176, 200, 232, 238n10, 280–281
  funding, 275–276
    appropriations for federal library and related programs, 277(table)
  government information, 278–279
  intellectual property, 281–282
  Library Services and Technology Act, 273, 274–275
  lobbying efforts, 280, 282
  NII and, 231–233

nonprofit organizations, 214, 280
postal issues; Kiosk Project, 279
SLA activities, 209–210, 214
telecommunications, 282, 283
term extension, 230–231
See also Government Performance and Results Act; Government Printing Reform Act of 1996; Higher Education Act; Library Services and Construction Act; Library Services and Technology Act; National Information Infrastructure; United States Information Agency
Legislation affecting publishing, 261, 284–291
AAP activities, 150–151, 284–291
ABA activities, 163
Alliance for Community Media, 155
antiterrorism, 287
antitrust lawsuit, 163
clarifications legislation, 285
Communications Decency Act, 154–155
copyright
  exemption for the blind, 284
  See also subhead fair use
education, 290–291
encryption, 288
fair use, 200, 232, 238n10, 286
FCC rule-making proceedings, 289–290
freedom of information, 286–287
intellectual property organization legislation, 285
Khawar v. *Globe International*, 155
National Defense Authorization Act, 286–287
NII and, 231–233
postal issues, 291
privacy legislation, online, 288–289
technologies, 288–289
term extension, 230–231
WIPO conference, 285–286
See also Elementary and Secondary Education Act; Government Performance and Results Act; Government Printing Reform Act of 1996; National Information Infrastructure
Legislative Branch Appropriations Act, 284
Leno, Jay, 604
Librarians and librarianship
  AASL's *Competencies for Prospective Teachers and Administrators*, 255
  automation, 533

bibliography for librarians, 533
exchange programs, *see* International personnel exchanges for librarians
future libraries, vision of, 240
placement services, *see* Placement
school library media specialists, 253–255
See also Council on Library Resources; Education for librarians and librarianship; Library/information science (LIS) education; National Librarians Association
Librarianship as a profession, *see* Librarians and librarianship
Libraries
acquisitions, *see* Acquisitions
administration, *see* Library Administration and Management Association; Library management
budget, *see* Funding for libraries
buildings, *see* Library buildings
collections, *see* Association of Research Libraries, collections services program; Collection development
customer service; bibliography for librarians, 531
depository, *see* Federal depository libraries
electronic, *see* Electronic libraries
funding, *see* Funding for libraries
international activity, *see* International library activity
legislation, *see* Legislation affecting libraries
See also Council of National Library and Information Associations; Council of Planning Librarians; Information industry; National Commission on Libraries and Information Science, *and* names of specific associations, countries, *and* subject headings, e.g., Library buildings
Library administration, *see* Library Administration and Management Association; Library management
Library associations and agencies
Canadian, 743–745, 750
cooperatives; NCES survey, 69
direct service to people, 422
electronic networking, 423
foreign, 767–777
international, 759–766
national and Canadian, 669–733

Library associations and agencies, *(cont.)*
  networks and cooperative organizations, 423, 639–668
  placement sources
    specialized associations and groups, 342–347
    state and regional, 348–349
  services to libraries, 421–422
  state, 347–348, 420–425
    administrative agencies, 746–749
    background, 420–421
    position in state government, 421
    school library media, 751–758
    services to libraries, 425(table)
    staffing, 424
  state and regional, 348–349, 734–745
  See also Association of Specialized and Cooperative Library Agencies; Council of National Library and Information Associations; International Federation of Library Associations and Institutions, *and* names of specific associations and countries
Library buildings, 461–477
  bibliography for librarians, 533–534
  college and research libraries
    additions and renovations, 467–472(table), 475–476(table)
    new buildings, 474(table)
    renovations, 477(table)
  LC restoration/renovation, 82, 267
  LSCA-funded construction, 329, 330–332(table)
  NARA's Archives II, 266
  public libraries
    new, 462–466(table)
    six-year cost summary, 473(table)
  school library media services
    renovation goals, 252
Library Education and Human Resource Development Program, 304–309, 306–307(table)
  fellowship grantees, (table), 304–305
  institute awards, 305, 307–309(table)
Library education, *see* Education for librarians and librarianship; Library/information science (LIS) education; Library Education and Human Resources Program
Library grants, *see* Grants; Higher Education Act; Legislation affecting libraries; Scholarships and fellowships

Library Journal (LJ)
  news report, 3–8
  placements and salaries survey, 360–371
  1997 Public Library Budget Report, 3, 240
Library Literacy Program, *see* Literacy programs, LSCA funding
Library management
  bibliography for librarians, 528–529
  See also International Council of Library Association Executives; Library Administration and Management Association
Library materials, *see* Preservation; School library media centers and services, *and* names of specific countries, *and* names of specific materials, i.e., Audiovisual materials
Library personnel
  education, *see* Education for librarians and librarianship; Library/information science (LIS) education
  employment, search for, *see* Placement
  exchange programs, *see* International personnel exchanges for librarians
  See also Librarians and librarianship; National Librarians Association; Placement; Salaries; Staffing
Library Research and Demonstration Program, 310–311
  holocaust survivor testimonies, 310
Library schools, *see* Education for librarians and librarianship; Library/information science (LIS) education; Placement
Library Services and Construction Act (LSCA), 312–334
  state-administered programs, 318–334(tables)
  Title I funding
    for the blind and physically handicapped, 322, 323(table), 324
    for the elderly, 324–326, 327(table)
    for the institutionalized, 326, 328(table), 329
  Title I funding
    for the limited-English speaking, (table), 320–322
    for literacy, (table), 320–322
    Public Library Services, 318–319(table), 318
  Title II funding; public library construction and technology enhancement, 318–319(table), 329, 330–332(table)

Title III funding
  interlibrary cooperation and resource sharing, 318–319(table), 318
  technology and networks, 333–334, 334(table)
Title IV; Library Services for Indian Tribes and Hawaiian Natives Program, 312, 313–315(table)
  basic grant awards, 313–315(table)
  special projects awards, 315–317(table)
Title VI; Library Literacy Program, 318
  See also Library Services and Technology Act
Library services and programs
  evaluation of; bibliography for librarians, 531
  See also Library Services and Construction Act; Library Services and Technology Act; National Commission on Libraries and Information Science, *and* names of special interest groups *and* specific countries
Library Services and Technology Act (LSTA), 4, 142, 273, 274–275, 303
Library standards, *see* International Organization for Standardization; National Information Standards Organization
Library statistics, *see* National Center for Education Statistics, Library Statistics Program; Statistics
Library/information science (LIS) education
  accredited master's programs, 373–374
  honor society, *see* Beta Phi Mu
  See also Education for librarians and librarianship; Library Education and Human Resource Development Program
Literacy programs
  AAP activities, 162
  ARL activities, 175
  LSCA funding, 318
  "Reach Out and Read," 162
  See also Center for the Book
Literary awards, *see* Awards
Lobbying
  by nonprofit groups, 280
  telecommunications issues, 282
Local Empowerment and Flexibility Act, 280
Louisiana
  networks and cooperative library organizations, 649
  school library media associations, 753

M

Machine-readable materials
  acquisition expenditures
    academic libraries, 438–439(table)
    government libraries, 442–443(table)
    public libraries, 436–437(table)
    special libraries, 440–441(table)
Maine
  networks and cooperative library organizations, 649
  school library media associations, 753
Make the Connection (Winfrey/Greene), 32, 33
Maps, 78, 79
Marsh, Brenda, 28
Maryland
  networks and cooperative library organizations, 649
  school library media associations, 753
Massachusetts
  linguistic minorities, 321
  networks and cooperative library organizations, 649–651
  school library media associations, 754
Media services, *see* School library media centers and services
Medical libraries, *see* Archivists and Librarians in the History of the Health Sciences; Association of Academic Health Sciences Library Directors; Medical Library Association; National Library of Medicine
Men Are from Mars, Women Are from Venus (Gray), 592
Mendelsohn, Jane, 31
Mexico; libraries, number of, 428–429
Michigan
  networks and cooperative library organizations, 651–652
  school library media associations, 754
Microforms
  acquisition expenditures
    academic libraries, 438–439(table)
    government libraries, 442–443(table)
    public libraries, 436–437(table)
    special libraries, 440–441(table)
  EDRS prices, 119(table)
  EROMM, 192–193
  Latin American Register of Microform Masters, 193
  preservation and, 179

Microforms, *(cont.)*
  prices and price indexes, 448(table), 458(table)
  See also Association for Information and Image Management; Association of Research Libraries; European Register of Microform Masters; National Register of Microform Masters
Miller, Bob, 16, 18, 19, 20, 21
Miller, John Ramsey, 605
Minnesota
  networks and cooperative library organizations, 652–653
  school library media associations, 754
Minorities
  affirmative action, 82–83
  1995 minority graduates
    salaries of placements by type of library, 368(table)
Mississippi
  networks and cooperative library organizations, 653
  school library media associations, 754
Missouri
  school library media associations, 754
  SLJ report, 9
Mitchard, Jacquelyn, 31, 592
Montana
  networks and cooperative library organizations, 654
  school library media associations, 754
Morrison, Toni, 32, 33
Moyers, Bill, 604
Multicultural issues, 250
Multimedia, educational, 235
Music
  libraries, *see* International Association of Music Libraries, Archives and Documentation Centres; Music Library Association
  licensing, 284
My Sergei (Gordeeva), 594

N

National Defense Authorization Act, 286–287
National Assessment of Education Progress, 13
National Digital Library Program (NDLP), 266
National Film Preservation Act, 81

National Independent Bookstore Week (NIBW), 171–172
National Information Infrastructure (NII)
  copyright and copyright law and, 152, 177, 231–233, 284
  fair use, 176, 200, 238n10
  intellectual property issue, 281
  libraries and, 74
  See also Citizens Internet Empowerment Coalition; Internet; World Wide Web
National Information Infrastructure Copyright Protection Act, 231–233
National Performance Review (NPR), 259–260
Native Americans, library and information services to
  LSCA Title IV, 312
    basic grant awards, 313–315(table)
    special projects awards, 315–317(table)
Nebraska
  networks and cooperative library organizations, 654
  school library media associations, 754–755
The Netherlands
  periodical prices and price indexes, 498
    Dutch (English Language), 501(table)
Networks and networking
  civic, *see* Civic networks
  community, *see* Civic networks
  international
    See also Internet; World Wide Web
  libraries and, 239–245, 408–409, 639–668
  library automation; bibliography for librarians, 533
  library service networks and Web site addresses, 244(table)
  LSCA funding, 333–334, 334(table)
  NAL activities, 103
  national, *see* Internet; National Information Infrastructure; National Research and Education Network; World Wide Web
  networks and cooperative library organizations, 423
  NLM, 111
  NPIN, 121
  regional, 240–241, 243, 245
  scholarly communication, 188
  security issues, 47
  state, 241, 423
  See also Information technology; National Information Infrastructure; National Research and Education Network *and*

names of specific networks, e.g., OCLC
Nevada
  networks and cooperative library organizations, 654
  school library media associations, 755
New Hampshire
  networks and cooperative library organizations, 654–655
  school library media associations, 755
New Jersey
  networks and cooperative library organizations, 655–656
  school library media associations, 755
New Mexico
  networks and cooperative library organizations, 656
New York
  Buffalo Free-Net, 321–322
  "little CDA," 154
  networks and cooperative library organizations, 656–657
  NYC textbook crisis, 161
  school library media associations, 755
  as TIIAP grant recipient, 276
Newspapers
  as placement sources, 337
  prices and price indexes, 493
    U.S. dailies, 458(table), 490(table)
NII/SUPERNet devices, 13
Richard M. Nixon presidential library, 54
Nixon, Richard M., 263
Nonfiction books, *see* Awards; Bestsellers; Books, best books
Nonprint materials, *see* Audiocassettes; Audiovisual materials; CD-ROM; Videocassettes
Nonprofit organizations, 280
North Carolina
  networks and cooperative library organizations, 657–658
  school library media associations, 755–756
North Dakota
  networks and cooperative library organizations, 658
  school library media associations, 756
The Notebook (Sparks), 31–32
Nutrition, 107

O

Ohio, 155

LJ report, 4
  networks and cooperative library organizations, 658–659
  school library media associations, 756
Oklahoma
  networks and cooperative library organizations, 659
  school library media associations, 756
Omnibus Consolidated Appropriations Act, 280
Online searching
  bibliography for librarians, 534
  See also Internet; World Wide Web *and names of specific networks*, i.e., MEDLINE
Online services, public library price index, 446(table), 448(table)
Oregon
  networks and cooperative library organizations, 659–660
  school library media associations, 756
  "Survival Spanish" program, 320
Outsourcing, 14–15

P

Paperback books
  bestsellers, 607
  children's, 624–628
  trade, 608–614
  prices and price indexes
    average mass market per-volume prices, 510(table)
    average trade per-volume prices, 511(table)
    U.S. mass market, averages, 488(table)
    U.S. trade, averages, 488(table)
  title output
    American trade production, 506(table)
    excluding mass market, 507(table)
    imported titles, 508(table)
    mass market, 507(table)
    trade; translations into English, 508(table)
  See also Association of American Publishers, Trade Division
"Parents as First Teachers," 10
Pennsylvania
  networks and cooperative library organizations, 660–662
  school library media associations, 756
SLJ report, 9–10

Periodicals and serials
　acquisition expenditures
　　academic libraries, 438–439(table)
　　government libraries, 442–443(table)
　　public libraries, 436–437(table)
　　special libraries, 440–441(table)
　bibliography for librarians, 536, 537–538
　prices and price indexes, 479, 490, 492
　　academic library, 457(table)
　　Dutch, 498, 501(table)
　　German academic periodicals, 498, 500(table)
　　Latin American, 502, 504(table)
　　library acquisitions, 458(table)
　　U.S., average, 480–481(table)
　　U.S. Serial Services, averages, 482(table)
　SLA publications, 208–209
　See also International Standard Serial Number; Newspapers
Petrocelli, Bill, 28
Placement, 337–359, 360–371
　1995 U.S. graduates, 364–365(table)
　by location, 369(table)
　minority, placement by type of library, 368(table)
　minority, salaries by type of library, 362–363(table)
　special placements, 367(table)
　status, spring 1995, 361(table)
　summary by region, 361(table)
　job hunting, 358–359
　joblines, 338–341
　national trends, 366–368, 371
　sources
　　federal employment information sources, 351–353
　　general and specialized jobs, 337–338, 353–354
　　Internet, 337–338
　　library and information studies programs, 349–351
　　newspapers, 337
　　nonlibrary uses of information skills, 356–358
　　overseas, 354–356
　　overseas exchange programs, 356
　　specialized library associations and groups, 342–347
　　state library agencies, 347–348
　　state and regional library associations, 348–349
　　temporary/part-time positions, 358

　　temp/part-time jobs, 366
　　traditional jobs, 366–368
Poetry, best books, 583
Poland, at Frankfurt Book Fair, 218–219
Popescu, Petru, 605–606
Pornography, *see* Censorship
Postal Reform Act of 1996, 159, 291
Preservation
　acquisition expenditures
　　academic libraries, 438–439(table)
　　government libraries, 442–443(table)
　　public libraries, 436–437(table)
　　special libraries, 440–441(table)
　ARL activities, 178–179
　bibliography for librarians, 534–535
　brittle books, *see subhead* deacidification
　CLR/CPA activities, 190–192
　copying for, 234
　deacidification, 190
　EROMM, 192–193
　FLICC activities, 91
　LC activities, 82
　microfilming, 179
　NAL activities, 105–106
　National Information Infrastructure Copyright Protection Act, 231–233
　NEH grants, 295–296
　See also Preservation Science Council
Presidential libraries, 54
　George Bush Presidential Library and Museum, 54
　Harry S. Truman; library and museum, 54
Prices and price indexes
　book prices, 507, 509
　public/academic libraries, 444–459
　U.S. and foreign published materials, 479–504
　using the price indexes, 502–503
　See also Academic books; Audiovisual materials; Books; CD-ROM; Hardcover books; Microforms; Newspapers; Paperback books; Periodicals and serials; Videocassettes *and* names of countries
Primary Colors (Klein), 31, 33, 592, 594
Prison libraries; bibliography for librarians, 537
Pro CD, 152
A Problem of Evidence (Bosco), 602
Public libraries, 190
　acquisition expenditures, 436–437(table)
　bibliography for librarians, 535

Canadian, 225
collections, 63
construction, see Library buildings
fund-raising, 6
interlibrary loan, 63
and the Internet, 239–245
Internet costs, 3–8, 273
LJ summary of budget changes, 6–8(table)
NCES survey, 60–64, 430–434
number of, 62
prices and price indexes, 444–451
  major component subindexes, 446(table)
  non-print media and on-line services, 448(table)
  operations expenditures, 445(table), 449(table)
staffing, 63
state rankings of selected data, 460(table)
statistics, 70–71
technology and, 189, 408–409
See also Collection development; Electronic libraries; Funding for libraries; Public Library Association, *and* specific states
Public schools, *see* School libraries; School library media centers and services
Public services; bibliography for librarians, 535
Publishers and publishing
  bestsellers and, 31–35
  booksellers and, 27–31
  coursepacks, 152
  education, *see* Education for publishing
  electronics
    See also PUBNET
  first sale doctrine, 232
  government, *see* Government Printing Office
  legislation, *see* Legislation affecting publishing
  merchandising, 24–25
  outsourcing, 14–15
  prices and price indexes, *see under* Academic books; Audiovisual materials; Books; CD-ROM; Hardcover books; Microforms; Newspapers; Paperback books; Periodicals and serials; Videocassettes
PW news report, 15–35
retail schedules, 27
sales, *see* Book sales
telephone numbers, toll-free, 539–572

See also Association of American Publishers; Federal Publishers Committee; Scientific, Technical and Medical Publishers *and* names of specific countries, e.g., Great Britain
Publishers Weekly (PW)
  bestseller lists, 593, 595–600
  news report, 15–35

R

"Reach Out and Read," 162
"Read More About It" project, 87
Reagan Library, 54
Reagan, Ronald, 263–264
Recession
  library buildings, *see* Library buildings
  placement and salaries, *see* Placement; Salaries
Recordings for children, notable, 587
Records management, *see* ARMA International; National Association of Government Archives and Records Administrators
Redfield, James, 591, 592
Reference services
  bibliography for librarians, 535–536
  FLICC activities, 91
  See also Reference and User Services Association
Reidy, Carolyn, 18, 19
Religion bestsellers, 594, 599
Religious libraries, *see* American Theological Library Association; Association of Jewish Libraries; Catholic Library Association; Church and Synagogue Library Association; Lutheran Church Library Association
Research libraries, *see* College and research libraries
Resnick, Faye, 602
Rhode Island
  networks and cooperative library organizations, 662
  school library media associations, 756
Rice, Anne, 607
Rodman, Dennis, 33, 594, 605
Romanos, Jack, 16, 18, 28
Rose Madder (King), 35
The Rules (Fein/Schneider), 33
The Runaway Jury (Grisham), 33, 594
Russia, 194

Russia, *(cont.)*
 Vologda conference, 199

S

Salamon, Julie, 594
Salaries, 360–371
 AAP survey, 162
 1995 U.S. graduates, 364–365(table)
 comparisons by type of library, 370(table)
 summary by region, 361(table)
 average salary index, starting library positions, 368(table)
 library price indexes, personnel compensation, 446(table), 456(table), 457(table)
 SLA survey, 208
 traditional vs. nontraditional graduates, 362(table)
 See also Fair Pay Act
Sargent, John, 28
Schneider, Sherrie, 32, 33
Scholarly books, *see* Academic books, prices and price indexes; Association of American Publishers, Professional and Scholarly Publishing Division; Textbooks
Scholarships and fellowships
 award recipients, 379–402
 HEA programs, (table), 304–305
 library scholarship sources, 375–378
 NEH programs, 297
 Soros Foundation-Library of Congress Librarian Intern Program, 108
 USIA Library Fellows Program, 147
School libraries
 bibliography for librarians, 536
 Canadian, 227
 See also American Association of School Librarians; International Association of School Librarianship; School library media centers and services
School Library Journal (SLJ) news report, 9–14
School library media centers and services, 9, 248–256
 accountability, 249–250
 availability of, 66
 bibliography for librarians, 536
 collection, 251–252
 diversity and community values, 250
 facility renovation goals, 252
 functions, evolution of, 251–255
 funding, 250
 historical overview, 66
 learning theory and information literacy, 250–251
 NCES survey, 65–66, 432–433
 resources, equity of, 250
 services and instruction, 253–254
 societal issues, 248–251
 staffing levels, 66
 standards for students' learning, 250
 state associations, 751–758
 technology, 249
 See also American Association of School Librarians; International Association of School Librarianship; School libraries
School library media specialists, 66–67, 253–255
The Search for Justice (Shapiro), 601–602
Sears, Barry, 592
Security measures, 47
 Library of Congress, 79
Seminars, *see* Conferences and seminars
Senior citizens, library services for
 bibliography for librarians, 536–537
 LSCA funding, 324–326, 327(table)
 See also Reference and User Services Association
Serials, *see* Periodicals and serials
Servant of the Bones (Rice), 607
Shapiro, Robert, 32, 601–602
Shinker, Bill, 16, 17, 19, 20, 21
Simple Abundance (Breathnach), 592
Simpson, O.J., 32, 601–602
Snow Falling on Cedars (Guterson), 33
Snowe-Rockefeller-Kerrey-Exon (SRKE) amendment, 283
Song of Solomon (Morrison), 32, 33
The Soul's Code (Hillman), 32
Sound recordings
 notable, for children, 587
 prices and price indexes, 458(table)
Sound recordings, *see* Audiovisual materials; CD-ROM (Compact Disc Read-Only Memory)
South Carolina
 networks and cooperative library organizations, 662
 school library media associations, 756–757
South Dakota
 LJ report, 4

networks and cooperative library organizations, 662
Physically Handicapped, Services to the, 324
Spain, World Book Day, 172
Spanish-speaking population, library services for, *see* REFORMA
Sparks, Nicholas, 31–32, 594
Special Libraries, 208
Special libraries
  acquisition expenditures, 440–441(table)
  bibliography for librarians, 537
  Canadian, 226–227
  See also Special Libraries Association, *and* names of specific associations, e.g., Music Library Association
SpeciaList newsletter, 208
Spielberg, Steven, 310
Staffing
  at GPO, 260
  bibliography for librarians, 528–529
  LC activities, 82–83
  NCES survey, 430–431
  public libraries, 63
  school library media centers, 66
  state library agencies, 424
Standard Address Number (SAN), 579–582
  assignment, 581
  check digit calculation, 580–581
  format, 580
  functions and suffixes, 581–582
  history, 580
Standards
  of learning, for students, 250
  library, *see* International Standard Book Number; National Information Standards Organization
NISO, 791–793
State humanities councils, 298–301
State libraries and library agencies, 347–348, 420–425
  administrative, 746–749
  background, 420–421
  NCES library statistics survey, 40–41, 69
  as placement sources, 347–348
  position in state government, 421
  school library media, 751–758
  services to libraries, 425(table)
  staffing, 424
  See also Chief Officers of State Library Agencies; Library associations and agencies; School library media centers, *and* names of specific states
Statistics
  ARL program, 181
  book sales, 23, 512–513
    AAP annual survey, 512–513
  government libraries, 410
  NCES library statistics program, 60–73
  NLM, 113(table)
  prices and price indexes, *see under* Academic books; Audiovisual materials; CD-ROM; College and research libraries; Hardcover books; Microforms; Newspapers; Paperback books; Periodicals and serials; School library media centers and services, expenditures for resources; Videocassettes, *and* names of specific countries
  state library agencies, 420–425
  See also Federal/State Cooperative System (FSCS) for Public Library Statistics; International Federation of Library Associations and Institutions; National Center for Education Statistics
Steel, Danielle, 591–592
Stine, R.L., 617
Survivors of the Shoah Visual History Foundation, 310

T

Technical services
  bibliography for librarians, 537
  See also Acquisitions; American Library Association, Resources and Technical Services Division; Association for Library Collections and Technical Services
Technology
  ALA initiatives, 144–145
  digital, 281
  FEDLINK activities, 94–95
  LSCA funding, 329, 333–334, 334(table)
  NLE Technology Resources Center, 137–138
  public libraries and, 189
  Public Libraries Survey and, 61
  in school library media centers, 249
  See also Electronics; Information technology; Office of Technology Assessment; Publishers and publishing, electronics

Telecommunications
　Canadian, 222
　computing and, 242–243
　discounted rates for libraries/schools, 175, 273, 283
　FCC rule-making proceedings, 289–290
　legislation, 282, 283
　lobbying, 282
　NII/SUPERNet devices, 13, 289
　rates, for public libraries, 3–4, 240
　RBOCs, 289–290
　universal service, 89
　See also Telecommunications Act of 1996; Telecommunications and Information Infrastructure Assistance Program; Telecommunications Reform Act of 1996
Telecommunications Act of 1996, 74, 167, 240, 273, 282, 283
Telecommunications Reform Act of 1996, 289
Telemedicine, 112
Telephones and telephone numbers
　LC, 83
　NLE, 140
　publishers' (toll-free), 539–572
Tennessee
　networks and cooperative library organizations, 662–663
　school library media associations, 757
Texas
　networks and cooperative library organizations, 663–664
　school library media associations, 757
Text digitizing, NATDP, 104
Textbooks
　coursepacks, 152
　NYC crisis, 161
　See also Academic books, prices and price indexes; Advisory Commission on Textbook Specifications; Association of American Publishers, Professional and Scholarly Publishing Division; Association of American Publishers, School Division
The University Licensing Program (TULIP), 410–411
Theological librarianship, *see* American Theological Library Association; Association of Jewish Libraries; Catholic Library Association; Church and Synagogue Library Association; Lutheran Church Library Association
Thomas, Barbara Bonds, 28
Translations, *see* Books, translation publishing
Truman, Harry S.; library and museum, 54

U

United States
　at Frankfurt Book Fair, 218
　book exports, 514(table)
　　compared to total book sales, 518(table)
　　to principal countries, 515(table)
　　trade in books, 518(table)
　　See also Books, exports and imports
　book imports, 508(table), 516(table), 516–518, 517(table)
　　from principal countries, 517(table)
　　trade in books, 518(table)
　　See also Books, exports and imports
　book trade associations, 779–782
　bookstores, 522, 523(table)
　Education, Department of, *see* Education, U.S. Department of
　government information, *see* Government information, access to
　libraries
　　number of, 426–427
　　in regions administered by U.S., 427
　postal service, *see* Postal Service, U.S.
　prices and price indexes, *see under* Academic books; Audiovisual materials; Books; CD-ROM; Hardcover books; Microforms; Paperback books; Periodicals and serials; Sound recordings; Videocassettes
　published materials, *see* Government Printing Office
　purchasing power abroad, 494
　See also Federal Publishers Committee; Government Printing Office; Interlibrary cooperation; Legislation affecting information industry; Legislation affecting libraries; Legislation affecting publishing; National Center for Education Statistics; United States Information Agency
University libraries, *see* College and research libraries
Urban libraries, *see* Urban Libraries Council

Utah
  networks and cooperative library organizations, 241, 664
  school library media associations, 757

V

Vendor services; FEDLINK, 96
Vermont
  networks and cooperative library organizations, 664
  school library media associations, 757
Videocassettes
  awards, 144
  bibliography for librarians, 534
  children's; notable, 588
  prices and price indexes, 448(table), 493–494
    academic libraries, 458(table), 459(table)
    averages, 490(table)
Vietnam, 158
Virgin Islands, networks and cooperative library organizations, 666
Virginia
  networks and cooperative library organizations, 664–665
  school library media associations, 757–758
Virtual libraries, *see* Electronic libraries
Visible Human World Wide Web site, 112
Vitale, Alberto, 18–19, 20

W

Wallace, David Foster, 32
Washington, D.C., *see* District of Columbia
Washington
  networks and cooperative library organizations, 665

PORTALS project, 311
  school library media associations, 758
West Virginia
  networks and cooperative library organizations, 665
  school library media associations, 758
Williams, Montel, 32
Winfrey, Oprah, 16, 17, 18, 31, 591, 592
Winton, Charlie, 16–17, 17–18, 20, 21
Wisconsin
  networks and cooperative library organizations, 665–666
  school library media associations, 758
  WISCAT, 333–334
Woodward, Bob, 602
World Book Day, 172
Wyoming
  networks and cooperative library organizations, 666
  school library media associations, 758

Y

Young adults, services for
  bibliography for librarians, 530
  NCES surveys on, 67–68
  reluctant readers; suggested titles, 589–590
  See also Children and young adults; Young Adult Library Services Association

Z

Z39 Committee, *see* National Information Standards Organization, Z39 standards
The Zone (Sears), 592